Yale Companion

to Jewish Writing

and Thought in

German Culture

1096–1996

Yale Companion

to Jewish Writing

and Thought in

German Culture

1096–1996

EDITED BY

SANDER L. GILMAN

& JACK ZIPES

Yale University Press   New Haven and London

Published with assistance from the Lucius N. Littauer
Foundation, gratefully acknowledged.

Designed by Sonia L. Scanlon.
Set in Garamond type by The Composing Room of
Michigan, Inc.
Printed in the United States of America by R. R.
Donnelley and Sons, Crawfordsville, Indiana.

A catalogue record for this book is available from the
British Library.

The paper in this book meets the guidelines for
permanence and durability of the Committee on
Production Guidelines for Book Longevity of the
Council on Library Resources.

10 9 8 7 6 5 4 3 2 1

Library of Congress Cataloging-in-Pubication Data

Yale companion to Jewish writing and thought in
    German culture, 1096–1996 / edited by Sander
    L. Gilman and Jack Zipes.
        p.   cm.
    Includes bibliographical references and index.
    ISBN 0-300-06824-7 (cloth)
    1. Jews—Germany—History. 2. Judaism—
Germany—History.   3. Jews—Germany—
Intellectual life.   4. Germany—Intellectual
life.   5. Germany—Ethnic relations.   I. Gilman,
Sander L.   II. Zipes, Jack David.
DS135.G3Y35   1997
943'.004924—dc21   96-49583
                                    CIP

Editorial Board

Contents

Index to Authors

The following alphabetical list is intended to help the reader quickly find chapters in which individual authors are discussed in detail. The first page of relevant chapters is provided here. For a more complete listing of individual authors and their works, please see the index.

Preface

The idea of a companion to Jewish writing in the German language arose out of the body of new and exciting critical and historical scholarship on the culture of Jews in Germany. This scholarship has grown greatly over the past two decades to form a scholarly field of its own. Departing from traditional fields such as literary history and social history, it now takes the complexity of Jewish experience in Germany, Austria, and other central European countries as a model for understanding the Diasporic experience of many peoples across many nations.

In developing this volume with our contributors, we endeavored to capture the manifold aspects of Jewish culture in German-speaking countries through a series of interlocking essays surveying its totality—but not exhaustively. We were primarily concerned with providing a new historical perspective on this Jewish culture by using an approach well known in modern scholarly reference tools. Consequently, this volume presents snapshots of moments and individuals in a changing culture and, through this kaleidoscope, affords the reader insight into the intricate transformations and contradictions of this culture. Not only is the object fragmented and shattered in the process, but also the voices that describe this object illustrate the wide range of means by which Jewish culture in German-speaking countries and Jewish writing in German can be approached.

This volume was the brainchild of our editor, Jonathan Brent. In the first stage it benefited greatly from the collaboration of our board of editors. Hillary Hope Herzog and Todd Herzog helped compile the complicated draft of the manuscript and provided (as noted) translations of selected essays. Julie Carlson did a most remarkable job of editing complex manuscripts, and Susan Abel added all the right finishing touches. The index that makes the volume truly useful was provided by Mary Jane Frisby.

Jewish Writing in German Through the Ages

The idea of "Jewish" writing in "Germany" is a conundrum wrapped in a confusion tied with a desire. How can one separate the writing of the Jews in German-speaking countries from the culture in which they wrote? How dare one amalgamate their writing with the cultural production of those so inherently hostile to them? Who are "they"? Where are "they"? Who and where were "they"? Who is, at the end of all of this, "Other," and who is "Self," "Jew," and "German"?

To compile the first guide to Jewish writing in German at the end of the twentieth century is a clearly impossible yet absolutely necessary task, and we and our contributors have proposed to do both the impossible and the necessary. We will not resolve the questions that are inherent in our quest but will endeavor, at least, to articulate them. The essays present a loose chronology of the flow of Jewish writing in German speaking countries. We have selected neither an implied "canon" nor "Great Moments" of Jewish writing in German. Each essay is a reflection on a moment in time: the texts presented capture an aspect of that moment, and the authors who wrote the texts present the moment's human face. In weaving these essays along a time line, the complexities and contradictions of our project become clear. No easy set of definitions helped us frame this project; thus this volume also makes no claim to completeness of coverage. The essays present a mosaic of Jewish writing covering a wide range of topics, but clearly not all topics, writers, or themes could be included. All of the essays, however, contain reflections on the question of what is "Jewish" about "Jewish" writing in "German-speaking countries."

"Jewish" can be and has been understood at different times and with different emphasis as a religious or religio-political designation, a political affiliation, a linguistic grouping, an ethnic identity, and an ethnographic or biological cohort or allele, as well as simply a term of praise or opprobrium. "German" has an equally complex history. Is it a political designation, a linguistic label for disparate and yet (in their own eyes) united groups of the speakers of a single language or group of mutually incomprehensible dialects? Is it an ethnicity or a superethnic designation, or an ethnographic or biological cohort or allele? Does it limit itself to the "Germans," and if so, whose Germans—those of Tacitus, of Charlemagne, of Luther, of Bismarck, of Lueger, of Franz Josef, of Hitler, of Adenauer, of Ulbrecht, of Waldheim, or of Kohl? When we link such impossible-to-define terms, even greater problems arise. These contradictions are reflected in the entries included here. Static definitions have been avoided, yet of course all definitions of "German," "Jew," and "writing" are by definition static and normative, as they need to be at each moment in the cultural history of Jews and Germans, German Jews, Jews in Germany, and so forth, as the relationships change and refocus in various times and places.

Thus the question of language seems important, because we are dealing with writing. (Here writing is understood not as high, low, mass, popular, theological, philosophical, scientific, or technical literature but rather as the written cultural record that includes all of these and more—film and even the use of language in art.) But what "real" language(s) are important? Certainly Hebrew, Yiddish, and German were all written by Jews in Ashkenaz, the medieval Jewish designation for the world between Cologne and Strasbourg that expanded as the Jews from this area moved south toward Rome, east toward Vienna and Lvov, and eventually from there west toward London and New York. But this was a world in which there were multiple German languages—historically ranging from Middle High and Low German through the various dialectic groupings running north to south and west to east. This world was peopled by readers of Latin—"real" Latin during the Renaissance as well as Church Latin and academic Latin—and the latter was used well into the nineteenth century. It was also a world of spoken and written French, the language of many of the minor and major "German" courts in which not only Jews functioned, but so did the French Huguenots in the seventeenth century and the French refugees from the French Revolution in the eighteenth century. All of these languages could also have been spoken and written by Jews ranging from the pious and simple to the powerful and courtly, from the widow-merchant to the journalist, from the memoirist to the biblical commentator. Many of these Jews were bilingual or even polyglot, as were many of their gentile neighbors. In addition, many of these Jews had a sacred language, Hebrew, that seemed to parallel the social role played by Latin throughout Germania until the time of the Reformation. And Hebrew had high status before and after the age of Luther. The Jews were the people of the Old Testament. This gave Hebrew a special place in the canon of peoples in Europe—but being special can also be dangerous. By the nineteenth century, Yiddish had vanished from the Ashkenaz, but it had not vanished from the Scheunenviertel in Berlin or the Second *Bezirk* in Vienna—where large numbers of Yiddish-speaking Jews from the East resided. These Jews, too, became part of the world of Jewish writing in the Ashkenaz. They brought with them the Yiddish high modernism of Warsaw, the culture of the socialist *Bund,* or the piety of the Hasids. All these influences mixed with new and different forces. Imagine the early 1920s in Berlin, when one might have spied on the same trolley car moving down Friedrichstraße the Prague German-Jewish writer Franz Kafka, the Hebrew novelist S. Y. Agnon, the socially critical Yiddish author I. J. Singer, and the Berlin Jewish writer Alfred Döblin—who returned to Berlin in 1945 wearing the uniform of the Free French. Jewish writing is found in multiple discourses. There are Jewish scientists and Jewish filmmakers, Jewish poets and Jewish journalists, all of whom reflect in one way or another their understanding of their writings as Jewish (or as not Jewish—significantly, much the same distinction). Language and discourse marked difference in various combinations or alone, as well as in a wide array of places and contexts.

And where is Germany? Or where is Germania (the designation in the Babylonian Talmud for "Gomer," the father of Ashkenaz)? It is perhaps best located in the world of the book—for the Jews are the people of the Book, and the imagined Germany resided for the longest time in the world of book culture. This was true in the splintered Holy Roman Empire after Charlemagne, in the multiple German states before 1871; it was true in Bismarck's Germany and the divided Germany immediately after World War I; but it was also true in the multicultural world of the Austro-Hungarian Empire, where the Jews became the best Austrians because, scattered in the eastern territories, they oriented themselves toward Vienna and German culture for their self-definition. In addition, the Jews of Switzerland and Liechtenstein read the journals and books published in Berlin and Vienna and saw themselves as loyal Swiss or true Liechtensteiners. Exile and flight in 1933 meant different things to different Jews in Germania. Many left for all corners of the world—and a few of them returned because they could not live without their language and culture. Some stayed and hoped that it would all be over soon. Many, many died in the camps, writing sketches, poems, and even operas right to the end. Some returned after the Shoah from Palestine, New York, or Shanghai. Some continued to think of themselves as Jewish writers in exile from a lost, never again to be, romanticized Germania. Some acculturated themselves into their new world and yet continued to think of themselves as Jewish writers in Germany once removed. All related to the idea of the mobile, expanding, internalized cultural space in which Jews, however defined, wrote.

The complicated world of language of the Jews in the original Ashkenaz was also a world always bounded by the tension between the notion of Jewish exile and that of Jewish achievement. The contradictory yet overlapping models of a Jewish Diaspora, as opposed to a Jewish Galut, informed Jewish understanding of what exile means. The voluntary dispersion of the Jews (Galut or Golah) is understood as inherently different from the involuntary exile of the Jews (Diaspora). These two models exist simultaneously in Jewish history in the image of the uprooted and powerless Jews on the one hand, and the rooted and empowered Jews on the other. It is possible to have a firm, meaningful cultural experience as a Jew in the Diaspora or to feel alone and abandoned in the Galut (as well as vice versa)—two people can live in the very same space and time and can experience that space and time in antithetical ways. Indeed, the same person can find his or her existence bounded conceptually by these two models at different times and in different contexts.

The notion of a dispersion of the Jews is inscribed in the Torah with negative, punishing overtones. This dispersion represents punishment for the transgression of specific boundaries. The idea of a textual model for the Diaspora rooted in the Torah and reflected in other writings is important to any comprehension of a Jewish articulation of the meaning of "exile." But the very assumption of the Diaspora is ambiguous and contradictory, even though it carries the force of divine revelation incorporated in texts. The Galut, on the other hand, is often understood as the experienced reality of being in exile—a real-

ity structured, however, by the internalization of the textual notion of the Diaspora tempered by the daily experience (good or bad) of life in the world. The Jew experiences the daily life of exile through the mirror of the biblical model of the expulsion—whether it be the expulsion from the Garden of Eden or the captivity in Egypt. If these two experiences are parallel—if life in the Galut is harsh and painful (as it often was), it seems a further proof of the validity of the model of the Diaspora. The South African–Jewish writer Sandra Braude has stated this succinctly: "But Jews tend to forget that there is only one promised land, and that they seldom are permitted to remain in any one place for longer than three generations" (Braude 1991, 79). If Jewish experience is contradictory to the expectations of the Diaspora model, as in the Golden Age of the Jews in Spain or during the "emancipation" of Jews in nineteenth-century Europe, the meaning of the models becomes muddled. It was the ultimate trial of the Diaspora Jew—the *Churban*, the murder of the six million—that seemed to make the relationship of Jews to the cultures of the Germans damned at their very outset. Yet as we shall see, the complexity of religious, ethnic, political, linguistic, and philosophical relationships was never straightforward. There was no single straight line from the Mainz of Rashi to the death camps, but there may have been a German "special relationship" that combined the complex, undecidable aspects of "German" and "Jewish" identity into a set of mutual needs and hates.

The biblical or textual model of the Diaspora centers on a geography that defines Jewish identity. The Jews are a chosen people in a divinely chosen land, and exile is a recurrent state that must be resolved by returning to that chosen land. Thus within the Torah there is an established textual tradition of the Diaspora. The exile in Egypt comes to serve as the ideal model for Babylonian exile, which in turn becomes the model for the exile from Spain and Portugal, and so forth. But Egypt was both a voluntary outgoing from the Holy Land, an experience of mutual benefit (cultural symbiosis) for Jews and Egyptians, and a cruel incarceration (a true Diaspora). The only answer for this series of false human steps that drew the Jews away from the Holy Land into the land of Egypt was divine redemption and the punishment of the "hosts of Egypt" who attempted to stop the Jews from leaving their Diaspora. These "hosts" violated their guests' *heimarmene,* the comfort always offered the stranger. The cruelty of the Egyptians was a breach of friendship, the transformation of a Galut experience into a Diaspora experience. And in the textual model, the Galut experience, the peaceful going out of Jews from their "appropriate" place into the world, is transformed in the Egyptian Diaspora into the torment of slavery, death, and loss of faith.

God's promise to the patriarchs is that their children would be "as the dust of the earth: so that if a man can number the dust of the earth, so shall their seed be numbered" (Gen. 13:16). But the Diaspora reading of that promise is tinged with the taste of the Diaspora: "As the dust of the earth is scattered from one end of the world to the other, thus your children will be scattered from one end of the world to the other, as the dust of the earth causes even metal vessels to wear out but exists for ever, so Israel is eternal but the nations of the world will come to naught . . . as the dust of the earth is threshed, so thy children will be threshed by the nations" (Gen. 41:9). Here the promise of fecundity is linked to the curse of exile in the sense of the Diaspora.

The Assyrian (722 B.C.E) and Babylonian (597 B.C.E) Diasporas were textually represented as very similar. The corruption in Israel became the rationale for predicting Nebuchadnezzar's capture of Jerusalem and his destruction of the Temple. Jeremiah's description of the Babylonian enslavement was cast in the terms of the Diaspora. The appropriate punishment was exile from the land of Israel. Here redemption means return: "I will gather you from all the nations, and from all the places whither I have driven you" (29:14). And for Jeremiah the promise of redemption is real: "After seventy years be accomplished at Babylon I will visit you, and perform my good word toward you, in causing you to return to this place" (29:10). Ezekiel makes a similar promise: "Yet will I leave a remnant, that ye may have some that shall escape the sword among the nations, when ye shall be scattered through the countries" (6:8).

It is of little wonder that the survivors of the Shoah, living in displaced-person camps in Germany, came to speak of themselves as the "She'erit ha-Peletah," the surviving fragment, the term for those who survived the Babylonian captivity and eventually returned to Jerusalem. The biblical model comes to define the Jewish experience as an experience in exile.

The alternative model is that of the Galut. Here the Jews are seen as ubiquitous and inherently nomadic. Their presence throughout the world is a result of their desire to live outside of their "appropriate" land. There is no land without its Jews in this model. As early as the second century B.C.E, the Hellenistic Sibylline oracle could sing not only that "every land is full of you, and every sea" but also that "it is thy fate to leave thine holy soil" (Or. Sibyl. 3:267). The Greek historian Strabo, in the first century, stated that there was not a place in the entire world into which the Jewish nation had not penetrated. And by the second half of the first century that was stated "among every nation are the dispersed of Israel according to the word of God" (Songs of Sol. 9:2). By the nineteenth century, successful, indigenous Jewish communities were found in China, India, and Africa as well as throughout those lands colonized by the European powers.

These Jews are seen as economically, culturally, and socially successful in this context, in spite of the oppression they encountered. Franz Kafka spoke of the power given to the Jews in this struggle for survival: "The Jewish people is scattered, as a seed is scattered. As a seed of corn absorbs matter from its surroundings, stores it up, and achieves further growth, so the destiny of the Jews is to absorb the potentialities of mankind, purify them, and give them a higher development. Moses is still a reality. As Abriam and Dathan opposed Moses with the words '*Lo naale!* We will not go up!' so the world opposes him with the cry of anti-Semitism. In order not to rise to the human condition men sink into the dark depths of the zoological doctrine of race. They beat the Jews and murder humanity" (Janouch 1953, 66–67).

Many Jews are integrated to one degree or another in Galut culture, yet they are seen and see themselves as separate from that culture because of the power of the Diaspora model, the biblical model of exodus and dispersion. This was as true for purely secular Jews as it was for religious Jews.

In addition, that dispersion into the world of Ashkenaz is a dispersion as complex as any in the history of the Jews. For as complex as the Jewish self-representation has become, so too is the self-representation of Germany and the Germans. Are they a nation or competing tribes? Are they one culture—inferior to the French, superior to the British, or vice versa? The weaker the notion of a single German identity was, the more culture came to be the place where that missing identity was worked out. Jews entering Germany entered also into the world of German culture—the world of textual production and of letters, film, theology, and public oratory (as little of it as existed). And all varieties of relationship took place over the eons. Jews were integrated into the Rhenish linguistic community and spoke Middle High German rather than the Spanish, Italian, or Hebrew they brought with them. This very sign of linguistic "acculturation" foreshadowed the isolation of the Jews in ghettos (an Italian invention) and came to isolate Jews in the Ashkenaz into their own linguistic community, where Middle High German melded with other fragments of older Romance and bits and phrases of Hebrew were transformed into Proto-Yiddish. But certainly the Jews who had been linguistically acculturated into the world of Middle High German speakers had also been bilingual (if they were literate at all), because they had at least memorized enough Hebrew to say the Psalms, if they could not read and write the language of Torah. Yet there were also certainly speakers who became assimilated into the fringe world of courtly culture and who saw themselves as little different from their non-Jewish contemporaries. But how were they seen? The anathema of the convert was two-sided. Hated by the Jews, he or she was considered untrustworthy by the Christians. The tale was told of the deacon of the medieval Cologne Cathedral who on his deathbed repented his conversion to Christianity and said that Jews were as unlike German Christians as the hare was unlike the dog.

If this pattern is traced across the ages, and we can see it appearing and reappearing in this complex volume, it is clear that the very concepts we are dealing with are much like the basic law of physics that states that if you focus on one variable all the others shift. This project is thus an attempt to address the complexity of Jewish writing in German, not an effort to resolve it. We are able to do so in 1997 because of a generational shift that is not unimportant to our tale.

In 1945 it would have been unthinkable to write a book about the "Jewishness" of German writing or about Jewish writing in German. At that time, Jews did not want to have anything to do with things German. Furthermore, it was commonly believed that Germany had eliminated most if not all of its Jews and that its Jewish culture had been annihilated. Certainly the Germans did not want to be reminded of what had happened to the Jews and were even less inclined to welcome a revival of Jewish thinking and art in German culture. It appeared that the "famous" German-Jewish symbiosis had come to an end. Nothing could be further from the truth, however.

Today, more than fifty years after the end of the Shoah, it is apparent that Jewish writers never stopped writing in German, even during the 1930s and 1940s, and that they continued to refer to a German cultural tradition, contesting and claiming this culture as part of their own identity. Within the concentration camps, in hiding, and in emigration, Jews used the German language to express their dismay, horror, anger, and chagrin about the barbarism that had taken hold in Germany (and elsewhere in Europe). Moreover, they employed this language to salvage the humanist tradition in Germany and to grasp their Jewishness in light of the Shoah. In this regard, the Jewish contribution and connection to German culture has never been totally broken, and it is our purpose in the present volume to study the entirety of Jewish writing in German from the Middle Ages through 1996. This body of Jewish writing represents a significant aspect of German culture, and just as Germany has marked this "Jewish body," Jewish writers have sought to question, change, and appropriate German culture as a body from the margins—beneath, below, and even from above. This Jewish "intervention" was still evident at the end of the Shoah and at the beginnings of what was to be a "new" Germany.

In a recent book, *Nach dem Holocaust: Juden in Deutschland, 1945–1950* (1995), Michael Brenner demonstrated that the 220,000 to 230,000 Jews who survived the Shoah in 1945 and were placed in camps for displaced persons in Germany quickly established communal organizations inside and outside these camps. Further, there was a resurgence of cultural life, albeit a very small one in comparison with what had existed in Germany. Nevertheless, newspapers, journals, plays, poems, diaries, memoirs, and political programs were produced from 1945 to 1950 as the 20,000 to 30,000 Jews who remained in Germany organized themselves into different communities. Because many if not most of these Jews had been born outside Germany and did not speak German as their native language, they did not consciously seek to restore a German-Jewish cultural continuity; rather, they were mainly intent on surviving in an alien country. Yet there were also numerous German Jews who had been either in camps or in hiding and who had returned to their "homeland" after 1945, and these Jews did consciously seek to reawaken Jewish cultural life in what they hoped would be a "new Germany." Indeed, there were major differences and conflicts between the Eastern European Jews and the native-born German Jews, but they gradually joined together to form various communities in postwar Germany, and their common source of identity was based on a painful question: How is it possible to define oneself as a Jew living in the land of one's murderers?

It is not by chance that when the gifted Jewish actor and director Fritz Kortner decided to return to Germany in 1946, this question was on his mind and behind the remarkable film *Der Ruf,* which he wrote and in which he starred. The film concerns a famous Jewish professor, an émigré in America, who accepts a "call" back to a German university only to find that the political climate is still rife with anti-Semitism and fascism. Nevertheless, he wants to struggle for the cause of

humanity and to establish his rightful place in Germany. In the end, after many disturbing experiences, he dies symbolically from a heart attack. But this notion of "Ruf," the call as a mission, is not negated by the ending of the film, for the Jewish professor passes on his hope for a humanistic future to his "German" son, who recognizes how he had been on a wrong path in the "new" Germany. To a certain extent, the film was a call to Germans to recognize the nature of National Socialism and the ramifications of this movement for Jews. It also was a challenge to Jews to reestablish a humanistic tradition that might help Germany recover from the devastating effects of fascism.

This is not to say that the Jews in postwar Germany were on some sort of mission to prove something to themselves or to the world. Yet it is important to realize that the Jews who remained in Germany accomplished something remarkable that has been neglected and even discredited by the general public in Europe and North America. For better or worse, they reasserted themselves into the German public sphere and cultural tradition, and they gradually created a Jewish presence that has helped revitalize German society in different ways. It is within a context of Jewish reassimilation and contestation in Germany that Jewish writing in German has assumed significance within the last half a century, and it is important to consider how Jewish writers have taken different stands on the sociopolitical developments in contemporary Germany to grasp why a book on Jewish writing in German could even become possible. In fact, the present volume is, in part, an outcome of a vigorous Jewish cultural renascence in Germany, the concerns by Jews living outside of Germany, and a renewed interest of Germans in all things Jewish.

In his essays and books about Jewish writers, Marcel Reich-Ranicki, one of the foremost and certainly most controversial literary critics in Germany, has often referred to Jewish artists as disturbers of the peace and provocateurs. Of course, it would be an exaggeration to maintain that the resurgence of Jewish writing in Germany during the last fifty years can be characterized entirely by provocation. At the same time, the most significant Jewish writing in Germany in the post-Shoah period has been provocative in some way, and it is through provocation that Jewish writers since 1945 have gradually forged a strong presence in Germany. Here it is important to review how this has come about, and why provocation in all sorts of modes and guises has remained central to Jewish writing in German. Though it is always difficult and dangerous to divide an epoch into clearly delineated periods, the following outline is intended to indicate how one might begin to depict the manner in which Jews have inserted themselves into German social, political, and cultural discourses.

1945–66: The Return of Outside Voices

Aside from the Jewish writing that continued within official Jewish organs and the publications of the various communities after 1945, there was a concerted effort made by the newly formed West German government in 1949 to encourage Jews to return to Germany. Reparation programs were instituted, and Jews were given certain legal privileges and entitlements. The situation was and remained different in East Germany, where Jews were harassed to such an extent that the majority left the German Democratic Republic by 1953. In the West, however, the "official" policies were openly philo-Semitic, and because most Jews at first refused German recognition, there was a tendency in the German public to pay homage to "dead" Jews, as if new Jewish writing were not extant and could not play a role in the rebuilding of German society. Yet, as we have already seen in the case of Kortner, Jews began writing their way back into German culture as soon as World War II ended. Some did this from outside the country, whereas many began returning and played central roles in the mass media and in the university within Germany.

Jewish poets were among the first to make their voices known in the postwar period. These authors included Nelly Sachs from Sweden, Erich Fried and Theodor Kramer from England, Ilse Blumenthal-Weiss, Rose Ausländer, and Alfred Gong from the United States, Paul Celan and Yvan Goll from France, and others who returned to Germany and Austria at some point—such as Hilde Domin, Stephan Hermlin, Mascha Kaléko, and Berthold Viertel. Most of these writers inverted Theodor Adorno's dictum that poetry was impossible after Auschwitz. They pointed to the necessity of writing poetry to combat barbarism and to claim Jewish continuity in the German language. Here Berthold Viertel's poem "Der nicht mehr deutsch spricht" (On refusing to speak German) is indicative of the disturbing tone that Jews developed among themselves and also in the German public sphere:

You say the German language is taboo,
Because of our rage and shame.
But how to speak then to your dead,
None of whom escaped with you?
To the friends who suffered for you,
Who were captured instead of you,
How to beg their forgiveness
If their words are no longer in you?

And however pure your English locution,
Those bastards wouldn't care:
You could swallow your original tongue,
They'd still concoct a final solution.
The spoiled child, sure he's right,
Who sulks, and punishes his mother
By refusing to eat, this is that:
Infantile; a tantrum, spite.

If Auschwitz defined, for both Jews and Germans, what it meant to be Jewish during a certain period of history, German-Jewish poets reacted by resisting the totalitarian way in which they had been defined, and they explored numerous possibilities for self-realization through the German language after the Shoah. Auschwitz is not an idée fixe in their poetry, but it is a leitmotif, just as German-Jewish poets of the nineteenth and early twentieth centuries wrote with a sense of being stigmatized. Even when assimilation laws had been decreed in the early part of the nineteenth century, German Jews were still ostracized, and Jews were never really integrated into German society on their own terms. Their status was always marginal, and if they became assimilated, the conditions that determined their acceptance in German society were never of their own making. Whether religious or assimilated, Jews led a marginal existence in German society and continued to live that way until the present. The *different* ways in which they have contended with this marginality can be seen in such important early postwar anthologies of Jewish poetry as *Jüdisches Schicksal in deutschen Gedichten* (1959), edited by Siegmund Kaznelson, *Menschheitsdämmerung* (1959), edited by Kurth Pinthus, and *Welch ein Wort in die Kälte gerufen* (1968), edited by Heinz Seydel. There is also Manfred Schlösser's collection, *An den Wind geschrieben: Lyrik der Freiheit,* which includes poems written from 1933 to 1945 that address the struggle for freedom and self-definition. The title of this book, "Written to the Wind," was taken from Paul Celan's short piece that reads: "There was a time when one could hear a song resonate in Germany as it had never been sung before. A chorale from a thousand voices, which the wind carried on its back through the land, invisible, intangible. A consolation for many, a terror for the rulers of power. The wind collected the songs of freedom from the prisons and cellars, from secret rooms and all remote places. It was the confidante of all the suffering people and did not sense that days would come in which a tiny shift in tone would annihilate its mission. Whoever raised their voices for the sake of freedom and justice wrote to the wind, and on the day that freedom came, it was forgotten. Time passed. The words were written in the wind."

Whether those words have indeed been forgotten is debatable. Certainly, the words of provocation kept coming from Jewish writers in the period from 1945 to 1967, and not only from the poets. In Austria, Ilse Aichinger produced her autobiographical novel, *Die größere Hoffnung* (1948), and Friedrich Torberg wrote his *Hier bin ich, mein Vater* (1948), a moving account of a Viennese Jew driven to suicide by the Nazis. In Germany, Jakov Lind published a significant collection of grotesque stories titled *Eine Seele aus Holz* (1962), which are reminiscent of Kafka. Other important works by Jewish authors were Stefan Heym's *Kreuzfahrer von heute* (1950) and *Die Kannibalen und andere Erzählungen* (1953), Wolfgang Hildesheimer's *Tynset* (1965), Günter Kuntert's *Im Namen der Hütten* (1967), H. G. Ad-

ler's *Panorama* (1968), and Hilde Spiel's *Rückkehr nach Wien* (1968). And, of course, Peter Weiss began to make his mark in German literature with two autobiographical works, *Abschied von den Eltern* (1961) and *Fluchtpunkt* (1962), which were followed by his political plays, *Marat / Sade* (1963) and *Die Ermittlung* (1965). The latter caused a great stir in Germany by focusing on the relationship of the Shoah to capitalism and by drawing parallels to contemporary developments in West Germany. But Weiss was not alone in trying to explore the connections between politics, culture, anti-Semitism, and economics. Two prominent writers of the Frankfurt school, Max Horkheimer and Theodor Adorno, had returned to Germany, and their book, *Dialektik der Aufklärung,* written in 1944 during their American emigration, sought to demonstrate how the tenets of the Enlightenment had become perverted and had served to rationalize socioeconomic relations in a way that made anti-Semitism and the Shoah possible. Their ideas had a tremendous effect on students during the 1950s and 1960s—as did the works of other returning Jewish intellectuals and survivors of the Holocaust, such as Günther Anders, Jean Améry, Hans Mayer, Ernst Bloch, Werner Krauss, Victor Klemperer, Peter Szondi, Alphons Silbermann, Ralph Giordano, and Marcel Reich-Ranicki (not to mention the translation into German of works by such authors as Saul Bellow, Bernard Malamud, and Philip Roth). Their works and viewpoints during this early period laid the basis for the future development of Jewish writing and thinking in Germany. In some cases, these Jewish writers appeared on the center stage of the German literary scene and continued a tradition of Jewish provocation within German culture.

An interesting case in point is the work of Victor Klemperer. A respected professor of French literature at the technical university in Dresden until 1934, Klemperer, whose wife, Eva, was Christian, remained in Dresden during the war, began writing an autobiography when he was dismissed from the university, and kept a clandestine journal about his daily struggles while doing forced labor. After the war, he resumed teaching at the technical university of Dresden and in 1947 published *LTI* (*Lingua Tertii Imperii*), one of the most significant analyses of how the Nazis transformed the German language as part of their ideological socialization and how this language played an important role in the everyday lives of Germans during the Third Reich. This book served as the starting point for many philological studies of Nazi language in the postwar period, and though Klemperer died in 1960, his autobiography, *Curriculum Vitae* (1989), and journals, *Ich will Zeugnis ablegen bis zum letzten* (1995) and *Und so ist alles schwankend* (1996), were published posthumously and have attracted a great deal of interest and discussion. Klemperer's works, by a Jew who thought that he was more German than Jewish, reveal how many Jews fought insistently to maintain German culture against the barbarianism of the Nazis. Jewish writers in contemporary Germany have picked up this "provocative thread."

1967–89 The Clash with Philo-Semitism

Whereas Jewish writers had been concerned mainly with the Shoah and its consequences in the first two decades after World War II, many began focusing on the question of Jewish identity during the next twenty years. A key turning point in Germany for Jews was the Six-Day War in 1967 between the Israelis and the Arabs. The victory of the Israelis led to greater respect for Israel by the Germans, who established stronger commercial and diplomatic ties to Israel and continued to cultivate philo-Semitic attitudes. At the same time, however, the image of a strong "Jewish state" led ironically to a gradual distancing of Germany from Israel during the 1970s. Here a threefold reaction can be discerned: (1) Christian Democratic voters and business leaders developed growing sympathies for the Arab states, which were becoming more important economically, especially during the oil crisis of 1975, (2) the Social Democrats, who had been supportive of Israel, began playing the Israelis against the Arabs in the armaments industry, especially under the administration of Helmut Schmidt, and (3) the independent Left switched from admiration of Israel's socialist tendencies to

a position that condemned Israel for its Zionism and "imperialist" expansionist policies.

As a result of these developments, most Jews, whether on the Right or the Left, became even more wary of German attitudes toward Jews and Israel than they had been during the 1950s and 1960s. In fact, during the 1970s there was an upsurge of new German publications and films about Hitler, as well as histories by Joachim Fest and Helmut Diwald that played down the extermination of the Jews. Despite the influence of Jewish thinkers of the Frankfurt school, especially Herbert Marcuse, and the messianic "philosopher of Hope," Ernst Bloch, radical students took a crass anti-Zionist position that contributed to anti-Semitic sentiments. Meanwhile, the West German government continued to harbor, tolerate, and support prominent ex-Nazis as important political leaders while maintaining an official philo-Semitic stance. Here the role played by the conservative Jewish community leaders in West Germany must be taken into account. The elected officials of the Central Council of Jews, such as Werner Nachmann, Heinz Galinski, and others, continually supported the philo-Semitic positions of the state, despite evidence that these positions were hollow. The official Central Council followed a policy of appeasement established in 1950, and some of its members publicly defended ex-Nazis. Though these "professional Jews," as they were called by their critics, sought to appear as if they represented all Jews in Germany, they rarely took into consideration the varied opinions of their constituency. Many assimilated Jews did not feel represented by the official organs of the Jewish communities, and the "silent" progressive Jews, especially those of the first generation, rarely made themselves heard.

All this began to change as the first generation of Jews in Germany came of age and as Germans sought to "normalize" their own history in the 1980s—that is, as they attempted to make it seem that the Nazi past and the Shoah were not unique in the course of history. Such "normalization" made Jews feel more paranoid and provocative in their criticism and writings about all things German. Some German Jews maintained that this trend toward normalization, which led

Jürgen Habermas to start the Historians' Debate in 1986, triggered a "new" awareness among Jews, especially after 1984. This new awareness was strengthened as Jews responded first to the putative anti-Semitic endeavor to produce Rainer Werner Fassbinder's provocative play, *The City, Garbage, and Death* (*Die Stadt, der Müll und der Tod*) in Frankfurt am Main, and second to the successful but disgraceful 1985 commemoration ceremony in Bitburg, where former president Reagan and Chancellor Kohl honored those German soldiers, including SS troops, who fought valiantly for the Nazis in World War II. Indeed, Micha Brumlik, one of the most perceptive Jewish intellectuals of the first generation, stated in his lecture "The Situation of Jews in Today's Germany," held at Indiana University in 1990, that the Fassbinder scandal, Bitburg, the Historians' Debate, and the proposal to establish a memorial for all the dead of World War II fostered a new critical consciousness among the Jews in Germany. As a result, in his view, they constituted themselves as a *self-conscious* minority.

Yet it is not entirely clear that Jews formed a truly "new" consciousness in Germany. Adjectives that may better describe Jewish self-awareness in Germany during this critical period are "heightened," "different," "shifting," or "defiant." New was the *behavior* of Jews from different backgrounds and generations who joined in protests against German discrimination and insensitivity during the 1980s. Also new was a more liberal stance in previously conservative Jewish communities that had been governed autocratically and whose interests had been linked closely to both the Bonn government and the state of Israel. The fact is that Jews in Germany had always been aware of their dilemma, but they had always reacted with anxiety and skepticism to the way the Jewish Question was treated. Emphasis should be placed on the word *reaction*. Instead of taking the initiative, which many Jews had tried to do between 1945 and 1950, most Jews who remained in Germany after the Shoah *reacted* to conditions determined by the German government and their own organizations, or they refused to have anything to do with the Jewish community. With few exceptions, Jews in Germany did not reveal much about their awareness or seek to articulate it until the end of the 1970s. The consciousness was there, but a fear of exposing themselves to anti-Semitic attacks and a lack of viable venues to voice what they felt and knew led most Jews in Germany to keep a low profile.

Brumlik pointed to the Fassbinder scandal and the Bitburg fiasco as turning points with regard to a new Jewish consciousness. Yet there were and are many kinds of Jewish consciousness, all sensitized by issues of anti-Semitism and attitudes toward the Shoah. These different kinds of Jewish awareness were tempered by self-restraint until the telecast of the American television series *Holocaust* in 1979. This film about the treatment of Jews during the Nazi period engendered a massive emotional response by hundreds of thousands of Germans and also moved many Jews to air their concerns in public, many for the first time. The most important books published during this time were *Fremd im eigenen Land* (1979), edited by Henryk M. Broder and Michel Lang, and *Dies ist nicht mein Land—Eine Jüdin verläßt die Bundesrepublik* (1980) by Lea Fleischmann. What was new in these works and in the public sphere was not so much the consciousness of these Jewish writers, but the manner in which they decided to articulate their consciousness and organize others. If indeed there was a *new* consciousness, it consisted in a conscious strategy that Jews were conceiving to guarantee a tolerable life in Germany. After all, by 1980 the Jews who were in Germany had made a decision to stay and to regard Germany as their country. Brumlik used the discreet term "Jews in Germany" in his lecture, rather than German Jews. A review of the demographics of Jews in Germany during the first three decades of the twentieth century, however, shows stunning similarities regarding the historical formation and mix of the Jewish population. Just as there are at present assimilated and religious Jews born in Germany, Eastern European Jews from all regions including Russia, Israelis who continually visit Germany, and Iranian Jews—all of whom live and seek to define themselves as Jews in Germany today—there were similar groups in Germany from 1900 to 1933. In other words, there never was a "pure" German Jew, nor is there one now. But there were and are German Jews, and they began playing a more provocative and visible role in 1980 to demonstrate *different* interests and experiences. Clearly, this new interventionism has added a significant dimension to the consciousness of German Jews and deepened their understanding of what it means to stay in Germany. They felt responsible (and guilty) for the way Germans as a nation acted in international affairs, they responded to Israel's policies as Jews in the Diaspora, and they were now quick to criticize in public offensive German actions. To make their concerns known, they employed various strategies through films, television, books, journals, and so forth. There were two distinct aims in these strategies that continue to play a role today: (1) to impress on Germans what it meant and means to be Jewish in Germany and thus to undermine Jewish stereotypes and expose new forms of German anti-Semitism and (2) to formulate what it means to represent Jewishness in Germany and whether it is meaningful to live in a perpetual dilemma.

The dramatic increase in the number and variety of publications by German Jews since 1980 is indicative of how crucial it became for German Jews to voice their views and insist that the Jewish perspective be included in public debates and official decision making. Some representative examples of this new literature include: (1) journals and magazines such as *Babylon: Beiträge zur jüdischen Gegenwart* (founded in 1986), which appears semi-annually and addresses an intellectual readership, and *Tachles* (founded in 1989), an independent quarterly that seeks to appeal to younger Jewish readers as a critical forum; (2) scholarly books that explore cultural problems and developments of German Jews, such as Klara Carmely's *Das Identitätsproblem jüdischer Autoren im deutschen Sprachraum: Von der Jahrhundertwende bis zu Hitler* (1981) and Günter Grimm and Hans-Peter Bayerdörfer's *Im Zeichen Hiobs: Jüdische Schriftsteller und deutsche Literatur im 20. Jahrhundert* (1985); (3) histories and documentaries of Jewish life in the Federal Republic, the German Democratic Republic, and Austria, such as Micha Brumlik, Doron Kiesel, Cilly Kugelmann, and

Julius Schoeps, eds., *Jüdisches Leben in Deutschland seit 1945* (1986), Günter Gorschenek and Stephan Reimers, eds., *Offene Wunden—brennende Fragen: Juden in Deutschland von 1938 bis heute* (1989), Robin Ostow, *Jüdisches Leben in der DDR* (1989), and Ruth Beckermann, *Unzugehörig: Österreicher und Juden nach 1945* (1989); (4) autobiographies by Jews of the older generation, such as Inge Deutschkron's *Ich trug den gelben Stern* (1983), which was also adapted by Volker Ludwig as a play for children entitled *Ab heute heißt du Sara* and performed by the famous Grips Theater of Berlin in 1990; (5) reportages such as Peter Sichrovsky's *Wir wissen nicht was morgen wird, wir wissen wohl was gestern war: Junge Juden in Deutschland und Österreich* (1985); (6) political analyses such as *Ist der Nationalsozialismus Geschichte? Zu Historisierung und Historikerstreit* (1987) edited by Dan Diner and *Ewige Schuld? 40 Jahre deutsch-jüdisch-israelische Beziehungen* (1988) by Michael Wolffsohn; (7) novels and stories such as Barbara Honigmann's *Roman von einem Kinde* (1986), Jurek Becker's *Bronsteins Kinder* (1986), Katja Behrens's *Von einem Ort zum anderen* (1987), Esther Dischereit's *Joemis Tisch* (1988), and Rafael Seligmann's *Rubinsteins Versteigerung* (1989); and (8) poetry such as Robert Schindel's *Im Herzen die Krätze* (1988), Matthias Hermann's *72 Buchstaben* (1989), and Helena Janeczek's *Ins Freie* (1989).

Most of these works were produced by Jewish writers born after the Shoah and raised in Germany and Austria. Given the difficult circumstances of their youth as children of survivors, one of their major concerns was to "come out" and define what their Jewishness has meant to them in revolt against the manner in which Germans sought to define Jews and the "Jewish problem." These younger writers were the first to depict in their fiction and poetry live Jews—that is, Jews who experienced what it meant to grow up in Germany and Austria in the post-Shoah period. This is not to imply that the older generation of Jewish writers had neglected to deal with Jewish identity in the post-Shoah period. In fact, one glance at Jürgen Schultz's *Mein Judentum* (1978), which contains fascinating autobiographical essays by Günther Anders, Jean Améry, Hilde Domin, Michael Landmann, Lily Pincus, Manès

Sperber, Hans Mayer, Wolfgang Hildesheimer, and Robert Jungk, among others, reveals that Jewish writers of the older generation continually provided the spark if not the frame for many writers of the younger generation, both Jewish and non-Jewish, who have sought to inquire into the meaning of Jewishness in light of the Shoah and German history.

Aside from the rediscovery of the Frankfurt school during the late 1960s and the growing importance of other German-Jewish philosophers such as Ernst Bloch, Hannah Arendt, Günther Anders, and Hans Jonas, there are five very different Jewish writers of this older generation who should be noted. These authors played a key role as provocateurs from 1967 to 1990 in confronting German culture from the Jewish margins and influenced the mainstream of German intellectual and political thought: Marcel Reich-Ranicki, Hans Mayer, Norbert Elias, Alphons Silbermann, and Ralph Giordano.

Born in Poland in 1920, Reich-Ranicki escaped from the Warsaw Ghetto and fought in the Jewish resistance movement during the 1940s. After the war, he worked for the Polish government and was active as a journalist and editor in Warsaw. In 1958 he left Poland and began working as a literary critic for different newspapers and journals such as the *Frankfurter Allgemeine Zeitung, Die Welt,* and *Die Zeit.* In addition to his work as a journalist, he was a literary critic for radio and television, and it would not be an exaggeration to say that Reich-Ranicki became the most renowned critic of German literature in the postwar period. A great essayist, knowledgeable and witty, he also made it a point to write in a German-Jewish tradition of irony and provocation reminiscent of Börne and Heine, two of his favorite authors. His book *Über Ruhestörer: Juden in der deutschen Literatur* (1973) was one of the first studies to deal with key writers in the German-Jewish tradition, and he has continually provided a forum for discussing the essence of the Jewish contribution to German literature in such other works as *Der doppelte Boden* (1992) and *Die Anwälte der Literatur* (1994).

Much in the same manner as did Reich-Ranicki, the equally prominent Hans Mayer

spent the Nazi period in Switzerland. Born in 1907 in Cologne, in 1946 he became professor of German literature at the University of Leipzig and was regarded as the foremost Marxist literary critic in the German Democratic Republic. In 1964, however, Mayer decided to leave East Germany and accept a position at the Technical University of Hannover. Already well known in the West, Mayer had a great influence in German literary circles, especially because he dared to raise sociopolitical issues in his writings, and he did so with an enormous breadth of knowledge and perspicacity. Like Reich-Ranicki, Mayer appeared often on television and was considered an authority on German literature, but he always favored the great writers on the margins of mainstream German literature. His books *Außenseiter* (1975) and *Der Widerruf: Über Deutsche und Juden* (1994), among others, point to the failure of the bourgeois Enlightenment to incorporate women, homosexuals, and Jews into its program. At the same time, Mayer's own program of recuperation reveals to what extent the marginal Jewish writers have invigorated German culture and continue to do so.

One of Mayer's major concerns departed from that articulated by Freud in *Das Unbehagen an der Kultur:* he continually investigated how writers did or did not fit into the "civilizing process" of Germany. This concern was shared by Norbert Elias, born in 1897 in Breslau. After studying with Karl Mannheim at the University of Heidelberg during the 1920s and teaching in Frankfurt, Elias emigrated to England in 1933, where he became professor of sociology at the University of Leicester. His major work, *Über den Prozeß der Zivilisation,* first published in 1938, was rediscovered during the 1970s and had a profound effect on German sociologists and literary critics. Though he was primarily concerned with the socialization of Jews during the reign of Louis XIV, Elias drew parallels to the authoritarian tradition in Germany, parallels that become most evident in his significant study *Studien über die Deutschen: Machtkämpfe und Habitusentwicklung im 19. und 20. Jahrhundert* (1989). Though he adopted an approach different from that of Mayer and the sociologists of the Frankfurt school, Elias shared the same goal of what might be called the "Jewish Enlightenment." As he stated in his autobiographical book, *Über sich selbst* (1990), "I earnestly believe that we live in a thicket of mythologies and that one of our major tasks today is to clean them out. The great spring cleaning—that's what has to happen."

Spring cleaning has been typical of Alphons Silbermann's work. Born in 1909 in Cologne, Silbermann studied law before he was forced into exile in 1935. After spending time in Holland and France, Silbermann emigrated to Australia, where he eventually became a sociologist of music and made a name for himself in this field. In 1964, he became a professor of mass communication and sociology at the University of Cologne, but he also turned his attention to the question of anti-Semitism in Germany and wrote numerous revealing essays concerning the development of anti-Semitism. Two of his most important works are *Was ist jüdischer Geist? Zur Identität der Juden* (1984) and with Herbert Sallen, *Juden in Westdeutschland: Selbstbild und Fremdbild einer Minorität* (1992). In these studies, as well as in his compelling autobiography, *Verwandlungen* (1989), Silbermann made full use of empirical research about the various forms that anti-Semitism assumed in post-Shoah Germany and made bold statements about the inability of the Germans to deal with this anti-Semitism. Such a critique endowed his work with an edge that made him an uncomfortable critic in West Germany.

The same could be said for Ralph Giordano. Born in 1923 in Hamburg, Giordano was subjected to discrimination by the Nazis because his mother was Jewish. Arrested by the Gestapo and tortured, he was released from prison in 1943 and survived the war in hiding. In 1946 he began working as a journalist in Hamburg, and from 1961 on, he was a news broadcaster for different television stations. A muckraking critic with enormous integrity, Giordano won many awards for his reports about the Third World and about contemporary political themes. In 1985 his autobiographical novel, *Die Bertinis,* became an international success and was made into a remarkable television film directed by Egon Monk. Two years later, he published *Die zweite Schuld oder Von der Last Deutscher zu sein* (1987), which accused the Germans of denying the Nazi past and passing on their sins to the younger generation. This book evoked such a strong reaction from Germans that Giordano's life was threatened several times. Nevertheless, he continued to voice his outspoken views in such other books as *Wenn Hitler den Krieg gewonnen hätte: Die Pläne der Nazis nach dem Endsieg* (1989), and he is still involved in numerous debates about Israel and the attitudes of Germans toward Jews.

Giordano's outspokenness is somewhat typical of the major Jewish writers of his generation; from 1967 to 1989 their voices became even stronger than before and more intent on dealing with their Jewishness and the normalization process. By the time the new German state was declared in 1990, these writers had helped prepare for an even greater Jewish cultural renascence based on outspokenness and provocation.

1990–96: The Resurgence of New Jewish Writers

In his literary history *Juden in der deutschen Literatur* (1992), Hans Schütz remarks that although the Jews do not play much of a political, economic, or cultural role in Germany, "the German-Jewish relationship is still precarious, especially since there is a latent anti-Semitism and an extreme right movement" (32). This statement certainly needs to be qualified. If we consider the manner in which the Frankfurt school and writers like Reich-Ranicki, Mayer, Silbermann, Elias, Giordano, Bloch, and others have shaped some of the major cultural and political debates in Germany, it is clear that these few Jewish writers and their questions have played an enormous role in Germany. Moreover, most of the major controversies in Germany have taken shape against the backdrop of the Shoah. In other words, Jewish writing has had an influence, visible and invisible, that has stamped Germany in incalculable ways. Further, Jewish writers have focused their attention more on what it means to be Jewish after the reunification of East and West Germany and have increased their productivity and intensity, especially as provocateurs who want Germans to realize that Jews are very much a part of Germany both today and into the future.

Perhaps the best way to gauge Jewish reaction to a united Germany is to read Henryk M. Broder's *Erbarmen mit den Deutschen* (1993). As the enfant terrible among Jewish journalists, Broder (b. 1946), the son of Polish immigrants who came to Cologne in 1958, has never been one to hold his tongue. After coediting *Fremd im eigenen Land* in 1979, he has become involved in almost every major debate concerning Germans and Jews, even though he purportedly emigrated to Israel in 1981. Writing in the tradition of Heine, Tucholsky, and Kraus, Broder has little tolerance for hypocrisy. If public awareness has been raised about the dilemma of Jews in Germany today, Broder must be given a great deal of credit. In *Der ewige Antisemit* (1986), he criticized the Germans' general assumptions that perpetuated false notions about Jews and kept anti-Semitism alive. In *Erbarmen mit den Deutschen,* Broder delivered a pessimistic prognosis of the future in Germany by demonstrating how foreigners, refugees, Jews, Turks, and homeless people have been brutalized in the new state and how strikes, corruption, and mismanagement are placing a great strain on democracy. Nor does Broder spare Jews who collaborate in the process, just as Rafael Seligmann—in his novel *Die jiddische Mamme* (1990) and his collection of essays *Mit beschränkter Hoffnung* (1991)—demands that Jews realize that they are part of Germany and that they must start taking themselves more seriously as German Jews to play a significant role in its future.

It appears that the major issue in Jewish writing since 1990 has been defining—to Germans and to Jews themselves—what Jewishness means in a post-Shoah context and, more specifically, in a changing Germany in which many new Jewish emigrants are settling and making their voices heard. Fiction writers such as Maxim Biller (*Wenn ich einmal reich und tot bin,* 1990, and *Land der Väter und Verräter,* 1994), Barbara Honigmann (*Eine Liebe aus Nichts,* 1991), Esther Dischereit (*Merryn,* 1992), Edgar Hilsenrath (*Josel Wassermanns Heimkehr,* 1993), Katja Behrens (*Salomo und die Anderen: Jüdische Geschichten,* 1993), Jean-

nette Lander (*Jahrhundert der Herren,* 1993), and Valentin Senger (*Die Buchsweilers,* 1994) are all concerned not only with the manner in which Germany has marked Jewish lives, but also with the way in which Jews assert themselves in a country that tries to deny their existence. This concern is also evident in the work of Jewish writers in Austria such as Peter Stefan Jungk (*Tigor,* 1991) and Robert Schindel (*Gebürtig,* 1992, and *Gott schützt uns vor den guten Menschen,* 1995) as well as in the plays of George Tabori (*Weisman und Rotgesicht,* 1990, and *Goldberg-Variationen,* 1991) and in the autobiographies of Andreas Sinakowski (*Das Verhör,* 1991) and Chaim Noll (*Nachtgedanken über Deutschland,* 1992). It is not too difficult to define exactly what the *Jewish* concerns of these writers are, though each of their perspectives and styles is unique.

It is much more difficult, however, to determine what constitutes the common Jewishness of these contemporary writers and their writings. Is there indeed something essentially Jewish about Jewish writing in German? Has there always been something clearly Jewish about Jewish writing in German that makes it recognizable? The point of the present volume is for us to explore both the Jewishness of Jewish writing in Germany and its Germanness without a predisposition to try to define any of our main terms. This is not a "post-modern" gesture. It is an acknowledgment that even the most negative definitions of "Jew," "German," and writing—those found between 1933 and 1945 under the Nazis—affected the self-awareness and identity of writers. Even more profoundly have other definitions in their infinite combinations shaped writers who have seen themselves as producing Jewish writing in German culture. This volume is dedicated to providing access to some of this complexity.

Bibliography

H. G. Adler, *Die Juden in Deutschland: Von der Aufklärung bis zum Nationalsozialismus* (Munich: Kösel, 1960); Adler, *Der verwaltete Mensch: Studien zur Deportation der Juden aus Deutschland* (Tübingen: Mohr, 1974); Adler, Hermann Langbein, and Ella Lingens-Rainer, *Auschwitz: Zeugnisse und Berichte,* 2d rev. ed. (Cologne:

Europäische Verlagsanstalt, 1979); Jean Améry, *Jenseits von Schuld und Sühne* (Stuttgart: Klett Cotta, 1976); Thomas Ammer, "Wandlungen im Verhältnis der DDR-Führung zum Judentum," *Deutschland Archiv* 21 (July 1988): 699–703; Günther Anders, *Besuch im Hades* (Munich: Beck, 1979); Hannah Arendt, *Eichmann in Jerusalem: A Report on the Banality of Evil* (New York: Viking, 1963); Arendt, *The Jew as Pariah: Jewish Identity and Politics in the Modern Age* (New York: Grove, 1978); Wilfried Barner, *Von Rahel Varnhagen bis Friedrich Gundolf: Juden als deutsche Goethe-Verehrer* (Wolfenbüttel: Lessing-Akademie, 1992; Göttingen: Wallstein, 1992); Zygmunt Bauman, "Exit Visas and Entry Tickets: Paradoxes of Jewish Assimilation," *Telos* 77 (fall 1988): 45–78; Bauman, *Modernity and the Holocaust* (Ithaca, N.Y.: Cornell University Press, 1989); Bauman, "Strangers: The Social Construction of Universality and Particularity," *Telos* 78 (winter 1988–89): 7–42; Ruth Beckermann, *Unzugehörig: Österreicher und Juden nach 1945* (Vienna: Löcker, 1989); Wolfgang Benz and Marion Neiss, eds., *Deutsch-jüdisches Exil, das Ende der Assimilation? Identitätsprobleme deutscher Juden in der Emigration* (Berlin: Metropol, 1994); Dietz Bering, *The Stigma of Names: Anti-Semitism in German Daily Life, 1812–1933,* trans. Neville Plaice (Cambridge: Polity Press, 1992); David Biale, *Power & Powerlessness in Jewish History* (New York: Schocken, 1987); Jean-Paul Bier, *Auschwitz et les nouvelles littératures allemandes* (Brussels: Université de Bruxelles, 1979); Dirk Blasius and Dan Diner, eds., *Zerbrochene Geschichte: Leben und Selbstverständnis der Juden in Deutschland* (Frankfurt a. M.: Fischer, 1991); Y. Michael Bodemann, *Gedächtnistheater: Die jüdische Gemeinschaft und ihre deutsche Erfindung* (Hamburg: Rotbuch, 1996); Achim von Borries, ed., *Selbstzeugnisse des deutschen Judentums, 1861–1945* (Frankfurt a. M.: Fischer, 1988); Hamida Bosmajian, *Metaphors of Evil: Contemporary German Literature and the Shadow of Nazism* (Iowa City: Iowa University Press, 1979); Leon Botstein, *Judentum und Modernität: Essays zur Rolle der Juden in der deutschen und österreichischen Kultur, 1848 bis 1938* (Vienna: Böhlau, 1991); Daniel Boyarin and Jonathan Boyarin, "Diaspora: Generation and the Ground of Jewish Identity," *Critical Inquiry* 19 (1993): 693–725; Sandra Braude, *Windswept Plains* (Cape Town: Buschu Books, 1991); Michael Brenner, *Nach dem Holocaust: Juden in Deutschland 1945–1950* (Munich: Beck, 1995); Brenner, *The Renaissance of Jewish Culture in Weimar Germany* (New Haven: Yale University Press, 1996); Henryk M. Broder, "Antisemitismus ohne Antisemiten: Über die jüngste Variante eines alten Vorurteils," *Tribune: Zeitschrift zum Verständnis des Judentums* 88 (1983): 75–

87; Broder, *Erbarmen mit den Deutschen* (Hamburg: Hoffmann and Campe, 1993); Broder, *Der ewige Antisemit: Über Sinn und Funktion eines beständigen Gefühls* (Frankfurt a. M.: Fischer, 1986); Broder, "Tote Seelen in Berlin oder: Die wundersame Wiederaufstehung der jüdischen Gemeinde Adass Jisroel als Familienbetrieb—eine deutsch-jüdische Posse aus der Wendezeit," *Die Zeit* 40 (Oct. 4, 1991): 16; Broder, "Die treudeutschen Dummheiten des Gesinnungsidioten: Interview mit Christian Ströbele," *Semit* 2 (1991): 10–12, 86; Broder and Michel R. Lang, eds., *Fremd im eigenen Land: Juden in der Bundesrepublik* (Frankfurt a. M.: Fischer, 1979); David Bronsen, ed., *Jews and Germans from 1860 to 1933: The Problematic Symbiosis* (Heidelberg: Winter, 1979); Micha Brumlik, *Der anti-Alt: Wider die furchtbare Friedfertigkeit* (Frankfurt a. M.: Eichborn, 1991); Brumlik, "The Situation of the Jews in Today's Germany" (Bloomington: The Jewish Studies Program of Indiana University, 1991); Brumlik, Doron Kiesel, Cilly Kugelmann, and Julius Schoeps, eds., *Jüdisches Leben in Deutschland seit 1945* (Frankfurt a. M.: Athenäum, 1986); John Bunzl, *Der lange Arm der Erinnerung: Jüdisches Bewußtsein heute* (Vienna: Böhlau, 1987); Erica Burgauer, *Zwischen Erinnerung und Verdrängung: Juden in Deutschland nach 1945* (Hamburg: Rowohlt, 1993); Klara Carmely, *Das Identitätsproblem jüdischer Autoren im deutschen Sprachraum. Von der Jahrhundertwende bis zu Hitler* (Königstein / Taunus: Scriptor, 1981); Detlev Claussen, *Grenzen der Aufklärung: Zur gesellschaftlichen Geschichte des modernen Antisemitismus* (Frankfurt a. M.: Fischer, 1987); Claussen, *Jüdisches Leben in Deutschland seit 1945* (Frankfurt a. M.: Athenäum, 1988); Michael Cohn, *The Jews in Germany, 1945–1993: The Building of a Minority* (Westport, Conn.: Praeger, 1994); Lucy Dawidowicz, *The War Against the Jews* (New York: Holt, Rinehart & Winston, 1975); Peter Demetz, *After the Fires: Recent Writing in the Germanies, Austria, and Switzerland* (New York: Harcourt Brace Jovanovich, 1986); Isaac Deutscher, *The Non-Jewish Jew and Other Essays* (Oxford: Oxford University Press, 1968); Dan Diner, ed., *Ist der Nationalismus Geschichte? Zu Historisierung und Historikerstreit* (Frankfurt a. M.: Fischer, 1987); Diner, ed., *Zivilisationsbruch: Denken nach Auschwitz* (Frankfurt a. M.: Fischer, 1987); Arnold M. Eisen, *Galut: Modern Jewish Reflection on Homelessness and Homecoming* (Bloomington: Indiana University Press, 1986); Norbert Elias, *Studien über die Deutschen: Machtkämpfe und Habitusentwicklung im 19. und 20. Jahrhundert* (Frankfurt a. M.: Suhrkamp, 1989); Elias, *Über sich selbst* (Frankfurt a. M.: Suhrkamp, 1990); Ismar Ellbogen and Eleanore Sterling, *Die Geschichte der Juden in Deutschland* (Frankfurt a. M.: Athenäum, 1988); Thomas Elsaesser, "West Germany's Inability to Commemorate: Between Bitburg and Bergen Belsen," *On Film* 14 (spring 1985); Bernd Engelmann, *Deutschland ohne Juden* (Cologne: Pahl-Rugenstein, 1988); Sidre Ezrahi, *By Words Alone: The Holocaust in Literature* (Chicago: University of Chicago Press, 1980); Lea Fleischmann, *Dies ist nicht mein Land: Eine Jüdin verläßt die Bundesrepublik* (Hamburg: Hoffmann and Campe, 1980); Fleischmann, *Ich bin Israelin: Erfahrungen in einem orientalischen Land* (Hamburg: Hoffmann and Campe, 1982); Saul Friedländer, *Reflections of Nazism: An Essay on Kitsch and Death,* trans. Thomas Weyr (New York: Harper & Row, 1984); Friedländer, *When Memory Comes,* trans. Helen R. Lane (New York: Farrar Straus Giroux, 1979); Peter Gay, *Freud, Jews and Other Germans* (New York: Oxford University Press, 1978); P. Gay, *Weimar Culture: The Outsider as Insider* (New York: Harper & Row, 1968); Ruth Gay, *The Jews of Germany: A Historical Portrait* (New Haven: Yale University Press, 1992); Mark H. Gelber, ed., *The Jewish Reception of Heinrich Heine* (Tübingen: Niemeyer, 1992); Sander L. Gilman, *Difference and Pathology: Stereotypes of Sexuality, Race, and Madness* (Ithaca, N.Y.: Cornell University Press, 1985); Gilman, *Jews in Today's German Culture* (Bloomington: Indiana University Press, 1995); Gilman, *Jewish Self-Hatred: Anti-Semitism and the Hidden Language of the Jews* (Baltimore, Md.: Johns Hopkins University Press, 1986); Gilman and Karen Remmler, eds., *Reemerging Jewish Culture in Germany: Life and Literature Since 1989* (New York: New York University Press, 1994); Ralph Giordano, *Wenn Hitler den Krieg gewonnen hätte: Die Pläne der Nazis nach dem Endsieg* (Hamburg: Rasch und Röhring, 1989); Giordano, *Die zweite Schuld oder Von der Last ein Deutscher zu sein* (Hamburg: Rasch und Röhring, 1987); Giordano, ed., *Deutschland und Israel: Solidarität in der Bewährung* (Gerlingen: Bleicher, 1992); Giordano, ed., *"Wie kann diese Generation eigentlich noch atmen?" Briefe zu dem Buch Die zweite Schuld oder Von der Last Deutsche zu sein* (Hamburg: Rasch und Röhring, 1990); Yitshak Goldkorn, *Heymishe und fremde: Literarishe etyudn* (Buenos Aires: Sevivah, 1973); Günter Gorschenek and Stephan Reimers, eds., *Offene Wunden—brennende Fragen: Juden in Deutschland von 1938 bis heute* (Frankfurt a. M.: Josef Knecht, 1989); Walter Grab, *Der deutsche Weg der Judenemanzipation, 1789–1938* (Munich: Piper, 1991); Grab, ed., *Gegenseite Einflüsse deutscher und jüdischer Kultur: Von der Epoche der Aufklärung bis zur Weimarer Republik* (Tel Aviv: Institut für deutsche Geschichte, 1984); Grab, ed., *Juden in der deutschen Wissenschaft: Internationales Symposium, April 1985* (Tel-Aviv: Universität Tel-Aviv, Institut für Deutsche Geschichte, 1986); Grab, ed., *Jüdische Integration und Identität in Deutschland und Österreich, 1848–1918* (Tel Aviv: Institut für deutsche Geschichte, 1984); Grab and Julius H. Schoeps, eds., *Juden in der Weimarer Republik* (Stuttgart: Burg, 1986); Mathias Greffrath, ed., *Die Zerstörung einer Zukunft: Gespräche mit emigrierten Sozialwissenschaftlern* (Reinbek bei Hamburg: Rowohlt, 1979); Günter E. Grimm and Hans-Peter Bayerdörfer, eds., *Im Zeichen Hiobs: Jüdische Schriftsteller und deutsche Literatur im 20. Jahrhundert* (Königstein / Taunus: Athenäum, 1985); Karl E. Grözinger, ed., *Judentum im deutschen Sprachraum* (Frankfurt a. M.: Suhrkamp, 1991); Frederic Grunfield, *Prophets Without Honor: A Background to Freud, Kafka, Einstein, and Their World* (New York: McGraw-Hill, 1979); Geoffrey Hartman, ed., *Bitburg in Moral and Political Perspective* (Bloomington: Indiana University Press, 1986); Jost Hermand and Gert Mattenklott, eds., *Jüdische Intelligenz in Deutschland* (Berlin: Argument, 1988); Deborah Herz, *Jewish High Society in Old Regime Berlin* (New Haven: Yale University Press, 1988); Renate Heuer, ed., *Bibliographia Judaica: Verzeichnis jüdischer Autoren deutscher Sprache,* 3 vols. (Frankfurt and New York: Campus Verlag, 1981–1988); Raul Hilberg, *The Destruction of the European Jews,* 3 vols. (New York: Holmes & Meier, 1985); Hans Otto Horch, ed., *Judentum, Antisemitismus und europäische Kultur* (Tübingen: Francke, 1988); Max Horkheimer and Theodor Adorno, *Dialektik der Aufklärung* (New York: Social Studies Association, 1944; Frankfurt a. M.: Fischer, 1969); Nicoline Hortzitz, *Der "Judenarzt": Historische und sprachliche Untersuchungen zur Diskriminierung eines Berufsstands in der fruhen Neuzeit* (Heidelberg: Winter, 1994); Annette Insdorf, *Incredible Shadows: Film and the Holocaust* (New York: Random House, 1983); Gustav Janouch, *Conversations with Kafka,* trans. Goronwy Rees (London: Derek Verschoyle, 1953); Martin Jay, *The Dialectical Imagination: A History of the Frankfurt School and the Institute of Social Research, 1932–1950* (Boston: Little, Brown, 1973); Walter Jens, *Juden und Christen in Deutschland* (Stuttgart: Radius-Verlag, 1989); Marion A. Kaplan, *The Making of the Jewish Middle Class: Women, Family, and Identity in Imperial Germany* (New York: Oxford University Press, 1991); Werner Keller, *Diaspora: The Post-Biblical History of the Jews,* trans. Richard and Clara Winston (London: Pitman, 1969); Elisabeth Kiderlen, ed., *Deutsch-jüdische Normalität . . . Fassbinders Sprengsätze* (Frankfurt a. M.: Pflastertrand, 1985); Hillel J. Kieval, *The Making of Czech Jewry: National Conflict and Jewish Society in Bohemia, 1870–1918* (Oxford: Oxford University Press, 1988); Victor Klemperer, *Curriculum Vitae,* ed. Walter Nowojski, 2 vols.

(Berlin: Rütten & Loening, 1989); Klemperer, *Ich will Zeugnis ablegen bis zum letzten: Tagebücher, 1933–45,* ed. Walter Nowojski with Hadwig Klemperer (Berlin: Aufbau, 1995); Klemperer, *LTI: Notizbuch eines Philologen* (Berlin: Aufbau, 1947); Klemperer, *Und so ist alles schwankend: Tagebücher Juni bis Dezember 1945,* ed. Günter Jäckel with Hadwig Klemperer (Berlin: Aufbau, 1996); Ruth Klüger, *Katastrophen: über deutsche Literatur* (Göttingen: Wallstein, 1994); Friedrich Knilli and Siegfried Zielinski, *Holocaust zur Unterhaltung: Anatomie eines internationalen Bestsellers* (Berlin: Elefanten Press, 1982); Gertrud Koch, "Corporate Identities: Zur Prosa von Dische, Biller und Seligmann," *Babylon* 7 (1990): 139–42; Koch, *Die Einstellung ist die Einstellung: Visuelle Konstruktionen des Judentums* (Frankfurt a. M.: Suhrkamp, 1992); Gustav Krojanker, *Juden in der deutschen Literatur: Essays über zeitgenössische Schriftsteller* (Berlin: Welt Verlag, 1922); Berel Lang, ed., *Writing and the Holocaust* (New York: Holmes & Meier, 1988); Lawrence L. Langer, *The Holocaust and the Literary Imagination* (New Haven: Yale University Press, 1975); Theodor Lessing, *Der jüdische Selbsthaß* (Munich: Matthes & Seitz, 1984, based on the first ed.; Berlin: Jüdischer Verlag, 1930); Heiner Lichtenstein, ed., *Die Fassbinder-Kontroverse oder Das Ende der Schonzeit* (Königstein: Athenäum, 1986); Solomon Liptzin, *Germany's Stepchildren* (1944; Cleveland: World, 1961); Dagmar C. G. Lorenz and Gabriele Weinberger, eds., *Insiders and Outsiders: Jewish and Gentile Culture in Germany and Austria* (Detroit: Wayne State University Press, 1994); Alfred D. Low, *Jews in the Eyes of the Germans: From the Enlightenment to Imperial Germany* (Philadelphia: Institute for the Study of Human Issues, 1979); Michael Löwy, *Redemption and Utopia* (Berkeley: University of California Press, 1992); Peter Märthesheimer and Ivo Frenzel, *Im Kreuzfeuer: Der Fernsehfilm 'Holocaust'* (Frankfurt a. M.: Fischer, 1979); Charles S. Maier, *The Unmasterable Past: History, Holocaust, and German National Identity* (Cambridge, Mass.: Harvard University Press, 1988); Gert Mattenklott ed., *Über Juden in Deutschland* (Frankfurt a. M.: Jüdischer Verlag, 1992); Hans Mayer, *Außenseiter* (Frankfurt a. M.: Suhrkamp, 1975); Mayer, *Der Widerruf: Über Deutsche und Juden* (Frankfurt a. M.: Suhrkamp, 1994); Lothar Mertens, "Jews in the GDR Today," *GDR Monitor* 20 (winter 1988–89): 43–56; Mertens, "Juden in der DDR: Eine schwindende Minderheit," *Deutschland Archiv* 19 (Nov. 1986): 1192–203; Judith Miller, *One by One: Facing the Holocaust* (New York: Simon and Schuster, 1990); Stéphane Moses and Albrecht Schöne, eds., *Juden in der deutschen Literatur: Ein deutsch-israelisches Symposium* (Frankfurt a. M.: Suhrkamp, 1986); George Mosse, *Germans and Jews* (New York: Howard Fertig, 1970); G. Mosse, *Confronting the Nation: Jewish and Western Nationalism* (Hanover, N.H.: University Press of New England, 1993); G. Mosse, *German Jews Beyond Judaism:* (Bloomington: Indiana University Press, 1985); Werner Mosse and Arnold Packer, eds., *Juden in Wilhelminischen Deutschland, 1890–1914* (Tübingen: J. C. Mohr, 1976); Donald Niewyk, *The Jews in Weimar Germany* (Manchester, Eng.: Manchester University Press, 1980); Robin Ostow, *Jüdisches Leben in der DDR* (Frankfurt a. M.: Athenäum, 1988); Anson Rabinbach, "German Intellectuals and the Gulf War," *Dissent* 38 (fall 1991): 459–63; Rabinbach, "The Jewish Question in the German Question," *New German Critique* 44 (1988): 159–92; Rabinbach and Jack Zipes, eds., *Germans and Jews Since the Holocaust* (New York: Holmes & Meier, 1986); Marcel Reich-Ranicki, *Die Anwälte der Literatur* (Stuttgart: Deutsche Verlags-Anstalt, 1994); Reich-Ranicki, *Der doppelte Boden: Ein Gespräch mit Peter von Matt* (Zurich: Ammann, 1992); Reich-Ranicki, *Über Ruhestörer: Juden in der deutschen Literatur* (Munich: Piper, 1973; 2d rev. ed., Stuttgart: Deutsche Verlags-Anstalt, 1989); Eva G. Reichmann, *Grösse und Verhängnis deutsch-jüdischer Existenz: Zeugnisse einer tragischen Begegnung* (Heidelberg: Schneider, 1974); Jehuda Reinharz, *Fatherland or Promised Land: The Dilemma of the German Jew, 1893–1914* (Ann Arbor: University of Michigan Press, 1975); Reinharz and Walter Schatzberg, eds., *The Jewish Response to German Culture: From the Enlightenment to the Second World War* (Hanover, N.H.: University Press of New England, 1985); Monika Richarz, ed., *Bürger auf Widerruf: Lebenszeugnisse deutscher Juden, 1780–1945* (Munich: C. H. Beck, 1989); Régine Robin, *L'amour du yiddish: Ecriture juive et sentiment de la langue* (Paris: Sorbier, 1984); Alvin H. Rosenfeld, *A Double Dying: Reflection on Holocaust Literature* (Bloomington: Indiana University Press, 1980); Rosenfeld, *Imagining Hitler* (Bloomington: Indiana University Press, 1985); Marsha L. Rozenblit, *The Jews of Vienna, 1867–1914: Assimilation and Identity* (Albany: State University of New York Press, 1983); Reinhard Rürup, *Emanzipation und Antisemitismus:* (Göttingen: Vandenhoeck & Ruprecht, 1975); Rachel Salamander, ed., *The Jewish World of Yesterday, 1860–1938* (New York: Rizzoli, 1991); Robert Schindel, *Gott schützt uns vor den guten Menschen: Jüdisches Gedächtnis—Auskunftsbüro der Angst* (Frankfurt a. M.: Suhrkamp, 1995); Johann N. Schmidt, "'Those Unfortunate Years': Nazism in the Public Debate of Post-War Germany" (Bloomington, Indiana: The Jewish Studies Program, 1987); Michael Schneider, *Den Kopf verkehrt aufgesetzt oder Die melancholische Linke* (Darmstadt:

Luchterhand, 1981); Julius H. Schoeps, ed., *Juden als Träger bürgerlicher Kultur in Deutschland* (Stuttgart: Burg Verlag, 1989); Gershom Scholem, *On Jews and Judaism in Crisis* (New York: Schocken, 1976); Rolf Schörken and Dieter Jürgen Löwisch, eds., *Das doppelte Antlitz: Zur Wirkungsgeschichte deutsch-jüdischer Künstler und Gelehrter* (Paderborn: Schönigh, 1990); Hans-Jürgen Schultz, ed., *Mein Judentum* (Stuttgart: Kreuz, 1978); Hans Schütz, *Juden in der deutschen Literatur: Eine deutsch-jüdische Literaturgeschichte im Überblick* (Munich: Piper, 1992); Dietrich Schwanitz, "Surrealpolitik oder die deutsche Reaktion auf den Golfkrieg im Spiegel der deutschen und internationalen Presse," *Semit* 3 (May-June 1991): 7–9; Valentin Senger, *Die Buchsweilers* (Frankfurt a. M.: Fischer, 1994); Senger, *Kaiserhofstraße 12* (Darmstadt: Luchterhand, 1979); Peter Sichrovsky, *Schuldig geboren: Kinder aus Nazi Familien* (Cologne: Kiepenheuer und Witsch, 1987); Sichrovsky, *Wir wissen nicht was morgen wird, wir wissen wohl was gestern war: Junge Juden in Deutschland und Österreich* (Cologne: Kiepenheuer & Witsch, 1985); Alphons Silbermann, *Verwandlungen: Eine Autobiographie* (Bergisch Gladbach: Lübbe, 1989); Silbermann and Herbert Sallen, *Juden in Westdeutschland: Selbstbild und Fremdbild einer Minorität* (Cologne: Verlag Wissenschaft und Politik, 1992); David Sorkin, *The Transformation of German Jewry, 1780–1840* (New York: Oxford University Press, 1987); Inge Stephan, Sabine Schilling, and Sigrid Weigel, eds., *Jüdische Kultur und Weiblichkeit in der Moderne* (Cologne: Bohlau, 1994); Frank Stern, "The Historic Triangle: Occupiers, Germans and Jews in Postwar Germany," *Tel Aviver Jahrbuch für deutsche Geschichte* 19 (1990): 47–66; Herbert A. Strauss and Norbert Kampe, eds., *Antisemitismus: Von der Judenfeindschaft zum Holocaust* (Bonn: Schriftenreihe für politische Bildung, 1985); Strauss and C. Hoffmann, eds., *Juden und Judentum in der Literatur* (Munich: dtv, 1985); Pierre-André Taguieff, "La nouvelle Judéophobie: Antisionisme, Antiracisme, Anti-impérialisme," *Les Temps Modernes* 520 (Nov. 1989): 1–80; Enzo Traverso, *The Jews and Germany: From the 'Judeo-German Symbiosis' to the Memory of Auschwitz,* trans. Daniel Weissbort (Lincoln: University of Nebraska Press, 1995); Eveline Valtink, ed., *Jüdische Identität im Spiegel der Literatur vor und nach Auschwitz* (Hofgeismar: Evangelische Akademie Hofgeismar, 1988); Verband der Jüdischen Gemeinden in der DDR, *Damit die Nacht nicht wiederkehre: Gedenken an die faschistische Pogromnacht vom 9. November 1938* (Berlin: Panorama DDR, 1988); Berthold Viertel, "Der nicht mehr deutsch spricht," *An den Wind geschrieben: Lyrik der Freiheit, Gedichte der Jahre 1933–1945,* ed. Manfred Schlösser (Darmstadt: Agora, 1960), p. 83; Shulamit Volkov, *Jüdisches Leben und Antisemitismus im 19. und 20. Jahrhundert* (Munich: C. H. Beck, 1990); Jacob Wassermann, *Deutscher und Jude: Reden und Schriften 1904–1933* (Heidelberg: Lambert Schneider, 1984); Wassermann, *Mein Weg als Deutscher und Jude* (Berlin: S. Fischer, 1921); Wassermann, *Selbstbetrachtungen* (Berlin: S. Fischer, 1933); Robert Weltsch, *Die deutsche Judenfrage: Ein kritischer Rückblick* (Königstein: Jüdischer Verlag, 1981); Erhard R. Wiehn, ed., *Juden in der Soziologie: Eine öffentliche Vortragsreihe an der Universität Konstanz 1989* (Konstanz: Hartung-Gorre, 1989); Robert S. Wistrich, *Austrians and Jews in the Twentieth Century: From Franz Joseph to Waldheim* (New York: St. Martin's Press, 1992); Wistrich, *The Jews of Vienna in the Age of Franz Joseph* (Oxford: Oxford University Press, 1989); Wistrich, *Socialism and the Jews: The Dilemmas of Assimilation in Germany and Austria-Hungary* (East Brunswick, N.J.: Associated University Presses, 1982); Michael Wolffsohn, *Ewige Schuld? 40 Jahre deutsch-jüdisch-israelische Beziehungen* (Munich: Piper, 1988); Yosef Hayim Yerushalmi, *Zakhor, Jewish History and Jewish Memory* (Seattle: University of Washington Press, 1982); James E. Young, *Writing and Rewriting the Holocaust: Narrative and the Consequences of Interpretation* (Bloomington: Indiana University Press, 1990); Jack Zipes, "Jewish Consciousness in Germany Today," *Telos* 93 (1992): 159–72; Zipes, "Die kulturelle Operationen von Deutschen und Juden im Spiegel der neueren deutschen Literatur," *Babylon* 8 (1991): 34–44; Zipes, *The Operated Jew: Two Tales of Anti-Semitism* (New York: Routledge, 1991); Harry Zohn, *Wiener Juden in der deutschen Literatur* (Tel-Aviv: Edition "Olamenu," 1964); Zohn, ". . . ich bin ein Sohn der deutschen Sprache nur . . . ": *Jüdisches Erbe in der österreichischen Literatur* (Vienna: Amalthea, 1986); Mosche Zuckermann, "The Curse of Forgetting: Israel and the Holocaust," *Telos* 78 (winter 1988–89): 43–54; Gerhard Zwerenz, *Die Rückkehr des toten Juden nach Deutschland* (Ismaning bei Munich: Max Heuber, 1986).

SANDER L. GILMAN AND JACK ZIPES

May–June 1096 Crusading assaults are launched against the Jewish communities of Worms, Mainz, and Cologne, the three great centers of late-eleventh-century life in northern Europe

On November 7, 1095, at the closing session of the Council of Clermont, Pope Urban II challenged the knights of western Christendom to take up arms, to exact revenge upon the Muslim world, and to liberate the sacred shrines of Christianity in the Holy Land. The crusading campaign called forth by Urban II ended at the walls of Jerusalem in June 1099 with a stunning victory for the entire Christian world. Inevitably, the pope's bold vision could not be realized in precisely the manner intended. Urban II envisioned an organized and well-equipped military force setting forth under the leadership of one of his lieutenants. The knights of Europe, however, were unwilling to subordinate themselves to the leadership of the Church. They preferred instead to organize their own armies—forces that sometimes worked in tandem and sometimes at loggerheads, forces that often diverged from their stated objective and carved out for themselves rich principalities throughout the Near East. But the crusading armies, for all their shortcomings, managed to fight their way eastward and, in June 1099, they successfully breached the walls of Jerusalem. The goal of the papal call had been achieved, although the means to this achievement differed radically from those projected by the ecclesiastical leadership that had set the movement in motion.

Exhilarated responses to Urban II's call to the crusade extended far beyond the knighthood of western Christendom. The papal challenge at Clermont evoked an unexpected but powerful reaction among broad segments of the populace. Biblical imagery of victory assured by the Lord to those of pure heart surfaced all across Europe (particularly in the northern areas) as popular preachers fanned the flames of enthusiasm. Just as the military expedition escaped the control of its papal instigator, so too did the popular movement set off in directions of its own. In many instances these directions were inimical to traditional Church thinking and practice. It is in this popular response to the papal initiative that the roots of the crusade-related anti-Jewish violence of 1096 are found.

More specifically, both Christian and Jewish writers note how many within the popular crusading ranks quickly and curiously transformed the crusading call into a rationale for immediate anti-Jewish violence. For example, one formulation of an anti-Jewish slogan rapidly emerged: "Behold we travel to a distant land to do battle with the kings of that land. We take our lives in our hands in order to kill and to subjugate all those kingdoms which do not believe in the Crucified. How much more so [should we kill and subjugate] the Jews, who killed and crucified him." This dangerous slogan, although clearly rooted in traditional Church teachings that preached Jewish culpability for the crucifixion of Jesus, diverged radically from accepted ecclesiastical

1

doctrine. The slogan was also vigorously repudiated by the leadership of the Second Crusade, who were fully aware of the potential for crusade-related anti-Jewish outbursts. In 1096, however, the organized Church was as yet unaware of the diverse distortions that the papal call would elicit.

The most effective of the popular preachers associated with the First Crusade was the enigmatic Peter the Hermit. Peter preached across the length and breadth of northern France, attracting followers by the thousands. There are no significant signs of anti-Jewish violence in northern France associated with the popular army that coalesced around Peter the Hermit, which is a tribute in all likelihood to Peter's own leadership and to the relative strength and stability of the northern French authorities. During the spring months of 1096, Peter and his followers—ill provisioned and poorly armed—set out for the East, confident of divine approbation and the support of those whom they would encounter on their sacred mission. In April, Peter reached the Rhineland, where he was able to gain requisite financial support, inter alia, from the Jewish community of Trier. On Easter Sunday, April 13, 1096, Peter preached in Cologne before a multitude. By this time, the pressure within the ranks of his followers to depart for the East was overwhelming. Many thousands of Peter's cohort headed eastward on Tuesday, April 15, with Peter and the remainder of his army departing at the beginning of the following week. In effect, Peter stirred up the same crusading ardor that he had generated in France but did not tarry long enough to take active command of those who responded to his message.

The French followers of Peter the Hermit were more than a little unruly, both in their everyday behavior and in their rejection of accepted ecclesiastical norms. The popular movement unleashed by Peter the Hermit in Germany was yet more anarchic. Miracles abounded among these unorganized German bands, and popular discontent with the Church manifested itself in a bizarre arrogation of ecclesiastical privileges. Particularly striking was the intensity of anti-Jewish animus. As reported by a Jewish observer, a re-

port spread that "anyone who kills a Jew will have all his sins absolved." In the Rhineland, the widespread and intense deflection of the crusading call into a rationalization for violence against the Jews lay at the heart of the outbreaks during spring 1096.

Distortion of the crusading message—the central catalyst for the violence of 1096—mobilized the German popular crusading forces against the Jewish communities of the Rhineland. The hostility rampant in these popular crusading bands was related to broad anti-Jewish animosity in the urban areas of the Rhineland. In general, northern European Jewry was a late-developing network of Jewish settlements attracted by the new economic opportunities available in this rapidly developing area and by the support and encouragement of key baronial and royal figures. The Jews of northern Europe faced considerable hostility because of their immigrant status, their unique circumstances as the only legitimate dissidents in an otherwise homogeneous society, their business endeavors, their firm alliance with the authorities, and the long legacy of Christian anti-Jewish teaching. Although this hostility can be noted all across northern Europe, the emergence of radical anti-Jewish doctrine among popular bands of German crusaders and the breakdown of imperial control in the Rhineland at this critical juncture paved the way for a limited, but vigorous and costly, outbreak of violence during the spring months of 1096.

A harbinger of what was to come occurred in the town of Speyer on Saturday, May 3. Plans were laid for an assault on the newly settled Jews of Speyer as they made their way from the synagogue of that town. Alerted to the danger, the Jews completed their prayers early and gained the safety of their homes. Frustrated in their designs, the attackers—a combination of crusaders and burghers—vented their rage upon a small number of Jews, killing eleven. The bishop of Speyer responded quickly and decisively, squashing the violence, punishing some of the burghers involved, and sequestering his Jews in fortified rural redoubts.

The same coalition, a combination of crusaders and burghers, threatened the older and larger Jewish community of Worms. The Jews of Worms, aware of what had befallen the neighboring community of Speyer, split into two segments, with the first group electing to seek safety in their homes and the second turning to the bishop, who gathered them in his palace. Neither effort was successful: the former group fell victim to the attackers almost immediately, on May 5, and the latter group held out for two weeks, only to succumb to the same fate on May 18. As a result of this double assault, the Jewish community of Worms was almost entirely destroyed. A subsequent Jewish account gave eight hundred as the number killed.

Larger and more distinguished yet was the Jewish community of Mainz. The same steady buildup of violence already noted manifested itself in Mainz as well. Tensions in the town, combined with the reports of the destruction of Worms Jewry, moved the Jewish leaders of Mainz to turn to their lord, Archbishop Ruthard, for advice and assistance. The counsel offered by the archbishop—and by the burgrave as well—was to utilize the major fortifications within the town, the episcopal palace, and the burgrave's palace, as centers of security. They advised that both Jews and Jewish wealth be gathered into these central refuges, which could be effectively protected. Unfortunately, when one of the largest of the German popular crusading bands, that of Count Emicho of Leinigen, appeared before the locked gates of Mainz, sympathetic burghers opened these gates, thereby paving the way for easy access to the Jewish refuges. At both sites, the same pattern manifested itself: siege, intense battling, crusader victory, and massive Jewish martyrdom, with large numbers of Jews electing to take their own lives and the lives of their spouses and children rather than to permit themselves to fall into the hands of their persecutors. Once again an entire Jewish community was wiped out; a later Jewish account put the number of Jewish losses in Mainz at eleven hundred.

The third of the great late-eleventh-century Rhineland Jewish communities was that of Cologne. Here the pattern of persecution was played out somewhat differently. The archbishop of Cologne chose to protect his Jews in the manner chosen by Bishop John of Speyer. Rather than attempting to secure Jewish safety in a fortified area within the town perimeter, the archbishop of Cologne gathered his Jews and moved them into a series of seven fortifications outside the city. Clearly, the theory was that the crusading bands, driven into the major towns by their need for supplies and assistance, would not make the extra effort required to hunt down Jews sequestered in out-of-the-way fortifications. Unfortunately for Cologne Jewry, the theory proved incorrect. The crusading forces did in fact abandon their ultimate goal long enough to seek out the Jewish enclaves and in the process wiped out the third great Rhineland center of early Jewish life in northern Europe. Although no figures are given by later sources for the loss of life among the Jews of Cologne, the number must surely have been something on the order of those already cited for Worms and Mainz.

Beyond these three great losses—of the outstanding Jewish communities of Worms, Mainz, and Cologne—there is no solid evidence of widespread calamity across northern Europe and no evidence whatsoever of assault on southern European Jewry. Although the attacks were relatively localized, the ferocity of these assaults, their relationship to the great crusading enterprise, and—in particular—the remarkable behavior patterns of the Jews exposed to crusade-related violence combined to elicit considerable subsequent Jewish concern with the events of 1096. Lists were compiled of the martyrs of 1096, dirges in their memory were composed, and a number of prose accounts highlighting both the attacks and the Jewish responses were written. The surviving prose accounts of the catastrophe of spring 1096 are of major significance for the evolution of medieval Jewish historical narrative and early Jewish writing in Germany.

We are fortunately provided with three extant Hebrew narratives concerning the First Crusade. Because the two most important of these narratives are obviously independent compositions and yet share almost their entire narration of events in Mainz, it seems highly likely that behind these extant accounts lies an earlier stratum of epistolary reports on each of the communities.

The third Hebrew narrative is derivative, an epitome of the longer of the two original compositions embellished with poetic dirges in memory of the communities whose demise is depicted.

Unfortunately, we have no real evidence of authorship or date of composition of either of the two original narratives. The shorter of the two (which I shall designate S) is exceedingly well organized. It opens with the call to the crusade and goes on to describe the evocation of anti-Jewish sentiment among the popular crusading bands in France, the movement of these crusading forces from France into Germany, the exploitation of Jewish anxieties for the solicitation of Jewish fiscal support, the arousal of burgher animosity against the Jews, and the emergence of the German popular crusading bands. All this is recounted sparingly, but effectively. With the Jews of the Rhineland beset by the dangers posed by the French crusaders, the German crusaders, and hostile burgher neighbors as his backdrop, the author proceeds to an account of the abortive assault on Speyer Jewry and its relatively positive outcome. This leads him in a natural way to the twin attacks on Worms, attacks that began only a few days after the events in Speyer. The largest part of this narrative is devoted to the fate of the Jews of Mainz. But after depicting most of the destruction of Mainz Jewry, S suddenly breaks off. We are thus deprived both of any observations of whatever else might have followed and of a general closing that might have helped identify either the author or the circumstances of composition.

The lengthier Hebrew narrative (which I shall designate L) is longer and richer, but less admirably organized. In fact, the precise dimensions of this narrative are far from clear, which complicates all efforts to analyze it properly. The narrative generally treated as the lengthier Hebrew account of the First Crusade assaults on Rhineland Jewry is embedded in a complex mélange of historical records, which in all likelihood stems from the late-twelfth-century Jewish community of Speyer. The opening comment of the editor of the mélange indicates that what we have presently is only a portion of what previously existed. It is likely that preceding what we have now was an extensive report on events in Speyer in May 1096. This lost section is succeeded by a brief portrait of events in Speyer and Worms that lacks the detailed depiction of the early development of the crusade and the buildup of tensions, as well as the full account of developments in Speyer and Worms provided in S. On the other hand, the report on Mainz is much fuller than that found in S and includes narration of some events that took place in the wake of the near-total destruction of Mainz Jewry on May 27, 1095.

From the reports on Speyer, Worms, and Mainz, the narrative proceeds to describe events in Cologne. Although it is generally assumed that the Cologne segment is simply a continuation of the Speyer-Worms-Mainz narrative, this is unlikely. There are striking differences of terminology and style between the Speyer-Worms-Mainz narrative and the account of events in Cologne. It seems highly probable, instead, that the Cologne segment was independently written and appended by the compiler of the comprehensive mélange. Identification of the Cologne segment as independent is important from a number of points of view. Most significant is the fact that the Cologne segment offers the only available evidence for dating the Hebrew narratives. Midway through the description of the pursuit of dispersed groups of Cologne Jews, the author cites the story of a Jewess who was saved from the carnage at Ellern and who, as a result of her traumatic experience, fasted regularly by eating only one meal per day "till now, the year 4900 [= 1140 C.E.]." What follows this date seems to be an auctorial identification: "I Solomon ben Simson transcribed this incident in Mainz." It seems clear, however, that the date supplied applies only to the Cologne segment of the mélange and tells us nothing with respect either to S or to the Speyer-Worms-Mainz composition. Likewise the name Solomon ben Simson, not really a known figure in any case, identifies merely the author of the Ellern report or—at most—the author of the Cologne segment. The independent Cologne segment is succeeded by a number of similarly independent accounts of attacks in Trier, Metz, Regensburg, and an unidentifiable locale.

It is clear that the twelfth-century author of the derivative narrative with its poetic embellishments had at his disposal the composite narrative as we now have it. By the latter decades of the twelfth century, the composite narrative had assumed its present form, which allowed a later Jewish author to shorten the lengthy story that he found therein and add his original poetic compositions. Recognition of the composite nature of what has often been seen as a unitary narrative expands the number of independent sources that we have at our disposal. That is to say, we have the writings of a number of different authors, each with his own distinctive focus and style, yet all share perceptions of both Christian and Jewish behaviors.

These diverse Jewish reporters of the events of spring 1096 had common objectives. In part, they wished to report with relative accuracy the events that had taken place in the Rhineland communities. Some of the authors may well have been eyewitnesses to the events that they describe; some may have heard oral testimony from eyewitnesses or from those who had heard directly from eyewitnesses; some may have depended on prior written materials. The quest for relative accuracy in depiction was influenced by a number of considerations. To some extent, the recorders of the events of 1096 wished to sketch out for their fellow Jews patterns of successful and unsuccessful lines of Jewish political negotiations and to enlighten their fellow Jews on the proper patterns of behavior when political negotiations fail. Much more significant was the desire to memorialize properly the martyrs of 1096. The post-1096 Jewish writers, like their Christian counterparts who memorialized the Christian heroes of the First Crusade, were convinced that the most effective technique for enshrining their subjects was to let their behaviors speak for themselves. That there was some embellishment of behaviors both Christian and Jewish is indisputable.

Wholesale fabrication would have constituted a serious disservice to the martyrs of 1096, however. Paradoxically, there was also a need to protect the Jewish hero figures from potential criticism. The acts of martyrdom—more specifically the acts that involved the taking of the lives of others, particularly children—were sufficiently unprecedented as to evoke possible objection. In particular, they lacked grounding in the Halakhah, the corpus of Jewish legal tradition. Thus, the authors of the subsequent reports of these Jewish behaviors had to present the acts of martyrdom in a manner that would obviate any criticism—and this could only be done by accurately reporting on the actual behaviors. Finally, this was a period during which both Christians and Jews in western Christendom became more fully committed to accurately observing and reporting both the world of nature and the world of human affairs. In part, the Jewish commitment to the accurate portrayal of the events of 1096 was shaped by this larger tendency.

Accurate depiction of the complex events of May–June 1096 was only part of the goal of the Jewish authors. Beyond accurate reportage, there were a number of key interpretive stances that these authors attempted—rather successfully—to advance. One has been hinted at already. In the face of potential criticism of some of the more extreme forms of Jewish martyrdom, the post-1096 writers sought to remove all possible doubt with respect to the martyrs. This was done by presenting martyrological behaviors in all their detail, by setting these acts in an interpretive framework that glorified them. The martyrs of 1096 see themselves and are seen by their recorders as belonging on the very highest plane of human existence. They are comparable to the greatest heroes of the Jewish past, such as the biblical patriarchs and the past martyrs to Greek and Roman persecution. Indeed, the martyrs of 1096 are recurrently portrayed as exceeding the heroism of the giant figures of the past. The greatness of the patriarch Abraham, for example, who has been extolled by Jews over the ages for his willingness to sacrifice his beloved son Isaac, was surely superseded by that of the Rhineland Jews of 1096—Abraham was merely willing to sacrifice one son; the Rhineland martyrs sacrificed hundreds of their beloved offspring. Out of this sense of terrestrial greatness came a parallel conviction that, in the afterlife, these eleventh-century heroes would sit at the very highest levels of blessing, among the pillars of Jewish life throughout the ages.

Beyond rationalization and indeed glorification of the martyrs, there was a far greater challenge: that of explaining the horrific contrast between Christian successes—in fact, after 1099, astounding Christian successes—and Jewish losses. The Christian milieu in which European Jewry found itself had long claimed, in general, that its victories reflected the truth of its vision and, in particular, that the contrast between Christian glory and Jewish degradation could only be understood as the truth of the one tradition superseding the other. Although this was a continual claim throughout the Christian world, the special circumstances of the late eleventh century sharpened the issue in an excruciating way. Repeatedly in the Hebrew narratives, Christians both hostile and friendly are made to argue to Jews the hopelessness of their circumstances and the meaning of this hopelessness. "Know and see that God does not wish to save you, for they [the Jewish victims of Worms] lie naked at the corner of every street, unburied." Thus argue a group of seemingly sympathetic Christians to a Worms Jewess as they attempt to persuade her to convert. In the heat of the moment, she refuses adamantly and perishes. When the tumult had died down, however, the surviving Jews had to face this painful issue, and the Jewish authors of our extant narratives surely, above all else, had to put the events of 1096 (the Jewish tragedy) and 1099 (the stunning Christian victory) in some sort of meaningful framework.

For the Jewish writers, the answer was to impose their own special historical interpretation upon the events of the closing decade of the eleventh century. The crusading venture is portrayed as devoid of all religious meaning, the aimless wandering of the cruel and the dissolute; the crusading venture certainly involved no real religious zeal or truth. The genuine hero figures of this otherwise shoddy episode were the Jewish martyrs. By their resolute behaviors, they provided the surest proof of the truth of the Jewish faith. More important yet, by their extraordinary

commitment they assured themselves of otherworldly bliss and their fellow Jews of redemption. On the surface, the events of 1096 and 1099 may have looked like a Jewish humiliation and a Christian victory, yet in truth, argued the Jewish writers, the opposite was the case. The Jews had won a major spiritual triumph, the result of which could only be punishment of persecuting Christendom and reward for its persecuted Jews. This was a brazen but powerful effort at historical interpretation aimed at reinforcing the conviction of victims that their rectitude would not go unrewarded.

Is it fair to see these Jewish writers as—at least in some sense—German? Ostensibly, the answer seems negative. Their writings are entirely in Hebrew, and the imagery that they conjure up is historically Jewish, rooted as it is in the rich legacy of biblical and rabbinic literature. Nonetheless, in significant ways, these authors were surely German, or, better for this point in time, European. Despite their profound hatred for the Christianity in the name of which the crusaders set forth and for the Christian society out of which the Crusade was spawned, the martyrs of 1096 and those who set about recording their actions and singing their praise shared profoundly some of the revolutionary thinking that lay behind the crusade and that was fated to have prolonged effects long after the ardor for crusading had diminished. The Jewish authors whose work we have been considering certainly shared with their Christian counterparts—those who extolled the crusaders and their achievements—a sense of the historic import of the events that they depicted. Both sets of authors saw their heroes as projected onto the highest plane of historic achievement. The Christian warriors were seen as taking up the cross of Jesus and following in his footsteps across the hills of Judea; the Jewish martyrs were seen as reconstituting the divinely ordained sacrificial ritual of the Temple mount. The sense of what was truly meaningful in individual and corporate existence was also shared: the conviction that humanity's ultimate purpose was to answer the divine summons and, in so doing, bear witness to the highest truth. For neither the first nor the last time in Christian-Jewish relations, parallel convictions were expressed in ways that set the two camps in profound conflict with one another. In this case, the conflict resulted in unanticipated Christian attacks upon Rhineland Jewry and in a response that was, for the Jewish world, every bit as remarkable as—indeed far more remarkable than—the subsequent Christian conquest of Jerusalem.

Bibliography

The three Hebrew narratives were published in Adolf Neubauer and Moritz Stern, *Hebräische Berichte über die Judenverfolgungen während der Kreuzzüge* (Berlin: Verlag von Leonhard Stein, 1892), and republished in Abraham Habermann, *Sefer Gezerot Ashkenaz ve-Zarfat* (Jerusalem: Tarshish Books, 1945). English translations are available in Robert Chazan, *European Jewry and the First Crusade* (Berkeley: University of California Press, 1987), and in Shlomo Eidelberg, *The Crusaders and the Jews* (Madison: University of Wisconsin Press, 1977), which presents an overview of Jewish fate and the narratives. Additional consideration of the narratives can be found in the following works.

Anna Sapir Abulafia, "The Interrelationship Between the Hebrew Chronicles of the First Crusade," *Journal of Semitic Studies* 27 (1982): 221–39; Robert Chazan, "The Facticity of Medieval Narrative: A Case Study of the Hebrew First-Crusade Narratives," *Association for Jewish Studies Review* 16 (1991): 31–56; Jacob Katz, *Exclusiveness and Tolerance* (Oxford: Oxford University Press, 1961), 82–92; Ivan G. Marcus, "From Politics to Martyrdom: Shifting Paradigms in the Hebrew Narratives of the 1096 Crusade Riots," *Prooftexts* 2 (1982): 40–52; and Alan Mintz, *Hurban: Responses to Catastrophe in Hebrew Literature* (New York: Columbia University Press, 1984), 84–101.

ROBERT CHAZAN

1150 The emergence of distinct intellectual schools changes the character of Jewish theology, esotericism, and mysticism

The emergence of Jewish mysticism in medieval Germany and northern France is closely connected with three major historical developments that characterized Jewish culture in the twelfth and thirteenth centuries. These three processes affected several aspects of Jewish creativity in this period, but their effect on mystical and esoterical writings is most meaningful. The developments relate to changes in the concepts of scholarship and language, as well as those of God, the creation, and divine revelation.

Until the second half of the twelfth century, Jewish creativity in the realms of thought, ethics, and esotericism was perhaps best described as individual writers working independently. Saadia Gaon, Ibn Gabirol, Judah ha-Levi, Bahya Ibn Paquda, Abraham bar Hijja, Abraham Ibn Ezra, and many others are isolated writers; we do not know who their teachers, colleagues, or disciples were. The concept of "schools," so deeply ingrained since ancient times in the study of the Halakhah, is completely absent in the first three centuries of medieval Jewish thought. By the thirteenth century, however, almost all the writers in this field are integrated into various "schools": the rationalists and the mystics of Provence and northern Spain, the Tibbonite school, the Kalonymus school in the Rhineland, the Unique Cherub circle (see below), and many others. This dramatic transformation, which occurred in the second half of the twelfth century, was influenced by the emergence of the Maimonidean school of theology. This shift changed the character of Jewish creativity in the fields of theology, esotericism, and mysticism and shaped their historical development. Jewish mysticism in Germany and France is a part of this process, having enhanced it and been shaped by it.

The second transformation occurred in the realm of language. The external evidence of this change includes the transition of Jewish creativity from Arabic into Hebrew and the emergence of Hebrew styles and terminologies dedicated to the expression of philosophical, esoteric, and mystical ideas. Many of the writers in this period had to invent new modes of expression because they had no Hebrew precedent or accepted tradition. Abraham bar Hijja, Abraham Ibn Ezra, Maimonides (in his Hebrew writings), the Tibbonites, and the Ashkenazi schools created styles and terminologies to suit their particular needs. Originality in language and style usually enhances originality in content as well, and this at least partially explains the unusual variety and power of Jewish thought in this period.

The external transition to Hebrew, which was the result of historical processes that brought many Jewish communities under Christian rule (and the Jews refused, for religious reasons, to accept Latin as a language, whereas they viewed Arabic as the secular language of a civilization and not only the language of Islam), had many other results, some of them affecting culture in subtle ways. One of the immediate consequences of this process was the strengthening of ties—related to both content and form—between Jewish medieval speculations and the world of the Talmud and Midrash. Pseudepigraphy in midrashic modes abounded, and midrashic language had a renewed effect on the thought of rationalists and mystics alike. At the same time, the ancient midrashic concept of language as an expression of the infinite wisdom of God was reinvigorated. The letters of the Hebrew alphabet were regarded not just as elements that combine to enable human communication, but as the sources of divine creative power (for God created the world by ten linguistic utterances, composed of these letters) containing infinite meaning. Language was regarded not as a means or a tool, but as the subject and ultimate purpose of speculation.

The third major historical process that shaped the emergence of Jewish mysticism in medieval Germany was the growing distance between rationalistic philosophy and the needs of everyday religious worship. God as described in the writings of Maimonides and his followers seemed remote from the everyday world, thus inaccessible and removed from religious experience. It seemed that the rationalists denied any possibility of actual divine revelation and made impossible any contact between the worshiper and transcendent divinity even in prayer: both revelation and the acceptance of prayer postulated a change in God, an exercise of his will. The "God of the Philosophers" seemed incapable of responding to human needs. This growing distance, which was expressed in Spain and Provence by the growing criticism of Maimonidean philosophy until the eruption of open controversy in 1232, motivated several Jewish thinkers in Germany and France two generations before the beginning of public controversy to seek other ways to portray the relationship between the Creator and his devoted creatures.

All three processes converged in the last few decades of the twelfth century to contribute to the emergence of several schools of esoterics and mystics in Germany and northern France. The earliest among these is probably the school of the Unique Cherub, which flourished in Germany and France from the second half of the twelfth century to the end of the thirteenth.

The earliest text of this circle is a pseudepigraphic work, the *Barayta of Joseph ben Uzziel* (Mss. Parma 1138, Paris 770, British Library 754). This brief treatise, which was written in medieval language without any serious attempt to imitate ancient language, holds in this geographic realm a position similar to that of the *Book Bahir,* the earliest work of the Kabbalah, in Provence and Spain. But while the attribution of the *Bahir* to a pseudepigraphic author, Rabbi Nehunia ben ha-Kanah, is clear (he is described in Hekhalot mystical texts as the leader of the school of ancient Jewish mystics), the attribution of the *Barayta* to Joseph ben Uzziel is perplexing. This name is known from only one source, the ninth-century collection of stories known as the *Alphabet of Ben Sira.* In this treatise, Joseph ben Uzziel is portrayed as the grandson of Ben Sira (Ecclesiaticus), who was, according to the anonymous author, both the son and grandson of the prophet Jeremiah. The *Barayta* and other treatises of this circle repeatedly claim that the secrets presented are those that "Jeremiah revealed in Babylonia" and that were transmitted from generation to generation. It is evident that the medieval mystic demands the recognition of his secrets as being rooted in biblical tradition (whereas kabbalists in Provence and Spain usually attributed their sources to the talmudic-midrashic period). But why did he choose Joseph ben Uzziel, when the narrative treatise in which he is mentioned is manifestly vulgar and heretical? This is an enigma to us even today.

The *Barayta* is essentially a presentation of the teachings of the ancient *Sefer Yezira* (The book of creation), which has been interpreted by many Jewish scholars since the tenth century as a work of science. It may be the first attempt to treat the *Sefer Yezira* as a source of esoteric and mystical knowledge (this was done also by the *Bahir* and by the first kabbalist, known to us as Rabbi Isaac the Blind of Provence, whose only extant treatise is a commentary on that work). The first paragraphs of the *Barayta* paraphrase the *Sefer Yezira* by including a prohibition on contemplating the secrets of cosmogony and cosmology. But the main spiritual innovation included in it is the description of the divine world as comprising three layers: the supreme Godhead at the top, the emanated divine glory next, and below these the image of the Unique Cherub, who is the subject of all anthropomorphic descriptions of God (including the ancient *Shiur Komah*). It is the Unique Cherub who sits on the throne of glory and is revealed to the prophets. The divine world includes, therefore, three distinct divine entities (compare these to the *Bahir,* sec. 127–28), which are connected by the process of emanation. In the writings of other treatises from this school, it becomes apparent that the divine glory is the hidden power that receives prayers and is responsible for miracles.

The literature of this circle includes a dozen treatises, all recognized by the centrality of the figure of the Unique Cherub, by the reliance on Joseph ben Uzziel as a source, and by other terminological and theological characteristics. The text of the *Barayta* is accompanied in most manuscripts by a *piyyut,* a theological poem that repeats some of the principles found in the *Barayta,* and in all the extant versions a commentary is appended to both texts. It is evident that a "school" of esoterics and mystics produced these writings, which served as a basis for the more elaborated and detailed works written subsequently.

The best known among these subsequent works is the pseudo-Saadia commentary on the *Sefer Yezira.* It was printed in an abbreviated form in the traditional editions of the *Sefer Yezira;* the complete treatise is found in numerous manuscripts. This text includes an introduction describing the creation of a golem by Ben Sira and his father (and grandfather) Jeremiah, and in the work itself there are detailed instructions concerning the creation of an artificial man. The work also includes many pages of medieval physiological and cosmological scientific material, and it is possible that the creation of a golem was regarded as a scientific, rather than a magical, enterprise. The alphabet is to be used in this endeavor, but the alphabet is also the source of all other creatures, as explained in the *Sefer Yezira.* The attribution of this work to pseudo-Saadia is unclear: a source often quoted in the work is iden-

tified by the acronym PRS, which was understood to mean "Rav Saadia commented." The material included in these quotations is not found in the Saadia Commentary in our possession, and it is possible that some mistake is the origin of this attribution. Other works of this circle do not mention Saadia or his commentary.

An important treatise of this circle is a brief *Pesak* called "Pesak ha-Yirah veha-Emunah" (Decision concerning faith and the fear of God, Mss. Leipzig 30, New York, Adler 1161, Oxford-Bodley 2575), which is extant in several manuscripts. It is directed toward every person who prays to God. It prohibits prayer to the Unique Cherub, who has a corporeal image, and insists that supplicants direct their prayers to the divine glory. This treatise represents one of the earliest attempts to connect esoterical and mystical speculations with daily rituals and to derive some practical conclusions from spiritual experiences concerning the religious meaning of prayers and other commandments. In later generations the connection between exoteric rituals and inner experiences and their textualization became one of the main subjects of Ashkenazi Jewish mystical discourse, a discussion that enabled the integration of these phenomena with the general religious culture of the communities in Germany.

From a historical point of view, the authors who produced the treatises of the Unique Cherub circle remained marginal, and their effect minimal. They chose complete anonymity and thus relinquished any ambition to influence the surrounding society and its culture. The one known writer who belonged partially to this school was Rabbi Elhanan ben Yaqar of London, who wrote two commentaries on the *Sefer Yezira* and a theological treatise also based on that ancient work, *Sod ha-Sodot* (Mss. Fulda 4, Paris 815, New York-JThS 838, 8118). He lived in the first half of the thirteenth century and studied with a disciple of the great tosafist Rabbi Isaac the Elder, in northern France. His works are anthological in character and serve as an important source for early Ashkenazi traditions concerning the nature of the divine world, especially those related to cosmological and scientific concepts that prevailed at that time.

The main school of Ashkenazi mystics and esoterics, that of the Kalonymus family in the Rhineland and elsewhere, developed its teachings in two parallel literary modes, one esoteric and one exoteric, and it assumed a position of spiritual leadership in the Jewish medieval community. The founder of this school was Rabbi Samuel ben Kalonymus, who was called "the pious, the martyr, the prophet" in the second half of the twelfth century, though no mystical works of his have reached us. His son, Rabbi Judah the Pious (d. 1217), was the main leader of this group, and his disciple, Rabbi Eleazar ben Judah of Worms (d. ca. 1230), was the most prolific writer. Their writings include important halakhahic works (like Rabbi Eleazar of Worms's *Rodeah*) and especially ethical ones (like Rabbi Judah the Pious's *Sefer Hasidim*). In addition to their esoteric and mystical treatises, they both wrote commentaries on the prayers and on the *piyyutim* (Rabbi Abraham berabi Azriel's *Arugat ha-Bosem*). They represent a meaningful historical transition in Ashkenazi Jewish culture in which the new ideas and concepts concerning the divine world, the mystical dimension of ritual, and the esoteric concept of the scriptures are interwoven. The Ashkenazi contribution to Jewish hermeneutics was one of the most influential aspects of their thought and had a lasting effect on Jewish esoterical and mystical speculations.

In his *Sefer ha-Hokhmah,* which he wrote in 1217 while mourning the death of his teacher, Rabbi Judah the Pious, Rabbi Eleazar of Worms presented a list of seventy-three "gates of wisdom" (the number is based on the numerical value of the word *haokhmah*), each of which constitutes one method for the exegesis of biblical verses. Later in this work he presented a detailed example of how many of these methods should be employed in interpreting one verse as the first verse of Genesis. Thus we have a clear example of this school's hermeneutical concepts.

Nearly fifty-five of these "gates" present techniques based on the external characteristics of the biblical text: the numerical value (*gematria*); acronyms (*notaricon*, both of the first and the last letters of a group of words); the various methods of *temurah* (transmutation of letters, or the exchange of letters by others according to a specific rhythmic method); the proximity of words to each other (*semuchim*); the interpretation of the vocalization marks (*nikkud*); the musical signs (*teamim*) and the adornments of letters (*tagin*); and the shape of the letters themselves. Several gates are dedicated to counting the number of words, letters, and holy names in a segment of a biblical text and to interpreting the meaning of that number (its correspondence to other segments which have the same numbers). Even an exegesis of the absence of certain letters from a verse or a group of verses is among the many offered.

These methods are essentially midrashic, and examples for them can be found in ancient literature. To some extent this list follows traditional lists of the ways by which the Torah is to be interpreted. There is no ancient example, however, of such a detailed and comprehensive presentation of the midrashic concept of language and hermeneutics. The theological basis of this methodology is the deep belief that language is of divine origin: it is essentially an expression of divine wisdom, and its use by human beings as a means of communication is a secondary, unimportant role. Language existed before the world was created, and creation itself is the result of divine speech. This concept demands that language have an infinity of meanings, because divine wisdom is infinite and can never be exhausted by human comprehension. The divine source also indicates that the exegete cannot distinguish between "important" and "not important" aspects of language, like saying that literal meaning is important whereas the shape of the letters or the vocalization marks is secondary. The biblical verse includes a full semiotic expression of divine wisdom in all aspects of its presentation, and divine meaning is hidden in every aspect of linguistic expression: visual, auditory, numerical, and semantic. The Torah existed before the creation of the world, so its structure, form, and meaning are independent of human needs and limitations. No interpretation can therefore exclude any other, and every possible meaning found in it can coexist with a multiplicity of other explanations. The meeting between the exegete and the verse is the meeting between a human mind and a divine one; human beings may discover more and more layers of meaning, but they can never exhaust them and cannot designate one kind of interpretation as inferior or superior to any other. The divine text is a picture of letters, marks, adornments, and so forth, as well as a combination of sounds, a hidden numerical layer, and many semantic messages, all of them of equal value and standing. Hermeneutics means, therefore, the infinite effort to discover more and more aspects of divine wisdom hidden in all the semiotic aspects of the verse: the pictorial, the sounds, the numbers, and the various meanings.

The semantic level is represented in the list of seventy-three gates by many subjects: prayer, the divine glory (*kavod*), the chariot, the soul, the angels, the divine name, the "secret," "faith," divine unity (*yihud*), and others. A second group of thematic gates is dedicated to ethical principles, the love of God, fear of God, piety (*hasidut*), repentance; a third group of themes is a list of texts the exegesis of which is to be combined with biblical hermeneutics: the *Sefer Yezira,* Talmud, Midrash, the prayer book, and the piyyut. The example that follows demonstrates the use of the technical as well as the thematic principles in the exegesis of the first verse of the Torah.

This list was not regarded by the Ashkenazi Hasidim of the Kalonymus school as theoretical, but as a structural directive for esoteric speculation. Of all the works we have from the Ashkenazi Hasidim of this school, several dozen treatises bear titles that are taken from this list; often chapters in works are also entitled by such terms. The collection of works by Rabbi Judah the Pious in Ms. Oxford 1566–67 includes thematic gates: the divine glory, the angels, and possibly the soul and the technical ones—semuchim, teamim, and tagin. Rabbi Eleazar's *Sodey Razaya* is a collection of five thematic ones: Creation, Chariot, Holy Name, the Soul, and the *Sefer Yezira.* Rabbi Eleazar's ethical chapters in the *Rokeah* include the gates of Piety, Love, Fear, and Repentance; another treatise by Rabbi Eleazar is a combination of "The Gates of Secret, Unity, and Faith." Other works from this circle and related circles demonstrate the same awareness of this list.

The ancient concept of the Midrash has been developed in this system of "gates of wisdom" into a comprehensive concept of language and hermeneutics that represents the full utilization of the Bible's divine message to Man in its infinite aspects and forms. The concept of the inexhaustibility of the meaning of divine language has been formalized and adopted as the basic approach to the hermeneutical treatment of ancient texts. It was used not only in the interpretation of the Bible, but also in the exegesis of the prayers, and the Ashkenazi Hasidim were described by contemporary and subsequent generations as those who "counted the words and letters," and thereby recognized the importance of this aspect of their teachings.

The two main avenues of mystical expression in this school were the concepts of prayer and of the holy name of God. Rabbi Judah the Pious developed in his commentary on the prayers (which has been lost, but many quotations survive) the idea that the language of the prayers reflects the intrinsic harmony among the divine and the earthly realms, the text of the scriptures and the text of the prayers, and human existence. This harmony was demonstrated mainly by numerical analysis of the words and letters through gematria. Rabbi Eleazar of Worms continued in this way, though in a less radical manner, in his commentary on the prayers (extant in three versions, Mss. Oxford 1204, Vienna 108, Paris 772). The mystical significance of the holy name is expressed in the most important esoteric work written in Germany during the thirteenth century, the *Sefer ha-Shem* (The book of the holy name, Mss. British Library 737, Munich 81). In this work Rabbi Eleazar developed the concept of the *havayot* (essences; this term was introduced at the same time by Rabbi Isaac the Blind in Provence), which is the semantic expression of the metalinguistic tetragrammaton.

These two circles—that of the Kalonymus family and the Unique Cherub writers—were not alone; around them were several other individuals and groups who developed their own concepts of the divine world and the secrets of the Torah. One of the most important among them was the anonymous author of the *Sefer ha-Hayim* (The book of life), a theological-scientific treatise written around 1200 that relied on the writings of Abraham Ibn Ezra; another is the *Sefer ha-Navon,* a commentary on the *Shema Yisrael* and on the *Shiur Komah.* Some radical traditions concerning the divine world and the holy name are found in our sources as quotations from the works of Rabbi Nehemia ben Shlomo, a contemporary of Rabbi Judah the Pious, and others. This intense activity evoked opposition: around 1200, Rabbi Moshe ben Hisdai Taku wrote a polemical work, *Ketav Tamim,* against these speculations, which accused their authors of heresy because of their attempt to understand forbidden secrets.

By the second half of the thirteenth century, meaningful connections had been established between the esoterical circles of the Ashkenazi Hasidim and the Kabbalah in Spain. Rabbi Isaac ben Jacob ha-Cohen of Castile, writing around 1260, claimed to have received many of his mystical traditions from disciples of Rabbi Eleazar of Worms. A legend developed in Spain that attributed the origins of the Kabbalah to the Ashkenazi sages; this was expressed mainly by Rabbi Shem Tov ben Gaon in his *Badey ha-Aron* (written in Jerusalem and Safed between 1315 and 1325). Hermeneutic methodologies and traditions concerning the holy name of God, formulated by Rabbi Eleazar in his *Sefer ha-Shem* (Mss. British Library 737, Munich 81) may have reached the circle of Rabbi Abraham Abulafia and influenced his Kabbalah of holy names.

In the opposite direction, Ashkenazi theological treatises of the middle and second half of the thirteenth century include references to the kabbalistic concept of the ten divine hypostases, the *sefirot.* These new traditions were interwoven and integrated with the Ashkenazi terms and ideas. Ms. Adler 1161 (The Jewish Theological Seminary) includes several such works attributed to Rabbi Judah the Pious. Some of the most important expressions of this integration are the treatises of Rabbi Moshe ben Eliezer, a great-grandson of Rabbi Judah the Pious; his commentary on the *Shiur Komah* includes an intense expression of mysticism of language, which quotes the *Sefer ha-Bahir* and uses some kabbalistic terminology (it also quotes the *Sod ha-Gadol,* identified by Scholem as one of the sources of the *Bahir*). An

important kabbalistic work of this period is *Keter Shem Tov* (A crown of good name), by Rabbi Abraham of Cologne.

Ashkenazi ideas and metaphors became a part of Spanish Kabbalah. The concept of the four "shells" (*kelipot*) surrounding the divine chariot, presented in several versions of an Ashkenazi treatise, *Sod ha-Egoz* (Secret of the nut), which probably derived from Hekhalot tradition, was accepted by Spanish kabbalists and was interpreted by the author of the Zohar as a description of the powers of evil surrounding the divine world. Other concepts and terms, mainly concerning the nature of prophecy, the meanings of the holy names, and the divine glory, were integrated in the works of Spanish kabbalists. From the fourteenth century onward, Ashkenazi mystics and esoterics traveled to southern Europe and became prominent among the schools of the kabbalists, like Rabbi David ("the son of Rabbi Judah the Pious") and Rabbi Abraham Ashkenazi. They may have brought with them some Ashkenazi traditions, which were interwoven into their kabbalistic writings.

Several Ashkenazi scholars became part of the Kabbalah in the late fourteenth and during the fifteenth centuries; one of the most important is Rabbi Menkhem Zioni, who wrote an extensive commentary on the Torah and other kabbalistic treatises like *Zefuney Zioni,* a treatise on the powers of evil based on Zoharic terminology. Several anthologies were composed in Germany that combined Ashkenazi Hasidic traditions with the teachings of the Kabbalah, like the great commentary on the prayers known as the *Yalkut Reuveni.*

Bibliography
Ashkenazi Hasidic Esoterical and Mystical Teachings

Joseph Dan, "The Ashkenazi Hasidic Gates of Wisdom," *Homage à Georges Vajda* (Louvain, 1980), 183–89; Dan, "Early Hebrew Source of the Yiddish Aqdamot Story," *Hebrew University Studies in Literature* 1 (1973): 39–46; Dan, "The Emergence of the Mystical Prayer," *Studies in Jewish Mysticism* (Cambridge, Mass.: Association for Jewish Studies Review, 1981), 85–120; Dan, "Das Entstehen der jüdischen Mystik im mittelalterischen Deutschland," *Judentum im deutschen Sprach-raum,* ed. K. E. Grözinger (Frankfurt a. M.: Suhrkamp, 1991), 127–172; Dan, "Prayer as Text and Prayer as Mystical Experience," *Torah and Wisdom: Studies in Jewish Philosophy, Kabbalah and Halacha in Honor of A. Hyman,* ed. R. Link-Salinger (New York: Shengold, 1992), 33–47; Dan, "Pseudepigraphy in Medieval Jewish Mysticism in Germany," *Fälschungen im Mittelalter,* vol. 5 (Hannover: Hahn, 1988), 519–31; Gershom Scholem, *Major Trends in Jewish Mysticism,* 3d ed. (New York: Schocken, 1954), 80–120; Scholem, *The Origins of the Kabbalah* (Princeton, N.J.: Princeton University Press, 1986); Haim Soloveitchik, "Rabbi Elezar of Worms' Hochmat ha-Nefesh," *Jewish Social Studies* 18 (1967): 65–78.

Studies on Sefer Hasidim and Ashkenazi
Hasidic Ethics

Tamar Alexander-Frizer, *The Pious Sinner: Ethics and Aesthetics in the Medieval Hasidic Narrative* (Tübingen: Mohr, 1991); I. Baer, "The Social and Religious Meaning of the Sefer Hasidim," *Binah: Studies in Jewish History,* ed. Joseph Dan (New York: Praeger, 1989); Nehemiah Brüll, "Beiträge zur jüdischen Sagen und Spruchkunde im Mittelalter," *Jahrbuch für jüdische Geschichte und Literatur* 9 (1889): 1–71; Joseph Dan, "Hasidei Ashkenaz," *Encyclopedia Judaica,* vol. 7, 1377–83; Dan, *Jewish Mysticism and Jewish Ethics* (Seattle: University of Washington Press, 1987); Dan, "A Note on the History of *Tshuvah* in the Teachings of the Ashkenazi Hasidim," *The World of Rav Kook's Thought,* ed. B. Ish-Shalom and S. Rosenberg (New York: AviHai, 1991), 271–82; Dan, "Sefer Hasidim," *Encyclopedia Judaica,* vol. 7, 1388–90; Ivan G. Marcus, "The Devotional Ideals of Ashkenazi Pietism," *Jewish Spirituality,* ed. A. Green (New York: Crossroad, 1986), 356–66; Marcus, "From Politics to Martyrdom: Shifting Paradigms in the Hebrew Narratives of the 1096 Crusade Riots," *Prooftexts* 2 (1982): 40–52; Marcus, "Hasidei Ashkenazi Private Penitentials," *Studies in Jewish Mysticism,* ed. Joseph Dan and F. Talmage (Cambridge, Mass.: Harvard University Press, 1982), 57–83; Marcus, "Hierarchies, Religious Boundaries and Jewish Spirituality in Medieval Germany," *Jewish History* 1 (1986): 7–26; Marcus, "Mothers, Martyrs and Moneymakers," *Conservative Judaism* 38 (1986): 34–45; Marcus, *Piety and Society: The Jewish Pietists of Medieval Germany* (Leiden: Brill, 1981); and Marcus, "The Politics and Ethics of Pietism and Judaism: The Hasidim of Medieval Germany," *Journal of Religion and Ethics* 8 (1980): 227–58.

JOSEPH   DAN

ca. 1200   *Sefer Hasidim* (The book of the Pietists) is written by a group of rabbinic authors who come to be known as *hasidei ashkenaz,* the Pietists of Germany

In the 1880s, Moritz Güdemann could observe that *Sefer Hasidim* is one of those books that are often quoted but almost never studied. In the last fifty years alone, dozens of studies have appeared to make up for that earlier neglect. And for good reason. *Sefer Hasidim* is the first book written by European Jews that is neither a commentary on an earlier work nor a collection of legal opinion or responsa—the two dominant genres for northern European Jews in the Middle Ages. A book that stands on its own, *Sefer Hasidim* expresses a distinctive world view concerning Judaism and medieval Christian society. It also offers a new, ascetic vision of the ideal Jewish personality and a program of Jewish religious exclusiveness that Jewish Pietists (Hasidim) are to follow in their everyday interactions with other Jews as well as with Christians.

In it we find allusions to knights and demons, princes and prices, Jewish-Christian debates, scribal practices, the transliterated Latin word *dialectica,* and the undercurrents dialectica reflects in contemporary Christian culture between the new style of learning of Peter Abelard and the reaction by monastic thinkers like Bernard of Clairvaux. In addition, there are references to prostitution, coin clipping, Jewish women occupied as weavers and moneylenders, and much more. *Sefer Hasidim* depicts the broad canvas of medieval German towns in the High Middle Ages.

It is above all the major pietistic work by a group of rabbinic authors who came to be called *hasidei ashkenaz* (the Pietists of Germany). The most significant authors who were directly responsible for writing down the pietist traditions are Rabbi Samuel ben Rabbi Qalonimos the Elder of Speyer (fl. mid-twelfth century) and R. Samuel's younger son, Rabbi Judah, known as *he-hasid* (the Pietist; d. 1217). The latter, in particular, was traditionally considered to have compiled the elements that became most of *Sefer Hasidim,* although later students and editors made contributions as well.

Father and son were members of the religious aristocracy of medieval European Jewry. They lent their charismatic authority to a regimen of extreme religious behavior that sometimes differed from the written classics of late antique and early medieval Judaism such as the Babylonian Talmud, which was compiled in early sixth-century Iraq. Writing in the towns of Speyer, Worms, and Regensburg in the late twelfth and early thirteenth centuries, the pietist authors were descended from the first families of early Germany Jewry, the Qalonimide and Abun clans. The Qalonimos clan in particular traced its origins to early medieval Italy. This clan ultimately carried on ancient Palestinian traditions, which were transmitted orally from generation to generation until Rabbi Samuel and his son Rabbi Judah the Pietist wrote down their customs and practices in the form of topically arranged collections of exegetical, liturgical, theological, and mystical comments.

The first sixteen paragraphs of the book are part of a short work called *Sefer ha-Yirah* (Book of the proper fear of God), which was written by R. Samuel ben Qalonimos the Elder. It stresses the pietistic ideal of ascetic self-denial, total direction of the will toward serving the complete will of God, and the discipline of seeking to discover and fulfill neglected religious commandments. The individual Pietist, rather than a social group or sect, stands at the center of R. Samuel's presentation of the pietist way, and he emphasizes how the Pietist must be trained to properly fear God in order to be rewarded in the world to come. Ignorance of God's secret will is no excuse before the day of judgment.

In marked contrast to this personalist focus of *Sefer ha-Yirah,* most of *Sefer Hasidim* presents the same ascetic ideal but formulates it not just as a regimen for the individual, but also as a rule for sectarian groups of Pietists organized under the spiritual leadership of charismatic leaders called *hakhamim* (sages). For R. Judah, the divine trial derives not only from the individual Pietist's sexual urges but also from the social pressures exerted by non-pietist Jews, whom he calls "the wicked." To be a member of the pietist sect requires choosing between loyalty to other Pietists and loyalty to other Jews, even one's family, who may not be members. Thus, for *Sefer Hasidim,* society is divided into three social groups: Christians; Jews who are Pietists and who are referred to as "righteous ones," "pure ones," "proper ones," or "God-fearers"; and other Jews, whom the authors call "wicked," "impure ones," "violent," and so on.

R. Judah's, then, is a social as well as a religious conception of the pietist ideal, and it affects choosing a marriage partner, giving to charity, selecting a teacher, and a host of other forms of social contact. Pietism as Jewish sectarianism was unprecedented in European Judaism, and it served as a model of Jewish religious fervor in medieval Europe and into the twentieth century—Jewish groups of religious zealots still study it and try to live by its exclusivistic teachings.

Among the most influential features of the pietist ideal described in *Sefer Hasidim* is R. Judah

the Pietist's penitential system of confession to a sage (*hakham*) and the latter's administering of penances to the contrite sinner. Despite some uncertainty as to how much this system of sage-atonement was implemented in R. Judah's lifetime, the norms and patterns of this form of atonement were internalized in Jewish life in Central and Eastern Europe and surface even in modern fiction such as Isaac Bashevis Singer's Yiddish story translated as "A Crown of Feathers" and S. Y. Agnon's Hebrew parable called "Aggadat ha-Sofer."

The *Sefer Hasidim* suggests that it was written by Pietists for other Jews who wanted to follow the higher teachings and rule of Pietism but lacked either a proper teacher or the ability to themselves derive the hidden requirements of Pietism from Scripture. Fiercely concerned with following what they defined as the will of God (*rezon ha-borei*), the book reflects the inner groups' efforts to use exegetical techniques to discover the hidden divine will or to express it in quasi-prophetic, charismatic intuitions.

The difficulty of discovering the hidden will of God is central to Pietism. Pietism is for the few, not the many, unlike the popular movement of Hasidism that developed in late-eighteenth- and nineteenth-century Eastern European Judaism. The medieval German-Jewish Pietists maintained that life consists of continual divinely ordained trials, by which the Pietist's loyalty to God is continually being tested in all he does, thinks, and feels. A primary source of the divine trial is a man's passions, such as his sexual attraction to women other than his own wife, or the drive to achieve personal honor and adulation.

The authors refer to such urges as the "evil impulse" (*yetzer ha-ra*), a term from classical rabbinic theology sometimes associated with the tempter or the accuser (Satan) in the Book of Job (for example, 1:6–12). The Pietist's trial by his passions is part of God's plan to reward those who successfully resist them. As R. Samuel ben R. Qalonimos says, "Is not the evil impulse good for man? If it did not dominate him, what reward would he earn for acting virtuously?" (*Sefer ha-Yirah,* par. 2). God's reward for the Pietist derives not only from his effort to search Scripture for

God's hidden commandments but also from his continuous resistance to the strong evil impulse. That effort, in turn, involves a constant self-examination of one's motives and feelings.

Because the Pietist's life requires resistance to all kinds of temptations of the flesh and ego, a tendency toward asceticism—in the sense of a commitment to disciplined behavior and strategies of self-denial—emerged. In accordance with the authors' focus on maximizing otherworldly reward by resisting temptations in this world, the Pietist is told to avoid all illicit physical or psychological pleasures during his life. For example, he should not play with his children. Judah the Pietist even goes so far as to prohibit an author from writing his own name in the introduction to a book he writes: his children might take pride in their father's work and thereby lose reward in the afterlife.

Within their ascetic regimen, Pietists made room for the Jewish religious commandment of marriage and procreative sex. Nothing compromised these and other related aspects of Jewish law for them. Nevertheless, they viewed themselves as constantly struggling to ward off temptations and even debated whether it was a virtue or a sin to expose themselves to temptation in an artificial way to test themselves. Was the risk of actually sinning worth the exercise of going up to the brink and straining not to fall off the precipice?

The inner struggle for dominance over the power of the passions is reflected in many of the sections of *Sefer Hasidim* that include *exempla* (examples). Among the most elaborate exempla written by R. Judah the Pietist himself is an elaborate story of three Pietists who come to sages to confess what they claim to be problematic behavior. They ask the sages not what their penances are but if they might in fact deserve a divine reward for having subjected themselves to a severe trial.

The first found out where someone had hidden some money, went there, took out the money, and exposed himself to the temptation to steal it. But instead of taking it, he put it back. Has he sinned, he asks the sage, or does he deserve a reward? A second Jew confesses that he has trouble controlling his temper and purposely got into an argument with an irascible neighbor. Outside the town limits, away from the neighbor's many relatives, the Pietist claims that he provoked his enemy to anger him. Moreover, the Pietist admits he was carrying a sword and was ready to kill his antagonist but despite his powerful urge to harm him, he restrained himself from doing so. Does he merit a reward or a punishment for coming so close to committing murder? Finally, the third Jew tells the sages that he was madly in love with his neighbor's wife. When his friend was out of town, he would become passionately involved with her. They kissed and embraced, and he was so aroused that he burned with desire for her. At the last minute, however, he stopped himself and did not have intercourse with her. He, too, wants to know: have I sinned or did I earn a reward? (*Sefer Hasidim,* ed. Parma, pars. 52–53, translated in Marcus 1990)

These tales are the most developed in *Sefer Hasidim* and point to the inner struggle that lay at the heart of the Pietists' system of religious merit and sin. To follow the commandments of Judaism may have been difficult for ordinary Jews who lived in the small towns of Christian Europe, but succeeding at that task did not make one a Pietist. To achieve that status, one needed to be under the urge to sin and resist it. Pietism was a dynamic process that combined an inwardness typical of twelfth century European Christian spirituality with the social dimension of Judaism that required public behavior, as well as thoughts or feelings, to be directed toward God.

The hidden divine will added to rabbinic Judaism myriad additional, often ascetic prohibitions and placed perpetual claim on the inner as well as the external performance of the Pietist. True motivation was as important as proper behavior, and illicit pleasure as well as deed were required to be atoned in proportional penances that remind one of the calculus in the Latin penitentials of the early Middle Ages.

In style, the book is more of an anthology of short traditions than a coherently written treatise. The impression it makes is of a kaleidoscopic mixture of midrash, homily, exegetical snippets, and hundreds of short and some lengthy narratives similar to the contemporary Latin *exempla* of Caesarius of Heisterbach, to whose *Dialogus miraculorum* (ca. 1220) *Sefer Hasidim* has sometimes been compared.

Although it lacks Caesarius's dialogue form, *Sefer Hasidim* is arranged according to a sequence of themes around which the *exempla* and other comments cohere. In both the long and short recensions (see below), a nearly identical table of contents exists as follows: Fear of God, Atonement, The Dead, Harmful Spirits, Prayer, Sabbath, Books, Study of Torah, Charity, Honoring Parents, Beginning of Pietism, Ritual Slaughter of Animals, Women, Trustworthiness in Business, Bans, and Oaths.

These categories, like the fourteen books into which Maimonides (1138–1204) divided his comprehensive code of Jewish law, the *Mishneh Torah,* represent an original taxonomy of Judaism that is not dependent on the topical arrangement of ancient Jewish classical texts such as the Mishnah and the Talmud. But whereas Maimonides focused primarily, though not exclusively, on law, R. Judah the Pietist organized his traditions and tales into categories of religious behavior that he understood to be superrogatory acts of Pietism that one must seek to perform *in addition to* the requirements of Jewish law and custom. In this regard, the pietist way of living for R. Judah should be compared not to Jewish law, which he took for granted as obligatory, but to the study of metaphysics, which Maimonides saw as a higher discipline than mere rabbinic learning and behavior.

Indeed, the religious program of *Sefer Hasidim* expresses one of several contemporary "meta-halakhahic" or meta-legal ideals of medieval Jewish culture in the twelfth century. At the same time that Maimonides proposed Aristotelian metaphysics as the acme of Judaism, R. Judah the Pietist conceptualized the highest form of Judaism to be living as a Pietist.

Similarly, in twelfth-century Provence, other Jews were writing down Jewish mystical traditions that they, in turn, believed expressed the true hidden, ancient meaning of the written Torah as ten divine emanations, or *sefirot,* which they exegetically connected with all of rabbinic and biblical lore and law—the Kabbalah.

In northern France, still other rabbinic Jews, the tosafists, or Talmud glossators, developed an ideology around the supreme value of studying the Babylonian Talmud, of probing its contradictions and resolving them dialectically by using a scholastic method similar to that used in Peter Abelard's theological writings; Gratian's synthesis of canon law in the *Decretum;* and Irnerius's achievement, even earlier in Bologna, of systematizing Roman law.

Each of these four competing claims about the true, higher meaning of Judaism took place in the atmosphere of "the renaissance of the twelfth century" in Latin Christendom, in which the recovery of ancient Greek and Latin texts was accompanied by a new sense of the value of reasoning and of individualism applied to the reappropriation of earlier traditions.

The same can be said mutatis mutandis about the four types of Jewish cultural revival just outlined. All four reappropriated earlier Jewish culture and transformed it. Maimonides was original in many ways, but in his code at least he reappropriated the language, scope, and style of the first document of rabbinic Judaism, Rabbi Judah the Prince's *Mishnah* from around the year 200 in Roman Palestine. The Talmudist glossators, too, were innovating but used the same dialectical tools that characterized the Talmud itself, edited six hundred years earlier: questions and answers, contradictions reconciled by distinctions. The Kabbalah claimed to be ancient rabbinic lore; the *Zohar,* the main work of this genre, poses as an ancient Midrash written by one of the earliest masters of rabbinic Judaism, Rabbi Simeon Bar Yohai. And, finally, *Sefer Hasidim* claims that its lore, far from being original to R. Judah, was revealed to Moses and a few gifted religious virtuosi at Mount Sinai and was transmitted secretly for generations among the worthy (or Pietists) until it reached Rabbi Judah who wrote it down.

Sefer Hasidim exists in two different versions or recensions. The short one was published in Bologna in 1538 and became the basis for all subsequent printed editions of the book until the discovery and publication in 1892 of the long recension. This long recension is based on a single manuscript. Edited by Jehuda Wistinetzky, it was published in Berlin in 1892 and reissued in 1924 in Frankfurt am Main with an important scholarly introduction by Aron Freimann. Because it is held today by the Biblioteca Palatina in Parma, Italy, this is sometimes called the Parma manuscript. Until 1984, the Parma manuscript was the only witness to the long edition. In that year a second manuscript, more condensed than the Parma manuscript, became available. Now held by the Library of the Jewish Theological Seminary of America, this shorter recension is referred to as the New York manuscript.

The relative size of the two recensions is reflected in the fact that the paragraphs in the short version number 1,178, whereas those in the long version reach, with some errors of numbering along the way, almost 2,000. A consideration of the relationship between the two versions indicates that there is older and later material in both and that neither is exclusively dependent on the other. Hundreds of parallel sections exist in both recensions, but they are arranged differently. Over the years, scholars have supplied indices to the parallel paragraphs that are found in both the Parma manuscript and the Bologna edition, but an index still needs to be supplied for the New York manuscript of the Bologna edition.

Despite the differences in size between the two recensions, and the different order in which parallel or similar subunits are arranged in them, the table of contents of both recensions is remarkably similar. This fact suggests that the structure of the book was of critical importance and that several efforts were made to collect traditions and exempla and fit them into the same topical form. The book was not composed by one author in any conventional Western sense; there was no original version or urtext from which the various manuscripts and printed editions descended. Rather, like many other northern European Hebrew compilations, authors or groups of individuals compiled multiple versions of the same work. Sometimes one author did this. The open-ended or indeterminate character of Jewish book writing in medieval France and Germany is very different from Jewish authorship in Hebrew or Arabic book composition in Muslim lands, where a single author wrote a book once and published it.

Apparently, Rabbi Judah the Pietist wrote down snippets of tradition, possibly on scraps of parchment left over or cut from the margins of other books, a practice well attested in Latin manuscripts. These fragments were later copied as separate paragraph units on conventional folio pages of parchment. By around 1300, the Parma manuscript existed, and sometime in the sixteenth century the small units were consecutively numbered.

This manner of composition and replication may account for the strange gaps of several lines found throughout the Parma manuscript that the scribe annotated: "Missing here" or "so many lines are missing here." These gaps may mean that the scribe's model from which he copied the book lacked some material because pieces had fallen out of the onetime bundles of parchment fragments.

In any case, the book's brief traditions were figuratively stitched together into topical units that, in turn, were combined into the book-length recensions that have survived. Altogether, they constitute the *Sefer Hasidim* and offer us a unique window through which to view religious virtuosi and everyday life in twelfth- and early thirteenth-century Germany.

Bibliography

Yizhaq Baer, "The Socio-Religious Orientation of *Sefer Hasidim*" [trans. and adapted by Jonathan Chipman] *Zion* 3 (1937): 1–50 (Jerusalem: Jewish Civilization University Series, n.d.); Abraham Cronbach, "Social Thinking in *Sefer Hasidim*," *Hebrew Union College Annual* 22 (1949): 1–147; Joseph Dan, "Rabbi Judah the Pious and Caesarius of Heisterbach: Common Motifs in Their Stories," *Studies in Agadah and Folk-Literature: Scripta Hierosolymitana,* ed. Joseph Heinemann and Dov Noy (Jerusalem: Magnes, 1971), 18–27; Monford Harris, "The Concept of Life in *Sefer Hasidim*," *Jewish Quarterly Review* 50 (1959): 13–44; Jacob Katz, *Exclusiveness and Tolerance* (New York: Schocken, 1961), 93–105; Ivan G. Marcus, *The Book of the Pietists: A Complete Annotated English Translation for the Yale Judaica Series* (in preparation); Marcus, "The Devotional Ideals of Ashkenazic Pietism," *Jewish Spirituality: From the Bible Through the Middle Ages,* ed. Arthur Green (New York: Crossroad, 1986), 356–66; Marcus, "The Historical

Meaning of Hasidei Ashkenaz: Fact, Fiction or Cultural Self-Image?" *Gershom Scholem's Major Trends in Jewish Mysticism: Fifty Years After,* ed. Peter Schäfer and Joseph Dan (Tübingen: Mohr, 1993), 103–14; Marcus, "Narrative Fantasies in Sefer Hasidim," *Rabbinic Fantasies: Imaginative Narratives from Classical Hebrew Literatures,* ed. Mark Mirsky and David Stern (Philadelphia: Jewish Publication Society of America, 1990), 215–38; Marcus, *Piety and Society: The Jewish Pietists of Medieval Germany* (Leiden: Brill, 1981); Marcus, "The Recensions and Structure of Sefer Hasidim," *Proceedings of the American Academy for Jewish Research* 45 (1978): 131–53; Marcus, *"Sefer Hasidim": A Critical Edition of the Parma Manuscript* (Jerusalem: Merkaz Dinur, 1985); Gershom Scholem, *Major Trends in Jewish Mysticism* (New York: Schocken, 1941); and Haym Soloveitchik, "Three Themes in the Sefer Hasidim," *Association for Jewish Studies Review* 1 (1976): 311–57.

I V A N   G .   M A R C U S

1250 During the latter part of the thirteenth century "Süßkind the Jew of Trimberg" is among the growing number of nonaristocratic *Spruchdichter*—poets writing on a wide range of social, religious, or political themes

For information on secular literature in German by Jewish writers in the High Middle Ages we are able to call on one witness and one witness only, and it must be made clear from the start that our single witness is both reticent and ambiguous. Hard facts about many of the poets of the later thirteenth century are very sparse indeed, and this is especially true of the poet called Süskint der Jude von Trimperg in the single manuscript in which his work is preserved, the Manesse Codex (also known as Minnesang Manuscript C), which is the great collection of Middle High German poetry compiled in the first decades of the fourteenth century in Zurich, and now in Heidelberg as Cpg 484. Nor, indeed, is the body of poetry ascribed to him extensive: Süßkind is not represented at all in other collective codices, although many similar poets appear in more than one. Under his name in the Manesse Codex we have twelve strophes of Middle High German verse, arranged, as is the custom in this codex, according to metrical forms. There are six different forms (we do not have the melodies), all with the tripartite (musically bipartite) structure found in medieval German lyric verse of a repeated initial section (the *Aufgesang*) and then a metrically distinct conclusion (the *Abgesang*). The strophes, the longest of which have fifteen lines, are in the main thematically independent, though sometimes those in the same form are linked. One feature of the rhyme schemes often (though not always) employed by Süßkind and found in others is the use of a final rhyme picked up from the first part of the poem. At the beginning of his group of poems, the marginal indication is the slightly varied *Suskint von trimberg ein jude,* and the opening initial *W* is decorated with a fanciful winged creature with a human head, wearing the distinctive Jewish hat.

It is highly questionable just how much may be extrapolated from the very limited material we have by this unique poet to help us form a general view of Jewish secular writing in German at this period. We are not even entirely sure that he was indeed Jewish. No matter how little we actually *know* about him, however, a great deal has been assumed and asserted with or without justification based partly on material in (or sometimes only imagined to be in) the poems, and partly on the full-page illustration that accompanies his work, one of the 137 magnificent pictures in the Manesse Codex. The poet cannot be associated with any historical personage (Jews named Süßkind have been identified in earlier and later documents, in 1218, and in the mid-fourteenth century), and even his place-designation (probably Trimberg near Schweinfurt, in Lower Franconia) is of little help, although the poet's language confirms this as his probable area of origin. It is indicative that modern material relating to this (at all events minor) medieval German poet ranges from a fascinating but strictly imaginative novel by Friedrich Torberg (*Süßkind von Trimberg*, 1972) to scholarly papers concluding that Süßkind, far from being the only known Jewish poet writing in German in the period, was not a Jew at all.

Even in recent literary histories and reference works, quite unequivocal statements may be found declaring that the poet *was* a Jew, and as many (by, for example, Raphael Straus, Helmut de Boor, and at least with a question mark, Chone Schmeruk) that he was *not*. Expressly Christian views have also been seen in some of his poems. The assumption that Süßkind was a Jew rests upon three clues: the name itself, with its accompanying designation in the Manesse Codex; the illustration in that manuscript, which shows a figure wearing the distinctive Jewish hat; and a reference in one of the strophes in which the poet states his dissatisfaction with singing at court and declares that instead he will turn his back on poetry and "will grow a long beard and gray hair, and will walk humbly in a long coat and large hat, like an old-style Jew." All of these points have been criticized as criteria for determining that he was a Jew. It has been argued that what might be no more than an image in the single strophe in question led the compilers of the Manesse Codex—whose hard information was scarcely better than ours—to assume that the poet (who was clearly not well known even in the fourteenth century) was himself a Jew, and to designate and then to depict him accordingly. It is, of course, always dangerous to draw biographical conclusions from a poet's oeuvre, especially when that poet uses a great number of highly conventional motifs, even though his writings probably do contain some reflection of reality. An early variation on the idea that the Jewish motif in that one poem is merely an image, incidentally, is the suggestion repeated in the original edition of the *Verfasserlexikon* in 1953 that the two strophes in that meter might be by another hand altogether.

The name Süßkind is a little more conclusive and can indeed be associated with Jews in the period, although again it is neither common nor exclusively Jewish, and many of the names of other nonaristocratic Spruchdichter of the period are unusual or descriptive, like Singûf (sing out),

or the two named Rûmslant (leave-the-land). The evidence of the Manesse Codex is, however, all we have, and the illustration, the purported picture of the poet, gives us no immediate help because it cannot be related to material in any of the poems and is, indeed, at variance with what is claimed in one poem about Süßkind's poverty. It is, of course, just possible that the very divergence of the scene from anything in the poems might indicate some extrinsic knowledge about Süßkind and that this might confirm that he was a Jew. The picture (by one of the supplementary illustrators), however, is itself stylized, with elements that can be matched on other illustration pages (especially those for Konrad der Schenk von Landeck or for the Burggraf von Regensburg). Whether there are specifically Jewish elements in Süßkind's verses other than his reference to "living like an old Jew" is a matter of debate.

Even where it is assumed that Süßkind von Trimberg was in fact a Jewish lyric poet writing in German in the later thirteenth century, two opposing judgments may serve to make it clear that the reception of such a poet can, in the absence of historical evidence, be a difficult matter. A widely circulated Nazi history book noted, for example, how "the Jewish Minnesänger Süßkind von Trimberg complained bitterly about being neglected" and then went on immediately to juxtapose, predictably enough, a point about moneylending. Against this, a history of the Jews (that by Solomon Grayzel, which was still in print in 1969) used precisely the same brief complaint-poem to support the view that the poet, "being a Jew, was kept out of many places and shabbily treated in others." The complaint expressed by Süßkind, though it sounds and may of course *be* realistic, is nevertheless commonplace in this sort of poetry and can be matched by examples from any number of other contemporary poets. In fact, he himself does not attribute the neglect to his being a Jew.

Even the illustration in the Manesse manuscript must be treated with care. Grayzel's *History of the Jews* reproduces the picture with a caption declaring it to show the poet "at the court of a bishop," adding that the reader should "note the figure pointing to the cross." Illustration 117 in the Codex actually shows a richly dressed Jewish figure (distinguishable again by the hat—the *Judenhut* prescribed after the Lateran Council in 1215—and the style of his beard) standing before a figure seated on a throne. The seated figure carries a crozier but has no other attributes of a bishop; he is equally richly dressed, but in secular clothing. Two other figures are present, and that they seem to be pointing (though not in any case at the cross) is a normal iconographic device to indicate that they are taking part in a discussion. Further, the cross (not in fact a Latin cross) is actually part of the banner of the city of Constance, not that of the bishopric. It is likely that the figure in the picture is involved in a business or political transaction. What it is we cannot tell, nor whether it represents something known about Süßkind.

Süßkind is frequently referred to as a *Minnesänger,* a love-poet, but this is also inaccurate. It is true that the *Kanzone* form, with its doubled Aufgesang and single Abgesang, is used both for courtly love poetry (*Minnesang*) and for the social-didactic and aphoristic lyrics known as *Spruchdichtung,* but of our poet's twelve strophes, only one (3:2) praises women, taking as a starting point the comment in Proverbs 12:4 that a virtuous woman is a crown for her husband. Because a permanent companion is also implied in the otherwise highly courtly description of the woman, there is nothing of the unattainability of the courtly love tradition.

Süßkind is a Spruchdichter whose poetic themes can virtually all be matched with those of his contemporaries or, indeed, with those of earlier poets, most notably Walther von der Vogelweide. One theme, for example, that recurs regularly in the works of later thirteenth-century poets, especially those who are not members of the aristocracy, is the nobility of character rather than of birth. Gottfried von Straßburg developed the point in his *Tristan,* and it has classical origins, but many of the Spruchdichter use it, too.

In the first strophe of those ascribed to Süßkind in the Heidelberg manuscript, the poet declares that he will accept as a nobleman only someone who behaves in a noble fashion; high birth is irrelevant, because such men can behave ignobly. This is a subsidiary motif, also a much-

used one, that the poet picks up again. The second strophe in the manuscript (there are three in the same metrical form, with a fairly complex rhyme scheme) is linked thematically with the first, in that it develops the theme of noble behavior. Süßkind plays here (and again the idea is not unique to him) with the notion of a medicine for use against wickedness. The medicine is made of five ingredients: the courtly virtues of good faith, breeding, generosity, bravery, and moderation (1:3). Other poets prescribe these virtues, sometimes as a group, though not always with the medicinal conceit. The final strophe in this metrical form (which is independent of the first two) can again be compared with the work of other poets, most notably Ulrich von Singenberg and Friedrich von Sonnenburg, who have written very similar passages. It develops the topos of a man's life—what he was, is, and will be toward a memento mori conclusion, in which the poet begs God ("full of grace") that his soul, too, should find that grace. De Boor considers this strophe to be Christian, and the final lines are indeed reminiscent of a liturgical collect or secret, perhaps in a mass for the dead—but there are echoes, too, of the Psalms, and there is no specifically Christian content. In neither case is the influence absolutely clear.

The second (less intricate) metrical form is represented by a single strophe only. The theme, again known in classical antiquity, is this time the notion that thoughts (the word itself is stressed anaphorically) are free, and the strophe ends with a series of proverbs. Süßkind's third meter is represented by two separate poems. The second of these is the poem of praise to a woman that has been referred to already, but the first (3:1) is religious in content. God is praised as the separator of day and night, for being the creator of the sun, the moon, and the stars, and as the giver of gifts that do not fade away; the influence of the first part of Psalm 148 is fairly clear in this case. There is a religious element, too, in 4:1 (the first of three strophes in this metrical pattern), when the poet takes up once again the theme of memento mori: no one knows the hour of his death, and (in a foreshadowing of the Everyman motif) friends, wealth, birth, and class are all powerless to help. There is a feeling of divine providence in the strophe that follows, however. Süßkind here uses the theme (yet again a conventional one) of acting according to nature, of remaining true to type, and he expresses the point in a series of proverbial phrases: if a donkey had horns, it would gore, and if the wolf had complete freedom, a lot of sheep would be lost. The third strophe, however, 4:3, makes a far clearer social point and is one of Süßkind's most interesting pieces. The rich are urged not to sneer at the poor because one day they might need the poor, who serve them anyway. The themes of both of these strophes may be linked with that of the sixth and final poem in the collection, a single strophe presenting a kind of fable. Animal imagery is extremely common among the Spruchdichter, and this poem is not remarkable in choosing a wolf as its central figure (although the choice has been taken as self-ironic on Süßkind's part to indicate a moneylending Jew). In it, the wolf complains that he is hunted as an outlaw, but that he is only following his nature, whereas many deceitful men go unpunished. "I am forced to steal to avoid hunger," says the wolf, "so why am I worse than a wicked hypocrite?" The admonition to the rich (who do possess a comfortable life and wealth) to behave properly is present once again.

The question arises, of course, as to how far if at all these poems can be related to the poet's life. Certainly the broad theme of supposedly noble men who act ignobly toward those less well-off might reflect the poet's own experiences, as it might those of any poet dependent upon patronage. Spruchdichter from Walther onward complain loud and long about being treated badly by the rich. Süßkind develops his own position more directly and on the surface at least more bitterly, however, in 5:1 and 5:2, which are cast as personal expressions. In 5:1 the speaker complains of how Herr Bîgenôt von Darbîân (Mr. Want from Sufferingsville) is his companion, and how her Dünnehabe (Mr. Short-Rations) lives in his house, causing his children to cry for food. He pleads with the rich to help him get rid of this unwelcome visitor. Nevertheless, the poem is a witty one that personifies misfortune, and once more the strophe can be compared with the writing of other poets who use similar devices. The almost equally enigmatic contemporary known just as "Tannhäuser" (also the subject of biographical speculation, though portrayed in the Manesse Codex as a Teutonic Knight), talks about how he is well acquainted with "Mr. Seldom-Rich," "Mr. Damage," and so on.

The second strophe is that referred to already, the only one in the oeuvre with an explicit reference to Jewishness. The whole matter of being a poet is a waste of time, the poet declares; and because the lords won't give him anything for his art, he will "flee their court, and live in old Jewish style." The formulation adopted by the poet is that of a threat; he is not already behaving in this manner—the phrase *ich wil* (I shall) is repeated three times. Once again, we do not really know with this poem either how much it reflects reality or how much it justifies critics referring to him as "a poor traveling poet" or, as some have said, "a poor wretch." His disgruntlement with the court seems real, it is true, and the image of himself as an old Jew is fully drawn, which bespeaks real knowledge, at least. But it is still a vision of the future, not of the present. Nor is there any special awareness of being an outsider in anything but the artistic sense; rather, there is the same feeling of existential precariousness encountered in so much Spruchdichtung, the same irritation with the court and with noble patrons expressed so vigorously by poets like Walther von der Vogelweide in his *Unmutston* poems ("poems of discontent") and elsewhere. Süßkind's contemporary, the poet known as Meister Stolle, for example, makes a strong attack on one patron's meanness in a poem in which he repeats *ern gît niht* (he gives nothing) anaphorically over and over again; and the poet known as hêr Geltâr also declares that he will give up singing at court. Similar discontent is expressed by many others. It is important to be consistent, too, in the evaluation of what little evidence we have about Süßkind. His editor, Carl von Kraus, felt that it was clear from the two strophes in meter 5 that Süßkind was genuinely a poor traveling poet, even though the judgment of poverty is not consonant with the illustration in the Codex (which certainly does not show a poor man). Interestingly, von Kraus also used this illustration as biographical evidence to prove that the poet was a Jew.

The sociology of the Spruchdichter of the later thirteenth century still requires research, even if the idea no longer holds that poetry, once a feudal, courtly pastime, fell gradually into decay and hence into the hands of the proletariat. Although many of these later poets were indeed not aristocratic, this does not represent a decline in or degeneration of an aristocratic activity that was not, in any case, exclusive. Nor, on the other hand, is that much-used term "wandering minstrel" or *Spielmann* an especially helpful one, given the potential for confusion with traveling *ioculatores* (entertainers of various sorts). Süßkind has also been seen as a Spielmann, and his very existence has been used to support the notion that there were other Jewish wandering minstrels. But the Spruchdichter are serious poets who have at least a pretension to learning, who are conscious of their art and aim at a high-level (court) audience with works that instruct rather than just entertain. Those who are not aristocratic—who are designated *Meister* in the manuscripts or who have no designation at all—are perhaps even more dependent upon patrons and their generosity than are the minor knights. Süßkind is indeed unique among these poets in being referred to as a Jew, but others seem to have different social roles—"the schoolmaster of Esslingen" is self-explanatory, the poet known as "Regenbogen" seems to have been a blacksmith. There is no real justification for the regularly expressed surprise that *even* a Jew should become a poet. If the Manesse illustration is of any documentary value, then Süßkind's status was higher than some. Legal restrictions would have been an inhibiting factor for a Jewish poet, but similar problems would have befallen others breaking away from their trades or their countries of origin (in which context we may recall the name Rûmsland).

Finally, "wandering" or "traveling" in this context is also a concept that needs to be handled with care. It need mean no more than appearing at a court away from the home area, and in the case of Süßkind, the court of Constance might be a possibility, given the illustration. How much

Süßkind traveled is also unclear, of course, and the smallness of his surviving work does not allow us to speculate. What his poems do not have is the contrast of *gast* and *wirt* (stranger and host) found in so many of the poets from Walther onward. The small amount of material ascribed to Süßkind remains a problem, of course. Whereas what has survived need not (and surely does not) represent the poet's entire literary output, Süßkind is still one of only a handful of the many late-thirteenth-century poets represented by a dozen strophes or less.

The evidence for Süßkind even as a Jewish writer, then, has to remain inconclusive, although the balance of probability is on the affirmative side. Old Testament allusions, however, especially to the Psalms—one of the first texts studied in the medieval schools—do not really help, and with such a small body of material it is simply difficult to reach any firm conclusions. What is important is that the corpus of poetry should be seen in the context of late-thirteenth-century Spruchdichtung as a whole. Here the religious elements do not stand out when set against those found in poets such as Friedrich von Sonnenburg, who like many others also praises God the Creator and refers to the Psalms.

It is even more dangerous to use this slender corpus to make judgments about a broader Jewish contribution to writing in German in the period or indeed about the specific treatment of the Jewish artist. Assuming that our poet was in fact a Jew, what we have are a few competent, well-turned, educated, but (in the context even of the Manesse collection) unremarkable and almost entirely conventional didactic verses, most of them conservative in their stress on the courtly ethical values of breeding, moderation, and especially inner nobility. An awareness of the transience of human life (another stock theme) is coupled with a desire for God's grace. With the sole exception of 5:2, all of these verses could be placed under the names of some other poet, and they would not stand out.

It is hard to find evidence in Süßkind's work of a specifically *Jewish* contribution or feeling; rather, we have a poet writing firmly within a conservative and highly conventionalized literary tradition. Even in the strophe (and there is only the one) in which the poet declares his intention to leave the court, it has to be stressed that the poet makes clear that it is his *art* that has been rejected and that this is once again a highly conventional response by a late-thirteenth-century Spruchdichter. What he does not say is that he has been spurned because he is a Jew, although that motif is developed by Torberg in his novel. Indeed, in some earlier studies of the poet (such as that by Albert Friedenberg in the *Jewish Quarterly Review* in 1902, which is factually unreliable in other respects and hence not included in the bibliography), that same assertion was made on the basis of a quite spurious translation of the poem in question, in which the speaker apparently claims that he "belongs to a race accursed." The version (from Karpeles's *Jewish Literature* of 1895) bears only a slight resemblance to the Middle High German.

Süßkind himself, then, tells us very little, and probably the first real evidence of Jewish German literary interaction in the Middle Ages must be sought elsewhere and later, in Judeo-German or proto-Yiddish (call it what we will) material, like the "Dukus Horant" of the Cambridge Codex TS-10 K 22, at the end of the fourteenth century. But it can be counted among the achievements of the nebulous medieval figure of Süßkind that he provided the basis for Friedrich Torberg's novel. Torberg constructs from the poems, which he translates in his text, a background for the poet and gives them an imaginative context. He makes the central figure a forceful personality determined to pursue his art though originally forbidden as a Jew to do so. This main character both speaks out against injustice and anti-Semitism and sings at different courts, but is aware of his position of being a Jew as well as a composer of German

songs. The poems are incorporated with skill, and the Manesse illustration even becomes a portrait. In an epilogue, the author draws the link between Süßkind, the Jew writing in German, and other Jews between two worlds, including himself, and so the novel becomes a memorial, but not just to the shadowy Spruchdichter. The work is an impressive one, but it remains a novel. This approach to Süßkind is probably the most appropriate and is certainly intellectually more honest than many others.

Bibliography

Helmut de Boor, *Die deutsche Literatur im späten Mittelalter I, 1250–1350* (Munich: Beck, 1962), 407–81; Kurt Franz, *Studien zur Soziologie der Spruchdichter* (Göppingen: Kümmerle, 1974); Carl von Kraus, *Deutsche Liederdichter des 13. Jahrhunderts,* ed. Hugo Kuhn (Tübingen: Niemeyer, 1958; 2d ed. by Gisela Kornrumpf, 1978), 2:421–25 and 2:513–16; Dieter Richter, "Ritterliche Dichtung," *Literatur im Feudalismus* (Stuttgart: Metzler, 1975), 9–40; G. Roethe, "Süßkind von Trimberg," *Allgemeine deutsche Biographie* (Leipzig: Bayer Akademie, 1875–1912), 37:334–36; Olive Sayce, *The Medieval German Lyric, 1150–1300* (Oxford: Clarendon, 1982), 408–41; Chone Schmeruk, "Can the Cambridge Manuscript Support the Spielmann Theory in Yiddish Literature?" *Studies in Yiddish Literature and Folklore* (Jerusalem: Hebrew University, 1986), 1–36; Hans J. Schütz, *Juden in der deutschen Literatur* (Munich: Piper, 1992); Karl Stackmann, "Süßkind von Trimberg," *Verfasserlexikon* (Berlin: de Gruyter, 1935–55), 4:350; Raphael Straus, "Was Süsskint von Trimperg a Jew?" *Jewish Social Studies* 10 (1948): 19–30; Friedrich Torberg, *Süßkind von Trimberg* (Frankfurt a. M.: Fischer, 1972); and Ingo F. Walther and Gisela Siebert, *Codex Manesse* (Frankfurt a. M.: Insel, 1988).

BRIAN MURDOCH

1286   R. Meir ben Barukh (Maharam) of Rothenburg, the leading rabbinic figure of his day, is arrested in Lombardy and delivered to Rudolph of Habsburg

The arrest, imprisonment, and death (in 1293) of R. Meir of Rothenburg signaled the end of the tosafist era. For close to two hundred years, rabbinic scholars in Ashkenaz (northern France and Germany) had been engaged in talmudic and legal (halakhahic) studies that were grounded in a dialectical method that revolutionized the nature of rabbinic interpretation. The study of rabbinic literature in the twelfth century was marked by sustained intellectual creativity, a hallmark of the larger twelfth-century renaissance that changed the face of scholarship in Christian Europe. Almost every section of the Talmud was subjected to close, critical analysis and compared with or contrasted to other relevant talmudic and rabbinic texts. Crucial to this process was the work of R. Solomon b. Isaac (Rashi) of Troyes (1040–1105), who attended the academies at both Mainz and Worms, the two major yeshivot of the pre-Crusade period. Rashi's running commentary to most tractates of the Talmud enabled his successors to apply new strategies of interpretation. The comments produced by Rashi's descendants and other students became known as *Tosafot,* or addenda. Given their wide scope on the one hand, and their attention to textual detail and nuance on the other, the comments were intended to complement or supplement the talmudic text itself as much as they were meant to probe or to enhance Rashi's commentaries. The scholars who composed the Tosafot were known as *ba'alei ha-Tosafot* (tosafists).

Traces of the dialectical method used by the tosafists can be found already at the academy of Worms in the last quarter of the eleventh century, although the possible influence of scholastic methods prevalent in the surrounding society must also be considered. The two most prominent tosafists in northern France in the twelfth century, Rashi's grandson R. Jacob ben Meir (known as Rabbenu Tam, 1100–1171) and a great-grandson of Rashi, R. Isaac b. Samuel of Dampierre (known as Ri), were exposed to this method by Rabbenu Tam's father, R. Meir, who had preserved samples of it from his student days at Worms. At the same time, Rabbenu Tam received Tosafot from an older contemporary who was perhaps the earliest German tosafist, R. Isaac ben Asher of Spires (Riba). The writings of the two major tosafists in twelfth- and early thirteenth-century Germany, R. Eliezer ben Nathan (Raban, a younger contemporary of Riba) and his grandson, R. Eliezer b. Joel ha-Levi (Rabiah), paralleled the developments in northern France, when the authors maintained contact.

There was, however, a significant difference in literary style. The German scholars composed free-standing books that presented halakhahic rulings, responsa, and other extracts according to the order of the talmudic tractates. The rabbis of northern France, on the other hand, offered comments that were closely attached to the talmudic text. These comments featured intricate textual analyses along with briefly stated legal conclusions. Moreover, they were usually compiled by students and reflect the fluidity of the study hall discussions that produced them. The Tosafot texts that became part of the standard editions of the Babylonian Talmud (along with Rashi's commentary) represent the teachings of many different tosafist masters. The teachings of one master were often transmitted to other tosafist study halls or academies where further discussion was incorporated or appended.

Regardless of its origins, the effect of tosafist methodology was far-reaching. R. Solomon ben Luria, a sixteenth-century Polish rabbinic scholar, wrote that "the tosafists . . . rendered the Talmud as a spheroid." As he goes on to explain, they successfully manipulated and maneuvered a corpus that appeared to contain passages that were irreconcilable, making it possible not only to resolve interpretational inconsistencies but also to utilize the Talmud more effectively as a primary resource and repository for halakhahic decisions (Luria 1968, introduction to *Hullin*). Indeed, during the thirteenth century, in addition to the compilation, organization, and expansion of twelfth-century Tosafot texts, there appeared a series of tosafist codes that were intended to summarize and to apply further, in practical legal contexts, the fruits of the prior century. Examples of these are R. Barukh of Worms's *Sefer ha-Terumah,* R. Moses of Coucy's *Sefer Mizvot Gadol,* R. Isaac ben Moses of Vienna's *Sefer Or Zarua'* (R. Isaac was a student of Rabiah and of other tosafist masters in both Germany and northern France), and R. Isaac of Corbeil's *Sefer Mizvot Qatan.*

The impetus to compose legal treatises was also generated in part by the German Pietists (*hasidei ashkenaz*) whose leaders, R. Judah the Pious of Spires and later Regensburg (d. 1217) and R. Eleazar of Worms, were active at the turn of the twelfth century. The Pietists stressed the importance of talmudic study that was geared primarily toward halakhahic conclusions. Dialectical argumentation was to be downplayed in favor of the more methodical collecting of legal decisions and customs. R. Eleazar of Worms's own *Sefer Roqeah* is a fine example of the pietistic approach. Four of the five tosafists just mentioned had connections to the Pietists. Although their

halakhahic works represented the results of tosafist dialectic, the urge to compose these codes may have come from German Pietism.

Another possible factor in the composition of Ashkenazic codes was the rapidly increasing awareness of the major pillars of Sephardic Halakhah, especially Maimonides' *Mishneh Torah* and R. Isaac Alfasi's *Hilkhot ha-Rif. Sefer Mizvot Gadol* bears the unmistakable imprint of *Mishneh Torah,* just as it (along with *Sefer Or Zarua'*) makes extensive use of *Hilkhot ha-Rif,* although the goals and approaches of the Ashkenazic codes remained markedly different from their Sephardic precursors. In the second half of the thirteenth century, the effect of Sephardic codes on tosafist writings advanced even further, especially in Germany. R. Meir of Rothenburg, who studied in both Germany (with R. Isaac Or Zarua) and, following an established pattern, in northern France as well (with R. Yehiel of Paris and R. Samuel of Falaise among others), elevated the writings of Maimonides and R. Isaac Alfasi beyond the first rank that had been accorded them by earlier tosafists. Although R. Meir and his students occasionally differed with Maimonides' conclusions, they considered his *Mishneh Torah* to be an inspired work, full of unquestionably authentic and accurate material. Moreover, several of the important commentary-codes of R. Meir's students—R. Asher ben Yehiel's *Perush ha-Rosh,* R. Mordekhai ben Hillel's *Sefer Mordekhai,* and R. Meir ha-Kohen's *Haggahot Maimuniyyot*—followed the order of or were based on *Hilkhot ha-Rif* and *Mishneh Torah.*

This dimension of Maharam mi-Rothenburg's approach to rabbinic literature should be linked with another. R. Meir dictated and composed Tosafot and novellae (*hiddushim*) to a number of talmudic tractates and edited collections of earlier Tosafot material. Nonetheless, his responsa (*she'elot u-teshuvot*) and legal decisions and customs (*pesaqim u-minhagim*) were his most copious (and best known) compositions. R. Meir was certainly not the only tosafist to author responsa and brief *pisqei halakhah.* He was the first, however, to preserve large numbers of his own responsa and legal decisions. Moreover, he was the first to compile the responsa of earlier Ashkenazic authorities, especially those of his teachers. Hundreds of R.

Meir's responsa were preserved and organized into collections by several of his immediate students.

These two unprecedented developments, the systematic preservation of responsa and decisions by R. Meir and his students, as well as the veneration of monolithic Sephardic legal codes, were most probably the result of deteriorating conditions in Ashkenaz, which shaped life in the thirteenth century from the 1230s onward. R. Meir was present for the so-called burning of the Talmud in Paris in the early 1240s. This tragic event was itself a consequence of the ill-fated Trial of the Talmud in 1240 at which his teacher, R. Yehiel of Paris, served as the main Jewish spokesman. R. Meir composed an elegy, "Inquire, you who have been consumed by the fire" (*Sha'ali serufah va-esh*; Habermann 1945, 183–85), in which he described the shock and pain felt by students of the Talmud. He intimates that despite their momentous loss, Ashkenazic scholars characteristically maintained their faith and continued their studies. Nonetheless, this incident contributed greatly to the heightened sense of intellectual insecurity and spiritual inadequacy that became evident in the Ashkenazic rabbinic literature as the thirteenth century progressed.

In response to a poignant question about an actual incident that occurred in Coblenz, R. Meir asserted that German Jewry and its rabbinic leadership had, from the days of the First Crusade in 1096, accepted and approved the practices of committing suicide and even killing others in the face of torture that might lead to forced conversion (*Kahana*, vol. 2, 54 [#59]). Those who died under such circumstances were considered martyrs. In another responsum (*She'elot u-Teshuvot*, Prague, #517), Maharam argued that once someone had made the decision to die as a martyr, he felt none of the pain of his death, regardless of the means of execution. R. Meir supported his contention on the basis of ancient mystical and rabbinic texts but saved his most striking proof for last: "There is no one in the world who will not scream when he touches fire with even the smallest finger or limb. Even if he tries to restrain himself he will be unable to do so. But we have seen many martyrs (*qedoshim*) who do not scream at all."

Temporal events had a noticeable effect on rabbinic literature. Legal decisions, preserved fully and authoritatively in the form of responsa, left little room for uncertainty, debate, or modification. By utilizing the works of Maimonides and Alfasi, which had been constructed to arrive at firm and undisputed legal decisions, Maharam and his students acquired additional stability and finality for their own rulings, a status that the difficult times demanded. Indeed, R. Asher ben Yehiel's son R. Jacob, born in Germany and influenced by R. Meir in his youth (prior to his family's flight to Spain to escape persecution), was the first rabbinic scholar trained in Ashkenaz to produce a full-fledged monolithic code, the *Arba'ah Turim*, which was in the mold of earlier Sephardic works.

This is not to suggest that R. Meir's considerable abilities as a halakhahist were limited to dealing with issues of tragedy or persecution. His responsa encompass all areas and aspects of Jewish law and have proven to be fruitful sources for the political, economic, and social history of medieval Ashkenazic Jewry. Despite the large number of Maharam's legal decisions, however, his tendencies toward strictness (*humra*) or leniency cannot be categorized firmly. For every programmatic statement that appears, one can find examples that contradict it. Nonetheless, R. Meir's proclivities in deciding matters of Jewish law and custom may be accurately described as conservative, especially when compared to the tendencies of earlier tosafists. In ritual matters ranging from the necessity of reciting certain blessings to the procedures for the burial of the dead on a festival, R. Meir attempted to offer solutions that would bridge opposing positions of his teachers and other predecessors so that the essential demands of both positions could be satisfied (*Kahana*, vol. 1, 298–99 [#531–35]; Katz 1984, 169). It is possible that R. Meir was swayed in this direction by the German Pietists, whose influence is clearly discernible in R. Meir's interpretation of liturgical and biblical texts, his appreciation of the efficacy of mystical praxis, and his approval (following his teacher R. Isaac Or Zarua' and others) of various pietistic modes of penitence and physical forms of penance (*tiqqunei teshuvah*) proposed by R. Eleazar of

Worms (Urbach 1980, 522, 547, 564; Elbaum 1992, 19–20, n. 3; 22, n. 9).

A similar approach is evident in matters of economic policy and even communal government. R. Meir's views on the rights of the majority and the minority in communal government amount to a nuanced amalgamation of the theories of Rabbenu Tam and Rabiah. Rabbenu Tam held that unanimous agreement of the communal board (*tuvei ha-'ir*), if not of the members of the community themselves, was required in all aspects of communal government. The more common practice in Franco-Germany, explicated thoroughly and approved unconditionally by Rabiah, was to follow the will of the majority.

R. Meir was able to interpret and apply these seemingly antithetical views and to develop an overarching theory of communal government that took both positions into account. In situations that involved communal regulation of social, economic, and religious life and practice (*migdar milta*), R. Meir maintained the more conventional view of Rabiah that a majority of the members of the community could set policy. He sided with Rabbenu Tam, however, in cases that involved the apportioning of tax encumbrances. In light of the increasingly harsh taxation demands that had become the rule in Germany at this time, individual members of a community stood to lose arbitrarily substantial amounts in the tax-collection process. For these matters, R. Meir ruled that it was necessary to bind the members of a community together on the basis of unanimous agreement. He also preferred that the communal board, which had the power to impose certain monetary fines and restrictions, be elected unanimously by members of the community.

Maharam's status as the leading scholar of his day (*gedol ha-dor*) accounted for the large number of questions that he received from near and far and for the unusually troublesome controversies that were brought to him for resolution. Occasionally, and without much success, R. Meir suggested that some of these matters might best be decided by the local rabbinic leadership. For the most part, however, R. Meir accepted his role willingly and without hesitation. He was partic-

ularly inspired when it came to matters of personal status (Urbach 1980, 529–34).

A high degree of empathy and sensitivity may be detected throughout Maharam's writings and practices. In several formulations, R. Meir stressed that a son's failure to provide support for his parents from specially designated funds (assuming that the son had the means to do so) and his choice to instead provide that support from charity funds constituted a desecration of the biblical requirement to show honor for one's parents (*Kahana*, vol. 2, 118–19 [#87]). R. Meir displayed great personal respect for colleagues and students. He apparently rose when his students entered the room. He offered encouragement to those who entered the nascent professional rabbinate and called repeatedly for rabbinic scholars to treat each other respectfully, even when they disagreed in matters of law and authority (Agus 1954, 143, 174–76).

In the last decades of the thirteenth century, Western European Jewry experienced dramatic increases in severe taxation measures and other threats to their livelihoods, as well as a steep rise in incidents of physical and religious persecution. Modern scholarship has debated whether the group of northern French and English tosafists who made their way to Israel in 1210–11 did so primarily in response to political, economic, or religious sanctions, or whether their *aliyah* was motivated by positive considerations of the spirituality of the land of Israel. There can be no doubt, however, that the eastward flight of R. Meir of Rothenburg and many others from Germany in the mid-1280s (perhaps with Israel as their final destination) was occasioned by restrictive policies of Rudolph of Habsburg, in addition to a series of blood accusations and murders. R. Asher b. Yehiel and other students of R. Meir fled Germany for Spain in the early years of the fourteenth century following the severe pogroms of 1298.

The precise details and reasons for R. Meir's capture and lengthy imprisonment have not been fully clarified, nor has the inability of German Jewry to ransom him prior to his death been explained sufficiently. Negotiations between Rudolph and German-Jewish rabbinic leaders and communities led to sums of money being paid and guaranteed, but not to R. Meir's release. R. Solomon Luria (1968, *Gitten* 4:66) maintained that R. Meir himself forbade the communities to pay any additional sums for his release. It is possible, however, that negotiations continued up until R. Meir's death in 1293, involving R. Asher ben Yehiel among others. R. Meir's body was ransomed finally from Albert I in the spring of 1307. During his imprisonment, in which he was held in at least two different locales, R. Meir had occasional access to rabbinic texts. He was also visited by students who were able to discuss legal and ritual matters with him.

The first half of the fourteenth century was a bleak period for Ashkenazic Jewry, as it was for Europe as a whole. The Jews of England were expelled in 1290, and the Jews of northern and parts of central France in 1306. German Jewry was rocked by a series of persecutions culminating in the decimation associated with the Black Death in 1348–49 and its aftermath. By the end of the fourteenth century, a number of older German-Jewish communities were able to stabilize themselves, and newer communities began to develop, especially in the eastern and southern regions. Although rabbinic leadership was centered initially in Austria, several important German rabbinic figures emerged by the late fourteenth and early fifteenth centuries. It is not surprising that policies and approaches of R. Meir of Rothenburg figured prominently in the literature of this period. As the last great tosafist master, and with a corpus that was relatively well preserved, R. Meir served as a strong link to the heyday of Ashkenazic rabbinic literature and thought and as a source of religious tradition and guidance. Moreover, R. Meir himself had dealt with issues that faced Ashkenazic Jewry in a period of difficulty and decline. In addition, his rulings in communal and economic matters were valued for their obvious balance and sense of fairness.

Maharam's responsa were cited in regard to a number of vexing situations faced by recovering communities in the period after the Black Death. R. Jacob b. Moses ha-Levi Moellin (Maharil, d. 1427), who was considered the foremost rabbinic authority and teacher throughout Germany, Austria, and Bohemia; his best student R. Jacob (Mahari) Weil (d. ca. 1450); and R. Moses (Maharam) Mintz, who studied with Mahari Weil in Germany and with R. Israel Isserlein in Austria all relied heavily upon a responsum of R. Meir of Rothenburg in the case of a community that was having difficulty electing the members of its administrative board and providing other key services. R. Meir ruled that the election, as well as the establishment of other services, could be accomplished through the acquiescence of the majority, despite his general preference that officers be elected unanimously. This ruling, which may have come to the attention of the fifteenth-century rabbis through its citation by R. Menahem of Merseburg (Saxony), who studied with a student of R. Meir's, was instrumental in allowing new or reconstituted communities to establish vital communal institutions with a minimum of difficulty. Rulings of Maharam were cited to the effect that individual Jews were barred from making any separate arrangement for the payment of taxes to the overlord unless the entire community agreed and every member could be compelled to contribute his share (Zimmer 1970, 19, 49–50).

R. Meir, extending a position of his father's teacher, the tosafist R. Simhah of Spires (which may itself have been based on the thought of the German Pietists), held that a habitual wife-beater should be punished severely, even by the amputation of his hand if necessary. R. Menahem of Merseburg applied this decision in the situation of anyone who had been heinously struck by a habitual attacker (R. Isaac b. Moses, *Sefer Or Zarua'*, vol. 3 [*Bava Qamma*], sec. 161; R. Meir b. Barukh, *She'elot u-Teshuvot*, Prague #81, Cremona #291; Zimmer 1970, 91–92). Maharam Mintz and other fifteenth-century rabbis referred to and prescribed pietistic tiqqunei teshuvah, which they associated with R. Meir. The approbation given to these practices by a halakhahist of Maharam's stature undoubtedly heightened their legitimacy in the eyes of fifteenth-century scholars, although there is a view within modern scholarship that suggests that some fifteenth-century rabbis resisted the use of these techniques. It should be noted that like their tosafist predecessors (and unlike several of their contemporaries in Prague / Bohemia), the rabbis of fifteenth-century Germany and Austria did not demonstrate any proficiency or interest in Jewish philosophy. There is, however, literary evidence for small circles around Cologne and elsewhere that were engaged in mystical or esoteric studies. It appears that Maharil, who expressed an interest in astronomy and liturgical music, was also familiar with certain mystical teachings.

The very nature of German rabbinic literature of the fourteenth and fifteenth centuries was closely related to the works of R. Meir of Rothenburg. The genre that R. Meir brought to prominence from a position of relative obscurity, the written responsum, became the favored literary vehicle. The responsa of Maharil, Mahari Weil, Maharam Mintz, R. Israel Isserlein (*Terumat ha-Deshen*) in Austria, and Mahari Weil's student R. Israel (Mahari) Bruna (d. 1480), are by far the most important and influential rabbinic works of this period. To be sure, the vicissitudes of the time diminished the literary output of rabbis generally and may have contributed to the reduced range of rabbinic writings as well. Indeed, recent research has revealed the existence of a number of important communal rabbis, such as R. Zalman Katz of Nuremberg, who remained almost completely unknown, either because they left no unified compositions or because their small treatises were lost (Yuval 1989, 48–58).

Lists, or full-fledged collections of the customs that leading rabbis followed (*sifrei minhagim*), formed another genre that became popular in the fifteenth century. Two well-known examples of this genre are *Minhagei Maharil,* which was compiled by his student, R. Zalman of the Rhineland community of St. Goar, a number of years after Maharil's death, and *Leqet Yosher* by R. Joseph b. Moses of Hoechstadt (Bavaria), which contains the customs and practices of his teachers R. Israel Isserlein and R. Jacob Weil, among others, together with selected responsa and pesaqim. This type of work had its principal antecedents among the students of Maharam. Both *Sefer ha-Parnas,* composed by R. Moses Parnas of Rothenburg, and the more widely cited *Sefer Tashbez,* compiled by the Boswell-like R. Samson ben Zadoq, pre-

sented in great detail the ritual, personal, and communal practices and customs of R. Meir. This genre became even more important after the turbulent fourteenth century, when it was no longer possible to establish customs consistently and accurately on the basis of what was done by the general populace in various communities. The best alternative was to disseminate the customs of the generation's greatest scholars, which could be adopted and followed by communities. A series of practical handbooks composed in fourteenth-century Germany dealt with topics such as scribal practices, circumcision, and other specialized ritual realms. These treatises, which were intended to standardize technical regulations and thereby provide guidance in areas where customs and traditions had been lost, also had their roots in works produced by students and other younger contemporaries of R. Meir of Rothenburg.

The status of rabbis in fifteenth-century Germany should also be considered in light of the life and times of Maharam, although in this instance the points of contrast are more significant than the commonalities. There is no evidence for a professionalized rabbinate in Ashkenaz (which meant the granting of both title and compensation) until the end of the thirteenth century. Even then, this institution seems to have begun slowly in outlying areas, and Maharam, as to be expected, was consulted when problems and questions arose. In addition to the upheavals of the fourteenth century, the desire of local rulers to appoint all spiritual leaders and the dearth of rabbinic leadership (which could still be found at the end of the thirteenth century even in the presence of Maharam and others), necessitated the formalization and expansion of the professionalized rabbinate (Breuer 1976, 18–20). Despite the formal appointment of and approbation for communal rabbis, however, their status and stature were perceived by both laymen and the rabbis themselves to be lower than those of their counterparts in earlier centuries. Mahari Weil discussed at length the tribulations that rabbis often endured in trying to retain their positions as communal leaders and heads of academies. Mahari Bruna was himself the target of abuse by vindictive laymen, overzealous colleagues, and competitors alike, and Maharam Mintz describes the excesses of both haughty heads of academies and disrespectful laymen. In addition, rabbinic decisions routinely expressed both trepidation and inadequacy in offering independent halakhahic rulings in certain kinds of cases (*yir'at ha-hora'ah*).

Strongly felt expressions of inadequacy as well as concern for their abilities and status as decisors can also be found with increasing frequency in the rabbinic literature of Ashkenaz in the late thirteenth century. Nonetheless, the rabbinic establishment at that time did not undertake any initiatives to strengthen or reinforce its position. Indeed, Maharam wrote that although according to talmudic law an individual scholar could place a ban against a layman who had wronged him personally or economically without recourse to a sitting rabbinic court, this should not be done in practice because members of the community might not abide by such a ban and the scholar's prestige would in fact be diminished. In the fifteenth century, this issue was raised anew. Whereas leading scholars such as R. Jacob Weil maintained that the privilege of imposing a ban was unavailable to scholars of his day, others including R. Israel Bruna disagreed (Yuval 1989, 406–8, 417–18). Rabbis of the fifteenth century found it necessary generally to utilize prerogatives that would enhance their status. Despite the deteriorating societal conditions at the end of the thirteenth century, the position of the rabbinic scholar was still essentially intact. The need to strengthen it was felt less strongly, and therefore less benefit was seen in any attempts to do so.

A similar pattern can be seen in regard to tax exemptions for scholars, for which there was justification within talmudic law. Leading Ashkenazic scholars, beginning with the pre-Crusade period and continuing through the twelfth and thirteenth centuries (including students of R. Meir of Rothenburg), maintained the ideal that Torah study should not be associated with any type of overt economic advantage; thus they did not accept tax exemptions. A more lenient position in regard to tax exemptions developed among rabbinic leaders in both Austria and Germany during the period following the Black Death, perhaps as a corollary to the formalized professional rabbinate.

As an heir to the legacy of Franco-German Jewry in the tosafist period, R. Meir of Rothenburg exhibited a remarkable and unending commitment to scholarship, piety, and community. His teachings and writings played a significant role in transmitting these values to the rabbinic leadership of Germany in the fourteenth and fifteenth centuries and beyond.

Bibliography

Irving Agus, *Rabbi Meir of Rothenburg* (Philadelphia: Dropsie College Press, 1947); Agus, *Teshuvot Ba'alei ha-Tosafot* (New York: Talpioth, 1954); Mordechai Breuer, *Rabbanut Ashkenaz Bimei ha-Benayim* (Jerusalem: Merkaz Shazar, 1976); Yedidyah Dinari, *Hakhmei Ashkenaz be-Shilhei Yemei ha-Benayim* (Jerusalem: Mosad Bialik, 1984); Jacob Elbaum, *Repentance and Self-Flagellation in the Writings of the Sages of Germany and Poland, 1348–1648* [Hebrew] (Jerusalem: Magnes, 1992); Simhah Emanuel, "Teshuvot Maharam mi-Rothenburg Defus Prague," *Tarbiz* 57 (1988): 559–97; Avraham Grossman, "Reshitan shel ha-Tosafot," *Rashi: Iyyunim be-Yezirato*, ed. Z. A. Steinfeld (Jerusalem: Bar Ilan University Press, 1993), 57–68; A. M. Habermann, *Gezerot Ashkenaz ve-Zarefat* (Jerusalem: Tarshish, 1945); R. Isaac b. Moses of Vienna, *Sefer Or Zarua'* (vols. 1–2: Zhitomir, 1862; vols. 3–4: Jerusalem, 1907); I. Z. Kahana, *Maharam mi-Rothenburg: Teshuvot, Pesaqim u-Minhagim* (Jerusalem: Mosad ha-Rav Kook, 1957–63); Ephraim Kanarfogel, "The Aliyah of Three Hundred Rabbis in 1211: Tosafist Attitudes Toward Settling in the Land of Israel," *Jewish Quarterly Review* 76 (1986): 191–215; Kanarfogel, *Jewish Education and Society in the High Middle Ages* (Detroit: Wayne State University Press, 1992); Kanarfogel, "Unanimity, Majority, and Communal Government in Ashkenaz During the High Middle Ages: A Reassessment," *Proceedings of the American Academy for Jewish Research* 58 (1992): 79–106; Jacob Katz, *Goy shel Shabbat* (Jerusalem: Merkaz Shazar, 1984); Ephraim Kupfer, "Li-Demutah ha-Tarbutit shel Yahadut Ashkenaz ve-Hakhameha ba-Me'ot ha-Yod Daled / Tet Vav," *Tarbiz* 42 (1973): 113–47; R. Meir b. Barukh of Rothenburg, *She'elot u-Teshuvot* (Cremona, 1557; Lemberg, 1860; Berlin, 1891; Pressburg, 1895); R. Solomon Luria, *Yam shel Shelomoh* (repr. New York, 1968); Haym Soloveitchik, "Three Themes in the Sefer Hasidim,"

Association for Jewish Studies Review 1 (1976): 311–57; Israel Ta-Shma, "Qavvim le-Ofiyyah shel ha-Sifrut ha-Rabbanit be-Ashkenaz ba-Me'ah ha-Yod Daled," *Alei Sefer* 4 (1977): 20–41; Ta-Shma, "Rabbenu Asher u-Veno R. Ya'aqov Ba'al ha-Turim: Bein Ashkenaz li-Sefarad," *Pe'amim* 46–47 (1991): 75–91; E. E. Urbach, *Ba'alei ha-Tosafot* (Jerusalem: Mosad Bialik, 1980); I. J. Yuval, *Scholars in Their Time: The Religious Leadership of German Jewry in the Late Middle Ages* [Hebrew] (Jerusalem: Magnes, 1989); and Eric Zimmer, *Harmony and Discord: An Analysis of the Decline of Jewish Self-Government in 15th Century Central Europe* (New York: Yeshiva University Press, 1970).

E P H R A I M   K A N A R F O G E L

1300 Near the end of the thirteenth century, a body of literature emerges to help acquaint children with the texts and traditions of Judaism

In the period between the beginning of the twelfth century and the middle of the fourteenth century, from the time of the First Crusade to the time of the Black Plague (1096–1350), technological developments did not allow the luxury of writing for children, and neither public nor private attitudes perceived a need for such a literature. The reason efforts were made to adapt the scriptural texts for children was that Jews as a group recognized a pressing need for children to undergo a process of group socialization connected to the literature and texts of the Jewish culture. Therefore, considerable efforts were made to introduce the children to the group's sacred texts, to create an intimate experiential connection between the children and the texts. In my opinion, it is possible to define these efforts as "writing for children," which can be seen as a sort of prelude to "children's literature." In other words, we cannot speak of a specific and separate body of writing aimed at children and stemming from a recognition of their unique needs, but a first step was made toward understanding that something appropriate and specific for children needed to be created. Research indicates that the Jewish group in this period had a definite perception of childhood, one that recognized the special characteristics of this age group and encompassed a clear understanding of how young persons should be treated. Jewish parents demonstrated great understanding, closeness, and emotional warmth and expressiveness toward their offspring, as well as a deep concern for children and their special needs: food, emotional and medical attention, and more. In Jewish sources we find the special attitude toward the unique period of childhood defined in the term "the way of children."

"The way of children" is the unique manner in which children understand the world. Their process of understanding is different, special, and one shaped by gradual development. They are very sensitive emotionally and of course physically. Young children are easily frightened, helpless, and pose a risk to themselves; they must therefore be supervised with extreme caution. This point of view created a special bond of physical and emotional intimacy between children and adults in general and children and parents in particular. We find expressions of great concern for infants in regard to their health and in regard to nursing, and descriptions of heartbreaking sorrow in cases of severe illness and child mortality. On the other hand, the swift process of introducing the child into the normative framework started immediately with the child's first encounter with education. This process began in accordance with the child's mental ability and had no connection to either his biological development or the chronological age defined in the Talmud as the age at which responsibility is first assumed (thirteen years and a day). The group perceived the child to be a responsible, thinking individual at a considerably earlier age and assigned him or her maximum duties and respon-

sibilities, which I will detail later. The explanation for this dual attitude toward childhood—on
the one hand, recognizing its special characteristics, and on the other hand, desiring the child's
inclusion in adult society—can be found in the
relationship of the Jewish community to the surrounding Christian society. The Jews were conscious that the Christians wanted to convert Jewish children to Christianity. Their concern was
based on active efforts on the part of both the
secular and church establishments to take over
their children. In order to counter this threat, the
community tried to construct a process of socialization that would crystallize the inner Jewish
group and make it resistant to the outer Christian
group with all its temptations and violence. The
children benefited from special attention but also
from a special preparatory education, in effect a
special socialization process that served to foster
the individual's identification with and internalization of the primary values of his or her group.

Among these primary values were the unique
religious practices of the Jewish people, which
find expression in the fulfillment of ritual commandments and a lifestyle different from that of
others. Behind these practices lay the idea of the
people of Israel's status as the chosen people. This
idea was emphasized in contrast to the Christian
claim of the truth of Christ's gospel and the concept that the Jewish people were then abandoned
by God in favor of the Christians. The concepts of
the chosenness of Israel and the primacy of the
Jews as a group constituted powerful tools for
convincing Jews that transfer into the outer
Christian group would cause a decline in one's
ethical stature.

The value system of the Jewish people can be
found within canonical literature: the Bible and
its exegesis, the Talmud and its commentaries,
and the prayer book (*Sidur*). In order for the socialization process to come to fruition, the group
needed to convince its members that small children could understand and internalize the society's values. Creating this awareness required a
fundamental change in the way small children
were perceived.

In the eyes of medieval people, every child had
a different mental capacity; hence it was futile to

attempt to define a chronological or biological
age at which a child was ready to adhere to the
ritual commandments: "As it is said everywhere,
everyone is not equal, rather each to his own."
The people instead defined a new age group:
"little, knowledgeable, and he who has arrived at
the age of education." A child who was "little"
(less than thirteen years and a day) but "knowledgeable" had "arrived at the age of education"
and thus had to be educated in certain ritual commandments even though he was not of an age to
be punished. The people of that period based
their beliefs on the Talmud, which describes
those children who have to fulfill certain commandments irrespective of chronological or biological age (the children were to be tested to determine whether they were of the right age).
Medieval people demanded additional tests in order to establish who was "little and knowledgeable." A child who could maintain personal hygiene and was careful not to enter the bathroom
with his phylacteries had to fulfill the mitzvah of
laying tefillin. The child was required to be well
versed in the rules governing the commandment
for wrapping the *talit* and for carrying the *lulav*
and, furthermore, the reciting of the *Shema*
prayer. In other words, the child who proved his
understanding of the commandments to a sufficient degree would be responsible for performing
them, because "everyone is not equal, rather each
to his own." This conception of children as capable of learning quickly called for mechanisms
that would afford children opportunities to access
knowledge and acquire it. Adapting fundamental
texts—for example, those recited in the synagogue—to a child's level of comprehension thus
became a central goal.

Throughout the liturgy there are many mechanisms intended to educate and guide children
and to draw their attention to the content. For
example, during the reading of the Book of Esther
on the holiday of Purim, a number of verses are
scattered throughout that the congregation re-
cites in unison, thus ensuring that the children's
attention does not wane. Efforts were made to
involve the children in the adult prayers in the
synagogue: in the middle of the thirteenth century Rabbi Isaak ben Moses wrote in his book *Or*

Zarua that a child "had reached the age of education" even under the age of thirteen if he could come up to the dais and read from the Torah just as an adult would. In other words, children were encouraged to participate in the principal ritual of reading from the group's most sacred text. Another example is the orphan's kaddish. Saying the kaddish over the dead has the power to benefit the departed soul in the hereafter. This vital task naturally fell to the children of the deceased. In the period in question, this task was assigned even to the "little" orphan—those under age thirteen.

The clearest expression of the adult status granted to children can be found in the discussion and argument over the custom of counting a child as a tenth man in the minimum of ten men, or minyan, required for public prayer. One of the earliest sources for this is R. Yitzhak Bar-Yehuda. While a fire was burning in his city, he gathered a minyan for prayer and could find only nine men of the age of mitzvah. So he brought a small boy holding a *Chumash* (the five books of Moses or Pentateuch) to pray as the tenth. Throughout the Middle Ages the other sages objected strenuously to this practice, and it would seem that those against it were opposing an existing custom. At any rate, circumstances defeated these opponents, as evidenced by their interdictions. The futility of their efforts was perhaps predictable given that the children who were included were over "the age of knowledge," had "arrived at the age of education," and were actively involved in fulfilling other duties in the synagogue. In the end, it is possible that the phenomenon became customary due to the limited population of the communities and the desire to allow a minyan and communal prayer during the day, but in any case children came to be seen as adults for the purposes of prayer.

The importance to the Jewish community of bringing the child close to the group's sacred text is expressed during the first day of school in the Introduction to Education ceremony. The child, who is typically between the ages of three and five, and the text (the Torah) are the central figures in the ritual. The members of the community participated in the ceremony, during which the child is symbolically transferred from his home to the synagogue (or the home of the teacher). The importance of the ritual stems from the fact that after the ceremony the child embarks upon his stage of learning, during which he is introduced to the mysteries of the group's actual worship. Even if subsequent to this ritual he is not considered an adult or completely responsible for fulfilling the ritual commandments, he is essentially considered a member of the group despite his young age. In fact, during the period in question, there was no other rite whose function was to pass the child from infancy and childhood to the age of beginning to assume responsibility, or to conduct him into the mysteries of the group's rituals. This ceremony has great significance because implicit in the ritual is the attitude toward the biblical text so important to the group and because the ceremony reveals how the group adapts its principal text for the use of children. The preparations for the ceremony included bathing the child and dressing him in clean clothes. In addition, special, symbolic foods are prepared for this momentous day. For the transferal of the child from his parents' home to that of the teacher, the child's parents seek out an additional person, one who is "important and wise." There is an emphasis on the need for the child to be covered while he is being carried from his home to the synagogue and back again. The ceremony is usually conducted in the synagogue, and the members of all age groups participate. Children are taught their first meaningful words and undergo a variety of rituals related to this day.

We can identify a variety of motifs that shape this ceremony. For instance, the entire ritual parallels the myth of receiving the Torah on Mount Sinai, which is described in Exodus 19: the synagogue becomes Mount Sinai; the congregation, especially the children, are the People of Israel gathered at the foot of the mountain; the "important and wise" man symbolizes Moses; and the introduction of the children to the mystery of reading is like the ceremony of God presenting his people with the Torah and making an eternal covenant with them. At the end of the ceremony, the board on which the letters of the Hebrew alphabet are written is coated in honey, and the child licks the honey. He then eats the alphabet-shaped cookies that have been specially prepared for him. The descriptions of pictures from this period that have survived validate all the details described in the written sources (Schultz 1987, 122–24, the picture from Leipziger Mahzor).

A child's reading education traditionally commenced with the first verses of Leviticus. It is difficult to understand why these verses were chosen rather than the creation stories and stories of the Fathers in Genesis, or the beginning of the instructions of the commandments in Exodus. The explanation given in the Talmud, in the name of R. Asi, is that pure infants should deal with the pure sacrifices. This is unquestionably an excuse for the trend after Bar Kochva's revolt of teaching the section about sacrifices in order to ensure that events connected to the destroyed Temple would not be forgotten. In the period under discussion, this excuse is presented but it is related to the children: "And why shall the beginning be *Torat Cohanim* in Leviticus? The Holy One Blessed be He said that the pure ones should come and study purity, and I consider it as if they had sacrificed to me." In *Sefer Hasidim* the consolidation of the in-group is emphasized in a discussion of the same biblical material: "And when he comes to learn at the age of five, they begin to teach him in the book of Leviticus 'when a man of you bringeth an offering unto the Lord' (Lev. 1:2), from among you is my portion, and not the other nations."

This theme of sacrifice is emphasized again and again in all of the verses taught to the child in his first reading lessons—starting with the first verse, which teaches about God choosing the people of Israel and the impossibility of a non-Jew making a sacrifice, through all the verses in the first chapters of Leviticus that relate to this theme. In addition, when the child celebrates the end of the first stage of learning to read, he does so by reading aloud in public a passage relating to sacrifices that ends with the words "It shall be a perpetual statute throughout your generations in all your dwellings, that ye shall eat neither fat nor blood" (Lev. 3:17). The explanation advanced by Jews of the period to this strange and public ending is astonishing: "Because of the children whose blood and fat were diminished because of studying Torah, I consider it as if you had sacrificed them to me." The *brit milah* is seen as similar to a sacrifice in that blood is spilled, and the child is seen as being like a sacrifice. "The world is sustained by the breath of children [learning Torah]," equal in merit to the sacrifices, and therefore "I consider it as if you had sacrificed them before God." Thus the commencement of learning is not given a pedagogical emphasis but rather a theological-social emphasis with the children at the center.

The language of study was Hebrew, and the sources were mainly the Bible and the Talmud. In his commentaries on the Talmud, Rashi refers as a matter of course to the children sitting in the synagogue and studying the Bible or repeating what they had learned while reading the Pentateuch. In *Masechet Megilla* he writes: "as the children were wont to read in the synagogue"; in *Masechet Shabat* he writes: "Sometimes the cantor doesn't know the place for the next day's reading, and he sees where the children are reading in the candlelight in the synagogue and he knows that this is the portion for the week." The fact that very small children who know how to read are present in the synagogue can also be inferred from the words of the author of *Kol Bo*. When he wants to emphasize that each man who enters the synagogue must recite a prayer or a portion of the Torah before he leaves, he writes: "He must either read one verse or tell one of the children to read one for him if he doesn't know how to read." This author also notes that one mustn't read an incomplete verse, except for the purpose of teaching children to read: "It is said that a verse shall not be interrupted, except in the teaching of babies."

Recent research indicates that elementary education in the earlier period did not take place in an organized, community-sponsored framework, but rather in the home. In the important families, basic teaching was done by the father, uncle, or brothers. In other families, an agreement was reached between the father and a private tutor, the *melamed,* and a course of study was set. In these latter circumstances, the material that is taught gains even greater importance, as does educational literature for children. Direct evidence of

Jewish concern for this issue can be found in a number of passages from *Sefer Hasidim:* instructions appear in the first passage that teach fathers how to hire a suitable teacher for their sons. The advice cited is to test the teacher's knowledge, especially his familiarity with the Bible and the Talmud, the principal books of instruction: "From the beginning when a man hires a tutor for his son he should be educated in the thing he is teaching, for if a man's sons are studying Bible and the Rabbi is well versed in the Talmud but an ignoramus in Bible studies, in what the boys need he should have knowledge 'for in all you acquire, acquire wisdom' (commentary on Prov. 4:7); he should have a teacher who knows that even though he's only studying Hebrew, he must understand what he's learning, and when he's studying Bible he should understand it." Further on, the subject matter emphasized is the Torah and Talmud.

The second passage (S.H.P., 176) reveals that people who were buying books sought Pentateuchs for small children as well as books of *Tosafot,* which are actually books that expand and elucidate the text of the Talmud didactically, with examples such as this one: "A man who is traveling abroad and has money to purchase goods, and finds books which are unavailable in his city, such as Perushim and Tosafot, or in the event that in his home town parchment is expensive and there aren't enough books for all the scholars or enough Pentateuchs for the children, it is a good deed, (a *mitzvah*) to buy books and sell them, but if they have sufficient books to meet their needs then he shall not trade in books."

The third passage (S.H.P. Saif, 358) confirms that the main material for teaching Talmud to children was the writings of the tosafists: "If one man has students he shall instruct them, and if another good rabbi has students as good as his, he shall instruct them as he does his own, and if he has the Tosafot and the other rabbi doesn't, he shall not say I won't lend them to him, so his students will come to me, for it is said your friend's honor shall be as dear to you as your own and it is written (Lev. 19:18) love your friend as you love yourself."

From the fourteenth to the sixteenth centuries, with the invention of printing, we find two central efforts intended to further writing for children. One effort in the educational field included publishing special collections of writings to aid in the teaching of the books of Halakhah. The other related to bringing children closer to the central texts of Judaism.

This first type of initiative took the form of a new kind of writing that consisted mainly of summaries of the Halakhah books; this writing appears from the fourteenth century onward. Although it is possible to view this literature as having been written for a dual purpose—namely, for teaching and as an aid in deciding the law—in my opinion these briefs were intended principally for students, because they seem designed for people who need to absorb a great deal of material in a short time.

The principal texts (listed in order of importance, not chronology) in this literary style to be found on the bookshelf of a Jewish scholar of the period were:

1. Jacob ben Asher, *Arba'ah Turim* (Four columns). This was a central *psika* book, compiled in the fourteenth century by Rabbi Jacob ben Asher who was originally from Ashkenaz, where he studied under his father, one of the most important of the sages of Ashkenaz. In the early fourteenth century, Rabbi Jacob moved to Spain. It was there he wrote his inclusive psika book about the mitzvoth customarily observed in his time.

2. The book of Mordechai, written by Rabbi Mordechai Ben Hillel at the end of the thirteenth century. This is essentially a commentary on the legal decisions of R. Yitzhak Alfasi according to the customs of Ashkenaz. His comments reflect the opinions of his Ashkenazi and French teachers, and in particular those of the Maharam of Rothenburg in the late thirteenth century. This book has been much revised, and it is difficult to estimate its original size.

3. Asher b. Yehiel's *Sheelot u-Teshuvot ha-Rosh* (Venice, 1552). This is a description of legal decisions and a collection of questions and answers. Yehiel was a student of the Maharam of Rothenburg who moved to Spain in the early 1500s.

4. The book of *Sha'arei Dura* (The gates of

Dura), which categorizes what is permitted and what is forbidden. Written by R. Isaak of Dura toward the end of the thirteenth century, the book is concerned with the laws governing the issue of forbidden foods and *Nida*. Its rulings are clear-cut and allow no give and take with the Halakhah.

5. Moses of Coucy's *Sefer Mizvot Gadol* (Venice, 1807), written at the end of the thirteenth century, after the burning of the Talmud in Paris. Two volumes of *aseh* and *lo taseh* ("thou shalt" and "thou shalt not") commandments, the 613 mitzvoth that appear in the Pentateuch, arranged by order of appearance.

6. Isaak ben Joseph of Corbeil's *Sefer Mitzvot Katan*, written at the end of the fourteenth century. A classification and clarification of the 613 mitzvoth divided into seven parts to allow each supplicant one prayer each day of the week.

The above literature became an authoritative text both for the study of Halakhah in the *yeshiva* (*Poskim* lesson) and as a basis for the literature of *Pilpul*. This library became study material by a process of copying and revising. It was copied by students who abridged and revised it endlessly while copying. There exist many copies of this literature with remarks in the margins that clarify, revise, and comment on the original contents of the page. These are known as *Hagahot*. Thus these books also became "summaries"—that is, adaptations of canonical texts for didactic purposes—which were revised in turn.

In order to demonstrate the meaning of this second form of writing for children, I will describe what happened to the Passover *Haggadah* with the early appearance of print, and explain why in my opinion it is possible to view the *Haggadah* as the shift to writing for children. The events of the Seder night and of course the central text of the evening—the Passover *Haggadah*— were arranged with a view to transmitting the messages of this important holiday to children. In this sense, Passover eve is an educational evening. The imperative for celebrating the Seder is the biblical injunction "and you shall tell your son on that day" (Exod. 13:8). There is a clear didactic purpose to the evening: in order to transmit the

message, and in order for the message to be internalized, the child's interest must be aroused. The child will ask, and thus he will remember and internalize the reply. Even the tool for transmitting the messages was already specified in the Torah. The child must ask so the father can answer him (Exod. 12:26, Exod. 13:14–15, Deut. 6:20–23). Thus was created the blueprint for the Passover *Haggadah*, into which were subsequently inserted midrashim and selected passages and prayers in order to meet the need to convey the messages to the children.

By performing unusual, illogical, and strikingly theatrical acts on Passover night, the adults encourage the child to ask questions. For example, the Talmud tells us that before the meal began, it was customary to carry the table outside so that the child would inquire as to the reason for this peculiar act, which would then be explained to him. This mechanism is similar to that of the four questions. These mechanisms to pique the child's interest were developed before the Middle Ages and during the period in question the practice was polished and improved so as to create a text clearly aimed at children.

During the Middle Ages, two particular refinements were made. The first was the introduction of songs at the end of the *Haggadah;* the second the addition of illustrations to the text, illustrations with a clear didactic intention. The songs "Had Gadya" and "Ehad Mi Yode'a," which were introduced no earlier than the fourteenth century, undoubtedly were inserted in order to recapture the children's attention toward the end of the Seder. "Ehad Mi Yode'a" was borrowed from a Christian song whose origin was a farmer's song. "Had Gadya" also has a German origin; the Aramaic is faulty. Both songs encourage children to continue to participate in the last part of the Seder, when they are tired. Similarly, the illustrations were intended to arouse the children's curiosity, to draw their attention to significant points, and to ensure that they stayed awake and alert throughout the long evening. One example of such an illustration is found in the 1526 Prague *Haggadah;* on pages 21 and 22 are two illustrations depicting Jewish children being harmed by the Egyptians, who are dressed as urban Christians. The Jewish children are shown being drowned in the river or grabbed by Egyptian soldiers, who are spilling their blood into the bathtub where the leprous Pharaoh is soaking. This illustration appears repeatedly in *Haggadahs,* presented as an ongoing story in three parts. In the 1590 Prague *Haggadah,* there is a written explanation: "Pharaoh is bathing in a bath full of the blood of the poor children of Israel, thus his leprosy might be cured."

In the Augsberg *Haggadah,* published in 1534, an illustration depicts the children seated across from their parents and pointing at the *pesach* and the bitter herbs (Yerushalmi 1975, plate 14). In the Augsberg *Haggadah,* under the words "pour the second cup" is an illustration of a man pouring wine (Yerushalmi 1975, plate 17).

The instructions for how to begin the Seder if it fell on a Saturday night were remembered by a mnemonic device, an acronym of the Hebrew words for: wine, kiddush, candle, and time: YAKNEHAZ. This term reminded German Jews of the German word for rabbit hunting, *Jagen-has,* and in the *Haggadah* there is an illustration depicting a rabbit hunt. Horsemen are on the left of the picture, preceded by hounds chasing the rabbits, while on the right side of the picture a net is stretched to trap the runaway prey. This is clearly a tool intended for children. The picture reminds them of the German term, which in turn reminds them of the Hebrew acronym, which then reminds them of the correct order in which the things are to be done. It is obviously aimed at children and not adults, because adults are well aware that on Saturday night the order of things is different. The illustration bore an additional educational message: in another picture the rabbits are seen escaping from the net, that is, the Jews are escaping their persecutors.

Sixteenth-century *Haggadahs* and *Books of Customs* are illustrated with explanatory pictures that instruct children in their particular duties: the Venice *Book of Customs* from 1600 has an illustration of a child searching for crumbs at his father's feet. The source for this picture was the *Haggadah* of Mantoba 1560, page 1. In addition, in the *Venetian Book of Customs* from 1593 *daf 19 amud bet* there appears an illustration of a child searching for crumbs under the table at his father's feet, or perhaps scattering crumbs. Thus it is evident that the inclusion of children in the illustrations of the *Haggadah* dates back quite far and had a definite purpose.

The 1606 Prague *Haggadah* clearly states, in Yiddish, that the pictures are included for the children's sakes, to keep them alert and awake on the Seder night. In my opinion, it is possible to view this trend of directing the *Haggadah* at children, which is evident as early as the sixteenth century, as the point at which writing for children became children's literature.

Bibliography

Simha Goldin, "Die Beziehung der jüdischen Familie im Mittelalter zu Kind und Kindheit," *Jahrbuch der Kindheit* 6 (1989): 211–33, 251–56; Solomon Grayzel, "Popes, Jews, and Inquisition, from 'Sicut' to 'Turbato,'" *Essays on the Occasion of the Seventieth Anniversary of the Dropsie University* (Philadelphia: Dropsie University Press, 1979), 151–88; Avraham Grossman, *The Early Sages of Ashkenaz* [Hebrew] (Jerusalem: Magnes, 1981), 299–300; Ephraim Kanarfogel, "Attitudes Towards Children and Childhood in Medieval Jewish Society," *Approaches to Judaism in Medieval Times* 2 (1985): 1–34; Kanarfogel, *Jewish Education and Society in the High Middle Ages* (Detroit: Wayne State University Press, 1992), 15–41; Elchanan Reiner, "The Yeshivas of Poland and Ashkenaz During the 16th and 17th Centuries," [Hebrew] *Studies in Jewish Culture in Honor of Chone Shmeruk,* ed. I. Bartal et al. (Jerusalem: Magnes, 1993), 21–22, n. 20; M. Schultz, "Feste Mit dem Kind, Feste um das Kind, Zur Geschichte jüdischer Kindheit in Deutschland," *Kinderkultur,* ed. Konrad Kostlin (Bremen: Focke-Museum, 1987); Chone Shmeruk, *The Illustrations in Yiddish Books of the Sixteenth and Seventeenth Centuries* [Hebrew] (Jerusalem: Akademon, 1986), 45–47, 49, 56; Israel Ta-Shema, "Children of Medieval German Jewry: A Perspective on Aries from Jewish Sources," *Studies in Medieval and Renaissance History* 12 (1991): 263–80; Ta-Shema, "Some Notes on the Origins of the 'Kaddish Yathom (Orphan's Kaddish),'" [Hebrew] *Tarbiz* 53 (1984): 559–68; and Yosef Hayim Yerushalmi, *Haggadah and History* (Philadelphia: Jewish Publications Society, 1975), 16, 25.

SIMHA GOLDIN

1382 An anonymous scribe completes the transliteration into Hebrew of a Germanic epic poem with the Yiddish title "Dukus Horant"

Other than a twelve-word Old Yiddish inscription in the Hebrew-Aramaic language prayerbook *Worms makhzer* dating from 1272, the "Dukus Horant" is the oldest surviving literary document in the Yiddish language. To substantiate this claim, I will explore both its secular and artistic merits.

Almost from the date of its first publication to the present, this literary text has been the source of considerable expectation and subsequent disappointment by Germanists as well as an object of controversy for all scholars concerned. After the initial publication of a few verses in 1954 in *The Field of Yiddish Studies,* the entire text became available in print in 1957. Leo Fuks's edition, entitled *The Oldest Literary Documents of Yiddish Literature, Circa 1382,* is based on the manuscripts housed in the library of the University of Cambridge, where it is referred to as Taylor-Schecter 10.K.22. The collection contains six poems resembling Central Middle High German transliterated in Hebrew characters. The manuscripts were purchased for the Cambridge library by Charles Taylor and Solomon Schecter from the Cairo Fostat Genizah in 1896. This *genizah* (secret hiding place) was located in a synagogue in Cairo that housed collections of religious works that were no longer usable. The texts were intended to be kept there prior to their ritualistic burial but were subsequently neglected and forgotten until their rediscovery by European tourists and collectors.

The date of the manuscript as indicated by the copier colophon appears twice, on plates 38 and 40, respectively. It is the third Kislev 143 (the first digit being omitted because it is understood), that is, the Jewish calendar year 5143. It corresponds to the years 1382–83 C.E. or exactly to November 9, 1382. This date is paleographically verifiable because it is consistent with other Old Yiddish documents of known provenance written in Hebrew-Ashkenazic cursive.

Four of the poems deal with Jewish biblical themes—specifically, the stories of Moses, Abraham, and Joseph, as well as a description of paradise. The fifth is a version of the Aesopian fable of a sick lion, and the last is the "Dukus Horant," a lengthy fragment based on material from the tradition of the German heroic epic. According to Eli Katz, one of several editors of the Cambridge Codex, as the manuscript will be referred to henceforth, the document is an early representative of the literary tradition that gave rise to Yiddish literature. Katz therefore coined the term Germano-Judaic for this tradition before linguistic differentiation can be determined. Much of the controversy has revolved around the question of taxonomy involving two diametrically opposed points of view. According to one, propounded mostly by Germanists and medievalists, the Codex is merely Middle High German transliterated in Hebrew characters; according to the other, it is an Old Yiddish text that is different from any text written in Roman characters and medieval German.

For the purpose of this discussion, we shall refer to the language of this document as Old Yiddish on the theory that it represents a phase of Yiddish that predates the period of its separation from all variants of New High German. In addition to the argument of its close proximity to medieval German to justify its designation as an example of Judeo-German, it has been pointed out that there are only a handful of instances in the Horant poem that point to Jewish authorship. In the absence of the German original for this text and any certain knowledge of its transmission either orally or in writing, we can only be certain that the Codex and its six poems were copied or adapted by a single scribe from one or several originals. One of the poems is signed by "der shrayber Abraham" (Abraham, the scribe) and three by "Isaac der shrayber" (Isaac, the scribe). The scribe or copier of the Horant remains anonymous.

There is insufficient evidence that the Horant was transliterated from a Latin letter source. In fact, the orthographic practices and system employed are consistent with those common in Yiddish of later periods. Furthermore, many of the inconsistencies noted by reviewers of the Fuks edition of the Codex turn out to be misreadings of the text or the result of a failure to recognize distinctions in the language that were faithfully recorded by the spelling system. Indeed, the graphemic evidence points to a Hebrew letter original, because there are many symbols used that are spelled differently in the German phonetic spelling convention. Even the seventeen instances of consonant doubling in the Codex do not prove the claim made by some linguists that the manuscript had a Latin letter source, because most of these doublings appear in order to avoid confusion with other phonemes in providing analogies for rhymes.

Although the "Dukus Horant" is based on the German tradition of a matchmaking epic, as a subcategory of the heroic epic, and despite its resemblance to the *Kudrun* and *König Rother* epics, it cannot readily be assigned to any one medieval German model. Moreover, the more popular among the German epics did not find their way into the Germano-Judaic (Old Yiddish) literature. In the fourteenth century, the two literatures overlap in areas of theme and motif but do not completely coincide. According to Eli Katz, it is possible that neither side influenced the other and that each derived certain motifs independently from a third source.

The "Dukus Horant" is de-Christianized. Because the Jews already had a literary tradition before they adopted Middle High German as their vernacular, it cannot be automatically inferred that the source or transmission of an Old Yiddish literary text was German as opposed to the normal process whereby oral transmission precedes the written document. The language of the Cambridge Codex is a Central German dialect. A possible explanation for the existence of Old Yiddish texts is that, among other things, they represent attempts at approximating the literary language of the German works with which the Jewish scribes were familiar and that these texts were far removed from the actual spoken Yiddish. The Codex illuminates the manner in which the four-hundred-year tradition of the German-speaking Jewish community acting as the chief bearer of Jewish culture, with Yiddish as the vehicle of literary expression, had its beginnings. The Codex seems to have two functions: namely, as a didactic means to entertain women and poorly educated men and as an artistic narrative device. The Jewish community has always been bilingual, functioning both in Hebrew, the holy tongue, and the vernacular or coterritorial language (or its Jewish variant).

As has been variously pointed out, the Germano-Judaic Horant is a mediator between two worlds and signals a good deal of cultural interaction between the Jewish and coterritorial realms. It thereby casts considerable doubt on the notion of a Jewish ghetto culture that insulated as well as excluded Jews from participating in or interacting with the German-speaking populace and society.

A more difficult problem that presents itself in connection with Old Yiddish literature in general revolves around the question of attribution. According to the prominent Yiddishist Khone

Shmeruk, the extant texts do not represent more than transcriptions, even if certain Christian references are expunged; that is to say, there is no evidence of a creative relationship to the source material on the part of the scribe. Specifically, he rejects a theory advanced by two highly visible and distinguished Yiddishists of the past, Max Weinreich and Max Erik, who propounded the so-called gleeman or minstrel theory, whereby Jewish minstrels created and transmitted epic and lyrical poetry. This theory arose naturally from the absence of an answer to the question of authorship. Weinreich and Erik followed German Romantic tradition that posits a *Spielmann* (gleeman) as the originator of lyrical poetry as well as heroic and other epic poems. Because of the nature of these minstrel-beggars, libertines, magicians, and clowns, it is highly doubtful that they could have been the authors of *König Rother, Herzog Ernst, Orendel, St. Oswald, Salman,* and *Morolf.* In the case of the "Dukus Horant," Hans Neumann's analysis makes a sharp distinction between the quality of the Jewish part of the Cambridge Codex and the trivialized form of the heroic epic as represented by the Horant. The real achievements of Old Yiddish literature rest with the adaptations of biblical and midrashic material such as the four (out of six) poems of the Codex.

Finally, it needs to be pointed out that an automatic assumption about the secular nature of Yiddish texts rests with an assumption of minstrel authorship. Because that is not provable, there exists no basis for the claim that biblical and midrashic epics are "secular" in their substance. It was, however, natural to come to such a conclusion for early Yiddish scholars in the 1920s in Eastern Europe, because they worked within a nonreligious, secular, enlightened atmosphere. The copyists and punctuators (men who added vowel points or diacritics to Hebrew manuscripts) belonged to a middle stratum of educated people proficient in Hebrew and midrashic literature. We know no more about the authors of the Cambridge Codex.

The story line of the duke's fragmentary tale contained on plates 41–84 of Taylor-Schecter is relatively simple and straightforward. At an unspecified time and place, sixteen-year-old king Etene ruled over all German lands: Lombardy, Sicily, Denmark, Spain, France, and Hungary. He is known for his physical strength and kindness. Three giants—Wate, Witolt, and Asprian—are there to serve him as the mighty arm of his power. Duke Horant of Denmark is his adviser, and he counsels Etene to take a wife. The king at first declines, but he ultimately relents and makes preparations for a big celebration to which all of his vassals are invited. Twelve kings and the three giants accept his invitation, as well as many others. The guests are treated royally. On the twelfth day of the festivities, Etene asks his company to make proposals for a suitable wife. A pilgrim tells of Hilde, beautiful daughter of Hagen, the very difficult ruler of Greece. The old man convinces Etene that Hilde's beauty rivals that of Isolde, daughter of the Irish king, and even that of the fabled Helen of Troy. The pilgrim issues a warning, however: Hagen will try to kill any suitors. Etene appoints Duke Horant as his matchmaker, counting on his beautiful voice to sway the princess. Although the duke at first refuses to go on such a dangerous mission, he relents and is promised the Danish crown as his reward. He is to be accompanied by his brother, Morunk, the three giants, and a party of two hundred men. The boat that is to carry them to Greece is well equipped and luxuriously appointed. The inside is lined with velvet, the main mast made of gold, the sails are silken, and the oars made of silver. He will take thirty thousand gold marks and magnificent horses with exquisite tack. The three giants agree to be his loyal servants.

Horant sets sail, and Etene prays for his men. Horant intones a prayer for God's help and protection. He sings so beautifully that the fishes and sea nymphs emerge from the bottom of the sea to listen. The crossing proves uneventful, and the voyage is completed in twenty-eight days. Once ashore, Horant begins to search for suitable accommodations. His men promise to behave themselves in his absence. Horant rides into town in his most resplendent attire, and his horse has a harness of gold. On his way, the duke is stopped by a splendidly dressed man, a merchant, who offers him his services. Horant claims that he and his retinue are refugees in search of shelter. The stranger offers him his house. Horant thereupon asks for a loan of thirty thousand marks, and the worthy citizen refers him to the wealthiest man in town. This man, a banker, even offers Horant a hundred thousand marks. Horant is skeptical and wants to satisfy himself as to the man's true wealth, which angers the banker. In the end, both ride down to the harbor to welcome Horant's men ashore. Upon seeing the giants, the merchant-banker has second thoughts about his generosity; the town's citizens are also in fear of the giants. But the merchant's wife welcomes them all most cordially and shows off her well-appointed mansion with its plumbing that supplies the house with water. Horant provides gifts for the poor in the city.

During Pentecost, Hagen stages a great festival to show off his might and the beauty of his daughter. There are twelve kings among the guests. The onlookers on the morning of Whitsunday also include Horant and his men. An incident, in the course of which Witolt hurls a young prince across the bodies of ten thousand men, attracts the attention of everyone. Horant is only barely able to assuage Witolt. All are told to avoid the ogres as messengers of hell. At one point Horant sings, and Hilde, who is listening, is deeply moved. She sends for him and offers him ten thousand gold coins and a concubine. Horant refuses but asks her to meet him under the linden tree of his banker host's mansion. She accepts and Horant, whose magnificent appearance had attracted her attention earlier, sings again, causing the birds to cease their singing and the boars to stop digging. After this, the two exchange rings and Hilde learns of the reason for his presence. He has to convince her that he is wooing her on behalf of his lord and master and that he himself is a happily married man. If she agrees to wed his liege lord, he explains, he will be her loyal servant and sing for her. She promises to follow Horant to Etene's court and insists that only death could stop her. Horant announces to the giants that he and they will attend his king's wedding. Horant, his brother, Morunk, and the giants are all in their respective resplendent attire. Horant orders that his horses be shod with golden shoes fastened only

with one nail so that the horses will lose them and the poor can pick them up. The ogres continue to inspire fear. Witolt wrestles and kills a lion. Hagen dubs the ogres the devil's companions. The festival proceeds, and everyone enjoys the jousting of the knights. In the course of the events, Horant makes a present of a beautiful horse to a minstrel. The minstrel shows the horse to Hagen and to Hilde. Impressed by Horant's generosity, the king sends for him. Horant offers his services to Hagen. Hagen can see, however, that Horant is no ordinary knight and declines. Instead, he offers Horant and his retinue his hospitality. Horant accepts. He returns to his abode with the linden tree, where he sits until Pentecost. At this point, the manuscript breaks off, becoming illegible. It is fair to assume, however, that Horant returns to Etene, his mission accomplished.

In addition to the already mentioned problems attending this narrative, there are numerous others destined to keep scholarly debate alive. The most obvious part of that debate has revolved around the question of the specific Jewish elements characterizing the narrative. Specifically, the occurrence of the word *tifle* (an impure place) for church has led to controversy because of its inconsistent use in lieu of the German word for church. One possible answer to the puzzle could be that the manuscript came to the copyist orally and he forgot that he had previously failed to correct the Christian reference. His alterations, however, appear to be limited to those areas he deemed unacceptable from a Jewish standpoint. Another striking feature is the consistent abbreviation for the deity's name *got* (God) as *giml* (g), in keeping with Jewish practice of avoiding taking the Lord's name in vain. Finally, there is the so-called pilgrim's song or anthem, which Horant intones as his ship gets under way: "And now may He who saved the Jews on the sea come to our aid today. We are sailing in God's name. We desire His grace" (plate 51, vv. 245–48). This reference to the exodus from Egypt (?) is said to be a substitution for the customary prayer in German medieval literature, whereby reference is made to Christ's sepulcher and the disciples. The Yiddish anthem is in rhymed couplets, as is the entire poem.

This nonetheless very limited evidence of de-Christianization confirms the theory that the scribe sought only to alter the original in very special instances. Because the remaining five poems of the Codex have *shrayber* (copyists, scribes; *soyfer* [copyist] and *shrayber* [scribe] are used synonymously in Yiddish), it is not unreasonable to assume that the transmitter of the "Dukus Horant" was also a shrayber—that is, a copyist performing a mechanical rather than creative task. Finally, the title of the epic features the Yiddish word for duke (*dukus*), the only time this is done in the entire fragment. Again, it is not possible to conclude from this that the original was a non-Christian version of a Germanic epic. It may only have been due to the imponderables of the transmission of a non-Jewish narrative to a Jewish audience. The fact that the copyist stopped short of eliminating all Christian references, such as Pentecost or the strictly aristocratic context and therefore non-Jewish practice of marriage brokering, merely confirms the likelihood of a copyist at work whose task it was to transmit—perhaps even to mediate—but whose knowledge of Jewish practices and law more than likely identifies him as a Jew (although some Germanists have doubted the Jewish identity of the writer).

As has been pointed out in the introduction to the Cambridge Codex in the Ganz, Norman, and Schwarz edition of the Horant, there is no question that the Jews had little or no knowledge of *galkhes* (Latin characters) prior to the eighteenth century, and all non-Jewish texts in Ashkenazic practice had to be transliterated. It is false, however, to assume a direct correlation between the Latin and Hebrew letters. The Yiddish orthographic and graphemic system had to be used to render a medieval German epic into Yiddish. Thus from the point of view of a graphemic argument alone, the "Dukus Horant" should be regarded as a text written in a language that is different from its Middle High German model. The linguistic interpretation of Taylor-Schecter is made very difficult by the fact that four single graphemes represent sixteen monophthongs in Middle High German and three Yiddish digraphs represent six Middle High German diphthongs. Thus no one can be certain about the phonetic values or vowels and semi-vowels in Taylor-Schecter: a determination of the epic's language by purely linguistic means is impossible.

In terms of grammar (morphology), syntax, and vocabulary, the Horant is identifiable as a late medieval German text of possibly Rhenish Franconian dialectical origin. In the absence of definitive knowledge of the phonetic values of Old Yiddish manuscripts and the fact that Middle High German has come to us only as a language of many dialects, ideology has crept into the debate in the form of definite colorations and assumptions underlying the text editions of the Codex, though their editors would deny it. Thus the question of the existence of Old Yiddish as a language separate from medieval German has remained a point of contention. Finally, there is the question of transliteration of Old Yiddish texts into Middle High German. In order to pursue the Jewish integrity of the text, it is important to allow only for transcriptions into modern Yiddish or Hebrew. This attitude then is consistent with the "ideological" position that there was such a language as Old Yiddish that differed from medieval German at the very least graphemically, and possibly also lexically and syntactically.

A closer reading of the text reveals similarities and differences between the Jewish and coterritorial cultures as well as the valorization of a matchmaking epic in a Jewish context. The epic poem fits the typical pattern of a German medieval matchmaking epic: the liege counsels his lord to marry; a vicarious courtship is carried out by a messenger; the courtship is won through cunning; the messenger and princess have a bedchamber scene; abduction is accomplished through a ruse; and the two are chased by the man who has authority over the hand of the princess. Horant, indeed, advises Etene to marry; Horant departs for Greece in the company of his brother, three giants, and two hundred men; three kinds of ruses are employed: Horant's beautiful voice, the tale of his banishment from Etene's court, and his generosity; the encounter between the emissary and the princess does not take place in her bedchamber but, at his request, in the courtyard of the banker's mansion (the meeting under the linden tree is a unique feature and departure from the standard possibly because he is a married man); and abduction through a ruse is hinted at but uncertain, because the concluding part of the epic is missing. Horant as a *shadkhen* (matchmaker) exercised a function highly respected in Jewish culture, because matchmaking was often performed by rabbis. Similarly, the two banker merchants would have met with approval by Jewish audiences, because moneylending was regarded as an honorable pursuit as long as religious laws and laws of fairness were observed. In non-Jewish societies, on the other hand, moneylending was held in low esteem.

Among the unconventional, though not necessarily (but possibly) Jewish features of the poem is the ring exchange episode. The problem is that the relevant couplets (705–16) are partially illegible; thus we cannot be certain who is the giver and who is the receiver. Traditionally it is the bride-to-be who presents the matchmaker with a ring as a token of her gratitude, in this instance for his extraordinary singing. The ring has magic qualities, and another possible reading of the episode is that Horant presents the ring to Hilde as a talisman to ward off the evil eye in accordance with Jewish folk belief.

In general, it can be said that the reception of an epic like the Horant involves a clash of two value systems: medieval knighthood and Jewish learning; knightly courage, leadership, romance, and religious obligations and Jewish ethical and religious tenets. There was rabbinical opposition to Old Yiddish literature, just as there were clerical opposition and condescension toward all Yiddish-language literature, which was regarded as "jargon" even by the educated among its native speakers until the emergence of a purely Yiddish literature in its own right. In addition to being a sign of the low esteem in which nonprivileged Jews were held by the rabbis, contemporary rabbinical opposition may also have been based on a fear of the threat of assimilation, and the rabbis frequently offered midrashic narratives or anecdotes as entertainment to counter the effect of Yiddish literature.

As to the possible date for the original Horant

epic, there are various indications that it belongs to the end of the period of the courtly epic, toward the conclusion of the thirteenth and early fourteenth centuries. The scene where Horant bids Etene farewell, the appearance of the figure of the *civis nobilis* (the wealthy merchant), the detailed architectural descriptions, the plumbing, and the carpeting of the street for the princess's walk to the church are examples of that style. Finally, the "Dukus Horant" epic is removed from the traditions of the gleeman epic, the heroic epic, and the orally composed epic by the presence of elements of a courtly tradition. Although there is only indirect evidence to support this assumption, it is commonly believed that the heroic epic continued to be popular in the form of a minor epic literature.

Bibliography

Solomon Birnbaum, "Old Yiddish or Middle High German?" *Journal of Jewish Studies* 12 (1961): 19–31; Manfred Caliebe, "Dukus Horant: Studien zur literarischen Tradition," *Philologische Studien und Quellen* 70 (1973): 5–147; Siegfried Colditz, "Das hebräisch-mittelhochdeutsche Fragment vom Dukus Horant," *Forschungen und Fortschritte* 40 (1966): 302–6; Max Erik, *Vegn altyidshn roman un novele: Fertsentn-sexhtsentn yorhundert* (Warsaw: n.p., 1926); Leonard Forster, "Dukus Horant," *German Life and Letters* 4 (1958): 276–85; Jerold Frakes, *The Politics of Interpretation: Alterity and Ideology in Old Yiddish Studies* (Albany: State University of New York Press, 1989), Leo Fuks, *The Oldest Known Literary Documents of Yiddish Literature,* 2 vols. (Leiden: Brill, 1957); Peter F. Ganz, Frederick Norman, and Werner Schwarz, *Dukus Horant* (Tübingen: Niemeyer, 1964); Heikki Hakkarainen, *Studien zum Cambridger Codex T-S.10.K.22,* vol. 1: *Text,* vol. 2: *Graphemik und Phonetik,* vol. 3: *Lexicon* (Turku: Annales Universitatis Turkuensis B 104, 174, 182, 1967, 1971, 1973); Eli Katz, "Six Germano-Judaic Poems from the Cairo Genizah," Ph.D. diss., University of California, Los Angeles, 1963; James Marchand and Frederic Tubach, "Der keusche Joseph: Ein mittelhochdeutsches Gedicht aus dem 13.–14. Jahrhundert. Beitrag zur Erforschung der hebräischdeutschen Literatur," *Zeitschrift für deutsche Philologie* 81 (1962): 30–52; Hans Neumann, "Sprache und Reim in den judendeutschen Gedichten des Cambridger Codex T-S. 10 K. 2," *Indogermanica: Festschrift für Wolfgang Krause*

(Heidelberg: Carl Winter Verlag, 1960), 145–65; Khone Shmeruk, "Can the Cambridge Manuscript Support the Spielmann Theory in Yiddish Literature?" *Studies in Jewish Literature and Folklore* (Jerusalem: Hebrew University Press, 1986), 1–36; Gabriele Strauch, *Dukus Horant: Wanderer zwischen zwei Welten* (Amsterdam: Rodopi, 1990); and Max Weinreich, "Old Yiddish Poetry in Linguistic-Literary Research," *Word* 16 (1960): 100–118.

ARTHUR TILO ALT

1689 Glikl of Hameln begins writing her memoir, which includes her distinctive yet representative view of the gentile world

Glikl of Hameln lived as a German Jewess externally subject to the will of local autocratic princes and to a frequently hostile surrounding populace. Her rich and colorful autobiography chronicles the many disasters and less frequent triumphs reflecting the precariousness of Jewish life in the seventeenth and early eighteenth centuries. A woman of the pre-Enlightenment *Judengasse,* she structured her "seven little books" to correspond roughly to the seven decades of her biblically allotted years. She lived in accordance with the Jewish calendar and in hope of messianic redemption.

Glikl cannot be said to have "come of age" at her marriage, nor at the birth of her first child. She was betrothed at twelve, married at fourteen, and gave birth to thirteen children, twelve of whom lived to adulthood. One cannot wonder that after twenty-nine years of what she describes as a happy marriage, with a new child arriving almost every other year, that Glikl spent her sleepless nights writing after her beloved Chaim's death. His untimely end, lamented by Glikl all her life, was nevertheless the major impetus for the creation of her narrative, which has long been considered the most significant cultural document of Jewish life of her era. For later generations of historians, linguists, folklorists, literary scholars, Germanists, and Yiddishists, Glikl comes of age in 1689, the year of Chaim's death, when Glikl was forty-two years old and began writing the only existing pre-modern Yiddish memoir by a woman.

Although Glikl's narrative is sui generis, it is nevertheless very much informed by the extensive ethical-didactic Yiddish literature for women that flourished from the sixteenth through the eighteenth centuries. Glikl's citations of exemplary tales and homilies from traditional Hebrew and Yiddish texts, however, are freely supplemented by stories from what she designates as heathen or idolatrous sources. Knightly romances and tales of Solon and Alexander the Great are only a few examples of Glikl's highly eclectic references. To this day, many of Glikl's sources have not been identified.

There are far fewer cruxes about her intended audience. Glikl clearly states that her twelve remaining children, six females and six males and their descendants, are the intended audience for her seven little books. Yet it would appear that children and descendants were not the only possible audience for her memoir. Glikl, for example, read the will of Pessele Ries and encouraged her children to read it. Because Pessele Ries was related to Glikl by marriage, it can safely be assumed that to the extent Glikl's document is like a will, she would have expected her audience to include extended family and perhaps even friends. The ethical will was an important document in Jewish literature beginning in the twelfth century. Glikl mentions such wills many times but is, I believe, constrained by gender and modesty from openly acknowledging as a model for her work a genre that was almost always written by a male in Hebrew. Nevertheless, the will is the subtext of Glikl's much more elaborate social, family, and life history. What is important is that it would not have occurred to Glikl and her contemporaries to publish a secular family document written in Yiddish by a woman, although her son-in-law, Kossman Gompertz, was associated with a printing establishment in Amsterdam. Given such an important, albeit limited audience, we may assume that Glikl would be extremely aware of posterity and, despite frequent demurrers of inadequacy, would wish to present herself as a religious and moral example to her descendants. At the same time, she is rhetorically addressing what is in essence an audience of intimates and, in a singularly inappropriate figure for a pious Jewish daughter, she can metaphorically let her hair down. Given the need to be an exemplary moral guide and yet preserve an intimate, motherly tone, her interaction with the surrounding Christian culture reveals much about the relationships between Jews and gentiles in early modern Europe.

In her very first chapter, when Glikl is earnestly urging the importance of prayer and admonishing her beloved children to support their wives and children honestly, she adds "and especially that you should do honest business with Jew or gentile lest by not so doing, God forbid, you desecrate the Holy Name." Glikl seems to have lived up to that pious injunction for some 150 pages, and ten years later she notes proudly that she left Hamburg owing not a single taler to Jew or gentile.

Constraints of space prevent me from citing each reference Glikl makes to her encounters with non-Jews. I will therefore confine my examples to those interactions that are most revelatory of Glikl's modes of discourse and those that might be considered representative of seventeenth-century Jewry. Absent in the early modern Glikl is a nationalist consciousness of herself as a German Jew, and she surely exhibits none of the German-Jewish symbiosis that Gershom Scholem posits is a one-way love affair. Significantly, the only reference Glikl makes to Germany is a linguistic one, when she contrasts the ordinary Yiddish that she was taught with the French that her new family in Metz speaks. Their *lingua franca* was the western Yiddish of Glikl's narrative. However, if Glikl is no nationalist, she, like most of the Jews of her time, was certainly a royalist; she negotiated more readily with rulers than with representative bodies.

A case in point occurs early in her narrative. Glikl tells us that in 1648, when she was not yet three years of age, the town council of Hamburg expelled all the German Jews from the city. Although Glikl's family had lived in Hamburg for more than three generations, they had to reestablish themselves in Altona, which was then under the jurisdiction of Denmark. In the 1640s a very limited number of German Jews had been granted temporary permission to live in Hamburg, whereas the Danish king had established rights of domicile for Jews as early as 1630. She recalls as well that when she was ten the Swedes invaded Altona and the Jews fled back to Hamburg, seeking shelter among the Sephardim, who had rights of domicile and worship in Hamburg, and with the citizens of the town. Unfortunately, the ever garrulous Glikl neglects to inform us whether her family fled to a Jewish or a gentile home. She further notes that with neither domicile nor religious rights, Jews could worship in Hamburg only on the sufferance of the town council who "looked through their fingers," but when the priests found out about Jewish worship the Jews had to return, in the well-worn simile, "like frightened sheep" to the little *shuls* in Altona. Glikl adds "and so it will be until the present day as long as the town council rules Hamburg."

Altona in those years was under the hegemony of the king of Denmark, whom Glikl states was rewarded by God because he was such a pious and righteous monarch who always treated Jews well. He was, according to Glikl, successful against the fierce Swedes because he had good advisers and subjects who gave their lives for him. Regarding relations between the Danes and the Swedes, Glikl writes that though they may be friendly and intermarry, they never remain on good terms very long. These are the generalizations about Christians and politics that Glikl makes in her maturity about events that occurred in her childhood. They reflect the Jewish leaning toward absolutism that Jonathan Israel cites, by which Jews trust their fate to the growing power of princes. Basic to Glikl's theodicy is the belief that Jewish persecution at gentile hands is meaningful and part of ultimate redemption. More mundanely, however, despite her theodicy and her negative remarks about the town council, Glikl is proud that her father interceded with the Hamburg authorities and was the first German Jew to get permission to return. He lobbied so successfully that eventually all the Jews who had fled to Altona were resettled in Hamburg.

Another insight into the accommodation of Jews like Glikl's father to authority, a major component of German-Jewish interaction, is revealed when she retells a family tale that occurred long before she was born. She uses the same fiction-like pointers she employs when retelling the many morality tales that are such an organic part of her narrative. She tells of her father's stepdaughter who "spoke French like water." A customer of Glikl's father, whom she describes as a nobleman, comes to her father's house to redeem a pledge. When the father leaves the room in order to get the pledged article, he leaves his French-speaking stepdaughter seated at the clavier, where she entertains the noble strangers. Even this tiny detail is revealing of Jewish-gentile relations, for by 1715 there was rabbinical legislation in Hamburg and Altona forbidding Jewish women merchants from entering the homes of non-Jews unless chaperoned. One may speculate that the threat of closer German-Jewish interaction may have frightened the religious establishment in the early eighteenth century but that some fifty years earlier there was enough civility in German-Jewish relations that Glikl's father allowed his young stepdaughter to entertain three gentiles when he left the room. As the stepdaughter plays, she overhears her distinguished guests plotting in French to abscond with the pledge upon his return, naturally without paying. She thereupon begins playing and singing loudly in Hebrew, warning her stepfather not to give up the pledged article. Her stepfather, realizing the situation, refuses to give up the pledge unless he receives the money. One of the nobles says, "We are betrayed—the whore knows French," and they

leave. The next day the noble returns to redeem the pledge properly and comments that "it was money well-spent to have your daughter learn French." The tale, which is structured like a moral fairy tale with the innocent virginal heroine triumphing over evil through cleverness or superior knowledge, is very much like the morality tales that are so much a feature of Glikl's narrative. It contains a moral as most of Glikl's tales do: it is well to educate one's daughters. We see thus the historic commercial interaction between the Jewish money lender and upper-class Christians, but we also see the peril of the interaction when Jews were exploited rather than protected by civil authorities.

Glikl employs the rhetoric of her time in complex, seemingly sycophantic ways. Glikl refers to the gentile as a lord, thereby ennobling her father's status by association. So noble were the clients that the daughter of the house is engaged to entertain them. Yet they ignobly attempt to cheat their Jewish creditor and call the daughter of the house a *hur* (whore), although Glikl calls her *b'sule* (a virgin). Whore and virgin are the terms used by Glikl in David Kaufmann's original Yiddish edition (1896) and not in the bloodless, euphemistic, and widely used standard German and English translations.

Glikl's ability to tell a story is again demonstrated in the tale of her drunken servant Jacob, who spent most of his time drinking with his fellow tippler, the deputy postmaster of Hanover, instead of safeguarding on a strenuous journey Glikl, her three small children, her maid, and her manservant. This story is significant for the boozy camaraderie of the two alcoholics, Jewish Jacob and gentile Peterson; for the courtesy extended to the entourage by humble postillions, toll keepers, coachmen, and innkeepers; and for Glikl's good humor throughout her ordeal.

The high point of Glikl's social interaction with gentiles takes place at the famous wedding between her daughter Zipporah and Kossman Gompertz in Cleve. Glikl delights in telling of the distinguished guests, especially the noble gentiles such as thirteen-year-old Frederick of Brandenberg who became Frederick I of Prussia, the prince of Nassau, and other lords and ladies.

Glikl naively assumes that these worthies came to see her daughter, the beautiful bride. But a more likely explanation may be princely curiosity about Jewish marriage customs and princely needs to honor a wealthy Jewish creditor. Because Glikl had twelve children who lived to marriageable age, and many weddings are described in her memoirs, it is significant that this wedding is both the only one that appears to have included royal guests and the only one described in detail. The differentiating factor here is, of course, the elevated social status of the important Gompertz family. The rest of Glikl's children were married off with much less pomp. Nevertheless, Glikl's vivid description of the guests, the setting, food and drink, and especially the entertainment point not only to the relationships between Jews and gentiles but also to the acculturation that was occurring among upper bourgeois Jews in the late seventeenth century (1674).

Glikl retells with pride how the young Prince Frederick was particularly taken with Glikl's five-year-old son and held his hand throughout the activities. The sumptuous food and wine were presented to the guests in order of rank in a large chamber with gilded leather walls. But the pièce de résistance was the entertainment: masked performers who presented an elaborate tableau culminating in the Dance of Death. This dance is of Christian origin and has its roots in the folk belief that joyous events like weddings are threatened by evil spirits.

Another incident that takes place at the wedding emphasizes the sycophantic aspect of Jewish-gentile relations where Jews were ever vulnerable to the caprices of princes. Glikl tells us that the groom's father, Elia Cleve, wanted to present the young prince with a very expensive watch brought by a Sephardic jeweler, but he was dissuaded. The young prince became Frederick the First, and Glikl writes that Cleve never forgave his friend for dissuading him from presenting the watch; he added that had he done so, the prince would never have forgotten it, for "these great princes do not forget such things." Glikl obviously believed in the gratitude and long memory of monarchs. She concludes, still basking in the glory of the wedding, that the presence of royalty

so enhanced the wedding that no Jew had been thus honored in a hundred years.

In contrast to the manifest social snobbery of the wedding, however, is her account of their difficult journey back to Hamburg. Glikl and her entourage, a party of eight including a baby, could not return by sea because of the danger of pirates; they were equally threatened on land by gangs of marauding soldiers. They procured safe-conduct passes and were able to complete their journey accompanied by a "faithful, loyal corporal" who was appointed by his general for the task. The journey took some weeks, and there were stopovers to allow the group to celebrate the holidays in Jewish homes. Glikl describes their stopping at a village inn on one occasion and sitting by the fire with the villagers. They were pleased to learn from one of the peasants, who was boasting that his lord had sent twelve thousand men to Holland, that they had finally reached Hanoverian territory where they would be safe. There, notes Glikl, the duke kept his lands in order, and a soldier dare not even disturb a chicken, to say nothing of any further transgression. The vignette of the Jewish merchants and the German peasants sitting, smoking, and talking around the fire at an inn, proud to be under the hegemony of an oligarchic ruler, is a rare glimpse into seventeenth-century social relations. The loyal corporal seems to have become part of the family; he is not only well rewarded for his services, but also asks to accompany them to Hamburg, a city he had never seen.

The sensational double murder case that Glikl describes in great detail in her fifth book is, in contrast, a grim instance of Jewish-gentile relations at their most volatile and dangerous. Because it offers many levels of interaction, it will be presented here in some detail. The Burgomaster of Hamburg allowed middle-class Jews of the Altona community to obtain monthly permits to trade in Hamburg. The poorer merchants who often risked going without a permit were frequently imprisoned and required ransoming by the Jewish community. By Glikl's account, the men left the synagogue in the morning, went to Hamburg (fifteen minutes away in those years), and returned to Altona toward evening when the gates were closed. She writes: "When they passed through the gates their lives were in continual peril from attacks by sailors, soldiers, idlers and all sorts of hooligans." In the Hamburg community each man also belonged to a study group that met after afternoon prayers. The men went home after studying with perhaps less peril but, lacking rights of domicile, were still reliant upon the goodwill of those they encountered. In 1684, a poor Altona money changer disappeared and, although his wife sought him all over Hamburg, he was not to be found: she was left a "living widow" with three children. Three years later a Hamburg money changer of comfortable means also disappeared, leaving another distraught "living widow" and four children.

This second widow and her missing husband had sufficient standing in the community so that the town council was pressured to proclaim that anyone who knew of the missing Jew should come forward and tell what he knew. For his information he would be rewarded with one hundred ducats and complete secrecy. There were no takers. The Jews of Hamburg and Altona who had business in the Hamburg bourse, however, began to suspect the son of the tavern keeper of the most famous tavern in Hamburg. The Mariner's Tavern, located near the bourse, was the place where Jewish and non-Jewish merchants came to settle their accounts and drink from silver goblets, and the tavern keeper was well respected. The situation would have resulted in yet another unsolved crime were it not for the tireless efforts of a clever and obstinate woman, Rebekah Lipman. Although her husband warned her not to say anything because they were without residential rights in Hamburg, Rebekah vowed to bring the murderer to justice. She persuaded other members of the Jewish community to accompany her to the president in Altona, who warned that if they could not prove their accusations, he would confiscate their goods. Rebekah countered that she would risk her life as well as her goods. The accused murderer refused to admit his guilt, however, and indeed threatened the Jews, who recognized too well the power of his prominent family. Rebekah pleaded with them, saying that God would help them. As if to but-

tress her belief, on the way back to Hamburg she encountered the servant of the murderer, who had been instrumental in luring the hapless Jews to their fate. In a maneuver worthy of a clever detective or attorney, Rebekah convinced the maid that her master and mistress had confessed to the murders and that she would do well to tell her version. Glikl assures us that Rebekah was a very persuasive speaker and the results seem to support her contention. Most important, the maidservant revealed the whereabouts of the corpse. The criminals, however, refused to confess. The president said he could not torture the tavern keeper's son and his wife on the word of a servant, and that the Jews should petition the town council of Hamburg for permission to search the house for the corpse. The Jewish community leaders employed some trustworthy soldiers and sailors and obtained permission to both search for the body and upon finding it to bury it in the cemetery in Altona. (Hamburg, of course, had no Jewish cemetery.) The council warned them to remember well that if they did not find the corpse they were all lost, because the council could not protect the Jews from the fury of the Hamburg mob. Meanwhile, there were outcries through the city, news had spread rapidly, and a huge crowd of artisans, apprentices, and others gathered at the house of the tavern keeper's son. The mob, says Glikl, spoke with one voice: If the Jews find the corpse, all will be well, but if they do not, there will not be a single Jew left. Fortunately, the corpse was indeed found where the maidservant said it was, and the Jews were "with tears in their eyes and joy in their hearts"—tears for the dead righteous young man of twenty-four and joy that the community was out of danger and could see the guilty punished. When the body of the young man was brought to the Altona cemetery, Glikl reckons that there were a hundred thousand people there including apprentices, artisans, and sailors but, she writes, no one said a word. The Jews, however, protested that the president in Altona had the right to try the murderer because he had him and his wife in custody.

It was well known that the other man missing previously had also been a frequenter of the Mariner's Tavern. Eventually, under threat of additional torture, the murderer admitted that he had killed the poor money changer and buried him in a pit in the cheese cellar of the tavern. Jewish community leaders went to the Hamburg council and again asked for permission to search. This time the community was in even more danger because of the distinguished reputation of the tavern; even more anti-Jewish feeling was evoked than in the first case. But again, the Jews were able to find and identify the body for Jewish burial. The case was a cause célèbre for the Jews of Hamburg and Altona who risked hostile mobs, loss of goods, and even death in order to follow Jewish law and find the bodies so that the young widows could remarry. Glikl vividly presents this historic event like a suspenseful Purim tale wherein a courageous woman saves the Jewish people. She utilizes fully those fictionalizing components that characterize her discourse throughout.

Glikl's rich narrative frequently mentions much Jewish-gentile commercial and governmental contact on all levels of society. Some contact may have been neutral, some even friendly, but much of Glikl's text conveys the perilous nature of life for the Jews of her era. Similarly the idea that Jewish suffering at gentile hands was meaningful and a temporary stage on the path to redemption is expressed by Glikl on countless occasions throughout her narrative. She eloquently relates the joyous messianic expectations evoked by Shabbetai Zevi and her own family's bitterly dashed hopes when he proved false. But she remains firm in her theodicy, convinced that Jewish exile will come to an end. What instead came to an end was the high degree of Jewish cohesion that, despite obvious class divisions, was characteristic of the age. What Glikl's remarkable text gives us is a look into a Jewish world still united by the single vision of messianic redemption at the very moment that the Enlightenment was setting the stage for the competing secular messianisms of the modern era. From Glikl's varied and complicated relations with the gentile world, we can see the beginnings of the cataclysmic changes that were to reverberate through the lives of those future descendants whom Glikl was addressing.

Bibliography

All Yiddish citations are transcribed according to YIVO conventions—for example, Glikl instead of Gluckel.

Beth-Zion Abrahams, *The Life of Gluckel of Hameln* (London: East and West Library, 1962); Dorothy Bilik, "The Memoirs of Glikl of Hameln: The Archaeology of the Text," *Yiddish* 8 (1992); Jonathan Israel, *European Jewry in the Age of Mercantilism, 1550–1750* (Oxford: Clarendon, 1985); David Kaufmann, ed., *Zikhrones mores Glikl Hamil* [Memoirs of Glikl of Hameln] (Frankfurt a. M.: Kaufmann, 1896); and Herman Pollack, *Jewish Folkways in Germanic Lands* (Cambridge, Mass.: MIT Press, 1971).

DOROTHY BILIK

1697   The earliest extant Yiddish purimshpil is traced to Leipzig

The Jewish holiday of Purim was, according to Esther 9:20–28, instituted by Mordecai to celebrate the deliverance of the Jews from Haman's genocidal plot to murder them all. The text of Esther is late, its overt religious content, and thus its theological authority, slight. Nonetheless, the holiday itself was well established by the second century C.E., when a tractate of the Mishnah (megillah) was composed to explain the details of its observance. The festival is a joyous one celebrating the divine protection of the Jewish people. The primary component of the celebration is the ritual reading of the Book of Esther. Although even some of the traditional practices observed during that reading are susceptible to humorous enactment (for example, the use of noisemakers—*grager*—by children during the reading in order to drown out the name Haman each time it is mentioned), outside the reading a carnival atmosphere obtains, with a meal as festive as circumstances allow. This merrymaking follows a directive from the early Babylonian teacher Rava (Meg 9a) to drink so much wine as to be unable to distinguish between cursing Haman and blessing Mordecai—as well as the traditional production of parodies of (especially) the Talmud and its disquisitional style not on theological matters but rather on trivial subjects such as drinking and the institution of a Purim rabbi who turns authority and sometimes propriety on its head. The Talmud itself mentions entertainments and buffooneries in connection with Purim (Sanh 64b; Meg 76).

The centrality of the reading of the relatively brief and already rather dramatic text of Esther and the general tendency toward a relaxation of strict standards of decorum may well have led to the development of dramatizations of selected parts of the Esther story separate from its ritual reading. There were medieval Jewish traditions in both Babylonian (gaonic) academies and the European communities of performing the Esther story in which Haman (represented by a dummy) was burned while jesters sang. At least as early as the Middle Ages, the traditional Jewish prohibition of theatrical performance was regularly circumvented, or simply deemed irrelevant, when it came to the celebration of Purim. As the tradition developed, other biblical narratives were also adapted and dramatized. The *purimshpil* (Purim play in Yiddish) can be generally defined as a play performed during the Purim holidays or thereabouts for the entertainment and/or edification of the Jewish celebrants of the holiday. In Frankfurt, the Purim season lasted from fourteen days before to fourteen days after Purim. There is no evidence from the early period that Jewish drama was performed outside of Purim and Hanukkah, and Hanukkah drama itself was rare. Thus, due to the cultural circumstances that at least discouraged theatrical performance except for purimshpiln, the early history of the Yiddish purimshpil in large part is the early history of Yiddish theater.

The earliest purimshpiln were usually performed in private dwellings with the roles taken by yeshiva students, who sometimes traveled from town to town performing. Such plays were produced for a chamber audience, with a mixture of the comic and the serious, and always with a didactic and moral purpose. The earliest form of this type of drama was probably a rhymed monologue in one act of the tale of biblical Esther, performed by a character in mask and/or costume. Over time, this simple presentation developed into more complex dramas that were based on well-known traditional narratives and that included parody, satire, and even obscenity as aspects of their comic form. Despite the historical setting of the plays, there was little or no attention paid to accuracy in the representation of that setting; in fact, the ancient narrative material was commonly adapted to contemporary conditions and topical references. The central figure is the *lets* (buffoon)—later the *marsalik* (jester)—who carries the monodrama and later is central to dialogic drama. This comic character was adapted from and common to European non-Jewish dramatic traditions of the time, named Pickelherring in Dutch, Jean Potage in French, Signor Maccaroni in Italian, Jack Puddin' in English, and Hans Wurst in German. This comic figure in the European theater was defined by his impudence, cynicism, disrespect, and obscenity; he was the focus of the play's comedy who forced his way into serious situations with respectable people and mocked them. In the further development of the purimshpil, there was often a character who narrated parts of the action or simply commented upon it: the *loyfer* (messenger) or *shrayber* (writer).

It is difficult to plot a chronological development from the simple private chamber performances on the holiday to the more complex and multifaceted productions that were designed for public performance during the month of Adar and were no longer exclusively—although still primarily—a component of the Jewish celebration of Purim. The one form often ran parallel to the other: private performances often disappeared in one locale while continuing elsewhere, and large-scale professional performance for obvious reasons never made it to all Jewish communities. The developing duality of performance site (private and public) and audience (solely Jewish or both Christian and Jewish) was also matched in a pair of contrasting literary styles available to the purimshpil: as the Christian biblical drama of the Reformation grew in prominence and the plays became more serious, the earlier folksy style influenced by the German theater gave way to a more learned prose and less prominent comic style, while continuing to include elements of both.

There are extant manuscripts of parodic and satirical but nondramatic Purim poems from the fifteenth century, and by the beginning of the sixteenth century printed versions were in circulation. Such Purim poems enjoyed great popularity, and it is in just such a poem, based on the Book of Esther, composed ca. 1555 by Gumbrecht of Szczebrzeszyn (Shebreshin) and now found in a manuscript in Budapest, that the earliest known use of the term *purimshpil* is found. One of the earliest extant Jewish Esther plays, specifically designed for theatrical production, appeared in Ferrara in 1567, when Salomon Usque, with the help of Lazaro Graziano (Gratianos), adapted the Esther tale to Spanish drama. This play and similar ones from the time were almost certainly for the general stage and not just for Jews or Purim. In 1598, however, a satirical poem in Yiddish indicates that at Tannhausen a play called *Shpil fun Toyb Yeklayn, sayn vayb, kendlayn un zeyere tsvey zinlikh fayn* was performed every Purim. While it is all but certain that the Yiddish purimshpil had existed for quite some time prior to 1598, no documentary evidence exists. It took almost a century after this initial mention of the *Shpil fun Toyb Yeklayn* for the play to be printed (1680), and even it has not survived.

The earliest extant purimshpil, the Leipzig *Akhashveyresh-shpil,* dates from 1697. Rather surprisingly, for almost a hundred years after that date, up to the last decade of the eighteenth century, there were in effect only five Yiddish purimshpiln, three of them from the twenty-year period immediately following 1697: two *Akhashveyresh-shpiln, Mekhires Yoysef,* and *Dovid un Golias,* and the brief sketch with the unlikely title *Moyshe Rabeynu Bashraybung* (Description of Moses, our rabbi). That is, however, not to say that Yiddish purimshpiln were infrequent, but rather that these plays, along with the Book of Esther itself, supplied the basis for myriad adaptations during the following century. It was in fact not until the advent of the anti-Yiddish Haskalah movement —with its reformist *Maskilim* comedies (in Yiddish!) that were represented especially by the works of Isaac Abraham Euchel (Itzik Eichl) and Aaron ben Wolf Halle (Aaron Wolfso[h]n) in the last decade of the eighteenth century—that the repertoire expanded. These anti-purimshpiln, intended to supplant the traditional purimshpil, never became part of the common repertoire.

The *Akhashveyresh-shpil,* because it is based on the foundation narrative of Purim—the Book of Esther—not surprisingly formed a core or family of dramatic texts in the eighteenth century. Authors and interpreters of this core of texts adapted, borrowed, and plagiarized within the textual family to the extent that any attempt to define lineage is difficult. Its earliest representative is the Leipzig text of 1697. The text comprises fourteen folios, written in Ashkenazic cursive script and bound into a folio volume with other texts, primarily letters from the collection of Johann Christoph Wagenseil. The play's text was copied in Altdorf by Johann Christian Jakob, *olim* Moyse Katz of Cracow, who was probably one of Wagenseil's convert helpers in Jewish studies. The second *Akhashveyresh-shpil* was printed in Frankfurt in 1708, but was prohibited by the Jewish authorities and—perhaps due to the play's obscenity—confiscated and burned. In 1720 in Prague a rather more serious and sophisticated Akhashveyresh play was performed, an anonymous *Akta Ester im Akhashveyresh,* of which there was a further edition in Prague in 1763, and yet another in Amsterdam in 1774. The title page claims the play was performed in Prague in a regular theater with trumpets and other instruments. The actors were all pupils of R. David Oppenheim of Prague, who gave his consent for the performance.

There are three rather striking aspects of the plots of many (not all) of the Akhashveyresh-shpil adaptations of the period: the action begins with the Esther story itself, omitting the Vashti episode altogether; Haman's monologue just prior to his execution and his conversation with his wife depict a sympathetic character rather than a monstrous, genocidal villain and show about the only genuine human emotion of the play; and the comic role of the fool, or Pickelherring, figure has been combined with Mordecai's character. Mordecai's role is also still improvised as in commedia dell'arte. Originally, the Yiddish clown figure was a character named Prince Mondrish, but as one moves from the earliest to the later versions, that role diminishes and becomes fused with the originally serious role of Mordecai, who then becomes the central figure. With the further passage of time, however, Mordecai's role tended to lose its comic features. The combination of the two roles in Mordecai may initially have derived in part from a need among strolling companies on Purim for economy in casting.

By the time of the Amsterdam version of 1718, the play had become far more complex than in the earliest extant texts, particularly in terms of its staging technique. If this text is a production text, Yiddish theater indeed came a long way in a short time. In any case, the quasi-stage directions indicate that this is no longer a chamber play as were the earliest purimshpiln; the language is sophisticated and includes many foreign words. This is already learned drama. Toward the end of the eighteenth century a version was published, *Mordkhe un Ester,* whose subtitle illustrates an early tendency toward musical drama in the purimshpil: "eyne komise operete in eynen oyf tsug. fun reb lib tsimbler in musik gezetst. di dekorasions fun eynen um bkantin" (a comic operetta in one act; set to music by Mr. Lib Tsimbler; set designer unknown).

The first edition of *Mekhires Yoysef* (printed by Joh. Wust in Frankfurt without date, ca. 1710) is a prime example of rationalistic drama. It was produced by the Hessian Jew Berman of Limburg. This edition was apparently destroyed in the fire of the Frankfurt ghetto of January 14, 1711. A second edition, by Löw Ginsburg, appeared in Frankfurt in 1713. There was also a third edition, which included a German translation. This play, alternating with the David drama (see below), was performed in Frankfurt (and later in Metz) by yeshiva students from Hamburg and Prague under the direction of Berman. The performances lasted for the entire month of Adar and drew such great interest from the public that two soldiers were assigned to ensure order and guarantee the public safety. Finally, when Christians began to attend the performance, it was simply prohibited by the civil authorities. The play was performed with full sets as a *Singspiel* and was well on the way toward being an opera. It continued to be popular and was performed in Minsk as late as 1858.

The anonymous comedy *Dovid un Golias* was printed in Hanau in 1717 (now fragmentary, but complementary copies are in the Bodleian Library in Oxford and the National Library in Jerusalem). The play is in fact an opera with twenty-four songs; the comedy is rather coarse. The clown figure is named Lizinski, the "rats-her" of Goliath; he is later called Hansvurst when he is sent as a spy to King Saul. The name Lizinski and some other vocabulary suggest an origin for the play in Bohemia.

The briefest of these plays, *Moyshe rabeynu bashraybung,* comprises only eight pages in a manuscript found in the British Museum. The date and place of publication are not specified, but on the basis of orthography and language, mid-eighteenth-century Germany is likely. The play is based on midrashic material and may well represent the first extant Yiddish play composed without recourse to non-Jewish material. There is an interesting use of stylistic register in the play for the purpose of characterization: Moses uses far more Hebrew expressions in his Yiddish than does Joshua, who more often uses a Germanic or Germanized expression for common merged and whole Hebrew lexical items. Such usage may reflect a contemporary characterization of older versus younger Jews (for example, *kol yisroel* versus *Geshlekht izrael*). In any case it corresponds to the characters of the two figures involved here.

The earliest extant material displays not just the Jewish cultural base that one would expect, but also the direct and profound influence of the dominant surrounding culture—in particular that of the German-speaking lands, but also, due to a peculiar set of circumstances, a secularized

British dramatic tradition (Slavic influence was negligible). There are elements and examples of improvised comedy in the style of the commedia dell'arte; the Latin *acta;* and German *Aktionen, Singspiele,* and enlightenment drama; and, in the purimshpil's earliest stages, there are obvious relations to the German *Fastnachtspiel* of the fifteenth and sixteenth centuries. The strongest influence on Yiddish drama of whole period, both technically and theatrically, was German drama, from medieval plays to the bourgeois theater of the Nuremberg Meistersinger.

Even so, there were clear limitations to the otherwise pervasive influence of non-Jewish drama on the purimshpil. Because the Christian biblical plays of this and earlier periods not surprisingly almost always theologized, especially in treating characters from the Hebrew Bible as prefigurations or allegories of characters and/or concepts from the Christian New Testament (for example, the sacrifice of Isaac as prefiguration of the crucifixion), Yiddish adaptations of such works were not desirable or even possible without compromising the entire point of the Christian original. On the other hand, Jewish adaptation of Christian secular epics was not obstructed, because they did not turn on essential aspects of Christian theology. Thus many medieval European epics were adapted for Jewish audiences, just as they were from one language to another for Christian audiences across the continent.

It was not until the end of the sixteenth century that non-Jewish secular drama appeared and exerted an influence on the incipient dramatic tendencies of the purimshpil. During the last decade of that century a troupe of British comedians first toured Germany with a largely secularized repertoire (even if still biblical, it was not theological or didactic). Itinerant English troupes continued to perform Esther plays in continental towns and for German princes for decades thereafter (certainly as late as a known performance in Dresden on July 3, 1626). Such troupes constituted in a significant sense a professional theater not based in or controlled directly by the church, and especially not by the Jesuits, as had earlier usually been the case. These troupes strongly influenced the development of Yiddish theater, both directly (especially in Holland) and through the mediation of contemporary German drama, which likewise underwent a secularizing development.

The actual techniques and means of Jewish adaptation of Christian theater from this early period are difficult to reconstruct and never transparent. This difficulty is due particularly to the fact that little or no contemporary German drama of the type adapted by the Jewish tradition has survived, primarily because the traveling troupes refused publication in order to avoid competition with other troupes, who might then have appropriated their repertoire. One aspect of this type of adaptation is clear, however, and reflects a similar practice in the adaptation of medieval (secular) Christian epic for Jewish audiences: motifs and scenes deemed inappropriate for Jewish audiences were omitted and often replaced by specifically Jewish material. These unique features were drawn especially from the wealth of material unavailable to Christian biblical literary adaptations: excerpts from the midrashic traditions, aggadic material, and the parts of works from earlier Yiddish and Hebrew literary traditions (for example, relevant passages from the Old Yiddish *Shmuel-bukh* were used to adapt *Dovid un Golias*).

Although the purimshpil originated in the Jewish community to fulfill a specifically Jewish cultural need—as a component of the celebration of Purim—the participation of the surrounding non-Jewish dominant culture was not confined to its profound intellectual and cultural influence on the development of the specific dramatic form of the purimshpil; it extended as well to overt political intervention. It was not always obvious, but the celebration of Purim, like other aspects of Jewish life in Christian Europe, was ultimately under the control of Christian authorities. That control as it extended to the regulation of Jewish theater is demonstrated in the municipal documents of many communities and perhaps most clearly in Amsterdam, which in the wake of the events of 1648 (Chmielnicki's revolt against Polish rule in the Ukraine, the massacre of tens of thousands of Jews, and the ensuing flight of thousands of survivors to Western Europe) experienced a rapid growth of its Ashkenazic commu-

nity. In 1683 the Amsterdam Jews requested permission for the public performance of purimshpiln; a similar petition from 1707 specifically indicates that such permission had been granted some years previously. The play was to be performed in the "language of the high German Jews," that is, Yiddish. Although the city council rejected this particular petition, the document nonetheless reveals an interesting bit of information—there was at the time already an operating Jewish theater in Amsterdam that staged performances three times a week during the Purim season to an audience of two to three hundred.

As noted above, beyond the mere regulation of Jewish theater, there were at various times and places explicit attempts—sometimes by Christian authorities, sometimes by their Jewish counterparts—to suppress purimshpiln altogether. The move to prohibit Jewish theater and circus attendance was widespread among religious Jews, but with the rise of the Enlightenment and the Jewish Haskalah, the antitheatrical movement was often also based on antipathy toward the Yiddish language (the linguistic medium of the theater), and on the view—both Christian and "enlightened" Jewish—that the Book of Esther was anti-Christian, especially in the hanging of Haman (the non-Jew and thus in this view quasi-Christian) as the sacrifice of a Christian or as a mockery of crucifixion or both. This was particularly volatile subject matter due to Purim's proximity to Easter. In Berlin in 1703, Christian authorities forbade purimshpiln so as to prevent the "violation" of the Christian Holy Week. The host in whose house any play was performed, all actors, and the host's guests (the audience) were to be arrested and fined. Compliance with and enforcement of the statute was made the responsibility of authorities within the Jewish community. Similar statutes were instituted elsewhere as well, and although purimshpiln persisted (whether clandestinely or not) in the smaller towns of Prussia into the nineteenth century, in the course of the eighteenth century they disappeared in Berlin. In the mid-eighteenth century the Jewish community authorities themselves often established fines for Jews who entered playhouses (comedy houses). Although it is not clear that such fines only applied to Jewish drama, all such ordinances are dated to Purim. The fact that one of the earliest printed versions of the *Akhashveyresh-shpil* was burned in Frankfurt by the Jewish authorities, and that the Hamburg Jewish community banned performance of all purimshpiln in 1728, may support the view of some scholars that the obscenity of the plays outraged the community, but it may also simply manifest the responsibility imposed on the Jewish authorities for the enforcement of the Christian ordinances.

The core repertoire of plays described above in various versions was produced countless times throughout the course of the eighteenth century (and later) both in German-speaking lands and the Slavic East. The older plays were adapted, revised, modified, and updated, and new ones were composed in Yiddish specifically for Purim celebrations in both the older folkloristic style (such as that found in *Akeydes Yitskhak, Yetsies mitsraim, Shloymemelekhs mishpet, Geshikhte fun Kinig Saul,* and *Moyshe rabeynu lebn un toyt*) and the more sophisticated literary style. In the nineteenth and twentieth centuries, with the massive emigration of Ashkenazic Jewry from Eastern Europe, Yiddish purimshpiln came to be performed in Jewish communities around the world. Even now, in the late twentieth century, Yiddish purimshpiln are still being composed and performed in Jewish communities in Brooklyn, New York, and Jerusalem (and perhaps elsewhere). Among the last Yiddish purimshpiln performed by Ashkenazic Jews in Germany were those that took place in displaced-persons camps by recent survivors of the Holocaust; in Landsberg in 1946 the Haman character was costumed and made-up as Hitler. Just like Mordecai's claim in *Mordkhe un Ester* to have attended yeshiva in Prague, this post-Holocaust performance practice demonstrates a recurring tendency in the purimshpil to make the ancient source material modern, topical, even overtly political.

Bibliography

Jean Baumgarten, "Le 'Purim-shpil' et la tradition carnavalesque juive," *Introduction à la littérature yiddish ancienne* (Paris: Cerf, 1993), 443–73; Ahuva Belkin, "'Habit de Fou' in Purim Spiel?" *Assaph: Studies in the Theatre* 2/c (1985): 40–55; Noyakh Prilutski [Noah Prylucki], "Purim-shpilen fun Noyakh Prilutskis zamlungen," *Zamlbikher far yidishen folklor filologie un kulturgeshikhte* 1 (1912): 125–88; 6 (1917): 143–57; Yankev Shatsky, "Der kamf kegn purim-shpiln in praysn in 18tn yorhundert," *Yivo-bleter* 15 (1940): 28–38; Shatsky, "Geshikhte fun yidishn teater," *Algemeyne entsiklopedie: Yidn b* (Paris: Dubnov-Fond, 1940; New York: Central Yiddish Culture Organization, 1948), cols. 389–414; Shatsky et al., "Purim-shpiler," *Leksikon fun yidishn teater,* ed. Zalmen Zilbertsveig (New York: n.p., 1959), III, cols. 1653–1756; Y. Shiper, *Geshikhte fun yidishn teater-kunst un drama fun di eltste tsaytn biz 1750,* 3 vols. (Warsaw: Kultur-lige, 1923–28); Chone Shmeruk, ed., *Makhazot mikrayim beyidish* [1697–1750] (Jerusalem: Ha-akademia le madaim, 1979); E. Shulman, *Sefat yehudit ashkenazit vesifrutah* (Riga: E. Levin, 1913), 172–77; Moritz Steinschneider, "Purim und Parodie," *Monatsschrift für Geschichte und Wissenschaft des Judenthums* 46 (1902): 176–87, 275–80, 372–76, 473–78, 567–82; 47 (1903): 84–89, 169–80, 279–86, 360–70, 468–74; 48 (1904): 242–47, 504–9; Yisroel Tsinberg, *Geshikhte fun literatur bay yidn,* vol. 6 (Vilna, 1939; New York: Sklarsky, 1943), 336–84; and Max Weinreich, "Tsu der geshikhte fun der elterer Akhashveyresh-shpil," *Filologishe shriftn (fun Yivo)* 2 (1928): cols. 425–52.

JEROLD C. FRAKES

1769 Lavater's attempt to compel the conversion of Moses Mendelssohn abuses the friendship cult surrounding Jewish and Christian intellectuals

I have the good fortune to count some excellent men, who were not my co-religionists, among my friends.

—Moses Mendelssohn

The dialectics of the friendship cult of the eighteenth century, especially between Christian and Jewish intellectuals, were captured rather dramatically in an image by the artist Moritz Daniel Oppenheim (1799–1882), who became famous through his *Bilder aus dem altjüdischen Familienleben* (1865). In 1856 he painted a genre scene that shows Mendelssohn and Lessing, who have been interrupted in their chess game by Lavater. Sitting opposite Mendelssohn, his right arm pushing the chess game aside and his left hand resting on the pages of an open book, Lavater argues with Mendelssohn—nay, he rushes upon him. His body language and his pale face characterize him as someone who does not seek a dialogue but proselytizes. Oppenheim has superimposed Lavater's conversion attempt of 1769 already onto their first meeting, which took place in 1763. Mendelssohn is sitting in the pose of a thinker, listening tolerantly and attentively as if already formulating his arguments. The discussion is observed by Lessing, who is standing behind the table and looking at the intruder with indignation. The triangular composition is as characteristic for the enlightened culture of disputation as the interior is for bourgeois respectability. A large bookshelf covers the back wall, and two tomes in the foreground rest against a desk—attributes of Mendelssohn's learnedness. Furniture, two small paintings, a curtain, tablecloth, and carpet provide an almost Biedermeier atmosphere. The sociability of the Jewish salon is underscored by the appearance of elegant Fromet Mendelssohn, who enters the room from the right to serve coffee for the gentlemen. Not much, if anything, points to a Jewish household; the Mendelssohns appear in Oppenheim's painting to be already integrated into the German *Bildungsbürgertum*.

Why is this stylized image of the past so typical for the friendship cult and the culture of discussion in the late eighteenth century? Johann Caspar Lavater, a young student of theology, stumbled into Mendelssohn's life as many others did: he wanted to make the acquaintance of the famous Jewish philosopher. What was unthinkable in previous centuries, namely a dialogue between Christians and Jews, became part of intellectual life during the Enlightenment. Although these interreligious discussions since the days of Eisenmenger's *Judaism Unmasked* (1711; *Entdecktes Judentum*) often had the purpose of converting the Jews, nevertheless the civility and sociability of the age brought Christian and Jewish intellectuals together in discussions. They started to speak to each other and to argue—much ink, but no blood was spilt. Lessing was not present during the first meetings of Mendelssohn and Lavater in 1763 and 1764, but it is a convincing invention of Oppenheim, because two tolerant Enlighteners are a stronger counterpart to one religious fanatic who wanted to offer Mendelssohn "a golden bridge" to Christianity. As was customary in those days, they took leave of each other as friends, soon exchanged friendly letters, and contributed in their way to the booming cult of friendship. But the danger of such enthusiasm for friendship in the eighteenth century was that it could lead to dubious or even false friends. The latter was the case between Mendelssohn and Lavater. Lavater characterized their discussions as candid and intimate; for Mendelssohn, however, the discussions were also private. In this belief he was badly mistaken.

How surprised must Mendelssohn have been when Lavater sent him in 1769 his abridged translation of Charles Bonnet's *Palingenesie philosophique* under the German title *Untersuchung der Beweise für das Christentum,* adding a printed dedication in which he demanded that Mendelssohn refute Bonnet's arguments—or convert. The private conversation in Mendelssohn's salon on the historical importance of Jesus had become an unsolicited offer to discuss *coram publico* the truth of both religions. For Mendelssohn, a "protected Jew" in Berlin, this indiscretion of a religious zealot was a dangerous provocation. But how to answer it? Mendelssohn could not ignore it; that could be misconstrued as an implicit acceptance of Bonnet's arguments. Nor could he attack these arguments, because this would have brought him into conflict with the Christian authorities. In his private notes and drafts of the answer one can still feel Mendelssohn's anger and the temptation to give a polemical answer. In his public response, however, he wisely circumvented the debate into which Lavater had pressured him. In the process of his writing, "Mendelssohn was forced to define his own image of the Jew in a public forum" (Gilman 1982). The Lavater affair truly became a "turning point" in Mendelssohn's life (Altmann 1973).

"I have read, compared, contemplated and taken sides," writes Mendelssohn in his *Schreiben an den Herrn Diaconus Lavater zu Zürich* (Berlin, 1770), and the result is his *Confessio Judaica:* "I am as thoroughly and irrefutably convinced of the essence of my religion as you, or Mr. Bonnet could ever be of yours" (*JubA* 7:10). This is without doubt a courageous confession within a Christian society on whose benevolence he depended. Deeply disappointed by Lavater's crude conversion attempt, which offended the decency of Enlightenment tolerance, Mendelssohn answered "with a multifaceted defense of toleration" (Sorkin 1996). From a philosophical perspective, he argued that philosophers should avoid religious controversies and discuss "only those truths that should be of equal importance to all religions" (10). The universality of natural religion as a moral axiom should lead to religious toleration as well, Mendelssohn asserted, because no religion can or should demand an exclusive claim to eternal felicity: "He who in this life leads men to virtue cannot be condemned in the next" (*JubA* 7:12). And finally, Mendelssohn assures his Christian adversary that Judaism—in contrast to Christianity—had no missionary zeal and was therefore in harmony with natural religion and with the principle of toleration: "In accordance with the principles of my religion, I am not obliged to convert anyone who was not born into our law" (7:15). Although Mendelssohn disappointed all those who expected a public debate on the merits of the two religions or at least an apology for Judaism, he had steadfastly defended his conviction and pleaded for the toleration on which the Jewish flock's well-being depended. Even if some critics of the whole affair saw their suspicions that Mendelssohn's defense of natural religion made him a Jewish deist supported, theological questions, on which Mendelssohn had written in Hebrew, were not discussed—and for good reason.

"I hate religious disputes and especially those which are conducted in the eye of the public. Experience teaches that they are useless, they lead more to hatred than to enlightenment," writes Mendelssohn (7:10). If we set aside for the moment Mendelssohn's justified fear that such religious controversies would sooner or later call up the Christian authorities, we can see that he also wanted to avoid the negative stereotype of the polemical or disputatious Jew. Nothing was further from Mendelssohn's mind than engaging with a Christian enthusiast in a theological argument on so touchy a matter as the exclusivity of Lavater's Christianity—least of all in the mode of a rabbinic disputation, polemical and hair-splitting like a *pilpul*. Mendelssohn intended to project the positive image of a reasonable and non-polemical Jew: "I hope to refute the contempt in which the Jews are held not through polemics but through virtue" (7:10). Therefore, he refused to accept Lavater's challenge and stressed the importance of those principles that all religions have in common.

Mendelssohn in no way responded to Bonnet's proofs of Christianity. Instead, he reserved a critical aside for the end. There he praised Bonnet as an excellent writer, but he dared to compare his apology for Christianity with German works that seem to be much more thorough and more philosophical. "Herr Bonnet is indebted in almost everything he wrote to German philosophers. When it comes to philosophical principles, the German has seldom to borrow from his neighbors" (*JubA* 7:15). These sentences can be read as Mendelssohn's second confession, namely to German language and philosophy. During his youth in Dessau he heard and spoke Yiddish, and in his rabbinical studies he learned Hebrew. When he came to Berlin, he learned German behind the back of his mentor, Fränkel, for it was still considered heresy to read or write German, and the Jewish community of Berlin could have even expelled him for this transgression. As an autodidact, he secretly and at great cost read every German book he could lay his hands on and slowly cultivated his German style to such perfection that his German is even today praised for its perspicuity. German became the exclusive language of Mendelssohn's philosophical and literary writings, whereas he reserved Hebrew for his theological and exegetical commentaries on Jewish subjects. When Lavater challenged him publicly, Mendelssohn had already established his reputation as the "Jewish philosopher of Berlin." Well read in the German philosophy of the Leibniz-Wolffian school, he had published such influential books as *Philosophical Conversations* and *Letters Concerning Perception* (both published anonymously in 1755); his treatise *On the Evidence of*

Metaphysical Sciences had won first prize of the Berlin Academy in 1763 (Kant came in second); and his *Phädon, or on the Immortality of the Soul* (1767) had made him one of the leading figures of the German Enlightenment. He was respected as a Jewish intellectual writing for a German audience and participated freely in the literary life of the time, as demonstrated by his literary criticism in two leading journals: *Briefe, die neueste Literatur betreffend* (1759–65) and *Allgemeine Deutsche Bibliothek* (since 1765). Mendelssohn had no intention of risking his reputation as a German philosopher and literary critic by engaging with Lavater in a public theological debate, which could have endangered both his civic life and his intentional separation of the Jewish religious from the German intellectual sphere.

The more Mendelssohn grew into German language and culture, the more he distanced himself from the language of the common people, Yiddish. What in 1769 was only indirectly noticeable in his praise for German philosophy became quite clear in 1782 when Mendelssohn advised the Prussian government on the so-called Jewish oath, an oath that was demanded of every Jew before he could testify in a German court. In his correspondence with the civil servant Ernst Ferdinand Klein, he insisted that the sanctity and dignity of the oath required that it be given in *pure* Hebrew or *pure* German: "Absolutely no intermingling of languages!" (*JubA* 7:279). He was strictly against the use of "the Jewish German dialect," and what followed was his strongest attack on Yiddish: "I fear that this jargon has contributed to no small degree to the immorality of the common people." In Mendelssohn's view, this corrupt and corrupting language had to be replaced by "the pure German dialect," because it had recently become customary among his fellow Jews. Whether Mendelssohn projected his own acculturation as a Jewish intellectual in Berlin onto all Jews, or whether he thought it practical for the Jews to become familiar with the language of the host country, he insisted, like most Jewish reformers, on the use of the German form of the oath and stressed the usefulness of the German language in everyday life. What he did not dare to dispute was the discriminating use of an oath *more judaico*. He accepted the law of the land and tried to uphold the dignity of the Jewish oath, but in the process he also accelerated the linguistic acculturation of the Jews in Prussia.

What slowly emerges is a new image of the Jewish intellectual in Berlin. Mendelssohn held steadfastly to Jewish tradition, but also intended to reform it in accordance with time, place, and circumstances, which bespeaks his historical understanding of culture. Knowing that his existence depended on the benevolence of the Prussian state, he pleaded for philosophical and religious toleration. In an effort to erase the stereotype of the disputatious or illogical Jew, he avoided public debates on religious issues that could upset the delicate balance of toleration. He advocated the use of pure German as a civilized language in everyday life and praised German philosophy and literature. And within a circle of Christian friends, he participated freely in the intellectual life of the German Enlightenment. Mendelssohn clearly moved in two different spheres: he upheld the Jewish tradition while he took part in the modern world of the Enlightenment. It is still hotly debated whether this type of new Jewish identity, for which Mendelssohn became the model, was the beginning of a "long slide of Western Jewry into the morass of confused self-identity" (Gilman 1982), or whether "his dualism was induced by external constraints rather than the internal needs of his philosophy" (Sorkin 1996).

Lavater's crude attempt to convert Mendelssohn was sharply condemned by many Enlighteners because he had violated one of the most important principles of the Enlightenment, toleration. His Christian chiliasm ran counter to the temper of the time, and Mendelssohn's Christian friends closed ranks around him. Mendelssohn's wise and cautious reply would not have deterred Lavater from continuing his mission had not public opposition forced him to retreat. Even Bonnet and some other theologians disapproved of Lavater's attempted public extortion. Because Mendelssohn did not engage in any polemics, he left it to his friends, especially his publisher, Nicolai, "the arch-polemicist of the Holy Roman Empire," to confront Lavater—and they did it with

gusto. Noteworthy is Georg Christoph Lichtenberg's pungent satire *Timorus* (1773), which exposed Lavater's missionary zeal to roaring laughter. When Lavater admitted his mistake and publicly apologized for his indiscretion (*JubA* 7:28), Mendelssohn remained magnanimous up to the end when he responded: "Come on, let us embrace each other spiritually. You are a Christian preacher and I am a Jew. What does it matter . . . are we not both human beings?" (*JubA* 7:337). This was almost too much! The Christian preacher wanted to convert a Jew at all costs, and the attacked Jew only wished to be respected as a human being and allowed to live quietly within a Christian society. To battle with such false friends must have seemed harder than to fight real enemies.

Mendelssohn entered the literary scene of the German Enlightenment under unusual circumstances. When Lessing published his comedy *Die Juden* in 1754, it was immediately criticized by Johann David Michaelis, the leading orientalist at the University of Göttingen. He argued that Lessing's noble Jew was not impossible, but all too improbable. In his rebuttal, Lessing used two arguments: one practical, the other tactical. The improbability would become superfluous if the Jew's living conditions were improved. What else was required for that other than wealth and education? Why should these cultivating prerequisites, which his Jew possesses, have less influence on him than on a Christian? To give authenticity to his argument, Lessing quoted from a letter of a Jew who felt deeply offended by Michaelis's critique. Lessing's use of a private letter of Moses Mendelssohn, written to his friend Gumpertz, can be construed as indiscreet if not dangerous, because he had dragged an angry Jew into an anti-Semitic argument. But by this time it was already common practice within the new friendship culture to circulate private letters and even publish them. Mendelssohn did not mind this indiscretion; to the contrary, it made him, a Jew, a public figure and introduced him into the literary life of the time. Henceforth he would be surrounded by, and in dialogue with, his Christian friends. Even Michaelis learned to respect Mendelssohn and often sought his advice, although he clearly distinguished between this exceptional Jew and "the rest of them," who were in his eyes uneducated, debased, and therefore unfit for integration into Christian society. In good humor, Mendelssohn later called him "the grey eminence of prejudice."

One should, however, not underestimate the mental reservations of an observant Jew in a circle of Christian intellectuals. As a learned Jew, Mendelssohn enhanced their discussions with his religious tradition, which was, by and large, alien to his Christian friends. In their circle he was truly a *Luftmensch*—aloof, different, and in many ways enigmatic. He certainly participated freely in their deliberations, but their differences came to the surface in debates of philosophical and religious issues of the Enlightenment. These productive tensions never threatened their friendships, but they have to be acknowledged and kept in mind in order not to paint too harmonious a picture of Mendelssohn's friendships. To give but one example: Mendelssohn's interest in and perspective on the developing discourse of the Enlightenment had nothing to do with Zöllner's original question of religious versus civil marriage in a Christian society. Nothing could have been further from Mendelssohn's mind than to interfere in a debate on so delicate a matter. As distinguished from Kant's famous essay "What Is Enlightenment?" which stressed maturity, independent thinking, and above all philosophical criticism, Mendelssohn's treatise emphasized concepts such as enlightenment as theoretical thinking, culture as practical knowledge, and *Bildung* as their synthesis. They all contributed to toleration, which guaranteed the well-being of Jews in a Christian society.

For all that, one should not overlook the new forms of sociability that brought Jewish and Christian intellectuals together in spontaneous discussions. Whether in private circles, reading societies, or coffee houses, these friends stimulated, provoked, and irritated each other in heated debates that carried over into their correspondences. The neutrality of these social gatherings made it possible to discuss religious, moral, or aesthetic issues beyond and across the religious divide of centuries. Here Christians and Jews associated with each other as if the old social barriers no longer existed. This new sociability, for which Moses Mendelssohn's house became famous, was a positive sign for the social acceptance of the Jewish intellectuals. It was "a kind of social Utopia" (Katz 1973) that anticipated the integration of the Jews into a Christian society. Mendelssohn, in an aside to the reader of his *Jerusalem* (1783), fondly remembers those meetings and the discussions he had with his "best friends" on matters of religion or philosophy: "Oh, who has had this experience in his lifetime and still can be intolerant or can still hate his fellow man, because he does not express or think in religious matters like himself, I don't want to have him as a friend; for he has lost his humanity" (*JubA* 8:135).

Reading the letters between Mendelssohn and his numerous Christian friends, one can still feel that openness and trust, respect and intimacy are the foundations of these friendships, but they are no longer an outpouring of the heart as was the style of Sentimentality. One has only to compare Gellert's primer for letter writing (1742) or Gleim's collection of *Freundschaftliche Briefe* (1746) with Mendelssohn's correspondence to his dearest friend Thomas Abbt (1766) to notice a stark difference in content and tone. Whereas the sentimental letters of Gleim's circle continually stress the emotional and moral value of friendship, Mendelssohn's correspondence with Abbt reads like a philosophical dialogue on the essence of life and man's destiny. This difference between sentimental and enlightened letter culture does not diminish the concept of intimate friendship. On the contrary, it only enlarges its depth and scope; it makes these correspondences an integral part of the literary sphere, where seemingly harmless and apolitical issues of ethics, aesthetics, and the arts were first discussed privately and then made public. One of the first instances in which the private entered the public sphere was the publication of *Briefe, die neueste Literatur betreffend*. Edited by Lessing, Nicolai, and Mendelssohn between 1759 and 1765, the *Literaturbriefe* stylized their reviews as a collection of letters to a "meritorious officer" who had been wounded during the Seven Years War. This fictitious situation provided the criticism with a familiar, conversational tone and also gave the critics an opportunity to discuss matters that transcended literature. In contrast to the secessionist tendencies of the age of Sentimentality, Mendelssohn and his friends were eager to find public outlets for their private discussions. For them friendship meant productive cooperation to enhance the process of enlightenment. Nicolai, whose publishing business existed for and because of the Enlightenment, provided his friends with the means to proliferate their ideas.

Friendship was no longer a private celebration of mutually assured sympathy, but a public discussion of the universal concerns of humanity. The discourse of enlightenment was grafted onto the firmly established cult of friendship. The friendships between Christian and Jewish intellectuals in particular did not limit themselves to an interreligious dialogue; rather, they contributed to the development of the major concepts of the Enlightenment, such as theoretical and practical knowledge, natural religion and toleration, aesthetics, and Bildung. To mention Bildung in this cluster of concepts seems to be an anachronism, because we usually connect this idea with German Idealism; it was Mendelssohn, however, who first promoted it and made it the capstone of enlightenment. Already in his letters to Abbt (1766) and later in his commentary on their correspondence (1783), he tried to circumscribe it. When Abbt asked him what the destination of man should be, Mendelssohn's belated answer defines his ideal of self-cultivation *in nuce:* "Development, cultivation and practice of all human faculties under the proper conditions of an assigned place" (*JubA* 6:42). The first part of this definition is familiar through its later refinement by Schiller, Goethe, and Wilhelm von Humboldt, but the second part sounds like a limiting proposition. It reminds us of Lessing's and Mendelssohn's defense of the plausibility of the rich and educated Jewish traveler in *Die Juden* against Michaelis's criticism. What in 1754 was merely a theoretical argument thirty years later still defined the practical limitations of Jewish self-cultivation. These limitations found their expression in the restrictive edicts as well as in the corresponding Christian prejudices. Only enlightenment, based on criticism of all prejudices and on a culture of toleration that permits otherness, can

prepare for the possibility of Bildung in which the Jews could also participate.

This is the hidden message of Mendelssohn's contribution to the debate of 1784, "What Is Enlightenment?" His answer is as original as Kant's and as typical for his practical thinking. *Expressis verbis,* he establishes Bildung as the centerpiece of enlightenment and, even more important, he makes it dependent upon the condition of the subject of the state as a human being and as a citizen. He understands the newly developed concepts of enlightenment, culture, and Bildung as "modifications of social life, effects of diligence and of man's efforts to improve his social condition" (*JubA* 6:115). Enlightenment provides the philosophical and theoretical foundation; culture aims at practical knowledge and improvement of life; and Bildung, the result of their interaction, finds its living expression in the individual as well as in a people. In Mendelssohn's words, "Enlightenment is to culture as theory is to practice, as theoretical is to practical knowledge" (115). Only the harmony of both can constitute the form of Bildung for which the Greeks are the classical example. But if the "conditions of an assigned place" are not in harmony with human destiny, this ideal cannot be reached: "Lamentable is the state which has to admit that the essential conditions of man are not in harmony with the essential rights of the citizen, that enlightenment, which is indispensable for humanity, is not disseminated equally among all classes of the state" (*JubA* 6:117). Here Mendelssohn breaks off his argument and replaces it with a gesture of silencing, if not despair: "In this case philosophy puts a hand over its mouth" (117). Mendelssohn, the Jew, who had pleaded since the beginning of his intellectual life for human rights as the smallest of concessions for the Jews, does not dare to demand civil rights at this point in his career, but the development of the argument and his *aposiopese* clearly point in this direction. He considers the process of enlightenment and its ideal of Bildung to be incomplete so long as the state neither provides conditions favorable to enhancing the pursuit of Bildung for all citizens nor grants civil rights to all. This is indirect criticism of enlightened despotism in the best tradition of the Enlightenment, although the Jewish philosopher has to speak with a muffled mouth. Even the friendships of the best minds of the age could not substitute for this want of freedom and self-cultivation. Bildung, as the essential element of enlightenment and human development, can flourish under the sun of friendship, but it requires above all self-determination, which was denied to the Jews. Here the cult of friendship finds its limits, even if Mendelssohn and his friends argued for emancipation.

And argue they did. It was certainly no coincidence that such important works as Lessing's *Nathan der Weise* (1779), Dohm's *Über die bürgerliche Verbesserung der Juden* (1781), and Mendelssohn's *Jerusalem* (1783) were all published within a short time span, when the political climate seemed ripe for reforms. Lessing's *Nathan* raised the literary discourse on toleration to a level never before achieved; Dohm's reform project anticipated the Prussian emancipation edict of 1812; and Mendelssohn's *Confessio Judaica* is embedded in an argument for the separation of church and state. These are signposts of a productive Jewish-Christian dialogue that transcended the reclusive sphere of friendship. What had started as private discussions on matters of philosophy, aesthetics, and literature led to joint critical enterprises and developed into civic debates on the major issues of the Enlightenment. Their public discussions on natural religion, toleration, and freedom of expression slowly paved the way for the reforms to come. Without friendship, dialogue, and cooperation between Christian and Jewish intellectuals, this would not have been accomplished. Mendelssohn had come a long way: from his simple plea that Jews too are human beings in his refutation of Michaelis's criticism (1754), to his masterful deflection of Lavater's conversion attempt (1769), and finally to his courageous statements of the 1780s in which he argued for reforms and emancipation.

More than his Christian friends, Mendelssohn must have felt the importance of these friendships. For them the private sphere was the foundation from which they could launch their indirect criticism of enlightened despotism; for him, his circle of friends was an island in a hostile world. Here, the Jewish outsider was accepted as an equal, integrated into an intellectual community, and able to participate in the literary endeavors of the culture at large. For Mendelssohn, friendship became a substitute for social connectedness. As long as the state denied him his basic rights and restricted his freedom, his circle of friends constituted a social utopia that anticipated a world without oppression, prejudice, and hatred—a world where human dignity and Bildung could flourish. An aphorism from 1781 best sums up what Mendelssohn meant by "human destiny": "To search for truth, to love beauty, to mean well, to do the best" (*JubA* 6:195).

Bibliography

Alexander Altmann, *Moses Mendelssohn: A Biographical Study* (Birmingham: University of Alabama Press, 1973); Sander L. Gilman, "'Hebrew and Jew': Moses Mendelssohn and the Sense of Jewish Identity," *Humanität und Dialog: Lessing und Mendelssohn in neuer Sicht*, ed. Ehrhard Bahr, Edward P. Harris, and Lawrence G. Lyon (Detroit: Wayne State University Press, 1982), 67–82; Jacob Katz, *Out of the Ghetto: The Social Background of Jewish Emancipation, 1770–1870* (Cambridge, Mass.: Harvard University Press, 1973); Moses Mendelssohn, *Moses Mendelssohn Gesammelte Schriften, Jubiläumsausgabe* [known as *JubA*], 22 vols. (Berlin: Akademie Verlag, 1929); George L. Mosse, *German Jews Beyond Judaism* (Bloomington: Indiana University Press, 1985); and David Sorkin, *Moses Mendelssohn* (Oxford: Oxford University Press, 1996).

KLAUS L. BERGHAHN

1779 David Friedländer and Moses Mendelssohn publish the *Lesebuch für jüdische Kinder*

It is notoriously difficult to identify a precise cultural turning point. In history there are neither events nor moments of dramatic change. Events are shaped by myriad occurrences that precede them and combine with others to confect the future. Given that "turning point" is understood as a metaphor, however—as a historical crossroad from which new processes can be clearly discerned and clearly distinguished—the publication in 1779 of *Lesebuch für jüdische Kinder* can be regarded as a turning point. The *Lesebuch* was edited by David Friedländer (though Friedländer's name does not appear on the title page), and it was partially translated and written by Moses Mendelssohn. Its importance was not its place in historical consciousness. Its publication was barely noticed during its day, and it neither reached a large reading public nor established a model for future Jewish children's texts to emulate. Indeed, within a short time, the *Lesebuch* had been all but forgotten. Its importance was primarily symbolic: for the first time in European Jewish culture, a book for a modern, nonreligious Jewish school was published. It concretely promoted the objectives of the Jewish Haskalah in Berlin and constituted a device for the actual implementation of Haskalah ideals rather than a mere intellectual airing of them. It also divulges to current readers the Haskalah's understanding of ideal relations between the German and Jewish cultures.

Although children were recognized as a discrete reading audience in the late Middle Ages and early Renaissance, this recognition did not become widespread until much later, at which point it prompted the large-scale production of books for children. Books that were written exclusively for Jewish children appeared even later. Only toward the end of the eighteenth century, almost a century after German culture began turning out such texts, did Jews do so themselves, and their production was episodic until the early nineteenth century. Since then, hundreds of books addressing Jewish children exclusively, written in Hebrew, German, and in a bilingual format, were published in German-speaking countries. This development played a major role in modernizing the Jewish community.

Clearly, children were used to reading nonreligious texts before the *Lesebuch*'s appearance in 1779. Nevertheless, books that served as popular reading material for children, such as Volksbücher, were not published exclusively for children (see Shmeruk 1986 and Shavit 1986), but rather for women, children, and laymen. Books addressed solely to Jewish children during the eighteenth century were mainly catechisms, primers on morality, and books of etiquette. They were not intended to constitute secular schooling; they were meant to teach children appropriate behavior and the basic principles of Judaism. Thus, the distinctive nature of the *Lesebuch* was twofold: it was the first secular book that officially addressed Jewish children, and it was the first book compiled to provide reading material for a modern Jewish education.

Friedländer's *Lesebuch* was created in a new cultural context and acquired its meaning from this context. These traits are reflected in its title: "For children" stemmed from the new awareness developing in western Europe since the seventeenth century of children as a separate reading public (Ariès 1962). The term *Lesebuch* indicates the newest permutation of the nonreligious textual model to emerge in Germany in the 1770s. It also implied that the purpose of the book was to serve the educational goals of the Jewish Haskalah in the new net of modern schools it founded in Germany (Büdinger 1831; Eliav 1960; Elboim Dror 1986; Stern 1928; Wechsler 1846).

It is true that many Jews had given their children nontraditional educations. But those were specific cases affecting only individuals whose parents had made private decisions. The Haskalah, by contrast, promoted modern education for all Jews. Despite its failures in various cultural endeavors, the Haskalah did manage to change the structure of Jewish education in Germany, even among the Orthodox. In 1778 David Friedländer, together with his father-in-law, Isaac Daniel Itzig, founded in Berlin the *jüdische Freischule,* which was based on the philanthropist schooling philosophy (Eliav 1960, 73; Lowenstein 1994, 52; Simon 1953). The school opened officially in 1781. The founding of the school under the rubric of the Haskalah created a demand for specialized schoolbooks. The new books were expected to express the social and cultural ideals promulgated by David Friedländer and the Berlin circle (Sorkin 1987). Because of the importance attributed to texts for children and adolescents in the process of education and socialization as a German Jew, books like the *Lesebuch* provide a unique perspective for the study of German-Jewish culture. Indeed, the *Lesebuch* reflects the complicated ideology of the Berlin Haskalah at the end of the eighteenth century. From this vantage point, I will analyze the *Lesebuch,* focusing on the following two issues:

1. Friedländer's mode for creating a Jewish *Lesebuch* based on the German model(s).

2. Criteria for selection of segments of the German culture on the basis of aspects with which the Haskalah was acquainted.

The *Lesebuch* did not arise in a vacuum. It had roots in the long tradition of contemporary German readers as well as in the Hebrew cultural heritage known to David Friedländer and Moses Mendelssohn, the mediators between the *Lesebuch* and both cultures. These scholars' perception of the desired relations between the German and the Jewish cultures determined which segments of the repertoire of both cultures would be included in the *Lesebuch,* and even more important, which would not. David Friedländer utilized various models of German readers, new and old, and thus created, perhaps unintentionally, a unique model of a reader. Unlike later Jewish authors, Friedländer endeavored to graft German culture onto the Jewish, thus Germanizing certain aspects of Jewish culture. This process of Germanization involved a reorganization of Jewish culture: substantial portions of it were given up, whereas some marginal components were revitalized. In addition, many parts were combined anew with the remaining components, which imparted them with new meanings and functions.

In implementing this program, Friedländer resuscitated forgotten elements. By loading them with functions borrowed from the German repertoire, he changed their original ones. For the most part, Friedländer identified in the traditional Jewish repertoire elements that resembled German components, stripped them of their original functions, and substituted new ones. Unlike later Hebrew readers, Friedländer's *Lesebuch* aimed to prove that one can find in the Jewish heritage the same elements that exist in the German. In this way, he drew parallels between the two and legitimized their interaction. To further this procedure, Friedländer appropriated non-German elements as well, drawing on Roman and Greek literature that was commonly included by the German readers. In his search for Jewish equivalents, Friedländer nearly exhausted those portions of the Jewish heritage that were ideologically amenable and with which he was acquainted.

The entire *Lesebuch* consists of only forty-six pages, but it still includes all the central components of German readers during this time. It is divided into eight units, the first of which contains a guide to the German alphabet, the vowels, the Latin alphabet, numbers, a short reading exercise, the Hebrew alphabet, and the Shema Israel prayer rendered in German translation in Hebrew letters. The second unit introduces Maimonides' thirteen principles of Judaism, followed by the Ten Commandments. The third unit consists of six fables by Berechiah Ben Natronai Ha-Nakdan; the fourth, of two moral tales from the Talmud; the fifth presents four contemporary German lyric poems; the sixth comprises "a prayer exercise" (a text by Moses Mendelssohn on the nature of divinity) and a "preparatory prayer" taken from Juda Halevi's poetry (the first part of his poem "God Against You All My Passion"); and the seventh is made up of epigrams and proverbs from the Talmud, followed by Lichtwer's poem "Die Laster und die Strafe." Finally, the eighth unit offers a selection of moral tales and sayings appropriated from Sulzer's reader (*Vorübung zur Erweckung der Aufmerksamkeit und des Nachdenkens,* 1771).

The choice to open the *Lesebuch* with the alphabet was standard for more traditional German readers. The Latin alphabet, however, was usually included only in German readers tailored to middle- and upper-class children, which tells us either that Friedländer had hoped to attract such a student body or that perhaps he simply was inclined toward a specific German model that included the Latin letters. This second possibility seems more likely, because his school was attended primarily by children from low socioeconomic classes rather than by the offspring of the Berlin Haskalah circle. In addition, Moses Mendelssohn was particularly close to Basedow, whose reader (*Kleines Buch für Kinder aller Stände,* 1771) did list both the German and Latin alphabets.

Newer German readers like those of Campe (1778) and Rochow (1776) did not usually include even the German alphabet. When they did, the readers appended illustrations, short texts, and exercises. Friedländer's *Lesebuch* offers just one exercise in the alphabet section. This typifies the book's entire tenor. Rules and generalizations abound, whereas exercises and examples are scarce.

What examples there are can be described as abstract and formal rather than concrete and colorful, with no detailed description or simple tales. Given this disparity between the *Lesebuch* and the German readers it followed, one is tempted to conclude that the author of the *Lesebuch* was perhaps more conscious of its status as a symbol for adults of the revolution in Jewish education than determined to create a practical tool for conducting the change. In addition, the book's first unit keeps quite a sanitary distance from matters Jewish. In the first seven paragraphs of text, which present the various items to be learned, there is neither a Hebrew word nor any reference to Judaism or the Jewish people. Endeavoring to avoid any similarity to the traditional Jewish catechism, Friedländer did not use the opportunity to compose a text with Jewish meaning; he preferred instead to include some general instructions about good demeanor.

Between the seventh and eighth paragraphs, Friedländer inserts the Hebrew alphabet, the first and last time the children will encounter Hebrew letters in the reader. Not only does the Shema Israel prayer appear only in German translation; it also occupies precisely the spot reserved in German readers for the Vater Unser prayer, implying equivalence between the two. Other texts taken from the Jewish tradition likewise appear only in German translation, such as Maimonides' thirteen principles in the reader's second unit, translated by Mendelssohn, and the Ten Commandments.

Having followed the traditional model of German readers in the first two units—setting forth the alphabet and the fundamentals of religion—Friedländer employs fables in the third unit, which the advanced pedagogical circles of his day considered as the most appropriate means for teaching children. Fables appeared in popular advanced readers such as Sulzer's *Vorübung zur Erweckung der Aufmerksamkeit und des Nachdenkens* (1771) and Weisse's *Neues ABC-Buch* (1773). However, rather than borrow fables from such German readers or from Lessing (see Toury 1993), Friedländer sought a Hebrew equivalent, which he found in Moses Mendelssohn's translation of Berechiah Ben Natronai Ha-Nakdan, previously published in *Briefe, die neueste Literatur betreffend*

(Mendelssohn 1759, 186–98). The tenor of these fables, rather enigmatic and complicated because they had been written in the thirteenth century, fits with the abstract and formalistic reworking of German models in the book's first two units. A typical fable chosen by Friedländer, that of the wolf, involves a person "accustomed to steal and to rob" violently seizing the property of others. The moral provided is that even if such a person swears to abandon his wicked habits, his oath is of no value. Undoubtedly, German pedagogues would judge such a moral as unsuitable for children. Morals of the fables in German readers were simpler and less sarcastic. But Friedländer had another audience uppermost in his mind: German and Jewish adults, to whom Friedländer wished to prove that Jewish culture was commensurate to the German.

Another stock-in-trade of German readers for children was the moral tale. In unit four, Friedländer supplied comparable stories adapted from the Talmud. Later generations of the Haskalah came to regard the Talmud as the lamentable source of Jewish cultural deformation. Friedländer's treatment of his talmudic borrowings foreshadows this development. The tales Friedländer omitted were more "Jewish"—they highlighted Jewish cultural singularity and cultural conflict with dominant peoples—whereas those he included had a streak of universalism. Friedländer chose two of the seven moral tales Mendelssohn had translated from the Talmud for Johann Jacob Engel's 1787 collection, *Philosophen für die Welt*. Friedländer's criterion of selection was, once again, not suitability for children, but whether the tales enabled him to make his point about the correspondence of German and Jewish cultures. Friedländer ignored such tales as that of Rabbi Akiva's determination to persevere in teaching Torah despite the Roman ban, which, as is well-known, cost him his life. Such a moral tale did not conform to the ideal of the Haskalah in regard to harmonious coexistence with a foreign government. In contrast to such a story, the tale about Alexander the Great (Margulies 1993, 618–23) served as proof for the universal character of the Jewish sources, as did one about Rabbi Meir and his wife (Yalkut Shimoni, Prov. 31:964).

The wish to strengthen the presence of the Jewish tradition was conditional upon the Jewish repertoire's capacity to supply equivalent components. When they were deemed absent, Friedländer refused to include Jewish elements. Thus, unit five consists of four German lyric poems rather than a translation of Hebrew poems. Both Friedländer and Mendelssohn apparently felt that the available medieval Jewish poetry, especially the piyyut and Shirat Kodesh, were too heavily burdened by religious baggage. Mendelssohn deigned to include in the *Lesebuch* only one Juda Halevi poem he had translated, which was incorporated into another section, and even there it was presented as a prayer and not as a poem.

The German poems that compose this section, "Auf einen Feldbrunnen" by Johann Nicolas Götz, "Der Vorwizt das künftige zu wissen" by Christian Felix Weisse, "Der Schäfer zu dem Bürger" by Johann Joachim Ewald, and "Die Grossmuth" (anonymous), were all lifted from a popular contemporary anthology, *Blumenlese,* which was edited by Ramler. Mendelssohn had printed a complimentary evaluation of Ramler's gifts as an editor (Mendelssohn 1759, 267–324), and Ramler composed an ode to Mendelssohn upon his passing (Zeitlin 1891–95, 399). It thus seems possible that collegial considerations and respect, in tandem with the aforementioned dismissal of Hebrew poetry, helped relegate the agenda of promoting Jewish culture in this unit.

In unit six, entitled "Andachtsübung eines Weltweisen" (a prayer exercise), Mendelssohn proffered his vision of maskilic Judaism. Emphasizing the universal nature of divinity in Judaism, he went on to give it a secular legitimation by describing religion as the fount of all branches of knowledge. Such a rendering of religion can be found in the German readers of Campe, Rochow, and Basedow. Indeed, Mendelssohn does not even refer to the Jewish religion or people by name. As might well be expected, the major difference between the German readers and Friedländer's *Lesebuch* lies in their implied assumptions about the addressee. Seen from the point of view of German pedagogical thought of the time, the Germans' treatment of religion is more rudimentary and lucid, and suits the juvenile addressees—unlike

Mendelssohn's text, which addresses an adult audience.

The next unit adduces concrete Judaic corroboration for Mendelssohn's deracinated apologetics: a poem by Juda Halevi framed as a "preparatory prayer." Originally, Mendelssohn translated some of Juda Halevi's poems for the periodical *Beschäftigungen des Geistes und des Herzens* (1755–56). Of the poems, including "Zion dost thou not ask for the peace of thy captives?" Friedländer chose the one that could pass as a prayer belonging to any religion. It deals only with the general relations between the divine being and the individual, especially divine omniscience and human fallibility.

The seventh unit most explicitly advances the *Lesebuch*'s project of proving that Jewish culture meets German standards, in that it crops maxims and proverbs from the two traditions together as if they were seamlessly one. The Jewish snippets come from the Talmud, with each passage presenting a widely held humanistic value. These are woven around a fable from Lichtwer (whose fables were praised by Mendelssohn in *Bibliothek der schönen Wissenschaften* [Mendelssohn 1762, 2:57–73]).

The pedagogic goal of this unit, like the corresponding units in German readers, is to instruct about the proper relations among individuals, between subjects and state, and between man and God. The ideological goal of this unit, however—to evince Jewish cultural affinity with Germans—generates a tone quite unlike that in the parallel German texts. In a typical saying borrowed from the Talmud toward this end, this part of the text seems to advocate "either companionship or death" (Babylon Talmud, Taanit, 23a). The difference between the *Lesebuch* and the counterpart German readers lies in the arcane aspect of many of the Jewish citations. Once again, Friedländer seems more preoccupied with convincing other adults of the sincerity of the universality of Jewish sources than with imbuing children with it.

The eighth and last unit is the only one that appropriates directly from a German reader, Sulzer's *Vorübungen zur Erweckung der Aufmerksamkeit und des Nachdenkens* (1768, 1771, and in 1780–82 a revised edition in collaboration with Meier-

otto). The reasons for Friedländer's appreciation of Sulzer's reader are clear. Sulzer and his collaborator Meierotto were intent on creating the quintessential humanistic and universalist reader. Friedländer borrowed from it two chapters especially cooptable for his own project, both of which strictly complied with John Locke's pedagogic theory stressing "example" (*Beispiel*) and "virtue" (*Tugend*).

The extraction of passages from these sections served two purposes: Friedländer could indicate his concurrence with Locke's methodology, which boosted his reader's universalist credentials, and he could easily exploit Sulzer's culling of passages from multifarious sources in Sulzer's own effort to demonstrate a common ethical thread. In addition, Mendelssohn and Sulzer were professionally close, and Sulzer had nominated Mendelssohn to an appointment to the Royal Academy in Berlin in 1771 (vetoed by Frederick the Great on account of Mendelssohn's religion), which implies that in this second unit of the *Lesebuch* to exclude Jewish material collegial concerns again seem to have outweighed the agenda of showcasing the parity of Jewish texts with their counterparts in German *Lesebücher*. Out of the copious passages in Sulzer, Friedländer had to limit himself to a select few, and naturally opted for those most congenial for his purposes. Out of sixty-one texts comprising the third chapter "Beispiele von Tugenden und Lastern," Friedländer chose only six; out of sixty-one short tales of the fourth, "Verstand und Unverstand," he chose just four. To further ecumenicize his *Lesebuch,* he preferred passages from the classical Greek tradition over German or French examples (with the exception of the tale of Ludwig XIV), and as usual preferred abstract passages to concrete ones. Thus, right to the end, Friedländer's work reads more like a manifesto of the Berlin Haskalah written in *Lesebuch* conventions than a practical *Lesebuch* for actual classroom use. But it is precisely in the text's awkward suspension between German and Jewish cultures—its ambivalent valorization of religious particularism, national integration, and universal aspirations—that Friedländer's *Lesebuch* marks a milestone in the evolution of German-Jewish identity.

As a working model, the text was a failure. Its reading public was not yet in existence, and could not be created at the time. Despite its historical significance and its revolutionary nature (or maybe due to it), the *Lesebuch* had a rather unfortunate history, in contrast to the popularity of the Hebrew readers that followed. Its anonymous publication, quite out of keeping with the practice of the Berlin Maskilim, adumbrates its swift relegation to oblivion. Historiographies of German readers stated at a rather early stage that they could not get hold of the book (Bünger 1898; Fechner 1882; Gutmann 1926). Even Heinrich Ritter, David Friedländer's biographer, related that he was unable to locate a copy of the book as early as 1861 (Ritter 1861, 46). On the other hand, the *Lesebuch* was already reprinted in Prague in 1781 by Johann Ferdinand von Schönfeld. Why a second edition was needed remains unclear.

Regardless of how it was received by contemporaries, its analysis provides us with a unique opportunity to reconstruct a cultural puzzle comprising the various parts of the Jewish maskilic world in Germany at the end of the eighteenth century. Despite its fragmentary character, this puzzle furnishes us with a unique picture of an attempt to tailor Jewish culture to the German by filtering it through the strainer of German culture. It discloses the actual agents and channels whereby the relations between the German and the Jewish cultures were made possible and materialized. It tells us about the nature of the Jewish acquaintance with the German: partial, filtered via several agents, eclectic, and to a certain degree also anachronistic.

The *Lesebuch,* like other texts for Jewish children and young people, played a leading role in the interaction between German and Jewish-Hebrew culture at the end of the eighteenth and the beginning of the nineteenth centuries. Friedländer and Mendelssohn contrived in the *Lesebuch* the various cultural options that were later engaged more systematically. Friedländer's attempt to draw from the two cultures simultaneously and his refusal to decide in favor of one of them might account for the text's failure to be a practical document impinging directly on the cultural life of German Jews. With all of its conflicting tendencies, the *Lesebuch* could never have served as the paradigm for a specific stream of Haskalah. As a collection of cultural prototypes its significance as an agent of cultural change cannot be overstated.

Bibliography

Alexander Altmann, *Moses Mendelssohn* (London: Routledge and Kegan Paul, 1973); Philippe Ariès, *Centuries of Childhood* (London: Jonathan Cape, 1962); Moses Büdinger, *Die Israelitische Schule, oder: Über die Vermengung der Kinder verschiedener Religionsparteien in Einer Schule* (Kassel: Verlag des Verfassers, 1831); Ferdinand Bünger, *Entwicklungsgeschichte des Volksschul-Lesebuches* (Leipzig: n.p., 1898); Rachel Elboim-Dror, *Education in Eretz Israel* [Hebrew], 2 vols. (Jerusalem: Yad Izhak Ben-Zvi Institute, 1986–1990), 1.1854–1914, 2:1914–20; Mordechai Eliav, *Jewish Education in Germany in the Period of Enlightenment and Emancipation,* [Hebrew] (Jerusalem: Jewish Agency / Leo Baeck Institute, 1960); Heinrich Fechner, *Die Methoden des ersten Leseunterrichts* (Berlin: n.p., 1882); Joseph Gutmann, "Geschichte der Knabenschule der jüdischen Gemeinde in Berlin (1826–1926)," *Festschrift zur Feier des Hundertjährigen Bestehens der Knabenschule der jüdischen Gemeinde in Berlin* (Berlin: Phönix Illustrationsdruck u. Verlag, 1926), 7–15; Jacob Katz, *Out of the Ghetto* (Cambridge, Mass.: Harvard University Press, 1973); Steven M. Lowenstein, *The Berlin Jewish Community* (Oxford: Oxford University Press, 1994); Mordecai Margulies, ed., *Leviticus Rabbah* (Jerusalem: Abbel, 1993), 27:1; Moses Mendelssohn, *Bibliothek der schönen Wissenschaften,* 2 vols. (Leipzig: n.p., 1762); Mendelssohn, comp., *Briefe, die neueste Literatur betreffend* (Berlin: n.p., 1759); Uriel Ofek, *Hebrew Children's Literature: The Beginning* (Tel Aviv: The Porter Institute for Poetics & Semiotics, 1979); Heinrich Ritter, *David Friedländer: Sein Leben und sein Wirken* (Berlin: n.p., 1861); Yaacov Shavit, *Athens in Jerusalem: Hellenism and Classical Antiquity in the Making of Modern Judaism* (Oxford: Littman Library of Jewish Civilization, 1996); Zohar Shavit, *David Friedländer Lesebuch für jüdische Kinder* (Frankfurt a. M.: Dipa, 1990); Z. Shavit, "The Function of Yiddish Literature in the Development of Hebrew Children's Literature in Germany" [Hebrew] *Ha-Sifrut* 35–36 (summer 1986): 148–53; Z. Shavit, "Interference Relations Between German and Jewish-Hebrew Children's Literature in the Enlightenment: The Case of Campe," *Poetics Today* 13 (1992): 41–61;

Chone Shmeruk, *The Illustrations in Yiddish Books of the Sixteenth and Seventeenth Centuries: The Texts, the Pictures and Their Audience* [Hebrew] (Jerusalem: Akademon, 1986); Ernst Simon, "Philanthropism and Jewish Education" [Hebrew] *Mordecai M. Kaplan Jubilee Book* (New York: Jewish Theological Seminary of America, 1953), 149–87; David Sorkin, *The Transformation of German Jewry, 1780–1840* (Oxford: Oxford University Press, 1987); Moritz Stern, "Aus Moses Mendelssohns und David Friedländers wiederaufgefundenem *Lesebuch* für jüdische Kinder," *Gemeindeblatt der jüdischen Gemeinde zu Berlin* 17 (1927); Stern, "Jugendunterricht in der Berliner jüdischen Gemeinde während des 18. Jahrhunderts," *Jahrbuch der Jüdisch-Literarischen Gesellschaft* 19 (1928): 39–68; Gideon Toury, "An Enlightened Use of Fable: Christian Fürchtegott Gellert in Hebrew Literature," *Turning Points in Hebrew Literature and Their Relationship to Contacts with Other Literatures,* ed. Ziva Shamir and Avner Holzman [Hebrew] (Tel Aviv: Tel Aviv University Press, 1993), 75–86; Bernhard Wechsler, *Über jüdische Schul- und Lehrer-Verhältnisse, ein Vortrag gehalten im Vereine zur Beförderung der Volksbildung in Oldenburg am 26. April 1846* (Oldenburg: Erhard Stalling, 1846); and William Zeitlin, *Bibliotheca Hebraica* (Leipzig: n.p., 1891–95).

ZOHAR SHAVIT

1781   The publication of Christian Wilhelm von Dohm's *On the Civic Improvement of the Jews* prompts widespread public debate on the Jewish Question by both Jews and gentiles

In the literature of the late eighteenth and early nineteenth centuries, efforts were made by both Jewish and non-Jewish writers to frame the "Jewish Question." These efforts manifested themselves from three points of view: assimilationism, monoculturalism, and multiculturalism. Assimilationism was an ambivalent point of view that advocated tolerance toward the Jews on the implicit condition that they give up their unique cultural identity, after which they could be absorbed into society. Monoculturalism was the philosophy of the anti-Semites who felt that Jews and gentiles were culturally incompatible, and therefore coexistence was not possible. Multiculturalism (a rare point of view that existed in the writings of Saul Ascher) stressed the differing cultures of Jews and gentiles but argued that coexistence between the cultures in their integral forms was perfectly viable.

Gotthold Ephraim Lessing, with his sympathetic portrayal of the Jew in *The Jews* (1749) and *Nathan the Wise* (1779), was one of the initiators of what has come to be known as the "tolerance debate." The tolerance debate was the effort of the Enlightenment to come to terms with the issue of framing the Jewish Question. Lessing portrayed the Jew as a purveyor of wisdom and sophistication and a person of superior moral character. Nearly all the Enlightenment writers who took part in the tolerance debate after Lessing, however, whether Jewish or non-Jewish, viewed or portrayed Jews as an infantile people in need of moral improvement as well as the guidance and protection of the dominant culture. (Saul Ascher was perhaps the sole exception.) This perspective was to have fateful results in terms of German society's efforts to come to grips with its own multiculturalism.

One of the earliest and most important of the participants in the tolerance debate was the Prussian public official Christian Wilhelm von Dohm, who wrote *On the Civic Improvement of the Jews* (1781). Underlying Dohm's many emancipatory suggestions was the implication that Jews were a backward people who needed the assistance of the dominant culture to progress morally and socially. Dohm's political tract helped bring the Jewish Question into the forefront both of public discussion and of concrete efforts for political and legal reform.

The first concrete legal step in the direction of Jewish emancipation was undertaken by the Austrian emperor Joseph II, who issued the Edict of Toleration in 1781. The provisions of this edict included abolition of the yellow badges that Jews were forced to wear outside of the ghettos and annulment of the dehumanizing body toll placed on Jews and their cattle. Other important provisions included granting Austrian Jews the right to send their children to public elementary and secondary schools. In fact, one means by which Joseph hoped to attain the total assimilation of Jews into German culture was by educating Jewish youth in German schools. School and study were seen as major avenues through which Jews would be Germanized (Low 1979, 22). Thus attendance at universities, which had never been forbidden, was now expressly allowed. Jews were allowed to frequent public places of amusement. Perhaps most dramatically of all, Jews were allowed to learn all trades and engage in wholesale business under the same conditions as Christian subjects and were permitted to establish factories (18–19).

Because of the Jews' newly acquired civic status, it became necessary to grant them family names. They were also made subject to military service. According to Alfred D. Low, Joseph II "wanted to have all Austrian subjects contribute to the welfare of the nation, without regard to nationality or religion." He approved of economic diversification of the Jews as a means of making them more useful to the state, much as Dohm had recommended. Joseph II rejected every "pressure of the conscience as harmful" and maintained that religion was a matter of personal convictions. Joseph examined alleged shortcomings of Jews— for example, their economic activity—and attributed these to harsh oppression. He believed that Jews had the capacity for moral improvement. Joseph's opening of agriculture to the Jews was done with the reasoning that they "should seize the hoe instead of the wallet" (20).

Although Joseph's tolerance edict was regarded by many as a striking change for the better for the Jews living in his kingdom, it was in fact at best a restricted religious tolerance (Barton 1981, 11). Joseph's reforms stopped short of granting full equality to Jews, and it was clear that the "tolerated" were to remain second-class citizens. Bureaucratic chicanery often made it clear that the Jews were subjected to mere forbearance and not to any modern standard of tolerance (33). The tolerance was of limited range because it had been granted by ruling powers who were convinced that they belonged to the sole true religion and administered by those who were equally convinced that they were religiously and morally superior (13). Nonetheless, Joseph's re-

forms were regarded by many in the Jewish community as a substantial improvement in their condition.

Literary history has recorded two sorts of Jewish reactions to the Edict of Toleration. The first position is exemplified by a Jewish author known to us only as Arenhof, who, in his short play, *Some Jewish Family Scenes* (1782), expressed jubilation over the new reforms. (A similar position was expressed by Naphtali Wessely in his *Worte der Wahrheit und des Friedens an die gesammte jüdische Nation,* published in Breslau in 1798.) The second position is exemplified by the Berlin bookseller, philosophy professor, and adherent of the Enlightenment Saul Ascher who, in his *Remarks on the Civic Improvement of the Jews* (1788), expressed skepticism over the ability of the reforms to grant full equality to the Jews and dismay over the decision to induct Jews into the military. We can describe these two positions as being respectively assimilationist and multiculturalist. Arenhof's position can be regarded as assimilationist, because his joy over the new reforms signals a desire to be absorbed into mainstream Austrian society. Ascher, on the other hand, is deeply concerned with maintaining Jewish cultural integrity.

The full title of Arenhof's play was *Some Jewish Family Scenes in Observation of the Freedoms Which the Jews Have Been Granted in the States of the Empire.* The play argues that the emancipatory reforms enabled the Jews to take their places as Germans without abandoning their Jewish identity. In its opening, the play portrays a Jewish father despairing over the fate of his people. He pleads with his son not to marry because he does not wish to inflict the scourge of Jewishness and the discrimination that accompanies it upon future generations: "Do you wish to give poor creatures life, who have to stoop and bend over in order to achieve an impoverished life, in which they will regret the existence of the one who gave them life with every tribulation, every tear of oppression?" (Arenhof 1782, 5–6). The father's statement is a reflection of the Jewish self-hatred that was the inevitable consequence of the Jews viewing their Jewishness, their very identity, as a burden and a curse.

The son defends his marriage plans with an argument that Joseph II has brought about a new age of tolerance and that the conditions that the father laments no longer exist: "It is no longer the barbarian time, where prejudices govern, now reigns Joseph the Great, who has seen through the prejudices with his eagle eyes, and brought about with a majestic wave of his hand . . . that only slaves of superstition or money endeavor to deceive or blind the best people through their prisma of prejudices" (6–7). Note the dual emphasis of the above statement. On the one hand, it is an assertion of Jewish self-consciousness: the speaker's espousal of the right to be free from the ill effects of bigotry, prejudice, and superstition. Together with this avowal of Jewish identity is an avowal of German identity: an assertion of loyalty and patriotism toward the Austrian state. The son trusts the state to protect his interests and rights as a Jew and as an Austrian. The father chimes in, giving homage to the Austrian state of Emperor Joseph: "Now in the golden age of Joseph's government, . . . every little worm can rejoice in his existence, as the pest of humanity, the prejudice, is banned" (7).

Arenhof's writing gives credence to Dohm's contention that Jews become more patriotic citizens when the state acts to defend their rights. For the son, the group identification with his immediate Jewish family is extended into a group/family identification with the Austrian state. The son urges his bride: "Thank our dear father, he finally assents to our union, or thank even more the father of all unfortunates, our most gracious monarch. He was touched by our unhappy history; he recognizes and treats us as human beings, breaks our shackles, grants our nation the freedom, and thereby changes us from miserable creatures to happy ones, and makes me the happiest" (7–8). The single Jewish family becomes a microcosm for the larger entity of the Austrian state— portrayed as one big, happy family.

Arenhof's criticisms of the excesses and prejudices of gentile society are enveloped in an expression of gratitude that these excesses have been relegated to the past. The play particularly celebrates the opening up of the professions to the Jews. The forced concentration of Jews in money

circulation is described as a terrible condition for the Jews because it draws such hatred upon them: "What a fortunate prospect for our descendants, because different means stand open for them to provide for themselves as honest men and good citizens and that no longer, as in the earlier time of fanaticism, all sources [of income] are sealed to us, so that usually only the sole miserable choice of money-handling remained. . . . And for that we had to endure the most bitter reproaches of usury" (13–14).

Because he is writing in German and not Hebrew or Yiddish, it seems likely that the intended audience for Arenhof's play is the Christian community. He wishes to communicate his gratitude for the new reforms to the dominant culture and at the same time signal the readiness of the minority to take its place within the dominant culture. Underscoring Arenhof's obvious jubilation is the expectation and the hope of inclusion. He signals his desire for inclusion by writing within the paradigm most popular with and accessible to the Christian readership: that of the bourgeois family drama. In asserting the unrelenting loyalty of the Jewish community toward the emperor, Arenhof gives voice to the desire of his Jewish coreligionists to be regarded as among the emperor's full-fledged subjects. He demonstrates that the Jews do not wish to be regarded as a state within a state.

The expression of such sentiments takes on a dialectical tinge: Arenhof casts a binary opposition between autonomy of identity and subjugation to the state. On the one hand, a certain Jewish pride underlies the submerged and often indirect assertions of human rights for Jews. On the other hand, the expressions of patriotic feeling toward the Austrian state show a willingness and an eagerness to procure inclusion in the broader society through submission to the authority of the emperor.

A diametrically opposed view of Joseph's reforms is expressed by Saul Ascher in his anonymously published *Remarks on the Civic Improvement of the Jews Occasioned by the Question: Should the Jew Become a Soldier?* (1788). Walter Grab rightly credits Ascher as being an important and undeservedly forgotten figure in the progressive tradition of German history (Grab 1977, 136). Ascher objects to Joseph's plans to induct Jews into the Austrian army, contending that this is premature in advance of their being granted full equal rights.

Ascher points to Joseph's war against the Turks as a motivation for making the Jews into soldiers. Although he concedes that the emperor can properly demand military service from his other subjects, he does not believe that such service can justly be demanded of Jews because Jews had not reaped the benefits that other subjects had received. Ascher maintains that there is no duty in the world that is so isolated that it does not engender another duty in return. A sovereign has responsibilities toward his subjects if they have responsibilities toward him. And because the emperor had not performed all his responsibilities toward the Jews in peacetime, he therefore could not demand such sacrifices from them during a war. In Ascher's view, to demand extra duties without corresponding rights is nothing less than slavery, despotism, and oppression.

Ascher next explores how military service could harm the Jews, with an eye toward the uniqueness of Jewish culture. To expect culture from contemporary Jews is a vain hope, he argues. They are an infantile people because they have been discriminated against for so long. No nation is more pursued, despised, and oppressed than the Jews. Because a Jew can count on little happiness in this world, he acts in respect to his eternal happiness by performing good deeds. Military service, in contrast, would spread disloyalty among the Jews toward the entire system by exerting a negative influence on their moral character. Enlightenment cannot take place without morality. The enthusiasm that the Jews have already begun to show for their sovereign has borne fruit, Ascher contends. The proposed reform, however, will not alter their civic status—only their religious status.

Ascher continues his argument by asserting that Jews do not possess the characteristics that the status of a soldier requires, and that the emperor should grant the Jews human rights in order to teach them to view the advantage of the state as being not isolated from their own. The

emperor would thus awaken in Jews an inclination toward patriotism and good citizenship, and in the process they could be educated toward becoming useful citizens.

Thus although Arenhof views Joseph's tolerance edict as an occasion for jubilance and renewed patriotism among the Jewish community, Ascher views it as a Trojan horse that instead of emancipating the Jews could very well bring about their enslavement. Writing seven years after the tolerance edict, Ascher sees the promise of emancipation as being largely unfulfilled.

One Christian writer who advocated full emancipation of the Jews was Heinrich Friedrich von Diez, the one-time Prussian ambassador to Turkey, in his essay *On Jews* (1783). Although he has largely been forgotten, Diez is well worthy of study in the present day, first because he was one of the most lucid exponents of the Christian deist viewpoint on the Jewish Question, and second because he was one of the few Christians of his time to call for full and unconditional emancipation of the Jews (see Reuss 1891, 37).

Diez condemns the pressure that had been placed upon the Jews to convert to Christianity. He sees a bitter irony in the wish to force Jews to abandon their own beliefs and take up the religious beliefs of their oppressors. He exposes the fallacy of the claim that this is only done to make them happier in the next life (Diez 1783, 4–5). He points to the absurdity of the notion that the Jews, whose religion is among the oldest, should be forced to convert to a more recent religion. It was insane, he argues, to believe that Jews would appreciate the teachings of those who made them objects of hatred and vilification.

Diez's admiration for the steadfast faith of the Jews in the face of adversity is evident in his account. As he describes it, spite, mockery, and oppression were the lot of the Jew. Placed in a position where they had to fear everything and bear everything, they came to consider misery to be a condition of life that could not be separated from it. They knew the teachings that were the ground for their oppression and secured themselves all the more firmly to their faith, as it became more difficult to adhere to it. Among would-be converters, they always remained the unconverted.

A follower of deism and natural religion, Diez briefly describes his own religious principles. He is an opponent of positive religion because he feels it can only reign at the cost of humanity. He is, however, convinced that the Jews were only able to preserve their faith in humanity in the face of oppression through faithfulness to their religious principles. In Diez's view, Jews were so humiliated and dehumanized that their religious principles were their only hold on life.

Diez maintains that it was a disgrace for barbarism and superstition to have dominated for so long and that hatred against Jews is one of the oldest of superstitions. Nonbelievers, he argues, long since pushed aside by both Jews and Christians, do not deny that both religions profess mutual love instead of oppression, because the one evolved out of the other. Even the more enlightened Christians disapprove of a hatred of which their God of Love could not approve. He also examines the contention that Jewish religion contains much that goes against the spirit of contemporary values and customs. He contends that people had prevented Jews from reconciling their religion with the intellectual currents of later centuries by isolating them from the mainstream. It is unfortunate that it was decided to integrate the Jews into civil society only after their conversion to Christianity, in his view; this inhumane policy promoted Jewish isolation by barring Jews from taking part in the continual redefinition of the dominant society.

Diez argues that the reformation of the Jews would not occur as long as public policy continued to make them martyrs and champions of their own religion. The first step toward breaking this vicious cycle was for princes and governments to make Judaism an officially sanctioned religion. This would ameliorate the blind zeal with which Jews clung to their religion. In time, Diez maintains, Jews would discover for themselves that "new truths are better than old errors" (Diez 1783, 13). In order to make human beings more similar to one another, one must only give them the opportunity to influence one another undisturbed.

The ultimate goal, according to Diez, is to supersede religion altogether. He feels, however, that although it is possible to intensify religious convictions, one can never forcibly reduce them. Diez contends that it is astounding that more than eighteen centuries were necessary to bring Christianity into proportion with other religions, with bourgeois society, and with reason. He predicts that Judaism would reform itself more quickly and bring itself more in line with the dominant pulse of society if the Jews were granted civil rights.

Diez next addresses the issue as to what is to become of Jews if they ceased to be Jews. Christians imagined that they will convert to Christianity, yet Diez maintains that it is an error to believe that an abandonment of Judaism would lead to Catholicism or Protestantism. Jews were destined to convert to natural religion or to rationalistic moral teachings, he believes. Diez promotes an assimilation concept in which both Christians and Jews give up the dogmatic underpinnings of their religions and meet on the common ground of natural religion. He felt, however, that this should occur in a natural, uncoerced manner. Neither states nor laws could make something be regarded as the truth if the subject regarded it as an error. No religious dissenter should be punished, but rather the person who cannot tolerate the dissenter. Despite his truly radical emancipatory rhetoric, one principle underlying Diez's essay is that Jews are a backward people who can be improved only if the dominant culture can have more opportunity to influence them. Diez's writing must therefore be viewed through a dialectizing optic that appreciates its emancipatory elements but at the same time acknowledges that Diez is not a prejudice-free advocate of Jewish culture.

Heinrich Friedrich von Diez's claim that Jews and Christians should seek common ground on a plane that is neither Jewish nor Christian was echoed by David Friedländer. Friedländer took over the intellectual and civic leadership of Berlin's Jewish community after Moses Mendelssohn's death. Friedländer advocated the founding of a Jewish-Christian sect on the basis of religious compromise by the Jews (Low 1979, 178). The state was in turn to reward the Jews' effort by extending civil equality to them. Friedländer was characterized by his desire for an improvement in the condition of Jews morally and politically.

There are large differences between Friedländer's conception of Judaism and that which had earlier been advanced by Mendelssohn. Mendelssohn viewed Judaism as being the most suitable religion for Jews because it was the one closest to the path of reason. Friedländer, on the other hand, viewed Judaism as having strayed from the path of reason and become steeped in mystical principles, making it no different from other religions.

Friedländer is very critical of many Jewish precepts because he felt that they were not only contrary to reason, but that they in fact kept Jews in an infantile condition. In his view, enlightened persons were humiliated because their religious precepts constrained them into a mode of thought that was contrary to reason and prohibited their fullest development. These conditions also limited the civic participation of the Jews. For Friedländer, the irrational and infantile elements within the Jewish religion itself were factors preventing the inclusion of the Jews in the broader society. Friedländer believed that the state should perform a tutelary function in bringing about the moral improvement of the Jews, who were under the influence of anachronistic religious precepts (Sorkin 1987, 74).

Friedländer asserts that the oppression and social disadvantages that Jews faced were valid reasons for them to subject their religious precepts to critical scrutiny and initiate reforms that would bring them closer to the Christian mainstream. In his view, Jews should have transformed their religion in order to make it more acceptable to the Christian majority. Contact with enlightened Christians could lead to a modernization and evolution of Judaism. Like Diez, Friedländer believed that Jews and Christians should meet on the neutral ground of rationalistic philosophy and that such a philosophy could have a modernizing influence on the Jews.

Through Jewish self-criticism and a push toward moral improvement, Friedländer hoped to increase the status of the Jewish people. He ex-pressed his ideas in the form of an anonymously published, open letter to the Protestant minister Wilhelm Teller. Teller rejected the proposals promoted by Friedländer, however, and insisted on the conversion of the Jews as a pretext for any extension of civil rights to them (Low 1979, 178). Signs of an assimilationist willingness to compromise on the part of Jews such as Friedländer only made clerics such as Teller feel all the more justified in their anti-Semitism. Both Friedländer and the gentile Diez argued in favor of religious developments that would erase the unique cultural identity of the Jews. In so doing, they inadvertently laid the foundation for an anti-Semitism contrary to their own emancipatory intentions.

At the outset of the eighteenth and the beginning of the nineteenth centuries, there was a rejection of Enlightenment philosophy that manifested itself in increasing anti-Semitism and monoculturalism. These tendencies are believed to have been fueled by the Wars of Liberation, which led to both a wholesale rejection of the Enlightenment (seen as a French import) and growing antagonism against the Jews (likewise seen as non-German). A manifesto of monoculturalism written during this time is Johann Gottlieb Fichte's *Contribution to a Justification of the Judgments of the Public over the French Revolution* (1793). Many analyses of Fichte have concentrated on the overt anti-Semitism of his pronouncements that the Jews constituted "a state within a state" and that Jewish identity was something both negative and immutable. His most notorious statement was that Jewish nature could not be changed without cutting the heads off the Jews and putting new ones in their place. There is a tendency on the part of some scholars to view this brief anti-Semitic diatribe as an anomaly in Fichte's thinking instead of placing it within the broader context of Fichte's monoculturalism.

Fichte believed that society was unified by a social contract (*Bürgervertrag*) and that belonging to the Christian religion was one of the requirements for that social contract. The purpose of religion was to provide society with social stability: diversity and change were part of the physical world, but sameness and unalterability were part

of the superior spiritual world. The churchly contract was to provide for a unity of religious belief
and bring false beliefs into line with true teachings. For Fichte, not to be a part of the officially
sanctioned church was to abandon the social contract. If one individual can withdraw from the
state, many can do so, and these individuals
would then stand in opposition against each
other. Unity of religion, he believed, was necessary for differing people to live in harmony with
one another.

Saul Ascher wrote a pamphlet attacking
Fichte entitled *Eisenmenger the Second* (1794). The
name *Eisenmenger* is a reference to Johann Andreas
Eisenmenger, the notorious anti-Semite of the
early eighteenth century. In this pamphlet,
Ascher complains that attempts were being made
to adapt Christianity to the spirit of the age at the
cost of other religions, particularly Judaism.
Ascher saw Fichte as a dangerous *moral* opponent
(as opposed to political or religious opponent) of
Judaism. For Ascher, political and religious opponents of Judaism could be dealt with, but
moral opponents were beyond endurance because
of their intolerance.

Ascher blamed Fichte for developing a system
of intolerance out of Kantian teachings. According to Ascher, if Jews constituted a state within a
state, that was the fault of the state itself: it happened under its authority. Ascher's last statement
is prophetic: "If he is to have such adherents as
this, then God preserve my nation and all of humanity" (Ascher 1794, 90).

Followers of Fichte included such people as
Carl Wilhelm Friedrich Grattenauer, who was,
ironically, a Prussian public official like Dohm.
Grattenauer again unearthed Eisenmenger's and
Fichte's false accusations against the Jews and
actually plagiarized them in many of his hate
pamphlets. Another of Fichte's followers was
Friedrich Buchholz, a purported deist who can be
characterized by his accusation that Moses Mendelssohn felt that the crucifixion of Christ was
justified. By imputing deicidal attitudes to Mendelssohn, the leader of enlightened Jewry, this
statement attempted to keep alive the charge that
Jews held an eternal collective guilt for the death
of Christ (Buchholz 1803, 264).

Even relatively secularized Christians often
maintained their hatred of the Jews at this time
because of the Jews' involvement in money circulation. This hatred is exemplified in the anonymous anti-Semitic drama of 1804, *Der wuchernde
Jude am Pranger (The usurious Jew in the pillory)*. The
anti-Semitic dramatists made use of a vicious
humor to differentiate themselves from the Jewish
out-group and strengthen their own group identity. This humor became a means for expressing
monoculturalist sentiments. Humor in all of its
forms is a vehicle for group formation. As Sigmund Freud pointed out, one cannot enjoy a joke
by oneself; a joke produces a need for someone
else's laughter. Humor creates its own group dynamic: "Every joke calls for a public of its own and
laughing at the same jokes is evidence of far-
reaching psychical conformity" (Freud 1963, 151).
The subscribers to a certain sort of humor constitute an in-group of sorts and therefore it should
come as no surprise that some groups will attempt
to foment humor by deriding the members of out-
groups. Such humor is a manifestation of the ag-
gressivity of the out-group toward all those who
deviate from its norms (Jurzik 1985, 38).

Humor of this nature had been attacked by the
dramatists and literary theorists of the Enlightenment. The comic theory of such authors as Lessing and Diderot was anathema to the notion that
comedy manifested itself in the production of
laughter at the expense of "lower" people (Berghahn 1991, 4). They were more interested in
teaching people how to laugh at themselves in
order to promote recognition of the comical in-
congruities of society. Lessing believed that comedy should ridicule social habits or moral failings
which are subject to being remedied: "Comedy
wants to improve through laughter but not
through derision" (Berghahn 1991, 12). However, the decimation of the philosophy of the Enlightenment through the rise of nationalism also
led in large measure to a jettisoning of the literary
conventions of the Enlightenment and the return
to derisory humor as a common element in the
theater.

The early nineteenth century was a time when
Germans and Christians reinforced their group
identifications. Derisory humor regained popu-

larity because of the largely subliminal nature of laughter, which made it an ideal means of appealing to the suggestibility of the individual. A coldness toward the victim is promoted by humor of this sort (Jurzik 1985, 38). Therefore, the laughter promoted by this sort of humor is an effective expression of the opposition between the larger collective and the nonconforming individuals whom the collective wishes to humiliate (44).

According to Detlev Claussen (1987, 39), a key concept of modern anti-Semitism is viewing the Jew as a synecdoche for money circulation. The Jews became a scapegoat for the economic woes of the entire populace. The author of *Der wuchernde Jude am Pranger* tried to elicit laughter from his audience by deriding the Jews for what was perceived to be their economic role. The peasant or burgher who was in fear for his economic well-being may find the opportunity to laugh at a designated culprit a welcome diversion from his troubles. At the same time, this laughter helped mobilize him against the maligned out-group by appealing to his suggestibility. The implication was clear: Jews should somehow bear responsibility for the economic troubles of this era. The Jews were portrayed as the willing and cheerful beneficiaries of contemporary economic conditions. By portraying Jews as wanton and usurious villains, the author endeavored to build a Christian in-group identification based on a common persecutor: the majority group is appealed to as being oppressed by a "powerful" minority.

In order to help members of his own Christian in-group appraise themselves favorably, the author draws a dichotomy between the bad Jewish banker Ruben Herz and the good Christian lawyer Müller. Ruben is, true to stereotype, unscrupulous and obsessed with money: "Whoever possesses money, the world smiles upon him" (8). He is devoid of sympathy for his fellow human beings and is a harsh taskmaster toward his debtors. Appeals to fear contributed powerfully to the effectiveness of any propaganda, and by convincing economically troubled Christians that Jewish creditors would subject them to unconscionable debt harassment, the author shrewdly plays on their fears.

The author attempts to deepen an "us-identification" with the majority group and deepen prejudices against the minority by portraying Ruben in his mistreatment of an impoverished widow. The portrayal of this situation is calculated to deepen paranoia against the social pariah by attributing heinous attitudes to him. Humor of this sort can best succeed by disparaging an object of repulsion while enhancing an object of affection (Wilson 1979, 136). In order to disparage his object of repulsion, the author introduces his object of affection as a contrast figure: the heroic lawyer Müller. Müller proclaims his own goodness by declaring what an evil man Ruben is and how he intends to put a stop to Ruben's wrongdoing. The author encourages his audience to think that they are justified in harboring prejudices against the Jews by portraying Jews as posing a danger to the welfare of Christian citizens. The only way the author can make this work amusing to a Christian audience is by having the Christian hero triumph over the Jew. Laughter thereby becomes a gesture of blind superiority. By having Müller trick Ruben into admitting his wrongs in front of witnesses, the narcissistic tendencies of the audience to favor their own gentile in-group were addressed.

The laughter of the anti-Semitic audience is elicited as Ruben stands in the pillory declaring: "I would like to die, because I have to see, / My money in strange hands / I would be glad to suffer scolding and mockery / If I could prevent this" (46). The fact that Ruben is more worried about the loss of money than the loss of his dignity made the audience feel justified in laughing about the loss of dignity and, at the same time, reinforced stereotypes that Jews were fixated on money.

Der wuchernde Jude am Pranger is formally in the tradition of German farce. Comedy, according to Lessing, is the genre in which human folly is laughed at and the possibility for self-improvement is diagnosed. However, by portraying a member of a socially disadvantaged group as the mainstay of folly and the object of laughter, the author of *Der wuchernde Jude* reinforced stereotypes and promoted a demeaning image of the Jews. In this way, he attempted to appeal to people's more negative instincts. In contrast to Lessing's comedy *Die Juden,* where prejudice is portrayed as the object of laughter and exposed as folly, *Der wuchernde Jude* promoted prejudice by portraying Jews as hard-hearted, powerful, and greedy. It falsely encouraged the image that most Jews had Christian debtors, and it projected upon the Jewish community a power that they could not possibly have had.

In *Der wuchernde Jude am Pranger,* the anti-Semitic author laughs at the Jews and thereby sides with the reactionary forces that reversed the progress of the Enlightenment in regard to Jewish emancipation. People who agreed with this reactionary author experienced a rekindling of those monoculturalist sentiments against which the Enlightenment philosophers had fought. They were encouraged to join a community of laughter that believed that a good society was only possible within an ideology of ethnic homogeneity.

Bibliography

Arenhof, *Einige jüdische Familienszenen* (Vienna: Rudolph Grässer, 1782); Saul Ascher, *Bemerkungen über die bürgerliche Verbesserung der Juden veranlaßt, bei der Frage: Soll der Jude Soldat werden* (Frankfurt an der Oder: n.p., 1788); Ascher, *Eisenmenger der zweite: Nebst einem vorangesetzten Sendschreiben an Herrn Professor Fichte in Jena* (Berlin: n.p., 1794); Peter F. Barton, "Der lange Weg zur Toleranz," *Im Lichte der Toleranz,* ed. Peter F. Barton (Vienna: Institut für protestantische Kirchengeschichte, 1981), 11–33; Klaus Berghahn, "Comedy Without Laughter: Jewish Characters in Comedies from Shylock to Nathan," *Laughter Unlimited: Essays on Humor, Satire, and the Comic,* ed. Reinhold Grimm and Jost Hermand (Madison: University of Wisconsin Press, 1991), 3–27; Friedrich Buchholz, *Moses und Jesus oder über das intellektuelle und moralische Verhältniß der Juden und Christen* (Berlin: Johann Friedrich Unger, 1803); Detlev Claussen, *Grenzen der Aufklärung* (Frankfurt a. M.: Fischer, 1987); Heinrich Friedrich von Diez, *Über Juden* (Dessau: Buchhandlung der Gelehrten, 1783); Christian Konrad Wilhelm von Dohm, *Über die bürgerliche Verbesserung der Juden* (1781–83; Hildesheim and New York: Olms, 1973); Johann Gottlieb Fichte, *Beitrag zur Berichtigung der Urteile des Publikums über die französische Revolution,* 1793 ed. Richard Schottky (Hamburg: Meiner, 1973); Sigmund Freud, *Jokes and Their Relation to the Unconscious,* trans. James Strachey (New York: Norton, 1963), 143; Freud, *Der Witz und seine Beziehung zum Unbewußten* (1905; Frankfurt a. M.: Fischer, 1973); David Friedländer, *Sendschreiben an Seine Hochwürden Herrn Oberconsistorialrath und Probst Teller zu Berlin von einigen Hausvätern jüdischer Religion,* (1799; Jerusalem: Zalman Shazar Center, 1975); Walter Grab, "Saul Ascher: Ein jüdische-deutscher Spätaufklärer zwischen Revolution und Restauration," *Jahrbuch des Instituts für Deutsche Geschichte,* vol. 6 (Tel Aviv: Institut für Deutsche Geschichte, 1977), 131–79; Carl Wilhelm Friedrich Grattenauer, *Erklärung an das Publikum über meine Schrift: "Wider die Juden"* (Berlin: Johann Wilhelm Schmidt, 1803); Grattenauer, *Wider die Juden: Ein Wort der Warnung an alle unsere christliche Mitburger* (Berlin: Johann Wilhelm Schmidt, 1803); Renate Jurzik, *Der Stoff des Lachens: Studien über Komik* (Frankfurt a. M.: Campus, 1985); Jacob Katz, *From Prejudice to Destruction: Anti-Semitism, 1700–1933* (Cambridge, Mass.: Harvard University Press, 1980); Robert Liberles, "Dohm's Treatise on the Jews: A Defense of the Enlightenment," *Leo Baeck Institute Year Book* 33 (1988): 29–42; Ellen Littmann, "Saul Ascher: First Theorist of Progressive Judaism," *Leo Baeck Institute Year Book* 5 (1960); Alfred D. Low, *Jews in the Eyes of the Germans: From the Enlightenment to Imperial Germany* (Philadelphia: Institute for the Study of Human Issues, 1979); Franz Reuss, *Christian Wilhelm Dohms Schrift: "Über die bürgerliche Verbesserung der Juden" und deren Einwirkung auf die gebildeten Stände Deutschlands* (Kaiserslautern: Blenk, 1891); Paul Lawrence Rose, *Revolutionary Antisemitism in Germany: From Kant to Wagner* (Princeton, N.J.: Princeton University Press, 1990); David Sorkin, *The Transformation of German Jewry, 1780–1840* (Oxford: Oxford University Press, 1987); Christopher P. Wilson, *Jokes: Form, Content, Use and Function* (London: Academic Press, 1979); and *Der wuchernde Jude am Pranger: Ein Drama in Versen* (Berlin: G. Hayn, 1804).

PETER R. ERSPAMER

March 23, 1782 ("Shabbat ha-Gadol," 5542)   Chief Rabbi Ezekiel Landau responds to the Austrian emperor's Edict of Toleration (*Toleranzpatent*)

On January 2, 1782, the emperor Joseph II issued the Edict of Toleration, one of the milestones in the process of Jewish emancipation. Although it was issued in the medieval tradition of legislation applying exclusively to Jews, its content was quite different from most medieval Jewry law and went beyond even the most liberal privileges in local and national charters. The underlying goal, stated in the preamble, was that all tolerated subjects should participate in common in the public welfare "without distinction of nationality and religion." To this end, many discriminatory regulations were repealed. There was to be no more requirement of distinctive marks on clothing; no more exclusion of Jews from residence in the city (although the Jews of Vienna were still not permitted to have a public synagogue); and no more prohibition against employing Christian servants, leaving home on Sunday mornings and holidays, or frequenting places of public amusement. The result was to "place the Jewish nation on an almost equal level with adherents of other religious associations in respect to trade and employment of civil and domestic facilities." Perhaps with the exception of Amsterdam, this was a principle that had hardly been implemented in the previous fifteen hundred years.

In addition to ending these forms of discrimination, the edict contained a positive program intended to encourage integration of the Jews into the wider society and enhance their usefulness to the State. This program included encouragement for Jews to learn crafts or trades as apprentices to Christian masters, as well as a mandate for Jewish children to attend standardized primary and secondary schools—the "normal schools"—"so that they have at least the opportunity to learn reading, writing and counting." In order to facilitate the mastery of the German language that would unify the empire and enable Jews to foster stable economic interaction with Christians, use of "the so-called Jewish language and writing of Hebrew intermixed with German" was abolished by fiat.

The Jewish response to this edict was, not unexpectedly, mixed. In circles favoring Enlightenment and urging the amelioration of Jewish civil status, it was enthusiastically welcomed. One of those deeply influenced by Moses Mendelssohn, Naphtali Wessely, quickly published a pamphlet in Hebrew called "Words of Peace and Truth" endorsing the edict's educational reforms. Wessely criticized Jews of central and eastern Europe for their ignorance of proper Hebrew. And if the foundation of the traditional Jewish curriculum was not being properly taught, "how much more are they ignorant of the purity of the tongue of the people among whom they live. Many of them do not even know how to read it or write it." Jews of Italy, England, and France speak the respective vernaculars correctly, Wessely continued; many Jews in Poland can speak Polish if necessary, and they can hardly be blamed for their substandard German for they do not live in an environment where it is spoken. But in his view, the Jews of German-speaking lands never learn German properly, a failing he attributes to the use of teachers from Poland in the Jewish school system. The result is an educational and cultural scandal.

In his treatise, Wessely repeatedly emphasizes the need for Jews to learn correct German. The practical benefits of helping Jews earn a livelihood are only the beginning. For Wessely, German is the key to general enlightenment; it enables Jews to discuss the Bible intelligently and engage in other meaningful conversation with non-Jewish intellectuals and it opens to Jews the literature of the surrounding culture. Mastery of the language can only redound to the prestige and honor of the Jewish people. He therefore welcomed the emperor's legislation with its educational reforms, arguing for the establishment of a primary school system in which Jewish children would learn the German language as well as Hebrew, and recommending Mendelssohn's translation of the Pentateuch as a means of teaching German to older Jews.

By contrast, traditional forces in Jewish society were highly suspicious of the edict. Although reluctant to speak out openly against the emperor, they vehemently attacked Wessely for his support of the edict's educational goals. In Vilna, Wessely's pamphlet was reportedly burned in the streets; in an anti-Wessely tirade delivered from the pulpit, a rabbi from western Poland endorsed this act, saying "Even though the Emperor's name and praises are mentioned numerous times in [Wessely's pamphlet], in my opinion justice was realized in Vilna." Wessely became kind of a lightning rod, attracting the discharged hostility and ambivalence of the traditional leadership about dramatic new developments they could not fully understand.

In this context of deep division, eyes were turned to the chief rabbi of the largest Jewish community of the empire, Rabbi Ezekiel Landau of Prague. He may have spoken about the edict not long after its promulgation in a sermon no longer extant, to which he later referred. But as the controversy ensued, the next major preaching occasion was on "the Great Sabbath" preceding the holiday of Pesach in 1782, a day when all rabbis were expected to deliver a major sermon. In addition to the exegetical and homiletic material traditionally expected in a sermon before Pesach, Landau could hardly avoid addressing the *Toleranzpatent* on this day.

He was not in an easy position. No matter what he may have thought, open criticism of the emperor or his edict from the pulpit was not a realistic option. Only sixteen months before, in his eulogy at the death of the empress Maria Theresa, Landau had praised Joseph in blatantly messianic terms: "God has bestowed upon him the spirit of wisdom and insight, the spirit of counsel and valor (Isa. 11:2). He shall judge the poor with equity and decide with justice for the lowly of the land (11:4). He will be a source of refuge for every one of his realms, the great eagle under whose wings all will find shelter and live securely." It would have been unthinkable, almost scandalous, for him to reverse himself and attack what was widely viewed as a progressive and enlightened policy toward the Jews. At the same time, Landau recognized the challenges to traditional Jewish society in the changes that Joseph was promoting. He certainly felt more in common with the rabbinical defenders of tradition than with the maverick reformer Wessely. His was a precarious tightrope to walk.

Near the beginning of his sermon, Landau makes it abundantly clear that his position on Joseph II did not change as a result of the edict. Joseph is placed in the category of heroic, beneficent sovereigns encountered by Jews in their history, the tradition not of Pharaoh but of Cyrus and Darius. "Our lord his Majesty the emperor has decided to help us and to raise us from our degradation." He has "removed from us the stigma of bondage, removed all externally recognizable signs of servitude. . . . May God reward him for his good deed and raise his ever higher!" At the same time, Landau begins to put the brakes on the process of integration. Despite the liberal sentiments embodied in the edict, Jews should remember that they are guests in a land not their own. Even if given legal parity, they should retain a sense of psychological submissiveness; they should never be arrogant, never think themselves fully at home, or fully free.

The preacher then targets Wessely, whose name or book he does not mention, but whose identity few would have missed: "An evil man has arisen from our own people and brazenly asserted that the Torah is not all important, that an animal carcass is worth more than talmudic scholars, that etiquette is more vital than the Torah. . . . He is worse than an animal carcass, and in the end his corpse will lie like dung upon the field!" At issue was Wessely's citation of a rabbinic hyperbole, "As for a scholar who lacks sense (*de'ah*), a carcass is better than he" (Leviticus Rabbah 1:15), to support his claim that rabbinic scholarship bereft of the social graces is of no benefit to anyone. Landau presents this as a paradigm indicating that Wessely believed traditional Jewish culture to be less important than the values and mores of the gentile world, and thereby denounces him as a traitor whom no Jew should take seriously.

But what about the substantive matter of educational reform? At the end of the sermon, Landau endorses the principle of "normal schools" in which Jews would learn a general curriculum from teachers not trained in Talmud. Such teachers must not, however, transmit any criticism of the Jewish tradition: "This would be against the desire of the exalted government, which established the position solely for the purpose of teaching children language, writing, mathematics, ethical behavior, and etiquette, not to speak calumnies against our religion. If in any town or city such a teacher should be found transgressing in this matter and acting with duplicity, pay him no heed whatsoever." Assuming good will on the part of the teachers, Landau believed, the institutional change could be accommodated.

In this sermon, rather than responding to the prohibition of a Judeo-German vernacular, Landau takes a positive position toward the mandate that Jews must learn the German language. He notes that the problem of linguistic corruption among Jews went back to the Bible itself, as seen in the Book of Nehemiah (13:24). Maimonides codified the rule that the profession of God's unity may be said in any language, provided that

that language be spoken correctly. "Do not think that you know how to speak the German language," Landau says to his listeners, probably in a German considerably less elegant than *Hochdeutsch*. "No one can be said to know a language unless he can speak grammatically." Therefore, "His Majesty the emperor has done us a great favor in commanding us to learn the language grammatically so that we can speak it properly." As a linguistic phenomenon with political implications, Germanization was a process he decided should not be resisted.

But literacy in a language such as German had cultural implications as well, and this is where Landau tried to draw the line. After attacking both Jews and Christians who subject the mysteries of faith to the searing scrutiny of reason, Landau issued a warning. "Fear the Lord and the king (Prov. 24:21): do the will of his Majesty our king, while remaining very careful to fear the Lord. For as you become accustomed to the [German] language, you will also want to read books that are not aids in learning the language but philosophical inquiries pertaining to matters of Torah and faith, which may lead you to harbor doubts about the faith, God forbid!"

Here is the crux of Landau's attempt to define a middle course. The German language was the key to improving the political and economic position of Jews in the empire. Yet it also opened up to Jews an entire library of philosophical work, rationalistic in approach and deistic in content, far removed from Landau's admonition that "the foundation of all is faith!" Jews who learned German would be able to read the writings of those "who cogitate and ponder with their confused intellects, darkening the religion of the Torah, whether they be Jews or from any other people, those who deny individual providence over the affairs of men, who deny the revelation of the Torah and supernatural miracles, who say that religion was not given by the Creator." Whether or not Landau had specific writers in mind (Lessing, or perhaps even Mendelssohn?) is uncertain, but the vehemence of his rhetoric indicates his belief that the danger was great.

In a later undated sermon for the Sabbath of Repentance, Landau pushed beyond the rhetoric of this sermon. There is a conventional complaint about neglect of traditional Jewish study (*bittul Torah*), a theme one can find in almost every generation. But there is also a recognition of inroads being made by a specific historical process against which the chief rabbi had warned: "They do not raise their children to [a life of] Torah. On the contrary, they remove their children from the [traditional Jewish] schools and make them familiar with other books, planting doubts in their hearts about all the signs and wonders of the Torah. At first they give the excuse that they must make their children familiar with the prevailing literature and language, but eventually they abuse the Torah, believing neither in God nor in His servant Moses. The Psalmist spoke of this in the verse, *They set their mouths against heaven; their tongues range over the earth* (Ps. 73:9), meaning, we need to make them familiar with the books and the tongues of the Gentile nations, but why have their set their mouths against heaven?"

Where Wessely had argued that the study of history, geography, and the natural sciences would lead to a fuller understanding of Torah and a strengthening of faith, Landau sees the new linguistic tool as a dire threat. Partly because of the nature of his position, partly because of a temperamental and ideological commitment to the authority of the emperor, Landau was in a bind, and he seems to be aware of forces beyond his control. We see at this moment the beginning of a policy and process that would rapidly transform the Jewish communities in German-speaking lands. A generation later, significant numbers of Jews could be described as knowing German well but little Hebrew; these supplicants therefore demanded to pray in the vernacular, which they understood. Two generations later, a leading rabbinic representative of German-Jewish traditionalism, Samson Raphael Hirsch, could wax eloquent in praise of Schiller and outline an educational curriculum that went beyond Wessely in its openness to German culture.

Landau's somewhat tortured effort to draw a line of demarcation between a language and a culture, encouraging the first but vigorously warning against the second, may have seemed a solution in its homiletic context. As a cultural policy, it was doomed to failure.

Bibliography

Alexander Altmann, *Moses Mendelssohn* (University: Alabama University Press, 1973); Mordechai Eliav, *Jewish Education in Germany in the Period of Enlightenment and Emancipation* [Hebrew] (Jerusalem: Jewish Agency Publications, 1960); Joseph Karniel, *Die Toleranzpolitik Kaiser Josephs II* (Gerlingen: Bleicher, 1986); Jacob Katz, *Out of the Ghetto* (Cambridge, Mass.: Harvard University Press, 1973); Ruth Kestenberg-Gladstein, *Neuere Geschichte der Juden in den böhmischen Länder* (Tübingen: Mohr, 1969); Ezekiel Landau, *Derushei ha-Tselah* (Sermons) (Warsaw: n.p., 1899); Paul Mendes-Flohr and Jehuda Reinharz, eds., *The Jew in the Modern World* (Oxford: Oxford University Press, 1980); Marc Saperstein, ed., *Jewish Preaching 1200–1800: An Anthology* (New Haven: Yale University Press, 1989), 359–73; and Naphtali Wessely, *Selected Writings* [Hebrew] (Jerusalem: Ever, 1952).

MARC SAPERSTEIN

1783 Moses Mendelssohn writes *Jerusalem, oder Über religiöse Macht und Judentum,* which addresses the relationship between state, church, and the individual and refines the notion of religious toleration

The concept of toleration first appeared in Europe as a demand for religious freedom leveled at church authorities and secular rulers. Although the definitions used in older encyclopedias to denote the concept of toleration tend to be rather general and trivial in character, such as "permission or conscious acceptance of things and actions of any kind," more recent reference works mostly focus on the problem of religious freedom and thereby define tolerance/toleration as "acceptance of divergent convictions." Modern history textbooks contain similar statements, which usually refer to the concept of toleration as the result and product of the Reformation era and the concomitant religious struggles. In this context, reference is made to the work of spiritualists active at the fringe of the Reformation movement, such as Sebastian Frank (1499–1542) and Sebastian Castellio (1515–63), or to leaders of the Baptist movement like Hans Denck, Dirck van Cornheert, or David Joris, who declared that religious coercion and violent suppression were irreconcilable with the Christian commandment of charity. To give an example: in 1534, the Moravian Baptist Kilian Aurbacher stated in a letter to the Reformer Martin Butzer, "I also know that it cannot ever be just to coerce anyone in religious matters; every man should be free in his beliefs, be he Jew or Turk."

The development of the concept of toleration was closely linked to the demand for acceptance of the Jews. In the era of religious wars, men like Paul Felgenhauer (1593–1677) preached religious toleration and at the same time advocated the cause of the Jews. Felgenhauer, a millenarian who out of enthusiastic love for all things Jewish named his son Israel and his daughter Hierosolyma, was a staunch opponent of church dogmas, which he fought in rough language; he called the church "Babylon" and the pope "father of all false prophets." His christology—his Christ was purely a celestial being invested with only divine, not human, nature ("the celestial flesh of Christ")—showed him a way to acceptance and toleration of Jews. "It would only be just," he remarked, "that we human beings should tolerate each other since God tolerates us all, irrespective of all our differences of belief and religion."

The really decisive impetus for the development of the concept of toleration, however, did not come from Christian mystics, spiritualists, or millenarians of any kind; neither did it result from the influence of Christian or neo-Stoic humanists (Erasmus, Reuchlin, Lipsius, Heinsius, and so forth). Rather, and above all, it was the gradually emerging theory of natural rights that enabled representatives of all religions and philosophies to meet and converse. Scholars like Jean Bodin, Johannes Althusius, and Hugo Grotius, each of whom advanced the "coming of the age of reason," contributed to this development. Bodin advocated the acceptance of the differences between religious creeds. Under the concept of "Politik" (politics), Johannes Althusius developed a systematic sociology that attributed all social life to man's original acceptance of "symbiosis," coexisting with others. Finally, Hugo Grotius—the "father of the law of nations"—presented a legal system based on the principles of equality between nations and reciprocity, which to this day is reflected in international political theory.

In the late seventeenth century a mass exodus of about 500,000 Huguenots from France was triggered by King Louis XIV's revocation of the Toleration Act of Nantes. This revocation also had an unexpected side effect, however: it strengthened the idea of toleration instead of weakening it. John Locke (1632–1704), for example, presented a program of toleration ("Letters Concerning Toleration," 1689) in which he advocated the freedom of all religious creeds and demanded toleration as a duty to be observed by church and state. In turn, Pierre Bayle (1647–1706), who was forced to flee from France and was a declared opponent of all forms of dogmatism, preached religious toleration on the part of the state—even vis-à-vis atheists, thus going beyond Locke. In Germany, Christian Thomasius (1655–1728) directed his criticism at the regional sovereigns' right to intervene in church matters and supported a strict separation of the matters of state and church; in this, he abandoned the basis of the doctrine prevalent in his time and effectively became a precursor of German Enlightenment.

In modern states, the concept of toleration became reality through a gradual process in the seventeenth and eighteenth centuries. The first change came about in the Netherlands, where Catholics and Lutherans, as well as Baptists, sectarians, spiritualists, and *conversos* (Jews expelled from Spain), found a new homeland. Next was England, where after fierce religious struggles the Act of Toleration—which granted full religious freedom to all dissenters outside the State church as long as they swore allegiance to the English king and rejected papal power—was passed in 1689 as the climax of the Glorious Revolution. Finally, there was the Bill of Rights of the United States, which provided a model for France and its

"droits naturelles et inscriptibles" advocated by the 1789 revolution.

Although Brandenburg-Prussia, which was celebrated as a model state of religious freedom, did have some tolerant princes, such as the Great Elector (the later King Frederick I, who opened his realm to Arians, Socinians, Mennonites, Huguenots, and Jews), it was not so much the spirit of religious toleration that made Brandenburg-Prussia a shelter for religious refugees; rather, it was a mentality of pragmatic statesmanship, of tangible interests that determined this immigration policy. In this process, ideas relating to *Peuplierung* (population policy), as well as financial motivations, played a key role. The Elector hoped that the newcomers would not only prove loyal subjects but also provide the necessary financial input to bring a commercial and economic boom to his country.

As a rule, we tend to overlook the fact that the Jews, contrary to other groups brought to Brandenburg, were not accorded full rights. The second section of the so-called Edict concerning 50 families of protected Jews, dated March 21, 1671, in which the Elector granted the Jews a qualified right to settle in his realm, contained the restriction "however, they may not have synagogues." Thus it was clear that the toleration of Jews was limited in those areas that might affect Christian beliefs and convictions. The Elector's successors, the Soldier King and the philosopher of Sanssouci, also did not pursue the idea of toleration and Christian charity in their attitudes toward the Jews, but rather were motivated by the stringencies of the tax and economic policies of their newly emerging mercantilist industrial state.

For decades, patriotic and edifying treatises and school textbooks have idealized the Prussian king Frederick II as an enlightened sovereign who followed the principle of toleration in questions of religious policy. A more recent, critical attitude toward the king and his era, however, demands a certain revision of this image. This new attitude asserts that it will not do any more to take his famous dicta at face value; rather, they should be correlated with the policy actually pursued by this *roi-philosophe*. For example, his side note on an appeal file, "All religions must be tolerated, and the Treasury should only make sure that none of them will impair the other; for here every man will have to find salvation in his own way," or his well-known reply to an inquiry of the directorate general, "All religions are of equal value if only the people professing them are honest" were statements and utterances corresponding to the spirit of Enlightenment but at the same time firmly grounded in the realities of the Prussian state and its inhabitants.

For Frederick II, toleration was not strictly a matter of convictions but also of practicability and raison d'état. In the end, for Frederick II all religions were "un système fabuleux plus ou moins absurde," which probably was the reason that he did not enact an Act of Toleration—contrary to the Catholic emperor Joseph II, who passed such a document for the Austrian crown lands on October 13, 1781. However, Joseph II was not any more "enlightened" than his Prussian adversary. He, too, wanted to curtail the role of Jews in the state. His Act of Toleration, which it was only in name, actually constituted a sophisticated system of regulations that in its twenty-three sections subjected the Jewish population to more duties than rights, thereby narrowing the Jews' freedom of choice in many ways. Critics of Joseph's legislative legacy thus have called this document an act of toleration dictated by obviously utilitarian considerations, which, under the pretense of reform and with recourse to the powers of a police state, actually aimed not only at eliminating the autonomy of Jewish communities but also attempted to suppress the language and national culture of Jews, in keeping with the motto "first depersonalize them as a nation, then grant them equal rights as citizens."

All this can hardly be called toleration in the modern sense. In those days, even many "enlightened" men were only conditionally willing to accept another person on his or her own terms or concept of self-definition. A typical example of this ambivalent attitude may be seen in the discussion regarding the civil rights of Jews, which was characterized by a complicated diversion created by the Jews' opponents to prevent their enfranchisement. The idea was to assert that Jews

should be principally granted individual civil rights as demanded—yet they should also stop being Jews. Put differently, this means that there was a certain willingness to emancipate Jews as human beings but not as Jews. A frequently quoted statement in this context is the dictum Count Clermont-Tonnerre made during the emancipation discussion in the French National Assembly in December 1789, "Everything for the Jews as individuals but nothing for the Jews as a nation," which later became the credo of all opponents of Jewish emancipation in Europe.

Nevertheless, the concept of toleration began to gain momentum under the influence of the picture of the "good Jew" drawn in the eighteenth century by numerous writers, including Johann Gottfried Schnabel, Christian Gellert, and in particular Mendelssohn's friend Gotthold Ephraim Lessing. Many treatises, magazine articles, novels, and plays preached toleration and tried to depict charitable and noble Jews. The good Jew was not only a literary character but, even more, became a kind of symbol of the author's enlightened attitudes and was understood as a parable for the struggle of a bourgeoisie dedicated to the principle of reason against all expressions of prejudice and intolerance.

The significance of Lessing's *Nathan der Weise* (Nathan the wise) for German Jewry should not be underestimated. This play encouraged Jews to define themselves and became a kind of reference point that not only provided a basis for the concept of toleration but also permitted the definition of a formula for the coexistence of Jews and Christians. The parable of the three rings given by the father to the sons argued that God the Father had given the genuine ring to each of his sons—that is, to the Jew, the Christian, and the Muslim, so that He was revealed in each of the three monotheistic religions. According to this parable, each religion in this image should be respected in equal measure. This message was handed down from one generation to the next. The veneration accorded to the author of *Nathan* brought about a veritable Lessing cult in the German-Jewish bourgeoisie, which led to some strange phenomena.

Unfortunately, however, Lessing's contemporaries did not—or did not want to—notice that Lessing's concept was shaky in itself because it relativized truth. "Oh, so all three of you are deceivers deceived!" the judge exclaims in the play. "None of your rings," he continues, "is the genuine one. The genuine ring was probably lost. To replace the loss, the father had these three rings made." So far, so good. However, the Jews of and after Lessing's time were not concerned with the ambiguity of the parable of the rings that has given generations of literary historians food for thought and inspired some of them to venture daring interpretations. What was much more important for them was the message—perhaps a little obvious today but closely linked with Lessing's name then—that modern man was faced with the question of "whether he should hold on to the space of intellectual freedom that had been won by the generation of 1800 who had blazed the trail from dogmatic controversy to a conversation about religious matters, thus establishing a new attitude towards religious and ideological opponents" (Schoeps 1979).

The enlightened public of the late eighteenth century was convinced that neither state nor church were entitled to tie the individual to any religious, ideological, or moral convictions. It is one of the great achievements of Moses Mendelssohn to have dealt with this issue in his book *Jerusalem, oder Über religiöse Macht und Judentum.* When first published in 1783, the book met with lively interest and soon was talked about everywhere. The fact that a disenfranchised Jew claimed the right to plead for his oppressed brethren in God was an unusual thing in itself. What caused general astonishment and admiration, however, was that this Jew dared to deal with the relationship between state and church openly and uninhibitedly and to speak in favor of freedom of conscience, justice, and toleration. This was unheard of.

Although Mendelssohn did accord the state the right to intervene in certain cases, this was to happen only if the ethical and social basis of the state was in jeopardy—if the authority of the state was endangered by atheism, epicureanism, or fanaticism. He was fundamentally convinced that the state must take a neutral position on religious issues. Neither should the church make use of the state's powers, Mendelssohn declared. According to him, attitudes, opinions, and convictions must never be restricted by state or church: "Principles are free; by their very nature, attitudes do not suffer constraint or corruption. . . . Thus, neither church nor state are entitled to subject the principles or attitudes of men to any form of coercion."

Mendelssohn's book was a plea for religious toleration and mutual tolerance. Inspired by the hope that the impediments opposing the political emancipation and social integration of Jews could be eliminated, Mendelssohn at the end of his discourse directly addresses the Christian nations and princes with the words, "Princes of the earth! . . . For the sake of your as well as universal happiness, *religious egalitarianism is not toleration* but rather the opposite of true tolerance! . . . Do not reward or punish any doctrine, do not tempt or bribe any one to embrace a religious creed! Whoever does not infringe public happiness, whoever honestly observes the civil laws, let him speak as he pleases, let him call to his God in his own way or the way of his fathers, and let him find his salvation where he hopes to find it."

In his plea for religious toleration and mutual tolerance, Mendelssohn never lost sight of the oppression of his fellow-believers and their demand for political emancipation and social recognition. Mendelssohn did not want the state to play any special role in enforcing this demand. This is easy to understand, because the state of Mendelssohn's era legally embodied the very position he opposed. Three generations later, the situation was completely different. Legally, the Jews were now emancipated, and the German Jews had come to regard the state no longer as an adversary but rather as the guarantor of their rights. At this point, the state's function was to safeguard freedom of conscience, justice, and toleration. "The state alone," the neo-Kantian Hermann Cohen stated in a 1917 lecture held in Berlin, "provides not only political security for religious communities, but also must ensure freedom of conscience and safeguard the independence of religious creed against outside impediments and handicaps."

The commitment to religious toleration and social tolerance was part and parcel of the basic principles of the German Jews before 1933. The creed conveyed by the friends Lessing and Mendelssohn, that is, that every person must have the right to profess his or her religion freely and without coercion and "find salvation in his own way" (Frederick II)—no matter whether Christian, Muslim, or Jew—was regarded by schools and families as a kind of sacred testament and thus cultivated and passed on to coming generations. The existence of a space in which the partners in a discussion could move and deal with each other on equal footing was perceived as a precious achievement of modern liberalism. The objective was to be able to speak the truth openly without having to worry about incurring personal risk. Coercion of any form was rejected.

In particular, any kind of intervention into religious matters was abhorred. "It does not make any sense," Johann Caspar Lavater remarked in his *Physiognomische Fragmente* of 1775, "to force a certain form of religion on the conscience of a nation, community, or society. Coercion can make people profess a faith outwardly but cannot make them embrace inner convictions." Lavater, a Swiss deacon who throughout his life strove for a rational apology of the Christian faith, at least once acted against his Christian maxims: several years earlier, he had tried to convert Moses Mendelssohn to Christianity—thereby engaging the rapt attention of the cultivated European public of his day. Lavater failed; Mendelssohn persevered. In their fervor to proselytize, Lavater and his sympathizers had overlooked that the demand made on Mendelssohn would have forced him to concede something that he simply could not concede. Besides, this demand—which Mendelssohn had to reject first and foremost to preserve his self-respect—was contrary to Lavater's own teachings, in particular his well-known ideas of religious toleration and mutual tolerance. But perhaps this ambiguity did not come about by chance. In a way, Lavater stands for a certain type of intellectual that can often be found even today. In this case, his attitude may be described as advocating toleration; yet at the same time the freedom of religion he demands is not of existential concern to him but only constitutes some arbitrary problem of conceptual theory. And this is not real toleration—the actual, practical everyday full acceptance of one's fellow men.

Bibliography

Hans Rudolph Guggisberg, ed., *Dokumente zur Geschichte einer Forderung* (Stuttgart-Bad Cannstatt: frommann-holzboog, 1984); Johann Caspar Lavater, *Physiognomische Fragmente* (Leipzig: Weidmanns Erben und Reich, 1775); Heinrich Lutz, ed., *Zur Geschichte der Toleranz und Religionsfreiheit* (Darmstadt: Wissenschaftliche Buchgesellschaft, 1977); Trutz Rendtorff, ed., *Glaube und Toleranz: Das theologische Erbe der Aufklärung* (Gutersloh: Gutersloher Verlagshaus G. Mohn, 1982); and Julius H. Schoeps, *Moses Mendelssohn* (Königstein / Taunus: Jüdischer Verlag im Athenäum, 1979).

JULIUS H. SCHOEPS

1783 The final volume of Moses Mendelssohn's edition of the Pentateuch appears

In 1783 Moses Mendelssohn published two works on Judaism. In May his German treatise *Jerusalem, or on Religious Power and Judaism* came off the press. Written in a matter of months in the heat of a polemic, the tract has become the chief source for the study of Mendelssohn's view of Judaism and his attempt to harmonize Judaism and the Enlightenment. Also in the spring of that year, the fifth and final volume of his edition of the Pentateuch appeared, *The Book of the Paths of Peace*. This work was the culmination of almost a decade of labor but, even more significant, the crowning product of some three decades of Hebrew writing. Mendelssohn had published consistently in Hebrew throughout his career, yet the definitive scholarship and prevailing view of Mendelssohn would give little indication that this was so.

Mendelssohn's manifest function as German Jewry's "patron saint" and the "ideal figure" of its subculture long encouraged the creation of a "German" Mendelssohn in whose oeuvre the *Jerusalem* was privileged over the Pentateuch edition and other Hebrew works. Indeed, the first edition of Mendelssohn's collected works (1843–45) made this view canonical by excluding all of the Hebrew works with the exception of the Pentateuch edition, which it successfully Germanized. Ironically, it is the ostracized extracanonical Hebrew works that in fact reveal the true extent and inner workings of Mendelssohn's effort to harmonize Judaism with the European Enlightenment. These works cast the *Jerusalem*, and the nature of Mendelssohn's self-understanding as a Jew, in a different light.

Mendelssohn's Hebrew works constituted a coherent effort to renew the traditions of Hebrew philosophy and biblical commentary that had practically disappeared from the curriculum of Central and Eastern European Ashkenazi Jewry. His works used an individual philosophy to express a specific version of Judaism in a selected literary form.

Mendelssohn developed his own understanding of Christian Wolff's philosophy. Inspired by Newton and the scientific revolution, Wolff had adopted the mathematical method for philosophy, hoping to attain the certainty of science. In his search for certainty, Wolff had identified "practical" with "theoretical" conviction: he thought a priori and a posteriori theoretical arguments that were persuasive engendered conviction and thus fell into the category of "vital knowledge." Mendelssohn dissented. He asserted that mere theoretical argumentation did not necessarily constitute vital knowledge. In metaphysics the most demonstrably certain proofs of God's existence were not always the most persuasive. Less certain arguments (for example, the "beauty and order" of the world, or physico-theology) were often more effective in securing convictions and thus constituted the vital knowledge that guided lives. This distinction between practical and theoretical knowledge informed Mendelssohn's philosophical works.

Mendelssohn's Judaism rested on his effort to revive the medieval Jewish tradition of practical rationalism, in which philosophy was a tool in the service of piety and observance. Despite the venerable phrase, "from Moses [Maimonides] unto Moses [Mendelssohn] there was none like Moses," Mendelssohn was not a follower of Maimonides. To be sure, Mendelssohn had a detailed knowledge of Maimonides' work and borrowed freely from it. Yet Maimonides represented the tradition of speculative rationalism that aspired to a systematic account of Judaism's beliefs and a thorough rationalization of its laws, which Mendelssohn eschewed. If Mendelssohn had a fundamental affinity with any one medieval Jewish thinker it was Jehudah HaLevi, the central exponent of practical rationalism.

The literary form Mendelssohn chose was commentary. Commentary was of course a central genre of postbiblical Jewish literature, yet it also fit Mendelssohn's views. Mendelssohn did not want to write a systematic account of Judaism. Rather, he chose to use commentary as a means to renew the discourses of Hebrew philosophy and biblical exegesis that were instruments of practical piety, observance, and morality.

Mendelssohn's first two Hebrew works were devoted to philosophy and logic. *Kohelet Musar* (The preacher of morals) was published sometime in the late 1750s. Mendelssohn chose the medium of a journal that was current in Germany at the time, the "moral weekly." The *Kohelet Musar* was thus the first modern journal in Hebrew. Mendelssohn used the journal as a way to address an audience of Talmud students and others adept at learning Jewish works on some of the same practical philosophical subjects he treated in his German works of the period: nature as a source of enjoyment or belief (physico-theology); evil and misfortune in daily life (theodicy); and the nature of relationships between man and man and between man and God. In his treatment of these issues, Mendelssohn repeatedly employed the same method. He formulated the philosophical issue using Wolffian categories; gave an example, usually drawn from Jewish texts, to which the categories were applied; quoted passages of rabbinic or Hebrew philosophical literature that confirmed the analysis; and ended with a peroration of Wolffian conclusions to be derived from it.

Wolff is never mentioned by name, but Hebrew equivalents are introduced for key terms of his philosophy.

In considering the ethical nature of friendship, for example, Mendelssohn used Wolff's definition of love as taking pleasure in another's increased perfection. His illustration was the friendship of David and Jonathan in the Bible. He pointed out that the rabbinic sages had seen this friendship as an "unconditional love" (Mishneh Avot 5:17). Mendelssohn asserted that whereas in human love pleasure arises from the other's achievement of perfection, in the love of God, because He is the embodiment of all perfection, pleasure arises out of obedience to His law: "Know that love of His holy name consists in pleasure in the knowledge of His perfection. From it will be born the desire to heed His voice and to obey His commandments. This is service (*avodah*) from love. . . . Pleasure in God and love of Him are one and the same."

Mendelssohn then cited a passage from the Babylonian Talmud that illustrates this point. This example demonstrates how Mendelssohn transformed the genre to suit his own purposes: whereas the German moral weekly purveyed natural philosophy, Mendelssohn used it to offer a revealed, if entirely reasonable, Judaism.

Mendelssohn's second Hebrew work was a commentary on Maimonides' *Milot Ha-Higayon* (Logical terms), written in 1760–61. Maimonides had written this succinct account of twelfth-century logical terminology for a layman. The book was at once an introduction to logic and a philosophical primer. Mendelssohn republished it with an introduction and a commentary. In his introduction Mendelssohn defended logic as an entirely pious pursuit that is necessary to correct belief. Without logic, he asserted, one can neither fathom God's creation nor distinguish right from wrong. Mendelssohn argued that to think without an awareness of logic is equivalent to using language without knowing grammar: one uses it willy-nilly, but it will be all the better if one understands it.

Mendelssohn asserted that speculative reason has distinct limits—an argument he also made in his German works—and he next discussed the

revealed philosophy that surpassed and complemented it. He argued that without Torah and
tradition we are "like a blind man in the dark,"
and that the true path to knowledge is the combination of Torah and logic. According to Mendelssohn, however far man's understanding may
go in comprehending God and divine truth, it is
only possible through the application of God-
given reason to Torah and tradition. Only the
prophet who has direct revelation can dispense
with logic—a fundamental idea of Jehudah
HaLevi's. Mendelssohn therefore recommended
that students study logic an hour or so per week
in support of their traditional textual studies.
Mendelssohn regarded logic as an instrument and
not as an end in itself.

Maimonides' exposition served Mendelssohn's
purposes, albeit with one exception. Maimonides'
method and philosophy were distinctly medieval.
His work pointed backward to medieval Jewish
philosophy; it did not point forward to eighteenth-century philosophy. Mendelssohn's commentary was intended to be the bridge between
these two times. At the end of each of the fourteen
chapters of his treatise, Maimonides provided a list
of the terms he had introduced. Mendelssohn used
these as a philosophical lexicon: next to each
Hebrew term he gave the equivalent in German
and in Latin (though in Hebrew characters). He
thereby attempted to renew philosophical discourse in Hebrew in a systematic manner by performing the same function for Hebrew that Wolff
had for German some four decades earlier. In his
early German philosophical treatises Wolff had
invented German equivalents for accepted Latin
terms.

Mendelssohn did not rest content with creating an up-to-date philosophical vocabulary. He
also introduced the substance of eighteenth-
century philosophy. Wherever Maimonides had
used Aristotelian or Platonic notions (for example,
that God had created form from an existing primordial matter), Mendelssohn corrected it with
the eighteenth-century Leibnizian-Wolffian view
(that is, God created both matter and form) that,
unlike the Aristotelian view, was not in conflict
with fundamental Jewish belief.

Mendelssohn's commentary was in keeping

with his emphasis on practical knowledge. As the
foundation of philosophy, logic was common to
both the speculative and the practical traditions
of medieval Jewish rationalism. This was a Maimonidean text Mendelssohn could use without hesitation.

Mendelssohn's subsequent Hebrew works
were devoted to biblical exegesis. In a commentary
on, and introduction to, the Book of Ecclesiastes
(1770), he reiterated his preference for practical
over speculative reason in a discussion that again
showed the harmony between his Wolffianism and
his Judaism. Mendelssohn's commentary focused
on the ideas of providence and immortality integral to natural religion and Judaism. He claimed
that the events of this world are illusory: "If I wish
to understand something of the ways of providence, it is necessary to become acquainted with
all of God's works, with what was and what will be,
in this world and the world to come. For no one can
grasp any aspect of the way of superior [that is,
divine] wisdom by considering only the actions
taken in this world. This would be like a dream
without an interpretation, a question without an
answer. One will not attain a true explanation of
events and the [divine] decree that informs them,
if one does not look beyond to include what occurs
in the world to come."

The recognition of providence and immortality affords escape from this seemingly inscruta-
ble world, from the "dream without an interpretation." Were there no world to come, the
God who sits in constant judgment would have
created intelligent beings only to condemn them
to witnessing insufferable injustice without hope
of redress. Because belief in immortality ultimately provides that redress, it is the foundation
of morality, the guarantee of justice, the key to
understanding, and the "source of life." Adopting
the technical language of his 1767 dialogue on
the immortality of the soul, *Phaedon,* Mendelssohn asserted that the soul is a simple imperishable substance that sets man apart from beasts,
and thus the loss of consciousness is the worst fate
a rational being can suffer. Providence and immortality constitute "genuine superior truth"
and enable man to pursue his God-given vocation, the quest for perfection.

Mendelssohn also aimed to renew, and defend, the tradition of Jewish biblical exegesis. Medieval Jewish exegesis posited four possible modes of interpreting any biblical text (literal, homiletic, allegorical, esoteric) that existed simultaneously without tension or contradiction. Since the seventeenth century, scholars such as Spinoza, Capellus, Morinus, and Richard Simon had developed a critical approach to the Bible in which they contested many venerable theological interpretations, including the rabbinic ones, which some of them derided as little more than homily or fantasy. Mendelssohn consequently introduced his commentary with a "natural" defense of all Jewish interpretation in keeping with both his philosophy and his Jewish faith.

Mendelssohn provided perhaps the first defense of Jewish exegesis on the basis of language. He argued that the multiple meanings that rabbinic exegesis presumes are inherent in the very use of language, and he employed Maimonides' categories of "primary" and "secondary" intention to explain how this is possible. The primary intention arises from the "context and connectedness of discussion." The speaker and listener are concerned with the sense the words convey rather than with the words themselves. The secondary intention, in contrast, does not emerge from the context of discussion—in fact, the two must not agree—but from the "close scrutiny of each and every word, each and every letter, and each and every jot." The natural speaker will use "wit and intelligence" to hint at a meaning that he does not desire to state explicitly.

Mendelssohn's natural defense of rabbinic exegesis was of a piece with his general thinking. He averred that multiple meanings are entirely in keeping with reason: "There are four methods of interpreting our holy Torah—the literal, homiletical, allegorical and esoteric—as is well known. All of them are the words of the living God and are in agreement. This does not contradict the laws of reason or inference, nor is it alien and disturbing to human reason." This is the case because the "superior wisdom" according to which God had created the world dictated that "one act served many ends." Mendelssohn argued by analogy with the physical world. Just as the

limbs of the body and the elements serve more than one purpose, so words can bear multiple intentions, an argument Mendelssohn corroborated with quotations from rabbinic and mystical literature.

Mendelssohn thus supported his natural defense of Jewish interpretation with an argument by analogy with creation. This sort of argument "from design" could easily have been drawn from any number of medieval rationalists, yet it was also a version of the German Enlightenment's physico-theology. It was thoroughly characteristic of Mendelssohn to use an argument from the heart of the Enlightenment, but it was especially poignant when he did so to defend rabbinic exegesis against its enlightened critics. When combined with the quotations from rabbinic and mystical literature, the argument recalled the *Kohelet Musar* in its demonstration of the convergence of Enlightenment and Jewish thought.

Mendelssohn continued his effort to renew biblical exegesis in his edition of the Pentateuch, which contained a translation into German (printed in Hebrew letters), a line by line commentary, notes on the Masoretic text, and a general introduction. Mendelssohn had been the guiding spirit and editor of the edition: besides producing the entire translation, he wrote the commentary to the first lection of Genesis (1:1–6:8) and the entire Book of Exodus, edited the commentaries to the other books, and wrote the introduction.

Mendelssohn's commentary was part and parcel of his practical rationalism. He regarded the Pentateuch as the primary source of practical knowledge for the Jews because it teaches truth by prescribing action in the form of law. His treatment of the nature of the commandments, for example, exemplified the fit between his general philosophy and his Judaism.

That the commandments are a form of practical and not theoretical knowledge is unmistakably articulated in Mendelssohn's commentary on the first commandments of the decalogue (Exod. 20:2). According to Mendelssohn, these commandments are not intended to teach the abstract truth of God's existence: they presuppose Israel's belief in His creation and providence and aim instead to teach Israel that it was a "chosen people" who had accepted "the yoke of His Kingdom and His government." God spoke to Israel not as the God of creation, but as the God of the Exodus from Egypt. As a result of that relationship and event, "God gave the Torah, commandments, laws and injunctions" to Israel "alone."

The distinction between practical and theoretical knowledge is of cardinal importance here because it lays the foundation for universal belief in God. By understanding the commandments to confirm rather than to confer belief, Mendelssohn posited the universality of theism. The God of creation—as distinct from the God of the Exodus—spoke a universal language. Israel had no monopoly on, or special knowledge of, any abstract truth. The other nations believe in Him but even more, their forms of worship are valid. Whatever the form of worship—be it idols, animals or the stars—the other nations thereby acknowledge a higher being and embrace God's rule: "In the judgement of reason there is no cause to forbid such worship to the sons of Noah." In contrast, such worship is forbidden to the sons of Israel because they have accepted the laws of the Torah. For the other nations such worship is a form of subjection to God's will and has practical value because it promotes virtue and prevents evil. Here is a plea for toleration: knowledge that has practical value is to be respected. With this argument Mendelssohn had secured the foundation of natural religion even as he delineated Israel's chosenness.

Mendelssohn in fact balanced these two elements in his discussion of Israel's election (Exod. 19:5–6). Mendelssohn stressed that although all humanity was dear to God, Israel had a special role: "For indeed all of the earth is Mine, all of the nations are Mine and the entire human race is dearer to Me than all of the lower beings, since it alone is the ultimate purpose of them all, as [the Rabbis] of blessed memory said: 'Beloved is humanity which has been created in God's image.' The saintly of the nations are without doubt cherished by Him. *But:* . . . All of the nations are like one people, and you are like the priests specially appointed for the worship of God, to instruct and teach the entire human race to call upon the name

of God and to worship Him." In Mendelssohn's translation the *aber* ("but") that connects the two clauses (Exod. 19:5, 6) shows the indissoluble link, yet also the immutable distinction, between them.

The law was the sign of Israel's election as a priestly people, and Mendelssohn emphasized that the law was a form of practical knowledge. On the dietary laws (Exod. 23:19) he commented: "It is not to be inquired why the Holy One blessed be He forbade us meat and milk, since He obligated us to many commandments whose explanation He did not reveal. It must suffice for us that we know that they are commanded by Him, may He be blessed. Since we have accepted for ourselves the yoke of his kingdom, we are required to perform His will. The purpose [of the commandments] is in their performance, not in the knowledge of their explanation."

In taking this position Mendelssohn identified with the medieval school of thought, represented by Jehudah HaLevi, that understood the commandments as essentially heteronymous: they are reasonable from the side of the divine legislator yet impenetrable to those for whom they were legislated. This view also informed Mendelssohn's insistence that the decalogue did not teach abstract truths otherwise unavailable to mankind, and that for Israel the Bible is a handbook of practical knowledge.

Just as in his introduction and commentary to Ecclesiastes Mendelssohn had offered a natural defense of the various forms of exegesis, in his introduction to the Pentateuch he defended the authenticity of the biblical text against the attacks of the "historical-critical school" as represented by the work of Johann Gottfried Eichhorn. Eichhorn treated the Bible as a human document by studying it with the methods that had been developed to study classical and profane literature. He rejected divine origins in favor of the "documentary" hypothesis: Moses had written the Pentateuch by weaving together earlier accounts. Although Eichhorn acknowledged that the text was genuine, he asserted that it had suffered "manifold and irremediable" corruption. Were Moses "to rise from the dead," Eichhorn claimed, he would hardly recognize what we know as the text of the Bible. The text we know, Eichhorn explained, emerged between the sixth and tenth centuries when Jewish students of the Bible—that is, the Masoretes—divided the words, introduced punctuation and accents, and in general attempted to fix the text. That effort prevented further corruption but was not authoritative: the corruption long predated the Masoretes' work and could not be corrected by it. Eichhorn argued that all existing methods of correcting mistakes were insufficient. The contemporary exegete must rely on his experience and historical sense to suggest emendations: this was the method of higher criticism.

Mendelssohn's account of the biblical text in his introduction is a restatement of Jewish tradition in the face of this higher criticism. Eichhorn had argued that the Bible had multiple sources. Mendelssohn, however, propounded the traditional Jewish argument that God had spoken every word of the Torah to Moses and that the text had been preserved as a result of the special oral nature of Hebrew and the Jewish tradition of scriptural transmission and notation. In the twelfth century Jehudah HaLevi had made the argument that Hebrew was a divine language distinguished by its oral quality. Mendelssohn amplified HaLevi's argument by asserting that the system of Masoretic notations or accents had a divine origin: God had vouchsafed them to Moses at Sinai. Moses had heard every word of the Torah from God, who pronounced the words with the full emotion, inflection, and intonation that made their meaning unmistakable. Moses duly noted all of these oral signs, transmitted them to Joshua, and from Joshua they were communicated through the ages. This process was possible due to the singular nature of Hebrew. According to Mendelssohn, Hebrew is not only the language of God and the primordial language of all mankind, but because of its system of accents, which record the full range of expression, it also has the singular ability to fully preserve utterances. All language was originally oral; Hebrew alone was able to remain so. The oral tradition had preserved the knowledge of the way God had spoken and thereby precluded the text's corruption. The peculiar endowments that enabled Hebrew to re-

tain its oral character also safeguarded the text from corruption.

Eichhorn's entire argument showed that the Bible was a profane book whose text had suffered corruption and therefore required emendation. Mendelssohn demonstrated that it was a sacred book that had escaped corruption by virtue of a singular oral tradition. Emendation was not only unnecessary but unthinkable. For Mendelssohn the exegete's task was not emendation but studying literal meaning in order to extract practical knowledge.

Mendelssohn's Hebrew writings show his effort to establish a fundamental harmony between Judaism and the Enlightenment—whether in his use of Wolffian philosophy or in such key ideas as natural religion and toleration. In addition, these writings show that the central ideas of his book *Jerusalem* had been developed in his earlier Hebrew works and were in keeping with his understanding of Judaism based on the tradition of practical rationalism. Mendelssohn's central argument in the *Jerusalem,* for example, was that Judaism consisted of a divine legislation, not a divine religion. "To state it briefly: I believe that Judaism knows of no revealed religion in the sense in which Christians understand this term. The Israelites possess a divine *legislation*—laws, commandments, ordinances, rules of life, instruction in the will of God as to how they should conduct themselves in order to attain temporal and eternal felicity. Propositions and prescriptions of this kind were revealed to them by Moses in a miraculous and supernatural manner, but no doctrinal opinions, no saving truths, no universal propositions of reason" (Mendelssohn 1983).

According to Mendelssohn, what distinguishes Judaism are the actions its laws prescribe. Judaism consists of a set of acts aimed at the will rather than a set of beliefs. These acts are to be found in the Pentateuch, which is a "book of laws containing ordinances, rules of life and prescriptions." The Pentateuch is more than a sourcebook of laws, however: it is also "an inexhaustible treasure of rational truths and religious doctrines which are so intimately connected with the laws that they form but one entity." The Pentateuch's laws form a bridge between the historical truths of Judaism and the eternal truths: they derive from God's relationship to His people. The laws "guide the inquiring intelligence to divine truths, partly to eternal and partly to historical truths. . . . The ceremonial law was the bond which was to connect action with contemplation, law with theory. All laws refer to, or are based upon, enduring truths of reason, or remind us of them, and rouse us to ponder them. Hence, our rabbis rightly say: the laws and doctrines are related to each other like body and soul." For Mendelssohn Judaism is the nonpareil religion of practical knowledge. Although its laws and actions impart practical knowledge, their performance also leads to eternal and historical truths.

The search for Mendelssohn's self-understanding as a Jew cannot be confined to his German works; his thirty years of Hebrew writing must be admitted to the canon. Once this is done, it becomes apparent that Mendelssohn was even more out of step with his contemporaries than he himself was willing to acknowledge. In 1785 Mendelssohn conceded that his philosophical views were at least ten years out of date. Moreover, as far as its understanding of Judaism is concerned, his *Jerusalem* could have been written almost half a century earlier. Mendelssohn's view of Judaism should not be compared to the neologists' approach to Christianity in the 1770s and 1780s, the figures with whom he is usually grouped, but rather to that of the "theological Wolffians" who attempted to rearticulate Protestantism using the categories of Wolffian philosophy between 1720 and 1750. Mendelssohn's formative period as a philosopher was in the 1740s and 1750s; in fact, one of the first books he read in German was *Considerations on the Augsburg Confession* (1733) by Johann Gustav Reinbeck (1683–1741), the most prominent theological Wolffian in Berlin. Mendelssohn's work in general has marked affinities to that of *the* theological Wolffian, Siegmund Jacob Baumgarten (1706–57), who was professor of theology at Halle. Mendelssohn can be seen as a Jewish theological Wolffian who attempted to do for Judaism what Reinbeck and Baumgarten had done for Protestantism.

Seeing Mendelssohn in this manner makes it clear that his self-understanding as a Jew is to be found at the nexus between his revival of the medieval tradition of practical rationalism and his version of Wolffian philosophy. His self-understanding turned on the rearticulation of Judaism through the categories of Wolffianism. He partook of none of the dilemmas of identity so common among German Jews from the 1790s onward. He had no doubts about who he was or what he believed; his Judaism was deeply rooted in internal traditions, and he regarded it with unwavering pride and honor. Mendelssohn was truly an ephemeral figure in the sense that his understanding of Judaism belonged to a particular moment of eighteenth-century culture that, just three years after the publication of *Jerusalem* and the final volume of *Book of the Paths of Peace*, died with him.

Bibliography

Alexander Altmann, "Moses Mendelssohn as the Archetypal German Jew," *The Jewish Response to German Culture*, ed. Jehuda Reinharz and Walter Schatzberg (Hanover, N.H.: University Press of New England, 1985), 17–31; Altmann, *Moses Mendelssohn: A Biographical Study* (University: University of Alabama Press, 1973); Allan Arkush, *Moses Mendelssohn and the Enlightenment* (Albany: State University of New York Press, 1994); Lewis White Beck, *Early German Philosophy: Kant and His Predecessors* (Cambridge, Mass.: Harvard University Press, 1969); Edward Breuer, "In Defense of Rabbinic Tradition: The Masoretic Text and Its Rabbinic Interpretation in the Early Haskalah," Ph.D. diss., Harvard University, 1990; Johann Gottfried Eichhorn, *Einleitung ins Alte Testament*, 2d ed., 3 vols. (Reutlingen: n.p., 1790); Meir Gilon, *Kohelet Musar le-Mendelssohn al Reka Tekufato* (Jerusalem: Israel Academy of Sciences, 1979); Steven M. Lowenstein, *The Berlin Jewish Community: Enlightenment, Family and Crisis, 1770–1830* (New York: Oxford University Press, 1994); Wolfgang Martens, *Die Botschaft der Tugend: Die Aufklärung im Spiegel der deutschen Moralischen Wochenschriften* (Stuttgart: Metzler, 1968); Moses Mendelssohn, *Gesammelte Schriften*, 7 vols. (Leipzig: Brockhaus, 1843–45); Mendelssohn, *Gesammelte Schriften: Jubiläumsausgabe*, 22 vols. (Stuttgart: Friedrich Frommann Verlag, 1971–); Mendelssohn, *Jerusalem or on Religious Power and Judaism*, trans. Allan Arkush (Hanover, N.H.: University Press of New England, 1983); Michael Meyer, *The Origins of the Modern Jew: Jewish Identity and European Culture in Germany, 1749–1824* (Detroit: Wayne State University Press, 1967); Johann Gustav Reinbeck, *Betrachtungen über die in der Augsburgischen Confession enthaltene und damit verknüpfte Göttliche Wahrheiten,* 2 vols. (Berlin and Leipzig: n.p., 1733); Peretz Sandler, *Ha-Biur le-Torah shel Moshe Mendelssohn ve-Siato* (Jerusalem: Mosad Bialik, 1940); Azriel Shohat, *Im Hilufei Tekufot: Reshit ha-Haskala be-Yahadut Germanya* (Jerusalem: Mosad Bialik, 1960);

David Sorkin, *Moses Mendelssohn and the Religious Enlightenment* (Berkeley: University of California Press, 1996); and Harry Wolfson, "Maimonides and Hallevi: A Study in Typical Jewish Attitudes Towards Greek Philosophy in the Middle Ages," *Studies in the History and Philosophy of Religion,* 2 vols. (Cambridge, Mass.: Harvard University Press, 1973) 2:120–60.

DAVID SORKIN

1783 The Haskalah begins in Germany with the founding of the Hebrew journal *Hame'asef*

Hebrew Haskalah (Enlightenment) marks a turning point in the history of the Jewish people and its culture and letters in modern times. It began in Germany in the 1780s as a group of aspiring Hebrew writers undertook a new and daring enterprise: the publication of an up-to-date monthly journal in the Hebrew language. *Hame'asef* (The gatherer), however, published during the periods 1783–96 and 1808–11, was more than just a literary journal patterned after the contemporary morality weeklies. The journal became the ideological mouthpiece of a literary and cultural movement that began a concerted effort to effect a cultural revolution among Jews in Germany and elsewhere. It also served as an organ that published the literary works produced by its circle of writers. Through their literary endeavor, these writers ushered in the modern era in Jewish history and started the modern trends in Hebrew letters.

From a historical perspective, Haskalah can be said to have emerged on the European scene as a reaction to both external and internal forces. Undoubtedly, it was a Jewish response to the new spirit generated by the European Enlightenment, yet it was certainly also an answer to a great need within the Jewish society for change. It came in the wake of inner strife within Jewish society resulting from messianic movements, a breakdown in the structure of the *Kehillah* (the organized Jewish community), and a decline in the authority of the rabbinate.

The ideas and ideals of Haskalah were neither totally innovative nor completely original. Drawing from European Enlightenment on the one hand and from medieval Jewish philosophy on the other, its ideology may be characterized as eclectic. Continuously in a state of formation, this ideology lacked a systematized code, and its proponents did not have a single, unified view on how to implement their goal. Nevertheless, they were united in their aim to enlighten their Jewish brethren and leaned heavily on Mendelssohn's definition of Judaism and its relations to the surrounding culture. Haskalah's facets, factions, and voices were many, and they varied from the extreme enlighteners to the more moderate ones. Regardless of their position on the Enlightenment scale, the Hebrew enlighteners—as distinguished from the German-Jewish enlighteners, who in general were more radical—had one thing in common: their desire to introduce changes in Jewish culture was coupled with loyalty to the Hebrew heritage.

The question of setting a date and place for the beginning of modern Hebrew literature is often discussed in this context. Haskalah scholars in both Hebrew literature and Jewish history have debated the criteria for discerning modernity and whether a certain writer, or group of writers, may be said to have started the modern trends in Hebrew letters. Two main theories on the beginning of modern Hebrew literature have emerged in the historiography of Haskalah. One stream has identified the beginnings with the German Hebrew Haskalah, which indeed is our approach, whereas the other has found earlier phenomena in Italian Hebrew writing.

The latter position, advocated by the literary historian and critic Yeruham Fishel Lachover, has selected Moshe Hayim Luzzatto (1707–47), an Italian Hebrew poet, moralist, and kabbalist, as the starting point of modern Hebrew literature. The former, espoused by the literary historian Joseph Klausner, has chosen Naphtali Wessely (1725–1805), a poet, biblical commentator, grammarian, and one of the leading figures of the Hebrew Haskalah in Berlin, as the author who signals the beginning of modern Hebrew letters. A third approach suggested by another literary historian, Hayyim Nachmann Shapira, proposed the writers and editors of *Hame'asef* as his choice. Outside the literary spheres, the figure of Moses Mendelssohn (1729–86) has been cited by historians such as Heinrich Graetz as the "father" of the Jewish Enlightenment and the person who signals the advent of modern times in the annals of Jewish history. Indeed, Mendelssohn had a seminal influence on these young Hebraists, who saw in him a model of Haskalah. He was thought to exemplify the symbiosis between Judaism and Enlightenment, adhering to both and allegedly making compromises to none. They recognized him as the initiator of a major Hebrew Enlightenment enterprise—namely, the commentary and translation of the Hebrew Bible into German—and as such, a figure to be emulated.

Discussion of modernism is more often than not relegated to the notion of secularism—that creeping change that is said to have affected the thinking, *Weltanschauung,* and behavior of young Jewish intellectuals known as *Maskilim* (Hebrew Enlighteners). Both modernism and secularism in our context are still a subject of continuous scholarly discussion, but are yet to be defined satisfactorily. Nevertheless, the contribution of the Hebrew journal *Hame'asef* and its writers to the growth of modern Hebrew literature by promoting both modernity and secularism (see below), has gained recognition in the past twenty-five years, as more scholars continued to produce critical assessments and analyses of literary works published by the Berlin Haskalah.

Haskalah scholarship has raised several methodological questions regarding some of its own basic tenets. For one, should a literary discussion on Haskalah be based solely on literary grounds, or may it also incorporate current trends in Jewish social and intellectual history? And second, should we distinguish between the two aspects of Hebrew Haskalah, namely, Haskalah as a literary movement and Haskalah as a social and perhaps a cultural movement? The fact that the two questions are interconnected, however, especially during Haskalah's inception in Germany, does help us solve the latter issue for the time being. The first question is actually resolved by the prevailing practices of ideas continuously flowing from the spheres of social and intellectual histories to literary histories and criticism, and vice versa. This interdisciplinary trend in Haskalah scholarship had been questioned by Avraham Holtz, who demanded a more literary approach to the study of Haskalah.

The works of social historians Bernard Weinryb, Azriel Shohat, and Jacob Katz, to name a few, have contributed insights to the understanding of the Haskalah phenomena. They pointed out that certain aspects of modernism, manifestations of trends toward secularism in Jewish society, and the dawn of the Enlightenment could be found earlier in that century in Jewish circles in Holland and in Italy. Thus they suggested that the Haskalah began earlier than had previously been thought. But even if one is to accept the notion that there were several writers and even rabbis who are said to have heralded the Haskalah prior to the German phenomenon, or even that there had been previous phenomena of secularism, as suggested above, it will be difficult to argue against the unique thrust of German Haskalah. It emerged as a group and as a movement in its collective energy, its centrality, and more important, in its unified effort to disseminate the ideology of the Enlightenment. It is in the activities of this group of young Hebraists, consisting of writers, educators, and even rabbis, that modern Hebrew writing has been reborn and the new trends of modern Hebrew letters began.

This group and its writings represent the beginning of modernism, which I identify and define as a strong awareness of the changing times, a desire to effect change, and a collaborative effort to disseminate ideas and establish tools for change. I have identified as modernism those subtle, covert signals in the writings of these Maskilim that are indicative of their sensitivities to the changes that were about to take place in Jewish society.

Hame'asef was not the first periodical to be published in Hebrew in that century. Thirty years earlier, in midcentury, Moses Mendelssohn initiated the budding of Haskalah by attempting to publish in about 1755 a Hebrew periodical entitled *Qohelet Musar* (Moral Ecclesiastes). He followed the trend of the morality weeklies that flourished in that century. His endeavor, however, was short-lived; only two issues of the periodical appeared. In spite of its brief appearance, the periodical signifies an important step toward the publication of a modern periodical in Hebrew. It is not insignificant that thirty years later, in the 1780s, the editors of *Hame'asef* republished the contents of one issue of *Qohelet Musar*. A religious periodical, *Pri Etz Hayim* (The fruit of the Tree of Life), had appeared in the 1720s, but it cannot be considered either modern or literary.

In advance of the publication of *Hame'asef*, the editors circulated a prospectus in 1783 entitled "Nahal Habesor" (The brook Besor, or Good tidings). In it, they outlined their plans for the new monthly periodical, by detailing its contents and literary and Enlightenment goals. It was an editorial statement that exposed their precarious predicament, which was characterized by a desire to advocate change, but it was disguised by their caution not to declare it in a provocative manner. In their desire not to alienate any of the rabbinic authorities or the moderate Maskilim, the editors maneuvered between hinting at their yearning for change and declaring their allegiance to traditional Judaism.

Thus their statement did not sound like a declaration of change and did not overtly propose too many new ideas. It openly declared the editors' choice of a general conservative (namely, traditional) attitude toward Judaism. Their announced plans for the contents and departments of the journal definitely show an inclination toward the new and contemporary scene, yet with a slant toward the conservative and traditional. The

journal, they wrote, would consist of five major departments: poetry; articles on language, Bible, knowledge and ethics, *Halakhah* (Jewish legal matters), and moral and physical education; biographies; news of contemporary events; and information about new books.

The editors seem to vacillate between the Bible and Halakhah on the one hand—ostensibly traditional subjects—and secular subjects like education and contemporary events on the other. At the same time, their aspiration to revive the Hebrew language and literature is manifested in their publishing of poetry and prose as well as articles on grammar and language.

The journal's launch was coupled with the formation of a new association, Society for the Seekers of the Hebrew Language, in keeping with the prospectus "Nahal Habesor." This cultural society proved to be quite enterprising. It founded a publishing house that had its own Hebrew and German typesetting and used the printing press of an established printer. Thus the new center for Hebrew literature was able to execute its cultural plans and disseminate its own books. Members were independent of the religious and the community authorities and thus were free to publish the literary production of Haskalah, including controversial books. One such book was Saul Berlin's *Besamim Rosh* (Incense of spices) in 1793. This was a pseudepigraphical work in the responsa genre, which the author attributed to Rabbi Asher ben Yehiel of the thirteenth and fourteenth centuries. The sum total of these publishing efforts is an impressive and diversified list of Hebrew books.

The emphasis that the authors of "Nahal Habesor" placed on the concept of establishing an active center of Hebrew literature and founding this society for Hebrew language is striking. To disarm any possible rabbinic attacks of this innovation "which is forbidden by the Torah" (*hadash asur min hatorah*), they quoted from the Hebraic sources the dictum that Torah may be studied only in groups. Obviously, the group was not formed to study Torah in the traditional sense— even though the authors were initially eager to describe themselves as educated both in Jewish and secular disciplines.

In addition to cultivating the cultural inclinations of Haskalah, the authors of "Nahal Habesor" also addressed certain social aspects of Jewish existence, such as Jews' attitude toward their host country and its citizens, their aim to become productive citizens of that country, and the like. And eventually they made an attempt to present an alternative to the existing structure of the Jewish *Kehillah* by establishing their own modern school and forming an "enlightened" burial society.

Visible manifestations of Enlightenment appeared in the pages of the journal. Overtly and covertly, the editors of *Hame'asef* endeavored to promote the ideology of the Enlightenment. Even in traditional topics such as the Bible and Halakhah, their position was far from traditional. Engaging in various Haskalah-related controversies, they advocated the positions held by Mendelssohn and Wessely in their respective social and cultural rifts with the traditionalist rabbis. They championed Wessely, for example, not only as the poet laureate of Haskalah, but also as an advocate of the modernization of Jewish education. The editors defended Wessely's position as expressed in his pamphlets, *Divrei Shalom Ve'emet* (Words of peace and truth; 1782–84). Following Wessely's dictate, they advocated the introduction of modern, secular education in Jewish schools.

In a like manner, the editors embraced the translation and commentary of the Hebrew Bible project, started by Mendelssohn and known as the *Be'ur* (The commentary on and translation of the Pentateuch). Advancing the cause of enlightened Judaism as they understood it they supported Mendelssohn's stand vis-à-vis the traditionalist rabbis in a halakhahic (pertaining to Jewish law) controversy concerning the Jewish custom of early and immediate burial of the dead. The German authorities demanded a modification of this Jewish custom, which the traditionalists could not accept. Mendelssohn was summoned by the Jewish community to intercede on its behalf, and in the process he endeavored to prove—using his typical rhetorical technique of tracing similar practices to talmudic sources—that there was nothing wrong with the suggested new burial practices. Thus the editors undertook to defend both Wessely and Mendelssohn against the attacks of their Orthodox rivals.

The editors were tenacious in publishing articles, fables, poems, and satiric pieces in support of their Enlightenment agenda. They disseminated their ideology by educating their public through variegated articles on natural sciences, world history, education, and biographies of meritorious personalities. They urged their readers to widen their horizons by becoming Maskilim in their world outlook, their conduct, and in their manners. All in all, the tenor of Haskalah was that of the Enlightenment: to learn, explore, doubt, question, and probe.

The contribution of this group of Haskalah writers to the rebirth of Hebrew language and Hebrew culture may be considered in a few major areas of endeavor, beginning with the use of the Hebrew language. In no other realm of their Enlightenment enterprise did the Maskilim face as difficult a task as in the area of language. They had to cope with the existing classical structures, forms, and idioms of historical Hebrew that were used continuously prior to the period of the Enlightenment in rabbinic responsa, halakhahic writings, philosophical, historical, and grammatical treatises, as well as in belles lettres.

The Haskalah was innovative in its concept of language and its approach to the use of Hebrew. First and foremost, writers who were a part of this movement expressed a strong pride in the Hebrew language and in its aesthetic qualities. They further emphasized their strong belief in its potential to be used for modern purposes. Thus they undertook to explore the modern linguistic capabilities inherent in that ancient language, although they still referred to it by the traditional term "the holy tongue."

In keeping with the prevailing notion of language and its effect on thought and morality, the Maskilim rejected Yiddish, which they considered a "corrupted language." Instead, they preferred either the "purity" of German as their vernacular and literary expression, or the revived form of Hebrew. They rejected the contemporary rabbinic idiom and its careless use of grammar. This rejection, however, was easier said than done. Many of them still resorted to the old rabbinic stylistic practices to which they were accustomed. Other writers rejected the rabbinic euphuism, a high lofty use of Hebrew, for yet another type of euphuism based on the Hebrew Bible.

These writers' first inclination was indeed to use the biblical idiom, which they considered to be the epitome of linguistic purity. Although they could employ the biblical idiom in timely poetry and in poetic drama, however, it lacked the vocabulary and linguistic forms adequate for philosophical or linguistic treatises, let alone for contemporary issues and modern ideas in secular subjects such as education, history, and the sciences. Trained in the medieval works of Jewish philosophy and theology (as autodidacts, to be sure), the Maskilim's natural inclination was to turn to medieval Hebrew for their nonbelletristic writings.

Reviewing some other literary traditions in the medieval Hebrew corpus, many of these Hebrew writers rejected the *piyyut* (liturgy) and its style of Hebrew. They could not accept the *paytanim*'s excessive use of poetic license in innovating new forms in Hebrew for the sheer need of a rhyme or for other aesthetic purposes. Their linguistic freedom in coining new words, regardless of grammatical rules, was severely criticized by the Maskilim.

As part of their concentration on the Hebrew language, they began to probe the historical and linguistic aspects of Hebrew and published voluminous works on Hebrew grammar. Many of their grammatical and biblical studies involving commentaries on the meaning of synonyms and obscure words in the Bible were published in *Hame'asef*.

The linguistic tension between biblical Hebrew, talmudic idiom, and medieval usage continued to be felt throughout the Haskalah period. It was finally synthesized by Mendele Mocher Sfarim (Shalom Yaakov Abramowitz, 1835/36– 1917) in the latter period of Hebrew Enlightenment, toward the end of the nineteenth century.

Simultaneous with its effort to revive the Hebrew language, the Haskalah launched a major drive to revive Hebrew culture and Hebrew literature. This literary endeavor was expressed in a number of areas of creativity in both the classical and contemporary spheres. It was published in *Hame'asef* and in separate books printed by the Maskilim's publishing house.

In terms of classical writings, the republication effort of the Maskilim emphasized a new edition of the latter books of the Bible and new editions of medieval works. Joel Brill, Isaac Euchel, and Aaron Wolfssohn published new editions of the biblical books (Brill, *Psalms,* 1785; Euchel, *Mishlei,* 1790; Wolfssohn and Brill, *The Five Scrolls,* 1807) with introductions, new commentaries, and translations into German. This project emanated from Mendelssohn's school of the *Be'ur.* Another Maskil, Juda Leib Ben-Zeev, published his *Introduction to the Scripture* (1810). Many pages of *Hame'asef* were devoted to reviews and assessment of the new translations, as well as to polemics in defense of Mendelssohn's enterprise and his followers.

Another major undertaking was the republication of medieval philosophical works, such as Judah Halevi's *Hakuzari* (by Isaac Satanow, 1795) and Maimonides' *Moreh Nevuchim* (Guide for the perplexed; 1796) with new, up-to-date commentaries written by the Maskilim. Similarly, they republished the inaccessible belletristic tome of Immanuel Haromi, *Mahberot Immanuel* (also published by Satanow, 1796). This creative Maskil, Isaac Satanow (1732–1804), was very active in the publication of other traditional books, such as the Book of Psalms (1794), the Book of Job (1799), and Passover *Haggadot* (1785). He also published Aristotle's *Ethics* (1790) in Hebrew. It was a modest beginning of a Jewish publication project that was to be proposed in the twentieth century by Hayim Nachman Bialik as the library of classical Jewish sources.

Another principal characteristic of Haskalah as a modern, up-to-date literature was manifested in its writers experimenting with a variety of new or revived literary genres. These genres were taken from the classical Hebraic corpus and from the surrounding European literatures. It was Isaac Satanow who undertook the task of reviving some classical Hebrew genres with a modern slant. He selected the genre of biblical wisdom writing as a model and patterned his *Mishlei Asaf* (Proverbs of Asaf; 1789–1802) on this classical form. Emulating the traditional façade of a published biblical text, he added his own commentaries below the core text, and to make things more attractive, he attributed the text to an ancient Levite. Satanow also revived the medieval genre of the religious disputation and composed a contemporary story, *Divrei Rivot* (Words of dispute; ca. 1800), patterned on *Hakuzari,* which he had published previously.

As another means of bringing Hebrew literature up to date, writers of the Hebrew Enlightenment emulated contemporary European literary genres and modes such as epistolary writing, travelogues, utopia, satire, biography, autobiography, and dialogues of the dead. Isaac Euchel (1756–1804), a prolific writer and editor of *Hame'asef,* is credited with introducing a number of European literary genres. He was indeed one of the literary innovators and a bridge builder between cultures. Following the pattern of Montesquieu's *Lettres Persanes,* he composed an original epistolary writing entitled "Igrot Meshulam" (The letters of Meshulam; 1790), which was published serially in *Hame'asef.* This is not the only early modern satiric piece in Haskalah literature, but it may be considered uniquely utopian in its portrayal of an ideal picture of a Jewish society of the past. Mixing genres was common in European literature of that century. Similarly, Satanow's religious disputation piece, *Divrei Rivot,* mentioned above, also contains a section with a utopian element. In it, the author envisions the righteous and enlightened king helping to build an ideal Jewish society that, guided by the ideas and ideals of the Enlightenment, achieves both cultural and social emancipation.

Another Maskil, Saul Berlin (1740–94), also wrote a satiric masterpiece, *Ktav Yosher* (An epistle of righteousness; 1795). He wrote it in defense of another Haskalah writer, Naphtali Wessely, who was engaged in a dispute with traditional rabbis concerning educational reforms. This satire contains some of the most bitter and critical remarks about contemporary Judaism and Jews.

Borrowing a popular genre from European literature, Aaron Wolfssohn introduced the dialogues of the dead to Hebrew literature. In his "Sihah Be'eretz Hahayim" (Dialogue in the land of the living; 1794–97), he enlisted the figures of Maimonides and the deceased Mendelssohn to argue with a fanatic rabbi and defend the ideals of Haskalah. This piece was serialized in *Hame'asef.* Another Hebrew Maskil, Tuvyah Feder (ca. 1760–1817), used the genre of the dialogue of the dead in his piece, *Qol Mehazezim* (Voices of the archers; 1853, written in 1813), as an invective against another Haskalah writer, Menahem Mendel Lefin (1749–1826), for his translation of *Mishlei* (Proverbs) to allegedly Yiddish-like German. Many other writers also published regular dialogues and didactic dialogue, which were used for educational purposes, as was customary at the time.

Another European literary genre, the travelogue, served the Italian Maskil Shmuel Romanelli (1757–1814) in depicting Jewish society in Morocco in the 1780s in his *Masa Ba'rav* (Travail in an Arab land; 1793). *Hame'asef* published a shorter travelogue by Euchel that described a trip back to his birthplace in Copenhagen. It was Euchel who contributed to the modern biography in his book-length portrayal of Moses Mendelssohn. This genre, too, served the purpose of Haskalah because it promoted the figure of the "Jewish Socrates," as Mendelssohn was called. Other biographies of Jewish luminaries, such as Isaac Abravanel and Moses Maimonides, were published in *Hame'asef,* which also serialized Euchel's biography. These personalities were selected for a biographical sketch because their philosophy was thought to have adhered to and supported Haskalah ideology. Their portrayal, too, served to exemplify the typology of an enlightened and openminded spiritual leader who is loyal to Jewish tradition.

Resorting to another popular genre, the enlighteners, some of them following contemporary European writers and others in the footsteps of the best of Jewish tradition, published hundreds of fables.

Needless to say, Hebrew writers also expressed their creative energy through some other types of writings concurrent with the above; some of them wrote allegorical dramas, biblical dramas, and biblical epics. The Hebrew novel is a phenomenon that was to appear only years later, in 1853, with the historical novel by Abraham Mapu, *Ahavat Zion* (The love of Zion). The short story, too, emerges in the second half of the nineteenth century, although some initial attempts may be found earlier.

The efforts of Hebrew Haskalah in Germany were geared toward reviving Hebrew culture. The major thrust of its activities was reorienting modern Hebrew culture toward the secular and the mundane, highlighting the utilitarian and practical, and emphasizing aesthetic values that were based on contemporary European standards. Revival of Hebrew was part of the Maskilim's attempt to revive the people and resuscitate the Hebrew culture. There was no conflict with their German orientation, and their adherence to Hebrew culture exemplified their perception that their Jewish identity could be presented in terms acceptable to their fellow German enlighteners.

Education was deemed by the Haskalah to be the most important tool for changing Jewish society. In their published essays on modern education, pedagogy, and curriculum, the Maskilim advocated introducing a modern secular curriculum and a revised religious teaching into the educational system. Toward this end, they published catechisms and numerous textbooks for use in Jewish schools. Informal education was also on their agenda, and they produced lengthy articles on world history, the history of other religions and cultures, science, nature, psychology, and ethics.

Hebrew Haskalah in Germany was short-lived. *Hame'asef* ceased publication in 1797 and resumed its appearance in 1808–9, only to shut down three years later. There had been great expectations upon its foundation in 1783, and a bitter desperation at its end. It was Euchel who in 1800 bemoaned the changing times in his florid style: "I have also tasted the dregs of the cup of trembling which came on the nation of Judea and its enlighteners. The days of love have passed, gone are the days of the covenant between me [or: between it, namely the Hebrew language] and the children of Israel. . . . They have run away, and they have gone!" The activities of *Hame'asef,* and this group's initial struggle for Haskalah, were continued, however, as other centers of Hebrew literature came into being in Eastern Europe.

Bibliography

Shmuel Feiner, "Yitzhak Euchel-Ha'yazam' Shel Tenu'at Hahaskalah Begermanyah," [Hebrew] *Zion* 52, no. 4 (1987): 427–69; Menuhah Gilbo'a, *Lexicon Ha'itonut Ha'ivrit Bame'ah* [Hebrew] (Tel Aviv: Tel Aviv University, 1986),, Meir Gilon, *Qohelet Musar Lemendelssohn Al Reka Tekufato* [Hebrew] (Jerusalem: Israel Academy of Sciences and Humanities, 1979); *Hame'asef* [Hebrew] 1783–1797, 1808–1811; Avraham Holtz, "Prolegomenon to a Literary History of Modern Hebrew Literature," *Literature East and West* 11 (1967): 253–70; Jacob Katz, *Tradition and Crisis* (New York: Schocken, 1977); Joseph Klausner, *Historiah Shel Hasifrut Haivrit Hahadashah* [Hebrew] (Jerusalem: Ahiasaf, 1952); Yeruham Fishel Lachover, *Toldot Hasifrut Haivrit Hahadashah* [Hebrew] (Tel Aviv: Devir, 1927, 1963); "Nahal Habesor," *Hame'asef* [Hebrew] (n.p., 1783); Moshe Pelli, *The Age of Haskalah* (Leiden: Brill, 1979), 185, n. 55; Pelli, *Bema'avkei Temurah* [Hebrew] (Tel Aviv: University Publishing Projects, 1988); Pelli, "Criteria of Modernism in Early Hebrew Haskalah Literature: Towards an Evaluation of the Modern Trends in Hebrew Literature," *Jewish Education and Learning,* ed. Glenda Abramson and Tudor Parfitt (Chur, Switz.: Harwood, 1994), 129–42; Hayyim Nachmann Shapira, *Toldot Hasifrut Haivrit Hahadashah* [Hebrew] (Tel Aviv: Massada, 1967); Aaron David Shohat, *Im Hilufei Tekufot* [Hebrew] (Jerusalem: Bralik Institute, 1960); Eisig Silberschlag, *From Renaissance to Renaissance* (New York: Ktav, 1973); David Sorkin, *The Transformation of German Jewry, 1780–1840* (New York: Oxford University Press, 1987); Shalom Spiegel, *Hebrew Reborn* (New York: Macmillan, 1930); and Meyer Waxman, *A History of Jewish Literature* (New York: Bloch, 1941).

MOSHE PELLI

1792–93 Salomon Maimon writes his *Lebensgeschichte* (Autobiography), a reflection on his life in the (Polish) East and the (German) West

In his essay "On Salomon Maimon" (1801), the well-known German-Jewish philosopher and mathematician Lazarus Bendavid recollects his first encounter with Salomon Maimon. It was in 1780, and Bendavid, only eighteen years old, was still living in his parents' house. He was celebrating the Purim feast with his family when, just as they had started with dinner, a stranger knocked at the door. During the Purim holidays, Jews who did not live in Berlin were allowed to enter the city and beg for money or a meal, but Maimon, the stranger in question, did not have simple begging in mind. It was his second visit to Berlin, and this time he hoped to find a sponsor and to extend the visit into a prolonged stay.

Maimon was a Polish Jew, and in 1780 he was about twenty-five years old. A rabbi and an expert on the Talmud since his early youth, Maimon had also begun to study mathematics and philosophy. For these new interests, Berlin seemed very much like a promised land. After all, this was the city of Moses Mendelssohn, the homeland of contemporary philosophy, and the capital of the German Enlightenment for Jews and non-Jews alike. And even if Maimon did not quite speak German yet, he had already begun to read German books voraciously. All he needed was a room (not necessarily one of his own), a minimum of food and drink, and, of course, a great number of books. Bendavid's family was willing to supply this stranger with what was needed, and Maimon's residence in Berlin began.

At about the same time, Karl Philipp Moritz, a teacher at the graues Kloster, one of the best known (and still existent) high schools in Berlin, contemplated a new scholarly discipline, the *Experimentalseelenlehre*. In an essay published in 1782, "Aussichten zu einer Experimentalseelenlehre," Moritz defines his subject as a pedagogical enterprise. He describes his experience of having entered the "youthful hearts" of his students for the purpose of gaining knowledge, and wonders whether it would be possible to observe the hearts of friends and strangers as well. Moritz wanted to publish these observations in a journal; they could serve as "mirrors" for its readers, who would then be able to reflect upon the lives of others as well as upon their own. In contrast to medical doctors, who had largely abstained from a discussion of individuals and individual psyches, Moritz's project would be true to the Enlightenment spirit and trace the general human mind via its peculiarities or aberrations.

Moritz's notion of the Experimentalseelenlehre derived from Johann Gottlob Krüger's study, the *Experimental-Seelenlehre* (1756), but Mendelssohn, interested in Moritz's ideas, was eager to suggest a change. Not the experiment, but the experience seemed to be of utmost importance here, and referring to a term used in Christian Wolff's *Psychologia empirica* (1732)—a work of rational philosophy to which Moritz's project would not be indebted otherwise—the title of the new journal was settled: *Gnothi sauton oder Magazin zur Erfahrungsseelenkunde.* The *Magazin* offered and encouraged empirical reports, the descriptions of and observations on the state of mind of individuals, and included self-reflections by its various authors. Published between 1783 and 1793 and received by a wide array of "educated" and "less educated" readers, it became the world's first journal of psychology and documented as well the establishment of the bourgeois citizen and his (or her) acceptable behavior.

Moritz ran his journal single-handedly until 1787, when he embarked on a trip to Italy. There, he proceeded to write essays on art and allegory that would supply Johann Wolfgang von Goethe, whose protégé he had become, with a theoretical framework for his own oeuvre. At home, another scholar and pedagogue, Carl Friedrich Pockels, functioned as a coeditor of the *Magazin,* and issued its fifth and sixth volume. Pockels, however, complemented the contributions with moralizing essays and commentaries. These lessons in morals were not the kind of pedagogy that Moritz had in mind. Upon his return, Pockels had to leave the *Magazin,* and the journal once more began to stress empirical case studies and documents of self-observation, as it had in its earlier years. By volume eight, however, the discipline of Erfahrungsseelenkunde was redefined again, and turned into a *Seelenarzneikunde,* the study of the soul as, and for the purposes of, therapeutic means. Thus, Erfahrungsseelenkunde openly complemented and sometimes even rivaled the medical sciences themselves. The person who provided this last shift from the pedagogical to the pharmaceutical became the journal's final coeditor and the publisher of volumes nine and ten: Salomon Maimon.

The Protestant teacher Moritz was a close friend of the prominent Jewish physician and *Hofrat* Markus Herz, who had studied philosophy with Immanuel Kant, and Moritz also had access to several other Jewish houses. But Moritz's social life hardly offers an explanation for Jewish readers' immense attraction to the *Magazin.* At a time when Prussian Jews themselves were deprived of citizenship, unable to reside where they wanted or even marry at will, a journal dedicated to the behavior and emotions of people perceived or perceiving themselves as outsiders seemed attractive indeed. Here was sought a knowledge that confirmed and even seemed to stretch the social boundaries. It was an Enlightenment project that not only included Jews, but that almost seemed to seek them out, and the list of its Jewish contributors is impressive. Mendelssohn supported Moritz's efforts; Herz and Bendavid supplied Moritz with material; and David Veit, a doctor who dabbled in poetry and philosophical writings, sent Moritz some of his observations. When Maimon took over the journal in 1792 as Moritz's collaborator, it had become another "first": the first German journal edited by a Jew that offered articles written by Jews for an integrated German readership.

Maimon's signed contributions to the *Magazin* were limited to reflections on human psychology and the illnesses of the mind that served as the outlines of Seelenarzneikunde, and became part of his general editorial work. In volume nine (1792) he published a case study of a delusionary Jew, reported by Bendavid, as well as the *Fragmente aus Ben Josua's Lebensgeschichte,* a sequence of unsigned articles reflecting on a Jew's life. The *Fragmente* were prefaced by Moritz, who assured his readers of the "literal" and "true" representation of these "real" events. These articles would provide an insight into the (at this point no longer youthful) heart of its subject, and would speak to the reader's heart as well. With seemingly uncensored candor, the author of the *Fragmente* proceeds to tell a life story as bildungsroman—to describe "B. J.'s" childhood in a Polish-Lithuanian village and comment on his love for science and scholarship, as well as his sexual desires.

Thus, the reader learns that B. J. was educated in a poor and impure oral language that consisted of Russian, Polish, and Yiddish expressions, but that he early on became an expert in Hebrew scriptures. Increasingly, writing rather than speech took center stage. B. J. developed a technique of alphabetic deciphering that enabled him to study German books as well as kabbalistic treatises. Although B. J. would later reject the study of the Kabbalah, the Germany encountered in his books became his adopted spiritual fatherland. Finally, B. J. discovers the writings of Moses Maimonides, whose *Guide of the Perplexed* would become the most influential text for B. J.'s search for knowledge and Enlightenment.

The *Fragmente* concentrates on B. J.'s early life and education; it is not necessary to report B. J.'s later achievements here to make his story interesting and to explain why it was fit for the *Magazin*. The success of these articles was soon followed by a book-length version of this tale, again published with an introduction by Moritz. This time, the author changed his voice from the third-person narrative that suggested an objective, scientific description to a first-person account of self-observation, a case study as autobiography. And he changed the name of his subject as well. The *Fragmente aus Ben Josua's Lebensgeschichte* turned into *Salomon Maimons Lebensgeschichte,* published in two volumes in 1792–93. As author and subject seemed to merge, the author had, apparently, found his name.

What's in a name? In Maimon's case, the choice of name is significant. Until 1812, Jews in Prussia had no legally established last names and were allowed to choose their names at will. Many referred to their father's name according to Jewish tradition; others referred to the place they came from to avoid confusion with Jews of the same first name who lived in the same town. Often, these names were changed; a man called Moses could be known as Moses Dessau first and Moses Mendelssohn later. If somebody was called Salomon, he had been given a biblical name that was probably carried by a deceased family member, and one that designated wisdom as well. If Salomon's father was named Josua, he would be called Salomon Ben Josua according to Jewish tradition. This is, indeed, the tradition in which B. J. had been raised before he exchanged his father's name for that of his chosen, intellectual father, Moses Maimonides. Thus, the difference between "Ben Josua" and "Maimon" is the difference between orthodox religion and free spirit, between tradition and Enlightenment, between East and West, and between past and present.

The revisions of the *Fragmente* as *Lebensgeschichte* tell, moreover, of the establishment of the author Maimon, under the signature of his new name. But the change of names confirms a paradox of Maimon's *Bildung* as well. As B. J. moves west to fulfill his dream of becoming a proper scholar, he is guided by the work of the medieval Jewish philosopher Maimonides rather than by any singular, modern German tome; it is Maimonides' philosophy that instigates B. J.'s final transformation from a poor, Orthodox, Polish boy into a German figure of the Enlightenment. As a German philosopher, he becomes Maimon, a second Maimonides.

In his introduction to the book, Moritz is eager to depict the early Maimon as a naïf, and to stage Maimon's life story as a pedagogical project and a lesson in therapeutic self-improvement. Maimon can stand for all poor and uneducated Jews who would find his tale exemplary—if only they were able to read and understand it. Mostly, however, Maimon's life story provides an engaging, albeit exotic account for a largely gentile audience largely unacquainted with Jewish rites or with the Eastern-Jewish wilderness. According to Moritz, moreover, the *Lebensgeschichte* offers a "neutral and unprejudiced representation of Judaism" that needs no further qualification. If Jews may appear to be a people without land, the realm of "Judaism" had clearly moved to the East. Situated within the context of Moritz's project of self-observation as a step toward understanding and possibly self-improvement, moreover, Maimon's work becomes an early instance in the series of treatises concerning the reformation of the "Jewish nation" written by David Friedländer, Christian Dohm, Friedrich Schleiermacher, and others—treatises that would engender much discussion at the turn of that century. For Moritz, the Jew is a foreigner in need of acculturation, and Maimon's search for knowledge prefigures the desire for Bildung of the *Bildungsbürgertum.* Maimon seems to agree. As Moritz suggests, Maimon is not only the subject of this book, but, as its author, his own ethnographer. For him, the East and his former life have turned into a wilderness as well. His subject may move from the East to the West, but the author can only look to and observe the East. His point of view seems firmly fixed in the West: only Maimon, not B. J., can tell this story.

Because Maimon's life should serve as an example, Moritz can avoid calling him by his name, and Moritz, indeed, does not mention it in his introduction. This is especially peculiar as Maimon had already achieved recognition under his chosen name. An ardent student of Kant, he had commented on and critiqued Kant's work and received his praise. Maimon had published a book on transcendental philosophy, *Versuch über die Transcendentalphilosophie mit einem Anhang über die symbolische Erkenntnis,* in 1790, his *Philosophisches Wörterbuch* in 1791, as well as several articles on logic and the nature of truth. Indeed, at the time of the publication of his memoirs, Maimon had already embarked on a vigorous publishing career that would eventually result in twelve books and fifty-eight articles. Several of his works are mentioned in the *Lebensgeschichte,* and Maimon alludes to the reaction of Mendelssohn, Bendavid, and Kant to his own work, as well as to his growing reputation as a scholar.

For Moritz, however, Maimon's *Lebensgeschichte* was, first of all, the case study of a man who tried to free himself from the shackles of poverty, ignorance, and superstition; one that resonated with the story of Moritz's own early life. Moritz had published this story, a description of bleak youth and deprivation, as a third-person narrative and "novel" in 1785–90; he had chosen the name Anton Reiser for his subject and the title of the book. *Anton Reiser* can be firmly placed within the tradition of pietistic introspection; a first version of the story appeared, however, as a case study of "Anton Reiser" and an exercise in Erfahrungsseelenkunde in the *Magazin* (1784). Although Maimon may represent to Moritz someone who has both come from a typical Jewish background and exerted exceptional efforts to leave it behind, Moritz's tale and the publication history of his autobiography serve as precedents for Maimon's story and Maimon's book.

Maimon's *Lebensgeschichte* does not commence with his birth. As a true ethnographer, he introduces the reader to Lithuania first, to his family's village, and his grandparents' life. These are the surroundings into which Maimon is born, in which he received his worldly and religious education, and from which there seems hardly any escape. But Maimon's tale of the continuity of families and lives is punctuated by accidents and unpredictable events. Pogroms had become part of Jewish life; thefts occur often and indeed both seem to structure experience. Most of the decisions made concerning his or his families' lives seem willful or arbitrary, and in many instances, there seems no justice at all. In this world, a boy grows up fast. Although eager to follow the path of Truth, Maimon was no innocent child himself; he stole a box from a young, wealthy friend, or hid books he was not supposed to read, because these were objects he desired. Deceit turned into the rule of survival. Destined to become a rabbi, the young Maimon was promised by his poor father to two brides at once; their families were supposed to support the fiancé in his life and studies. Clearly, it was vital that Maimon learn how to take advantage of any given situation. On his way to find Truth, Maimon protested corruption but adjusted to it.

Maimon finally married one of his fiancées at a very young age. His later move to Germany as a young man was perhaps motivated by his search for knowledge, but it appears to be a flight as well, because he abandoned his young family and the stifling life that he felt unable to change (many years later, his wife and son would journey West, too, but only to ask him for a divorce). The promised land, however, was not always able to fulfill its promises, if it had, indeed, many to make. Maimon's first attempt to gain residence in Berlin failed, and he settled temporarily in Posen. Although he tried to escape his former Orthodox surroundings, he seemed most successful in finding financial support as a rabbi or talmudic scholar; most religious tutors hired by German-Jewish families at that time came from Poland and the East. As a rabbi, however, Maimon offended his community with his unorthodox views and was soon suspected of being a heretic. Later, in Berlin, he had difficulties participating in that city's more polished social life and exasperated his Jewish and non-Jewish friends and supporters alike. He was a philosopher who enjoyed drinking and gambling. He shaved his beard and changed his clothes according to gentile fashion, but he was unable to lose his accent or assimilate completely. Although he turned away from Orthodox Judaism, he was unwilling to convert to Christianity. The Enlightenment, not Germany, proved to be his destination, and even if Judaism could be located more in the East, the geographical mapping of Enlightenment seemed somehow more elusive. At various times, Maimon left Berlin again to travel to Silesia or to journey further west. But where, indeed, does the West begin? In Posen? In Berlin? Or in the Netherlands?

When Berlin's Jewish community offered to fund Maimon's studies of *Arzneiwissenschaft* (pharmacy), he accepted the fellowship but decided not to pursue this field. Instead, he entered the gymnasium; during this time he read, translated, wrote books on philosophy, and travelled. Thus, Maimon had been most successful in losing his former home, family, and past convictions, and less successful, or not successful yet, in the matter of "true" gains. His Bildung does not translate into bourgeois achievement; Bildung and knowledge seem to part. Indeed, Maimon proves Moritz wrong, as well as Mendelssohn, who insisted on cultural "polish" as a means of social adjustment. Bildung is not what Maimon desires. He wants knowledge, the apprehension of Truth, but he is unable to attain it. For Maimon, however, this has been the Enlightenment's true promise, and he pursues this Truth with mathematical logic and psychological theory, with the instruments of geometry and talmudic rigor and an *Erfahrung* dependent on travel (*fahren*). True light, however, remains elusive. Maimon's *Bildungsgeschichte* is a history of longing, and a profoundly melancholy one. Either by choice or circumstance, Maimon, obsessed by his quest, remains alone, and thus provides a negative foil for that praised invention of the eighteenth-century: individuality.

For the chronically impoverished author, the *Lebensgeschichte* provided a slight, and only temporary, financial windfall—the expected royalties were perhaps another reason for its publication. In his last years, following the publication of his *Lebensgeschichte,* Maimon was supported by an aristocrat, Graf von Kalckreuth, who had admired this autobiography. Maimon lived on Kalckreuth's estate in Glogau, and when Maimon died in 1800, he was buried outside of the Jewish cemetery, deprived of Christian as well as of Jewish rites. Perhaps it is a final irony that, when borders changed after the World War II, this final resting place in Silesia became part of the Polish state.

In his introduction to the *Lebensgeschichte,* Moritz insists not only on the authenticity of Maimon's tale, but on Maimon's "authentic" language as well. Thus, the first printing of the *Lebensgeschichte* offers grammatical errors and stylistic imperfections. The text seems to capture Maimon's oral speech rather than represent the written word. Maimon, in turn, pursues his task of documenting the events by insisting on various details while refraining from offering any dates. In the *Lebensgeschichte,* time cannot be confirmed or measured. Memory cannot be secured by history, and as his own birth date remains unknown—he probably never knew it—so do the dates of his marriage, his entry to Berlin, and his meetings with various people. Maimon's journey is a specific, "authentic" tale, but one that seems timeless as well, and often allegorical.

The narrative, moreover, is not straightforward. There are many digressions, and stories within stories abound. Moritz's *Anton Reiser,* moreover, does not seem to provide the only model for the *Lebensgeschichte.* Elaborate chapter headings turn the model of a *Schelmenroman* (picaresque novel) into the novel of a schlemiel. Maimon's search for truth is clearly influenced by Jean-Jacques Rousseau's *Confessions.* The *Lebensgeschichte* may insist on its author and subject's moral ideals as he attempts to bare his heart, but several incidents reported by Maimon seem to be previously experienced by Rousseau. In his *Confessions,* for example, Rousseau stresses the significance of real or purported thefts, as Maimon does, and Augustine did before him. Which confession or conversion is, however, at stake? Does Maimon's life mirror Rousseau's, does he steal those scenes from Rousseau, or does he provide an allegory to his tale? And what about the other, countless, equally unmarked references to the

Bible, the Talmud, or works by authors like Christoph Martin Wieland and Jonathan Swift, references that not only comment upon, but often provoke events? Although Maimon travels in the West, his studies are reflected in a patchwork of implicit quotations that seem to force the question of whose life is narrated here, and in which voice he is able to write. Gain and loss, a matter of gambling as well as of theft, become an educational matter, too, as Maimon documents his life—and the coming into existence of Salomon Maimon—by literal (as well as social) alienation.

And if accident and discontinuity mark his life, they are made to mark his book also. In the most radical instance, Maimon interrupts his story to embed, in the middle of his book, an explication and treatise on the work of Maimonides. As Maimon insists, the reader will profit from a knowledge of Maimonides' projects, and will view it as an Enlightenment endeavor. The *Guide of the Perplexed* should not only explain Maimonides' influence on this particular life, but with luck inspire Maimon's reader as well. At this point, Maimon's pedagogy rejects the case study to provide a model for a philosophical lesson. Literally placed in the center of Maimon's life, it comments on the author as a Jew and German. Although Maimon had moved to the West, the reader will have to move to the East if he or she wants to understand him—or to conceive of the proper Enlightenment. Maimonides and Kant do not provide alternatives, but pursue a common agenda.

Once the significance of Maimonides' central placement has been recognized, the reader will be able to perceive his effect beyond any individual textual allusions. Indeed, the accidents that seem to govern Maimon's life are a structuring principle of Maimonides' text. The *Guide of the Perplexed* cannot be read straightforwardly; it calls for a decoding and for a reading that moves back and forth between individual passages in the book. Maimon's *Lebensgeschichte* resembles Maimonides' book in this respect, as do most of Maimon's philosophical works that offer gaps in the arguments and many repetitions. What may, at first glance, seem unstructured follows an established model as well. Maimon's treatise on the *Guide of the Perplexed* in the *Lebensgeschichte* is not simply an excursion to, or an interruption of, his life's story. It is also more than an expression of the author's interests, or a commentary of the significance of this philosopher for the author's thought. Maimon's treatise turns his narrative of his life into a new *Guide of the Perplexed,* providing a last transformation of Seelenarzneikunde into the therapeutics of philosophy.

In his *Confessions,* Rousseau refers to an aristocratic woman, who, being immersed in a reading of the *Nouvelle Héloïse,* misses a ball. Maimon includes in his *Lebensgeschichte* a brief allegory on the nature of metaphysics and the history of philosophy. In this allegory, philosophy is personified; she is a woman, and ready to dance. Not only pursuing philosophy, but trying to "live" it, Maimon's *Lebensgeschichte* is a contemplation of metaphysics come to life, and of Kant's *Kritik* by practical example. The *Lebensgeschichte* takes its place next to Maimon's *Streifereien im Gebiete der Philosophie,* published in 1793, or his *Versuch einer neuen Logik oder Theorie des Denkens,* published in the following year, 1794.

None of Maimon's philosophical work is widely read now. Although some critics refer to Maimon as a significant Jewish philosopher, others view him as an explicator of Kant's works. These scholars thus keep a peculiar division between the Jew and the German that can only barely capture the attraction of Kant's philosophy for many Jews of Maimon's (and later) time. Maimon's work includes an idiosyncratic philosophical dictionary, an introduction to logic, reinterpretations of idealistic philosophy, reflections on Kant's treatises, and a contemplation on talmudic tales and examples that he names "rabbinical fantasies." But when Goethe eagerly questioned his Jewish visitors, such as Veit, about Maimon's fate, he referred to the author of the *Lebensgeschichte,* a project that Goethe would soon succeed with his own life's story of talent and of privilege. And the *Lebensgeschichte* has remained the book on which Maimon's fame rests today.

Thus, readers today are more interested in Maimon's tale of becoming a philosopher than in his philosophy itself. But the resulting split between philosophy and confession, between the philosopher and the man of letters, was instigated less by Maimon than by his later publishers. It is interesting to note that editors of the subsequent editions of the *Lebensgeschichte* have been eager to improve on Maimon's style and delete his philosophical essays as digressions. Thus, they have completed the task of acculturation that Maimon himself seemed to attempt. Maimon became the author of a "proper" autobiography. Gone with these revisions are important signs of a resistance to this acculturation, those insisted upon by Moritz as well as those that were part of Maimon's own philosophical agenda. Although Maimon's life may not appear straightforward, he was thus able to issue a straightforward narrative, one that could truly stand between *Anton Reiser* and *Dichtung und Wahrheit* as a peculiar classic.

Moritz's insistence that Maimon's book would tell the truth about "Jewish" life has been easily maintained, for the philosopher turned not only into the writer, but into the Jew par excellence. A few years after his death, Wilhelm Friedrich Grattenauer referred to Maimon in his pamphlet *Wider die Juden: Ein Wort der Warnung* (1803), and described him as a man "of sharp intelligence" ("mit großem Scharfsinn," 15) who lacked practical wisdom as well as taste. For Grattenauer, Maimon was still a philosopher primarily, although one who had turned transcendental philosophy—quite possibly, a Jewish ploy itself—into an economic currency. Grattenauer did not define poverty as a characteristic of the Jew, but a *Verstand* (reason, intelligence) that could be translated into wealth; this Verstand as *Scharfsinn* could turn, however, into the Jew's final downfall, as the term itself assumed the derogatory properties of an anti-Semitic slur. Almost a century later, George Eliot's Daniel Deronda would pick up a copy of the revised and translated *Lebensgeschichte* in a London book stall, and Maimon's autobiography would help him discover his own Jewish roots. It is neither Moritz's insistence on poverty and superstition (something that Jews should overcome), nor Grattenauer's stress on *Scharfsinn* (something that Jews can never overcome) that are emblematic for Daniel Deronda's understanding of Jewish life, but the story of the Jew as social outsider and the

tale of an individual's suffering. That Maimon had been a philosopher seems incidental. In Eliot's novel, Maimon's life is romanticized, and his story serves as a means to undo acculturation, now viewed as the more inappropriate and plainly undesirable path. Maimon's social rebellion and his search for Truth became finally Deronda's (unavoidable) return to, and his embrace of, Jewish faith and fate.

If Moritz's Erfahrungsseelenkunde had envisioned social integration, Eliot's novel provides a happy end that confirms the power of one's birth. Moritz's subject may have been an unhappy man, but he was not supposed to lose his belief in the possibility of acculturation. Eliot's subject begins as an acculturated one: only to learn about the determination of his Jewish fate. Despite the novel's happy end, it is perhaps Eliot's vision that proved more disastrous when taken to its extremes. Somewhere between Erfahrungsseelenkunde and *Daniel Deronda*, however, rest the options for German Jews in the nineteenth century—and the contemporary options for interpreting Maimon's life and *Lebensgeschichte* as well.

Bibliography

Samuel Atlas, *From Critical to Speculative Idealism: The Philosophy of Solomon Maimon* (The Hague: M. Nijhoff, 1964); Zwi Batscha, "Nachwort," *Salomon Maimons Lebensgeschichte: Von ihm selbst geschrieben und herausgegeben von Karl Philipp Moritz*, ed. Zwi Batscha (Frankfurt a. M.: Insel, 1984), 331–92; Lazarus Bendavid, "Über Salomon Maimon," *National-Zeitschrift für Wissenschaft, Kunst und Gewerbe in den preußischen Staaten, nebst einem Korrespondenz-Blatte* 1 (1801): 91–93; Samuel Hugo Bergman, *The Philosophy of Solomon Maimon*, trans. Noah J. Jacobs (Jerusalem: Magnes Press, 1967); Achim Engstler, *Untersuchungen zum Idealismus Salomon Maimons* (Stuttgart-Bad Canstatt: Fromann-Holzboog, 1990); Sander L. Gilman, *Jewish Self-Hatred: Anti-Semitism and the Hidden Language of the Jew* (Baltimore, Md.: Johns Hopkins University Press, 1986), 124–32; Salomon Maimon, *Gesammelte Werke,* ed. Valerio Verra, vols. 1–4 (Hildesheim: Olms, 1965); Karl Philipp Moritz, ed., *Gnothi Sauton oder Magazin zur Erfahrungsseelenkunde als ein Lesebuch für Gelehrte und Ungelehrte: Mit Unterstützung mehrer Wahrheitsfreunde,* 1–10 (1783–93; no volume appeared in 1790), reprint, ed.

Anke Bennholdt-Thomsen and Alfredo Guzzoni (Lindau: Antiqua, 1979); Günter Niggl, *Die deutsche Autobiographie im 18. Jahrhundert* (Stuttgart: Metzler, 1977), 141–44; Nathan Rotenstreich, *Experience and Its Systematization: Studies in Kant* (The Hague: Nijhoff, 1965), 100–110; Liliane Weissberg, "Erfahrungsseelenkunde als Akkulturation: Philosophie, Wissenschaft und Lebensgeschichte bei Salomon Maimon," *Der ganze Mensch: Anthropologie und Literaturwissenschaft im achtzehnten Jahrhundert,* ed. Hans Jürgen Schings (Stuttgart: Metzler, 1994), 298–328; Ernst Peter Wieckenberg, "Juden als Autoren des *Magazins zur Erfahrungsseelenkunde:* Ein Beitrag zum Thema 'Juden und Aufklärung in Berlin,'" *Zeitschrift für Litera-* *turwissenschaft und Linguistik,* Beiheft 14 (Göttingen: Vandenhoeck & Ruprecht, 1987), 128–40; Conrad Wiedemann, "Zwei jüdische Autobiographien im Deutschland des 18. Jahrhunderts: Glückel von Hameln und Salomon Maimon," *Juden in der deutschen Literatur: Ein deutsch-israelisches Symposium,* ed. Stéphane Moses and Albrecht Schöne (Frankfurt a. M.: Suhrkamp, 1986), 88–113; Ralph-Rainer Wuthenow, *Das erinnerte Ich: Europäische Autobiographie und Selbstdarstellung im 18. Jahrhundert* (Munich: Beck, 1974), 101–9; and Sylvain Zac, *Salomon Maimon: Critique de Kant* (Paris: Les Editions du Cerf, 1988).

LILIANE WEISSBERG

1804 Madame de Staël pays a visit to the Berlin salons of the lucky Jewish dilettantes

In April 1804, Germany's intellectuals were flattered to receive a visit from the notorious, opinionated, important, and self-important Madame Germaine de Staël. If they later happened to read her book reporting on her visit, however, they might well have felt that their esteem had been misplaced, for she cast a disdainful eye on the social life of most of the country. Berlin was for her a significant exception. There, she rejoiced at the "wide diversity" of men who gathered in the salons. But, she went on, "This happy mixture is not yet extended to the society of the women" in Berlin. She found some women whose "talents and accomplishments" were considerable. She argued, however, that "at Berlin, as well as throughout the rest of Germany, female society is not as well amalgamated as that of the men." But in spite of their failure to "amalgamate" as a "happy mixture," she concluded that the German women "were superior to the men." She saved her most painful sting for the end, when she concluded that "there is nothing more clumsy, more smoke-filled in the moral as in the physical sense, than German men" (Staël-Holstein 1914, 166).

Madame de Staël's views can hardly be attributed to her ignorance of the city's leading *salonnières*. On that April visit, she had dinner with the Duchess Dorothea von Courland and spent an entire day chatting with Rahel Levin. De Staël's special Frenchwoman's eyes may have made it hard for her to judge the Berlin women in the correct national setting. Wealthy, educated women could enjoy considerable cultural influence in France, but such influence was enormously difficult for wealthy women to achieve in Germany. Even by the first years of the nineteenth century, Germany remained thin in female intellectuals. To be sure, the sheer number of women publishing in Germany was steadily increasing in these years. But when they did publish, German women still found it difficult to translate those printed words into public influence. Thus precisely because their very appearance as salon hosts was unusual then in Germany, de Staël's disappointment in the Berlin salonnières is puzzling. Should posterity, too, find them wanting?

The salon era in Berlin began in 1780, when Henriette Herz began hosting the city's first real salon. Some twenty-six years later, when French troops marched into the city in October 1806, the salon years passed into history, almost overnight. First the privations of the French occupation made relaxed sociability impossible. Then, as political resistance to French domination grew stronger, salons and their Jewish leadership came to be seen as suspect, French, foreign. But during the quarter century between 1780 and 1806, my collective biography has uncovered a total of sixteen

This essay is a very much revised and shortened version of chapter 6 of my *Jewish High Society in Old Regime Berlin* (New Haven: Yale University Press, 1988).

salons, which provided some one hundred partici-pants a special sort of social life indeed. There were sixty-nine men and thirty-one women among the total guests at all sixteen salons. But because ten of the thirty-one women led their own salons, this left only twenty-one women to be "merely" guests at other salons. Surviving con-temporary reports confirm the picture provided by the numbers. One observer actually com-plained that very few women could be found at Rahel Levin's salon. Dorothea Veit, another Jew-ish salonnière, lamented that women were not encouraged to join the discussion at Henriette Herz's salon. Dorothea von Courland was appar-ently the only salonnière who had a sizable num-ber of female guests at her salon. Contemporaries explained this by her elevated social position as a duchess. Her place at the summit of the social hierarchy offered von Courland the freedom to invite as many women as she wished. So if Ma-dame de Staël was looking for an all-female circle in the salons, that she certainly would not have found.

When we look at just which women partici-pated in salons, we are left to puzzle over de Staël's disappointment that the salon women were not a more diverse group. Her complaint that the salon women were not as much of a "happy mixture" as the salon men were may well have been a reaction to how few Christian com-moners there were among the thirty-one salon women. Whereas over half of the sixty-nine men in salons were Christian commoners, only seven salon women, well under a fifth of the women, were neither noble nor Jewish. It follows that female salon society was proportionately denser in Jews and nobles than was male salon society; there were twelve Jewish and twelve noble women in salons. Now this noble-Jewish mixture among the women was every bit as unusual for Germany in those years, perhaps even more un-usual than was the noble-commoner mixture among the Christian salon men that pleased de Staël so much. The absolute numbers of noble and Jewish women were obviously tiny, but the sym-bolic implications in contemporary Berlin were volatile. Perhaps we would be well to let the mat-ter rest by concluding that de Staël must have

considered the leading role of Jewish women in Berlin society odious rather than happy.

But let us return to her positive reactions. When de Staël praised the salon women's "talents and accomplishments," we would be mistaken to assume that she meant publication. That would be to miss the historical point altogether. For it was precisely women who did not publish who were able to use the salon to play a public cultural role, a public role that was difficult for un-published women in other times and places to fulfill, especially in Germany. These female dilet-tantes made the salon world go round. In terms of sheer numbers, they dominated; two-thirds of the women in salons were dilettantes. But their importance went beyond numbers. The whole notion of being influential without publishing defined the salon's uniqueness as an institution. A well-informed dilettante who worked at making learned conversations more witty and sophisti-cated was playing an important role in a national intellectual life whose ambiance had long been provincial and professorial. Moreover, some salon women's ambitions went beyond the evanescent pleasures of urbane discourse. They intended to make a far more important contribution to high culture, for they had in mind that salon dialogues would improve their male guests' written style as well. Madame de Staël would certainly have ap-proved of this endeavor! Perhaps if the Berlin salonnières had been more successful in this aim, Berlin's male intellectuals might have appeared less "clumsy" and "smoke-filled" than de Staël found them during her 1804 visit.

Dilettantes born into the nobility were central indeed in female salon society, although they usu-ally exercised their power without hosting their own salons. This shows how different the Berlin salons were from most salons in the European past. In many past salons, the central figure had been a queen or a princess who inspired the male authors and literally dispensed the patronage. Thus when Jewish women not only assumed the leading role in Berlin but prominent nobles also accepted their cultural and social leadership, this was new, unusual, notable. But not all noble-women were equally open to mixing with Jewish women, however high their social position had become. Noblewomen who either themselves belonged to the ruling family, or were close to court circles, tended to keep their distance from the Jewish salons. We know from their letters, however, that these courtly noblewomen made sure to be very well-informed about what went on there.

Noblewomen married to state officials, in contrast, often developed real friendships with Jewish salonnières. A famous example was Caroline von Humboldt, the wife of the very important scholar and statesman Wilhelm, who for a time was intimate with Rahel Levin. But this particular friendship later came to a painful end in the Napoleonic years, when Caroline, following the prevailing mood in Berlin, turned anti-Semitic. There was also a more rebellious sort of noblewoman whose unconventional behavior surpassed even the rather permissive sexual practices enjoyed in these years by many in the Prussian nobility. When bold, iconoclastic noblewomen such as Josephine von Pachta and Katherine von Schlabrendorff befriended the Jewish salon women, they very much helped to legitimize the Jewish women's leadership role. These friendship patterns show that Jewish women were drifting into the fringes of noble society through intimacies with noblewomen long before they actually married into the nobility.

The presence of even a few Christian commoner dilettantes in female salon society shows its difference from male salon society. Among the men, only nobles enjoyed the privilege of coming to salons without having published. Thus all of the Christian commoner and Jewish men in salons had succeeded in getting their work in print. For men, salon participation seems to have been a reward for quiet accomplishment at the desk. Not so for the women, who did not need to publish to participate in salons. The four commoner dilettantes among the salon women had no counterparts whatsoever among the men. Three of the four were actresses. (This classification of actresses as dilettantes clearly illustrates that in this group I include anyone who did not publish, not just those about whom we know that they wrote "literarily significant" letters.) The actresses' presence in salons shows how dramatically their standing had improved in Germany. Like the

Jewish women, they too must have been honored to mix with nobles. And like the Jewish women, the actresses were often romantically involved with prominent noblemen in salons. Across the wide social divide that separated actresses from nobles, both circles seem to have shared an emancipated sensual style. Perhaps this is one reason why contemporaries sometimes complained that salons contributed to Berlin's reputation as a "loose" city in those years.

The remaining eight dilettantes among the salon women were Jewish. They were altogether central, for six of the eight led their own salons. The intellectual level of the Jewish dilettantes was very high, often higher than that of the Jewish women authors. That dilettantes could be smarter and enjoy more social power than authors rings absolutely true for the salon setting. The individual whose life best illustrates this truth was Rahel Levin. Her conversations, letters, and aesthetic judgments earned her the admiration of many important male intellectuals. However much she may have had posterity in mind when she wrote her thousands of letters, she did not seem to think that publication of those letters was the only route to contemporary or even posthumous fame.

Rahel Levin may well have been especially smart and especially charismatic, but she definitely was not the only example of her type. The two Meyer sisters, Sara and Marianne, used their mastery of French, their character sketches, their letters, and even their advantageous intermarriages to good advantage in attracting prominent noble guests to their salons. When it became known that Marianne Meyer was corresponding with a writer of no less stature than Johann Wolfgang von Goethe in Weimar, her status in Berlin obviously skyrocketed. Philippine Cohen was popular with a younger set, the intellectual friends of her children's Christian tutors. But her ability to host this circle in style disappeared overnight when her extremely wealthy husband went bankrupt in 1804 and fled Berlin to escape his creditors.

Amalie Beer's sophisticated beauty; her husband's wealth; her sons' literary, scientific, and musical talents; and the elegance of her home all contributed to her success as a salonnière. Sara Levy was known to be a fine pianist, and although her conversational skills were apparently somewhat dull, her home in the center of town continued to be frequently visited well into the nineteenth century. These two Jewish salonnières are especially interesting, because both remained married to their Jewish husbands. This practice was definitely not typical for this set, for most of the salon women converted and married Christians. That these two women could lead salons without converting and marrying Christians indicates that it was not absolutely necessary to exit Judaism in order to host a salon.

These eight Jewish dilettantes were lucky. They exercised considerable cultural influence without suffering the stress and loneliness of writing for publication. Nor was this their only gift from fate. They also were the rare Jews (of either gender) who found a way to social prominence at a time when Jews in Germany did not yet enjoy civic emancipation. The complete absence of male Jewish dilettantes in salons reveals this opportunity as "gendered." Another way to see the luck of the Jewish dilettantes is to ponder Fanny Lewald's picture of Rahel Levin's life. Fanny Lewald was a prolific Jewish novelist of the next generation in Berlin, who wrote a historical novel based on Rahel Levin's life. The novel is suffused with nostalgia for Levin's many friendships with nobles, especially with Prince Louis Ferdinand of Prussia. That Lewald, who achieved the authorship that Levin did not, would so envy Levin is the best illustration of the apparent impossibility only one generation later of achieving what Rahel Levin had achieved. That Levin paid for her prominence with insults from her powerful friends is not the point. The point is that she had the chance to choose to pay in pain for her social glory.

Still, there were other Jewish women in salons who did endure the sufferings and sometimes reaped the rewards of writing for publication. Some clearly needed the money, some probably craved that sort of respect, and all of them, at some level, no doubt enjoyed the intellectual challenges. However their motives for publishing differed, the barriers that female authors of the salon world confronted were remarkably similar, regardless of social rank or religion. Although some salon women were trying to create a subculture that would aid the lives and work of their male guests, they do not seem to have provided each other with practical aid or intellectual inspiration, either in or out of the salon setting. The men they met in salons were actually a more frequent source of patronage for them. But even this male aid could not solve the central dilemmas of their lives and their work, which lay mainly in the private world. For the truth was that family wealth in itself by no means guaranteed education. Some salon authors, especially the noble and Jewish ones, were born to wealth. Still, a daughter bent on an intellectual life usually had to fight against her family to obtain an education.

Perhaps more important, arranged marriages, which made the wife's intellectual work difficult or even impossible, were a problem that cut across the social hierarchy. Upwardly mobile arranged matches with men indifferent, if not hostile, to their wives' intellectual projects disrupted the lives of almost all of the Christian authors. And even though the Jewish authors were all quite wealthy and were often socialized in a culture that valued intellectual achievement, they too had problems reconciling authorship and marriage. For three of the four Jewish authors, breaking away from early arranged marriages was a major life event. Sometimes their divorces made possible a life richer in intellectual and emotional experiences. Yet like the divorced Christian authors in salons, for most of the Jewish authors life after divorce brought new kinds of pain—pain that did not necessarily enhance their literary productivity.

In terms of the sheer magnitude of her father's intellectual stature, Dorothea Veit, Moses Mendelssohn's daughter, was the luckiest of the four authors. Her second husband, Friedrich Schlegel, also ranked among the intellectual stars of the next generation. Yet in spite of, or perhaps because of, her relationship to these two famous men, the sum of her own literary achievements hardly constituted a satisfying intellectual career. Her early training ranked among the most thorough of any young girl who came of age in eighteenth-century Germany. Yet in her early married years, at least until she was thirty, her unusual training did not result in any publications. She herself seems to have hoped that her 1798 break with her kindly but dull first husband, Simon Veit, might have been the chance to fulfill herself intellectually. Indeed, Friedrich Schlegel was impressed with Dorothea's intellect, and he had taken a public position in support of female education. But Dorothea's intellectual life after her separation turned out to be an ironic one indeed. Her motive for publishing seems to have been principally financial; Friedrich Schlegel was a poor provider. And all of her publications were literally in Schlegel's name!

Moreover, Schlegel's personal style limited rather than enhanced her quality of life. She was abandoned by her family and even most of her Christian friends after she left Veit to move in with Schlegel when she was still legally married to Veit. This radical step was not the only reason for her subsequent isolation, for Friedrich alienated otherwise sympathetic friends with his brittle personality. It may be argued that Dorothea's alliance with Friedrich did stimulate her to intellectual productivity, in that the couple's meager finances prompted her to publish. But this view can only be adopted in retrospect. At the time, the whole situation must have been very difficult for her, because Dorothea's work conditions were very challenging. Her time to write and publish (even under Schlegel's name) was limited by the burden of more domestic labor than the typical salon woman had to endure. She was also the copyist for all of Friedrich's manuscripts and edited many of the essays published in his various aesthetic journals. Still, some critics subsequently judged Dorothea to have been a better novelist than Friedrich was. She enjoyed the esteem of several prominent male authors, some of whom worked to help her find writing assignments.

Through it all, Dorothea Veit, eventually Dorothea von Schlegel, was enthusiastic about being Friedrich Schlegel's "journeyman." Observers have found her subordination to him dismaying. Her two religious conversions—to Protestantism in 1804, and their conversion as a couple to Catholicism in 1808—were viewed by critics then and later as signs that she lacked personal integrity. This seems harsh and unhistorical. Dorothea risked a great deal when she left Veit in 1798. Her extreme loyalty to Schlegel may well have been a necessary force to enable her to leave the intense orbit of Jewish family and Jewish friends. Her subsequent isolation no doubt exacerbated her dependence on Schlegel. It may seem quite horrid today that Veit published under her husband's name. But even that was an accomplishment in the terms of her own day. That she was able to write a novel, translate many essays, and complete scores of her own essays and reviews is a testimony to her early education, as well as to her talent and tenacity.

Henriette Herz's difficulties in becoming a published author seem to have more internal than those faced by Dorothea Veit. Altogether, her life was far easier and more harmonious than Veit's or Rahel Levin's. Perhaps that very harmony limited her creativity. Herz never suffered a sharp break with the Jewish world, and unlike Veit, she enjoyed great social success. She never had to balance the consolations and the demands of a Friedrich Schlegel, who offered release from a traditional community at the price of serving his many needs. Then, too, Herz did not lose an intellectual mentor when she left her family home to wed Markus Herz, a leading physician, at the age of fifteen. He took over her training when they married and concentrated on her great strength, the acquisition of languages. He aided her intellectual development in other ways, too. His income, connections, and natural science lectures were useful, perhaps indispensable, as she opened her own salon in 1780. The couple remained childless, so motherhood posed no conflicts with authorship.

In addition to these crucial supports from her mate, Herz's close friend, the prominent preacher Friedrich Schleiermacher, nurtured her writing and continually encouraged her to devote herself more ardently to publication. With Schleiermacher's daily assistance, Herz completed two translations of English novels. Later, toward the end of her life, she wrote her memoirs, which were eventually published. But when Herz was a widow strapped for funds, she did not seek publication as a source of income. After Markus died in 1803, her social life collapsed overnight because they had spent his considerable income on entertaining and little was left to support her in the style to which she was accustomed. In the lean years of her early widowhood, Herz sought out governess positions and hosted boarders in her home but did not attempt to live on income earned by publication.

Esther Gad, a third author among the salon women, was born into a far more obscure family than either Veit or Herz. Nor did she ever achieve the notoriety the other two women enjoyed. Yet in her own modest way Gad's conflicts were similar to those experienced by Dorothea Veit. Gad was born and raised in Breslau, and as a girl she worked to learn secular subjects on her own. By the time she was ten, she often stayed up all night engrossed in a book. Her older brother agreed to teach her what he had learned on a daily basis. When he went off to Dresden for a time, she taught herself French to surprise him on his return. She subsequently taught herself Italian and then English. In 1791, when she was twenty-one, Gad achieved her first publicity with a poem she wrote for a Jewish school that opened that year in Breslau. That same year, Gad married Samuel Bernhard, a rich Jewish businessman from Frankfurt an der Oder. The couple moved to Berlin, where Esther, now Frau Bernhard, made friends with several salon women, Jewish and Christian alike.

While in Berlin, she began publishing poetry and essays. A 1798 article devoted to the theme of women's talents as authors earned her a reputation as a "second Wollstonecraft." Gad had not been in Berlin long before she made decisive changes in her personal life. In 1796, she divorced Samuel Bernhard, and in 1800, she became a Protestant. Two years later, when she was thirty-five, Gad married again, this time to a Christian physician from England. Throughout her second marriage she continued to write and publish, working zealously on a novel. Unfortunately, the volume lay unfinished when she died at fifty-three in 1823.

Rebecca Friedlaender, the youngest of the four

Jewish authors in salons, was certainly the most prolific, at least in terms of the sheer volume of novels she published—her final count was sixteen. Her first novel appeared in 1808, when she was twenty-five. A second novel, *Schmerz der Liebe* (The pain of love), which appeared in 1810, focused on the romantic entanglements in a supposedly fictional salon circle. Rahel Levin, Friedlaender's closest friend in those years, became angry when she read the novel. Levin was convinced that the main character was based on her, and she felt that this character had been portrayed negatively. The novel received a devastating reception. Her publisher had advertised the volume as being full of "lively situations," proclaiming that her "character descriptions" were the work of a "feminine sensibility" and that the book could count on the approval of the "elegant reading world." But few readers from that "elegant world" seem to have agreed. A year after the novel appeared, Karl August Varnhagen von Ense, Rahel Levin's eventual husband, published a damning review of three of Friedlaender's recent novels. He began by blaming the rush of "mediocre women's writing" on their "participation in intellectual interchanges," which led some of the women to believe that they themselves were intellectuals. Varnhagen concluded by wishing that the author would enjoy "in other circles all of the happy success which is denied to her in this one." Later Friedlaender's own nephew Paul Heyse, himself a distinguished writer, portrayed his aunt as lacking any talent whatsoever, and considered it a "riddle" how her "wretched products could have found a publisher at all."

It is not clear how much money Friedlaender earned from her novels, or how much money she actually needed. Moses Friedlaender, the husband she divorced, was, after all, the son of a rich banker and entrepreneur, and divorcing him had not left her in poverty. But even if publishing brought her neither praise nor wealth, literature did seem to have been an interest that helped her become more intimate with several noblemen. During 1805 and 1806 Friedlaender's chief literary adviser was Count von Egloffstein, whom she hoped to marry. This dream was not realized, and she next fell in love with a French noble officer stationed in Berlin. But he too declined to marry her. Some years later, Friedlaender, who had already been publishing and traveling under the name Regina Frohberg, converted to Christianity. But she never did remarry. Her story illustrates well that publishing in itself could mean little in this setting. Bright, charismatic dilettantes like Rahel Levin seemed to go further in this world than mediocre authors like Rebecca Friedlaender.

In the Berlin social world in the decades before Napoleon, literary work, published or unpublished, proved useful for entering high society. Sometimes this same literary work also helped make possible more private changes in Jewish women's lives. Nine of the twelve Jewish salon women converted; five divorced their Jewish husbands, and six married Christians. Four of these intermarriages were to nobles. These intermarriages can properly be interpreted as the culmination of the intricate process of using intellectual skills—as well as money, beauty, and whatever else one could—to improve one's social position. Then and now, some have criticized these women's lack of Jewish loyalty. Yet in their own place, in their own time, the salon women who left Judaism seem to have seen this departure as necessary for their emancipation as women, especially as women with intellectual ambitions. In that world, where caste lines were still so very rigidly drawn, their conversions, divorces, and intermarriages were experienced by all involved as exceptional. A mere handful of individuals were involved, to be sure. But because the symbolic implications were great, these women became notorious in Berlin and beyond, admired by some and despised by others. Their steps toward radical assimilation were the most extreme version of the complex social exchanges that bound the wider group of diverse salon participants together.

But none of this could be seen in the 1770s, while the women were still single and living with their families. Even a decade later, when they were still married to Jewish husbands, observers may well have judged that they were managing a successful balance of innovation and tradition. It was not until they had been mixing in salon circles for a few years that this balance unraveled into divorce, conversion, and intermarriage. The classic explanation of the salon women's eventual departure from Judaism is that unlike their brothers they received too little traditional Jewish education and too much merely "decorative" secular education. But this account overstates the difference in male and female education in Jewish Berlin during these decades. It is of course true that the women did not receive a serious Jewish education, but few of their brothers were given such training; women, however, often did receive a good secular education. Nor is it so clear that the girls' secular learning was frivolous. Even their own testimony must be interpreted carefully. Rahel Levin, for example, complained that she grew up like a "wild savage." Yet she learned a passable French from tutors, and beginning at age eighteen she used her correspondence with David Veit, a young Jewish medical student, to improve her German. She studied mathematics with a tutor; she read Voltaire, Rousseau, Kant, and Fichte. Her anger at her lack of a rigorous secular education may have been more a reflection of the high goals she set for herself than of a particularly deficient training for those times.

We must also remember the distinctive setting of Berlin in these years, for comparing Berlin to other cities further weakens an explanation that focuses on the women's early education. In other Central European cities, wealthy Jewish girls also learned French and read novels, but they did not mix socially with Christians, convert, and marry Christians as often as the Berlin women did. The point is that the key juncture in the women's journeys away from Jewishness actually came later in their lives, when they were already married and socializing in salons. It was then, when they were in their early twenties, that their lives became so different from the lives of their brothers. Educated Jewish men in Berlin found both salons and the city's intellectual clubs largely closed to them, and eventually, they had to make do by forming their own all-Jewish clubs. One key reason why the women departed from their Jewish world once they achieved social success in salons was because their marriages had been arranged when they were quite young.

There was a powerful historical logic to these arranged marriages. It followed from the wealth of their fathers, and the castelike character of the Jewish plutocracy, that marriage was a central event in preserving familial power. Early and arranged marriages were crucial if the alliance was to be made with precisely the right family. The coincidence of affluence and legal insecurity in the Jewish community made carefully chosen marriages critical.

It would be wrong to think that the salon women had resisted entering these marriages in the first place. During those years, married women were generally considered to lead freer lives than single women. With their husband's social and financial backing, they could entertain in style. For instance, Henriette Herz remembered how enthusiastic she had been to marry at fifteen. She was eager to end the privations of being a dependent daughter and begin to enjoy the privileges of being a wife. She later remembered that she was content to marry an older, unknown man if it meant being able to buy new bonnets and have her own hairdresser. But later, once they became intimate with Christian women and especially Christian men in salons, the Jewish salon women had an incentive to vote with their feet against the system of arranged marriages. That they had not married for love no doubt weakened their feelings of family loyalty as soon as Christian men seemed ready to provide the ultimate ticket into the much-desired elite of Berlin society.

We must also keep in mind that the whole story unfolded in the early days of the romantic literary movement, when personal freedom and sensual pleasure were highly valued by young intellectuals. In the end, to truly explain just why the Berlin salonnières had the chance to achieve social integration through intermarriage requires an examination of the various resources each partner brought to these intermarriages. Indeed, a person-by-person reconstruction accounts very well for the temperamental, economic, and even cultural motives individuals had for marrying across the wide divide that separated Jew from Christian in the Berlin setting. But unfor-

tunately, space will not allow even a brief summary of this more detailed account of the Jewish women's marriages.

Before they embarked upon the radical disjunctures of divorce, conversion, and intermarriage, the Jewish salon women had used their literary skills to enter a glittering gentile world. When they went on to leave their Jewish husbands and the Jewish world, they gained tremendous personal freedom. Unfortunately, perhaps inevitably, with this freedom often came condescension, even hostility, a hostility that was not always latent, from those same friends on whom they depended to build this new life. With few exceptions, it is not the women's published words that provide us the record of their poignant stories. Most of the salon women lacked the training, the support, and perhaps most notably, the incentive to publish. The texts they have left us are their lives. What excites both empathetic admiration and true historical wonder is that fate gave them the chance to venture beyond a balanced acculturation into a heady, if very risky social integration.

Bibliography

Barbara Hahn and Ursula Isselstein, eds., *Rahel Levin Varnhagen: Die Wiederentdeckung einer Schriftstellerin*, vol. 14: *Zeitschrift für Literaturwissenschaft und Linguistik* (Göttingen: Vandenhoeck & Ruprecht, 1987); Steven Lowenstein, *The Berlin Jewish Community: Enlightenment, Family, and Crisis, 1770–1830* (Oxford: Oxford University Press, 1994); Anne Luise Germaine Staël-Holstein, *Germany*, 3 vols. (London: n.p., 1914); Carola Stern, *"Ich möchte mir Flügel wünschen": Das Leben der Dorothea Schlegel* (Reinbek bei Hamburg: Rowohlt, 1990); Stern, *Der Text meines Herzens: Das Leben der Rahel Varnhagens* (Reinbek bei Hamburg: Rowohlt, 1994); Heidi Thomann Tewarson, *Rahel Levin Varnhagen mit Selbstzeugnissen und Bilddokumenten* (Reinbek bei Hamburg: Rowohlt, 1988); and Petra Wilhelmy, *Der Berliner Salon im 19. Jahrhundert (1780–1914)* (Berlin: de Gruyter, 1989).

DEBORAH HERTZ

1812 The German romance with *Bildung* begins, with the publication of Rahel Levin's correspondence about Goethe

Rahel Levin is credited with having founded the "Goethe cult" that spread from her salon to the rest of Germany. She particularly admired Goethe's *Wilhelm Meisters Lehrjahre* (1796; Wilhelm Meister's apprenticeship), which focused on the *Bildung* of a young man and is probably the most important bildungsroman in German literature. Although Bildung, an often used and frequently contested term, can be traced over five hundred years of German history, Rahel's embrace of Goethe, who came to represent the symbol of Bildung for Jews and other Germans alike, serves as a starting point for the German-Jewish romance with Bildung.

The German word *Bildung,* loosely translated as "self-formation" or "self-cultivation," combined the concept embodied in the English word "education" with a belief in the primacy of culture and the potential of humanity. Originally a theological term, in the mid-eighteenth century "Bildung" took on a new meaning that merged redemption with education. By the early nineteenth century, a secular Bildung capable of promoting morality came to replace religion in certain circles. In linking reason and education with moral development, character formation, and self-improvement, Bildung described a cultured, well-bred personality—an autonomous, harmonious person of aesthetic appreciation, ethics, and gentility.

The German bourgeoisie, well before its actual socioeconomic ascendance, had made culture a defining character of class and had used Bildung to distinguish itself from its "betters," the nobility, and its "inferiors," the peasantry and emerging working class. Class and gender specific as it was (see below), Bildung also contained an egalitarian aspect: theoretically everyone could take part. As a result, during the struggle for Jewish legal emancipation in the nineteenth century, when an economically mobile Jewish population that eagerly sought civil and political rights joined the ranks of the German bourgeoisie, bourgeois liberals urged Jews to develop their characters and intellects as a way of integrating into the middle class and into the nation. Adapting enthusiastically, Jews were "emancipated simultaneously into the age of Bildung and middle class respectability" (Mosse 1983, 69).

Emancipation, however, presumed a degraded Jewry, one that would be rewarded with citizenship after having achieved moral regeneration by acquiring Bildung. Defined by the various German states, emancipation usually presupposed reforms of Jewish occupational and community structures, religion, education, and manners. For the minority group, therefore, Bildung encompassed not only education and cultivation, as in the majority population: their legal transformation from a discriminated corporate community to a confession depended on their "improvement." Bildung and emancipation were thus inseparable and, as David Sorkin has shown, the ideal of

Bildung increasingly came to be synonymous with emancipation.

Bildung appealed to Jews because it could transcend differences of religion or nationality through the development of the individual personality. Moreover, the Jewish ideologues of emancipation (David Friedländer, David Fränkel, Joseph Wolf, Mendel Hess) embraced Bildung as compatible with elements of Judaism. Further, Bildung denoted learning through interpretive interaction with venerated texts, a process familiar to traditional Jews. Whereas the ideology of Bildung created serious controversies within Jewish communities over religious and educational reform in the early nineteenth century, individual Jews believed their own display of Bildung would enhance their roles as citizens and allow them to associate with their equally respectable middle-class neighbors. They clung to this interpretation of Bildung long after it had become nationalized and narrowed.

For newly emancipated German Jews, then, the educated bourgeois (*Bildungsbürger*) became the ideal. Jewish men could acquire the attributes of Bildung by adopting the German intellectual and scholarly traditions of the nineteenth century: by showing appreciation of intellectual and cultural pursuits, by cultivating their own personalities, and by attending schools and universities. By the 1840s Jewish men were twice as heavily represented in the universities as their proportion of the population. The Jewish student population grew rapidly. By 1886, Jews in Prussia were eight times as heavily represented as their proportion of the population and made up 10 percent of all students. During the second half of the nineteenth century, many Jewish men made careers in fields related to Bildung, becoming prominent in the theater and music, as well as in publishing, law, and medicine. They also succeeded as writers, journalists, critics, and scholars. Even businessmen could display Bildung in their support of the arts and philanthropy. Moreover, their continued adulation of Goethe made Jewish men the leading publishers, scholars, and promoters of his work.

Although it enticed women, this prominent and public version of Bildung focused on men.

Historians, too, have placed great emphasis on the male educational and intellectual elements of Bildung. Because nineteenth-century liberals did not consider women in a concept of the individual, even George Mosse's profound contribution to our understanding of Jewish identity excludes women. Mosse wrote of Wilhelm von Humboldt, Prussian minister of education (1809–10), that he provided the model for German citizenship for newly emancipated Jews: "Through fostering the growth of reason and aesthetic taste, each man would cultivate his own personality until he became an autonomous, harmonious individual. This was a process of education and character building in which everyone could join regardless of religion or background; only the individual mattered" (Mosse 1987, xiii)—only the male individual. German governments and educators ignored women's intellectual needs, excluding them from the universities (with some exceptions) until 1908. Serious self-cultivation, too, was a perilous path, offensive to a society that expected a smattering of intelligence and polish—but no more—from its women. Ute Frevert (1988) concludes: "It was never intended that female persons would take part in either a general or specialized Bildung. All . . . reform energies and theoretical insights stopped short before the barriers of gender." "Everyone" could not join the process of education and character building, because women were barred from serious study, and character was based on a male model.

Nevertheless, as was the case with many liberal concepts, Bildung expanded beyond its original boundaries. Bildung appealed to the universal by encouraging the self-cultivation of the individual—a clear invitation not only to Jews, but also to women. In addition, Bildung implied far more than simply an appropriate intellectual stance or an appreciation of high culture. It also meant manners and breeding and, therefore, included women in a private but powerful way: they were to raise a family steeped in Bildung.

In a society in which proper behavior, public and private, differed according to class, the middle classes distinguished themselves through their singular devotion to legitimation through the display of Bildung in the family. The very notion of a "bourgeois family" implied the combination of Bildung and family. Typical of the European and American bourgeoisie of the period, family and breeding signified respectability. Symbolically and practically, the familial aspect of Bildung was as important as an advanced education to bourgeois Germans of all faiths. It was of particular importance to most German Jews— male and female—who could not achieve the academic and professional heights open to a growing number of Jewish males. Their social and cultural education, however, could proceed apace within an exemplary and refined family. Culture did not begin and end with the university or the German classics. It included the creation of a model home life. Jews were conscious of the "familial" side of their cultural project of enlightenment and *embourgeoisement* from the very beginning.

Jewish women set the tone and style of this family incarnation of Bildung by affirming, and sometimes contesting, its values, roles, and relationships. They contributed to the highly prized tranquillity and steadiness of the bourgeois family, to its literate conversations, its *Gemütlichkeit* (homeyness), manners, cleanliness, orderliness, and pretensions. They created cultivated and respectable families, displaying their similarity with others of their class. Thus, Jewish women were crucial to the Bildung component of bourgeois class formation and Jewish integration. To highlight women's participation in the construction of Bildung, then, is to emphasize the significance of the family to acculturation, because a bourgeois profile was synonymous with the only "German" identity available to Jews.

Like the modest strata of German civil servants and the *Bildungsbürgertum,* Jews measured their respectability more and more in terms of their consumption patterns and their private lives. Women had to mediate between German popular culture—in the forms of music, literature, and social engagements—and their families. Women were responsible for the behavioral and cultural attainment of the family, for its Bildung. When German Jews remarked that quotations from Goethe were part of every meal, they were not only emphasizing a Jewish allegiance to

Goethe as a symbol of a progressive, enlightened tradition or as "a bridge toward acceptance through identification with Germany's cultural hero" (Mosse 1983, 45)—they were also pointing to the family context in which cultural transmission took place. A family of Bildung, discussing Goethe during a meal, constituted a German-Jewish bourgeois identity. Respectable middle-class homes demonstrated that Jews had the moral fiber to be equal citizens.

Bildung served a dual purpose for Jews, not only as their entrée into cultured German society, but also as a complement to their religiosity. For example, in the *Sulamith,* the first journal that Jews published in German (1806), religion and Bildung (including refinement of morals, civil improvement, and distinctive bourgeois gender roles) were closely connected. Later in the nineteenth century, Bildung became for many Jews "synonymous with their Jewishness." Merging Jewish traditions with German forms, "Bildung . . . was transformed into a kind of religion—the worship of the true, the good, and the beautiful" (Mosse 1983, 11). Bildung blended the Jewish tradition of learning with its secular counterpart: an appreciation of German language, literature, and etiquette. And many German Jews were predisposed to accept Bildung, as Sorkin has noted, because the Jewish ideal of man, the *talmid hakham* (talmudic scholar) as embodied in the rabbinate, had lost its attractiveness. Bildung provided a new secular ideology of learning to hold the Jewish community together. United by a yearning for Bildung, nonreligious Jews affiliated in clubs, organizations, and friendship circles, creating a dense network of Jewish social affiliations even as religious practices declined.

The familial side of Bildung was also an essential part of being Jewish. This ideal preceded embourgeoisement. Later in the nineteenth century, the family often became an extension of religious life and, increasingly, a substitute for it. The portrait of a comfortable family life became not only, as mentioned earlier, a class emblem and vehicle toward integration, but an important element of Jewish ethnic identity. Like the German middle class, Jews developed their identities around domestic values. A family of Bildung exemplified both Germanness *and* Jewishness to its members.

By the 1880s, Jews also had special issues to confront on their climb into the bourgeoisie. Increasing anti-Semitism and an influx of Eastern European Jews created new conditions. Sparkling domesticity and cultivation served not only to confirm their bourgeois credentials, but to create a huge distance between themselves and their more "backward" Eastern European coreligionists. Anti-Semites as well as some German Jews assailed the filth and stench in which Eastern European Jews ostensibly lived. Both gentiles and Jews believed that dirt could lead to decadence, but for German Jews, it could also lead to the dreaded identification with other proletarian, eastern, unacculturated Jews living in the ghettos of Berlin and other major cities. German Jews focused on eliminating dirt and smell—class symbols—from their lives. That is, they tried to translate anti-Semitism against eastern Jews into class terms, assuming—and hoping—that their own spotless and *gebildete* families and, therefore, their Jewishness, would be acceptable to bourgeois, non-Jewish Germans. Ironically, it was Germany's reputation as the land of Bildung that attracted a number of Eastern European Jews in the first place, although their loyalty was to Schiller.

German Jews also had to restrain their children from behavior attributed to Jewish children by anti-Semites. The latter depicted Eastern European Jewish children, but by implication, all Jewish children, as dirty, undisciplined, unathletic, and unmannerly—in other words, *ungebildet*. Anti-Semites castigated "Jewish" national or cultural attributes. They were quick to hurl the epithet "just like in a Jewish school" or "Jewish haste" in their disdain, and Jews were eager to show by their calm and mannerly bearing that these slurs had no semblance of reality. Jewish leaders cautioned self-control and warned against using *Jargon* (in this case, Yiddish). Niceness, gentility, and civility—Bildung—became the hallmark of Jews who sought to refute anti-Semitic stereotypes. It is no wonder that in asserting their claim to German culture—in an era spanning the careers of the early-nineteenth-

century liberal proponent of emancipation, Christian Wilhelm Dohm (who saw Jews as degenerate) and the late-nineteenth-century anti-Semite and popular historian Heinrich von Treitschke (who depicted Jews as "nothing else but German-speaking Orientals")—Jews clung to Bildung, acquiring educations and enforcing "a modulation of tone, a lowering of the decibel level" (Ascheim 1982, 9) upon themselves and their children.

Even as Jews held to the original ideals of Bildung, by the mid-nineteenth century the original sense of it became transformed. For many, Bildung had come to be identified with *Besitz* (property): those with Bildung and without it corresponded to those with means and those without. In fact, Bildung became Bildung als Besitz—as a form of intellectual and social capital, as a kind of status or pretension, as a step on a career path. Moreover, Bildung became hotly contested: it was open to all in theory but was class- and gender-specific in practice; its humanism clashed with its nationalist and statist overtones. By the late nineteenth century, the mandarins, professors, and gymnasium teachers who defended the existing order redefined and controlled the ideal. They preferred patriotism, duty, and discipline: "Prussian army barracks adorned with Doric columns and Corinthian capitals" (Ludwig Marcuse in Mosse 1983, 13).

As the concept of Bildung changed, stressing conformity and compromising with the new nationalism rather than stressing individual growth, Jews were increasingly isolated. Many remained faithful to the older version of Bildung as the concept further eroded after World War I into educational arrogance seasoned with nationalism and racism. Throughout the Nazi era, Jews maintained their steadfast devotion to the ideals of Goethe, which provided some with (false) assurances of an "other" Germany. Even in 1942, Goethe provided solace. Cora Berliner, a leader of the Reichsvertretung der Juden in Deutschland and the Jüdischer Frauenbund, met with her friend immediately before her own deportation. The friend wrote: "C. and our other friends took books along. They agreed on the selection. To my knowledge C. took *Faust* I and an anthology. When I went to visit them on the last day, shortly before their departure, they were sitting in the sun in the courtyard reading Goethe."

Bibliography

Steven E. Aschheim, *Brothers and Strangers: The East European Jew in German and Jewish Consciousness, 1800–1923* (Madison: University of Wisconsin Press, 1982); Wilfried Barner, "Jüdische Goethe-Verehrung vor 1933," *Juden in der deutschen Literatur: Ein deutsch-israelisches Symposium,* ed. Albrecht Schöne and Stéphane Moses (Frankfurt a. M.: Suhrkamp, 1986), 127–47; Werner Conze and Jürgen Kocka, *Bildungsbürgertum im 19. Jahrhundert,* vol. 2, *Bildungsgüter und Bildungswissen* (Stuttgart: Klett-Cotta, 1990); John Murray Cuddihy, *The Ordeal of Civility: Freud, Marx, Lévi-Strauss, and the Jewish Struggle with Modernity* (New York: Delta, 1974); Ute Frevert, ed., *Bürgerinnen und Bürger Geschlechterverhältnisse im 19. Jahrhundert* (Göttingen: Vandenhoeck & Ruprecht, 1988); Jürgen Kocka, ed., *Bürger und Bürgerlichkeit im 19. Jahrhundert* (Göttingen: Vandenhoeck & Ruprecht, 1987); Reinhart Koselleck, "Einleitung-Zur anthropologischen und semantischen Struktur der Bildung," *Bildungsbürgertum,* vol. 2, 11–46; George Mosse, *German Jews Beyond Judaism* (Bloomington: Indiana University Press, 1983); Mosse, "German Jews and Liberalism in Retrospect: Introduction to Year Book XXXII," *Leo Baeck Institute Year Book* (London: Secker & Warburg, 1987), xiii–xxv; Mosse, "The Secularization of Jewish Theology," *Masses and Man: Nationalist and Fascist Perceptions of Reality,* ed. George Mosse (New York: Howard Fertig, 1980), 249–62; David Sorkin, "The Impact of Emancipation on German Jewry," *Assimilation and Community,* ed. Jonathan Frankl and Steven Zipperstein (Cambridge: Cambridge University Press, 1992), 177–98; Sorkin, *The Transformation of German Jewry, 1780–1840* (Oxford: Oxford University Press, 1987); Rudolf Vierhaus, "Bildung," *Geschichtliche Grundbegriffe: Historisches Lexikon zur politisch-sozialen Sprache in Deutschland,* ed. Otto Brunner, Werner Conze, Reinhart Koselleck, vol. 1 (Stuttgart: E. Klett, 1972), 508–51; and Shulamit Volkov, "Die Verbürgerlichung der Juden in Deutschland: Eigenart und Paradigma," *Bürgertum im 19. Jahrhundert: Deutschland im europäischen Vergleich,* ed. Jürgen Kocka (Munich: Deutscher Taschenbuchverlag, 1988), 343–71.

MARION KAPLAN

1818   Ludwig Börne begins his professional career as a freelance German journalist and editor of *Die Wage*

Early in 1818 the Frankfurt senate received a request from one Juda Löw Baruch, "son of the merchant Jew in money-changing Jakob Baruch," to change his name to Ludwig Börner. The request, which gave no reasons for the change, was denied. A second request, submitted "in extreme submission and devotion," explained that the petitioner "wish[es] to start a national journal that will be dedicated primarily to administrative and political matters. Since not only the desire to express myself but also the need to establish a source of income has led me to this publishing venture, I must take all precautions to eliminate any obstacles and barriers to this end." The recipient of this request put the matter more clearly to his senate colleagues—"he needs above all a name that doesn't sound Jewish" and noted that the name "Börner" was denied him "because an investigation revealed the existence of four citizens with that name already living in Frankfurt." A modified form of the name, without the final "r," was finally approved by the senate (Estermann 1986, 39; Jasper 1989, 66).

Endowed with this German name, which at once included him in the Christian community of Frankfurt while orthographically cordoning him off from its members, Dr. Ludwig Börne founded *Die Wage* (The scale), a journal that, as its subtitle announced, would be dedicated to bourgeois life, science, and art. These two events of 1818—Börne's name change (which included conversion to Protestantism) and the founding of *Die Wage* under his new name—mark a seminal episode in the history of modern Jewish culture in Germany: nothing less than the *professional* entry of Jews into the realm of public German discourse. Although other Jews before Börne had of course written in German, Börne was the first to make his living and establish a national identity through his work as a German writer and critic, first in his native Frankfurt, then as a "foreign correspondent" in his immensely successful *Letters from Paris* (1831–34). Börne paved the way for Heine, who followed him not only to Paris but also into the genre of cultural commentary that was made popular by Börne and would later become known as the feuilleton. A journalist with high moral and aesthetic standards, Börne used the ideas of Kant and Schiller to criticize the affairs of bourgeois daily life, whether the tyranny of local officials or the tremor in the voice of a popular soprano. He saw his role as that of a mediator between truth and public opinion (*Der Vermittler* was in fact the name of an earlier journal he had unsuccessfully sought to publish), or as that of a "money-changer" who transforms the "gold bars of truth" into coins for everyday use: "[For] copper, which is brought to the people by the daily papers, is worth more than all the gold contained in books" (1818).

Börne's history is entwined in the larger context of the emergence of the German bourgeoisie and the emancipation of German-speaking Jews at the end of the eighteenth century. Born into the Frankfurt ghetto in 1786, the son of Jakob Baruch was twenty when Napoleon's army defeated the Prussians in Jena and Auerstädt. The subsequent dissolution of the "Holy Roman Empire of the German Nation" led to the formation of an alliance between sixteen Rhineland dukedoms under the protection of Napoleon, whose legal code established equal rights for Jews. Although this emancipation would prove to be short-lived, it allowed Börne to pursue a career in the Frankfurt administration, which until then had been closed to Jews. He abandoned the study of medicine and enrolled in 1808 in the University of Giessen, where he took his doctorate in public administration and business. Three years later he obtained a position in the Frankfurt government as "Polizeiaktuar," or police records-keeper, a position of some responsibility that required him to wear a uniform and dagger on official occasions. In 1815, however, following Napoleon's defeat and the conservative policies of the Vienna Congress, the city of Frankfurt reverted to the "Judenstättigkeit" that had regulated Jewish life in the city since 1616. Then thirty years old, "Dr. Baruch" lost his job and most of his pension, and was forced to make his living as a freelance critic, editor, and journalist.

This aborted emancipation of the Rhineland Jews had a fundamental effect on Börne's subsequent development, as indeed it did on the development of other young Jews of the region, including Heine and Karl Marx. Reluctant to pursue the "Jewish" professions of their fathers but barred from careers as civil servants (which included university professors), they often sought an alternative in freelance work as professional writers, especially journalists. Politically, their hearts beat for the French republicanism that had briefly granted them equality.

Had Börne not lost his civil rights, he might well have remained a devoted servant of Frankfurt and a Sunday poet with no particular ax to grind. But because he had been banished from his post by a reactionary and anti-Jewish authority, he became instead a full-time writer and critic of the state. Börne's youthful ardor for the principles of the French Revolution developed into a lifelong passion—Heine would label it an obsession—for the cause of German freedom and national unity. When the "bourgeois revolution" of 1830 in France promised to reinstate the liberal principles of 1789, this "patriot without a fatherland" (Reich-Ranicki 1986) decided to leave the parochial and censor-ridden Frankfurt for Paris, where his democratic liberalism became radical and even more outspoken. He died there seven years later and was buried in the Père Lachaise cemetery. He had become a moral icon for generations of German patriots, democrats, and political exiles.

Theoretically, Börne had stopped being a Jew in 1818 when he changed his name and converted to Protestantism. But in the anti-Semitically charged years of the "Holy Alliance," during which Börne made his mark as the leading critic in (and of) Germany, he never stopped being considered a Jew. "It's like a miracle!" he exclaimed in his seventy-fourth "Letter from Paris": "I've experienced it a thousand times and yet it remains eternally new. Some people criticize me for being a Jew; others forgive me for being one; a third even praises me for it; but all are thinking about it. They are as if caught in the spell of this magic Jewish circle—no one can escape from it" (February 7, 1832). Although Börne sometimes displayed traces of an anti-Jewish sentiment, using Judaism as a trope for capitalism and economic exploitation generally (Rose 1990), he never denied his origins. Indeed, when conservative readers in Germany questioned his "Jewish" republicanism, he boasted of his dual identity, turning his humble origins into a source of moral and political superiority. "I know how to appreciate the unearned fortune of being both a German and a Jew," he wrote in the same letter from Paris of 1832, adding that he strove to attain "all the virtues of the Germans without sharing any of their faults." The famous conclusion to this thought resounded through the century; it was at once a provocation and a declaration of love to his "unliberated" fellow Germans: "Yes, because I was born a servant, I love freedom more than you. Yes, because I tasted slavery, I understand freedom better than you. Yes, because I had no fatherland at birth, I wish for a fatherland more ardently than you, and because my birthplace wasn't bigger than the *Judengasse* and because the ghetto gate marked for me the beginning of a foreign country, a single city is no longer enough for me as fatherland, nor is a territory or a province. Only the entire, magnificent fatherland will satisfy me, as far as its language is spoken."

Later in the century, nationalists with a racial understanding of the "Volk" would malign the critic who did so much to further the cause of German national unity and political freedom. But in the three years of *Die Wage*'s existence, Börne was acclaimed by non-Jews and Jews alike for his outspoken, witty, and courageous defense of civil freedom generally, of which Jewish emancipation was one important though subordinate part. The chief problem facing Germany in the wake of Metternich's restoration politics, he claimed in the advertising brochure announcing his new journal, was the lack of a public sphere where "bourgeois life" could be freely presented and discussed. The *Geist* or "spirit" of public life, he challenged, "is far from adequately refreshing all limbs of the German body of state, least of all in those territories lying between southern and northern German confessions" (1818). Börne's interests were decidedly secular: *Die Wage* would focus not on religion or philosophy, or even on art as an autonomous entity, but on what he defined as the "holy unity" of "bourgeois life, science and art." Conscious of the historical importance of his age—"a developmental stage which humanity is now traversing [and whose significance] will reappear only after centuries of immobility"—Börne described *Die Wage* as a "diary of the times" that would let no aspect of bourgeois public life pass unnoticed. Indeed, he wished that the daily newspapers could become "hourly newspapers" for there can never be enough "observing looks" or "reports of actual events." He pledged to speak openly, to create a forum for multiple opinions, to dare to call things (and people) by their real names and thereby test the limits of the press's freedom. ("Wage," it should be noted, refers not only to the "scales" of truth but also to the critic's audacity or "daring": *ich wage*.) "Only the suppressed word is dangerous," he concluded in a phrase anticipating both Marx and Freud. "The censored word avenges itself, the freely spo-

ken word is never in vain. . . . What public opinion earnestly requests will be denied by no one; if its request is turned down, then only because it was made half-heartedly."

Between 1818 and 1821 Börne published thirteen issues of *Die Wage*. He wrote most of the articles himself and assumed virtually all duties connected with editing, printing, and distributing the journal. Offered at the modest price of 3 florins and 45 kreuzer for a year's subscription, *Die Wage* counted six hundred subscribers in 1819—an astonishing number when one considers that even daily newspapers in that period rarely surpassed a circulation of 1,500. In the journal's first issue, Börne took up the politically sensitive issue of "Freedom of the Press in Bavaria": "Public opinion is a lake," he admonished. "If it is dammed up, [it will] rise continually until it rushes over its barriers, floods the land and pulls everything along in its path." In the second issue, published in August 1818, he expounded on his hope that Prussia would take the course of monarchic constitutionalism. Whereas Austria is the "China of Europe," fearful of "every popular movement," the Prussian King should mediate between the aristocracy and popularly elected officials, thereby ensuring a kind of two-chamber parliamentary government. Camouflaging his criticism of German political life in satire, caricature, and quotations from foreign periodicals, Börne nonetheless clashed almost immediately with the German censors. As early as December 1818, a spy in the German Confederation advised authorities in Vienna to suppress *Die Wage* because "Börne seems to echo the liberals in France or at least to represent their liberal views in Germany" (Jasper 1989). And in 1820 he was briefly imprisoned when informants discovered in his office "two forbidden caricatures representing freedom of the press and the Zeitgeist." Börne also maintains, they went on to report, "that Prussia's demise must be near, since it blindly follows Austria's wish and is completely against the principles of liberalism" (119).

Börne's commitment to the frank discussion of German public life not only set him against the ruling authorities, it also marked a definitive break with German classical and romantic notions of the writer. Goethe had already coined the term *Zeitschriftsteller* (literally: "time-writer") to disparage the new form of journalistic writing that had become increasingly popular after the French Revolution. In his introduction to the first issue of *Die Wage,* Börne wore the term as a badge of honor: the Zeitschriftsteller in his sense was to be a writer "of and for the times," a scholar-journalist who uses knowledge to "move" readers who themselves are caught in the movement, the ebb and flow, of bourgeois life. People in the modern world have no time for books, he wrote: "die Welt ist auf Reisen," the world is traveling. Against a classical aesthetics of the finished, autonomous artwork of his time, Börne readily conceded the ephemeral, unfixed, brief, and provisional nature of his writing, the bulk of which in fact consists of letters, aphorisms, and journalistic essays. "I haven't written any works," he protested in the introduction to his *Gesammelte Schriften* in 1828, "I have only tried out my plume, now on this, now on that sheet of paper." At the same time he abhorred the German pedant who has gotten lost in the "Idea" and failed to see the connection between theory and praxis. One of his earliest essays, "On the Spirit and Purpose of Academic Life," insisted that scholars "strive to encompass the entire realm of life" (1805). Especially in Prussia, he noted in 1808, historical developments had erected "a wall between life and science" ("Das Leben und die Wissenschaft," 1808; in Börne 1964–68).

Börne's notion of writing as "traveling with one's time" thus set him against the Weimar classicists, who insisted on the autonomy of art—as well as against the romantics, who tended to eschew direct political engagement. One of his favorite metaphors for his journalistic writing concerns the realm of *Verkehr,* of "traffic" or "travel": "a journal departs like a post carriage at specific times and dates," he writes; a "journalist is only the coachman of science and history" (from the announcement of *Die Wage,* 1818). But Verkehr also implies financial and commercial transactions, the "commerce" of modern urban life: "All knowledge is nothing more than the metal with which life pays for itself," he proclaimed in a passage particularly rich in mercantile allusions. "But the [gold] bars of truth, set down in great works by the wealthy in spirit, cannot be used to take care of the small daily needs of the unmoneyed. Only knowledge that has been *turned into coin* ["nur das *ausgemünzte* Wissen] can be used in this way" (*Die Wage,* 1818, Börne's emphasis). Like Heine, who also daringly employed metaphors of commerce to talk about art, Börne, the son of a Frankfurt money-changer, insisted on the relationship between art and money, between morality and the material needs to sustain it, between an ideal truth and a useful one. Both writers would be accused of sullying the purity of German art with "Jewish" considerations: money, commerce, and the physical needs of the body. For the young writers of their generation, however, Börne's attachment to life made him a leader of Junges Deutschland, Young Germany, the movement that ushered German literature into the modern world with a commitment to the realistic representation of social conditions, including those of the poor and disenfranchised.

This divorce between traditional and revolutionary generations became acute in Börne's famously drastic opposition to Goethe on moral and political grounds. "Goethe had an unbelievably restrictive force," he lamented, calling the Weimar poet a "cataract in the German eye" and a "servant of despots": "Ever since I have felt, I have hated Goethe; ever since I have thought, I've known why" (Estermann 1986, 61). Styling himself the "anti-Goethe" (Marcuse 1967), an attitude that reveres as well as blasphemes, Börne complained that Goethe embodied the German tendency toward servility on the one hand and autocratic rule on the other: "The Germans cannot do without giving orders and obeying them, and it's hard to tell which gives them the most pleasure." Quoting Goethe's lines from *Faust* (spoken by Mephistopheles) "You must rule or serve / Be the anvil or the hammer," Börne maintained that this "pithy saying" in fact contains a "great lie" and a "disgusting libel of human nature." Human beings are, in his classic Enlightenment formulation, "born to freedom"; identity and behavior are a task, a constant struggle, not fixed in an immutable human nature (*Aphorisms,*

1829). Although this opposition to Goethe made Börne a leader for young, more politically inspired writers of Young Germany, it proved to be a thorn in the eye of many German Jews who revered German culture and *Bildung,* especially in works such as *Faust* and *Wilhelm Meister.* Börne of course recognized Goethe's importance—in 1818 he had written to Weimar asking for a contribution to *Die Wage* (a request that Goethe left unanswered)—but, as with his later quarrel with Heine, he refused to allow for a poet's aesthetic freedom from politics. For Börne, writing meant intervention in *this* world, the human world of governments, prisons, censors, and newspapers—not an attempt to rise above it or make it more beautiful.

One of the innovative features of *Die Wage* that made it, in Rahel Varnhagen's words, the "most intelligent and witty writing today," was its regular theater reviews. Like Schiller, Börne saw the theater as an essential organ of a democratic nation, as a workshop for the developing sense of public life, civic responsibility, and national unity. Although plays were offered in abundance—Börne counted no fewer than "324 larger and smaller plays" for the year 1820 in his *Letters from Frankfurt*—theater reviews were a novelty, and neither actors nor playwrights were accustomed to public criticism, especially criticism delivered with Börne's sarcastic, uncompromising wit. "In the Frankfurt National Theater," writes a modern biographer, "Börne had a permanently reserved seat at the right of the stage. There he stood in the glare of flickering oil lamps, wearing a coat and scarf in winter since the theater was unheated. On strips of paper attached to the leaden stage lamps he would scribble his critical notes, to the terror of all participants" (Jasper 1989, 113). In essence these reviews constituted the beginning of the feuilleton, or cultural section of a newspaper, which still is a regular feature of the German press. (The term stems from the French *Journal des débats,* which around 1800 started to publish its theater reviews—previously printed on separate sheets, or "feuilles"—on the same page with political news, but separated from the news by a line.)

In Börne's hands these articles became the site for witty, frank, and often controversial discussions of larger political and social issues. A performance of Schiller's *Wilhelm Tell* in 1818 became an occasion for Börne to rebuke the Frankfurt censors for having removed the word "Austria" from the play, "without regard for verse meter," so that "no one could tell whether the term 'foreigners' (which had replaced 'Austrians') meant Christians or Hottentots" (Oct. 1818). In a later review on the "character" of Wilhelm Tell, Börne famously derided the then heroic model of patriotism and liberty as bearing "all the traits of the German philistine"; incapable of autonomous action, Tell was "the model of servility" (1828). His review of Shakespeare's *Merchant of Venice* was similarly unconventional. "We detest the money devil in Shylock," he wrote, "but we pity the tormented man, and we love and admire the avenger of inhumane persecution." Shakespeare's design is not to preach or lecture, but "if he ever wished to be a schoolmaster, in the 'Merchant of Venice' he certainly had more lessons to give to Christians than to Jews." Börne concluded with the regret that his own age lacked a Shakespeare to describe "our Shylocks," that is, the modern capitalists who reap enormous profit without regard for the enormous human suffering they bring about. "What did the Venetian Shylock do?" he queried in a rhetorical broadside against the financiers of the Turkish occupation of Greece. "Three thousand ducats for a pound of poor Christian flesh—at least it was good money for his wish. But our Shylocks, of the Old and the New Testaments, would drown all of Hellas for a few percentage points as if she were a blind kitten" (1828).

Börne was playing with fire when he labeled capitalism a "Jewish" matter, but so convinced was he that Judaism and capitalism would fall by the wayside in the march toward ever greater human liberty that he confidently linked the two, as would Heine and Marx in their "left-wing" critiques of their fathers' religion (Rose 1990). But Börne's relation to the question of German-Jewish assimilation cannot simply be reduced to an anti-Jewish stance. Throughout his career he repeatedly wrote in support of Jewish civil rights: in 1808 when the city was in the process of revising its statutes on Jews ("Bold Remarks on the Restrictions and Protection of the Jews in Frankfurt am Main"), in 1816 after the repeal of the Napoleonic Civil Code ("The Jews in the Free City of Frankfurt and Their Enemies"), in 1819 following the "Hep-Hep!" riots ("For the Jews"), in 1821 in response to a purportedly scholarly study of "The Wandering Jew," and on numerous other occasions in his letters and reviews. Nonetheless, Börne's simultaneous allegiance to the Jewish community, to French liberalism, and to the cause of German national unity proved increasingly difficult to reconcile. Here too he is an exemplary figure for the history of German-Jewish assimilation, both for his own published reflections on his problematic status between diverse groups as well as for the anti-Semitic stereotypes used against him by later German nationalists who wished to link him with a Franco-Jewish spirit.

In his essay "For the Jews," which was published in 1819 in the Frankfurt journal *Die Zeitschwingen,* Börne begins by noting that the initial steps toward Jewish civil equality taken in Germany in the late eighteenth century and during French rule encountered slight popular opposition. But when Napoleon fell and Germany was liberated, a number of writers in northern Germany began publishing anti-French and anti-Jewish tracts, which led Frankfurt "to pull the old rights of the Jews, or rather their previous status without rights, from the dust of the archives." Because Germany had suffered under French tyranny, he wrote, "the drive for freedom and the hatred of the French were fused together in a single sentiment." And because one tends to mistrust even the beneficial aspects of a hated regime, so the Germans started to consider the emancipation of the Jews, introduced by the French, as something negative—a view supported by the Jews' friendly relation to the French. Rejecting as so much "theatrical noise" the racial arguments of the anti-Semites who wanted Germans to be "as they had emerged from the forests of Tacitus, with red hair and light blue eyes," Börne insisted on a historical explanation that would justify the prejudice against Jews as a "pardonable weakness" in the German struggle for freedom. Be-

cause all the struggles of the German people had been directed at the aristocracy, he argued, it was only natural for the Jews to be targeted as well: "For the Jews and the nobility, i.e. money and authority, i.e. material and personal aristocracy, constitute the two last foundations of the feudal system. They stick together. For the Jews, threatened by the people, seek protection from the nobility, while the latter, terrified by the specter of equality, seek weapons and castle walls in money." Here Börne saw popular prejudice against the Jews (who are "threatened by the people"), whereas in his first explanation he claimed that this prejudice was imposed on the people "from above" in reaction to French tyranny. Both explanations, however, tend to justify the historical animus against the Jews, which Börne freely acknowledged because he was convinced that the greater issue of general civil equality and freedom would prevail. In a miscalculation that seems astonishing to contemporary readers, he concluded that because all Germans knew what they were fighting for, hatred of the French had disappeared and the writers who had spread the teachings of Jew hatred were silent.

Börne was the first victim of this misjudgment: he lost a fatherland that was never quite his. The Prussian authorities did not adopt the liberal program he had championed; anti-Semitism in Germany increased rather than faded away, and the local Frankfurt censors became so harsh that Börne was forced to cease publishing *Die Wage* in 1821. After several trips to Paris during the 1820s, he moved there permanently in 1830, convinced that the July Revolution would usher in a new era of political freedom in France (he also knew that his career as a freelance journalist in Germany had become impossible). Nonetheless, it was here that Börne composed his three collections of *Letters from Paris* (1831, 1833, 1834), which constitute his major critical opus and, with his Frankfurt pieces, the beginning of what Jost Hermand has called a "liberal *Belletristik*" (Estermann 1986, 199–210): a witty, subjective, and yet accessible form of commentary that definitively changed political and cultural writing in Germany. These works established Börne's unimpeachable moral reputation for German liberals throughout much of the nineteenth century. Even such an unforgiving anti-Semite as Richard Wagner, in his pamphlet "Judaism in Music" (1850 and 1869), praised Börne as a shining example of assimilation, by which he meant that Börne had radically purged himself of his Judaism. But there was the rub. Börne's early experience in Frankfurt, which had granted him citizenship only on condition that he remain isolated within it, stands as a troubled legacy for the subsequent history of German-Jewish assimilation. Only a year after leaving Germany, Börne came to regret the sacrifice of his religious identity on the altar of a presumed civil equality. "In the end," he lamented in his sixty-third "Letter from Paris," "I wished someone would give me back the three gold pieces I paid the clergyman for my Christianity. It's been eighteen years since I was baptized and it hasn't helped me a bit. Three gold pieces for a tiny corner in the German nuthouse! What a foolish waste of money" (1831).

Bibliography

Ludwig Börne, *Sämtliche Schriften,* ed. Inge and Peter Rippmann, 5 vols. (Düsseldorf: Melzer, 1964–68); Alfred Estermann, ed., *Ludwig Börne: Zum 200. Geburtstag des Frankfurter Schriftstellers* (Frankfurt: Buchhändler-Vereinigung, 1986); Sigmund Freud, "A Note on the Prehistory of the Technique of Analysis" (1920), in *The Standard Edition of the Complete Psychological Works,* ed. James Strachey, vol. 18 (Toronto: Hogarth, 1955); Willi Jasper, *Keinem Vaterland geboren: Ludwig Börne. Eine Biographie* (Hamburg: Hoffmann and Campe, 1989); Ludwig Marcuse, *Ludwig Börne: Aus der Frühzeit der deutschen Demokratie* (Hamburg: J. P. Peter, 1967); Marcel Reich-Ranicki, "Ein Genie der Formulierung-ein Patriot ohne Vaterland" in Estermann, *Ludwig Börne;* Paul Lawrence Rose, *German Question / Jewish Question: Revolutionary Antisemitism from Kant to Wagner* (Princeton, N.J.: Princeton University Press, 1990); and Richard Wagner, "Das Judentum in der Musik," trans. as "Judaism in Music" in *Richard Wagner's Prose Works,* trans. William Ashton Ellis, vol. 3: *The Theatre* (London: K. Paul, Trench, Trubner & Co., 1907).

MARK M. ANDERSON

1833   Rahel Varnhagen, *salonnière* and epistolary writer, publishes *Rahel: Ein Buch des Andenkens für ihre Freunde,* a collection of letters and diary entries

The unusual work, bearing only the author's first name in the title, was both a modest and daring endeavor. It left open the question of authorship while at the same time alluding to the biblical Rachel. Clearly intended to memorialize Rahel and edify a readership that had known and admired her, this volume and other posthumous publications of Rahel's writings soon began to assume overt political meanings. As the congeries of more or less retrograde German states evolved into the autocratic and hegemonic German Empire, Rahel's commitment to reason, tolerance, and human progress stood not only in stark contrast to a reactionary age but also as an example of the best that Enlightenment thought had produced. At the same time, the life and writings of this Jewish woman chronicle nearly half a century of aspirations for emancipation and assimilation. These efforts ended exactly one hundred years later with Hitler's ascent to power. In her biography, *Rahel Varnhagen, the Life of a Jewess* (1957), all but completed before her emigration in 1933, Hannah Arendt presented Jewish assimilation as a failed experiment.

Encouraged by the response of the initial publication, Varnhagen brought out, barely a year later, an expanded three-volume edition of *Rahel: Ein Buch des Andenkens,* again arranging *Rahel's* texts in chronological order. In time, the small but unusual *Rahel* oeuvre comprised many volumes: volumes 1–3 constituted the *Buch des Andenkens* (1834); volumes 4–6 contained Rahel's correspondence with Karl August Varnhagen (1874–75), and volume 7 that with her friend David Veit (1861); and volume 8 (in the present *Collected Works*) includes love letters to and from Rahel and diary entries (1877), as well as her commentaries on the writings of Angelus Silesius and Saint-Martin (1849). This work, in part conceived and shaped by Rahel herself, remains unique. Yet it evolved from the tradition of epistolary writing practiced by both men and women, notable and ordinary, since the beginning of the eighteenth century. To understand the distinct place of Rahel's letters within this context, it is important to briefly survey the modern epistolary tradition in Germany.

The eighteenth century might well be designated the epoch of the letter. As the middle classes assumed a greater role in the economic, social, and intellectual life of their countries, there emerged a distinctly bourgeois consciousness guided by Enlightenment thought. The private or intimate letter, because it was usually informed by a subjective viewpoint, served as an important medium in this process. Letter writing was also intimately connected both to the cult of friendship, underpinned by utopian notions of the uniqueness of the individual, and to the emerging belief in romantic love.

Furthermore, this form of writing permitted women to participate in the literary world for the first time. Christian Fürchtegott Gellert, in his treatise on the letter, presented women as exemplary letter writers. In his view, women most successfully fulfilled his demand for naturalness, liveliness, and literary agility, as well as for a pleasing style. But although women excelled at letters, epistolary writing did not at that time evolve into a genre unique to women. Rather, men embraced previously derogated feminine qualities and used the private letter to express and explore their inner lives and sensibilities. The importance of the letter in the bourgeois imagination is further demonstrated by the appearance toward the end of the century of a new literary genre—the epistolary novel. Richardson's *Pamela,* Rousseau's *Julie ou La Nouvelle Héloïse,* Choderlos de Laclos's *Les liaisons dangereuses,* Sophie von la Roche's *Das Fräulein von Sternheim,* and Goethe's *Die Leiden des jungen Werthers,* to name but the most acclaimed, were no longer action novels. Instead, they drew their subject matter almost entirely from the protagonists' emotional states, feelings, and thoughts.

If the eighteenth century was important for the popularization and perfection of private letter writing, the nineteenth was notable for the publication of a great variety of correspondences and epistolary collections. In fact, printing private letters became so popular that by the second half of the century one can speak of a veritable explosion of such publications, among them the epistolary exchanges of kings and queens, princes and princesses, political figures, men of learning, artists, composers, women of note, and so forth. At the same time, serious reservations arose about the practice. In 1804, for example, a dispute erupted over Wilhelm Gleim's literary estate and the publication of correspondences contained therein. Similarly, Dorothea Mendelssohn Schlegel's decision to burn most of the letters in her possession with the intent of preventing their future publication further illustrates a critical attitude about the propriety of bringing private matters into print. (She encouraged others, including Henriette Herz, to do likewise.)

The central questions were whether private letters qualified as publishable literature and whether communications that were intended for the eyes of an intimate friend or at most a small circle of acquaintances ought to be released to the wider public. Modern notions of authorship (that is, who is entitled to "authorize" a work) thus conflicted with the public's appetite for such reading material. During the eighteenth century no sharp distinction existed as yet between the private and the literary spheres of writing. The absence of such a division is precisely what encouraged the flowering of epistolary writing. To the considerable extent that friendship became an essential factor in the lives of the literate classes and letter writing was turned into an art, the demand for published letters grew.

Around the same time, Goethe narrowed the definition of literature to three main genres—poetry, drama, and epic prose. He thus excluded or, more precisely, marginalized epistolary writing, until then an integral part of belles lettres (both in France and the German states). Goethe nevertheless attributed great value to this kind of writing: "Letters are among the most important memorials the individual can leave behind." Like many of his contemporaries, he carried on wide-ranging correspondences with prominent men. But, as the quotation indicates, he appreciated letters primarily for their historical and documentary value. They served as a key to a person's life and work and, in his case, as material for his literary efforts.

Letters, like memoirs and diaries, differ from other literary genres in several respects. They are much more vulnerable than texts expressly written for publication. Not only subject to being lost or burned, they are also very much dependent on the intermediary role of a collector-editor. Furthermore, the very openness of this form of writing allows for a great many possibilities of presentation: as correspondences between two or more persons, as collections of letters by one writer or as selections by several, with entries arranged chronologically or around a theme, excerpted or presented in their entirety, and so forth. From the great number and variety of nineteenth-century epistolary publications, three stand out as formative, influential, and illustrative of the aesthetic and didactic potential of such publications. The first is by Goethe, the luminary who for half a century dominated the literary and cultural stage;

the second, a seminal first work, is by the romantic writer Bettina von Arnim. The third is the epistolary work of Rahel Levin Varnhagen, which is also the focus of this essay.

The *Briefwechsel zwischen Schiller und Goethe* (Correspondence between Schiller and Goethe; 1828–29) exemplifies Goethe's views and the position he assigned to letters within his oeuvre. Prepared and published by the author himself toward the end of his life, it quickly became, like so many of Goethe's endeavors, the standard for subsequent epistolary publications. The letters Goethe had exchanged with Schiller between 1794 and 1804 clearly were of great importance to him. Theirs was an epistolary conversation prompted not by a meeting of kindred souls but by common literary and aesthetic concerns. Besides documenting a most interesting discourse regarding their current literary projects, the correspondence testifies to the two authors' lofty efforts to set up criteria for a German national literature and theater modeled on but also differentiated from Greek classicism. It traces the evolution of their ideas on questions of form and shows how these inquiries went far beyond their narrow confines to address the much more encompassing task of finding the literary means to adequately represent the modern world. Thus, it can be claimed that these letters were from the beginning intended for publication, as an elucidation of Schiller and Goethe's other formal aesthetic writings.

In 1835, less than ten years later and three years after Goethe's death, another work appeared: *Goethes Briefwechsel mit einem Kinde: Seinem Denkmal* (Goethe's correspondence with a child). It was written by Bettina von Arnim, who used the letters she had exchanged with Goethe and his mother, Frau Rath Goethe, mostly between 1807 and 1811 and intermittently until 1832. The actual letters, however, form but a small part of a work of over five hundred pages, which may be more accurately termed an epistolary novel. Like Goethe, Bettina von Arnim published her book for a specific reason: to memorialize the poet she revered throughout her life and to honor their unusual relationship, in which she portrayed herself as his muse and inspiration. Additionally, she

intended it as a memorial to a time that enabled someone like Goethe to conceive and depict a more daring idea of man and human relations. As such, the book represents an implicit criticism of the repressive Period of Reaction (1815–48). Although a young woman rather than a child at the time of the actual letter exchange and a mature woman at the time of composing the novel, the author's posing as a child created an effective literary device. It permitted her to disregard convention; to speak freely, even bluntly; and to juxtapose the retrograde real with the free and often fantastic world of her imagination. A combination of Enlightenment thought and romantic exaltation of nature, art, and love informs the book.

Additionally, *Goethes Briefwechsel mit einem Kinde,* although it contributed to the Goethe cult then on the rise, is an early female bildungsroman, or artist's novel. Bettina von Arnim, who also exhibited considerable talents as a composer, sculptor, and artist, explores in this and subsequent epistolary novels her own development as a creative individual from the vantage point of the mature woman and writer. A distinguishing feature of her writing is the dialogic form that characterizes all of her works: in the epistolary novels, she speaks *with* poets—Goethe, Caroline von Günderode, and her brother, Clemens Brentano—whereas her political books are addressed *to* King Frederick William IV, who reigned in Prussia at that time.

If Goethe took great care in preserving the documentary value of his correspondence with Schiller, and Bettina von Arnim freely fictionalized them, Rahel embodies a third approach that was never repeated. Although she published little and only anonymously during her lifetime, it is now quite well known that she carefully prepared parts of her wide-ranging correspondence for posthumous publication. Almost from the beginning she collected and preserved her own letters and those written to her, whether they came from notables, friends, members of her family, or her servants. At the same time, Karl August Varnhagen's role in this project cannot be overestimated. With acuity and vision, he created a collection of autographs that remained unparalleled in his century and even now ranks among the best with regard to variety and comprehensiveness. The repository of some six thousand letters written by and to Rahel represents a most valuable component of the Varnhagen collection. Recent research has shown the often maligned Varnhagen as an unusually conscientious and careful editor whose changes and omissions were, for the most part, intended to protect the privacy of the living or dictated by the repressive spirit of the times. Nonetheless, his editorial principles had far-reaching consequences for almost all subsequent editions and anthologies of Rahel's writings until World War II. Even today, the historical critical editions now in progress will draw from Varnhagen's copious notes on many now forgotten persons with whom Rahel corresponded. Equally influential was Varnhagen's focus on Rahel as an outstanding personality rather than on her achievements as a writer and salonnière. Moreover, because they preferred not to do battle with Rahel's notoriously cryptic handwriting, most scholars and authors relied on the neat copies her husband made of a large number of her letters in preparation for future publication. These, however, also bear his mark because he standardized her idiosyncratic grammar and orthography and frequently replaced her spirited or even coarse expressions with more neutral and diplomatic ones. All this indicates that Rahel's literary oeuvre cannot be separated from the history of the way it was edited and published. In fact, it is doubtful that it would exist in anything approaching its present form without Varnhagen's loving devotion and dedicated efforts. In important respects, therefore, Rahel's literary legacy represents the result of a collaborative undertaking by a husband and wife team as well as a fortuitous understanding between gentile and Jew. Their editorial manipulations notwithstanding, Rahel's letters hold their own as literary texts of great originality and authenticity.

As an author Rahel distinguished herself from all others in making the letter, this recently marginalized genre, her almost exclusive literary means. It was indeed an appropriate vehicle, for she was marginal: a woman and a Jew, unmarried until age forty-three. We may justifiably ask what qualifies these letters as literature of a distinct genre. For one, there is the sheer volume, indicating that here was an author who dedicated a good part of her life to writing and for whom writing constituted an existential necessity. The *Gesammelte Werke* (Collected works) of ten volumes (eight of them facsimile reprints) are being supplemented at present by a critical edition of six more of mostly unpublished material (three featuring Rahel's correspondences with women, two presenting family letters, and one containing her diaries and other writings). Like any artistic oeuvre, Rahel's epistolary work evolved in terms of both style and content.

Second, although Rahel never aspired to become a novelist or poet and maintained that she could write only letters, she incorporated many other genres within the letter: aphorisms, epigrams, anecdotes, poetic passages, travel reports, diary entries, literary criticism, philosophical "treatises," literary and music reviews, dream recordings, and essays on a great variety of general topics, such as education, women, political developments, society and sociability, and progress. Although Rahel, an intellectual woman, had at best an eclectic education and was subject to frequent interruptions, she employed these minor forms effectively to convey a wealth of ideas, and they served her well.

Third, Rahel displayed a high degree of sensitivity in regard to formal, stylistic, and linguistic aspects of writing. She was familiar with the current literary debates as well as the tradition of epistolary writing. She particularly admired the letters of Madame de Sévigné, Ninon de Lenclos, Voltaire, Mirabeau, and Gotthold Ephraim Lessing. But early on she began to formulate an epistolary theory of her own—one dictated by the needs of her specific situation as an extraordinarily intelligent woman, a Jew, and a salonnière of renown. In devising her writing strategies, she pursued a path that differed from the classicist principles established by Goethe and Schiller. This may be surprising, given the fact that the significance of Goethe was for Rahel at least as momentous as for Bettina von Arnim. Indeed, the effect of his work (rather than his personality) was such that her being and thought cannot be understood without considering her apperception and appreciation of Goethe (Hamburger 1983). His mature works in particular became her lifelong avocation and subject of study, from which she drew consolation, strength, and inspiration, as well as confirmation for her own thoughts and feelings. Today, she is acknowledged as one of the first of many Jewish interpreters of Goethe. That she did not emulate him in her writing points to her own self-possession and to her awareness that his kind of artistic perfection could be attained only by a man of genius, secure in his personal, social, and artistic identity and able to draw and build on established traditions. In contrast to the many women novelists attempting to conform to the norms of classicist literature, Rahel chose the letter, an infinitely flexible genre, and adapted it to her needs as an author without a tradition or accepted identity.

The overriding characteristic of Rahel's written communication is her insistence on dialogue. "I do not like to write monologues, but rather want to write conversations such as they animatedly occur within the individual." Speeches or monologues, she claimed, tended to be presented "like a herbarium, according to an ever lifeless order" (Varnhagen 1979, 3:183). Her writing was thus never self-contained but reached out in its continual struggle toward genuine communication. The letter is of course inherently dialogic, but Rahel pursued the dialogic form with a purposefulness that far surpassed most other epistolary writing, including Bettina von Arnim's. Not only did she respond to letters in great detail and point by point, adjusting the tone and level of argument to the sensibilities and capabilities of the recipient, she demanded the same from her partners. Admonitions such as, "Answer me!" or "I want answers," can be found throughout her letters. The writer Jean Paul (1763–1825) early on appreciated the "artist" in Rahel, but he also perceptively added that she could write only if she wrote to someone.

Rahel thus intentionally practiced a style of writing that approximated spoken conversation by aiming for spontaneity, naturalness, and the illusion of immediacy and physical presence. In later years, she liked to situate a letter not only with the date and place but also with a detailed weather report, explaining that this served to excuse her unmethodical way of writing. The weather constituted at least in part "the situation of the day" for her, and she intended the recipient to be aware of the frame of mind in which she wrote the epistle. She wanted a letter to "be a portrait of the moment in which it is written." This attempted spontaneity largely precluded the kind of aesthetic refinement and idealization demanded of literature at the time.

Implicitly referring to Goethe, Friedrich de la Motte Fouqué, Friedrich Gentz, and others whom she admired for their elegant ways with language, Rahel carefully distinguished between herself, a "storm-tossed soul" and "rebel," and those fortunate individuals endowed with methodical and measured minds who "have no mood, no weather! or rather! their moods are the music of a beautiful state of mind; and their weather is sunshine in the purest, mildest air." Endowed with such innate harmony, they were able to fulfill the demands of idealization in the very act of creation, whereas Rahel had to contend with the task of exactly rendering "the moment," regardless of any unresolved dissonances and contradictions (Varnhagen 1979, 3:55). In her case, then, truth took precedence over aesthetic perfection and idealization. In her letters, she frequently referred to her love of truth and truthfulness. Just the same, Rahel placed both her conversations and her writing within the realm of art, as each was guided by what she considered to be defining artistic criteria—arrangement and self-knowledge.

The commitment to truth and authenticity is also evident in Rahel's astonishing appraisal of her idiosyncratic use of language: "Language is not at my service, not even my own, German; our language is our lived life; I have invented my own [life]; I could therefore make less use than many others of the existing phrases, that's why mine are often rough and in many ways faulty, but always genuine" (Varnhagen 1979, 1:337). Rahel's many reflections on writing, scattered throughout her letters, almost invariably relate language, style, and form to personal and social provenance. As both an outsider and a pioneer, she knew that for her, writing entailed a different set of demands. And although she was familiar with the rules of aesthetics, she refused to let her writing be dictated by them. Instead, she turned her new and unprecedented situation into the wellspring of her written expression. The famous passage to David Veit, a fellow Jew, on the effects of anti-Jewish slander, may serve as an example: "I have a strange fancy: it is as if some supramundane being, just as I was thrust into this world, plunged these words with a dagger into my heart: 'Yes, have sensibility, see the world as few see it, be great and noble, nor can I take from you the faculty of eternally thinking. But I add one thing more: be a Jewess!' And now my life is a slow bleeding to death. By keeping still I can delay it. Every movement is an attempt to staunch it— new death: and immobility is possible for me only in death itself. . . . I can if you will, derive every evil, every misfortune, every vexation from that. . . . This opinion is my essence" (7:79). Although leading Jews had always protested the conditions under which they and especially their poorer coreligionists suffered, they tended not to dwell on the psychological hurt. Rahel's written explorations of the effects of social discrimination on the self were thus new and startling. Moreover, in her case, it concerned a self that was extraordinarily sensitive and socially aware. In the process, she fashioned a language for expressing the psychological and emotional conflicts that the newly emancipated Jews confronted in their struggle to find a place in the larger society.

The "blemish" of Jewishness, for this was how she viewed her origins, stayed with her throughout her life, in spite of her efforts at assimilation, including marriage to a gentile and the required baptism preceding it. The gentile world, even some of its most enlightened leaders such as Wilhelm von Humboldt, continued to react with hostility to her aspirations. The many passages of despair and outrage scattered throughout the letters bear testimony to the lifelong discrimination Rahel encountered. Nevertheless, she refused to accept society's judgment of her. This refusal further defined her writing. It was motivated, on the one hand, by an attitude of defiance and, on the other, by a compulsive need to explain and define

herself to others. She never tired of wishing to disclose herself to others "as one opens a cupboard and, with one movement, shows the things, ordered, on the shelves. People would surely be satisfied; and, as soon as they saw it, also understand" (Varnhagen 1979, 1:135). Her self-portrayals ranged from grandiose to self-deprecatory or pathetic, but a close reading reveals them also as surprisingly objective. Thus, depending on the situation, she could define herself as "the first critic" or "as unique as the greatest phenomenon of this earth. The greatest artist, philosopher, or poet is not above me" (260). At other times, she acknowledged the reality of her precarious position in society. In one of her most startling self-appraisals, she acknowledged the untimeliness of her person and aspirations in a retrograde society by defining herself as a "paradox." By this she meant a truth that had as yet no established place in the world, which nevertheless pressed "forward forcefully, albeit with a contortion" (400).

By means of her vast epistolary network and her salon, Rahel established and maintained contact with many notables of the time. These included the more progressive-minded members of the royal family and aristocracy, leading state officials and public servants, the philosophers and theologians responsible for German Enlightenment and Idealist thought, representatives of the classical and romantic literary movements, and even some who were associated with the politically oriented Young Germany. Additionally, many of the revered composers, musicians, singers, actresses, and actors of the day attended her salon and corresponded with her. Her letters, therefore, even if they are not explicitly political, trace a most eventful period in European history, from the French Revolution through the Napoleonic Era to the Congress of Vienna and the ensuing Period of Reaction. They offer both an astonishing array of cultural history and an outstanding record of sustained reflections and original insights. The letters, moreover, disclose the degree to which Rahel assimilated the achievements of one of Europe's most fertile periods in the history of ideas and the arts and the competence with which she responded to many of the pressing issues of the day. At the same time, her comments differ in important ways from those of other observers, because they came from someone not in a position to make or even influence the events of the day. Hers was a marginal voice using a marginal genre to judge the actors on both the cultural and the political stages. Firmly committed to the idea of progress and human perfection, she had much to say about her fatherland and about human issues that revealed an unusually astute, almost clairvoyant sense of history.

In one important respect Rahel's published epistolary work has remained deficient, although it constitutes almost a third of the repository of the six thousand letters at the Varnhagen Archive: her correspondence with women. Although a good number of Rahel's letters are contained in the *Buch des Andenkens,* those written by her friends have for the most part not been published. Many of these women were Jewish. Several corresponded, like Rahel, with prominent men and women, especially the authors they revered, including Goethe, Jean Paul, and Friedrich Schlegel. Some also wrote in other literary genres, such as novels, novellas, essays, and travelogues. Once these correspondences are published in the volumes edited by Barbara Hahn and Ursula Isselstein, they will reveal much about women's lives and writing efforts. Rahel may remain be the most prominent and prolific of nineteenth-century epistolary writers, but she may not stand so alone.

Rahel's legacy was not passed on in the form of epistolary writing, the genre that suited her so well and that she made so uniquely her own. Instead, the generations of writers that followed paid homage to her in novels, poems, pamphlets, essays, biographies, anthologies, and personal testimony. Moreover, these authors concentrated on her personality and thought rather than on her writing strategies. For the Young Germans, she became a model for their notion of the emancipated woman. To many women both outside and inside the women's movement, she served as an inspiration in their various struggles for independence and self-realization. Rahel herself appoin-

ted the poet Heinrich Heine, fellow Jew and fellow rebel, to carry on her struggle for truth and social justice through writing.

Bibliography

Hannah Arendt, *Rahel Varnhagen: The Life of a Jewish Woman,* rev. ed., trans. Richard and Clara Winston (New York: Harcourt Brace Jovanovich, 1974; first published in 1957 as *Rahel Varnhagen: The Life of a Jewess);* Bettina von Arnim, *Goethes Briefwechsel mit einem Kind* in *Werke und Briefe,* ed. Walter Schmitz and Sibylle von Steinsdorff, 4 vols. (Frankfurt a. M.: Deutscher Klassiker Verlag, 1992); Arnim, *Der Briefwechsel zwischen Schiller und Goethe,* ed. Siegfried Seidel, 3 vols. (Munich: Beck, 1984); Christian Fürchtegott Gellert, *Briefe, nebst einer praktischen Abhandlung von dem guten Geschmacke in Briefen* (Leipzig: Wendler, 1751); Barbara Hahn, *Antworten Sie mir! Rahel Levin Varnhagens Briefwechsel* (Frankfurt a. M.: Stroemfeld / Roter Stern, 1990); Barbara Hahn and Ursula Isselstein, eds., *Briefwechsel mit Freundinnen,* 3 vols. (Munich: Beck, 1996–); Käthe Hamburger, "Rahel und Goethe," *Rahel-Bibliothek: Rahel Varnhagen; Gesammelte Werke,* ed. Konrad Feilchenfeldt, Uwe Schweikert, Rahel E. Steiner, 10 vols. (Munich: Matthes & Seitz, 1983), 10:179–204; Ursula Isselstein, *Studien zu Rahel Levin Varnhagen* (Turin: Tirrenia Stampatori, 1993); Heinrich Mohr, "'Freundschaftliche Briefe'—Literatur oder Privatsache? Der Streit um Wilhelm Gleims Nachlaß," *Jahrbuch des Freien Deutschen Hochstifts* (Tübingen: Niemeier, 1973), 14–75; Solveig Ockenfuss, *Bettina von Arnims Briefromane: Literarische Erinnerungsarbeit zwischen Anspruch und Wirklichkeit* (Opladen: Westdeutscher Verlag, 1993); *Rahel-Bibliothek: Rahel Varnhagen; Gesammelte Werke;* Marianne Schuller, "'Unsere Sprache ist unser gelebtes Leben': Randbemerkungen zur Schreibweise Rahel Varnhagens," *Rahel-Bibliothek: Rahel Varnhagen; Gesammelte Werke,* 10:43–59; Heidi Thomann Tewarson, *Rahel Varnhagen mit Selbstzeugnissen und Bilddokumenten* (Reinbek: Rowohlt, 1988); and Rahel Varnhagen, *Briefwechsel,* ed. Friedhelm Kemp, 4 vols. (Munich: Winkler Verlag, 1979).

HEIDI THOMANN TEWARSON

1834 The Jewish historical novel helps to reshape the historical consciousness of German Jews

The process of forming and reshaping historical consciousness and historical images can be enhanced by the creation of "high" historical texts as well as by the production of "para-historical" literary texts, as demonstrated in the case of the nineteenth-century German-Jewish historical novel. In the nineteenth century, with the awakening of national consciousness and the wide interest in national history, the historical novel flourished in Europe and penetrated modern German-Jewish literature. Following in the wake of modern German-Jewish nonreligious journalism in the 1830s, Jewish writers began writing popular historical novels that, together with "high" and "popular" historiography and various other genres, constructed a new perception of the past and shaped a new vision of the future.

Dozens of popular historical novels were written at this time by a rather small group of authors, educators, rabbis, and community leaders in Germany. Men like Ludwig Philippson and his brother, Phoebus Philippson; Markus Lehmann; Moses Wassermann; and Herrmann Reckendorf wrote in German, for a Jewish reading public, mostly youth and families. The first novels came from the liberal camp: Phoebus Philippson's *Die Marranen,* which was published in installments in the *Allgemeine Zeitung des Judentums* in 1834, then in book form in 1850; various of Ludwig Philippson's early stories like *Hispania und Jerusalem* (1848); and Reckendorf's *Geheimnisse der Juden* (1856–57). The neo-Orthodox movement countered with its own version of historical novels, written mostly by Markus Lehmann, a leading figure in this movement. *Bostanai* (1870), *Der Fürst von Coucy* (1872), and *Akiba* (1881) are only a few examples of Lehmann's most popular novels, whose sequels were followed with "glowing cheeks and pounding hearts" by thousands of Jewish youngsters (Lehmann 1910, 79).

Most of the novels were first published in German-Jewish periodicals: in the widely read Reform organs *Allgemeine Zeitung des Judentums* and *Jüdische Volksblatt* (both edited by Ludwig Philippson), and in the neo-Orthodox journal, *Der Israelit* (edited by Markus Lehmann). They were then published in book form, sometimes distributed gratis to the subscribers of these periodicals, and then republished in various volumes of collected works.

The contribution of these novels did not lie in their high literary value, nor were they written by or for a literary-cultural elite, yet they played a major role in constructing what modern research into Jewish nationalism terms the "precursors" of modern Jewish national consciousness. Rather than formulating clear and systematic "national" thought, they expressed the more vague emotions and longings of their authors (and, to a great extent, of their readers)—sentiments that often clashed with the principles formulated in nonbelletristic writing.

Most of these historical novels were later translated into Hebrew and enjoyed great success in Eastern Europe, so that they played a major role not only in Jewish culture in Germany but in the Hebrew culture developing in Eastern Europe. Their translations/adaptations were also published in Hebrew periodicals in Palestine (*Ha'havazelet,* for instance, from 1870 to 1882), where they later shaped models for and formed part of a repertoire of Jewish heroes in children's literature and in primers produced in Israel. Testimonies from the period maintain that these works were read by children and adults with equal enthusiasm, and some readers went so far as to assert that the historical novels had influenced their practical actions, as a factor determining their decisions to emigrate to Israel, for instance. Most of the translations/adaptations are still available in Israel's libraries for young children.

The emergence of a Jewish historical novel was neither "natural" nor self-evident. Critics espousing Hebrew Enlightenment norms, which still dominated Jewish culture throughout the first half of the nineteenth century, perceived the historical novel as "trivial" nondidactic literature. Toward the middle of the century, however, internal as well as external conditions arose that brought about the acceptance of the historical novel. Yet even then, the writers of historical novels were forced to legitimize their works as informative and educational literature and to present the genre as a "familiar" model.

The stages of the acceptance of the historical novel indicate the role of external and internal "pressure": the German-Jewish historical novel was adopted after the enormous popularity of the historical novel in German culture, which, after the initial stage of massive translation from the English, subsequently took a national form that rejected "foreign" elements and adopted Germanic themes unacceptable to Jewish culture. The acceptance of the German-Jewish historical novel, first by the Reform movement and much later by the neo-Orthodox one, was accelerated by the fear that German-reading Jewish youth, in search of lighter forms of reading, would turn to this German literature. Its acceptance was a reaction to other popular Jewish (and German) models describing the present.

It should be noted that these stages did not coincide with the development of the genre in German culture. In fact, in every stage of the process a somewhat outdated model was adopted. This chronological gap could have been a result of the reluctance with which the popular novel was admitted into Jewish culture, as well as of the necessity of simultaneously adapting the literary model to this reading public and reshaping the reading public according to the ideology of the texts. The formation of this broad yet clearly defined reading public may have been partly assisted by the establishment of the various ideologically oriented periodicals.

Reading the Jewish historical novel within the context of its function in Jewish culture exposes the complex processes that Jewish culture was undergoing in nineteenth-century Germany and the way popular literature was mobilized in the cause of external emancipatory and internal (reformatory) struggles. The German-Jewish historical novel reflects the need to reshape thinking patterns concerning the past, to "update" tradition and to alter the Jewish image, both in Jewish and in non-Jewish eyes. It particularly reflects the duality with respect to the national aspect of Judaism characteristic of German Jews affiliated with the two major ideological camps. This duality is expressed in the clash between, on the one hand, the effort to efface any trace of nationality and to stress the universalist (and even confessionalist) aspect of Judaism, and, on the other hand, the strong national feeling emerging almost involuntarily, perhaps even unconsciously, from the romantic (Herderian) recognition of the uniqueness of the Jewish people, the value of its spiritual and cultural heritage, and its contribution to world culture.

This duality, appearing as a conflict between the rationalist formulation and the belletristic-romantic presentation, is illustrated by the fact that the same rabbis, educators, and community leaders who wrote historical novels because they recognized the need for these novels and wanted to exploit the various possibilities they offered also wrote using "higher"—historiographic, religious, or polemical—literary forms. Moreover, their writing in each case was significantly different, even when the subject matter was identical.

The later success of the German-Jewish historical novel in Eastern Europe, within the context of the Hebrew Revival, indicates that most novels shared a component that could, with proper adaptation, be read as national. In the process of translating the German-Jewish historical novels into Hebrew, the novels were rewritten according to the needs of Hebrew culture in Eastern Europe and in Israel. Thus the analysis of these translations/adaptations reveals the change in the portrayal of the past, in the new historical images that ensued, and in the new vision of the collective future. Yet the Hebrew translations did not "append" to the Jewish novel traits that were absent from the original. Rather, they accentuated and developed traits inherent in it. Thus the reading of the translations/adaptations themselves, as well as their "retrospective" reading, throws additional light on the uniquely problematic texture of the German-Jewish historical novel in the nineteenth century.

Theoretically, the writers of the German-Jewish historical novel had access to the rich repertoire of European literatures. In practice, in view of the needs of Jewish culture, the options were limited. Since the eighteenth-century Hebrew Enlightenment, German-Jewish culture had reacted to developments in German culture and had evolved in correlation to it. Due to the special development of the Jewish culture and the direction that German culture was taking, however, adoption of the historical novel proved to be problematic. The German-Jewish historical novel began to appear in the 1830s at a low point in the popularity of the German historical novel, when the German historical novel à la Walter Scott had reached a point of stagnation and the political-literary *Jungdeutschen* movement demanded that literature deal directly with the *Zeitroman* (present). At this stage there was no compatibility between the two cultural systems, and the needs of Jewish culture were only partly answered by a former stage in German culture.

Later, from the middle of the nineteenth century onward, there seemed to be a simultaneous engagement between the two cultures, mainly due to the revival of the German historical novel at a time when the German-Jewish historical novel began to flourish. This apparent simultaneity was mostly illusory, however, because this was the period of the crystallization of the German "national" historical novel, which was mobilized consciously and unconsciously to reinforce Bismarck's efforts toward the unification of Germany and the establishment of the Reich. In this period, most of the activities of the cultural systems in Germany united in the effort of turning Germany into a nation by recreating and distributing "German" myths and "common" traditions, and by recovering the German *Eigentümlichkeit* or *Volksgeist*. Historiography, high literature, and popular literature were duly mobilized. Periodicals joined in the effort with the *Feuilleton-Romane,* novels published in sequences in family journals like the *Gartenlaube,* which was established in 1853 *Kolportageromane,* small cheap editions of novels that were sold door-to-door, played a significant role in the process due to their wide distribution among all strata of the rising bourgeois class. The German historical novel was also mobilized, because its immense popularity offered tremendous possibilities for the popularization of ideas and philosophies of history and for the implementation of the notion of German history. This process was accomplished with the unification of Germany and the establishment of the Reich in 1871. After this time, the nineteenth-century German historical novel died out, whereas the Jewish historical novel was still at the peak of its success.

The main ideological camps in German-Jewish culture regarded themselves as partners in the formation of German national identity and in Bismarck's *Kulturkampf,* but sought to join it as unique citizens with individual cultural assets. They looked for ways to stress that there was no contradiction between devotion to the German *Vaterland* and a sense of the unity of the Jewish people, defined by Fraenkel and others as *Stammesgenossen.* But there was no room for a separate Jewish culture within this German culture as it developed its national consciousness. Thus, when the historical novel finally made its way into Jewish culture, it could no longer borrow themes from German culture. It could, for instance, adopt the general idea of seeking pride in "glorious" periods of the past, but it had to turn to Spain for examples of glory, because although the German national culture preferred periods like the Middle Ages in central Europe, these were considered problematic in the Jewish collective memory. In the same way, the Jewish historical novel refrained from seeking its "roots" in antiquity; Jewish historiographers tended, for different reasons, to avoid describing periods like the First Temple period or even prior ones.

Models from European culture, though available, were also not an option. Even if Jewish culture was aware of occurrences in European literature, borrowing was chiefly accomplished through the mediation of German culture, and the main condition for acceptance was "permission" from German culture. Since the Hebrew Enlightenment, French literature (in German mediation) had been a natural source for models, but when it lost its status in German culture it ceased to be a real option for Jewish writers. Jewish leaders like Ludwig Philippson, who considered themselves true German patriots, joined in the general chorus of criticizing the French influence and glorifying the German "genius," as exemplified for them, not accidentally, by Lessing. Moreover, the French historical novel itself was developing mostly along national and adventurous lines, which could hardly serve the German-Jewish culture as a proper source of imitation. German-Jewish literature primarily had to adopt models that had been accepted by German culture, that had passed its censorship, and that would not be branded trivial. Thus Jewish writers adopted elements from the French "social" historical novel, represented by Eugene Sue, whose novels were widely acclaimed, translated, and imitated in German culture.

English philo-Semitic literature, which enjoyed great popularity in Europe and Germany, continued to present available models (through the mediation of the German). These novels included the works of the Jewish writer Grace Aguilar, the novels of the converted Disraeli, and the novels of the philo-Semitic George Eliot. Such texts, however, presented a problem for German-Jewish culture, because they suggested territorial solutions to what had begun to be termed, innocently enough, the Jewish Problem. Such solutions were a source of embarrassment for German Jews, who had been suffering from the image of a state within a state and felt compelled to prove that they deserved to be called loyal German citizens.

This type of elimination of available models accounts for the fact that the Jewish historical novel borrowed only selected elements from the general repertoire of German, French, and English literatures. It borrowed the idea of writing historical novels for ideological needs from German literature. With this idea came a number of suitable ideological elements: rewriting popular history with the aim of proving the continuity of Jewish existence; using this continuity as a source of encouragement and pride; and correcting the wrong image of Jews and Jewry by highlighting heroic moments of Jewish history. From neighboring cultures (via the mediation of the German), the Jewish historical novel could borrow other, carefully filtered elements, whether structural (a Sue-like description of twenty-two generations of the house of David), thematic (the Marranos), or repertorial (the model of the proud Sephardic Jew, in perfect harmony with his environment). It also adopted contradictory elements from other models, like polemic elements from the Zeitroman of the Young German movements. It was this rather general framework that the writers of Jewish historical novels sought to fill with German-Jewish themes according to the varying needs of each different ideological camp.

Two major conditions brought about the acceptance of the German-Jewish historical novel: (1) a growing interest, shown by German Jewry since the Enlightenment and especially since the foundation of Wissenschaft des Judentums in Jewish history, Jewish historiography, and its place in world history; and (2) the possibility of translating the historical novel at every stage in terms of a familiar "safe" model, and of legitimizing it as such. Both conditions helped to secure the historical novel as an acknowledged model in Jewish culture. For instance, under the didactic mask of teaching Jewish history to Jewish youth, it was possible to justify the writing of such "trivial" literature for youth. The historical novel was also able to present itself as a biographical novel. This explains why the German-Jewish historical novel tended to recount the lives of famous historical protagonists, whereas the original (English and German) historical novels rejected the use of historical personae as their focus. The historical-biographical neo-Orthodox novel, which focused on a series of famous Jewish *Schtadlanim* (Rabbi Josselmann v. Rosheim, Süss Oppenheim) best illustrates this trend.

The historical novel was accepted in a period marked by the growing need to shape, and to some extent invent, an updated Jewish tradition and a new set of historical images to suit the needs of the modern German Jew. This reform effort is known to have divided German Jewry into two main camps, the liberal (or Reform) camp and the neo-Orthodox one, which differed in their views over the need for, type of, and extent of reform. Each camp sought to anchor its new or renewed system of concepts in precedents from Jewish history. To this end, each camp was, in its own way, preoccupied with "discovering" history as well as "activating" it—that is, with seeking in past occurrences legitimation for new present images, and at the same time projecting these new images of the present onto the past. The historical novel was conceived as a tool for distributing these new images among wider strata of the Jewish public, officially among youth, with youth literature serving as a pipeline to the rest of Jewish society.

Side by side with the reform struggle, the *emancipatory* struggle sought, among other goals, to change the image of the German Jew and to eliminate any sign of the "Ghetto Jew." Within this framework, the historical novel struggled against Jewish and German novels of the present, sometimes termed *Ghettogeschichten,* which were written by Jewish authors like Aron Bernstein, Leopold Kompert, and Karl-Emil Franzos, and by German authors like Wilhelm Raabe, Gustav Freytag, Karl Gutzkow, and even Berthold Auer-

bach in his *Dorfgeschichten.* These writers tended to describe traditional Jewish figures and customs in caricature-like fashion, which enjoyed a certain amount of success among assimilated and non-Jewish readers. The Jewish historical novel defined itself primarily in opposition to this literature and was written with the doubly idealistic aim of embellishing and correcting this image of Jews and Judaism. But because it was not meant for a German public, one must assume that the main effort was directed at re-forming—and reforming—the concepts of Jews and Judaism from within.

The creation by the historical novel of a new repertoire of heroes played a vital role in this process of forming a new Jewish image. This repertoire selected or invented past personae for the purpose of creating a "new" Jew, a "new" Jewess, and a "new" Jewish family to comply with nineteenth-century needs. To achieve this goal, it selected and brought together images from the Hebrew Enlightenment and from the nineteenth-century German bourgeoisie.

To counter a frustrating sense of rejection from German culture, the proponents of emancipation saw the need to prove the unique importance of Jewish culture. This need, whether a reflection of an apologetic attitude in the face of antagonism or of the internal awareness, legitimized by German Romanticism, of the uniqueness of Jewish culture, found an expression in the historical novel. The rewriting of history stemmed from the need to describe the breadth and depth of Jewish culture in the past, so as to provide the modern Jew with a *billet d'entrée* (admission ticket) to European culture in general and to German culture in particular, *as an equal partner.* This billet d'entrée, as opposed to the one suggested by Heine, aimed at preserving the Jewish character and drawing pride from it.

This new conceptual model sparked the recognition that the sense of identification and affinity experienced by the Jewish people stemmed not only from external rejection or a common fate, but from the very uniqueness of Jewish culture. In this context, the acceptance of the historical novel resulted from an acknowledgment that the historical novel had been a major factor in shaping collective consciousness, identity, and affinity. This acknowledgment was borrowed from German polemics over the function of the historical novel and echoed through the introductions to historical novels throughout the nineteenth century. Following the renewed sense of unity came the need to recover and rediscover national symbols cast aside by the Enlightenment in favor of integration. One of the roles of the historical novel in this respect was to reshape these signs of symbolic nationality and bring them back to consciousness.

In addition to these needs, common to the Jewish historical novel of all ideological hues, the historical novel also gained acceptance out of a recognition of the possibilities it offered as a valuable tool in the inner struggle between the two main opposing camps in German Jewry. The neo-Orthodox camp at first showed preference for the novel of the present, mainly out of fear of what might prove to be a "dangerous" inquiry into historical material that could lead to a scientific investigation of sacred texts. This camp was particularly averse to the idea of using the Bible as background material for trivial literature. Moreover, the priorities of this camp did not lie in exploring the past, but in helping the Jew, who was struggling with his surroundings, to solve the problems and avoid the dangers of the present. In opposition to the Reformists, this camp was also eager to demonstrate a total lack of "inferiority" concerning the self-image and / or public image of the Jew, and therefore did not shy away from descriptions of the "Ghetto Jew" abhorred by its opponents. However, in counter-reaction to the popularity of historical stories among the Reform public (and probably out of apprehension that youngsters might read "adverse" literature), the neo-Orthodox camp also adopted the historical novel in an effort to shape the image of a new neo-Orthodox Jew.

The liberal camp, on the other hand, demonstrated a modern, scientific interest in historical research and a marked aversion to novels describing the present. After more than fifty years as editor of the *Allgemeine Zeitung des Judentums,* Ludwig Philippson reacted with growing scorn to contributions of Jewish writers to popular family magazines like the *Gartenlaube* and its Jewish imitators. As late as 1874, he still referred to the popular novel of the present in didactic, Enlightenment terms. He contrasted it with the "higher" genres of poetry and drama as "a flood of dirty water" that wastes the reader's time, distracts his mind, and excites his imagination with "unhealthy" scenes, thereby preventing him from dedicating his spiritual energy to "serious" matters. In opposition to this, Philippson described the historical novel as a "marriage" between "science" and "poetry." His conscious choice of the historical novel expresses his recognition of its importance in shaping the new historical images of the Reform camp.

The different attitude of the various ideological camps to the Jewish historical novel reveals how these two aspects, the external presentation of a more favorable view of Jews and Judaism and the internal reform of Jews and Judaism, functioned as the two major ideological axes. The German-Jewish historical novel held a double dialogue—an outward one with German culture, and an inner one within the opposing Jewish camps. Through the selection and manipulation of the historical "data," each camp presented new images, re-formed a new vision of the past, and created a new repertoire of Jewish heroes. Not only did each use various techniques to achieve legitimation, but they also enlisted this legitimation as a disguise for introducing new patterns of thought.

Analysis of the German-Jewish historical novels of the various ideological camps shows that their principal resemblance lies in their understanding of the historical novel as an ideological vehicle; their differences lie in how this understanding is applied, in terms of the new themes and the new historical images each sought to shape and convey. The novels share the basic recognition of the power of the novel and its liberty to present new concepts with an immediacy that religious, polemic, or historiographic writing can hardly achieve, and to disseminate them more easily through the "back door" of youth literature. Their common characteristics stem from their adherence to Hebrew Enlightenment norms, in the double—and seemingly contradictory—use of bona fide Enlightenment conventions, and as a disguise for introducing innovations.

This double use of Enlightenment norms can be described on three levels. First, the historical novels adhere to Enlightenment norms in their motivation, their legitimation, and their "activation" of history. The motivation to use historical material emanates from the wish to teach and to educate, to present Jewish history in the context of universal history, and to make Jewish history a source of pride for the Jew while approaching history and historiography critically. The need of these novels for legitimation is expressed by the urge to apologize for writing popular novels and for using historical sources, and by the attempts to justify both with respect to Enlightenment norms. Their "activation" of history is indicated in the way the authors select periods or personae from the past because these suit certain needs, while at the same time applying current concepts and ideologies to the past in order to justify and legitimize them.

Second, all texts use accepted Enlightenment-oriented justifications and styles to camouflage the introduction of new concepts. Authors made these new ideas conform with the changes that occurred in German-Jewish culture of the nineteenth century, in terms of both the modern historical material selected and the ideological needs this material was mobilized to serve.

Third, generally speaking, all texts draw from historical "materials" that, more often than not, contradicted each other in several ways: in fact, they represent simultaneous uses of Enlightenment historiography and scientific historiography, universal historiography and national (or supposedly national) historiography. Extreme examples of this use of ideologically incompatible texts can be seen in the use of the works of Markus Jost and Heinrich Graetz, which are based on ideologically contradictory concepts in their perception of the past, their periodization of Jewish history, and their vision of the present (and future) of the Jewish people and its historical mis-

sion. Such historiographies also differed in their presentation of the role of the historiographer and the extent of his emotional involvement in his subject matter.

The novels differ, of course, in their manipulation of the historical "data" to achieve the various ends of their respective ideological programs. The license granted to them by the poetic form enabled their authors to apply a wide range of principles of selecting, presenting, and rewriting history—principles denied them in the "higher" forms of writing. Close reading reveals that the most significant difference is not necessarily between novels from the Reform camp and the neo-Orthodox one (L. Philippson's *Sepphoris and Rom* and Reckendorf's *Geheimnisse der Juden* versus Lehmann's *Akiba,* for instance), but rather between novels based on extreme Reform ideology and novels representing the mainstream of the opposing camps. *Geheimnisse der Juden* stands out for its attempt to present a comprehensive popular history of the Jewish people based on an extreme Reform-oriented historical approach that is different from that of the main camps of Jewish culture.

But even in this respect, the novels of all ideological hues exhibit some similarities. These similarities stem from a problematic shared by German Jews with respect to their loyalty to the German Vaterland, a problematic conveyed by the tension between the ideology and the demands of the romantic (basically German) model: the attempt to undermine the national character of Judaism and justify and idealize the Diaspora, and the wish to enhance national pride through the selection of periods, heroes, and symbols from the "national" repertoire.

This apparent contradiction was irrelevant for the enthusiastic readers of the Jewish novels in Eastern Europe, where the translators emphasized the "national" element and abolished the ambiguity. Thus, it seems that the success of the German-Jewish historical novels in Eastern Europe should be ascribed to a factor with which their writers had not consciously intended to invest them: the national factor potentially embedded in them. That is, by their very selection of Jewish history as a unifying element and source of pride, and in their preoccupation with past myths and symbols like "the Land of the Forefathers" or "the House of David," the authors of these works inadvertently made their works more attractive to Eastern European readers than they otherwise would have been. In fact, retrospectively, and in spite of the writers' efforts to undermine it, a national character could be read into all the German-Jewish novels, just as it could be read into Enlightenment historiography.

It may be claimed, therefore, that the German-Jewish historical novel played a double role in Jewish culture: within the Jewish culture that originally gave it birth, it played a vital role in establishing new historical images and values, in giving expression to unformed and ambivalent emotions, and in forming new literary models. In the Hebrew culture that adopted and adapted it, in Eastern Europe and later in Israel, it played a major role in the creation of a new national ideological system.

The question of the processes of forming a new consciousness of the past has lately been dealt with, rather intensively, within the historiography of Jewish culture, but it has barely been studied in the context of the German-Jewish historical novel. Through its contribution to the formation of new historical images and a new awareness of the past among nineteenth-century German Jewry, the "trivial" historical novel was responsible for enhancing the new historical images no less—and perhaps even more—than "higher" texts written at the time.

The writers of historical novels devoted as much time to their "higher" writing as to their popular, or so-called marginal writing. They did so both within the context of their struggle for equal rights and political and social integration in Germany, and as part of their attempt to form a universalist concept of Judaism and to dispose of the "bonds of national particularism." Yet it was their popular writing that, perhaps because of its very ambivalence, fueled the struggles and dilemmas of a large stratum of German Jews.

The historical novel, in its broad cultural context, is to be regarded as a vehicle for expressing ambivalent positions, both emotional and spiri-

tual, that had not yet found theoretical formulation. Studied as such, the implications of this phenomenon for the growth of a Jewish culture in Germany—as well as its effects on the growth of a parallel Hebrew culture in Eastern Europe and the budding national consciousness that resulted from the contacts between them—become obvious.

The conclusions drawn from reading the historical novel in this context reveal from a new angle the special ambivalent situation of German Jewry in the nineteenth century. These analyses emphasize the continual tension between the attempt to undermine the national aspect of Judaism and the contradictory effort to awaken pride in the national heritage and in Jewish history, an effort that eventually, largely in spite of the conscious intentions of its initiators, resulted in the growth of a new national feeling. The new concept of the past was significant in the formation of modern Jewish consciousness, and the historical novel played a major role in this process.

Bibliography

Mordechai Breuer, *Jüdische Orthodoxie im Deutschen Reich, 1871–1918* (Frankfurt a. M.: Leo Baeck Institut, 1986); David Bronsen, *Jews and Germans from 1860–1933: The Problematic Symbiosis* (Heidelberg: Carl Winter, 1979); Harmut Eggert, *Studien zur Wirkungsgeschichte des deutschen Romans, 1850–1875* (Frankfurt a. M.: Klostermann, 1971); Hans Vilmar Geppert, *Der "andere" historische Roman* (Tübingen: Niemeyer, 1976); Heinz Mosche Graupe, *Die Entstehung des modernen Judentums: Geistesgeschichte der deutschen Juden, 1650–1924* (Hamburg: Leibniz, 1969); Hans Otto Horch, *Auf der Suche nach der jüdischen Erzählliteratur: Die Literaturkritik der "Allgemeinen Zeitung des Judentums" (1837–1922)* (Frankfurt a. M.: Peter Lang, 1985); Ruth Horovitz, *Von Roman des Jungen Deutschen zum Roman des Gartenlaube* (Breslau: Marcus, 1937); Otto W. Johnston, *Der deutsche Nationalmythos: Ursprung eines politischen Programms* (Stuttgart: Metzler, 1990); Marion A. Kaplan, *The Making of the Jewish Middle Class: Women, Family & Identity in Imperial Germany* (Oxford: Oxford University Press, 1991); Jacob Katz, *Out of the Ghetto* (Cambridge, Mass.: Harvard University Press, 1973); Jon Lehmann, *Dr. Markus Lehmann* (Frankfurt a. M.: Kauffmann, 1910); Michael Meier, *Response to Mod-*

ernity (Oxford: Oxford University Press, 1988); Jehuda Reinharz, *Fatherland or Promised Land* (Ann Arbor: University of Michigan Press, 1975); Itta Shedletzky, *Literaturdiskussion und Belletrisik in den jüdischen Zeitschriften in Deutschland, 1837–1918* (Jerusalem: Hebrew University, 1986); Anthony D. Smith, *National Identity* (London: Penguin, 1991); Jacob Toury, *Soziale und politische Geschichte der Juden in Deutschland,* *1847–1871* (Düsseldorf: Droste, 1977); Shulamit Volkov, *Die Erfindung einer Tradition: Zur Entstehung des modernen Judentums in Deutschland* (Munich: Stiftung Historisches Kolleg, 1992); and Henry Wasserman, "Jews and Judaism in the Gartenlaube," *Leo Baeck Year Book* 23 (1978): 47–60.

NITSA BEN-ARI

1840 Heinrich Heine's ghetto tale "The Rabbi of Bacherach" is published

Heine was a master of provocation. The appearance of nearly every one of his works immediately elicited an almost boundless number of reviews, polemics, and counter-statements, which betray a thinly veiled fascination even in the most virulent critiques. It is therefore all the more peculiar that Heine's tale "The Rabbi of Bacherach," which dealt quite openly with the history of his "people" and excoriated an anti-Semitic pogrom committed by a "Christian mob," drew far less attention than did his *Travel Sketches,* his *Book of Songs,* or his *Germany: A Winter's Tale.* Why did it remain somewhat obscure? After all, this tale is as irritating as can be imagined. It opens with a deeply felt, religiously tinged portrayal of a small Jewish community in Bacherach on the Rhine, but this stirring chapter is followed by a humoristic, almost ironic depiction of the Frankfurt ghetto and the sudden appearance of a Sephardic Jew who has repudiated Judaism. Perhaps this contrast was too overdrawn, too crass, to challenge contemporary readers to voice a clear opinion. Not only Jews but also Christians were confused, even unsettled, by this story. Some even wondered where Heine's sympathies really lay in this tale: did he identify with the pious but timid Rabbi Abraham of Bacherach, or with the free-minded but somewhat superficial Don Isaak, who likes Jewish food but dismisses the religious rules of these people as a medieval specter? Don't these two figures, drawn by Heine with equal empathy, stand at opposite extremes? How could he simultaneously sympathize with Jewish Orthodoxy and on the other hand ridicule it? Was Heine really moved by the content of this story, or did he relate it with a tone of ironic distance? Or are we dealing here with two fundamentally different stories?

In order to explain these contradictions, interpreters to date have usually taken as their starting point the complex circumstances under which "The Rabbi of Bacherach" was written. We have long known that the first part of this story was written during Heine's student days in Göttingen, about 1824–25, and that the second part was not added until fifteen years later in Paris. Critics have therefore tried to attribute all these discrepancies to the major shifts in Heine's political, religious, and cultural views between these two periods. They have generally drawn the conclusion that Heine did not succeed in melding these contradictions into a convincing synthesis, and that as a result the work remains unsatisfying. Therefore, we read over and over again, this tale is not a novella at all but a succession of disjointed segments with which Heine simply wanted to fill out the fourth volume of his *Salon.*

Indeed, this thesis cannot be rejected out of hand. The intentions of the first and second parts strike us—at first glance—as radically different. The parts written in Göttingen are marked by a romantic tone that includes moments of melancholy and pain. Despite his fury with the German anti-Semites, Heine eschewed a critical, programmatic voice and instead sought to imitate the mood of historical novels, a genre that had become popular through Sir Walter Scott and German late romanticism. In order to avoid any ill-informed inventions, Heine studied a number of detailed source works dealing with the history of the German Jewry in the fifteenth century, and thus gave his narrative due authenticity and the necessary local color. With his "Rabbi," Heine aimed not at "vain glory," as he wrote to Moses Moser on October 25, 1824, but instead at lighting "an eternal lamp in God's temple" (Heine 1970, 20:176).

Despite these ambitious intentions, the actual writing lagged. Indeed, after a few months, Heine actually gave up on the project altogether. There were several reasons for his decision. First, Heine was scheduled to defend his doctoral dissertation in Göttingen a short time later, for at that time he still expected to take up a career as a lawyer and he feared ruining his prospects by any public display of his Jewishness. In addition, he was already coming to realize that the late romantic mood of his "Rabbi of Bacherach" did not suit him as well as did the humoristic tone of his *Harz Journey,* which he was writing at the same time. Finally, he secretly converted to Lutheranism in the spring of 1825 and was eager to distance himself from Judaism. To be sure, Heine did not throw away the parts of his "Rabbi" that were already finished. Only a short time later, he was forced to confront how little his baptism had helped him with his "Christian brethren." In a moment of regret he even considered including the "Rabbi" fragment in the second volume of his *Travel Sketches,* for he felt that he had nothing more to lose in the world of Christendom. In the following years, however, we hear about this work only once. In a letter to his friend Friedrich Merckel (Heine 1970, 20:39) written in Paris on August 2, 1832, he said that he wanted to "pitch" the "Rabbi of Bacherach" into the second volume of his *Salon.* He did not carry out this plan, either.

It was not until 1840 that the "Rabbi" resurfaced in Heine's correspondence. Heine again needed a filler to reach the required number of pages for the fourth volume of his *Salon,* and he told his publisher, Julius Campe, that he was thinking of adding this "portrayal of medieval manners and morals written fifteen years ago"

(Heine 1970, 21:370). Moreover, he remarked, it would now be an "addendum bearing on current events," and this time he finally decided in favor of the "Rabbi." He regarded this work as newly pertinent in the summer of 1840 because of a horrific event. In this year, the French consul in Damascus had accused the local Jews of murdering a Capuchin monk and of drinking his blood during the Passover seder. Charged with ritual murder, the Jews were subjected to court-ordered torture, and the inaction of the French government in Paris deeply embittered Heine. Therefore he finally dared to publish his long-withheld "Rabbi of Bacherach" with a new, added concluding section, even though it contained such "arch-heretical views" that it was certain to unleash "a huge hue and cry" from both Jews and Christians (Heine to Julius Campe, July 21, 1840, in Heine 1970, 21:370).

Although his contemporaries were largely speechless when confronted with the text's glaring discrepancies, the interpretation of "The Rabbi of Bacherach" has sparked many heated controversies in succeeding generations. German nationalists regarded this work as a forthright admission of Heine's Jewishness, a step with which he had allegedly left the German people once and for all and exposed himself as a "Yid outsider." Literary critics claimed that Heine had no "narrative talent" because the tale had neither coherence nor a sensible conclusion, requirements of any well-crafted novella. The liberals, who definitely liked the story's open, freethinking conclusion, were vexed by its opening passages, which struck them as overly reverent. And the Orthodox Jews praised only the beginning of the tale; they were silent on the last part.

The critiques of these four groups can be challenged with the following arguments. In regard to the nationalistic objections, it can be said that in his "Rabbi of Bacherach" Heine never attacked Germanness per se but only its pernicious connection with Christianity in the form of fanaticized, mob-ruled pogroms. In regard to the literary critique, it can be said that Heine never intended to write a formally closed work of art in either this or any other prose piece. He was no one-sided aesthete committed to the formal closure so typical of the writings of the classical-romantic "age of art," as he mockingly liked to call it. On the contrary, in accordance with Hegel's thesis of the "end of art," he aimed to replace well-rounded stories with critical reflection. And as far as the liberal and Orthodox critiques of "The Rabbi of Bacherach" are concerned, it can be said that Heine in this story was a partisan of neither one nor the other camp. Indeed, he rejected any simplistic, black-and-white contrast and instead tried to depict these two standpoints as the major forms of Judaism that had developed over time.

But even if one rejects the counterarguments offered here, the story is still riven with a contradiction that can only be overcome with deeper and more sophisticated arguments. To do so, it is necessary to take up once again Heine's Jewishness in general and the disturbing elements in his "Rabbi of Bacherach" in particular. Only then can the hidden meaning behind these puzzling contrasts be decoded and the intellectual status of this story be discerned.

Heine's relationship with Jewishness in the years 1824 and 1825 can be characterized in the following way. After his childhood in his parents' home in Düsseldorf, which was marked by a precarious balance between Jewish tradition and Enlightened thought, Heine was carried along by the trend toward assimilation as a student in Bonn and even became deeply involved with the German-nationalist fraternity league (*Burschenschaft*). A short time later, as a student in Göttingen, he was expelled from this league because of his Jewishness. During his semesters in Berlin, he therefore avoided any contact with German-nationalist students and even began ridiculing them. He now became a member of the Association for the Culture and Science of Judaism, to which his friends Eduard Gans and Moses Moser also belonged. Like the other members of this association, he even seems to have considered emigrating at this point, first to the United States, then to Paris, in order to turn his back on the German anti-Semites once and for all.

It was on the basis of this outlook that Heine developed the plan for his "Rabbi of Bacherach." The projected story about the pious Rabbi Abra-

ham and the apostate scholar Isaak Abarbanel was to take place in the year 1489 and to open with the threat of a pogrom. Rabbi Abraham and his wife, Sara, are forced to escape from Bacherach, and they flee to the Frankfurt ghetto, where Abraham, who studied in Spain as a young man, meets his earlier friend Isaak Abarbanel. The text written during this initial phase of Heine's work was suffused with a tone of rebuke and pain at the atrocities inflicted upon the Jews, and the overall project was intended as a novel about the life and martyrdom of the Jews in late medieval Germany. On the one hand Heine aimed to offer a painstakingly accurate depiction of Jewish manners and morals, whereas on the other hand he employed the stylistic devices of romantic enthusiasm with those of the Middle Ages—such as dream sequences; the nocturnal journey on the Rhine; and allusions to knights, dwarves, water sprites, and enchanted princesses. Indeed, at certain points he even blended the Jewish with the romantic by equating the murmurs of the Rhine with the melodies of the Jewish liturgy.

At such points it becomes apparent how much Heine was trying to evoke a mood that was simultaneously poetic and popular, romantic and anti-Christian, committed and aestheticizing. Much of this effort was clearly heartfelt. Other parts, however, seem freighted with details from his source studies. One senses that in these passages Heine was not dealing with familiar material and that he had acquired his knowledge through diligent reading. Although Heine was writing as a private person, he was also writing as a spokesman of an outlook that in its religious form was somewhat foreign to him. But he felt obligated to continue this undertaking not only because he had promised his Berlin friends in the Association for Culture and Science of Judaism to write a novel about the medieval persecutions of the Jews, but also because of the German pogroms in the summer and fall of 1819. During these pogroms, the anti-Semitic call of "Hep-Hep" resounded, Jewish stores were plundered, and synagogues were set on fire.

Unfortunately Heine's aims, however well-intended, were not sufficient to complete his romanticizing and simultaneously "gloomy song of martyrdom." Heine finally set the project aside not just because of the personal reasons already cited, especially his impending baptism, but certainly also because of aesthetic misgivings. In this tale, Heine had evoked a historicizing, romantic-medieval tone that struck him as incompatible with the individualism and present-orientedness of his liberalism. Although in letters up to January 1826 he continued to assure his friend Moser that he would someday complete his "Rabbi," this day never came (Heine 1970, 20:192).

When Heine took up this "fragment" again in 1840, he was confronted with an almost impossible task. We will not deal here with the question of whether he had completed two chapters or just one at this point. It can be stated with some certainty, however, that in the passages written or rewritten in 1840, there is an entirely new tone, one that is devoid not only of the poetically romantic but also of any effort to extol the old Jewish faith. In the meantime Heine had already spent nine years in Paris, and his involvement with Saint-Simonism and his consequent aversion to anything "Nazarene" within the Judeo-Christian tradition—already manifest in his *History of Religion and Philosophy in Germany* and then in his *Memorandum* on Ludwig Börne—was increasingly leading him away from anything that had to with Jews and Jewishness.

The passages that take place in Frankfurt, those at the beginning of the second part, are therefore marked by a decidedly lighthearted tone. The "gloomy song of martyrdom" is no longer to be heard. The very first two Jews whom Abraham and Sara encounter, the gatekeepers Jäckel and Nasenstern, have droll traits and are not as solemnly treated as are the pious Jews of the first chapter. The other ghetto dwellers are also depicted humorously rather than reverently. In the Frankfurt synagogue scene, "the sense of worship" among the men "begins to fade rather quickly." Some "take their ease," and others whisper "with their neighbors about worldly matters." Just as impious are the women in the synagogue's gallery, whose devotions "diminish" even more rapidly. Instead of listening to the cantor, they engage in "chatting and laughing." Special wit is devoted to the figure of the Schnapper-Elle,

the owner of a small eatery who attracts attention among the assembled women with her outlandish attire and obstreperous behavior.

The following scene is even louder, as Abraham and Sara mix with the crowd on the street and suddenly encounter Don Isaak Abarbanel, a lady-killer who immediately pays the most flattering compliments to the beautiful Sara. Conceived by Heine in 1824–25 as a "Spanish Jew" who had "converted because of an extravagant impulsiveness," Don Isaak becomes in this passage a mouthpiece for that "Hellenic" spirit that Heine, in his Börne *Memorandum*, had diametrically opposed to the "Nazarene" spirit. "Yes, I am a heathen," Don Isaak tells the horrified Rabbi Abraham, "and I find the gloomy, guilt-ridden Nazarenes just as repulsive as the dried-up, joyless Hebrews." Asked why he is still drawn to the Jews, Isaak replies that his sole reason is the "exquisite fragrance" of Jewish cooking. "Traffic with God's own people is otherwise not my hobby," he declares, "and I visit the Judengasse to eat, certainly not to pray." Rabbi Abraham can only capitulate in the face of so much witty forthrightness. Obviously Heine, too, no longer knew how to continue, for he simply broke off the story after this exchange.

Almost all interpreters have usually reacted to the contrast between the story's gloomy, reproachful opening and its ironic closing with exasperation or total confusion. But what did these critics expect from Heine: a straightforward, perhaps even nostalgia-tinged ghetto tale, or an equally straightforward story of emancipation with the major emphasis on freethinking and the denial of God? Granted, both possibilities were open to Heine. But to write a one-sidedly reverent ghetto tale, as would become quite popular among German-Jewish writers in the second half of the nineteenth century, would have deeply contradicted Heine's own urge to also assimilate his emphatically liberal, even rebellious outlook. He was neither religious nor romantic enough for such an approach. But it was equally impossible for him to write a one-sided emancipation story that tended intellectually toward Jewish assimilation within the "superior" culture of the West. To be sure, such stories did already exist at that time. The earliest of these tales, Karl Gutzkow's "The Sadducean of Amsterdam" (1834), had actually appeared prior to Heine's "Rabbi." It deals with the fate of Uriel Acosta, who tries to rebel against Amsterdam's Orthodox rabbinate but twice recants because of his love for the beautiful and pious Judith. He even accepts the most appalling punishments and tortures of the Orthodox Jews until he realizes that Judith loves another man, whereupon he shoots both her and himself. In this story there is, as in every "proper" novella, a clear beginning and a clear ending. But a high price is paid for this formal coherence: first, the tale employs a black-and-white approach typical of pulp fiction in its portrayal of Orthodox Jews as dastards and freethinkers as victims; and second, it promotes a linear view of history that approves only of development toward agnosticism while it demonizes all older forms of religion as fanatical.

But matters were not so simple for Heine. A dialectical thinker, he realized from the outset that for Jews in the diaspora—in contrast to the members of other nations—there is not just one identity, be it the strictly Jewish or that taken on from contact with the host society. For Heine, the Jew was always both the one and the other. Viewed in this way, "The Rabbi of Bacherach" stands as one of the most telling accounts of pre-Zionist Jewry. Because they still lacked any hope of a new Eretz Israel, these Jews lived in a constant inner contradiction: they sought to maintain the old beliefs even though they simultaneously longed for Western liberalism. Heine felt this contradiction more clearly than most of his Jewish or non-Jewish contemporaries, who favored either one or the other alternative. He knew that the Enlightenment's rationalism and cosmopolitanism had set into motion a process that brought not just gains but also losses for all existing peoples, cultures, and religions. As a good Hegelian, he saw that the old cannot always be dismissed as "bad" and the new embraced as "good." Instead, every step forward entails a step backward in other areas. His Don Isaak is indeed superior to Rabbi Abraham in intellectual agility, but he has less of the earnestness, the soulfulness, that distinguishes the latter. Heine knew all too well that the dialectic of liberalization contrib-

utes not only to emancipation, but also to growing superficiality, which means the loss of national and human identity. For this reason Heine was not taken in by any facile optimism about progress, and he endorsed both the old and the new in their good senses rather than simply playing off one against the other. Deeply aware of the long and painful history of Jewry, he would have regarded it as an act of betrayal to forget the sufferings of his people—to switch over blithely from the world of the ghetto into the liberated, secularized world of modern Enlightenment and lapse into a comfortable amnesia.

In this light, Heine's "Rabbi of Bacherach" is the story par excellence of Jews both persecuted in the diaspora and simultaneously striving toward assimilation. This master narrative is set in the year 1489, to be sure, but it also takes place in the following centuries, and even in Heine's own time. It demonstrates that Jews have long lived in the nonsynchronicity of Orthodoxy and emancipation. They were continually forced to relive their earlier history, which cannot be narrowly localized or historicized. Thus we read that several pogroms took place in Germany in the year 1489, at a time when the Jews in Spain still enjoyed their chartered tolerance. But the historically aware reader knows full well that a scant three years later the Jews were driven out of Spain. We also know that Germany was the scene of renewed pogroms in 1819—indeed, that in 1840, as the final parts of this story were being put to paper, barbaric persecutions of Jews were again occurring in Damascus, which were later followed by even more horrible pogroms in Russia, Poland, and Nazi-occupied Europe.

With his Jewish ancestry, Heine was likewise rooted in the fifteenth as well as the nineteenth centuries, and he could therefore empathize with both Rabbi Abraham and Don Isaak. In the character of Rabbi Abraham, he expressed his pain over the injustices visited upon the Jewish people. Through Don Isaak, he voiced his allegiance to a cosmopolitanism for which humanity stands higher than obedience to time-honored laws. As a self-consciously German-Jewish author who wrote this story out of a profound sense of personal involvement, he felt for the one as well as the other. With this dual identity, he was in a position to forge a stronger bond to humanity than if he had committed himself to a one-sided outlook.

"The Rabbi of Bacherach" thus stands as the story of that Jewry whose history was still open-ended at Heine's time. Embedded in an ongoing dialectic of perseverance and emancipation, this history could only be portrayed as an unfinished fragment. There can be no end to this tale, because the Jews depicted here live in a social setting that is not yet willing to tolerate their difference. Accordingly, Heine—despite his emphatic drive toward emancipation—clung tenaciously to his Jewish distinctiveness. He was of the conviction that Jews should never relinquish their otherness until the surrounding society has moved beyond all national, racial, and religious divisions, and thereby beyond all claims to domination. Only then, in Heine's view, can Jews arrive at a truly enlightened cosmopolitanism.

Bibliography

Rainer Feldmann, "Heinrich Heine: Der Rabbi von Bacherach," Ph.D. diss., Paderborn, University of Paderborn, 1984; Lion Feuchtwanger, "Heinrich Heines 'Rabbi von Bacherach,'" Ph.D. diss., Munich, University of Munich, 1907; Heinrich Heine, *Säkularausgabe* (Berlin: Akademie Verlag, 1970–95); Hartmut Kircher, *Heinrich Heine und das Judentum* (Bonn: Bouvier, 1973), 200–210; Hartmut Kircher, ed., *Heinrich Heine: Der Rabbi von Bacherach* (Stuttgart: Reclam, 1983); Erich Loewenthal, "Der Rabbi von Bacherach," *Heine-Jahrbuch* (1964): 3–16; Ludwig Rosenthal, *Heinrich Heine als Jude* (Berlin: Ullstein, 1973), 165–82; and Jeffrey L. Sammons, "Heine's 'Rabbi von Bacherach': The Unresolved Tensions," *German Quarterly* 37 (1964): 26–38.

JOST HERMAND

TRANSLATED BY JAMES STEAKLEY

1843 Berthold Auerbach's first collection of *Dorfgeschichten* appears

Berthold Auerbach, unlike any other German-language writer until the last third of the nineteenth century, can be taken as representative of the development of the German-Jewish relationship in general and of the Jewish contribution to German literature in particular. To make such a claim may seem provocative in the face of the international literary significance of Heinrich Heine or the (at least) European influence of Ludwig Börne, especially if one takes into account the considerable distance in aesthetic quality between Auerbach and the other two, which more than any other factor is probably responsible for the rapid neglect of Auerbach after his death. Nevertheless, it is not the most outstanding but rather the middlebrow writers who are best known for having a vision that is limited to their own epoch and its progressive possibilities. For this reason, they are capable of leaving their signature upon the period. And if one compares the life and work of Auerbach with that of Heine, it becomes immediately clear that the former was much more in the mainstream as far as the actual evolution of the relationship between Germans and Jews is concerned. Heine was always innovative and galvanizing in the manner in which he proclaimed the universal emancipation of humanity in his works. Though Auerbach subscribed to the same fundamental values of freedom and equality as Heine, he felt that they could be realized only by means of compromises with the emergent (albeit belated) German nationalist movement that became more questionable to the Jews during the latter part of the nineteenth century.

It was precisely this attitude that won Auerbach the praise of similarly minded Jews. Hence, upon Auerbach's death, the philosopher and rabbi Ludwig Stein (1859–1930) distinguished Auerbach from Heine and Börne, extolling Auerbach's accommodating national liberal (*nationalliberal*) views that were in no way contingent upon his being Jewish: "Heine and Börne were Jews in their writings, but not in their lives. Berthold Auerbach, on the other hand, lived as a Jew, but did not write as one" (Stein 1882, 8). Even though this evaluation has its limitations, it still reveals both the public perception of the writer and his own private ideal: the triad of Swabian origins, Jewishness, and Germanness was seen as the right mixture for overcoming latent or manifest social exclusion and for fashioning a literary oeuvre. It was precisely this orientation that, generations later, evoked the rage of anti-Semites with their idée fixe that all mixed identities, especially those with a Jewish component, were reprehensible. In the second edition of *Semi-Kürschner,* consequently, Auerbach was deemed worthy of an extensive article that closed with a quote by B. Saphra (that is, Benjamin Segel) from the Jewish journal *Ost und West*. For Saphra, all of Auerbach's books were Jewish, "the most Jewish being those that weren't about Jews" (Segel 1929, 333). What an advocate of a Jewish Renaissance saw as positive was seen by anti-Semites as proof for the validity of their indisputable racist instincts.

The life of Berthold Auerbach spanned the rise and fall of German-Jewish integration. In 1812, the year he was born, the first Prussian emancipation laws set an idea in motion that—with a delay of two generations—was realized in the constitutions of the Norddeutscher Bund (northern German federation) in 1869 and the German Empire in 1871. When Auerbach died in 1882, Jews had already secured legal rights, but an intensified campaign of anti-Semitism began to dispute Jewish attempts to integrate socially—a campaign that in effect prefigured the extermination of German and European Jewry in the Third Reich. In light of these developments, Auerbach's lament "I have lived and worked in vain!" voiced in a letter to Jakob Auerbach (November 23, 1880), his friend of many years, is a succinct formulation of the experiences that shattered his hopes that Jews might achieve full integration as German citizens. Auerbach's oeuvre—from the tales and novels to the critical essays and *Kalendergeschichten*—relates in its autobiographical undercurrent, overtly and covertly, the precarious attempt to bring his identities as a free-thinking Jew, a staunch southern German, and a patriotic liberal *Kleindeutscher* into a viable, acceptable equilibrium.

Decisive in Auerbach's view of himself was the situation in his hometown of Nordstetten near Horb, a village in the Black Forest where a large number of Jews lived among Swabian peasants in apparently tolerable social and religious conditions. Auerbach went on to idealize Nordstetten in his *Schwarzwälder Dorfgeschichten* (Black Forest village stories) as a national model of German-Jewish harmony, the epitome of *Heimat*. The accommodationist tendency of this admittedly utopian design looked like a "coerced reconciliation" (to cite Theodor W. Adorno's criticism of Georg Lukács' interpretation of Realism) in view of the not infrequent clashes between Christians and Jews that Auerbach recounted in private.

Auerbach's socialization as a Jew at the outset of the nineteenth century was not atypical. Moses Baruch Auerbacher (Berthold Auerbach's name until it was changed in 1830) was born February 28, 1812, the ninth child of the merchant Jakob Auerbacher and his wife, Edel (née Frank). His birthplace of Nordstetten had formerly been part of Austria and was still typically Josephinian in its dual composition of Catholics and Jews. He was first exposed to the world beyond the village sphere after Bernhard Frankfurter—an especially capable Jewish teacher who later collected some material for the first Dorfgeschichten—was assigned to Nordstetten. The young Auerbach was supposed to become a rabbi, like his grandfather after whom he was named, and was sent off to the traditional yeshiva in Hechingen at age thirteen. Just two years later, however, he left the Talmud-Torah school, which he evidently found oppressive, due to lack of funds. He was only too glad to move into an uncle's house in Karlsruhe, where he prepared himself for the Stuttgarter Gymnasium; after failing the first test, he was eventually admitted in the summer of 1830. In 1832 Auerbach began to study law in Tübingen, but political circumstances brought him in 1833 to Munich. There, suspected of being a *Burschenschaftler* (member of students' association), he was arrested, questioned, and returned to Swabia on the orders of the district superior court in Tübingen. After being expelled from the university there at the end of 1833, Auerbach registered at the university of Heidelberg. Although he continued to be officially enrolled as a student of "Jewish theology"—which did not keep him from attending lectures in any number of disciplines (particularly in philosophy, history, and literary studies) or from declaring in an 1831 letter to Frankfurter that he was not suited to the rabbinate (Bertelheim 1907, 56f.)—Auerbach had already begun to write fiction. He was presumably not unhappy that his Burschenschaft affiliation made it impossible for him to take the rabbinical examination. Like so many other Jews who had sought acculturation, he embraced German and European literature as his new religion (87). At the end of 1836, he was prosecuted as a demagogue and was sentenced to two months in the Hohenasperg prison. Yet the incarceration did not in any way diminish his resolve to establish himself as a freelance writer. He used the opportunity to write his first novel about the renowned philosopher and apostate Spinoza.

It was not until the 1840s that Auerbach discovered that model of a national but universal-humanistic "Heimatliteratur" exemplified in the realistic Dorfgeschichte, a model that made him famous and became his trademark in literary history. Yet prior to that time, Auerbach had tried for a number of years to make a name for himself as a professing Jewish writer, not just to appeal (as one might expect) to the unmistakably tiny Jewish audience, but also to familiarize the general reading public with Jewish issues. His attempts to reflect Jewish life in a period of crisis and transition—for example, the essay "Das Judenthum und die neueste Literatur" (1836), the historical novels *Spinoza* (1837) and *Dichter und Kaufmann* (1840), and a planned "Ghetto" cycle—all proved to be disappointments, however. In "Das Judenthum und die neueste Literatur," Auerbach countered the materialism and sensualism of Junges Deutschland (particularly with respect to Heine), while opposing Wolfgang Menzel's condemnation of the politically harassed liberals as "Junges Palästina." At the same time, he was perceptive enough to recognize how ambivalent many liberal non-Jewish literati were toward the Jews, to the point of demanding that the latter discard all traces of Jewishness before they could be embraced as allies. In his *Spinoza* novel, Auerbach wrote a masked and wishful autobiography. The historical figure of Spinoza (of whom Auerbach had already translated and written a biography) becomes the exemplar of anti-Orthodoxy and religious tolerance under the banner of an enlightened Reform Judaism as embodied in his friend Abraham Geiger. *Dichter und Kaufmann,* on the other hand, depicts the life of Moses Ephraim Kuh, the first Jewish poet to write in German. Kuh represents the substantial difficulties Jews faced in the first phase of emancipation as they tried to break out of their inner and outer ghettos and become free citizens together with Christians, who were also victimized by absolutism. *Bildung* is the sole motto here, not—as still was the case for the traveler in Lessing's early comedy *Die Juden*—Bildung and property. For the young Auerbach (not unlike Ludwig Börne), the pecuniary disposition of Jews and Christians alike seemed to epitomize a *gegenbürgerlich* (anti-civic)

spirit that had to be transcended if an ideal commonwealth was to emerge.

The fact that both of his Jewish novels were unsuccessful was a sore point for Auerbach. Until the end of his life he made plans to write various *Judenerzählungen* (Jewish tales) and a *Judenroman* (Jewish novel) that would also cover the present, yet he never produced anything more than fragmentary notes. Auerbach's decision to proceed with the Dorfgeschichte after 1840 (the first collection appeared in 1843) can be seen, at least in part, as an attempt to translate the German-Jewish predicament into the more general dialectic of the exotic and the Heimat (familiar) that he would elucidate in *Schrift und Volk* (1858), a book that resonated with young Hegelian ideas. The writer is compared to a journeyman who returns home after years of travel: "He was cut off from himself, his exceptional soul surrendered to another place; he had achieved opposition, separation and thus the capacity to mediate. While away he felt at home, and now at home he feels removed and yet still at home. What is familiar and what is not become intertwined and form for him a new home [*Heimat*]" (Auerbach 1864, 28).

The writer described here points to that peculiarly Jewish discrepancy of feeling both safe and exposed wherever one might live. Auerbach's restless travels are in many ways the real test of this theory, and a trace of this can definitely be found in Alfred Wolfenstein's later identification of the modern Expressionist poet with the Jewish intellectual. Yet Auerbach had already located the specific Jewish elements of the broader existential predicament prior to the twentieth century. Whereas the human condition was addressed in the early novels as it appeared in Jewish milieus, the later works do the opposite, taking up the cause of the Jews in a non-Jewish setting. At stake here are not religious questions: Auerbach did not claim to be a devout Jew, but thought of himself as belonging to a historical community of traditions and fate (*Traditions- und Schicksalsgemeinschaft*) and therefore saw religious customs in a positive, even sentimental light. In the pre-1848 *Dorfgeschichte,* humanity and rationality are exemplified by the minor characters who are Jews. But even a non-Jewish figure like Vefele (in *Des Schloßbauers Vefele,* 1843), stigmatized by both her physical impairment and her status as the daughter of the village outsider, elucidates the socio- and pathogenesis of intolerance. It is no coincidence that it is the *Handelsjude* (trader Jew) Marem who does a favor for her before she commits suicide. Jewish issues and other social problems are similarly linked in *Die Sträflinge* (1846) and in *Ivo, der Hajrle* (1843), where the debate surrounding Orthodox Judaism is mirrored in the opposition of a Catholic initiate who manages to resist the dogmas of positive religion with the help of enlightened universalist piety. Finally, the tale "Der Lauterbacher" (1843), in according high status to concrete cultural practice and correspondingly relativizing abstract idealism, suggests how prejudice toward both peasants and Jews can be eliminated.

At the same time, Auerbach deliberately used the program of detail-bound early Realism, as embodied in the genre of the Dorfgeschichte, to propagate the idea of German-Jewish integration. He continued to hold this view even after the failed Revolution of 1848, which he had championed among other reasons as an important opportunity to improve the position of the Jews. The growing tendency to idealize the village world, though attacked by critics as an escapist pipedream, can also be seen as a renewed appeal to finally "bring home" all outsiders, Jews as well. The village was only in the most ideal sense the place where social harmony might be achieved. The reality—an exclusionary society—looked far less humane. The fictional victims of ostracization are usually non-Jews, such as the Black Marann and the orphans Amrei and Dami in Auerbach's most famous postrevolutionary Dorfgeschichte *Barfüßele* (1856). Even in their own village the three characters behave as though they were "drifters in a foreign land." The decision by the orphans to emigrate to the Alsace illustrates the Jewish subtext, for Jews were being granted civil rights there as well as in the rest of France. If discrimination against the Jews was truly on the wane in the majority Christian society as this story and Auerbach's didactic *Kalendergeschichten*

were appearing between 1846 and 1869, the situation had changed radically by the time he published his last collection of Dorfgeschichten (*Nach dreißig Jahren,* 1876) and his very last village story ("Brigitta," 1880). Despite having achieved legal equality a few years earlier, Jews were being subjected to a level of social injustice hitherto unseen in modern Germany. In the face of it, recurring narrative evocations of a communal spirit seemed rather illusory.

Auerbach's turn to the *Zeit- und Gesellschaftsroman* (the novel of contemporary society) was prompted by the failure of the *Bürgerliche Revolution* (middle-class revolution) of 1848–49. Yet Auerbach remained aesthetically indebted to the model of the Young German *Reflexions- und Ideenroman* (novel of ideas). As a result, his efforts come off as anachronistic when measured against the paradigm shift to programmatic Realism then taking place. Though unable to build upon his success with the Dorfgeschichte, Auerbach's novels take up central issues of post-1848 society. *Neues Leben* (1851) considers the bourgeois humanist enterprise in the context of exile and the postrevolutionary German countryside. *Auf der Höhe* (1865) deals with the question of religious freedom and resolves conflicts between the nobility, the bourgeoisie, and the peasantry by recourse to the notion of the "good man." In *Das Landhaus am Rhein* (1869) the problem of integrating minorities and strangers (Huguenots, Jews, and blacks) is addressed. And in *Waldfried* (1874) Auerbach formulates the parable of the Jewish "stepchild in a step-fatherland" (vol. 3, 83) to suggest how Jews and non-Jews might grow together (*zusammenwachsen*) in the process of national unification.

The words of a Jewish supporting character in this novel—that educated (*gebildet*) Jews are "not so much Jews as non-Christians" (vol. 3, 85)—shows the extent to which Auerbach's concept of a secularized Judaism had become drained of religious substance, and the objection of the liberal reformist rabbi and journalist Ludwig Philippson to this sentence is best understood in this context. The Jewish reformer saw it as an expression of Auerbach's increasing allegiance to "non-denominationalism" (*Confessionslosigkeit*), an allegiance that distinguished him clearly from educated Jews who subscribed to a philosophical idea of monotheism (Philippson 1875, 466). That Auerbach's works were positively received by the larger educated public may well have been due to this nondenominational stance. Yet, for all the respect shown Auerbach by middle- and upper-class readers, the author was continually reminded of his outsider status among his aristocratic patrons. An anti-Semitic review journal of the Prussian Junker Party defamed him as a "court Jew" (letter to Jakob Auerbach, December 25, 1860), and his former liberal comrade Heinrich von Treitschke, after the author's death, accused him of creating Jews disguised as peasants (Auerbach 1876). Auerbach, however, was hesitant in drawing the consequences of these developments in his own writing. Although he attacked the rise of newfangled Jew-baiting in numerous articles after 1875 (to the point of accusing Theodor Billroth in an open letter of December 31, 1875, of wanting to banish the Jews yet again into a new "exile of foreignness"), and even though he never minced words in his letters to Jakob Auerbach, he did not waver from his standard literary practice of addressing German-Jewish integration only in passing, indirectly, in the mask of "disguised symbolism" (to borrow a term from Erwin Panofsky). He pointedly invoked the spirit of Nathan at the 1881 celebration of Lessing, a spirit that had earlier guided his *Studien und Anmerkungen zu Lessings Nathan der Weise* (1858): "The Jew, because he is not directly involved in the great events of world history, his social status being 'questionable,' functions as a barometer of humanity. The way in which nations (*Völker*) and collectives (*Genossenschaften*) that truly set the course of world events think and behave towards him indicates their stage of human development" (Auerbach 1858, 256).

Auerbach's reiterated appeals to Lessing could not conceal the fact that the Enlightenment utopia of a reconciled society sounded hopelessly anachronistic at this point in time, just as anachronistic as it sounded half a century later in 1929 at the two-hundred-year anniversary commemoration of Lessing and Mendelssohn. The incommensurability between a fiction of conciliation and an (at least partial) understanding of historical realities was bound to have fatal consequences in the aesthetic realm. It was no accident, then, that more notable contemporary writers like Gottfried Keller, Theodor Fontane, and Wilhelm Raabe accused Auerbach of producing obscurantist kitsch. This verdict, however, revealed an utter ignorance of Auerbach's specific ethical and social situation, of how in fact Jewishness, as a matter of religion, tradition, and fate, could be sublated (in the Hegelian sense of *aufgehoben*) into an identity that was culturally and politically German. Jewish identity was not to be negated, but would be integrated into the greater whole when elements were relinquished that seemed superfluous, a process that would ultimately shape and enrich that whole. What Auerbach longed for was a German-Jewish symbiosis that he believed to have been almost realized from time to time. His position was in sharp contrast to that of Gershom Scholem, who, writing after the Shoah, felt the need to see such a symbiosis as doomed from the start. In this manner, Auerbach was truly representative of his epoch in his idealistic notion of a German-Jewish community, a notion that proved to be a grim illusion.

Bibliography

Berthold Auerbach, "An Professor Billroth in Wien," *Die Gegenwart* 9 (1876): 17f.; Auerbach, *Barfüßele* (Stuttgart: Cotta, 1856); Auerbach, *Briefe an seinen Freund Jakob Auerbach. Ein biographisches Denkmal,* 2 vols. (Frankfurt a. M.: Rütten & Loening, 1884); Auerbach, *Deutsche Abende* (Stuttgart, Augsburg: Cotta, 1858); Auerbach, *Dichter und Kaufmann: Ein Lebensgemälde,* 2 vols. (Stuttgart: Krabbe, 1840); Auerbach, *Die Genesis des Nathan: Gedenkworte zu Lessings 100jährigem Todestag* (Berlin: Aug. Berth. Auerbach, 1881); Auerbach, *Das Judenthum und die neueste Literatur: Kritischer Versuch* (Stuttgart: Brodhag, 1836); Auerbach, *Schrift und Volk: Grundzüge der volksthümlichen Literatur angeschlossen an eine Charakteristik J. P. Hebels* (Stuttgart: Gotta'scher Verlag, 1858); Auerbach, *Schwarzwälder Dorfgeschichten,* 2 vols. (Mannheim: Bassermann, 1843); Auerbach, *Spinoza: Ein historischer Roman* (Stuttgart: Scheible, 1837); Auerbach, *Waldfried,* 3 vols. (Stuttgart: Cotta, 1874); Anton Bettelheim, *Berthold Auer-*

bach: *Der Mann—Sein Werk—Sein Nachlaß* (Stuttgart, Berlin: Cotta, 1907); Irene Stocksieker Di Maio, "Berthold Auerbach's *Dichter und Kaufmann:* Enlightenment Thought and Jewish Identity," *Lessing Year Book* 19 (1987): 267–85; Hans Otto Horch, "Gustav Freytag und Berthold Auerbach: Eine repräsentative deutsch-jüdische Schriftstellerfreundschaft im 19. Jahrhundert," *Jahrbuch der Raabe-Gesellschaft* (1985): 154–74; Nancy A. Kaiser, "Berthold Auerbach: The Dilemma of the Jewish Humanist from Vormärz to Empire," *German Studies Review* 6 (1983): 399–419; Jacob Katz, "Berthold Auerbach's Anticipation of the German-Jewish Tragedy," *Hebrew Union College Annual* 53 (1982): 215–40; Margarita Pazi, "Berthold Auerbach and Moritz Hartmann: Two Jewish Writers of the Nineteenth Century," *Leo Baeck Institute Year Book* 18 (1973): 201–18; Ludwig Philippson, "Berthold Auerbach über die Juden," *Allgemeine Zeitung des Judentums* 39 (1875): 465–67; Thomas Scheuffelen, *Berthold Auerbach, 1812–1882, Marbacher Magazin Sonderheft* 36 (1985); Benjamin Segel, *Sigilla Veri* (Ph. Stauff's *Semi-Kürschner*) [Article on Berthold Auerbach], 2d ed. (1929): 297–333; David Sorkin, "The Invisible Community: Emancipation, Secular Culture, and Jewish Identity in the Writings of Berthold Auerbach," *The Jewish Response to German Culture from the Enlightenment to the Second World War,* ed. Jehuda Reinharz and Walter Schatzberg (Hanover, N.H.: University Press of New England, 1985), 100–119; and Ludwig Stein, *Berthold Auerbach und das Judenthum* (Berlin: Driesner, 1882).

HANS OTTO HORCH

TRANSLATED BY DAVID BRENNER

1843   Fanny Lewald's novel *Jenny* treats
the issue of discrimination against the Jews
in nineteenth-century Germany

Fanny Lewald was born in Königsberg, East Prussia, where she grew up in a fairly well-to-do Jewish merchant family as the oldest of eight children. Like many other bourgeois women of her time, she spent much of her youth waiting for a suitable husband. As the years went by, this turned into an increasingly frustrating and humiliating experience for the young woman. When her father, Marcus Lewald, staged a last attempt to marry off his oldest daughter to a mediocre suitor many years her senior, it took all of Lewald's remaining willpower to refuse her father's wish. The incident caused her to feel guilty for many years.

By age thirty, Lewald had resigned herself to what seemed her inescapable fate: spinsterhood. Convinced that most of her active life was over and feeling unwell physically, she started dressing in darker and more subdued colors. In an act of desperation, and stricken with guilt because she considered herself an ungrateful daughter, she sat down one afternoon and started pouring her frustrations and sentiments about arranged marriages (*Konvenienzehen*) and their unhappy consequences into what would become her first novel, *Clementine*. The act of writing, as she later remembered, was accompanied by intense heart palpitations and feelings of anxiety. Unsure of herself, she asked one of her brothers to critique her work, and after he had "corrected" her writing with "legal precision" (*juristischer Akribie*) and her father told her that her novel was "quite nice" (*ganz hübsch*), she felt an immense rush of happiness and accomplishment. Two years later her second novel, *Jenny* (1843), was published, in which Lewald decided to expose yet another social wrong, the "discrimination against the Jews on the grounds of their different religious beliefs."

Both *Clementine* and *Jenny* had to appear anonymously because Lewald's family felt uncomfortable with the idea that their daughter should be associated with such a frivolous and dubious enterprise as the writing of fiction; besides, her sisters had urged her not to reveal her identity in public, fearing that this would seriously impinge on their chances of getting married.

Two decades later, and against considerable odds, Fanny Lewald had become one of the most widely read female writers of popular fiction in nineteenth-century Germany. People compared her to Britain's George Eliot, and she was frequently referred to as the "German George Sand." A younger colleague, the poet Paul Heyse, proclaimed her the "most profound (*geistvoll*) German woman writer," and an 1874 review blankly stated that Fanny Lewald "indisputably" ranked first among her female contemporaries. Just how popular her novels were is perhaps best reflected by the fact that they were available in more than eight hundred libraries throughout the country and that all of her later novels first appeared in serial form in such widely circulating journals as

Deutsche Zeitung, Kölnische Zeitung, and *Deutsche Romanbibliothek,* where they were read by thousands of people. Finally, her six-volume autobiography, *Meine Lebensgeschichte* (The story of my life; 1861–62), was widely read and viewed as an outstanding document even by her contemporaries.

At the end of her life, Fanny Lewald had achieved what very few women had achieved before her: she had gained financial independence, established an outstanding literary career for herself, and carried on the tradition of women like Rahel Varnhagen, Henriette Herz, and Sarah Levy by establishing one of the most famous literary salons in Berlin. It had not been an easy achievement. In fact, Fanny Lewald had violated numerous social rules along the way. In 1843, shortly after the publication of her second novel, she did what was then unheard of: she left her hometown of Königsberg and moved to Berlin, where she rented a flat and discovered the joys as well as the burdens of being on her own. It was at that time that she decided to give up her anonymity, and soon afterward a Berlin publishing house approached her and commissioned a third novel. The novel, which she called *Der Dritte Stand* (The Third Estate; 1844), focused on the social conflicts between the nobility and the bourgeoisie, a theme that was to run throughout most of her future work.

In 1844, shortly after finishing *Der Dritte Stand,* Lewald decided to leave Berlin and embark on a journey to Italy, an adventure that was to change her life forever. For the first time, she felt truly liberated from the narrow constraints of her family life in Königsberg, and the thought dawned upon her that she might still be able to enjoy life and feel young. Spending most of her time among a tightly knit circle of German artists and scientists in Rome, she came into her own and realized that she was no longer the woman whom everyone pitied for not finding a husband but rather a mature woman who was judged on her own merits and considered an aspiring artist in her own right. Not surprisingly, it was at that point in her life that she fell in love with the classicist Adolf Stahr, a married, non-Jewish man much older than she. After almost a decade of

agonizing separations, secret meetings, and frequent travel to be with him, she married Stahr in 1855. Lewald ended up raising his oldest son but never had any children of her own.

Much has been said about the strangely symbiotic relationship between the sickly Stahr and the resolute Fanny Lewald, and many people, including her own family, ostracized her for "selfishly" pursuing her own happiness in the manner she had. Still, without any doubt, Lewald's marriage to Stahr provided the background for one of the most creative periods of her life during the 1860s and 1870s. During that time she wrote close to thirty novels, an equal number of novellas and short stories, and numerous essays on current events, as well as literary sketches of various famous contemporaries such as Heinrich Heine, Wilhelmine Schröder-Devrient, and Franz Liszt. Although most of her literary work has fallen into oblivion, today Fanny Lewald is still remembered for two things: writing one of the most remarkable autobiographies of a woman in the nineteenth century, and poignantly expressing the dire need for women to become better educated and to emancipate themselves.

Let us now take a closer look at Lewald's second novel, *Jenny* (1843), which in many ways holds the key to a closer understanding of Fanny Lewald herself. There we see how she tried to come to terms with her upbringing in an assimilated Jewish household, and how she attempted to construct her own identity, as a woman and as a Jew in nineteenth-century Germany. Whereas Fanny Lewald's first novel, *Clementine,* had been an attempt to justify the fact that she had rejected her father's chosen marriage candidate, Lewald's *Jenny* clearly transcended the realm of the merely personal. It was a novel written with an explicit purpose and a social agenda, that of fighting a common prejudice: the "hatred that Christians feel toward Jews." With that statement Lewald put herself into the tradition of the *Jungdeutsche Literatur* or *Tendenzliteratur,* whose most prominent proponents were Heinrich Heine, Karl Gutzkow, Heinrich Laube, and Gustav Kühne. Literature, according to this school of thought, had to be tendentious, to serve a certain cause and effect change within a society. According to many of the Jungdeutsche, Goethe, with his emphasis on aesthetics and style, was the incarnation of everything that had been wrong in the past.

Although Lewald's attitude toward literature certainly changed over the years, to a point where she eventually became a resolute admirer of Goethe's and emulated his writing style, Lewald's first novels, in particular *Jenny*, were clearly written in the Jungdeutsche tradition. They were guided by the idealistic vision of effecting social change and rigorously exposing certain moral wrongs. As we shall see, the novel's characters bear a close resemblance to the people in Fanny Lewald's life.

Jenny Meier is the daughter of a wealthy Jewish merchant in a town that is a barely disguised Königsberg. She is an independent young woman who is described as intelligent, beautiful, funny, and desirable, but most of all as a freethinking spirit who does not believe in any religious dogmata, be they Jewish or Christian. It is a mystery for Jenny how anybody would draw strength or comfort from religion. As the novel moves along, Jenny's brother Eduard introduces his sister to a friend of his, Reinhard, who happens to be a student of theology and the son of a Lutheran preacher. Despite their apparent differences— one of them being that Reinhard comes from a very modest background—he and Jenny fall in love. When things start getting serious and their engagement is announced, Jenny decides that the most appropriate step would be to convert to Christianity. It is at this point that her father, the prosperous merchant Meier, voices his distaste for the situation and makes it clear why he finds the idea unacceptable. These are the words Lewald puts in his mouth: "Jenny is one of the wealthiest girls in town. . . . Such a girl should have brought me a different son-in-law, somebody who would bring honor to my house. . . . I simply cannot understand that my only daughter wants to get engaged to a student or candidate of theology, . . . who in the end might even take pride in sacrificing or doing me a favor by marrying a Jewish girl, such a pearl of a young woman."

After Jenny goes through a devastating and soul-searching crisis, which is induced by her conversion, she realizes that her father is right and that her principles as well as her family's honor are at stake. In the end she decides not to marry Reinhard. Although there is a brief glimmer of hope for Jenny when a Christian nobleman declares his love for her and the two get married, their happiness only lasts a short while before the forces of bigotry and prejudice set out to destroy them. Disgusted by the nobleman's distasteful choice of a former Jew for a wife, a fellow nobleman challenges him to a duel and kills Jenny's husband. Jenny herself dies of septic shock after she is poisoned from touching her husband's dead body. Except for the overly dramatic ending, the resemblance between Jenny Meier in the novel and the real Fanny Lewald is striking, although the fictitious Jenny is much less a creature of her father's will than was Lewald.

Like Jenny Meier in the novel, Fanny Lewald was the first-born daughter of a well-to-do Jewish merchant in Königsberg. But unlike the Lewald family, who seemed to have gone through several economic ups and downs over the years, the fictitious Meier family is the incarnation of economic stability and prosperity, a family that all the while draws strength and pride from their Jewish heritage. In reality, however, the religious indifference displayed by the young Jenny Meier closely mirrors the attitudes of Lewald's father. Like many other assimilated German Jews of his generation, he no longer obeyed any religious laws, nor did he adhere to any of the Jewish traditions. Being a true child of the Enlightenment, he had no taste for anything religious or speculative and rejected everything that was not firmly grounded in rational thought. In her autobiography, Fanny Lewald proudly tells us that her father was reading Kant's *Die Kritik der Reinen Vernunft* with her at a very young age. It was during such readings that he explained to his daughter, among other things, the meaning of the categorical imperative.

Lewald grew up in a household that was entirely devoid of any religious elements. It was not until she was five that she found out about her background from a Jewish neighbor, who also explained to her that the reason her parents did not want her to know about this was because "other people were not very fond of Jews." When

Lewald asked her father to confirm this rumor, his reply to her was that she was their child and that she should not concern herself with any further questions. Like many Jews of his time, Marcus Lewald no longer considered his Jewish background to be relevant.

Lewald's mother, on the other hand, had deeply rooted apprehensions regarding the family's minority status. Keenly aware of her family's lack of belonging to any particular community, she considered it a misfortune to have been born Jewish and had only one wish: that her husband would allow their children to convert as soon as possible. Marcus Lewald, however, was in no particular hurry to allow such a change because he was primarily concerned with practicalities. To be sure, it made perfect sense for his two sons to convert when they were about to enter the university, because he felt that nothing should distinguish them from their Christian peers. He even went to the trouble of changing his family name from Marcus to Lewald, dryly commenting that he did not see how a Jewish name could be of any use to his sons. As far as he and his wife were concerned, however, a conversion would not have been good for his business, which relied to a large extent on connections with mostly East European Jews. For Fanny, finally, he did not see any immediate need for a conversion. His rationale was that she could always convert should she decide to marry a Christian, but it would be foolish to dissuade marriage proposals from Jews by encouraging her to convert before marriage.

Like Jenny Meier in the novel, Fanny Lewald was briefly in love with a student of theology, Leopold Bock, whom she had met when she was sixteen. As time went by, everyone in her family, including herself, started seeing Leopold as her future husband. It therefore came as a complete surprise when her father precipitately, and without any explanation, ordered Fanny to return Leopold's books and forbade her to see him again. Devastated, Fanny tried to find out from her father the reasons for his behavior, but Marcus Lewald only looked at her "sadly" and replied with a "mild voice" that it had never before been necessary for him to explain his motives. Incredulous as it may sound, Lewald was never given the real reason behind her father's decision. It took her many years to come to terms with this disappointment, and in many ways *Jenny* was the most obvious attempt to rationalize her father's behavior, which so drastically altered her life.

In her novel, Lewald carefully portrays Jenny's resolution not to marry Reinhard as her own decision and not as something she was ordered to do. She also has Meier explain to Jenny in great detail why he is so opposed to the idea of his daughter marrying Reinhard. He is proud to belong to a distinguished Jewish family, and he simply does not see why Jenny should marry somebody who might think he is doing the family a favor. No doubt this was the kind of explanation that Lewald wished her father had given her but never did. Curiously, shortly after the breakup she was finally allowed to convert, an act that she came to view with extreme ambivalence throughout her life. Coupled with the notion of not being in charge of her own life, it was the same ambivalence that lay at the basis of much of her future writing and her continuing preoccupation with the theme of emancipation.

Throughout her autobiography, Fanny Lewald points to the ways in which the discriminating laws against Jews profoundly influenced her family's history. To her, one of the most striking arguments against the way the modern state dealt with the Jewish Question was that it simply was devoid of all reason (*Staatsraison*). Why, she asked again and again, were Jews admitted into the Christian states, and why were they expected to share all the responsibilities and burdens, if they were not given the rights that came along with these burdens?

Equally rational in tone was her reaction toward the anti-Semitic events in Berlin at the end of the 1870s and the beginning of the 1880s, the so-called Berlin movement, in which Adolf Stoecker played a major role. Whereas many of Lewald's Jewish friends, among them the writer Berthold Auerbach, saw the movement as a devastating setback and terrible disappointment, Lewald tried to rationalize the events and even went as far as criticizing her fellow Jews' reactions. There simply is no point in fretting and complaining time and again, she remarked coolly. Instead, why not look for the real causes of these periodically recurring anti-Semitic epidemics? At the very heart of the problem, according to Lewald, were the Jews themselves and their "typical Jewish lamenting." She also suggested that Jews "polish" their "unbearable dialect" and do away with their "unseemly facial expressions and gestures," which to her were signs of an uneducated mind and therefore had to be eradicated. Why, she asked, were the Jews not increasing their "mental capital" and why were they not trying to emulate such outstanding personalities as Moses Mendelssohn, Henriette Herz, Rahel Varnhagen, Sarah Levy, David Veit, and David Friedländer? In her opinion, Sarah Levy and Rahel Varnhagen had done an invaluable service to the cause of Jewish emancipation, but much to Lewald's chagrin, their successors had not been able to keep up this admirable tradition. Without a doubt, Lewald's famous literary salon in Berlin is to be seen in exactly this context.

Despite all her criticism, Lewald never thought that quick assimilation was the solution to the problem. On the contrary, throughout her life she remained extremely critical of the attempts in her father's house to silence and suppress their Jewish origin. In her opinion, the "prejudiced individual as well as the prejudiced society" had a "right" to "despise" Jews as long as Jews did not have respect for themselves. Jews needed to stop being ashamed of their roots and instead assert themselves as different, yet equal.

In many of her novels Fanny Lewald brought these thoughts to life. In her monumental *Von Geschlecht zu Geschlecht* (From generation to generation; 1866), which chronicles the fate of two families through several generations, she portrays the Jewish merchant Fließ as a noble, educated, honorable family man who has gained his fellow citizens' respect because of his integrity and noble character. He has freed himself from any exaggerated facial expressions and gestures otherwise associated with Jews. Even more important, he has rid himself of any subservience and instead assumed a "quiet composure" that to the nobleman whose affairs he manages makes him appear like a "stranger."

In the persona of the Jewish doctor Bernhard, featured in *Der Dritte Stand* (1845), Fanny Lewald gives us a vivid portrait of the proud, self-confident, and liberal free-spirited Jew. Through his own efforts, Bernhard has already achieved the kind of emancipation that most of his fellow Jews can only hope for: "Born as a Jew, the Doctor had retained from his first years the memory of an oppressive poverty. . . . He was gifted with that iron perseverance, with that indefatigable patience, which forms a main characteristic in the nature of the Jewish people."

When we compare descriptions of such liberal Jewish freethinkers to her first novels, it becomes obvious that the religious element has disappeared completely. Like Lewald herself, these emancipated Jews are advocates of a humanistic religion that takes into account many of Spinoza's ideas, and they subscribe to the idea of an ever-progressing humanity in general.

The Jewish emancipation that Lewald promoted consisted of two pillars: the legal recognition and equality of the Jews within the German state, and the emancipation of the Jews from themselves, meaning their various "faults" (*Fehler*) and "bad habits" (*Unarten*). Such a view was influenced to a large extent by the nineteenth-century premise that education was the key factor in the emancipation process. Assuming that it was the environment that had made the Jews into what they were, it was entirely feasible that they could be "re-educated" under better conditions and transformed into useful members of society.

This kind of thinking inherently assumed that the final goal consisted of a gradual assimilation within German society, toward which legal equality provided merely the first step. The question of what defined the Jews as a group, a question that seems obvious to us today, was one that Fanny Lewald left unanswered. It might have been a question that she thought would become obsolete with time, because she believed true religion was to be found in a religion of humanity through which everyone would eventually emancipate themselves. It is this understanding of emancipation that also played a major role in her views on women's emancipation.

The two central essays on the issue of the emancipation of women were the *Osterbriefe*

(Easter letters; 1863) and the letters *Für und Wider die Frauen* (For and against women; 1870), both of which have been called some of the most poignant, although not the most radical, assessments of women's situation at the time. Whereas in the ten *Osterbriefe* Lewald concentrates on the question of how society should improve the fate of the uneducated female workers (*hand-arbeitende Stände* or *vierter Stand*), the fourteen letters *Für und Wider die Frauen* center on the question of how the more educated women of the bourgeoisie should emancipate themselves toward "work and earning a living" (*Arbeit und Erwerb*).

Like many other women of her time, Fanny Lewald grew up in a strictly patriarchal household in which everyone—including the mother and siblings, as well as coworkers, employees, and servants—obeyed the father. Lewald's relationship to her father, a principled and strict patriarch, was ambivalent. On the one hand she admired, idolized, and loved him; on the other, she deeply resented the way in which he had suppressed any sign of emotion or weakness not only in himself but also in her. This, according to Lewald, made it extremely difficult for her to express any kind of emotion in her writing.

Whereas Marcus Lewald did everything to further his sons' advancement in life by sending them to the gymnasium and later to the university, the education he offered his daughter was haphazard, unsystematic, and very short, not unlike that of most women of her time. Deprived of any mental stimulation—because of a sudden outbreak of cholera she had to leave the private school she was attending at age thirteen— Lewald was doomed to wait at home for a suitable husband, an experience she found utterly humiliating. It is this "time of sorrow" (*Leidenszeit*), as she referred to it throughout her later life, that lies at the very heart of her scathing critique of women's upbringing and education.

In order to avoid the degrading experience she had gone through and to enable women to take care of themselves, she demanded that all women have equal access to education. Her immediate goal was twofold: she wanted to establish well-functioning public primary schools for girls from age seven to eighteen, and at the same time create vocational schools for women, which she saw as forerunners for *Realschulen* (middle schools) and *Gymnasien* (high schools). Only once a certain economic independence had been achieved did she see the point in giving women voting rights or admitting them to universities.

Many of these ideas are reflected in Lewald's novels, several of which have maidservants as protagonists, such as *Die Kammerjungfer* (Maidservant; 1856) and *Das Mädchen von Hela* (The girl from Hela; 1860), and several of which center around female artists, such as *Adele* (1855), where the protagonist is a writer, and *Die Erlöserin* (The female savior; 1872), where she is an actress. Again, as with the emancipation of the Jews, for Lewald the issue of women's emancipation was to be viewed within the wider context of the social improvement of society as a whole. Women should emancipate themselves primarily in order to transform themselves into more useful members of society and thus contribute to the overall goal of the emancipation and betterment of humankind. It was precisely this ideal that lay at the heart of many of Lewald's works, and it was one class in particular that was to play a major role in bringing about these changes: the bourgeoisie, or Third Estate.

Although throughout her writing career Fanny Lewald portrayed numerous characters from all walks of life, it was the *Bürger* (burgher or bourgeois), and in particular the merchant, who took center stage in many of her books. It is here that her descriptions are most vivid and authentic, mainly because she had personally experienced many facets of that particular life. It was the *Dritter Stand* (Third Estate) that for her embodied all the fine qualities that could propel society forward toward a better future.

In earlier novels like *Der Dritte Stand* (1845), *Wandlungen* (Changes; 1855), and *Von Geschlecht zu Geschlecht* (1866), her burghers were defined mainly in class terms and favorably contrasted with the decadent nobility. Lewald had been an enthusiastic witness of the 1848 revolution, and she was a fervent supporter of the democratic movement, which considered the republic the ideal form of government. The bourgeoisie was to play a major role in advancing these democratic goals, because for Lewald it embodied many of the virtues that were essential for building a new society: a spirit of enterprise, a sense of civic duty and responsibility, and a willingness to shape one's future through personal achievement rather than through a reliance on privileges associated with birth.

Two decades later, Lewald's attitude toward class issues had changed significantly. Many of her hopes for the bourgeoisie had become reality in Bismarck's Imperial Germany, and it no longer seemed relevant to lobby for the rights of this particular group and contrast it favorably with the aristocracy. Although the political reality under Bismarck was far from the democratic society Lewald had dreamed of during the 1848 revolution, her attitude toward Bismarck had changed considerably over the years: from a harsh condemnation of his undemocratic way of governing in the 1860s to unconditional admiration of his strong leadership during the Franco-Prussian War and the subsequent creation of the German Reich.

One of her last big novels, *Die Familie Darner* (The Darner family; 1887), poignantly reflects how Lewald's attitude changed over the years. The emphasis had slowly moved from the politi-cal to the personal, from issues of *Stand* (class) to issues of individual integrity and virtue. *Bürger,* as Lewald used the term during her later years, no longer referred to a particular class, but rather connoted an enlarged concept of civic responsibility, political maturity, and the willingness to contribute to the general progress of society. Like many of her Jewish contemporaries, Fanny Lewald had always believed in the bourgeoisie as the engine of social change and democratization. She was confident that when this goal was achieved, the Jewish Question would eventually solve itself.

Bibliography

Fanny Lewald, *Clementine* (Leipzig: Brockhaus, 1843); Lewald, *Für und Wider die Frauen* (Berlin: Janke, 1870); Lewald, *Jenny,* 2 vols. (Leipzig: Brockhaus, 1843); Lewald, *Meine Lebensgeschichte,* 6 vols. (Berlin: Janke, 1861–62); Lewald, *Osterbriefe für die Frauen* (Berlin: Janke, 1863); Brigitta van Rheinberg, *Fanny Lewald: Geschichte einer Emanzipation* (Frankfurt a. M.: Campus, 1990); and Marieluise Steinhauer, "Fanny Lewald, die deutsche George Sand: Ein Kapitel aus der Geschichte des Frauenromans im 19. Jahrhundert," Ph.D. diss., University of Berlin, 1937.

BRIGITTA VAN RHEINBERG

1843 Heinrich Heine and Karl Marx meet for the first time in Paris

A striking illustration of the contribution of the Jewish community to German culture is provided by the examples of Heinrich Heine and Karl Marx. When they met for the first time in Paris in December 1843, Heine was already one of the most brilliant and controversial of German writers, and Marx was soon to become the most influential German Socialist thinker of the late nineteenth century. The relationship that developed between Heine and Marx has fascinated and perplexed observers of nineteenth-century German culture ever since. Moreover, its interpretation rapidly became a political minefield.

The treatment of the relationship between Heine and Marx demonstrated the highly political nature of the reception of Heine's work in Germany. There can be little doubt that the political bias of literary critics frequently colored their appreciation of Heine's work. Heine's reception in Germany was contentious for various reasons. As a fiercely oppositional writer who pitted himself against the political establishment and flirted with progressive political movements such as Saint-Simonism and Communism, Heine was suspect to conservatives. His uncompromising rejection of German nationalism led to charges that he was unpatriotic, and in some quarters these charges were fueled by anti-Semitism. Moreover, many critics mistook Heine's often vituperative satire and wit for flippancy, and others were uncomfortable with the manner in which he expanded the accepted boundaries of literary genres by producing political poetry, travel writing, and social and political commentaries of the highest literary quality.

Marxist literary critics from Walther Victor and Hans Kaufmann to Gerhard Schmitz and the cultural representatives of the German Democratic Republic traditionally highlighted Heine's highly quotable political poetry of the 1840s, often to the detriment of an appreciation of the full range of his work, which also included the memorable lyric poetry of his early phase and the great poetic reckoning with the suffering of his later years. The fact that Heine and Marx appeared to have worked together for a brief period from 1843 to 1844 provided an opportunity to appropriate Heine's controversial, but nonetheless great, reputation for the cultural heritage of the East German state. Critics, echoing the work of the nineteenth-century Marxist critic Franz Mehring, emphasized that the proletariat had done more to defend Heine's writings than any other class in German history, and several sought to stress the service done to the Germans by the Soviet Union in making Heine's work accessible once more after its suppression by the National Socialists. Furthermore, the credibility of Karl Marx could be boosted even further by the claim that this young man of twenty-five succeeded in crucially influencing the greatest of nineteenth-century German writers. Heine and Marx were typically portrayed as comrades engaged in a common battle against oppression. Directives from the cultural bureau of the Socialist Unity Party maintained that Heine's greatest political poetry, including his verse epic *Germany: A Winter's Tale* and the famous poem *The Silesian Weavers,* had emerged under the tutelage of Marx. In a similar vein, Walther Victor insisted that Marx educated Heine in political and even on occasion in literary matters and that Heine remained a passive recipient of Marx's intellectual bounty. Heine's highly ambivalent attitude toward Communism and revolution was generally ignored or dismissed as temporary doubts that Heine would undoubtedly have revised had he been granted the opportunity. Not all East German critics towed the official party line, however, and some openly admitted that close cooperation between Heine and Marx must remain a matter of speculation.

By contrast, up until the late 1960s, non-Marxists in the West tended to play down or even ignore Heine's relationship with Marx and much of his politically committed poetry of the 1840s. New research has changed this. Not only has it led to a greater appreciation of Heine's political poetry, but it has also produced a more differentiated picture of the forces that drew Heine and Marx together and the influence they exerted on each other's work.

One reason that the relationship between Heine and Marx is so susceptible to misinterpretation is that evidence about it is scarce. Only one letter from Heine to Marx and three from Marx to Heine exist in addition to scattered references in their work and the correspondence and recollections of Marx's daughter Eleanor. What we do know is that Heine and Marx probably met for the first time in Paris in December 1843. Heine had been living in Paris since 1831 and had just returned from his first visit back to Germany in twelve years. Marx had arrived in Paris in October 1843 after the suppression by the Prussian government of the *Rheinische Zeitung,* which he had edited. He established contact with the sizable German community in Paris and was introduced to its most prominent member, Heine. The writer soon became a regular guest at the home of Marx and his wife, and Marx promptly succeeded in securing contributions from Heine for the new political journal, the *Deutsch-Französische Jahr-*

bücher, which he planned to edit with Arnold Ruge. The journal, which contained Heine's *Eulogies on King Ludwig,* duly appeared for the first and last time in March 1844 due to lack of subscriptions and suppression by the Prussian government. Undaunted, Marx joined the editors of the political journal *Vorwärts,* to which Heine was persuaded to contribute the most important of his political poetry of 1844, including *Germany: A Winter's Tale* and *The Silesian Weavers.* Heine, for his part, sought Marx's assistance in publicizing *Germany: A Winter's Tale. Vorwärts* proved too controversial for even the French authorities to tolerate, and in January 1845, as a result of pressure from the Prussian government, Marx was expelled from Paris—but not before expressing the wish in a parting letter to Heine that he might pack the writer in his suitcase and take Heine with him. Heine was allowed to remain in Paris by virtue of the fact that he had been born in Düsseldorf during the French occupation of the town and was thus entitled to the residence rights of a French citizen. Marx's subsequent attempts to extract contributions from Heine for the *Rheinische Jahrbücher, Album,* and the *Neue Rheinische Zeitung* met with no success. They met again briefly in 1848 and 1849 and remained in contact until Heine's death six years later.

It would be misleading to argue, as some do, that a common interest in literature, Hegelian philosophy, and family life rather than politics sealed the bond between these two. The timing of their encounter was crucial. Marx's thought was still in flux. His Communist ideas were still in their infancy, and he had only just begun to turn his attention to a study of political economics. Heine's visit to Germany had radicalized his writing, and he sought an outlet and a sympathetic ear for his increasingly devastating political satire. Naturally, they found each other useful. Heine's contributions increased the standing of Marx's journals, and Marx provided Heine with useful publicity and contacts. The relationship cannot be reduced to one of expedience, however. By all accounts the genuine friendship between Heine and Marx was unusual by the standards of either man.

More important, although Heine and Marx

may have disagreed about the solutions to be applied to the iniquities of contemporary political life in Germany, common enemies drew them together. As Jews, albeit baptized—Marx along with the rest of his family at the age of six, Heine at the age of twenty-seven—both men were especially sensitive to the oppressive and unjust nature of the German, and particularly the Prussian, political system. They longed to see the power of the aristocracy broken and a new meritocratic social order created. The concept of the Christian State embraced by Frederick William IV and his circle—the ideal state was a Christian totality and that subsequently no non-Christians could participate in its administration—was a particular anathema to them, and both shared a skeptical attitude to orthodox religion. Indeed, Marx declared himself an atheist. For similar reasons, both detested the burgeoning nationalist sentiments exploited by governments and embraced by the liberal opposition in Germany. Moreover, they both recognized the future significance of tensions between socioeconomic groups in society and believed that a thoroughgoing social upheaval rather than a mere political revolution was required to achieve their aim of the emancipation of humanity. Their shared discontent was cemented, as Jeffrey Sammons has perceptively pointed out, by their passionate unwillingness to compromise in any way with existing conditions in Germany. Yet although the experience of exile sealed their friendship, Germany remained their homeland and the focus of their respective hopes for the future.

The myth, perpetuated by many Marxist critics, of Marx's allegedly great influence on Heine's thought and writings has been largely dispelled by recent research. Arnold Ruge's claim in a letter of 1870 that it was he and Marx who first gave Heine the idea of writing political satire is disproved by the simple fact that several of Heine's political poems of this period were written before he ever encountered the editors of the *Deutsch-Französische Jahrbücher*. Similarly, far too much has been read into the claims of Marx's daughter Eleanor that Heine involved her father in his work on the poetry he published in 1844. Although one can only speculate on the stylistic

alterations suggested by Marx, it is clear that his political theories had little effect on the content of the work. Contrary to the assertions of many Marxist critics, neither *Germany: A Winter's Tale* nor *The Silesian Weavers,* the most significant verse of this period, deals with the theme of class conflict. Heine's satire targets the Prussian state, political romanticism, and nationalism—not the bourgeoisie. In essence, these works provide a concentrated recapitulation of ideas developed by Heine more than a decade before. Heine's one surviving communication to Marx, concerning plans for the publication of *Germany: A Winter's Tale,* has been put into context by Ronald Nabrotsky, who has demonstrated that Marx was simply one of many contacts, including François Wille, Johann Hermann Detmold, and Georg Eckermann, to whom Heine turned for help in assessing and securing publicity for the work. That is not to say that the young Marx had no influence on the revered writer. But the influence Marx exerted appears to have been in the realm of style rather than substance. It is easy to imagine that Marx's brilliance and ambition inspired Heine. Even if Marx could contribute few new ideas to a writer whose opinions were well established, he appears to have succeeded in strengthening Heine's views and, as Nigel Reeves has pointed out, in confirming Heine's belief in the revolutionary potential of ideas and poetry. A fragment written by Heine in 1844 calling for the emergence of new "productive poetry" that would be capable of altering the world can be seen in this context. The sharply polemical tone of the poetry written in 1844 may well have been encouraged by Marx, and his willingness to publish such controversial material played no small part in increasing the scope of Heine's satire.

Heine never actually converted to Marxism or Communism, but several isolated comments by Marx and Friedrich Engels led some to believe he had. In 1844 Engels announced in *The New Moral World* that "Henry Heine, the most eminent of all living German poets, has joined our ranks, and published a volume of political poetry which contains also some pieces preaching socialism." A year later, on February 1, 1845, Marx wrote to

Heine asking for more contributions for another journal and observed: "You will surely not turn this down, for we must use every opportunity to establish ourselves in Germany itself." The conspiratorial nature of the remark was taken by some critics to indicate that Heine was fully converted to their cause. In fact, Heine turned down Marx's request, and his comments on Communism resonate fear and foreboding rather than acceptance and approval. In the French preface of 1855 to *Lutetia,* Heine recalled his prediction of the early 1840s that the future belonged to the Communists:

This confession that the future belongs to the Communists was made in a tone of the deepest fear and anxiety and oh! this tone was in no way feigned. Indeed it is only with dread and horror that I think about the time when these gloomy iconoclasts will attain power; when their heavy hands will smash to pieces all the marble statues of my beloved world of art. . . . They will chop down my laurel groves and plant potatoes in their place, and the lilies, which neither spin nor toil and yet are more magnificently clothed than King Solomon, will be rooted up from the soil of society unless they take up the spindle; it is no better for the roses, those idle brides of the nightingales; the nightingales themselves will be driven away as useless singers, and oh! my book of songs will be used by the grocers to make paper bags in which to put coffee or snuff for the old women of the future.—Yes, I foresee all this, and unspeakable grief comes over me when I think of the destruction with which the victorious common multitude threatens my verses, which will sink into the grave with the whole ancient romantic world. Yet despite this, I publicly confess that this Communism, which is so inimical to all my interests and inclinations, exerts a magic influence on my soul from which I cannot defend myself. Two voices in its favor move my heart . . . the first voice is that of logic. . . . The second imperative voice which ensnares me is far mightier and more demonic than the first, for it is the voice of hate—of the hate which I feel for a party whose most deadly enemy is Communism, and which from this common ground is our common foe. I speak of the party of the so-called representatives of nationality in Germany, of those false patriots whose love for their native land consists only of idiotic aversion to all foreign or neighboring races. . . . Out of hatred for the Nationalists I could almost love the Communists.

How can these heartfelt fears be reconciled with Heine's friendship and cooperation with Marx in 1844? They can if Heine's understanding of Communism is examined more closely. In the first place, for Heine the concept of Communism was not synonymous with Marxism. As Wolfgang Schieder has demonstrated, by Communism Heine understood not a specific doctrine but rather a broad class ideology that sought to satisfy the requirements of the proletariat. Heine applied the term to a whole range of French proletarian groups that embraced the ideas of diverse individuals such as Louis Blanc and, most significantly, François Babeuf. Second, the fears expressed by Heine in 1855 reiterate those he articulated as early as 1841, in other words well before his encounter with Marx. As Leo Kreutzer has argued, Heine's misgivings about Communism centered on his rejection of the egalitarianism preached by followers of Babeuf, the Communist executed in 1796 for his part in a conspiracy against the French revolutionary government, the Directory. His ideas were popularized by Filippo Buonarroti, who published a documentation of Babeuf's life and teaching in 1828. Neo-Babouvism rapidly captured the imagination of leaders of the French proletariat, and in 1837 the Society of the Seasons was founded to propagate Babouvist ideas among French workers. Heine abhorred the puritanical philistinism of Babeuf's egalitarian Communism. In an article of December 11, 1841, for the *Allgemeine Zeitung*, Heine reported on developments in Paris and offered his views on the French Communist groups: "The destructive doctrines have too much of a hold on the lower classes in France—it is no longer a case of the equality of rights but the equality of pleasure on earth and in Paris there are about 400,000 rough fists which are only waiting for the password in order to turn the notion of absolute equality, which is brewing in their coarse heads, into reality. . . . The propaganda of Communism possesses a language that every people understands: the elements of this universal language are as simple as hunger, envy and death."

Yet in the mid-1840s it appears that Heine was temporarily willing to suspend his hatred of Communism and to give it a chance, especially as he recognized that they shared common enemies. The egalitarian Communism preached by French proletarian groups may have been anathema to him. But the Communism advocated by German thinkers such as Marx, Engels, Karl Grün, and Moses Hess was a different proposition—the more so because Marx was himself highly critical of Babeuf's crude egalitarianism. In his *Economic and Philosophical Manuscripts* of 1844, Marx was scathing about the aim of the neo-Babouvists to revert to a primitive society untouched by civilization, and four years later in *The Manifesto of the Communist Party* he condemned their "asceticism" and "coarse egalitarianism." Heine's belief that these German thinkers might lend Communism a new, more noble quality did not represent a conversion to the cause, however. He did not rate their chances of success very highly and admitted to being more impressed by the logic of their thought than the content of their ideas.

Several factors prevented Heine from throwing in his lot with Marx and the German Communists. Quite apart from his strong individualism, which throughout his life prevented him from committing himself firmly to any group or organization, Heine appears to have had little concrete interest in questions of political economics. He never embraced Marx's theories, promulgated in Heine's lifetime, of the alienation of man under capitalism and of historical materialism. Heine was unable to accept that the industrial proletariat would be the agent of radical change and the emancipation of humanity, and the idea that the proletariat would emerge as the ruling class horrified him. Although he defended the right of all to be properly fed and educated, Heine remained an elitist at heart. In Jeffrey Sammons's memorable phrase (1979), Heine was a "poet against the people's enemies," rather than a poet of the people. Like many liberals of his day, Heine had a positive attitude toward the people

(*Volk*) in the abstract but recoiled in horror at the reality of the masses (*Pöbel*). The social revolution envisaged by Heine would put some form of intellectual elite in power and certainly not the industrial proletariat. Moreover, Heine was perfectly prepared to countenance the idea that a monarch would rule over his utopian society of the future. The aristocracy rather than the monarchy was Heine's bête noire. He firmly believed that the monarch could successfully represent the views of the people once he was no longer impeded by the selfish machinations of the aristocracy.

Above all, Heine never overcame his fear that Communism, be it of the French or German variety, would destroy the achievements of civilization and debase the value of art. He regarded Communist egalitarianism as a recipe for philistinism and mediocrity. Reluctantly, he came to believe that the political status quo would more readily defend the intrinsic value of aesthetics. As Leo Kreutzer has demonstrated, Heine was consistent in his hostility toward any movement he regarded as puritanical and antagonistic to art. Referring to the ascetic French revolutionary leader, Heine fought what he regarded as "the Robespierre element" in groups ranging from Ludwig Börne and his republicans, Wilhelm Weitling and his craft-worker Communists, and the German political poets of the 1840s to the neo-Babouvists. Instead, Heine defended the intelligence, elegance, amusement, and adroitness that he associated with the French philosopher Voltaire. These fears fueled Heine's outbursts against the Communists in the last years of his life. Curiously, these outbursts display little evidence that he had ever differentiated between the Communist groups of the French proletariat and the Communism preached by Marx. Instead he conflated the two to conjure up a vision of impending doom. Seemingly, Marxism had failed to enable Heine to overcome his long-standing and deeply ingrained fear of Communism.

The unsuccessful revolution of 1848 in Germany and his debilitating illness sorely tested Heine's traditional optimism. Unlike Marx, he appears to have lost faith in the concept of revolution and in the inexorable progression of humanity. His view that a proletarian revolution was nevertheless inevitable gave him little comfort. Quite the opposite: it filled him with foreboding. Finally, Heine's rejection of Communism took on a new dimension in the period after 1848 as he came increasingly to identify it with atheism. Heine had never professed atheism but pantheism, the belief that God and the universe are identical, which denies the personality and transcendence of God. Pantheism was not enough to support him through his last difficult years of illness and disillusionment, however, and although he never became reconciled to organized religion, he developed a belief in a personal God. It was from this new vantage point that he castigated the atheism of the Communists in general and of his friend Marx in particular. Referring to the biblical character King Nebuchadnezzar, whose pride caused him to be struck down by God, Heine noted in 1852 in the foreword to the second edition of *On the History of Religion and Philosophy in Germany*: "How often have I thought since about the story of that Babylonian king who believed himself to be God but plunged down wretchedly from the summit of his pride, crawled on the ground like an animal and ate grass (I expect it was lettuce). This legend is to be found in the grandiose and magnificent Book of Daniel and I recommend it not only to the good Ruge, but also to my much more obstinate friend Marx, not to mention Messrs Feuerbach, Daumer, Bruno Bauer, Hengstenberg and whatever their names may be, these godless self-gods, as an edifying tale which they should heed."

The shared Jewish heritage that played some part in drawing Heine and Marx together at the outset finally drove them apart intellectually, as Heine returned to the notion of a personal God and the old testament of his fathers. The friendship survived, however, not least because Marx proved unusually willing to tolerate what he regarded as Heine's political weaknesses.

Ultimately then, Marx's influence on Heine was quite limited, which is hardly a surprising conclusion if one bears in mind that they were separated in age by a generation. As Nigel Reeves has shown, it is in fact more fruitful to consider Heine's influence on Marx, and here some inter-

esting conclusions can be drawn. In the first place, as a writer Heine had a significant effect on Marx's polemical style. Marx greatly admired Heine's work. The influence of Heine's *Pictures of Travel* and his *Ideas: The Book of le Grand* can be discerned in Marx's fragmentary novel of 1837, *Several Chapters from Scorpion and Felix,* and it is clear that Marx plundered Heine's writings for inspiration for his polemics that appeared in 1848 in the *Neue Rheinische Zeitung.* More significant, however, is the role played by Heine's political interpretation of Hegelian philosophy in Marx's conversion from idealism to materialism. Hegel had dominated early-nineteenth-century German philosophy, and Heine had personally attended his lectures as a student in Berlin. Hegel's vision of the onward dialectical progression of history toward perfection in accordance with the demands of reason greatly influenced Heine as well as radical thinkers such as Marx two decades later. Yet it was Heine who first articulated the practical implications of Hegel's philosophy of history in his 1834 work *On the History of Religion and Philosophy in Germany.* Hegel argued that individuals would be free when the objective world was rationally organized and when they were free to act in accordance with the universal law of reason and morality. Contrary to common assumptions, he did not explicitly claim that Prussia represented this final stage in the development of human history. But he failed to spell out what turn this development should take next. Heine refused to reconcile the final stage of Hegel's model with existing conditions in Germany and interpreted Hegel's philosophy as a demand for a better world that would allow humans to develop their full potential and become reconciled to society. The philosophical revolution must give way to a practical revolution. In this way, he actually anticipated the arguments of Marx himself. The aim of such a revolution would also be to release individuals from a state of self-division and enable them to enter a new harmonious and fully human state.

Heine's concept of the "self-division" of the individual, or the separation of the spirit from material affairs (the body from the soul), also anticipated to some extent Marx's concept of alienation. Furthermore, by focusing on religion as a meaningless consolation for injustices endured on earth, Heine also preempted Marx's observations in his 1844 *Introduction to the Critique of Hegel's Philosophy of Right* on the social role of religion as the "opium of the people." Heine would later retract this view. Heine may also have indirectly influenced Marx's infamous essay of 1844, "On the Jewish Question," by associating Jews in *The Baths of Lucca* with an acquisitive society concerned only with the worship of money. Unlike Marx, however, Heine emphasized the historical constraints that had forced Jews into securing their livelihood through trade and finance.

As these views suggest, neither Heine nor Marx were given the opportunity to feel at ease with their Jewish identity. Yet the heightened sensitivity that emerged from their position as outsiders in Prussian society yielded two of the most significant contributions to the literature and intellectual history of nineteenth-century Germany.

Bibliography

Peter Demetz, *Marx, Engels and the Poets: Origins of Marxist Literary Criticism* (Chicago: University of Chicago Press, 1967); Leo Kreutzer, *Heine und der Kommunismus* (Göttingen: Vandenhoeck & Ruprecht, 1970); Ludwig Marcuse, "Heine und Marx: Eine Geschichte und eine Legende," *Essays, Porträts, Polemiken aus vier Jahrzehnten,* ed. Harold von Hofe (Zurich: Diogenes, 1988), 41–59; Franz Mehring, "Heine an Marx," *Aufsätze zur deutschen Literatur von Klopstock bis Weerth* (Berlin: Dietz, 1961), 465–71; Ronald Nabrotsky, "Karl Marx als Heinrich Heines politischer und poetischer Mentor: Die Legende von Marx' Mitarbeit an Heines 'Wintermärchen,'" *Sprache und Literatur: Festschrift für Arval L. Streadbeck,* ed. Gerhard P. Knapp and Wolff A. von Schmidt (Bern: n.p., 1981), 129–40; Nigel Reeves, "Heine and the Young Marx," *Oxford German Studies* 7 (1973): 44–97; Ritchie Robertson, *Heine* (London: Holban, 1988); Jeffrey Sammons, *Heinrich Heine: A Modern Biography* (Princeton, N.J.: Princeton University Press, 1979); Wolfgang Schieder, "Heinrich Heine und der 'Kommunismus,'" *Heinrich Heine, 1797–1856,* ed. Klaus Brieglebs (Trier: Karl-Marx-Haus, 1981), 120–33; and Manfred Windfuhr, "Heinrich Heine zwischen den progressiven Gruppen seiner Zeit," *Zeitschrift für Deutsche Philologie* 91 (1972): 1–23.

ANITA BUNYAN

1844 After a self-imposed exile in Paris, Heinrich Heine writes *Deutschland: Ein Wintermärchen*

On October 25, 1843, Heinrich Heine crossed the border into Germany—twelve years after his last visit to the country he had left in 1830 to live in exile in revolutionary Paris. Eleven months later, in September 1844—and after a second, longer trip to his publisher Campe in Hamburg—Heine published an account of this reencounter with his fatherland, entitled *Deutschland: Ein Wintermärchen* (Germany: A winter's tale; 1844). The twenty-eight chapter, two-thousand-verse epic poem appeared first in conjunction with the poetry collection *Neue Gedichte* (New poems)—in order to circumvent the precensorship that affected any writings longer than twenty sheets—and shortly thereafter as a separate volume and in a second edition, with a biting preface by the author. The "rhymed travel pictures" (*versifizierte Reisebilder*), as Heine himself called the *Wintermärchen,* are his satirical *Abrechnung,* his settling of accounts with his former home. Considered by many to be Heine's most poignant political satire, *Germany: A Winter's Tale* gives vivid expression to his ideological convictions and scruples and to his struggles over the idea and reality of a German nation. Together with its companion pieces "Anno 1839" and "Nachtgedanken" (1843), both of which appeared in *Neue Gedichte,* the poem attests to Heine's *Zerrissenheit,* to the inner conflicts arising from his multiple identities and multiple allegiances: as a German-Jewish writer living in French exile, writing mostly in German and publishing in both countries; as a "radical liberal" caught between republicanism à la Börne and Prussian absolutism and at odds with any totalizing system of thought; and as an assimilated Jew and converted Christian who rejected both Judaism's and Christianity's "asceticism" (*Nazarenertum*).

As Heine retells his travels through German towns and landscapes in late fall—from Aachen to Hamburg and back—he creates an imaginary itinerary through space and time, adding places he never visited (the Arminius monument in Teutoburg Forest; the Kyffhäuser mountain in the Harz, where the legendary emperor Barbarossa resides; and the bishop's seat, Paderborn), and reversing the order of the actual trip. "Germany" emerges as a chain of associations that link observation with dream, experience with memory, history with myth. The narrative I in turn assumes shifting positions and disguises, slipping into the roles of the prodigal son or revolutionary "wolf," the suffering "missionary" or martyr (Christ and Prometheus), or the erring Odysseus or Wandering Jew, depending on the particular constellation or issue Heine wants to address. Caught between fatherland and adopted *patrie*—between *Heimweh* for German language, food, and forests, and identification with the emancipatory traditions of his chosen home, France—the poet poses at once as persecuted and persecutor, mediator and prophet. The *Wintermärchen* thus becomes a symbolic voyage through both Germany's and Heine's past and present, or rather, through Heine's past and present relationship with what Walter Hinck called—in analogy to Adorno's "die Wunde Heine"—"die Wunde Deutschland," Germany the wound.

In 1843, Germany existed only as an idea, the idea of a *Kulturnation* bound by a common language and common cultural traditions. The thirty-seven sovereign principalities and four free cities that were loosely connected in the German Federation of 1815 had only recently begun to grow together under Prussian hegemony as the German Customs Union (1833). By 1844, most German states had joined the union, with the exception of Hamburg, Bremen, Holstein, and Mecklenburg. Whereas the political unification process proceeded slowly and in leaps and bolts, nationalism—that is, the desire for German national unity and identity—had been growing exponentially since the Wars of Liberation. A series of political and cultural events in the 1840s fomented the rise of more virulent brands of chauvinism: the assumption of the Prussian throne by the reactionary romantic-Christian King Frederick William IV (1840); the Oriental Crisis (1839–1841) and the ensuing controversy with France over the "German" Rhine (*Rheinliedkontroverse*); the renewal of the construction of Cologne's gothic cathedral as a symbol of the unity of crown and altar and of the "medieval" roots of the *Reich* (*Kölner Dombaufest;* 1842); and the celebration of the millenary of the German Empire (843–1843; ironically, the first date, that of the Treaty of Verdun, marks both the reconciliation of church and crown under Otto I and the division of the Carolingian empire).

As German officials and German writers created a movement toward unification and an ideology of an exclusive national identity grounded in a mythic medieval Reich, Heine parodied and deconstructed this Germanic identity by mimicking and mocking the various discourses that dominated public debates in the 1840s and the symbols to which they clung: from "Father Rhine" to "Emperor Barbarossa" and from "Hermann der Cherusker" (the Germanic chieftain Arminius of the Cherusci tribe who defeated the Romans in the battle of Teutoburg Forest in 9 C.E.) to "Charlemagne." Heine's voyage through Germany is marked by well-known signposts

along the way—figures of speech familiar to those who know his earlier writings—that not only create an aesthetic unity between the individual chapters of the poem, but also establish dialectic tension between opposites: the tension between unifying forces and the desire for freedom; between control and resistance, "renunciation" (*Entsagung,* spiritualism, religious longings) and gratification (*Sensualismus,* aesthetic pleasure, material well-being), provincialism and cosmopolitanism, tradition and innovation; and between father state and mother tongue, hatred and love. These tensions are reworked over and over again in the poet's mind, yet they remain unresolved. The image of the grand synthesis, the "marriage" between the Virgin Europe and Freedom invoked in chapter 1, ends in the miasma of Charlemagne's chamber pot and in the frustrated union between the castrated poet and the prostitute Hammonia, the allegorical embodiment of Hamburg.

Heine's "Germany"—that is, the Germany he conjures up and debunks—is represented by two poles, Prussia and Hamburg. To the poet, Prussia is the omnipresent enemy, the embodiment of postrevolutionary Restoration: the symbol of its power, the Prussian eagle ("the ugly bird"), greets the traveler at the frontier and at every official building. Prussian fortifications, soldiers, bureaucrats, and censors extend Prussian hegemony ever farther to the west, excluding or fending off anything that might undermine its prerogative. Prussian militarism, its authoritarianism and arrogance ("der eingefrorene Dünkel," chap. 3), precludes the development of an open society with room for political dissent, for a constitution, and for critical assimilated Jews like Heine. As Heine ironically remarks, the inner and outer unification of a Prussia-dominated new Germany is cemented by the "material unity" achieved through the Tariff Union and by the "spiritual unity" enforced through censorship and mind police:

"The Customs Union," he opined,
"will be our people's foundation,
and make the divided fatherland
into a single nation.
"This outward unity is our first

since the empire of you-know-when, sir.
The higher unity of ideas
is the task we leave to the censor.
"Yes, the inner unity is his job,
we must all think as he allows us.
Germany one, without and within—
that's the ideal to rouse us."

In Heine's hatred of Prussian rigidity and exclusivity, personal and collective disappointments blend, from his disappointment over the Prussian authorities' refusal to accept him into Prussian civil service after his conversion to Christianity (1825) and his anger over Prussian prohibition or censorship of his books to his general disgust over the betrayal of enlightened traditions after 1815 (Prussia's revocation of the Jewish Emancipation Edict in 1816) and again, after 1840. As Klaus Briegleb states, "Prussia stands for Germany, whenever 'the state' impinges on the freedom of the writer."

By extending its hegemony to the Rhine, the Prussian eagle had sullied an area with very different traditions, a region that was particularly dear to Heine, because he was born there and because, for some time at least, the French revolutionary administration had guaranteed civic rights and Jewish emancipation in the Rhenish provinces. Now, in the 1840s, the Rhine river had become an object of contention, a "frontier" for a literary-political feud triggered by the so-called Oriental Crisis. In 1840, the Quadruple Alliance formed by Austria, Russia, England, and Prussia had taken on the protection of Turkey against the pasha of Egypt, who was supported by France. In retaliation, and in order to deflect attention from the crisis in the Orient, France demanded the left bank of the Rhine. A national outcry ensued: all over Germany, writers produced xenophobic songs claiming the Rhine as their own and vowing to defend it "until death." The most famous of these songs was Nikolaus Becker's martial *Der deutsche Rhein* of 1840 ("They shall not, shall not have it / Our free-born German Rhine"); they culminated in what became the German national anthem, Heinrich Hoffmann von Fallersleben's *Lied der Deutschen* (1841). The anti-French tendency of Becker's popular

song and its many sequels provoked French writers such as Alphonse de Lamartine and Alfred de Musset and German poets of the opposition such as Herwegh and Gottschall to compose their own protest Rhine songs, a movement that Heine partakes of and departs from when he sings to a very different Germany ("Deutschland!" 1840–42) and when he declares his *Wintermärchen* a "new song, a better song"—in parodic imitation of the "new beautiful song" composed by a Becker acolyte, a certain Carl Gerber.

To the avowed Rhinelander Heine, "Father Rhine" does not mark the German frontier but a crossroads, an area of cultural mixing where German traditions ("Eyerkuchen mit Schinken," egg pancakes with ham) are modified by Roman-(esque) influences: the Rhine wine in the "Römer" glasses that fires up the poet's imagination (another aside against Becker's "stupid song," in which the "Feuerwein" was reserved for Germans only) and the freer French culture that dominated Rhenish provinces during the Napoleonic years.

As Heine becomes painfully aware, the Rhineland, the liberal counterpart to Prussia, is no longer a liberated territory. A symbol of the return to repressive practices is the Cologne Cathedral, which in Heine's representation stands for medieval intolerance and religious persecution. Again, a concrete "event" triggers Heine's wrath and releases his creative antinationalist energies: the mixed emotions raised by the renewed efforts to complete the construction of the Dom. For centuries, the gothic cathedral had remained incomplete; during the French occupation, it had even served as stables. With the ascent of the romantic nationalist Frederick William IV, demand grew for the completion of what would be a symbol of the reconciliation between the Catholic Church and the Protestant-Prussian administration. In 1842, a society for the reconstruction of the cathedral (*Dombauverein*) was founded that collected money for the restoration of this national monument. Heine himself had joined the Paris branch of the society and had contributed toward the Dom's reconstruction. In 1844, however, as it became clear that the Dom issue was being used to further Prussia's hegemonic goals, Heine withdrew from and ridiculed the project.

The cathedral came to represent for Heine the epitome of the marriage between state and church and became a symbol of Christian intolerance. It associated, in the poet's mind, state censorship with the Inquisition, and more recent outbreaks of Prussian anti-Semitism with the burning of Jewish books in the fifteenth century. Again, Heine's own trajectory, his suffering from Prussia's literary "inquisition," formed the backdrop for his attack on German conditions at that time.

If the restoration of the Cologne Cathedral had inspired Heine to voice his critique of the unholy alliance of church and state in contemporary Prussia and the tradition of intolerance shared by both Catholic and Protestant churches, two other symbols of nationalism permitted him to take issue with the concept of a German Empire founded on exclusivity and a mythic millenarianism: the *Hermannsdenkmal* (the monument to Arminius, the "liberator of the Germans" [Tacitus], in construction since 1838), and *Barbarossa* (the legendary German emperor who had died in the Crusades and who supposedly sleeps in the Kyffhäuser mountain, whence he will one day emerge to reestablish the German Empire). To Heine, the cult of Hermann is just another incident in the teutomania he abhors. If Hermann had not won the battle, Heine muses, there would not be liberty à la Germany—nay, "we would have become Romans!" In a whole series of "what if" situations, Heine imagines the devastating effect of a Romanicization on German culture—mediocre poets like Freiligrath would have become Horaces, asses, donkeys (*usini*). "Thank God," the poet concludes, tongue-in-cheek, "that Hermann won the battle, the Romans were driven away, Varus and his legions perished, and—we remained Germans!"

Whereas Hermann embodied the teutomania and xenophobia of the various nationalist movements in the 1840s (the *Burschenschaften* or student associations, the gymnastics movement started by Turnvater Jahn), "Barbarossa" speaks to the romantic dream of an empire rooted in the Middle Ages and ruled by a populist father figure who can resolve all divisions between the Germanic tribes—a dream that had been reactivated and instrumentalized by Frederick William IV for Prussian dynastic purposes. In contrast, in the figure of the old emperor, Heine creates a bearded fuddy-duddy neither prepared nor eager to assume power. As the narrator says to his face in chapter 16: "Herr Rotbart—rief ich laut—du bist / Ein altes Fabelwesen, Geh, leg dich schlafen, wir werden uns / Auch ohne dich erlösen!" (Mr. Redbeard, I loudly called, you are an old legend—go sleep, we can save ourselves!) and "Bedenk ich die Sache ganz genau, / So brauchen wir gar keinen Kaiser!" (If I think this thing through, we don't even need an emperor!). Heine's radical break with the feudal past and with dreams of imperial glory under iron Prussian rule contains the option for a radically different Germany: a more democratic nation open to cultural influences from outside, a Germany whose identity does not depend on martial symbols and legends from the past and whose liberty does not just reside in its philosophies and dreams.

In opposition to stuffy, retrograde, law-and-order Prussia, reigned by the stick and smelling of cabbage and old leather, the "free city" of Hamburg seemed to offer greater attractions to the returning poet. Hamburg is the place of childhood reminiscences and support; where he is fed by his "mother," supported by his uncle Salomon, the banker, and nurtured and sustained by his publisher Campe—a place of physical gratification, sensual pleasures, material well-being, integration, and incorporation, in which Jews and gentiles can live and reign in happy union. And yet this image of plenty, embodied by the luscious matron Hammonia, who offers her services to the poet, is undercut by reference to her very profession: as a prostitute and streetwalker, she becomes a symbol of the city's overemphasis on commerce, on the commodification of the individual, on material wealth. Through Hammonia, Heine denounces Hamburg's Biedermeier quietism and snugness, its proneness toward corruption and ultimate sellout to Prussia (if it joined the dreaded German Customs Union).

Neither the Prussian capital Berlin, it seemed, nor the free city of Hamburg provided the returning poet with a place of refuge, a home. The former, with its aggressive militarism and evocation of mythic models to veil its imperialist intentions, could not accommodate a free thinker like Heine. The latter, with its emphasis on apolitical materialism, did not appeal to his combative, profoundly political nature, his desire for all-out emancipation. If "Prussia" was bound by its repressive system, "Hamburg" was mired in apathetic hedonism. So what remained? In one of the last images of the *Wintermärchen,* Heine created a devastating vision of Germany's future: the goddess Hammonia permits the poet a glance into Charlemagne's chamber pot—to presage, like the priests of classical antiquity, the fate of the nation from the excrements of the past. But the odors wafting off the German miasma make the poet faint.

In view of Heine's scathing indictment of Germany under Prussian rule, it is tempting to consider *Germany: A Winter's Tale* nothing but a biting satire, an expression of the insurmountable antagonism between the poet Heine and his country of origin. By representing Prussia and Hamburg as parental spaces, however—the disciplining father Prussia, the indulgent mother Hamburg—Heine suggests for himself the position of son, a rebelling or prodigal son, but a son nevertheless. (A similar distinction between the paternal and the maternal appears in "Nachtgedanken" and in the poem "Zur Beruhigung," in which fathers and fatherland are associated with the masters, the absolutist rulers of the state.) Heine presents himself both as a son whose love was rejected, who was not accepted into the fold of the "family," and as a renegade son who has forsaken his fatherland because he can no longer tolerate its reactionary politics. The love for Germany, the nostalgia and homesickness to which the poet admits (chap. 24), are nurtured by bittersweet memories: olfactory and culinary memories (the smells of the countryside, the tastes of local foods), as well as memories of comfort (the nurturing support he received from mother and uncle) and of suffering (the *via crucis,* "Leidensstationen," of his youth, which he does not further elaborate). This love extends to romantic German literature—the "nightingales" and "beech groves" of its poetry—and to idealist philosophy—the "blue smoke" of freedom that emanates from German chimneys and disappears into thin air.

When he returns to France, however, Heine has left it all behind, literally and figuratively. Heine clearly distinguishes between love of fatherland (*Vaterlandsliebe*), "this stupid longing" from which he continued to suffer until his death, and "patriotism," the ostentatious show of allegiance for a Germanic nation he abhors. Because the fatherland can no longer provide him with a home, Heine locates his home in his mother tongue, the German language. Hence, the last chapter of the *Wintermärchen* is a hymn to the powers of language: it is here that the poet can create the visions of a new reality and imprison those who, like the Prussian king, make empirical reality inhospitable.

In Heine's literary oeuvre, *Deutschland: Ein Wintermärchen* constitutes a major turning point. Until his trip to Germany, he had still clung to the idea that German conditions, although deplorable, could change for the better. Afterward, however, he realized fully the "deutsche Misere," the apathy and stagnation, as well as the degree of political repression and economic hardship in the German lands (articulated in his poem *The Silesian Weavers;* 1844). Whereas the story of the poet's "return" effectively closed the doors to his German home—the Prussian government shortly thereafter issued a detention warrant if Heine dared to cross the border into Prussian-controlled territories—the settling of accounts with "Germany" freed him to explore different contexts and allegiances. Subsequent poems and prose pieces—particularly those written after the failed 1848 Revolution—delve further into the past, the collective past of European Jewry and Heine's position within it (see, for example, the "Hebrew Melodies" of the *Romanzero* [1851] and the *Confessions* and *Memoirs* [1854]). Although the poet became increasingly immobile, confined to his "mattress grave," he expanded, in his writings, the geographic horizon to include visions of worldwide suffering and annihilation, from the expulsion of the Moors and Jews in fifteenth-century Spain to the massacres of Amerindians and African slaves in the New World ("Der Mohrenkönig," "Vitzliputzli," "Das Sklavenschiff").

Although the *Wintermärchen* focuses on German politics, Heine's dis-ease with Germany was not just motivated by political disagreements. The sense of exclusion he felt was intimately tied to his identity as an assimilated German Jew—to the agony of conversion and the rejection he has suffered because of his origin. Whereas in the *Wintermärchen* questions of Jewish identity, exclusion or assimilation, persecution or emancipation lead a somewhat submerged life, emerging only in small asides, they are the main focus of his "Ludwig Marcus: Denkworte" (1844), a necrology for a former member of the Berlin "Society for the Culture and Science of Judaism" to which Heine had belonged from 1822 to 1823. If read in conjunction with the *Wintermärchen*, the *Denkworte*, as well as selected articles Heine composed for the *Augsburger Allgemeine Zeitung* during those years, reveals the full extent of his preoccupation with the so-called Jewish Question, even in his supposedly most "political" satire. Thus his scruples over his own conversion (and Prussia's failure to honor it by providing him with a civil-servant position) are reactivated when he hears of Felix Mendelssohn's employment as a concertmaster at the Prussian court in 1841. The ironic tribute to Mendelssohn's possibly pecuniary motivation for his conversion in the *Wintermärchen* (the "little guy Felix . . . made headway in Christiandom," chap. 16) ties in with both former and later critiques of "tactical" conversions, such as that of Eduard Gans, another member of the society. Heine's short references to the Christian church's anti-Semitic record (chap. 4) in turn echo the publicity around a supposed ritual murder in Damascus, whereas his substitution of "hatred of Jews" (*Judenhasse*) with the more general "religious hatred" (*Glaubenshasse*, chap. 4) indicates less a concern over censorship than an intense involvement with the debate over the nature of Jewish emancipation in a Christian state.

The so-called affair of the Jews of Damascus brought to the fore the intensity of European anti-Semitism under the veneer of enlightened "tolerance." In February 1840, a Capuchin monk and his servant were assassinated in Damascus. The French consul in Syria distributed an anti-Semitic pamphlet that drew the hatred of enraged Muslims to Jews as possible culprits of a "ritual murder." The Muslims then initiated a pogrom among Damascus's Jewish population: seven were arrested and tortured without evidence of their guilt. The ensuing controversy in the press over the consul's actions (a controversy to which Heine contributed) and the blatant anti-Semitic overtones of some of the voices revived Heine's memories of his own encounters with anti-Semitism—from the Hep-Hep riots in 1819 to insidious critiques of his "Jewish" style—and renewed his interest in the history of Jewish-German relations.

In theory, Heine expressed serious doubts about Judaism as a religion. Indeed, Heine seemed to have doubts about religion in general, perhaps due to the influence of Bruno Bauer, whose writings Heine owned and who was one of the first recipients of the printed *Wintermärchen*. Bauer, a radical atheist theologian and a former member of the Young Hegelians in Berlin, had published two essays on the so-called Jewish Question: *Die Fähigkeit der heutigen Juden und Christen, frei zu werden* (The capacity of today's Jews and Christians for emancipation; 1843) and *Über die Judenfrage* (On the Jewish Question; *Deutsche Jahrbücher* 1842, 1843). In these essays, Bauer had argued that Jews were rightfully denied political equality because religion and emancipation are mutually exclusive. Jews should demand instead that *all* religion—that is, all servitude—be abolished; only if obsolete traditions (Christian or Jewish) were sacrificed, he argued, could true emancipation be achieved: "Not just the Jews, but we, too, will no longer be satisfied with the chimera; we too want to become a real people, real peoples." Bauer's stance stemmed not just from his rejection of religion, but from an essentialist conception of Jews as bound up with nature, with the world of senses, and as such unable to become "free" citizens. To grant them political equality, he believed, would release their sensuousness and tear apart the fabric of civil society. Bauer's provocative essays raised vehement objections. Orthodox Jewish leaders bemoaned his contempt for Jewish religion and culture. The young Karl Marx, himself an assimilated Jew, challenged Bauer by claiming that society needed to be emancipated not from religion—which would survive separately from the state because it responded to a spiritual need for overcoming the alienation of civil society—but from the "Jewish spirit," the pursuit of money and self-interest (Marx 1975). Jews will not be socially emancipated, Marx argued, until society as a whole is emancipated from the rule of money and man achieves an unalienated civil life. "Therefore we do not tell the Jews that they cannot be emancipated politically without radically emancipating themselves from Judaism, which is what Bauer tells them. We say instead: the fact that you can be politically emancipated without completely and absolutely renouncing Judaism shows that *political emancipation* itself is not *human* emancipation" (226).

Heine, it seems, was caught in the middle of the debate. His "Ludwig Marcus: Denkworte," written in April 1844, as Heine established a close friendship with the young Marx and as he composed his *Wintermärchen,* can be read as *his* comments on "that emancipation . . . which these days is sometimes talked about in such a disgustingly unintelligent way" (Heine 1962, 294). Emancipation will have to be granted sooner or later, Heine affirms, "from a sense of justice, from foresight, from sheer necessity" (292). Although he shared Bauer's skepticism toward the institution of religion and, to an extent, his atheism, he rejected Bauer's belief in a Jewish (inferior) essence. And although Heine apparently alludes to Marxian ideas when he blames anti-Semitism on "resentment against the overweening power of capital" among the "lower classes," he does not, like Marx, equate Judaism with huckstering and use it as a metaphor for the ills of civil society. Instead, he focuses on the psychology of orthodoxy, irrespective of religion. Reactionary governments should be glad to have devout Jews in their midst, he says, somewhat tongue-in-cheek, for these are the "Swiss Guards

of Deism," pillars of faith in a faithless world. "Don't insist on the Jews' baptism," he admonishes Protestant Prussia, "that's just water and water dries fast. Encourage circumcision instead, for it is faith cut into the flesh, when it can no longer be carved into the mind" (293). In other words, because religious traditionalism breeds authoritarian behavior, authoritarian governments should embrace it. Implicit in Heine's "good advice" to authorities was his own opposition to any religious, ethnic, or national fundamentalisms and the expectation that economic interests would soon supersede old divisions and create new "brotherhoods":

Our nationalists, so-called patriots, who carry only race and full-blood and other such horse-breeding thoughts in their heads, these relics from the Middle Ages will soon encounter adversaries who will put a terrible end to all their dreams of a Germanic, Romanic or Slavic identity, so that they won't even dream of picking on the German character of Jews. I am specifically speaking of the brotherhood of the workers of the world, of the wild army of the proletariat that will eliminate all that nationality's business in order to pursue a common goal in all of Europe, the realization of true democracy. And is there indeed such a great ethnic difference between the German Jews, who for 1500 years have lived in Germany, and their Christian compatriots? Indeed, no. (Heine 1962, 294)

The international proletariat, on the one hand, and the international finance capital on the other would, Heine speculated, make religious differences between Protestant and Jewish Germans obsolete.

Heine even went so far as to postulate an "elective affinity" between Germans and Jews: "Miraculous coincidences in the mentality of both peoples: the bravest hatred against Rome, a sense of personal liberty, morality" (Heine 1962, 294). Again, this statement must be read dialectically; it is meant both facetiously and seriously. In view of Heine's philo-"Roman" remarks made simultaneously in the *Wintermärchen,* the hatred against "Rome" that Germans and Jews supposedly shared referred not just to Prussia's recent battles with the Catholic Church, the Prussian Wars of Liberation against Napoleon, or Israel's resistance against Roman occupation; it was also directed at the cultural rigidity and exclusivity Heine bemoaned in both nations. Within the context of Heine's oeuvre, however, the insistence on an elective affinity between Germans and Jews also attests to his continued desire to "own" a borderland between the two peoples (see the foreword to *Wintermärchen*), that is, to be recognized as a hyphenated German, as a Jewish-German poet over and beyond religious, national, or ethnic divisions. Once again, the statement encapsulates Heine's hate-love relationship with Germany, the country he left behind and from which he could never escape.

Bibliography

Gisela Benda, "'Dem Dichter war so wohl daheime . . .': Heines verhaltene Deutschlandliebe," *Heine-Jahrbuch* 11 (1972): 117–25; Karlheinz Fingerhut, *Heinrich Heine: Deutschland. Ein Wintermärchen* (Frankfurt a. M.: Diesterweg, 1992); Wilhelm Gössmann and Winfried Woesler, *Politische Dichtung im Unterricht: Deutschland. Ein Wintermärchen* (Düsseldorf: Schwann, 1974); Walter Grab, *Heinrich Heine als politischer Dichter* (Frankfurt a. M.: Büchergilde Gutenberg, 1982–1992); Heinrich Heine, *Deutschland: A Winter's Tale,* trans. T. J. Reed (London: Angel, 1986); Heine, "Ludwig Marcus: Denkworte," *Heinrich Heine: Werke und Briefe,* ed. Hans Kaufmann (Berlin: Aufbau, 1962), 7: 283–300; Heine, *Sämtliche Werke, Düsseldorfer Ausgabe (DHA),* vol. 4, *Atta Troll: Ein Sommernachtstraum. Deutschland: Ein Wintermärchen,* ed. Winfried Woesler (Hamburg: Hoffmann and Campe, 1985); Jost Hermand, "Heines 'Wintermärchen'—Zum Topos der 'deutschen Misere'," *Diskussion Deutsch* 8 (1977); Walter Hinck, *Die Wunde Deutschland: Heinrich Heines Dichtung im Widerstreit von Nationalidee, Judentum und Antisemitismus* (Frankfurt a. M.: Insel, 1990); Gerhard Höhn, *Heine-Handbuch: Zeit-Person-Werk* (Stuttgart: Metzler, 1987); Hans Kaufmann, *Politisches Gedicht und klassische Dichtung: Heinrich Heine. Deutschland. Ein Wintermärchen* (Berlin: Aufbau Verlag, 1959); Joseph A. Kruse, "Heinrich Heine, der Deutsche, und die Deutschen," *Bulletin des Leo Baeck Instituts, Jerusalem* 71 (1985): 3–19; Karl Marx, "On the Jewish Question," *Karl Marx: Early Writings,* intro. Lucio Colletti, trans. Rodney Livingston and Gregor Benton (New York: Vintage, 1975), 211–41; Marx, "Zur Judenfrage," *Karl Marx: Die Frühschriften,* ed. Siegfried Landshut (Stuttgart: Kroner, 1953), 171–207; and Edda Ziegler, *Heinrich Heine, Leben-Werk-Wirkung* (Zurich: Artemis & Winkler, 1993).

SUSANNE ZANTOP

January 31, 1850   Conversion to Judaism is protected under the constitution of the North German Confederation

The *Jüdisches Lexikon* (1930), under the entry "Proselyt" (proselyte), notes that "statistics concerning numbers and motivations of conversions during modern times are not yet available." Whereas Jewish conversion to the Christian denominations was not only common but actually expected in nineteenth-century Germany, Christian conversion to Judaism by comparison remained a limited phenomenon, one regarded with suspicion by the Christian majority as well as by some Jewish commentators. Conversion to Judaism in nineteenth-century Germany, as opposed to conversion in antiquity, was embedded in the context of centuries of Jewish history in a Christian society. Until well into the eighteenth century, throughout Christian Europe both converts and Jews involved in the conversion process faced the death penalty. During the first half of the nineteenth century, conversion to Judaism, which in principle was guaranteed by the Prussian Legal Code of 1794 with its decree of freedom of religion (*Religionsfreiheit*), was in practice frequently prohibited by anti-Jewish legislation. Frederick William III, for example, in his cabinet orders of 1814 and 1834, revoked the right to convert to Judaism. Under penalty of law, the king ordered the Jewish communities not to admit any convert who had not obtained an official release from the Christian community— and forbade Christian leaders to grant secession from Christianity. The constitution of the North German Federation finally instituted freedom of religion in 1850, which was extended to all of Germany in 1871. Austria granted freedom of religion in 1868, and Hungary followed as late as 1895. Jewish scholars such as the Berlin schoolteacher Nathan Samter, who often addressed the subject of conversion to Judaism, situate this particular relationship between Jews and Christians in the larger framework of Jewish legal and social history in Germany.

It was not until the early twentieth century that German-Jewish communities began to include conversions to Judaism in their population statistics; for Germany, the data collected by the regional Protestant churches pertaining to conversions from Protestantism constitute the most comprehensive nineteenth-century source. According to church records, 126 conversions took place in Berlin between 1872 and 1894; in the city of Dresden, nine Protestants converted to Judaism between 1886 and 1903. In Austria, with its significantly higher rate of conversion, the Jewish communities did compile statistics on conversions to Judaism: in Vienna between 1868 (the year in which freedom of religion was granted in Austria) and 1903 more than 2,300 people converted, with women outnumbering men almost two to one. Given that the foremost motivation for conversion was (and is) marriage between Christian-born women and Jewish men, the ban of interfaith marriages in Austria, which was in effect throughout the nineteenth century, explains the comparatively high numbers as well as the overwhelming predominance of female converts. For the year 1903, the *Zeitschrift für*

Statistik und Demographie der Juden (Journal for statistics and demographics of the Jews) reports twenty conversions to Judaism in all of Germany, excluding Berlin. Although there are no separate figures for baptized Jews who returned to the "religion of the fathers" (*Religion der Väter*), their conversions are treated as specific cases involving the reavowal of an affiliation that has never been fully severed, rather than the adoption of a new religion. Commentators on conversion statistics generally welcomed (re)conversions to Judaism (*Übertritte*) as gains and regretted conversions from Judaism (*Austritte*) as losses to Judaism.

Reaching well beyond its relative numerical insignificance, conversion to Judaism triggered a vital public debate in the second half of the nineteenth century. This issue also has some importance in autobiographical literature as well as in fiction and popular history. In the larger contexts of general secularization and Jewish assimilation, German anti-Semitism, and Zionism, Christian conversion to Judaism marks a critical intersection between Jewish-German and Christian-German identity positions. The Jewish debates surrounding the desirability of converts and the conditions of conversion speak to the larger question of definitions of Jewishness and Judaism in the modern world.

The popular and critical success of Wilhelm Herzberg's epistolary novel *Jüdische Familien-papiere* (Jewish family papers; 1868, Eng. trans., 1875) illustrates public interest in an increasing diversity of Jewish identities in nineteenth-century Germany, which the novel depicts as the result of a growing liberalization in Jewish-Christian relationships. Herzberg's protagonist, a young man born to Jewish parents who died in England on their way to America, was raised in the Christian faith by an Englishman. The novel shows him during an extended visit in the house of his uncle, a neo-Orthodox rabbi. As a demonstration of his gratitude, young Samuel, in an early letter to his adoptive father, renews his vow to devote his "earthly life to the poor lost sheep of Israel" (7). Contrary to the protagonist's missionary intentions, religious disputes between uncle and nephew ensue, during which the young man experiences a religious crisis, confesses to his

adoptive father his rejection of Christian dogmas, and affirms his Jewish identity. Questions of Jewish identity occupy a central position in this novel, whose protagonist characterizes his conversion as one of conviction rather than as simply a return to the religion of his parents. The rabbi defines a "good Jew" as one who "strictly adheres to the ceremonial laws" (12), but he extends this delineation by suggesting the existence of a Jewish "Nature" that cannot be erased by a Christian "Education" (147). Herzberg affirms the reality of a Jewish essence through an insertion: immediately preceding the letter that relates Samuel's return to Judaism, he relates a lengthy story about a Moroccan Jewess who reveals her Jewish essence by choosing death over forced conversion to Islam. Although on the surface it defines Jewishness as the religious observance within the social community into which the individual is born, the novel simultaneously acknowledges the precariousness of Jewish identity toward the beginning of the second half of the nineteenth century and, through its minor characters, allows for Jewish identity positions outside a purely religious framework. In a contradiction of the rabbi's assertion that Jewish "Nature" guarantees Jewishness, in his own family he suffers the loss (and return) of his oldest son, who, despite the father's dedicated efforts to provide him with a profound Jewish education, married a Christian woman; in a desperate attempt not to lose his younger son to a Christian actress, he begs his son's prospective bride to abandon her profession and convert to Judaism. To maintain the traditional Jewish family unit, the rabbi reluctantly resorts to opening his house to a convert. The actress respectfully declines his invitation, explaining that of the rabbi's two requests, to give up her profession is the one that she cannot fulfill. Even though the erotic relationships between the rabbi's sons and Christian women ultimately fail, Herzberg's novel, which the critics praised as a strong statement in favor of traditional Judaism, in fact probes the boundaries of traditional Jewish society. Conversion to Judaism in this novel is a response to an increase in Jewish-Christian relationships and a counterargument against Jewish conversion to Christianity.

The distinction between "good" and "bad" Jews, as made by Herzberg's rabbi, expresses his regret that in the nineteenth century birth to Jewish parents can no longer be assumed to be positively synonymous with religious observance. Until about 1870, observance of ceremonial law, including circumcision, figures centrally in the Jewish reception and appreciation of converts. Between the years 1843 and 1875, the *Allgemeine Zeitung des Judentums* (*AZJ*) reports more than twenty individual and multiple cases of conversions to Judaism. Although these brief notices contradict each other in their assessment of the commonness or rarity of Christian conversion, without exception the convert's motivation is of central interest to the authors. Strict observance of Jewish law, which in some cases is said to precede the actual act of conversion by decades, represents the most persuasive indication of the convert's sincerity to become a "good" Jew. Observance of Jewish rituals and dietary laws testifies to the Jewishness of those born into Judaism as well as converts. In the journalistic conversion narrative, the traditionally required recitation of Jewish ceremonial laws, which serves to deter the potential convert, is conventionally followed by the convert's solemn refusal to refrain from conversion. The mention of circumcision and the convert's conduct during the "conversion operation" ("Bekehrungs-Operation") (*AZJ* 30 [1866]: 198) emerge as standard narrative elements designed to illustrate the male convert's integrity; self-circumcision or the new Jew's willingness to bear the financial burden of the medical care necessary for his recovery elicit even higher admiration. The eagerness of a convert to submit to circumcision as a sign of sincerity, as it emanates from the pages of *Allgemeine Zeitung des Judentums* or *Der Israelit,* aims to confirm Judaism's inherent attractiveness perhaps more to the Jewish readership than to prospective converts.

By comparison, reports on female conversions, which commonly attribute the motivation to change religion to the convert's desire to marry a Jew, tend to discredit these conversions as secondary in merit to male religious convictions. In practice, the valuation of conviction over marriage as two distinct motivations translates into the tendency to place male converts above females. In a letter dating back to 1865, Ludwig Philippson, rabbi in Magdeburg and founding editor of the *Allgemeine Zeitung des Judentums,* who insisted that his willingness to accept converts did not contradict his principal objection to seeking proselytes (*Proselyten-Macherei*), treated conviction and marriage as mutually compatible when he explained that he converted a number of people to Judaism upon having "convinced himself that a complete and honest conviction had taken root . . . even if the first motive was marriage" (*AZJ* 79 [1915]: 403). Until well into the second half of the nineteenth century, the convert's ability to demonstrate through observance the integrity of his or her religious belief was believed to reflect converts' self-understanding of Jewish identity as a traditional religious identity.

Around 1870, liberal Jews begin to reexamine the question of converts with the general goal of facilitating conversion. The two issues at the center of this controversy, male circumcision and the presence of men during the ritual bath of women converts, are expressions of a larger development among the Jewish communities away from the primacy of ceremonial law and toward the proclamation of the universal humanist monotheism, which was expected to secure a space for Judaism and Jewish identity within a modern world. Hoping that a "fresh air stream" from America might enliven Judaism in Germany, the great scholar and liberal rabbi Abraham Geiger reported extensively in his *Jüdische Zeitschrift für Wissenschaft und Leben* (Jewish journal for science and life) on the 1869 rabbinical conference in Philadelphia and its deliberations concerning circumcision of proselytes. Reversing the prevalent contention that circumcision serves to deter undesirable converts, Bohemian-born rabbi Isaac Mayer Wise argued that mandatory circumcision, because the procedure was not explicitly required of born Jews, on the contrary might keep away serious converts and attract those with ulterior motivations. It was not until 1892, however, that the Central Conference of American Rabbis passed a resolution to the effect that circumcision did not constitute a requirement for converts; in Germany, circumcision remained an obligation for converts throughout the nineteenth century. Nevertheless, the challenge to make circumcision imperative for male converts, which Ludwig Philippson had considered "indispensable" less than ten years earlier (*AZJ* 26 [1862]: 86), aimed at lowering the boundaries between Jews and Christians and illustrated the self-understanding of Reform Judaism as an integral part of German and European culture. By uncoupling conviction from ritual observance, the Reformers adjusted the conversion process to the dwindling reality of this once decisive difference between Judaism and Christianity and integrated the convert into their understanding of a Jewish identity grounded in spirituality, philosophy, and scholarship.

Concerning the question of female proselytes, the Second Israelite Synod, the 1871 convention of liberal rabbis in Augsburg, again at the initiative of Abraham Geiger, pronounced that two trustworthy Jewish women could serve as witnesses of the ritual bath. Although the brief discussion revealed that, in actual practice, standard rules of moral conduct prevented male presence, the main argument in favor of the motion, the perceived necessity to raise the status of women within Judaism, shows the close connections between the issue of conversion and a reform of Judaism as envisioned by liberal Jews. The Association of Liberal Rabbis of Germany officially adopted the Augsburg decision in 1899.

From the mid-1880s into the first decade of the twentieth century, the history of conversion to Judaism was a topic of interest to a number of Jewish writers. In particular the stories of "famous" converts and their individual cases appeared in both the weekend supplements of Jewish family journals and Jewish "house calendars" (*Haus-Kalender*), and in scholarly journals. Expressions and products of a late-nineteenth-century German-Jewish identity, these narratives no longer questioned the desirability of converts or pondered the requirements for conversion. Rather, the figure of the outstanding proselyte exemplified the attractiveness of Judaism in light of the obstacles and risks that the act of conversion entailed within the convert's particular historical context. The evidence of Christian conver-

sion became a sensitive measuring device for the legal and social position of Jews in European Christian society. The interest in conversion as a specific aspect of Jewish-Christian history was also a response to the contemporary context of anti-Semitism. Because of its plea for tolerance and emancipation, the Enlightenment serves today as the historical referent and positive counterpart to anti-Semitic prejudice, and the French Revolution is celebrated as a liberating turning point in Jewish history.

Among the canonical cases of famous converts, which include Count Potocki, the Polish nobleman who allegedly was burned at the stake in Vilna in 1749, and Anna Constanze von Cosel, mistress and prisoner of the Saxon King August the Strong, the story of Joseph Steblicki drew perhaps the most extensive attention. An educated man and a public figure in his native Nikolai (Silesia), Steblicki converted from Catholicism to Judaism in 1785. His case marks a decisive change in the official treatment of converts because valid law, which called for the death penalty, was overruled by a legal council in Berlin in accordance with the proclamation of freedom of religion under Frederick II. Eduard Biberfeld, who published the transcripts of the Steblicki case in the *Magazin für die Wissenschaft des Judenthums* (Magazine for the science of Judaism) in 1893, drew a connection between the Enlightenment period and his own time when he wrote in his introduction: "And what would be more befitting to the understanding of the general cultural development of a period than its treatment of the Jews? . . . Especially in our time, which is so contaminated by the spirit of hate" (183). A year prior to Biberfeld's historical documentation, Marcus Brann in his *Jüdischer Volks- und Hauskalender* (Jewish people's and house calendar) had evoked the Steblicki case to contrast the anti-Semitism of contemporary "German Christianity" with the unprejudiced attitude of the Enlightenment. Similarly, Louis Neustadt in his 1894 monograph on Steblicki distinguishes between the Enlightenment spirit of Frederick II and late-nineteenth-century anti-Semitism. Narrative accounts of historical cases such as Steblicki's pursue an additional strategy: the con-

vert's courage to follow his or her religious convictions is meant to throw a critical light on the
status of Jewish-Christian relationships. At the
turn of the century, most writers introduced their
interest in Christian conversion to Judaism with
at least implicit references to the spread of anti-
Semitism.

Among the "outstanding converts" enumer-
ated in encyclopedia entries and monographs on
the subject of conversion, Nahida Ruth Lazarus's
name figures prominently as one of the most important and honored converts in late-nineteenth-
century Germany. Her conversion took place in
early 1895 in Freiburg under the supervision of
Rabbi Adolf Lewin. Because the majority of converts to Judaism were women, whose conversions
were generally assumed to be motivated by marriage to a Jew, Lazarus's example is both representative and unique. The cases of, for instance,
Paula Beer-Hofmann, who converted in 1898 and
became the wife of the Austrian writer Richard
Beer-Hofmann; Paula Buber (née Winkler), a
born Catholic who converted prior to marrying
Martin Buber in 1901; and Nahida Lazarus, who
after her conversion married her teacher of many
years, Moritz Lazarus, the cofounder of ethno-
psychology, are similar to the degree that all three
women married prominent men. The prevailing
assumption that marriage provided the sole incentive for their conversions, however, obscures
any sovereign motivations. Nahida Lazarus—in
contrast to Paula Beer-Hofmann, whose writings
concerning her conversion remain unpublished,
and Paula Winkler Buber, who wrote only a short
journal article about her conversion—related the
story of her conversion before public audiences
and published a 220-page autobiographical narrative. Its title, *Ich suchte Dich!* (I sought you!;
1898), describes the autobiographer's search,
which reaches its completion in the act of conversion and her affirmation of a single God. Lazarus's
autobiography is as much the story of her conversion out of the Christian religion as it is the narration of her conversion to Judaism. Her gradual
rejection of Christianity, which takes up the major part of the autobiography, draws on two lines
of argumentation: the dogmatic insistence on supernatural phenomena in Christian belief (the

conventional contention that is central also to
Herzberg's novel, whose influence Lazarus acknowledges in her autobiography), and the base
position of women in the New Testament. In
engaging her older male Christian educators in
religious disputations, young Nahida not only
confronts Christian dogma but also asserts herself
as a woman with a Jewish voice of her own. In her
narrative, Lazarus strictly separates her resolve to
convert from her subsequent marriage to Moritz
Lazarus, who appears in the autobiography as her
teacher long before he becomes her husband.
Lazarus appropriates the model of conversion
that the contributors to the *Allgemeine Zeitung des
Judentums* had reserved for male converts: her autobiography privileges religious conviction as an
independent motivation. The conversion was already scheduled to take place in Geneva when
her decision to marry Moritz Lazarus was brought
about by a visit to him on her way to Switzerland.

Lazarus's understanding of her Jewishness as a
female convert draws on several different traditions. The autobiographical statement that, prior
to her conversion, in her "heart (even if entirely
unconsciously) she had long been a Jewish
woman" (213) uncouples Herzberg's idea of a
Jewish essence from Jewish birth and defines Jewishness as a spiritual constitution based solely in
faith. The comparative discussions of Judaism
and Christianity in the tradition of the dispute
over the true religion, however, do not lead to
immediate conversion. Not having undergone
Christian confirmation, Lazarus remained without religious affiliation for several years. In her
autobiography, she explains her initial interest in
Judaism not as a result of her disenchantment
with Christianity, but as a response to the ascent
of the anti-Semitism she observed in Berlin in the
1880s. Her desire to defend the Jews against their
German attackers led her to the scholarly study of
the Jewish religion, history, and people in the
tradition of Leopold Zunz (*Wissenschaft des Judentums*), with conversion as the natural outcome of
her occupation with Jewish culture, in particular
the role of women. Lazarus's path to Judaism
combines the traditional quest for religious fulfillment with modern scholarship, both of which

are principally open to the sincere male student regardless of the religious community into which he was born. Her academic pursuits against anti-Semitism thus double as a struggle for the recognition of women as intellectuals.

Decrying the decline in religiosity among Jews, enthusiastic critics recommended the convert Nahida Lazarus as an ideal to all born Jews, in particular to Jewish women. In contrast to the perception of converts as foreign elements and a threat to a distinct Jewish identity, Lazarus's reviewers used her example to strengthen a modern yet religious Jewish identity. A former Christian and a woman, the figure of Nahida Lazarus confirmed to her Jewish contemporaries the value and validity of a spiritual Jewishness. At the end of the twentieth century, Lazarus's hope that scholarly proof of Jewish cultural accomplishments could enlighten racial anti-Semites seems perhaps naive. Her positive reception as a scholar and autobiographer by many Jewish historians well into the twentieth century, however, suggests how much her voice was appreciated.

Paula Winkler, a Germanist by training and among the first women to enroll at the University of Munich at the turn of the century, found her way to Judaism through Zionism. In the Zionist weekly *Die Welt,* Winkler, who subsequently published novels and stories under the pseudonym Georg Munk, described her relationship to Jews and the Jewish people and assessed her position as a convert within the Zionist movement in an article entitled "Confessions of a Philozionist" ("Bekenntnisse einer Philozionistin"; 1901). Merging Jewish history with her own family history, Winkler traced her exceptionally positive attitude toward Jews back to her childhood and, importantly, to the stories of her mother, to whom Jewish culture provided intellectual and emotional stimulation as a young woman. The attractiveness of Jewish culture to Christian women is based on the perception that Jewish women enjoy a higher social status than Christian women, a notion that is also central to Lazarus's conversion narrative. Winkler insists that her community knew no anti-Semitic discrimination against Jews but that she failed to understand the special position of Jews (*Sonderstellung*) within

Christian society. Both Winkler and Lazarus associated Jewish identity with Christian persecution; subsequently, both writers traced their motivation to convert to Judaism to memories of witnessing such acts of aggression. For Winkler, Zionism provided the means not only to end Jewish suffering but also to preserve Jewishness: "in differentiating lies all your beauty" ("im Unterscheiden liegt all Deine Schönheit," 6), she writes, addressing the Jewish people. Emphatically downplaying her own "value, sense, or meaning" (6) to the Zionist movement, Winkler stresses the strength with which Zionism endows her own life. Winkler met her future husband, Martin Buber, at the Third Zionist Congress in Basel in 1899, where she listened to his speech. In her article, she recapitulates this encounter as a turning point in her life—without mentioning Buber's name or the fact that she was married to him by the time she wrote this text. One of only two short texts she published under her own name, Paula Winkler's conversion narrative occupies a special position within her work.

Jewish writing on conversion, whether literary or carried out in the pages of journals, whether autobiographical or scholarly, responded to shifts in the relationship between the dominant Christian majority and the Jewish minority. Jewish emancipation, Reform Judaism, Zionism, and the continuous struggle for new definitions of Jewish identity in an increasingly anti-Semitic Germany shaped nineteenth-century discourses on Christian conversion to Judaism.

Bibliography

Eduard Biberfeld, "Joseph Abraham Steblicki: Ein Ger Zedek des 18. Jahrhunderts," *Magazin für die Wissenschaft des Judenthums* 20 (1893): 181–98; David Max Eichhorn, ed., *Conversion to Judaism: A History and Analysis* (New York: Ktav, 1965); Ismar Elbogen, Georg Herlitz, Bruns Kirschner, eds., *Jüdisches Lexikon* (Berlin: Jüdischer Verlag, 1927–30); Wilhelm Herzberg, *Jüdische Familienpapiere: Briefe eines Missionärs* (Hamburg: Meissner, 1868); Bernhard Koenigsberger, "Proselyten im Judenthum," *Jeschurun: Organ für die geistigen und sozialen Interessen des Judenthums* 1 (1901): 571ff.; Nahida Ruth Lazarus, *Ich suchte Dich! Biographische*

Erzählung von Nahida Ruth Lazarus {Nahida Remy} (Berlin: Siegfried Cronbach, 1898); Louis Lewin, "Jüdische Proselyten in Grosspolen," *Jahrbuch der Jüdisch-Literarischen Gesellschaft,* vol. 7 (1910): 375–78, vol. 9 (1912): 498–503, vol. 11 (1916): 268–71; Louis Neustadt, *Joseph Steblicki: Ein Proselyt unter Friedrich dem Großen* (Breslau: Schatzky, 1894); Jacob Raisin, *Gentile Reactions to Jewish Ideals, with Special Reference to Proselytes,* ed. Herman Hailperin (New York: Philosophical Library, 1953); Nathan Samter, *Judenthum und Pros-* *elytismus: Ein Vortrag* (Breslau: Wilhelm Jacobson, 1897); Samter, "Sollen die Juden Mission treiben?" *Allgemeine Zeitung des Judentums* 59, no. 40 (1895): 471–74; no. 41 (1895): 457–89; Samter, "Der Übertritt zum Judenthum: Eine rechtsgeschichtliche Studie," *Allgemeine Zeitung des Judentums* 58, no. 43 (1894): 509–11; and Paula Winkler, "Bekenntnisse einer Philozionistin," *Die Welt* 36 (1901): 4–6.

KATHARINA GERSTENBERGER

1857 Abraham Geiger's epoch-making book *Urschrift und Übersetzungen der Bibel in ihrer Abhängigkeit von der inneren Entwicklung des Judentums* disseminates the Jewish version of the origins of Christianity

German-Jewish thought displays a fascination with Christianity that was central to Judaism's own self-definition in the nineteenth and early twentieth centuries. Rather than a new or superior religion, Christianity, according to many German-Jewish thinkers, was entirely unoriginal, serving as a mere extension of Judaism. Indeed, it was Christianity's mission to carry Jewish monotheism to the pagan world; meanwhile Judaism, by remaining aloof from the world, could preserve its pure monotheism from the dilution of pagan associations.

In defining the message of Judaism and Christianity as essentially the same, the question of the difference between the two religions arose. Although German liberal Protestantism had rejected the dogma and miracles of conservative Christianity, German-Jewish theologians doggedly portrayed Christian theology as a welter of supernatural claims inconsistent with modern rationalism. Judaism, they argued, made no such claims, but was rooted in an ethical monotheism thoroughly compatible with modernity.

Jesus became a central figure of dispute in the self-definition of Jewish and Christian theologians. Jewish theologians imaged him as a pious, observant Jew, falsely cloaked in the garb of Christian dogma, rather than the founder of a new religion. Christian theologians described Jesus as a spiritual genius who transcended the religious sterility of Judaism to found Christianity.

German Jews' ideological construct of Christianity was both an effort to assimilate and a construction of a counterhistory. In carving out a place for Judaism within the Christian culture, Jewish theologians consistently inverted the traditional Christian portrayal of the relationship between the two religions and depicted Christian civilization as a deviant branch of the tree of Judaism. Not Christianity, but Judaism, they argued, was the font of Western civilization, the mother of its two daughter religions, Islam and Christianity, and, through its intellectual open-mindedness, the driving force behind modernity.

Jesus became a particularly crucial figure for leaders of Reform Judaism. By questioning the authority of Jewish law, they realized they had come precariously close to Jesus' and Paul's own rejection of the law. Reform Judaism's task was to clarify the difference between its own view of Jewish law and that of Christianity, placing the question of the Jewishness of Jesus and Paul at the center of Jewish theological self-definition.

In one of the earliest statements concerning Jesus, Jacob Emden, one of the most powerful Orthodox rabbis of the late eighteenth century, asserted that Jesus had no intention of abolishing Jewish law, nor had made any claims to divinity (Emden 1757). In the 1870s, Moses Mendelssohn, under an uncomfortable challenge from Christian theologians, described in two letters to Lavater written in 1769 and 1771 his respect for Jesus as a moral personality, provided no supernatural claims were attached to him (Mendelssohn 1843, vol. 3, pp. 42, 105). Indeed, according to Mendelssohn, viewing Jesus as a moral teacher was in accord with Jesus' own self-understanding, because he never claimed divinity nor attempted to found a new religion or overturn Jewish law.

Neither Emden nor Mendelssohn wrote extensive public works about Jesus or Christianity; their views were confined primarily to private correspondence. Yet their brief remarks suggested an interpretation that became normative for subsequent Jewish thinkers and overturned centuries of Jewish tradition concerning Jesus. Prior to the modern era, Jesus was portrayed in Jewish texts in a consistently negative light. Scattered talmudic references present Jesus as illegitimate, and in some passages of the Talmud he is presented as a heretic whose punishment in the afterlife is to boil eternally in a vat of dung. These rabbinic condemnations affirm the basic Christian premise that Jesus rejected Jewish law and sought to found a new religion. In the Middle Ages, the popular collection of Jewish folktales concerning Jesus, the *Toldot Yeshu,* similarly elaborates his wickedness as a heretic who, as the son of a whore, maliciously defiled the Temple in Jerusalem, performed miraculous healings, spurred his followers to acts of wickedness, and justifiably deserved the Jewish-imposed death penalty. Even the great medieval philosopher Maimonides portrayed Jesus as an impostor who never intended to found a new religion (1172).

By the nineteenth century, the image of Jesus as a moral teacher without supernatural attributes came to predominate in Jewish writings, but an explanation was sought for the Christian break with Judaism. Isaak Jost, in his first multivolume survey of Jewish history (published during the 1820s), argued that although Jesus "outwardly observed the old law," he actually wanted to bring about a break with Judaism (Jost 1820, 57). Jesus' motivation, according to Jost, was the degenerate state of Judaism in his day. Jost describes the Pharisees of the first century in the traditional language of Christian polemicists: as religiously corrupt, hair-splitting, legalistic hypocrites who had Jesus put to death because his religious reforms threatened their power. Indeed, Jost blames the Pharisees for bringing about the Roman destruction of Jerusalem in 70 C.E. and argues further that most Jews in modern Europe are followers of Pharisaic legalism.

Like Jost, Joseph Salvador, one of the first Jewish authors to compose a biography of Jesus, assigns the Jews responsibility for the death of Jesus but justifies his death on the grounds that Jesus spoke of himself as a god and preached new religious teachings that were, in fact, heretical (Salvador 1838, vol. 1). Salvador portrayed Jesus as an Essene who had studied magic in Egypt and had aroused the antipathy of the Pharisees as a result of his violation of biblical commandments and his identification of himself as a god. Jesus, according to Salvador, preached an individualistic, effeminate religious message, in contrast to the community-oriented, masculine religion of the Pharisees.

Neither Emden, Mendelssohn, Jost, nor Salvador saw anything radically new in the actual content of Jesus' preachings; he was simply preaching the moral principles of Judaism. The difference lay, for Mendelssohn, in later Christianity's attribution of dogma to Jesus' person, inventing a "son of God"; for Jost, in the degenerate state of first-century Judaism, which placed Jesus' preaching in high moral relief; and for Salvador, in the "feminine" style of Jesus' "gentle" teachings, which contrasted with the "masculine" style of the rabbis' power of judgment and sense of rectitude (Salvador 1841, 192).

During the 1840s, the Hegelian Jewish philosopher Samuel Hirsch went a step further, suggesting that Christianity's break from Judaism also constituted a break with Jesus. Hirsch, who wrote two books comparing the two religions, presented Jesus as a pious and loyal Jew and blamed the break between Christianity and Judaism on Paul (*Das*

System der religiösen Anschauung der Juden und sein Verhältnis zum Heidentum, Christentum und zur absoluten Philosophie, 1842). Jesus and Judaism are synonymous, he argued, and any deviation from Jewish tradition found in the Gospels must have been a later interpolation by gentile Christians. It was Paul, according to Hirsch, who deviated from Jesus' own teachings and transformed Jesus into a "metaphysical entity."

Jewish discussions of Christianity received their most influential formulation in the writings of Abraham Geiger (1810–74), whose work was widely read by Christian, as well as Jewish, theologians. Geiger, one of the founders of Reform Judaism, was a noted historian and prolific leader of the Wissenschaft des Judentums. In his *Urschrift,* Geiger first began to elaborate a systematic Jewish version of Christian origins, further elaborated in his later writings, primarily *Das Judentum und seine Geschichte* (Judaism and its history; 1865). Geiger answered Christian anti-Judaism by presenting the Pharisees as the democratic, progressive leaders of their day who attempted a liberal reform of Judaism, in contrast to their opponents, the conservative, literalist Sadducees. Going further, Geiger transfigured Jesus himself into one of the Pharisees by demonstrating parallels between Jesus' teachings and actions and those attributed to the Pharisees in mishnaic and other rabbinic sources. Far from being the founder of a new faith who bore an original religious message, Jesus, for Geiger, was thoroughly unoriginal; he was simply a pale imitation of his teacher, the rabbi Hillel. Moreover, the only way to understand the New Testament was to see it in the context of rabbinic teachings, because nothing attributed to Jesus was unique or original: "Jesus was a Jew, a Pharisaic Jew with Galilean coloring, a man who joined in the hopes of his time and who believed that those hopes were fulfilled in him. He did not utter a new thought, nor did he break down the barriers of [Jewish] nationality. . . . He did not abolish any part of Judaism; he was a Pharisee who walked in the way of Hillel" (Geiger 1865, 117–18). Although he followed Hillel, Jesus, according to Geiger, actually took a stricter position in regard to Jewish law:

for example, he forbade divorce. And though Jesus' historicity remains problematic, "Hillel was a fully historical man."

In denying the originality and uniqueness of Jesus, Geiger asserted the primacy of Judaism and claimed that Christianity, in all of its positive elements, was derived from it. He had already presented a similar argument about the derivative nature of Islam in *Was hat Muhammed aus dem Judentum aufgenommen?* (1833; What did Muhammed take from Judaism?), but his claims regarding Christianity were far more controversial, at least among Christian theologians. Still, his definition of the Pharisees, Jesus, and Paul became the normative view of Christianity adopted by nearly all subsequent German-Jewish thinkers. His views were disseminated in the Jewish press, in the popular histories of the Jews, and in scholarly Jewish publications by writers such as Felix Perles, Leo Baeck, Kaufmann Kohler, and Ismar Elbogen.

Redefining the Pharisees as the liberalizers of their day allowed Geiger and other leaders of Reform Judaism to present their efforts as a way of continuing the principles of rabbinic Judaism, rather than of rejecting them. Reform of Judaism, in their self-representation, preserves the spirit of the Talmud, if not strict adherence to immutable laws. Presenting Jesus as a Pharisee not only neutralized the Gospels' polemics against the Pharisees by making them intrapharisaic debates, but also suggested that the faith *of* Jesus was Judaism, whereas the faith *about* Jesus was Christianity.

Geiger's writings appeared at a propitious time in German Protestant theology. Emerging from the distractions of the Tübingen school, with its focus on the postapostolic Christian movement, theologians returned by the 1860s to a renewed interest in the historical figure of Jesus. Claiming that their goal was recovering Jesus' faith, rather than the dogma about him, they moved in two directions: toward a reconstruction of the historical setting of first-century Palestine, and toward a description of the subjective religious consciousness of Jesus. In both cases, Geiger's work served as an unpleasant hurdle to their conclusions.

Although flaws and biases in Geiger's writings were found by Christian scholars, they found the thrust of his argument difficult to refute. The parallels he identified between the sayings of Jesus and those of the Pharisees made the Jewish content of his message indisputable. Claims to Christian originality and uniqueness were difficult to establish, particularly because liberal Protestants were unwilling to root their theology in the miracle stories and traditional dogma. Christians' only recourse was to develop the category of Jesus' personal religious subjectivity and give it a role within theological arguments comparable to the role of supernatural miracles—that is, a unique, superhuman quality unattainable by anyone else. Jesus' sublime religious subjectivity became the central principle in the sudden spate of lives of Jesus written during the 1860s by Ernst Renan, Daniel Schenkel, Theodor Keim, and Adolf Hausrath, among others. Jesus' spiritual uniqueness was further heightened by contrasting it with a highly negative portrayal of a degenerate first-century Judaism, a depiction that became increasingly common in Christian scholarship after the 1870s, most predominantly in the work of Emil Schürer and Julius Wellhausen. Whatever the parallels Geiger had drawn between Jesus and rabbinic Judaism, the actual "life under the law" of the Pharisees was sterile and devoid of religious meaning.

The effort to preserve Jesus as a good rabbinic Jew was modified somewhat during the 1860s by Heinrich Graetz, who portrayed Jesus as an Essene, rather than as a Pharisee. According to Graetz, Jesus lived with the Essenes, and from them he learned mysterious medicinal healings, an ascetic lifestyle, and an urgent striving to hasten the messianic era. Jesus' preaching was useful, Graetz claimed, because it inspired Jews with piety and fervor, belief in God, and the value of humility. His message, however, attracted followers primarily from Galilee, a region whose inhabitants, according to Graetz, were intellectually unsophisticated, superstitious, and susceptible to charlatans and false messiahs.

Graetz's portrayal placed Jesus within the context of Judaism, but somewhat at its edges, in the bizarre, marginal sect of the Essenes. In Graetz's

depiction, the Pharisees and rabbis, whom he presents in glowing, hagiographical terms, shaped what became the powerful normative Judaism of subsequent centuries, whereas the Essenes, who simply disappeared from Jewish life, left no traces of influence.

For both Geiger and Graetz, the discussion of Christian origins helped explain the roots of centuries of Christian persecution of Jews. Graetz, who began nearly every chapter of his multivolume *Geschichte der Juden* (History of the Jews; 1853–70) with a description of Christian hatred of Jews, had little positive to say about Christianity. For Geiger, Christian intolerance toward Jews was the reason that Judaism's initially liberal rabbinic tradition ultimately developed into a narrow-minded, rigid orthodoxy of the Talmud. Whatever was positive about Christianity was derived from Judaism, Geiger argued, and all that was negative resulted from Christian corruption at the hands of paganism.

Many Christians in Germany considered the writings of both Geiger and Graetz to be an assault on Christianity. Conservatives and liberals published a flurry of pamphlets in the 1860s and 1870s asserting that Christianity was under assault from Jewish theologians, who showed particular contempt for the figure of Jesus. Franz Delitzsch attacked Geiger for calling Jesus a Pharisee, claiming it was equivalent to Christian anti-Judaism and a justification for it. Graetz's writings on Christianity became a central example in Heinrich von Treitschke's notorious 1879 anti-Semitic articles of what Treitschke described as Jewish arrogance and aggression against Germany's Christian values.

At the turn of the century, debates about the Jewishness of Jesus intensified. Jewish writers, including Moritz Lazarus, Hermann Cohen, and Martin Schreiner, polemicized against Christianity's allegedly impure monotheism and its reliance on miracles and dogma concerning Jesus' divinity. Christian theologians such as Schürer, Wellhausen, and Wilhelm Bousset responded by claiming that early Judaism's monotheism had been rendered worthless by its sterile, degenerate legalism. Whereas liberal Jewish theologians saw Jesus as a typical example of the prophets and rabbis, liberal Protestants saw Jesus as having restored classical prophecy after it was smothered by Judaism's priestly and rabbinic traditions.

Ultimately, by the early twentieth century, Christian theologians and scholars, for example, Adolf von Harnack, Wilhelm Herrmann, Wilhelm Bousset, and Eduard Meyer, conceded that Jesus' moral message was derived from Judaism. But they immediately insisted that it was precisely a sign of Jesus' extraordinary religious genius that he was able to extract moral teachings from the sterile legalism of his day. Harnack enshrined this idea in his classic statement of liberal Protestantism, *Das Wesen des Christentums* (Essence of Christianity; 1902), in which he wrote that although the religious message Jesus proclaimed was not original but had already been stated by the Pharisees, nonetheless the Pharisees "were in possession of much else besides. With them [religion] was weighted, darkened, distorted, rendered ineffective and deprived of its force by a thousand things which they also held to be religious and every whit as important as mercy and judgment. . . . The spring of holiness . . . was choked with sand and dirt, and its water was polluted." With Jesus, "the spring burst forth afresh, and broke a new way for itself through the rubbish" (30–31). For Harnack, then, it does not matter that Jesus' teaching was not original; only that it was pristine.

Jewish reaction to Harnack's book was anger—both at its negative depiction of Judaism and at its denial of a positive link between Jesus and the Pharisees. In their responses to Harnack, Leo Baeck, Joseph Eschelbacher, and Martin Schreiner returned to Geiger's arguments concerning the liberal nature of Pharisaism and reaffirmed the derivative status of Jesus' teachings. Citing passages from the Bible, Midrash, and Talmud, they argued that Jesus was no unique spiritual figure, but simply experienced the religiosity taught by rabbinic Judaism. Eschelbacher insisted that Christian doctrine concerning Jesus as the "son of God" was entirely pagan and violated Judaism's pure monotheism. The legalism of Judaism portrayed by Harnack was countered by Baeck, who distinguished between Jesus' criticism of Pharisaic Judaism and Paul's rejection of

rabbinic law. Christianity, by following Paul, violated Jesus' own adherence to the law and created, in Baeck's words, a "romantic religion" of mysticism in which human beings remain trapped by their sinful nature, passively awaiting salvation through grace. Christianity, Baeck argued, fails to foster moral responsibility, in contrast to the masculine "classical religion" of Judaism, which places ethical commandments at the forefront and demands no belief in irrational dogma.

During the Weimar period, Martin Buber and Franz Rosenzweig were the only major Jewish thinkers sympathetic to Jesus and Christianity. For Buber, Jesus was an exemplar of the highest reaches of Jewish spirituality, a figure who linked Jews and Christians. The negative attitudes toward the law espoused by Jesus and Paul were no problem for Buber, because he, too, espoused antinomianism as essential for an experience of God. Rosenzweig was far more sympathetic to Jewish law and less interested in the figure of Jesus. Although Christianity is clearly inferior to Judaism within the architectonic of his *Stern der Erlösung* (The star of redemption; 1921), in Rosenzweig's view it does provide a viable path to God, and ultimate judgment regarding its validity will only be revealed in the messianic era.

The question of Jesus' Jewishness took on important political connotations during the Third Reich in the German Christian movement (the Protestant effort to synthesize Christianity with Nazism). Although Houston Stewart Chamberlain was the first to give widespread popularity in Germany to the notion that Jesus was an Aryan (*Grundlage des neunzehnten Jahrhunderts*, 1899; Foundations of the nineteenth century), Christian theologians themselves did not begin to debate the issue in earnest until the latter years of the Weimar Republic. As the German Christians gained control of the Protestant churches during the Third Reich, they called for the de-Judaization of Christianity. This process entailed eliminating the Old Testament from the Christian canon, eradicating Hebrew words from the hymnal and New Testament, and declaring that Jesus was not a Jew but an anti-Semite, most probably an Aryan. Jesus' alleged goal of destroying Judaism served as a pretext for Christian support of Nazi persecution of the Jews.

The efforts at reconciliation between Christians and Jews in Germany following World War II have revived Jesus' Jewish identity as a vehicle for common ground between Jews and Christians. Pinhas Lapide and Schalom ben-Chorin have been the leading Jewish representatives who describe their spiritual brotherhood with Jesus. Among Christian theologians, Friedrich Wilhelm Marquardt has identified Christ as the indwelling presence of Israel, arguing that a repudiation of Judaism is necessarily a repudiation of Christianity (*Das christliche Bekenntnis zu Jesus, dem Juden* [The Christian declaration of belief in Christ, the Jew, 1990]).

From the outset, as liberal Protestants sought the historical man Jesus, rather than the Christ of theological dogma, they were faced with a Jew. The more the historical context of Jesus' life was examined, the more attention had to be paid to the Jewish setting of first-century Palestine. Yet how could Jesus the Jew support the religion of Christians? How could Christians follow the faith of Jesus, if that faith was Judaism? The construction of the historical Jesus carried dangerous theological implications, because historical study had demonstrated the conventional Jewishness of Jesus' teachings. The theological claims of Christian faith, on the other hand, demanded that Jesus the Jew be transformed into Jesus the Christian. Balancing historical scholarship with Christian theology gave Jesus a deliberately blurred identity—a Jew dressed as a Christian, a kind of religious transvestite.

For Jewish theologians, the problems were no less complex. Reform of Judaism during the nineteenth century focused primarily on challenging the binding authority of talmudic law and changing the practice of Halakhah. Yet the challenges to Halakhah seemed uncomfortably similar to the rejection of the law formulated by Jesus and Paul. The transformation of Jesus from a Christian critic to a Jewish rabbi was an effort to save Reform Judaism from charges of straying too close to Christianity. Yet even while insisting that Jesus had said nothing original but had drawn his entire message from Pharisaic Judaism, Geiger

and his Reform colleagues were reorganizing the synagogue and its worship service after the model of liberal Protestant churches. Who was imitating whom?

Bibliography

Leo Baeck, "Romantische Religion," *Festschrift zum 50jährigen Bestehen der Hochschule für die Wissenschaft des Judentums* (Berlin, 1922): 1–48; Wilhelm Bousset, *Die Religion des Judentums im neutestamentlichen Zeitalter* (Berlin: Reuther und Reichard, 1906); Franz Delitzsch, *Christenthum und die jüdische Presse* (Leipzig: n.p., 1882); Delitzsch, *Jesus und Hillel* (Leipzig, 1866); Jacob Emden, *Lehem Shamayim* (Hamburg: n.p., 1757); Joseph Eschelbacher, *Das Judentum im Urteile der modernen protestantischen Theologie* (Leipzig: Fock, 1907); Eschelbacher, *Das Judentum und das Wesen des Christentums* (Berlin: Poppelauer, 1905); Abraham Geiger, *Das Judentum und seine Geschichte* (Breslau: Schlettersche Buchhandlung, 1865); Geiger, *Urschrift und Übersetzungen der Bibel in ihrer Abhängigkeit von der inneren Entwicklung des Judentums* (Breslau: Julius Hainauer, 1857); Heinrich Graetz, *Geschichte der Juden* (Breslau: n.p., 1853–70); Adolf von Harnack, *Das Wesen des Christentums* (Berlin: J. C. Hinrichs, 1902); Samuel Hirsch, *Die Religionsphilosophie der Juden, oder, Das Prinzip der jüdischen Religionsanschauung und sein Verhältnis zum Heidenthum, Christenthum und zur absoluten Philosophie* (Leipzig: H. Hunger, 1842); Isaak M. Jost, *Geschichte der Israeliten seit der Zeit der Maccabäer bis auf unsere Tage* (Berlin: Schlesinger Buchhandlung, 1820–29); Moses Mendelssohn, *Gesammelte Schriften* (Leipzig: Brockhaus, 1843); Felix Perles, *Boussets "Religion des Judentums im neutestamentlichen Zeitalter" kritisch untersucht* (Berlin: Wolf Peiser, 1903); Franz Rosenzweig, *Stern der Erlösung* (Frankfurt a. M.: J. Kauffmann, 1921); Joseph Salvador, *Jesus-Christ et sa doctrine*, 2 vols. (Brussels: Hauman et compagnie, 1838; Ger. trans. *Das Leben Jesu und seine Lehre*, 1841); Martin Schreiner, *Die jüngsten Urteile über das Judentum* (Berlin: Cronbach, 1902); Emil Schürer, *Geschichte des jüdischen Volkes im Zeitalter Jesu Christi* (Leipzig: J. C. Hinrichs, 1898); Uriel Tal, *Christians and Jews in Germany*, trans. Noah Jacobs (Ithaca, N.Y.: Cornell University Press, 1975); Julius Wellhausen, *Pharisäer und Sadducäer: Eine Untersuchung zur inneren jüdischen Geschichte* (Greifswald: L. Bamberg, 1874).

SUSANNAH HESCHEL

1872 Leopold Zunz declines an invitation to the inauguration of the Hochschule für die Wissenschaft des Judentums

To understand why Leopold Zunz is considered one of the founders or even *the* founder of the Science of Judaism, one has to go back to the time when he was a student. Zunz had spent several years at the Samsonsche Freischule of Wolfenbüttel, where he was given a Jewish education. This education was at first traditional, but it was later modernized by the work of Samuel Meyer Ehrenberg. Further, Zunz had entered the gymnasium of Wolfenbüttel before he registered at the University of Berlin in 1815. There he attended, among others, the lectures of August Boeckh and Friedrich August Wolf. The influence of philology, as it was elaborated in Wolf's *Altertumswissenschaft* (Science of antiquity) and in Boeckh's *Encyclopädie und Methodologie der philologischen Wissenschaften* (Encyclopedia and methodology of the philological sciences) was essential for Zunz, who twice conceived drafts of an introduction to the Science of Judaism that were strongly inspired by Boeckh's model.

At age twenty-three, still a student, Zunz wrote his work *Etwas über die rabbinische Literatur* (A few words about rabbinic literature), which was published in 1818 and is considered one of the founding texts of the Science of Judaism. In this text he demands a scientific and nondogmatic study of rabbinical literature, which he would rather call Jewish literature or modern Hebrew literature. In addition, according to Zunz, this literature—despite the inferiority of his era to biblical times, when the Jewish people had raised their culture to the level of universality—belonged to the cultural heritage of humanity. In this same text, Zunz listed Jewish contributions in such various fields as medicine, ethics, geography, and astronomy. The greatest merit of this work was the fact that it opened up a field of research: it offered an outlook on everything that existed, in order to promote studies allowing to "know and sort what is old and usable, what is out of date and harmful, what is new and to be wished for."

Already in this first work one can note that Zunz is not a theorist. Even if the influence of Johann Gottfried Herder can be felt, one can see above all the way Zunz, by borrowing the rules used to study antiquity and certain national literatures and applying them to the rabbinical literature, tries to renew the approach of the traditional texts and place it under new principles. One of these principles is that one should not try to find in these texts a rule of life but rather should strive to place them in their historical or even geographical contexts.

An oft-quoted (and misunderstood) statement taken from this first work asserts that the time had come to prepare for a time in the near future when rabbinical literature would no longer exist. According to this scenario, the Science of Judaism would act as an inventory and a tribunal of Jewish literature. Because of this comment, Zunz has been compared to Moritz Steinschneider, who was to speak a few years later of the decent burial that should be given to Judaism. Zunz's statement, however, should be understood in connection with the situation at that time. Zunz pointed out that fewer and fewer Hebrew books could be found on the market and that ever more Jews no longer understood Hebrew. Moreover, as one can read in his writing on Hebrew manuscripts in Italy (*Die hebräischen Handschriften in Italien: Ein Mahnruf des Rechts und der Wissenschaft;* 1864) he worried that the last material prints of the Jews' past were vanishing. He expressed anger and sadness when complete libraries with valuable Hebrew manuscripts were scattered or went abroad because they found no purchaser in Germany.

In short, Zunz did not believe that Judaism had the linguistic or national future articulated by Zionism and the idea of a state of Israel. This doubt, however, did not prevent him from struggling for a "Jewish consciousness" based upon historical consciousness and Jewish culture. Zunz was one of the most active members of the Verein für Cultur und Wissenschaft der Juden (Society for the culture and the science of Judaism), which was officially founded in 1821. Among its members were Eduard Gans, Heinrich Heine, Moses Moser, and Ludwig Marcus; Lazarus Bendavid and David Friedländer were considered honorary members. This society, which is often called today Kulturverein, defined its main task as supporting the scientific study of the culture of Judaism and thereby reestablishing its good name in the eyes of both Jews and Christians. This society was unique in that, although it kept tight links with the circles of the Reform, it was not grounded upon a religious tendency but on Jewish culture.

The Kulturverein published a journal, the *Zeitschrift für die Wissenschaft des Judentums,* edited by Zunz. The society also offered scholarships to penniless Jewish students; gave courses, which in particular inspired Salomon Munk, one of the main representatives of the Science of Judaism in France; and tried to establish links in Germany and abroad. Later a scientific institute was also founded, which was directed by Zunz. This institute organized lectures and planned long-term projects—for instance, a new translation of the

Hebrew Bible into German, a goal that was finally met in 1838 under Zunz's leadership.

In spite of all these plans, the Kulturverein was dissolved in 1824. Zunz was greatly disappointed; although he continued to pursue the goals of the group, he was one of only a few members to do so. This year also marked Zunz's first conflicts with the Jewish authorities—for instance, when he gave up his position at the new Beer synagogue, where he had preached between August 1821 and September 1822. In his sermons, given in German, Zunz exhorted his listeners to a higher morale and to a more authentic religious life. He also accused the Jewish authorities of being too weak. The main source of conflict was his criticism of synagogues and Jewish schools; his opponents considered his reproaches extreme.

What is usually pointed out in Zunz's first writings, *Etwas über die rabbinische Literatur* and the three articles published in the *Zeitschrift,* is that Zunz shows there an interest for a rabbinical corpus, whereas he proves otherwise to be hostile toward rabbis (or at least rabbinism). In an anonymous article written after the publication of a book that included the judgments of twenty rabbis on the change of prayer ritual and the introduction of organ and German into the religious service, Zunz scathingly criticized the conservative positions of the rabbis of his time, who according to him constituted an "institute of ignorance, arrogance and fanaticism." He nonetheless made a clear distinction in this same article between those rabbis whom he qualified as barbarians, and those rabbis of the period before the Lutheran reform, whom he qualified as scholars (*Ankündigung eines Werkes: Geist der Rabbiner,* 1819).

It was on this rabbinical corpus that Zunz carried on his work with his book *Die gottesdienstlichen Vorträge der Juden, historisch entwickelt* (Historical exhibition of predication and liturgical readings of the Jews) published in 1832. In this book, the historical description resulting from Zunz's meticulous work on various sources and on many manuscripts proves that the forms of liturgy had changed as time passed—by, for example, adapting themselves to the different countries. Zunz tried to defend in this demonstration the cause of the Reform, which he believed to be the natural continuation of the historical evolution and the only chance of survival for Judaism.

Other later books carried on this project of writing the history of the synagogue and of the literature associated with it, for instance *Die synagogale Poesie des Mittelalters* (The synagogal poetry of the Middle Ages), published in 1855. The first part of this work contained the well-known chapter on the Jews' sufferings, through which he tries to explain the particular nature of certain Jewish prayers; the second part, published in 1859, concerns the synagogue rites. *Literaturgeschichte der synagogalen Poesie* (History of literature of the synagogal poetry), published in 1865, is another example. It chronologically presents the different forms of prayers with a few translations, as well as descriptions of their authors and the context in which the prayers were written.

Zunz's main contribution, however, was not the theory of a new science nor a deep reflection on the Jewish condition, but his role in establishing a new use of the term *Judentum* by giving it an ever richer content. As handwritten notes prepared for a course of lectures on the Science of Judaism held in 1852–53 prove, Zunz used this term by analogy with *Deutschtum* (Germanness) and *Griechentum* (Hellenism)—rather than only as the counterpart of *Christentum* (Christianity)—because the Judaic religion was for him only one aspect of Judentum.

The restatement of this concept of Judaism dates from Immanuel Wohlwill's article "Über den Begriff einer Wissenschaft des Judentums" (About the notion of a science of Judaism), on which Zunz is supposed to have closely collaborated and which was published in the first issue of the Kulturverein journal. There *Judentum* is no more defined as the Jewish religion, but as the whole set of the cultural aspects of Jewish life. Wohlwill also proclaimed these aspects of organic unity, in which the idea of Judaism would express itself and develop. This idea of Judaism is, according to an idea borrowed mainly from Hegel, the unity of the divine, and it constitutes

the fundamental contribution of Judaism to the history of humanity. Zunz himself did not try to develop this reflection; his life's work lay in classifying the historical material into periods.

The organic unity of the Jewish culture was thus affirmed. Further, the linguistic tools with which it was understood enabled scholars to analyze Jewish culture: to speak about it using the same language used to describe other cultural entities, and to compare and relate it to those others. Furthermore, once the ancient Hebrews had been "rehabilitated" and Judaism had been placed on the level of universality, Zunz was able to assess that the Hebrew tradition was the foundation of the Christian state. In other words, as soon as the lineage had been scientifically constituted, Zunz tried to show that the continuous exchange between the Jewish culture and its environment—even at the time of the ghetto, when exclusion and withdrawal perhaps dominated that exchange—was nevertheless mutually enriching. This insistence on exchange is to be found particularly in his pamphlet on the names of the Jews (*Die Namen der Juden,* 1836), which was written to defend the Jews' right to have Christian names, and in *Die gottesdienstlichen Vorträge der Juden.*

One can see in this use of the term *Judentum* an attempt to search for a strengthening of Jewish unity and solidarity not only in religion, the force of conviction of which seems to have diminished during that period, but also in the memory of Jewish history, understood historically and no longer only through worship, at a time when the end of the ghetto and the crisis of religions seemed to jeopardize this solidarity.

Until 1850, when the Jewish community of Berlin granted him a pension, Zunz was in charge of several jobs that kept him quite busy. He spent all his leisure time on research, however, which explains why his dedication and his voluntary work became legendary. Between 1823 and 1850, Zunz worked at the *Haude und Spener'sche Zeitung* as editor, at the school of the Jewish community of Berlin as director, and after a short stop at the Society for the Improvement of the Israelite Worship in Prague, he became director of the seminar that prepared the teachers of Jewish primary schools in Berlin. During all this time his resentment grew against the German university (which did not let him practice as a professor); against the Jewish authorities and their plots; against the Jewish community of Berlin, which did not acknowledge him for his true value; against the financial Jewish aristocracy; and against the salons, which in his eyes did not care enough for the cause of the Science of Judaism.

Added to these resentments were political disappointments. Zunz, who had become a Prussian citizen in 1821 and exhibited patriotic feelings for Prussia, sometimes ostentatiously, invested himself in German political life, especially in 1848–49, and again after 1860 on the liberals' side. For a long time he believed in Germany, which was, according to him, going to make the first move in the field of emancipation, and in which he hoped to find a kind of second Spain, according to the "myth of Sephardic supremacy," which was brought to light by Ismar Schorsch (*The Myth of Sephardic Supremacy*, 47–66). In this work, the Jews, being quite well assimilated and transcending their particularism, reintroduced Judaism into the history of universal thought. This dream, however, like his other aspirations for Germany, never materialized. Moreover, these disappointments experienced by Zunz turned his hopes and the rather revolutionary messianism of his youth into a dark messianism, to such a point that at the end of his life, when he had become a celebrity, he remained bitter and derived no pleasure from the honors which were paid to him. As a result of his disillusionment, he did not share the enthusiasm of younger representatives of the movement for the progress made by the Science of Judaism, which perhaps by this time was not exactly what Zunz would have wished it to be.

This bitterness may explain why on May 6, 1872, Zunz, then seventy-eight, preferred to stay home rather than attend the inauguration of the Hochschule für die Wissenschaft des Judentums (University for the Science of Judaism) under Abraham Geiger's patronage. This Hochschule was designed to be both a Jewish university institution and a liberal rabbinical seminary.

Ismar Elbogen, a leader of the Hochschule between 1910 and 1940, wrote in an article in Leopold Zunz's honor (*Leopold Zunz zum Gedächtnis*, 1936) that he did not believe the anecdote commonly told about Zunz, which was that he had refused to come because he did not want science to be confined into a new ghetto. But even if Abraham Geiger himself, a friend of Zunz's, doubted this quip and even if this assertion comes, according to Ismar Elbogen, rather from Moritz Steinschneider, it seems nonetheless that Zunz's refusal cannot just be explained by his irascible nature, for which he was already infamous. Even if Zunz did not openly show hostility to the project and to the Hochschule activities, and even if the meaning of this refusal should not be exaggerated, this date can be considered as a break—a line of demarcation between Zunz's intentions for the Science of Judaism and what it had actually become in the cultural context of 1872.

Zunz had always made a point of inserting his work and his research into the general context of German and European academic life, and his demand to the Prussian authorities in 1848 to create a chair of Jewish history and literature at the University of Berlin remains famous. This demand was based on his conception of science, which was for him, in all its forms, one of the driving forces of progress and one that was intended to open a new era for humanity. Zunz had clearly inherited this view from the Enlightenment.

In chronologies on the history of humanity that Zunz made for his own use and that are today in the Zunz archives in Jerusalem, he noted among the main dates of the history of humanity those of the foundation of the great European universities, along with those of the great scientific and technical discoveries and those of the various revolutions considered as leading humanity toward an increasing emancipation.

Zunz considered Jewish emancipation to be an event that should be included in the general context of the emancipation of nations, and the idea of revolution was essential for him. He was an enthusiastic supporter of the French revolution and of the revolution of 1848, and he gave a speech in 1865, titled "Revolution," in which he raised the latter up to the level of a principle of historic evolution. For him this was not inconsistent with his reformist positions in other respects. This partly explains why he conceived the role of the new science—or rather of this new branch of science that he intended to found, the Science of Judaism—as revolutionary.

This new science was to be founded by a kind of double revolution: revolution against the Christian prejudice, as it appeared in the Christian works on the Jewish tradition, and revolution against the rabbinical dogmatism. This second goal should not be neglected, even if Zunz is well known for his piety and his faithfulness to the Jewish religion. The "revolutionary" vocabulary used by Zunz confirms the spirit of his intentions. In a letter dated October 13, 1818, to Samuel Meyer Ehrenberg, his old master and friend, he writes: "So long as the Talmud has not been overthrown, nothing can be done."

For Zunz the university was the place where Judaism would emancipate itself, and for him, who had taken the sentence "the true science begets action" as a motto, emancipating the Jews especially meant emancipating the Science of the Jews. This meant first of all fighting the dogmatism among the Jews themselves and inciting them to a new vision of tradition, and second, giving to Judaism the right to figure among the great civilizations and to be studied as part of the cultural heritage of humanity in universities—that is, as Zunz wrote, awarding it "the right to be part of the world of mind and reason."

And so when he realized that the German university perpetuated in a certain way the Christian prejudice by refusing Jewish history and literature the right to be part of its curriculum, Zunz used again the "revolutionary" vocabulary. Addressing Prussian minister of education Eichhorn during a visit, Zunz told him (as he reported in his diary) that "the science he excludes will break the ring he has built, i.e.: the branches of studies at the Christian university."

In opposition to this universalist concept of science, the creation of the Hochschule testified effectively to a certain withdrawal in itself from pursuing the inclusion of Judaic studies at German universities, surely necessary if the Science of the Jews really wanted to be established as a branch of studies, even if that was to be done outside the German state university. As time passed, this focus seemed to go along with a kind of move toward theology, which impelled Ismar Elbogen in 1918 to criticize the term *Wissenschaft des Judentums* as too vague and to offer to replace it with *Jüdische Theologie* (*Neuorientierung unserer Wissenschaft,* 1918). This proposed change in terminology, however, might have seemed contrary to Zunz's efforts to establish precisely a branch of studies that would posit Judaism as a cultural entity and not only as an object for theology.

Around 1850 the Science of the Jews started to develop on a significant level in Germany within the Hochschule für die Wissenschaft des Judentums; the Breslauer Seminar founded in 1854 and conducted by Zacharias Frankel; the Akademie für die Wissenschaft des Judentums, born from Franz Rosenzweig and Hermann Cohen's joint initiative; and in important journals such as the *Monatsschrift für die Geschichte und Wissenschaft des Judentums* (Monthly review of the history and science of the Jews). The movement also seemed to gain momentum elsewhere in Europe and the United States. The Science of the Jews not only founded its own institutions but also played an important role even in the Orthodox rabbinical seminaries.

The Science of the Jews experienced a great "ideological" success in Germany, to such an extent that it was often considered as a feature of the German-Jewish attitude. In this way it came to arouse strong controversies in which it was often identified with the assimilationist position, which in this context was considered as ruining Judaism's last hopes of survival. Therefore the Science of the Jews was usually opposed to Zionism, which was considered to be based upon a more popular and active culture. Gershom Scholem evoked the tomblike feature of this science (*Wissenschaft vom Judentum einst und jetzt,* 1960), and it is true that the question that has been the center of these debates and of the Science of the Jews itself is the question of the perpetuation and of the life of a culture. How had Judaism survived, when all that seemed to have guaranteed this perpetuation—that is, the ghetto, the religious convictions, the traditional rabbinate, and the mastery of ancient Hebrew—had changed so dramatically?

This concern for the continuity of Judaism may be the reason why translations have played an essential role of transmission and conservation for this first generation of the Science of the Jews. And if the concern was to conserve the treasures and the teachings of the tradition under another aspect and by considering them from another point of view, it seems that the whole project of the Science of the Jews could be seen as one of translating the Jewish heritage into the historical and critical "language of modernity."

This interpretation of their project fits then the one through which Shulamit Volkov has tried to define the constitution of modern Judaism in Germany—that is, the invention of a tradition. One could add that for the Science of the Jews a tradition was invented within a new system of thought in which the transmission and the conservation of knowledge and of collective memory did not work the same way and did not follow the same rules as in the old rabbinical tradition.

The Science of the Jews on the whole and the efforts of these pioneer members of the Kulturverein are considered today to represent the start of Jewish historiography. For this same reason the Science of the Jews is the ancestor of Jewish Studies, such as it exists today in universities; in fact, the latter may be closer to what Zunz wished than was the Hochschule für die Wissenschaft des Judentums.

Bibliography

Julius Carlebach, ed., *Wissenschaft des Judentums: Anfänge der Judaistik in Europa* (Darmstadt: Wissenschaftliche Buchgesellschaft, 1992); Ismar Elbogen, *Der jüdische Gottesdienst und seiner geschichtlichen Entwicklung* (Leipzig: Fock, 1913); Nahum N. Glatzer, *Leopold Zunz and Adelheid Zunz: An Account in Letters (1815–1885)* (London: East and West Library, 1958); Glatzer, *Leopold Zunz. Jude, Deutscher, Europäer. Ein jüdisches Gelehrtenschicksal des 19. Jahrhunderts in Briefen an Freunden* (Tübingen: Mohr, 1964); Ismar Schorsch, "Breakthrough into the Past: The Verein für Cultur und Wissenschaft der Juden," *Leo Baeck Institute Year Book* 33 (1988): 3–28; Schorsch, "From Wolfenbüttel to Wissenschaft," *Leo Baeck Institute Year Book* 22 (1977): 189–208; Schorsch, "History as Consolation," *Leo Baeck Institute Year Book* 37 (1992): 33–45; Shulamit Volkov, "Die Erfindung einer Tradition: Zur Entstehung des modernen Judentums in Deutschland," *Historische Zeitschrift* 253 (1991): 603–628; Luitpold Wallach, *Liberty and Letters: The Thoughts of Leopold Zunz* (London: East and West Library, 1958); Kurt Wilhelm, ed., *Wissenschaft des Judentums im deutschen Sprachbereich* (Tübingen: Mohr, 1967); Leopold Zunz, *Etwas über die rabbinische Literatur* (Berlin: In der Mauerschen Buchhandlung, 1818); Zunz, *Die gottesdienstlichen Vorträge der Juden, historisch entwickelt* (Berlin: Asher, 1832; 2d ed., Frankfurt a. M.: n.p., 1892); Zunz, *Die Ritus des synagogalen Gottesdienstes, geschichtlich entwickelt* (Berlin: Springer, 1859); Zunz, *Die synagogale Poesie des Mittelalters* (Berlin: Springer, 1855); Zunz, *Gesammelte Schriften*, 13 vols. (Berlin: Gerschel, 1875–76); Zunz, *Literaturgeschichte der synagogalen Poesie* (Berlin: Gerschel, 1865); Zunz, ed., *Zeitschrift für die Wissenschaft des Judentums* (Berlin: Trowitsch, 1821–23).

CÉLINE TRAUTMANN-WALLER

1873 Samson Raphael Hirsch oversees the secession of Jewish Orthodoxy in nineteenth-century Germany

The place is Berlin. The year, 1873. The German Empire, united at last, is being ruled by Bismarck with an "iron fist." The last enemy to be overcome is the Catholic Church, which takes orders from a foreign power, the Vatican, and which thereby impairs German sovereignty. In order to assert the state's supremacy over the Church, Bismarck launches a series of legislative measures that are assured safe passage through parliament by the conservative-liberal coalition backing Bismarck's campaign, known as the *Kulturkampf*. In May the Prussian House of Representatives passes a law allowing Catholics to secede from their church without renouncing their adherence to the Catholic religion.

As soon as he heard this news, Rabbi Samson Raphael Hirsch (1808–88) in Frankfurt am Main prepared to travel to Berlin. He was head of an Orthodox Jewish congregation that had been struggling for many years against the despotic rule of the elders of the local Jewish community. The elders were followers of the Reform movement and had been managing the affairs of the community without regard for Jewish law and tradition. Hirsch's congregation had attained recognition by the city government, yet its members were obliged to pay their annual dues to the community—in short, they were being forced to give financial support to the same reformed institutions in protest against which they had set up their congregation. Secession from the community was out of the question, because Jews in Prussia and in most other German states were compelled by law to be members of the local community; they could thus leave the community only by conversion to another religion. This is what made Samson Raphael Hirsch board the train to Berlin soon after secession from the Catholic churches had been made legal.

Hirsch was then an aging man of sixty-five. He had devoted his life to leading the struggle of Orthodoxy against Reform, on both the communal and the cultural levels. In the face of the Reform movement's claim that Orthodoxy was a hindrance to emancipation, Hirsch redefined traditional Judaism so as to demonstrate its compatibility with modernity. He developed a system of religious philosophy that lent a new and meaningful significance to many Jewish laws and customs; he built a school for all grades and both sexes where Jewish and general subjects were taught on an equal footing; and he headed a synagogue where all the traditional prayers and rituals were conducted within a setting pleasing to the modern ear and eye.

Hirsch's days in Berlin were exceedingly busy. They were filled with audiences with senior government officials, whom he tried to convince that his call for a supplementary secession law to allow for the establishment of nonconformist Jewish congregations was just and equitable. He spent his nights studying official documents and minutes as well as reference literature so as to be able to enlist the most effective arguments to promote his cause. Nevertheless, when a Lithuanian rabbi sent word that he wished to pay him a visit, Hirsch immediately invited him to come. The rabbi's name, Israel Lipkin (a.k.a. Salanter, of Salant where he was born), was well known in traditionalist Jewish circles. He knew of Hirsch's achievements and had come to consult him on how to ensure the future of Jewish Orthodoxy in Russia. R. Israel Salanter (1810–83), an outstanding talmudist, was the founder of a "moralist" movement (*Mussar*), through which he hoped to invigorate Orthodoxy by putting it on a foundation of ethical perfection. It was hoped that this would prove an effective response to the challenges of Haskalah and other secularizing trends in Russian Jewry. Salanter was convinced that the only effective way to combat Haskalah in Russia was to bring about a vigorous religious movement that would instill a new and lively spirit into an Orthodox tradition that had become stale and unattractive. Thus both Hirsch and Salanter were Orthodox innovators, motivated by similar quests to make Orthodoxy viable in a modern environment and enable it to confront an increasingly secular world.

The uninitiated onlooker would probably regard the meeting of Hirsch and Salanter as a meeting between "new" and "old" Orthodoxy. In the nineteenth century, however, there was hardly any "old" Orthodoxy left in Europe, if by that term we mean the Jewish tradition as lived and expounded in the ghettos and shtetel before the inroads made by both the state and Enlightenment. True, Jewish society in Eastern Europe was still by and large a traditionalist society, but both Hasidism and the Mussar movement were innovations that introduced new emphases and unprecedented practices. Even the excessive conservatism and militancy of Hungarian Orthodoxy was not identical with old-time mainstream Orthodoxy. R. Israel Salanter was a radical modernizer. During his prolonged stay in Berlin, he pursued various secular studies so as to be able to bring about a "spiritual revolution" in Russian Jewry; these studies were also motivated by his hope of becoming eligible for a Russian passport. Salanter also studied the German language and grammar so that he might be able to read German

newspapers. He had close relations with some of the leading figures of Jewish Orthodoxy in Germany. He doffed his Lithuanian Jewish garb and dressed like the German Jews.

At one point during the visit, Salanter pointed out that whereas Hirsch had had to start from scratch because German-Jewish youth had already been largely estranged from traditional Judaism, in Russia there was still "much to lose"; one had to be careful not to destroy existing structures by setting up new ones. It was agreed that as a first project Hirsch's *Nineteen Letters* should be translated into Hebrew and Russian. The Russian translation never materialized; several Hebrew translations, however, have been published, the first coming out in Vilna (1891), together with the German text in Hebrew characters. We will come back to this historic meeting, but let us first consider why the book *Nineteen Letters* was singled out for confronting Haskalah in Russia.

Nineteen Letters (1836) was the first publication by S. R. Hirsch but not his literary first fruits. He had ready for publication a voluminous treatise expounding the full range of Jewish laws with a novel system of philosophical support. When he offered his manuscript to a Christian printer in Altona, he was advised to publish a slight volume of Jewish thoughts first. On the basis of the public response to the smaller work, the printer would decide whether to take the risk of publishing the treatise, entitled *Horeb,* which eventually ran to eight hundred pages. Presumably, the printer's hesitation was prompted not only by the size of the manuscript but also by its subject matter. Enlightenment and Reform had made educated Jews familiar with the idea that the essence of Judaism is its theological and cogitative content, not its laws and customs. The printer hoped that if Hirsch's meditations found a market, his readers would then try his legal discourse as well. The result pleased him. *Nineteen Letters* became something close to a best-seller and was certainly a sensation. Joseph Carlebach (1882–1942) did not exaggerate when he wrote that these letters signified a turning point in the religious history of German Jewry.

The effect of the *Nineteen Letters* in educated Jewish circles was immediate and profound. The

Hamburg librarian Meyer Isler (1807–88) wrote to Leopold Zunz (1794–1886) on April 5, 1836: "The *Nineteen Letters on Judaism* have caused a sensation here and on the whole have met with approval, even from opponents. I hear that in Berlin there is also much talk about it." In 1839 the historian I. M. Jost (1793–1860) published a very critical review of *Horeb* in his *Israelitische Annalen,* but this is what he wrote twenty years later about Hirsch's early publications in his *History of Judaism and Its Sects:* "The determination with which he defended a cause that had already been thought to be lost, the enthusiasm and eloquence with which he presented it, did not fail to generate a measure of enthusiasm in this direction. The manner in which Hirsch vindicated the historical basis of Judaism drew respect even from his opponents." To many young Jews who were wavering between adherence to tradition and its abandonment for the enticing promises of modernity, Hirsch's *Nineteen Letters* relieved them from gnawing doubt and reconciled them to Orthodoxy in a new package. To one gifted young man, Heinrich Graetz (1817–91), who lived in the faraway Posen province, the book came as a revelation, prompting him to write to its author and ask him to be allowed to come to Oldenburg, where Hirsch served as rabbi, and study with him. Hirsch consented, and Graetz became a member of the Hirsch household for a number of years, serving as an assistant to the rabbi and as a domestic teacher to his children. Subsequently they parted ways, and the master-disciple relationship changed into one dominated by antagonism.

Another close associate of Hirsch who turned from friend to foe was Abraham Geiger (1810–74). He studied with Hirsch at the University of Bonn, and while serving as rabbi in Wiesbaden and emerging as a leader of the Reform movement, he published a journal in which he printed several articles on Hirsch's first two publications. Geiger "stretched out his hand from afar to shake the hand of the noble and highly respected" author, but he was utterly disappointed. His critique bears out the incipient misgivings of the Altona printer. Geiger could not put up with Hirsch's total and unconditional acceptance of the "yoke of the precepts" and found the system of religious philosophy underlying the precepts tasteless and hopelessly outdated. He was unable to accept the fact that a highly educated and cultured person should earnestly enlist his intellectual and rational powers to justify and affirm the minute observance of the ritual laws in their entirety. A sentence like "The Torah is a given fact to be explored like nature: both are divine revelations" was for Geiger an occasion for scorn and disgust.

In the last of the nineteen letters, Hirsch made by implication a personal statement of considerable significance. He wrote: "In a time when opposites face each other and truth is on neither side, he who belongs to no party, having nothing in mind but the cause he works for and serves, cannot expect approval from either side." Hirsch was conscious that he was an outsider in the religiopolitical constellation of Jewry in Germany, which was split between Orthodoxy and Reform. He was critical of Orthodoxy as much as of Reform, though on totally different counts. Reform, in his view, denied the fundamentals of Judaism, whereas Orthodoxy had, through the contingencies of life in the ghetto, given way to a disfigurement of Judaism's outward appearance. Thus it was to be expected that his first publications would meet with disapproval from the Orthodox side as well. In fact, in Hirsch's own circle doubts were raised about the advisability of making his manuscripts available to the public. Isaac Bernays (1792–1849), the chief rabbi of Hamburg and Hirsch's former teacher and master, is reported to have voiced his opinion against the publication of the *Nineteen Letters.* Bernays, although he certainly adhered to strict Orthodoxy, was himself an innovator in more than one respect; Hirsch possibly had him in mind when he wrote that in taking the route he had chosen, "only one star" had guided him at the outset.

The other person close to Hirsch who took exception was none other than his own father, and his criticism comes to light in a letter by his son dated May 1, 1835: "I have long pondered over your objection to the appearance [of *Horeb*] in German script. My very first intention had in fact been to publish the book in Judeo-German, not because I was afraid of something that would be caused by its publication in German but generally, because I find it desirable that purely Jewish affairs should be dealt with exclusively within the Jewish orbit. However, I very soon dropped the idea." Hirsch gave several reasons for his decision: half of those for whom the book was intended would not open it were it written in Hebrew characters; and even if they did, half of the intended effect would fade because of their lack of practice in reading Hebrew. "A large proportion of the entire young generation can hardly read Hebrew or have not read anything in Hebrew letters since their school days and are from the first prejudiced against everything Jewish," he wrote. Finally Hirsch emphasized with great pathos that because the opponents of Orthodoxy published their attacks in German and in German journals, the defenders of Orthodoxy had no choice but to do likewise. Father Hirsch agreed and the books appeared in German.

This correspondence is significant, for it shows that in the fourth decade of the nineteenth century, roughly a hundred years after the beginning of the Enlightenment among Jews in Germany, the public use of the German language and script in matters of Jewish concern was still apt to be challenged even by enlightened traditionalists like Hirsch's father. It almost goes without saying that Hirsch's persistence in writing and publishing in German was later censored by such Jewish and Hebrew scholars as S. D. Luzzatto (1800–65) and M. Steinschneider (1816–1907). Yet it would be erroneous to infer, as has been done occasionally, that Hirsch had no strong feeling of attachment to the Hebrew language. On the contrary, his love of Hebrew was deep, genuine, and sincere. It stemmed from three sources. First and foremost, it sprang from his deep religiosity, Hebrew being the vehicle through which, traditionally, God created the world. A second factor was the legacy of the Hebrew branch of the Enlightenment, one of whose centers was in Hamburg, embodied by the *Me'assefim* who brought about a short-lived Hebrew renaissance that they considered to be a way to Jewish regeneration. Hirsch's uncle, Moses Mendelssohn (1782–1861, not to be confused with the Berlin

philosopher), author of several Hebrew books, was one of them, and so was Wessely (Weisel, 1725–1805), who was held in high esteem in the Hirsch family. Finally, Hirsch's attachment to the Hebrew language was a feature of his Jewish pride: he admonished the readers of the *Nineteen Letters* to be proud of their Jewishness, in opposition to the prevailing trend of the time to conceal one's Jewish identity.

The diction of Hirsch's Hebrew writings and letters discloses his indebtedness to the Hebrew Enlightenment. Among the three layers of Hebrew-biblical, mishnaic-talmudic, and rabbinic-medieval, he inclined heavily toward the biblical. The Enlightenment had discarded rabbinic Hebrew for the biblical as part of an aesthetic approach that considered the language of the sages as inferior. Moreover, rabbinic Hebrew is replete with associations from the world of the Talmud, and many, though not all, men of the Enlightenment wished to distance themselves from that world. That this did not deter Hirsch from demonstratively embracing rabbinic Hebrew in view of his spirited defense of rabbinic Judaism illustrates his detachment from both the parties. Biblical Hebrew also appealed to him for another reason: both his own uncle and his father's uncle (R. Judah Leib Frankfurter) wrote commentaries on the Pentateuch, and according to Hirsch's own testimony the Bible was his father's "second soul." He thus seems to have grown up in a home where the study of the Bible played an important role.

Hirsch's biblicism was also part of his romanticism. It flowed from a deep longing for the simple and homely life of the ancient Hebrews, guided by prophets, sages, and priests who conveyed to them the word of God. Hirsch adopted the philosophic approach to language and its structure and development as expounded by the romantic school, and on this basis he developed a speculative etymology. This method rested on the principle of phonetic relationships, which Hirsch applied to explore the basic connotations of Hebrew roots. In his view, this method, which dealt exclusively with the inner workings of the Hebrew language, freed biblical studies from the secular approach of comparative philology, which he considered un-Jewish. "Let us read the Bible as Jews," was his slogan. Yet the Jews thus addressed had by and large ceased to be fully conversant with the Hebrew language, and Hirsch, as we have seen, had to write in German if he wished his works to have an effect on his readers. So he joined the handful of German-speaking and partly university-trained rabbis who in those years inaugurated an enormous Orthodox Jewish religious literature consisting in large measure of translations from the Hebrew. To be sure, during the ghetto period many Jewish books had appeared in Western Yiddish, and Yiddish translations had been added to many Hebrew texts. These translations, however, had been intended primarily for women, who rarely were given formal Hebrew schooling, whereas the Orthodox German literature of the nineteenth century was in demand by men and women alike. A similar phenomenon had occurred only once before, when a printer from among the Marrano refugee families from Portugal in Ferrara, Italy, published in the mid-sixteenth century a considerable number of Hebrew religious texts translated into Portuguese and also original Portuguese works on Jewish subjects. In fact, many members of the new Orthodoxy in Germany were in a religious situation comparable to that of the Marranos: they had been estranged from tradition and had been won back to it, largely through the leadership and works of Hirsch and his friends. No wonder R. Israel Salanter turned to Hirsch in his search of remedies for the growing secularization of Jewish youth in Russia.

Hirsch's love of Hebrew did not diminish his deep involvement with the German language and literature. This is one of several apparent contradictions in his intellectual makeup, visible also in the communities that looked to him for guidance. One of his most loyal followers once declared: "The language of our thoughts and poetry, our love and loyalty, the language to which we are attached with every fiber of our being, remains for us German Jews our mother tongue, our beautiful German language." The fact that strictly Orthodox Jews could feel that there was a well-balanced union of German culture and traditional Judaism loses some of its strangeness, not to say absurdity,

if we consider that Hirsch postulated the existence of a fundamental agreement between Judaism and every "true" culture, of which classical German literature and art was exemplary. Long after Schiller's plays had lost their predominant position in the German theater, leaders of Orthodoxy still recited his lines over and over again, hailing the poet as a mouthpiece of true Jewish values. In his German translation of the Pentateuch (1867–78), Hirsch endeavored to mold the German language in a manner that would faithfully render the subtleties and intricacies of biblical Hebrew. In this procedure he did not flinch from creating complex and daring neologisms if the accurate meaning of the Hebrew word or phrase could thereby be preserved.

Never before had such a linguistic symbiosis of Hebrew and German been attempted. Many years later Martin Buber (1878–1965) and Franz Rosenzweig (1886–1929) adopted the same method, which they applied far more extensively. Orthodoxy, it seems, could well afford this symbiotic relationship with the German language, for contrary to Reform it was never in danger of losing its Jewish identity, due to its tenacious adherence to Jewish law and custom. Of course, Orthodoxy's "affair" with the German language had no effect whatsoever on German culture. Its religious literature was almost totally ignored by German academics, Bible scholars, and others, because German universities, with very few exceptions, took no notice of Jewish scholarship. Only one scholar of note, Professor Carl Hilty (1833–1909), lecturer in public law and moral philosophy at Berne University, left traces in his writings indicating that he had studied and, incidentally, did appreciate, Hirsch's oeuvre—but then he was a Swiss. There seems to have been only one German-language Orthodox author who can be said to have made a contribution to German culture, and that was Hirsch's grandson Isaac Breuer (1883–1946). Breuer read Kant "Jewishly," and some of his philosophical and legal essays were noted by German academics.

In the moral philosophy that underlay Hirsch's ethical writings and his rationale of the laws of the Torah, the footprints of Kant and Mendelssohn are unmistakable. The centrality of the notion of duty—to God, to fellow men, and to one's ancestors—clearly bears the Kantian stamp, and in stressing that law and not faith is the essence of Judaism, Hirsch himself acknowledged his debt to Mendelssohn. In a marginal note in the *Nineteen Letters,* he hinted that in undertaking the literary enterprise of his *Horeb*—by expounding the spirit of Jewish laws on a purely rational basis—he was in fact following Mendelssohn's lead, and if the philosopher had carried through this idea himself, the entire subsequent religious development of Jewry in Germany would perhaps have been different—that is, it would have forestalled the rise of Reform Judaism.

Did Hirsch perhaps ponder over this and similar memories while listening that night in his hotel room to Israel Salanter's account of the dangerous situation in which Jewish Orthodoxy in Russia found itself and his description of its inability to remedy itself with the powers at its own disposal? Looking back on his career, Hirsch had every reason to be thankful to providence. Together with some like-minded colleagues, such as Esriel Hildesheimer (1820–99) in Berlin and Markus Lehmann (1831–90) in Mainz, he had succeeded in consolidating Orthodoxy by establishing a modernized version of traditional Judaism that combined strictest observance of Jewish law and custom with an affirmative approach to the culture and civilization of contemporary society. Even during Hirsch's stay in Berlin, Hildesheimer had just opened a rabbinical seminary designed to train a new type of modern-Orthodox rabbi, thus marking the culmination of a process of transition from old to neo-Orthodoxy (a term that was, to be sure, disliked by Hirsch yet was borne out by subsequent developments). Hirsch's own school in Frankfurt was a far cry from the old educational establishments, both in terms of its curriculum and in the fact that girls were taught on an equal footing with boys, though in two separate departments. Hirsch could also be pleased with the literary achievements of a regenerated Orthodoxy. Besides his own publications, including fifteen volumes of a monthly journal *Jeschurun* (1855–69), there had sprung up a new Orthodox-oriented narrative literature linked with such names as Lehmann and Salomon Kohn of Prague (1825–1904) and an Orthodox press (Israelit founded in Mainz in 1860, Jüdische Presse in Berlin as of 1870) whose combined readership was not less than that of the central organ of liberal-oriented Jewry, the *Allgemeine Zeitung des Judentums.*

During his long talk into the night with R. Israel Salanter, the question may have occurred to Hirsch how he had managed, despite his universal recognition as the pilot of Western European Orthodoxy, to stay aloof from party affiliation, just as he had presented himself in his *Nineteen Letters.* While he served as chief rabbi of Moravia in Nikolsburg (Mikulev), his neo-Orthodoxy had confounded both the progressive and the conservative segments of the community. The former welcomed his assuming leadership of the movement for Jewish emancipation during the 1848–49 revolution; the latter were pleased with his providing for the minute requirements of ritual law. The combination, however, raised eyebrows everywhere: the conservatives wondered that a conscientious Orthodox rabbi had time for political activities, and the progressives sneered at a communal leader who in critical times cared about such trifles as issuing instructions to Torah scribes on circumcision and on repairing the defects of a *Mikve* (ritual bath). Ever since his first public appearance, Hirsch had defied easy classification, and so had neo-Orthodoxy in general. The rationalism dominating his exposition of the spirit of Jewish law was evident and so was his avoidance of drawing from the treasures of kabbalistic literature, yet in view of his delving into the minutest particulars of the ritual, he was deprecated as a "mystic." His students marveled at the complexity of his public character. Despite his reputation for rigidity and intolerance, he was the most tolerant of teachers. Kaufman Kohler, the American Reform rabbi (1843–1926) who had studied with Hirsch in his youth, remembered that although he lived himself in a closed world of thought, the rabbi was remarkably receptive to new ideas put forward by his pupils: "He made us think independently, though his own system of thought was peculiar" (Kohler 1931).

Another incongruity, which to recent research appears to be the most glaring one, may not have come to the minds of S. R. Hirsch and his visitor that night, although the occasion should have brought it to mind. Hirsch was immersed in his campaign for a Jewish secession law; Salanter asked for his opinion on how to withstand the onslaughts of modernity on traditional Judaism in Russia. These topics represented the two problems Hirsch was most concerned about at that time. How did they square with each other? According to the account of the conversation between the two rabbis, the communal problem was also brought up, and Hirsch asserted apodictically, using a talmudic phrase: "We stick to ours, and they stick to theirs." Salanter nodded in assent. Apparently neither of the two questioned the congruency of Hirsch's strictly—not to say fanatically—sectarian approach in the communal sphere, on the one hand, and his tolerant moderation toward non-Jewish culture and art, which not so long before had had no place in the Jewish home and school, on the other. Upon reflection, this should be less intriguing than it appears. Both Hirsch and Salanter considered formal separation of Orthodoxy from Reform as much a vital necessity for the survival of Orthodoxy as was the integration of general knowledge into the curriculum of the Orthodox school. Furthermore, they both were almost obsessively devoted to truth and honesty. The name of the journal edited by Hirsch was derived from the Hebrew root denoting honesty and sincerity. One must not compromise with untruths, he declared, and adapt to crookedness. For this reason he proclaimed the necessity of secession from a community that was not based on Torah, and for the same reason he strove to mold young Jews into human beings who would be true to themselves and whose Judaism would absorb all the truth, beauty, and goodness in the world. To deny the ethical and spiritual merit of the cultural achievements in the gentile world—of his time—seemed to him a denial of truth.

"Honesty (*yosher*) comes before ritual perfection (*kosher*)," was one of Hirsch's maxims. Presumably, R. Israel Salanter concurred.

Bibliography

Isaac Breuer, *Concepts of Judaism,* ed. J. S. Levinger (Jerusalem: Israel University Press, 1974); Mordechai Breuer, *Modernity Within Tradition: The Social History of Orthodox Jewry in Imperial Germany* (New York: Columbia University Press, 1992); M. Breuer, *The "Torah-Im-Derekh-Eretz" of Samson Raphael Hirsch* (Jerusalem: Feldheim, 1970); Samson Raphael Hirsch, *Nineteen Letters of Ben Uziel: Being a Spiritual Presentation of the Principles of Judaism,* trans. Bernard Drachman (New York: Funk and Wagnalls, 1899); *Historia Judaica* 10, no. 2 (1948), Kaufmann Kohler, *Personal Reminiscences of My Early Life: Studies, Addresses and Personal Papers* (New York: Alumni Association of the Hebrew Union College, 1931); Moses Mendelssohn, *Jerusalem and Other Jewish Writings,* trans. and ed. Alfred Jospe (New York: Schocken, 1969); Alan L. Mittleman, *Between Kant and Kabbalah* (Albany: State University of New York Press, 1990)

MORDECHAI   BREUER

1893 Hugo von Hofmannsthal worries about his Jewish mixed ancestry

Beginning in the 1880s, Austrian liberalism as a political force was replaced in German-speaking Austria by the populist mass movements of the Christian Socialists and the Social Democrats, and by the Pan-German Nationalists. These movements were able to organize the discontent of the middle and lower classes into powerful political organizations that toppled the elitist liberals who had failed to come to grips with the growing conflicts between the nationalities of the Habsburg Empire and the effects of social and economic dislocation generated by rapid industrialization. In terms of racial politics, the anti-Semitism espoused by the Christian Socialists and the German Nationalists increasingly dominated the Viennese and Austrian sociopolitical climate in the 1880s and 1890s and led, by reaction, to the development of Herzl's Zionist movement.

The disintegration of liberalism with its ideological core of Germanophile Austrian nationalism and capitalism left its traditional ally, the assimilated Viennese-Jewish bourgeoisie, isolated and an easy target for antiliberal politicians. Whereas Viennese anti-Semitism was at that time almost completely ambiguous, it also pervaded every aspect of daily life. Under the leadership of Karl Lueger, the Christian Socialists employed religious, social, and economic anti-Semitism to mold a mass movement out of ideologically, socially, and ethnically diverse groups that found their common denominator in being anti-Jewish. Lueger's infamous phrase "I decide who is a Jew" illustrates the kind of cynical use he made of anti-Semitism in his politics. It also highlights a difference between his brand of anti-Semitism and the rabidly racial anti-Semitism of the German Nationalists that was grounded in pseudoscientific theories of evolution. Whereas the possibility of assimilation was at least partially acknowledged among some of the Christian Socialists, the German Nationalists denied that there could ever be successful integration of Jews into a "host-culture." To them, there was no escaping one's race. Even though the German Nationalists never had the broad popular support enjoyed by the Christian Socialists, university teachers and student groups were among the Nationalists' staunchest followers—and thereby poisoned the very environment that had provided one of the main routes of Jewish assimilation in Vienna: education and participation in the professions.

In this racially charged environment, Jews were forced to confront the failure of their assimilation into German-speaking Austrian society. This experience challenged the very core of individual and group identity and compelled Jews to respond in a particularly forceful way to the modern crises of liberal individualism and its institutions. It is no surprise then, that fin-de-siècle Viennese culture was closely—though obviously not completely—associated with the experiences and traditions of Jews, assimilated Jews, and people of mixed ancestry who were viewed by non-Jewish Viennese as being "Jewish." Looking back at the time, Stefan Zweig wrote in his autobiography *Die Welt von Gestern* (The world of yesterday; 1944), "Nine tenths of what the world celebrated as Viennese culture in the nineteenth century was promoted, nourished, or even created by Viennese Jewry" (22).

Hugo von Hofmannsthal (1874–1929), his title notwithstanding, was born into the milieu of cultured upper-class liberal bourgeoisie. His grandparents, as he would later like to point out, were of Jewish, Italian, Austrian, and German extraction, his paternal grandfather having converted from Judaism to Catholicism. Hofmannsthal's paternal great-grandfather, Isaak Löw Hofmann, had played a major role in the development of the silk industry in the Habsburg lands, was ennobled by Ferdinand I, and had chosen the mulberry leaf and stylized Mosaic tablets as his insignia. Hugo von Hofmannsthal was raised as a Catholic, and no records show that he possessed any kind of formal learning about the Jewish tradition. The Viennese environment in which a person's ethnic background was officially registered, however, compelled him to confront the "Jewishness" of his heritage. It also provided some of the racist stereotypes that Hofmannsthal applied when reflecting on his own family's history, his disassociation from his bourgeois background, and the fragile construction of his own identity as a writer.

To study the Jewish aspects of Hofmannsthal's writings, then, is not to distill some sort of Jewish essence out of his works, thereby legitimating racial determinism. Rather it is to show how Jewishness, both as constructed by the environment and by Hofmannsthal himself, figures in his responses to the cultural crises of liberal-humanist individualism, for which the philosopher Ernst Mach coined the formula of the "unsavable self," the *"unrettbare Ich."* Hofmannsthal, like many others in his generation, experienced these crises not only as social disintegration, as anomie, but equally as a challenge to the integrity of his own personality. He responded by developing strategies to save *his* self, and it is in the cultural critiques he outlines and in his works that "Jewishness" attains a certain importance. At the same

time, "Jewishness" is only one of a number of interrelated concepts that Hofmannsthal employs when describing his problems as a modernist writer and possible solutions to these problems; some of the others are "aesthetism" (*sic*), "life," "nostalgie du passé," "decadence," "dilettantism," and "the allomatic." Their origins in Hofmannsthal's readings of Friedrich Nietzsche, Paul Bourget, Ferdinand Maack, and others need not concern us here. When foregrounding "Jewishness," however, one has to be aware of the danger of a reductionist approach that traces all of Hofmannsthal's creative impulses to a single origin.

When Hofmannsthal rejected intimations that his Jewish background held any significance in his thinking—in a letter of August 2, 1919, to Hermann Bahr, for example, he wrote that the problem of being Jewish "has never penetrated my inner being, neither in my youth nor later" (quoted by Rieckmann 1993b, 474)—he either suffered from self-deception or avoided the truth. Whereas his published works contain few references in this regard, his private papers and letters, especially those unearthed by Jens Rieckmann, provide a quite detailed picture of Hofmannsthal's attitudes toward his Jewishness and their place and import within his artistic thinking.

As early as 1887, when he was thirteen, Hofmannsthal began to reflect about the position of Jews in Viennese society. After seeing a Burgtheater staging of Hermann Mosenthal's *Deborah,* he penned a long letter to his friend Gabriele Sobotka, in which he takes an impassioned stand against anti-Semitism (Rieckmann 1993b, 474–475). He even criticizes Mosenthal because he failed to reject the anti-Semitic slur that portrays Jews as the archetypical materialists. Hofmannsthal's extensive and very involved discussion of Mosenthal's play shows that even at this early stage he was very much aware of some of the historical roots of the anti-Semitic attacks that plagued his environment. It also indicates that he was quite conscious of his partially Jewish background and saw in it a major component of his own identity.

There is other, albeit sporadic, evidence of

Hofmannsthal's continuing engagement with Jewish topics. In 1891, for example, there is—among a number of other projected works—the plan for a story that was to explore the life of a young man with a mixed Catholic-Jewish background similar to Hofmannsthal's. The few notes on this plan (Rieckmann 1993b, 475f.) suggest that Hofmannsthal wanted to represent the problematic nature of assimilation and the roots of anti-Semitism in the resentment of Christians toward the perceived ethical superiority of the Jews.

Beginning in the 1890s, Hofmannsthal's comments about his Jewish background become increasingly ambiguous. In his diary of 1893, we read, "What if all my inner developments and quarrels were nothing but agitations of my inherited blood, insurrections of the Jewish drops of blood (reflection) against the Germanic and Romanic and reactions against these insurrections?" (quoted in Rieckmann 1993a, 214). Employing the stereotype of cultural anti-Semitism that reflection and rational thinking are attributes of Jewishness, he casts these against the Germanic and Romance nature of thinking—which in Hofmannsthal's mind were apparently contributed by his Italian and German roots. By implication, the integrity of Germanic and Romance thinking is threatened by reflexive, "Jewish" intellectualism. In a letter of February 24, 1899, to his (Jewish) future brother-in-law and former schoolmate, Hans Schlesinger, Hofmannsthal reiterates and broadens this view. There, Hofmannsthal ascribes to the "Jewish type of thinking" a "tendency towards reflection, towards 'critical' 'historical' 'objective,' imitative and second-hand" thinking "that has about it something so horribly bloodless and unfit for life, and over time even something that voids the ability to experience life [*Erleben*]" (quoted in Rieckmann 1993b, 477).

Although formulated in the terminology of racist sociobiology of the late nineteenth century, these comments point to the central conflict of both the person and the artist Hofmannsthal. Struggling to answer the nihilist challenge of the modern disintegration of the self so forcefully stated in Mach's empirio-criticism and Nietzsche's critique of decadence, Hofmannsthal strove to create a bridge between self and world that would promise both to stabilize or "save" his own identity and to open the possibility of an artistic expression that could escape the dangers of aesthetic solipsism. His early lyrical dramas and poetry mirror the tension between a yearning to participate in a full and rich life and community and a simultaneous attraction to the intellectual and aesthetic thrills of snobbish antibourgeois decadence and aloof aestheticism, of "artistry of words," of *Wortkunst* (Hofmannsthal 1945–59, 3:493). These early writings resolve this tension by balancing a formal aestheticism with a subjective impressionism in which the magical word authenticates the participation of the self in the world.

The problem of bridging the divide between self and world, "aestheticism" and "life," solipsism and community, was for Hofmannsthal the problem of modern man. In his essays and reviews, especially on Henri-Frédéric Amiel, Gabriele d'Annunzio, Algernon Swinburne, Henrik Ibsen, Paul Bourget, and Maurice Barrès, he tries to capture the spirit of the age and define his own stance. The problem of reaching into "life" remains a constant in Hofmannsthal's works, even as his thinking about the best way to achieve this bridging changed radically over time. Through all the changes, this problem remains interwoven with Hofmannsthal's thinking about Jewishness; divisive thinking seemed to him, as he wrote to Pannwitz in 1917, to be "disintegrating everything, tattling everything to pieces"—threatening even the possibility to experience life fully (Hofmannsthal 1994, 56). And throughout this time, the problem remains attached to Hofmannsthal's ambiguous attitude vis-à-vis his own mixed ancestry, of possessing "as mixed a blood as is possible" (56). This ambiguous attitude, however, was not limited to his Jewish background. In another letter to Pannwitz, written toward the end of World War I, for example, he states matter-of-factly: "I am not at all German, neither by blood nor in spirit, at least not a 'present-day German'" (94). It is precisely the amalgamation of all these areas in Hofmannsthal's often introspective comments about "Jewishness" that makes it at times difficult to distinguish blatantly anti-Semitic remarks from those that employ a racial or ethnic typology typical for his time to address serious artistic and personal questions.

This point is accentuated by a close reading of Hofmannsthal's angry rejection in 1922 of an essay by his friend Willy Haas for the collection *Juden in der deutschen Literatur* (Jews in German literature; 1922). Haas explains all of Hofmannsthal's writings up to *Der Schwierige* (The difficult man; 1921) as the work of a "Jewish artistic genius" (156). The methodological thrust of Haas's essay is to apply "Mendel's principles of heredity to matters of the spirit" (Hofmannsthal 1968, 110). In his response to this "drivel" (47), Hofmannsthal provides a brief genealogy of his family and insinuates that—if this information would not change the thesis of the essay—there may be some racist impulse behind its conception. "Against that, of course, I would be without defense" (47). But Hofmannsthal did not stop there. As if to dispel the "Jewishness" of his work, he gave a self-interpretation of his creative production, describing it as "a difficult, peculiar assertion of the self" that is based on "an extremely consistent, natural creative process" (47), and insisting that his works have to be viewed in their totality—that is, as something that has developed *away* from its origin.

Hofmannsthal's two-pronged argument indicates the peculiar position of "Jewishness" within his thinking. By providing his genealogy, Hofmannsthal questioned and at the same time validated the importance of the Jewish component; by emphasizing the evolution of his literary production, he suggested that he had moved away from his "Jewish" beginnings, that is, from the reflection and narcissistic aestheticism of his early works. The "assertion of the self" became the signature of a sort of liberation poetics in which the truly artistic imagination functioned as an agent of emancipation for the self—both from outside forces that are beyond the individual's control (that is, his ancestry) and from an imprisonment in aesthetic self-referentiality radically disconnected from and unable to reach into the world. Within this context, "Jewishness"— as a cipher for an external predetermination of the individual and for aesthetic solipsism—is ac-

knowledged as that which has to be overcome. Thus, Hofmannsthal's letter to Haas lays out *in nuce* a plan for an assimilation through artistic imagination, an assimilation that would find its fulfillment in a work in which the total realization of the artistic self coincides with its complete participation in the world. Ultimately, Hofmannsthal's response does not primarily concern itself with the rejection of the "Jewishness" of his background, but rather insists that to view his artistic accomplishments solely from a "Jewish" perspective is faulty precisely because it emphasizes only *one* aspect of a complex and ultimately ineffable individuality and artistic imagination. The final words of the letter stress this point, when Hofmannsthal writes that he is "sorry about the imprecision and arbitrariness" (47) that he finds in Haas's essay.

Hofmannsthal was particularly sensitive in this respect, and his defensiveness was by no means limited to rejecting a "Jewish" interpretation of his work. We find a similarly enraged dismissal of an essay by Hofmannsthal's friend Rudolf Borchardt that was part of *Eranos,* a book published in celebration of Hofmannsthal's fiftieth birthday. Borchardt's essay praises Hofmannsthal's early writings but shows little understanding for his dramatic and operatic works. After receiving the volume, Hofmannsthal chided Borchardt: "It has become the *mot d'ordre* of the mean spirited and otherwise annoying literati to tie me down to my early works, and to ignore insolently and consciously my accomplishments since then; they are, after all, something" (Borchardt and Steinert 1954, 185f.). Again, Hofmannsthal sees a denial of his achievements as an individual artist and of his development away from his early aestheticism.

Juxtaposing these two responses, it becomes clear that Hofmannsthal's irritability had its basis in a perceived threat to his own artistic identity, a point that is further supported by numerous notes he made about this issue. It is wrong, Hofmannsthal wrote as early as 1904, "to view every work of art as something definitive. . . . Correct: to view the works of art as continual emanations of a personality. . . . Correct: to take the striving for individual style as the only possibility to feel eternal" (Hofmannsthal 1945–59, 3:451). To tie artistic identity to a single principle, "to name" (451) every aspect of artistic production, would deny complexity to the individual and to the world. This would make the artist radically deficient in achieving the confluence of subjectivity and the "muddled being [*Dasein*]" (451) that was, for Hofmannsthal, the sign of true art.

The obvious parallel between these notes and the "liberation poetics" laid out in the Haas letter highlights the fact that Hofmannsthal's thoughts concerning his Jewishness played an important, but not the dominant, part in his broader reflections about the challenges of the modernist experience. In fact, his notes and letters (at least those accessible to scholars) show relatively few references to "Jewishness"—a fact that need not be explained as a sign of Hofmannsthal's "repression" of his Jewishness. Nevertheless, Hofmannsthal's attempt, through the power of art, to bridge the divide between self and world in order to provide "harmony" (451) to both and to allow full participation of the individual in what Hofmannsthal called "life," repeats, as an analogy, the drive of his Jewish ancestors to assimilate into German-Austrian society. This "second assimilation" (Broch 1955, 132–39), however, is not intrinsically that of a Jew, but rather that of a modernist artist.

Hofmannsthal's response to the challenge of modernism and the cataclysmic event of World War I was conservative and ultimately reactionary. Like many other conservative intellectuals of the time, the Thomas Mann of the *Betrachtungen eines Unpolitischen* (Reflections of a nonpolitical man; 1918) among them, he searched for new bounds that would guard against the dissolution of the self and the breakdown of the social fabric. He called for a "creative restoration" (Hofmannsthal 1945–59, 4:243), or, as the better known phrase from his late speech *Das Schrifttum als geistiger Raum der Nation* (Literature as the spiritual realm of the nation; 1927) has it, for a "conservative revolution," a "countermovement against the revolution of the spirit the two aspects of which we call the Renaissance and the Reformation" (413). Hofmannsthal's ideas in this regard were

heavily influenced by the messianic Nietzsche-follower Rudolf Pannwitz and the ethnographic-racist literary historian Josef Nadler, among others. But they were also in line with his artistic development, which had led him to reject his aestheticist notions in favor of an ethical understanding of art.

The most famous document of this reorientation is *Ein Brief* (A letter; 1902), a fictitious letter by a Lord Chandos to Sir Francis Bacon that connects the description of Chandos's identity crisis as a writer with a critique of language. The artistic word and form no longer guarantee a unity between self and world. Although the expressiveness of language is not questioned, language itself disjoints the individual from the meaning of "life," imprisoning Chandos in a "horrible loneliness" (Hofmannsthal 1945–59, 2:13). Unlike Claudio, the main character in the early lyrical drama *Der Tor und der Tod* (1893), who is led by the artist in the guise of death from isolated individuation to a full experience of life, Chandos remains barred from his surroundings precisely by the words that had ensured Claudio's ultimate realization of life's meaning through death. Not words but rather a mystical silence is the cipher of Chandos's experience of the mystical immanence of individual and world, the "harmony that interweaves both me and the world" (17).

Hofmannsthal himself did not remain in this realm of mystical silence. For him, it held the same danger of solipsistic disconnection from life as did his early aestheticism. "The mystical experience [is] degraded to masturbation if it does not search for the strictest reference to life," he proclaimed (Hofmannsthal 1945–59, *Dramen III,* 493). The challenge for Hofmannsthal, then, was to find new modes of artistic expression that would allow him to *show* the mystical connectedness between world and individual, configured in Hofmannsthal as a transhistorical collective unconscious. Hofmannsthal found them in the theater, "the only great social [entity] that we still have" (Hofmannsthal 1994, 95). The stage provided the space where the sensibilities of the artist and the public could intersect, where the fluidity of the actors' position between reality and play could invoke and transmit a feeling of participation that was not completely dependent on words, where the totality of the play's production would become a celebration of a community that did not repress or exclude anyone. As Hofmannsthal wrote, "The theater postulates that everyone who gets involved with it is a social person" (Hofmannsthal 1945–59, 4:95).

For Hofmannsthal, this new view of language as participatory meant a move away from the esoteric artistry of his earlier works toward more accessible forms, a diversification of language levels through the inclusion of dialects and sociolects, and a branching out into nonverbal forms of expression like pantomime, ballet, set design and lighting, and, of course, music. It also meant intensive collaborations with theater director Max Reinhardt and composer Richard Strauss to create dramatic and operatic *Gesamtkunstwerke* that celebrated, in different ways, the inclusiveness of the stage as a festival for all. Hofmannsthal attempted to show on the stage a sort of alternative world order that could actually reveal the "harmony" between the individual and the world—a harmony that rested beyond the threat of violent historical change—and ultimately transcend these limited points of view. Hofmannsthal himself called his development his "way to the social" (Hofmannsthal 1945–59, 3:610) and he thought he had reached it in his comedies. "The achieved social: the comedies" (610), he notes in his autobiographical notes *Ad me ipsum* (posthumously 1930 ff.). The "social" was linked, though, to the full realization of the self: "The route to the social as the route to the self" (610). It seems, then, that Hofmannsthal's own interpretation of his artistic development toward the "social" corresponds with the "liberation poetics" sketched in his letter to Haas—that is, that the theater is the place where full realization of the self coincides with its complete participation in the world. The merging of self and world, however, binds and ultimately negates both within an essentially aesthetic conception of "wholeness" and harmony that does not allow for deviation. The "deliverer" (Hofmannsthal 1945–59, 3:451) of this harmony is the artist who defines the "social" in premodern terms: not as conflict-laden struggles between divergent individual and group interests, but as

participation in a unified and ritualized collective, which is accessible only through aesthetic revelation, not through rational discourse. This is the reason why Hofmannsthal calls for a creative restoration of premodern times before the discovery of individuality in the Renaissance and Reformation. Hofmannsthal's "Salzburg" miracle plays, *Jedermann* (Everyman; 1913) and *Das Salzburger große Welttheater* (The Salzburg great theater of the world; 1922), reach back to the universalist Catholic baroque tradition and present—in a combination of psychological individuality and allegorical form—the grand and "natural" order of the world, configured in such a way that every person has the place that is inherently the most suitable and appropriate within the "harmony" of the world. This natural order counteracts social change.

The conception of the Salzburg Festival, developed by Hofmannsthal and Max Reinhardt, has a strong supranationalist thrust that was meant, in part, as an "Austrian" counterweight to the "Germanness" of the Bayreuth Festival of Wagnerian musical drama. This "Austrian" inclusiveness, embodied for Hofmannsthal in a mythologized Habsburg Empire that no longer existed, is based on a premodern, nonpolitical understanding of a collective rooted in a cultural and ethnic chthonic intactness that comes dangerously close to a *völkisch* understanding of community. Within this context, Salzburg is synonymous with a celebration of the *Mitte,* of individual and community, of a cultural nationality and "Europeanism" (Hofmannsthal 1945–59, 4:94), and of the cultural-geographic myth of *Mitteleuropa* (Central Europe), epitomized in Salzburg, "the heart of the heart of Europe" (92).

Hofmannsthal's development toward an increasingly reactionary, nonpluralistic understanding of culture goes hand in hand with an increasingly distanced attitude toward his Jewish background. A partial explanation for Hofmannsthal's public distancing from anything "Jewish," at least in his earlier years, may be that it was a defensive move against commentators who saw in Viennese modernism an attempt by Jews to undermine wholesome German culture and who had, for example, derided Hofmannsthal's *Oedipus und die Sphinx* (Oedipus and the sphinx; 1906) as being written "in a Jewish German" way (quoted by Beller 1989, 205). (This criticism is, by the way, an indication that, at least in the eyes of anti-Semites, Hofmannsthal was a "Jew.") But the deeper reason for this distancing lies in the dichotomy between Hofmannsthal's racial typology of "Jewishness" as divisive, historical, reflexive, unoriginal, and rational—in short, modern—and the antimodern understanding of culture that he developed in response to the modernist challenge. Hofmannsthal himself seems to suggest as much, when in a letter to Pannwitz he rants, in his ugliest anti-Semitic diatribe, against "a certain intellectual Viennese-Jewish milieu," this "true *vermine du monde*," "this world of mollusks and parasites" that is "the true and absolute opposite to the society . . . postulated and assumed (*supponiert*) in my writings . . . which, at least in its elements, is my world and is the Austrian world" (Hofmannsthal 1994, 56). This is almost a textbook example of "Jewish" self-hatred, especially because earlier in the letter Hofmannsthal emphasizes that he is himself of partially Jewish ancestry and therefore knows what he is talking about. But even this hateful deprecation of Jews points to the fact that his own "Jewishness" continued to play an important role in Hofmannsthal's identity, and—precisely because he rejects it so vehemently—in his artistic thinking. "His" world, the "Austrian" world, included him as the "quarter-Jew." But Hofmannsthal's "Austria," the imaginary space of the full social participation of the individual regardless of his background, was a construct of his artistic imagination, almost devoid of "reality"—a reality that soon proved deadly.

There is a sadly ironic epilogue that highlights the trepidations of studying the importance of "Jewishness" in Hofmannsthal's works: *Juden im deutschen Kulturbereich* (Jews in German culture; 1959), a book that was scheduled for delivery in 1934 but was confiscated by the *Staatspolizei* of Berlin and only published in 1959, includes a section on Hofmannsthal by Arthur Eloesser. In the same volume, Paul Landauer states that

Hofmannsthal combines Jewishness and Viennese traditions "to a wonderful end" (908). In 1938, the *Reichsschrifttumkammer* declared that because Hofmannsthal had only one Jewish grandparent, his works would not be considered Jewish literature and shipment of his books could continue.

Bibliography

Steven Beller, *Vienna and the Jews, 1867–1938: A Cultural History* (Cambridge: Cambridge University Press, 1989); M. L. Borchardt and H. Steinert, eds., *Hugo von Hofmannsthal—Rudolf Borchardt: Briefwechsel* (Frankfurt a. M.: Fischer, 1954); Renate Böschenstein, "Mythos als Wasserscheide: Die jüdische Komponente der Psychoanalyse," *Conditio Judaica II,* ed. Hans Otto Horch and Horst Denkler (Tübingen: Niemeyer, 1989), 287–310; Hermann Broch, *Dichten und Erkennen,* ed. Hannah Arendt (Zurich: Rhein, 1955); Willy Haas, "Hugo von Hofmannsthal," *Juden in der deutschen Literatur,* ed. G. Krojanker (Berlin: Welt Verlag, 1922); Hugo von Hofmannsthal, *Gesammelte Werke,* ed. Bernd Schoeller, 10 vols. (Frankfurt a. M.: Fischer, 1979–80); Hofmannsthal, *Hugo von Hofmannsthal—Rudolf Pannwitz: Briefwechsel, 1907–1926,* ed. G. Schuster (Frankfurt a. M.: Fischer, 1994); Hofmannsthal, *Hugo von Hofmannsthal—Willy Haas: Ein Briefwechsel,* ed. Rolf Italiaander (Berlin: Propyläen, 1968); Hofmannsthal, *Sämtliche Werke,* ed. Rudolf Hirsch, 38 vols. (Frankfurt a. M.: Fischer, 1975–); Hofmannsthal, *Werke in Einzelausgaben,* ed. H. Steinert, 15 vols. (Frankfurt a. M.: Fischer, 1945–59); Siegmund Kaznelson, ed., *Juden im deutschen Kulturbereich* (Berlin: Jüdischen Verlag, 1959); Hans-Albert Koch, *Hugo von Hofmannsthal* (Darmstadt: Wissenschaftliche Buchgesellschaft, 1989); Jacques Le Rider, *Modernity and Crises of Identity,* trans. Rosemary Morris (New York: Continuum, 1993); Mathias Mayer, *Hugo von Hofmannsthal* (Stuttgart: Metzler, 1993); Jens Rieckmann, "(Anti)-Semitism and Homoeroticism: Hofmannsthal's Reading of Bahr's Novel 'Die Rotte Kohras,'" *German Quarterly* 66 (1993a): 212–21; Rieckmann, "Zwischen Bewußtsein und Verdrängung: Hofmannsthals jüdisches Erbe," *Deutsche Vierteljahresschrift* (1993b): 466–83; and Carl E. Schorske, *Fin-de-Siècle Vienna: Politics and Culture* (New York: Knopf, 1980).

PETER C. PFEIFFER

1895 The author, feuilletonist, and renowned foreign correspondent Theodor Herzl turns toward Zionism and writes the manifesto *The Jewish State*

In the rise of Zionism to an international politics and mass movement bound up with the "idea of the state of Israel," the life and work of Theodor Herzl took on historical significance. Through the founding of the state of Israel in 1948, Herzl's political activity was carried through in a way unforseeable to contemporaries. On September 3, 1897, a few days after the First Zionist Congress, Herzl noted in his journal: "At Basel I founded the Jewish State. If I said this out loud today, I would be answered by universal laughter. Perhaps in five years, and certainly in fifty, everyone will know it" (Herzl 1960, 2:581). Herzl's portrait hanging in the Knesset in Jerusalem is the iconographic confirmation of this comment.

The author, journalist, and politician is reflected most clearly in his literary self-representations: Herzl's journals, conceived as a chronicle of the beginnings of political Zionism, as well as his journalistic and fictional texts, speeches, and letters (the relevance of which was first recognized only in the latter half of the twentieth century), are at once poetry and politics, autobiography and prophecy. They demonstrate the transformation of a concept into reality, as well as the all-consuming struggle of the man who sought to carry it out. In spite of the historical relevance of these works, the assessment of his biographer Alex Bein, that Theodor Herzl's personal uniqueness "hardly penetrated the consciousness of the present" (Bein 1940, 1:11), is still valid.

If Holocaust and war provide historical justification to Herzl's life's work, they also deprive him of an objective historiographical treatment. Seen through this lens, interpretations of Herzl's Zionist activities polarize representations of his life and work: the acknowledgment of Herzl's achievements is anathema to the anti-Zionist perspective, which ignores or takes a fragmentary or distorted view of his works and literary remains. In this respect, every biography of Herzl reflects the attitude of its author toward the state of Israel.

Herzl's ancestry, family, and education hardly prepared him for the historical accomplishments of his life. Born on May 2, 1860, as the first child of Jakob and Jeannette (née Diamant) Herzl in Budapest, he grew up in a family whose primary orientation was toward the values of the Jewish-liberal haute bourgeoisie. Members of this class, largely protected from anti-Semitism, anticipated the gradual victory of Enlightenment and liberalism and, with it, their own progressive assimilation.

Herzl's mother's conception of education, shaped by the German language and culture, had a strong influence on his youth and upbringing. His knowledge of Jewish tradition and spirituality remained rather modest, and it is characteristic of this German-speaking family that the invitation to the thirteen-year-old's Bar Mitzvah party announced the occasion as a "confirmation."

Herzl's attachment to his parents intensified when the family moved to Vienna in 1878 after the death of their only daughter, Pauline. Herzl studied law in Vienna and graduated in 1884 with a doctorate in jurisprudence. The cultural atmosphere in the Austrian capital decisively impressed the young man; it shaped his aesthetic sensibility and awakened his passion for theater and opera. His mastery of several languages, characteristic of the Austro-Hungarian Jewish middle class, lent him cosmopolitan versatility: along with German, which was his mother tongue and the language in which he wrote, Herzl spoke French, Hungarian, Italian, and English and had some knowledge of Greek and Latin. The liberalism of the 1880s influenced the development of his personality and strengthened his wish for far-reaching social assimilation. Like most Jewish students in Vienna, Herzl was an admirer of Bismarck and the united German Empire. Accordingly, he modeled his personal values and external appearance on the aristocracy. As late as 1895 Herzl stressed, "If there is one thing I should like to be, it is a member of the old Prussian nobility" (Herzl 1960, 196).

Yet Herzl conceived of himself above all as a writer: he made his first attempts at writing as a schoolboy and displayed a lively literary productivity by the time he began his legal studies. After training in 1884–85 as a law clerk, he realized that he could never become a judge because the state judiciary did not offer Jews the prospect of promotion. For this reason, he determinedly began his literary career: educational travels in Europe, which he undertook in 1883–84 and again in 1887–88, were intended to promote his literary creativity. He also cultivated relationships with the authors of the Young Vienna circle, who, however—with the exception of Arthur Schnitzler—remained distanced from him.

In spite of Herzl's extensive literary production, public recognition did not materialize for a few years. Herzl sought success above all in the theater. Between 1880 and 1904 he wrote sixteen plays, which were either never published or were not reissued, and hence are difficult to access. With the exception of *Das Neue Ghetto* (The new ghetto), these are comedies of a satirical social-

critical nature that do not offer profound worldly wisdom; instead they are populated with one-dimensional heroes who have elegant love affairs and embittered spouses. Herzl came too late to the genre of social comedy: most German-language theaters had broken away from the tradition of French society plays and were dominated by a new realism and a soon-to-begin naturalism.

Herzl's feuilletons provided his first literary success. He composed these pieces while traveling, and their publication in Viennese newspapers made a name for him. A volume of travel pieces and short prose, *Neues von der Venus* (News from Venus), appeared in 1887, accompanied a year later by *Das Buch der Narrheit* (Book of folly). Herzl then became a freelance writer for the esteemed *Neue Freie Presse,* and the theater began to take notice of his dramatic production, if only for a few years. *Seine Hoheit* (His highness), a satire on the power of money, was performed in 1888 in Prague, and later that year the play *Wilddiebe* (Poachers), about three playboys on the hunt for women, was successfully introduced under a pseudonym at the Burgtheater. *Der Flüchtling* (The refugee; written in 1887) was also performed there under Herzl's name. In 1890, Herzl's plays were staged at approximately seventeen theaters in Austria and Germany. Nevertheless, the author began to distance himself as early as 1893 from his no longer successful dramatic works and wanted to let all of his plays be "buried" (Herzl 1982–83, 1:526).

Public success, which appeared to guarantee an economically secure career, gave Herzl the confidence to marry Julie Naschauer, the daughter of an oil millionaire. The marriage ceremony was performed on June 25, 1889, by Dr. Adolf Jellinek, well known as a rabbi and founder of the Beth ha Midrasch (school). It certainly required no particularly astute observer to ascertain that the sought-after heiress, who was eight years Herzl's junior and who tended toward nervous emotional outbursts, and the intellectual author, who was characterized by his outsider status and melancholy nature, had little in common. The antifeminist satire *Was wird man sagen?* (What will people say? performed in 1880 in Prague), which already began to take shape during the honeymoon, compares an engagement with a visit to the dentist; the bride appears as an immature child, and the groom dreams of flight. Even the children—Pauline (1890), Hans (1891), and Margarethe (1893), all of whom Herzl deeply loved—had little effect on the conflicts and inner alienation of husband and wife.

Herzl worked over his existential problems more and more in a literary medium, in which he distanced himself from the problems and reflected anew. In the process, his primarily intellectually determined creativity shifted effortlessly back and forth between the discursive and the fictional realms. He often conceived of ideas as literary plans in order ultimately to realize them as political plans, and vice versa.

Herzl received his long-awaited professional recognition at the beginning of October 1891, when he became the Paris correspondent to the *Neue Freie Presse*. With this appointment, his years of apprenticeship began.

Herzl was long protected from a direct encounter with anti-Semitism. Yet he did not avoid the conflict. He read Eugen Dühring's inflammatory pamphlet *The Jewish Question as a Racial, Ethical, and Cultural Question* (1881), one of the most widely discussed publications on the new pseudoscientific racism that had begun to spread rapidly, and which promoted the social exclusion of Jews and the abolition of their civil rights. Although the twenty-two-year-old Herzl reacted with anger and bitterness, he tried to look at the "infamous book" in a detached manner: "Despite its exaggerations and obvious hatefulness it is still informative and every Jew should read it" (Herzl 1982–83, 1:611). As a member of the dueling student fraternity Albia, which he had joined in 1881, Herzl experienced anti-Semitism in a more personal manner: the occasion was a turbulent memorial for Richard Wagner at which Hermann Bahr, also a member of the fraternity, gave a virulent anti-Semitic speech. The fraternity did not distance itself from Bahr's statements, as Herzl had expected, but endorsed them, and consequently Herzl resigned. If Herzl could still largely ignore the new, public manifestations of anti-Semitism in Vienna, Paris confronted him unavoidably with the problem: the

ugly debates in the French parliament revealed the political dimension of the problem and forced the adoption of a personal position. Herzl was in the midst of a two-year developmental process, which manifested itself in theatrical public acts and literary works. Looking back, Herzl reported that he had wanted to challenge the leaders of Austrian anti-Semitism—Karl Lueger (later mayor of Vienna), Georg von Schönerer (leader of the German National movement of Austria), and Prince Alois Liechtenstein (a member of parliament)—to a duel, in order to direct the conscience of the world toward the fate of European Jews. This anecdotal remembrance indicates that Herzl, in 1893 at the latest, was ready to put his own existence on the line for Jewish concerns. Nevertheless, he declined the invitation to join the Viennese Society to Combat Anti-Semitism, and stressed that his relationship to the Jewish Question was a "paradoxical play of colors." Although he acknowledged the political dimension of anti-Semitism, he emphasized its educational function, the need to draw lessons from it. Although he recommended for the younger generation a collective conversion, he rejected this notion for himself: "For in the age of consciousness, one may not leave the 'Faith of the Fathers,' even when one does not have it" (Herzl 1982–83, 1:511).

As a correspondent for the *Neue Freie Presse*, Herzl nonetheless maintained his distance from Jewish issues. His daily dispatches over political developments and debates in Paris, as well as French society and literature—which were widely read and had a significant impact throughout all of Central Europe—show that Herzl had to concern himself with a broad spectrum of topics. He complained of the "heavy news" of the foreign correspondent, in which one practiced "cool reflection and rapid action," which, in his view, was of value to a future politician, but hardly of use to him as "a Jew in Austria!" (Herzl 1982–83, 1:526).

Herzl channeled his unease over the Jewish Question into a play in October 1894, which he endowed with the didactic intention that it should function as "a Jewish sermon . . . a bit of Jewish politics" in the theater. *Das Neue Ghetto* (The new ghetto), however, actually revealed

Herzl's then still "paradoxical" relationship toward Jewry. The central argument of the play is that even the modern Jew lives as if behind invisible ghetto walls. The protagonist, Dr. Jakob Samuel, an ethically motivated lawyer of modest means, marries the daughter of a wealthy businessman, although he rejects the profit-oriented mentality of merchants and speculators. His selfless representation of exploited miners leads to a duel, which he accepts as a representative of the honor of all Jews. Mortally wounded in the duel, the dying man states, "Juden, meine Brüder, man wird Euch erst wieder leben lassen-wenn ihr . . ." (My Jewish brothers, one will first allow you to live again—when you . . .). Left unspoken is the line, "when you know how to die" (Bein 1940, 52). Here Jewish spectators are challenged to earn public esteem through discretion and courage, and, if necessary, through self-sacrifice. Non-Jewish spectators, in contrast, were to become aware that ethical values and behavior are tied to neither religion nor birth. This dual intention, however, is difficult to realize in a play whose Jewish characters partially embody anti-Semitic preconceptions: the stock-market speculators, for example, define their self-worth through the state of the stock market and a dubious business coup. Others feel spiritually and socially exiled in a new ghetto. "The ghetto is the seclusion that I do not want, that sickens me, and that I should bear," argues Samuel, railing against the prejudices of others and also against his own essential qualities, which in his eyes embody Jewish negativity (55).

The central metaphor of the ghetto signifies the perceived otherness of the Jews, all of the negative qualities projected onto them, which they accept as their identity and which separate them from the dominant society. This negativity should, however—according to the message of the play—be overcome through ethical sublimation and aristocratic ideals. The absurdity of this ultimately anti-Semitic command is demonstrated by the protagonist, in that he looks to fulfill the command through indirect self-obliteration. The words of the dying man, "Out-of-the-ghetto!" (Bein 1940, 124), should stand as a Jewish imperative to ethical self-overcoming, but must be read today as the most extreme self-negation, illustrat-

ing the unconscious self-deception of the author, who identifies with his protagonist. Just as illusionary were his hopes that the play would exert a "healing effect," that it would serve to "lead the Jews out of the ghetto" (Herzl 1982–83, 4:41). This anti-Semitic scope approaches the "Jewish self-hatred" frequently identified by scholars examining the turn of the century (Gilman 1986, 238–40), the difference being that Herzl later grasped and articulated its sociological suppositions: "There are more mistaken notions abroad concerning Jews than concerning any other people. And we have become so depressed and discouraged by our historic suffering that we ourselves repeat and believe these mistakes" (Herzl 1946, 134). Only when one compares Herzl's play of 1894 with his later statements regarding Jewry and anti-Semitism can one observe the spiritual and intellectual dimensions of his Zionist transformation, which took place over a period of years and encompassed many paradoxes.

This dramatic self-expression did not bring the clarification Herzl had hoped for. Instead, his engagement with the Jewish Question intensified as he shifted between the literary and political spheres. Although the play was initially turned down by all theaters (it premiered on December 27, 1897, in Vienna), he decided to continue unwaveringly on his "new path" as a writer and planned four or five similar plays for the coming years (Herzl 1982–83, 1:570). The Zionist idea prompted a literary plan to create characters who succeed in "discovering the promised land, more appropriately: in grounding it" (Herzl 1982–83, 2:51).

From 1893 to 1895, Herzl went through another renewed turn toward Jewish reality: he paid more attention to the life of French Jews. He visited a synagogue for the first time in many years and read the two-volume anti-Semitic tract *La France juive* by the journalist E. A. Drumont. His political education intensified with the Dreyfus Affair, which began in the fall of 1895 with the arrest of French Army Captain Alfred Dreyfus on fabricated charges of high treason and his subsequent life sentence handed down by the military court. When Dreyfus was publicly humiliated in the beginning of January 1895, shortly before his deportation to Devil's Island, Herzl was affected above all by the anti-Semitic statements of the masses, and his reports emphasized the remarkable "resolute character of the dishonored soldier." Although Herzl was not convinced of Dreyfus's innocence until later, the accused seemed to him to be a paradigm of the modern Jew. The Dreyfus Affair altered Herzl's opinion of anti-Semitism: he recognized that this anti-Semitism of the fanatic masses was neither a social question, as he had earlier believed, nor an ethical test that the Jews could withstand by educating themselves. Rather, anti-Semitic attitudes and rhetoric were, it seemed, becoming more and more accepted in political life: in the Austrian provinces, parliamentarians attacked the rights of Jews, while in Vienna the supporters of Lueger's anti-Semitic party gained strength, as did the anti-Semitic factions in the Reichstag in Berlin.

Herzl experienced the life-changing turn toward Zionism in "Paris Around Pentecost, 1895." This subtitle of his diaries denotes an inspiration—distinctly not Jewish—that prompted the event. Herzl himself pointed to several different meanings: the most autobiographical and most thorough describes a quasi-mythical experience that appears as "a work of infinite grandeur" and "a mighty dream" (Herzl 1960, 1:3).

In the year 1899, Herzl—now an internationally recognized Zionist politician—argued against this characterization, stating that "the Dreyfus trial made me a Zionist" (Herzl 1934–35, 1:374). The autobiographical piece written a year earlier for the *Jewish Chronicle* (London), however, does not contain a single reference to Dreyfus (11–16). Presumably the following statement also follows from this admission not to be able to point to the life-changing event: "How I proceeded from the idea of writing a novel to a practical program is already a mystery to me, although it happened within the last few weeks. It is in the realm of the unconscious" (Herzl 1960, 1:13).

The diary entries that begin at this point are unique in their style and often masterfully written. They also serve as the autobiography of the founder of Zionism: posterity knows him mostly through his self-presentation, because the diaries written between 1895 and 1904 have served as the most important source for Herzl's biographers. These entries also help document the beginning of Zionism, in which the historical events are written from the point of view of their main actor. Herzl remained throughout a thoroughly critical observer; he noted his grand strategies as well as the small details, his technical reasoning as well as his fantastic plans for the future.

The diaries show better than any other document that Herzl's historical accomplishment of turning the Zionist idea into an international political movement in just nine years rested at least partially on his ability to integrate fiction with the principles of action or to compensate for the multiplicity of reality through the medium of fiction: "If my conception is not translated into reality, at least out of my activity can come a novel. Title: The Promised Land!" (Herzl 1960, 1:3). A later entry, which reads, "tense moments of the serial novel of my life" (694), reveals that Herzl saw himself as a fictional character. Such statements about the compensatory function of literary formulation appear like leitmotifs throughout the diaries. Fiction supplies Herzl's own situation with meaning, serving as a means to overcome reality and provide encouragement or to provide inspiration for political advances. As in much post-Kantian philosophy, "as if" is used to overcome barriers to thought. Therefore, Herzl denied accusations that his plan for a Jewish state was utopian. Instead, he compared it with the presentation of a state budget, which, despite estimates made with assumed figures, is not labeled fantasy. Herzl's fictional thought broadened his own imagination and led, when it concerned the future of European Jews, to a frighteningly exact prognosis: "Will it be a revolutionary expropriation from below or a reactionary confiscation from above? Will they chase us away? Will they kill us? I have a fair idea that it will take all these forms, and others. . . . In Germany they will make emergency laws as soon as the Kaiser can no longer manage the Reichstag. In Austria people will let themselves be intimidated by the Viennese rabble and deliver up the Jews. There you see, the mob can achieve anything once it rears up. It does not know this yet, but the leaders will teach it. So they will chase us out of these countries, and in the countries where we take refuge they will kill us" (131–32). The diaries show the transformation of the journalist and writer into a politician for whom the future of his people became a question of existence. Herzl's diaries show that his transformation into a Zionist spokesman was accompanied by an increasing reduction of his personal life: introspection and emotional reactions to people and events became increasingly less common as political events moved into the foreground, and finally even these became quite fragmentary. In the weeks before his death, one finds only copies or sketches of letters written in concern for "the fact that our masses are perishing in misery" (Herzl 1960, 4:1631).

Herzl's turn to political Zionism early in 1895 fundamentally changed his opinions on anti-Semitism: the new pseudoscientific racism not only demonstrated for him that humanism and the Enlightenment had failed, it also represented in his eyes a threat to the Jews of Europe, who were approaching the unavoidability of a natural law. Herzl accepted this insight as a personal responsibility. He was convinced "that there is no more important purpose for my life than for me to take up the cause of the Jews, but in a different manner from how it has previously been done—freer, higher, more personally" (Herzl 1982–83, 4:41). Herzl continually maintained that he knew nothing of his predecessors—such as Moses Hess, Leo Pinsker, and Nathan Birnbaum—and that this was an advantage that provided him with complete freedom of thought and action.

The important outcome of Herzl's turn to Zionism remains the political thought, for the first time since the destruction of the temple, that all Jews are one people. In October 1894, Herzl noted that the return of the Jews to Palestine would defeat itself, because if they "returned home one day, they would discover . . . that they are no longer one people. For centuries they have been rooted in diverse cultures and nationalisms, different from each other, group by group" (Elon 1975, 122). Counter to that, he wrote in the summer of 1895 in *The Jewish State:* "Thus, whether we like it or not, we are now, and shall henceforth remain, a historic group with unmistakable characteristics common to us all. We are one people—our enemies have made us one without our consent, as repeatedly happens in history" (92). And Herzl identified with the Jewish people: "Our community of race is peculiar and unique, for we are bound together only by the faith of our fathers" (92).

The Jewish State: An Attempt at a Modern Solution of the Jewish Question (1896) is the political manifesto that declares all Jews to be one people and defines the Jewish Question as "a national question, which can only be solved by making it a political world—a question to be discussed and settled by the civilized nations of the world in council. We are a people—one people" (76). Assimilation seemed to Herzl to be neither possible nor desirable, for "the distinctive nationality of Jews neither can, will, nor must be destroyed" (79). A Jewish state, therefore—though geographically not yet fixed—emerged as a necessity that became technically realizable at the end of the nineteenth century.

For the majority of Central European Jews Zionism meant a revision of their standard of moral values and expectations for the future. The public reacted in general with criticism, opposition, and scorn. Herzl countered them with historical perspective: "But a man who is to carry the day in thirty years has to be considered crazy for the first two weeks" (Herzl 1960, 1:300). This certainty of standing in the service of a historical task allowed the last decade of Herzl's life to become the history of Zionism (see *The Zionist Movement in Germany and Austria*). It only remained to be pointed out the extent to which his Zionist activities—the building of the organization and the international-political discussion—influenced his relationship to Judaism and his writing.

The keynote address Herzl delivered at the First Zionist Congress on August 29, 1897, in Basel was both an address and a personal testimony: "Zionism is our return to Judaism even before our return to the Jewish land" (*Gesammelte Zionistische Schriften* 1:176). Herzl came to understand the multiplicity of the Jewish people from the Jews of Eastern Europe, whose religiosity and suffering he encountered during the Zionist congresses, committee meetings, and his travels to Turkey and Russia. At the same time he developed an attitude of unconditional toleration vis-à-vis other faiths and ethnicities. This tolerance is, for Herzl, the precondition for all human co-existence—although opponents of Zionism so often deny him this thought. Toleration was for him a lesson learned from the fate of European Jews: "We have learned toleration in Europe" (Herzl 1946, 147). If in the diary entries from the summer of 1895 the contemporary European attitude of superiority is still present, religious and political toleration are characterized in *The Jewish State* as the foundation of the state: "And if it should occur that men of other creeds and different nationalities come to live amongst us, we should accord them honorable protection and equality before the law" (146). Herzl hoped to prevent Zionism from turning into a new type of intolerance.

Herzl's literary contributions in the service of political Zionism and as feuilleton editor of the *Neue Freie Presse* are extensive: his correspondence fills five volumes, his diaries take up two volumes, and he wrote a novel and four plays. In 1897 he founded *Die Welt,* the official weekly of the Zionist Organization, which within one year reached a circulation of 10,000. As president of the Zionist Organization, Herzl held an office with global influence and was responsible for countless details. A style of leadership that others complained of as authoritarian seemed necessary to him to achieve in just a few years all that was possible.

Herzl undertook travels to foreign governments and audiences with heads of state without considering the accompanying professional risks or expectations of his family. As early as 1896, he spoke with the archduke of Baden, whom he held in high esteem. This paved the way for audiences with the chancellor as well as with Emperor Wilhelm II, who received Herzl in 1898 in Constantinople and Jerusalem. Herzl was in Constantinople three times for meetings with the Turkish government and finally with Sultan Abd al Hamid II. At the beginning of 1903 he led proceedings in Cairo, and a few months later he met with the Russian ministers Plevhe and Witte

in Moscow. In that same year, he spoke with Pope Pius X and King Victor Emmanuel III in Rome. Herzl's diaries contain colorful vignettes about conferences and conferees, the decorum and ambiance. Through these descriptive entries, he mastered the genre of memoir writing.

Although most of these discussions did not lead to direct successes, they nevertheless resulted in Zionism's becoming an international political issue within just a few years. Herzl's meetings with the British government had, however, a big effect on the future, and in 1903 the foreign office gave the Zionist Organization permission to establish an autonomous Jewish colony in Uganda. Herzl considered the potential settlement in British East Africa to be only "a temporary result," which, however, one had no right to deny to the "suffering masses." But as the battle over the question "Uganda or Palestine" threatened to divide the movement at the Sixth Zionist Congress, Herzl, who was haunted by the fear of death, was able to restore unity only with the greatest diplomatic fortune. The effect of Herzl's charisma was never greater than at the end of his closing remarks when he swore the oath in Hebrew: "If I forget thee, oh Jerusalem, may my right hand lose its cunning" (Elon 1975, 388). Politically, the British offer of a settlement in Uganda meant the recognition of the Jewish national struggle by a European power; it was the first step on the path of Zionism to the state of Israel.

When Herzl realized that he would not survive to see the realization of his political plans, he presented his conception of the Jewish state in his utopian novel *Altneuland* (1902), in which he emphasized confessional and ethnic toleration and sought to demonstrate through detailed description that the foundation of the state becomes realizable through scientific and technical progress.

Years of Zionist activity, along with the strain and excitement associated with it, brought Herzl to the point of complete exhaustion. More and more frequently, the forty-four-year-old man reflected on his own accomplishments with the distance of historical perspective: "By what I have done I have not made Zionism poorer, but Jewry richer" (Herzl 1960, 4:1548). Herzl now saw himself as the originator of a movement that would doubtless achieve its goal. The request that one day the Jewish people should transfer his remains to Palestine documents his assurance. On July 3, 1904, Theodor Herzl died of cardiac sclerosis in Edlach bei Wien. In 1949, his remains were flown to Israel. His grave on Mount Herzl is close to the Holocaust Memorial Center Yad Vashem; it overlooks the city of Jerusalem.

Bibliography

Alex Bein, *Theodore Herzl: A Biography,* trans. M. Samuel (Philadelphia: Jewish Publication Society of America, 1940); Gisela Brude-Firnau, "Der Toleranzbegriff Theodor Herzls," *Seminar* 19 (Feb. 1983): 20–32; André Chouraqui, *A Man Alone: The Life of Theodor Herzl* (Jerusalem: Keter Books, 1970); Israel Cohen, *Theodor Herzl: Founder of Political Zionism* (New York: Thomas Yoseloff, 1959); Amos Elon, *Herzl* (New York: Holt, Rinehart, Winston, 1975); Sander L. Gilman, *Jewish Self-Hatred: Anti-Semitism and the Hidden Language of the Jews* (Baltimore, Md.: Johns Hopkins University Press, 1986); Leah Hadomi, "Jüdische Identität und der zionistische Utopieroman," *Bulletin des Leo Baeck Instituts* 86 (1990): 23–66; Andrew Handler, *Dori: The Life and Times of Theodor Herzl in Budapest* (Birmingham: University of Alabama Press, 1983); Theodor Herzl, *Alt-neuland* (Vienna: Harz, 1900); Herzl, *Briefe und Tagebücher,* ed. Alex Bein et al., 6 vols. (Berlin: Propyläen, 1982–83); Herzl, *The Complete Diaries of Theodor Herzl,* ed. Raphael Patai, trans. Harry Zohn, 5 vols. (New York: Herzl Press and Thomas Yoseloff, 1960); Herzl, *Gesammelte Zionistische Schriften,* 3d ed., 5 vols. (Berlin: Jüdischer Verlag, 1934–35); Herzl, *The Jewish State: An Attempt at a Modern Solution of the Jewish Question* (New York: American Zionist Emergency Council, 1946); Rudolf Kallner, *Herzl und Rathenau: Wege jüdischer Existenz an der Wende des 20. Jahrhunderts* (Stuttgart: Ernst Klett, 1976); Jacques Kornberg, *Theodor Herzl: From Assimilation to Zionism* (Bloomington: Indiana University Press, 1993); Peter Loewenberg, "Theodor Herzl: A Psychoanalytic Study in Charismatic Political Leadership," *The Psychoanalytic Interpretation of History,* ed. Benjamin B. Wollman (New York: Harper and Row, 1973); Josef Patai, *Star over Jordan: The Life of Theodore Herzl,* trans. Francis Magyar (New York: Philosophical Library, 1946); Julius Schoeps, *Theodor Herzl: Wegbereiter des politischen Zionismus* (Göttingen: Musterschmidt, 1975); and Meyer W. Weisgal, ed., *Theodor Herzl: A Memorial* (1929; New York: Hyperion, 1976).

GISELA BRUDE-FIRNAU

TRANSLATED BY
HILLARY HOPE HERZOG
AND TODD HERZOG

February 1896 Publication of Theodor Herzl's *Der Judenstaat* begins a diverse tradition in Central Europe of Zionist writing in German

A substantial share of Zionist writing in Central Europe consists of polemics in support of the creation of "a national home for the Jews in Palestine" under the auspices of the Zionist movement, beginning with the publication of Theodor Herzl's *Der Judenstaat* in February 1896. Zionist writing nevertheless encompasses a broad spectrum of content: from the far left wing(s) of the movement to the far right wing; from the traditionally religious to the self-consciously, irreverently secular. It also exists in nearly every form imaginable: poetry—from the insipid to the profound   prose, novels, plays, short stories, journalism, and technical-scientific and economic reporting. The Central European Zionist oeuvre includes illustrated fables for children (to inspire them to donate their extra *Pfennig* to the Jewish National Fund); humor magazines; journals aimed at specific constituencies such as university students, youth, and women; writings based on social science and statistics; sophisticated essays on political philosophy (such as in Buber's interwar journal *Der Jude*); Buber's recasting of Hasidic tales; Leo Motzkin's research on the wave of pogroms in Russia; Gershom Scholem's first soundings in the history of Jewish mysticism; and Hannah Arendt's analysis of the Berlin salon Jewesses.

Following Herzl's precedent, Zionist tracts were frequently issued as pamphlets, but the movement also became known and spread its views largely by means of its press, notably *Die Welt* (1897–1914), which was the main organ of the Zionist Organization before World War I, and the *Jüdische Rundschau* (1902–38), which was the paper of the German Zionist Federation. *Die Welt* originated as Herzl's personal instrument and was staffed initially by Viennese university students; it suffered from amateurism, even though Herzl and other contributors were writers of distinction. In time, the journal that Herzl had proclaimed would carry the appellation "Jew Paper" with pride became truly respectable; its editors included Buber, Berthold Feiwel, and in its last years, Kurt Blumenfeld. The *Jüdische Rundschau* also matured into a solid and complex party organ; it is a surprisingly rich source of material not only about the Zionist movement, but of the Jewish world in general, and it sheds light on various aspects of Jewish culture and politics in the interwar years. Even after it was harshly censored by the Nazis in the 1930s, the journal sustained its vitality with a tighter focus on British politics and Palestine and on cultural matters that were deemed politically innocuous by the German authorities. Its longtime editor, Robert Weltsch, penned one of the most famous pieces in the history of the European Jewish press in response to the onset of the Nazi anti-Semitic campaign: "Tragt ihn mit Stolz, den Gelben Fleck" (Wear it with pride, the yellow badge; *Jüdische Rundschau,* April 1, 1933).

The publishing house Jüdischer Verlag (established 1902), although not officially in the domain of the Zionist organization, was the brainchild of a group of young

Zionists enamored of the idea to forge a new, secular, national Jewish culture. It became a major source of books on Zionist and Zionist-related themes, including translations from Hebrew and Yiddish; its mission would eventually overlap considerably with the Schocken Verlag, which was founded in 1931. The Jüdischer Verlag was responsible, albeit inconsistently, for publishing the stenographic protocol of the Zionist congresses (twenty of which were held in Europe between 1897 and 1938) as well as selected writings, speeches, biographies, and memoirs of the movement's leaders, and literary products of those identified with the movement. As early as 1903, the Jüdischer Verlag released a volume devoted to the Hebrew essayist and inter-Zionist critic Ahad Ha'Am by none other than the peripatetic Mathias Acher (Nathan Birnbaum). Jewish art and photographs pertaining to the Zionist and Jewish world also were reproduced as pictures and postcards in great quantity by the Jüdischer Verlag, as it styled itself, to promote a wide range of Jewish culture.

As much as Zionism has been noted for its relatively reactionary posture regarding the non-Zionist German-Jewish community, and despite German Zionism's reputation for intense dedication to *aliya* (emigration to Palestine), particularly after overheated resolutions were passed in 1913 and 1920, Zionist writing in Germany and Austria did not constitute a singular, Palestino-centric discourse. It is true that overall the emphasis was on developments in Palestine and Jewish politics pursuant to the realization of the national home. Still, Zionist writing evinced multiple discourses about the possibilities of Jewish identity and renewal, which involved refractions of the contemporary Jewish scene as well as forays into the Jewish past and future in innumerable guises. Furthermore, most Zionist writing implicitly accepted the persistence of Jewish life in Central Europe (and elsewhere in the Western Diaspora) until the late 1930s and accommodated itself to it. Perhaps the most striking evidence of the resilience of Diaspora thinking within Zionist writing is that the *Jüdische Rundschau* from around 1935 onward contained a number of articles to acquaint its readers—who

were supposedly poised to go to Palestine—with other places they might call home, such as Australia, South and Central America, and the United States. On Kristallnacht, that day's issue of the *Jüdische Rundschau* featured an article entitled: "Can You Learn English on Your Own in the United States?"

More significantly, though, as the recent work of scholars such as Michael Brenner, Mark Gelber, Jeffrey Grossman, and David Brenner makes clear, Zionist writing in Central Europe had a hand in carving out a new cultural space for German-speaking Jews that went beyond Jewish-confessional or parochial Zionist concerns. No doubt inadvertently, Zionism provided a springboard or forum for subjects that intersected specifically Jewish tensions—including discussions of modernism in art and literature. Although it would be inaccurate to label figures such as Franz Kafka and Walter Benjamin Zionists, their work to no small extent was received in the context of Zionist writing. In some respects this reception is highly ironic, because the original leading lights of Zionism—Theodor Herzl and Max Nordau—were less than open themselves to modernism and quite conservative in their literary and artistic temperaments. Their own plays, such as *Dr. Kohn* (Nordau) and *The New Ghetto* (Herzl), are fascinating means for probing the psyche of their authors, but they are of little aesthetic interest. What is of paramount importance is that Herzl sought to fashion a movement that would include as much of the Jewish world as possible. Surely the written word that came to be associated with Zionism reveals his genuine commitment to what would now be recognized as pluralism within the Jewish sphere.

There are at least three components of Zionist writing in Central Europe that distinguish it from the products of other political, social, and religious groups. The first is that Zionist writing had its own terminology, often in Hebrew transliteration. The most common of these terms are: *Chaluz* (pioneer), *Aliya* or *Alija* (emigration to the *Erez Israel* [the Land of Israel]), and *Yishuv* or *Jischub* (the Jewish settlement in Palestine). Selected parties and institutions in the movement also were known by their Hebrew names: the

Keren Kayemet L'Israel (Jewish National Fund), the first comprehensive Zionist fundraising body, and Brith Shalom (Covenant of Peace), an interwar caucus that advocated a Jewish-Arab binational state in Palestine, are two of many possible examples. Although the number of such terms is not immense, it is difficult to read Zionist writing after World War I without such a vocabulary. Overall, German Zionist writing contained a noticeable practice of "language mixing"—primarily of Hebrew and Yiddish, but occasionally of French and English. Predictably, the British Mandate for Palestine spawned a number of Anglicisms in the Zionist lexicon, such as "High Commissioner."

Second, perhaps the most distinctive feature of Zionist writing was that it was conspicuously accompanied by illustrations—that is, portraits, photographs, drawings, charts, graphs, and maps. In Central and West European Zionist discourse, the visual elements were as important as the written word. There were a number of periodicals composed primarily of pictures, such as *Palæstina-Bilder-Korrespondenz,* and the mainstream Zionist press contained far more illustrations than most Jewish papers. Scores of travelogue-type books and pamphlets, and especially promotional materials for fundraising, disseminated selected images of the new Jewish life in the Old / New Land of Israel. This dimension of the Zionist project is only beginning to be explored.

The third distinguishing aspect of Zionist writing is the unusual degree of criticism of the Zionist movement that was apparent in its own literature. It is widely noted that Ahad Ha'Am was the most important and galvanizing internal critic of the movement; certainly he inspired a good deal of the scraping against the grain of mainstream Zionism. But the movement also was called to task in other quarters. In Zionism's early years it supported a satirical magazine called *Shlemiel,* which wielded a sharp tongue at the movement's rivals while simultaneously pointing to serious faults and contradictions in Zionism. *Shlemiel* was revived briefly in the interwar years, cast in a more avant-garde and somber, if not sardonic tone. In addition, the Zionist press, such as the *Jüdische Rundschau,* delved into satire from time to time to take aim at the movement's sacred cows. The allowance for criticism of the movement within the organs of Zionism, however, suffered a drastic setback with the installation of the unwieldy fundraising instrument, the Keren Hayesod (Palestine Foundation Fund) under the control of Chaim Weizmann in 1920–21. "Dissent" from "loyalty" to the fund was deemed impermissible as the Keren Hayesod was erected over the strenuous objections of Louis Brandeis and others. One of the little-noticed consequences of the "Brandeis/Weizmann conflict" was a change in the discourse of Zionism, in which denunciations of fellow Zionists for "treasonous" speech reached a previously unmatched virulence. This type of unrestrained invective would become most prevalent in the attacks hurled at the Zionist administration by the right-wing Revisionists, led overall by Vladimir Jabotinsky and in Germany by Richard Lichtheim.

It furthermore should be acknowledged that writing in the German language was not simply incidental, but extremely important to Zionism's development. In the wake of the Holocaust, however, it is understandable that few commentators have reflected on the centrality of German in early Zionism. Moreover, the place of German is obscured because Zionists were very successful in propagating the myth that the Hebrew language was a most effective, if not the most effective, cohesive force in the movement. Nevertheless, from 1897 to 1938, the idea that Hebrew should and could be a vital rallying point for a regenerated Jewish nation was never an unchallenged goal in Zionism, and a disproportionate share of Zionist writing appeared in the native tongue of Zionism's Central European founders, German.

German was the language of the annual and biennial Zionist congresses and its main periodicals; it was crucial, as well, because it provided a cultural tie to the largely Yiddish-speaking Jewish masses and the Eastern Jews who had recently migrated westward. Furthermore, for assimilated Jews in Central Europe, the use of German promoted the perception that Zionism occupied "high" cultural ground. In light of the movement's goals, it seems that no other language could have been as constructive as German; it was the only language in which disparate Zionist constituencies could speak to each other—both literally and figuratively. Moreover, the use of German in official Zionist circles helped to tone down the divisive Zionist *Kulturdebatte*. It is necessary to briefly revisit this clash over language and culture in order put the role of German in perspective.

From 1897 to 1902, the Kulturdebatte in Zionism was essentially a dispute between two distinct factions in the movement: the first was referred to as the "cultural Zionists," or *Kulturisten,* who maintained that Zionism should take a prominent role in developing and propagating a secular national culture, featuring the revival of the Hebrew language. The most outspoken adversaries of the Kulturisten were among the small phalanx of Orthodox Jews who had joined Zionism; they would later form Mizrachi, the initial Orthodox-Zionist party. The Orthodox feared that the Kulturisten wanted to dominate Zionism as part of a greater scheme to replace traditional Judaism with a modern, secularized Jewish ideology and way of life.

In Zionism's early years, Herzl deftly managed to sidestep this conflict by keeping the movement's official position on a national language and culture as vague as possible. He wished not to offend or alienate the few Orthodox who had declared themselves in favor of the movement, and he sought to prevent the erection of barricades that might keep the masses of East European Orthodox—who generally opposed Zionism—from rallying to the movement in the future. Despite this careful effort at damage control, sparks continually flew over the *Kulturfrage,* "the problem of culture."

However much the Kulturdebatte afforded some of the more raucous scenes in the Zionist congresses and bitter polemics (and is still being played out in the state of Israel), the Orthodox might not have been present at all if the meetings were not held in German. Had the congresses' discussions been in Hebrew, most of the rabbis would have considered it impolitic to enjoin the debate, and most Jews, particularly in Central and Western Europe and the United States, never would have listened. Using Yiddish as the official

language of the congress was unworkable for several reasons. Ideologically, many Zionists disparaged Yiddish as a corrupt jargon (although the movement was ambivalent about it), and practically, many of the assimilated Western leaders did not know Yiddish. There was little chance that the world press and established governments would have paid much attention to a movement that conversed primarily in Yiddish—or Hebrew. Even though the "real" business of the congress may have transpired in the hallways and hotel lobbies in a multitude of tongues, the German addresses and responses, later published in newspaper reports and stenographic protocols, were an essential touchstone of Zionist writing from which many other discussions derived.

In effect, then, it was by default that German was significant in this regard because it largely precluded the official use of Hebrew in the movement's first decades. There is little doubt that a greater stress on Hebrew would have constrained Zionism even further. In addition, though, German is important because it allowed Zionism to distance itself from both Yiddish and Hebrew. Conventional wisdom divides Jewish national politics between proponents of Hebrew and those of Yiddish; yet the actual boundaries were never so clear. Yiddish also counted some ardent champions in the Zionist camp, and in Diaspora Zionism, German, and then English actually reigned supreme.

In the Zionist context, direct attacks on the German language occurred mostly in Jewish Palestine. Shortly before World War I, a dispute known as the "Language War" broke out over which language should be used in the technical college in Haifa—Hebrew or German. A wave of enthusiasm for Hebrew erupted in Palestine, which prompted impressive demonstrations in Europe. By 1913, the myth of the regenerative power of Hebrew was firmly entrenched in Zionism, and in reality, Hebrew had developed tremendously. Decades later, upon the arrival of waves of German-Jewish refugees to Palestine in the 1930s, hostility and even violence were unleashed against German speakers and the German-language press in the Yishuv. Tom Segev has characterized this unfortunate episode as part of a larger clash of cultures between the "Yekkes" (German Jews) and the emigrants to Palestine from Eastern Europe.

From the inception of Zionism until the Holocaust, German supplied an instrumental, respectable common ground and provided a critical distance from both Hebrew and Yiddish in Zionist discourse. It also was important as a language of the movement in its own right. However much the contributions of Hannah Arendt and Walter Benjamin were peripheral to Zionist writing, their very presence under the Zionist tent contributed to an intellectual richness and complexity that transcended programmatic, nationalist statements and sentiments. Despite a polemical stance that encouraged denigration of the Diaspora, German Zionist writing was anything but unworldly and rigidly Palestine-oriented. Zionist writing might have helped even non-Zionist Jews in Central Europe to imagine a legitimate, intellectually vital, national community of their own, as they were increasingly affected by the racist nationalism that would infiltrate their former homelands.

Bibliography

Almanach, 1902–1964: Jüdischer Verlag (Berlin: Jüdischer Verlag, 1964); Schmuel Almog, *Zionism and History* (Jerusalem: Magnes Press, 1987); Michael Berkowitz, *Zionist Culture and West European Jewry Before the First World War* (Cambridge: Cambridge University Press, 1993); Michael Brenner, *The Renaissance of Jewish Culture in Weimar Germany* (New Haven: Yale University Press, 1995); Arthur Cohen, ed., *The Jew,* trans. Joachim Neugroschel (Tuscaloosa: University of Alabama Press, 1980); Volker Dahm, *Das Jüdische Buch im Dritten Reich,* 2 vols. (Frankfurt a. M.: Buchhandler-Vereinigung, 1979); Harriet Freidenreich, *Jewish Politics in Vienna, 1918–1938* (Bloomington: Indiana University Press, 1991); Mark H. Gelber, "The jungjüdische Bewegung," *Leo Baeck Institute Year Book* 31 (1986): 105–19; Gelber, "Theodor Herzl, Martin Buber, Berthold Feiwel, and Young-Jewish Viennese Poets," *Turn-of-the-Century Vienna and Its Legacy,* ed. Jeffrey Berlin, Jorun Johns, and Richard Lawson (Vienna: Atelier, 1992); Theodor Herzl, *The Jewish State,* trans. Harry Zohn (New York: Herzl Press, 1970); Herzl, *Zionist Writings,* trans. and ed. Harry Zohn, 2 vols. (New York: Herzl Press, 1973 and 1975); Dagmar Lorenz and Gabriele Weinberger, eds., *Insiders and Outsiders: Jewish and Gentile Culture in Germany and Austria* (Detroit: Wayne State University Press, 1994); George L. Mosse, *Germans and Jews* (New York: Howard Fertig, 1970); Stanley Nash, *In Search of Hebraism: Shai Hurwitz and His Polemics in the Hebrew Press* (Leiden: E. J. Brill, 1980); B. Netanyahu, ed., *Max Nordau to His People* (New York: Scopus, 1941); Jehuda Reinharz, "Ahad Ha'Am, Martin Buber, and German Zionism," *At the Crossroads: Essays on Ahad Ha'Am,* ed. Jacques Kornberg (Albany: State University of New York Press, 1983), 142–55; Reinharz, *Dokumente zur Geschichte des deutschen Zionismus 1882–1933* (Tübingen: Mohr, 1981); and Jacob Toury, "Herzl's Newspapers: The Creation of *Die Welt,*" *Studies in Zionism* (autumn 1980): 159–72.

MICHAEL BERKOWITZ

1897 Herzl draws international attention to Zionism, and the Young Vienna circle flourishes

Stefan Zweig, in his autobiography, *The World of Yesterday,* expressed most memorably the meaning for Viennese culture of the Jews, who never constituted more than about 10 percent of the city's population. After making the point that the Jews replaced the somewhat jaded Austrian aristocracy as the carriers of cultures and the patrons of the arts, Zweig wrote: "Nine-tenths of what the world celebrated as Viennese culture in the nineteenth century was promoted, nourished, or even created by Viennese Jewry." Such a rosy picture of the nostalgically remembered Vienna of Zweig's youth must be viewed in the context of his depression and despair shortly before his suicide in 1942. Vienna also had a role to play in the development of Martin Buber's thought. Several of Vienna's important literary figures and particularly the great Burgtheater had a formative influence on Buber, Theodor Herzl's occasional associate, when he returned from Poland to his native Vienna as an eighteen-year-old student. As his biographer Maurice Friedman has pointed out, Buber discovered in and associated with Vienna "the spokenness of speech . . . the life of dialogue . . . [the] reality of speech-as-event."

Jakob Wassermann, however, a native of Franconia who came to Austria in 1898 and decided to settle there, sounded an alarm. He found the banks, the press, the theater, the literature, and the social organizations of Vienna in Jewish hands. In his autobiography, *My Life as German and Jew,* first published in German in 1921, he severely criticized the Jews of fin-de-siècle Vienna for their servility, their lack of dignity and restraint, and their self-seeking opportunism—qualities that Theodor Herzl had also identified as being part of a ghetto mentality. At that time, however, salvation was found in greater adaptation and assimilation, even conversion, and thus Herzl's historic Zionist quest found few champions among Viennese Jewry, though it had many adherents in other countries, particularly the Jewish communities of Eastern Europe.

The poets, storytellers, dramatists, and essayists of fin-de-siècle Vienna, who were typically born in the 1860s and 1870s, are often grouped together as the *Jung Wien* (Young Vienna) circle, possibly in slightly ironic analogy to the *Jung-Deutschland* (Young Germany) movement that succeeded German romanticism in the 1830s and 1840s. In an article entitled "The Old Age of Young Vienna," however, Victor A. Oswald, Jr., complains that this designation reminds him too much of *Alt-Wien* (Old Vienna), the "beautiful blue Danube," and other clichés. He points out that those rather dissimilar writers were too divergent to form an enduring association and that their most mature works were produced after the turn of the century. With the exception of Hermann Bahr, the Nestor and chief theoretician of the circle, these writers were Jews, or at least of Jewish birth or descent. They included—in addition to Bahr—Stefan Zweig, Theodor Herzl, Hugo von Hofmannsthal, Arthur Schnitzler, Felix Salten (born in Budapest as Signund, or Zsiga, Salzmann), Richard Beer-Hofmann, Felix Dörmann (originally Biedermann), Leopold von Andrian-Werburg, Peter Altenberg, and Raoul Auernheimer. Many of these men of letters came from patriarchally structured Jewish families from which they, the gifted sons, broke away at the earliest opportunity, spurning the business opportunities provided by the self-made father in favor of a literary career. Cases in point are Karl Kraus, Theodor Herzl, Felix Salten, Stefan Zweig, and Siegfried Trebitsch in Vienna and Franz Kafka and Franz Werfel in Prague.

The assimilation and Jewish attenuation of Austrian Jewry are exemplified by the cloth and silk merchant Isak Löw Hofmann, who became Edler von Hofmannsthal in 1835 and, thus ennobled, proceeded to cofound the Kultusgemeinde (Jewish Community Council) of Vienna. His son was already baptized, and his great-grandson, Hugo von Hofmannsthal, was a Catholic, though hardly parochial, writer and thinker who once referred to his grandfather's conversion as "stepping out of an isolation that no longer made sense." One has to look hard for vestiges of Jewish sensibilities in Hugo's writing. In his *Terzinen über Vergänglichkeit* (1894, Eng. trans. 1957), a group of poems about evanescence, Hofmannsthal writes: "I existed a hundred years ago, and my ancestors in their shrouds are as related to me as my own hair." In another poem, "Manche freilich . . . " (1895, Eng. trans. 1957, I, 22), we find these lines. "I cannot brush off from my eyelids the weariness of completely forgotten peoples." Presumably these are references to the poet's Jewish ancestry, but why should the Jewish people have been "completely forgotten," except perhaps in Hofmannsthal's own consciousness? At any rate, in 1905 the precocious poet expressed the *Lebensgefühl* (sense of life) of fin-de-siècle Vienna when he wrote: "We must take leave of a world before it collapses. Many know it already, and an indefinable feeling makes poets out of many."

It was a rich literary scene. At one end of the spectrum were self-hating Jews like Arthur Trebitsch and Otto Weininger (though the label "Jewish self-hatred" has been attached to Karl

Kraus as well, and not without reason). Weininger shot himself in 1903 in the house in which Beethoven had died. He had been a newly minted doctor of philosophy at age twenty-three and the author of a very original, sensational, and influential book called *Sex and Character* in which he managed to attack both Jews and women. At the other end of the spectrum is the only *homo judaicus* of the Young Vienna circle, the patriarchal figure of Richard Beer-Hofmann. His orientation may be regarded as a protest against the assimilated, feckless Jewry of his time, and to this end he invoked the heroic biblical period of the Jewish people in a grandly conceived but fragmentary cycle of poetic plays about King David. Beer-Hofmann perceived the biblical king to be the embodiment of the Jewish psyche in all its ambivalence, and through this figure he wished to explore the mysteries of divine grace and Jewish chosenness as well as the age-old moral mission of the Jewish people. In his best-known completed play, *Jaákob's Traum* (Jacob's dream; 1900, Eng. trans. 1927), he gave shape to two biblical episodes: the conflict between the sensitive dreamer Jacob and the earthbound realist Edom (Esau), as well as Jacob's covenant with God and the assumption of the name (and obligation) Israel. "I am fully Jewish in substance," said Beer-Hofmann, "fully Austrian functionally." He achieved early fame in 1897 with his "Schlaflied für Mirjam," a philosophical lullaby for his first-born and a paean of praise to paternal love. (Another rare kind of love bound Beer-Hofmann to his much younger wife, Paula Lissy, a Catholic whom he met in 1895 and who converted to the Jewish faith—as did Martin Buber's Paula Winkler a few years later.) Although the first three stanzas of this beautiful poem do express the melancholy, fin-de-siècle feeling that life is impenetrable, disconnected, and evanescent—that we are unable to communicate our deepest feelings and experiences even to those dearest and nearest to us and that each generation is doomed to recapitulate the past with its errors and sorrows—Beer-Hofmann opens up a new perspective in his concluding stanza by assuring us that we may derive solace and support from our ancestral community, that there is a definite continuity of existence with enduring values *l'dor vador* (from generation to generation), and that the voices of our ancestors can guide us to a more meaningful, purposeful existence. This widely admired "Lullaby," which has been set to music a dozen times (though never notably), betokened Jewish dignity even to Rainer Maria Rilke, who was no particular friend of the Jews. Among the several English versions of the "Schlaflied," the one by the poet's younger daughter, Naëmah, may be regarded as the most authentic, though it is flawed by the inconsistent use of "you," "thee," and "thine."

Sleep, my child, it's late, go to rest.
Look how the sun sets in the west,
Over the mountains its last dying breath.
You—you know nothing of sun and of death,
Turning your eyes to light and to shine.
Sleep, so many more suns are thine.
Sleep, my child, my child, go to sleep.

Sleep, my child, the evening wind blows.
Nobody knows whence it comes, where it goes.
Dark and hidden the ways are here
For you, and for me—and for all of us, dear!
Blindly we wander and wander alone,
No companion for you—or for me here below.
Sleep, my child, my child, go to sleep.

Sleep, my child, and don't listen to me,
Meaning for me is but sounds for thee,
Sounds like the wind, like the falling of rain

Words—but maybe a lifetime's gain.
All that I've reaped will be buried with me.
None can to none an heir here be.
Sleep, my child, my child, go to sleep.

Mirjam—my child, are you asleep?
We are but shores, and blood in us deep
Flows from those past to those yet to be,
Blood of our Fathers, restless and proud.
All are within us, who feels alone?
You are their life—their life is your own.
Mirjam, my life, my child, go to sleep.

"Aging," another of Beer-Hofmann's scant two dozen poems, expresses his unquenchable faith in God and his conviction that the seeming harshness of our earthly lot is preordained and indeed divine. If the fate of man is doom-laden, it

can be mastered if the bonds of isolation are broken. Life is neither absurd nor a process of decay; there can be a dialogue with God and a feeling of oneness with Nature. Clearly, Beer-Hofmann's vibrant Judaism helped him overcome his own dandyism and decadence, his passivity and pessimism. In his novel *Der Tod Georgs* (George's death; 1900) the protagonist's reveries and stream-of-consciousness reflections on his aesthetic existence lead him to an affirmation of life and of his Jewish heritage. His new awareness of his Jewishness frees him from narcissistic dreams and unproductive delusions. Paul thinks of "ancestors in their peregrinations, rejected even by the lowliest persons but never rejecting themselves . . . and behind them was a people that did not beg, Jews who always earned the blessing of their just God who suffused their feelings the way the blood coursed through their veins. And he shared their blood."

Beer-Hofmann's first drama, *Der Graf von Charolais* (The Count of Charolais; 1900), a tragedy of fate based on *The Fatal Dowry* by Philip Massenger and Nathan Field, includes "Der Rote Itzig" (Red Isaac), a figure reminiscent of the legendary Wandering Jew. The dramatist's first biographer, Theodor Reik, has commented about him as follows: "In 'Red Itzig' the author shows not only a Jew the way he *is* but also how he has become so" (1912). Itzig, the Jewish spokesman for the creditors, delivers himself of a Shylock-like speech presented here in Ludwig Lewisohn's unpublished translation (which does not attempt to reproduce Itzig's Judeo-German patois—which is ostensibly Yiddish as imagined by a cultivated Viennese Jew).

An evil man! "And why
Should I ever be kind to you? Give me one
      reason—
A single one! Or do you think I should
Be kind because all human beings should
Be kind unto each other? First, my Lord
Tear out this heart contracted and convulsed
By the infliction of a thousand wrongs;
Put out these eyes and give me other eyes
That are not wounded by too much of weeping;
Smooth out my back that's bent to crookedness

With bowing down in enforced humbleness;
And give me other feet unwearied
By the eternal wandering of exile:
Crash through my skull, tear out the brain
  beneath
So that I may forget; and last of all,
Cut me these veins and let my blood run out
That nothing's left that was my father's or
My father's father or his own or his—
No drop of all that blood, of all that woe—
And when you have done all that, my Lord
  Count,
And I am still among the living—
then
I'll speak with you right humanly—I mean
As a good man should speak unto his brother!
—Till then let me be what to you I am
And should be though I were I know not what:
A Jew, a Jew, a common vulgar Jew!

In 1897 Karl Kraus's first book (or pamphlet) appeared, a literary satire entitled *Die demolierte Literatur* that had appeared in a journal the preceding year. (An English translation, "The Demolished Literature," may be found in Segel's *Vienna Coffeehouse Wits*.) This witty diatribe, so rich in innuendo and invective, achieved five editions by 1901 and netted its author a bodily attack and a challenge to a duel. Kraus starts with the memorable line "Wien wird jetzt zur Großstadt demoliert," meaning that the wrecker's ball is turning Vienna into a metropolis. Kraus's satire is actually an obituary of the legendary Café Griensteidl on Michaelerplatz, which was the favorite gathering place of the Young Vienna writers, most of whom Kraus lampoons (without mentioning any names). With the exception of Kraus's lifelong target Hermann Bahr, the "gentleman from Linz" who is depicted on the cover as being dragged off, kicking and screaming, by two attendants, Kraus's attitude toward these writers was ambivalent. Those "aristocratic" poets whose nobility has already encompassed several "degenerations" seem to have chosen dying as their main theme. In them Kraus diagnoses a curious inbreeding and inactivity, a narrow horizon, and a great shallowness. Arthur Schnitzler is treated relatively gently as the man "who has plunged

deepest into this shallowness and is the most deeply immersed in this emptiness." Others satirized include Felix Salten, Beer-Hofmann (as a poet who writes sparingly and dresses nattily), Leopold von Andrian-Werburg, the painter-poet Ferry Beraton, and Bahr's discovery, Hugo von Hofmannsthal ("Goethe on a school bench").

Also in 1897 Kraus wrote an unfavorable review of Herzl's *Das neue Ghetto* (The new ghetto), "a play that presents an altogether corrupt Jewish society but disappoints with its unexpected emphasis on one noble-minded Israelite, which cost the author the sympathies of authoritative anti-Semitic circles." In *Eine Krone für Zion* (A crown for Zion), a twenty-eight-page pamphlet written the following year, Kraus, who was erroneously listed as a delegate, lampoons the First Zionist Congress, its official minutes, and the delegates' preoccupation with Jewish nationalism and their messianic pathos. "It took narrow-minded Zionism," he writes, "to enable these gentlemen, who have hitherto been occupied only with their nerves, to feel that they, too, are of this day and age." Internalizing the millennial pain of Jewry has permitted them to shed their coffeehouse aestheticism, adopt Hermann Bar-Kochba as their idol, and replace the perfumed atmosphere of bourgeois salons with the fata morgana of earthy agricultural schemes. "One can hardly assume that this time the Jews will enter the Promised Land with dry feet; another Red Sea, Socialism, will block their way there." For the rest, "when Zionists share a rather skimpy weltanschauung with anti-Semites, it must soon be exhausted." Curiously enough, Herzl did not mention Kraus and his diatribes in his voluminous diaries. Although some of the satirist's arguments differed little from the strictures and gibes heaped upon Herzl and his Zionist quest by many of his Viennese contemporaries, Kraus's early prominence and the incisiveness of his attacks should have made this longtime foe of the *Neue Freie Presse* worthy of the attention of its cultural editor.

William H. Hechler, an eccentric British clergyman who supported Herzl's Zionism because he believed that a Jewish homeland had been prophetically foretold, once called 1897 "one of the critical years." Indeed it was, and Herzl, a political amateur and a poor prophet in many things (particularly the attitude of the Arab population of Palestine), was right on the mark when he wrote in his diary on September 3, 1897: "At Basel I founded the Jewish State. If I said this out loud today, I would be answered by universal laughter. Perhaps in five years, and certainly in fifty, everyone will realize it." His essay "The Menorah," written that year, is of distinct autobiographical significance. In the form of a poignant parable about a *baal teshuvah,* a man who returns to the Jewish fold, Herzl wrote of the symbolic beauty, growth, and acceptance of the Zionist idea as the darkness of suppression, superstition, and a ghetto mentality (he wrote in a diary entry, March 24, 1897, "The Viennese Jews are, like most of our people, ghetto types who are glad if they get off with only a black eye") giving way to the splendor of Jewish auto-emancipation and a new Jewish homeland. Most of Herzl's thirty plays, which are predominantly witty but lightweight drawing-room comedies, have not stood the test of time: the only play still worth attention is *Das neue Ghetto,* which was written in Paris in 1894 and published by the Verlag der Welt in 1897. Its theme is the plight of the Jews in the Diaspora and the tragic incompleteness of Jewish emancipation. Written on the eve of the development of political Zionism, it is Herzl's "farewell to his assimilatory past" (L. Lewisohn 1955) and marks his transition from a self-styled "writer of sorts with limited ambitions and petty vanities" to a leader with great vision and selfless devotion to his cause. Soon after writing this play, Herzl took his friend Schnitzler into his confidence and asked him to submit it to theaters under the nom de plume Albert Schnabel. It was premiered at Vienna's Carltheater in January 1898 and performed to mixed reactions on some twenty German and Austrian stages that year. Herzl also published several volumes of stories and essays. "His essays," wrote Stefan Zweig, "are still enchanting in their wealth of keen and oftentimes wise observations, their stylistic animation, and their aristocratic charm. Whether light or critical, they never lost their innate nobility; they were the most cultivated in journalism and the

delight of a city that had schooled itself to every subtlety" (Zweig 1943).

In 1897 Karl Lueger, having been elected mayor of Vienna three times, was finally confirmed and installed in that office by Emperor Franz Joseph. His reputation as a Jew-baiting demagogue and manipulator was such that the emperor had refused to ratify the first two elections. Two years earlier, Herzl had found himself in front of a polling place for municipal elections, and upon catching sight of "handsome Karl," a man in the cheering crowd said, "Das ist unser Führer" (That is our leader). "These words," wrote Herzl in his diary on September 20, 1895, "showed me more than all the declamation and abuse how deeply anti-Semitism is rooted in the hearts of these people."

Though Herzl's Zionist quest met with little sympathy in his own city, his ideas and activities did produce a new Jewish awareness, as evidenced by the formation of discussion groups, courses for students and adults, and sports associations. Of the Young Vienna writers, only Beer-Hofmann evinced a complete understanding of Herzl's Zionist quest. In a letter hailing the appearance of *The Jewish State* he wrote: "I appreciated what was *behind* your book even more than what was *in* it. At last there is a man again who does not bear his Jewishness resignedly as a burden or a misfortune but is proud to be a legitimate heir of an age-old culture." When Herzl assured Beer-Hofmann that the Jewish state would have a university and an opera house and that the dramatist would go to the latter wearing full dress with a white gardenia in his buttonhole, Beer-Hofmann replied: "Oh no! When the time comes, I will appear in a silken burnoose and deck myself out with many chains and a turban with a diamond clasp."

The prevalence of anti-Semitism and the challenge of Zionism also found expression in the writings of Arthur Schnitzler. From 1899 to 1912 he worked on his play *Professor Bernhardi,* in which he highlighted the highly controversial social issue of anti-Semitism as well as the problem of euthanasia and its religious considerations. In this play, a simple act of mercy on the part of a Jewish doctor is trumped up by prejudice-ridden clerical Vienna and inflated into a cause célèbre. The dramatist gives a cheerless picture of Viennese society and weaves into it the many social, political, ideological, and religious cross-currents that were leading to its disintegration. The *Diskussionsroman* (novel of discussion) entitled *Der Weg ins Freie* (The road to the open) that Schnitzler wrote between 1902 and 1907 betrays the influence of Herzl and his largely unsuccessful attempts to win Schnitzler's support for the Zionist cause. It presents a whole typology of Austrian Jewry floundering between the Scylla of anti-Semitism and what to the author appeared to be the Charybdis of Zionist endeavors. Schnitzler did not believe that roads to freedom—from prejudice, erotic entanglements, artistic frustration, and other aspects of an unfulfilled life in a constricting atmosphere—could be traveled with others. Dr. Schnitzler's only prescription seems to have been that everyone search his soul and find that inner road for himself. He considered it proper that Jews should be a kind of ferment in the brewing of humanity (a position close to that of Stefan Zweig, that great believer in the Diaspora) and that what Herzl called *Judennot* (Jewish misery) should be borne by them proudly, with dignity, and without yielding to the blandishments of any party, ideology, or movement that promised a panacea.

In 1897 the prestigious S. Fischer Verlag of Berlin issued the second collection of short prose pieces by Peter Altenberg. (The first collection had materialized the preceding year after Altenberg's friend and patron Karl Kraus had gathered loose sheets into a volume entitled *Wie ich es sehe* [As I see it].) The pieces in *Ashantee* (Altenberg 1897) were inspired by the author's frequent visits to an authentic African tribal village that had been installed in the Vienna Zoo. Altenberg befriended the young women and children in residence there. He delighted in their beauty, naturalness, and honesty, which brought home to him the virtues of living in harmony with nature and of shedding the excesses, superfluities, and absurdities of the European lifestyle.

Born into a Viennese Jewish family in 1859, Richard Engländer became known as P. A., or

"Der Peter." The forced gaiety, amorous dalliances, and unheroic passivity of this eccentric bohemian and Viennese Socrates and Diogenes rolled into one (though he thought of himself as a "Verlaine d'Autriche"), are a poignant reminder of a bygone age. This confidant of poets and prostitutes, however, also prefigured the beatniks, hippies, and flower children of the 1960s. Spurning the stuffy attire of his time and place, he pioneered in what later became the more respectable leisure clothing, trudging through the streets of Vienna with an alpenstock; wearing Franciscan sandals without socks, loose-fitting raglan coats or capes over checked shirts and trousers, brightly colored homespun jackets, and "artists'" neckties; and covering his bald pate with floppy hats or tweed berets. Having been declared neurologically unfit for regular employment, P. A. became dependent on the generosity of his family and friends, though his prolific writings later earned him some income.

A master of the "small form"—impressionistic feuilletons, sketches, dialogues, and aphorisms—P. A. endeavored to present "extracts of life," to characterize a landscape in one word, to describe a human being in one sentence and an emotional experience on one page. He wished to "turn a nothing into a something, a something into an everything." A latter-day "Frauenlob," an early male feminist who was concerned with the spirituality, grace, and psychic needs of women and who idolized teenagers, this denizen of the fabled Café Central remained a confirmed bachelor. His nervous hypersensitivity and mental instability caused him to be frequently institutionalized in sanatoriums and mental hospitals. Altenberg was an idiosyncratic "natural" food faddist and a preacher of a "natural" lifestyle, as well as an alcoholic and a drug addict. According to Otto Basil, P. A. was an *enfant terrible, who experienced the splendor and misery of the Habsburg monarchy,"* and a "sage who played the fool in order to lead the world *ad absurdum*." In 1900 Altenberg converted to Catholicism, reportedly on the advice of Karl Kraus (who secretly took the same step a decade later).

P. A. rarely commented on his Jewish heritage, and when he did, it was usually in negative terms. During World War I, for example, he unaccountably criticized the Jewish practice of sitting shiva—the seven days of intense mourning during which the family of a deceased person is required to stay home and be comforted by visitors. Nevertheless, critics have discerned Jewish qualities in P. A.; thus Richard von Schaukal (1966) speaks of his "*schlemiel* humor." In 1922, a few years after Altenberg's death, another Austrian-Jewish writer, Albert Ehrenstein, attempted to integrate him into their shared tradition: "He was quintessentially Viennese and yet homeless. . . . Like the Eternal Jew he wandered from one hotel room and café to another. His wit was antithetical, upsetting, self-revealing—but his rage was prophetic and his wrath Old Testament–like. He made a strong case for the constancy of the Jewish race [sic]. His words are as imperishable as those of any Biblical poet" (1921). The contemporary critic Ernst Randak (1960) has compared Altenberg with his own literary contemporaries: "Altenberg never presented Judaism like Beer-Hofmann, he did not discuss it like Schnitzler, he did not suffer because of it like Weininger, and yet it was there, in everything he did and wrote, as the messianic element that also existed in Karl Kraus. Both had the fanatical belief that they had to help redeem others."

An undated letter by Arthur Schnitzler found in 1942 may serve to sum up the attitude of most of the Young Vienna writers:

Neither Jewish-Zionist resentment nor the stupidity and impudence of German nationalists will make me doubt in the least that I am a German writer. . . . I would not want Zionism eliminated from the world's political scene of today or from the soul-economy of contemporary Jewry. As a spiritual element to elevate one's self-reliance, as a possibility for reacting against all sorts of dark hatreds, and especially as a philanthropic action of the highest rank, Zionism will always retain its importance even if it should some day prove to have been merely a historic episode. I find it proper that authors whose language is Hebrew should call themselves Hebrew writers or Jewish writers. Neither could I object if poets of Jewish background who have hitherto written in another language became outraged at the stupidity and vulgarity of anti-Semitism, which would deny them membership in a nation on whose territory they were born, in whose speech they were reared and which they even helped to shape; and if, as a result, these poets abjured the beloved language hitherto employed by them and turned to Hebrew as the medium for their creative works. Such poets would thereby have obtained the right to designate themselves as Jewish poets. But as long as they continue to write in German, they must call themselves German poets. . . . They are German poets as surely as Heine, Börne, Gundolf, and a hundred others of Jewish origin are German; as surely as Brandes is a Danish writer and Proust a French writer. Just ask any genuine living German poet, ask Heinrich Mann, Thomas Mann, Gerhart Hauptmann, Hesse, Unruh, whom they feel to be more German: Wolzogen, Dinter, and that crowd, or Wassermann, Werfel, Beer-Hofmann, and a dozen others of Jewish origin that I could name.

Bibliography

Peter Altenberg, *Ashantee* (Berlin: Fischer, 1897); Richard Beer-Hofmann, *Der Graf von Charolais* (Berlin: Fischer, 1900); Beer-Hofmann, *Jaákob's Traum* (Berlin: Fischer, 1900; New York: Kessin, 1927); Beer-Hofmann, "Schlaflied für Mirjam" (Berlin: Fischer, 1900); Beer-Hofmann, *Der Tod Georgs* (Berlin: Fischer, 1929); Steven Beller, *Vienna and the Jews, 1867–1938* (Cambridge: Cambridge University Press, 1989); George Berkley, *Vienna and Its Jews* (Cambridge, Mass.: Abt Books, 1988); Donald Daviau, ed., *The Correspondence of Stefan Zweig with Raoul Auernheimer and with Richard Beer-Hofmann* (Columbia, S.C.: Camden House, 1983); Albert Ehrenstein, *Wien* (Berlin: Rowohlt, 1921); Esther Elstun, *Richard Beer-Hofmann* (University Park: Pennsylvania State University Press, 1983); Josef Fraenkel, ed., *The Jews of Austria* (London: Vallentine, Mitchell, 1967); Hugo von Hofmannsthal, *Ausgewählte Werke,* ed. Rudolf Hirsch, 2 vols. (Frankfurt a. M.: Fischer, 1957); Alan Janik and Stephen Toulmin, *Wittgenstein's Vienna* (New York: Simon and Schuster, 1973); William M. Johnston, *The Austrian Mind: An Intellectual and Social History, 1848–1938*

(Berkeley: University of California Press, 1971); Lothar Kahn, *Between Two Worlds: A Cultural History of German-Jewish Writers* (West Lafayette, Ind.: Purdue University Press, 1993); Alexander King, *Peter Altenberg's Evocations of Love* (New York: Simon and Schuster, 1960); Jacques Kornberg, *Theodor Herzl: From Assimilation to Zionism* (Bloomington: Indiana University Press, 1993); Ludwig Lewisohn, *Theodor Herzl: A Portrait for This Age* (Cleveland: World Publishing, 1955); Sol Liptzin, *Germany's Stepchildren* (Philadelphia: Jewish Publication Society of America, 1948); William O. McCagg, Jr., *A History of the Habsburg Jews, 1867–1938* (Bloomington: Indiana University Press, 1989); Ivar Oxaal et al., eds., *Jews, Antisemitism, and Culture in Vienna* (London: Routledge & Kegan Paul, 1987); Ernst Pawel, *The Labyrinth of Exile: A Life of Theodor Herzl* (New York: Farrar, Straus and Giroux, 1989); Ernst Randak, ed., *Peter Altenberg oder das Genie ohne Fähigkeiten* (Graz: Siasny, 1960); Theodor Reik, *Richard Beer-Hofmann* (Leipzig: Eichler, 1912); Richard von Schaukal, *Über Dichter* (Munich: Langen, Müller, 1966); Carl E. Schorske, *Fin-de-Siècle Vienna* (New York: Alfred A. Knopf, 1980); Harold B. Segel, *The Vienna Coffeehouse Wits, 1890–1938* (West Lafayette, Ind.: Purdue University Press, 1993); Hilde Spiel, *Vienna's Golden Autumn* (London: Weidenfeld & Nicolson, 1987); Jakob Wassermann, *Mein Weg as Deutscher und Jude* (Berlin: Fischer, 1921), trans. Salomea Neumark Branin (New York: Coward-McCann, 1933); Robert S. Wistrich, *The Jews in the Age of Franz Joseph* (Oxford: Oxford University Press, 1989); Wistrich, ed., *Austrians and Jews in the Twentieth Century: From Franz Joseph to Waldheim* (London: Macmillan, 1992); Harry Zohn, *Karl Kraus* (New York: Twayne Publishers, 1971); Zohn, *Austriaca and Judaica* (New York: Peter Lang, 1995); Stefan Zweig, *The World of Yesterday* (New York: Viking Press, 1943).

HARRY ZOHN

1898   Sigmund Freud's Passover dream responds to Theodor Herzl's Zionist dream

Sigmund Freud was not a Zionist. Despite Theodor Herzl's proximity in Vienna, Freud remained so aloof from Zionism that he hardly ever expressed himself concerning individual or national Jewish identity. Although on rare occasions he did acknowledge his Jewishness, he renounced nationalistic ideas. Developing a personal solution to the "Jewish Question," Freud never explained his views at length; Freudian methods of analysis suggest that this near-total silence derived from an avoidance or a disavowal (*Verneinung*). One of Freud's dreams is a "royal road" to his ambivalence toward Judaic traditions.

The decisive encounter with Zionism came in January 1898, three weeks after Freud lectured to the B'nai B'rith Society in Vienna and only a few months after the First Zionist Congress convened in Basel. At that time Freud saw Herzl's play *Das neue Ghetto* (The new ghetto); his reaction took the form of a dream, which he recorded in *The Interpretation of Dreams*. Usually called the dream of "My son, the myop," this might also be known as Freud's "Passover dream." The manifest content of his dream is essential, for it responds to and interprets Herzl's play.

Over the past sixty years, numerous scholars have discussed Freud "as a Jew" or have compared his writings to Jewish sources. I will not retrace this uneven history of reception, because I do not share its basic assumptions; I am not concerned with those deliberate statements of Freud that affirmed his Jewishness while rejecting all religious beliefs. Nor do I insist that Freud directly borrowed psychoanalytic concepts or methods from ancient Jewish sources, although there is evidence of indirect influence. Rather, what interests me is Freud's ambivalence and the distortions it produces in his work. Yet my intention is not to criticize Freud for remaining something of a crypto-Jew, because his suppression of the Judaic component in psychoanalysis was virtually inevitable given the Viennese cultural and scientific contexts.

Biographical writers and psychohistorians have prepared the way for a literary interpretation of Freud's Passover dream as a reaction to Herzl's early play and later Zionist dream. For example, they cite a letter Freud wrote to Herzl in 1902, when he enclosed a copy of *The Interpretation of Dreams* for possible review in *Die Neue Freie Presse*. In this letter, Freud asked Herzl to keep the book "as a sign of the esteem in which I—like so many others—have for years held the poet and fighter for the human rights of our people." We need not take this letter at its word, but it serves well as a preface to Freud's more complex, and partially unconscious, message to Herzl.

In *The Interpretation of Dreams*, chapter 5, Freud discusses the materials and sources of dreams. He demonstrates that recent experiences are incorporated into their manifest content and gives the example of his own dream "that a teacher whom I know at our university says: *My son, the myop (Mein Sohn, der Myop)*" (*Td* 273 / *ID* 303). The German word *Myop* signifies a nearsighted person, hence this phrase alludes to a son's inadequate vision. The dream consists of three parts; the second part is a dialogue, followed by a third scene in which Freud and his sons appear (ibid.). Freud fails to mention a number of relevant "day's residues" and postpones interpretation of this dream until a later passage.

Chapter 6, on the dream work, illustrates the mechanisms of distortion that purportedly give rise to dreams. At every turn, Freud intimates that the distortions bear meaning, like figures of speech expressing literal contents. Hence the subdivision heading, "Absurd Dreams," is a misnomer awaiting correction: even the most apparently absurd dream has meaning, or may be given meaning, with the help of the dreamer. The Passover dream is an intriguing example in which Freud uncovers meanings of an apparently meaningless mental product, which he calls "an absurd and incomprehensible word construction." Specifically, one linguistic innovation stands like a palimpsest over buried formations. Freud reveals certain associated materials, yet he merely begins the work of interpretation. Without claiming to have discovered the exclusive meaning of Freud's dream, we may extrapolate further from his associations. The present analysis focuses on significations linked to the intertextual relationship between Freud's Passover dream and Herzl's drama.

This dream report, together with other dreams and letters, has led a recent critic to speculate on Freud's "Rome neurosis." For Freud, Rome was a place of exile in the Christian era, as Egypt was for Joseph and as Babylon was for Daniel after the fall of the First Temple in Jerusalem. Freud recounts his dream:

As a result of certain events in the city of Rome, it is necessary to evacuate the children, which also takes place. The scene is then in front of a gateway, a double door in the ancient style (the Porta Romana in Sienna, as I am already aware during the dream). I sit on the edge of a fountain and am very dejected, close to tears. A female person—an attendant or nun—brings the two boys out and delivers them to their father, who was not myself. The older of the two is clearly my eldest; I do not

see the face of the other one. The woman who brought out the boy requests a kiss from him in parting. She is remarkable for having a red nose. The boy refuses her the kiss, but while reaching out his hand in parting says: *Auf Geseres,* and to both of us (or to one of us): *Auf Ungeseres.* I have the notion that the latter signifies a preference. (*Td* 426 / *ID* 477–78)

In his first interpretive gesture, Freud provides two literary associations. He mentions *The New Ghetto* and quotes the scriptural words "By the waters of Babylon, we sat and wept." Both allusions conceal as much as they reveal. Nowhere in his interpretation does Freud discuss the play *The New Ghetto,* nor does he even name its author. And although he cites Psalm 137 (from Luther's translation), he never discusses its exilic sentiments.

Freud explicitly states that "this dream is constructed upon a tangle of thoughts which were provoked by a play seen in the theater, *The New Ghetto*" (*Td* 427 / *ID* 478). This remark names an unusual "day's residue" of *thoughts*—rather than characters, images, or events—that were incorporated into the dream. Freud specifies that "the Jewish Question, concern over the future of children to whom one cannot give a fatherland, concern about raising them so that they may become independent [*freizügig*], are easy to recognize in the corresponding dream thoughts" (*Td* 427 / *ID* 478). The present example, which involves dream thoughts that respond to a mental conflict, differs from most instances in which the manifest dream alludes to recent occurrences. Freud cannot have been entirely comfortable with this, because his overarching dream theory conceives the dream as "*the (disguised) fulfillment of a (suppressed, repressed) childhood wish*" (*Td* 175 / *ID* 194). Mature, rational reflections on the Jewish Question should not enter into the latent dream thoughts, and according to Freud, such conscious ideas play an indifferent part in the manifest content. Nevertheless, this particular concern draws from emotional conflicts and from a childhood source: "The dream situation, in which I rescue my children from the city of Rome, is incidentally distorted by its reference back to an analogous occurrence from my childhood. The sense is that I envy relatives who, many years ago, were given an occasion to relocate their children on another soil" (*Td* 429n / *ID* 481n). Freud envies those who escaped earlier with their children.

Freud also mentions a related experience, associated with the mental asylum that he saw in Sienna: "Shortly before the dream I had heard that a person of my faith had to give up his strenuously obtained position at a public mental asylum" (*Td* 427 / *ID* 478). In recalling this event, Freud alludes to the anti-Semitic policies of Karl Lueger, mayor of Vienna from 1897. Herzl's drama and the experience of Freud's acquaintance place in question the standing of Jews in turn-of-the-century Vienna. We know from other contexts that Freud worried about his own prospects and whether they might be hindered by his "Mosaic" descent.

Freud concentrates his interpretive efforts on discovering the significance of the seemingly meaningless words *Auf Geseres* and *Auf Ungeseres*. Confronted by these "absurd" phrases, Freud acts like a classical philologist, but one who subjects his own mental product (rather than an ancient text) to analysis. He also follows the traces left in his dream language, much as etymologists analyze collective linguistic phenomena. Beneath the layer of modern German, taking the place of *Auf Wiedersehen, Auf Geseres* reveals affinities to Yiddish, Aramaic, and Hebrew. Freud's manner of dealing with this linguistic plurality elucidates his relationship to these languages, and his associations indicate his troubled sense of the modern Jewish condition.

In attempting to gloss *Geseres,* Freud does not rely exclusively on his own knowledge. He enigmatically refers to unnamed sources: "According to the information that I have received from biblical scholars, *Geseres* is a genuine Hebrew word, derived from a verb *goiser,* and may be best conveyed by 'commanded suffering, doom.' According to the use of the word in Yiddish [*im Jargon*], one might think it meant 'weeping and wailing'" (*Td* 427 / *ID* 478).

Freud simultaneously claims and disavows knowledge of the Hebrew and Yiddish his dream employs. Through Yiddish, *Geseres* had entered Austrian slang. Freud himself recalls having heard the word used in this way, and he considers one incident a source for the dream: "Many years ago, when this son of Professor M.—who today is an independent thinker—was still in school, he became ill with an eye infection which, the doctor declared, aroused concern. . . . 'Why are you making such a *Geseres?*' he prevailed upon the mother" (*Td* 428 / *ID* 480). The "absurd" *Auf Geseres,* then, echoes an expression meaning "to make a fuss" (*machen ein Geseres*), specifically in relation to an illness of the eyes or a deficiency of vision. The initial "concern over the future of children" reemerges as a concern lest they become shortsighted or one-sided—like the Cyclops. Although Freud suggests that this particular memory is the main impetus for his verbal innovation, his philological observations point to deeper determinants.

Freud begins to gloss *Geseres* by disclaiming responsibility for the explanation: "According to information that I have received from biblical scholars [*Schriftgelehrten*]. . . ." Here the standard English translation is particularly misleading, for it renders *Schriftgelehrten* as "philologists." Had Freud consulted the leading Christian philologist of his time, in fact, he would have discovered that *Geseres* is *not* a "genuine Hebrew word"; it is, rather, an Aramaism. The Aramaic word *gezerah* signifies a decree; by extension, Yiddish *gesere* came to mean "evil decree" and, by association, "misfortune." It derives from the Hebrew root *Gimmel-Zayin-Resh* (meaning to cut or separate). Although Freud attributes his slightly inaccurate information to a rabbinic source, he cannot deny knowing enough to know that his dream employs Judaic materials. Unconsciously, Freud carries an awareness of the Hebrew language, which he learned as a child. He also knows a number of Yiddish words and is familiar with the Passover ritual, one of the few Jewish customs that his parents retained in Vienna. Significantly, the Aramaized meaning of the Hebrew root *Gimmel-Zayin-Resh* occurs in the Passover ritual, when the Maggid recalls that Pharaoh "decreed [*gazar*] only against the males."

In the process of interpreting his dream, Freud evokes the flight from Egypt and the matzoth that Jews eat in memory of the Israelites' hasty departure. He paraphrases: "During their flight from *Egypt,* the children of Israel did not have time to allow their dough to rise, and even today at Easter-time eat unleavened bread in memory of this" (*Td* 427 / *ID* 479). Freud's association derives in part from the similarity he hears between *Ungeseres* and *ungesäuertes Brot,* unleavened bread. What is the meaning, then, of *Auf Geseres* when spoken by Freud's eldest son? Freud himself suggests that his child confirms a theoretical position associated with Wilhelm Fliess by *"acting, as it were, in consideration of bilateral symmetry"* (*Td* 429 / *ID* 480). This far-fetched interpretation screens other meanings. Freud concludes that, in general, "the dream is often most profound where it appears most mad" (ibid.); bizarre elements assume meaning when placed in the context of associations. Yet Freud does not complete his interpretation of *Auf Geseres,* because of his own "myopic" perspective. Placing greater emphasis on the Greek allusion to one-eyed Cyclops, Freud deemphasizes Judaic components.

Freud's one-sided reading of his Passover dream occurs in several stages. From the outset, he diminishes the importance of Herzl's play in producing the dream. Although he writes that this dream "is constructed upon a tangle of thoughts which were provoked by a play," he neither acknowledges its Zionist author nor discusses any aspect of *The New Ghetto.* Prior events may, however, be more than incidental precipitants of the manifest dream content; a dream may respond to recent experiences, as the dream of Irma's injection responds to Freud's (and Fliess's) unfortunate dealings with Emma Eckstein. Dreams do not exclusively represent repressed *childhood* wishes: as contemporary theorists have suggested, the meanings of dreams are often more immediate.

Freud's Passover dream responds both directly and indirectly to Herzl. Because Freud's dream confronts central issues in *The New Ghetto,* the question arises: How does Freud's dream interpret Herzl's play?

On about January 5, 1898, Freud was among the first to see Herzl's play *The New Ghetto* in Vienna. Because Herzl had become known as the organizer of the First Zionist Congress in August 1897, his play naturally awakened Freud's "concern about the future of children to whom one cannot give a fatherland" (*Td* 427 / *ID* 478). Nevertheless, Herzl's early play is not Zionistic; it merely raises the issues that Zionism later sought to resolve.

Herzl's title alludes to several discussions within the play. "The new ghetto," according to the protagonist Jacob Samuel, has invisible walls. In spite of the Jewish Enlightenment, which enabled Jews to leave the old ghetto, another ghetto with subtler boundaries remained. Jacob states that "the ghetto is the separation which I do not want, which pains me and which I am supposed to bear" (II.v.). During the same scene, after Jacob is snubbed by his Christian friend, he paraphrases the message he has received: "Away, Jew! Back to the ghetto!" Throughout the play, Jacob strives to escape this ghetto, implicitly aiming at assimilation as a solution to the Jewish Question. He discovers that this resolution is impossible, however, and is destroyed by his quest.

Jacob Samuel, the protagonist of *The New Ghetto,* is a young and idealistic lawyer who marries at the start of the play. His wife's circle of Jewish financiers contrasts with that of Jacob's non-Jewish university friends. Known to defend workers, Jacob is approached by a representative of the coal miners; he agrees to take on their case as they prepare to strike. Because the coal mine is jointly controlled by Jews and non-Jews, Jacob makes special efforts to prevent a scandal that would result in anti-Semitic retaliations. When he tries to act as mediator, he falls victim in the financial battle between Count Schramm and two Jewish businessmen. Early in the play, a local rabbi anticipates Jacob's death by telling a medieval tale. The legend of Moses of Mainz functions as a parable of the Jewish condition in Europe: "Moses was an honest youth, son of a merchant, and wished to become a scholar. One summer night he sat with the ancient books of our sages and studied. Suddenly he heard a call for help in the night. He leaned out of the windows; it was not in the ghetto. Someone was crying outside, in front of the ghetto. The wailing became ever more horrible. Deeply moved to pity, he stood and went out. . . . When he did not return and his mother was consuming herself in anxiety, she also stood and went out to look for him. . . . The next morning Moses was found stabbed in front of the opened gate to the ghetto, and near the corpse sat his mother, smiling happily. . . . She had become insane" (III.iv.; my ellipses).

In attempting to save a life, Moses of Mainz loses his own. Anti-Semitic murderers lure their victim outside ghetto walls only to murder him. This story corresponds to Jacob's self-perception at the close of Herzl's play. Like Moses, Jacob has sought to be of assistance beyond the ghetto walls and is mortally wounded in a duel with Count Schramm. "Tell the Rabbi," Jacob says on his deathbed, that he has died "like Moses of—Mainz!" (IV.vii.). One may add, in light of the fact that Herzl wrote this play in Paris in 1894, that Count Schramm's anti-Semitic actions resonate with the contemporaneous Dreyfus Affair. Moreover, Jacob follows the example of the biblical Moses, who led the Jews out of their Egyptian servitude, and he consequently falls victim of opponents who wish to prevent Jews from leaving the new ghetto. His final words reaffirm the collective ambition: "Jews, my brothers, one will only allow you to live again—when you. . . . Why are you holding me so tightly? . . . (Murmurs.) I want—out! . . . (Very loudly.) Out—of—the—ghetto!" (IV.viii.; ellipses in original). In responding to the Jewish Question, this play is evidently more assimilationist than Zionist. According to Herzl's drama, however, turn-of-the-century Vienna does not permit Jews to escape the new ghetto. Jacob's struggle to escape, like Moses of Mainz's attempt to save a life, is suicidal. Herzl's play shows his evolving commitment to the Jewish cause, and Freud identified with the predicament of its protagonist.

The social standing of Yiddish in Freud's Vienna is apparent from its place in Herzl's drama: only the rabbi and the unmannered character named Wasserstein use the so-called Jewish *Jargon*. Wasserstein asks whether Jacob Samuel is meshugge enough to refuse his relatives' financial support (I.iii.). Later, anticipating Herzl's Zionist rhetoric, the rabbi refers to God's role in leading the Jews out of *Mizrajim* (I.viii.). Both *me-*

shugge and *Mizrajim* (like *Auf Geseres*) have Hebrew origins but were incorporated into colloquial Viennese speech through Yiddish. Unlike Wasserstein and the rabbi, the more assimilated and educated characters in Herzl's play never lapse into Yiddishisms. Although he adopts the metaphors of Egypt and Zion then, in his later writing Herzl predictably decrees: "The stunted and oppressed *Jargons*, which we now employ—these ghetto languages—we will give up [*abgewöhnen*]." In fact, Yiddish was already a repressed subtext for German-speaking Jews, many of whom had Yiddish-speaking parents, and their language was one of the most complex knots of ambivalence. Hence it is not surprising that Freud's published essays seldom employ Yiddish idioms, whereas his private letters to Martha Bernays in the 1880s and to Wilhelm Fliess in the 1890s contain numerous Yiddish words. The exception among Freud's published papers is *Jokes and Their Relation to the Unconscious (Der Witz und seine Beziehung zum Unbewußten)*, in which Freud analyzes a wide range of Jewish jokes containing Yiddish.

In June 1897, the summer of Herzl's First Zionist Congress, Freud wrote to Wilhelm Fliess: "I'll admit that recently I have been planning a collection of profound Jewish stories." *The Interpretation of Dreams*, published less than three years later, contains some examples and a further reference to Jewish anecdotes that "conceal so much profound and often bitter wisdom about life" (*Td* 206 / *ID* 227). Freud printed the Jewish stories he had been collecting in *Jokes and Their Relation to the Unconscious*, together with other materials that disguise the earlier design. In many respects, the joke book is a second dream book: when studying dreams, Freud resorts to his own dream reports, and when studying wit, he refers to his favorite jokes—those of Jewish popular tradition. His theories demonstrate that both dreams and jokes have a manifest content that conceals deeper meanings, and both employ condensation, displacement, reversal, and wordplay. As Freud wrote fragments of an implicit autobiography based on his dreams, he later sketched scenes from Jewish life and embedded these collective self-portraits in his psychoanalysis of wit.

Freud's jokes and anecdotes characteristically reveal something (a *Tendenz,* or tendentious message) that has been hidden. Much like the dream work, according to Freud, the mechanism of jokes involves a transformation that disguises covert obscenity, aggression, or criticism. A second-order disguise is at work in Freud's discussion of such disguises. If we wish to interpret the concealed layer of meaning in his book on jokes, two passing phrases provide points of departure. When Freud begins to relate Jewish jokes, he apologizes for their source: "We ask for no proof of nobility from our examples; we do not inquire into their descent, but only into their efficacy" (*W* 49 / *J* 49). In another context, Freud regrets that he has not been able to "divest" (*entkleiden*) a story of Yiddish. The socially disadvantaged language recurs at several stages, specifically acknowledged as a source of humor (*W* 103, 108 / *J* 108, 114).

Freud remains somewhat uneasy with the folk humor and Yiddish "Jargon" he embeds in an analysis of mental processes. The suppression of socially inferior Yiddish is apparently integral to one story Freud tells. This joke allows the teller to expose what assimilated Jews have concealed; namely, meaner origins. Presumably a converted Jew, the baroness of this story knows (as did Freud) a smattering of Yiddish:

The doctor, who has been asked to attend the Baroness at her delivery, declares that the moment has not yet come, and therefore suggests to the Baron that they play a game of cards in the neighboring room. After a while the Baroness' cry of pain reaches the ears of the two men. "*Ah mon Dieu, que je souffre!*" The husband leaps up, but the doctor counters, "It's nothing; let's go on playing." A little while later one hears the woman in childbirth again: "*Mein Gott, mein Gott, was für Schmerzen!*"—"Don't you want to go in, Herr Professor?" the Baron asks.—"No, no, it is not yet time."—Finally, from the neighboring room one hears the cry of an unmistakable: "*Ay, vey, vey*"; then the doctor throws down his cards and says, "It's time." (*W* 78 / *J* 81)

Freud only partially analyzes this anecdote. He writes that the woman's pain gradually breaks through the layers of her cultivated manner, until her "original nature" (*ursprüngliche Natur*) finds expression. French culture cedes to German as the pain intensifies, and finally Yiddish slips out. The baroness's origins are revealed, not by an inchoate primitive wail, but by an Eastern European accent; her "original nature" was Jewish. Assimilated Jews may laugh in comfort at this circumstance that acknowledges pretensions and the suppressed past. Freud himself declines to discuss the Yiddish his joke contains; nor does he deal with issues surrounding the assimilated or converted Jew in modern European culture.

Most relevant to the issue of collective identity is a submerged allusion to Zionism. Freud leaves the political and ethnic dimensions untouched when he analyzes this anecdote: "Itzik has been declared fit for the artillery. He is obviously an intelligent fellow, but inflexible and not interested in the post. One of his superiors who is well-inclined toward him takes him aside and says: 'I want to give you a tip: *Buy yourself a cannon and make yourself independent*'" (*W* 56 / *J* 56).

We know that this independent artillery man is Jewish from the Yiddishized form of his name, Itzik. The anecdote plays on stereotypes of Jews' aversion to military service and resistance to authority. Because Itzik cannot subordinate himself to the artillery unit, his superior ironically suggests that he start his own army. This is a patently ridiculous idea, exaggerating the tendency that is evident in Itzik's behavior. While it obliquely satirizes Zionist aspirations, the joke reflects Freud's own concern with independence. In this context, one may recall a post-Freudian witticism that is popular among Yiddishists: "What is the difference between a language and a dialect? A language has an army and a navy." Power and authority have, indeed, always given German priority over Yiddish in Western culture.

In 1905, the Itzik joke assumed special pathos. Many Jewish Socialists participated in the failed revolution of 1905, and following Herzl's death the Zionists continued to struggle for the Jews' political independence in a Jewish homeland. Both the Socialists and the Zionists sought to assert themselves, with or without weapons. In fact, there were almost no Jewish artilleries, not to mention armies or navies, during the period from 135 C.E. until 1948. Instead of military cannons, Jews had only textual canons.

Herzl's early play and later Zionist dream understandably provoked Freud's reflections on the future of his children. In the analysis of his Passover dream, Freud cautiously states that he wishes to raise (*erziehen*) his children in such a way "that they may become independent [*freizügig*]" (*Td* 427). Alexander Grinstein notes that this central phrase may also mean to "become . . . liberal minded." In the standard edition of Freud's works, however, James Strachey translates *freizügig* as being able to "move freely across frontiers" (*ID* 478), which emphasizes the territorial problem of the Jews. This alternate translation resonates with Herzl's play, which also arouses thoughts about Jews' potential freedom to move—beyond the walls of the new ghetto.

At a rare moment in Herzl's play, a Jewish woman addresses herself to an aristocratic non-Jew. Jacob's sister-in-law expresses concern over the upbringing of her children and asks Count Shramm to make inquiries about a certain governess: "I will of course take only a person who has served in good houses. . . . You understand: it's important with children. One really wants to give them a finer education [*Erziehung*]" (I.vii.). She would like her Jewish children to receive the same genteel upbringing as aristocratic Viennese. The non-Jewish governess in question reappears in the Passover dream, perhaps conflated with Freud's own childhood nanny, as the "attendant, nun" who cares for his children in Rome. This passage also recalls the moment when Jacob's mother explains: "I accustomed myself to a better way of speaking than Jewish-German [*Judendeutsch*], so that he [her son] would not have to be ashamed of me" (I.iv.). She thus sets herself apart from the socially backward Wasserstein.

Despite supervision by a Christian attendant, in Freud's dream the eldest son reverts to Yiddish, or at least compounds Viennese German with layers of Yiddish, Aramaic, and Hebrew. Freud's hope that his children may become *freizügig,* independent or liberal-minded, does not mean that they must become Christian. Fulfilling in a disguised manner Jacob Samuel's wish to escape "the new ghetto" of modern anti-Semi-

tism, Freud's children are evacuated from Christian Rome. They benefit from the "finer education" a non-Jewish attendant provides, but they also part from her while expressing a preference for Freud in something like the ancestral mother tongue.

This returns us to the enigmatic words *Auf Geseres* and *Auf Ungeseres*. Freud refuses to read the decree that these words pronounce. He guesses that the Yiddish signifies "weeping and wailing," although *Gezeres* more accurately refers to ordinances or edicts, typically directed against Jews. Gezeres were linguistic events, pronouncements that determined the fate of the European Jewish community. In 1421, for instance, the Vienna *Geserah* led to the execution and expulsion of the Jews. Such a catastrophe in exile pervades the atmosphere of Freud's dream, starting with his allusion to the Babylonian exile as lamented in Psalm 137.

Freud limits his imaginative creation, then, by declining to honor the manifest dream thoughts. As the Babylonian Talmud asserts, "A dream that is not interpreted is like a letter that is not read" (Tractate Berakhot 55b). Although Freud says that he treats the dream as a "holy text" (*Td* 492–93 / *ID* 552), he does not probe the deeper meanings of the *gezerah* his son utters; nor does he discuss his pained sense of the Jews' precarious position in their Viennese exile. Myopic in his own way, Freud chose to underestimate the crisis Herzl perceived and dramatically depicted in *The New Ghetto.*

We must, then, reinterpret the words of Freud's eldest son. Saying *Auf Geseres* and *Auf Ungeseres* means, as Freud himself indicates, allotting leavened bread (*gesäuertes Brot*) to the nun and unleavened bread (*ungesäuertes Brot*) to himself. As if to assert the difference and repudiate assimilationist hopes, Freud's son affirms his awareness of Passover customs. His "finer education" has not eliminated all traces of Jewish tradition. Furthermore, *Auf Geseres* and *Auf Ungeseres* are condensations of fuller statements that might read: *Auf Ihnen—Geseres,* "Upon you [nun]—decrees," and *Auf dir—Ungeseres,* "Upon you [father]—the negation of decrees." The son's supposed consciousness of bilateral symmetry might then emerge as an awareness of Jewish-Christian antipathies. Freud's dream further responds to the Jewish Question by recalling both a history of persecution and the central ritual of Jewish memory, the Passover Seder. In his assimilated Viennese context, however, Freud never employs the word *Passah* (or *Pesach*), but instead refers to Passover as *Osterzeit,* Easter-time. This linguistic quirk aptly reflects Freud's cultural dilemma, which demands euphemistic self-denials. In any case, Freud gives meaning to his apparently meaningless verbal combination by associating it with the Jewish practice of eating unleavened bread in memory of the Exodus. This association is all the more reason for his concern that his children become independent.

Freud's Passover dream represents and responds to the uneasy position of assimilated Jews in turn-of-the-century Vienna. Confronted by anti-Semitic policies such as those of Karl Lueger, the post-Enlightenment version of ancient and medieval gezeres, Freud's dream work sought a solution. At the same time, repressed Yiddish and Hebrew signifiers remained present, awaiting expression. Because it was impossible to escape "the new ghetto," as Herzl's play showed dramatically, Freud's dream found a linguistic compromise. In the dream, his son employs an "absurd" expression that posits continuity with the Jewish condition and ritual, and which casts him as an opponent of persecution. This act and its consequences differentiates Freud's son from Freud's father, whose public humiliation Freud never forgot (*Td* 208 / *ID* 230).

Before his marriage, Freud considered conversion but remained a Jew. In Herzl's play, this path is represented by a Dr. Bichler who has attempted to escape "the new ghetto" through conversion. The ingenuous Emanuel Wasserstein asks why he converted, to which Dr. Bichler responds, "What I did is the individual solution of the question. . . . Or rather, an attempt at a solution. . . . For—between us—it solves nothing" (I.i.). Freud apparently also reached this conclusion.

Freud experienced ambivalence toward the antithetical options of assimilation and separatism that Herzl presents in his early play. *The New*

Ghetto initially aims at the former solution to the Jewish Question; on his deathbed, Jacob still cries out that he wants to escape the ghetto. In spite of his and others' efforts at assimilation, however, the problematic separation remains. The story of Moses of Mainz epitomizes the hazardous position of European Jews: a single step beyond ghetto walls may expose one to murder. The technical "bilateral symmetry" Freud discusses might, hence, suggest a delicate balance between Christianity and Judaism. His dream of *Auf Geseres* and *Auf Ungeseres* neither cedes to the assimilationist temptation nor embraces Herzl's Zionism. The Passover dream confronts contemporary perceptions of the Jewish exile and, in the absence of a Moses to lead the return to Palestine, seeks an elusive equilibrium.

Bibliography

References to Sigmund Freud's *Die Traumdeutung* (*Td*) are in the edition of the *Studienausgabe,* ed. Alexander Mitscherlich, Angela Richards, James Strachey, vol. 2 (Frankfurt a. M.: S. Fischer, 1972). Although the translations are my own, for the benefit of the English reader I include corresponding page references to *The Interpretation of Dreams* (*ID*), trans. James Strachey (New York: Avon, 1965). Freud's *Der Witz und seine Beziehung zum Unbewußten* (*W*) was originally translated into English by A. A. Brill as *Wit and Its Relation to the Unconscious* (New York: Moffat, Yard, 1916); it later appeared as *Jokes and Their Relation to the Unconscious* (*J*). All quotations in the present context are based on the German text contained in the *Studienausgabe,* ed. Alexander Mitscherlich, Angela Richards, James Strachey, vol. 4 (Frankfurt a. M.: S. Fischer, 1970). Translations are my own; page numbers refer first to the German edition and then to the corresponding pages of *Jokes and Their Relation to the Unconscious,* trans. James Strachey (New York: Norton, 1963). See also the following references.

Harold Bloom, "Freud: Frontier Concepts, Jewishness, and Interpretation," *American Imago* 48 (1991): 135–52; José Brunner, "The (Ir)Relevance of Freud's Jewish Identity to the Origins of Psychoanalysis," *Psychoanalysis and Contemporary Thought* 14 (1991): 655–84; Jerry V. Diller, *Freud's Jewish Identity: A Case Study in the Impact of Ethnicity* (Rutherford, N.J.: Fairleigh Dickinson University Press, 1991); Ken Frieden, *Freud's*

Dream of Interpretation (Albany: State University of New York Press, 1990); Sander L. Gilman, *The Case of Sigmund Freud* (Baltimore, Md.: Johns Hopkins University Press, 1993); Gilman, *Freud, Race, and Gender* (Princeton, N.J.: Princeton University Press, 1993); Gerard Haddad, *L'enfant illégitime: Sources talmudiques de la psychanalyse* (Paris: Point hors ligne, 1990); Ulla Haselstein, "Poets and Prophets: The Hebrew and the Hellene in Freud's Cultural Theory," *German Life and Letters* 45 (1992): 50–65; Jacques Le Rider, *Modernité viennoise et crises de l'identité* (Paris: Presses Universitaires de France, 1990), 197–222; and Yosef Hayim Yerushalmi, *Freud's Moses: Judaism Terminable and Interminable* (New Haven: Yale University Press, 1991).

KEN FRIEDEN

1901   Nineteen-year-old Stefan Zweig publishes his first volume of poetry

Stefan Zweig's mother came from a bankers' family that lived in Hohenems, Austria. She had grown up in Ancona, Italy, and therefore spoke Italian fluently. His father, Moriz Zweig, owned a textile factory at Liberec (Reichenberg), today Czechia, but managed his enterprise from his Vienna office, knew English and French, and is said to have played piano fairly well. He was typical of the Viennese-Jewish fin-de-siècle bourgeoisie. Somewhat younger than Arthur Schnitzler and Hugo von Hofmannsthal, Stefan Zweig grew up in late-nineteenth-century Vienna. It was a city that had changed its face since the middle of the century, above all in the construction of the impressive *Ringstraße,* which had replaced the medieval wall, and in the building of the two great museums, the house of parliament, the city hall, the university, and the cultural jewels of the new Vienna—the Hofoper and the Hofburgtheater.

On the one hand Vienna in the course of the late nineteenth century had gained openness and had become a melting pot of the nationalities gathered in the Austro-Hungarian monarchy; on the other hand, there was a growing anti-Semitism and xenophobia. Zweig barely recognized this in his world of childhood privilege, as he revealed in his autobiography *The World of Yesterday (Die Welt von Gestern).* He was developing a mania for German (including Austrian) and international literature while being bored in his classes in classical literature at the Wasa Gymnasium in the capital's ninth district, a district with a comparatively high percentage of upper-middle-class Jewish pupils.

Young Stefan used to spend his afternoons in coffeehouses reading French, British, and German magazines such as the *Mercure de France* and the *Burlington Magazine.* At the age of nineteen he published his first works, among them a volume of lyrics, *Silberne Saiten* (1901). In the same year a novella, *Im Schnee* (Escape), found its way into print in the newspaper *Die Welt* (Vienna) and was reprinted in Berthold Feiwels's *Jüdischer Almanach* in 1904. It is a tale about the imagined life among the Jews in the East. The inhabitants of an Eastern European shtetel are warned that they might be invaded by rioters and that they should prepare themselves to resist. But they are too frightened, and while fleeing from the anticipated pogrom they freeze to death. Such images of the weak Jew as victim were located by Austrian writers of the time, such as Karl Emil Franzos, in this fabled world of the Eastern Jew.

Like other second sons of the Vienna's Jewish bourgeoisie, Stefan Zweig continued his efforts to assimilate into Viennese society by concentrating on culture and science. Both father and son were frequent customers of the Burgtheater and other theaters. When the famous actress Charlotte Wolter died, the whole family fell into deep mourning, indicating the important role the world of theater played also in the emotional life of the Viennese-Jewish bourgeoisie. Zweig studied French literature and philosophy at the capital's university, spending one semester in Berlin. Although his main interests were already writing poetry and prose, he finished his studies with a dissertation on the French positivist philosopher Hippolyte Taine.

Having satisfied his parents by getting an academic degree, "Dr." Zweig concentrated fully on writing poems, dramas, narrative texts, and feuilletons and was a prominent contributor to Vienna's best-known liberal paper *Die Neue Freie Presse*. He became "a model and victim of the impressionistic lifestyle of the fin de siècle" (Daviau 1986). It remains uncertain how much Zweig was encouraged to write feuilletons by Theodor Herzl, who was the founder of the Zionist movement and then a leading journalist in Vienna. As a writer, Zweig tried to gain wider knowledge and experience by traveling. He not only went to places in such Western European countries as Germany, France, and Belgium but also traveled to India and New York. Devoting one's life to literature for Zweig also included an intensification of powerful emotional and personal relations with other writers. He developed a love for the works of the Belgian author Emile Verhaeren. He translated his works, wrote a book on him, and even tried to copy his elder colleague's "Bejahung," a philosophical concept Verhaeren had created to master his crisis while being ill in London.

Zweig also established close contacts with the Swedish educator Ellen Key, with the Belgian wood engraver Frans Masereel, and with the famed Viennese Jewish *Jugendstil* illustrator Ephraim Moses Lilien. Because of the Viennese emphasis on drama as the highest form of art, Zweig tried to make his way in the theater; like many other Austrian authors before him, he was eager to have his work performed at the Burgtheater. He succeeded—his play *Das Haus am Meer* found its way on to this world-famous stage in 1912. Yet although he wrote plays until the end of his life, Zweig's main field in literature definitely was not drama. It became apparent as his career continued that he was a gifted narrator and that it would be his fiction that would earn his fame.

After 1910 Zweig found a new friend and mentor, the French author Romain Rolland, who later won the Nobel Prize for Literature. He was impressed by the French author's literary efforts, especially by his novel *Jean Christophe*. Rolland had intended this novel to transcend the national borders between the German and the French. Meanwhile Zweig had become a famous author himself: a volume of novellas, *Erstes Erlebnis: Geschichten aus Kinderland* (1911) had impressed both critics and the reading public. Yet World War I destroyed the world Zweig was used to, and above all the Austro-Hungarian monarchy. In summer 1914, at the outbreak of the war, he was to be found among the chauvinist propagandists. But by early 1915, having been sent as a special agent to Galicia (today western Ukraine) to collect pamphlets the Russian army had left after its withdrawal, he was shocked to learn what cruelties the soldiers had committed against the Jewish population.

In the same year he started writing his antiwar drama, *Jeremias*. Zweig remained in Vienna and lived with the writer Friderike von Winternitz; it has to be assumed that she, who later became his wife, influenced him in changing his mind about war. Once, on a short trip to Salzburg, they discovered the Paschingerschlößl on the Kapuzinerberg and decided to buy the estate for postwar times. But still he was obliged to write "patriotic" stories ("Heldenfrisieren") every day until 3:00 P.M. at the Kriegsarchiv, after which he went home and continued his work on *Jeremias*. Knowledge about Zweig's pacifist efforts, especially concerning his play, impressed some and appalled many. In 1917 Zweig, accompanied by Friderike von Winternitz, was allowed to move to Switzerland as a special correspondent of the *Neue Freie Presse* as well as to assist in rehearsing the setting of *Jeremias*. The first performance of the play was to take place at the Zürcher Schauspielhaus in February 1918, when World War I was still far from its end.

Returning from Switzerland into small postwar Austria for the couple meant changing their domicile from Vienna to Salzburg. Soon afterward, Zweig and Friderike (whose last name had since changed to Burger, after her divorce from Felix von Winternitz) married. Stefan dedicated himself to peace and to the unification of Europe, by writing and giving lectures, and Friderike contributed to these causes by organizing meetings of a women's league. During this period Zweig became world famous as a narrator and as an author of portraits of famous men in literature such as *Drei Meister: Balzac—Dickens—Dostojewski* (Three masters; 1921, Eng. trans. 1930) and *Drei Dichter ihres Lebens: Casanova—Stendhal—Tolstoi* (Adepts in self-portraiture; 1928, Eng. trans. 1928), as well as psychology—*Die Heilung durch den Geist: Franz Anton Mesmer—Mary Baker-Eddy—Sigmund Freud* (Mental healers; 1931, Eng. trans. 1932). He took his figures from different European nations in each of these volumes.

The twenties brought Zweig a surge of literary and financial success, but only marginal acceptance in the town where he lived. Salzburg, which had become a festival site dominated by Max Reinhardt and Hugo von Hofmannsthal, had gained an international flair in the summertime. It was dull and packed with a conservative Catholicism the rest of the year. Zweig suffered from being ignored by the city, its festival, and the festival crowds, and in the summers he tried to escape from Salzburg by traveling abroad or by withdrawing to Thumersbach, a cozy place near Zell am See about sixty miles away from his home. Yet on the whole he was very content living in his Paschingerschlößl on the hillside of Salzburg's Kapuzinerberg, which was much more a representative residence than an ordinary house, being shadowed by a wood but still only five minutes to walk to the Basar, his favorite café downtown. He spent his days not only writing literature but also dictating an enormous number of letters—in the process probably neglecting his wife and his two stepdaughters more and more.

The author claimed that the position of Salzburg in the net of European railways had been one of the main reasons for his decision to live there. Now he intensified his traveling activities into Western Europe, where he met with friends, read his works in public, and lectured about the efforts for peace. The first translation of his complete works was into Russian, with a preface by Maxim Gorky. Rabindranath Tagore, Eugen Relgis,

publisher Anton Kippenberg, Romain Rolland of course, and many others visited the Zweigs in their "Villa Europa," as the house on the Kapuzinerberg began to be called. Zweig started acting as a mentor for authors of the young generation by arranging translations, providing publishers, or simply encouraging them to keep writing.

Toward the end of the twenties Austria and especially the Weimar Republic approached a critical stage that left little room for ideas for a united and democratic Europe. On the one hand Zweig reacted to this development with a romantic biography entitled *Joseph Fouché: Bildnis eines politischen Menschen* (Joseph Fouché: The portrait of a politician; 1929, Eng. trans. 1930), which was written as a warning against the rising National Socialist Party. But the Nazis, as Zweig himself stated in *Die Welt von Gestern,* read that book with enthusiasm and found Fouché an interesting person.

Two of the heroes of his subsequent biographies were royal heroines: *Marie Antoinette: Bildnis eines mittleren Charakters* (Marie Antoinette: Portrait of an average woman; 1932, Eng. trans. 1933) and *Maria Stuart* (Mary, queen of Scotland and the Isles and the queen of Scots; 1935, Eng. trans. 1935). Sexuality and partnership played a much more important role in these works than in Zweig's corresponding writing about men. In the scenes depicting the relations between partners, where Zweig shows his special biographic technique most convincingly. The writer comments on situations by comparing them with similar episodes throughout history and in an Olympian fashion claims inside knowledge of intimate detail and emotion. Critics have called this manner a "keyhole perspective." It is significant that *Triumph und Tragik des Erasmus von Rotterdam* (1934; Erasmus; Erasmus of Rotterdam) was the last manuscript Zweig could and would publish with Insel-Verlag. It is interesting that he chose as the subject for this work Erasmus, the great humanist, who would not take anyone's part in the conflict of Catholics and Protestants—although it is hard not to recognize Adolf Hitler in Zweig's portrait of Martin Luther in the same volume.

The intensity and complexity of the relationship between Zweig and Kippenberg has been known for only a few years. The latest scholarship reveals Zweig's role not only as the more important author of the team but also as the more important mediator in the acquisition of manuscripts and translations. The end of the collaboration must have been painful for Kippenberg, and even more so for Zweig. Kippenberg changed to a small publisher in Vienna, Herbert Reichner. Zweig, continuing his part as a manager in the business of literature, discovered young Elias Canetti and others. In *Castellio gegen Calvin: Oder, ein Gewissen gegen die Gewalt* (The right to heresy: Castellio against Calvin; 1936, Eng. trans. 1936), Castellio, the hero, tries to resist the dictator, Calvin, but finally is burned at the stake. Commenting on both the *Erasmus* and the *Castellio* in a letter to Joseph Roth, Zweig stated that the hesitating Erasmus was the man he was and that the upright Castellio was the man he would have liked to be.

Zweig's two-volume work about the French novelist Honoré de Balzac has to be viewed apart from Zweig's other biographical work, because the nineteenth-century master had fascinated and disturbed him almost since the beginning of his life and would continue to do so until Zweig's death. *Balzac* (1946) was completed posthumously by his friend Richard Friedenthal.

Men in history who had left Europe behind and continued Christopher Columbus's efforts in discovering the world increasingly began to occupy Zweig's mind. Toward the end of the decade this fascination may be seen from the titles of the biographies he wrote during these years: *Magellan: Der Mann und seine Tat* (Conqueror of the seas: The story of Magellan; Magellan, pioneer of the Pacific; 1938, Eng. trans. 1938) and *Amerigo: Die Geschichte eines historischen Irrtums* (1944; Amerigo: A comedy of errors in history, 1942). The two discoverers, like Zweig some centuries later, had left Europe and had gone westward, to Ibero-America.

Zweig also wrote novellas full of tension and exotic flair during the period between the two wars. Delving into the human psyche, especially into the psyche of women, Zweig created characters who were driven to passion and despair. The hero of *Der Amokläufer* (Amok; 1927) is a German medical doctor in India. He falls desperately in love with a lady who asked him to perform an abortion and indirectly causes her death. Accompanying her coffin on a sailing vessel, he tells his story to the narrator in the darkness of a tropical night. *Verwirrung der Gefühle. Private Aufzeichnungen des Geheimrates R.* (Confusion of sentiments; 1927) deals with a triangular relation between a homosexual professor, his wife, and one of his students. *Vierundzwanzig Stunden aus dem Leben einer Frau* (Twenty-four hours in the life of a woman; 1927) brings to life a middle-aged woman who is surprised by her own outbreak of passion. *Kleine Chronik,* a small volume of narrative texts, belongs to the same period and is no less interesting than the well-known novellas. The texts that appear in that book focus on a few men who failed to rise to the challenges of the postwar world. Knowing Zweig, it is not astonishing that most of these men are Jewish. In one of these brief texts, the narrator pays a visit to a collector of antiquities he has known for a long time. In post–World War I Germany the collector, who has become almost blind, has realized neither the German loss of Alsace and Lorraine nor the loss of the war and his antiquities: his family has sold his valuables piece by piece to provide for their basic needs and has replaced them with worthless copies (The invisible collection; *Die unsichtbare Sammlung,* 1929, earlier in *Neue Freie Presse,* 1925).

In *Buchmendel* (1929), it almost seems as if Zweig had intended to write a caricature of himself. The Jewish hero, because he has emigrated from Russia years before the outbreak of the war, does not read papers or even possess an identity card, and seems to live apart from place, time, and regulations. Jakob Mendel is a living universal bibliography who does nothing except deal with second-hand books in one of Vienna's cafés; yet by denying the existence of politics, he gets involved with the authorities during World War I, is taken into a civilian camp, and lives and dies in deplorable conditions.

The "Geheime Kommissionsrat" Salomonsohn, another of Zweig's creations (*Untergang eines Herzens,* 1929), does not survive his encounter with modern European society inside his family: his Jewish wife and daughter are both intent on assimilating and modify accordingly their general behavior as well as their sexual and moral actions. The old man turns away from his family to work, silence, and religion and dies from an operation.

Zweig himself was different from most of his literary figures in the *Kleine Chronik*. He was coping with the new situation: the New World on the other side of the Atlantic started opening for him. During the early thirties his works were translated into Spanish (in Argentina) and into Portuguese (in Brazil). In *Sternstunden der Menschheit: Fünf historische Miniaturen* (The tide of fortune; 1927, Eng. trans. 1940, rev. ed. 1943) Zweig collected important moments in the history of civilization as a way of providing a counterweight to the aggressive tendencies of war literature and Nazi politics. The range of these collections reaches from the conquest of Constantinople to Napoleon's Waterloo to Walter Scott's expedition to the South Pole. Most of these little stories deal not with victors and victories but with losers and defeats. The *Sternstunden* used to be read regularly in German secondary schools, but in recent times their Eurocentric conception has been criticized.

After the Nazi Party seized power in Germany in January 1933, Zweig was shocked but thought his fame would protect him. His books were banned like those of many others, however, and were burned at the first Nazi book burning on April 1933. In Austria the conservatives had dismissed the parliament and were turning into a fascist government. The Nazi takeover in Germany spread its shadows also over Salzburg, only a few miles away from the German-Austrian border. Due to these political developments as well as to his private situation, Zweig moved to London in the fall of 1933.

Zweig was conscious that a German occupation of Austria was a mere question of time. Moreover, the *Stürmer* portrayed Zweig as being one of the arch-Semitic physiognomic prototypes. In spite of this discrimination, Zweig renewed his collaboration with Richard Strauss, president of Third Reich's chamber music, and

wrote the libretto *Die schweigsame Frau*. As has recently been discovered, Zweig even continued his collaboration with the composer after the Nazis seized power: two more librettos for Strauss, officially signed by Joseph Gregor, were in reality written mostly by Gregor's friend Stefan Zweig.

Zweig not only had written thousands of letters to writers, painters, politicians, composers, and others by his fiftieth birthday but also had received even more. He had sent a collection of his autographs to the Jewish Library at Jerusalem in January 1934. This indicates that he had already planned to emigrate from Salzburg to London at this time. The depiction by some of Zweig's biographers that the writer left Austria because the police had searched his Salzburg house for weapons in February 1934 thus has to be doubted. In fact, there is no proof of Zweig's intentions except Zweig's own version—a version that turned out to be very useful for brushing up his slightly damaged reputation, especially among his strictly anti-fascist French friends.

In London, Zweig lived with his former secretary Lotte Altmann. When Nazi air raids started striking the city, the couple retired to the rural and ancient Roman town of Bath in Somerset. The fact that he was rated as an "enemy alien B" for some time, simply because he had been an Austrian citizen, depressed Zweig deeply. During his stay in London, his Salzburg estate was expropriated by the Nazis. Stefan and Lotte Zweig became citizens of the British empire soon afterward, a rather rare exception, and they of course were given British passports. But the proximity of war in Britain, the interference of British authorities, and last but not least the Brazilian offer of a permanent visa for Zweig, convinced Zweig to continue his emigration into the New World.

Because of his move, Zweig had to cancel his contract with the publisher with whom he had been cooperating for almost three decades, Anton Kippenberg and his Insel- Verlag. Yet he continued to write intensively: a series of big biographies, the best known perhaps being *Triumph und Tragik des Erasmus von Rotterdam;* the novel *Ungeduld des Herzens* (Beware of pity; 1938); and a legend, *Der begrabene Leuchter* (The buried candelabrum; 1937, Eng. trans. 1937). In 1936 Stefan Zweig had attended the PEN world congress in Buenos Aires and had also paid a visit to Rio de Janeiro, where he had been welcomed heartily by members of the government. In 1941, when Nazi air raids struck Great Britain, he remembered his Brazilian permanent visa and moved to Petropolis with his second wife, Lotte.

Stefan and Lotte lived in a small house in Petropolis, the former residence of the Brazilian emperors, about fifty miles from Rio de Janeiro, in the hills. The Zweigs lived alone, cut off from Stefan's beloved Europe and from many friends: Joseph Roth had died in Paris before the Nazi conquest, Ernst Weiss had committed suicide when the German armies marched into the city, and Romain Rolland was far away in the literal and the personal sense. Zweig was very pessimistic about the further development of the world war. He went to Rio very rarely, and only for a few hours each time. The few friends he had in his final resort were Jewish, among them his Brazilian publisher, Abrao Koogan, and his lawyer, Bernard Malamud. For Zweig, finding his way into new surroundings always had entailed reading, investigating, and finally writing about the new situation. So when he was encouraged by President Getulio Vargas, fascist dictator of Brazil and an admirer of Zweig, to write a book on Brazil, he started this work immediately and tried to get a quick look at northern parts of the country by hopping from town to town by airplane.

The book (*Brasilien: Land der Zukunft*), however, was not a success. Zweig had meant to praise the country by pointing to its history, its picturesque and exotic glamour, and its racial integration. But the Brazilians had expected more emphasis on the growing industry of a "modern" Brazil, and critics from outside, especially from the United States, complained that Zweig had missed an opportunity to analyze the undemocratic character of the regime. After the Japanese took over Singapore, he dreamed that the nightmare of the war would soon seize South America. Zweig fell into despair and in 1942 committed suicide together with Lotte. The Brazilian government arranged a state funeral for the couple.

Certainly Zweig cannot be considered a Zionist or even a writer who had been constantly aware of his Jewish identity. But in a sort of tangential movement Zweig approached (or was approached by) very conscious Jewish writers, artists, and thinkers such as Martin Buber, Walter Rathenau, and Hermann Broch; he also revealed some sympathy for the forthcoming state in Palestine. In addition, he was confronted with the persecution of Jews in Galicia and in the Third Reich. Despite his yearning for assimilation, the rise of the Nazi regime had made Zweig realize that his Jewish identity counted much more in the eyes of the dominant powers than he had ever thought. After 1945 Zweig remained a popular author all over the world, especially in France and the United States, but also in the Soviet Union, China, and Japan. It may be due to his book on Brazil and to his suicide that his popularity has suffered in this very Catholic country and is only now beginning to revive. To determine Zweig's popularity within the German-speaking countries, one has to distinguish between the reading public and the critics and academic scholars. Zweig has continued to be read but has been widely ignored in the field of literary criticism.

Bibliography

Donald Daviau, ed., *Stefan Zweig, Paul Zech Briefe, 1910–42* (Frankfurt a. M.: Fischer, 1986); Mark Gelber and Klaus Zelewitz, eds., *Stefan Zweig: Exil und die Suche nach dem Weltfrieden* (Riverside, Calif.: Ariadne, 1995); Randolph J. Klawiter, *Stefan Zweig: An International Bibliography* (Riverside, Calif.: Ariadne, 1991); Donald A. Prater, *Stefan Zweig: Das Leben eines Ungeduldigen* (Munich: Hanser, 1981); Stefan Zweig, *Brasilien: Ein Land der Zukunft* (Stockholm: Bermann-Fischer, 1941); Zweig, *Erstes Erlebnis: Geschichten aus Kinderland* (Leipzig: Insel, 1911); Zweig, *Jeremias* (Leipzig: Insel, 1917); Zweig, *Kleine Chronik* (Leipzig: Insel, 1929); Zweig, *Der begrabene Leuchter* (Vienna: Herbert Reichner, 1937); Zweig, *Die Welt von Gestern* (Stockholm: Bermann-Fischer, 1937).

KLAUS ZELEWITZ

1903 Gustav Mahler launches a new production of *Tristan und Isolde,* Otto Weininger commits suicide shortly after his *Geschlecht und Charakter* is published, and Max Nordau advocates the development of a "muscle Jewry"

In 1903, Gustav Mahler and Otto Weininger undertook actions that today appear paradigmatic for the late-nineteenth-century Jewish reception of Wagner and Nietzsche in the German-speaking world in general, and in Vienna in particular. Mahler, with his Nietzschean Third Symphony completed, and having converted to Catholicism in order to be named director of the Vienna Opera in 1897, launched a new production of Wagner's *Tristan und Isolde,* and thereby became one of the most prominent Jewish artists (for Viennese society continued to regard him as such) of the Austro-Hungarian Empire to actively champion both Nietzsche's and Wagner's works. Weininger—whose misogynist and anti-Semitic *Geschlecht und Charakter* (Sex and character), penned under the sway of Nietzsche's and Wagner's writings, constituted the publishing event of the year—took his life only a few months after his book's appearance in the house of Wagner's beloved German forebear, Beethoven. Thus, these men, both avid Wagnerites and admirers of Nietzsche, embraced the only two options that Wagner had implied were available to the modern Jew in his infamous essay "Das Judentum in der Musik" (Jewishness in music; 1850). In his concluding remarks, Wagner claimed that the solution to the tension between Germans and Jews lay in the Jew's *Untergang,* a term that, because of its evocative vagueness, could mean either assimilation or death (Wagner 1911, 13:29). However translated, its message was clear: Jewishness for Wagner, and for the Wagnerites that followed, had to "go under," to be abandoned, given up, and eradicated. At the turn of the twentieth century, virtually no Jew in German-speaking Europe could ignore the interpretation of his "race" that Wagner's writings and works had so forcefully promulgated in his society, nor those of his philosopher friend and rebellious acolyte, whose writings, though critical of Wagner, were imbued nonetheless with the repertoire of images from a culture that labeled the Jew a degenerate, a dangerous parasite, and the German's racial opposite.

In a host of public pronouncements and in his aesthetic writings and social criticism—especially "Das Judentum in der Musik," "Was ist deutsch?" (What is German? 1865, first published in 1878), "Aufklärungen über 'Das Judentum in der Musik'" (Elucidations on "Jewishness in music"; 1869), "Modern" (1878), "Wollen wir hoffen?" (Shall we hope? 1879), and the addenda to "Religion und Kunst" (Religion and art), "Heldentum und Christentum," and "Erkenne dich selbst" (Heroism and Christianity, and Know thyself; both 1881), Wagner made it clear that he viewed Jews as a pernicious influence on the modern world, an influence responsible for a purported loss of communal spirit through the forces of industrialization and through the financial institutions the anti-Semitic imagination so closely associated with those it despised. In

"Was ist deutsch?" Wagner characterized the position of Jews in German society as an "invasion of [the] German essence by an utterly alien element" (Wagner 1983, 10:91), and in "Das Judentum in der Musik" he described the Jew in terms gleaned from a pervasive repertoire of anti-Semitic imagery deeply entrenched within nineteenth-century European society: "In everyday life the Jew strikes us first of all by his external appearance which, no matter what European nationality we belong to, has something unpleasantly foreign to this nationality: we desire instinctively to have nothing to do with a person who looks like that" (Wagner 1911, 13:11).

Central to his critique of Jews was Wagner's association of the foreigner with what he perceived to be the failings of the modern age, which were characterized for him within the aesthetic realm by the shortcomings of modernism: a purported lack of rootedness within the community; emphasis on the individual over the collective; the arbitrary exchangeability of the particular within the whole belying an organic cohesiveness that would justify the individual (in the *völkisch* society) or the aesthetic detail (in the work of art); and a decay, nervousness, and degeneration typical for Wagner of both the physiological makeup of the Jew and, metaphorically, of the modern work of art furthered by the institutions (such as the Grand Opéra) of the Jewish culture industry. These beliefs formed the basis for the characterization of his own works as "total art works" (*Gesamtkunstwerke*) and "art works of the future," as opposed to the mediocre products of the modern age made up of disparate, particularized details reflecting the heterogeneity of a multiracial and supranational modern audience.

Many of Wagner's celebrated works for the stage were understood in his own time to convey metaphorically these ideas, for despite their settings in myth and legend, they contain obvious parodies of Jews based on the repertoire of anti-Semitic imagery of his age. Such popular imagery functioned as a vehicle to represent Wagner's critique of the modern world as controlled by Judaized culture. This is precisely how both Weininger and Mahler understood *Siegfried,* the third drama of the *Ring* cycle. In *Geschlecht und Charak-* *ter* Weininger described the figure of the young Teutonic hero as "the most un-Jewish thing imaginable" (408), and just five years earlier Mahler had penned a letter to Natalie Bauer-Lechner in which he claimed that "No doubt with Mime [the Nibelung dwarf in the drama whom Siegfried murders], Wagner intended to ridicule the Jews (with all their characteristic traits— petty intelligence and greed—the jargon is textually and musically so cleverly suggested)" (quoted in de la Grange 1973, 1:482). When *Die Meistersinger von Nürnberg* was first performed in Mannheim and Vienna, the Jewish communities of both cities protested vehemently because they recognized in the figure of Beckmesser in particular, and in Wagner's works in general, a derisive attack on the Jewish race (Cosima Wagner 1978– 80, 1:120; Fischer-Dieskau 1974, 64). Thus, already in the nineteenth century, Wagner's controversial and increasingly popular musical dramas had become signs in the collective public imagination—and especially in the Jewish community—for his racism and German nationalism.

Because so much of the music of *Die Meistersinger* and the *Ring* constituted parodies of purportedly Jewish speech patterns and physiology, it was often difficult for Wagner's audience— both German and Jew alike—to divorce Wagner's aesthetic production from the traits that for him defined the Jew. Already in 1876 Heinrich Porges, a sycophantic, exceedingly devoted Jewish Wagnerite, had written a detailed account of the rehearsals for the first complete performance of the *Ring* at Bayreuth in which he drew attention to the felicity of Wagner's racist parodies (Porges 1983, 30, 82). Nietzsche's polemics against Wagner—especially in *Der Fall Wagner* (The case of Wagner; 1888) and *Nietzsche contra Wagner* (1888)—excoriated the composer for his anti-Semitism and leveled against him the very criticisms Wagner had directed at the Jews: Nietzsche called Wagner's works decadent, nervous, degenerate, and quintessentially modernist (Nietzsche 1967–95, 6:3, 4, 15–23). When Nietzsche implied that Wagner's father may have been a Jew (not Carl Friedrich Wilhelm Wagner, but Ludwig Heinrich Christian Geyer, whom

Wagner's mother married nine months after the death of her first husband and whom the composer suspected of being a Jew), he was not only posthumously exploiting a fear of Wagner's, but perpetuating, perhaps unwittingly, the cultural assumption of Jewish identity as inferior (6:3, 35n.). Following Nietzsche's lead, Weininger, himself suffering from the "Jewishness" of his body, his being, and his art, viewed the works of the Teutonic composer he so revered as evincing purportedly Jewish traits, as he made clear in *Geschlecht und Charakter:* "But even Richard Wagner—the deepest anti-Semite—is not innocent when it comes to undertones of Jewishness, even in his art, though indisputably he, next to Michelangelo, is the greatest artist of all time, though most likely he represents for all mankind the artist per se. . . . Thus, even his music . . . can be accused of containing aspects that are obnoxious, loud, and vulgar" (408). Such passages suggest that both Wagner's admirers and detractors based their arguments on a common cultural vocabulary that viewed Germans and Jews as fundamental opposites, and the Jew as inferior.

Some intellectuals, beginning with Nietzsche, took the attack one step further and sought to deride not only Wagner, but his followers as well (including Jews) by maintaining not only that the very features Wagner had characterized as Jewish were discernible in his own aesthetic production but that these failings also explained the attraction he held for the "sick" and "decadent" masses who championed his works. In *Der Fall Wagner* Nietzsche had claimed that a degenerate pallor was a characteristic feature of the composer's admirers: "Just look at these youths—rigid, pale, breathless! These are the Wagnerians" (Nietzsche 1967–95, 6:3, 23). Max Nordau's famous *Entartung* (Degeneration; 1892) had characterized Wagner's and Nietzsche's works as symptomatic of their own physiological and spiritual degeneration, and though he was extremely critical of Nietzsche, Nordau repeated the philosopher's remarks when he argued that the "degenerate," and indeed even "insane," followers of Wagner were attracted to his music dramas, especially to *Tristan* and *Parsifal,* because they "agitated the mind" (Emmerlin 1990, 205–8). Such

an explanation made sense even to those it affected, such as Weininger, who accepted Wagner's anti-Semitism, recognized traits of Jewishness in the German composer's musical dramas, and believed himself to be irredeemably afflicted with the curse of the Jewish race, which constituted, for him, a spiritual and aesthetic disease made manifest in the inferior makeup of his physiology. Weininger's discourse even characterizes such inferiority as "feminine," and thereby takes up a motif discernible in Wagner and Nietzsche. Wagner's racist image of the male Jew harbored the antithetical notions of the foreigner as sexually rapacious and, at the same time, as effeminate and inferior—notions that are represented on the one hand by the figure of the Nibelung dwarf Alberich and on the other by the high-voiced roles of Beckmesser and Mime. This conflation of the feminine and the Jew was also central to the vocabulary of anti-Semitism found in Nietzsche's life and works, as seen in *Die Geburt der Tragödie* (The birth of tragedy; 1872), and to the culture of the early twentieth century that received both men's writings (Nietzsche 1967–95, 1:3, 66). Weininger's misogynous self-hatred simply drew upon and perpetuated the equation of disease, the feminine, and the Jew that was already firmly entrenched within the culture reflected in the works of Wagner and Nietzsche.

The Jewish Wagnerite was thus locked in the vicious circle of an intractable racist logic: if even Wagner's staunchest critic (Nietzsche) based his vilification of Wagner on the assumption that the composer's failings were idiosyncratically Jewish and that this accounted for his success, those Jews who sought redemption from their status through the glorification of their most relentless critic were twice doomed. If they believed Wagner, they constituted that element of society responsible for and representative of the failings of the modern world. Yet as intellectuals in a culture in which no tenets were more widely discussed than those of Nietzsche, their very adoration of Wagner constituted a manifestation of the "weak" and "degenerate" nature that had presumably drawn them to the German composer in the first place. Any Jew accepting Wagner's beliefs would have to desire redemption from such a curse. On the other hand, though Wagner defined the German by contrasting him with the Jew and Nietzsche's works perpetuated such polarization (albeit in a rhetorically dazzling fashion designed to attack Wagner), most of the Jews of the German-speaking European intelligentsia understood their cultural identity to be *German* and sought to distance themselves from the stereotypes that they, as part of that culture, accepted as valid. Mahler chose the path of conversion that implied assimilation (and that, moreover, suggested a shift from the stereotype of the Eastern to that of the Western Jew), even though Wagner had ridiculed Heine for having sought such redemption from his Jewishness; Weininger (like the Jewish Wagnerite Joseph Rubinstein before him) chose the more violent manifestation of Wagner's solution (Cosima Wagner, 1978–80, 1:1078). Both men, however, were responding to the same interpretation of the Jew as a foreigner that was central to Wagner's culture, writings, and art, and to their own image in fin-de-siècle culture.

Nietzsche's writings were themselves fraught with the ambivalence of the culture that he attacked and upon whose repertoire of imagery and beliefs he drew. Some of his works, such as *Jenseits von Gut und Böse* (Beyond good and evil; 1886) contain passages overtly directed against the Jews, such as the following: "That Germany has amply *enough* Jews, that the German stomach, the German blood has trouble (and will still have trouble for a long time) digesting this quantum of 'Jew' . . . that is the clear testimony and language of a general instinct to which one must listen, in accordance with which one must act. 'Admit no more Jews! And especially close the doors to the east (also to Austria)!'" (Nietzsche 1967–95, 6:2, 201).

Some, such as *Morgenröte* (Dawn; 1879), contain both anti- and philo-Semitic statements, whereas others—*Zur Genealogie der Moral* (On the genealogy of morals; 1887), *Der Antichrist,* and *Ecce Homo* (both 1888)—are so replete with pro-Jewish sentiment (such as "Jews among Germans are always the higher race—more refined, spiritual, kind"; see Aschheim 1992, 95n.) that only the most dogged anti-Semite could ignore them in favor of Nietzsche's pronouncements in *Also*

sprach Zarathustra (Thus spake Zarathustra, 1883–92). This latter work extols the *Übermensch* and strength-pronouncements that, to the racist imagination of the time, implied glorification of the German and a denigration of the Jew.

Many of Nietzsche's non-Jewish detractors of the early twentieth century dismissed the philosopher in anti-Semitic terms that affected the Jewish reception of Nietzsche as well. Theodor Fritsch and Karl Kynast, for example, rejected the notion that Nietzsche was German, claiming instead that his was a "Polish" or even "Mongolian" mind—claims that resonated within the vocabulary of racism and disease that identified Jews with the eastern borders of the Austro-Hungarian Empire and that characterized them as "Oriental" and degenerate. Not only Fritsch and Kurt Eisner (in his *Psychopathia Spiritualis* of 1891) maintained that disease permeated Nietzsche's writings and led to widespread suicide among his readers; Emil Kraepelin, in his *Psychiatrie* of 1903, also warned of Nietzsche's ill mind, thereby repeating the concluding statement of Paul Julius Möbius in his *Über das Pathologische bei Nietzsche* of the year before (cited in Aschheim 1992, 26 n.38). Not coincidentally, the notion that Wagner's music was damaging to the nerves was commonplace in the late nineteenth century and was found throughout literary depictions of his work. The theme of disease thus links the figures of Wagner and Nietzsche to their followers and is closely associated with widely held beliefs in the physiological inferiority and pathology of the Jews with whom both men were identified in the public imagination.

But just as Jews living in the fin-de-siècle intellectual world sought to define themselves by openly accepting or rejecting the racist images of Jews as diseased that were widely interpreted to be at the center of Wagner's and Nietzsche's works, so too were the followers of the two men themselves polarized in their understanding of these texts. The Austrian Wagnerite Georg von Schönerer organized his right-wing, pan-German, and anti-Semitic movement along the lines of Wagner's postrevolutionary writings and the composer's (unrequited) apostrophes in the late 1860s and early 1870s to Bismarck and to the powers that led to the formation of the German Reich while, at the same time, such leftist thinkers as those in the Pernerstorfer circle—Viktor Adler, Heinrich Friedjung, Siegfried Lipiner, Mahler, and Engelbert Pernerstorfer—could emphasize the earlier, revolutionary Wagner who in 1848 had stood on the barricades in Dresden with the anarchist Mikhail Alexandrovich Bakunin in a losing battle for the rights of the common man (see *Dionysian Art and Populist Politics in Austria*). Just as Wagner was to some a German and to others a Jew, so he was also, to both groups, either a reactionary nationalist or a leftist revolutionary, depending on one's own identity and desired goals. The same was true of Nietzsche's followers. Both Ferdinand Tönnies and Georg Simmel, for example, distinguished between the early figure, in their opinion a populist and Socialist, and the later, purportedly elitist Nietzsche, who was contemptuous of the masses (Aschheim 1992, 39–43). Already by the end of the nineteenth century, Nietzsche could be embraced by both those opposed to and those accepting of Jewish presence in the German-speaking world. Liberal Jews like Theodor Lessing might later interpret the rampant anti-Semitism of their age through the Nietzschean concept of resentment (as seen in his *Deutschland und seine Juden*), and thus would use the philosopher's ideas against their own detractors, whereas others, such as Friedrich Blach, adopted Nietzsche's occasionally racist vocabulary and, recalling Wagner, advocated Jewish self-immolation, calling it "a free and joyful suicide. For I no longer want to be the self that I was born. 'Die at the right time: thus spake Zarathustra'" (Blach 1911, 42). Weininger had acted on that belief only eight years earlier. No wonder the cult of the Wagnerites and the champions of Nietzsche attracted as much attention from the Jewish intelligentsia at the turn of the century as did the two figures themselves; these followers embraced their mentors' diverse pronouncements with such willful fervor that their actions appeared as caricatures of the very works they sought to glorify. In his prominent journal *Die Fackel,* Karl Kraus derisively referred to "the super-apes of the coffee-house," to the modern, fin-de-siècle instantiations of Nietzsche's and

Wagner's "superman," in a formulation that lampooned contemporary pretensions to racial superiority modeled on the writings of the German masters (Kraus 1900, 22). But their followers were legion, and to ignore them would be to disregard a fundamental component of intellectual life at the turn of the century in German-speaking Europe.

The legacy of both Wagner and Nietzsche played an important role in the development of the Zionist movement, which in some ways may be deemed, ironically, a kind of corollary to the separatist and utopian currents in Wagner's works. It was while attending a performance of *Tannhäuser* in 1895 that Theodor Herzl, the founder of the movement, had the nearly epiphanic realization that the only answer to the irrational forces of völkisch politics lay in the establishment of an independent Jewish state (Herzl 1922–23, 1:44). Herzl's hope would be to apply Wagner's notion of the *Gesamtkunstwerk*—an all-encompassing conception of the social realm as an ideologically defined aesthetic accomplishment—to the realm of politics, but to use it as a model for the salvation of the Jews. Here again, as in Nietzsche, the culturally pervasive belief in the irreconcilability of Jews and Germans was not called into question, but only reversed, emerging on both sides of the racial spectrum. Nordau, another key figure in the Zionist movement, was also influenced by Wagner, albeit in a different fashion. After claiming in *Entartung* that Wagner's and Nietzsche's works were the results of diseased minds and attractive to degenerates, Nordau offered a counter to Wagner's and to his own culture's image of the Jew by claiming in articles from 1900 to 1903 that Jews needed to rid themselves of their illness by transforming themselves into more powerful and muscular men—into a "muscle Jewry" (Nordau 1903, 137; Nordau 1902, 2). Thus Nordau, too, did less to question the assumptions concerning the anti-Semitic imagery of his culture found in Wagner and Nietzsche—indeed, he seemed to accept them—than to adopt the image of the Jew's racial opposite for the Jews themselves.

Much of Wagner's and Nietszche's influence on Jewish writers emerged through the reception of the two figures by both German and Jewish musicians. The cultural criticism, including anti-Semitism, of Hans Pfitzner, for example, as well as the makeup of his music, constituted a perpetuation of the Wagnerian tradition and of ideas discernible in Nietzsche. The same can be said of the music of Pfitzner's colleagues Richard Strauss, Mahler, and the Jewish composer of *Lieder,* Felix Wolfes. (Nietzsche's and Wagner's role in modern music was openly discussed in a host of contemporary publications, as demonstrated in articles in *Die Zukunft* from 1897 to 1905.) Franz Werfel's *Verdi: Roman der Oper* (Verdi: A novel of the opera; 1923), though overtly critical of Wagner, also lampoons the Wagnerian legacy through a surreptitious parody of Pfitzner's musical drama *Palestrina* and of various tenets central to Pfitzner's conservatism; this work thereby attacks both the nineteenth- and the twentieth-century racist composers. It was no coincidence that the epigonic Jewish writer Ludwig Hirschfeld, a figure from the circle associated with Arthur Schnitzler, chose Mahler as the conductor of a performance of *Die Walküre* in his novel *Jupiter in der Wolke* (Jupiter in the clouds; 1913), a story highly reminiscent of Thomas Mann's "Wälsungenblut" (Blood of the Volsungs; 1905) (which lampoons Wagner's dramatic paean to racial purity). Both texts concern the role of the Jew in the fin-de-siècle world and represent the tension between Germans and Jews through musical signs—through the figures of Wagner and Mahler, an especially poignant choice given Wagner's association of Jews with modernism and Mahler's prominent role in the development of modernist music. Owing to the pervasive appearance of Wagnerian and Nietzschean motifs in the literature of the time, such Jewish writers as Hirschfeld were also responding to specific German literary models, as well as to the position of Wagner and Nietzsche in the culture of the German-speaking world in general. This was the case with Arthur Schnitzler, whose novel *Der Weg ins Freie* (The road into the open; 1908) both expanded upon Wagner's role in earlier works of Fontane, von Saar, and Thomas Mann, and used the figure to evoke topical issues of racism and German nationalism in the contemporary Austro-Hungarian Empire. Schnitzler's novel portrays the life of the fictitious Georg von Wergenthin (whose name pointedly recalls Georg von Schönerer), an anti-Semitic dilettante composer enamored of Wagner and distrustful of Jewish influence in the arts and modern society. Toward the end of the novel, Schnitzler has his protagonist attend a performance of *Tristan* at the Vienna Opera and, though the contemporary reader must have assumed that Mahler would conduct the performance, Schnitzler's brilliantly narrated monologue never mentions the converted Jewish musician. It depicts instead the workings of von Wergenthin's anti-Semitic imagination as he dreams only of a grandeur similar to the German's and represses the Jew from his fantasy of a racially pure, homogeneous socioaesthetic realm (Schnitzler 1970, 920–21). It is a testament to the historical sensitivity and accuracy of Schnitzler's ideological criticism that in the very year of his novel's publication, an angry Wagnerite and fledgling artist, Adolf Hitler, arrived in Vienna with his own thoughts on the Jewish Question. Hitler's plan for *der Untergang,* however, would not be put into practice for more than thirty years, by which time Mahler's assimilationist interpretation of Wagner's ambiguous advice to the Jews would no longer be an option.

Bibliography

Steven Aschheim, *The Nietzsche Legacy in Germany, 1890–1990* (Berkeley: University of California Press, 1992); Friedrich Blach, *Die Juden in Deutschland* (Berlin: K. Curtius, 1911); Bruce Emmerlin, "Nietzsche Among the Zionists," Ph.D. diss., Cornell University, 1990; Dietrich Fischer-Dieskau, *Wagner und Nietzsche: Der Mystagoge und sein Abtrünniger* (Stuttgart: Deutsche Verlags-Anstalt, 1974); Henri-Louis de la Grange, *Mahler,* 3 vols. (New York: Doubleday, 1973); Theodor Herzl, *Theodor Herzls Tagebücher, 1895–1904,* 3 vols. (Berlin: Jüdischer Verlag, 1922–23); Ludwig Hirschfeld, *Jupiter in der Wolke* (Leipzig: Xenien Verlag, 1913); Karl Kraus, *Die Fackel* 51 (Aug. 1900): 19–22; Theodor Lessing, *Deutschland und seine Juden* (Prague: Neumann, 1933); William J. McGrath, *Dionysian Art and Populist Politics in Austria* (New Haven: Yale University Press, 1974); Paul Julius Möbius, *Über das Pathologische bei Nietzsche* (Wiesbaden: J. F. Bergmann, 1902); Friedrich Nietzsche, *Werke: Kritische Gesamtausgabe,* ed. Giorgio Colli and Mazzino Montinari (Berlin: de Gruyter, 1967–95); Max Nordau, "Muskeljudentum," *Jüdische Turnzeitung* 8 (1903): 137–38; Nordau, "Was bedeutet das Turnen für uns Juden?" *Die Welt* 31 (1902): 2–3; Heinrich Porges, *Wagner Rehearsing the "Ring": An Eye-Witness Account of the Stage Rehearsals for the First Bayreuth Festival,* trans. Robert L. Jacobs (Cambridge: Cambridge University Press, 1983); Arthur Schnitzler, *Die Erzählenden Schriften,* 2 vols. (Frankfurt a. M.: S. Fischer, 1970); Cosima Wagner, *Diaries,* ed. and annotated Martin Gregor-Dellin and Dietrich Mack, trans. and intro. Geoffrey Skelton, 2 vols. (New York: Harcourt Brace Jovanovich, 1978–80); Richard Wagner, *Dichtungen und Schriften,* ed. Dieter Borchmeyer, 10 vols. (Frankfurt a. M.: Insel, 1983); Wagner, *Gesammelte Schriften,* ed. Julius Kapp, 14 vols. (Leipzig: Hesse & Becker, 1911); Otto Weininger, *Geschlecht und Charakter: Eine prinzipielle Untersuchung,* 25th ed. (Vienna: Wilhelm Braumüller, 1923); and Franz Werfel, *Verdi: Roman der Oper* (Vienna: Paul Zsolnay, 1924).

MARC A. WEINER

1904 Bertha Pappenheim establishes
the Jewish Women's Federation in Germany

Bertha Pappenheim (1859–1936), an experienced organizer and social activist, was to head the Jewish Women's Federation for twenty years. After she had moved from Vienna to Frankfurt am Main in 1888, she took an active part in the organization of social work in Germany and helped establish dozens of sewing schools, which gave women an opportunity to learn a craft that could help them make a living. In addition, Bertha Pappenheim was instrumental in establishing orphanages and preschools, and she headed a home for female orphans for twelve years. Finally, she joined efforts with other emancipated women from Frankfurt, including Henriette Fürth, Hella Flesh, Anna Edinger, and Jenny Apolant, in order to realize basic political and social goals of the German women's movement, such as the establishment of preschools, orphanages, and various institutions for the education of women, as well as health care and welfare services. One of the major achievements of the Zentralstelle für Gemeindeämter der Frau, a Frankfurt-based section of the German Women's Federation, was the attainment of women's right to vote in the municipal elections of 1919. Two years prior to the establishment of the Jewish Women's Federation, Pappenheim had founded the Jewish Women's Union, Weibliche Fürsorge, which she described as a "school for social Jewish thinking and activity." In 1907 she established the Isenburger Heim, a home for women and children who were deprived of financial assistance and could not make it on their own. The home helped orphans, illegitimate children, pregnant unwed women, and single mothers without a source of income. The Isenburger Heim embodied political and educational tenets that Pappenheim had detailed. These tenets appeared in numerous articles and lectures published by the *Blätter des jüdischen Frauenbundes,* the organ of the Jewish Women's Federation; in Pappenheim's study *Zur Lage der jüdischen Bevölkerung in Galizien* (1904), which describes the poor living conditions of Jewish communities in Galicia; and in the two volumes of her *Sisyphus-Arbeit* (1911, 1922), a response to society's unwillingness to fight white slave traffic.

From her first essays on Jewish women's education published in the 1890s to her last articles against prostitution written shortly before her death in 1936, Pappenheim tried to bridge the abyss between women's emancipation and an Orthodox Jewish conviction, thus attempting to solve what seemed to be a contradiction in terms. For centuries, the Orthodox Jewish community had denied women an active role in the public sphere. In their quest for self-realization, Jewish women struggled to evade the restrictions imposed upon them by Orthodox Judaism. Many, therefore, turned their backs on Jewish communities and embraced the ideas of the surrounding gentile society, which gave them more social and political rights. Pappenheim tried to reverse this process and improve the status of women within Jewish communities by reforming Judaism in such a way that it became a source of support and strength for women—an institution that helped them overcome the social and political barriers of their time. But Pappenheim did not share the familiar exegesis of the Talmud. In her opinion, YHWH's commandments called upon individuals, both men and women, to assume responsibility for their actions as well as for society at large. God's grace was a commandment to care for others. Time and again Pappenheim's prayers asked God to give women the strength to find a meaning in life by caring for other people. In Pappenheim's view, her interpretation of the Talmud and the Jewish Law was much more plausible than the misreadings propagated by some Orthodox rabbis. As Margarete Susman points out in her introduction to Pappenheim's prayers, the leader of the Jewish Women's Federation hoped to reconcile the Jewish Orthodox belief with women's emancipation. Despite all of her feminist objectives, Pappenheim remained a practicing Jew.

In her essays about the education of women, Pappenheim used arguments that even an Orthodox Jew could accept. In Orthodox Jewish homes, women were in charge of the household and the education of their children. But they could not fulfill these tasks if they were uneducated, Pappenheim argued. Hence the education of women was a necessity and not a choice. To insist that a woman's education should benefit only her own children would be mere egoism, she wrote. Pointing to Maimonides' notion of the Jews' commitment to welfare as a constitutive element of Jewish religion, she underlined the moral obligation of Jewish communities to give all children a chance to become the beneficiaries of women's education. Hence women's activities as teachers and social workers were in accordance with Jewish religion. Again and again, Pappenheim stressed that the education of women—both secular and religious—was a crucial step toward their emancipation and self-realization.

In Pappenheim's view, the goal of the Jewish Women's Federation was to give Jewish women a mission in life. Hence she fought against the traditional education of girls from wealthy families, who were doomed to lead an idle life, get married, and please their husbands. Middle-class women spent their days visiting friends, giving reception, going to concerts, and sometimes engaging in welfare activities. Bertha was critical of such a lifestyle, as well as of parents who treated their daughters like princesses. She also fought against those parents from lower-income classes who deprived their daughters of any education. In all her pamphlets and essays, Pappenheim pleaded for the emancipation of women through work rather than through acculturation. Women should become aware of their duties in society; they should gain self-confidence and responsibility by performing tasks they chose or were designated. She even succeeded in convincing women from wealthy families to help the "fallen daughters" of the Jewish community. The training of women as teachers and social workers constituted a major part of Pappenheim's pedagogical program.

The relationship of the Jewish Women's Federation to the German Women's Federation was often marked by mutual sympathy and support, but sometimes also by tension. The Jewish Women's Federation constituted the largest sister organization of the German Women's Federation. Representatives of the German Women's Federation had little understanding of Orthodox Judaism and favored the integration of Jews into society on the condition that they were willing to give up their Judaism. It is for this reason that the representatives of the Jewish Women's Federation kept arguing that their organization was similar in nature to the Catholic and Protestant Women's Federations. They considered themselves to be Germans of Jewish belief. In fact, as a result of their love for Germany and the German people, leading representatives of the Jewish Women's Federation tended to ignore the danger of rising Nazism in the 1920s and 1930s. But despite her bond to German culture and the German women's movement, Pappenheim did not hesitate to attack Helene Lange when she made anti-Semitic remarks. After the controversy with Lange, Pappenheim withdrew from the German Women's Federation.

The Isenburger Heim was the practical realization of Pappenheim's educational tenets. The home, which was financed by the family of Pappenheim's mother, as well as by the Rothschilds, was modeled after Dr. Bernardo's Homes for the

Protection of Women, the Charcroft House, and the Roseford Garden—as well as the Shepherd's Bush Rescue and Training Home for Unwed Jewish Girls and Women, which was established by the Jewish Association for the Protection of Girls and Women in 1889. The Isenburger Heim attempted to show women a path toward self-realization by educating them and promoting their socialization through a very strict educational program. The daily schedule began at 6:15 A.M. and ended at 10:00 P.M.; every hour of the day was devoted to different activities; and even the time of leisure was structured. Both children and adults were required to stick to the schedule. Pappenheim hoped that eventually the outer order would turn into an inner psychic order. By providing outer protection and security, she hoped to enable her students to gain an inner harmony as well as the strength to fight for their status in society. Pappenheim was very strict, but she loved her disciples, to whom she read poetry, stories, and prayers. She celebrated the Jewish holidays with them and created a family-like atmosphere in the Isenburger Heim, which added warmth to the restraints imposed by the strict order.

Asceticism and a Spartan way of life made up the educational program for women, who were perceived as "endangered." In a strict sense, this word referred to sexual and moral endangerment. In a broad sense, it alluded to any deviation from the Jewish law, the way it had been handed down from generation to generation and had come to constitute the basis of human behavior. The conscious suppression of vanity, eroticism, and sexuality in the home was a means to undo the clichés of the woman, in particular the Jewish woman, as a potential prostitute by juxtaposing it with the traditional image of the Jewish woman as a mother and responsible educator of her children.

As the two volumes of Pappenheim's *Sisyphus-Arbeit* show, she was well aware of the hard times Jewish women went through in the Eastern European and Russian ghettos. She had traveled extensively in Eastern Europe and Russia, as well as in northern Africa, and had seen how Jewish women from the shtetel and from low-income classes fell victim to white slave traffic. Lured to foreign countries through promising newspaper advertisements, they left their homes in the hope of finding a better life and a source of income. Upon arrival in Western Europe, and Germany in particular, they were forced into prostitution and often locked up in brothels. Because they had no passports, no residence permits, and no civil rights, these women could not approach any organization for the protection of women, and certainly not the police. Among the prostitutes, Jewish women were the outcasts of all outcasts. For the society of that time, these prostitutes confirmed the anti-Semitic cliché of Jewish women as the wild, perverse, sexual beings whose lust undid the hegemony of the man.

Some representatives of the Jewish community tried to fight these prejudices and prevent Jews from getting involved in white slave traffic. In 1897, Gustav Tuch, the head of the B'nai B'rith in Hamburg, pointed to the existence of Jewish slave traffic extending from Eastern Europe to South America. The B'nai B'rith established a Jewish committee, whose representatives tried to protect single women, the potential victims of white slave traffic, by assisting them in train stations and harbors. Although they uncovered some aspects of this traffic, they did not succeed in convincing Jewish communities to join their efforts in fighting against white slave traffic. Many Jews refused to believe that their coreligionists were capable of such perversions; they therefore failed to assist the victims of such criminals.

Pappenheim turned the struggle against white slave traffic into a prime goal of the Jewish Women's Federation. The organization established shelters and assistance services for women traveling alone, put up posters against white slave traffic in all major train stations and harbors, and sent social workers to Eastern Europe to inform the Jewish communities about the fate of girls forced into prostitution. It also uncovered some of the causes for the Jewish involvement in white slave traffic: the extreme poverty of Jews in Eastern Europe, which forced parents to sell their children.

Pappenheim warned Jewish communities, which were reluctant to acknowledge the problem and fight it, that anti-Semites could take the existence of Jewish prostitutes and pimps as a pretext to attack the entire Jewish community. In the 1920s, the Rockefeller family financed a commission that traveled all across Eastern and Western Europe as well as North Africa and investigated white slave traffic. This commission prepared a secret report for the League of Nations in Geneva, a report that presented a myth in a scientific way: the legend of the Jew's responsibility for the establishment of the international white slave traffic. By using statistics, which were considered then the climax of scientific objectivity, the Rockefeller Commission proved that in all countries many pimps were Jews and that many brothels were owned by Jews. It did not mention, however, that the victims were mostly Jewish women. In addition, the causes for the prostitution remained unexplored. Although Pappenheim showed that many phrases used in the report were anti-Semitic, she and a few of her supporters were the only ones to question the impartiality of the commission, which published its findings in a second, shortened report. As Pappenheim predicted, the Nazis later misused the allegations of the Rockefeller Commission to "prove" the perversity of Jews and to legitimize their anti-Semitic campaign.

Bertha Pappenheim's political and educational tenets were based on her own life and experience. She had grown up in an Orthodox Jewish family in Vienna at a time when women were given some access to basic education but were doomed to lead an idle life, stay at home, and wait for a future husband. Pappenheim, who attended a private Catholic school, was fluent in several languages, played the piano, embroidered, and even went horseback riding but, unlike her brother, was not allowed to study at the University of Vienna. There was no outlet for her energy and fantasy creativity except in stories, which she did not write down but acted out in her imagination. This imaginary theater became a source of comfort.

When Pappenheim's father became seriously ill, she helped her mother take care of him. This gave her life a new meaning. She soon came to realize that her father's illness was terminal. As she gradually understood that she was going to lose not only a beloved parent, but also the person who had given her life a direction, she became ill herself. The physicians of that time did not understand the causes of her hallucinations, paralysis, and depressions. They could not detect any physical illness and diagnosed her as hysteric. Only Josef Breuer, one of the leading Viennese physicians of that time, was able to help her, first by using hypnosis and later by listening to her account of the incidents that in her view triggered her physical condition. This form of therapy, which she called "chimney sweeping" and "talking cure," was to become the basis of the later psychoanalytical treatment used by Sigmund Freud. Although a leading physician of the time, Breuer did not recognize Pappenheim's actual problem: the discrepancy between her secular education and the futility of her existence determined by her Orthodox Jewish upbringing. Breuer's intensive endeavors to help Pappenheim—his visits, which occurred twice a day; his refusal to stop seeing Pappenheim even on his wife's insistence and after her subsequent attempt to commit suicide—all suggest that his feelings for Bertha were more than mere sympathy for a patient. Pappenheim in turn had become very attached to her physician, who had improved her condition. As the family pressure to give up the treatment of this patient grew, however, Breuer told Pappenheim one day that he believed she was cured and advised her to go on a summer vacation with her parents. He was planning to leave on a second honeymoon with his wife. But that same night, Pappenheim's mother called on Breuer, asking him for help. When Breuer arrived at the Pappenheim home, he found Bertha fantasizing that she was in labor; it was his child that she was giving birth to, she insisted. Breuer was shocked. After hypnotizing Bertha into a state of slumber, he took his hat and coat and left the Pappenheim home forever.

As an entry in Freud's diary shows, Breuer told him about Bertha's "talking cure" on November

18, 1882; Freud underscored that it was on this very day and thanks to Bertha's case that he finally understood the effect of the unconscious on human behavior. It took Freud several years to persuade Breuer to describe Pappenheim's illness, which became known as the "Anna O." case in their later *Studien über Hysterie* (1895). In his report, Breuer uncovered the ways in which the "talking cure" helped Anna O. but claimed that he had not noticed any interest in sexuality on Bertha's part. In fact, he considered her to be an asexual being. For Freud this case provided an insight into the phenomenon of counter-transference. The actual identity of Anna O. did not become known until 1953, when Ernst Jones, in his biography of Freud, betrayed the secret, thus stirring up the emotions of both psychoanalysts and feminists. Many psychiatrists and psychoanalysts were unable to understand how a person who had been so ill could later become the leader of the Jewish feminist movement in Germany. By contrast, the feminists, in particular Pappenheim's friends, were concerned that the knowledge of her illness would affect the interpretation of her later work.

Little is known about Bertha Pappenheim's life between 1882 and 1888. She spent some time in a Swiss sanatorium and later returned to Vienna, where she wrote stories for children, *Kleine Geschichten für Kinder,* which appeared anonymously in 1888. Her subsequent novel *In der Trödelbude* (1894), published under the male pseudonym Paul Berthold, projects her story upon a male protagonist and the broken objects that he collects. The novel consists of a series of stories told by these damaged objects in an old curiosity shop owned by the protagonist. Each object details the inevitable circumstances that led to its damage. The protagonist's fate is similar, for he was once a promising talent but due to hostile circumstances became a loser. The novel, however, has a happy ending. It is through caring for other people, in particular for his daughter, whom the protagonist succeeds in finding and bringing back home, that he attains a new meaning in life.

Bertha Pappenheim inscribed her own fate into the novel, which is a response to the treatment received from Viennese physicians and their misinterpretations of her emotional problems. Her illness had not been of her own making, but was caused by a society that prevented educated women from using their talents and expertise in any meaningful way. Writing must have had a therapeutic effect on Pappenheim; it must have helped her understand that social work was a way out of her illness and a means of self-realization.

Pappenheim's later literary works focus on social and feminist questions. In her play *Frauenrecht* (1899), also published under the pseudonym Paul Berthold, she criticizes the violations of law committed in order to oppress women. A recurrent motif in her collections of stories, entitled *Tragische Momente* (1913) and *Kämpfe* (1916), is the attempt to reconcile women's emancipation with Orthodox Jewish beliefs. But Bertha Pappenheim was not only the author of stories, poems, and prayers—she was also an excellent translator. She translated Mary Wollstonecraft's *A Vindication of the Rights of Women* (1792) from English into German (*Verteidigung der Rechte der Frau;* 1899). She wrote a German adaptation of Glückel von Hameln's autobiography written in Yiddish. This book, which appeared under the title *Die Denkwürdigkeiten der Glückel von Hameln,* was the very first autobiography of a Jewish woman living in Germany (1645–1724). As a brave and well-respected widow who had to make a living on her own and care for her thirteen children, Glückel became a model for Pappenheim by showing her a way to reconcile Orthodox Judaism with women's emancipation. In this way, Glückel was Pappenheim's ancestor. The leader of the Jewish Women's Federation also translated the Woman's Bible, *Zennoh Rennoh,* and the *Maásse Book, Allerlei Geschichten,* from Yiddish into German. These translations, along with her stories, her political and pedagogic studies, and her translations, appeared under her actual name, which signaled her growing self-confidence.

Anna O., Paul Berthold, and finally, Bertha Pappenheim. These three names mark the development of a German-Jewish feminist who succeeded in leading a life as both a religious Jew and an emancipated woman despite all the prejudices and social barriers of her time.

Bibliography

Blätter des jüdischen Frauenbundes: Für Frauenarbeit und Frauenbewegung (Berlin: Biko-Verlag, 1924–38); Dora Edinger, ed., *Bertha Pappenheim: Leben und Schaffen* (Frankfurt a. M.: Ner-Talmid-Verlag, 1963); Marion Kaplan, *Die jüdische Frauenbewegung in Deutschland: Organisation und Ziele des jüdischen Frauenbundes, 1904–1938,* trans. Hainer Kober (Hamburg: Hans Christian Verlag, 1981); Bertha Pappenheim, *Gebete,* intro. Margarete Susman (Berlin: Philo Verlag, 1936); Pappenheim, *Kämpfe: Sechs Erzählungen* (Frankfurt a. M.: J. Kaufmann, 1916); Pappenheim, *Sisyphus-Arbeit: Reisebriefe aus den Jahren 1911 und 1912* (Leipzig: P. E. Lindner, 1924); Pappenheim, *Sisyphus-Arbeit: Zweite Folge* (Berlin: n.p., 1929); Pappenheim, *Tragische Momente: Drei Lebensbilder* (Frankfurt a. M.: J. Kaufmann, 1913); and Pappenheim and Sara Rabinowitsch, *Zur Lage der jüdischen Bevölkerung in Galizien: Reise-Eindrücke und Vorschläge zur Besserung der Verhältnisse* (Frankfurt a. M.: Neuer Frankfurter Verlag, 1904).

AMY COLIN

1905 Karl Emil Franzos's masterpiece *Der Pojaz* is published posthumously

The questions surrounding the reluctance of the successful and prolific writer, editor, and journalist Karl Emil Franzos (1848–1904) to publish his most significant novel for a German readership during his lifetime, although it was ready for publication in 1893, have not been completely answered. To be sure, anti-Semitism had been growing in the German-speaking world, and some of it was directed at him personally. Thus the hostility toward Franzos on the part of Orthodox East European Jewish circles, and the failing health of the author (due largely to years of overwork), have been suggested as reasons, but none of these explanations is entirely satisfactory. Curiously, Franzos had not objected to the novel being published in a Russian translation; it was first serialized in the St. Petersburg journal *Voskhod* in 1894 and printed in book form in 1895.

Der Pojaz (The clown; *pojaz* is the Yiddish version of the word *Bajazzo*) relates the life of Sender Glatteis, who is prevented by his ghetto environment from developing his one talent—acting. He thus never realizes his one dream, and ultimately he dies as a result of the stifling atmosphere of the ghetto. It has become something of a cliché to allude to *Wilhelm Meister* in discussing Franzos's work. *Der Pojaz* contains all the major characteristic themes and ideas put forward in all of Franzos's literary works: in each, the Eastern European Jew's one hope for enlightenment, liberation, and even survival hinges on his acquiring German education and culture; the ghetto provides an intellectually asphyxiating life under the crushing tyranny of the fundamentalist Hasidic rabbis; and all the main characters refuse to consider outright baptism and conversion.

Franzos has been the subject of numerous post-1945 dissertations and articles in both the United States and Germany, although this attention has not seemed to increase significantly the numbers of his readers. Most German writers of dissertations and articles somewhat coyly sidestep the reason for the disappearance of the names of Jewish writers during the 1930s and 1940s, seeming to imply that the disappearance of their books was due to the natural loss of interest in these authors on the part of the German readership. In Franzos's case they ignore the great popularity of his works during his lifetime, a popularity amply attested by the numbers of reprints and editions of those works up to the 1930s and even beyond.

Karl Emil Franzos was born on October 25, 1848, in what was then Russian Podolia, and he spent his childhood in Czortków—the "Barnow" of his stories—in what was then Galicia. He died on January 28, 1904, in Berlin. The son of an enlightened and assimilated German-Jewish district doctor who inculcated in his son the fact that he was first a German and then a Jew, he was treated as an apostate and outsider by the local sectarian Hasidic Jewish population in the Polish-Jewish town. He thus actually had very little immediate contact with Orthodox Jews while growing up. It was from his father that Franzos absorbed the conviction—reflected throughout his works—that only by adopting the German language and German cultural values could the Eastern European Jews deserve and gain enlightenment and equality.

After attending the Dominican school in Czortków at the wish of his father (who died in 1859), Franzos was enrolled in the German gymnasium in Czernowitz, where after 1862 he had to support himself. Franzos first wanted to study philology at the university, but as a Jew he could not qualify for the necessary state support. From 1867 to 1871 he successfully studied law in Vienna and Graz. But due to his involvement with the Verein der Deutsch-Nationalen (Club of German Nationalists) on the occasion of the Prussian victory in the Franco-Prussian War and his resultant legal problems with the Austrian authorities, he was excluded from the expected legal career in state service. In order to earn a livelihood for himself, his mother, and his two disabled sisters, he turned to journalism. In 1872 he became a correspondent for the Viennese *Neue Freie Presse*. In 1872–73, he wrote for the Budapest newspapers *Ungarischer Lloyd* and *Pester Lloyd,* and from 1873 to 1876 he contributed to various periodicals, mostly in Vienna.

In Graz, Franzos had experienced an unfortunate love affair with a Christian girl, who had ultimately rejected him only because he was a Jew. He sublimated his disappointment into the short story "Das Christusbild" (The Christ picture), which was to form the nucleus of the collection *Die Juden von Barnow* (The Jews of Barnow; in book form, 1877). This book was to establish his name as a major belletristic writer. Already the year before, however, Franzos's first collection of travel sketches was published in Leipzig in book form and in German. Some of these sketches had earlier been published in the periodical press, and a pirated Danish version of these had already appeared as a book. This collection, *Aus Halb-Asien: Kulturbilder* (From Semi-Asia: Cultural pictures; 1876), first introduced Franzos to an international readership. It was to be followed by two sequels, *Vom Don zur Donau: Neue Kulturbilder aus Halb-Asien* (From the Don to the Danube: New cultural pictures from Semi-Asia; 1878) and *Aus der großen Ebene: Neue Kulturbilder aus Halb-Asien*

(From the great plain: New cultural pictures from Semi-Asia; 1888). In these "cultural pictures," as in *The Jews of Barnow,* Franzos habitually focused on the appalling backwardness and shocking living conditions in towns and villages of the Slavic and Rumanian territories of Eastern Europe. By doing so, he inevitably evoked counterattacks, especially from the Poles on one side and the Orthodox Jews on the other.

In 1877 Franzos married Ottilie Benedikt, the daughter of a cultured and assimilated Viennese family, who was herself to become a writer, using the pen name "F. Ottmer." The couple lived for several years in Vienna. In 1879 Franzos became famous as the rediscoverer of Georg Büchner, publishing in that year his edition of Büchner's *Sämmtliche Werke und handschriftlicher Nachlaß* (Complete works and unpublished literary remains), including his reading of Büchner's manuscript of *Woyzeck.* During these Vienna years Franzos published a stream of works. *Junge Liebe* (Young love; 1879), *Moschko von Parma* (1880), *Die Hexe* (The witch; 1880), *Stille Geschichten* (Quiet stories; 1880), *Ein Kampf ums Recht* (For the right; 1882), *Mein Franz* (My Franz; 1883), and *Der Präsident* (The chief justice; 1884). In addition, he edited the volume *Deutsches Dichterbuch aus Österreich* (German book of poetry; 1883). During this period he was also busy as a popularly acclaimed touring lecturer. Himself a member of several literary clubs or associations, he wanted to establish a *Verein für jüdische Literatur* (society for Jewish literature) in 1885, but this plan was never realized. Another of his ideas that he was unable to carry out was a project to publish a collection of the writings of German-Jewish authors, similar to the *Deutsches Dichterbuch aus Österreich.*

From 1884 until 1886 Franzos edited the Vienna weekly *Neue Illustrierte Zeitung,* and in spite of the extremely heavy work load this position entailed, he was able to continue his own imaginative writing, publishing *Die Reise nach dem Schicksal* (Journey to destiny; 1885) and *Tragische Novellen* (Tragic stories; 1886). Now Franzos had the chance to edit his own literary journal. He eventually succeeded in taking over the failed periodical *Deutsche Dichtung* (German fiction) and establishing it in Berlin, permanently settling in that city in 1887. A factor in his decision to leave Vienna was undoubtedly the growing and increasingly aggressive anti-Semitism in Austria.

Franzos continued to edit *Deutsche Dichtung* until his death, successfully publishing significant literature, including lyric poetry, of contemporary writers. He also included articles of broader general interest. During this last period of his life, Franzos also established his own Berlin publishing firm, Concordia. In addition, he continued both his popular public lecturing and his own writing. His last belletristic works included *Die Schatten* (The shades; 1888), *Judith Trachtenberg* (1891), *Der Gott des alten Doktors* (The old doctor's God; 1892), *Der Wahrheitssucher* (The truth seeker; 1893), *Ein Opfer* (A sacrifice; 1893), *Ungeschickte Leute* (Inept people; 1894), *Der kleine Martin* (Little Martin; 1896), *Leib Weinachtskuchen und sein Kind* (L. W. and his child; 1896), *Allerlei Geister* (All kinds of spirits; 1897), *Mann und Weib* (Man and woman; 1899), and *Neue Novellen* (New stories; 1904). (*Der Pojaz* appeared posthumously in 1905.) In addition, Franzos edited and contributed a story to *Die Geschichte des Erstlingswerks* (The history of the first work; 1894, a collection of various authors' stories of their own first published literary works), and published two further collections of travelogues—*Aus Anhalt und Thüringen* (From Anhalt and Thuringia) and *Aus den Vogesen* (From the Vosges mountains)— under the common title *Deutsche Fahrten: Reise- und Kulturbilder* (German excursions: Travel and cultural pictures; 1903–4). Owing apparently to a great extent to the mounting anti-Semitism throughout the German-speaking lands, Franzos encountered increasing difficulty in finding publishers for literature that expressed attitudes favorable toward Jews. As a result, many of his later works were published by his own firm, Concordia.

The only imaginative works of Franzos that are read at present—and these are not read by many—are those centered around Jewish themes and material. Besides the masterwork *Der Pojaz,* even the Jewish works still read to any extent are

limited to the collection of short stories *Die Juden von Barnow* and the novel *Judith Trachtenberg.* These three books, as well as *Aus Anhalt und Thüringen* and a collection containing "Zwei Retter" from *Die Juden von Barnow,* "Schiller in Barnow" from *Aus Halb-Asien, Ein Opfer,* "Matthias Zenner" from *Neue Novellen,* and "Martin der Rubel" from *Vom Don zur Donau,* have been recently reprinted: *Der Pojaz* (Königstein: Athenäum, 1988); *Die Juden von Barnow* (Reinbek: Rowohlt, 1990); *Judith Trachtenberg* (Berlin: Verlag der Nation, 1987); *Aus Anhalt und Thüringen* (Berlin: Rütten & Loening, 1991); and *Erzählungen aus Galizien und der Bukowina* (Berlin: Nicolai, 1988).

In writing the ghetto stories that make up *Die Juden von Barnow,* Franzos was by no means inventing a new genre; he was following a tradition, if a young one, established in German by Leopold Kompert (1822–86) in his collection of stories *Aus dem Ghetto* (From the ghetto; 1848). Franzos personally knew and esteemed Kompert, and he dedicated the first edition of his own collection of ghetto stories to the older writer. Franzos also wrote a moving tribute to Kompert on the latter's death in 1886 (published in 1906 in the *Jahrbuch für jüdische Geschichte und Literatur*). Between the time of Kompert and his copioneer in the genre of the German-Jewish ghetto story, Aaron David Bernstein (1812–84), and the period when Franzos was writing, there had been several other writers in the genre, with whose works Franzos must have been familiar and upon which he built. Although there were several other writers in the genre who followed Franzos, he, along with his contemporary Nathan Samuely (1847–1921), developed the ghetto story form into an art not equaled before or since.

Although Franzos's ghetto stories make up only a very small part of his prodigious literary production, as an artistic achievement Franzos equaled them only with *Der Pojaz,* and never surpassed them. The popularity of *Die Juden von Barnow,* with non-Jewish as well as Jewish readers, is attested by the fact that its eighth printing appeared in 1907. As has been pointed out, Franzos, like Kompert but unlike the other ghetto story writers, has been recently reprinted. The collection contains the stories "Der Shylock von Barnow" (The Shylock of B.), "Nach dem höheren Gesetz" (According to the higher law), "Zwei Retter" (Two rescuers), "Der wilde Starost und die schöne Jütta" (The wild "Starost"—a powerful local tyrant—and the beautiful Jütta), "Das 'Kind der Sühne'" (The "Child of Atonement"), "Esterka Regina" (a nickname), "Baron Schmule," "Das Christusbild" (The Christ picture), and "Ohne Inschrift" (Without epitaph). "Das Christusbild" and "Zwei Retter" have been reprinted in Jost Hermand's anthology *Geschichten aus dem Ghetto*.

The best of the stories in the collection represent the highest literary achievements that Franzos was ever to attain. Virtually all the themes used by Franzos—and by almost all the other ghetto story writers as well—are to be found in Kompert's works. "Der Shylock von Barnow" takes up Kompert's theme of the seduction of the daughter of a prosperous, pious Jew by a Christian (or an apostate Jew) and her eventual penitential return to her father's home. In fact, Franzos borrowed the strikingly effective motif of the barking dog announcing the return of the errant daughter directly from Kompert's "Die Jahrzeit" (The memorial day). Franzos's mouthpiece (here as elsewhere) is a Jewish district doctor (presumably modeled on his father), who blames the girl's downfall on the narrow-minded fanaticism of the ghetto that made it a sin to read a German book, for example, and that boasted an almost religious rule to educate girls only "to cook, to pray, and to reckon"; then they would "know enough for the house, for heaven, and for life."

"Nach dem höheren Gesetz" presents the reverse side of "Der Shylock von Barnow"; the cycle of tragedies caused by the Jewish custom of forced and early marriages is broken by a magnanimous Jewish husband who releases his wife from their marriage so that she can follow her own emotional inclinations. "Der wilde Starost und die schöne Jütta" treats the tragic love between a Christian nobleman and a Jewish girl. Prejudice and hatred on both sides lead to universal tragedy

and destruction. Franzos pleads here for the precedence of love and understanding over religious creed. "Das 'Kind der Sühne'" is another indictment of the superstition and ignorance of the Jewish sectarianism that controlled the lives of the Eastern European Jews in the area where Franzos spent his childhood, with its tyrannical "miracle-working" Hasidic rabbis.

"Esterka Regina" is a romantic tale of frustrated love, but at the same time it is an attack on rigid orthodoxy, which imprisons women in ignorance and forces them into loveless marriages, all in the name of religion. "Das Christusbild," which according to Franzos's preface was the first ghetto story he ever wrote, was completed in 1868. It is another tragic love story of a Jew and a Christian, and in the story the Christian countess paints an ironic portrait of her love, a Jewish doctor, as Jesus Christ. "Ohne Inschrift" is Franzos's most powerful condemnation of the ignorance and fanaticism of the Hasidic sect predominant in the Eastern European Jewish settlements. The title refers to tombstones without names that were customarily placed over the graves of those who had gravely transgressed against the so-called sacred laws of the community. The story contains a line summing up Franzos's view of Jewish life in Eastern Europe—he calls the Jewish cemetery (which the Jews of Eastern Europe called "the good place"—"der gute Ort") "the only place where neither the Pole's whip nor the greedy hand of the 'wonder rabbi' reaches" ("das einzige Plätzchen . . . wohin weder die Peitsche des Polen reicht, noch die gierige Hand des Wunderrabbi"). The story identifies one such gravestone "without epitaph" as that of a woman whose only transgression was that she, with her understanding husband's concurrence, had kept her own hair after marriage when the Eastern European Jewish custom, sanctified by custom to the rank of a holy commandment, was to shear, or even shave, a woman's head before the wedding; thereafter for the rest of her life she had to wear an ugly wig or head covering.

Judith Trachtenberg is an elaboration on the theme of the almost inevitable tragedy resulting from a mixed marriage between Jew and Christian at the time. Though now it is probably read—if at all—simply as a love story with a tragic ending, it is better read as a sociological picture of the time as well. If not a great work of literature, it is still an important work of a sensitive, observant, and talented artist.

Der Pojaz, Franzos's masterpiece, goes beyond the simple ghetto story, and although it may be considered as an outgrowth of the subgenre of the Jewish artistic genius in conflict with Eastern European Jewish conservatism, it has attained a universality lacking in the ghetto stories. Sender Glatteis's tragedy is a universal human tragedy, not one limited to the ghetto. Into this novel Franzos has distilled all the vital points he had made throughout his major works, including his travel books. These include his revulsion for the various forms of anti-Semitism encountered in their worst forms in Eastern Europe, his equal hatred of the tyranny exercised by the Hasidic "wonder rabbis" over the population of the Eastern European shtetel, and his apparently unshakable belief in the power of German culture, once acquired by the Jews, to cure all the ills afflicting them. In hindsight, it is all too easy to castigate Franzos for his preoccupation with German culture, but at the time the only alternative, Zionism, seemed absurdly undesirable or out of reach to most enlightened Jews.

Clearly, Karl Emil Franzos was a complex personality, and his best works are likewise too complex to be susceptible to a quick and simplified analysis. Such an analysis, however, used cautiously, is an essential first step toward the appreciation of the works of this extraordinary writer. Franzos's unpublished literary remains are preserved in the Stadt- und Landesbibliothek, Vienna.

Bibliography

Claudia Albert and Gregor Blum, "Des Sender Glatteis neue Kleider: Judentum und Assimilation bei Karl Emil Franzos (1848–1904)," *Die Horen* 30 (1985): 68–92; Martha Bickel, "Zum Werk von Karl Emil Franzos," *Juden in der deutschen Literatur: Ein deutsch-israelisches Symposion,* ed. Stéphane Moses and Albrecht Schöne (Frankfurt a. M.: Suhrkamp, 1986), 152–61; Ludwig Geiger, "Karl Emil Franzos," *Jahrbuch für jüdische Geschichte und Literatur* 11 (1908): 176–229; Mark H. Gelber, "Ethnic Pluralism and Germanization in the Works of K. E. Franzos (1848–1904)," *German Quarterly* 56 (1983): 376–85; Jost Hermand, *Geschichten aus dem Ghetto* (Frankfurt a. M.: Athenäum, 1987); Hermand, "Karl Emil Franzos: *Der Pojaz* (1905)," *Unbequeme Literatur: Eine Beispielreihe* (Heidelberg: Lothar Stiehm, 1971), 107–27; Sybille Hubach, *Galizische Träume: Die jüdischen Erzählungen des Karl Emil Franzos* (Stuttgart: Hans-Dieter Heinz, Akademischer Verlag, 1986); Maria Klanska, *Problemfeld Galizien in deutschsprachiger Prosa, 1846–1914* (Vienna: Böhlau, 1991); Margarita Pazi, "Die frühen Erzählungen von Karl Emil Franzos," *Die Bukowina: Studien zu einer versunkenen Literaturlandschaft* (Tübingen: Francke, 1990), 49–62; Pazi, "Karl Emil Franzos' Assimilationsvorstellung und Assimilationserfahrung," *Conditio Judaica: Judentum, Antisemitismus und deutschsprachige Literatur vom 18. Jahrhundert bis zum Ersten Weltkrieg* (Tübingen: Niemeyer, 1988–89), 218–33; Egon Schwarz and Russell A. Berman, "Karl Emil Franzos: *Der Pojaz* (1905): Aufklärung, Assimilation und ihre realistischen Grenzen," *Romane und Erzählungen des Bürgerlichen Realismus: Neue Interpretationen* (Stuttgart: Reclam, 1980), 378–92; Fred Sommer, *"Halb-Asien": German Nationalism and the Eastern European Works of Karl Emil Franzos* (Stuttgart: Akademischer Verlag Heinz, 1984); and Carl Steiner, *Karl Emil Franzos, 1848–1904: Emancipator and Assimilationist* (New York: Peter Lang, 1990).

KENNETH H. OBER

1906 The discipline of *Sexualwissenschaft* emerges in Germany, creating divergent notions of the sexuality of European Jewry

In 1906, the Berlin Jewish physician Iwan Bloch (1872–1922) coined the term *Sexualwissenschaft* to designate the body of scientific knowledge about sexuality that had been accumulating for about half a century. The "science of sexuality" had emerged out of mid-nineteenth-century criminology from reflections on the connections between criminality and sexual proclivities. At first, following a long theological tradition, it was argued that masturbation lay at the roots of perverse sexual behavior. But as criminologists such as Cesare Lombroso claimed that the "criminal mind" was inherited rather than acquired, forensic medicine began to consider sexual perversion as equally inborn. Gradually separating from criminology, the investigation of sexuality was now taken up by physicians specializing in neurology.

With the publication of Richard Krafft-Ebing's *Psychopathia Sexualis* in 1886, sexology gained its most definitive taxonomy. Krafft-Ebing shared with other physicians of his time the assumption that sexual pathology was a product of degenerate nerves, a congenital defect provoked by modern civilization (Krafft-Ebing's position was therefore closer to Lamarckian than Darwinian biology). By using the already established Latin term *Psychopathia Sexualis* for the title of his classic work, Krafft-Ebing canonized the medical monopoly on sexuality. The study of sexual practices was to be an arcane science, limited to experts and defined by a concept of pathology. By implication, the students of these phenomena remained outside the object of study because they were, presumably, healthy doctors, immunized by the scientific jargon of their craft from infection by the pathologic agent. Indeed, Krafft-Ebing engaged in linguistic immunization by encoding his more titillating tales in Latin. Sexual pathology was to be divorced in this way from the erotic.

Krafft-Ebing's disciples, including Bloch, never broke from the master in this general scientific tendency. Yet by referring to the new branch of medicine not as *Psychopathia Sexualis* but as the German equivalent of "sexology," Bloch and his contemporaries subtly shifted the emphasis away from pathology and toward universal human drives. Although the practitioners remained overwhelmingly physicians, the shift from Latin to German signaled the possibility of a science that might address the general human condition. Normal sexuality, including the sexual practices of other peoples, increasingly became the focus of study alongside the sexual pathology of fin-de-siècle Europeans. If, as Bloch argued in his anthropological studies, all peoples exhibited the same range of sexual practices and pathologies, then the presumed sexual difference (whether positive or negative) of modern Europeans from all non-European others might be erased.

By universalizing the study of sexuality, the new Sexualwissenschaft also implicitly shifted the framework for thinking about the sexuality of Europe's own Other, the Jews. In his *Textbook of Insanity,* Richard Krafft-Ebing had claimed that Jews exhibit "abnormally intensified sensuality and sexual excitement that leads to sexual errors that are of etiological significance" (English ed., 1904, 143). Krafft-Ebing held that Jewish sexual neurosis was a product of degeneration, the "modern" condition that was widely believed to be over-represented among Jews. Both popular anti-Semitic culture and the dominant medical opinion of the fin de siècle considered Jews to be a neurologically diseased people whose pathology was inextricably linked to perversion and hypersexuality.

Yet Krafft-Ebing's position should not be automatically labeled "anti-Semitic," because there is no evidence that he advocated any political consequences for the Jews as a result of his diagnosis. On the contrary, his politics appear to have been liberal and tolerant, especially with respect to those ostensibly suffering from "degenerative" disorders. The congruence of medical with anti-Semitic opinion does not mean that one should necessarily be reduced to the other. Yet even if medical opinion was not automatically anti-Semitic and was indeed shared by many Jews, physicians, and nonphysicians alike, it nonetheless gave the prejudices of the anti-Semites "scientific" legitimation.

Many, although not all, of the generation of sexologists who followed Krafft-Ebing were Jews. Notable among these were Bloch himself, Magnus Hirschfeld, Max Marcuse, Alfred Moll, Alfred Blaschko, and, of course, Sigmund Freud. Most of these were sons of families that had migrated from the East to cities like Berlin and Vienna. Some, like Hirschfeld and Blaschko, were sons of physicians. Many were politically left-wing and had ties to utopian and Socialist movements. It was not uncommon for Jewish physicians to take up marginal specialties, and it is perhaps no surprise that the creation of a new medical discipline, such as sexology, might be the product of those already on the professional margins.

For these Jewish sexologists, Krafft-Ebing's pathologizing of Jewish culture had to have posed a serious challenge, especially because he had virtually canonical status in the field. I wish to think about the way in which Jewish sexologists responded to Krafft-Ebing's overall hypotheses in light of the Jewish issue that he himself raised. I do not claim that they necessarily formulated their theories as conscious "Jewish" responses to the problem of presumed Jewish pathology. On the contrary, few wrote as self-identified Jews. Magnus Hirschfeld's protest against the anti-Semites for identifying him as a Jew was typical of most of these assimilated Jewish physicians (Herzer 1992, 25). To be a scientist at the turn of the century meant that one at least theoretically belonged to a fraternity in which identity played no role. Yet in light of the cultural context in which the sexologists operated, silence often spoke as loudly as speech. The unsettled debate over what can be ferreted out of Freud's Jewish identity from his psychoanalytic writing demonstrates how effective science could be in both obscuring such questions and at the same time drawing attention to the questions themselves. Among the Jewish sexologists, we will find a variety of strategies for both addressing the question of Jewish pathology and, simultaneously, deflecting away personal questions of identity.

We begin with Iwan Bloch's *Beiträge zur Aetiologie der Psychopathia sexualis* (1902–3). Iwan Bloch undertook an anthropological account of human sexuality that was explicitly aimed against Krafft-Ebing and his theory of congenital degeneracy. Although Krafft-Ebing had claimed that modern society exhibited more sexual pathology than did "primitive" societies, Bloch argued that all peoples were equally susceptible to the full range of sexual practices and perversions: "The nature of the sex impulse and of its anomalies is simply independent of all culture, and exhibits the same characteristics among primitive and civilized peoples" (Bloch 1933, 9). At the same time, Bloch rejected any hereditary or racial cause of sexual difference, the second pole of Krafft-Ebing's theory. Bloch's explanation of difference was reminiscent of Montesquieu, for it was based primarily on the effects of climate, altitude, and other environmental factors. Thus, subscribing uncritically to the Orientalism of his day, he speaks of the "tremendous prevalence of sexual perversions among the Semites living in the Orient (Arabs) who spread them everywhere" (39), as a result of factors other than race or culture, presumably those related to the heat of the Middle East. On the other hand: "If it is thought in Aryan Europe that the Semite is especially sensual, the opinion may be based on prejudice rather than on factually established race distinctions. Among the Jews, at least, unnatural vice is of conspicuously rare occurrence" (39). Bloch therefore subscribes to the prejudices of "Aryan Europe" about the Semites living in the Middle East, but excludes the "Semites"—the Jews— who live in Europe. Indeed, he singles the Jews out as those who seemingly exhibit none of the sexual characteristics that he elsewhere claims to be eternal.

By universalizing sexual pathology, Bloch implicitly defended the Jews against Krafft-Ebing's degeneration theory: all people, not only the hyper-modern Jews, are driven by the same sexual impulses and suffer the same defects. At the same time, however, he explicitly excluded the Jews from universal sexuality: only the Jews are sexually "pure." In a peculiar way, then, Bloch's theory retains a kind of doctrine of the chosenness or exceptionality of the Jews.

Bloch grounds this position in what appears to be a contradiction in his argument that culture plays no role in sexual proclivities. Against this hypothesis, he claims that religion—surely a type of culture—is the cause of much of sexual pathology: "every kind of sexual perversion and anomaly known to us may be of religious origin" (Bloch 1933, 110, see also 115). He attacks the theological treatment of sexual questions, especially through the confessional, as a kind of aberrant precursor of Sexualwissenschaft that promoted rather than cured perversion. Although he notes that both Islam and Judaism—as well as every other religion—contain "sexual casuistry," his primary target is Christianity. Indeed, he blames Christianity for the persecution of witches, which he considers a product of sexual pathology. But then he notes that "only the Jews—perhaps because of cruel persecution—remained uninfected by the hysteria." He quotes Curt Müller, a historian of the persecution of witches in Germany, who argued about Jews that "They have to thank for [the fact that they were free from superstition against witches] their fundamentally sane religion which has not suffered so many alterations and schisms" (Bloch 1933, 109).

Thus, whereas all religions have more or less the same "sexual admixture," only Judaism remained "virtually uncontaminated even in the Middle Ages by the monstrous sexual aberrations prevailing all around them" (Bloch 1933, 64). This purity they owed to their religion, which fostered an "exemplary family life and profoundly intimate concept of marriage, since their dispersion into all countries." This "intense family life" was unknown in biblical times, but was instead produced by the "sufferings" of dispersion. One might add that the Jews, as a dispersed people, were no longer susceptible to the effects of the particular climatic geography of the Middle East; perhaps their very lack of rootedness explained how they escaped the sexual fate of all other nations.

Bloch's argument followed a well-established Jewish apologetic in Germany that claimed uncommon sexual purity for the Jews as a result of their family life. The Jews, according to this position, were the prototypical bourgeois—more bourgeois than the Christians in their sexual values. But here this homiletical commonplace had infiltrated a seemingly scientific study of sexuality. Far from a degenerate race suffering a higher degree of sexual pathology, the Jews now emerged as the most healthy. In a sense, this argument recapitulated one of the major debates over Jewish emancipation: were the Jews "modern" enough to be emancipated? What Bloch claimed was that, at least in terms of sexuality, no real distinction could be drawn between modernity and earlier ages, but that the Jews were much farther along the road toward a perfect future than any other people.

A related but somewhat differently argued position was that of Otto Rank, who wrote in 1905, shortly after his conversion to psychoanalysis, an essay in which he dealt with Jewish sexuality.

Rank defined "the essence of Judaism" as its "stress on primitive sexuality," which the Jews were forced to repress as a result of exile (Rank 1981, 171). For Rank, as for Bloch, Jewish sexuality is somehow healthier than that of the non-Jews, but its healthy phase was in the biblical rather than the exilic period. Once again, the Jews offered the best model for modernity, but only if they returned to their biblical roots.

Freud's position on the Jews also shared much with Bloch's, although it was less systematic and explicit. Freud was well aware of the possible consequences for Jews of a theory of degeneration. As he wrote in his early *Studies in Hysteria,* "We should do well to distinguish between the concepts of 'disposition' and 'degeneration' as applied to people; otherwise we shall find ourselves forced to admit that humanity owes a large proportion of its great achievements to the efforts of 'degenerates'" (Breuer and Freud 1957, 104). The theory of degeneration had argued for the creativity of degenerates and Freud surely was thinking of the consequences for his own self-identity as a creative Jewish scientist when he wrote these lines. Indeed, it has often been argued that Freud's universal theory of sexuality served to generalize and therefore obscure the specific Jewish cultural context in which he worked.

Freud's views of the relationship of Jews to sexuality, insofar as he directly expressed them, were contradictory. On the one hand, in some of his early writing, he appears to argue that Jews suffer less "cultural hypocrisy" around this issue and that, as a Jew, he was better equipped to give sexuality an open, scientific treatment (Freud 1959, 5:170). On the other hand, in later works—especially *Moses and Monotheism*—he stressed the way monotheism created a renunciation of the instincts. Here, the Jews are cast as superior because they were the first to sublimate their desires. In both cases, as with Bloch and Rank, Jewish sexuality becomes a kind of model for the modern world.

The rejection of the theory of degeneration led to several alternative possibilities besides Bloch's anthropology. On the one hand, sexual variety, if not determined by genetic predisposition, might be the result of some chance event such as child-hood trauma. This was the "seduction" theory of Binet (as well as of Charcot and Magnan) to which the early Freud subscribed. On the other hand, as Alfred Moll (1862–1939) and Freud himself came to argue, sexual variety might be the result of different patterns within normal childhood development. Moll did not discover childhood sexuality, but he gave it its most systematic developmental scheme; he argued that the object of children's sexual desire was undifferentiated until adulthood. In his *Libido Sexualis* (published in 1897), Moll found evidence for childhood sexuality in early childhood. Moreover, he argued that sexual "perversions" in childhood were not predictive of abnormal adult sexuality.

Moll thus opened up a new field in the study of normal sexuality. Here, too, one might argue that this new theory had consequences for the widespread beliefs about Jewish sexuality, even though neither Moll nor Freud ever explicitly drew them. Both Moll and Freud wrote at a time when the blood libel was enjoying a resurgence in Central Europe. The accusation that Jews kill Christian children for their blood appealed to the same fears as those aroused by a fear of childhood seduction. That is, both sets of beliefs were grounded in images of innocent children severely at risk from depredations by adults. The similarity in appeal of blood libel and childhood seduction traumas is most evident in arguments in contemporary culture regarding the satanic abuse of children, the motifs of which are frequently identical to those of the blood libel. By arguing that it was not childhood seductions but rather variations within childhood sexuality that determined later pathology, the new theory at once made children less innocent and undermined the belief in widespread, actual abuse. With Freud, seduction became imagined, just as the Jews argued, in self-defense, for a psychological explanation for blood accusations. I am not trying to assert here that it was fear of the blood libel that caused such Jewish sexologists as Moll and Freud to develop their accounts of childhood sexuality and the role of the unconscious; rather I suggest cultural parallels between the arguments.

A similar kind of claim can be made about homosexuality. There was already a lively debate in the early decades of the century about the number of Jewish homosexuals. Many anti-Semites, starting perhaps with Eugen Dühring in 1897, connected Jews to homosexuality, and such Jewish sexologists as Magnus Hirschfeld and Benedict Friedländer who campaigned for homosexual rights were regularly attacked as *hebräische Arzte* (Hebrew doctors). Not only anti-Semitic propagandists adopted such arguments; there were also physicians who claimed a high incidence of homosexuality among Jews. Curiously enough, given the prevailing theory of homosexuality as neurasthenia and a lack of virility, such an association of Jews with homosexuality contradicted the equally prevalent belief in Jewish hypersexuality.

The Jewish defense against such charges commonly took one of two forms. Alfred Moll, for example, argued in his important early work on homosexuality, *Die konträre Sexualempfindung* (1891), that there were an equivalent number of Jewish and Christian homosexuals (151). Iwan Bloch, on the other hand, disputed Moll with the statement: "Not only have I been unable to round up one single homosexual among the Jews; I have been assured by other experienced physicians that homosexual Israelites were of the greatest rarity" (Bloch 1933, 64). One wonders whether Bloch had consulted with his colleague Magnus Hirschfeld on this point, although Hirschfeld never openly declared his homosexuality.

Hirschfeld himself (1868–1935) offers a striking example of the cultural parallels between debates over homosexuality and debates about the Jews. Hirschfeld was closer to the biological, hereditary model for sexual diversity than were Bloch, Moll, or Freud. He subscribed to Ulrich's "third sex" theory of homosexuality. This "intermediate" sex consisted of a female soul in a male body and was determined, following Steinach's hormonal theory, by a difference in the hormone balance of the testicles. Homosexuals exhibited effeminate behavior and had different physical features than heterosexuals.

On the basis of this theory, Hirschfeld argued for homosexual rights on the same grounds as for the rights of women: each of the three sexes was the product of biology, and culture should not discriminate among them. The psychological health of homosexuals could only be guaranteed by allowing them free expression of their nature. Yet Hirschfeld constructed homosexual subjectivity in a restricted way that appealed for compassion more than it did for true equality. In his view, the "Urning" was, *by nature*, weak and effeminate and was therefore implicitly to be pitied by a culture that privileged male virility.

It was precisely on this point that Hirschfeld's colleague and then opponent, Benedict Friedländer, broke with Hirschfeld and participated in the formation of a different view of the homosexual. According to Friedländer, the true homosexual is virile and aggressive; he is a male in all respects and, in fact, the male "bonding" of homosexuals is superior to all other social forms. Homosexuality was therefore not a third sex but the apotheosis of the male sex. This theory was expounded by a number of non-Jewish homosexuals as well, including the *Wandervogel* ideologue Hans Blüher. In its assertion that homosexuals exhibited aggressive tendencies and its endorsement of male camaraderie, this position on homosexuality stood much closer to German nationalism, and some of its advocates (including Friedländer) were anti-Semitic as well.

This tension within the homosexual movement mirrored the contemporary debates among Jews, and between Jews and their opponents, over emancipation and assimilation. Were the Jews to be emancipated out of compassion for their disabilities or because they were truly the same as non-Jews? Or, conversely, were they superior in some way? Was the assimilated Jew outwardly like the Christian, but inwardly different? If so, this difference might be based on a body-soul dichotomy like that advocated by some of the third-sex theorists, such as Ulrich, about homosexuals. On the other hand, if homosexuals had visible bodily characteristics, as Hirschfeld had argued, perhaps the same might be said about Jews. In short, even if these discourses did not fully overlap, the similar standing of Jews and homosexuals as partly visible, partly invisible "Others" generated similar structures of argument. In both cases, much of the defensive work of the theories was directed against the degeneration model, which condemned Jews and homosexuals to a pathological status.

There were, of course, those Jewish physicians who accepted the degeneration theory for the Jews and prescribed a variety of cures. Perhaps the best known of these was Max Nordau, who was trained in neurological medicine, although he was not a student of sexuality. Nordau gave the classic expression to the theory of degeneration in his book of that name, which created a sensation when it was published in the 1890s. According to Nordau, of all the components of degeneration, sexual pathology was perhaps the most pervasive, but it was a curiously contradictory pathology: "The emotionalism of the degenerate has, as a rule, an erotic coloring, because of the pathological alteration in their sexual centers. The abnormal excitability of these parts of the nervous system can have as a consequence both an especial attraction towards woman and an especial antipathy to her. The common element connecting these opposing effects of one and the same organic condition is the being constantly occupied with woman, the being constantly engrossed with presentations in consciousness from the religion of sexuality" (Nordau, *Degeneration,* 167–68). The "sexual centers" rule the "erotomaniacal" degenerate: "He feels that he cannot resist the exciting influences proceeding from the woman, that he is her helpless slave. . . . He necessarily, therefore, sees in woman an uncanny, overpowering force of nature, bestowing supreme delights or dealing destruction." Obsessed by women, the degenerate either falls into promiscuity or flees to the opposite extreme of celibacy. Healthy sexuality, on the other hand, involves cool detachment, and marriage should be contracted not to satisfy the libido but as a social arrangement.

Nordau applied these theories to the Jews in his Zionist writings, and he clearly conceived of Zionist culture as a cure for Jewish degeneracy. His vision of "Judaism with muscles" included sexual health as well. Zionism would save the Jews from the dual consequences of sexual degeneracy: promiscuity and celibacy.

Other Zionists developed Nordau's theories in greater detail. The physician Rafael Becker wrote two essays, in 1918 and 1919, about the nervous diseases of the Jews; he attributed these diseases to Jews' political status as a minority and their skewed occupational structure, as the result of which they tended to marry late (a theme taken up by Jewish demographers as well). Late marriage thus became a believed cause of degeneration because the period when sexual desire is greatest is spent in frustration. And as a consequence of degeneration, the argument continued, Jewish fertility had fallen drastically. For Becker, like Nordau, Zionism was the answer to these sexual dilemmas, because it addressed the root causes of Jewish degeneracy both by bringing about greater sexual restraint and by increasing fertility.

This obsession with the problem of Jewish fertility, which paralleled a similar obsession about German fertility, was already at least a decade old when Becker wrote his treatises. In 1911, Felix Theilhaber had published his *Der Untergang der deutschen Juden* (The decline of the German Jews), in which he predicted the demise of the German-Jewish community as a result of demographic factors. Chief among these was late age of marriage, which led to low fertility. Theilhaber's argument was profoundly conservative: in previous ages, the Jewish family had effectively protected the Jews from sexual disease. Jewish sexual health was assured because "the Jews never had a real eroticism" (Theilhaber 1911, 151). Jewish sexuality was controlled by religious imperatives that effectively de-eroticized the culture. But in modern times, this ethic had broken down and especially Jewish students, apprentices, and travelers had become susceptible to all kinds of degenerate behavior and disease. Theilhaber also attacked feminism for destroying the family. He advocated a new Jewish ethic of procreation in order to counter these trends.

Some, like Walter Rathenau, argued that the only hope for the Jews was intermarriage and that, paradoxically, Jews would survive only by assimilating. In Rathenau's opinion, Jewish inbreeding had produced a kind of degeneracy. This view was linked to the anti-Semitic accusation that the Jews engaged in incest. Yet a contrary medical view held that mixed marriages tended to produce fewer children than either marriages among Jews or between Protestants and Catholics. Racial theorists argued that this was proof that Jews were of such a different race that they could not mix biologically with non-Jews; such marriages were, of necessity, sterile. Against this view, the sexologist Max Marcuse wrote in 1920 that the low rate of fertility among mixed married couples had nothing to do with biology and everything to do with culture. Marcuse denounced such marriages as a betrayal of the Jewish people, but his defense of the Jews, interestingly enough, was not religious. Jews, for Marcuse, as well as for many others of the period, were to be defined as a *Stamm*, a tribe—or what would today be called an ethnic group. This position reflected a kind of nonbiological racialism.

There was, then, no such thing as *a* Jewish sexology, for the Jewish sexologists occupied all possible positions on the scientific map. Yet, as Sander Gilman has argued, the invention of a "science of sexuality" precisely at the time when the sexuality of the Jews had become such a central issue meant that the work of these physicians, even if they were silent on the Jews, resonated loudly against the Jewish Question. At times, the presumed sexual maladies of the Jews were seen as evidence of normal diversity. In other contexts, however, the Jews were held up as a model for sexual health in a degenerate world. In either case, whether intentionally or not, the Jewish sexologists who followed Krafft-Ebing persistently shaped or revised their teacher's theories in ways that acquire an additional dimension when placed in this Jewish context. Sexology in Central Europe was in no sense a "Jewish" science, despite the preponderance of Jews in its ranks; rather it was a science that can be fully understood only in the larger picture of Jewish-German relations at the beginning of this century.

Bibliography

Iwan Bloch, *Beiträge zur Aetiologie der Psychopathia sexualis* (Dresden: H. R. Dohrn, 1902–3), Eng. trans. of vol. 1, *Anthropological Studies in the Strange Sexual Practices of All Races in All Ages* (New York: Anthropological Press, 1933); Bloch, *Das Sexualleben unserer Zeit* (Berlin: L. Marcus, 1906); Josef Breuer and Sigmund Freud, *Studies on Hysterics* (New York: Avon, 1957); John Fout, "Sexual Politics in Wilhelmine Germany: The Male Gender Crisis, Moral Purity, and Homophobia," *Journal of the History of Sexuality* 3 (Jan. 1992): 388–422; Sigmund Freud, *Collected Papers,* trans. Joan Riviere (New York: Basic Books, 1959); Freud, *Moses and Monotheism,* trans. Katherine Jones (New York: Vintage Books, 1939); Sander L. Gilman, *The Case of Sigmund Freud* (Baltimore, Md.: John Hopkins University Press, 1993); Gilman, *Freud, Race, and Gender* (Princeton, N.J.: Princeton University Press, 1993); Gert Hekma, "'A Female Soul in a Male Body': Sexual Inversion as Gender Inversion in Nineteenth-Century Sociology," *Third Sex, Third Gender: Beyond Sexual Dimorphism in Culture and History,* ed. Gert Hekma (New York: Zone Books, 1994), 213–40; Manfred Herzer, *Magnus Hirschfeld: Leben und Werk eines jüdischen, schwulen und sozialistischen Sexologen* (Frankfurt a. M.: Campus Books, 1992); Magnus Hirschfeld, *Die Homosexualität des Mannes und des Weibes* (New York: Walter de Gruyter, 1984); Hirschfeld, *Sexual Pathology,* trans. Jerome Gibbs (New York: Emerson Books, 1940); Richard von Krafft-Ebing, *Psychopathia Sexualis* (Stuttgart: F. Enke, 1886); Krafft-Ebing, *Textbook of Insanity* (New York: F. A. Davis, 1904); Max Marcuse, *Über die Fruchtbarkeit der christlich jüdischen Mischehe* (Bonn: A. Marcus und E. Webers, 1920); Alfred Moll, *Die konträre Sexualempfindung* (Berlin: Fischers Medicin Buchhandlung, 1899); Moll, *Ein Leben als Arzt der Seele* (Dresden: Carl Reisner, 1936); Moll, *Untersuchungen über die Libido sexualis* (Berlin: Fischer, 1897); George Mosse, *Nationalism and Sexuality* (New York: H. Fertig, 1985); Max Nordau, *Degeneration* (New York: Appleton, 1895); Otto Rank, "The Essence of Judaism," *Jewish Origins of the Psychoanalytic Movement,* trans. Dennis Klein (New York: Praeger, 1981); James Steakley, *The Homosexual Emancipation Movement in Germany* (New York: Arno Press, 1975); Frank Sulloway, *Freud, Biologist of the Mind* (New York: Basic Books, 1979); Felix Theilhaber, *Der Untergang der deutschen Juden* (Munich: E. Reinhardt, 1911); Paul Weindling, *Health, Race and German Politics Between National Unification and Nazism, 1870–1945* (Cambridge: Cambridge University Press, 1989); Annemarie Wettley, *Von der 'Psychopathia sexualis' zur Sexualwissenschaft* (Stuttgart: F. Enke, 1959); and Charlotte Wolf, *Magnus Hirschfeld* (London: Quartet, 1986).

DAVID BIALE

1908 Prussian universities allow women to matriculate for the first time

In the fall of 1908, Prussian universities finally opened their doors to women, admitting them as regular students in nearly all faculties except for theology. Austrian universities had already begun accepting women students a decade earlier in 1897, whereas the universities of Baden started allowing them to enroll in 1900 and those in Bavaria began admitting women in 1903. But 1908 was an important date for German women, especially German-Jewish women, because henceforth, with the proper preparation, they could attend the university of their choice and not have to go far from home. Formerly, women who wished to pursue advanced study had to go to Switzerland or to one of the few German universities that would tolerate them as special students or auditors.

University education enabled women to expand their horizons and become twentieth-century "new women." Middle-class girls no longer had to restrict themselves to segregated female education, which prepared them for traditional roles as wife and mother or trained them as elementary school teachers, nurses, or social workers. They could now aspire to enter previously all-male professions and become physicians, high school teachers, economists, scientists, and, after World War I, even lawyers and academics. Woman were given the chance to attain intellectual self-fulfillment through the study of philology, art history, philosophy, or physics, even if they did not plan to pursue a career. Their path would not be easy, but the opportunity for study and for professional careers was now available.

Even before 1908, Jewish women, including many from Eastern Europe, were very visible among the pioneering generation of female students in Switzerland, as well as in Germany and Austria. Middle-class Jewish families in Central Europe in the nineteenth century had generally provided their daughters with the finest girls' education available, often in private schools or through governesses at home. As soon as universities offered them access, Jewish girls and young women sought special tutoring and flocked to the cram courses and the brand-new girls' gymnasia where they could learn Latin, Greek, mathematics, and physics in order to prepare for their matriculation (*Abitur* or *Matura*) examination. Jewish women were particularly drawn to medical schools because, as Jews, their employment opportunities as high school teachers were extremely limited and because women teachers were generally not permitted to marry;

The database to which I refer throughout is part of a larger ongoing project of mine, a collective biography of Central European Jewish university women in the early twentieth century. This analysis is based on information gleaned primarily from published and unpublished memoirs, biographies, and biographical dictionaries, as well as questionnaires and interviews. It focuses on a study population of 420 Jewish women who attended university in Central Europe before the Nazi era.

in addition, women were not admitted to the bar in either Germany or Austria until after World War I.

Jewish women were attracted to universities in disproportionately large numbers. In 1908, Jewish women made up 40 percent of the female student population at the University of Vienna and 60 percent of the women students in the faculty of medicine. On the eve of World War I, Jews constituted 11 percent of the women students at Prussian universities and 30 percent within the medical schools. During the interwar years, the absolute numbers of Jewish women attending universities continued to increase, although their relative numbers declined due to the increasing popularity of higher education among Protestant and Catholic women. In 1931, Jewish women still composed 7 percent of all German university women, including 14 percent of the women studying law and 12 percent of those in medicine. In Austria, at the University of Vienna in 1933, they amounted to almost 20 percent of the women students overall, and in particular 38 percent of those in medicine, 20 percent of those in law, and 13 percent of the women studying philosophy.

To what extent did these university women contribute to the written legacy of German-Jewish women? *Bibliographia Judaica* lists 788 Jewish women who published works in German, 593 of whom were born between 1870 and 1920 and hence theoretically had the opportunity of attending Central European universities before World War II. Of these, slightly over 200 had earned doctorates; others attended universities without completing their degrees. Thus, more than one-third of the German-Jewish women writers born in the late nineteenth and early twentieth centuries were among the first two generations of Central European university women.

Within a database of 420 women of Jewish origin who attended German or Austrian universities before the Nazi era, more than half have publications to their credit aside from their doctoral dissertations, including scholarly, literary, and journalistic works. Although most of these writings are in German, many are in English and

some are in other languages, including Hebrew and French. At least seventy Jewish university women have written memoirs or autobiographies of varying lengths. Andreas Lixl-Purcell has identified more than 400 memoirs by Central European Jewish women; university-educated women contributed almost 20 percent of this total.

Although only a small minority of university women have left written accounts of their lives, their memoirs provide many insights into their shared experiences and the making of the Jewish "new woman." Nearly all of these memoirs begin with a nostalgic description of an idyllic childhood in a middle-class, often upper-middle-class, Jewish family before World War I. Their fathers were usually successful businessmen or professionals and their mothers were highly cultured housewives (or sometimes widows). Fathers proved much more likely than mothers to serve as their daughters' role models; many of these women were rebelling against following in their mother's footsteps. Most of these memoir writers came from large urban centers and associated primarily with other Jews, especially during their school years. Those from smaller towns tended to have more close friendships with non-Jews. Few of them recall anti-Semitism as affecting their childhood years, except in the form of social segregation.

German *Bildung* played an important role in their upbringing, whereas Jewish observance, in most cases, had been declining for several generations. Relatively few of these memoirs were written from either an Orthodox or a Zionist perspective, although Rahel Straus's *Wir lebten in Deutschland* (My life in Germany; 1961) proves a notable exception. Although some women mention synagogue attendance and the Friday night dinners of their childhood, many of these university women were raised in highly assimilated households where Christmas was more likely to be celebrated than the High Holy Days or Passover Seders. Some of these women, especially those who later became academics, were baptized as children; others, including Alice Salomon and Edith Stein, were baptized as adults. Interestingly enough, Edith Stein's memoir, which she wrote while already a Catholic nun, was entitled *Life in a Jewish Family* (1986). Two rather exceptional women, Emilie Melchior Braun and Margarete Sallis-Freudenthal, who were raised as Christians, describe in their memoirs how they later returned to the fold. Quite a few of these writers, including Käte Frankenthal, Käthe Leichter, Toni Sender, Marie Langer, and Genia Quittner, were actively involved in either Socialist or Communist parties and eventually left the Jewish community, but they do not always mention this in their memoirs. Most university women of Jewish origin remained at least nominally within the Jewish community, although their Jewishness often did not play an important role in their lives before the advent of Hitler.

The memoirs indicate how common an early immersion in German literature and culture was in Jewish households. Many writers recall being exposed to German classics, as well as art and music, in their homes at a very young age, with parents and sometimes grandparents reciting Goethe and Schiller to them before they could even read. Others developed a love of reading by having unrestricted access to their fathers' extensive libraries. Some wrote poetry and began publishing essays in local newspapers while still in high school. One did not learn to write at the university; one acquired such skills at home on one's own or else in school. A degree was by no means a prerequisite for writing literature, and quite a few university women who later wrote novels or poetry probably would have done so regardless of their degrees. Indeed, most of the best-known German-Jewish women writers of belles lettres, including Else Lasker-Schüler, Nelly Sachs, Vicki Baum, and Gertrud Kolmar, never attended universities.

Young women who chose to continue their education at the university level, especially the pioneering generation before World War I, often encountered obstacles along the way. Although some women received strong encouragement from their families, others met with serious opposition from parents who did not want their daughters to become "bluestockings." Many parents feared that if their daughters attended universities, they would never marry or produce grandchildren. In some cases, these fears were

indeed warranted: among the 420 university women in my database, 26 percent never married (mostly by their own choice); 30 percent eventually married but remained childless; and only 44 percent had children. Among the 200 women within my sample who published nonautobiographical works, slightly over a third remained single, and of the approximately two-thirds who married, only a little more than half had children. University women were often striving for independence from families and rebelling against traditional women's lifestyles; for many, careers and writing served as child-substitutes. The first generation, those who entered universities before World War I, were less likely to marry and more likely to publish than those who studied during the interwar years.

The memoir literature illuminates not only the conflicts within families over whether or not a woman should be allowed to study, but also the trials and tribulations involved in passing the Abitur examination and the hostility that women often encountered from both professors and male students once they reached the university. But rather than focusing on discrimination, most memoirists emphasize the newly found freedom for those living away from home, the excitement of friendships with both men and women, and the intellectual stimulation they discovered in lectures and seminars—as well their appreciation for the professors who served as their mentors. Although women students from large cities tended to live at home during most of their university years, many took advantage of the common practice of transferring from one university to another for one or more semesters. These young women were thereby freed from parental supervision and chaperones; their university experiences helped transform them into independent, if not economically self-sufficient, "new women."

The memoirs also shed light on the effect of World War I on women; on the one hand, they met with deprivations, but on the other hand, new job opportunities opened up, at least temporarily. These sources also increase our understanding of the effects of the inflationary spiral on upper-middle-class Jewish families. Women students who before the war would have received full financial support from their fathers increasingly found themselves working as tutors and at other part-time jobs to help put themselves through school. Paid employment, which had previously been socially unacceptable for respectable women, now became an economic necessity for many. The memoirs chronicle careers and marriage through the 1920s and into the Nazi era. Many of them, especially those written in the late 1930s or 1940s, end with descriptions of the emigration of the authors and their families from Central Europe.

Nearly all of the memoirs of Central European university women were written by émigrés. Very few autobiographies exist of women who perished during the Holocaust. Among them are Edith Stein's work written in a convent in 1935 and Käthe Leichter's memoirs written in 1938 in a Viennese prison. This account of the Austrian Social Democratic activist's life ends abruptly after her university years (Steiner 1973). An important unpublished memoir is Elise Richter's *Summe des Lebens.* Richter, the first woman professor in Austria, who taught Romance philology at the University of Vienna from 1907 to 1938, wrote her life story in 1940 at the age of seventy-five, before being deported to Theresienstadt. Several Holocaust survivors who remained in Europe, particularly those who spent the war in France (such as Lotte Eisner, Lydia Ehrenfried, and Recha Rothschild), have written memoirs. Among the 10 percent of the women writers within my database who returned to Germany or Austria after the war, only a few have published their memoirs. Most memoirs by Central European university women, however, were written from a distance, whether in the United States, England, Israel, or Latin America. The spate of autobiographies written since 1970 often discusses adaptation to life in emigration in considerable detail, as well as the authors' experiences in Europe before and during the Nazi era.

Some university women put their memories on paper in mid-life because of a special project, like the 1939 Harvard University essay competition on "My Life in Germany Before and After 1933," which was won by two physicians, Käte Frankenthal and Hertha Nathorff. But most women who wrote their memoirs generally did so relatively late in life; often they were writing primarily for the benefit of their children or grandchildren, rather than for the general public. For thirty of the seventy memoirists, their life stories represented their only literary efforts and many of these memoirs remain unpublished, whether in private hands or in archives such as the Leo Baeck Institute in New York or the Houghton Library in Boston. The majority of university women who wrote memoirs, however, also published other works.

Although these published and unpublished memoirs provide an important source of information about the lives of Jewish university women and, indeed, the lives of Central European Jewish women in general during the early twentieth century, they are by no means the only, or even the most important, written legacy of women with higher education. Roughly 20 percent of the published authors can be classified as writers by profession, including journalists, novelists, poets, dramatists, film critics, editors, and translators. For these women, many of whom explored several genres, writing provided either a primary or a secondary income in Europe and, in some cases, in the countries to which they emigrated as well. Three-quarters of these women had earned the title of doctor of philosophy; most of the remainder attended universities for several years but never wrote dissertations. Included among the rather lengthy list of university women who became significant literary figures as essayists, poets, novelists, or dramatists are Gertrud Kantorowicz, Grete Meisel-Hess, Anna Seghers, Hilde Domin, Elisabeth Freundlich, Hilde Spiel, Margarete Kollisch, and Gabriele Tergit.

Journalism was only beginning to emerge as a separate field of study at German universities during the interwar years. For the most part, those university women who became journalists or editors received their academic training in other fields. Their ranks included Margaret Muehsam-Edelheim, one of the first women to receive a law degree in Germany in 1914, who wrote for various German and German-Jewish papers both in Europe and in the United States; Lotte Eisner, a journalist and film critic, first in

Germany and later in France, who had a degree in art history; Marie Papanek-Akselrad, who studied agriculture in Vienna but then worked for the newspaper that her father edited; and Martha Wertheimer, who earned a doctorate in philosophy and who wrote a regular advice column and other articles for the *Offenbacher Zeitung* from 1920 to 1933 and then worked as feuilleton editor for the *Israelitisches Familienblatt*.

For many of these professional writers, emigration posed an almost insurmountable language problem. Journalists had a particularly difficult time adapting to a foreign language. Some, like Margaret Muehsam-Edelheim in the United States and Margarethe Turnowsky-Pinner in Israel, continued to write primarily for German-language publications while away from their countries of origin. Several writers, like Anna Seghers, Hilde Spiel, and Elisabeth Freundlich, returned to Germany or Austria to continue their careers. Vera Lachmann, a school director in Germany and a professor of classics and camp director in the United States, always wrote her poetry in German, even though her audience was limited. Some younger poets proved more successful in making the transition to a new language: for example, Hilde Marx, who became a recognized American poet, and Lea Goldberg, one of the best-loved Hebrew poets in Israel. Hebrew, which very few of these university women had learned during their childhood, presented a much greater barrier as a written language than did English, French, or Spanish.

Most of the publications by university women tend to be related to their academic training. The vast majority of these Jewish university women did not write literary works but instead published scholarly and professional articles and books in a wide range of fields. A remarkably large proportion of the women who held academic appointments as untenured associate professors or lecturers in Germany or Austria before the Nazi era were of Jewish origin. Most of them were highly assimilated, if not baptized. This list of recognized women scholars, all of whom had been published extensively, primarily in German, includes among others: Elise Richter in Romance philology and Charlotte Malachowski

Bühler in psychology at the University of Vienna; Lise Meitner in nuclear physics, Lydia Rabinowicz-Kempner in bacteriology, and Hedwig Guggenheimer Hintze in history at the University of Berlin; Emmy Noether in mathematics at Göttingen; and Margarete Bieber in classical archeology at Giessen.

Women who did scholarly research in Germany or Austria were generally paid poorly, if at all. Many held unpaid assistantships in research institutes, taught in untenured (hence unsalaried) faculty positions, or worked as freelance writers. In most cases, their fathers or husbands provided the necessary financial support; women writers who did not have this support barely earned enough to eat. Both Lise Meitner, the cofounder of nuclear fission who recently had a chemical element named in her honor, and Emmy Noether, the abstract algebraist who is perhaps the foremost woman mathematician of the twentieth century, lived very frugally on minimal pay. Tilly Edinger, one of the foremost women paleontologists, received no pay for her research work before her emigration. Nevertheless, these women, and others who are less known, published important scientific and mathematical works and papers.

Women who identified themselves strongly as Jews and were interested in pursuing Jewish research could sometimes write their doctoral dissertations on Jewish topics but could never find academic positions in Europe. At least one such published dissertation, Paula Odenheimer-Weiner's *Die Berufe der Juden in Bayern* (The occupations of the Jews in Bavaria; Munich, 1917), is still cited as a standard work in Jewish economic history. Even though their work achieved considerable acclaim, women scholars such as historian Selma Stern-Täubler, political philosopher Hannah Arendt, and political scientist Eva Reichmann could only find research positions outside of, or else on the fringes of, academia, both in Germany and in emigration. The same holds true for the biblical scholar Nehama Leibowitz and the Arabist-by-training Trude Weiss-Rosmarin, both of whom emigrated soon after receiving their doctorates and became noted Jewish educators and writers—Leibowitz in Palestine / Israel and Weiss-Rosmarin in the United States.

Married university women who were not employed in their own fields often served as their husbands' coresearchers or editors, but they rarely received credit for the publications to which they contributed. One exception was the social psychologist Marie Jahoda, who published the classic study on unemployment, *Die Arbeitslosen von Marienthal* (The unemployed of Marienthal; 1933) with her husband Paul Lazarsfeld. Companionate marriages and shared research interests helped some women continue to publish in high-level journals even while raising children. One example is the Viennese art historian Erica Tietze-Conrat, who was a prolific freelance writer and married to another art historian. When asked how she managed to do her research and publish so many books and articles while fulfilling her responsibilities as a wife and mother of four children, she supposedly replied: "It's easy. I just go away" (Sherman 1981, 305). For most women with children, the solution was not quite so simple, even though housekeepers and child care were common in most middle-class Jewish families. The women within my sample who published nonautobiographical works are divided fairly evenly into three categories: never married, married but childless, and married with children. Single and childless women are thus overrepresented among the writers, but a significant number of women with children were able to publish, whether in Central Europe or in the countries to which they emigrated.

About 25 percent of the Jewish university women within my database had medical degrees, as did one quarter of the women with publications. Thus women who trained as physicians were as likely to publish as those whose had doctorates in the humanities, social sciences, or sciences. Some of these women, including Rahel Hirsch and Selma Meyer, were in medical research. Many others, among them Helene Rosenbach Deutsch, Margaret Schönberger Mahler, Frieda Fromm-Reichmann, Therese Benedek, and Hilde Bruch, became prominent psychiatrists or psychoanalysts. These women, who were among the pioneers in the development of psychoanalysis, published widely, especially in the United States. Both in their writing and their teaching they made extremely important contributions, particularly in the subfields of the psychology of women and child analysis.

Because all of these émigrés spoke with accents, many of them needed editing in their new countries. Quite a few of these women showed considerable linguistic adaptability, however. They sometimes thought, taught, and wrote in different languages. Klara Blum of Vienna, later known as Dshu Bai-Lan, translated from Russian into German while in the Soviet Union, lectured in Chinese in China, and continued to publish articles in German in East Germany. Helen Silving-Ryu, born in Galicia and educated in Vienna, taught in Spanish in Puerto Rico and wrote articles, law textbooks, and her memoirs in English. Several women taught and wrote in French, even though some of them never lived in French-speaking countries. More commonly, émigrés wrote professional articles and books in the language of the land in which they were living, usually English, occasionally French and, more rarely, Hebrew or Spanish. Relatively few women continued to publish scholarly works in German after they had left Central Europe.

The Jewish women writers who received their university education in Germany and Austria proved to be a remarkable group with an impressive range of publications. Their work made its mark in a wide variety of fields, ranging from memoirs to literature and journalism, from science and mathematics to medicine and psychology, and from the social sciences through the humanities. They have left a rich written legacy, but unfortunately their works are not generally known except to specialists in their areas of expertise. If Central European universities had not opened up to women by 1908, German-Jewish literature would have been significantly poorer as a result, because it would have been missing the important contributions provided by Jewish women with higher education.

Bibliography

Christine Backhaus-Lautenschläger, *. . . und standen ihre Frau: Das Schicksal deutschsprachiger Emigrantinnen* *in der USA nach 1933* (Pfaffenweiler: Centaurus, 1991); Renate Heuer, ed., *Bibliographia Judaica,* 2 vols. (Frankfurt a. M.: Campus Verlag, 1981); Andreas Lixl-Purcell, ed., *Erinnerungen deutsch-jüdischer Frauen, 1900–1990* (Leipzig: Reclam, 1992); Elise Richter, "Summe des Lebens," unpub. memoir, Landes- und Staatsarchiv, Vienna, 1940; Claire Richter Sherman, ed., *Women as Interpreters of the Visual Arts* (Westport, Conn.: Greenwood Press, 1981); Edith Stein, *Collected Works of Edith Stein,* ed. L. Gerber and Ramies Leaven, vol. 1 (Washington, D.C.: Institute of Carmelite Studies, 1986); and Herbert Steiner, ed., *Käthe Leichter: Leben und Werk* (Vienna: Europa Verlag, 1973).

HARRIET FREIDENREICH

1910 Ernst Bloch and Georg Lukács meet in Heidelberg

Born in the same year (1895), Ernst Bloch and Georg Lukács are among the more outstanding figures of the romantic and utopian, revolutionary current of the Jewish-German culture. The romantic *Weltanschauung*—as a cultural protest against the disenchantment of the world and the quantification of social values in the modern capitalist and industrial civilization—was dominant in German culture at the turn of the twentieth century, not only in literature and the arts, but also in the *Geisteswissenschaften* (humanities). Although it often assumed conservative and regressive forms, the romantic *Zivilisationskritik* (critique of civilization) could also be progressive and utopian; not surprisingly, most of the writers belonging to the revolutionary pole of the romantic spectrum were of Jewish origin.

The Max Weber Circle in Heidelberg—a group of friends that met regularly at the house of the great German sociologist from 1908 until 1918 and that included people such as Georg Simmel, Ferdinand Tönnies, Werner Sombart, Robert Michels, Ernst Troeltsch, Ernst Bloch, and Georg Lukács—was one of the main informal centers of this romantic culture in the Geisteswissenschaften. It is there, during the years 1910 and 1916, that Bloch and Lukács became friends and wrote their first important works, *Spirit of Utopia* (1918) and *The Theory of the Novel* (1916). It is also during these Heidelberg years that they became interested, for a short period of time, in Jewish culture and religion.

The Jewish German sociologist Paul Honigsheim described the ethos of the Max Weber Circle (of which he also had been a member) in a highly illuminating testimony in his book of memories *On Max Weber* (1968): "Even before the war, from more than one quarter there had been a trend away from the bourgeois way of life, city culture, instrumental rationality, quantification, scientific specialization, and everything else then considered abhorrent phenomena. Lukács and Bloch were part of this trend. This neo-romanticism, if one may call it that, was connected to the older romanticism by means of many, if concealed, little streams of influence. Neo-romanticism in its various forms was also represented at Heidelberg, and its adherents knew on whose door they should knock—Max Weber's door."

Georg Lukács was the son of a rich Jewish banker of Budapest, Joseph Löwinger. There was little Jewish background in his family, and Lukács's cultural *Bildung* was mainly German. He was fascinated by romanticism, and between 1907 and 1908 he outlined the draft of a book to be entitled *Nineteenth Century Romanticism*. His first publication, the collection of essays *Soul and Form* (1910), focused primarily on writers linked to romanticism or to "neo-romanticism"—Novalis, Theodor Storm, Stefan George, and Paul Ernst.

Ernst Bloch was born in the German industrial town of Ludwigshafen, headquarters of IG Farben, but he often wandered into the neighboring city of Mannheim, an old cultural and religious center. As he later said in an interview, the contrast between his native town, which showed "the ugly, naked, and uncaring face of late capitalism" (a symbol of the "railway-station nature" [*Bahnhofshaftigkeit*] of our modern life) and the old city on the other side of the Rhine (inheritor of the "most shining medieval history") had made a deep impression on him. An avid reader of Schelling since adolescence, Bloch studied in Berlin under Georg Simmel. Although he had met Lukács before in Berlin and Budapest, it was after 1910, when both moved to Heidelberg (following a proposal by Bloch), that an intimate friendship developed between them.

During their years in Heidelberg (1910–15) a kind of "ideological symbiosis" united the two young "symphilosophers" in a common ethical and messianic utopianism. Circulating in Heidelberg at that time was a very amusing epigram coined by the neo-Kantian philosopher Emil Lask that admirably captured the common *Geist* of the two: "What are the names of the four evangelists? Matthew, Mark, Lukács, and Bloch." Lukács was responsible for initiating Bloch into the religious universe of Meister Eckhart, Kierkegaard, and Dostoevsky—three key sources in Bloch's intellectual evolution. But contemporary observers sometimes had the impression that Bloch was the guiding figure. Paul Honigsheim, for instance, described the two in the following terms: "Ernst Bloch, the semi-Catholic apocalyptic Jew, with his follower at the time, Lukács." Marianne Weber, in the biography of her husband, mentioned Lukács, with much respect and admiration, as a young philosopher "moved by eschatological hopes on a new emissary of the transcendent God," and seeking salvation "in a socialist social order created by brotherhood"; she also refers to Bloch, in more ironical terms, as "a new Jewish philosopher, who obviously believed that he was the precursor of a new Messiah" (Weber 1926). Honigsheim defined Bloch's ideas as "a combination of Catholic, gnostic, apocalyptic, and collectivist economic elements."

According to Bloch (in an interview), at that time his views and those of Lukács were such that the two philosophers were like communicating vessels: they learned from each other and the few disagreements they had were artificially kept in a sort of "wildlife preserve."

To what extent were both Bloch and Lukács part of a specific Jewish-German culture? Although strongly assimilated and hardly related at all to the Jewish tradition, one can find in their writings and correspondence from those years some significant elements of Jewish messianism and mysticism that certainly contributed to the apocalyptic and utopian, revolutionary quality of their thought. Although the Jewish components tend to disappear in their later Marxist writings, one cannot understand their attraction to Marxism and the Russian Revolution without this messianic background. To some extent one could say that Jewish messianism was *aufgehoben* (in the Hegelian sense of sublated, negated, conserved, superseded) in their later Marxist oeuvre.

Like many other intellectuals in Central Europe, Lukács discovered the spiritual universe of mystical Judaism through Martin Buber's books on Hasidism. In 1911, Lukács wrote to Buber, expressing admiration for his work and in particular for *The Legend of the Baal Schem* (1908), which he hailed as an "unforgettable" book. Their correspondence continued until 1921 (when Lukács was already an exiled leader of the Hungarian Communist Party!), and their letters from November and December 1916 suggest that they met in Heppenheim, the German village where Buber lived at the time. In 1911, Lukács published an article on Buber's books in a Hungarian journal of philosophy, where he compared the Baal-Schem to Meister Eckhart and Jakob Böhme. This piece, entitled "Jewish Mysticism"—the only one that Lukács ever wrote on a Jewish topic (and he never had it translated or republished)—attributed great significance to Hasidism in the modern history of religions: "The Hasidic movement, whose first major figure was the Baal-Schem, and whose last one was Rabbi Nachman, was a primitive and powerful mysticism, the only great and authentic movement since the German mysticism of the Reformation and the Spanish mysticism of the Counter-Reformation."

Evidence of Lukács's interest in Buber and in the relations between Hasidism and messianism can also be found in his personal notebooks from these years. But the most interesting testimony on Lukács's Jewish and messianic inclinations is the diary of one of his best Hungarian Jewish friends, Béla Balázs, which has the following entry in 1914: "Gyuri's [Lukács's] great new philosophy: *Messianism*. Gyuri has discovered the Jew in him! The search for ancestors. The Hasidic sect, the Baal-Schem. Now, he, too, has found his ancestors and his race, but me, I am alone and abandoned. . . . Gyuri's theory on the emergence or re-emergence of a Jewish type, the anti-rationalist ascetic, the antithesis of what is usually described as Jewish."

Like other German-Jewish intellectuals, Lukács was primarily attracted by the "romantic" elements of the Jewish tradition, as opposed to the rationalist image of Judaism conveyed by the Haskalah, the liberal Jewish establishment, and the German sociologists (such as Weber and Sombart). In his remarkable "Notes on Dostoevsky" (1915), he paid special attention to "heretical" Jewish messianic movements, like Sabbatai Zevi and Jakob Frank—the very ones that were to fascinate Gershom Scholem a few years later.

It would be wrong to view these messianic inclinations of young Lukács as exclusively Jewish in origin. His knowledge of Jewish texts other than the Old Testament was very limited, and his apocalyptic tendency owed as much, if not more, to Slavic mysticism and to Dostoevsky. But Balázs's comment ("Gyuri discovered the Jew in him") is interesting because in Lukács's many autobiographical writings and conversations he always denied any link between his thought and Judaism.

Max Weber, who often discussed ethical and religious issues with Lukács, placed him (in a letter from December 1913) within the German spiritual context as "one of the types of German 'eschatologism,' at the opposite pole from Stefan George," the conservative bard of German ancestry.

Lukács's apocalyptic sense was heightened by World War I, which he saw as the lowest point in the abyss, "the age of absolute sinfulness" (*Zeitalter der vollendeten Sündhaftigkeit*), to use Fichte's

expression, which appears in *The Theory of the Novel* (1916). In one of the notes on Dostoevsky written at that time, Lukács linked Fichte's expression to the Jewish doctrine that "the Messiah could come only in an age of absolute (*vollendeter*) impiety." Although *The Theory of the Novel* did not speak of the Messiah, its last chapter (dealing with Tolstoy and Dostoevksy) was illuminated by utopian hope, presented, in a typical romantic way, as the restoration of the epic form—which corresponded to an age of absolute harmony between individual and community, man and universe. Lukács perceived the great Russian writers as prophets and forerunners of a new harmony and a new *epos:* "In Tolstoy, intimations of a breakthrough into a new epoch are visible; but they remain polemical, nostalgic and abstract. It is in the works of Dostoevsky that this new world is drawn for the first time as a seen society. He belongs to the new world. Only formal analysis of his work can show whether he is already the Homer or the Dante of that world. It will then be the task of historico-philosophical interpretation to decide whether we are really to leave the age of absolute sinfulness or whether the new has no other herald but our hopes" (Lukács 1971).

The war also provoked a growing political estrangement between Lukács and the Heidelberg Circle, whose main leaders, such as Max Weber, supported German imperialism. Georg Simmel, for instance, in a letter to Marianne Weber dated August 14, 1914, complained about Lukács's antimilitarism, explaining it in terms of his "lack of experience."

Ernst Bloch also was hurt by the patriotic reaction of the Heidelberg sociologists at the outbreak of the war. Both Lukács and Bloch left Heidelberg a few months later. During the war years Bloch wrote his first major book, *Spirit of Utopia* (1918), one of the most significant manifestations of modern revolutionary romanticism. Critics have often deplored the hermetic, esoteric, and above all Expressionist writing of this book. The style is, however, inseparable from its content. As Adorno once commented, Bloch's philosophy is Expressionistic in its protest against the reification of the world. *Geist der Utopie* also shares with Expressionism the explosive combination of a radical Zivilisationskritik, a "modernist" artistic sensitivity, and a social-revolutionary utopian tendentiousness.

The first aspect is most striking: from the very start of the book: there is a bitter critique of machinery and "technological coldness," responsible for the "murder of imagination" (*Phantasiemord*) and for a lifeless and subhuman mechanical production. This is followed by a hymn to the glory of Gothic art, that "lofty spirit" that becomes "organic-spiritual transcendence," superior to Greek art itself, because it makes of man as Christ "the alchemical measure of all construction."

Bloch used words charged with religiosity to develop his aesthetic, philosophical, and utopian views. His religious spirituality drew its inspiration from Christian sources—the Apocalypse, Joachim de Flore, and the mystics and heretics of the Middle Ages—as well as from Jewish texts such as the Old Testament (notably the prophetic visions of Isaiah), the Kabbalah, Hasidism, and the writings of Buber. The first edition of *Geist der Utopie* (1918) contains numerous references to kabbalistic concepts (Schechina, Adam Kadmon), as well as to Jewish (Meir ben Gabbai) or Christian (Franz Joseph Molitor) kabbalists.

Bloch's attitude toward Judaism was complex. One of the rare texts in which he explicitly developed his views is the chapter "Symbol: Die Juden," which was published in the first edition of *Spirit of Utopia*. Curiously enough, he deleted it from the second edition of the book (1923) but included it in the collection *Durch die Wüste* (Through the desert), also from the same year. In that text, Bloch rejected both the assimilationism of the free-thinking, nonreligious Jewish bourgeoisie and the preservation of the traditional ghetto in Eastern Europe. As for Zionism, he considered it worthless because, "in using the concept of nation-state—which had rather fleeting currency in the nineteenth century—it wanted to change Judea into a sort of Asiatic Balkan State." Bloch did, however, value the historical continuity of the "people of the Psalms and of the prophets," and he was delighted by the recent "awakening of Jewish pride." In his view, the Jewish religion had the essential virtue of

"being built on the Messiah, on an appeal to the Messiah." He therefore assigned to the Jews, along with the Germans and Russians, a crucial role in "preparing for the absolute era," as these three peoples were destined to receive "the birth of God and messianism."

The romantic anticapitalist and antimilitarist political message of the book was mainly concentrated in the last chapter, "Karl Marx, Death and the Apocalypse," in which he denounced the world war as a product of capitalism—"a naked businessman's war"—and hoped for a social revolution that would "tear the paper of life from the mouth of the Golem of European militarism." He hailed the Russian workers and soldiers councils, the soviets, of February 1917 (the book was written before the October Revolution) as the destroyers of the money economy and of the "mercantile ethics"; "the crowning of all that is wicked in man"—a surprising political intuition in an author who was more familiar with the various doctrines of the transmigration of souls than with the programs of the various socialist movements.

After a short period of hesitation, both Lukács and Bloch became enthusiastic supporters of the October Revolution—a commitment that lasted throughout their lives. For both of them this decision was intimately related to their messianic hopes and romantic, utopian aspirations.

Unlike Lukács, Bloch never joined the Communist movement, but he was sympathetic to its aims. In 1921, when Germany still seemed on the eve of a new upsurge, he published *Thomas Münzer, Theologian of the Revolution,* which celebrated the Russian Revolution as the inheritor of the past heretical and millenarian movements and figures, from the Catharists to the Hussites, and from Münzer to Tolstoy—including the sixteenth-century Kabbalists of Safed who, north of Lake Tiberias, waited for "the messianic avenger, the destroyer of the existing Empire and Papacy, the restorer of *Olam-ha-Tikkun,* the true Kingdom of God" (Bloch 1960).

By resurrecting this German revolutionary tradition—Thomas Münzer and the sixteenth-century peasant wars—Bloch hoped to contribute to the future social revolution in Germany, which he perceived in messianic terms. The concluding pages of the book refer to "the time that is to come" in Russia and Germany, and to the "new messianism in preparation." In a curious visionary and allegorical language of Jewish inspiration, he wrote of the "Princess Sabbat" hidden behind a thin, cracked wall, while "from on high, upon the rubble of a civilization in ruins will rise the spirit of an ineradicable utopia." Bloch's faith in the imminence of the millennium is the focal point of his political and religious views: "It is impossible for the time of the Kingdom not to come now; it is for that time that a spirit shines in us, a spirit that refuses to resign, a spirit that will never be disappointed" (Bloch 1960).

Thomas Münzer is a romantic book not only because of its heretic, millenarian spirituality but also because of its reference to an idealized communitarian past. Like the Anabaptist peasants, Bloch celebrates in this work the "free communities" of the early Middle Ages, which were rooted in the ancient Germanic tradition and formed "a sort of agrarian Communism, quite adequate to the Christian requirements." In opposition to the communitarian aspirations of the sixteenth-century rebel peasants, Calvinism represented, "as Max Weber brilliantly showed," the beginnings of a capitalist economy that had been "totally liberated, detached, emancipated from all the scruples of primitive Christianity." Weber's sociology of Protestantism, which Bloch surely studied in Heidelberg, is here taken completely out of its context and put at the service of a Communist, Christian damnation of capitalism.

Lukács's road to Marxism is equally complex and unfolds through the mediation of Dostoevsky and Sorel. During 1918, probably under the influence of the Russian Revolution, Lukács's messianism became more political and linked with his revolutionary ideas. In a lecture from 1918 entitled "Conservative and Progressive Idealism," he paid homage to the Anabaptist movement (the same that had inspired Bloch's *Thomas Münzer*), and made his own its categorical imperative: "Bring the Kingdom of God down to earth at this very moment." Finally, in December 1918, Lukács published an article, "Bolshevism as a Moral Problem," in which the proletariat is pre-

sented as "the bearer of social redemption for mankind" and the "Messiah-class of world history." Messianism, thus "secularized," merged with social revolution, which Lukács then conceived as total upheaval on a worldwide scale.

A few weeks later, Lukács joined the Hungarian Communist Party, and became, during the short-lived Hungarian Councils Republic (1919), people's commissar for education and culture. Exiled in Vienna and Germany after the defeat of the revolution, he published in 1923 what is generally considered to be his most important work, *History and Class Consciousness*. Ernst Bloch wrote a sympathetic review of his friend's opus, which emphasized their intellectual affinity: "The global metaphysical theme of history is discovered in Lukács' book through other ways, but its content is entirely in accordance with *Spirit of Utopia*." This formulation is certainly exaggerated, but it is true that there were some common elements between the two books, among which was the romantic critique of industrial civilization. The main topic of Lukács's book, the analysis of capitalist reification (*Verdinglichung*) in all spheres of social life—economical, political, juridical, and cultural—is an original blend of Marxist economic theory with the "neo-romantic" German sociology of the Heidelberg Circle of Tönnies, Simmel, and Weber. For instance, in writing that Calvinist ethics—which supposes the complete transcendence of the objective powers that shape human destiny (*Deus absconditus* and predestination)—"represents, in a mythological way, but in its purest form, the bourgeois structure of reified consciousness" (Lukács 1971), Lukács was in fact reformulating Weber's classic thesis (as he acknowledges in a footnote). Like Bloch, he freely made use of the "value-free" Weberian analysis to put forward a Marxist critique of capitalism.

After the 1920s, the roads of the two friends diverged. Whereas Bloch's future works—including his monumental opus, *The Principle of Hope* (1954–59)—still contained much of that unique combination of romantic Zivilisationskritik, Judeo-Christian mystical speculations, and Communist utopia found in his first writings, Lukács developed a more classic and orthodox conception of (Marxist) philosophy and aesthetics, one that led him to a "self-critical" rejection of *History and Class Consciousness* as "idealistic." During the 1930s, public debate set them at odds about the meaning of the Expressionist movement, which was hailed by Bloch as progressive and rebellious and damned by Lukács as "petty-bourgeois" and reactionary. Only much later, in the 1960s, was there to be a sort of reconciliation between the two *symphilosophers* of Heidelberg.

Bibliography

Andrew Arato and Paul Breines, *The Young Lukács and the Origins of Western Marxism* (New York: Seabury Press, 1979); Béla Balázs, "Notes from a Diary: 1911–1921," *New Hungarian Quarterly* 47 (1972): 124–26; Ernst Bloch, *Durch die Wüste* (1923; Frankfurt a. M.: Suhrkamp, 1964); Bloch, *Geist der Utopie* (1918–23; Frankfurt a. M.: Suhrkamp, 1964); Bloch, *The Principle of Hope* (1954–59; Cambridge, Mass.: MIT Press, 1986); Bloch, *Thomas Münster, Theologe der Revolution* (Frankfurt a. M.: Suhrkamp, 1960); Bloch, *The Utopian Function of Art and Literature: Selected Essays,* trans. and ed. Jack Zipes and Frank Mecklenburg (Cambridge, Mass.: MIT Press, 1987); Andrew Feenberg, *Lukács, Marx and the Sources of Critical Theory* (Totowa, N.J.: Rowman and Littlefield, 1981); Agnes Heller, ed., *Lukács Revalued* (Oxford: Basil Blackwell, 1983); Paul Honigsheim, *On Max Weber* (New York: Free Press, 1968); Frederic Jameson, *Marxism and Form* (Princeton, N.J.: Princeton University Press, 1971); Michael Löwy, *Redemption and Utopia: Libertarian Judaism in Central Europe* (Stanford, Calif.: Stanford University Press, 1992); Georg Lukács, *Die Seele und die Form* (1910; Berlin: Luchterhand, 1971); Lukács, *History and Class Consciousness* (1923; London: Merlin, 1971); Lukács, *The Theory of the Novel* (1916; Cambridge, Mass.: MIT Press, 1971); Lukács, *Political Writings, 1919–29* (London: New Left Books, 1968); Lukács, "Zsido miszticismus," *Szellen* 2 (1911): 256–57; Arno Münster, *Utopie, Messianismus und Apokalypse im Frühwerk von Ernst Bloch* (Frankfurt a. M.: Suhrkamp, 1982); and Marianne Weber, *Max Weber, ein Lebensbild* (Tübingen: J. C. B. Mohr, 1926).

MICHAEL LÖWY

1911 Julius Preuss publishes *Biblisch-talmudische Medizin,* Felix Theilhaber publishes *Der Untergang der deutschen Juden,* and the International Hygiene Exhibition takes place in Dresden

Science without religion is lame; religion without science is blind.

—Albert Einstein

When discussing the relationship of the Jews to science in Germany, we are primarily concerned with a social phenomenon that began in the last third of the nineteenth century and ended in 1933 with the Nazi seizure of power. The entrance of Jews into the various branches of science, a marker of their legal emancipation, was coterminous with Germany's rise to scientific and industrial preeminence after the founding of the Second Reich in 1871.

The pursuit of science also marked the collective departure of German Jewry from traditional patterns of Jewish culture, especially education. Modern science, with its heuristic basis in empirical investigation rather than religious truths, is not a product of Jewish culture. It lies outside the epistemological paradigm of text-based rabbinic culture, which maintained a belief in the perfect correlation of divine revelation and worldly existence; the duty of every Jew to study Torah as an expression of faith and as a practical guide to upright living; and finally, that God's will and purpose will become manifest through loyalty to Torah. By contrast, the ethos of modern science, according to Robert K. Merton, is made up of universalism, communism, disinterestedness, and organized skepticism, features that are radically different from the faith-affirming, ethnocentric civilization of rabbinic Judaism. Perhaps only "communism," which Merton describes as "social collaboration," is applicable to a culture in which individualism is subsumed by the primacy given the collectivity. But the goal of "social collaboration" in modern science and Judaism is different: the former strives for it in order to arrive at a predictable norm; the latter has adopted it to ensure group survival.

From a purely intellectual point of view, it was science's very universalism that made it so attractive to young Jews who were no longer in pursuit of a Torah education. Still inspired by the traditional Jewish emphasis on the acquisition of formal education, secular Jewish students in Germany attended the universities as enthusiastically as they had once entered yeshivot. Socially, the opportunities afforded by the attainment of scientific expertise in Germany's expanding and modernizing economy led Jews in search of a university education to flock to the science faculties. With anti-Semitism barring Jews from holding prestigious positions in the Prussian officer corps and civil service, Jews turned to science as a means of ascending the social ladder. In particular, Jews were most heavily represented in medicine, chemistry, physics, and mathematics, composing approximately 20 percent of all practitioners in these fields at the fin de siècle. Jews at this time made up roughly 1 percent of the total population.

The immediate problem before us is to analyze the writing of Jewish scientists in Germany from the Enlightenment to Einstein. And this in turn raises another problem—one of definition. If the objective is to examine the science writing of Jewish scientists, one is immediately confronted with the impossible task of extracting the Jewish "essence" from particular scientific texts. To look for this quotient is to accept the Nazi standard that such a thing as "Jewish," as opposed to "Aryan," science exists. Such a premise is clearly unacceptable.

Nevertheless, it is worthwhile to highlight the general scientific contributions of German Jews because they form an important chapter in the story of Jewish integration into German society. A glance at Jewish recipients of the Nobel Prize for the sciences, a universally accepted indicator of high achievement, demonstrates the disproportionate contribution and representation of Jews in the various fields of scientific endeavor.

Prior to World War II, German Jews, or Germans of Jewish descent, were frequently recognized for their achievements by the Swedish Academy of Arts and Sciences. The first Jew to win the prize was Adolphe von Baeyer in 1905, for organic chemistry. Others in chemistry included Otto Wallach (1910), Richard Willstätter (1915), and the baptized Fritz Haber (1918). The areas of physiology and medicine count among their winners Paul Ehrlich (1908), Robert Bárány (1914), Otto Meyerhof (1922), Karl Landsteiner (1930), Otto Warburg (1931), and Otto Loewi (1936). Finally, physics saw Nobel Prizes awarded to Albert Einstein (1921), James Franck (1925), and Gustav Hertz (1925).

But what are we to make of these contributions in light of the current discussion? Neither Willstätter's work on plant pigments, especially chlorophyll; Paul Ehrlich's on hematology, immunology, and chemotherapy, and his signal contribution to treating syphilis; nor Einstein's theory of relativity are the products of Jewish culture. The textual form in which these scientists presented their theories does not make them Jewish texts, just because of the birthright of the authors. To claim that these ideas are Jewish is to deny the universal nature of science, even taking into account science's culturally determined artifice.

Beyond the Nobel laureates there is a galaxy of Jewish Germans who made enormous contributions to science. But again, it is a gross misunderstanding of science to claim that there is anything intrinsically Jewish about the mathematics of Georg Cantor (1845–1918), other than the fact that his notations of transfinite cardinal numbers were represented by the Hebrew letter aleph. Similarly, the brilliant Emmy Noether (1882–1936) did not arrive at her theory of ideals, which made her one of the most important algebraists of the modern period, by being influenced by earlier Jewish mathematicians such as Johann Kepler's and Tycho Brahe's friend, David Gans (1541–1613). Finally, the Hanover-born Sir William Herschel (1738–1822), who discovered the planet Uranus in 1781, was not inspired by the midrashic astronomical notion that the horizon is that place where heaven and earth "kiss each other." These people did not conduct "Jewish" experiments, perform "Jewish" calculations, nor practice a particular "Jewish" science. They did not operate as Jews. Rather, they worked as scientists, bound not to the laws of tradition, but to those which governed the natural laws of the universe.

Among German-Jewish scientists, however, it is possible to locate Jewish themes, concerns, and tropes embedded in the narrative structures of science if we confine ourselves to the only branches of science that permit such an investigation: medicine and physical anthropology. At the fin de siècle, the texts produced by scholars in these two fields and published in learned journals and monographs could and often did retain a literary quality that created space for a narrow, nonuniversal language. Moreover, despite the mathematization of both areas in the nineteenth century, medicine and physical anthropology were sciences unlike physics and chemistry. The practice of both was not laboratory-based, neither was it experimental or as objectively quantitative as other branches of natural science. Rather, they were highly subjective, informed more than the other sciences by such categories as nationalism, class, gender, and aesthetics.

In Germany, Jewish scientists who wrote scientific texts on overtly Jewish topics generally did so in the context of a larger debate within German society—namely, the Jewish Question. The question revolved around accounting for the physical, cultural, and social differences between Jews and Germans. The central issue was why, after their initial emancipation in 1812 in Prussia, their subsequent integration into German society, and their adoption of German culture, the Jews remained a distinct, visible, and easily identifiable group. Why had they failed to shed themselves of their Jewishness—that rarely described, but often observed, essence?

The Jewish Question, which engaged the intellectual energies of some of Germany's (and Europe's) most distinguished scientists, peaked when Jews began to enter the sciences in large numbers. In Germany, for example, Jews were particularly well placed to take part in such debates given their predominance in the medical profession; Jews made up about 16 percent of all Germany's doctors. What we have, then, is a case of an informed Other using the methodology of the adversary to confirm or deny claims of racial difference.

The unique constellation of forces in Germany—anti-Semitism, advanced Jewish acculturation, national scientific pre-eminence, and disproportionate Jewish participation in the sciences—led to the development of a particular genre of "Jewish" science writing in that country. For example, many Jews sought to employ science as a justification for the retention of ancient, seemingly outmoded and "Oriental" customs such as dietary laws and ritual circumcision. Those rituals came under scrutiny and criticism from gentiles who thought them atavistic practices from a less enlightened time, and from Jews who felt that they were rituals not befitting a recently emancipated and modernizing community. By contrast, Jewish physicians and rabbis who wished to preserve tradition attempted to defend ancient practices by presenting arguments that spoke to the prophylactic qualities of Jewish ritual and the hygienic farsightedness of the rabbis.

Although Maimonides and Abraham ibn Ezra

had already given hygienic explanations for the dietary laws in the Middle Ages, the tendency to defend such rituals on the basis of science first finds expression in Germany during the eighteenth-century debates on Jewish emancipation. In his book dealing with the illnesses of the Jews, *Von den Krankheiten der Juden* (1777), the Jewish physician from Mannheim, Elkan Isaac Wolf, argued for the therapeutic quality of many aspects of traditional Jewish law. Wolf thought highly of the dietary laws; he was convinced they promoted good health, and, in fact, he parted with the traditional view that certain foods were prohibited solely because of Divine commandment, and wondered whether "our holy Laws had not eternally banned [the consumption] of pork just for [health] reasons." Other positive aspects of Jewish law for Wolf that had direct bearing on the body were prohibitions against drunkenness and licentious and excessive sexual intercourse, fasting, and the laws concerning female ritual purity. For Wolf, all of these laws had a beneficial effect on the "morals, health, and propagation of the Jews." He also noted that circumcision, "although a painful operation," was not, in his observation, a cause of illness. "On the contrary," he wrote, "it is ultimately useful for propagation." Within Wolf's Weltanschauung, ancient traditions, provided they could be given a rational and scientific justification, were not to be considered obsolete.

Throughout the nineteenth century, rabbis and physicians continued to defend dietary and hygiene laws not only as compatible with the modern age but as initially instituted and informed by a higher sense of the scientific worth of those laws. The slaughtering of animals according to Jewish law (Halakhah) came under fire in the nineteenth century from antivivisectionist forces, who proclaimed the cruelty of the method—and by extension revived, or confirmed for some, a belief in the particular cruelty of the Jews as a people. In his volume of rabbinic response entitled *Matte Levi,* the Orthodox community rabbi of Frankfurt, Marcus David Horovitz, noted that it was incumbent upon Jews to inform the government of the nature and efficaciousness of the ritual slaughter of meat.

In his encyclopedic reference work *Biblisch-talmudische Medizin* (1911), the physician and medical historian Julius Preuss explained that he included a discussion of biblical dietary laws under the chapter entitled "Hygiene" "solely because *we* can conceive of no other reason than sanitary for their ordination."

Also in 1911, the International Hygiene Exhibition was held in Dresden. The Jews were just one of many groups exhibiting the culture of health and well-being among their people. The confluence of German anti-Semitism and Jewish assimilation in the period before World War I meant that the Jewish booth constituted an apologia on display. One of the most important collaborative pieces of Jewish science writing ever produced in Germany came out of that conference: the volume edited by the rabbi, historian, and folklorist Max Grunwald. Comprising articles by leading medical and rabbinical authorities, *Die Hygiene der Juden* (1911) is a wide-ranging discussion of traditional Jewish customs, ceremonies, dietary laws, and life-cycle events such as circumcision and burial practices. Both the exhibit and the accompanying volume were presented to the German and (assimilated) Jewish public as examples of the farsightedness of the rabbis and of the prophylactic nature of traditional Jewish life.

Around the turn of the century, Jews became involved in contemporary anthropological and medical debates concerning the "racial qualities" of the Jewish people. These studies sought to determine whether the Jews were a pure race and what, if any, peculiarly Jewish physiological and psychological traits they possessed. The effort of these Jewish scientists was impelled by the need to respond both to the rise of scientific racism in the late nineteenth century and to popular racial anti-Semitism. In addition, the enterprise of the Jewish scientists was driven by specifically internal Jewish concerns. Race science, with its emphasis on statistics, was employed, especially by Zionist physicians, to fully examine the social and biological condition of the Jewish people for the purpose of implementing a rational plan of Jewish national improvement. This is clear in the pronouncement of Max Nordau, neurologist and

leader of the World Zionist Organization, who declared at the movement's fifth congress held in Basel in 1901: "We must know more. We must reliably learn how a people is composed (*wie das Volksmaterial beschaffen ist*), with what it is we have to work. We need an entire anthropological, biological, economic and intellectual statistic of the Jewish people." This statement is a clear reiteration of the goals laid out by the leading figure of the *Wissenschaft des Judentums,* Leopold Zunz, who in 1822 published his programmatic essay, "Outline for a Future Statistics of the Jews." Zunz's thirty-nine-point thesis amounted to a call to scholars to examine all aspects of contemporary Jewish life.

Like Zunz before him, Nordau called for the study of the physical qualities of the Jewish people. He sought answers to the following questions: How are the Jewish people physically constituted? What is their average size? What are their anatomical particularities? What are their figures for sickness and mortality? Furthermore, he was of the opinion that censuses should be taken, presumably to compare differences among and between diverse Jewish populations.

In 1904, eighty-two years after the publication of Zunz's "Outline," an institution was established in Berlin to defend emancipation, stem the tide of assimilation, and combat anti-Semitism through the use of statistics. Attempting to present the sociology of Jewish life according to the methodology proposed by Zunz and the philosophy of Wissenschaft des Judentums, the Bureau für Statistik der Juden was responsible for collecting and publishing in its journal, the *Zeitschrift für Demographie und Statistik der Juden,* all manner of statistics pertaining to the Jewish present. The articles in the journal were primarily written by physicians, anthropologists, and statisticians.

The bureau was the brainchild of the Jewish statistician Alfred Nossig, who in 1902 founded the Association for Jewish Statistics. The whole enterprise of gathering Jewish statistics and searching for a scientific melioration of the Jewish problem was given impetus by the Zionist movement. As Nossig himself noted, "the nationally minded Jews have been, until now, the most eager sponsors of the work of the Association for Jewish Statistics" (Nossig 1903, 2). In fact, Louis Leopold, the first general-secretary of the Association for Jewish Statistics, clearly acknowledged the union between scientific objective and political design when he wrote that "the purpose of the Association is, on the one hand scientific, and on the other practical, in that through its efficiency, the fundamental information required for an improvement in the situation of the Jewish masses will be produced" (147).

In the journal, scientists debated such purely anthropological issues as the morphological differences among the Jews. The great conundrum for physical anthropology at the fin de siècle was as follows. It was often assumed that the Jews were a pure race and that they were Semites; thus they were thought to have originally looked similar to modern-day Arabs, brunette and dark-complectioned. How, then, are there blond-haired, blue-eyed Jews, or black, Indian, and even Chinese Jews? These questions led to wide-ranging and often vociferous debates among Central European Jewry (and non-Jewish anthropologists) in the early years of the twentieth century. Nor were these merely professional debates with little resonance outside of the academy. The most important books on the subject, such as I. M. Judt's *Die Juden als Rasse* (1903), Ignaz Zollschan's *Das Rassenproblem* (1910), Arthur Ruppin's *Die Juden der Gegenwart* (1911), Felix Theilhaber's *Der Untergang der deutschen Juden* (1911), and Fritz Kahn's *Die Juden als Rasse und Kulturvolk* (1921), went through multiple editions. Moreover, they were often popularized by the authors in the Jewish press and were always reviewed by newspapers and periodicals representing every religious and political stream in German Jewry. The physicians and scientists who debated the Jewish Question are largely forgotten today, but were, in their time, public figures in the scientific and Jewish worlds.

Medical doctors also wrote in both learned journals and the popular Jewish press about the pathology and the psychopathology of the Jews. In particular, mental illness among the Jews was one of the most widely discussed themes in Jewish scientific literature. Mainstream psychiatry held that the Jews were racially predisposed to certain forms of insanity—especially schizophrenia, hysteria, and that most nineteenth-century of mental illnesses, neurasthenia. This was a view that was perpetuated by assimilated German-Jewish psychiatrists such as Hermann Oppenheim in his tendentious article "Zur Psychopathologie und Nosologie der russisch-jüdischen Bevölkerung" (*Journal für Psychologie und Neurologie* [1908]), and Moritz Benedikt in "Der geisteskranke Jude" (*Nord und Süd* [1918]). These men subscribed to the Haskalah formulation that identified the traditional Jew, especially the one from Eastern Europe, as the mentally unsound Jew, a victim of his own religious fanaticism who prayed himself into what the maskilic physician, Isaac Elkan Wolf, had called "a constant *Delirio*."

By the turn of the twentieth century, young Zionist psychiatrists challenged this view. They maintained that it was the Western European Jew, the assimilated Jew who was stripped of his ethnic identity and whiled away his day in coffee lounges, who suffered from an inferiority complex referred to by the young Swiss-trained Russian Zionist psychiatrist Rafael Becker, in his *Die jüdische Nervosität* (1918), as the *jüdische Complex*. In contrast to Western European Jewry there stood the traditional or Eastern European Jew, who, although poverty stricken and in poor physical shape, was regarded as a paragon of mental health because his Jewish identity was intact.

Psychiatrists such as Becker; Martin Engländer in his *Die auffallend häufigen Krankheitserscheinungen der jüdischen Rasse* (1902); and Daniel Pasmanik in his *Die Seele Israels. Zur Psychologie des Diasporajudentums* (1911) saw the efficacious effects of Zionism as something that would benefit *Westjudentum* even more than it would *Ostjudentum*—a radical departure from the principles of early German Zionism.

So widespread were discussions of Jewish psychopathologies that the interlocking themes of Jewish identity and mental illness among Jews were even raised in popular form in the Jewish press. Felix Resek, writing in *Der Israelit,* the leading periodical of German Orthodoxy, found inadequate Rafael Becker's assessment that there were only two ways to cure the insanity of the

Jews: assimilation and their ultimate extinction, or Zionism and their "strengthening" in Palestine. For him, only traditional religious observance would soothe soul and psyche. The simple modesty and piety of the Fathers were the roots of their happiness, and the source of their capacity to resist all obstacles that were placed before them. Accordingly, a readoption of these time-honored principles, plus a general return to the "village-soil and garden-city" (not necessarily in Palestine), would lead to the contemporary psychological and religious recovery of the Jews.

In 1919, *Der Israelit* continued to push the link between Jewish mental health and religious observance. In a short feuilleton, Hermann Seckbach told the story of a young Jewish woman who is committed to an asylum after receiving notice that her husband had been officially declared missing during the war. Recounting her experience, the woman says: "It grips me with horror today when I have to say this word [asylum]. . . . In addition, there was the agony of my soul when I realized I was in a non-Jewish house. I wanted to die of shame when they removed the *Scheitel* [wig] from my head and I almost went crazy, when out of hunger, I had to dig into the non-kosher food." Happily, the story ends on a note of personal joy. But more important, it concludes with a resolution designed to benefit Jewish society as a whole. As luck had it, the woman's husband had not been killed but only taken prisoner of war, and had returned home. She concluded her story: "Then the first Friday evening we were together in unspeakable happiness, I decided to strive for, as much as it was in my power, the many Jewish welfare institutions [that existed]. But now the most important task was the establishment of Jewish mental asylums."

In conclusion, Jewish scientists did indeed write science that was methodologically universal, secular, and conformed to Merton's categories of what constitutes modern science. Yet because of the nature of medicine and physical anthropology, as well as the passion and intimacy they brought to their work, German-Jewish doctors were, from the Haskalah of the eighteenth century until the twentieth, also able to write science from a parochial and ethnic perspective. It is a tragic irony that when German Jewry met its demise, it was the most nonparticularistic, value-free practitioners such as Albert Einstein, Max Born, and Lise Meitner who were accused of practicing science infected with the Jewish spirit.

Bibliography

John M. Efron, *Defenders of the Race: Jewish Doctors and Race Science in Fin-de-Siècle Europe* (New Haven: Yale University Press, 1994); Sander L. Gilman, *The Case of Sigmund Freud: Medicine and Identity at the Fin de Siècle* (Baltimore, Md.: Johns Hopkins University Press, 1993); Max Grunwald, ed., *Die Hygiene der Juden* (Dresden: Verlag der Historischen Abteilung der Internationalen Hygiene-Ausstellung, 1911); Max Nordau, *Zionistische Schriften* (Berlin: Jüdischer Verlag, 1923); Alfred Nossig, ed., *Jüdische Statistik* (Berlin: Jüdischer Verlag, 1903); Julius Preuss, *Biblisch-talmudische Schriften* (Berlin: S. Karger, 1911); Monika Richarz, *Der Eintritt der Juden in die akademischen Berufe* (Tübingen: J. C. B. Mohr, 1974); Charles Singer, "Science and Judaism," *The Jews: Their History, Culture and Religion,* ed. Louis Finkelstein, vol. 2 (New York: Schocken, 1960); Felix Theilhaber, *Der Untergang der deutschen Juden* (Berlin: Jüdischer Verlag, 1911); Elkan Isaac Wolf, *Von der Krankheiten der Juden* (Mannheim: C. F. Schwan, 1777); and Ignaz Zollschan, *Das Rassenproblem unter besonderer Berücksichtigung der theoretischen Grundlagen der jüdischen Rassenfrage* (Vienna: Wilhelm Braumüller, 1910).

JOHN M. EFRON

1912 The publication of Moritz Goldstein's "The German-Jewish Parnassus" sparks a debate over assimilation, German culture, and the "Jewish spirit"

In March 1912, a young Zionist, Moritz Goldstein, published an explosive article, "The German-Jewish Parnassus." There he proclaimed that: "We Jews are administering the spiritual property of a nation which denies our right and our ability to do so." (Goldstein was a literary scholar, a Germanist, who, as he later ironically put it, was himself "by profession, an 'administrator' of the spiritual property of the German nation.") Jewish cultural domination, he argued, was multisphered and permeated the worlds of German literature, theater, journalism, and so on. Non-Jewish resentment over this state of affairs, Goldstein insisted, had to be acknowledged and its implications honestly confronted. Such a situation could be remedied, Goldstein wrote, only through a form of German-Jewish cultural disengagement and the construction of a new, specifically "Jewish" culture in Germany.

Anti-Semites had long been espousing the view that over the course of the nineteenth century Jews had taken over the economics, culture, and, indeed, the very inner life of Germany. But no Jew—not even militant German Zionists ideologically predisposed to uncover the duplicities of assimilation—had openly pronounced this before. What made Goldstein's challenge to the tacit liberal agreement to pass over such sensitive matters in discreet public silence particularly provocative was the fact that his analysis appeared in the prestigious *Der Kunstwart* (The art guard), a cultural journal whose editor, Ferdinand Avenarius, was an avowed German nationalist and whose literary critic, Adolf Bartels, was a notorious anti-Semite. (Previously, and for obvious reasons, Goldstein's piece had been rejected by the quintessentially liberal, and Jewish-owned, *Berliner Tageblatt*.)

To be sure, Goldstein castigated the *ressentiment* of anti-Jewish forces—those "German-Christian-Teutonic envy-ridden fools" who had brought about this state of affairs. But the "worse" enemy, he insisted, were "those Jews who are completely unaware, who continue to take part in German cultural activities, who pretend and persuade themselves that they are not recognized" when, in effect, their cultural creations were widely viewed as un-German: instead of being fused with the spirit of *Deutschtum* (Germanness), non-Jewish Germans regarded them as imbued with essentially foreign, "Asiatic," "Jewish" characteristics. Assertions of this kind predictably delighted anti-Semites (one such, Ph. Stauff, contributed a vicious piece to *Der Kunstwart*) and outraged liberals (especially Jewish liberals). The two sides rendered inevitable a protracted and heated debate that spread well beyond the pages of *Der Kunstwart*.

There was, of course, nothing new in either the critique or the defense of assimilation. What was perhaps novel (apart from airing the issue in public) was Goldstein's advocacy of the creation of a separate Jewish culture on German soil—a recommendation that, like the article itself, was occasioned by the perception of a persisting anti-Jewish feeling in Germany and channeled by a radicalized "post-assimilationist" sensibility characteristic of second-generation German Zionists. Indeed, Goldstein's plea was comprehensible only in terms of a prior vaunted "Jewish renaissance" whose seeds were already planted at the fin de siècle. His thoughts were as much a product of that development as was a call for its public recognition.

If this proposed radical cultural disjunction between Germans and Jews was unthinkable for Jewish liberals—the well-known critic Julius Bab dubbed the very attempt as a deliberate act of retrogression—the same held for the first generation of German Zionists. In 1910—only two years before Goldstein dropped his bombshell—Franz Oppenheimer defined the original German-Zionist relation to culture thus: "We are collectively German by culture . . . because we have the fortune to belong to cultural communities that stand in the forefront of nations. . . . We cannot be Jewish by culture (*Kulturjuden*) because the Jewish culture, as it has been preserved from the Middle Ages in the ghettos of the East, stands infinitely lower than modern cultures which our [Western] nations bear. We can neither regress nor do we want to."

But for Goldstein and others the new culture (conceived upon essentially organic assumptions) would resolve a problem that liberals and older Zionists either denied or sidestepped: it would re-create a condition of authentic wholeness for essentially bifurcated, fragmented Jews. To be sure, the exact contours and nature of this "Jewish" culture were, as Goldstein himself admitted, exceedingly vague. What would constitute the framework and content for such a revival? Apart from the Zionists, other radical circles—such as the one associated with the journal *Der Freistaat*—joined the debate and proposed different solutions. Like the Zionists, they believed that the creative Jewish instincts were repressed under the dictates of a "foreign culture" and that authentic expression was possible only in a Jewish milieu suited to the structure of the Jewish soul. But they went beyond Zionism in arguing not for

some vague, utopian Jewish culture of the future in Palestine but for the immediate union (*Anschluss*) of German Jewry with existing Eastern European Jewish culture. For these disaffected Zionists—most prominently Fritz Mordecai Kaufmann—the culture of *Ostjudentum* (Eastern Jewry) was synonymous with Jewish culture itself.

But more than its vagueness, Goldstein's posited solution—as well as his mode of diagnosis—revealed a kind of bewildered despair. It is here that the document retains its compelling historical interest. Perhaps, indeed, it should be read as a classic and pained restatement: a symptomatic expression of the ongoing and unresolved issue of the modalities and dualities of Jewish identity within German culture, a problem that both preceded and postdated his ruminations.

If the essay was informed by a Zionist sensibility, its tone was more confused than it was triumphalist. For Goldstein, the psychohistorical tragedy of acculturated Jews was to be found in their persistent condition of duality and fragmentation. The creation of a full Jewish, Hebrew-speaking culture was possible only in Zion, he wrote, but that was not really an option for the present generation of German Jews, those who had "left the ghetto, we lucky-unlucky beneficiaries of West European culture, we eternal-halves, we excluded and homeless." The cultural condition of German Jewry was thus was part blessing, part curse. For although Goldstein proposed the creation of a distinct culture in which Jews would work unconditionally *as Jews,* it did not mean that the deeply ingrained German inheritance had to—or could or should—be simply jettisoned: "We cannot cast it off as one exchanges a garment. We do not want to give this all up; it means draining the blood of our life." (Ironically, some later radical Zionists were convinced that German Jews were so thoroughly acculturated, their German "spirit" so deep, that they were *incapable* of inhabiting a Jewish one. Thus, in 1917 a student Zionist, G. Wollstein, proposed that in order to prevent the "Berlinization" of the future Jewish state, German Jews should marry only Eastern European Jews and refrain from writing in Hebrew journals, for their contributions could consist only of Jewish words wrapped in the German spirit!)

Forty-five years after the appearance of his *Kunstwart* piece, Goldstein reflected on the insolubility of the Deutschtum-Judentum nexus: his piece had been (mis)understood as "a programme for action whereas I merely wanted to free myself of a tormenting trouble by ventilating it." There was, indeed, even something cloying in the cliché-ridden, romantic mode in which he described the relation of German Jews to German culture and their sense of being slighted by their exclusion from it: "The German spring is our spring, as the German winter is for us winter. . . . Were we not raised on German fairy tales? . . . Is not the German forest alive for us, are we not also allowed to behold its elves and gnomes, do we not understand the murmur of its streams and the song of its birds?" (Goldstein 1957).

But of course his article was not received as a testament to German patriotism, nor even as an expressive document of cultural bewilderment. Ernst Lissauer (1882–1937), the Jewish author of the famous World War I "Hate Song Against England," insisted at the end of his indignant reply to Goldstein that the dualities over which Goldstein struggled could be straightforwardly resolved (Lissauer 1912). A simple decision had to be made: either to "become German" or to leave the country.

The polemics occasioned by this piece produced rather formulaic responses and have been thoroughly analyzed elsewhere. What has gone less remarked is the degree to which the discussion—indeed, the wider debate around Deutschtum and Judentum, the possibilities and limits of assimilation and of cultural creativity in general—employed a peculiar species of discourse that turned upon a hypostatized conception of "essences," of visible and hidden, external and internal characteristics taken to be profoundly determinative of "Jewishness." These characteristics were represented as both markers of a distinct identity and the "content" of such Jewishness, the inward and outward manifestations of an elusive but powerful Jewish being and "spirit," which assimilation in the last analysis could neither repress nor dissolve.

Goldstein, for instance, couched his arguments on the basis of what he regarded to be "inherited, ineradicable characteristics" of the Jews. Other participants in the debate spoke as if this were an unproblematic given of a constitutive Jewish "national substance" (Strauss 1912). It is significant that even the liberals, who were most obviously opposed to such essentialist thinking, were forced to construct their arguments within these terms, if only to dismiss the determinative role of such categories. Thus Lissauer, who categorically denied the existence of an inherent Jewish "national substance"—what one meant by that term, he argued, was simply the collectively acquired characteristics of ghetto life that were constitutive of East European Jews—noted that assimilation was a slow process and admitted that German Jews (already a quite distinct species from their East European branch) still exhibited some recognizable physical and mental signs of that past existence. But this was because they were still in a transitional phase. What one took to be inherent characteristics of the Jewish physique and psyche were simply products of their historical and sociological—and thus alterable—contexts. To speak of such an inborn substance, Lissauer exclaimed, was to speak in precisely those racial terms employed by enemies of the Jews.

This underside of the debate, we should point out, merely refueled and underlined an intuition of an evasive yet palpable Jewish "otherness" that had been sensed and discussed throughout the period of modern German-Jewish acculturation. This was a sentiment that was shared even though it was evaluated and deployed in radically different terms—by Jews, non-Jews, and anti-Semites alike. Hannah Arendt has suggested that the dynamic governing the notion of an indistinct, yet powerfully felt, Jewish "spirit" or inner essence was embedded in the logic of emancipation, in the very terms of the assimilationist pact: "Instead of being defined by nationality or religion, Jews were being transformed into a social group whose members shared certain psychological attributes and reactions, the sum total of which was to constitute 'Jewishness.' In other words, Judaism became a psychological quality and the Jewish Question became an involved personal problem for every individual Jew" (Arendt 1958).

It was this hypostatization of some invisible but determinative inner essence that from the late eighteenth century increasingly characterized both Jewish and non-Jewish perceptions. Indeed, with the passing of time it became increasingly definitive of Jewish identity itself: as the overt signs of Jewish difference receded, this simultaneously elusive yet ultimately constitutive internality (whether viewed approvingly or with distaste) became of paramount importance. Heinrich Heine provided some of the earliest and most powerful expressions of both the positive and negative psychological valences of a "Jewishness" experienced both as a kind of mental defect— "Incurable deep ill! defying treatment. . . . Will Time, the eternal goddess, in compassion / Root out this dark calamity transmitted from sire to son?"—and as an expression of "the genuine, the ageless, the true": it was the "character of the Jewish people," he wrote, that was the "cause," the key agent in the moralization of the West (Heine 1948).

Goldstein's assertion of ineradicable inherited Jewish characteristics was, then, not simply a passing fancy, the mutterings of a whimsical eccentric, but part of a larger cluster of convictions that seemed, if anything, to become more pronounced during this period. As moderate a German-Jewish journal as *Ost und West* announced in its 1901 opening statement that, the apparent differences notwithstanding, all Jews "shared the same inherited characteristics." Like others involved in the fin-de-siècle Jewish renaissance, it implied, rather remarkably, that genetics somehow doomed the politics and culture of assimilation.

Strikingly, the debate did not center around the issue of external characteristics. It focused instead on the question of internal content, of the corresponding Jewish "spirit"—because there was, more or less, general agreement that Jews did indeed possess physically distinguishing features and mannerisms. Liberal Jews like Lissauer recognized that there were painfully obvious physical landmarks of Jewishness, but they asserted that these were hangovers from the ghetto and would disappear with the successful completion of the assimilation process. Similarly Ludwig Geiger, the editor of the *Allgemeine Zeitung des Judentums,* elsewhere admitted the existence of this external dimension, but he did not quite know what to do with such an awkward perception. Jews, he wrote, were easily identifiable by the way they moved, by the shape of their noses, and by other bodily cues, but he drew no cultural or sociological conclusions from these observations. Still other liberal Jews of the time were often shocked by what appeared to be an "instinctive," physical recognition of kinship. Wrapped in a scarf so that only his eyes were visible, the playwright Richard Beer-Hoffmann was shocked when a caftan-clad *Ostjude* stopped him and said, "My good sir is one of us. . . . He will tell me how I can get to the Nollendorfplatz?"

Many identifying German Jews claimed that they too possessed this instinctive capacity for mutual recognition. The radical anarchist Gustav Landauer, for instance, was convinced that he could identify fellow Jews merely by looking at them. At the same time, for those interested in escaping their historical fate, Judaism could be regarded as a physiological defect. Thus, the famous linguist Fritz Mauthner experienced it as a kind of "duct" in the brain, a disease he was afraid to contract.

Like Goldstein, it was yet another young Zionist and Germanist (perhaps such people most sharply and paradoxically experienced the tensions between Deutschtum and Judentum), Ludwig Strauss, who did most to radicalize and polarize the debate and who—on the basis of popular physiognomic and racial wisdom—sought to derive internal conclusions and content from these external characteristics, thereby providing a literal and unified psycho-physiological form to the notion of a Jewish "national substance." In Strauss's conception, Jewish identity was locatable by external signs that betrayed an inner life. "The obvious bodily differences between Jewish and non-Jewish Germans," he exclaimed, "is necessarily connected to an inner difference, a dissimilarity in national substance."

If such notions did not exactly mimic, they

seemed at least to parallel—even if deployed for quite different, positive purposes—a long-standing, anti-Jewish discourse that linked the external to the internal, the physiological to the spiritual and cultural. Richard Wagner's 1850 essay "Judaism in Music," for instance, explained the roots of an "instinctive," "involuntary repellence" to the Jew in terms that equally emphasized Jewish physical and spiritual structure (and the interdependence between them). The most extreme articulation, partly expressive and partly satirical, of this physiocultural discourse was contained in Oskar Panizza's nightmarish short story "The Operated Jew" (1893). Panizza's tale relates the desperate attempts of a stereotypical Jew, the culturally and physically deformed Itzig Faitel Stern, to alter his inner and outer nature and turn himself into a modern Aryan-Christian. This physiocultural transformation—which included a number of excruciating surgical procedures on the repellent Itzig's entire skeletal framework in order to bring about the required metamorphosis—ultimately fails. The grotesque denouement moves from his cultural regression—the lapse into his ugly Jewish accent and stereotypical mannerisms—to his quite literal reversion from normal to Jewish physiology: "Faitel's blond strands of hair began to curl. . . . Then the curly locks turned red, then dirty brown and finally blue-black. . . . His arms and legs which had been stretched and bent in numerous operations could no longer perform the newly learned movements. . . . A terrible smell spread in the room . . . [the surgeon] Klotz's work of art lay before him crumpled and quivering, a convoluted Asiatic image in wedding dress, a counterfeit of human flesh, Itzig Faitel Stern." The assimilationist project was revealed in all its interrelated cultural and genetic absurdity.

In order to draw a similar conclusion but from a quite different source and for different purposes, Strauss explicitly employed the Buberian model of a Jewish essence that assimilation could perhaps hide and distort but never fully eradicate. This was a notion that Martin Buber developed in his influential 1909 "Bar Kochba" lectures, in which he portrayed the "community of blood" as the profound core of Jewishness, "the deepest,

most potent stratum of our being . . . our innermost thinking and our will are colored by it." Buber drew upon the common racial coinage of his day, obviously not as a tool for domination of others, but as a potent—some would argue merely as a metaphorical—device to imagine or conjure up a concealed but still pulsating Jewish essence. Ultimately, he proclaimed, Jewish belonging would be decided in terms of this community of blood rather than by the external "community of experience," those spheres and fields of assimilation to which Jews only apparently and superficially belonged.

It was on such Buberian premises that Strauss proceeded to argue that the greater the attempt to integrate into an alien (*fremdartig*) mode, "the 'national substance' becomes increasingly deeply repressed and hidden inside." In a startling confirmation of anti-Semitic and racial theses and couched in a similar organic discourse, Strauss proposed that to the extent that the "foreign" mixed with the Jewish soul, it would be apprehended as alien and a generalized Jewish ethnic distinctiveness (*Stammeseigenart*) would so assert itself in the individual that the instinct of survival would push him back toward his own ethnic particularity.

To be sure, Strauss emphasized, after such a long dispersion it was not simple to locate and identify this essence (Buber, some time before, had described assimilation as an ongoing form of Jewish self-alienation), but no matter how vague it was, the feeling of something substantial, essential (*wesentlich*) was sufficient. The content of this essence would be clarified through diligent work; this was the most urgent and binding Jewish obligation of the moment. Affirmation of Jewishness as the informing center of one's life, thought, and deeds would render bifurcated Jewish lives whole again.

But Strauss was extreme in his physiopsychic fusion of identity. The importance of the *Kunstwart* affair for certain Jewish intellectuals who were not affiliated with religious or official communal life yet who felt, in some vague yet deep way, "Jewish," was that it brought out the conviction that there were, indeed, real limits to assimilation and that these had to be explained not merely in terms of external antagonisms but also by acknowledging the intangible yet powerful inner sense of Jewishness. In a private correspondence with Strauss over the issue that Goldstein had raised, the young Walter Benjamin voiced his enthusiastic support for the idea of a new Jewish (German-language) journal that would encourage, as Strauss put it, "conscious Jews to delineate the nature of the Jewish spirit clearly and credibly." But although Strauss sought to formalize and channel this "Jewish spirit" into explicitly Jewish frames, for Benjamin its value consisted in the absence of formal definition. The essence of Jewish, or Western European Jewish, identity was contained in this peculiar "sensibility" and should in no way, therefore, be harnessed to any fixed framework.

For Eastern European Jewry, Benjamin declared, Zionism provided a solution of sorts—whereas for Western European Jews it was an irrelevance. Strauss's suggestion of creating an autonomous center of Jewish culture in Germany linked to the spiritual center that would arise in Palestine was objectionable because Jews in the West were at the forefront of a larger process that transcended parochial boundaries and activities. They were at the forefront of such a project because their ethnic-national bonds created a kind of shared spiritual and mental sensibility—never an end in itself—that rendered Jews an "elite in the party of intellectuals," "the most eminent bearer and representative of matters spiritual and intellectual." Strauss also proposed an inner essence, but at the same time programmatically advocated what Paul Mendes-Flohr has called an "exoteric" conception of Zionism and Judaism—the formation of explicitly Jewish cultural forms and the conscious practice of Jewish deeds. For Benjamin, Judaism was an "esoteric" matter: its power derived from the fact that it was both ill-defined and yet self-understood. He was certainly not alone. For many intellectual Jews, the importance of Jewishness lay in its implicit nature; it was not a formal commitment or series of obligations but a hidden sensibility that powerfully informed one's spiritual and mental life.

In the years following the *Kunstwart* affair

there were, nevertheless, numerous positive, "exoteric" developments in the direction that Goldstein had advocated. World War I and the years of the Weimar Republic witnessed the appearance of divergent, self-affirming "Jewish" journals of high intellectual quality, such as Martin Buber's *Der Jude* and the Centralverein's *Der Morgen* (under the editorship of Julius Goldstein); a virtual cult of the "Ostjuden" (or at least a serious reassessment of the East-West Jewish relation among various circles of German Jewry); an outburst of "Weimar" Jewish intellectual and theological creativity that blossomed in diverse directions—and included the work and thought of Hermann Cohen, Franz Rosenzweig, and Gershom Scholem (and even the "esoteric" Walter Benjamin).

But of course the tensions, ambiguities, and casuistic definitions concerning Deutschtum and Judentum continued unresolved. Indeed, they were definitive, perhaps the source of much that was creative in German Jewry through 1933. Beneath all these exoteric redefinitions there remained a persistent, positively evaluated experience (indeed, an ideology) of an elusive, indefinable, yet radically determinative inner Jewish essence. Jewishness, as Franz Rosenzweig put it, was "no entity, no subject among other subjects, no one sphere of life among other spheres of life; it is not what the century of emancipation with its cultural mania wanted to reduce it to. It is something inside the individual that makes him a Jew, something infinitesimally small yet immeasurably large, his most impenetrable secret, yet evident in every gesture and every word—especially in the most spontaneous of them."

Sigmund Freud, too, regarded Jewishness and its "many dark emotional powers" as "all the more powerful the less they could be expressed in words," as "the clear consciousness of an inner identity, the familiarity of the same psychological structure." This insistence on a Jewishness that resists definition, or as Yosef Hayim Yerushalmi has put it, the intuition of a distinct sensibility, essence, or character deprived of any particular content, did not only play an important role for intellectual German Jews. We may, indeed, dub it a prevailing ideology of our own times, a way in which countless contemporary secular Jews approach articulating their own persistent but difficult to locate sense of a "Jewish self."

Bibliography

Hannah Arendt, *The Origins of Totalitarianism* (New York: Meridian, 1958), esp. chap. 3; Steven E. Aschheim, *Brothers and Strangers: The East European Jew in German and German-Jewish Consciousness, 1800–1923* (Madison: University of Wisconsin Press, 1982); Julius Bab, "Assimilation," *Der Freistaat* 1 (1913–14): 172–76; Walter Benjamin, *Gesammelte Schriften,* ed. Rolf Tiedemann, vol. II, bk. 3 (Frankfurt a. M.: Suhrkamp Verlag, 1977), 836–44; Paul Breines, "The Jew as Revolutionary: The Case of Gustav Landauer," *Leo Baeck Institute Year Book* 12 (1967); Martin Buber, "Judaism and the Jews," *On Judaism,* ed. Nahum N. Glatzer (New York: Schocken, 1967), 11–21; Ludwig Geiger, "Zionismus und Deutschtum," *Die Stimme der Wahrheit: Jahrbuch für wissenschaftlichen Zionismus* (Würzburg: n.p., 1905); Sander L. Gilman, *Jewish Self-Hatred: Anti-Semitism and the Hidden Language of the Jews* (Baltimore, Md.: Johns Hopkins University Press, 1986); Julius Goldstein, "Moritz Goldstein's 'Deutsch-jüdischer Parnass,'" *Im deutschen Reich* 10 (Oct. 1912): 447–48; Moritz Goldstein, "Deutsch-jüdischer Parnass," *Der Kunstwart* 25 (1912): 281–94; M. Goldstein, "German Jewry's Dilemma: The Story of a Provocative Essay," *Leo Baeck Institute Year Book* 2 (1957): 236–54; Heinrich Heine, "The New Israelite Hospital in Hamburg" (1841) and "Moses" (1854), *The Poetry and Prose of Heinrich Heine,* ed. Frederic Ewen, trans. Margaret Armour (New York: Citadel, 1948), 285, 665–66; Ernst Lissauer, "Deutschtum und Judentum," *Der Kunstwart* 25 (1912): 6–12; Paul Mendes-Flohr, "The German-Jewish Parnassus," *A Land of Two Rivers: The German-Jewish Vision of a New Babylon* (forthcoming); Franz Oppenheimer, "Ost und West," *Ost und West* 1 (1901); Oppenheimer, "Stammesbewußtsein und Volksbewußtsein," *Jüdische Rundschau* 15 (Feb. 25, 1910); Oskar Panizza, "The Operated Jew," trans. Jack Zipes, *New German Critique* 21 (fall 1980): 63–79; Jehuda Reinharz, *Fatherland or Promised Land: The Dilemma of the German Jew, 1893–1914* (Ann Arbor: University of Michigan Press, 1975); Franz Rosenzweig, "On Being a Jewish Person," *Franz Rosenzweig,* ed. Nahum N. Glatzer (New York: Schocken, 1962); Ph. Stauff, "Die Juden in Literatur und Volk," *Der Kunstwart* 25 (1912): 251–59; Ludwig Strauss (Franz Quentin), "Aussprache zur Judenfrage," *Der Kunstwart* 25 (1912): 236–44; Strauss, "Ein Dokument der Assimilation," *Der Freistaat* 1 (1913–14); Richard Wagner, "Judaism in Music," *Richard Wagner's Prose Works,* trans. William Ashton Ellis, vol. 3, *The Theatre* (London: K. Paul, Trench, Trubner, 1907); Gershon Weiler, "Felix Mauthner: A Study in Jewish Self-Rejection," *Leo Baeck Institute Year Book* 7 (1963); G. Wollstein, "Neue Kompromisse," *Der Jüdische Student* 15 (Jan. 1917); and Yosef Hayim Yerushalmi, *Freud's Moses: Judaism Terminable and Interminable* (New Haven: Yale University Press, 1991)

STEVEN E. ASCHHEIM

1913 After two hundred years in which virtually no work by a Jewish woman writer has appeared in Prague, Babette Fried writes two collections of ghetto stories

Today, when many people are looking for previously unknown women writers and when unknown male writers from Prague at the time of Kafka continue to be discovered, the question about whether there were significant German-Jewish women writers in Prague is bound to be raised. Although none are mentioned in German literary histories or other German reference works, Jewish sources point to some Jewish women writers from Prague—although, to be sure, in a much earlier period.

From a combination of three sources, *The Universal Jewish Encyclopedia,* M. Kayserling's *Die jüdische Frau in der Literatur und Kunst,* and Otto Muneles's *Bibliographical Survey of Jewish Prague,* we learn that there were at least five Jewish women in Prague in the seventeenth and early eighteenth centuries by whom belletristic work was published in Judeo-German. The earliest was a song of praise of God's wonders by Bathseba (Petschel) Hurwitz in 1602. Next seems to have been "A Beautiful Song" of five pages, in the last line of which the name of the author, Taube Pan, is mentioned. This latter work was published in Prague in 1609. In the same year a book of ethical rules for women appeared by Ribka bat Meir Tiktiner, and in 1686 a "Beautiful New Song" dealing with the Ten Commandments appeared by Sheindl the Wife of Gershon. It was followed in 1705 by *The History of the House of David* by Bella Chasan. If Kayserling says that she "edited" it, he no doubt means that she did not invent it, but closely followed sources she found. Chasan also wrote a prayer that is to be sung on the Day of Atonement. The most important work written by women about that time was *A Beautiful Story,* on which Bella Chasan collaborated with Rachel Porges. It is a legend about the arrival of the first Jews in Prague.

Although Kayserling, whose format allows for more subjectivity than our other sources, insinuates that women's names may have been cited as authors to attract buyers, the fact that about that time there seems to have been a good deal of literature written, edited, or translated for female readers makes it plausible that some of them, too, produced works of the same kind. It was, after all, a literature that in content and form adhered closely to the literary traditions, gentile as well as Jewish, of that time. Without exception and in contrast to almost all the women who wrote in the late nineteenth and early twentieth centuries, all of them came from very pious and learned families and presumably continued in that tradition.

According to Kayserling's account, it seems that in the seventeenth and eighteenth centuries there was a somewhat more sophisticated literature written by Jewish women in Germany, Italy, and Spain. It was followed in Germany by a wave of participation by women in Jewish scholarship, which seems to have been lacking in Prague. We do not know why literary activity by Jewish women in Prague ceased, but the absence of Jewish salonnières there around 1800, in contrast to Berlin and Vienna, may be a function of the city's reduction to a provincial capital.

When another woman writer appeared in Prague, after a hiatus of two hundred years, hardly anybody took note of her. Babette Fried, born in Ckyn in southern Bohemia as the daughter of a rabbi, wrote fiction with Jewish themes in Prague in the early twentieth century. Her two small books, written in the style of old-fashioned ghetto stories, are *Der Unessane Tokef,* published in 1913, and *1001 Nacht in der Jeschiwa,* n.d. We know nothing about the author other than that she lived in Prague as a widow with eight children; additionally, we presume that in the latter book she portrayed herself in the young girl who complains bitterly about not being allowed to read, study, and be present at talmudic discussions.

The fact that there were not more Jewish women writing in German in Prague around the turn of the twentieth century does not seem particularly remarkable if one thinks of cities such as Berlin and Vienna, which had much larger German-speaking populations but likewise few Jewish women writers. Similarly, one would find that in the German-gentile population of Prague, comparable in size to the German-Jewish one, only perhaps one or two women writers are known by name.

But how can we explain that Prague Czech society, which had only recently developed a middle class and was still close to its rural roots, had at that time such a strong female literary presence that the literary historian Antonin Mestan was able to write: "The Czech novel of the second half of the nineteenth and of the first half of the twentieth century is to a considerable degree the work of women writers"?

I would like to suggest that Czech society had a much more encouraging attitude toward women intellectuals, including writers, than did German, including German-Jewish, society in Prague. Several factors contributed to this attitude: the admonitions to Czech women at the time of the Czech national revival earlier in the century to cultivate the Czech language and to help enrich it; Vojta

Noprstek's extensive women's library with its public lectures for women from the 1860s on; and Minerva, the first women's gymnasium in Central Europe, which was founded in 1891. Besides, perhaps the very fact that Czech society was so new meant that it was less settled in traditional bourgeois and noble grooves than was its German counterpart, which in many ways served as a model to the growing Jewish middle and upper classes.

During that period and on into the twentieth century, newly prosperous Jewish families discouraged their daughters from devoting their lives to anything other than entering into a suitable marriage, running a household in keeping with their husband's status, and having an education adequate for raising children and for making a suitable impression at social and cultural gatherings. Eventually some women attended university, but usually only until they found a husband. There were deviations from this pattern, mainly in the area of premarital and extramarital sex.

The novels by the writers of the Prague circle that portray women from their own background, such as Max Brod's *Jüdinnen,* Oskar Baum's *Die böse Unschuld,* and Hermann Ungar's *Die Verstümmelten,* to mention a few, describe women as uninteresting, not very bright, and focused on marriage and gossip. Was this really true of their own sisters and perhaps also their wives? From Kafka's letters to his sister Ottla we know that he felt that she understood him, but—like most women's letters to famous men—her letters to Franz have not been preserved.

My research turned up, sometimes by accident, some evidence of literary activity by women of that generation, such as the well-written introduction to Zdeněk Nejedlý's monograph *Bedřich Smetana,* by Elsa, Max Brod's wife; we know that she translated several books in addition to this one. Was this introduction her only attempt at writing? We also do not know how many women who were engaged in literary activities never saw their names in print. Oskar Baum's daughter-in-law, for example, believed that her mother-in-law did much more for her blind husband's works than transcribe them.

The archives of the Leo Baeck Institute in New

York, which have an extensive collection of unpublished memoirs, contain two remarkable manuscripts relevant in this connection. The earlier is the thoughtful, highly sophisticated family history of Ottilie von Kahler, who died around 1940 in her eighties. In the other, Else Bergmann, the wife of the philosopher Hugo Bergmann, collected the reminiscences that had been handed down in her family. A considerable part of the manuscript is devoted to her own memories of her mother, Berta Fanta.

Little is known about Else. She was active in a Zionist women's organization and worked as a pharmacist in her father's pharmacy before emigrating to Palestine with her husband, who later left her for another woman. Her proud remark about her grandfather, who financed the building of the large Vinohrady synagogue, can be considered an instance of identification with Jewishness. She tells even more proudly, however, of an earlier ancestor in a Bohemian village who lent his copy of Kant's *Critique of Pure Reason* to Gottfried Seume.

Her mother Berta Fanta (née Sohr), born in Libochowitz near Prague in 1866, was probably the most visible Jewish woman in Prague in her time. Both she and her sister Ida (Freund) received good educations and were provided by their parents, hard-working business people, with ample money to establish their husbands in their professions, as well as with a villa in a Prague suburb where they spent their summers. Berta gathered around her the most prominent German and German-Jewish intellectuals who lived in and passed through Prague. Her salon was famous for its lectures, mostly in philosophy, but there were also evenings devoted to themes in literature and in the arts. Else Bergmann writes in her reminiscences that although her aunt Ida was primarily a painter, her mother wrote poetry. It seems that none of the poetry has been preserved, however. Possibly it was destroyed along with parts of her diary by her husband, who evidently deleted portions of it that he considered frivolous. In Berta's diary, accounts about the life of the family alternate with reports about trips abroad to study art and architecture, and with her

thoughts about ideas to which she was exposed, for example, anthroposophy. She also lectured in the Verein Frauenfortschritt, but not even the titles of those lectures can be found.

Of the women mentioned here, none distanced herself as much from the limited horizon of the older generations in her family as did Berta Fanta. She studied various religions and the works of philosophers seriously, but mentioned no Jewish ones, not even Buber, who played such a central role among the Prague intellectual Zionists and perhaps most of all in the thinking of her son-in-law Hugo Bergmann. In 1918 Fanta decided to abandon the life she had been leading for one of useful physical activity in Palestine, but she died before she could realize that plan. Because her diary contains no references to Zionism, it seems that she had decided to go to Palestine to be close to Hugo.

If our search for Jewish women who wrote and published German literature in Prague is not very successful, the picture is a good deal less bleak if we consider women who left Prague, mostly for cities in Germany, and pursued careers abroad. The most successful of them by far is Auguste Hauschner. Born in Hôrice in Bohemia in 1851 and taken to Prague at age one, she was at least a generation older than the writers of the Prague circle. Although Hauschner did not begin writing until after her husband's death in 1890, twenty years after she moved to Berlin to marry him, the stifling atmosphere that she described in *Die Familie Lowositz*—the novel she wrote another twenty years later about her own Prague background—makes it clear that she was glad to leave that society.

Hauschner's many novels, now largely forgotten, succeed in depicting the richness of social interactions during her time by means of the language of different social strata in various regions. From a collection of letters to Hauschner published after her death, and from reviews of her books, we know that she was esteemed by a great variety of writers, artists, and other intellectuals. As she was a very private person, we find glimpses of her personal views and relationships only in her largely unpublished correspondence, which she carried on for many decades with two principal correspondents: her relative, the philosopher Fritz Mauthner, to whose German national conservatism her democratic liberalism provided an opposite pole, and Gustav Landauer, the murdered anarchist who for many years was the recipient of her generous financial support and, perhaps unbeknownst to him, the object of her fervent love.

Chronologically the second Jewish woman from Prague who had a career elsewhere was Grete Meisel-Hess (b. 1879). Like most of the women who interest us, she came from the family of a well-to-do industrialist. From her autobiographical fiction we gather that as a rebellious child she was sent to a progressive boarding school in the Bohemian forest—a school that seems to have had a decisive influence on her later development. We do not know exactly when the family moved to Vienna, but we find her there in time to have audited a variety of courses at the university, to have begun contributing articles to the feminist *Dokumente der Frauen,* and to have married an irresponsible young man—all by the age of twenty. Her main aim was to live by her talents as a writer of fiction and articles on women's issues, unlike her mother, who let herself be compelled into marriage with Grete's authoritarian father, who seems to have been a twin in the spirit of Herman Kafka, Franz Kafka's notorious father. Although Grete's marriages and other liaisons were disastrous—the first ended in divorce after about a year—she was successful as a writer first in Vienna and especially later in Berlin, where her books on marriage and sexuality and her novels and novellas were praised highly for a time.

Fairly suddenly in the early 1910s, critics began to see the inconsistencies and the repetitiveness in her theoretical works, as well as a sudden turn to conservatism on women's issues. As loneliness and financial worries increasingly dominated her personal life and she no longer was able to write with the exuberance of her earlier years, Grete's life became a desperate search for guidance among many ideologies and cults, but the idea of turning to Judaism does not seem to have

crossed her mind, or the minds of her troubled, originally "Jewish" protagonists in her novel *Die Intellektuellen.* Her involvement with spiritism led, in her own opinion, to the mental illness from which she suffered during the last several years of her life. Her death, on her forty-third birthday in 1922, may have been a suicide.

Why did Grete Meisel-Hess fail? A lack of guidance, of role models, comes to mind, but could that not have been provided by others such as her coworker Helene Stöcker and Hauschner, who was known to be eager to help younger colleagues and lived in Berlin at the same time? Although neither Hauschner nor Meisel-Hess liked Prague, it seems that neither left the city primarily in order to seek better career opportunities elsewhere. Although, as is generally believed, decreased financial support of German writers by the government of the newly established Czechoslovak Republic may have been a factor in the decision of some German-Jewish writers to move abroad, I believe that the women who made that decision left more because, in view of the social attitudes toward women, they did not expect to be successful there.

Grete Fischer, born in 1893, also as the daughter of a Prague Jewish manufacturer, was a teenager when she wrote in her diary that she would like to leave Prague. Already in high school she was interested in literature, published a poem at the age of fifteen, and organized with her friends "literary teas" and "published" a literary magazine of which, to be sure, only one copy was produced each time. At social gatherings she met several members of the Prague circle—for example, Max Brod, Willy Haas, and Egon Erwin Kisch—but according to her own testimony, she behaved so self-consciously that no continuing relationships developed. Grete so dreaded not excelling that when the prestigious editor Paul Wiegler rejected the play she submitted to him at the age of sixteen but suggested that she write some feuilletons for his newspaper, *Bohemia,* she angrily stomped out of his office.

Realizing that she could no more rely on writing for a reliable income than did most writers, Grete hoped for a career that would allow her to use her musical talent and training as well as her literary interests. She wanted to accept the invitation of Lothar Wallerstein, a renowned opera director, to accompany him to Germany as his assistant. To her parents, however, this plan was unthinkable because of what it would do to her reputation. Thus Grete had to wait until she was in her twenties to be allowed to go to Berlin and look for a position as editor in a publishing company. In Berlin Grete Fischer worked for Paul Cassirer and then for Ullstein, editing works by Bertolt Brecht, Else Lasker-Schüler, Erich Maria Remarque, and many other celebrities, in addition to teaching music, playing the violin in concerts of chamber music, being the music critic of the *Berliner Börsenkurier,* and writing the novel *Nicht traurig sein,* which appeared in installments in the same paper.

Although Prague still seemed like a safe haven from the Nazis in the mid-1930s, and although she felt very attached to her family, who still lived there, Grete, after completing a literary assignment in Palestine (evidently she never considered staying there), emigrated to England; here she supported herself with various types of work, such as writing radio addresses that were broadcast to Germany and practicing as a very successful self-taught child therapist. As the author of several books—including an extensive autobiography, *Dienstboten, Brecht und andere Zeitgenossen in Prag, Berlin, London*—and of lyric poetry, she became a very respected member of the PEN club of German authors abroad.

Grete Fischer seems to be the only writer from Prague, male or female, who had fond memories of the religious instruction she received as a schoolchild, but Jewish religion seems to have played no role in the rest of her life, not even during the many years of loneliness in Berlin, when she desperately searched for comfort.

Another woman to whom leaving Prague was of vital importance is Alice Rühle-Gerstel. Born in 1894, she belonged to the same generation and had a background similar to that of Grete Fischer. But unlike Grete, Alice early became a Marxist, rejected the bourgeois values of her family, and wrote scholarly books and articles on Adlerian psychology and sociology, often as related to

women, as well as belletristic works and articles on literary subjects. With her husband Otto Rühle, whom she met while working on her doctorate in Munich and who shared her interests, she lived in Buchholz near Dresden. After they fled to Prague in 1934, her writings were destroyed along with the other contents of their house in Germany. Her main belletristic work, *Der Umbruch oder Hanna und die Freiheit,* which was finally published by Fischer in 1984, is based on her observations and experiences during her years of exile in Prague.

From 1937 on, Alice and Otto lived in Mexico City, where they were close to Trotsky (without agreeing with his political views), but associated with none of the German Communist émigrés. The day of Otto Rühle's sudden death in 1943, Alice, despondent about the state of the world, committed suicide. She is forgotten, as are most, perhaps all, of the women I have here assembled, but perhaps a remark by Manès Sperber, made over forty years after he last saw her, will arouse some readers' curiosity about her: "She was the most intelligent and probably the smartest woman I have ever met."

The last of the Jewish writers from Prague, none of whom we can designate in this way entirely without hesitation, is another nonconformist. Ruth Klinger's memoirs, *Zeugin einer Zeit,* self-published in Zurich in 1977, are not only unusually frank and well written, they are also a very valuable document of her time. After she completed them in her seventh decade, however, she found no publisher for them. An abbreviated version of the book was published under the title *Die Frau im Kaftan.*

Ruth Klinger was born in 1906 as the daughter of a Prague Jewish couple that worked hard to make a living in their dry goods store. From an early age, she had several strikes against her, including her lively imagination, which seemed to have convinced her father, the powerful head of the family, that Ruth—originally Trudl—was mentally not quite normal. The Klingers lived in quarters that were a constant embarrassment to their daughter; what especially shook Ruth's sense of security, however, was a violent anti-Semitic attack directed against her family in

1919, which resulted in the death of her mother in the following year. In her teens, Ruth found a sense of belonging in the Zionist sports organization Blue-White. Because her acting talent was recognized early, she was able, while still in her teens, to start out on a promising career at the prestigious German theater in Prague. Her first lover, however, persuaded her to move to Berlin, where her career and her personal life for some years can be compared to a roller-coaster. In Berlin, on the road in much of Europe, and from 1933 on in Palestine, Ruth stumbled from one unfortunate love affair and marriage to another, sometimes successful in her profession and sometimes eking out a precarious existence.

After the war she accepted her sister's invitation and moved to Prague, where she felt very much like a stranger. That feeling was intensified when the Communists came to power. But this was also the time when Ruth finally found herself. After being a reporter for an Israeli paper, she worked her way up to a responsible position in the Israeli embassy in Prague, and later in the Israeli diplomatic service in Switzerland.

After her childhood, Jewish religion no longer seems to have played a role in her life. But was Ruth a Zionist? She announced in 1952 in Prague that she was going "home, to Israel," but the fact that she spent the many years of her retirement in Switzerland suggests that she may have had mixed feelings about Israel.

In view of the meager gleanings of our search for German-Jewish writers in and from Prague, let us take another moment to speculate about the possible causes. Were there so few talented women or was the ostracism and ridicule to which women with intellectual or artistic ambitions were exposed a deterrent to many? According to the books *WahnsinnsFrauen,* edited by Sibylle Duda and Luise Pusch, and *Handbuch für WahnsinnsFrauen,* edited by Luise F. Pusch, neither of which discusses women from Prague, women in different societies who did not conform to the conventional rules were often considered just a little bit crazy at best, or were driven to insanity or even suicide. Bohemian Jewish society had such precisely circumscribed rules of behavior for women, and deviations from them were so strictly

punished and mainly so carefully hushed up, that the many whispered reports about "melancholy" women and attempted and successful suicides by those who could not stand the pressure to conform can usually not be investigated adequately.

It seems that for Prague-Jewish women modernity had many unfortunate consequences. As increasing numbers of Prague Jews in the second half of the nineteenth century became more prosperous, it became customary for families to live some distance from their businesses and factories. This meant that women were increasingly restricted to being in charge of households where much of the work was done by maids. As housekeeping became simplified generally, and as Jewish dietary laws were no longer obeyed, there were fewer demands on their time. Thus, as their involvement in organizations caring for the sick, the poor, and the dead also decreased, there was a void that only the very imaginative and the very fortunate were able to fill.

In what ways were these women Jewish? Although they did not hesitate to refer to themselves as Jews, these women were minimally observant. Comparing their autobiographical writings with those of their counterparts in Germany, one is struck by how rarely they mention Jewish Holy Days, for example, or religious food laws. They may in different contexts have referred to themselves as Germans, Austrians, or Jews and not have been aware of a conflict. What did it then mean to them to be Jews? By 1900, it meant to be located somewhere along the spectrum of the middle class, but striving upward economically and educationally; in general to be thrifty until one arrived in the upper class; to sacrifice for one's children's future; to value family cohesiveness; and to be aware of the persecution of Jews, past and contemporary.

During Ruth Klinger's generation and after, there were no more German-Jewish women writers in or from Prague. Otto Muneles's *Bibliographical Survey of Jewish Prague* listed no women authors, Czech or German, for that period. Neither are there any in Ruth Schwertfeger's *Women of Theresienstadt,* which includes an anthology of writings by inmates in German. This absence can partly be explained by the hostility of the Czech prisoners against anyone using the language of the enemy.

After the war, there were forty years during which Jews had to keep a low profile, and the use of the German language was taboo for them. Since the revolution of 1989, converted gentiles, people of half-Jewish descent, and Jews who had been "passing" have been joining the formerly moribund Jewish community, which had consisted largely of concentration camp survivors, many of them from various countries.

The continuity with the prewar Prague-Jewish community with its strong German component has been broken; the names of most of the men of the Prague circle of writers have become a faint memory, and the names of the women writers are not even that.

Bibliography

Oskar Baum, *Die böse Unschuld* (Frankfurt a. M.: Rütten and Loenig, 1913); Else Bergmann, "Erinnerungen an meine Mutter Berta Fanta," unpub., Leo Baeck Institute, New York, n.d.; Elsa Brod, "Friedrich Smetana," introductory essay to her translation of Zdeněk Ne-jedlý's monograph, *Bedřich Smetana* (Prague: Orbis, 1929); Bella Chasan and Rachel Porges, "Eine schöne Geschichte," trans. Ruth Kestenberg-Gladstein, ed. Ferdinand Seibt, *Die Juden in den böhmischen Ländern* (Munich: Oldenbourg, 1983); Sibylle Duda and Luise F. Pusch, *WahnsinnsFrauen* (Frankfurt a. M.: Suhrkamp, 1994); Grete Fischer, *Dienstboten, Brecht und andere Zeitgenossen in Prag, Berlin, London* (Freiburg: Olten, 1966); Babette Fried, *Der Unessane Tokef* (Prague: Brandeis, 1913); Fried, *1001 Nacht in der Jeschiwa* (Prague: Brandeis, 1897); Auguste Hauschner, *Die Familie Lowositz* (Berlin: Fleischel, 1909); Ottilie von Kahler, "Ein Beitrag zu einer Familiengeschichte des Hauses B. Teller," unpub., Leo Baeck Institute, New York, Svinare, 1930; Ruth Klinger, *Zeugin einer Zeit* (self-published in Zurich, 1977); Grete Meisel-Hess, *Die Intellektuellen* (Berlin: Osterheld, 1911); Antonín Měštan, *Česká literatura 1785–1985* (Toronto: Sixty-Eight Publishers, 1987); Otto Muneles, *Bibliographical Survey of Jewish Prague* (Prague: Orbis, 1952); Luise Pusch, *Handbuch für WahnsinnsFrauen* (Frankfurt a. M.: Suhrkamp, 1994); Alice Rühle-Gerstel, *Der Umbruch oder Hanna und die Freiheit* (Frankfurt a. M.: Fischer, 1984); Hermann Ungar, *Die Verstümmelten* (Berlin: Suhrkamp, 1923); and *Universal Jewish Encyclopedia*, 10 vols. (New York: 1969).

WILMA A. IGGERS

1913 Karl Kraus writes "He's a Jew After All," one of the few texts in which he directly confronts his Jewish identity and suggests how it has affected his satirical writing

There can scarcely be a twentieth-century German-Jewish writer whose work has more often been vilified and dismissed as a product of "Jewish self-hatred" than the satirical writer Karl Kraus (1874–1936). In his classic but controversial essay published in 1930, Theodor Lessing singles out Kraus as "the most radiant example of Jewish self-hatred" and the "avenger and judge of the age," but he nevertheless predicts that nothing more will remain of Kraus's anti-journalistic work than a "mountain of printed paper" (Lessing 1930, 43). By this "mountain" Lessing certainly meant the *Fackel* (Torch), the radical journal of literary, social, and cultural criticism that Kraus founded in Vienna in 1899 and, beginning in 1911, wrote single-handedly until his death in 1936. The *Torch,* whose contributors included many distinguished Jewish and gentile writers and artists such as Frank Wedekind, Adolf Loos, Arnold Schönberg, and Else Lasker-Schüler—as well as a few compromising anti-Semitic thinkers such as Houston Stewart Chamberlain—proved to be much more than a paper mountain. It eventually served Kraus not only as a first venue for the aphorisms, essays, and dramas revised and collected in his books; it also coalesced into a carefully structured, monumental text in itself. Although the *Torch* has been valued for its incisive exposure of sexual hypocrisy, for its satirical critique of the legal system, and, above all, for its brilliant analysis of the press's insidious distortion of reality, the journal's complex and often problematic treatment of the Jewish Question has received relatively little attention. But the *Torch* contains what has been called a "gigantic discourse" (Wagner 1987, 387) on Jewish matters that focuses on the extremes and painful contradictions of Viennese particularities and, by extension, of the entire Central European *conditio judaica* between the turn of the century and the advent of the Holocaust.

It is an undeniable, regrettable fact that the intermittent congruence between Kraus's anti-Jewish satirical rhetoric and the worst anti-Semitic jargon of the conservative Christian press in Austria and Germany compromised some of his most important critical insights. In an early issue of the *Torch,* for example, he belittled what he called the fairy tale of "ritual murder" but insisted on the real danger of "ritual robbery" (*F* 100 [1902]: 1). Repeatedly, he employs this reprehensible pun, which evokes the worst clichés about "Jewish" finance, to castigate the corrupt journalism of Moriz Benedikt, the editor-in-chief of the *Neue Freie Presse,* one of the most highly regarded liberal newspapers of the era. Kraus was also capable of undermining Benedikt's Jewish pieties in more subtle ways that suggest considerable religious ambivalence on the part of the satirist. Alluding both to the *Neue Freie Presse*'s practice of silencing him by suppressing his name and to the prohibition on uttering the name of God, Kraus claimed that Benedikt's "faith stands and falls on two names that he will not take in vain, not even for

serious money. He fears me and maintains absolute silence concerning Adonai" (*F* 341–42
[1912]: 27). In the absence of a reliable biography, it is difficult to know how to relate such
satirically formulated statements to Kraus's own
beliefs. We do know that he left the Jewish religious community in 1899 and was baptized in
1911. His conversion remained entirely secret,
however, until he made sensational use of it in
1922 by announcing that he was leaving the
Catholic Church in protest over Max Reinhardt's
staging of theatrical productions in the Salzburg
Cathedral.

Contrary to psychological explanations emphasizing a neat "dualism" (Timms 1986, 173)
between the satirical persona and the private person, comparisons between Kraus's public and private remarks suggest instead an irresolvable tension. In an unpublished letter written in 1904 to
Alfred von Berger, a gentile colleague, he stooped
to exposing a former friend's Eastern Jewish origins by decrying his "shabby behavior, Galician-
style" (Kraus Archive, Vienna City Library). By
contrast, in 1929 Kraus gently but firmly repri-
manded the Baroness Sidonie von Nádherny, his
longtime, intimate companion, when she complained about the "provokingly Jewish faces" of
the accompanists who played the piano at his
readings (letter of Mar. 11–12, 1929, in Kraus
1977, 1:608). A similar ambivalence marks
Kraus's attitude toward the Yiddish-inflected
German spoken by many Viennese Jews. Although the typical Yiddish expression "chutzpah" is used in the *Torch* consistently to impugn
the unethical tactics of the liberal press, Kraus
was capable in private conversation of rein-
terpreting the term positively to characterize his
own satirical aggression. In 1913, he responded
to an acquaintance's wonder at the contrast between his combative writing style and his gentle
demeanor by saying that his chutzpah never surfaced until he sat down at his desk (*Kraus-Hefte* 37
[1986]: 11). Kraus's stylistic exploitation of Jewish German—referred to variously as "Jargon,"
"jüdeln," or "mauscheln"—is so complex and extensive that a published glossary of terms (*Kohn*)
barely scratches the surface of this important aspect of the *Torch*.

The degree to which Kraus's work originates
in his ambivalence toward Judaism may be measured by the fact that *Eine Krone für Zion* (A crown
for Zion; 1898), the second of the two pamphlets
he published before founding the *Torch* in 1899,
takes to task Theodor Herzl's idea of a Jewish
state. Although Kraus does not conceal his assimilationist sympathies, he is more interested in
revealing puns and in self-incriminating quotations from official Zionist reports than in cogent
political argumentation. His satirical deconstruction of the movement begins with the title, which
refers not only to the shekel—here pointedly exchanged for the basic unit of Austrian currency—
demanded of every card-carrying member of the
Zionist association. The crown also ironically
honors Herzl, the "King of Zion," who presumes
to negotiate with the crowned heads of Europe for
a Jewish settlement in Palestine. Finally, it even
signifies Kraus's own contribution: instead of the
official shekel that he had donated on the condition of anonymity, he offered this satirical text
with which he aggressively "crowns" the movement.

From Kraus's perspective, Zionism has the
same effect as anti-Semitism. It creates an undesirable Near Eastern detour for what seemed like
a straight, if narrow, path for Jewish assimilation
in Europe; and it leads only to a dead end of false
hopes for the poor Jewish masses, who would do
better to act in solidarity with the proletariat of
other races and nationalities. Instead of concluding with a typical Socialist exhortation, however,
Kraus resorts to a biblical metaphor. He predicts
that the Jews will not enter the Promised Land
with dry feet, but will instead be caught up in the
political promises of Social Democracy, that
"other red sea" (Kraus 1979, 314).

Clearly, history has shown that Kraus was
dead wrong, but that does not make it right to
read scorn for Eastern Jewry into this text, as
many commentators have done. Kraus explicitly
states that he is not writing as the advocate of
those assimilants who turn their newly won social
status against their underprivileged fellow Jews.
Moreover, he wittily rebukes the idle sons of such
families, "who have joined their Aryan sports
comrades in cultivating inner emptiness and

an aristocracy of manicured nails" (Kraus 1979, 312).

Many of the stylistic effects of *A Crown for Zion*, which is formulated as a journalistic correspondence from the Kaiser's summer retreat at Bad Ischl, point to the influential model of Heinrich Heine's *Travel Pictures*. When Kraus describes the reluctance of wealthy Viennese Jews to decide between assimilation and Zionism, he reprimands these "people of Ischl" (Kraus 1979, 313), an act that figuratively reduces them to confused descendants of the people of Israel. It is not surprising that such subtly satirical portraits of the Jewish bourgeoisie should have prompted a contemporary critic to dub Kraus "the Ischl Heine" (quoted in Lensing 1992, 98). Even less surprising is the fact that this praise should lead to an "anxiety of influence" for which Kraus would later compensate by aggressively rejecting this writer, who for German-Jewish cultural circles at the turn of the century was "the first great Jewish poet in Germany" (96).

In the very first issue of the *Torch*, Kraus himself had objected to the reduction of his famous predecessor's legacy to the "wretched punning paired with pitiful verse" (*F* 1 [1899]: 17) that characterized the work of a local librettist of Hungarian-Jewish origins hailed as the Viennese Heine. For the next decade, Kraus continued to defend Heine not only against Jewish imitators, but also against anti-Semitic detractors, including the proto-Nazi literary historian Adolf Bartels, whose reputation is dismissed as "the Germanic endurance with which he relieves himself at Heine's grave" (*F* 217 [1907]: 30). It therefore came as a shock to many of Kraus's admirers, particularly those on the cultural and political left, when he published *Heine und die Folgen* (Heine and the consequences; 1910). Ostensibly an attack on Heine's journalistic posterity, which Kraus perceives as corrupted by its forebear's skill in ornamenting reportage with poetic diction, the essay also criticizes the facile rhymes and cynical eroticism of Heine's early poetry as well as his polemical exploitation of his opponents' private lives.

Despite Kraus's attempts to downplay the Jewish subtext of the essay, there are also subtle

and not so subtle allusions to Heine's Jewishness. By referring to the "mosaic of this [Heine's] work" (Kraus 1986–, 4:193) that the poet's imitators are dismantling piece by piece, Kraus not only appropriates a pun that Heine himself had wielded against the Protestant-inspired liturgy of reform synagogues; he also implies that it is the "Mosaic" or Jewish element in Heine's writing that results in a fragmented rather than an organic literature. Near the conclusion of the essay, Kraus is more explicit. Alluding simultaneously to Heine's Rhenish origins and to the allegedly artificial nature of his poetry, Kraus identifies him as a "Moses who struck the rock of the German language with his staff" (Kraus 1986–, 4:209) only to have eau de cologne gush forth instead of water.

Finally, Kraus rejects what he interprets as the exaggerated male pose in Heine's writing. Not only has Heine set a baleful precedent by exploiting August von Platen's homosexuality; he has also "so loosened the bodice of the German language that every little salesman can finger her breasts" (Kraus 1986–, 4:190). This drastic formulation reflects the satirist's abhorrence not only of Heine's influence on journalistic discourse, but also of the poet's sexual sensibility. Furthermore, it helps to explain why the lyrical female voice of Else Lasker-Schüler is pointedly contrasted in the *Torch* with the ironic male voice of Heine. When Kraus finally takes stock of his own attitude toward Judaism, it is Lasker-Schüler and Peter Altenberg, whose literary otherness was often interpreted in terms of femininity, who are held up as the ideal of the German Jewish writer (*F* 386 [1913]: 6–7).

The short but explosive text "Er ist doch ä Jud" (He's a Jew After All; 1913) takes its title from a letter to the editor of the *Torch*. Kraus is asked to explain how the Jewish members in the audience of his famous readings could fall completely under his rhetorical sway only to mutter about him being no better than any other Jew as they leave the lecture hall. In an initial gloss on this question, Kraus stresses his identification with another misunderstood figure who had to submit to having "He's a Jew after all" whispered behind his back—Jesus of Nazareth (*F* 384–85

[1913]: 29). By provocatively aligning himself with Jesus, in Otto Weininger's words "the only Jew who succeeded in overcoming Judaism" (quoted in Viertel 1921, 60), Kraus indicated how seriously he intended what has generally been understood as a polemical retort to importunate reminders of his Jewish background. Without denying his race, Kraus succeeds in establishing himself as a category of one, a satirical provocation reflected most precisely in the original title of the essay when it was first read in manuscript: "I and Judaism" (F 386 [1913]: 9).

The final text of "He's a Jew After All" begins with a letter from another reader who asks whether Kraus believes he exhibits Jewish character traits and whether he agrees with Lanz von Liebenfels's dictum that a person cannot leave his race (the way one leaves the church). Kraus's aphoristic answer constitutes a crucial statement about his Jewish identity: "I believe I can say about myself that I go along with the development of Judaism up to the Exodus, but that I don't participate in the dance around the Golden Calf and, from that point on, share only in those characteristics which were also found in the defenders of God and the avengers of a people gone astray" (F 386 [1913]: 3). Here Kraus quite consciously adopts the role of the Old Testament prophet that his later admirers will often claim for him.

Kraus goes on to state his belief that an old whiskey seller in a caftan represents a higher form of culture than a (Jewish) member of the German-Austrian Writers Association in a tuxedo, an attitude that places him much closer to Martin Buber's contemporaneous rediscovery of the culture of Eastern Jewry than either of them would have been willing to admit. Although it is true that Kraus then delights in confounding his liberal readers by citing the characterization of himself as a "blond Jewish type" who together with Spinoza represents a synthesis of outstanding intellect and noble ethics, he deftly avoids any affirmation of Lanz von Liebenfels's "Aryan-Germanic" racial categories. Instead, Kraus concludes this witty, antagonistic text with an allusion that suggests just the opposite. He declares that it could be a Jewish characteristic to destroy

a double issue of the *Torch* because he has discovered "a question mark grimacing at the world rather than an exclamation point confronting it with the rod of chastisement" (F 386 [1913]: 8). This is much more than another of Kraus's much maligned battles over misplaced commas. Not only do the anthropomorphized punctuation marks suggest an almost kabbalistic transformation of German into Hebrew characters, but the allusion to the practice of Torah scribes destroying an entire manuscript because of a single transcription error also makes it clear that for Kraus secular writing had become the equivalent of a sacred task.

This startling appeal to the scriptural authority of the Hebrew Bible makes it all the more understandable that when Kraus, breaking the self-imposed silence he had maintained since the outbreak of war in August 1914, finally resumed his public readings in November, he gave prominence of place to passages from Isa. 1, 2, and 3 and from Jer. 8 (F 404 [1914]: 20). But these texts, in which the prophets take Israel to task for its idolatrous, warlike behavior, anticipate the problematic analogy that Kraus will pursue with single-minded fury in the controversial poem "Gebet an die Sonne von Gibeon" (Prayer to the sun over Gibeon; 1916). Although the poem is dominated by a powerful apocalyptic vision of the natural world triumphing over a corrupt humanity, it also engages in a searing critique of the chauvinist brutality of the Book of Joshua that is subtly but firmly linked to the pseudo-religious rhetoric of Wilhelm II's wartime speeches. In act 3, line 14 of *Die letzten Tage der Menschheit* (The last days of mankind; 1922), Kraus has the Grumbler, his fictionalized alter ego, articulate this connection in no uncertain terms. Here the "intellectual connection between Hindenburg [the commander in chief of the imperial German army] and Joshua" (Kraus 1986–, 10:353) is firmly established. In addition, the parallels between modern Germany and ancient Israel, supposedly the only two peoples of historical significance who have considered themselves worthy of a "national God" (Kraus 1986–, 10:353), are pursued relentlessly. Even if Kraus intended to lend to this devastating analysis of German militarism the mythopoeic force of biblical archetype while at the same time circumventing the censor, the references to Israel could easily be construed as singling out the complicity of German and Austrian Jews (cf. Timms 1986, 340). As Arthur Schnitzler, the other major Jewish writer to have emerged from fin-de-siècle Vienna, confided to his diary on June 25, 1916: "in a reading held in Zurich [which included "Prayer to the Sun over Gibeon"], Karl Kraus—the paragon of renegade cowardice—blames the Jews for the World War" (Schnitzler 1983, 298).

When *The Last Days of Mankind,* Kraus's gigantic antiwar documentary drama, finally appeared in revised form in 1922, even Schnitzler recognized its brilliant, occasionally "poetic" satire and felt compelled to grant Kraus the right to "exaggerations and injustices" (Schnitzler 1993, 334). The drama does indeed contain many exaggerated, even unjust depictions of characters that are identifiably Jewish—their names, their use of German-Jewish jargon, or even their fictional embodiment of the satirist's contemporaries reveal their background. Heinrich Friedjung, the German-Nationalist historian of Jewish extraction, for example, is shown in a compromising scene, as is Hugo von Hofmannsthal, who was descended on his father's side from a distinguished Viennese-Jewish family. In both cases, however, it is not their race, but rather their patriotic blindness and complacency that are at issue. There are also purely fictional characters such as the court functionary Schwarz-Gelber and his socialite wife, whose assimilationist self-deception in the service of war propaganda provides the basis for their satirical treatment. Their Dickensian name, which means "Black and Yellow," cleverly combines the Habsburg imperial colors with a recognizably Jewish name that was actually borne by a well-known dynastic apologist and which, in retrospect, seems extremely improbable: Adolf. Considerably more problematic are the use of obviously caricatured Jewish names such as Fressack and Naschkatz for the two "hyenas with human faces" in the expressionistic epilogue "The Last Night." Dancing a tango over the bodies of fallen soldiers, these grisly journalistic hybrids speak macabre verse sprinkled with Yid-

dish phrases as they pay homage to the "Lord of the Hyenas," who is unmistakably based on Moriz Benedikt.

Casting the Jewish editor of the *Neue Freie Presse* in the role of the Antichrist in this apocalyptic drama could not help but encourage the kind of anti-Semitic reading that Kraus expressly wanted to avoid. He clearly tries to compensate for this problem by basing Benedikt's appearance in the expressionistic epilogue on a documentary source, a rare photograph of the notoriously camera-shy journalist that had been published in the *Torch* in 1911. A more critically convincing use of documents occurs in Benedikt's only scene in the play proper. In act 1, line 28, the audience hears his voice dictating an actual editorial in which he had smugly reported that marine life in the Adriatic was getting fat off the corpses of Italian sailors killed in battle. As convinced as Kraus was that the liberal press, particularly its Jewish contingent, bore responsibility for the impoverishment of the imagination that had made the war possible, he cannot be accused of sparing non-Jewish participants and instigators. Indeed, both the German and the Austrian Kaiser are given significantly more substantial scenes in the drama than Benedikt himself. Franz Joseph appears improbably, but quite comically, performing a long, self-incriminating operetta in his sleep (Kraus 1986–, 10:519–25), and Wilhelm II is depicted as a hysterical carnivore howling like a wolf as he prances around his headquarters slapping his staff on the behind and grabbing them between the legs (536). In the revised edition of *The Last Days of Mankind* (1922), Kraus both omitted some negative references to Jews and added scenes showing that conservative Christian journalism, represented by the Viennese *Reichspost,* was no less guilty of warmongering than the supposedly Jewish liberal press.

Viewed under the dark shadow cast backward by the Holocaust, the treatment of many of the negatively drawn Jewish characters in *The Last Days of Mankind* seems highly objectionable. By contrast, the biblical motifs in the drama with which Kraus transformed contemporary characters and events into apocalyptic signs have, if anything, gained in their power to persuade. The names of Gog and Magog, for example, two Berlin war profiteers in act 5, line 50, shown enjoying freedom from military service in Switzerland, are taken from both an Old and a New Testament source. These surrealistically imagined "gigantic balls of fat" (Kraus 1986–, 10:660), who talk business as they take in the view from a cable car, provide grotesquely comic versions of the barbaric invaders from the North described in Eze. 38 and 39 and in Rev. 20:8. An even more striking use of a religious motif is used at the very end of the drama. The text concludes not with the Voice of God quoting Wilhelm II's infamous line "I did not want this"—as many commentators have claimed—but rather with a photograph of a crucifix on an unidentified battlefield. Actually, the cross itself has been destroyed by an artillery shell, leaving intact a Christ figure with its arms raised to a dramatically clouded sky. This image is in fact a pictorial quotation cut out of an illustrated magazine and sent to Kraus by Kurt Tucholsky. Lacking even the original caption that Kraus had edited for its initial publication in the *Torch,* the figure is no longer bound in its new context by the traditional iconography of the Crucifixion. Through the elimination of the quintessentially Christian symbol of the cross with which the early Church distanced itself from the temporally oriented ethics of its Jewish origins, the image becomes richly ambiguous. Ironically liberated from the cross and pleading with the warring nations for peace, this unusual documentary image of Jesus can be understood as the positive representation of the "arch-Jew" that Berthold Viertel saw embodied in Kraus's satirical negativity (58).

Written rapidly while Kraus was still revising *The Last Days of Mankind, Literatur oder Man wird doch da sehn* (Literature or we'll have to see about that; 1921) has often been understood as an intemperate response to the crude caricature of the satirist that Franz Werfel interpolated into his Expressionist drama *The Mirror Man.* Yet Kraus's text contains considerably more than one side of the personal literary quarrel between two of the most influential German-Jewish writers of the early twentieth century. Kraus's "Magic Operetta in Two Parts" pursues a variety of satirical themes

as it cuts Werfel's "Magic Trilogy" down to size. First and foremost, it deflates the play's pretentious pastiche of *Faust* and Eastern mystical ideas by having the main characters fracture the blank verse of German classical drama with Yiddish phrases and the clichéd inverted syntax of stage Jews (Scheichl 1986, 128–32). Second, it passes a devastating judgment on the complicity of the young Expressionist generation in the propaganda that supported World War I. Third, and most controversially, it suggests that the much touted father-son conflict in Expressionism is more a literary fashion than an existential problem; a conflict, in fact, that evaporates as the once revolutionary writers subordinate their literary ambition to the profits promised by the culture industry.

Literature is one of Kraus's wittiest texts. Its most irresistible line consists of a single word, in which Jewish-German slang and Expressionist Orientalism undergo an unforgettable synthesis. Parodying the excessively solemn moment in *The Mirror Man* when the hero Thamal saves himself by uttering the mystical ejaculation "Om!!!!!," Kraus has the Grandfather, who has dozed throughout the entire play, awaken at the end only to utter laconically "Oi" (Kraus 1986–, 11:75). Kafka, one of Kraus's most precise readers, was fascinated by *Literature,* which he discussed at length in a letter written to Max Brod in June 1921 (Kafka 1983, 336ff.). Kafka particularly admired the play's comic language and its revealing if symptomatic depiction of the increasingly untenable position of German-Jewish writers within the German literary tradition. More clearly than Kraus himself, Kafka saw the satirist implicated in his own polemics. Despite such reservations, he praised the "truth" in Kraus's text, which, he wrote, "is as substantial as the truth in my writing hand—and as clearly and frighteningly physical" (336). Perhaps only Kafka, who later, alluding to the well-known motif from Genesis, described the *Torch,* as "this sweet dessert made of all good and evil instincts" (380), could have sensed the horror implicit in this ostensibly comic text.

The *Third Walpurgis Night,* whose title suggests an apocalyptic sequel to the first two Walpurgis nights depicted in Goethe's *Faust,* represents Kraus's attempt to come to terms with the surrender of German culture to the primitive barbarism of the Third Reich. This dense, highly allusive text begins with what is perhaps the most misunderstood quotation in modern German literature: "When I think about Hitler, nothing comes to mind" (Kraus 1986–, 12:12). Inexplicably, many later critics have taken this to mean that Kraus had nothing to say. Actually, this deceptively casual opening, the shortest sentence in the text, effectively reduces the Führer's inflated self-importance to a nullity. What follows, however, is an astonishing tour de force of some three hundred pages that thoroughly documents the propaganda of a "dictatorship that has mastered everything except the language" (13). Although Kraus cannot bring himself to express solidarity even with such deserving fellow German-Jewish satirists as Kurt Tucholsky, he does devote considerable space to exposing the intellectual collaboration of two gentile darlings of German modernism. The poet Gottfried Benn is subjected to a detailed deconstruction, sentence by sentence, of his pro-Nazi radio speech; and the philosopher Martin Heidegger, in an uncanny anticipation of the revelations that have recently done so much to tarnish his image, is caught using such compromising metaphors as the "military service of the mind" (71). At the same time, Kraus ironically acknowledges that his own German style does indeed owe much to the "language of the Jews" (cf. Gilman 1986, 241). Frustrated and no doubt embarrassed by the absence of his works from those destroyed in the book burnings of May 1933, he defiantly accepts the new regime's directive that all works by German Jews be labeled translations and asserts that his renderings of Shakespeare's sonnets are "actually a translation from the Hebrew" (Kraus 1986–, 12:159).

Kraus also takes the opportunity in *Third Walpurgis Night* to come to the defense of Jacques Offenbach, whose operettas had in the meantime been banned in Nazi Germany. The musical works of this German-Jewish composer from the Rhineland whose creative life took place in Paris both provided an alternative to the cultural forebear Kraus had rejected in Heine and formed—

together with Shakespeare's plays—the bulk of the repertoire for the satirist's unconventional "Theater of Poetry." Between 1926 and 1935, Kraus created one-man performances with piano accompaniment of fourteen different works that he repeated on some 120 theatrical evenings. In November 1935, Kraus pointedly added *The Creole Woman* to his repertoire. Because the Nuremberg Race Laws had gone into effect on September 15, 1935, the title alone constituted a provocation to the Nazi state. Kraus underscored the satirical point, however, by referring to the Paris revival of the operetta with Josephine Baker (whom he had met in Vienna in 1928) in the title role, "which she can play without make-up" (*F* 916 [1935]: 2). As had been his practice for readings of Nestroy and Raimund as well as for Offenbach performances, Kraus also composed "Zeitstrophen" (Timely stanzas) for *The Creole Woman* that provided satirical commentary on the political situation. For one of these, he created a parody of the Nuremberg Race Laws by substituting "Negro" for "Jewish" in every statute (quoted in Wagenknecht 1991, 2–3). This satirical affirmation of a negative equation that had often been used to denigrate blacks and Jews alike must have seemed too incendiary, for Kraus failed to used it in the only two performances he gave. He did, however, explain in the "foreword" to his adaptation of the operetta that it was necessary to perform Offenbach as the "antithesis" (Kraus 1986–, 12:43) of the overblown Wagnerian *Gesamtkunstwerk* cultivated by the new German regime. Alluding to the Führer's favorite opera, Kraus declared that "Offenbach has triumphed in the demonic joke that at the most recent parade for Hitler, the orchestra, at the sight of the cavalry, did not feel inspired to play the March from *Tannhäuser,* but instead struck up the Infernal Cancan, the one from the underworld [from Offenbach's *Orpheus in the Underworld*]" (*F* 916 [1935]: 6).

The revival of Offenbach's racially subversive *opéra comique* made it possible for Kraus not only to write and perform again and to comment obliquely on current events; it also provided the opportunity to engage in a selective affirmation of the German-Jewish cultural heritage that he had subjected to such devastating critiques during most of his writing life. After Hitler's rise to power, Kraus had maintained a strategic silence in much the same way that he had in 1914. During this time, he did write *Third Walpurgis Night*, but he suppressed its publication for fear that reprisals would be taken against friends in Germany. Instead, he published the ironically titled issue 890–905 of the *Torch* "Why the *Torch* Is Not Being Published," a 315-page reckoning with the terrible times, into which he integrated substantial sections from *Third Walpurgis Night* and devoted considerable space to answering the critics who had denounced his silence in face of Hitler. In a crucial passage that appears in both texts, Kraus singles out the "natural force of an incorruptible Judaism" in his work "that he gratefully acknowledges and loves above all else" (F 890–905 [1934]: 38).

In his infamous extempore *The Ape of Zarathustra,* even as unsympathetic a critic as Anton Kuh ironically confirmed the Jewish subtext in Kraus's work by ridiculing the "faithful Aggadah readers of the *Torch*" (18) and impugning the journal itself as a "Talmud of Allusions" (38). More precisely and entirely without irony, Gershom Scholem recalled how he and a small circle of friends, including Walter Benjamin, had discussed "the derivation of Kraus's style from the Hebrew prose and poetry of medieval Jewry— the language of the great halakhists and of the 'mosaic style,' the poetic prose in which linguistic scraps of sacred texts are whirled around kaleidoscopelike and are journalistically, polemically, descriptively, and even erotically profaned" (Scholem 1981, 107). Clearly, the juridical impulse of Kraus's work, especially its tendency to marshal the most minute linguistic evidence toward the goal of satirical conviction, is much closer in spirit to the Halakhah than to the illustrative storytelling of the Aggadah.

The poet and theater director Berthold Viertel, Kraus's close friend, also stressed Jewish precedents for the satirist's fanatical devotion to the radical criticism of language. He claimed that Kraus's "philosophy of language" was not a "theory" but rather a "religious cult" comparable to the Hasidim's mystical belief in the power of the word (Viertel 1921, 61). A recent critic has even speculated that the idea of an ideal congruence between language and essence may have come to Kraus through his reading of Herder, Hamann, Jean Paul, and other writers of the Age of Goethe, whose interest in language mysticism and veneration of Hebrew as the "Divine Language" earned them the designation of the "Second Cabbala" (Dürr 1991, 384–88). It is quite conceivable that in the spirit of contradiction on which he thrived, Kraus himself might have pointed to a less sublime source: the travesties of classical theater with musical interludes. Kraus frequented such performances by the Yiddish Theater in Vienna with Adolf Loos and a young Oskar Kokoschka (Kokoschka 92). In a similar vein, Walter Benjamin, arguably the most incisive commentator on the Jewish aspect of Kraus's work, found a circus metaphor to explain this complex phenomenon. Objecting to the notion of Kraus's first biographer, Leopold Liegler, that the satirist had to suppress his Judaism in order to write authentically, Benjamin suggested instead that Kraus had performed the "truly Jewish *salto mortale*" of revering "the image of divine justice as language itself—even German" (Benjamin 1977, 349). Like Kafka, Benjamin sensed the desperate intellectual acrobatics behind Kraus's attempts to justify his satirical mission.

A less prominent but equally careful reader and listener cannot be blamed, then, for supposing that the satirist was working on something else other than the Shakespeare project mentioned in his last letter to Sidonie von Nádherny, written less than a month before his death on June 12, 1936 (Kraus 1977, 687). In February of that year, Camill Hoffmann, a member of the Czech Legation to Nazi Germany who would later die in the concentration camp at Theresienstadt, wrote from Berlin to inquire about Kraus's latest project. Hoffmann confided to Kraus that when he imagined what the satirist might be working on, he thought it would have to be "a new Book of Job" (unpublished letter, Kraus Archive, Vienna City Library). With this reference to Job, Hoffmann acknowledged the threads of narrative continuity running through the thousands of pages of the *Torch* and thus proved himself to be a "faithful Aggadah reader" in the best sense. In the central text devoted to his relationship to Judaism, "He's a Jew After All," Kraus had suggested that it might be a Jewish character trait to find the Book of Job worth reading. It is not difficult to imagine the satirist in 1936 thinking that a new Book of Job might be worth *writing*.

Bibliography

Walter Benjamin, "Karl Kraus" (1931), in *Gesammelte Schriften*, vol. 2, pt. 1, ed. Rolf Tiedemann and Hermann Schweppenhäuser (Frankfurt a. M.: Suhrkamp, 1977), 334–67; Volker Dürr, "Karl Kraus: Sprachmystik, Kabbala und die deutsche Sprache als 'Haus des Seins': Zum Essay 'Heine und die Folgen,'" *"Die in dem alten Haus der Sprache wohnen": Beiträge zum Sprachdenken in der Literaturgeschichte. Helmut Arnzten zum 60. Geburtstag* (Münster: Aschendorff, 1991), 375–90; Sander L. Gilman, *Jewish Self-Hatred: Anti-Semitism and the Hidden Language of the Jews* (Baltimore, Md.: Johns Hopkins University Press, 1986), 233–43; Peter Horwath, "'Wer Karl Kraus je gesehen hat . . .': Kraus im Lichte der Lanz von Liebenfels'schen Arioheroik," *Literatur & Kritik* 249–50 (1990): 461–78; Franz Kafka, *Briefe, 1902–1924,* ed. Max Brod (Frankfurt a. M.: Fischer, 1983); Georg Knepler, *Karl Kraus liest Offenbach: Erinnerungen, Kommentare, Dokumentationen* (Vienna: Löcker Verlag, 1984); Caroline Kohn, "Der Wiener jüdische Jargon im Werke von Karl Kraus," *Modern Austrian Literature* 8 (1975): 240–67; Karl Kraus, *Briefe an Sidonie Nadherny von Borutin,* ed. Heinrich Fischer, Friedrich Pfäfflin, et al., 2 vols. rev. ed. (Munich: dtv, 1977); Kraus, *Dritte Walpurgisnacht* [1933] (Munich: Kösel-Verlag, 1952); Kraus, "Er ist doch ä Jud," *Die Fackel* 386 (1913): 1–8; Kraus, *Die Fackel,* 1–922 (1899–1936): cited as *F;* Kraus, "Gebet an die Sonne von Gibeon," *Die Fackel* 423–25 (1916): 58–64; Kraus, *Heine und die Folgen* (Munich: Albert Langen, 1910); Kraus, *Eine Krone für Zion* [1898] in *Frühe Schriften,* ed. Johannes J. Braakenburg, vol. 2 (Munich: Kösel, 1979), 293–314; Kraus, *Die letzten Tage der Menschheit* [1918–19], as special issues of *Die Fackel,* rev. ed. (Vienna, Leipzig: Verlag "Die Fackel," 1922); Kraus, *Literatur oder Man wird doch da sehn: Magische Operette in zwei Teilen* (Vienna, Leipzig: Verlag "Die Fackel," 1921); Kraus, *Schriften,* ed. Christian Wagenknecht, 20 vols. (Frankfurt a. M.: Suhrkamp, 1986–); Anton Kuh, *Der Affe Zarathustras (Karl Kraus): Eine Stegreifrede* (Vienna: Verlag J. Deibler, 1925); Leo A. Lensing, "Heine's Body, Heine's Corpus: Sexuality and Jewish Identity in Karl Kraus's Literary Polemics Against Heinrich Heine," *The Jewish Reception of Heinrich Heine,* ed. Mark Gelber (Tübingen: Niemeyer, 1992), 95–112; Theodor Lessing, *Der jüdische Selbsthass* [1930] (Munich: Matthes and Seitz, 1985); Sigurd Scheichl, "Der Stilbruch als Mittel bei Karl Kraus," *Karl Kraus in neuer Sicht,* ed. Sigurd Scheichl and Edward Timms (Munich: Text & Kritik, 1986), 128–42; Arthur Schnitzler, *Tagebuch, 1913–1916* (Vienna: Österreichische Akademie der Wissenschaften, 1983); Schnitzler, *Tagebuch, 1920–1922* (Vienna: Österreichische Akademie der Wissenschaften, 1993); Gershom Scholem, *Walter Benjamin: The Story of a Friendship,* trans. Harry Zohn (Philadelphia: Jewish Publication Society of America, 1981); Jochen Stremmel, *"Dritte Walpurgisnacht": Über einen Text von Karl Kraus* (Bonn: Bouvier, 1982); Edward Timms, *Karl Kraus, Apocalyptic Satirist: Culture and Catastrophe in Habsburg Vienna* (New Haven: Yale University Press, 1986); Berthold Viertel, *Karl Kraus: Ein Charakter und die Zeit* (Dresden: Rudolf Kaemmerer Verlag, 1921); Christian Wagenknecht, "Karl Kraus: Zu Offenbachs 'Kreolin,'" *Kraus-Hefte* 59 (July 1991): 2–4; Nike Wagner, "Incognito ergo sum—Zur jüdischen Frage bei Karl Kraus," *Literatur & Kritik* 219–20 (1987): 387–99; Robert Wistrich, *The Jews of Vienna in the Age of Franz Joseph* (Oxford: Oxford University Press, 1990); and Harry Zohn, "Karl Kraus: 'Jüdischer Selbsthasser' oder 'Erzjude,'" *Modern Austrian Literature* 8 (1975): 1–19.

LEO A. LENSING

1914 Franz Rosenzweig writes the essay "Atheistic Theology," which critiques the theology of his day

In early 1914, Franz Rosenzweig (1886–1929) penned an essay bearing as its title the striking oxymoron, "Atheistic Theology." It was a bold critique of what he regarded to be the overarching tendency of religious thought since the Enlightenment to remove from its horizon the concept of revelation, and thus in effect to entertain the absurdity of a godless theology. This essay was to mark Rosenzweig's debut as a Jewish religious thinker. Submitted to a volume on Jewish renewal, it was rejected by its editor, Martin Buber (1876–1965), who presumably found it inappropriate. Buber may have detected in the essay, which was first published posthumously, the enthusiasm of a neophyte, of one who had only recently affirmed his ancestral faith after a dramatic reversal of an earlier decision to convert to Christianity. The essay may have also hit a raw nerve. At the time Buber—like many of his contemporaries—was beholden to a form of romantic mysticism, and although this mysticism celebrated the primordial religious sensibilities of the Jews, it muffled the revelatory voice of a transcendent God.

Rosenzweig presumably anticipated Buber's response, for he was keenly aware of the radical nature of his call for both a reaffirmation of the concept of revelation and a return to a theocentric Judaism. After having been virtually eliminated from modern Jewish discourse, God—the living God to whom traditional Jews prayed, to whose grace and love they submitted themselves—suddenly reappears with Rosenzweig at the center of the Jew's theological imagination. With his characteristic humility, he ascribed the beginnings of this theocentric shift in modern Jewish thought to Hermann Cohen (1842–1918), who founded the Marburg school of neo-Kantianism, and who toward the end of his life elaborated an inspired exposition of Judaism as religious system. To illustrate his contention, Rosenzweig was fond of telling the following story. On the occasion of one of his last lectures at the University of Marburg, Rosenzweig relates, the esteemed professor of philosophy spoke of "the concept of God," which he viewed as a rational construct that guaranteed the eternity of the physical world and thus provided the necessary condition for the eternal moral tasks imposed by reason on rational humanity. At the conclusion of the lecture, Cohen was approached by a simple Eastern European Jew—that is, a traditional Jew unaffected by the sophistication and critical self-consciousness of the Western Jew. In halting German, this visitor from the East admitted to the professor that he did not understand much of his learned discourse, but nonetheless he had one question: "Herr Professor Cohen, in all your talk of God where is *ribbono shel ha'olom,* the Master of the Universe"—the God of traditional Jewish prayer? Stunned by the question, the elderly Cohen—who had been raised as a traditional Jew by his father, a *hazan* (cantor) in a German village near the Polish border—is said to have bowed his head in contrition and begun to cry. This moment of truth, according to Rosenzweig, points to Cohen's incipient shift from a rigid rationalism and philosophical idealism to a type of religious existentialism that allowed him to acknowledge the ontological significance of religious emotion and experience. It has, however, been cogently shown that this anecdote and similar ones that Rosenzweig related about the man whom he regarded as his spiritual mentor instruct us little about Cohen's actual intellectual development; rather, they are patently projections of Rosenzweig's spiritual fantasy that offer us profound insight into his own religious orientation.

On the conceptual and theological level, Rosenzweig's point of departure was what he called *Offenbarungsglaube*—a belief based on revelation. Genuine religious belief, he maintained, affirms the reality of revelation—both the factual reality of the historical revelation at Sinai and the possibility of its renewal as an existential event in which God turns to individuals in the here and now and addresses each by his or her "first and last name"—that is, acknowledges the individual in his or her contingent being—thereby freeing them from the curse of finitude. The God of Revelation, Rosenzweig emphasized, is the God of Abraham, Isaac, and Jacob, the sovereign Creator of the World and the Heavens—it is this God who from the heights of his utter transcendence addresses humankind with gracious words of commandment and love. Such an Offenbarungsglaube, Rosenzweig averred, must become once again the ground or "heart" of Judaism, otherwise it perpetuates the scandal of an atheistic theology, which has drained the faith of Israel of all its spiritual and intellectual vitality.

To be sure, Rosenzweig pointed out, this flight from the God of Revelation was shared by both Jews and Protestants who since their entry into the modern world have increasingly found it to be a most uncongenial concept. This discomfort with what was the founding concept of Judaism is already discernible with Moses Mendelssohn (1729–86), who in his valiant attempt to demonstrate Judaism's allegiance to the autonomous rule of reason restricted revelation to the narrow realm of God's "legislation" to Israel governing its liturgical and ritual duties. His noble intentions notwithstanding, Mendelssohn's restrictive definition eclipsed the mystery and power of the traditional Jewish experience and understanding of revelation. And when nineteenth-century liberal Jews dared speak of revelation, they most often joined the lofty term as a metaphor for some human effort of a unique quality. Abraham Geiger (1810–74), the most respected name among the founders of Reform Judaism in Germany, for instance, employed the term as the equivalent of the "creative [moral] genius" of Israel. And even in his posthumous work, *Religion of Reason* (1919), which Rosenzweig acclaimed as a breakthrough to religious existentialism, Hermann Cohen declared rather apodictically that "revelation is the creation of reason."

Rosenzweig's own turn to Offenbarungsglaube was preceded by a profound spiritual crisis attendant to a disaffection with the neo-Hegelianism he had adopted as a student. This occurred while he was working on a dissertation on Hegel—which he wrote under the supervision of Friedrich Meinecke and which was later published by the Heidelberg Academy of Sciences as a two-volume book, *Hegel und der Staat* (1920). The trajectory of his journey from Hegel to religious faith was anticipated in a letter written in 1910, in which Rosenzweig explained to a fellow student that Hegel had erred in ascribing to history an ontological status. History, he reasoned, is not the unfolding of Being, rather it is but the discrete act of humans (*Tat der Täters*): "We see God in every ethical event, but not in one complete Whole, not in history." Indeed, history, which takes shape in the phenomenal world, cannot serve as a vessel of divinity: "Every human act becomes sinful as it enters history," because although the actors may have intended otherwise, the morality of an act is neutralized *eo ipso* by the material world of necessity. We are, Rosenzweig noted, left with only one possible conclusion: God redeems humanity not through history but—*es bleibt nichts anders übrig* (there remains nothing else)—through religious faith. This was not a statement of faith, but a philosophical proposition, a logical deduction. He would adopt a living faith, grounded in the concept of revelation, but only three years later.

Attendant to his affirmation of revelation,

Rosenzweig also asserted the centrality of Creation and Redemption—again categories that modern religious thought in German had tended to ignore or treat "poetically," that is, as metaphors bereft of genuine theological content. Each of these concepts—Revelation, Creation, and Redemption—teaches us, according to Rosenzweig, not only about God's gracious involvement in the world but also about the structure and meaning of existence. It is thus the exigent task of theology to rescue the phenomenological and theological significance of these concepts (as well as the ancillary and, alas, similarly obfuscated notions of miracle, providence, and divine love). To this sublime task, Rosenzweig dedicated his *Star of Redemption* (1921)—a volume that he essentially wrote on military postcards and stationery and mailed to his mother while serving on the Balkan front in the Kaiser's army.

Rosenzweig's endeavor to revalorize the central categories of classical (indeed, biblical) theology does not, of course, mean that he advocated a romantic return to a pristine, traditional Jewish faith untouched by the modern experience. On the contrary, Rosenzweig remained firmly rooted in modern culture and philosophical discourse. Even a casual reading of *The Star of Redemption* and his other writings will readily indicate his abiding commitment to the Western cultural enterprise, particularly as it was expressed in Germany. He was quick to acknowledge that a dual allegiance to Judaism and German culture engendered a tension, but it was a tension that must be embraced with love because, in his view, the tension served to ennoble one as both a Jew and a German. Moreover, he taught, to deny the tension or to seek to nullify it would do violence to the existential reality of the German Jew. Hence, in affirming Judaism, Rosenzweig attested with greater conviction than anyone before or since him to the vision of the German-Jewish symbiosis. As he confessed in a letter to a friend: "I am perhaps especially innocent with respect to the problem of *Deutschtum* and *Judentum*. I believe my return to Judaism (*Verjüdung*) has not made me a worse but a better German. I do not in any way whatsoever view the generation before us as better Germans. . . . Were someone to suspend me

between tenterhooks, tearing me in two pieces, I would surely know with which of these two halves my heart . . . would go; I also know that I would not survive the operation."

Indeed, what Rosenzweig's contemporaries found compelling about his teachings is precisely that he did not suggest that a reappropriation of authentic Jewish faith and religious practice required that one undergo some sort of mental lobotomy, a ruthless discarding of all "alien" culture from one's inner universe. Such a practice, Rosenzweig contended, would not only be preposterous but also profoundly injurious to the supreme effort of renewing Judaism.

This argument is certainly one of those implied in his frequently quoted letter to Rabbi Jacob Rosenheim (1871–1965), a leader of Orthodoxy in Germany. Alarmed by the claims of modern scholarship, especially as represented by the documentary theory of Julius Wellhausen (1844–1917), which held that the Bible is the literary creation of several hands, Rosenheim followed the beaten path of Samson Raphael Hirsch (1808–88). Hirsch, the founder of German neo-Orthodox Judaism, sought to secure the integrity of the Torah by fortifying it behind a fundamentalist faith—that is, by dogmatically proclaiming its unique status and divine authorship. From the bastion of this faith, the Jew should with defiant pride reject the scandalous claims of modern biblical scholarship. In a letter dated April 1927, Rosenzweig, who at the time was working with Buber on a translation of the Hebrew Scripture into German, wrote Rosenheim criticizing what he regarded to be his obscurantism:

Where we differ from Orthodoxy is in our reluctance to draw from our belief in the holiness or uniqueness of the Torah, and in its character as revelation, any conclusions as to its literary genesis and the philological value of the text as it came down to us. If all of Wellhausen's theories were correct and the Samaritans really had the better text, our faith would not be shaken in the least. This is the profound difference between you and us—a difference which, it seems to me, may be bridged by mutual esteem but not by understanding. I, at least, fail to understand the religious basis of Hirsch's commentary [to the Bible]. . . . Still, how does it happen then that our translation is more closely akin to that of Hirsch than to any other? . . . We too translate the Torah as a single book. For us, too, it is the work of one spirit. Who this spirit was, we do not know; that it was Moses we find difficult to believe. Among ourselves we call him the symbol which critical science is accustomed to use as a designation for [the Bible's] redactor: R. By this symbol R we expand not into Redactor but into *Rabbenu* (Hebrew: "our teacher"). For he is our teacher; his theology is our teaching.

Just as it would be fatuous to give up belief in revelation because of Wellhausen's scholarship, Rosenzweig gently suggested, so Orthodoxy's desperate obscurantism is equally inane, for it creates a brittle basis for an enduring, vibrant faith. To be sure, Rosenzweig observed in his letter to Rosenheim, Jewish tradition refers to Moses as *rabbenu*, as our teacher of God's Torah, but even as critical scholarship suggests, this does not necessarily imply that the theology of the redactor was not inspired by God. Thus, for Rosenzweig (and Buber), the redactor, the human hand that apparently spliced the various literary elements of the Hebrew Scripture together, is also rabbenu, "our teacher" who, guided by the spirit of God, conveyed to us the Torah, whose theological unity and sacrality may be affirmed without assuming an uncritical antagonism to modern critical scholarship.

German Orthodoxy's fundamentalism was, in Rosenzweig's judgment, an extreme form of the defensive, "apologetic" attitude that characterized much of modern German-Jewish thought. German-Jewish thinkers, he observed, be they liberal or Orthodox, were forever trying to parry the diverse and often invidious criticisms of Judaism posed by the philosophers and scholars of Germany. Responding to a specific challenge, Rosenzweig observed, the answer given by a Jewish apologist is perforce selective and distortive. A nonapologetic Jewish philosophy, such as pursued in *The Star of Redemption*, would philosophize about Judaism from within Judaism itself, thereby systematically clarifying the principles and practices of the faith. A nonapologetic method of theological interpretation of Judaism further requires that Judaism be regarded as separate from not only the polemical circumstances of the historical hour but even from life itself; Judaism must be adjudged not in opposition or contrast to life but as an a priori modality of life.

This Archimedean point from which a genuine, nonapologetic Jewish way of thinking must begin seems to have had not only methodological but also substantive significance for Rosenzweig. The consideration of Judaism as a modality of life apart from life appears to be dialectically related to his view of Judaism—which he preferred to call "the Synagogue"—as a metahistorical fact. Content with its unique relationship with God of Eternity and standing beyond history—namely, politics and war—the Synagogue exemplifies the Messianic promise and thereby prods the Church, enmeshed in history, to lead history beyond itself to the eschaton. Meanwhile, the perspective of the Synagogue is to look inward in blissful seclusion from the world.

There is compelling sublimity to this perception of Israel's destiny, but many also found it profoundly distressing, for it suggests that isolation from the world is an intrinsic quality of traditional Jewish spirituality. Notwithstanding his ascription of a dialectical, eschatological significance to the Synagogue's seclusion, Rosenzweig's celebration of a studied indifference to history was deemed offensive by his contemporaries, who were immersed in the urgencies of Jewish and world history. Here Rosenzweig's friend, Buber, despite—or perhaps because of—his weakness for "apologetic thinking," proved a more eminent guide.

Rosenzweig, on the other hand, proved an effective counselor to a generation of German Jews eager to break the spell of assimilation and reintegrate their lives into the fabric of Jewish tradition. Rosenzweig taught this generation of post–World War I Jews how to read the sources of Jewish tradition, to encounter these sources without surrendering one's intellectual integrity, and to engage them as religious texts that speak to one's mind and soul. He also taught them that in order to appropriate the spiritual reality of Jewish tradition one had to know it from within—that is, as he once put it, to know it "hymnically." Mere intellectual acquaintance, hence, is insufficient. For Judaism is, after all, a mode of life, and as such it entails the praxis of Judaism, the life of Torah and its mitzvoth (commandments). To be sure, Rosenzweig conceded, from the perspective of the observer, the life of Torah and mitzvoth seem to be but a heteronymous legalism—impositions, as Buber for one suggested, that shackle the Jew's spontaneous relationship to God. But as experienced from within its hymnical reality, the world of Torah and mitzvoth may in fact quicken the Jew's relationship to God and His or Her revealed presence: this was the challenge Rosenzweig posed to his generation.

The grim irony of the spiritual renewal of Judaism inspired by Rosenzweig is that it came as the dark clouds of barbarity began to gather over Germany. The endeavor of that generation to create anew out of the midst of assimilation an intellectually and spiritually vital Jewish religious community was to be cruelly aborted. This tragically unfulfilled task, so singularly associated with the name of Franz Rosenzweig, is perhaps the most enduring legacy of German Jewry.

Bibliography

Luc Anckaert and Bernhard Casper, eds., *Franz Rosenzweig: A Primary and Secondary Bibliography* (Leuven: Bibliothek van der Faculteit der Godeleerdheid van de K. V. Leuven, 1990); Else Freund, *Die Existenzphilosophie Franz Rosenzweigs* (Leipzig: Felix Meiner, 1933); Freund, *Franz Rosenzweig's Philosophy of Existence: An Analysis of "The Star of Redemption,"* ed. Paul Mendes-Flohr, trans. S. Weinstein (The Hague: Martinus Nijhoff, 1979); Nahum N. Glatzer, *Franz Rosenzweig: His Life and Thought* (New York: Schocken Books, 1953); Paul Mendes-Flohr, ed., *The Philosophy of Franz Rosenzweig* (Hanover, N.H.: University Press of New England, 1988); Stéphane Moses, *Système et Révélation: La philosophie de Franz Rosenzweig* (Paris: Editions du Seuil, 1982); Moses, *System and Revelation: The Philosophy of Franz Rosenzweig,* trans. C. Tihanyi (Detroit: Wayne State University Press, 1992); Franz Rosenzweig, *Das Büchlein vom gesunden und kranken Menschenverstand,* ed. Nahum N. Glatzer (Dusseldorf: Joseph Melzer, 1964); Rosenzweig, *Hegel und der Staat,* 2 vols. (Munich and Berlin: R. Oldenbourg, 1920); Rosenzweig, *Der Mensch und sein Werk: Gesammelte Schriften,* 4 vols. (The Hague: Martinus Nijhoff, 1979–83); Rosenzweig, *The Star of Redemption,* trans. William W. Hallo (New York: Holt, Reinhart & Winston, 1970); Rosenzweig, *Der Stern der Erlösung* (Frankfurt a. M.: J. Kauffmann, 1921); Rosenzweig, *Understanding the Sick and Healthy: A View of the World, Man, and God,* trans. T. Luckman (New York: Noonday Press, 1953); and W. Schmied-Kowarzik, ed., *Der Philosoph Franz Rosenzweig (1886–1929),* 2 vols. (Freiburg: Karl Alber, 1988).

PAUL MENDES-FLOHR

1914   Kurt Tucholsky withdraws from the Jewish community

On July 1, 1914, at the age of twenty-four, Kurt Tucholsky officially resigned his membership in the Berlin Jewish community. Tucholsky (1890–1935) was a Berlin journalist whose political satires written during the Weimar Republic continue to be popular among millions of readers in Germany and throughout the world. Did his withdrawal from the Jewish community reflect a wish to erase his Jewish identity altogether? In a letter to Arnold Zweig written on December 15, 1935, four days before his suicide, Tucholsky recollected that he had renounced his Jewish affiliation and commented: "I know that this is impossible to do" (Tucholsky 1962, 333). He correctly anticipated that regardless of how he saw himself, others ranging from National Socialists to Jews would not accept his decision. They would continue to regard him as a Jew who did not like Jews and did not want to be one. Tucholsky maintained that Judaism did not interest him, that he knew little about it and seldom dealt with it in his writings. Even so, literary historians persistently describe him as a *Jewish* essayist of the Left. Thus, in surveying his life and works we may justly raise the question whether it is even possible to "cancel" one's "Jewishness" and may also ask: what, if anything, is "Jewish" about Tucholsky?

Tucholsky was born in Berlin-Moabit as the oldest son in an affluent, assimilated upper-middle-class Jewish family and was educated accordingly at excellent secondary schools: the French gymnasium, where wealthy Jewish families sent their children because it had a reputation for being liberal, and the Royal Wilhelms Gymnasium. He disliked them both. Though the French gymnasium conducted its classes in French, it still inculcated the usual Prussian patriotism and discipline. Tucholsky was bored with what he later recalled as uninspired teaching. His transfer to the Royal Wilhelms Gymnasium in 1903 brought no improvement. In 1907, he flunked out and had to complete his university entrance exam with the help of a tutor. In retrospect, he said that he recalled his secondary schooling with indifference. But when Tucholsky became indifferent to something, this was a sign that he utterly despised it, that he considered it beneath contempt. His first reaction to hearing Hitler's voice, for example, was a physical revulsion followed by indifference.

Tucholsky began his law studies at the University of Berlin in 1909. During the following year, he spent a semester at the University of Geneva. Though he did his course work in Berlin, he submitted his law dissertation to the University of Jena, where it was finally accepted in February 1915.

Tucholsky had a cordial relationship with his father, who was a successful businessman and banker with a flair for music and a sense of humor that may have influenced his son's literary style. After his father died in 1905, Tucholsky found himself increasingly at the mercy of his mother's tyranny, and this was not without consequences for his development. Moving out of her compulsively clean apartment did not lessen her psychological hold over him. Perhaps he welcomed his conscription into the army in April 1915 not so much out of patriotic fervor as out of a desire to escape her control. No doubt there was also some connection between the tensions with his mother and his inability to enter into monogamous relationships. His writings and letters reflect a condescending, negative view of women that was influenced by Weininger and Schopenhauer. His two marriages and his love affairs with Lisa Matthias, Hedwig Müller, Aline Valangin, and Gertrude Meyer broke down in part because he could not take on the responsibility of committing himself fully to a relationship and was unable to give up his lifelong practice of maintaining liaisons with several women simultaneously.

The substantial allowance that his father bequeathed him provided Tucholsky with the means to live a life that, if not lavish, was extremely comfortable. His clothing was immaculate, expensive, and stylish. He ate well and was slightly corpulent. On his travels he always had the finest accommodations. When the inflation of 1923 undermined the value of his inheritance and of his considerable earnings as a journalist, he had such difficulty adjusting to his reduced circumstances that he took a job as an apprentice and personal secretary to the banker Hugo Simon, who had formerly served as the Prussian finance minister. It was this bank milieu that provided models for the *Wendriner Geschichten* (Wendriner stories)—biting caricatures of an opportunistic, conservative, Berlin businessman that Tucholsky published in *Die Weltbühne* between 1922 and 1930. Tucholsky had a lifelong fear of poverty. In 1933, when the Nazis canceled his German citizenship, banned his books, and thereby cut off his income, he was faced with the dismal prospect of cashing in his life insurance and then living off the kindness of his Swiss beloved, the physician Dr. Hedwig Müller. This financial insecurity was one of many factors that contributed to Tucholsky's suicide in 1935.

Although Tucholsky published his first article in the Berlin paper *Vorwärts* in April 1911, it was his story "Rheinsberg" that attracted the attention of the wider public when it appeared in November 1912. Daring for its time, "Rheinsberg" describes a young Berlin student couple in love and longing for love who spend a few blissful days in the country in an erotic union that defies and parodies Wilhelminian social convention.

The turning point in Tucholsky's journalistic career was his meeting with Siegfried Jacobsohn (1881–1926), who became a father figure and mentor for him. (Before the friendship with Jacobsohn, the writer Max Brod had had a similar relationship to Tucholsky: Brod introduced Tucholsky to Kafka in Prague in 1911, and he made editorial corrections when Tucholsky sent him the manuscript of "Rheinsberg.") Jacobsohn had begun as a theater critic writing for *Die Welt am Montag* from 1901 to 1904. In his book *Das Theater der Reichsstadt* (The theater of the imperial city; 1904), he called for a new form of folk theater, a synthesis of classical and modern forms epitomized in the productions of Max Reinhardt. In 1905, in the wake of a scandal over supposed plagiarism in his book that threatened to end his career, Jacobsohn founded his own theater journal, *Die Schaubühne*. Tucholsky submitted his first article to Jacobsohn in 1913. Jacobsohn both encouraged and criticized Tucholsky, sometimes cowriting articles with him. Soon every issue had several contributions from Tucholsky. In the beginning, these were usually book, cabaret, and theater reviews—a hundred of these were published within the first year of their collaboration. Tucholsky also published political articles, satire, and poems in other journals and newspapers such as *Vorwärts, Simplicissimus, Frankfurter Zeitung,* and *Pan*. This was the start of a journalistic career in which he went on to publish over 2,900 articles in nearly one hundred newspapers. Tucholsky was invited gradually to assume some of the editorial responsibility for *Die Schaubühne,* and under his influence the focus began to shift to political affairs. In 1918, the journal was renamed *Die Weltbühne: Zeitschrift für Politik /Kunst /Wirtschaft*. Its focus was to be dogma-free discussion among pacifist, left-wing intellectuals. It challenged anti-Semitism and exposed the failure of the Weimar Republic to establish democratic institutions. In its 1918 manifesto, it called for freedom and justice, which was to be maintained by an appointed Council of the Wise who would govern like Plato's philosopher kings together with an elected parliament. Even at its peak, *Die Weltbühne* never went beyond a circulation of 15,000. Its readership overlapped with that of the other major left-wing journal, *Das Tagebuch*, which was also published in Berlin between 1920 and 1933. The audience for both journals was thus a small but devoted elite located primarily in Berlin. The *Weltbühne* had a particularly intense relationship with its readers, who were so devoted that they formed reading circles to discuss its articles.

Tucholsky began publishing his articles under several pseudonyms. He did this in order to avoid the impression that *Die Weltbühne* was dominated by one author, and also as a way of concealing his personality and expressing opposing views and character traits within himself. The biting political criticism fell to Ignaz Wrobel, a redheaded hunchback who wore glasses. Theobald Tiger was responsible for much of the material in verse and for cabaret songs. Peter Panter, a rotund little fellow, reviewed books and theater. Kaspar Hauser, named after the figure portrayed in Jakob Wasserman's novel, directed satires at institutions of the German middle class. Hauser's bewilderment when confronted with the political turmoil of Weimar Germany and his melancholy nature may have most closely reflected Tucholsky's own character.

Tucholsky is remembered as a German "Cassandra" because of his prophetic warnings of the impending course of German politics, some of which were accurate (in 1925 he predicted the exact course of World War II) and many of which were not (he vastly underestimated the potential of the Nazis to stay in power and transform German society). He is also remembered for his ability to capture the spirit of his times in his poems, chansons, and cabaret skits, and in his journalistic writings, which attacked with scathing satire the war profiteers, the judiciary, and especially the military establishment during the Weimar years. In addition, Tucholsky's background in law equipped him to write devastating critiques of the corrupt legal system.

Tucholsky's objections to the military did not interfere with his army service in World War I, perhaps because, much to the chagrin of his fellow soldiers, he managed through connections and accommodation to obtain the maximum comforts his situation allowed. Despite his theoretical objections to war, he himself was guilty of the kind of corruption he criticized. He was actually considering the military as a career and hoped for the sake of his personal advantage that the war would continue. He was stationed first on the Eastern Front where, after some initial discomfort and hardship, his status as a privileged intellectual enabled him to construct fortifications and do secretarial work instead of fighting. Then, in 1916, he was moved even farther from the military action when he was stationed at a flying school in Alt-Autz (Kurland). He became a noncommissioned officer and enjoyed a comfortable lifestyle, with good food, many parties, visits to Berlin, and the leisure to take up his writing again, from which he had desisted since his conscription. (In 1915 he published only one article in *Die Weltbühne;* in 1916–17 he was able to write twenty-three more.) He courted his future wife, Mary Gerold; ran the library, and edited a military newspaper, *Der Flieger,* for which he was decorated. In May 1918, he was transferred to duty in the military police at Turn-Severin, Romania. It was in this setting that he had himself baptized a Protestant in order to further his military aspirations. He converted in July and by October had been promoted to the position of police commissioner in Calafat with five men under his command.

Tucholsky's articles denouncing war as an institution, written before he entered the military, stand in marked contrast to his opportunistic enjoyment of the advantages he gained from his service. While in the army, he even submitted a poem to a contest for slogans encouraging people to buy war bonds. Perhaps this was an early expression of a repeated pattern in his life, in which there was often a contradiction between the lofty ideals of the official ideological stance he expressed in his writings and the realities of his everyday behavior. For example, despite his negative descriptions of the German educational system, when he undertook to earn some extra money by tutoring students he resorted to Prussian discipline and used a switch on his pupils. And despite his outcries against the financial corruption of the Weimar Republic, when it was a matter of his own personal gain, he did not always adhere to his publicly proclaimed moral principles. For the sake of a handsome salary, he worked in 1920–21 as the editor of *Pieron* (Polish for thunder), a vulgar anti-Polish propaganda paper financed by the Weimar government to win support among the German population of Upper Silesia, when this territory was being contested by Germany and Poland. At the same time, he wrote an article in another paper denouncing this sort of propaganda and the people who made a living from it.

After his release from the army, Tucholsky returned to Berlin, and from December 1918 until April 1920 he took over the editorship of *Ulk,* the weekly satirical supplement to both the widely read liberal democratic paper *Berliner Tageblatt* and the leftist *Berliner Volkszeitung.* Mary Gerold followed him to Berlin in January 1920, but within a month they had decided to separate again. In May of that year, Tucholsky married the physician Else Weil, whom he had known before he met Mary. Unhappy in this relationship, he experienced severe depressions and a painful sinus inflammation that plagued him for the rest of his life. He attempted suicide before finally divorcing in February 1924.

Already in August 1920, eight months after his marriage, he was again cultivating his relationship with Mary Gerold, and six months after his divorce, on August 30, 1924, they married. Within a year, their relationship had degenerated. Tucholsky's correspondence reveals little concern for her as a person. His peculiar practice of addressing her in the third person, masculine form might be interpreted as a compliment of sorts, in that he elevated her to what he regarded as the superior status of a male, but it was also a way of maintaining distance that was similar to his practice of giving a nickname to all of his friends. Mary served as a passive springboard for Tucholsky's epistolary reflections. As a lover, her role was to provide inspiration for his writing but

not to compete as an intellectual. As a wife, she was to provide domestic comfort and relieve him of trivial everyday chores in order to facilitate his career, but she was not to work herself. Even though they separated, they did not divorce until after the Nazis came to power in 1933. She was not Jewish, and he feared their marriage might jeopardize her safety. In his last letter to her before his death, he asked for her forgiveness and proclaimed that she was the only one he ever really loved.

In April 1924, Tucholsky moved to Paris as a foreign correspondent for *Die Weltbühne* and a number of other publications. He sent Jacobsohn reports filled with ecstatic praise for the French lifestyle in contrast to that of the Germans. Many of his articles published in *Die Weltbühne* were taken from such letters to Jacobsohn, but in this case Jacobsohn prudently refrained from publishing the material. Tucholsky was later grateful for this omission, because in retrospect his enthusiasm for France and French politics was replaced by cynicism and disappointment over their appeasement of Germany.

For several years Tucholsky had been the target of vicious anti-Semitic threats sent anonymously by mail; thus his move to France was prompted both by his concern for his safety and his general disillusionment with Germany. Even so, when Jacobsohn died on December 3, 1926, of suffocation during an epileptic seizure, Tucholsky returned to Berlin and reluctantly agreed to take over the editorship of *Die Weltbühne.* By the summer of 1927, Tucholsky transferred this responsibility to his fellow author and staff-worker Carl von Ossietzky and was able to return to France. There followed a period of restless travel throughout Europe, during which he began his love affair with Lisa Matthias, who served as the prototype for the "Lottchen" stories that appeared in *Die Weltbühne.* In 1930, upon the advice of his doctor, he moved to Sweden in the hope that his health would benefit from the seaside climate. He rented a house in Hindas near Göteborg but continued to travel widely. The house in Hindas remained his permanent residence until his suicide on December 21, 1935.

Tucholsky ceased any further publishing in

September 1932. This was partly a sign of protest and resignation, but it also reflected his recognition that he had lost his readership in Germany and felt burned out as a writer. His letters and *Q-Tagebücher 1934–1935* (Nonsense diaries; 1978) document his life and thoughts during this period. Although they contain much tormented self-criticism, the diaries do not support the widely held notion that Tucholsky committed suicide out of despair over the political developments in Germany or because of his failing health. In fact, there are contradictions surrounding the circumstances of his death: varying speculations include not only suicide but also such possibilities as an accidental overdose of barbiturates, the revenge of a jilted mistress turned informant, or political murder by Nazi agents. His final letter of farewell to Mary Gerold strongly suggests that he did indeed commit suicide.

Although Tucholsky was not a systematic, consistent political thinker, his writings can be grouped chronologically into periods that reflect his changing political views. In the years immediately following the war, he tended to the Left, but he attacked the extremists on the Left and the Right with equal vehemence. In 1920, he joined the Independent Social Democratic Party of Germany (USPD), which had broken off from the SPD during the war. Although a member of the USPD, Tucholsky used the SPD publications as a platform for his writing. He joined the USPD not because he advocated everything it stood for, but rather as a gesture of support for the democratic system and because this party was radically opposed to militarism. This was also a means of underscoring his belief that one could take a leftist political position as a democrat and anticapitalist without joining the Communist Party.

Throughout the 1920s, Tucholsky became first sympathetic and then increasingly opposed to Marxism. He was too much of an individualist and adherent of Freudian theory to sympathize with Marxist collectivism and Communist Party dogma. In the mid-1920s he shifted toward a belief in economic determinism, but by the early 1930s he had rejected this: his study of Freud had convinced him that changing the economic structure of society would not alter man's inherent aggressive and possessive nature. Although he saw the Communists as allies in the struggle against the Right and published in the Communist press, in his later essays "Gebrauchslyrik" (Utilitarian poetry; 1928) and "Die Rolle des Intellektuellen in der Partei" (The role of the intellectual in the party; 1929), he made it clear that he deplored the basic anti-intellectualism of the Communist Party. He rejected the party line on the role of intellectuals, who were expected eventually to merge their identity with that of the proletariat but ended up being only second-rate intellectuals playing the role of workers. He became particularly disillusioned with the Soviet Union, because Stalin gave nominal support to the German Communists while simultaneously courting business deals with the Nazis.

Tucholsky searched for an ideological anchor between the prevailing extremes of Marxist materialism on the one hand and capitalism allied with irrational fascism on the other. This typifies what George Mosse has described as the dilemma of Jewish left-wing Weimar intellectuals such as Kurt Hiller, Hermann Cohen, Kurt Eisner, and Leonard Nelson (Mosse 1971). Tucholsky's essays written during the early 1920s contain contradictory political positions. He is torn between his desire for spiritual reform and his rejection of violent revolution as a threat to traditional values. Thus he seems both to admire and to be repelled by the leaders of the extreme Left. As he indicated in his programmatic essay "Wir Negativen" (We negative ones) in March 1919, he initially wanted to overthrow the corruption of the Weimar system with a nonviolent intellectual-spiritual revolution. At this point, he favored the enlightened rule by a democratically elected intellectual elite who would seek to establish international peace, freedom, and the rights of the individual. Although the Weimar Republic often seemed to be a perpetuation of the earlier Wilhelminian style of governmental bureaucracy and the glorification of militarism and power, the aim of Tucholsky's criticism in the earlier articles, songs, and cabaret skits was not revolution but rather democratic reform and the abolition of war. During the early 1920s, he spoke at antiwar demonstrations that attracted 80,000–100,000 people.

The assassination of the Jewish foreign minister Walther Rathenau in 1922 deeply distressed Tucholsky. He did not agree with Rathenau's politics, but he deplored the use of violence. He responded with aggressive political satire and criticism. The election of monarchist field marshall Hindenburg to the German presidency in 1925 marked a shift to right-wing nationalism and militarism that caused Tucholsky to question the parliamentary system and to revise his position: he thereafter called for resistance to the enemy on the Right, using not only words but whatever means were necessary, including force. Because of his articles, Tucholsky was faced with several lawsuits for insulting the military, for blasphemy, and for libel. The corrupt judicial system that he bitterly attacked in his writings blatantly supported the political Right. Tucholsky was fortunate that at least some of the suits were dismissed. In 1928, however, he lost a libel suit and had to make a public apology and pay an enormous fine. The most spectacular lawsuits involving Tucholsky were filed against Carl von Ossietzky in his capacity as editor of *Die Weltbühne* for printing articles, including one by Tucholsky, that were considered traitorous and offensive by the state. Tucholsky was acquitted, but in 1932 Ossietzky received an eighteen-month sentence. Ossietzky was arrested again in 1933 after the Nazis came to power. As an outspoken pacifist and secretary of the "German Peace Society," he was, along with Tucholsky, a much-hated opponent of the Nazis. They were both among the first writers and intellectuals whose books were burned and whose German citizenship was revoked. Ossietzky was never released, not even when he received the Nobel Peace Prize in 1936. Despite international efforts to obtain his freedom, he died in internment in 1938. The imprisonment of Ossietzky tormented Tucholsky and was a major factor in his decision to cease publishing. For the sake of his safety, Tucholsky had decided not to return to Berlin in 1932 to face the charges against him. He did send material to be used for the defense, and he continued privately to urge prominent figures to protest. When he finally acquiesced to Ossietzky's pleas that he continue to fight for him in the public arena, the article he wrote on his behalf for the *National Zeitung* in Basel was rejected.

Throughout his life Tucholsky vacillated between euphoric idealism and bitter resignation followed by retreat, either into the world of books or by removing himself from the field of conflict. He retreated first into his voluntary exile from Germany and then even further with his refusal to publish. Tucholsky was a successful writer in the sense that his works were best-sellers. But he felt he had failed to influence public opinion. When *Die Weltbühne* in Berlin was replaced by successor exile publications in Prague, Zurich, and Vienna, Tucholsky had already given up the battle. Before he fell silent, he contributed one last article to the Viennese *Weltbühne* in September 1932, calling for solidarity among the workers opposed to the armament industry.

During his lifetime, Tucholsky published a number of anthologies collected from his articles: *Mit 5 PS* (At five horsepower; 1927), *Das Lächeln der Mona Lisa* (Mona Lisa's smile; 1928), and *Lerne Lachen ohne zu weinen* (Learn to laugh without crying; 1931). His anthology *Deutschland, Deutschland über Alles* (Germany, Germany above all; 1929) on which he collaborated with photographer John Heartfield (1891–1968), contained mostly previously published materials and photomontages with provocative captions that attacked social and political institutions and incited the wrath of the public and the reviewers. This book, which was printed by a Communist publishing house, contributed to the legend that Tucholsky and other leftist intellectuals helped bring about the collapse of the republic by undermining it with their criticism. This view vastly overestimates the political influence of the Jewish essayists of the Left in Weimar Germany. Tucholsky also published a volume of travel memoirs, *Ein Pyrenäenbuch* (A Pyrenees book; 1927), and a comedy, "Christoph Columbus," which was written with Walter Hasenclever and premiered in 1932.

Though Tucholsky was most comfortable writing shorter prose pieces, his novel *Schloß Gripsholm* (Gripsholm castle; 1931) was a popular and artistic success that sold 100,000 copies in the year it was published. In 1929, Tucholsky spent six months in Sweden, living near Gripsholm Castle. He used this as the setting for the book, and he based some of the characters on people he knew, such as his mistress Lisa Matthias and his friends Erich Danehl (Karlchen) and Hans Fritsch (Jakopp). Much of the book consists of loosely connected plot threads presented in witty and realistic dialogues and conversations, including sections in low German. There are also descriptive passages that focus on nature and parody the style of popular literature, a playful account of a ménage àtrois, and a gruesome fantasy sequence on victims being torn apart by animals in the Roman arena. This fantasy underscores a central theme of the book: brutal, sadistic power unleashed on innocent, helpless victims. The book is a parable on political developments in Germany, and the symbol of power is Frau Adriani, the director of a boarding school who beats and torments the children entrusted to her. When the narrator and his friends encounter one child who has run away, they intervene and are able to remove the child from her control.

Tucholsky's novel illustrates his own response when he encountered persecution and the abuse of power. He felt that if it is hopeless for the victims of persecution to fight back, then they should attempt to remove themselves from the oppressive situation. This brings us back to our initial question regarding Tucholsky's Jewish identity and his attitude toward Jews and Judaism. The docile response of the German Jews after Hitler's seizure of power, their accommodation, and their failure to fight back or leave unleashed Tucholsky's unmitigated ire. Tucholsky abhorred what he regarded as the ghetto mentality of the German Jews, who bowed to Nazi harassment and did not opt for the freedom and dignity of emigration because they did not want to forfeit their property. Of course, the German Jews had no way of anticipating the scale of the coming Holocaust. For centuries accommodation had been an effective means of survival. Nor did Tucholsky suspect what was to come. If he had, he would never have said that the Jews got what they deserved for not resisting or leaving Germany.

Though Tucholsky explicitly denied being an anti-Semitic Jew, taken at face value, his furious tirades against the German Jews might seem to be examples of Jewish self-hatred. (It is perhaps more accurate to speak of his self-hatred, but not his *Jewish* self-hatred, because on one level he did not perceive himself as a Jew.) Tucholsky was fond of Jewish humor, and Jewish humor has an element of self-deprecation. But Tucholsky's attitude goes beyond this simple explanation. His descriptions of Jewish women combine his condescending attitude toward women with his distaste for Jews and read like passages from the Nazi *Stürmer*. Some of his statements sound like a form of Darwinian, pseudo-Nietzschean Nazi doctrine: the stronger should prevail and destroy the weaker race of slaves, who deserve their subjugation. A master race could not tolerate this situation and would offer heroic resistance and be extinguished, but the Jews cooperate and subsist. Tucholsky's popular fictional character Herr Wendriner was seen by some readers, including the Nazi propagandists, as an anti-Semitic caricature. Wendriner is clearly Jewish. In his stream-of-consciousness musings he uses Yiddish expressions and refers to non-Jews as "goys." But Tucholsky insisted that Wendriner's Jewishness was incidental. Wendriner, in Tucholsky's view, is a typical German authoritarian personality who bows to his superiors and oppresses his inferiors. Tucholsky's primary interest was to depict a political reactionary and anti-Communist, a German Babbitt, a banal, egotistical Weimar bourgeois businessman who could just as well have been a Christian. This presumably is the reason Tucholsky rejected a proposed illustration in which Wendriner looked "too Jewish." It would seem that Tucholsky both loved and hated his fictional creation Wendriner, and this same ambivalence characterized his attitudes toward both Germans and Jews.

The Jewish scholar Gershom Scholem (1976, 39) called Tucholsky's writings on German Jews "sinister," but other Jewish writers such as Kurt Hiller (1985, 8–10) and Arnold Zweig (in Hepp 1993, 290) correctly perceived that despite his disclaimers, on a deep emotional level Tucholsky did identify with and care about the German Jews. That is why he was so enraged at them. He did not agree with the Nazis that Jews as a race are biologically inferior and deserve to be destroyed. In his comments on the Jews, he is saying that he wishes they would fight back against the Nazis and that if they are too docile and intimidated to do so, then they have lost their own self-respect and his respect for them. Tucholsky did not want the Jews to be persecuted. Anticipating Bruno Bettelheim's argument that victims share in the responsibility for their persecution, Tucholsky was angry with the Jews for letting themselves be persecuted. Tucholsky favored assimilation, and this is presumably the reason he had no sympathy for Zionism as a first response to persecution. Recognizing that assimilation had failed, Tucholsky stressed that he deeply admired the Jews whose sense of dignity compelled them to migrate.

Many German Jews were assimilated to the point that they thought of themselves as Germans and, like Tucholsky, had little connection with the Jewish tradition. This also accounts for their inability to appreciate their precarious situation. There were, however, certain limits to Tucholsky's belief in assimilation. He was horrified by the reactionary elements within the Jewish community who celebrated their participation in the military and who would have supported the Nazis if anti-Semitism had not excluded them.

There is much in Tucholsky's life and works that is recognizably Jewish, in the sense of both ethnicity and religion. As a young man, he described his external appearance in a few ironic lines of verse as that of a "Jewish type" (Tucholsky 1989, 9). His second wife, Mary, also recalled him as identifiably Jewish. Tucholsky's immaculate dress and impeccable good manners may have been a reflection of his mother's obsession with order and cleanliness, but there may also have been some compensation here, a reaction to the negative stereotypes about Jews. In his letter of December 15, 1935, to the Jewish novelist Arnold Zweig, Tucholsky took great pains to argue that he had never experienced anti-Semitism firsthand except in the press. In other words, he had managed to pass, at least on occasion, as a non-Jew (Tucholsky 1962, 333). His Jewish background was generally known, and as a result

he was the target of violent and vulgar attacks in the Nazi press. After one of his public lectures in Wiesbaden in 1929, a mob of Nazis set out to attack him but beat up the wrong man by mistake. Tucholsky's statement that he had not experienced anti-Semitism reflects perhaps more of a wish than a reality.

Like his mentor and editor Jacobsohn, Tucholsky drew his intellectual inspiration and especially his sense of justice from the extreme Left reform movement of the German Jewish "educated middle class" (Bildungsbürgertum). Its ideals were grounded in the Classical Humanism of the French Enlightenment and in absolute ethical imperatives. It is perhaps a bit misleading to say that Tucholsky's ethical stance was shaped by Judaism, by the emphasis on individual responsibility, and by the utopian vision of a Messianic Age. He was as much shaped by Christian conceptions: his writings contain many more references to Christianity than to Judaism, and of course Christian ethics are essentially Jewish.

Tucholsky's conversion to Christianity appears to have been one of convenience, and was based more on indifference to Judaism than on Christian convictions. Even so, he maintained his close associations with Jews. It is not usual for assimilated, nonreligious Jews, including those who share Tucholsky's antipathy for Orthodox Jews to nonetheless form many of their most intimate interpersonal relationships with others of Jewish origin. Tucholsky's first wife, Else Weil, was Jewish, and so was his mistress Lisa Matthias, his secretary and lover Gertrud Meyer, and his most important friend, Siegfried Jacobsohn. The familial tone of Jacobsohn's letters to Tucholsky, with their occasional sprinkling of Yiddish words, is that of one Jew to another. In addition, Tucholsky chose to become a journalist, a profession that was open to and dominated by Jews. He started as a theater critic, a profession where the censorship was lax, there was room for lightly veiled political protest, and Jews were particularly active. Jacobson's Weltbühne was primarily a Jewish enterprise. Two-thirds of the staff were Jewish, and they formed a closely knit clique, in which, like Jacobsohn, they spoke their own special jargon flavored with Yiddish expressions.

Carl von Ossietzky was not Jewish. And when he became Tucholsky's editor, he did not follow Jacobsohn in establishing a close bond with Tucholsky. Mary Gerold, who was the great love of Tucholsky's life, was not Jewish, but Tucholsky's Jewish identity did play a role in his attraction to her. His letters reveal that he was fascinated by her blondness, the emblem of her non-Jewish identity, to which he refers repeatedly in contrast to his own darkness.

The style of Tucholsky's social and political satire was shaped by his identity as a Jewish outsider who looked from a distance at a society and institutions that did not accept him. This ironic distance, which one also finds in Jewish humor, has prompted some critics to compare him to other Jewish social satirists such as Karl Kraus (1874–1936) or Heinrich Heine (1797–1856), another disillusioned socialist idealist who like Tucholsky both loved and hated Germany, and who also retreated into exile in France. Both writers fall into the European tradition of the mobile Jew who is never at home in one place and is exiled and particularly conscious of language because of the need to learn and use new languages. Tucholsky himself resisted the comparison to Heine, on the grounds that his own writing was not as important.

Tucholsky was highly aware of nuances in language. In his writing, he mimics the patterns of current slang and uses various dialects, most notably Berlin jargon. Perhaps his persistent striving for syntactic accuracy and stylistic perfection under the tutelage of his mentor Jacobsohn came at least partly in response to the prejudices of those Germans who regarded Jews as foreigners. Today Tucholsky is indeed considered a master of modern German prose.

Bibliography

Irmgard Ackermann, "'Wir andern-auch wir suchen': Kurt Tucholsky und das Christentum," *Tucholsky heute: Rückblick und Ausblick,* ed. Irmgard Ackermann and Klaus Hübner (Munich: Iudicium Verlag, 1991); Fritz Hackert, "Die unkundbare Rolle: Kurt Tucholskys Verhältnis zum Judentum," *Im Zeichen Hiobs: Jüdische Schriftsteller und deutsche Literatur im 20. Jahrhundert,* ed. Gunter E. Grimm and Hans-Peter Bayerdörfer (Königstein/Taunus: Athenäum, 1985), 243–57; Michael Hepp, *Kurt Tucholsky: Bibliographische Annäherungen* (Reinbek bei Hamburg: Rowohlt, 1993); Kurt Hiller, "Kurt Tucholsky und der Selbsthaß," *text+kritik* 29 (1985): 8–10; Siegfried Jacobsohn, *Briefe an Kurt Tucholsky, 1915–1926* (Munich: Knaus, 1989); George L. Mosse, *Germans and Jews: The Right, the Left, and the Search for a "Third Force" in Pre-Nazi Germany* (London: Orbach & Chambers, 1971); Hans-Harald Müller, "'Im Grünen fings an und endete blutigrot': Kurt Tucholsky—Portrait eines vielseitigen Schriftstellers," *Literarische Profile: Deutsche Dichter von Grimmelshausen bis Brecht,* ed. Walter Hinderer (Königstein/Taunus: Athenäum, 1982), 338–51; Margarita Pazi, "Das 'ungelebte Leben' Kurt Tucholskys," *Juden in der deutschen Literatur,* ed. Stéphane Moses and Albrecht Schöne (Frankfurt a. M.: Suhrkamp, 1986), 293–315; Fritz J. Raddatz, *Tucholsky: Eine Bildbiographie* (Munich: Kindler Verlag, 1961); Marcel Reich-Ranicki, "Kurt Tucholsky: Deutscher, Preuße, Jude," *Juden und Judentum in der Literatur* (Munich: Deutscher Taschenbuch Verlag, 1985), 254–72; Gershom Scholem, "Jews and Germans," *On Jews and Judaism in Crisis,* ed. Werner J. Dannhauser (New York: Schocken, 1976), 71–92; Kurt Tucholsky, *Ausgewählte Briefe,* ed. Mary Gerold-Tucholsky and Fritz J. Raddatz (Reinbek bei Hamburg: Rowohlt, 1962); Tucholsky, *Gesammelte Werke,* ed. Mary Gerold-Tucholsky and Fritz J. Raddatz (Reinbek bei Hamburg: Rowohlt, 1993); Tucholsky, *Ich kann nicht schreiben, ohne zu lügen: Briefe 1913 bis 1935,* ed. Fritz J. Raddatz (Reinbek bei Hamburg: Rowohlt, 1989); Tucholsky, *Die Q-Tagebücher 1934–1935,* ed. Mary Gerold-Tucholsky and Fritz J. Raddatz (Reinbek bei Hamburg: Rowohlt, 1978); Tucholsky, *Unser ungelebtes Leben: Briefe an Mary,* ed. Fritz J. Raddatz (Reinbek bei Hamburg: Rowohlt, 1982); Elsbeth Wolffheim, "Mich haben sie falsch geboren: Tucholskys Exiljahre," *text+kritik* 29 (1985): 76–88; Arnold Zweig, "Lieber Kurt Tucholsky," *Die neue Weltbühne* (June 2, 1936), quoted in Hepp 1993, 290; and Gerhard Zwerenz, *Kurt Tucholsky: Biographie eines guten Deutschen* (Munich: C. Bertelsmann, 1979).

THOMAS FREEMAN

1915 In *Deutschtum und Judentum* Hermann Cohen
applies neo-Kantian philosophy to the
German Jewish Question

We live in a time of such German patriotic excitement that the unity between Germans and Jews that has been under way in the entire history of the Jews will now finally be realized as a cultural-historical truth in German politics, life, and identity. When this war clears away the last shadows that darken the inner German unity, then the international spirit of German humanity, grounded on the basis of German nationality and German uniqueness in science, ethics, and religion, will become the recognized truth of world history, overcoming all barriers of religions and peoples.

When Hermann Cohen wrote these lines in 1915, he was already seventy-seven years old and, having left the University of Marburg three years previously as an emeritus professor, was teaching at the Berlin Academy for the Science of Judaism. The founder of the Marburg School of neo-Kantianism had originally undertaken rabbinical studies in Breslau with Zacharias Fränkel but had switched to studying philosophy in Berlin. After a *Promotion* in Halle and a *Habilitation* in Marburg, he taught for about thirty years before leaving in 1912. Hermann Cohen was the only unbaptized Jew to hold a full professorship in the Wilhelmine empire. In a series of works on Kant and Plato that culminated in the standard systematic works *The Logic of Pure Recognition* (1904) and *The Aesthetics of Pure Feeling* (1912), he developed a philosophy that would later be labeled "neo-Kantianism." Cohen located his philosophy, as did Immanuel Kant himself, in the constructive principles of mathematics.

Cohen was also concerned with ethical questions. As the only well-known Jewish professor in the German Empire, he had to be affected by the anti-Semitic invectives of the important national liberal historian Heinrich von Treitschke (1834–96), who, in 1879—in the middle of the crisis of the founding of the Bismarckian empire— supported the Christian Social anti-Semitism of the Berlin court chaplain Adolf Stoecker (1835–1909), who publicly lamented that "the Jews are our misfortune" (Boehlich 1965).

Treitschke's anti-Semitically laced attack applied, despite all protests to the contrary, not only to the Jewish immigrants from Central and Eastern Europe, but also to those few German Jews who had with great difficulty achieved public recognition and reputation. "Among the leading figures in art and science," wrote Treitschke, "the number of Jews is not very large, making all the stronger the industrious group of second-rate Semitic talent" (Berding 1988, 114).

Due to his singular status and unquestioned recognition among German-speaking scholars, Cohen must not have felt personally attacked. He replied to Treitschke in a conciliatory manner hardly understandable today. Writing "not as a spokesman for a Jewish party, but rather as a representative of philosophy at a German institute and a believer in Jewish monotheism" (Cohen 1924, 74), Cohen declared in his "Confession on the Jewish Question" that racial questions could not be resolved through debate and that therefore the issue at hand was to defeat Treitschke's argument that Judaism was merely the national religion of a foreign tribe. Cohen held that this line of thinking was a barrier to reaching a real understanding of the problem.

Despite his bold declaration, Cohen approached Treitschke argumentatively, but generally accommodated his opponents more than was necessary. Because Cohen, as a philosopher interested in natural science, did not wish to wholly deny the persuasiveness of racial theory, his only recourse was to underscore the true universality of Judaism. In this respect, Cohen's 1880 response to Treitschke can be regarded as the original version of his posthumously published "Religion of Reason from the Sources of Judaism." In both texts, Cohen presents historical Jewish monotheism as a religion marked by the idea of the spirituality of God and the messianic promise, as a historical prototype of mankind's endeavors in the philosophy of history. Significantly, Cohen took up this argument during the 1880s, a decade characterized by the rejection of all—and especially Hegelian—philosophies of history.

Cohen's theory of Jewish universalism, conceived as a defense against Treitschke's enmity toward the Jews, again takes up the rejected philosophy of history. Cohen reformulates Hegel's questions as How is it possible for reason to become actualized in history? and How must we behave? These were the challenges posed to Hegel by liberal and socially responsible thinkers like Cohen's patron, the academic materialist F. A. Lange, who did not wish to believe that the Prussian state was the embodiment of reason. What appeared in Hegel's thinking as backward-looking reflection was adopted by the neo-Kantians as a political task. The return to Kant in the last quarter of the nineteenth century brought with it a revival of the teachings of just, correct behavior and ethics and a corresponding renunciation of the Realpolitical cynicism of the Bismarckian empire. The articulation of this position—including its appeal to Kant—seemed

particularly to catch the attention of philosophers of Jewish origin. It was no accident that Cohen saw himself as part of a long line of Kant's Jewish students dating back to Marcus Herz—students and readers who recognized an affinity between Kant's practical philosophy and the practice of Judaism. Hermann Cohen formulated this profound as well as historically immediate affinity with the following: "This idealistic meaning of morality, which we Germans honor as the sacrosanct teaching of Kant, in which all interpretations are reconciled, and which we hold up to all modern peoples as the greatest treasure of German national wisdom, appears historically unheralded from the depths, from closeness to God, from the glow of the moral enthusiasm of the Prophets. The imperative of Kantian ethics concurs in substance with Jewish ethics, with the Haggada, that part of the Talmud dealing with ethics" (Cohen 1924, 77).

Hermann Cohen, who was never baptized, nonetheless found himself obliged to fall back on Christian motifs in order to unfold the affinity between Kantianism and Judaism. The necessity of this line of argumentation was impressed upon Cohen through the formulation of a question posed by the Christian-influenced philosophy of German idealism. "How is it possible," the Kantian Cohen asked himself, "that a supposedly divine, general moral law of reason arises from a finite, if also morally free, essence, without in the process ascribing divinity to the finite human being?" From the generally accepted Hegelian philosophy of the first third of the nineteenth century in Germany came the answer: through mediation.

So the answer to Treitschke's diatribe is the simple comment that the modern Kantian Israelites share the fundamental assumptions of modern Christianity. Admittedly, the cost of this defense was the surrender of the theoretical autonomy of Judaism. It also granted the Christian religion systematic leadership in determining the validity of prophetic ethics: "Only one point has not come to full expression in this absorption by the Idea of God, a point whose dogmatic arrangement distinguishes Christian from Jewish monotheism. It is this fundamental thought, deriving from the association of modern peoples with the Greek spirit for the creation of a new culture: the idea of the relationship of man and God becomes spiritualized in the becoming-human of God, and fulfills in the dogmatic form of the humanization of God the cultural-historical mission of the humanization of religion" (Cohen 1924, 76).

Cohen argued along the same lines as David Friedländer (1750–1834), the Jewish reformer, Kantian, and student of Mendelssohn, who argued in his 1799 "Hausväterbriefen" against liberal theologians like David Friedrich Schleiermacher. More than a half-century later, Cohen used similar arguments against an illiberal and anti-Semitic historian like Heinrich von Treitschke in calling for a Christianity without Christ.

Cohen accepted this line of argumentation in order to secure for the Jews their place in a Christian-German society: "I hope to have demonstrated," Cohen writes at the close of this passage, "that the religious substance of Jewish monotheism is compatible with a historically conceived Christianity and is sufficient for a *Volksgemeinschaft*" (Cohen 1924, 78).

Naturally the task of mediating between Jewish and German could not be exhausted with the thought of a Christianity without Christ. It needed to be grounded in the concrete: the existing German state.

The population of this state, the Bismarckian empire, appeared to consist primarily of Protestants and other "pure" Germans, but it also included various nationalities and even various races. For this reason, Cohen found himself forced to go beyond his systematic theological arguments into racial theory and examine the meaning of race for nation building. In making this move, Cohen distanced himself sharply from the Jewish founder of "folk psychology," Moritz Lazarus (1824–1903), who had an aversion to all theories of blood. For Lazarus, racial concepts were useless in explaining the essence of a *Volk*. Cohen's remarks regarding the racial question, however, clearly assign an explanatory function to race: "With a healthy feeling of humanity, one answers the question of whether racial unity in a people is desirable and on a minimal scale neces-

sary with an unhesitating yes. . . . We must recognize that the racial instinct is by no means simple barbarism, but rather a natural, nationally justified longing. Barbarism becomes national feeling if it degenerates into the political and national exclusion of such fellow citizens who neither have nor wish for another Fatherland" (Cohen 1924, 84).

Cohen believed that Treitschke would have to admit that all Jews desired a Germanic appearance; he therefore constructed a social rapprochement, a marriage, that would finally bring about the assimilation of racial differences. There was for him no doubt that "we Jews must acknowledge that the ideal of national assimilation must from generation to generation be more consciously striven for" (Cohen 1924, 88).

Because Cohen stood on principle against conversion to Christianity, he finally had to endorse a way of life that could be characterized from the perspective of the time as a German-Jewish symbiosis, namely support of interfaith marriages in which the partners came from enlightened cultural Protestant or ethical monotheistic Jewish traditions. In such cases it was never necessary to speculate on the future. A simple assessment of real existing Jewry in Germany since the French Revolution was thoroughly sufficient for creating the religious service as well as for the teaching of German Judaism: "Our Jewish religion, as it inspires us today, has really entered into a cultural-historical relationship with Protestantism; not only in that, like any tradition of the Church, we have cast aside those who read the Talmud more or less plainly and directly, but also in that we feel and consider all spiritual questions of religion much more deeply in the Protestant spirit" (Cohen 1924, 93).

It is obvious here, in this quotation, the extent to which the German Jew and Kantian Hermann Cohen, without realizing or reflecting upon it, bought into the philosophy of the founding of the Bismarckian empire. Without giving a thought to the fact that there were also Catholics in the empire, without mentioning the actual conditions of one ethical Socialist, and without considering that there is also an atheistic universalism (Cohen 1970, 45–84), he took the relationship with German Protestants as the core of his political thought and his interpretation of Judaism. Cohen's writings to American Jews published at the beginning of World War I reveal that he continued to hold to these thoughts from the 1870s. Rejecting Zionism just as much as chauvinistic nationalism, Cohen ultimately chose a bizarre universalist-messianic creed for Germany's path in World War I and became thereby one of the leading representatives of the "Ideas of 1914" (Cohen 1974, 171), formulated in opposition to 1789. In a piece entitled "You Should Not Go Along as a Slanderer—An Appeal to the Jews of America," he stated plainly: "Not every Jew knows it, but every Jew should know it: we have Germany alone to thank for the inner religious development of our Religious-Constitution" (Cohen 1974, 233). These insights, Cohen thought, should swing every Jew in the world to the side of Germany in the war, which, with its weaponry and its realization of the practical interests of the Jews, would fulfill its world-historical, messianic mission: "Dear brothers in America: You will understand me if I now tell you that every Western Jew, along with his political fatherland, must recognize, honor, and love Germany as the motherland of his modern religious beliefs, his aesthetic strength and the center of his cultural convictions. I am convinced that this piety for German culture is also alive in every educated Russian Jew. And I am also confident that he must welcome our German war with Russia with his whole Jewish heart" (235).

Cohen justified the war against Russia from a Jewish perspective, principally because of the oppression of the Russian Jews, who were not granted even the basic right to send their children to school. Cohen countered the appeal of an English Jew to fight with the Russian Jews against Germany with only slightly tempered prophetic wrath. He saw the war as a historical moment at which the final judgment could fall on Russia, "not least out of consideration of the undisguised measures for the extermination of the Jewish people. Every Jew who is convinced of the cultural strength and therefore of the right of his religion to exist must count himself lucky if his patriotism imposes on him at least neutrality in

this war. He would have to envy us German Jews," Cohen stressed, "that we fight for our German Fatherland, carried at the same time by the pious confidence that we will fight with the greater part of our co-religionists for their human rights. Germany, the Motherland of Western Jewry, the land of spiritual freedom and moral education, will with her victory establish justice and peace among peoples of the world. On that point," Cohen thus closed his appeal to the Jews of America, "we can renounce diplomatic assurances. We trust the logic of our destiny and our history" (Cohen 1974, 235–36).

On the basis of these assumptions, that is to say, on the basis of a peculiar mixture of rigorous, universalistic morality, partial concession to racial thinking, and an interpretation of prophetic Judaism that in a sense had to accept the dispersion among peoples as the metahistorical meaning of Jewish destiny, Cohen could only reject the Zionist thinking of someone like Martin Buber that was emerging at the time. The gathering of the Jews and the confinement to a religiously inspired founding of the nation-state in Palestine had to be seen according to this perspective as a betrayal of prophetic messianism. Through this argumentation on two fronts—against the views of Moritz Lazarus, who appeared to him as relativistic, and who, in his rejection of racial thinking, seemed to surrender important materialist insights, and also against Martin Buber's particularism—Cohen maintained the thought of a Jewish nation as a worldwide cultural nation. This persistence depended on, as did his stand for the warring Germany, an idea one could characterize as "historical consciousness," which, however, in Cohen's variation was little more than a variation of a historical-philosophical faith in progress. When, at the end of his appeal to the American Jews, Cohen speaks of the "logic" of the destiny and history of the Jews, it is not a matter of a careless *façon de parler,* but rather a well thought out historical-philosophical argument.

Religion was for Cohen a part of the general cultural development of humanity, a development that follows its own natural laws. Cohen rejected Zionism not because it was oriented too much toward utilitarian aims for a happier life and too little toward the rigor of moral law, but rather on the grounds of an historical-philosophical conviction that behind the thoughts of the prophets lay a moral universality. Whereas Theodor Herzl posited the necessity of a Jewish state arising out of the anti-Semitism of the Dreyfus Affair, Cohen testified to the "historical meaning of the conclusion of the Dreyfus Affair:" "We may be certain that our suffering is coming to a glorious end: glorious not only for us, but for all of mankind. There will have to be justice on Earth; and justice must mean more than simply grace and tolerance. To the French martyrs, our brothers in faith in the French army, honor will again be returned because holy justice demands it; so may we hope for a similar fate for all martyrs. And for our religious totality we recognize with optimism the connection between our martyrdom and the triumph of the truth and the true moral salvation of mankind" (Cohen 1974, 359).

Now, to apply political and religious opinions to the whole of nineteenth-century German Jewry was anything but unusual. The question of a new formulation of a philosophy of history is clearly presented in the 1883 "Principles of the Infinitesimal Method and Its History." Inasmuch as Judaism developed like every other religion in history, and insofar as "religion" and "history" are concepts and all concepts originate systematically in reason, the task of a timely philosophy of religion can only be to defend "the concept of religion through the religion of reason" (Cohen 1978, 5). Hardly different from Hegel in his philosophy of history, Cohen adhered to the practice of a construction of history guided by reason, in which a reasonable concept of religion finds in the realm of historical development exactly the elements that it could systematically construct anyway. Does the historical, cultural, and religious material thereby become a shining illustration of an independently constructed moral truth? This is not the case for the later Cohen, because on the basis of his assumption, human reason is always already at work in history and thus brings to light nothing more than its effects. For this reason alone, Cohen believed it legitimate to construct the religion of reason precisely out of the origins of Judaism: "This generality, which becomes ac-

cordingly the fundamental condition for the religion of reason, appears as things now stand to contradict that which we derive from the sources of Judaism: that which lends historical reality to the individual forms of appearance in the face of necessity is precisely the generality that in spite of all social impediments and in spite of the shortcomings in a people's history is nonetheless able to prevail. And in this revelation of the effects of progress and continuity, in which the meaning of history is established, history becomes a history of reason" (9).

Cohen's strongest argument for this historical-philosophical approach thus consists in his acceptance of the psychic, social, and thus real effects of a generalizing reason and of the agencies of the law. The essence of reason consists for Cohen in what he characterizes with a term borrowed, rather unfortunately by today's standards, from the Old Testament, "lawfulness." This "lawfulness," that is, the human capacity to formulate general concepts and to formally test for inconsistencies, would delineate the link between human reason and another reason. Certainly only a conceptually guided examination of religion can explain anything about this reason. Cohen thus proceeds realistically and inductively from content and scope, both of which he defines as "human"—a decision of grave consequences (Cohen 1978, 13). Thus a way is shown to wrest from man, as Cohen phrased it, his "empirical ambiguity" (16). In this way, Cohen demonstrates that he is well aware of the difference between "God" and "religion," as well as of the difference between "religion" and "ethics." Both are based on and relate to humans. Accordingly, the contribution of ethics is to strip away man's individuality and to submit him to a self-reflection that culminates in thought and point of reference in "humanity."

According to this standard of ethics, the individual recognizes himself first in humanity and humanity is fulfilled in individuality. That humanity alone cannot be a complete symbol of individuality, but rather takes on here a mediating transitional significance, was a common thought among German-Jewish philosophers still influenced by Hegel: "All methodological danger is now removed from ethics. The individuality of humans, which they establish in humanity, is released of all appearance of paradox: the state mediates between the empirical individual and the idea of humanity, of which man becomes the representative. In the individuality of the state, in which the empirical man takes interest with every fiber of his heart and whose rhythm the beating of his own pulse follows, this miracle is realized as the source of the ethical teachings of humanity as the fulfillment of man" (Cohen 1978, 16).

Had Hermann Cohen left it at that, we would not be able to say where the deviation from Hegel's philosophy of law and of history lay, nor could we locate the specific contribution of the sources of Judaism to Cohen's thinking.

The mediation between the individual and humanity in the form of the state depends upon the fact, which was for Cohen quite obvious, that a single individual requires, along with the vertical mediation vis-à-vis humanity, a second mediation, in which man appears not merely as an autonomous individual, but rather as a concrete, sensuous fellow man, afflicted by suffering—as a being whose moral education and development operate under preconditions over which he has no control. Here Hermann Cohen discovers, long before the dialogic philosophy of Martin Buber and long before Franz Rosenzweig's linguistic philosophy of existence, "man as fellow man" (Cohen 1978, 131).

Through his reflections on the problem of theodicy, the metaphysical reality of suffering and the substance of language, Cohen was able to conceive of Judaism as an ethics of intersubjectivity. In this respect the influence of Schopenhauer cannot be overlooked alongside that of Hegel and Fichte, though Cohen does not mention him; for even before Hegel, Schopenhauer devised an intersubjective theory of recognition in his "Foundations of Natural Law According to the Principles of the Teachings of Science" (1796).

The undisguised and unabridged form of intersubjectivity is developed through an analysis of language and its personal pronouns, a reflection that Martin Buber would later take up in his work "I and Thou." By the clues of language

given in the construction of difference between participants and the perspectives of the observer, Hermann Cohen gains insight into intersubjectivity, which supports the Kantian ban on instrumentalization in relation to other human beings: "Next to the I the He imposes itself as different from It: is He only the other example of I, whose thoughts were already established through the I? Language guards against this error: it places the Thou before the He. Is the Thou just another example of the I and does it not require its own discovery of the Thou, even when I am already aware of my I? Perhaps it is the other way around, that first the Thou, the discovery of the Thou, might be able to bring me an awareness of my I, a moral recognition of my I" (Cohen 1978, 17).

Cohen based this departure from the methodical solipsism of a Kantian principle-testing ethics on the sources of Judaism, especially on a reading of the prophetic writings. In these writings, a view of the world developed that was different from the classical neo-humanism cultivated in Germany. This new world view was neither tragic nor aesthetic, but rather sympathetic and engaged. In its monotheism, it was already oriented toward the universal. This sympathetic view of the prophets requires the acceptance of their view that the relationship of man to God was the first test for the study of relationships between men, providing for the rediscovery of man: "The prophet becomes an ethicist of practice, a politician and a judge, because he wants to put an end to the suffering of the poor. And it is not enough for him to take up only these several occupations. Rather, he must also become a psychologist: he must make sympathy the primary emotion of man, at the same time find man in sympathy, fellow man and mankind itself" (Cohen 1978, 166).

The rediscovery of the concept of mankind, indeed the rediscovery of mankind itself, through the prophets—the cleverness of Cohen's turn-of-the-century thought, in its provision for the historicity of all ethics and simultaneous corroboration of the truth of its regulating ideas—can be appreciated when it is not naively seen only in relation to the "Jewish Humanism" of Buber and Rosenzweig. The attempt, first undertaken by

Cohen, to found a philosophical ethics not only on the basis of classical thought or the idea of an autonomous self-consciousness, but also from the writings of the Hebrew Bible, led to a philosophical paradigm shift. A reading of the experiences of suffering shown in the Bible, with its ethics grounded in the dialogue between God and man and the extension of prophetic universalism, enabled the consciousness-oriented Kantian Hermann Cohen to overcome a methodological solipsism and to conceive of a universalist ethics, which gave up its formal character and directed itself concretely toward the ethical organization of state and society. The Jews, as a historical minority, were particularly suited to support these messianic tendencies in modernity, because they could not form a nation in the classical sense: "For the development of monotheism we must maintain a national individualism, because monotheism has stamped us with an historical singularity, and since this nationality cannot be bound by our own state, it is protected from the fate of the materialization of its national idea" (Cohen 1924, 296).

Hermann Cohen paid a high price for maintaining the purity of the idea of a Jewish people as a people of priests and judges of nationalism. This thinker who, like no one else in modernity, stood for the purest prophetic universalism, for a non–materially grounded program of social justice, and for a worldwide order of justice, saw these goals fulfilled in of all things, Germany's entrance into the war. As clear and reasonable as this Jew and philosopher seemed, Hermann Cohen acted blindly in his German patriotism.

Bibliography

Helmut Berding, *Moderner Antisemitismus in Deutschland* (Frankfurt a. M.: Suhrkamp, 1988); Walter Boehlich, ed., *Der Berliner Antisemitismusstreit* (Frankfurt a. M.: Insel, 1965); Hermann Cohen, *Deutschtum und Judentum* (Gießen: Topelmann, 1915); Cohen, *Jüdische Schriften,* ed. B. Strauß (Berlin: Schwetschke, 1924); Cohen, "Kant," *Marxismus und Ethik, Texte zum neukantianischen Sozialismus,* ed. Hans-Jörg Sandkühler and Rafael de la Vega (Frankfurt a. M.: Suhrkamp, 1970); Cohen, *Religion der Vernunft aus den Quellen des Judentums* (Wiesbaden: Dreieich, 1978); J. G. Fichte, "Grundlage des Naturrechts nach den Principien der Wissenschaftslehre," *Fichtes Werke,* vol. 3 (Berlin: W. de Gruyter, 1971); and Hermann Lübbe, "Die philosophischen Ideen von 1914," *Politische Philosophie in Deutschland* (Munich: dtv, 1974).

MICHA BRUMLIK

TRANSLATED BY
HILLARY HOPE HERZOG
AND TODD HERZOG

1916 The first issue of Martin Buber's German-Jewish journal *Der Jude* appears

There is an interesting discrepancy between the memory of the elderly Martin Buber and the evidence at hand concerning the genesis of *I and Thou,* the seminal text that has earned him a secure place in the written records of twentieth-century religious thought. In a short autobiographical sketch penned in 1954, Buber recalled that he had originally formulated a plan for *I and Thou* as early as 1916. That is a very early *terminus ad quem* in this particular case. The first draft that can be documented dates back only to 1919, not 1916 as he later remembered, whereas the first published edition of *I and Thou* appeared in 1922. Virtually every study or consideration of Buber and *I and Thou* indicates that he was not mentally prepared to conceive of the "dialogical existentialism" of *I and Thou* until the termination of World War I and as a result of his enriching, intellectual encounters with the writings of Ferdinand Ebner and the thought and person of Franz Rosenzweig. Although an extended "gestation period" preceded the specific conceptualization of the text, there is apparently no documentation that might fix the start of that period as early as 1916. Nevertheless, that Buber's memory linked *I and Thou* in retrospect with the year 1916 serves to illuminate a personal, "inner truth" concerning the experiential and intellectual background of the achievement represented by the text, to the extent Buber reflected it in his utterances. This memory may also be a key to identifying the major aspect of his considerable contribution to German-Jewish culture as a whole, as far as he comprehended it in terms of his life's work.

World War I signalized a crisis and turning point in the intellectual orientation of many German-Jewish writers and intellectuals. It functioned as a catalyst that helped bring complex, underlying questions pertaining to national and Jewish identity and the self to consciousness and expression. External forces, represented by larger social, political, and military developments, appeared to compel in many a reevaluation of the Jewish and German components of identity, although the nationalistic and cultural-religious implications of the war waxed and waned in importance over time. Lukács once argued cogently in another context that the French Revolution, owing especially to the rapidity and intensity of public events affecting masses of people across large geographical spaces, occasioned a new way of perceiving history and the historical process altogether. In the same vein, World War I was credited with stimulating a new phase in the understanding of Jewish identity in Central Europe, owing to the particular manner in which the intense fighting and widespread hardships caused by the war directly affected Jews or were perceived by Jewry across national boundaries, especially as the battle line shifted back and forth on the Eastern Front, causing exile, death, and disaster for masses of Ostjuden.

Buber, who was never drafted and spent the war years safely in Germany, was nevertheless no exception in terms of his immersion and participation in this process. A direct result of his involvement was his determination to publish a new, independent German-language journal, which was to have a seminal effect on German-Jewish self-perception. In 1916 the first number of Buber's *Der Jude* appeared, and it came to be widely regarded in a very short time as the single most influential German-Jewish periodical of its time. Of course, "influence" in this sense cannot be measured precisely, but numerous sources testify to the singular and diverse effect of this publication, as well as to the loyalty and devotion of its readership.

Der Jude established a new phase or a new direction in terms of the presentation of Buber's public self, which he had been developing purposefully since a few years before the war. The feverish pace of his university years at the turn of the century in Vienna, Leipzig, Zurich, and Berlin were long behind him, although he had acquired the requisite basis and the fundamental methodological training and intellectual orientation that were to serve him later on. The early poetical and journalistic endeavors in Polish and German on topics ranging from art history, literary criticism, folklore, and poetry to philosophy and sociology may have also seemed a sort of preparation for this new phase. Likewise, his tempestuous period of association with the nascent, modern Zionist movement, his identification with a neo-romantic variety of Jewish nationalism and cultural Zionism, and his abandonment of the movement in 1903–4, were all in the past, especially after he marked his return to Zionist affiliation by means of three influential, annual lectures to the Bar Kochba Zionist group in Prague, beginning in 1909. These appeared to have steeled him for the work of the next decade, starting with the outbreak of the war. Also, his immersion in the study of Hasidism at the start of the century, as well as his meditation on the "Tales of Rabbi Nachman" and the "Legends of the Baal Shem," lent his myriad endeavors, beginning already before the outbreak of the war, a certain transcendental quality, no matter what area or genre of expression he chose for himself at any given time.

In addition, the fact that *Der Jude* came to be regarded so highly by a fairly large and mostly highbrow audience—the fact that a widespread, deep-seated, and loyal identification with this publication is traceable, especially on the part of a young readership faithful to Buber—says much about the particular strivings for group identity on the part of the intellectual wing of German Jewry, which was in the process of being cultivated and propagated at a fateful phase of its history. Given the fact that only a precious minority of Central European Jewry was officially or actively affiliated with Jewish nationalism or the Zionist organization, the broad-based enthusiasm for *Der Jude* may be the result either of sympathy from a distance and a projected longing for new identities more nationalist in their accent, or else the result of a curious process of recognizing belatedly—that is, well after the Nazi period and Shoah—that the orientation of this journal was indeed cogent or sensible. With the advantage of hindsight, and taking into account the rise of Nazism in Europe, the devastation of the Shoah, and the establishment and centrality of Israel in modern Jewish life, *Der Jude* may appear more compelling today than it was at the time of its publication. In any case, the multidimensional functions of this journal as a locus for understanding an ideal of Jewish culture in the collective consciousness of German Jewry, as well as the notion of Buber's self-cultivation in directing the publication, are worthy of serious consideration. As it turns out, this is perhaps the best place to seek the inviolable kernel of Buber's conception of a German-Jewish symbiosis, in view of the rising anti-Semitism in Germany during the war years.

The war might be viewed as an agent that served to spur Buber to action within the context of community while the painstaking, introspective process of identity reevaluation continued apace. His changing opinions about the war and about the relationships of the German and Jewish peoples to it is of secondary importance in this context. With the outbreak of the war, Buber was one of the founders of the Jewish National Committee, which worked chiefly on behalf of Eastern European Jews under German occupation on the Eastern Front. At about the same time, he made the final arrangements to launch *Der Jude*. Buber's idea of a publication called *Der Jude* was not a new one; it dates backs to his active involvement with "Young Jewish Movement," the Jewish Renaissance, and German cultural Zionism at the turn of the century. Berthold Feiwel, E. M. Lilien, and Buber had discussed more than a decade earlier the founding of a literary and artistic journal, to be called *Der Jude,* that would disseminate the finest cultural products of the young Jewish art movements and give credence to the idea of the vitality of modern Jewish culture. This project was never actualized. Nevertheless, when the proposal was finally realized by Buber during the war, its shape was markedly different from the original conception. In part, this was due as much to the developments that had taken place within Zionism in the interim as it was to the specific path Buber had followed since that time. In effect, the space envisioned for literary and artistic projects—that is, for the "cultural Renaissance," which was originally conceived as the dominant, in fact almost exclusive component—was significantly restricted in the final conception of *Der Jude.* Now, the political, historical, historiographical, economic, linguistic, educational, and sociological aspects of the Zionist enterprise, on one hand, and the East-West dialogue within Jewry, on the other, came to dominate the journal. After the publication of the first issues of *Der Jude,* Buber received letters from sympathetic readers and friends, Stefan Zweig to name but one, asking him to consider enlarging the literary-artistic component of the publication. But even if Buber did increase slightly the number of literary pieces, he decidedly avoided transforming *Der Jude* into a literary magazine, and this fact needs to be appreciated within the context of his greater purpose and ultimate achievement. Buber no longer aimed to gather and present Jewish culture, but rather to sketch the outlines and map the future course of the living Jewish nation as it progressed inexorably to its true spiritual destiny.

In his introductory remarks to the first number of *Der Jude,* Buber articulated a view of the contemporary Jewish dilemma, which had been unduly exacerbated by the war. According to his view, the war, because of its chaotic nature and its potential to cause spiritual fragmentation, had impinged on the condition of the Jewish *Volkseele.* Even in times of relative calm, the Jewish "folk soul" existed more or less in a state of abnormalcy or virtual crisis. Owing to their precarious diasporic existence, the Jewish people were perhaps the most vulnerable national group in Europe. Consequently, they were highly susceptible, in an inner and spiritual dimension, to the drastic changes and dramatic external forces unleashed by the war. The divisiveness among individual Jews and national Jewries, living and opposing each other across national borders, had become so palpable that it appeared that the Jewish national enterprise as a whole might be seriously endangered. Jews had become painfully aware of the negative, transcendent implications of the diasporic condition and their rootlessness. At the same time, the experience of the war indicated the powerful beneficiality of *Gemeinschaft,* Jewish belonging, and a greater sense of the living community. The war had made crystal clear to the "atomized" Jews of the West how forlorn their "decontextualized" condition of alienation from the holy *Volksgemeinde* (community of the people) was, and it impelled them, in an act of inner liberation, to join ranks with their brothers and sisters in the East, who desperately needed this bonding and unity at a seminal moment in the life of the nation. As Buber phrased it: "The illusion has been destroyed that it might be possible to truly live at a time like this, by viewing the life of the 'Gemeinschaft' from the outside, or that one might take part in the life of the 'Gemeinschaft' by nominally professing to be part of it." Whoever wishes to be serious about his existence on earth, claimed Buber's stentorian voice, must be serious about his relationship with the Gemeinschaft in terms of feeling responsible. That is, the new unity of Jewry would be forged through stimulating common feelings of responsibility for the fate of the community. *Der Jude* would serve ideally as a rallying point to advance this notion of responsibility, which would encourage Jews to take on the additional, consequential responsibility for their own future among the nations of the globe.

Buber managed to collect in *Der Jude* a rhetorically and conceptually sophisticated variety of intellectual expression, almost all of it Jewish national and Zionist in nature, and he pressed the totality of it purposefully into Jewish national service. This was to a degree an editorial strategy characteristic of cultural Zionism at the turn of the century. Buber was able to utilize it and refine it by providing the sense of a greater context beyond nationalism, within which Jewish national expression was ultimately viewed as a tool of internationalist cooperation and mutual understanding between the nations. As a rule, Eastern Jewry and the Eastern Jewish contributors were idealized or lionized in turn, mostly as the anchored component of the nation. Yiddish and Hebrew contributions were translated into highly stylized and elevated German prose, whereas Yiddish and Hebrew were conjointly promoted in German-language articles as the primary linguistic instruments of the nation. This somewhat paradoxical affirmation of linguistic diversity was nevertheless a strategy or form of inclusivity, and it projected national unity. As the Western contributors and readers struggled to disentangle themselves from their German cultural allegiances, they were to be uplifted and fortified by their intellectual engagement with the refreshing and vibrant reservoir of Eastern Jewry. And the Zionist enterprise, the establishment of a spiritually potent commonwealth in the Middle East, was to be enriched from both sides. Yet all of these efforts purportedly served higher, inner-Jewish and external, supranational goals in the end, although the parameters of these goals were not always articulated clearly. In any case, Buber never saw the creation of a Jewish community in the land of Israel or a Jewish state as an end in itself.

Buber succeeded in attracting to *Der Jude* a variety of outstanding contributors, many of whom resided or were rooted in Galicia, Rumania, and Russia, and their essays purported to bridge the divide between East and West. They included Hugo Bergmann, Max Brod, Adolf Böhm, Markus Ehrenpreis, Fritz Kaufmann, Jakob Klatzkin, Gustav Landauer, N. M. Gelber, Arno Nadel, Gershom Scholem, Robert Weltsch, Hillel Zeitlin, Micha Josef bin Gorion (Berdycewski), Kurt Blumenfeld, Arnold Zweig, Simon Dubnow, Julius Bab, S. J. Agnon, Georg Brandes, Margarete Susman, Franz Werfel, Nahum Goldman, and Franz Kafka.

Buber utilized the figure and thought of Ahad Ha'Am as a kind of banner for the publication or as a presiding spirit. This cultural Zionist intellectual and champion of the renaissance of Hebrew letters, who had been one of the early mentors of German cultural Zionism, was well represented and repeatedly feted in *Der Jude* by different contributors, who wrote from both Eastern and Western viewpoints. He was featured as a personification of the best qualities of enlightened, nationalist East European Jewry. In fact, it is fair to say that the first issues of *Der Jude* were saturated with Ahad Ha'Am. In the first year of the journal's appearance, Ahad Ha'Am's inaugural letter to *Der Jude*, entitled "Ost und West" was printed. Hugo Bergmann published an essay on Ahad Ha'Am's national significance. K. Baruch wrote on the "Jews of the West in the Judgment of Ahad Ha'Am." Markus Ehrenpreis wrote on "Ahad Ha'Am as an Educator." Schear Jaschub wrote on "Ahad Ha'Am's Zionism." And Rafael Seligmann contributed on Ahad Ha'Am's person. This preoccupation with the man and with his cultural-spiritual tenets was the setting for a debate about the future of Jewry, as much as a testimony to his stature and significance for Jewish nationalism. Of primary importance was Ahad Ha'Am's underlying faith in the singular capabilities of a Jewish cultural elite. Possibly, the contributors to *Der Jude*, by participating in the idealization or cult of Ahad Ha'Am, were at the same time fashioning images of themselves according to the model he presented. Rooted in Hebrew and in the prophetic-messianic tradition, Ahad Ha'Am argued singlemindedly for the establishment of an elitist, spiritual center in the land of Israel, whose spiritual and ethical power would radiate throughout the Jewish diaspora and effect its transformation.

From this point of view, *Der Jude* represented a preliminary stage in the founding of this Jewish-national spiritual center, albeit from a distance. The journal functioned as a prototype or blueprint of the creative, intellectual discourse that the Jewish-national elitist forum could be expected to produce. However, in theory it had to fall short of the ideal Jewish-spiritual wholeness, which might be attained by a subsequent, parallel endeavor undertaken in the land of Israel and in the Hebrew language. This theoretical position was part of Ahad Ha'Am's neo-romantic legacy and his emphasis on creative unity and was characteristic of his cultural Zionist thought. Buber's famous "debate" with Hermann Cohen, and other related essays printed in *Der Jude,* indicate that Buber aimed not only to establish himself as a founder of the spiritual center at an early stage of its development, but also to preserve an independent realm for himself within the arena of the Jewish national dialogue of the time. In other words, although he resolutely opposed Cohen's anti-Zionist Germanism, he distanced himself subtly from Scholem's youthful, strident, and to a degree limiting variety of Jewish nationalism, as well as from Landauer's cultural Germanism-cum-internationalism. By doing so, Buber utilized *Der Jude* in order to formulate a singular, individualized nationalist humanism, by developing a dialogue with "Otherness." Perhaps here is the intellectual connection to the subsequent conception of *I and Thou,* which was founded on the dialogical principle of a dynamic confrontation of the self with the human other and the divine other, in order to map the parameters of existential being.

Der Jude, viewed as perhaps the seminal Jewish national project in Buber's career, represented his attempt to draw strength for his developing position by reorienting the discussion of Jewish nationalism among German-speaking Jewry in two distinct ways. First, the implicit readership of *Der Jude* consisted first and foremost of Jewish youth—that is, the young, energetic cadres of an idealistic, intellectual elite, a vanguard with the potential to actualize the ideal form of Jewish community he so fervently desired. When Buber

failed to emigrate to Palestine after World War I, it appeared to at least some members of his committed, youthful following that their leader had betrayed them. Second, the reorientation was affected by Buber's consistent, unremitting concern for the Jews of the East. *Der Jude* included a plethora of different types of presentations on a wide range of Eastern Jewish issues in order to recenter the focal point of Jewish-national concern decidedly eastward. For Buber personally, the inclusion of these presentations may have been part of an effort to construct and present a unified self by returning to the scene of his childhood in Eastern Galicia, when he was separated from his parents—a way of salvaging that part of the untainted childhood self by integrating it finally into his new understanding of his adult self. For Jewry, though, it represented a concerted, if idealistic, effort to reinvigorate those parts of Jewry that had become enervated by processes of diasporic acculturation and assimilation while combining potent Jewish "folk" forces for the sake of humanity.

Bibliography

Martin Buber, *I and Thou* (New York: Scribner, 1970); Buber, *Der Jude* (1916–24); Buber, *Der Jude und sein Judentum: Gesammelte Aufsätze und Reden* (Cologne: Joseph Melzer, 1963); Maurice Friedman, *Martin Buber's Life and Work* (New York: E. P. Dutton, 1981); Rivka Horwitz, *Buber's Way to "I and Thou"* (Heidelberg: Lambert Schneider, 1978); Hans Kohn, *Martin Buber: Sein Werk und seine Zeit* (Cologne: Joseph Melzer, 1961); Graete Schaeder, ed., *Martin Buber: Briefwechsel aus sieben Jahrzehnten,* 3 vols. (Heidelberg: Lambert Schneider, 1972, 1973, 1975); and Schaeder, *Martin Buber: Hebräischer Humanismus* (Göttingen: Vandenhoeck and Ruprecht, 1966).

MARK H. GELBER

1916 The German army orders a census of Jewish soldiers, and Jews defend German Culture

Jubilant masses moved through the streets of Berlin and Paris, Vienna and London during the first days of August 1914. In Germany, the enthusiasm over the beginning of the war was greater than anywhere else. After the Kaiser's long saber-rattling, here finally was the long-awaited adventure that would interrupt the tedious everyday life of the ordinary person and encourage applause by even the most intelligent and liberal thinkers and politicians. If Max Weber initially believed that "this war is really great and wonderful beyond expectation," and the Social Democrats declared the defense of German culture as their utmost goal during the hour of war, who then would call for peace?

Certainly not German Jews. To be sure, like many non-Jews, not all of them were happy about the war, and there were a few dissenting voices expressing their deep concern—including Albert Einstein and the young Gerhard (Gershom) Scholem. But the vast majority of German Jews cherished high hopes for the coming events. The Kaiser's famous promise that from now on there would be no differences between classes, parties, and religions was greeted enthusiastically by the Jewish population. What peace had not achieved—the full social integration of Jews into German society—war would establish. The bonds of solidarity among Christian and Jewish soldiers, fighting together and dying in the same trenches, would eliminate the remaining barriers and stereotypes.

Like Max Weber, the philosopher Hermann Cohen, the most prominent German-Jewish thinker, felt pride in living to see Germany's heroic hour. In his essay *Deutschtum und Judentum* (Germanness and Jewishness; 1915), he expressed his conviction of the validity of a cultural German-Jewish symbiosis. In times of war it was, according to Cohen, the special task of German Jews to spread the supremacy of German culture among their coreligionists in other European countries. Once they recognized the specific affinity between Jewish ethics and German philosophy, even the Jews of France and England, Russia and the United States would conceive of Germany as "their spiritual motherland." With less emphasis on the spirituality of the war, the nationalist German-Jewish poet Ernst Lissauer turned his energies to the composition of war songs, such as his infamous "Haßgesang gegen England" (Hymn of hate against England; 1915). The support of the war was not restricted to Jewish liberals and German nationalists, but included most Orthodox and Zionists as well. Just as Social Democrats submitted themselves to the emperor's call for weapons, German Zionists, too, left no doubt that they would do their duty as German soldiers. A group of Zionists even returned from Palestine to fight for their German fatherland.

Indeed, World War I brought forth a decisive change in the development of German-Jewish relations, but it was not the change German Jews had envisioned.

Instead of resulting in the social acceptance of the Jews, the war led to their brutal disillusionment. Many German Jews recalled the anti-Semitism in the trenches as a lasting war experience. For some, this experience led directly to Zionism. Those who were already Zionists and had initially welcomed the war, like the writer Arnold Zweig, expressed increasing doubts about their commitment to a German state that had made its Jewish soldiers subject to a specific census, the so-called Jew-count, in 1916. Most significantly, liberal Jews like the writer Georg Hermann had their belief in successful assimilation shattered. In a moving essay, the author of *Jettchen Gebert* (1906)—the enormously popular novel about an assimilated Berlin Jewish family—confessed that his lifelong identification with Germanness had been an illusion. "Whether we want it or not," Hermann wrote a year after the war, "we had to rediscover our Judaism. . . . We experienced a great disappointment with the Germans and we continue to do so" (Hermann 1919, 400). With similar frustration, Ernst Toller adapted his own war experience for his drama *Die Wandlung* (The transfiguration; 1919), in which the assimilated Jew Friedrich remains the "alien" for his non-Jewish comrades, even after winning the Iron Cross.

The initial war enthusiasm of German Jews and their gradual disillusionment is best illustrated in the annual retrospectives of the yearbook of the Union of the Associations for Jewish History and Literature (*Jahrbuch für jüdische Geschichte und Literatur*), which had been founded in 1893 as a central agency to spread Jewish knowledge and literature among acculturated German Jews. In 1915, the author of the retrospective, Martin Philippson (1915, 11–12), spoke of "the liberalizing and elevating effect of the war," referring specifically to the equal standing granted to Jewish army chaplains. One year later, Philippson noted proudly that for the first time Jews had become officers in the Prussian army. Thus, "in general, the Kaiser's word that there are no longer differences between parties and religions, has materialized" (2–3). In 1917, Philippson's successor as the author of the annual retrospective, Ismar Elbogen, expressed the first signs of disappoint-

ment; among the "ugly phenomena caused by the long duration of the war," Elbogen perceived a revival of anti-Semitism and a shattering of the "community of the trenches." The author of the postwar retrospective, Isidor Landau, no longer hid his disillusionment; after the "Jews' census" not much had remained from the great expectations set in motion by the war. And for the immediate postwar period, Landau had even harsher words; for German Jews confronting a dimension of anti-Semitism, it was "the most cursed, detestable of all times, damned as no other year from time immemorial" (Landau 1920, 3–5).

German Jews had entered the war with high hopes of gaining recognition as integral parts of the German *Volksgemeinschaft*. Even the toll of 12,000 Jewish lives in the battlefield, however, was not sufficient to create the "community of the trenches" envisioned by Isidor Landau. Instead, the war experience strengthened the ties of many acculturated German Jews with the Jewish community. Only a few weeks after the outbreak of the war, Martin Buber anticipated the strengthening of *Gemeinschaft* (communal solidarity) among German Jews in a speech later printed as the opening essay in his journal *Der Jude*: "In the tempest of events the Jew has had the powerful experience of what *Gemeinschaft* means. . . . It was not the most essential weakness of the Western Jew that he was 'assimilated,' but that he was atomized; that he was without connection [to the Jewish community]; that his heart no longer beat as one with a living *Gemeinschaft* . . . ; that he was excluded from the life of the people and their holy *Gemeinschaft*. Judaism was no longer rooted, and the uprooted roots [*Luftwurzeln*] of his assimilation were without nourishing force. Now, however, in the catastrophic events which he experienced with his neighbors, the Jew discovered with shock and joy the great life of *Gemeinschaft*. And [this discovery] captured him" (Buber 1916–17, 1–2).

One of the major characteristics of the new sense of Gemeinschaft was the gradual detachment of German-Jewish thinkers from the optimistic belief in human reason and progress. Nonrational concepts such as messianism, mysticism, and divine revelation, which had been widely removed from Jewish theology in the nineteenth century, now reentered the works of such different thinkers as Franz Rosenzweig, Leo Baeck, and Isaac Breuer.

The "cleansing" of nonrational elements from Judaism in the course of the nineteenth century had found its clearest expression in the posthumously published work of Hermann Cohen, *Die Religion der Vernunft aus den Quellen des Judentums* (The religion of reason out of the sources of Judaism; 1919). The neo-Kantian philosopher of Marburg, who in his last years taught at the Liberal rabbinical seminary in Berlin, represented a position that had been established by the first generations of *Wissenschaft des Judentums* scholars. In their view, the emphasis on religious concepts originating beyond human reason constituted an aberration from the rational course of Jewish history and the rational essence of Judaism.

In contrast to Cohen, the most original German-Jewish philosopher of the younger generation, Franz Rosenzweig, a former student of the historian Friedrich Meinecke, deviated considerably from traditional Wissenschaft des Judentums and historicism during the war years. In the three sections of his *Stern der Erlösung* (Star of redemption; 1921), begun in the trenches of the Balkan front, he stressed the subjectivity of truth at which the individual can arrive only by his own personal experience, analyzed the continuous relationship between man and God on the basis of revelation, and juxtaposed the temporality of "the nations" with the messianic temporality of the Jews. *The Star of Redemption* was perhaps the most profound and innovative approach to Jewish philosophy during its time, but as Rosenzweig himself acknowledged, it was hardly read and little known among contemporaries.

The emerging leader of Liberal Judaism in Germany, Rabbi Leo Baeck, signaled the changing spirit of Liberal German Judaism in his second edition (1922) of *Das Wesen des Judentums* (The essence of Judaism), which was originally published in 1905 as a reply to Adolf von Harnack's *The Essence of Christianity*. Whereas in the prewar edition Baeck basically adopted the rational framework of Cohen's philosophy, the second edition bore significant modifications. Although

he never entirely refuted his rationalist outlook, his revised version emphasized those religious forces that remained beyond human reason. Baeck's prototype in Jewish philosophy was not the rationalist Maimonides, who was celebrated by Baeck's predecessors, but the nonrational Yehuda Halevi. Baeck's publications after World War I concentrated increasingly on topics of Jewish mysticism. When he wrote an obituary for the Orthodox Frankfurt rabbi Anton Nehemias Nobel, Baeck lauded first and foremost Nobel's reintegration of mystical elements into the rationalized nineteenth-century version of Judaism.

The apocalyptic vision of the war, so drastically illustrated in the art of the German-Jewish Expressionist Ludwig Meidner, also led to the development of a modern Jewish messianism by radical thinkers such as Walter Benjamin and Ernst Bloch. Although they rejected the violence of the war, they shared the notion of witnessing a "constructive destruction" that would ultimately lead to the foundation of a new and just order.

Among the Orthodox voices, a more conservative concept of Jewish messianism gained new strength. Typical of such an approach was Isaac Breuer, descendant of the leaders of Frankfurt neo-Orthodoxy and himself a spokesman for the secessionist Orthodox Jewish communities. Although Breuer was never able to realize his early student dream and become a professional writer, his publications are more numerous than those of any other representative of Orthodox German Jewry in his generation. They include political pamphlets, religious polemics, novels, children's literature, and an autobiography. His book *Messiasspuren* (Traces of the Messiah; 1918) interpreted the previously unknown dimension of a universal war as the birth pangs of the Messianic Age—the war between the two mythical powers Gog and Magog. (A few years later Martin Buber began his Hasidic novel *Gog und Magog,* which was translated into English as *For the Sake of Heaven.*) "A messianic breeze fans mild air to the burning pains of humankind," wrote Breuer (1918, 12–13), "Elijah, the annunciator of the Messiah, sends his messenger." In order to advance the advent of the Messiah, Breuer proposed the foundation of a Jewish state, to be governed by the traditional laws of Jewish religion.

In his postwar novels, *Ein Kampf um Gott* (A struggle for God; 1920) and *Falk Nefts Heimkehr* (The return of Falk Neft; 1923), Breuer combined harsh criticism of German Orthodoxy with genuine praise for the Eastern European Jewish world. The deeper cause for the alienation from Judaism among young German Jews in those novels is the superficial Orthodoxy practiced by their fathers. When, in the end, those young Jews find their way back to tradition, it is only with the help of Eastern European Jews.

The wartime encounter with Eastern European Jewry was perhaps the most decisive moment in the strengthening of Gemeinschaft among German Jews; it reached far beyond the Orthodox segment. When in 1925 Alfred Döblin wrote that on a visit to Poland he met there for the first time Jews, he only reiterated what many German-Jewish soldiers had experienced a decade earlier: the conviction that "genuine" Judaism was to be found only in the East.

The result of this encounter was a massive glorification of Eastern European Jewish life in war and travel accounts. The most vivid descriptions of Jewish life in Eastern Europe as seen by German-Jewish soldiers were Arnold Zweig's *Das ostjüdische Antlitz* (The Eastern Jewish countenance; 1919) and Samy Gronemann's *Hawdoloh und Zapfenstreich* (Havdalah and Taps; 1924). Zweig's best-selling novel *Der Streit um den Sergeanten Grischa* (The case of Sergeant Grischa; 1927) was a late reflection of his experiences on the Eastern Front. Both Zweig and Gronemann belonged to the same administrative unit of the German army, the Bezirk Oberost in Lithuanian Kovno, as did the artist Hermann Struck, who illustrated *The Eastern Jewish Countenance*. Whereas Zweig's style was full of pathos, and his character studies evoke the world of Eastern European Jews with such sentimentality that they are often reduced to caricatures, Gronemann, a former editor of the satirical Zionist journal *Shlemiel,* composed a humorous book full of anecdotes and epigrams about his activities as a Yiddish interpreter for the German army in Russia. In spite of their different literary styles, the two

accounts shared the same essential message: only in the East could one find "Jewish Jews," while in the West Jews had become "non-Jewish."

Zweig and Gronemann used almost the same words to express the contrast between Western and Eastern Jews. According to Zweig, "The Jew in the West was on his way to a torpid denomination, a feeble, desperate piety, . . . which threatened to decline daily and crumble away gradually. . . . The old Jew of the East, however, preserved his face" (Zweig and Struck 1920, 14). For Gronemann, the son of an Orthodox German rabbi, even Orthodox Jews in Germany practiced nothing more than "a stiff *Ersatzjudentum,"* whereas Eastern European Jews "lived their peculiar life, just as Germans or Englishmen." Gronemann, who regularly attended Orthodox services in Germany, came to the conclusion: "Since I have gotten to know the synagogue of the East, I have been disgusted with the temple of the West and its service. This relates to many Orthodox synagogues as well as to Liberal ones—seen from the perspective of a Lithuanian prayer house, there is only a minimal difference between the two" (Gronemann 1984, 60).

Unlike Arnold Zweig, Stefan Zweig (Arnold's Austrian namesake) was no Zionist and not active in organized Jewish affairs. He, too, however, was deeply affected by the wartime encounter with Eastern European Jewry. As he wrote later in his autobiographical account, *The World of Yesterday* (1943), it was a journey to Galicia that determined his decision to write a biblical drama during World War I. "In choosing a biblical theme," Zweig concluded, "I had unknowingly touched upon something that had remained unused in me up to that time: that community [*Gemeinschaft*] with the Jewish destiny whether in my blood or darkly founded in tradition." The result was the publication of the pacifist drama *Jeremias* (Jeremiah; 1917), which Thomas Mann called "the most significant poetic fruit of this war," and which Zweig himself regarded as "the first of all my works that mean something to me" (1943, 253). Widely read by the general public and staged by Jewish youth groups in the Weimar Republic, its effect on postwar German-Jewish culture was matched only by one other biblical play of a different Viennese-Jewish writer, Richard Beer-Hofmann. His *Jaákobs Traum* (Jacob's dream; 1918), performed simultaneously at the Vienna Burgtheater and the Berlin Deutsches Theater in 1919, led the highly acculturated editor of the *Weltbühne,* Siegfried Jacobsohn, to exclaim: "I am enough of a Jew to perceive 'Jacob's Dream' as a national poem and to admit that I was totally spellbound by it. . . . Especially in our time I welcome a kind of literature for which one has to be a Jew in order to understand it and sympathize with it" (Jacobsohn 1919, 641). The influence of those two German-Jewish plays reached far beyond Central Europe. In the 1920s they constituted the basis for a biblical repertoire of the newly founded Hebrew theaters: *Jeremias* for the Ohel Hebrew theater company of Tel Aviv, and *Jaákobs Traum* for the better-known Moscow-based Habimah troupe.

Those German Jews who did not go East had the opportunity to meet Ostjuden in Germany. Between 1916 and 1920, 70,000 Eastern European Jews moved to Germany as industrial workers or small merchants and artisans, and they brought with them their own Jewish culture. The immigration of Eastern European Jews radically transformed the face of Germany's Jewish community. Non-German citizens constituted about a quarter of Berlin's Jewish community and formed the majority in other communities, especially in Saxony. In many communities the Ostjuden, who were still deeply rooted in Jewish traditions, contributed decisively to a renaissance of Jewish culture. At the same time the encounter with Eastern European Jews served as the main stimulus for overcoming the internal divisions among German Jews. All major trends within German Jewry interpreted the encounter profoundly, but each did so differently. For Liberal Jews, the Yiddish-speaking Ostjuden represented a cultural outpost of Germanness; for Zionists they embodied authentic Judaism; and for the small segment of Orthodox German Jews, Eastern European Jewry served as the main source of religious inspiration. Although the *Burgfrieden* (civic truce) declared by the emperor proved short-lived for Jews just as for other segments of German society, a more lasting Burgfrieden was

reached within the German-Jewish community, with Eastern European Jews functioning as a bridge between the various streams.

The first phase of such a development dates back to well before the war years. The title of the journal *Ost und West* (East and West), which began to appear in 1901, gives evidence of the new importance Eastern European culture had gained among German Jews at the turn of the century. When on the eve of World War I the writer Fritz Mordechai Kaufmann founded a "Pan-Jewish Magazine" (*Die Freistatt;* 1913), its main purpose was the promotion of Eastern European culture. Transcriptions of Yiddish texts and translations of Hebrew sources occupied an important place in the journal. In his programmatic outline, Kaufmann defined his journal as a vehicle for overcoming the divisions among the various factions separating German Jewry. To reach this aim, he invited representatives of all religious and political streams, but especially "outsiders and heretics," to contribute.

Although the *Freistatt* never lived up to Kaufmann's hope of becoming a pan-Jewish journal (it folded after only two years), two journals, established in 1916, proved more successful. The most significant was Martin Buber's monthly, *Der Jude,* which was originally conceived in 1904 but realized twelve years later. During the eight years of its existence, *Der Jude* emerged as the major intellectual forum of modern German-speaking Jewry. To get an impression of its quality, one need only look at the second volume that appeared in 1917, where Franz Kafka published for the first time two of his animal stories ("Jackals and Arabs" and "A Report for an Academy"), the writer Arnold Zweig contributed "from the battlefield" on Jewish and European issues, the anarchist Gustav Landauer reflected on Strindberg and Shakespeare, and the leader of Socialist revisionism, Eduard Bernstein, described "How I Grew up as a Jew in the Diaspora." Buber, who a decade earlier had introduced the Ostjude as a literary figure to German-Jewish readers, endeavored to present the "real life" of Eastern European Jews in his journal by publishing statistics and accounts of contemporary political developments in Eastern Europe.

Der Jude was clearly Zionist-oriented, but as the above list shows it was open to all Jewish intellectuals. Like Kaufmann, Buber's main concern was to overcome the deep divisions that separated the various streams of German Jewry. In the preface of the first issue of *Der Jude* in 1916, Buber uttered his conviction that "our time . . . is the beginning of a genuine concentration and unification" for German Jewry. By providing German Jewry with a first-rate intellectual platform, *Der Jude* was to further this process. It was not the only journal founded in World War I with such high ambitions.

Almost synchronously with *Der Jude,* the twice-monthly *Neue Jüdische Monatshefte* (New Jewish monthly) began to appear in October 1916. It was also dedicated to the creation of a united German-Jewish Gemeinschaft. This aim was not only explicitly expressed in its subtitle (*"Ein offener Sprechsaal für jedermann"* [An open auditorium for everyone]), it also became clear from its list of editors. The *Neue Jüdische Monatshefte* was the only German-Jewish journal edited jointly by leading Liberal Jews and Zionists. Its five editors were the Liberal philosopher Hermann Cohen; the chairman of the Central-Verein, Eugen Fuchs; the moderate Zionists Adolf Friedemann and Franz Oppenheimer; and the translator of Hebrew and Yiddish literature Alexander Eliasberg.

Such an unprecedented collaboration was possible only because of the specific situation of the war. In 1916, the major German-Jewish organizations formed a common framework for the first time by creating the Komitee für den Osten (KfdO). This organization (enlarged to the Vereinigung jüdischer Organisationen Deutschlands—VIOD—in 1918), which aimed both at assisting Eastern European Jews suffering the miseries of war and at furthering specific German war interests in the East, published the *Neue Jüdische Monatshefte*. It was only natural, then, that Eastern European Jews were the dominant topic during the five years of the journal's existence. More than a third of its articles (122 out of a total of 347) were devoted to cultural, historical, or political issues of Eastern European Jewry. But the journal also became a central vehicle for the promotion of German-Jewish culture. Thus

Franz Rosenzweig's open letter to Hermann Cohen, which would later lead to the establishment of the Akademie für die Wissenschaft des Judentums, was published by the *Neue Jüdische Monatshefte* in 1917.

The *Neue Jüdische Monatshefte* was also a forum for prominent acculturated Jews who usually would not publish in a Jewish journal. Among them were four Jewish members of the Reichstag. Apart from the liberal Ludwig Haas, they were all Socialists analyzing the new situation for the Jews in Europe during and after the war. Most remarkable was the contribution by the grand old man of German Social Democracy, Eduard Bernstein. On the basis of their unique situation of dispersion and their participation in every European army, this pacifist called on the Jews to become mediators among the nations and thus put an end to the war. Although they were preoccupied with different questions, those three Jewish Social Democrats shared the same message. Analyzing the rise of anti-Semitism in the East, the task of Jews as mediators in wartime, and the significance of Zionism, they agreed that even acculturated Germans could no longer deny the existence of a Jewish nation. The question dividing Liberal Jews and Zionists was whether German Jews formed part of such a Jewish nation, or if this nation was only composed of Jews from Eastern Europe.

In 1919, when Zionists wanted to convene a Jewish congress as a nationwide assembly demonstrating the unity of German Jews, the Liberals refused to participate after protracted negotiations. Thus, the old divisions began to reappear after the war. The KfdO and the VIOD dissolved, and the *Neue Jüdische Monatshefte* had to suspend publication due to the inflation in 1920. The personal losses were no less significant. Hermann Cohen died in 1918, and Gustav Landauer, who had contributed to Buber's journal *Der Jude* and opened the Jüdisches Volksheim (the most important meeting place for Eastern European Jews and German-Jewish intellectuals) in Berlin, was killed as one of the leaders of the short-lived Bavarian Soviet Republic.

The Burgfrieden within the German-Jewish community did not survive the war, but it had decisively changed the community's face. During the war years German Jews for the first time formed a nationwide organization representing their common interests. Two journals of high intellectual standard created a new basis for a broad discourse on Jewish culture. The war experience and the postwar disorders reminded German Jews that anti-Semitism was not confined to the past, and the immigration wave during and after the war had transformed the social and demographic complexion of the Jewish communities.

Those changes left a clear mark upon German-speaking Jewish writers in the Weimar years. Only against the backdrop of the war and its aftermath is it possible to understand why their Jewish origins began to play an increasing role both in their works and in their lives during the 1920s. In Imperial Germany many of these writers had been able to ignore their specific situation as Jewish writers in Germany; in Weimar, they had to come to terms with their dual identities. The classic expression of this often painful process was Jakob Wassermann's *Mein Weg als Deutscher und Jude* (My life as a German and a Jew; 1921). Less known, but no less representative for many highly acculturated German Jews, was the return to Judaism by the widely read novelist and biographer Emil Ludwig, who had been baptized in 1902.

The ambiguous path of German Jewry became conspicuously manifest at the turning points of German history. As in 1871, the year 1918 both furthered the integration of Jews into German society and made them conscious of their distinctiveness. As Jews rose to the ranks of ministers and officers, anti-Semitic agitators experienced unprecedented success. But unlike 1871, this time the forces separating German Jews from the larger German society proved stronger than the simultaneous integrative tendencies. Thus Martin Buber's prophecy of 1916 had fulfilled itself by the early days of Weimar: "From all the letters I received from the front, from all talks with those who returned home, I got the same impression—one of a general strengthening of ties with Judaism. . . . Some will defect from Judaism. . . . But those who remain true to Judaism will be attached to it more strongly than before: more seriously, more actively, more responsibly" (Buber 1916–17, 1–3).

Bibliography

Steven Aschheim, *Brothers and Strangers: The East European Jew in German and German Jewish Consciousness, 1800–1923* (Madison: University of Wisconsin Press, 1982); Michael Brenner, *The Renaissance of Jewish Culture in Weimar Germany* (New Haven: Yale University Press, 1996); Isaac Breuer, *Messiasspuren* (Frankfurt a. M.: Hammon, 1918); Martin Buber, *Gog und Magog, eine Chronik* (Heidelberg: L. Schneide, 1949); Buber, "Die Losung," *Der Jude* 1 (1916–17): 1–3; Ismar Elbogen, "Rückblick auf das Jahr 1916," *Jahrbuch für jüdische Geschichte und Literatur* 20 (1917): 1–16; Samy Gronemann, *Hawdoloh und Zapfenstreich: Erinnerungen an die ostjüdische Etappe* (Königstein: Jüdischer Verlag, 1984); Georg Hermann, "Zur Frage der Westjuden," *Neue Jüdische Monatshefte* 3 (1919): 400; S. J. [Siegfried Jacobsohn], "Bibel-Ersatz," *Die Weltbühne* 15 (1919): 639–41; Isidor Landau, "Rückblick auf das Jahr 1919," *Jahrbuch für jüdische Geschichte und Literatur* 23 (1920): 1–13; Werner E. Mosse and Arnold Paucker, eds., *Deutsches Judentum in Krieg und Revolution* (Tübingen: J. C. B. Mohr, 1971); Martin Philippson, "Rückblick auf das Jahr 1914," *Jahrbuch für jüdische Geschichte und Literatur* 18 (1915): 1–14; Philippson, "Rückblick auf das Jahr 1915," *Jahrbuch für jüdische Geschichte und Literatur* 19 (1916): 1–17; Ernst Simon, *Brücken: Gesammelte Aufsätze* (Heidelberg: Lambert Schneider, 1965); Egmont Zechlin, *Die deutsche Politik und die Juden im ersten Weltkrieg* (Göttingen: Vandenhoeck & Ruprecht, 1969; Arnold Zweig and Hermann Struck, *Das ostjüdische Antlitz* (Berlin: Welt, 1920); and Stefan Zweig, *The World of Yesterday* (New York: Viking, 1943).

MICHAEL   BRENNER

1918 This year of the dissolution of the Austro-Hungarian Empire marks a crucial historical and symbolic change for Joseph Roth

For Joseph Roth (1894–1939), one of the outstanding Jewish writers of fiction to emerge from the Austro-Hungarian Empire, the year 1918, which saw the empire's dissolution, had a historical and, moreover, a mythic significance. The empire provided its Jewish citizens with a focus of loyalty that enabled them to sidestep the increasingly bitter nationalist conflicts of the empire's last decades. Its disappearance obliged them to accept the precarious status of citizens of such successor states as Czechoslovakia, Poland, Hungary, and "German Austria." Though born in the town of Brody in the remote province of Galicia, a few miles from the Russian frontier, Roth was enabled by a legal loophole to become an Austrian citizen in 1921 (Timms 1994). But his imaginative allegiance was to the vanished Austro-Hungarian Empire, to whose last years he gave a compelling mythic form in his novel *Radetzkymarsch* (Radetzky march; 1932), and to the poor Jews of Galicia, whose piety he celebrated in *Hiob: Roman eines einfachen Mannes* (Job: Novel of a simple man; 1930).

Myth and history stand at opposite ends of Roth's imagination. He loved to romanticize his life, and he claimed to have been brought up in a poor community of Eastern Jews, to be of mixed Russian and Austrian descent, and to have spent World War I as a Habsburg officer and as a Russian prisoner of war. His biographer David Bronsen has uncovered a more prosaic reality. Roth's mother, abandoned by her husband (who subsequently went mad and vanished into obscurity) before the boy's birth, brought him up in modest comfort and in virtual isolation from the rest of Brody. After studying German literature at Vienna University, Roth volunteered for the army in 1916 and was assigned to the information service. This started him on the journalistic career that he pursued with great distinction in postwar Germany. Between 1923 and 1929 he worked for the outstanding liberal paper the *Frankfurter Zeitung,* which sent him to France, Russia, Poland, and Albania. Later years were overshadowed by the insanity of his wife, Friederike ("Friedl") Reichler, by exile from Nazi Germany, and by alcoholism and depression. Yet his many friends acknowledge not only the storytelling gift that made him a successful novelist, but, perhaps paradoxically, his deep truthfulness and talent for precise and honest observation. To understand how Roth could be both a maker of myths and an observer of history, we must look first at his copious journalism, which is now at last available in a virtually complete edition, and then turn to the novels that shape history into myth and, at their deepest, explore its metaphysical and religious implications.

Though Roth published extensively in Socialist papers like *Der Neue Tag* (The new day) in Berlin (1919–20) and the SDP's Berlin *Vorwärts* (Forward; 1922–24), his Socialism seems to have been emotional, not ideological (Westermann 1987, 108; cf.

Schweikert 1974)—an expression of the sympathy for the poor that is a keynote of his writings. He conducted interviews with such "street types" as an eighty-year-old Jewish beggar and a blind violinist; a Hungarian refugee whom, with 50,000 fellow victims, the well-off demonize as "the peril from the East"; and homeless immigrants from Russia who take shelter in a Berlin hostel. He seldom wrote about workers except to deplore their lack of cultural ambitions. He opposed profiteering, nationalism, and, at this stage, monarchism. Visiting Schönbrunn Palace, which is today open to the public, in 1919, he showed no emotion on seeing the simple iron bedstead on which the old emperor died. His amusing reports from Burgenland, the western Hungarian province assigned to Austria by the Treaty of Saint-Germain, were skeptical about German national feeling.

The brilliance of Roth's early journalism can be illustrated from the sequence *Berliner Bilderbuch* (Berlin picture-book), which was published in Leipzig in 1924 in *Der Drache* (The dragon), a satirical magazine. The densely written opening piece juxtaposes an incident in which a drunken Berliner beat up an Indian woman (thinking, Roth surmises, that she was a Jew); a six-day bicycle race where spectators particularly enjoy the cyclists' accidental collisions; and the pompous ineffectuality of the Reichstag. Motifs of violence, greed, and drinking unify the piece. A verbal counterpart to a Grosz caricature, it rivaled the journalism of Heine, Kraus, or Tucholsky.

The sequence continues with prescient reports on the machinations of the far Right, whom Roth expects to be governing Germany "tomorrow or the day after." He notes that the police cooperate with their rallies and that the *Protocols of the Elders of Zion* have become their "Aryan Bible." He explains the appearance of the far Right as a multiplication equation: "German politics $\times$ German schooling $\times$ petty-bourgeois world-view." He both mocks and acknowledges their mythic appeal by reporting that "Attila's castle has been burnt down" in a fire on the set of Fritz Lang's *Die Nibelungen,* a film intended to manifest the German spirit. After a fine parody of nationalist cli-

chés, he evokes the real social issues that nationalism tries to obscure: poverty illustrated by the death of a match seller; class bias in the administration of justice; and the hypocrisy that makes prostitutes and unmarried mothers the scapegoats for social evils. On a positive note, he visits the house, now a museum, of the recently assassinated Rathenau, where the sight of a hymnbook alongside a Jewish law-code, the *Schulchan Aruch,* inspires the ecumenical conclusion: "He was indeed a wise man of Zion, Walther Rathenau. He belonged to that small group of the wise of Zion whose president was called Jesus Christ."

These articles already show the sympathy with the poor and downtrodden so characteristic of Roth's writing. He usually identifies poor people by name, obliging the reader to see them as individuals. Describing the higher classes, however, he moves from the individual to the type. Reporting in 1922 on the trial of Rathenau's assassins, he shows a keen eye for details, like the monocles and patronizing voices of the defense lawyers or the clichés uttered by the defendant Ernst von Salomon, features that identify these people as typical members of right-wing social groups. This interest in the type will underlie Roth's practice as a novelist.

The development of Roth's political outlook and of his sympathy with the poor can be illustrated by two later outstanding journalistic works: *Reise in Rußland* (Journey in Russia; 1926) and *Juden auf Wanderschaft* (Jews on their wanderings; 1927). He spent August to December 1926 in the Soviet Union, visiting Moscow, Leningrad, the Ukraine, and the Caucasus, and reported on his impressions in the *Frankfurter Zeitung* (Turner 1991). These reports are an exceptionally balanced and judicious picture of the USSR's most promising phase, when the New Economic Policy (NEP) allowed limited private enterprise, Stalin was not yet supreme, and forced industrialization and the collectivization of agriculture were still over the horizon. Roth finds much to praise: the welfare state, the equal treatment of Jews, the autonomy granted to nationalities (though he fears this may promote a narrow nationalism), and the education of the peasants. But he discusses also the drawbacks of these measures. Through education, the USSR was trying to create an informed public opinion, but it had only reached the stage where everyone mouthed slogans. Rejecting most of European culture as "bourgeois" and its own religion and literature as "reactionary," it, according to Roth, had been left with a belief in progress, technology, and statistics that could be described as "American." In his view, the "new sexual morality" reduced love to hygienic, emotionless coupling. In addition, in opposing religion with naively materialistic arguments, the USSR replaced the average Russian's primitive religiosity with a no less primitive atheism (Roth had no Rilkean belief in the devout Russian peasant). It was creating a new bourgeoisie, Roth believed, whose worst representatives were the unscrupulous NEP-man and the careerist petty bureaucrat. Besides offering an acute analysis, Roth developed during this period a critique of a soulless modernity that is located in America as well as in Russia.

If *Reise in Rußland* looks skeptically at modernity's beneficiaries, *Juden auf Wanderschaft* turns to its victims. Roth set out to correct many stereotypical views of Eastern Jews held in the West, where they were often denigrated as unproductive traders, celebrated as miracle-working rabbis, or demonized as a mass of immigrants threatening to invade and subvert Western society. Roth, by contrast, emphasized their hard work, their piety, their poverty, and the deep conservatism of their proletariat. Far from idealizing their life, he stressed its narrowness, dirt, poverty, and beggary; represented Orthodox Judaism as the worship of a punitive and pleasure-hating deity; and—in a phrase even more shocking than he intended—calls the shtetel a "concentration camp." Yet he also commended Eastern Jews for upholding "true and warm tradition." Purporting to describe a typical shtetel, he based his account on Brody, which in fact had an unusually high proportion of Jews in its population. This description heightened the contrast with the tour Roth then undertook through the Jewish quarters of Vienna, Berlin, and Paris, where he evoked the Jews' continual struggle with bureaucracy and their efforts to earn a living as peddlers or traveling salesmen. He also reported how the Jew who left for America could end up languishing in quarantine.

Juden auf Wanderschaft is plainly filled with ambivalence, indeed contradictions. Roth's commitment to truthful, understated description conflicts in this work with a schematic opposition between the shallowly materialistic West with its "deadly, hygienic boredom" and the traditional East with its suffering, its human greatness, and "the dirt that everywhere accompanies suffering." He saw three ways in which Jews could escape from poverty and anti-Semitism. They could assimilate to Western civilization and turn their religious services into a feeble imitation of Protestantism; they could become absorbed into the new society of the USSR; or as Zionists they could adopt modern nationalism at the cost of perpetual warfare with the Arabs. All three courses meant different kinds of surrender to a modernity that Roth was increasingly disposed to reject.

This rejection of modernity is enacted in Roth's novels, which fall into three groups. His novels of the 1920s, all readable though uneven, evoked modernity as experienced by discharged soldiers ("Heimkehrer") whose stable pasts vanished in 1918. Then came the two novels that are acknowledged as Roth's major achievements, *Hiob* and *Radetzkymarsch,* in which Roth goes back before 1918 to conduct ambivalent explorations of the supposedly intact worlds of Eastern Jewry and the Habsburg Empire. Last comes the fiction of Roth's "Catholicizing" phase, inaugurated by his strange polemic *Der Antichrist* (1934).

Roth's characters are usually types rather than individuals. His early novels have unremarkable heroes whose function is merely to observe or exemplify postwar anomie and the inexplicable injustice of the world. Their very names—Theodor Lohse, Gabriel Dan, Andreas Pum, Franz Tunda, and Friedrich Kargan—are colorless, without obvious national or lexical associations. Characters in his late fiction often came close to allegorical personification, especially the satanic figure of Jenö Lakatos. Increasingly during his writing career, he also reintroduced characters in successive novels. Kapturak, who smuggles deserters across the Russian border, appears frequently, and the Trotta and Chojnicki families from *Radetzkymarsch* also figure in *Die Kapuzinergruft* (The imperial vault; 1938). But although in Balzac or Trollope recurring characters may suggest a solidly real world, in Roth their reappearances make his fictional world seem more obviously an artificial construction (especially because he sometimes forgot important details, such as when Mendel Singer from *Hiob* reappears in *Das falsche Gewicht* (The false weight; 1937) with a different profession, wife, and family. Roth's simple, understated style is rare and welcome in modern German fiction. In the 1920s he was often associated with the Neue Sachlichkeit, or New Sobriety, but in 1930 he criticized this movement's overestimation of documentary data, arguing that these needed to be transmuted into art. Though he maintained that only a speaker of Yiddish could write good German, he owed much to the French of Flaubert and Stendhal (Bronsen 1974, 122, 274–75). His descriptions were formulaic: thus the Galician landscape is constantly evoked by the croaking of frogs and chirping of crickets. When he described people, physical features consistently acquire symbolic values: thus in *Radetzkymarsch,* especially, the beard worn by the emperor, the *Bezirkshauptmann,* and elderly Jews came to symbolize traditional loyalty—whereas representatives of modernity were clean-shaven (Timms 1990).

From *Das Spinnennetz* (The spider's web; 1923) to *Rechts und Links* (Right and Left; 1929), Roth focused on ex-soldiers who had lost the hierarchy and discipline of the army and were adrift in an unstructured, unstable, and cynical world. These characters illustrated for Roth the dictum of Nikolai Brandeis (in *Rechts und Links*) that "people do not develop, but change their natures." Thus Paul Bernheim is made successively a playboy, a pacifist, a soldier, and a businessman, while his brother Theodor moves from membership of illegal right-wing organizations to working as a journalist on a Jewish-owned liberal paper. Franz Tunda in *Die Flucht ohne Ende* (The flight without end; 1927) moves from Siberian imprisonment through revolutionary Russia and the sham culture of Western Europe and returns, disillusioned, to Siberia. Inevitably, politics are

prominent: *Das Spinnennetz* is set in the proto-Nazi underworld, whereas *Hotel Savoy* (1924) reveals Roth's Socialist sympathies by depicting a brush factory whose workers generally die of tuberculosis at the age of fifty because hygiene regulations are ignored and where a strike contributes to the novel's catastrophe. As another example, *Der stumme Prophet* (The dumb prophet; 1929) focuses on a humane Bolshevik who is eventually exiled by "Savelli" (Stalin). Roth, however, is not interested in political analysis, but rather in depicting postwar disorientation and exploring its human and, increasingly, its metaphysical implications (Amann 1990). The latter make a first, rather callow appearance in *Die Rebellion* (1924). Here the disabled ex-soldier Andreas Pum is described with kindly irony that modulates into pathos when a callous bourgeois, by denouncing cripples as "impostors," provokes Pum into a violent rage that leads to his imprisonment and premature death. Pum's rebellion, however, described in an unfortunate caricature of the Last Judgment, is not only against an unjust society but against God.

The most successful of these novels are *Hotel Savoy* and *Zipper und sein Vater* (Zipper and his father; 1928). In the former, the "Heimkehrer" Gabriel Dan breaks off his journey in Lodz, amidst Jewish poverty and urban squalor, and visits wealthy Jewish relatives whose son, the playboy Alexander, embodies a late stage in Western decadence. Metaphysical overtones are far subtler than in *Die Rebellion* (Wunberg 1991). The American millionaire Henry Bloomfield returns annually to Lodz to visit the grave of his father, Jechiel Blumenfeld, and his coming is awaited by the populace with almost messianic eagerness. The hotel itself is a symbol almost as multivalent as Kafka's castle. With the poor crowded into its upper stories while the rich live in comfort below, the hotel symbolizes an unjust, hierarchical society. Its mysterious, unseen owner Kaleguropulos finally proves to be identical with the lift-attendant Ignatz, who perishes when the hotel is burned down amid revolutionary chaos. Like the emperor in Kafka's *The Great Wall of China,* he suggests both a discredited ruling class and a God whose authority has vanished.

Zipper und sein Vater is Roth's first exploration of family relationships. In Zipper senior, an unsuccessful small businessman and autodidact who invests extravagant hopes in his sons, Roth portrays a rounded, seriocomic character who "had something of the sad clown about him." His son Arnold, gifted, sensitive, and weak, undergoes a painfully thorough education that proves useless in the postwar world. Disappointing his parents' expectations, he works as a minor civil servant and then abandons his job to become the hopelessly devoted husband of a self-willed actress (based, apparently, on Elisabeth Bergner) who refuses to consummate their marriage; discarded by her, Arnold makes a living as a clown. In the narrator's eyes, Arnold becomes a replica of his father except that, whereas the old man is happy in his obtuseness, Arnold has enough self-knowledge to realize that he is an absurd failure.

In *Hiob* it is a father, nor a son, who occupies center stage. The world of the Eastern Jews is contrasted with the modernity of New York, to which the main character emigrates, and the very title proclaims a theodicy—an inquiry into God's governance of the world. The new Job is a simple, devout Talmud teacher called Mendel Singer, whose misfortunes begin when his youngest son, Menuchim, turns out to be an imbecile. A Hasidic *tsaddik* prophesies that Menuchim will be cured and become a wise and good man. In the meantime, however, Mendel becomes estranged from his wife; his elder sons fight on opposite sides in World War I, and one is declared missing and the other is killed; Mendel's wife Deborah dies of grief; and their daughter, Mirjam, becomes promiscuous and subsequently insane. Overwhelmed, Mendel blasphemes against God and rejects the facile consolations that his friends offer in conscious imitation of Job's comforters. But the story ends with an apparent miracle: a famous conductor who visits New York turns out to be Menuchim, cured by Russian doctors, so that the tsaddik's prophecy is fulfilled.

This ending has divided Roth's readers: his friend Ludwig Marcuse thought it an unconvincing parallel to the story of Job (Bronsen 1974, 386); it has been taken as expressing a flight into fairy tale motivated by Roth's skepticism about

secular change (Magris 1974, 113; Hüppauf 1985); and his biographer defends it as "a mystery-play in Eastern European Jewish guise" (Bronsen 1974, 387). Although the story owes much to nineteenth-century models of ghetto fiction (Robertson 1991), Jewish tradition is woven into its texture (Shaked 1986; Horch 1991). The key position of the tsaddik indicates how much the novel owes to Hasidism and its stress on humankind's childlike trust in God's love. When Mendel crosses the ocean, we are reminded that God's terrifying plaything Leviathan, described in chapter 41 of the Book of Job, lurks in its depths. And Menuchim first reappears as a guest at Passover, hinting (less ironically than Bloomfield in *Hotel Savoy*) at the coming of the Messiah.

Because Roth's next novel, *Radetzkymarsch*, is often regarded as the supreme expression of the Habsburg myth (Magris 1966), it is important to stress the novel's emotional complexity. In the persons of the emperor and the *Bezirkshauptmann* (local administrator) who is his near-double, it celebrates a dogged, conscientious devotion to tradition; but the emperor knows that the empire is doomed to disintegrate into national states and feels fatalistically that this cannot be averted. Furthermore, the novel conveys deep doubt about whether the empire was worth saving. After all, the heroism of the Bezirkshauptmann's father, who saved the emperor's life at the battle of Solferino, was falsified by the history books so that he left the army in disgust; and the army in which the Bezirkshauptmann's son Carl Joseph von Trotta serves is pervaded by malice, debauchery, and national enmities. The real Austria seems present only when the band plays the Radetzky March on Sunday afternoons.

The novel's intense sadness comes from the interweaving of imperial decline with a narrative of personal failure. Carl Joseph is a mediocrity who gets through military school only because of his family connections. His upbringing, and indeed the whole Habsburg order, displays a rigid discipline amounting to paralysis. Only at rare, and correspondingly moving, moments do father and son manage to break through their emotional armor-plating and exchange tight-lipped words conveying affection. These momentary breakthroughs prepare us for the Bezirkshauptmann's success in penetrating court protocol and obtaining an audience with the emperor in order to have his son relieved from debt and dishonor; their meeting has faint overtones of divine grace.

Carl Joseph's life is overshadowed by bitterness and death. He is brought up without a mother; his sexual relationships are with older women, the first of whom dies during childbirth; his only friend in the regiment, the Jewish Dr. Demant, is killed in a duel; he has to shoot at factory workers who are demonstrating against exploitation; and the debts he incurs are mostly those of a fellow officer who commits suicide. In 1914, he buries a priest and two peasants who have been hanged as supposed spies, then is himself killed when fetching water for his troops under fire. The Bezirkshauptmann dies in 1916, on the day of the emperor's burial.

During his years in exile, from 1933 on, Roth described himself as a monarchist, a Catholic, and a reactionary. "I believe in a Catholic Empire, German and Roman in character," he told Stefan Zweig in a letter of July 24, 1935, "and I am close to becoming an orthodox, perhaps even a militant Catholic." Like Franz Werfel, another Austrian Jew attracted by Catholicism, Roth stopped short of conversion; and his zeal for the restoration of the Habsburgs struck even them as unrealistic. Horrified by the Third Reich, which he called "an outpost of hell on earth," he resorted at times to an unbalanced denunciation of modernity. His polemic *Der Antichrist* surveys the modern world, using a parabolic style in which, for example, a newspaper editor is "the lord of a thousand tongues"; it blames the Antichrist for perverting humankind's divine gift of reason into technical progress and impious pride; and, strangely, it finds the worst aspect of modernity in the cinema, etymologizing Hollywood as "Hölle-Wut" (hell-rage). Its literary counterpart is *Die Kapuzinergruft,* one of Roth's weakest novels, in which the last of the Trottas vents his spleen self-pityingly on the postwar world, abstract art, lesbians, Hungarians, and other pet hates of Roth's; the hero's wife naturally ends up in Hollywood. These works embarrassingly recall the polemics against modernity and the nostalgia for feudal hierarchy

common within the political Right in the interwar years (Marchand 1974). Roth's nostalgia sometimes resembles the confusion of social with theological issues in Hofmannsthal's *Das Salzburger große Welttheater* (The Salzburger great theater of the world; 1922).

In Roth's later fiction, however, politics are less important than religion, and we find a fascinating mingling of Jewish and Christian motifs (Steinmann 1984). *Tarabas* (1934) evokes the millennial suffering of the Jews but centers on a Russian soldier who assaults a pious Jew, makes him drop his Torah rolls in the mud, and tears out part of his beard, for which offense Tarabas does penance by becoming a beggar (he eventually dies in a monastery). Golubtschik in *Beichte eines Mörders* (A murderer's confession; 1936) succumbs to the devilish promptings of Jenö Lakatos and becomes a spy for the Russian secret police; as an illegitimate son of a prince, he is motivated partly by resentment against his lowly social position, and his main targets are the prince's legitimate son, whom he tries but fails to murder, and a selfless Jewish revolutionary whom he betrays.

More elaborate is *Die Geschichte von der 1002. Nacht* (The tale of the 1,002d night; 1939). Its humorous orientalizing framework provides the fairy-tale element that is increasingly prominent in Roth's late work. The Shah of Persia, on a state visit to Vienna, causes consternation by demanding the sexual services of a noblewoman; the situation is saved by Baron Taittinger, who substitutes a look-alike, the prostitute Mizzi Schinagl by whom he has had an illegitimate son. This act of procurement leads to Taittinger's downfall: the embarrassed authorities send him to a provincial garrison where he takes to drink and squanders his limited resources. His misfortunes, however, produce the beginnings of spiritual growth. Previously Taittinger was an empty-headed man about town, like Schnitzler's Anatol, who classified people merely as "charming," "indifferent," or "boring." Roth tells us matter-of-factly that his passions are imaginary, that his heart is atrophied, and that he loves only himself. Visiting Mizzi in prison he feels pity for the first time. But no transformation occurs: Taittinger is compelled to leave the army, falls among rogues (whose petty vileness is described with a calm acerbity unusual in Roth and more reminiscent of Horváth or Canetti), and commits suicide. Yet he is treated forgivingly by the narrator: at the beginning and end of the story he is "poor Taittinger."

Roth's late masterpiece is *Das falsche Gewicht,* a discreet parable about the relations between law and love. It concerns a Habsburg official of Jewish descent, Anselm Eibenschütz, who becomes an inspector of weights and measures in a Galician frontier town. When his wife has an illegitimate child by his clerk, Eibenschütz displays a harsh justice by banishing her lover and ignoring her and the child; meanwhile he himself is tempted by the gypsy Euphemia Nikitsch, who appears to him as the embodiment of sin. As Eibenschütz sinks into drunkenness and self-loathing, he masks his own unhappiness by applying the law with inhuman rigor. Finally he is murdered by Euphemia's long-term companion, the Jewish innkeeper, and in his dying moments he imagines himself being judged mercifully by his divine counterpart, the "Great Inspector." This ending is a far superior reworking of Andreas Pum's death in *Die Rebellion.*

Two late novellas, *Die Legende vom heiligen Trinker* (The legend of the holy drinker; 1939) and *Der Leviathan* (1940), also deserve special mention. The former adopts the genre of the saint's legend, used already by Kleist and Keller with a similar unstable, humorous, teasing irony. Roth's sympathy for the poor attains perhaps its finest expression in this story of a Polish tramp in Paris for whom the gift of two hundred francs by a generous Christian initiates a series of improbable strokes of good fortune: the tramp is reawakened from drunken oblivion to moral awareness, convinced of divine grace, and enabled to make a good death (Pikulik 1989). Its companion piece concerns an upright Jewish dealer in coral necklaces who becomes obsessed with the sea, the domain of Leviathan, from which the coral comes. Tempted again by Jenö Lakatos, the personification of corrupt modernity, he mixes fake beads with genuine ones; but he loses his customers, takes to drink, and sets out for Canada but is drowned on the way—or, as the narrator puts it, finds his true home on the ocean bed: "May he rest in peace there alongside Leviathan until the coming of the Messiah."

In these two stories especially, Roth blends realism with allegory, affectionate irony with deep respect for his characters, to produce a voice unique in German-Jewish literature, though not wholly unlike the kindly but searching irony of Kafka's last story, *Josefine the Singer or the Mouse Folk.* Like *Josefine,* they too turn on the acceptance of death; and their tone of grave playfulness contrasts strangely with the profound sadness that, as we have seen, dominates Roth's fiction.

Bibliography

Klaus Amann, "Die 'Verlorene Generation' in Joseph Roths frühen Romanen," *Literatur und Kritik* 247–48 (Sept.–Oct. 1990): 325–34; David Bronsen, *Joseph Roth: Eine Biographie* (Cologne: Kiepenheuer & Witsch, 1974); Fritz Hackert, *Kulturpessimismus und Erzählform: Studien zu Joseph Roths Leben und Werk* (Bern: Herbert Lang, 1967); Hans Otto Horch, "Zeitroman, Legende, Palimpsest: Zu Joseph Roths 'Hiob'-Roman im Kontext deutsch-jüdischer Literaturgeschichte," *Germanisch-Romanische Monatsschrift,* n.s., 39 (1989): 210–26; Bernd Hüppauf, "Joseph Roth: 'Hiob.' Der Mythos des Skeptikers," *Im Zeichen Hiobs: Jüdische Schriftsteller und deutsche Literatur im 20. Jahrhundert,* ed. Gunter E. Grimm and Hans-Peter Bayerdörfer (Königstein/ Taunus: Athenäum, 1985), 309–25; Claudio Magris, *Der habsburgische Mythos in der österreichischen Literatur,* trans. Madeleine von Pasztory (Salzburg: Müller, 1966), Magris, *Weit von wo: Verlorene Welt des Ostjudentums,* trans. Jutta Prasse (Vienna: Europaverlag, 1974); Wolf R. Marchand, *Joseph Roth und völkisch-nationalistische Wertbegriffe: Untersuchungen zur politisch-weltanschaulichen Entwicklung Roths und ihrer Auswirkung auf sein Werk* (Bonn: Bouvier, 1974); Lothar Pikulik, "Joseph Roths Traum von Wiedergeburt und Tod: Über die 'Legende vom heiligen Trinker,'" *Euphorion* 83 (1989): 214–25; Ritchie Robertson, "Roth's 'Hiob' and the Traditions of Ghetto Fiction," *Co-Existent Contradictions: Joseph Roth in Retrospect,* ed. Helen Chambers (Riverside, Calif.: Ariadne Press, 1991), 185–200; Joseph Roth, *Briefe, 1911–1939,* ed. Hermann Kesten (Cologne: Kiepenheuer & Witsch, 1970); Roth, *Das falsche Gewicht* (Amsterdam: Querido, 1937); Roth, *Werke,* ed. Klaus Westermann and Fritz Hackert, 6 vols. (Cologne: Kiepenheuer & Witsch, 1989–91); Hartmut Scheible, *Joseph Roth:*

Mit einem Essay über Gustave Flaubert (Stuttgart: Kohlhammer, 1971); Uwe Schweikert, "'Der rote Joseph': Politik und Feuilleton beim frühen Joseph Roth," *Joseph Roth,* ed. Heinz Ludwig Arnold (Munich: Text & Kritik, 1974), 40–55; Gershon Shaked, "Kulturangst und die Sehnsucht nach dem Tode: Joseph Roths *Der Leviathan*—die intertextuelle Mythisierung der Kleinstadtgeschichte," *Joseph Roth. Interpretation-Kritik-Rezeption,* ed. Michael Kessler and Fritz Hackert (Tübingen: Stauffenberg, 1990), 279–98; Shaked, "Wie jüdisch ist ein jüdisch-deutscher Roman? Über Joseph Roths *Hiob, Roman eines einfachen Mannes,*" *Juden in der deutschen Literatur,* ed. Stéphane Moses and Albrecht Schöne (Frankfurt a. M.: Suhrkamp, 1986), 281–92; Esther Steinmann, *Von der Würde des Unscheinbaren: Sinnerfahrung bei Joseph Roth* (Tübingen: Niemeyer, 1984); Edward Timms, "Citizenship and 'Heimatrecht' after the Treaty of Saint-Germain," *Austrian Studies* 5 (1994): 158–68; Timms, "Doppeladler und Backenbart: Zur Symbolik der österreichisch-jüdischen Symbiose bei Joseph Roth," *Literatur und Kritik* 247–48 (Sept.–Oct. 1990): 318–24; David Turner, "'Überwältigt, hungrig, fortwährend schauend': Joseph Roth's Journey to Russia in 1926," *Co-Existent Contradictions: Joseph Roth in Retrospect,* ed. Helen Chambers (Riverside, Calif.: Ariadne Press, 1991), 52–77; Klaus Westermann, *Joseph Roth, Journalist: Eine Karriere, 1915–1939* (Bonn: Bouvier, 1987); and Gotthart Wunberg, "Joseph Roths Roman *Hotel Savoy* im Kontext der Zwanziger Jahre," *Joseph Roth. Interpretation—Kritik—Rezeption,* ed. Michael Kessler and Fritz Hackert (Tübingen: Stauffenberg, 1990), 449–62.

RITCHIE ROBERTSON

1918   German-speaking Jewish writers visit the Soviet Union and encounter and report on Eastern Jewry in light of Lenin's decree abolishing anti-Semitism

Through the Bolshevistic experiment Russia had become for all thinking persons the most fascinating country of the postwar period, enthusiastically admired and at the same time fanatically hated without having any exact knowledge. Nobody knew for sure what was happening there—thanks to the propaganda and an equally rabid anti-propaganda. But it was well known that something completely new was being tried, something that could be decisive for the future state of our world either in a good or in an evil sense.

These lines of Stefan Zweig (1955, 299–300), an Austrian-Jewish author who described himself as "deeply" detesting "the political and dogmatic," shed light on the background of the enormous travel boom among Jews and non-Jews alike set off by the Russian Revolution. For Jewish intellectuals in Germany and Austria, the young Soviet Union, together with Palestine, became the most preferred travel destination in the 1920s and 1930s. Included among those who visited the country of the October Revolution—either through their own initiative or on assignment from a newspaper or an institution—were the already mentioned Stefan Zweig, Arthur Holitscher, Walter Benjamin, Egon Erwin Kisch, Ernst Toller, Friedrich Wolf, Otto Heller, Alfons Goldschmidt, Ismar Freund, Arthur Ruppin, Berta Lask, Emil Gumbel, Bertha Pappenheim, and Joseph Roth.

After 1918 about 3.5 million Jews were living in the Soviet Union. Until the revolution, the living conditions for them were more miserable than anywhere else in the world. Emancipation had not taken place, and under the czars anti-Semitism had been so strong that Russia had earned the dubious title of the "world center of anti-Semitism." After the revolution, Jews were formally liberated and granted equal rights. In 1918, Lenin signed decree 158, stating: "The Council of the People's Deputies orders all councils of the worker's deputations to extinguish the anti-Semitic movement with all means. People who organize pogroms or propagate them, are outside the law." Thus the Russian Revolution was of historical significance for the Jewish population. It is therefore surprising that among the intellectuals traveling to the Soviet Union who commented on the living conditions of the Jewish population, one finds many non-Jews, such as Dorothy Thompson, Alexander Wicksteed, Lili Körber, Panait Istrati, and Theodor Seibert, but very few Jews. In most cases these were visitors who had an interest in Jewish affairs for very specific professional reasons—such as Arthur Ruppin, the founder of the sociology of Jewry; Ismar Freund, a coworker of the Jewish Community in Berlin; or Bertha Pappenheim, an active Jewish social worker. In contrast, one finds almost no mention of the political, economic, and social conditions of the Jews either in the publications of Ernst Toller, Arthur Goldschmidt, Friedrich Wolf, and Arthur Holitscher or in the travel reports of Egon Erwin Kisch and Walter Benjamin (whose friends would all become victims of the Stalinist anti-Semitism). Though these authors might have had different and specific reasons for their silence, their shared origins and left-wing political interests suggest similar and thus comparable motives. There is one subject Toller, Goldschmidt, Wolf, and Holitscher did write on: the Jewish theater in Russia. But why did they keep silent on the social-political, economic, and religious conditions of Eastern Jewry?

It seems unlikely that these authors had remained untouched by their Jewish heritage. Willingly or unwillingly all of them grappled with being Jewish. All of them were contemporaries of the pervasive discussion about the *Ostjudenfrage* (Eastern Jewish Question), which had arisen with the immigration of around 85,000 Eastern Jews to Germany during and after the war. Not only the situation of the Eastern Jews who had moved to the West, but also the living conditions of those who stayed in the Soviet Union, were of high interest to the German-Jewish press. On the one hand, the liberation of the Jews was welcomed; on the other hand, it was feared that this recognition was likely to add fuel to the widespread fear of Jewish-Bolshevist world domination. Therefore, the bourgeois Jewish press emphasized the Jewish opposition to Communism. Though it declared its solidarity with the Russian Jews, it nevertheless feared that growing economic difficulties in Russia would induce a mass emigration to Germany. Thus an amelioration of the plight of Soviet Jewry living in the Soviet Union was in their own interest. The Jewish travelers were not only likely to be aware of the German-Jewish public's interest in the developments in the Soviet Union, but were at the same time observers, if not victims, of the growing anti-Semitism in Germany.

Yet other than their Jewish descent there were few if any links at all between them and the Russian Jews. Whereas German Jews were mostly assimilated and more or less prosperous, the majority of Russian Jewry was orthodox and poor. A high percentage earned their living as traders and entrepreneurs, a social structure that the *Jüdische Lexikon* described with noticeable distance and caution as "peculiar." Taking the historical significance of the revolution for the Russian Jewry into account, as well as the importance given to this subject by the German-Jewish press, it may be assumed that Jewish travelers from Germany who didn't write on the situation of their Eastern "brothers and sisters" more or less consciously pursued a complex strategy of avoidance by omitting the subject. There are various possible reasons for this strategy. Apart from the stated social and religious differences, the political situation in Germany must also be considered. One of the most pervasive anti-Semitic stereotypes in Germany depicted Jews as "unproductive elements" and as revolutionaries. Descriptions of Russian Jewry ran the danger of reinforcing these stereotypes and thus also the hatred against Jews in Central Europe, who were often identified with Eastern Jews. Avoiding the topic was therefore a way to protect oneself and the Jewish population in Germany from possible anti-Semitic attacks.

Most of the Jewish travelers to the Soviet Union were politically oriented toward the Left. From the orthodox Marxist perspective, the plight of the Jewish population presented itself as a mere socioeconomic problem that would be solved through the implementation of Socialist policies. Thus a description of the social and political situation of Russian Jewry separate from the general situation would not have been in accordance with Marxist views. On the other hand, German-Jewish travelers could have easily used the granting of equal rights and the official prosecution of anti-Semitism as arguments in favor of Socialism. But only Friedrich Wolf (1967) made use, in "Mit eigenen Augen in dem Sowjetunion," of this opportunity when he briefly recalled the pogroms under the czars.

Even though travelers like Toller, Goldschmidt, Wolf, and Holitscher had no ties to Judaism as a religion, they might have understood "Judentum" as something more than what Marxism declared it to be. Thus they were likely to have been disturbed by the persecution of the Jewish (and non-Jewish) faith. This attitude is revealed in reactions to Otto Heller's highly controversial book *Der Untergang des Judentums* (1931), in which he describes the situation of the Jews in the Soviet Union from a Marxist perspective. Sympathetic with Socialism but outraged and obviously disappointed by the developments in the country of the October Revolution, Eva Reichmann-Jungmann (1932) wrote in a review in *Der Morgen:* "Now, when for the first time in any place in the world the attempt is being made to realize Socialism, when out of this center new power currents merge into the social movements of the world, . . . at this point, the socialistic attempt turns against the Jewish culture." Though she does not explain her understanding of Jewish culture, it is evident that it does include the Jewish religion.

Reichmann-Jungmann's statement reveals the dilemma of the German-Jewish intellectuals of the Left. On the one hand, they hoped the Soviet experiment would be successful; on the other hand, they were shocked to see how the implementation of Socialism, with its anti-religious policies, was likely to destroy what had been fundamental to Jews in Russia. In addition, the economic and social conditions of the Eastern Jews after the revolution reveal a remarkable discrepancy between the revolution's intention to ameliorate the situation of the Jewish population and the reality of poor living conditions and limited political rights. Though the government had granted equal rights to the Jews, the prohibition of private commerce in 1920 had a tremendous negative effect: over a third of the Jewish population not only lost its economic base, but also became part of the déclassé who were not allowed to vote.

Viewed in this context, the silence of the Western Jewish intellectuals about the social, political, and religious situation of Russian Jewry becomes understandable as an attempt to avoid confrontation with the realities of Socialism, which created an asymmetrical experience for the Soviet Jews: all previous restrictions were lifted, but at the same time they had to suffer severe economic and political disadvantages and were hindered in practicing their religion. In writing on the Jewish theater, Toller, Goldschmidt, Wolf, and Holitscher had found a politically less sensitive topic and at the same time a "bridge" between West and East, as they, like many Jewish intellectuals in Germany, defined Judaism in cultural terms.

In their silence, the publications of the German-Jewish intellectuals are just as articulate as those written by Jewish writers who *did* address the subject, like the Austrian Joseph Roth, himself an Eastern Jew. In a series of articles based on travels in 1926 he proves to be rather critical of the overall development in the Soviet Union. In his eyes, the revolution had, in large part, already failed because of its bourgeois tendencies and bureaucratization. But in his article entitled "Die Lage der Juden in der Sowjetrußland" (The situation of the Jews in the Soviet Union; in Roth 1990) Roth praised Soviet policies toward the Jews: "The history of the Jews knows of no other example of such a sudden and complete liberation. . . . *Today,* the Soviet Union is the only country in Europe which despises anti-Semitism, even though it has not yet ceased completely. . . . In the new Russia anti-Semitism remains a disgrace. Public disgrace will kill it." Here Roth touches on a topic that in Germany is highly controversial. Whereas the journalist L. Wolff agreed with Roth's judgment, Georg Popoff and Karl Kautsky, as well as Panait Istrati and Dorothy Thompson, estimated the danger of anti-Semitism to be much higher. It is hard to tell who came closer to reality. Looking at Roth's statement, it is remarkable that he gives a rather simple explanation for the decline of the hatred against Jews. Further, it is worth mentioning that he leaves out the anti-Semitic resentments against those who profited from the New Economic Policies (NEP)—which Toller, Thompson, and Wolff had observed—although he is very critical of the NEP-men. The NEP abolished the prohibition of small trade, a change that had hit the Jewish population particularly hard.

Seen within the context of czarist anti-Semitism, Roth's optimistic view of the development of hatred against the Jews seems understandable. But a further observation gives one reason to pause. Roth does mention the closing down of synagogues, but he obviously tries to conceal the consequences of these measures, as well as the discrimination against Zionists and the lack of voting rights for a high percentage of Jews. Although Roth then doubts that the Jews can be made into a national minority like any other and although he gives a comprehensive explanation for the failure of Russian "nationality politics" vis-à-vis the Jews, he ultimately refers to the success of the Russian case as a starting point: "If the Jewish Question is solved in Russia, it is halfway solved in all countries" (Roth 1990). He does not, however, ask the decisive question of whether the conditions in Russia could be applied to other countries. The probable answer would have been no.

Following his own prophecy about the successful resolution of the Jewish Question, Roth notes: "The faith of the masses is decreasing rapidly, the stronger religious barriers are coming down, and the weaker national [barriers] are a bad replacement. If this development continues, the age of Zionism, the age of anti-Semitism—and maybe even the age of Jewry—will be over" (Roth 1990).

Otto Heller, who traveled to the Soviet Union in 1930, also foresees the decline of Judaism in his book, *Untergang des Judentums,* but for different reasons. Departing from the thesis that Jewry is only the ideological superstructure of a commercial caste, he concludes that Russian Jews will merge with the general population through their successful integration into agriculture. The impressions collected during his journey confirm this concept. Repeatedly, he points to the lack of knowledge of young Jews concerning religious questions and emphasizes that the inhabitants of a village he visited were "real farmers. If they had not spoken Jewish [sic], one would not have suspected that they were Jews." This satisfaction corresponds to his criticism of "the small remains of Jewish *Ghettogelehrsamkeit* [ghetto erudition]," which creates in young Jewish colonists the desire to study agronomy. Heller's book displays so much enthusiasm for the disappearance of Jews, Judaism, and Jewishness that one gets the impression that the author's fascination for Communism results from his desire to deny his Jewishness, which he perceives as stigmatizing.

Although Roth does not appear as euphoric as Heller, he declares that one could either welcome or regret the integration of the Jews into the Russian population, "but everyone must respectfully observe how one people is liberated

from the shame of suffering and another from the shame of mistreating" (Roth 1990). Roth thereby affirms the assimilation he had criticized so heavily in the earlier chapters of his essay *Juden auf Wanderschaft* (1927), of which his report on the situation of the Jews in the Soviet Union forms a part. The prophecy that anti-Semitism would disappear with the integration of the Jews into the general population contradicts the experience of German-speaking Jews: in the West, assimilation did not, as Roth knew, in fact lead to the overcoming of anti-Semitism. His rather uncritical analysis of the situation of Soviet Jews could lead one to suspect his article as a piece of propaganda. But his critique of the Russian Revolution in other articles and Walter Benjamin's judgment of this critique remove this suspicion. Benjamin wrote in his *Moskauer Tagebuch* about an encounter with Roth: "In a conversation . . . I quickly urged him to show his true colors. What turned up can be described in a word: he came to Russia as an (almost) convinced Bolshevist and is leaving it as a royalist." Even if this pointed formulation exaggerates the influence of the Soviet experience on Roth's political development, it clearly grasps the poles of his political positions.

The reasons for the uncritical image Roth depicts of the situation of Russian Jewry are twofold. Whereas anti-Semitism is condemned in the Soviet Union, "in the West," he states, "it has become a 'science,' the thirst for blood a political 'Gesinnung' [ideology]." In light of growing hatred against the Jews in Germany, Roth's positive picture of Soviet policies toward Jews is to be read as a criticism of the de facto sanctioning of anti-Semitism in the Weimar Republic and as a utopian model for Germany.

The second motif in Roth's positive picture of the state of Russian Jewry, as well as the surprising coolness with which he confronted the dissolution of Russian Jewry, are seen in his turning to the Catholic faith, which is revealed in his travel book *Die weißen Städte* (in Roth 1990), written the year before he traveled to the Soviet Union. The Jewish community regarded the movement toward the Christian religion as a threat and criticized converted Jews as traitors. By predicting the dissolution of the entire Jewish community,

Roth preempted such an accusation. If there were no more Jews left, there would also be no one to betray. In his coverage of Russian Jewry, this author tries to grasp a facet of Soviet reality that many of his colleagues ignored. But his article reveals more about himself than about the living conditions of Eastern Jewry. Ultimately, even if Roth did write about Jews, he also pursued a strategy of avoidance, albeit for different reasons than those authors who circumvented the topic altogether.

Bibliography

Walter Benjamin, *Moskauer Tagebuch,* ed. Gary Smith (Frankfurt a. M.: Suhrkamp, 1980); Alfons Goldschmidt, "Das jüdische Theater in Moskau," *Das Moskauer jüdische akademische Theater* (Berlin: Buchvertrieb W. Stolle, 1928), 17–21; Otto Heller, *Der Untergang des Judentums: Die Judenfrage / Ihre Kritik / Ihre Lösung durch den Sozialismus* (Vienna: Verlag für Literatur und Politik, 1931), Arthur Holitscher, *Drei Monate in Sowjetrußland* (Berlin: S. Fischer Verlag, 1921); Holitscher, *Stromab die Hungerwolga* (Berlin: Vereinigung internationaler Verlagsanstalten, 1922), Holitscher, *Das Theater im revolutionären Rußland* (Berlin: Volksbühne Verlag und Vertriebs-GmbH, 1924), 31–32; Panait Istrati, *La Russie nue* (Paris: Rieder, 1929); *Die Judenpogrome in Russland,* ed. the commission appointed by the Zionist fund to investigate the pogroms (Leipzig: Jüdischer Verlag, 1909); Hans-Wolfgang Kaiser, *Palästina: Erez Israel. Deutschsprachige Reisebeschreibungen jüdischer Autoren von der Jahrhundertwende bis zum Zweiten Weltkrieg* (Hildesheim: Olms, 1992); Egon Erwin Kisch, *Zaren, Popen, Bolschewiken* (Berlin: Reiss, 1927); Kisch, *Asien, gründlich verändert* (Berlin: Reiss, 1932); Lili Körber, *Eine Frau erlebt den roten Alltag* (Berlin: Rowohlt, 1932); Trude Maurer, *Die Ostjuden in Deutschland, 1918–1933* (Hamburg: Christian, 1986); Berta Pappenheim, "Bemerkungen zur Arbeit des Agrojoint in einigen jüdischen Kolonien Sowjetrußlands," *Der Morgen* 4 (1918): 189–94; Eva Reichmann-Jungmann, "'Der Untergang des Judentums,'" *Der Morgen* 7 (1932): 64–72; Joseph Roth, *Werke,* ed. Klaus Westermann, vol. 2: *Das journalistische Werk, 1924–1928* (Kiepenheuer und Witsch: Köln, 1990); Arthur Ruppin, *Die jüdische landwirtschaftliche Kolonisation in Rußland* (Berlin: Jüdischer Verlag, 1918); Theodor Seibert, *Das rote Rußland* (Munich: Knorr & Hirth, 1931), 41–47; Dorothy Thompson, *The New Russia* (New York: Holt, 1928); Ernst Toller, "Gruß an das Jiddische Staatstheater," *Das Moskauer jüdische akademische Theater* (Berlin: Buchvertrieb W. Stolle, 1928), 7–8; Toller, *Quer durch: Reisebilder und Reden* (Berlin: Kiepenheuer, 1930); Alexander Wicksteed, *Ten Years in Soviet Moscow* (London: John Lane, 1932), 166; Friedrich Wolf, *Werke in sechzehn Bänden,* ed. Else Wolf and Walter Pollatschek, vol. 15 (Berlin: Aufbau Verlag, 1967), 193–95; and Stefan Zweig, *Die Welt von Gestern: Erinnerungen eines Europäers* (Frankfurt a. M.: S. Fischer Verlag, 1955).

KATHARINA L. OCHSE

1919 The Bavarian Soviet is proclaimed, in a Socialist attempt to fuse cultural and political liberation

The year 1919 is an extraordinary date in Germany history. It brought the democratic revolution of 1918 abruptly to a close and opened the door for what would in 1933 become the Nazi seizure of power. It is a year cloaked in myths of personal martyrdom and political betrayal. Too often forgotten, however, is the paranoia that gripped Germany during 1919. Inspired both by the bitter reality of defeat on the battlefield and the radical specter of Bolshevism, this paranoia produced a subtle shift in the common understanding of anti-Semitism and the fears motivating the anti-Semite. Indeed, 1919 was the year in which the preoccupation of the right-wing press with the "Jewification" (*Verjudung*) of German society made way for the vision of a "Jewish-Bolshevik conspiracy" (Traverso 1992, 48).

The *Protocols of the Elders of Zion,* which had been forged in Russia, had already made its appearance in Europe during the Dreyfus Affair about twenty years earlier. Anti-Semites also continued to bemoan the Jews' alleged dominance in certain professions, including banking. Reference was still made to Adolf Bartels, the noted nineteenth-century philologist, and his list of eight hundred Jewish writers who were supposedly displacing German writers from their culture (Pachter 1982, 262). But the war and subsequent revolutions transformed older concerns. The Jews were now not merely considered profiteers, the worst sorts of capitalists, but also traitors working against the national interests of Germany and conspiring with the international Communist revolution. This change in the anti-Semitic world view made it possible to speak of Weimar democracy as a "Jew republic."

Was this new order not the product of defeat on the battlefield, dominated by moneylenders, led by Socialists, and willing to accept the provisions of the humiliating Treaty of Versailles? The November Revolution of 1918 had begun with the abdication of the Kaiser and the returning troops, who were disgruntled, without hope for the future, and whose plight was so well described by Erich Maria Remarque in novels like *The Road Back* and *Three Comrades*. A power vacuum arose with the fall of the monarchy and the German Social Democratic Party (SPD), which was filled under the leadership of the prowar "majority" faction led by Friedrich Ebert, Philipp Scheidemann, and Gustav Noske.

Accompanying the rise to power of the SPD came strikes and mass disturbances, of which the uprising initiated by a group of sailors in Kiel was the first. The aristocracy and bourgeoisie feared for their status and their property, and the military and bureaucracy felt betrayed by the defeat; meanwhile, peasants and the petty bourgeoisie embraced what soon enough became the legend of the "stab in the back" perpetrated by Jews and Communists on the home front. The situation was perilous, and the possibilities of civil war were real.

Social Democracy had always held forth the promise of a republic, but it was now in a terrible position (Rosenberg 1961, 5ff.). The SPD could either compromise with the antidemocratic and reactionary classes of the Wilhelmine monarchy and introduce a "republic without republicans" or risk civil war and possible invasion at the hands of the victorious allies by taking a more radical course. This course would involve purging the military and state bureaucracy, liquidating the estates of the reactionary aristocracy in the East, and dealing with an insistent minority of the proletariat seeking a genuinely "socialist" republic based on the spontaneously erupting "workers' councils" (*Räte*) or "soviets," if not the more authoritarian tenets of Bolshevik theory. The Social Democrats chose the less dangerous option and turned on the Left, whose most important proponents wished to chart a more radical, if somewhat inchoate, course.

None of this meant much to the far Right. Its ideological attachment to xenophobia, militarism, authoritarianism, and anti-Semitism created the philosophical context in which Jews could appear as the root of the problem: the Jews' lack of principle and national roots made it possible for them to dominate the liberal bourgeoisie, Social Democracy, and international Communism as well. To the Right, the Jews were thus at once capitalists and "reds," and the right-wingers saw no contradiction in their claims that the Jews were controlling the "Jew Republic" and behind the revolutionary uprisings to bring it down.

Rosa Luxemburg was clearly the dominant figure among the Jewish revolutionaries. Born in 1871 in the city of Zamosc, Poland, to a middle-class Jewish family, Luxemburg became a revolutionary while still in high school. Hunted by the police, she fled to Zurich before entering a marriage of convenience in order to enter Germany and work with the jewel in the crown of international Social Democracy.

Various writers have emphasized the effect of Luxemburg's identity as both a Jew and a woman (Arendt 1973, 36ff.; Dunayevskaya 1981, 79ff.). She always hated bigotry of any sort and insisted on equality. Her thought grudgingly allowed for "national cultural autonomy" (Luxemburg 1976,

251ff., 303ff.), and she saw Social Democracy as the natural home for the oppressed. But the argument originally made in her dissertation, the *Industrial Development of Poland* (1894), with its critique of the nationalism embraced by leaders of Polish Social Democracy like the future dictator Josef Pilsudski, extends by implication to any form of particularism. Luxemburg consistently opposed any ideology capable of compromising proletarian unity, the struggle against imperialism, and what she considered the internationalist assumptions of Marxism.

Her principles were well known, but these early writings were not. Luxemburg's ascent in the world of international Social Democracy began with a contribution to what became known as "the revisionist debate" of 1898. Initiated by Eduard Bernstein with a set of articles, which were reworked into a book entitled *The Preconditions of Socialism,* orthodox Marxism was charged with ignoring the manner in which capitalism had stabilized and the fact that the "inevitable" proletarian revolution anticipated by Marx was no longer on the agenda. Thus, emphasizing that "the movement is everything and the goal is nothing," Bernstein called upon Social Democracy to surrender its "revolutionary phraseology" and foster a policy of compromise with non-proletarian classes to ensure economic reforms so that socialism might gradually "evolve."

Social Reform or Revolution (1899) was the finest contribution to the debate made by any critic of "revisionism," which included the most famous theoreticians of orthodox Marxism like Karl Kautsky and Georgii Plekhanov. In this pamphlet, Luxemburg explained how crisis was endemic to capitalism and expressed her fears that an unrestricted politics of class compromise might justify any choice by the party leadership and shift power to the trade unions. She also argued that there were limits to reform and that it could never transform the production process or eliminate the prospect of imperialism and political crisis. Without a political revolution, she argued, reforms granted under one set of conditions can be retracted under another. A simple emphasis on economic reforms would thus result only in a "labor of Sisyphus." Indeed, without an articulated Socialist "goal," she believed that the SPD would increasingly succumb to capitalist values and so surrender its sense of political purpose.

Just as Luxemburg rejected the idea of a democratic mass party run by experts and basically concerned with incremental reforms, her *Organizational Questions of Social Democracy* showed how she equally opposed the idea of a "vanguard" party based on blind obedience and dominated by revolutionary intellectuals. Lenin and Bernstein were, for her, flip sides of the same coin insofar as both sought to erect an "absolute dividing wall" between the leadership and the base. If Socialism was to transform workers from "dead machines" into the "free and independent directors" of society as a whole, she argued, then they must have the chance to learn and exercise their knowledge. Consequently, it only makes sense that the Russian Revolution of 1905 should have inspired what is arguably her finest theoretical work, *Mass Strike, Party, and Trade Unions* (1906). This pamphlet placed a new emphasis on the innovative talents of the masses in organizing society. It spoke of connecting economic with political concerns. It also articulated her organizational dialectic between party and base, which would gradually build the "self-administrative" capacities of workers by continually helping them develop new democratic institutions.

This radical democratic vision stayed with Rosa Luxemburg during World War I, which she spent in a tiny prison cell. There she wrote various responses to her critics, translated *The History of My Contemporary* of her beloved Korlenko, and—under the pseudonym Junius—produced the great anti-war pamphlet, *The Crisis in the German Social Democracy* (1916), which mercilessly assaulted the SPD for its willingness to support the Kaiser's war, its obsession with votes, its cowardice in the face of public opinion, and its betrayal of working-class interests.

Also written in jail were her beautiful letters to friends and lovers. They portrayed her diverse interests, her courage, and her deep sense of humanity. A small volume of the more personal letters was published in 1922 by Sonja Liebknecht—the wife of Luxemburg's fellow Social-ist martyr Karl Liebknecht—and another followed a year later edited by Luise Kautsky. Interestingly enough, these letters served a political purpose. Their publication was meant to build sympathy for the woman who was now castigated both by Social Democracy and by a Communist movement undergoing "bolshevization" and attempting to rid itself of what its former leader Ruth Fischer called "the syphilitic Luxemburg bacillus."

There was good reason why this increasingly authoritarian movement should have turned on the first president of the German Communist Party (KPD). In jail, while ill and with little information other than newspapers, Rosa Luxemburg wrote what was surely her most prophetic and intellectually daring work. *The Russian Revolution* (1918) exposed the compromises that would ultimately undermine the Soviet experiment. Opposed to Lenin's agrarian policy and continuing to reject the use of slogans implying the "right of national self-determination," her analysis is best known for its demand that the revolution produce an extension of both formal and substantive democracy, as well as the justly famous words: "Freedom only for the supporters of the government, only for the members of one party—however numerous they may be—is no freedom at all. Freedom is always and exclusively freedom for the one who thinks differently. . . . Its effectiveness vanishes when 'freedom' becomes a special privilege."

Paul Levi, her lawyer and successor as leader of the KPD, convinced Luxemburg not to publish the piece for fear of aiding the opposition. She reluctantly agreed. She may not have had the strength to refuse. Alfred Döblin described her in his lengthy novel, *Karl and Rosa,* as suffering a nervous breakdown in prison. Following her release in 1918, her hair had turned white and she had become frail and thin. Nevertheless, she extended her support to the Spartacus group—which would serve as the nucleus for the KPD—and publicly advocated the creation of soviets.

Despite their almost legendary stature, however, the Spartacists never received the support of a proletarian majority—and Rosa Luxemburg knew it. She warned against setting loose the

revolution in Germany and, after initially opposing the idea of a national assembly, ultimately
called for participating in the elections of the
nascent Weimar Republic. But she was outvoted.
The Spartacist Revolt broke out in 1919, and
Rosa Luxemburg decided to remain in contact
with the masses. Article after article in the bourgeois press called for her death, and even the Socialist *Vorwärts* printed the ditty: "Hundreds of
proletarian corpses all in a row—proletarians! /
Karl, Rosa, Radek and company / None on show,
none on show—proletarians!"

Luxemburg alone, if not for her untimely
death, might have been able to counteract—if
ever so briefly—the power of Lenin and the Bolsheviks on the international Left (Borkenau 1962,
148ff.). She also warned that a "military dictatorship" would soon supplant the Weimar Republic.
But the forces of order got their wish. Rosa Luxemburg and Karl Liebknecht were brutally murdered at the hands of proto-Nazi thugs employed
by the Socialist government of Ebert and Gustav
Noske, and the phony investigation into their
deaths caused a sensation. But the murderers of
Liebknecht and "bloody Rosa, the Jewish sow,"
got off easy. They served little jail time, and all
became heroes in the Third Reich.

An organized anti-Communist witch-hunt accompanied the birth of the Weimar Republic.
Bavaria, which sought to preserve its independence and which remained relatively free from
the influence of the Ebert-Noske government in
Berlin, witnessed uprisings like so many other
cities in Germany. The reformist politician Kurt
Eisner—a Kantian pacifist and longtime Socialist parliamentarian, a newspaper editor as well as
a writer of Socialist lyrics and fairy tales—wound
up leading a demonstration of 200,000 people
and then, in the aftermath of the monarch's flight
from Germany, heading a minority government
that introduced numerous progressive reforms.

Eisner was the first of the "five literati" who
would dominate the Munich events of 1918–19.
His assassination while on the way to hand in his
resignation, coupled with the emergence of the
short-lived Hungarian Soviet, generated the desire for a Bavarian soviet. Many on the international Left believed that a soviet in Bavaria would

have induced the Austrians to form one of their
own (Carsten 1972, 219). Thus, the summary
declaration of a Bavarian soviet on April 7, 1919,
made a certain degree of political sense even if the
material conditions for its success were lacking.

The Bavarian Soviet was initially ruled by independent Socialists like Ernst Toller, along with
a sprinkling of anarchists like Gustav Landauer
and Erich Mühsam in coalition with representatives of the SPD. But the independents were organizationally weak, and the majority Socialists
were increasingly disgraced by the actions of their
comrades in Berlin. And so, subsequently, this
regime found itself supplanted by a Communist
government whose most visible leader was Eugen
Leviné. Communist rule, however, lasted only
two weeks. It was displaced by a new "dictatorship of the natives" led by Toller and his friends,
which lasted only a few days before capitulating
to the forces of right-wing reaction.

The Bavarian Soviet never had a chance. Its
base in the working class ran up against the capitalist class, the petty bourgeoisie, and the peasantry. The new soviet was also a perfect target for
the "philistines." Munich was, after all, a center of
the Expressionist avant-garde before World War
I. Perhaps for this reason, especially at the beginning, the Bavarian "soviet" was strongly influenced by representatives of the literati. And these
intellectuals did not make the best politicians.
The Bavarian Soviet never produced leaders on a
par with Luxemburg, Liebknecht, or Levi. Its foreign minister, in fact, was a certifiable lunatic by
the name of Franz Lipp who—in all seriousness—decided to declare war on the pope. Nevertheless, for better or worse, the Bavarian Soviet
was unique in attempting to fuse cultural with
political liberation.

Its guiding spirit was undoubtedly Gustav
Landauer, who withdrew from active participation when the Communists took power. He was a
pacifist and an anarchist whose nobility and commitment were noted by everyone who knew him.
Born in 1870 in Karlsruhe, Landauer entered politics very young. "I was an anarchist," he liked to
say, "before I became a Socialist." And that was
true enough. Landauer may have joined the Social
Democratic movement and edited a journal

called *The Socialist* around 1900. But from the start, he had little use for the reformism of the SPD and quickly became a leading figure of an ultra-left faction known as "the young ones," which was summarily expelled in 1894.

Proudhon and Kropotkin would always play a far greater role in the thinking of Landauer than Marx. His anarchist vision was directed less toward the institutions of the economy and the state than toward the human condition. He became interested in the "life reform" movement, and by 1902, his work had already influenced those concerned with founding the journal *New Community*, to which a number of major Jewish intellectuals would contribute. Indeed, this also was around the time Landauer formed what would become a lasting friendship with Erich Mühsam.

Landauer was more than a political figure or a bohemian. He was also a noted historian of literature who wrote an extraordinary study of Shakespeare, and a novelist whose works like *Macht und Mächte* brought him a wide measure of acclaim. His wife, Hedwig Lachmann, translated Oscar Wilde and Rabindranath Tagore. Landauer spoke of himself as a German and a Jew in essays like *Der werdende Mensch* (1913). But he deemed the whole of his personality more than the sum of its parts—just as humanity was, for him, more than the various nationalities and ethnic communities composing it. His ethics were informed by a presumption of human goodness, a striving for a utopian condition of harmony, and respect for the individual and the community. These beliefs also played a role in his somewhat less notable political writings like *A Call to Socialism,* which envisioned economic equality along with a new direct form of democracy whose control by a newly educated working class would make violence dispensable.

Marta Feuchtwanger—the wife of the great realist writer Lion Feuchtwanger—wrote an account of the end of Landauer's life. Apparently, after being arrested following the collapse of the Bavarian Soviet, he started talking to the soldiers escorting him to prison about the goodness of humanity when, suddenly, they grew tired of walking and summarily beat him to death

(Feuchtwanger 1984, 133). Baron von Gagern, the officer responsible, was never punished or even brought to trial. This story, which speaks volumes about the judiciary in the Weimar Republic, also provides a deep insight into Landauer.

Landauer always considered himself an educator and spoke to the best in people. His concern was less about institutions than the ways people treated one another. His aim was to provide the working class with a new consciousness and a new democratic world view. And, as minister of education in the Bavarian Soviet, Landauer attempted to introduce a set of radical reforms, ranging from allowing any eighteen-year-old to become a full-time student at the University of Munich to setting up a "students' soviet" and abolishing examinations. His general perspective, in fact, becomes abundantly clear from his striking claim: "Every Bavarian child at the age of ten is going to know Walt Whitman by heart. That is the cornerstone of my educational program."

Rimbaud had called upon his generation to "change life." Erich Mühsam heartily agreed. And why not? Mühsam was for Germany what Rimbaud was for France (Souchy 1984, 10). Born in 1878, the son of a Jewish pharmacist in Berlin, he was expelled from high school for Socialist agitation. Mühsam felt himself an "outsider" from the beginning and naturally gravitated to the anarchist circles of Berlin and Munich. Max Nordau described him as an inveterate sponger during these early years (16ff.). But in 1904 *The Desert,* his first collection of poems, was published, and soon enough Mühsam began making his name as the author of cabaret songs, anecdotes, and sketches. He riddled Social Democracy with sarcasm in poems like "Die Revoluzzer," and important journals like *Die Weltbühne* and *Simplicissimus* began publishing his work.

"Let us make room for freedom" was a line in one of his poems. And that was what he sought to do when, in 1911, Mühsam became the editor of *Kain,* which he described as a "magazine for humanity." It was, of course, nothing of the sort. This Munich-based journal was sophisticated and avant-garde. Mühsam wrote like his Viennese friend and counterpart, Karl Kraus, the editor of *The Torch.* Mühsam advocated pacifism, sexual liberation, and an apocalyptic notion of revolution. He defended his friends and castigated the status quo. When World War I broke out, he published a collection entitled *Deserts, Craters, and Clouds,* in which he made the plea: "drink, soldiers, drink."

In keeping with his pacifist convictions, Mühsam refused to either serve in the army or register as a conscientious objector, and for this he was jailed. He came out against the national assembly following his release and sought to found an association of international revolutionaries in Munich, which came to little. Their program was somewhat unclear, and organizational questions bored Mühsam. Never particularly concerned with the class struggle, in keeping with Landauer, he spoke to the "exploited" and even attempted to proselytize among the *Lumpenproletariat.* Mühsam's vision of Socialism, like that of Landauer and Toller, was essentially aesthetic and visionary.

Mühsam was taken alive after the fall of the Bavarian Soviet and condemned to fifteen years of hard labor. The sentence was commuted to five years. He continued his anarchist activities after his release, but grew more sober. His new journal, *Fanal,* no longer criticized Social Democracy as the main enemy; instead, the Nazis were targeted. Mühsam spoke out against the abuses of the Weimar judicial system and supported organizations like *Red Aid,* which raised money for political prisoners and sought their liberation. He wrote a play, *Reason of State,* about Sacco and Vanzetti, as well as an account of the Bavarian Soviet entitled *From Eisner to Leviné: A Reckoning.* These works reveal Mühsam's humanistic values and hopes for the Bavarian Soviet, as well as his view of the arrogance and stubbornness of the Communists. Nevertheless, even here, Mühsam could not adequately deal with the shortcomings of his own political voluntarism or the institutional and social reasons for the failure of the Bavarian experiment.

Few were hated with the same degree of passion by the nationalist Right, and its advocates continued to vilify Mühsam during the years of the Weimar Republic. Henry Pachter even suggested that Hitler probably remembered the young bohemian playing chess in the famous Café Megalomania in Munich after the war and making fun of the future chancellor's drawings (Pachter 1982, 252). In any event, the philistines ultimately had their revenge. Following the Nazi seizure of power, Mühsam was immediately captured and transported to Oranienburg, where he died in 1934 after being slowly and systematically beaten to death.

Within the Socialist movement, however, Mühsam was one of the best-loved figures of the Bavarian Soviet, and there are numerous reports of workers and soldiers shouting his name and even carrying him on their shoulders. He never showed favoritism toward any party, and he acted responsibly as a leading politician of the Bavarian Soviet. Mühsam sought unity, proved willing to compromise with the Communists, and even appeared as their spokesman on one or two occasions. He accomplished all of this without surrendering his principles or his various utopian ideas for reform. He knew who he was, and his "identity" was never a problem for him. Thus, Mühsam could write: "I am a Jew and will remain a Jew so long as I live. I never denied my Judaism and never even walked out of the religious community (because I would still remain a Jew and I am completely indifferent under which rubric I am entered in the state's register). I consider it neither an advantage nor a disadvantage to be a Jew; it simply belongs to my being like my red beard, my weight, or my inclinations" (Mühsam 1984, 2:422–23).

It wasn't much different for Ernst Toller. The most famous and perhaps prototypical leader of the Bavarian Soviet was born in Posen in 1893, and his autobiography, *I Was a German,* speaks elegantly of anti-Semitism in Germany. But still he joined the military in a mood of "emotional delirium" to fight in World War I. After his release in 1916, in the wake of a nervous breakdown, he soon became a staunch pacifist and ultimately a Socialist. After studying at Munich and Heidelberg, where he came to know Max Weber and various other distinguished academics, Toller wrote his deeply autobiographical play, *Transfor-*

mation (1917). Dream sequences, abstract figures, and various other Expressionist techniques are employed in this work whose main character experiences any number of "transformations," each of which liberates him from a prior ideological prejudice, until finally he finds "redemption" (*Erlösung*) in a utopian vision of "revolution." Based on a fundamental "faith in humanity," concerned less with workers than with an image of the oppressed, this "revolution" would necessarily prove nonviolent and effect a change in the very "essence" of "man" beyond all externalities.

Toller, like Eisner, was a member of the Independent Social Democratic Party (USPD), which had split from the SPD in 1916 over the latter's prowar policy. The USPD, small and poorly organized in Munich, had aligned itself with the Räte movement. Toller quickly became a leading figure in the Bavarian Soviet. His supposedly remarkable oratorical abilities surely did not hurt; indeed, it was said that "he carried the people by the force of his own convictions. . . . They wanted a mission in life; Toller supplied them with one" (cited in Flood 1989, 4).

The creation of the Bavarian Soviet was accompanied by the planting of freedom trees, the singing of Jacobin songs, and a great deal of libertarian rhetoric. The contemporary German writer Tankred Dorst, in fact, has argued that Toller identified the events of 1919 with the Expressionist apocalypse his works depicted. Whether that is true remains an open question. But it is true that Toller knew nothing about economics and not much more about institutions. His grasp of political priorities was also somewhat suspect. While Bavaria was experiencing a food shortage, in the aftermath of the Allied blockade, Toller's first speech to the soviet concerned the new forms of architecture, painting, and drama by which humanity might express itself more fully. Administrative services collapsed and the organization of revolutionary soldiers was a shambles; indeed, with a mixture of affection and sarcasm, Max Weber once remarked: "God in his fury has turned Toller into a politician."

But, in fact, Toller remains a great symbol for Socialist libertarians. He was brave and humane.

He fought courageously with the defenders of the Bavarian Soviet against the reactionary forces and saved many hostages from the revenge sought by various Communist leaders like Rudolf Engelhofer. Toller was captured with the downfall of the Bavarian Soviet and spent five years in prison. There he wrote his beautiful collection of poems entitled *The Swallow-Book,* which attempted to unify respect for the individual with solidarity in works like *Man and the Masses* (1924), and *Broken-Brow,* which concerns an impotent war invalid abandoned by society.

The pathos in the work of Toller increased along with his despondency. And yet, following his release, he joined *The German League for Human Rights* and participated in various pacifist organizations. Even while writing for prestigious journals like *Die Weltbühne,* which published his prison writings, and using an innovative Expressionist style, he always considered himself a "people's poet" (*Volksdichter*). He was another, like Mühsam, who bravely castigated the criminal justice system for its right-wing bias, and *Hooray! We're Alive* remains one of the most trenchant criticisms of the materialistic and chauvinistic underside of the Weimar Republic. Toller was also, along with Mühsam, one of the very few intellectuals who immediately realized the danger posed by the Nazis and what differentiated them from other "bourgeois" and even "reactionary" parties.

Toller fled Germany when the Nazis came to power, moving from Switzerland to France, England, and finally to the United States. But he hated exile. He never made it in Hollywood, and feeling his powers diminishing, he despaired as Hitler won victory after victory. Toller, the pacifist and humanitarian, committed suicide in New York in 1939. He never saw the end of the regime he so despised.

But if Toller died too early, his Communist competitor for power in the Bavarian Soviet— Eugen Leviné—died just in time. He would certainly have perished even more cruelly under Stalin. Leviné was not quite the saint Rosa Leviné-Meyer portrayed in her biography. But he incarnated the best of the Bolshevik spirit. He was unyielding and dogmatic, but an honest intellectual and totally committed to the most radical utopian ideals of international revolution.

Born on May 10, 1883, in St. Petersburg into a wealthy Jewish family, Leviné was brought up in Germany, where as a youth he actually fought a duel against someone who had made an anti-Semitic remark (Leviné-Meyer 1973, 6ff.). He returned to Russia in 1904. There he gained revolutionary experience and participated in the Revolution of 1905 before being arrested. Leviné was apparently severely beaten, and after bribery secured his release, he moved back to Germany. There he worked as a propagandist for the SPD and naturally gravitated to the circle around Rosa Luxemburg before ultimately finding his way into Spartacus.

Leviné soon enough found himself in disagreement with Luxemburg. Enthralled by the Russian Revolution of 1917, in contrast to Luxemburg, he took a genuinely ultra-left stance. He was critical of the alliance between Spartacus and the USPD. But even more importantly, he vigorously opposed participating in the national assembly and ultimately embraced Lenin's new Communist International. Believing the masses would follow an inspired vanguard, in keeping with the Bolshevik example of 1917, he and his close comrade Max Levien were instrumental in causing the defeat of the more moderate proposals of Luxemburg and the leadership of Spartacus, thereby exacerbating the ill-prepared revolutionary events in Berlin.

But, for all that, Leviné acquitted himself valiantly during the uprising. The police hunted for him, and at the urging of Paul Levi, the new leader of the German Communist Party, Leviné was sent to Munich, where he was to put the small and disorganized party cell into order. Leviné's first article warned workers not to engage in any "precipitous" actions, and he opposed forming a Bavarian soviet. When the soviet was proclaimed anyway, Leviné, appalled by its circus-like character, successfully convinced the KPD to remain in opposition. He feared working with representatives of the SPD and, perhaps more fully than any other of its prominent figures, recognized the lack

of support—especially among the peasants—garnered by the soviet.

The question is why Leviné should have called upon the Communists to reverse their position. He knew the soviet was doomed. Perhaps his new stance derived from a desire to take power and use the occasion to make propaganda and identify the Communists with the soviet. His policy surely did not find its source in Moscow; indeed, no Bolshevik emissaries were active in Munich. Most likely, following Rosa Luxemburg, Leviné had decided to preserve the soviet ideal and "stay with the masses" in the face of the reaction.

Leviné was, interestingly enough, no less utopian than his opponents. His Communists may have introduced censorship, but they too sought to revamp the schools and proclaimed the famous *Frauenkirche* a "revolutionary temple." All this was a desperate attempt to mimic what has been described as the "heroic period" of "war Communism" in the Soviet Union. Communist workers, however, soon enough turned against the disastrous policy of Leviné, and his heritage is tainted by the senseless shooting of hostages and arbitrary confiscations carried out by members of his own party. Nevertheless, Leviné remained true to his beliefs. He participated in the street fighting, and his defiant death before a firing squad only testified to his nobility of character. Indeed, with the dying cry of "Long Live the World Revolution!" the tragicomedy of the Bavarian Soviet came to a close along with the most radical hopes of 1919.

The Jewish revolutionaries of 1919 were a motley crew. Mühsam and Toller were leading figures of the Expressionist avant-garde; but the first was an anarchist and the second a left-wing Socialist. It was the same with Eisner and Landauer, even if both were influenced by Kant. For their part, whatever the differences between them, Leviné and Luxemburg were Marxists who had little use for moralism and less for bohemians. These Jewish revolutionaries spanned the spectrum of radicalism, and there was apparently very little uniting them.

Judaism never figured prominently in either their writings or their political activities. It seems to offer little of value in explaining their choices and belief systems. All of these revolutionaries were assimilationists and cosmopolitans inflamed by a passionate yearning for secular justice and a regeneration of humanity. Nevertheless, in terms of these very concerns, a certain strain of Judaism—itself derived from a mixture of the Jewish Enlightenment and the Old Testament—might well have indirectly affected their world views.

The Jewish revolutionaries of 1919 were prophets of justice, equality, and democracy without much sense of the institutions necessary to sustain these values. Each condemned the decadence of the status quo and genuinely identified with those whom, in biblical language, Ernst Bloch liked to call "the lowly and the insulted." Each prized the moment of action and sought to provide the masses with a new sense of their own possibilities. Each was also exceptionally brave and remained true to his or her convictions. In short, each, after his or her fashion, incorporated the idealism and romanticism with which to challenge an alienation whose source lies with the story of Adam and Eve. Each sought to realize utopia.

Now only the vaguest memories of these remarkable individuals remain. Barely visible is the alternative that each offered both to the impoverished cultural landscape of contemporary capitalism and to what increasingly became a Socialism of grayness. But this is precisely what makes it important to preserve their visions and contest the darkness. In the beautiful words of Erich Mühsam: "Who will remember me when I am dead? The sad day has snatched my youth. Evening came too soon. Rain fell. Happiness passed me by; I remained a stranger. My poor heart has its fill of suffering. Soon comes the night which has no stars."

Bibliography

Hannah Arendt, *Men in Dark Times* (Middlesex, Eng.: Penguin, 1973); Franz Borkenau, *World Communism* (Ann Arbor: University of Michigan Press, 1962); F. L. Carsten, *Revolution in Central Europe, 1918–1919* (Berkeley: University of California Press, 1972); Raya Dunayevskaya, *Rosa Luxemburg, Women's Liberation, and Marx's Philosophy of Revolution* (Atlantic Highlands, N.J.: Humanities Press, 1981); Kurt Eisner, *Sozialismus als Aktion: Ausgewählte Aufsätze und Reden,* ed. Freya Eisner (Frankfurt a. M.: Suhrkamp, 1979); Marta Feuchtwanger, *Nur eine Frau* (Munich: Knaur, 1984); Charles Bracelen Flood, *Hitler: The Path to Power* (Boston: Houghton Mifflin, 1989); Gustav Landauer, *Aufruf zum Sozialismus* (Vienna: Europa Verlag, 1967); Rosa Leviné-Meyer, *Leviné the Spartacist* (London: Gordon and Cremonesi, 1973); Rosa Luxemburg, *The Letters of Rosa Luxemburg,* ed. Stephen Eric Bronner (Atlantic Highlands, N.J.: Humanities Press, 1992); Luxemburg, *The National Question: Selected Writings by Rosa Luxemburg,* ed. Horace B. Davis (New York: Monthly Review, 1976); Luxemburg, *Rosa Luxemburg Speaks,* ed. Mary-Alice Waters (New York: Pathfinder, 1970); Luxemburg, *The Russian Revolution, and Leninism or Marxism?* (Ann Arbor: University of Michigan Press, 1962); Luxemburg, *Selected Political Writings of Rosa Luxemburg,* ed. Dick Howard (New York: Monthly Review, 1971); Erich Mühsam, *Briefe, 1900–1934,* 2 vols. (Darmstadt: Topos, 1984); Mühsam, *Prosaschriften,* ed. Gunther Emig, 2 vols. (Berlin: Verlag Ideen, 1978); Max Nomad, *Dreamers, Dynamiters, and Demagogues: Reminiscences* (New York: Waldon, 1964); Henry Pachter, *Weimar Etudes* (New York: Columbia University Press, 1982); Arthur Rosenberg, *Geschichte der Weimarer Republik* (Frankfurt a. M.: Europäische Verlaganstalt, 1961); Augustin Souchy, *Erich Mühsam: Sein Leben, Sein Werk, Sein Märtyrertum* (Reutlingen: Trotzdem Verlag, 1984); Ernst Toller, *I Was a German,* trans. Edward Crankshaw (New York: Paragon, 1990); Toller, *Seven Plays* (London: J. Lane, 1935); Toller, *The Swallow-Book* (New York: Haskell House, 1974); and Enzo Traverso, *Les juifs et l'Allemagne: De la "symbiose judéo-allemande" à la mémoire d'Auschwitz* (Paris: Découverte, 1992).

STEPHEN ERIC BRONNER

1919 German-Jewish writers begin to give literary expression to memories of the Munich Revolution of 1918–19

Few events provide a better point of departure for the *Problematik* of being Jewish in Germany in the twentieth century than the Munich Revolution of 1918–19. Indeed, its immense importance can hardly be overstated for Jews as well as Germans. Although the revolution failed in the end to achieve any of its major goals, it did expose many otherwise undetected wounds that afflicted German society after four years of warfare—especially those that would be consequential for Jews.

In Munich, Jews had played critical roles as leaders of the revolution in each stage of its unfolding, from its nonviolent inception on the sunny afternoon of November 7, 1918, to its savage conclusion six months later in the first days of May 1919. This involvement of Jews was wholly disproportionate to their numbers in either Germany or Munich. The reasons for this statistical abnormality defy any simple explanations, but undoubtedly derive from the social and political position of Jews in the last years of the German *Reich*. Contemporary observers remarked on the peculiarity of so many highly visible Jewish revolutionary leaders, whereas anti-Semitic writers and demagogues such as Hitler feasted on it. Historians have addressed the matter in a wide variety of ways ever since.

Given Jews' involvement in the uprising, it is not surprising that the Munich Revolution should have resonated frequently and deeply with Jewish writers. As participants, observers, highly literate and politically active citizens of the Weimar Republic, and ultimately as casualties of Nazi anti-Semitism, circumstances virtually compelled German Jews to reflect on the events of their recent past, prominent among which was the Munich Revolution and its leading personalities.

That Munich, famed in pre-war days for its tolerance and liberality, should have become the haven for reactionary and anti-Semitic groups following the revolution gave Jewish writers even more reason to ponder the revolutionary events. The Bavarian state government that followed the failure of the revolution in 1919 encouraged such organizations and even embraced their views when it expelled Eastern European Jewish immigrants who had not attained German citizenship in the early 1920s. Nor was it mere chance that prompted Hitler to launch his assault on the Weimar Republic in the same streets where Socialist and anarchist revolutionaries, many of them Jewish, had recently preceded him.

The forms that such writing took—letters, plays, memoirs, novels, and political polemics—varied as widely as did the political perspectives of the authors. Many of the earliest pieces were written by Munich Jews who experienced the revolution as anxious and sometimes anguished bystanders and who were frequently appalled by the radical politics of their coreligionists. Following the collapse and suppression of the revolution, the revolutionary leaders who survived—people such as Ernst Toller, Felix Fechenbach, and Erich Mühsam—ruminated in Bavarian prisons and wrote prolifically about the meaning of their experiences. The aftermath of the revolution also inspired a wide spectrum of other works by Jewish writers, from a widely acclaimed novel by the writer Lion Feuchtwanger to a highly controversial exposé of reactionary bias in the Bavarian and Weimar judiciary by the scholar Emil Gumbel. Also included in this brief overview is a description of the writings of an apostate Jewish writer, Paul Nikolaus Cossmann, who wrote and fostered anti-Semitic invective following the revolution in the pages of his highly influential Munich review, the *Süddeutschen Monatshefte*. Additional works this essay might have included are the eulogies and moving justifications written by relatives and friends for those Jewish leaders such as Kurt Eisner, Gustav Landauer, and Eugen Leviné who died in the revolution.

The reactions of most of Munich's indigenous Jews—those who were not directly involved in the revolution—invariably focused on the possible consequences of having so many highly visible Jewish radicals in the city. At the time, the Jews of Munich numbered about 10,000, or about 2 percent of the city's 500,000 inhabitants. Yet they in no way formed a single community or voiced a unified point of view. If the Jews of Munich shared a common identity as Jewish, they shared little else. Even their sense of Jewishness split them into factions. Generally, those families with older German lineages had assimilated themselves more completely than had more recent immigrants from Eastern Europe. The former, who made up approximately two-thirds of the Jews, had frequently become Reform in their religious observance, if they observed their religion at all, whereas the latter tended to be Orthodox and more clannish than their coreligionists.

But these generalities did not always hold true. The forebears of the writer Lion Feuchtwanger provide one example. Feuchtwanger could trace his Bavarian lineage to middle Franconia in the sixteenth century, yet the family had remained devoutly Orthodox down to the generation of the author himself, who finally rebelled against his rigid religious upbringing. Feuchtwanger recalled that his father was so deeply a part of both worlds that he prayed in a Hebrew that carried a heavy Bavarian accent.

Most of the writing by the Munich Jews took the form of either contemporary articles and letters, or memoirs written in exile in the 1940s to 1950s. Although many of these do not commonly qualify as "literature," they deserve to be included in a German-Jewish literary anthology because they not only are highly literate, but also amplify our understanding of the position of German Jews who generally prided themselves on their ability to assimilate and embrace the German concept of *Bildung*.

Yet these writings also reveal the fragility of this symbiosis. A recurrent theme of these highly personal works is a fear of jeopardizing the position of Jews as exemplary Germans. A similar sense of anxiety had impelled leaders of this same Jewish community to reject the offer by Theodore Herzl in the summer of 1897 to convene a congress of Zionists in Munich. Herzl eventually found a warmer reception in the Swiss city of Basel.

This feeling of foreboding found its most forceful expression in a large advertisement published by the Munich chapter of Germany's largest Jewish organization in Munich's leading daily newspaper on April 11, 1919, during the chaotic days of the Munich Soviet Republic (*Räterepublik*). Addressed to "all honorable fellow citizens" (*alle ehrlichen Volksgenossen*), the advertisement reminds readers how much Jews have shared the hardships of the war as good Germans and how much they are also suffering under the revolution. The authors of this ad then warn their compatriots against being misled by the "many Jewish sounding names among the leadership of the Independents and Communists." The majority of these, the ad continues, have ceased being Jews and have no connection with any Jewish group. There is no reason, therefore, to afflict an already tormented people with the additional hardship of religious and racial hatred. Munich Jews, the ad concludes, want only to share "the burdens and duties" of these troubled days with their fellow citizens.

Virtually all contemporary accounts by Jews reflect this anxious concern; for many this was their recurrent nightmare becoming reality. For example, the industrialist and member of the Bavarian Ministry of Trade and Commerce, Sigmund Fraenkel, directed a passionate public appeal to several revolutionary leaders of Jewish descent urging them to relinquish their political fantasies. Basing his plea on being a member of the Jewish community "to which you yourselves or your parents once belonged," Fraenkel too sought to distance Munich Jews from the actions of the revolutionaries, maintaining that "our hands are uncontaminated by the horrors of chaos and of the misery and suffering that your politics will inflict on the future development of Bavaria. You alone and only you bear the full responsibility for this." Presumably in an effort to appeal to the Jewish consciousness of the revolutionaries, Fraenkel, an Orthodox Jew, pointedly dated his letter, "April 6 at 11 pm on the eve of Passover 5679" (Lamm 1959).

Yet not all members of the Munich Jewish community who wrote about the revolution shared these reactions to Jewish revolutionary leaders. The lawyer Philip Löwenfeld, for example, writing his memoir as a refugee in New York in the early 1940s, recalled that many of his fellow Munich Jews had urged Kurt Eisner and other Jewish revolutionaries not to stand at the forefront of the revolution, because they might thereby provide anti-Semitic agitators with pretexts for their accusations. But Löwenfeld emphatically rejected this contention, insisting that the slurs of anti-Semites should never determine how Jews behaved (Richarz 1982).

Clearly, from the perspective of Munich Jews, as revealed by their writers, possible repercussions of the revolution for the Jewish community were their primary concern. German Jews from elsewhere who happened to be in Munich reflected a similar dread. Nor was this fear without foundation, as the constantly escalating activities of anti-Semitic groups and individuals seemed to confirm. Yet in turning to more ambitious literary works by Jewish writers resulting from the

revolution, this preoccupation with the precariousness of being Jewish in Germany assumes a lesser role. Although the plays, novels, and memoirs by people like Ernst Toller, Lion Feuchtwanger, and Erich Mühsam still bear witness to this dilemma, ethical issues such as justice, the use of violence, and the righteousness of revolution became primary instead.

More than any other German-Jewish writer who experienced and wrote about the Munich Revolution, Ernst Toller has captivated scholars and literati since his suicide in a New York City hotel room in 1939. He has been the subject of innumerable academic pieces and the protagonist of a celebrated play in 1968 by Tankred Dorst, which stimulated a new generation of young Germans to identify with his life and tribulations. Not that Toller had not already achieved renown. He was not yet thirty when his second play, *Masse-Mensch,* opened to critical acclaim in Berlin on September 18, 1921. At that time, Toller was languishing in solitary confinement in the Bavarian prison at Niederschönenfeld. By 1922 the play had been translated and published in French, English, Polish, Yiddish, Russian, Hungarian, and Lettish. It opened on Broadway in 1924 as *Man and the Masses,* and was accompanied by a full-size drawing of the author's tormented face on the cover of *Theatre Arts.*

Toller's path to the Munich Revolution had followed a psychological passage not uncommon for a young German Jew. Born in Posen in Prussia, he had been raised an Orthodox Jew among ardent German patriots who excluded him from their circles. Toller later vividly described his experiences as an "outsider" in his autobiography, *Eine Jugend in Deutschland* (1933), and explained how he resolved his identity conflict by rejecting the beliefs of his parents for the creed of the Fatherland. In 1914 he culminated his assimilation by joining the ranks of young Germans rushing to the Front; he recalled that "as a soldier, no one asked if he were Jewish."

Toller's second metamorphosis occurred in a machine-gun post in France, where the carnage of war resulted in his complete breakdown and his utter rejection of patriotism for the universal religion of humanity. His first and least successful play, *Die Wandlung* (Transfiguration; 1917), recounts these experiences and concludes with its hero, Friedrich, leading a spiritual uprising against patriotism and war. This prefigured Toller's own role in the Munich Revolution, in which, unfortunately, messianism led to demagoguery, and pacifism led to violence. Toller survived the bloodbath of the counterrevolution in May 1919, but was later captured and sentenced to five years of confinement in Niederschönenfeld.

At age twenty-six, Toller's life of action ended and his life of reflection began. He tormented himself during these years of enforced solitude with the moral dilemmas engendered by the revolution. In *Masse-Mensch* he dramatized his own conflict as a leader of the revolution. In this play, Toller's alter ego is The Woman, a visionary intellectual who rejects her bourgeois background to become the leader of a Socialist revolution. When the revolution fails, she is imprisoned and sentenced to die. When she learns of a plot for her escape, she rejects it because it will cost the life of a prison guard. "I have no right to gain my life by this man's death," she announces, "I should betray the Masses. Who acts may only sacrifice himself. Hear me: no man may kill men for a cause. Unholy every cause that needs to kill."

Toller wrote two additional plays in prison in which he explored the moral complexities of revolution and nonviolence. In neither play, however, did he again confront the question of a Jewish intellectual becoming a revolutionary. In *Die Maschinenstürmer* (The machine wreckers; 1922), he dealt with the Luddite rebellion against industrialization in early nineteenth-century England. Jimmy Cobbett, who undoubtedly embodies Toller in this play, warns his revolutionary counterpart, "The man who arouses the baser instincts of the masses is overwhelmed by their fury." And in *Hinkemann* (1923), his most dreary and depressing play, Toller disputes the optimism of potential revolutionaries by telling his audience, through the emasculated Eugen Hinkemann, that the scars of a corrupted society are so deep that no revolution can heal them.

If Toller used the stage as his platform to confront the moral issues raised by the Munich Revo-

lution, so too did his fellow revolutionary Erich Mühsam and the writer Lion Feuchtwanger. Like Toller, Mühsam and Feuchtwanger stemmed from Jewish households; Mühsam came from the northern German city of Lübeck, whereas Feuchtwanger was a native of Munich and, as already noted, could trace his Bavarian-Jewish lineage to the sixteenth century. Being both fledgling playwrights and of Jewish background, however, was about all Mühsam and Feuchtwanger had in common.

Like Toller, Mühsam wrote *Judas* (1920) in prison following the failure of the revolution, but unlike Toller, Mühsam's play evidenced no waning of his revolutionary ardor and optimism. Regarded by most observers as the prototype of the Schwabing, coffeehouse anarchist, and characterized admiringly by Else Lasker-Schüler as a "wilder Jude," Mühsam had championed the idea of a soviet republic (*Räterepublik*) during the revolution. Although a staunch critic of Marxism, Mühsam also steadfastly opposed representative parliamentary government in favor of a more direct council system. Referring at times in his play to concrete revolutionary events, Mühsam modeled many of his characters on actual people—for example, Professor Mathias Seebald, who closely resembled Mühsam's martyred mentor, Gustav Landauer. In the end, however, Mühsam's theatrical revolution succeeds on stage; it is the imprisoned author's reverie of the way events should have gone.

Feuchtwanger, on the other hand, as a nonparticipant in the revolution, used his unusual play, *Thomas Wendt*—he called it a "dramatic novel"— to depict the dilemma of a writer who chose to distance himself from revolutionary events. Wendt, the protagonist, follows Feuchtwanger's path and rejects all political action, not necessarily to stand above the conflict, but to retain a more universal perspective. Whereas Toller and Mühsam had abandoned the apolitical stance usually associated with German writers and confronted their failed revolution, Feuchtwanger followed the more traditional, detached role and could now justify it.

More important for Feuchtwanger's career than *Thomas Wendt*, however, was his novel,

Erfolg (Success; 1930), in which he dealt with the aftermath of the revolution. *Thomas Wendt* had marked Feuchtwanger's transition from dramatist to novelist (the genre in which he earned his greatest fame); it also had been his first attempt to write about contemporary events in an epic form, an effort that came to fruition in *Erfolg*.

As an epic, *Erfolg* is so rich in character and plot that it defies easy summary. Its locale is Feuchtwanger's native Munich during the years of reaction following the revolution. In this massive work, the author mixes cynicism about his Bavarian compatriots with rare touches of affection. Feuchtwanger even employed statistics to prove how much more violent and less intelligent Bavarians are than other Germans. "Brains were a rare commodity in Bavaria," he confidently asserts, and "Bavaria's percentage of crimes of violence was the highest among German states." He then reinforces this claim: "Of congenital idiots and cretins, there were in Germany, 36,461, of whom 11,209 were in Bavaria."

It is among these primitive people that Feuchtwanger described the atmosphere in which postrevolutionary politics permitted and encouraged the rise of the demagogue, Rupert Kutzner (that is, Hitler), and his anti-Semitic party. Well-known Bavarian politicians, as well as Hitler, were thinly disguised by Feuchtwanger in *Erfolg*, which, when published in 1930, became one of Germany's first anti-Nazi novels.

Yet given the overall purpose and scope of *Erfolg*, it lacks any genuine heroes; the closest any figure comes to that role is the Jewish lawyer and scholar, Dr. Siegbert Geyer. Geyer's commitment to "justice" as well as the fact that he is Jewish cause him to be shunned by other lawyers and politicians in reactionary and postrevolutionary Munich. In the same vein, Feuchtwanger also devoted a chapter to describing in detail how the revolutionaries Kurt Eisner and Gustav Landauer were brutally murdered by reactionary assassins. The concluding words of this cruel chapter mirror the mood of the entire book: "The city hymn of Munich continued to assert after these unhappy events as before them: as long as the Isar runs green through the town, you'll find jolly good fellows in Munich."

Feuchtwanger's portrayal of Siegbert Geyer may not have been fashioned on any actual figure, yet Geyer bears a resemblance in several significant respects to the real-life scholar Emil Julius Gumbel. In Feuchtwanger's novel, Geyer's obsession is the completion of his work in progress, "A History of Injustice in Bavaria from the Armistice of 1918 to the Present Day." Like the fictional Geyer, Gumbel was also a Munich Jew who spent the early 1920s collecting judicial data to show that justice in Bavaria and all of Germany had become a tool of the political Right. The two works that derived from this research, the pamphlet "Zwei Jahre Mord" (1921) and its book-length successor, *Vier Jahre politischer Mord* (1922), do not generally figure in any history of German literature, but should be included in an essay on German-Jewish literary works emanating from the Munich Revolution.

Gumbel's academic training had been in the field of statistics rather than jurisprudence, yet his exposé of German "justice," however statistical, reflects none of the dry tedium usually associated with this field. Gumbel used statistics to demonstrate that a decided right-wing bias existed in the German judicial system in when and how offenders were punished. This bias, Gumbel established, defied any statistical norms and could only have resulted from a right-wing political conspiracy.

Although Gumbel employed statistical tables to prove his point, his text is both polemical in tone and lurid in its detailed examples. Furthermore, in citing the major motives of the political Right, Gumbel listed anti-Semitism—specifically, the driving of Jews from all positions of influence and power in Germany. He used a significant portion of the book to describe the counterrevolutionary situation in Munich. Gumbel strove to do with statistics what Feuchtwanger employed an epic novel to achieve. They both portrayed postwar and postrevolutionary Germany as dangerously permeated by right-wing extremism and anti-Semitism.

Even before the Nazis came to power, Gumbel suffered for his views, as well as for his Jewish heritage. In a celebrated and notorious case, he was designated and then denied a professorial post at the University of Heidelberg in 1931, when Nazi-dominated student groups forcefully protested and dissuaded the faculty from following its expressed preference for Gumbel as a colleague. Given Gumbel's political stance as an anti-Nazi pacifist and his high visibility, he took refuge in France, where he was lecturing when the Nazis came to power in 1933, rather than return to Germany; later he fled to the United States, where he lived until his death in 1966.

If a conspiracy of the Right to undermine the Weimar Republic did exist in the early 1920s, as Emil Gumbel contended, then Paul Nikolaus Cossmann was the man who furnished the conspirators with their most compelling pretext for their deeds. As editor of the monthly journal the *Süddeutschen Monatshefte,* and as one of its most frequent contributors, Cossmann had first helped to create and then had become the leading publicist of the so-called *Dolchstoss* (stab-in-the-back) theory.

Under Cossmann's direction, the *Monatshefte* had become a "respectable" forum for Bavarian counterrevolutionary views. In its pages, reputable conservative and reactionary academics and literati published harangues against the *Novemberverbrecher* (November gangsters) and the Versailles peace treaty. Cossmann personally promoted the theory that the German armies had not been defeated on the battlefield in 1918, but had been betrayed by the Socialists and other revolutionaries at home; thus the Dolchstoss. By 1925, he was no longer content merely to promote this belief in the *Monatshefte,* but carried it into a broader public realm by bringing a sensational civil suit against the editor of Munich's Social Democratic newspaper, *Münchner Post,* for historical slander and falsification. The *Post* had purportedly published lies about Germany's defeat in the war.

The Dolchstoss and the *Dolchstossprozess* (Dolchstoss trial) quickly became central to the litany of the Right and gained broad currency among many less political Weimar Germans. For some anti-Semites such as Hitler, the Jews were as much the perpetrators of the Dolchstoss as were the "Bolsheviks." Hitler made this charge repeatedly in *Mein Kampf,* which he wrote in 1924.

Who was this Cossmann and why is he included in this compendium? Born in Moscow in 1869, Cossmann was an assimilated Russian Jew whose father was a well-known cellist and teacher in the conservatory. Paul Nikolaus came to Munich in 1890 as a student and remained. His own musical gifts provided him with access to intellectual and literary circles in the Bavarian capital, where, in 1904, he collaborated in the founding of the *Süddeutschen Monatshefte.* Initially the mission of the journal was cultural: to provide a southern German counterweight to northern German cultural domination. With the outbreak of war in 1914, however, Cossmann's chauvinistic views made the *Monatshefte* ever more political. The journal's postwar reactionary crusades were a continuation of this policy.

Cossmann had, however, converted to Catholicism in 1905. Whether to include apostate Jews in a collection on German Jews such as this has been a problem for every writer addressing the subject. In his recent work on *Jews and the German State* (1992), for example, Peter Pulzer noted that: "The last unbaptized member of the Mendelssohn banking family died in 1888, but that did not stop that banking house from being considered Jewish, or their members from being aware of their Jewish heritage." In addition to the Mendelssohns, luminaries such as Heine and Mahler, to mention only two, dot the historical landscape. Cossmann certainly did not consider himself Jewish, and he frequently published anti-Semitic pieces in the *Monatshefte* in the years immediately following the Revolution, yet his fate became that of a Jew when the Nazis came to power. Ultimately, Cossmann, despite numerous interventions on the part of his non-Jewish friends, was consigned to a ghetto in Munich, then sent to Theresienstadt, where he died of infirmities on October 19, 1942, at age seventy-three. Had he lived longer, this publicist of the Dolchstoss legend that helped bring Hitler to power might well have fallen victim to the gas chambers of Auschwitz.

The Munich Revolution unquestionably represents a pivotal point in the tangled history of Germans and Jews. Yet its full importance cannot be gauged merely by assessing the events of the

Revolution and its aftermath. We have learned that what people think happened is as important as what really happened. The meaning of the Munich Revolution derives not only from what happened in the streets, cafés, and beer halls of the city in 1918–19 and immediately thereafter, but also from what occurred in the consciousness of those who recounted and analyzed these events, especially in the minds of the German Jews who were most deeply affected by it.

Bibliography

Paul Cossmann, *Der Dolchstoss-Prozess in München, Oktober–November 1925: Eine Ehrenrettung des deutschen Volkes. Zeugen-und-Sachverständigen-Aussagen, eine Sammlung von Dokumenten* (Munich: G. Birk & Co., 1925); Tankred Dorst, *Toller* (Frankfurt a. M.: Suhrkamp, 1968); Dorst, ed., *Die Münchner Räterepublik: Zeugnisse und Kommentar* (Frankfurt a. M.: Suhrkamp, 1969); Lion Feuchtwanger, *Erfolg* (Berlin: Gustav Keipenheuer, 1930), also published as *Success* (New York: Viking, 1930); Feuchtwanger, *Thomas Wendt* (Munich: Georg Müller Verlag, 1920); E. J. Gumbel, *Vier Jahre politischer Mord* (Berlin-Fichtenau: Verlag der Neuen Gesellschaft, 1922); Hans Lamm, *Vom Juden in München: Ein Gedenkbuch* (Munich: Ner-Talmid-Verlag, 1959); Rosa Meyer-Leviné, *Leviné: The Life of a Revolutionary* (Farnsborough, Hampshire: Saxon House, 1973), also published as *Leviné: Leben und Tod eines Revolutionärs* (Frankfurt a. M.: Fischer, 1974); Erich Mühsam, *Judas, Arbeiter-Drama in fünf Akten,* 2d ed. (Berlin: Malik Verlag, 1924); Peter Pulzer, *Jews and the German State: The Political History of a Minority* (Oxford, Eng.: Blackwell, 1992); Monika Richarz, ed., *Jüdisches Leben in Deutschland: Selbstzeugnisse zur Sozialgeschichte, 1918–1945* (Stuttgart: Deutsche Verlags-Anstalt, 1982); Ernst Toller, *Eine Jugend in Deutschland* (Amsterdam: Querido Verlag, 1933), also published as *I Was a German: Autobiography of Ernst Toller* (New York: William Morrow, 1934); Toller, *Prosa, Briefe, Dramen, Gedichte* (Reinbek bei Hamburg: Rowohlt Verlag, 1961); and Toller, *Seven Plays* (New York: Liveright, 1936).

STERLING FISHMAN

October 29, 1920 Paul Wegener's *Der Golem: Wie er in die Welt kam* debuts in Berlin

During the early years of the Weimar Republic, the urban masses were deeply affected by the volatile political situation, the postwar economic decline, and the heterodox cultural climate, which together produced a potentially explosive atmosphere. "In the streets of Berlin," wrote Siegfried Kracauer in an early article on cinema in the *Frankfurter Zeitung,* "one is not seldom struck by the momentary insight that one day all this will suddenly burst apart. The entertainment to which the general public throngs ought to produce the same effect" (Kracauer 1963, 315). As the "theater for the little people" (Döblin) or "the psychoanalytic couch for the poor" (Guattari), the cinema has frequently been seen as a medium that bespeaks the collective desires, wishes, dreams, anxieties, and nightmares of the mass audience. Early Weimar cinema, with its predilection for haunted, mysterious, and faraway settings, often operates in this way, concealing the tensions of the contemporary and real within the fictional, removed cinematic space. An especially threatening horror film of 1920 offers a particularly rich historical text because it builds both on the social and psychological constellation constituting the moment in which it was conceived and on the cultural and historical constructs it projects.

When the sold-out Berlin premiere of Paul Wegener's third and final golem film, *Der Golem: Wie er in die Welt kam* (The golem: How he came into the world), opened at the Ufa Palast am Zoo on October 29, 1920, the German audience likely had at least some familiarity with the golem legend, having been exposed over the previous decades to numerous renditions. Aside from Wegener's first two golem films, *Der Golem* (1914–15) and *Der Golem und die Tänzerin* (The golem and the dancer; 1917), there had been a great number of early twentieth-century literary treatments of the golem myth: from Arthur Holitscher's *Der Golem: Ghettolegende in drei Aufzügen* (The golem: A ghetto legend in three acts; 1908) and Gustav Meyrink's *Der Golem* (1915) through Chayim Bloch's *Der Prager Golem: von seiner "Geburt" bis zu seinem "Tod"* (The golem of Prague: From his "birth" to his "death"; 1919), German culture of the 1920s had encountered its share of adaptations of the ancient Jewish legend. And yet, in exploring the complexities of Wegener's 1920 film, what is most significant is not the familiarity of the past adaptations, but rather how the legend now fit into the Weimar discourse on German-Jewish identity formation, into the broader understanding and widely shared perceptions of Jews at the time the film was produced.

Opening with the banishment of the Jews from the empire, the first scenes of *The Golem* speak immediately to the lingering Jewish Question. As the film's fictionalized documentary insert—the *Dikret wider die Juden* (Decree against the Jews)—reads: "We can no longer neglect the many grave complaints against the Jews, who crucified our Lord: they despise the holy Christian ceremonies; they endanger the lives and property of their fellow-men as well as non-Jews; they practice black magic. We decree that all Jews must abandon the city [Ghetto] before the new moon" (Wegener 1921, 13). Indeed, the guise of sixteenth-century kabbalistic legend assumed in the film merely serves as an allegory of the feared threat of urban domination. For in this light Rabbi Loew's mystical talents poignantly underscore his ability to transform the city, whereas his construction of a mechanical robot strikes a highly resonant chord in the then contemporary discourse on industrial production. "The creation of the Golem," remarks Kabbalah scholar Gershom Scholem, "is then in some way an affirmation of the productive and creative power of Man" (Scholem 1971, 337). As Rabbi Loew works in his study creating his mystical and, indeed, technological wonder—a scene that Fritz Lang's figure Rotwang of *Metropolis* (1927) undoubtedly cites—the consummate modernist asserts his productive powers. He operates on his own expressive terms, creating the mechanical object of horror and the ultimate symbol of modernity.

Not unlike the rabbi himself, the automated golem additionally serves as an embodiment of the urban metropolis. He is the commodity and instrument of exchange produced by the Jewish engineer and as such appears as the cause of both fear and desire. It is in the golem that the rabbi transforms the biblical Adam, referred to in talmudic legend as a "golem," into the modern Jewish robot. The blurred boundaries separating the ancient legend from the contemporary realm of political and cultural life around 1920 elicit a variety of questions on the Jewish position as producer or technician, necromancer, "strange magician," and mad scientist. How, for example, does the *Wunderrabbi* and technological mastermind Loew cultivate and wield his authority? Why, in a climate of great instability, do the Jews of the city pose a threat both to the German Empire within the film and to its contemporary counterpart, the Weimar Republic at large? And how does a Judeo-Christian myth of creation resonate with the myth-based construction of Jewish identity?

Though Wegener's film is set in the sixteenth-century ghetto, Rabbi Loew masters the economy of the city far more like a Weimar industrialist (à la Walther Rathenau) than a premodern alchemist. Considered in the wake of the Versailles treaty, as well as Hitler's formal announcement of his twenty-five-point party program for the Deutsche Arbeiter-Partei (German Workers' Party, the precursor to the Nazi party), Loew's negotiating power over the Jews in the German Empire appears to comment on the territorial struggles of the republic; indeed, as arbitrator between the German Empire and the ghetto world, Loew functions as foreign minister of the ghetto Jews. The images of past and present form a multilayered constellation. To be sure, the glimpse of the past in *The Golem,* evoked in the sixteenth-century ghetto setting, casts light onto the now, circumscribing the Jew's threatening presence in the German city. In a brief essay from 1915, "Schauspielerei und Film" (Acting and film), Wegener points precisely to this effect he had hoped to achieve in his *Golem* project. "Here everything is tailored to the image," he declares, "to the merging [*Ineinanderfließen*] of a fantasy-world of past centuries with everyday life" (Greve 1976, 116). As if to anticipate Benjamin's observations on the dialectical relationship between past and present, the images in Wegener's film produce an analogous type of antilinear, polyphonic constellation. The nature of the physical world blends with the fantasies of the cinematic world, revealing perhaps one of the cinema's greatest affective potentials. In terms of the relation that such celluloid images have to the common notions of Jewish identity, the liminal realm separating reality from fantasy provides an indeterminate space for communicating myth in the name of history.

One of *The Golem*'s central scenes, in which the rabbi visits the emperor's rose festival, illustrates the visual conflation of twentieth-century industrialism and ancient fantasy. Known to the court as the "strange magician," Rabbi Loew premieres his golem creation to the audience of the emperor's palace, boldly displaying his aesthetic power. Inside the lavishly decorated court, the wizard-like rabbi appears both submissive, as he kisses the emperor's ring, and almighty, as he orchestrates the spectacle. While the camera focuses on Loew's position among the audience at the emperor's court, the dimly lit "strange magician" takes on increasingly amplified dimensions. Not unlike Robert Wiene's *Das Kabinett des Dr. Caligari* (The cabinet of Dr. Caligari; 1920)—which premiered only months before Wegener's *Golem*, and in which the mad scientist and side-show performer Caligari exhibits his somnambulist Caesare before an eager crowd of spectators—Loew stands prominently framed alongside his golem "show" as the guests of the court curiously observe. Just as Caligari maintains control over his monster on display, Loew manipulates the movements of his robot-figure, withholding the secrets of his act. In fact, the rabbi himself asserts, "He is my servant and my creation, called golem, more I may not tell you" (Wegener 1921, 46).

In Rabbi Loew, Wegener characterizes the Jew as master of the power over the spectacle—over the aesthetic medium—a power that is repeatedly emphasized throughout the film. Indeed, the subsequent series of scenes at the rose festival further affirms this trait. In a remarkable metacinematic gesture, the rabbi conjures a film-within-a-film sequence of the biblical Exodus story through which his individual technological mastery as well as the status of the Jews forced to flee their homeland are duly invoked. Masses of Jews walk across the screen, mirroring ancient doubles of Loew's fellow ghetto inhabitants. Amidst the Jewish procession a lone figure reaches the center of the screen, abruptly turning toward the court spectators. Although one might at first glance recognize this figure as Moses, in the expository script published by the filmmaker in 1921, Wegener addresses him as "Ahasverus, the eternal Jew" (Wegener 1921, 50). In the role of "eternal Jew," the bearded mythical figure feigns a portrait of the exiled condition of the Jews in the emperor's city who likewise face expulsion from their non-Jewish domain. By invoking the figure of Ahasverus, not only does the Jewish Question return to the foreground, but the mythical foundation of the film also expands: the golem legend, the Exodus passage, and the citation of the "Wandering Jew" render the film's narrative both culturally and historically famil-

iar and yet fantastically remote. The audience, clearly exposed to the stock motifs and metaphors of *The Golem*, as well as to the Faustian and biblical inflections, can identify the cinematic rendition in terms of its rootedness in German culture while nonetheless distancing themselves from the bizarre (that is, Jewish) miracles on the screen.

Analogous to the interaction of the golem narrative with the present, the skewed Exodus citation embodied in Ahasverus resonates with the story that Wegener's film tells. Both the figures from Loew's "show" and the figures in Wegener's narrative must flee from their home—the Exodus Jews from the ancient homeland and the ghetto Jews from the German city. Both face persecution in their respective host countries and therefore must seek freedom. The blurred configuration of genres, time periods, and images conveys a jumbled composite of history, fiction, aesthetics, and myth. By introducing the biblical passage in the film, the past reemerges in the form of narrativized myth, imbricated with the historical immediacy of the modern Jewish Question. As witnessed in Hans Karl Breslauer's film of 1924, *Die Stadt ohne Juden* (The city without Jews), and less overtly in F. W. Murnau's *Nosferatu, eine Symphonie des Grauens* (Nosferatu, a symphony of horror; 1922), the question of expelling the unwanted inhabitants of the city provoked a wide range of responses in the years surrounding Wegener's production.

The aesthetic production of the biblical scene and the creation of the golem also implicate the theological problem of profanely imitating the divine—that is, the iconoclastic disavowal of the paramount Jewish biblical commandment against the creation of images resembling God or anything in the heavens or on earth (Ex. 20:4; Deut. 5:8). As the Jew, the artist, and the producer, Rabbi Loew creates iconoclastic images of sacred figures, thereby defying the biblical proscription of images (*Bilderverbot*) that prevents him from this enterprise. In the intertitle announcing the rabbi's intentions, Loew instructively states, "Allow me to show you, dear ruler, the fathers of my people" (Wegener 1921, 47). Loew's "show" offers precisely the mimetic photo-quality representation of the Jews against which he is proscribed. As Theodor W. Adorno remarks, "The Old Testament prohibition of graven images can be said to have an aesthetic aspect besides the overt theological one. The interdiction against forming an image of something in effect implies the proposition that such an image is impossible to form" (Adorno 1984, 106). Adorno's statement critically underscores the destructive nature of the film aesthetic. Unlike Benjamin, whose notion of cinema envisions a potentially redemptive aesthetic, Adorno insists on film's lack of autonomy and fetish character. When considered in light of Wegener's *Golem,* Adorno's thoughts point to a double fetishization, because the Jew on the screen creates a further projection of the biblical passage. In his earliest reflections on anti-Semitism, "Elemente des Anti-Semitismus" (Elements of anti-Semitism; 1944), written in collaboration with Max Horkheimer and Leo Löwenthal, Adorno implicitly comments on the fetishization and desecration of Jewishness: "The morbid aspect of anti-Semitism is not projective behavior as such, but the absence from it of reflection. When the subject is no longer able to return to the object what he has received from it, he becomes poorer rather than richer. He loses reflection in both directions: since he no longer reflects the object, he ceases to reflect upon himself, and loses the ability to differentiate" (Adorno and Horkheimer 1972, 189). The masses of Jews projected onto the screen in *The Golem* cannot possibly reflect the individuality of the living Jew. Rather, as Adorno would argue, they merely represent one-dimensional replicas of the absent object that can never be fully reproduced.

To understand the implications of Wegener's version of the golem legend for the identity formation of Jews both on and off the screen, it is important to note the film's predilection for myth-based, caricatured constructions of Jewishness. Shown variously at work, at prayer, in the streets, and in acts of intrigue and conspiracy, the Jews of the ghetto city exude an all but desirable air. Among Wegener's repertoire of Jewish figures, the viewer encounters a series of threatening characters: Rabbi Jehuda, the elder of the community who must be consulted in the decision to act with power against the emperor's banishment; Famulus, the rabbi's scheming, vengeful assistant, who turns the golem loose only to run amok after the rabbi has already thwarted the plan for Jewish expulsion; and the rabbi's unruly daughter Miriam, whose oversexed gaze lures the gentile court messenger Florian into the ghetto, resulting in his death and the near destruction of the city. As in the caricatured portraits of Jews widely appropriated for German and Austrian political campaigns in the years surrounding the film's production, and as in the 1920 publication of the German edition of the *Protocols of the Elders of Zion,* the film's depiction of Jewishness reveals a strong bent toward a feared invasion.

Just as the film's *Dekret wider die Juden* declares that Jews "work black magic" and "endanger the lives" of Christians, *The Golem*'s portrayal of the main Jewish characters confirms these claims. In his own right Rabbi Loew mysteriously produces the robot-like golem out of clay—a scene stylized with thick clouds of smoke, wizard's garb, and pseudo-kabbalistic sorcery—while his manipulatory "show" before the gentile court persuades the emperor to fearfully retract his decree. Such ominous affinities attributed to the Jew foster a clear division between the dark, mysterious ghetto and the enlightened empire, between Jewish sorcery and German culture, between the perceived threat of Jewish power and the vulnerable German state. In their unmediated affective capacity, the images conveyed in Wegener's film schematize, stereotype, and graft characteristics onto the Jew, shaping his identity as defined in opposition to the German. In this sense Wegener's film presents an iconography of Jewishness that far exceeds the mythical foundation of the golem story, thus highlighting the disparate contemporary issues beyond the legend.

Finally, one of the most salient issues underlying Wegener's golem story is the problem of Jewish masses in the city. As was well known at the time, after the German defeat in World War I Eastern European Jews migrated in waves, in unprecedented numbers, heightening the already acute awareness of the Jewish presence. The approximately 90,000 Eastern European Jews who lived within German borders prior to the war nearly doubled as another 70,000 new immigrants joined their countrymen in the West. If, as Georg Lukács claimed already in 1913, the cinema is to present a visual documentation of "everyday activities in the streets and markets," then *The Golem*'s focus on the crowds that occupy the ghetto city serves to foreground this new awareness of the Jewish masses. A 1920 review of Wegener's film appearing in *Der Kinematograph* notes this imperceptible line separating the cinematic from the real world: "The crooked buildings, the twisty alleys of the ghetto which appear in near inexhaustible fullness, indeed even the people who live in them are without any distortion of a non-reality [*Unwirklichkeit*] far removed from everyday life" (Greve 1976, 120). The Jewish setting, the *Kinematograph* critic suggests, along with the Jews portrayed on the screen, correspond to the common images of Jews in Weimar society. Indeed, as representatives of Weimar mass-society, the Jews paradoxically evoked at once capitalistic dominance, political prowess, and scientific insight on the one hand, and stifling swarthiness, exotic practices, and ghetto sensibilities on the other.

Signifying a meeting ground for the Jewish city-dwellers, the streets in Wegener's film fuse together with the masses, becoming a unified symbolic expression of the stylized setting. The amorphous crowds of Jews, swarming through the various passages of the ghetto city, resemble the arteries of an urban body. Like so much of the late nineteenth- and early twentieth-century reactionary discourse on Jewish identity, the Jews in *The Golem* are perceived as the quintessential urban *Volk*. By combining the Jewish and urban metaphors, Wegener obscures the differentiation of the Jewish masses immersed in the animated quality of the city. "It is not Prague," explains Wegener in a *Film-Kurier* interview introducing the film, "that my friend, the architect [Hans] Poelzig, has erected. Rather it is a poem of a city [*Stadt-Dichtung*], a dream, an architectural paraphrase of the golem theme. These alleys and city squares should not call to mind anything real; they should create the atmosphere in which the golem breathes" (Andrej 1920, 2). Given the remarkable visibility of the Ostjuden occupying

the postwar German city (most prominently in the Scheunenviertel of Berlin) and the Eastern Jewish swarms occupying Poelzig's fantasy city, the critique of the historical problem, whether willful or inadvertent, cannot be overlooked. Poelzig himself expressed the desire to make the ghetto buildings speak Yiddish—he once claimed, "wenigstens sollten die Häuser mauscheln" ("at least the buildings should jabber")—which only affirms the artfully constructed bond of Jew and city, a bond that discursively runs from the nineteenth century through the postwar period.

Because in silent cinema nothing speaks in audible terms, everything speaks in visual terms. As Hans Poelzig had hoped, the buildings that were to communicate in Yiddish thus do in fact conjure an air of *Yiddishkeit*. The distorted shapes, dark cavities, and hunchback structures all serve to characterize the figures who occupy its expressive space. Small wonder that the film's earliest critics both in Germany and abroad invariably noted the dynamic architectural mystique of Poelzig's ghetto city. Paul Westheim's review in the *Kunstblatt* recalls the aesthetic tension projected between the ghetto walls and the synagogue, which conveys what he pronounces a "strongly expressive unity of scenery," whereas Hermann Scheffauer's American critique observes an "eerie and grotesque suggestiveness" of the houses and streets in the golem's city. "The will of this master architect," Scheffauer continues, "animating façades into faces, insists that these houses are to speak in jargon and gesticulate" (Scheffauer 1960, 84). The physiognomy of the Jew—a subject that at the time of the film's debut was being widely explored in literary, popular, and *völkisch* writings—emerges in Wegener's film in the architectural construction of Jewishness. As attested by the creators of the film and their critics alike, the contemporary face of the Jew emanates from the historical surface of the ghetto buildings.

The unusual quality of this ethnically encoded architecture, or cinematic production of *Jewish* space, also finds expression in the advertising materials printed for the film. In the 1920 poster for *Der Golem: Wie er in die Welt kam,* reportedly designed by Poelzig, the profiles of the dark Jewish figures reflect the oblique shapes of the city buildings towering above. As in the film's representation, the Jews in the advertisement vividly mark the city's physiognomy. Huddled beneath the monstrous ghetto buildings, the ghetto inhabitants in the publicity poster bear the posture of the architecture itself. Like the Ostjuden portrayed in the political caricatures of the 1920s, these Jews connote dark, scheming, and intrusive elements that threaten to invade the German body politic.

Well before Wegener's production, the threat of cultural exchange between the German and Jew had long been a topic of popular literature and the visual arts. In the new wave of anti-Semitic writing following the brief boom at the end of the nineteenth century, Artur Dinter's bestselling novel *Die Sünde wider das Blut* (The sin against blood; 1918) warned the German Volk against the doomed fate of racial mixing. Pitting German and Jew against each other, Dinter argued that German-Jewish procreation results in an evil revenge manifest in the so-called sin against blood. In the cinema, this topic would be picked up again only two years after Wegener's *Golem* in F. W. Murnau's *Nosferatu* of 1922, a film that, when viewed against the historical backdrop of Eastern Jewish migration and the discourses of parasitism, insanity, and sexuality, clearly reveals an acute fear of Jewish invasion. The plague-bearing Eastern capitalist in Murnau's *Nosferatu,* played by the Jewish actor Max Schreck, buys up the property in the gentile city, an act that results in the near extinction of the dominant population. He destroys all who enter into his path, conspires with the (Jewish) pathological real estate dealer (played by the Yiddish theater actor Alexander Granach), and engages in sexual intercourse with the Western gentile Volk. As in *The Golem,* the ostensibly Jewish figures in *Nosferatu* are portrayed as swarthy, threatening creatures who inhabit dark, haunted spaces.

To explore the ways in which Jews are filmically portrayed during the 1920s is not to suggest that these images travel a course that teleologically leads to Nazism, the destruction of the Jews, and mass barbarism. Weimar cinema does *not,* as Kracauer claims in *From Caligari to Hitler,* provide a key to uncovering the alleged psychological disposition of a nation. Rather, the poignancy of such representations lies in their role in defining an identity, one that was constructed and continues to be constructed through memory and fantasy, history and myth.

Bibliography

Theodor W. Adorno, *Aesthetic Theory* [1970], trans. C. Lenhardt (London: Routledge & Kegan Paul, 1984); Adorno and Max Horkheimer, *Dialectic of Enlightenment* [1944], trans. John Cumming (New York: Seabury Press, 1972); Andrej, "Ein Gespräch mit Paul Wegener," *Film-Kurier* 244 (Oct. 29, 1920); Emily D. Bilski, ed., *Golem! Danger, Deliverance and Art* (New York: Jewish Museum, 1988); Sander L. Gilman, *The Jew's Body* (New York: Routledge, 1991); Ludwig Greve, ed., *Hätte ich das Kino! Die Schriftsteller und der Stummfilm* (Stuttgart: Ernst Klett, 1976); *Jüdische Lebenswelten im deutschen Film* (Berlin: Freunde der Deutschen Kinemathek, 1992); Gertrud Koch, *Die Einstellung ist die Einstellung: Visuelle Konstruktionen des Judentums* (Frankfurt a. M.: Suhrkamp, 1992); Siegfried Kracauer, "Kult der Zerstreuung" [1926], *Das Ornament der Masse* (Frankfurt a. M.: Suhrkamp, 1963), 311–17; Elfriede Ledig, *Paul Wegeners Golem—Filme im Kontext fantastischer Literatur* (Munich: Verlegergemeinschaft, 1989); Roger Manvell, ed., "The Golem," *Masterworks of the German Cinema* (New York: Harper & Row, 1973), 18–51; Hermann G. Scheffauer, "The Vivifying of Space" [1920], *Introduction to the Art of the Movies,* ed. Lewis Jacobs (New York: Noonday, 1960), 76–85; Gershom Scholem, "Die Vorstellung vom Golem in ihren tellurischen und magischen Beziehungen," *Zur Kabbala und ihre Symbolik* (Zurich: Rhein-Verlag, 1960), 209–59; Scholem, "The Golem of Prague and the Golem of Rehuvot" [1965], *The Messianic Idea in Judaism* (New York: Schocken, 1971), 335–40; *Sequenz: Film und Pädagogik* 7 [special issue: *Der Golem*] (Nancy, France: Goethe Institute, 1994); and Paul Wegener, *Der Golem: Wie er in die Welt kam. Eine Geschichte in fünf Kapiteln* (Berlin: August Scherl, 1921).

NOAH W. ISENBERG

November 16, 1920 Czech nationalists occupy the German Landestheater / Ständetheater in Prague

The occupation of the Landestheater / Ständetheater (since 1948 called Tylovo Divadlo, today Stavovské Divadlo) by Czech nationalists in 1920 and its official annexation by the Czech National Theater in December of the same year can be seen as symptomatic for the setting in which the Prague school of German writers evolved. It was an event highlighting one of the basic catalysts—the linking of cultural and political warfare—that led to a phenomenon possibly unparalleled in European history: the creation of an important literature by an ethnic minority (Jewish) using the culture and language of another minority (German) that had experienced oppression, after a period of domination. The Jewish minority then shared this oppression with—and paradoxically was at the same time rejected by—the German minority.

For both sides, the Czech and the German, the theater was the visible expression of dominance and national pride. In 1787 when Mozart came to Prague for the premiere of his *Don Giovanni* in the Landestheater (it was then called, after its patron, the Gräflich Nostitz'sche Nationaltheater, and after 1798, the Ständetheater), the Czechs and Germans still celebrated such events together. One of Mozart's closest friends (who was obliged to lock him up in his villa Bertramka so that he would finish composing the overture on time) was the Czech composer and piano virtuoso Franz Xaver Dušek. Bohemia still had the potential for becoming another Switzerland of Central Europe, a model for the peaceful coexistence of three cultures: in this case, Czech, German, and Jewish. But although this dream surfaced as an idea once in a while, history followed the opposite course. The gap between the cultures increased steadily during the nineteenth century. The Czechs revolted against the oppression by the Germans, who had upheld their economic and cultural superiority over the centuries. After the Germans—who still maintained their majority in the Bohemian parliament—had rejected the Czech request for more theater privileges in the early 1800s, a national grassroots movement was undertaken to ensure the building of a Czech theater. This was completed in 1881 on a prominent site on the banks of the Moldau: Národní Divadlo. The Germans responded with a similar effort, and in 1888, the Neues Deutsches Theater (today Státní Opera) adjacent to the Stadtpark was finished.

The Charles University, the oldest university of Central Europe, had also just split in 1882; the invisible wall between the two cultures was becoming a reality. Friedrich Jodl, an outsider from Munich who had accepted the chair of philosophy at the German half of Charles University, characterized the situation in 1885 well: "Czechs and Germans are divided by an impenetrable wall. . . . Social life here is permeated totally by politics and if one is not interested in going along with it, the only alternative possible is withdrawal" (Jodl, 1920, 17–19).

Egon Erwin Kisch, "der rasende Reporter" who raised the genre of reportage to the level of an art form, vividly described some of the concrete results of such a separation as they affected the fortresses of national culture, the Czech and German theaters: "What was obvious to any citizen of Prague and must have seemed incredible to anyone else—especially when one considers the role the theater played at that time—was this: no Czech citizen ever visited the German theater and vice versa. If the *Comédie Française,* the Moscow Artists' Theater or a famous singer made a guest performance at the Czech National Theater, the German press took not the slightest notice and it would not have occurred to the critics, who day in and day out juggled with the names like Coquelin, Stanislawski, or Chaliapin, to attend such a performance. On the other hand, if the performances were at the German Theater, regardless of whether it was the Viennese Burgtheater ensemble, Adolf von Sonnenthal, or Enrico Caruso, they received no recognition in the Czech press" (Kisch, 1957, 86).

The third ethnic group in Prague, the Jews, was divided. After their emancipation had begun, many Jews, compelled by adverse conditions, assimilated by identifying themselves with the Germans, who seemed to guarantee a more secure economic future. The German language was much more useful for international trade, and, with all their educational and cultural institutions, Germans had more to offer than the Czechs. Therefore, at the turn of the century, the Jews had become the backbone of German culture in Prague. Paul Leppin, one of the few non-Jews of the "Prague Circle" (although he was regarded by many as a Jew and was later arrested by the Nazis), expressed this view in an article entitled "A Jewish Colony" in the collection of essays *Das jüdische Prag,* published in 1917 by Selbstwehr. He had doubts whether "it was at all possible to speak about a culture of the German Prague" because the "Deutschtum" in Prague consisted in his opinion only of political parties. The Jews were the real contributors to German culture. Certainly, this was true for the theater. For years Angelo Neumann was director of the Neues Deutsches Theater, and Heinrich Teweles, a

friend of Theodor Herzl, was his dramatic critic until he became director himself. The list of performers and performances is impressive. It shows that the history of the Neues Deutsches Theater cannot be ignored in the history of German theater. And a look at the Prague school of German writers—most of whom were Jewish—also confirms Leppin's view.

Actually, the term "school" might be misleading. It implies a similarity between the members of this school and suggests a "master" who served as a model. But neither situation existed. Even Max Brod, who would come closest to being such a head of a school, would certainly have rejected the title. He was simply very active in helping other writers get started by encouraging them and aiding them in their search for publishers. It is perhaps best to follow the description in his account of the "Prague circle" and see him as the center around which various groups of writers and artists assembled like the skins or layers of an onion. The inner layer or, as he called it, the inner Prague circle consisted of Brod, Felix Weltsch, Oskar Baum, Franz Kafka, and after Kafka's death, Ludwig Winder. It was a group of friends who shared their experiences with one another, discussed old and new ideas, and read each other's work. Outside of this circle were many other small groups, as well as individuals without any real affiliations. Yet all of them can be included in the Prague school or the "wider Prague circle"— for instance, Ernst Weiss, Rudolf Fuchs, and Otto Pick, as well as Brod's immediate predecessors, the writers and artists of "Young Prague": Paul Leppin, Oskar Wiener, Viktor Hadwiger, Hugo Steiner-Prag, and Richard Teschner. Next is the important "layer" consisting of Willy Haas, Franz Werfel, Hermann Ungar, Franz Janowitz, Hans Natonek, Grete Fischer, and such younger writers as Johannes Urzidil, Karl Brand, Hermann Grab, Gustav Janouch, Franz Baermann Steiner, Georg Kafka, Hans Kolben, Franz Wurm, and Hanna Demetz. Other configurations are possible—many names have not been mentioned here. H. G. Adler lists eight different groups in his survey "Die Dichtung der Prager Schule."

These groups had little in common other than

a shared or similar cultural experience shaped by the political situation in Prague. And their attitude toward their surroundings was comparable. They did not fit the standard mold. They were the outsiders who resisted the cultural division and played an important role in trying to bridge the existing gap that separated Czech and German culture. In so doing, these writers did not live in isolation, in a "threefold ghetto"—German, German-Jewish, and bourgeois—as was often stated. Among others, Margarita Pazi, when expanding on remarks by Max Brod, convincingly rejected this notion by Pavel Eisner (himself one of the very active translators), which has haunted many an article. Real isolation would not have permitted them to be mediators. Eisner's remark also overlooks the fact that almost all of the younger generation of German writers spoke Czech and had Czech relatives or friends. Many of them also lived emotionally between the cultures. Pazi writes: "In his 'personal-political confession' of 1918, Max Brod characterized to a large extent the thoughts of many of his friends: 'I do not consider myself as belonging to the German people, however, I am a friend of *Deutschtum* (the essential German spirit) and, besides, through language and upbringing related to the traditional values of *Deutschtum,* I am a friend of the essential Czech spirit (*Tschechentum*) and yet in essence this spirit is culturally foreign to me.' In 1920 Kafka wrote to Milena Jesenska: 'German is my mother tongue and thus it comes naturally to me, but to Czech I have a stronger sense of affection'" (Pazi 1978, 22).

Max Brod's role in popularizing Czech culture is well known, especially his discoveries of Jaroslav Hašek and Leoš Janáček, which guaranteed them European fame. In addition, because of his efforts, Rudolf Fuchs's and Otto Pick's contributions as translators of Czech poetry have been recognized, as well as the work of many others, such as Pavel Eisner. Another bridge between the two cultures was the *Herderblätter* (its name already implying its program of cultural understanding), published in 1911–12. Its last issue contained Otto Pick's article "Czech Poetry," which was intended to help Czech literature achieve international recognition. But other writers who are forgotten today, such as Paul Leppin, were also praised at the time for demonstrating, as poets as well as citizens, that a peaceful and beneficial coexistence of the Czechs and Germans was possible without relinquishing one's cultural identity. In this way, Leppin may serve as the paradigm for all other Prague writers who have not yet been mentioned. He was not a prolific translator, but he wrote several articles—such as "Tschechische Literatur," "Tschechische Malerei," and "Die Tschechen"—to introduce his German audience to Czech literature and the arts; he had close contacts to the Czech literary avant-garde who were published in the Czech *moderní revue* and befriended several Czech artists, especially Jiří Karásek ze Lvovic; and his brother Josef was married to a Czech woman and raised his children bilingually. Leppin is another witness who pointed out that, in spite of all the official walls between the two nations, places such as the coffeehouse Arco, the meeting place of the German writers during Franz Werfel's time, were also frequented by their Czech friends. This list of contacts and collaborations could easily be extended. Rudolf Illový expressed the attitude of many Czech artists when he wrote in 1913: "They [the Germans] are young intellectuals who are watching the struggles of the Czech people and its cultural endeavors without prejudice and participating in Czech life as observers, in order to become acquainted with its different facets. . . . The hope that these young people will break down the barrier of prejudice and bias that opposes everything Czech in Germany and among Germans in Austria is both real and justified. They will then be in a strong position to promote the establishment of peace between the two peoples inhabiting this land" ("Němečtí básníci pražští a Češi," *Veřejné mínění* 1913, 2).

A glance at the various biographies also makes it clear that the supposed isolation of the Prague German writers from the rest of German culture is vastly overrated. As mentioned above, Angelo Neumann had turned the Neues Deutsches Theater into an active center of the arts with performances by the newest playwrights and composers. And there was a constant flow of exchange of ideas between the main German-speaking cultural centers: Prague, Berlin, Vienna, and Munich. No single new idea was floated anywhere without it also being picked up in Prague.

The distinguishing feature of the German writers in Prague was their precarious situation in a cultural amalgam of a city: they found themselves rejected by their own people whose culture they shared. Yet they could not simply abandon this essential part of themselves and replace it with their ethnic roots—that is, Judaism. The result was a sense of alienation, an identity crisis that they would not have experienced in any other place. In spite of all their personal friendships, the German writers could not escape the atmosphere of intolerance that grew increasingly stronger. They became victims of the anti-German attitude of the Czech populace, as well as of the anti-Semitism that increased on both sides, the German and the Czech.

At the end of the nineteenth century, when Jodl wrote about the political situation, he remarked: "Only two items are indispensable: There can be no flirting with the national character of the Slavs and no anti-Semitism. The German society here depends on both for its very existence" (Jodl 1920, 19). German liberalism was still strong in Prague, and Jews and Germans were aware of their interdependence; without the German-speaking Jews, the German decline would have been even more obvious. In a short time, the Germans had lost the majority in Prague, and at the turn of the century fewer than 10 percent of the city's citizens—most of them Jews. Prague had become a young Czech city. Therefore, these German-Jewish writers had learned in their youth to regard the Germans as their protectors during the anti-Semitic and anti-German street riots, chiefly in 1897 after the collapse of the Badeni government and its language reform, which had tried to establish official bilingualism. Max Brod wrote at that time, "How soothing it finally was for the anxiously pounding hearts of the children to hear the firm footsteps of the military clearing the streets" (Brod 1921, 29). It was the German military that was identified with security. Soon this too would change because of the Aryan movement that was to sweep through Austria and Germany.

In 1887, the Viennese fraternity Teutonia was the first to accept the Aryan article in its constitution. The Jewish students in Germany and Austria followed suit, as well as those in Prague. In 1893, a Jewish-national fraternity, Makabäa, was founded to raise Jewish national awareness. In light of the political and cultural atmosphere described above, it is not surprising that it was organized primarily by Czech-speaking Jews. But after a few years spent in seeking an identity, and after it had fallen under the control of the Zionist movement, the organization continued as "Verein jüdischer Hochschüler in Prag 'Bar Kochba,'" with increasing numbers of German Jews joining it. Their first cultural home, the liberal society "Lese und Redehalle der deutschen Studenten," founded originally to further German culture, had lost its importance. After the German nationalistic students had left this society and had established their own organization that did not allow membership for Jews, it was clear that the German-Jewish symbiosis had ended. In 1907 the Prague Zionist weekly paper *Die Selbstwehr* was founded. Felix Weltsch became editor in 1918. This was the time when most of the "Prague Circle" also became active. These writers had experienced rejection by the Czechs as well as the Germans and now found themselves in the situation of finding a new identity: their own roots were alien to them, and their relationship to German culture became more and more one of unrequited love.

This new situation was the basis for the feeling of alienation that became one of the outstanding features of the Prague school of writers. They had been robbed of their home—of the culture with which they had grown up. Even if some, like Brod, could find new intellectual roots in Zionism, a certain void remained. Although the new culture was ethnic, and thereby offered some emotional depth, it was to a large extent only cerebral. As Pazi notes, "Until his death, Max Brod, the convinced Zionist and patriot of the state of Israel, had the telephone book from Prague from the year 1939 on his desk" (Pazi 1978, 38), a reminder not only of his German past but also of the pain caused by this culture.

For the Czech writers, Prague was the embodiment of hope, the city in the process of ascension, the place where the prophecy of the mythological queen Libuše (Libussa) would be fulfilled: "I see a large city whose fame will reach to the stars." For the German writers, however, Prague was the embodiment of decay, as Norbert Frýd expressed eloquently in "The End of an Island." The "home," the security, had been proven to be an illusion. The individual was forced to rethink his or her existence, and partially buried ethnic knowledge had to be exhumed. Thus this process of searching, the intense intellectual discussions, the cultural cross-fertilization, the heightened sensitivity, and the constant awareness of the other created a feeling of questioning—but also of belonging—and provided a new basis for life and work. Such an intense intellectual atmosphere led to very personal, and therefore varied, written expression. This was the backdrop for the unique phenomenon of the Prague school of German writers, which absorbed and nourished itself from three cultures.

The paradoxical situation of the writers of the "Prague Circle" became even more so when the political tide changed again and the German "liberators" arrived in Prague. Although the writers who had stayed in Prague had been able to continue their mediation between the cultures under the new Czech government, the German liberation forced them into exile and death. The culture they had represented and had made their own and to whose renown they had contributed so much was perverted by the so-called defenders of German culture, the Nazis.

Bibliography

H. G. Adler, "Die Dichtung der Prager Schule," *Im Brennpunkt: Ein Österreich,* ed. Manfred Wagner (Vienna: Europaverlag, 1976), 67–98; Max Brod, *Adolf Schreiber: Ein Musikerschicksal* (Berlin: 1921); Brod, *Der Prager Kreis* (Stuttgart: Kohlhammer, 1966); Brod, *Streitbares Leben, 1884–1968,* rev. ed. (Munich: F. A. Herbig, 1969); Pavel Eisner, *Franz Kafka and Prague* (New York: Golden Griffin Books, 1950); Norbert Frýd, "Vom Ende einer Insel: Die deutschen Dichter Prags," *Im Herzen Europas* 3 (1959): 4–6; Eduard Goldstücker, ed., *Weltfreunde* (Prague: Academia, 1967); Dierk O. Hoffmann, *Paul Leppin* (Bonn: Bouvier, 1982); Margarete Jodl, *Friedrich Jodl: Sein Leben und Werk* (Stuttgart: Cotta, 1920); *Das jüdische Prag: Eine Sammelschrift* (Prague: Selbstwehr, 1917); Egon Erwin Kisch, *Marktplatz der Sensationen* (Berlin: Aufbau, 1951); Margarita Pazi, "Franz Kafka, Max Brod und der Prager Kreis," *Franz Kafka und das Judentum,* ed. Karl Erich Grözinger, Stéphane Moses, and Hans Dieter Zimmermann (Frankfurt a. M.: Jüdischer Verlag/Athenäum, 1987), 71–92; Pazi, *Fünf Autoren des Prager Kreises* (Frankfurt a. M.: Peter Lang, 1978); Pazi, "Der Prager Kreis-Judentum und zionistischer Gedanke," *Emuna Israel-Forum* 2 (1977): 46–51; Pazi and Hans Dieter Zimmermann, eds., *Berlin und der Prager Kreis* (Würzburg: Königshausen und Neumann, 1991); Pavl Petr, "Franz Kafkas Böhmen: Tschechen, Deutsche, Juden," *Germano-Slavica* 6 (fall 1981): 377–99; Richard Rosenheim, *Die Geschichte der Deutschen Bühnen in Prag, 1883–1918. Mit einem Rückblick, 1783–1883* (Prague: Heinrich Mercy, 1938); Jürgen Serke, *Böhmische Dörfer: Wanderungen durch eine verlassene literarische Landschaft* (Vienna: Paul Zsolnay, 1987); Christoph Stölzl, *Kafkas böses Böhmen* (Munich: edition text + kritik, 1975); Hans Tramer, "Prague: City of Three Peoples," *Year Book of the Leo Baeck Institute* 9 (1964): 305–39; Gertrude Urzidil, "Zur Quadratur des Prager Kreises," *literatur + kritik* 99 (Oct. 1975): 528–36; and Harry Zohn, "Participation in German Literature," *The Jews of Czechoslovakia: Historical Studies and Surveys* 1 (1968): 468–522.

DIERK O. HOFFMANN

1920 The Free Jewish School is founded in Frankfurt am Main under the leadership of Franz Rosenzweig

"You will already have read in the newspaper of the terrible blow that has struck us here," Franz Rosenzweig (1886–1929) wrote to Martin Buber (1878–1965) on January 25, 1922. "Part of the basis of my life has been snatched from underfoot. . . . It may be no accident that, in the last hour of that good fortune I have lost, you and I have had that dark and seemingly hopeless conversation that nevertheless compels further steps— though also into the darkness. . . . Stay with us, stay in this world for me!"

The sudden disaster of which Rosenzweig so movingly wrote to Buber was the death at the age of fifty-one of Rabbi Nehemiah Anton Nobel (1871–1922), the spiritual father of a remarkable group of young German-Jewish intellectuals who gathered at the Free Jewish School (Freies Jüdisches Lehrhaus) in Frankfurt am Main. Rosenzweig himself had come to Frankfurt in 1920 from his native Kassel to head the newly founded school at Rabbi Nobel's behest; now it was clear that it would have to struggle to survive the death of its guiding spirit, and Rosenzweig hoped Buber would help. It would prove, for reasons both internal and external to the Lehrhaus, to be a daunting task.

Born in Hungary, Nobel had been a defender of Orthodox against Reform Judaism, but he nonetheless had a serious training in academic philosophy: he wrote his doctoral dissertation at the University of Bonn on Schopenhauer's theory of beauty, later studied with the great neo-Kantian Hermann Cohen (1842–1918), and was renowned as a Goethe scholar. He also had a remarkable gift for inspiring younger disciples. One of their number, Leo Lowenthal (1900–1993), who was also to become a founding member of the Frankfurt Institute for Social Research, would remember him many years later as representing "a curious mixture of mystical religiosity, philosophical rigor, and quite likely also a more or less repressed homosexual love for young men. It really was a kind of 'cult community.' He was a fascinating speaker. People flocked to hear his sermons. He kept his house open to all, and people would come and go as they pleased" (Lowenthal 1987).

Nobel's goal was to reinvigorate an Orthodoxy that he thought had grown sclerotic and overly concerned with legalistic ritual. His enthusiasms were intense and varied; not only did he vigorously support the German war effort (as did Cohen, Buber, and most other German Jews), but he was also a fervent Zionist and a campaigner for women's suffrage. And he shared in the postwar idealization—some called it a cult—of the Eastern European Jews (the Ostjuden), whose evident piety, strong communal identification, and dogged resistance to Westernization seemed to offer a powerful alternative to the feckless assimilation and bourgeois values of most German Jews.

It was the rebellious sons of those assimilated parents who were gripped by Nobel's rhapsodic sermons in the heady days after the calamitous end of World War I, at a time when messianic and apocalyptic currents of all kinds swept through Central and Eastern Europe. When Nobel turned fifty, a *Festschrift* was presented to him with essays by some of the most gifted young Weimar intellectuals, many of whom later gained international fame, including Rosenzweig, Buber, Lowenthal, Siegfried Kracauer (1889–1966), Erich Fromm (1900–1980), Ernst Simon (1899–1988), Leo Baeck (1873–1959), Eduard Strauss (1876–1952), Richard Koch (1882–1949), and Nahum Glatzer (1903–90). It was from this group that the core of the experiment in adult education that was the Frankfurt Lehrhaus was formed.

Although superficially comparable to other German *Volkshochschulen,* the Lehrhaus was designed from the beginning to provide more than mere intellectual fare. A modern version of the traditional *Beth ha Midrasch,* it was "free" in the sense that it was open to everyone without an examination. Rather than serving as an outreach program of the scholarly and "objective" Wissenschaft des Judentums or a seminary for the propagation of the Halakhah (law), it sought to foster what Rosenzweig in his inaugural address of October 11, 1920, "On Jewish Learning," called a restoration of Judaism as a whole way of life. It would encourage, he argued, "a learning that no longer starts from the Torah and leads into life, but the other way round: from life, from a world that knows nothing of the Law, or pretends to know nothing, back to the Torah" (Glatzer 1961). Echoing the then fashionable— and often right-wing—terminology of *Heimat* as an antidote to modern alienation, he exhorted the members of his congregation to "turn into yourself, return home to your innermost self and to your innermost life." But it was to be a home in which dialogue with others and the practical embodiment of faith took precedence over pure interiority.

The Lehrhaus was thus to be what one commentator later called "an existential meeting-place," a place where adults could find their way back to a totalizing Jewish experience that went beyond the external observation of the law. "Judaism," Rosenzweig (1935, 425) explained, "is not a law. It makes law. But it is not identical

with such law. Rather it means 'being' Jewish." The key term was thus "experience," which was counterposed to the exaggerated reliance on intellect and disputation characteristic of an older model of Jewish learning. Significantly, of those who taught there, only 15 percent were rabbis; the remainder were a combination of professional scholars and learned amateurs.

It is, however, important to understand the specific meaning the leaders of the Lehrhaus gave to the vexed term "experience." Before the war, the German word *Erlebnis* (variously translated as inner or lived experience) had enjoyed an extraordinary cachet in the vocabularies of those thinkers associated with the Philosophy of Life (*Lebensphilosophie*), notably Wilhelm Dilthey and Georg Simmel. Among Jewish thinkers, Buber was most enamored of this term, which he counterposed to the purely reflective, overly intellectual experience of the neo-Kantian tradition he identified with *Erfahrung.* His exuberant discovery of the Hasidic communities of Eastern Europe, which anticipated the postwar cult of the Ostjude, was based on the assumption that membership in a "blood community" was a prerequisite for such lived experience.

Buber's exaltation of experience in the sense of irrational, ecstatic inwardness—his *völkisch Erlebnismystik,* as it was called by his opponents— did not, however, survive the war, perhaps, it has been conjectured, because of the scathing criticism to which it was subjected by his friend, the anarchist Gustav Landauer (1870–1919). By the time he joined the Lehrhaus, he had moved to a more dialogic notion of experience, which became known, following the book he published in 1923, as the philosophy of "I-Thou." Not only did this turn imply a greater respect for actual social relations, it also entailed a strong emphasis on communicative interaction, or more precisely on spoken language as a locus of the sacred, where impersonal law (*Gesetz*) could be received as personal commandment (*Gebot*). Rabbi Nobel's stirring sermons were evidence that speech might produce the level of existential intensity that betokened the holy.

Rosenzweig's own thought at this time was moving along parallel lines, despite certain subtle differences in his understanding of the relationship between law and revelation (Buber's position has been called "metanomian" because of his greater hostility to law). Alerted to the central importance of spoken language through his friendship with the Christian thinker Eugen Rosenstock-Huessy (1888–1973), Rosenzweig also thrilled at Nobel's sermons, which he once described as revealing "a rapture of the whole man, so that one wouldn't be surprised if he took wing in the end and disappeared . . . he prays the way one thinks of people praying only thousands of years ago when the great prayers originated; he speaks to the people as one thinks only the prophets should have been allowed to speak" (Rosenzweig 1935, 411).

After abandoning the idealist and historicist philosophy that had inspired his 1912 doctoral dissertation on "Hegel and the State," written for the historian Friedrich Meinecke, Rosenzweig began to articulate what he called "the New Thinking" in the masterpiece he composed in the trenches on the Balkan front during the war, *The Star of Redemption,* published in 1921. In this remarkable work, which developed a theistic mysticism grounded in a messianic reading of the interaction between creation, revelation, and redemption, Rosenzweig argued against a religion based simply on emotional conviction and inner experience. Despite the vital importance of his own internal struggles—in 1913, he had even seriously contemplated conversion to Christianity—Rosenzweig emphasized the need to combine systematic philosophy with theology, as had been recognized by Hermann Cohen at the end of his life: divine truth, Rosenzweig liked to say, must be implored "with both hands." But ultimately both theology and philosophy should be in the service of religious experience, albeit experience identified as an Erfahrung that went beyond subjective inwardness to include public discussion through speech, "the *organon* of revelation." Along with his other speech-related activities, most notably the new translation of the Hebrew Bible into German he began with Buber in 1925, Rosenzweig hoped the Lehrhaus would be a space in which the spirit of redemption might somehow come existentially alive for those

who joined its fellowship. Here, he believed, a truly dialogical, nonhierarchical relationship between teacher and student would be realized. Here a true *jüdisches Volk* (Jewish people) would begin to replace mere *Judentum* (Jewry as a confessional community defined by the state). Here the century-long German-Jewish adoration of abstract, universalist, humanist *Bildung* would be replaced by a renewed commitment to a concretely Jewish way of life.

Inevitably, so grandiose a hope was bound to be frustrated, and Nobel's premature death was only one of the reasons. The Lehrhaus, to be sure, did at first attract a remarkable group of participants to its seminars and lectures, many of whom were not professional intellectuals. All three of the Frankfurt rabbis took part, as did a range of others—from the Zionist politician Richard Lichtheim (1885–1963) and the political philosopher Leo Strauss (1899–1973), to the novelist and later Nobel Prize winner S. Y. Agnon (1888–1970), to the historian of the Kabbalah, Gershom Scholem (1899–1982). Some ninety lecture series and 180 seminars, discussion meetings, and study groups were held between 1920 and 1926, the lion's share dealing with classical (biblical) and historical (talmudic) Judaism, as well as theology, mysticism, and ethics. Many classes were devoted to the mastery of Hebrew and the reading of religious texts in the original language. During its fourth year (1922–23), the enrollment reached a peak of 1,100 students.

But potential for misunderstanding was high, especially considering the unselective quality of the Lehrhaus's constituency. Rosenzweig himself admitted in a letter that "to work with this *crêpe de Chine* audience [bourgeoisie with a taste for fine food as well as culture] is terribly unrewarding and yet necessary" (Rosenzweig 1935, 466). "There was something tragic," his loyal disciple Glatzer later wrote, "in the situation of a man who so fully believed in the power of the dialogue and the discussion to be doomed to a monological, one-sided activity" (Glatzer 1956, 109). In his memoirs, Scholem recalled the dubious following of one of the Lehrhaus's most charismatic speakers, the chemist Eduard Strauss, whose popularity he remembered as greater than even Buber's: "His equal was hardly to be found in Jewish circles but only among Christian revival movements. His crowded Bible lessons were speeches of an 'awakened one' who spoke out of the spirit. If one may be permitted to use the language of Christian sects, they were pneumatic exegeses, and to this day I do not know whether anyone took them down, for he himself spoke quite spontaneously. His listeners were spellbound, as though they were held by a magic circle; anyone who was not susceptible to this kind of talk stopped coming, and this is what happened with me" (Scholem 1980).

Scholem's sour recollection of the questionable effect of the charismatic Strauss was anticipated by a similar protest made by Ernst Simon in November 1923 in a letter to Buber, which responded to the latter's seminar on Hasidism, in which Simon detected an unhealthy aura of "pietistic idealism." "Direct testimony," Simon warned, "is possible in the narrowest circle, in which the audience is precisely known—that is to say, in the true I-Thou relation between man and woman, between friend and friend. But this relation—in the unmessianic world!—may not simply be assumed naively; rather it must be verified in every single case. In a totally chance company such as that at the Lehrhaus, where, along with a good deal of seriousness, hysteria and religious sensationalism (the worst thing of all) are widespread and would like to wallow, only *indirect* communication should be the rule. If the material does not speak, the holy material, then evidently it is not intended to speak" (Glatzer and Mendes-Flohr 1992). Buber and Rosenzweig understood his qualms, but insisted that if a *minyan* could be made out of any ten believers, no matter how pious, so the Lehrhaus could somehow transform its mixed audience into a genuine community.

A similar critique of the first volume of the Buber-Rosenzweig translation of the Bible was leveled in the *Frankfurter Zeitung* in 1926 by Siegfried Kracauer. By then no longer connected with the Lehrhaus, Kracauer argued that the principles on which it was based assumed too easy a transition from the original word of God to the modern listener's ear. Complaining that the his-

torical conditions for such a reception were not ripe, he contended that Buber and Rosenzweig had wrongly believed that spiritual regeneration could take place in a social and economic vacuum, through a direct relationship between God and man. The prophetic tone and elevated diction of the translation thus betrayed a neo-romanticism reminiscent of mythologizing *völkisch* thought (tellingly, even the non-Zionist Rosenzweig had embraced Buber's notion of the Jews as a "blood community" in *The Star of Redemption*). In private correspondence with Buber, Scholem also expressed reservations about its tonality of pathos, although without adopting Kracauer's more socially based reasoning.

By the time of Kracauer's critique, he and other members of the original circle around Nobel, like Lowenthal and Fromm, had drifted away from the Lehrhaus, indeed from any serious engagement with Judaism. If they retained its messianic impulse, they now expressed it more in terms of a Marxist critique of capitalism than as a hope for a purely religious redemption. Those who remained staunchly defended the translation. Interestingly, Simon was one of them—and by extension so too was the mission of the Lehrhaus itself. But by the mid-1920s, it was clear that the project was losing its momentum.

A primary reason for this decline was another personal tragedy, perhaps even more painful to endure than the sudden death of Rabbi Nobel: the progressive deterioration of Rosenzweig's health. In 1922, Rosenzweig had been diagnosed as suffering from amyotrophic lateral sclerosis— what would soon become well known in America as Lou Gehrig's disease. With a cruel irony, which Buber later recognized, the philosopher of speech found it harder and harder to communicate without extraordinary effort. Although death was expected within a year, Rosenzweig managed to survive in an ever-worsening condition until December 1929. His remarkable courage and perseverance against extraordinary odds contributed to the aura of spiritual strength that surrounded him as the "suffering servant" of God.

Rosenzweig's ability to lead the Lehrhaus, however, inevitably diminished. In August 1922, Rosenzweig put the best face on his decision to relinquish the directorship in a letter to his mother: "I am very happy. The Lehrhaus, whose dissolution, or more likely and worse, normalization (according to Buber, in a confidential remark to some Zionists, it is the only distinguished cultural institution today among all of Western Jewry) I had considered inevitable, is to be continued: [the art historian and archeologist] Rudi [Rudolf] Hallo is to 'substitute' for me. Thus its main direction (non-specialist, non-rabbinical, non-polemical, non-apologetic, universalist in content and spirit) has been assured. It's not going to be a committee affair but will retain its personal features. Moreover, as long as I'm still here, I can speak and act through this prophet" (Rosenzweig 1935, 442).

Hallo, however, remained as director for only a year because of differences over his willingness to adopt a fully traditional Jewish way of life. He was replaced by a four-man administration, consisting of Buber, Koch, Strauss, and Rosenzweig (Simon had declined for the reasons outlined in his disappointed letter to Buber cited above), with the young lawyer Rudolf Stahl acting as executive secretary (to be followed a year later by the medical student Martin Goldner). Rosenzweig was still able to respond to activities at the Lehrhaus—in November 1924, he wrote a long letter reacting to discussions of his thoughts on law in *The Builders* and in 1925 an essay reaffirming his commitment to the revival of "Jewish learning"—but he was no longer himself an active participant.

By the mid-1920s, moreover, the general climate for messianic projects in the Weimar Republic had cooled. In artistic circles, Expressionism had been succeeded by the sober and disillusioned *Neue Sachlichkeit;* politically, the republic seemed stable after its early paroxysm of revolutionary effervescence. The postwar cult of the Ostjude lost some of its allure, as a more realistic appreciation of their situation replaced the romantic idealization of the initial years of contact. By 1925, some 3,500 refugees from the East were struggling to survive in Frankfurt; they were no longer so easily transformed into examples of a vital Jewish *Gemeinschaft*. Although Zionism made some headway among German Jews, most remained wedded to the liberal assimilationist model, which was based on a reverence for secular German Bildung that Nobel, Rosenzweig, Buber, and other leaders of the Lehrhaus had found so vacuous. Of the some 30,000 Jews in Frankfurt, it has been estimated that only 4 percent were involved in one way or another with the Lehrhaus, and many of them—like Kracauer, Fromm, Lowenthal, and Scholem—only passed through on the way to other intellectual destinations.

As an institution, the Frankfurt Lehrhaus officially survived until Rosenzweig's death in 1929, although its program was effectively terminated in 1926. It had inspired similar houses of learning in Stuttgart, Cologne, Wiesbaden, Mannheim, Karlsruhe, Munich, Breslau, and Berlin. Then, in a sad afterlife, it was revived under Buber's leadership in November 1933, as a kind of cultural center for Frankfurt's beleaguered Jewry and a source of spiritual resistance to Nazism—only to be closed for good after the horrors of Kristallnacht five years later. Among those who participated was Abraham Joshua Heschel (1907–1972), who later became a leading liberal voice in American Jewish life. Buber and Simon, who had courageously returned from Palestine to Germany to help with the effort, left in 1938 to take up permanent residence in Jerusalem.

But even as a "failure"—and what else in German-Jewish life could not be ultimately called a failure?—the Lehrhaus must be accounted a remarkable moment in that long and convoluted history. Or rather, it was a heroic, if in the end vain, attempt to rise above history itself and provide a space for a more direct encounter between the Jewish believer and the Jewish God, an encounter shared by a community of the faithful. Under Rosenzweig's leadership, the Lehrhaus sought to free itself from the entanglements of history and politics—from assimilation, we might say, to anything outside of Jewish life—in order to foster a positive, spiritually meaningful experience of Judaism that was contemporaneous rather than in some imagined future. Thus Rosenzweig kept his distance both from political Zionism and liberal Bildung because he felt they were compromises with forces that would dilute such an experience. He was equally unmoved by the task of defending against anti-Semitism in an active way; in so doing, Jews would allow their lives to be dictated by the animosities and misconceptions of others, and their positive self-esteem would be reduced to apologetics. Tellingly, even the revered Rabbi Nobel could be criticized, as he was in a letter Rosenzweig wrote in January 1922, for "toying with Christian and pagan ideas."

In the end, so pure an ideal of realized Jewish experience could not withstand the pressures of the larger context in which it was situated. The profane history that Rosenzweig thought could be kept at bay insistently intruded. The personal links forged by charismatic leaders like Nobel and Rosenzweig could not withstand the more powerful impulses unleashed by other charismatic leaders in German politics, who would soon destroy the possibility of a renewal of Jewish life in Frankfurt as well as virtually everywhere else in Europe.

In his remarkable letter of November 2, 1923, to Buber, the letter in which he protested against the pitfalls of unearned immediacy, Ernst Simon also charged his teacher with lacking a "feeling for *the tragic aspect,* which is something different from melancholia. Our humanness is *constituted* by the fact that we have eaten from the Tree of Knowledge, of Good and Evil: the tragic aspect of *knowledge* is now our portion. . . . We do not live in the 'kingdom of God' in which the Halakhah—even you hold this not—may cease and in which every person is a Thou to an I" (Glatzer and Mendes-Flohr 1992, 300–301). In 1920, the messianically charged year in which the Lehrhaus was founded, tragedy was a far less prominent star in the heavens than redemption; in 1938, the year it was finally closed, the star of tragedy was shining so brilliantly in the firmament of Jewish life that even the light of redemption was obscured from human view.

Bibliography

Erich Ahrens, "Reminiscences of the Men of the Frankfurt Lehrhaus," *Leo Baeck Institute Yearbook* 19 (London: Secker and Warburg, 1974); Maurice Friedmann, *Martin Buber's Life and Work* (New York: Dutton, 1983); Nahum N. Glatzer, "The Frankfurt Lehrhaus," *Leo Baeck Institute Yearbook* 1 (London: Secker and Warburg, 1956); Glatzer, *Franz Rosenzweig: His Life and Thought* (New York: Schocken, 1961); Glatzer and Paul Mendes-Flohr, eds., *The Letters of Martin Buber,* trans. Richard Winston, Clara Winston, and Harry Zohn (New York: Schocken, 1992); Rachel Heugerger, "Orthodoxy Versus Reform: The Case of Rabbi Nehemiah Anton Nobel of Frankfurt am Main," *Leo Baeck Institute Yearbook* 37 (London: Secker and Warburg, 1992); Werner Licharz, *Der Philosoph Franz Rosenzweig, 1886–1929* (Freiburg: K. Alber, 1988); Licharz, ed., *Lernen mit Franz Rosenzweig* (Frankfurt a. M.: Haag und Herchen, 1984); Leo Lowenthal, *An Unmastered Past: The Autobiographical Reflections of Leo Lowenthal,* ed. Martin Jay (Berkeley: University of California Press, 1987); Paul Mendes-Flohr, ed., *The Philosophy of Franz Rosenzweig* (Hanover, N.H.: University Press of New England, 1988); Franz Rosenzweig, *Briefe,* ed. Edith Rosenzweig (Berlin: Schocken, 1935); Wolfgang Schivelbusch, *Intellektuellendämmerung: Zur Lage der Frankfurter Intelligenz in den zwanziger Jahren* (Frankfurt a. M.: Insel, 1982); Gershom Scholem, *From Berlin to Jerusalem: Memories of My Youth,* trans. Harry Zohn (New York: Schocken, 1980); and Ernst Simon, "Franz Rosenzweig und das jüdische Bildungsproblem," *Brücken: Gesammelte Schriften* (Heidelberg: Lambert Schneider, 1965).

MARTIN JAY

1921 Walter Benjamin writes the essays "Critique of Violence" and "The Task of the Translator," treating the subject of messianism he discussed with Gershom Scholem during the war

By 1921 it was a matter of record that the past was gone. It had vanished in a double sense: in the material disappearance of old regimes, legitimated social hierarchies, and expansionist expectation; and in the waning of the conception of history possessed by those fading regimes and cultures. By 1921, in other words, the epistemologically available past no longer could be understood as the continuum that produced the present. In this way, the Great War marked the European twentieth century as the century of rupture. For all Germans, the shaky parameters of the Weimar Republic demanded the continuous reinvention of politics and culture. German identity was being reinvented to correspond to a modernity that had left the nation in shock. For German Jews, this predicament carried a double intensity.

For German Jews, the military and home fronts of World War I and the sudden redefinitions of politics and civil society created a deep and evident paradox. In its nationwide *Kulturkampf* and in its heavy use of Jewish officers, the war had seemed to celebrate in blood the arrival of a true German-Jewish symbiosis. Ecumenical services were held on the fronts, and photographs of evangelical, Catholic, and Jewish clergy posing together were issued as postcards by a nationalist and assimilationist Jewish publisher. But nationalist ideology is defined precisely as a radical exclusionism posing as a radical inclusionism. The idea of the pure nation is always a phantom, and thus always based on the purging of some aspect of the real. Thus the same nationalist solidarity that fueled the war effort also fueled the final blow to the claims of symbiosis. The agitated nationalism of 1914–18 proved to be the agent at once of solidarity and exclusion.

Not only were specific, inhabited identities needy of reinvention, but the very notion of identity was not stable. The past that no longer generated the present no longer generated the possibility of identity. Identity finds its etymology and meaning in an assertion of sameness—the sameness of the subject over time, and the sameness of a subject and an object world. Modernity—defined as the state of mind that places subjectivity in a position contingent on history and time—places a spin on the possibility of sameness and stasis, a spin whose arrestation spurs the energy of anti-modernity. The displacement of history, understood as a rupture in the continuum of history, thus raises the stakes of modernity and renders implausible the formulations of identity as sameness. This is true for Jewish identity, for German identity (a reality that nationalists suppressed with the production of newly intense scapegoating, the most virulent among which was anti-Semitism), and for German-Jewish identity in all its formulations, as it is true for the notion of identity itself. Faced with this situation, post-1918 intellectuals found a horizon marked only by necessity.

By 1921 that horizon had been drawn by one text more than any other. As Walter Benjamin remarked in *The Origin of German Tragic Drama,* the publication that year of Franz Rosenzweig's *Star of Redemption* reoriented German-Jewish self-consciousness to the demands of the age. It sent that self-consciousness into the interiority of language, and to the reconfiguration of history through language as the site of the materialization of experience.

The dialogue between Walter Benjamin and Gershom Scholem, which produced two careers full of mutually engaged writing, originated in a shared opposition to the Great War. Their friendship dates from 1915, but Scholem's first exposure to Benjamin was as a fourteen-year-old listener to the twenty-one-year-old Benjamin in 1913, when Benjamin was giving an anti-Zionist address to the Zionist youth group "Jung-Juda." In his 1975 memoir of their friendship, Scholem wrote that he no longer remembered the argument of Benjamin's anti-Zionism (Scholem 1975, 10). No informed reader will let this remark go by easily; this is the most crucial issue in their friendship. Scholem was able logically to make the transition from anti-nationalism in the German context to nationalism in the Zionist context. Benjamin was not. Whereas Scholem's view of politics was utilitarian, Benjamin's was poetic. This poetic view carried a double dimension. On the one hand, it rejected the aesthetic ideology inherent in auratic politics, in the politics of reenchantment. This rejection produced Benjamin's famous definition, in "The Work of Art in the Age of Its Technical Reproducibility," of fascism as the aestheticization of politics. On the other hand, Benjamin could never believe or enact what he spent his life arguing: namely, that politics could really exist out of the realm of the symbolic and the sublime. The result was his refusal of all practical politics, including Zionism, for their sublime and auratic baggage. The messianic at once grounds and destroys the possibility of humane politics. Benjamin is symptomatic of that aspect of modernity for which the

cultural loss of the divine results in melancholy rather than mourning—in other words, in a Sisyphean sentence to repeat the experience of loss rather than to work through it.

For Scholem, Zionism was a political answer to a political predicament. For Benjamin, this rationalization of the political begged the question of what in Heideggerian language is Being. Scholem systematically rejected the scope of existential questioning. His reasons were good, and they saved his life. Benjamin, on the other hand, fought Being from within the claims of its ideological scope. He countered its ideology with the allegorical history of modernity, and in this category his work and Scholem's found a decisive common denominator.

History, for Benjamin, is a two-way street. The recovery of history involves the recovery of materiality and specificity. The past is indeed gone; it can be engaged through reference—which means an operation different from and opposed to representation. Representation involves the appropriation of the subject position of the represented object; reference marks the object-world's distance. Benjamin grounds this distinction in his work with allegory. When Benjamin addresses the baroque, the Second Empire, and the fight against fascism, he addresses concrete historical epochs. These three epochs, one of which is his own, share crucial qualities and conflicts. Recognition of these shared qualities enables the historian or critic to activate certain fragments of the life of the past. This dialogue among epochs retains its dependence on specificity but provides a presentism, a necessity of facing the present, that explodes any scholastic tendency toward antiquarianism. What Benjamin does not do, in his discussion of the baroque, or of the nineteenth century, is provide an inventory of tropes whose principal function is to provide contemporary criticism with a universalist agenda replete with a rich array of costumes. The demands Benjamin makes on historical consciousness will thus keep it a crucial step ahead of the political actors in *The Eighteenth Brumaire of Louis Bonaparte,* whose bodies wear costumes of the past while their minds are encumbered by the weight of the dead. Inspired historian that he is, Benjamin has a vital interest in sixteenth- and seventeenth-century Germany and nineteenth-century France because their traces form dimensions of the present and because he felt a sense of responsibility to the dead. At stake is not a Foucauldian genealogy of the present but a pattern of returns, repetitions, and responses within the political dialectic of totality and fragmentation. The present, in turn, maximizes self-awareness by recognizing patterns of repetition. The present moment began for the mature Benjamin with the Great War. It is defined decisively by fascism, which in his vocabulary includes National Socialism. (Fascism, to repeat, is defined famously as the aestheticization of politics.) The aesthetic gains cultural power as the instrument that inherits from religion the task of the reenchantment of the world.

In this way, historical reasoning becomes allegorical reasoning: Benjamin's historical practice becomes a critique of allegorical reason. Benjamin's revalorization of allegory, against the higher status that a century of German criticism had accorded its favored sibling, the symbol, is based in allegory's historicity and specificity. Allegory is limited. In its linguistic as well as cultural operations, signs refer to other signs. The baroque refers to the Second Empire; baroque totality to the temptations of fascism. Goethe, Schelling, and the brothers Schlegel also saw the limitations of allegory and preferred a secularized Christian practice of symbolism as a window on the universal. A. W. Schlegel asserted that, in symbols, the infinite is brought to the surface. Coleridge imported this predilection to England and to other stations of nineteenth-century sensibility. For Coleridge, the symbol is "characterized by a translucence of the special in the individual, . . . above all by the translucence of the eternal through and in the temporal" (Schlegel 1817; Coleridge 1953).

Here Benjamin says no. Among the romantics and their symbology, Benjamin is closest to Goethe, who tied to his love for the universalizing symbol a stringent critique of representation. This is the thrust of his *Faust, Part Two,* five acts of historical allegory that cannot become symbol because only in Heaven can reference become representation: "Alles vergängliche ist nur ein Gleichnis" (Everything temporal is but a likeness). The universal referent of the symbol implies the transcendence of history. The romantic transcendence of history in the name of universality gives way to the claim of universality over the autonomy of particulars. With the symbol, and in spite of Goethe, reference gives way to representation. Benjaminian allegory, unlike traditional allegory, is a discourse of reference rather than representation.

The Kantian and mystical Jewish tenets that groomed Benjamin early on stay with him to warn austerely that the limitation of human consciousness is the only ethical absolute the mind can allow itself. The later and equally serious engagement with Marxism joins in this austerity, and in the refusal to confuse historical work with utopianism. Universals are always unattainable, and therefore unrepresentable, even by implication. In their unavailability, the promises of Marxism and Messianism remain cosmological horizons: heuristic necessities but forbidden realities. Obviously, Benjamin took these things seriously; because he takes them seriously, he frames them with care and fear. An arrogance of representation leads to political disaster when the field of cultural manipulation is translated from the page or the canvas to society itself. The definition of fascism as the aestheticization of politics is grounded in these concerns.

The primacy of allegory is rooted in the absence of God: it is a Spinozan trope, one might say: Jewish, Protestant, and modernist. In its philosophical lineage in the early twentieth century, it is also neo-Kantian—a tradition Benjamin battles but never abandons. Hermann Cohen and his student Ernst Cassirer probably remain the clearest representatives of two generations of German-Jewish intellectuals who defended critique and civilization with a carefully honed neo-Kantian sensibility. Seen from our side of the postmodern divide, neo-Kantianism can be too easily associated with the hegemony of the subject. But if Kantianism can be described according to the thinking subject's command of the object, Cohen and Cassirer find dignity in subjectivity through its devotion to the object world. In their ethical-epistemological discourse, neo-Kantianism could also mean the plurality of subjects and the hermeneutic divide between the experiencing, interpreting subject and the object world. The varieties of neo-Kantian discourse posit a certain ethical and temporal distance between the two leviathan claims of subject-object convergence that form their philosophical past and future: Hegel's Spirit and Heidegger's Being.

The standard narrative of twentieth-century continental philosophy, told in terms of the victory of phenomenology over neo-Kantianism and symbolized by the Davos debate between the tired Cassirer and the ascendant Heidegger in 1929, is not entirely accurate. More accurate is an understanding of neo-Kantianism's continuation by other discursive and stylistic means. Philosophy's choice rested on the question of the possibility of ethics. As Leo Strauss later remembered that choice, Cassirer "did not face the problem" of philosophy's ethical incompetence, whereas Heidegger triumphed by declaring the impossibility of ethics (Strauss 1989). What really happened (says the historian!) is that philosophy once again went underground, as it had done with Spinoza and Nietzsche, to preserve the possibility of ethics.

The first step in this process was political diffusion, which was embodied in the divergent careers of Hermann Cohen's students Cassirer and Paul Natorp. Cassirer engaged a principle of distance to grow suspicious of nationalism; Natorp embraced both nationalism and the Great War as the defense of German culture. It is Natorp who brought Heidegger to Marburg in 1916. But there is also the question of philosophy pursued by other means, the alliance of neo-Kantian distance with Nietzschean form. (Neo-Kantianism and Nietzsche had converged before, in their shared attention to values as modernity's answer to the claims of universalism.) Here we have the early Benjamin's world. For Leo Strauss, the philosophical program necessitated by his diagnosis of Weimar's crisis of the ego was a reassertion of a strong identity principle. His embrace of Spinoza functioned, by his own account, to provide a strong model of masculine, Jewish identity that would counteract the soft negotiationalism

of Hermann Cohen. In differing guises, then, the result was an outpouring of rigorous argument toward the reconfiguration of modern experience. Rigor is a leitmotif for the "early Benjamin"— that is, from the wartime essays on language to the *Origin of German Tragic Drama;* it has an ethical purpose, and that is the defense of dialogical subjectivity and experience.

It was in 1921, several years before the Marxian turn, that Benjamin wrote the two essays that most explicitly engage the themes of messianism that he had absorbed from his wartime discussions with Scholem. These are the "Critique of Violence," written early in the year, and "The Task of the Translator," written between March and November. The earlier Kantian essay "On Language as Such and the Language of Man" (1916) and the "Theologico-Political Fragment" (ca. 1920–21) should be included as well in this context of critical thought. This five-year period represents the period of Benjamin's maturation and of the attendant, intransigent Kantian position of the unavailability of absolute language, knowledge, and hence of absolute moral or political action. In opposition to the neo-Kantianism characteristic of the discourse of late Jewish assimilation—as in the work of Hermann Cohen— Benjamin arrived at the rejection of all claims to philosophical and political resolution or synthesis.

In 1919–20 Benjamin wrote a dissertation for the University of Bern entitled "The Concept of Aesthetic Theory [*Kunstkritik*] for the Early Romantics." This work supplanted an intended project on Kant and Hermann Cohen and earned him a doctorate summa cum laude. Here it becomes clear how he linked his neo-Kantian separation of consciousness and world to a critical reception of Friedrich Schlegel's theory of the literary fragment. Benjamin was adamant in the distinction between aesthetic theory and the *concept* of an aesthetic theory, which is his topic. Critique functions as a distancing strategy to get a hold on what he will later call the truth content rather than the material content of the work of art. A year or so later, probably through his engagement with the work of Baudelaire, Benjamin refined this valorization of the fragment into his valorization of allegory over symbol. From Baudelaire's great "tableau parisien," "Le Cygne," Benjamin lifted the line "Tout devient allégorie" and placed it as an epigraph in his sketch "Paris, Capital of the Nineteenth Century." The elevation of allegory constitutes a departure from the aesthetic of the Athenäum circle (including both Schlegel brothers), where the fragment evoked a universal. Schlegel, Benjamin observed, honed his critical method on Goethe's *Wilhelm Meister* novels; Benjamin repeated the pattern with his work on *Elective Affinities.*

The resulting essay, "Goethe's *Wahlverwandtschaften,*" brought Benjamin his greatest professional success. Hugo von Hofmannsthal published it in his conservative, Catholic journal *Neue deutsche Beiträge,* under the assumption that it argued for the restoration of a community of *Gebildeten* (cultivated people). He was wrong. He fell into the essay's rhetorical trap. Its argument proceeds from the basic distinction between what Benjamin calls *Wahrheitsgehalt* (truth content) and *Sachgehalt* (material content). At first reading, this distinction suggests a Cartesian opposition of the absolute and the essential against the transitory and the historical. But the opposite is the case. Benjamin wrests Goethe's novel from the projections of its admirers, above all from those associated with Stefan George and Friedrich Gundolf (né Gundelfinger), and reshapes it into a spoof. In so doing, he reveals the meaning of his own leading categories to be the opposite of what the reader will first surmise. Gundolf had Wagnerized Goethe, heroicizing him by rendering his works into autobiographical refractions. In *Elective Affinities,* in this reading, the character of Eduard must be the author's reflection, his dalliance with Ottilie the master's infatuation with a young girl soon after his marriage to Christiane Vulpius in 1806. In Benjamin's sly hands, Goethe's novel becomes a parody of literary and moral convention; Benjamin's Goethe study becomes, mimetically, a spoof of criticism and the model for a new kind of critical writing. He shows how within and outside the novel, Goethe deliberately fashions a *tableau vivant,* a static picture of figures who have confused artifice with life—who have confused Sachgehalt with Wahr-

heitsgehalt. This is the tyranny of aesthetic theory over the aesthetic life. The error plays itself out in the character, and body, of Ottilie. Lifeless in life, possessed of a dead beauty, she is the object of this novel's and the nineteenth century's first renowned description of a performance of a tableau vivant. (From George Eliot to Edith Wharton, the Victorian imagination seized on this practice to show the staticization of women.) Ottilie's death is not only foreshadowed but also foreshadowed as beautiful. Benjamin writes: "For it is not an exaggeration to suggest that interest in the novel depends on the belief in Ottilie's beauty. For the duration of the novel's world, this beauty cannot vanish: the coffin in which the girl rests remains open."

In their alliance against the conceits of German aesthetic theory, Benjamin and Goethe take the categories of Wahrheitsgehalt and Sachgehalt and switch their meanings against the expectations of the reader. The truth is valued, but it moves, it exists in life, experience, and history, and not in the aestheticization of life. In such aestheticization play is dangerous, because the tableau vivant returns as the corpse. Benjamin's gloss on Ottilie's beauty prefigures his later position on the power and danger of the aura in modern life. Through Goethe and with Goethe, Benjamin reconfirms the Baudelairean aesthetic of modernity. The transitory, the fleeting, and the contingent are its hallmarks, as opposed to the absolute and the immutable. In this dynamism is found the Sachgehalt, the truth content, of history.

Modernity's historical contingency and temporality resist the impulse to static and to totalizing representation. The work of art, Benjamin argues, has an ethical position only in its self-conscious status as a fragment, in its refusal to claim totality. Such self-consciousness is revealed by a dimension of silence—of the unexpressed: "das Ausdruckslose." Again from the essay on *Elective Affinities:* "The unexpressed is that critical power which on its own cannot separate appearance from essence in art, but which prevents them from joining. It possesses this power as a moral word. The unexpressed reveals the exalted power of the true, as it determines the language of the real according to laws of the moral world. This in fact shatters what survives as the heritage of chaos in every representation of beauty: false, arrant totality—the absolute. The artwork is only completed as it splinters into fragment, into fragments of the true world, into the torso of a symbol."

The last line of the essay on *Elective Affinities* admonishes: "Hope is given to us only for the sake of those without hope" (201). The statement holds a key to Benjamin's sense of history: that of the activation of the past. Thus the demands of history rest in a responsibility—and provide an intellectual option—that Nietzsche did not see in his "Uses and Disadvantages of History for Life." For Nietzsche, it is a question of *my* life; for Benjamin, of the life of the world that includes me.

Historical investigation enables the representation of what Benjamin calls "Fragmente der wahren Welt" (fragments of the true world)— the phrase from the *Wahlverwandtschaften* essay that can serve as a leitmotif for the historicization of the German baroque. This becomes Benjamin's subsequent major project. The study of the origin of German tragic drama, *Ursprung des deutschen Trauerspiels,* appears as the third major work in his effort to formulate a modern German historical criticism. At this point, the tendency of historical criticism to become critical history was realized. Its distinguishing features were the Protestant baroque and its tendencies to modernity and fragmentation and the Catholic baroque and its tendencies to reaction and totality.

The fundamental political and cultural problem, which the practice of tragic drama strove to work through and which, through the invocation of the culture of *Trauerspiel* Benjamin faces anew, is the problem of sovereignty and legitimacy in a disenchanted world. This is the problematic engaged by Carl Schmitt, whose recently published book *Political Theology* (1922) had jolted varieties of Weimar theorists who shared his fear of the weakening German political ego. The Reformation crisis of sovereignty, legitimacy, and cosmology thus became an antecedent of Weimar uncertainty, and Benjamin seized on the connection. Again he reveled in the confounding of expectations. With Schmittian language, he worked out

an anti-Schmittian politics. At stake again was the power of the subject—in the philosophical sense, not the political one. The subject here is the sovereign, and the discussion makes the transition from an epistemological-ethical discussion of the subject in the world to a political discussion of power and representation.

The Origin of German Tragic Drama is divided into a massive theoretical introduction followed by two major sections. The first of these is dedicated to an explication of the difference between *Trauerspiel* (the lamentation play) and tragedy, between a practice and a form. The baroque cultural practice at stake for Benjamin is the collective negotiation of the dissipation of sovereignty, that is, legitimate—divinely legitimated—rule. This is the northern and largely Protestant baroque of the Reformation period, the period of fragmentation that heralds modernity. As such it might be described as the anti-baroque, in that the Catholic baroque world as the period's theatrical cosmology had first claimed control of representation and hence of politics and had reasserted these same principles with a vengeance in Counter-Reformation culture. The lamentation play mourns the loss of totality but makes no attempt to restore it. Tragedy, on the other hand, attempts a communitarian restoration through the very act of representation through form. Poetic form becomes a metaphor of social cohesion. Through his attention on Trauerspiel versus tragedy and on Protestant practice versus Catholic formal practice, Benjamin in effect unwrites *The Birth of Tragedy* here: against the aestheticist early (first edition) Nietzsche who would reform society according to the communitarian principles of Greek tragedy, Benjamin analyzes the baroque lamentation play as a crucible of early modern cultural fragmentation.

To illustrate the argument, along with its historical and political stakes, we can draw on a passage that generates much of the argument of the "Trauerspiel and Tragedy" chapter.

Whereas the modern concept of sovereignty amounts to a supreme executive power on the part of the prince, the baroque concept emerges from a discussion of the state of emergency, and makes it the most important function of the prince to avert this. The ruler is designated from the outset as the holder of dictatorial power if war, revolt, or other catastrophes should lead to a state of emergency. This is typical of the Counter-reformation. With the release of the worldly and despotic aspects of the rich feeling for life which is characteristic of the Renaissance, the ideal of a complete stabilization, and ecclesiastical and political restoration, unfolds in all its consequences. And one of these consequences is the demand for a princedom whose constitutional position guarantees the continuity of the community, flourishing in feats of arms and in the sciences, in the arts and in its Church. The theological-juridical mode of thought, which is so characteristic of the century, is an expression of the retarding effect of the overstrained transcendental impulse, which underlies all the provocative worldly accents of the baroque. For as an antithesis to the historical idea of restoration it is haunted by the idea of catastrophe. And it is in response to this antithesis that the theory of the state of emergency is devised. (Benjamin 1977, 65–66)

The restorative spirit of the Catholic baroque returns in the contemporary era. This is the "theological-juridical mode of thought" to which Benjamin refers, and the Catholic, restorative political theory of Carl Schmitt is the prime contemporary example. Carl Schmitt is a residue from the Counter-Reformation. This is a historical relationship: history creates its allegories, its dialectical images and identities. The task of the historian, in a charge we might attribute to Benjamin, is to uncover such historically constituted allegories.

In 1921, Benjamin attempted a translation of Baudelaire's *Fleurs du Mal,* and in conjunction with that effort wrote a meditation on language called "The Task of the Translator." The esoteric argument of this meditation held that the act of translation negotiated not so much between language x and language y, but between the forbidden idea of the absolute, original language and its pale refractions in human language—that is, the language of God versus the language of man. Benjamin argued that the unavailability of the absolute reduces human representation to the realms of history and allegory. The temptation to cross that boundary of the available produces the counterparts to history and allegory: myth and symbol. In the study of tragic drama, Benjamin added a third pair of oppositional terms: Trauerspiel, which is historical and allegorical, versus tragedy, which is mythical and symbolic.

Baudelaire's cauldron of Second Empire Paris, modernity, and allegory generated Benjamin's consuming project on "Paris, Capital of the Nineteenth Century," known through its 2,000 pages of fragments as the Arcades Project or the *Passagenwerk*. The dialectic between fragmentation and totality with which the modernist baroque fought the Counter-Reformation finds a gargantuan counterpart in the modernist / baroque juxtapositions of the Second Empire. As the project continued into the 1930s, into a period of Parisian exile that was no longer elected but rather was forced upon him, Benjamin added twentieth-century fascism to his instrumentarium of ideologies of totality. Thus the cultural history of modernity is the history of the desire to reformulate subjectivity in a disenchanted world where the energies of reenchantment spell political disaster.

In 1666 the baroque world from London to Smyrna was shaken and seduced by the messianic campaign of Sabbatai Zevi. The figure and history of this false messiah was the core of Scholem's lifelong scholarly project to restore the mystical side of Jewish history. This was a scientific restoration, not a redemptive one. The phenomenon of Sabbatai Zevi, Scholem argued, was made possible by the culture of the Kabbalah, by its cosmology and by its expectations. Scholem's study, *Sabbatai Zevi: The Mystical Messiah* was published in Israel, in Hebrew, in 1957. It remains, however, a Weimar project, a product of the dialogue with Benjamin. It is, one might say, Scholem's analogue to *The Origin of German Tragic Drama,* with the loss of Benjamin himself figuring in the book's own account of loss and shame. At the same time, the book's enormously complicated voice proceeds from its vantage point in post-1948 Israel, within the established Jewish state, which no longer is exile. Does the book contain a posture of exile? Is that posture transcended, or perhaps suppressed? That the book's imprimatur announces the place and ideological standpoint of the returned Jew, the Israeli scholar, is one of its most interesting complications.

Midpoint in his extraordinary study *Kabbalah and Criticism,* Harold Bloom described the desire of the Kabbalah—and, *a fortiori,* of acts of criticism as he sees and wants them to be—to reform and relegitimate aesthetic experience from a new vantage point, not the vantage point of the claims of Being but of the reality of exile: "Are not the *Sefirot* [heavenly spheres and stages] also, and all of Kabbalah, an incarnation of the desire for difference, and for an end to Exile? *To be different, to be elsewhere,* is a superb definition of the motive for metaphor, for the life-affirming deep motive of all poetry" (Bloom 1975; the translation of *Sefirot* is from Scholem 1941, 13).

For Scholem, the Lurianic Kabbalah is itself an elaborate myth of exile. Isaac Luria's sixteenth-century compilation of the interpretative tradition that originated in twelfth-century Provence emanates from Palestine in the aftermath of the Spanish expulsion. The vantage point of exile returns in Scholem's life's work on Jewish mysticism, as it was first conceived in Germany during and following World War I and after, and realized throughout a long career in Palestine, later Israel.

At the crux of Scholem's essay "Isaac Luria and His School," which was first published in 1941, comes an account of the Lurianic myth of the breaking of the vessels:

The Breaking of the Bowls, of which we find exhaustive descriptions in the literature of Kabbalism, is the decisive turning point in the cosmological process. Taken as a whole, it is the cause of that inner deficiency which is inherent in everything that exists and which persists as long as the damage is not mended. For when the bowls were broken the light either diffused or flowed back to its source, or flowed downwards. The fiendish nether-worlds of evil, the influence of which crept into all stages of the cosmological process, emerged from the fragments which still retained a few sparks of the holy light—Luria speaks of just 288. In this way the good elements of the divine order came to be mixed with the vicious ones. Conversely the restoration of the ideal order, which forms the original aim of creation, is also the secret purpose of existence. Salvation means actually nothing but restitution, reintegration of the original whole, or *Tikkun,* to use the Hebrew term. (Scholem 1941, 269)

This is one of two founding kabbalistic myths in which the creation of the world is described in terms of the exile of God. The deepest symbol of exile, deeper than the breaking of the vessels, is the doctrine of *Tsimtsum:* the creation of the physical space of the world in terms of the shrinkage and contraction of God. "According to Luria," Scholem writes, "God was compelled to make room for the world by, as it were, abandoning a region within Himself, a kind of mystical primordial space from which He withdrew in order to return to it in the act of creation and revelation" (Scholem 1941, 261). Tsimtsum is thus a doctrine of inner exile, whereas the breaking of the vessels describes the external exile of God. Both are myths of the origins of evil as a realm separate from God. Tsimtsum describes the creation of an autonomous space for evil; the breaking of the vessels resulted from the "cathartic cause": the necessity of cleansing waste products and their demonic forces from the pure substance of *Din* or "sternness" (267).

The answer to these myths of exile and fragmentation is the myth of redemption, and the doctrine of *Tikkun:* "the restitution of cosmic harmony through the earthly medium of a mystically elevated Judaism" (Scholem 1941, 287). This myth of restoration is thus the counterpart to the myth of the breaking of the vessels. It contains, according to Scholem, "a strictly utopian impulse," because the "harmony which it reconstitutes does not at all correspond to any condition of things that has ever existed even in Paradise" (Scholem 1971, 13)—in other words before the breaking of the vessels. Its resolution occurs through messianic agency. The problem lies in the question of the "earthly medium" that connects exile and human thought to messianic action and cosmic restoration. The historical con-

sequent to Lurianic kabbalism is the phenomenon of the false Messiah in the person of Sabbatai
Zevi. In Scholem's *Major Trends in Jewish Mysticism,* the chapter on Luria is followed by the chapter "Sabbatianism and Mystical Heresy," and the
work to which Scholem turned on the completion of this book became his largest and most
celebrated: *Sabbatai Zevi: The Mystical Messiah,
1626–1676.* It seems to me that this connection
is crucial to the principle of moral philosophy
inherent in Scholem's work, despite, or rather
because of, his consistent and modest posture as
historian or "mere" chronicler of tradition. The
historical passage from mystical messianism (the
myth of Tikkun) to the phenomenon of false messianism resonates in Scholem's writing with an
implicit moral warning against the temptation of
messianic discourse.

One can surely speculate that this fear of messianism intensified Scholem's mistrust of Marxist
discourse and fueled his sense of betrayal as his
childhood friend Walter Benjamin, with whom
he had first discussed his budding interest in Jewish mysticism, began to think in terms of Marxian categories in the mid-1920s. The problem of
the relation of Marxism to secular messianism is
complicated—more complicated than Scholem
thought it was—and will not be addressed here,
short of the assertion that it was Benjamin's recognition of the problems in that association, if
anything, that made him a good Marxian. Inherent in Marxian discourse, in other words, is the
anti-utopianism that prevents the intellectual
from anticipating and representing the future,
which must first be materially constituted. Marxism as a theoretical discourse is thus a separate
phenomenon from Communism as either a theory
of political practice or a practice in itself.
Throughout Benjamin's career, and inherent in
his Marxian turn, the key element in the connection of Communism and messianism remains
their shared identities as forbidden discourses.

The models for Scholem's ethical and political
treatment of messianism are Benjamin and Spinoza. Sabbatianism erupted a few years after Spinoza's excommunication from the Amsterdam
Jewish community in 1656. Spinoza's reaction to

the phenomenon appears in the *Theologico-Political Treatise.* In Yirmiyahu Yovel's summary: "*historia sacra* is a myth and messianism is a delusion"
(Scholem 1973, 25).

Scholem traces meticulously the trajectory
and dissemination of Sabbatian movement from
its origins in Palestine in 1665 to its whirlwind
European tour of 1666–67, where it touched
down perhaps most forcefully in Amsterdam and
Hamburg. In Hamburg its chief interlocutor,
first as supporter and then as vehement antagonist, was Jacob Sasportas. In Amsterdam, historians like to trace the reaction of Baruch Spinoza a
decade into his excommunication from the Jewish community. His reaction is little known,
however, save for two powerful pieces of circum-
stantial evidence: letters from his London colleague Henry Oldenburg, and the detailed position taken for rational politics and against the
belief in miracles in the *Tractatus theologico-poli-
ticus,* published in the wake of Sabbatianism in
1670.

Henry Oldenburg in London, interested in the
political restoration of the Jews, wrote to Spinoza
in December 1665: "As for politics, there is a
rumor everywhere here concerning the return of
the Jews, who have been dispersed for more than
two thousand years, to their native country"
(543). Spinoza's reply has not survived.

At the end of the third chapter of the *Theologico-Political Treatise,* Spinoza suggests that the
temporal restoration of the Jews is possible. Messianism, however, is not the method of that restoration, because it is inconsistent with the rejection of miracles. Jewish state building must
proceed without a messianic politics. Scholem's
historical practice is allegorical. The majesty of
Sabbatai Zevi is one of trope, not scope. The subject claimed Scholem's attention for thirty-five
years before the publication of the book. Its introduction suggests austerely the awesome two-
faced nature of the project: not only the account of
a "great and tragic chapter in Jewish history" but
even more a historical analysis of "the deep, dangerous, and destructive dialectics inherent in the
messianic idea" (Scholem 1973, ix, xii). The messianic idea is a historical absolute, a phenomenon

that visits the Jewish people through the trauma of Sabbatianism. But the agony of the book lies in its recognition of the moment of Jewish vulnerability to the messianic idea per se, the same phenomenon that visited the world in the form of National Socialism. Political messianism is the category Jacob Talmon used to describe twentieth-century fascisms, the political realizations of the organized drive to Freud's oceanic feeling.

Scholem inscribes his text with the Benjaminian principle of historical allegory. Declared here is the emancipation of allegory, and with it the emancipation of writing. In Benjaminian allegory, Scholem has found a key to emancipation of writing, exactly the opening Leo Strauss declared did not exist when he fastened onto the Marrano principle of persecution and the art of writing.

This allegorical instance assures the book's overwhelming tension. Scholem draws unmistakable lines between the mystical politics of the seventeenth century and the politics of reenchantment of the twentieth. But he refuses to judge Sabbatianism: he declares it the product of kabbalistic teachings and culture. Kabbalah is itself not false doctrine. It triumphed, writes Scholem, "because it provided a valid answer to the great problems of the time" (Scholem 1973, 20).

But if Scholem does not condemn messianic politics, he clearly does not present it as a model for Jewish state and nation building for the baroque or for the present. This issue is paramount for the book's voice—which was crafted in Hebrew, in Israel, after 1948. The key figure here, the voice through which Scholem's own comes closest to being allegorized, is that of Jacob Sasportas. Scholem describes Sasportas as he might have described himself: "The story has an obvious moral. If a shrewd, sober, and arrogant observer like Sasportas could be carried away, albeit for a short while only, and be persuaded of the truth of the reports, then it is not surprising that the Jewish masses saw no reason to doubt the good news which, all their minor discrepancies and contradictions notwithstanding, agreed on the main point: salvation was at hand" (Scholem 1973, 579).

Sabbatianism was, is, in the end, too big: it claimed and offered two levels of redemption: cosmic and political. The book's allegorical position suggests that in Scholem's view, the founding of Israel in 1948 must be understood as a political necessity and without an aura of cosmic redemption. Or, perhaps, as a modern version of the notion of Tsimtsum: the creation [of the Jewish state] as precisely the shrinking of the messianic.

If the lesson of false messianism is the need to separate secular from cosmic politics, then the understanding of the messianic phenomenon in politics demands a new kind of rationalism. This is the rationalism of Spinoza rather than that of Graetz: the reasoning that comes from looking into the abyss rather than from ignoring it. What it provides, via Spinoza, Kant, and Benjamin, is a measure of moral self-preservation through the ethical and epistemic insistence on the permanence of exile.

Bibliography

Walter Benjamin, *The Origin of German Tragic Drama*, trans. John Osborne (London: New Left Books, 1977); Daniel Bensaid, *Walter Benjamin, sentinelle messianique à la gauche du possible* (Paris: Plon, 1990); Harold Bloom, *Kabbalah and Criticism* (New York: Continuum, 1975), 52; Momme Brodersen, *Spinne im eigenen Netz: Walter Benjamin, Leben und Werk* (Buhl-Moos, Germany: Elster, 1990); Susan Buck-Morss, *The Dialectics of Seeing: Walter Benjamin and the Arcades Project* (Cambridge, Mass.: MIT Press, 1989); Buck-Morss, *The Origin of Negative Dialectics: Theodor W. Adorno, Walter Benjamin and the Frankfurt Institute* (New York: Free Press, 1979); Margaret Cohen, *Profane Illumination: Walter Benjamin and the Paris of Surrealist Revolution* (Berkeley: University of California Press, 1993); Samuel Taylor Coleridge, "Statesman's Manual," *Political Tracts of Wordsworth, Coleridge, and Shelley* (Cambridge: Cambridge University Press, 1953), 25; Susan Handelman, *Fragments of Redemption: Jewish Thought and Literary Theory in Benjamin, Scholem, and Levinas* (Bloomington: Indiana University Press, 1991); Michael William Jennings, *Dialectical Images: Walter Benjamin's Theory of Literary Criticism* (Ithaca, N.Y.: Cornell University Press, 1987); Birgit Recki, *Aura und Autonomie: Zur Subjektivität der Kunst bei Walter Benjamin und Theodor*

W. *Adorno* (Wurzburg: Königshausen & Neumann, 1988); A. W. Schlegel, *Vorlesungen über dramatische Kunst und Literatur* (Heidelberg: Schneider, 1817), 91; Gershom Scholem, "Isaac Luria and His School," *Major Trends in Jewish Mysticism* (New York: Schocken, 1961), 13; Scholem, *On Jews and Judaism in Crisis: Selected Essays,* ed. Werner J. Dannhauser (New York: Schocken, 1976); Scholem, *Sabbatai Zevi: The Mystical Messiah, 1626–1676,* trans. R. J. Z. Werblowsky (Princeton, N.J.: Princeton University Press, 1973); Scholem, "Toward an Understanding of the Messianic Idea," *The Messianic Idea in Judaism and Other Essays on Jewish Spirituality* (New York: Schocken, 1971), 13; Scholem, *Walter Benjamin* (New York: Leo Baeck Institute, 1965); Gary Smith, ed., *On Walter Benjamin: Critical Essays and Recollections* (Cambridge, Mass.: MIT Press, 1988); Rudolf Speth, *Wahrheit und Ästhetik: Untersuchungen zum Frühwerk Walter Benjamins* (Wurzburg: Königshausen & Neumann, 1991); Leo Strauss, "An Introduction to Heideggerian Existentialism," *The Rebirth of Classical Political Rationalism: An Introduction to the Thought of Leo Strauss,* ed. Thomas Pangle (Chicago: University of Chicago Press, 1989), 28; and Yirmiyahu Yovel, *Spinoza and Other Heretics: The Adventures of Immanence* (Princeton, N.J.: Princeton University Press, 1989).

MICHAEL P. STEINBERG

1921 The staging of Arthur Schnitzler's play *Reigen* in Vienna creates a public uproar that draws involvement by the press, the police, the Viennese city administration, and the Austrian parliament

Arthur Schnitzler's attitude toward his own Jewishness and the situation of the Jews in Vienna can be best reconstructed on the basis of his autobiography, which was published posthumously but covers only the first twenty-five years of his life; his diaries, which he kept from his adolescence until a short time before his death; and certain Jewish themes and characters in his voluminous oeuvre. Schnitzler lived in a period during which the Jews reached great heights in the economy and culture of the Austro-Hungarian Empire but at the same time became targets of a virulent anti-Semitism that ultimately led to the Holocaust.

The story of his family conforms in many details to a sociohistorical pattern: emigration from the shtetel or ghetto in Poland, the Bukovina, or Hungary to the capital; rise from the retail or manual trades into the higher spheres of business; and marriage with the daughter of an already emancipated family who sees to the education of her children and instills in them a love of the German language and literature. The offspring of such unions typically dedicate themselves to the expansion of the family business or with equal frequency to a profession such as medicine or the law. Their children in turn often become intellectuals, musicians, or writers. As this last stage indicates, this process is accompanied by a mental reorientation: the loss of Orthodoxy, indeed of almost the entire Jewish heritage; abandonment of Yiddish as a means of communication and of Hebrew as the sacred language; adoption of Western models of behavior; acculturation; and assimilation.

As he tells it in his autobiography *Jugend in Wien* (Youth in Vienna), Schnitzler's paternal family lived in Nagy-Kanizsa, Hungary. His grandfather was a carpenter who spent all his life in modest, indeed in meager, circumstances. Schnitzler's father, however, was able to study medicine, first in Budapest, then later in Vienna, where he became a renowned laryngologist whose clientele was made up of members of the theatrical and operatic world, as well as the aristocracy. As a young man he harbored literary ambitions, wrote plays, and regarded his talent as equal to that of his son (Schnitzler 1968, 16–19).

Schnitzler's mother was born in Vienna, the daughter of a wealthy, established family. Her father, a doctor of medicine and philosophy, was the grandson of a Viennese court jeweler. Maternally there were also Hungarian connections, but with an apparently wealthy, in part ennobled, family of bankers, officers, scholars, and landowners. Some were "originals . . . in whom a type of Jewish patriarch and aristocrat, business agent and cavalier were peculiarly intermingled" (Schnitzler 1968). The following sentence is instructive: "Some of the younger and youngest scions distinguish themselves from the descendants of old aristocratic families at the most by a bit more of wit and the propensity toward self-irony which is typical of the race." Here Schnitzler reveals a great deal of his attitude: the consciousness of a far-reaching cultural integration, but also the remnants of a psychic alterity and the characteristic tendency of the times to attribute mental traits to "racial" causes.

In spite of such expressions that are part of the then dominant discourse, it is clear that Schnitzler developed an early skepticism about the pressures of ethnic identification. A visit to his paternal grandparents impressed upon him the enormous cultural abyss that separated him from them. He proclaims: "One thing is certain . . . had I been forced to live temporarily or for a more durable sojourn in the city where my grandparents had their home and my father was born I would have certainly felt like a stranger or perhaps even an exile. Thus I might be tempted already at this point to take issue with the questionable view according to which someone, born, raised and permanently active in a certain country, is supposed to regard another country as his true home—not where decades ago his parents and grandparents had settled, but a country where his great-great-ancestors had been at home thousands of years ago—not merely for political, social, economic reasons (which might at least be debatable) but also for emotional reasons" (Schnitzler 1968).

Schnitzler also touches upon his family's relationship to the Jewish religion. Here we notice the strong current of secularization that was by no means restricted to Jews but swept across the entire turn-of-the-century culture. The Day of Atonement, the highest Jewish holiday, was observed in his grandmother's house. But only a few subjected themselves to the prescribed fast; "the more free-thinking male members of the family" did not. "The most pious, perhaps the only truly pious one," Schnitzler reports, was the good grandmother herself. All others "celebrated the day of repentance mainly for her sake and continued after her death only from a sense of devotion." But even for her this fasting and eating un-

leavened bread at Passover were "the only rituals which she performed with strictness." Schnitzler himself draws the inevitable conclusion: "In spite of sometimes defiantly emphasizing their tribal allegiance the following generations exhibited indifference toward the spirit of the Jewish religion and resistance, sometimes even mockery, against its external form" (Schnitzler 1968). Here we gain the same impression as before: far-reaching but not total adaptation to the general milieu had occurred, but a vague feeling of distance remained, no matter what was meant by "tribal allegiance."

Schnitzler lived through momentous transformations in his society. The Jews were identified with the speculative capitalism and the rapid industrialization that took place in Austria and Hungary. A modern anti-Semitism was born that differed from the old Judeophobia in several ways: it mixed the customary religious and economic accusations with racial ones; it unified those threatened or disadvantaged by the industrial revolution into a mass movement; and it served as a weapon to wrest power and privileges from the successful. This new hatred was so dynamic and infectious that it mobilized large populations, infiltrated entire institutions such as the Catholic Church, and basically left no one unaffected—not even the victims themselves. The self-hatred thus generated among the Jews occupied Schnitzler's psychological curiosity a great deal. He even joked about it, saying that "anti-Semitism lacked both respectability and success until the Jews themselves took it over" (Schnitzler 1968, 154).

These developments occurred in various European societies, but in Austria they were especially poisonous because of the many hostile minorities living in the empire and the great masses of Jews who, partly under the pressure of persecutions and partly because they were lured by the cultural and economic opportunities of the capital, had migrated to Vienna from their eastern settlements. All this, of course, happened not overnight but in a slow process. Nevertheless, if one wishes to remember a symbolic date, the great stock market crash of 1873 could be regarded as a turning point. It robbed many people of their life savings, plunged the country into a prolonged recession, and deprived the expansive capitalism of the "Austrian founding years" of whatever prestige it had had. Because many Jews had been involved in the failed speculations, the demagogues found it easy to blame all Jews for the disaster and to identify them with all the evils of the century.

It is no wonder then that Schnitzler (1968) paid close attention to this increasingly aggressive anti-Semitism in his autobiography. He confesses not to be "primarily interested in the social but preponderantly in the psychological aspect of the Jewish Question," but a meticulous psychologist is capable of revealing a great deal about the social conditions to which his psyche reacted. One phenomenon with both social and psychological repercussions that he records is the anti-Semitism of the university students, which culminated in the exclusion of Jews from the fencing fraternities. In a mass gathering the students adopted a resolution that Schnitzler quotes: "Every son of a Jewish mother, every person in whose veins flows Jewish blood is by birth without honor, devoid of delicate feelings. He cannot distinguish between filth and purity. Ethically speaking, he is a lowly character. Thus contact with a Jew is dishonorable; every communion with Jews must be avoided. A Jew cannot be insulted, therefore a Jew cannot demand satisfaction for insults suffered" (152).

This pseudo-aristocratic language is an indication that the historians who detected a "re-feudalization" of Austrian society have a point. Being excluded from the anachronistic code of dueling at that time meant relegation to a second-class status in society. Schnitzler adds only that the frame of mind from which this declaration emanated "triumphed in every respect."

"In every respect" includes Schnitzler's literary production. It is astonishing that a writer as retiring from the limelight of publicity as he, purely because of his gift of observation and his commitment to truthfulness, should have so often come into conflict with his society; that a writer who was accused in his youth of not only describing but also sharing the decadence and hedonism of his social class and, after the war, of

trying to resuscitate a "bygone world," should be involved in a perennial struggle with censorship and public opinion. The reason, of course, was that Schnitzler touched upon social and psychological taboos, the exposure of which proved painful to several social groups. No wonder Freud called Schnitzler a depth psychologist as truthful and intrepid as any.

Schnitzler's play *Professor Bernhardi* (1905–12), in which he confronted the new political anti-Semitism, was banned and could not be performed until the end of the monarchy in 1918. The censor justified his verdict by saying that Schnitzler portrayed a society characterized by a lack of integrity, as well as by social climbing, hypocrisy, and idiocy. Whether this portrayal was true did not enter into his reflections.

Schnitzler's play *Freiwild* elicited attacks from the anti-Semitic press because it dared call into question the favorite Austrian fetish, the "duel." "Leutnant Gustl" of 1900, a brilliant short story and the first in the German language to use interior monologue, caused a protracted scandal. The army felt offended and ultimately deprived Schnitzler of his officer's patent because he neither responded to attacks in the press nor appeared before a military tribunal to justify himself.

The story of Schnitzler's literary production is one simultaneously of great public triumphs and of public defamations and prohibitions. That his many difficulties with the censors, the press, and the politicians had little to do with morality or art but a lot to do with anti-Semitism is evident from the reception of his *Reigen* (La Ronde). The events surrounding this most notorious of his works have been well documented because this reception not only kept the Austrian parliament, police, and newspapers in suspense but also foreshadowed the country's political future. Here only the barest facts can be recorded. Schnitzler knew what dynamite the ten dialogues contained. Even though he completed them in 1896, he waited until 1900 before issuing a private edition of two hundred copies, which he distributed among friends. The riots caused even by attempts to *read* the farce in public convinced him of the continued impossibility of seeing it performed. When it was finally staged in Berlin in 1921, there was not only the usual uproar but both the director and the actors were also dragged before a court of law.

In Vienna the waves surged even higher. The most powerful figures of the time—politicians like Seipel, Reumann, Seitz, Schober, Schmitz, and many others who played a decisive role in the First Republic—were involved. There ensued a tug-of-war between the Viennese city administration, which was Social Democratic, and the federal government, which was dominated by conservative forces. The constitutional court had to occupy itself with the affair, interpellations were introduced in the national council, stormy scenes enlivened parliamentary sessions, protest rallies were held in the city hall, and street demonstrations were organized. The theater itself became a battlefield; stink-bombs were thrown, furniture was destroyed, and police and spectators were injured. The play was forbidden but reinstated under massive police protection. The true motives behind this insanity were articulated by the public voices of politicians and journalists. I shall quote a few representative phrases in order to characterize the mental climate in which Schnitzler had to function. A pamphleteer by the name of Karl Paumgartten called the *Reigen* "the vilest bordello piece" written to "arouse the lascivious prurience of Asiatic invaders," meaning the Jews. According to another newspaper, the *Volkssturm,* however, the work's purpose was to "unchain the drives and carnal pleasures of the *Aryan* [my emphasis] people in order to turn them into the spineless slaves of Judah's unbridled passions." The police contingents that had to be deployed to protect the performances were attributed by the *Deutsch-österreichische Tageszeitung* to "the enormous financial influence of a Jewry risen to power through profiteering and racketeering." The article indignantly raises the question whether perhaps "the federal army was also to be called up in order to secure the erotic enjoyments of a gang of perverse Jews." The Social Democratic city administration that wished to guarantee the performance of the *Reigen* in the name of free speech was accused of overzealousness "in protecting the rights of drones and exploiters" and of being "the protectors of the scum

of mankind." Lest one think that such vituperations were the excesses of a lunatic fringe, it must be reported that the prelate and later prime minister of the republic, Ignaz Seipel, also lent his voice to this chorus, dubbing the work a "filthy piece from the pen of a Jewish author" (all quotations from Pfoser, Pfoser-Schewig, and Renner 1993, vol. 1).

It made little difference in the face of the public outcry that the best academic critics adopted the opposite view: "It is incomprehensible," one of the most renowned literary historians said, "that this play could have been denounced as immoral. Far from whetting the appetite for amorous activity it is much better suited to spoil it thoroughly. This is the work of a moralist, not of an epicurean, a work of demasking, of disenchantment, merciless and deadly serious" (Urbach 1974, 160).

Small wonder then that among the factors that determined his fate Schnitzler singled out two as "greatly complicating matters": "Being Austrian, being Jewish." Judging his "situation in the world without paranoia," he conceded that "of course all artists of consequence are misunderstood," but that such a lack in his case "was for the greatest part due to my Jewishness" (January 1, 1919). Schnitzler went so far as to complain that "the clamour of the anti-Semitic rabble" had made him into "the most abused author in the German language since the invention of the printing press" (1917). References to the Jewish Question abound in the intimate pages of his diary. He seldom forgets to identify his visitors as Jews, non-Jews, or "Jew baiters" (1880). As early as 1883, more than a decade before Karl Lueger's election, he realized that a *social movement* was slowly evolving from the germ of anti-Semitism, "that monstrosity concocted of envy and baseness."

During World War I, Schnitzler's outrage rose to new heights. Much space generally is taken up by the case of a Jesuit priest by the name of Abel "who declared that the Jews were the only ones who did not do their duty in the war; they are responsible for all the misery, they must be exterminated." Such hate mongering must have sounded especially perfidious to the ears of someone who had to record the battlefield deaths of so many acquaintances. Schnitzler wished for *"legal action on the part of the Jewish officers against Abel;* summoning the Emperor, the War Minister as witnesses" (July 1918). But he knew that there was no remedy. His ultimate insight: "The anti-Semites can act with impunity, they are unassailable" (November 1903). After recording several such unwarranted attacks on the Jews he asked rhetorically, "Can this country still be saved?" And a particularly outrageous manifestation of anti-Semitism escalates his indignation: "Of what concern can this country still be to us?" (May 19, 1915). But it is Schnitzler's dilemma that he is also Austrian. The very next day he professes to feel "the destiny of this country as deeply as others, perhaps more deeply. How rooted one is in the country of one's birth! What do I care in the end about the citizens, the diplomats, the monarchs! The country! The homeland!" (May 20, 1915). It is clear that the Jew and the Austrian in Schnitzler lived in a tension that he could not resolve.

Schnitzler knows of course that there are two sets of players in the deadly game of anti-Semitism, anti-Semites and Jews, and the latter engage his scrutiny as much as the former. Veritable portrait galleries of Jewish types can be found in his works and diaries, and even though it is quite obvious that Judaism did not mean much to him in either a religious or a national sense, he is nevertheless extremely sensitive to the "snobbish" Jew. This is a code word in his vocabulary that indicated a widespread propensity among assimilated Jews to deny their Jewish origins and to cuddle up to or cringe before the Christian majority. Whether it is the "cowardice and snobbishness" of the "liberalizing Jew press," which helped the reactionaries "deflect in pogrom-like fashion the despair, the wrath of the people toward the middle class" (November 4, 1917); the "Byzantinism" of the Jewish Fischer Verlag, Schnitzler's own publishing house, "toward its Christian authors"; or a Jew who tries to escape his Jewishness by means of conversion, he did not cease railing against the "renegades." Worse than anti-Semitism is the inappropriate leniency toward it (1930), and the worst offenders are the Jewish anti-Semites. Schnitzler unleashed the full

force of his irony against such Jewish antics. A Jewish critic panned Hugo von Hofmannsthal's play *Elektra,* whereupon Peter Altenberg wrote: "A Jew cannot understand this play." Schnitzler commented with devastating logic: "He himself a Jew, Hugo of Jewish extraction, the director a Jew, the loudest fans Jews—the madness of anti-Semitism" (1904).

Did Arthur Schnitzler, the rational diagnostician, the keen psychologist, remain unaffected by this ubiquitous insanity? Not quite. Often he noted that someone is "very" or "all too" Jewish, deprecated another for being "a Jew boy" or "Jew girl" (1922), or remarked that one visitor, the director of a museum in Jerusalem, whom he otherwise finds interesting, "unfortunately spoke strong Jargon"—*Jargon* being the supercilious term of Western Jews for Yiddish. Such weaknesses are the tribute to the tenor of the times that no one, not even a sage, could avoid paying.

Schnitzler's profound understanding of anti-Semitism—his observations of the various, often contradictory reactions of the Jews to the psychic and social complexity of their situation—found expression in *Professor Bernhardi,* a play he called a comedy despite its tragic undertones, and the novel *Der Weg ins Freie* (1903–8), which one could translate as "the road into the open" or "the way to freedom." Anti-Semitism and the Jewish Question are touched upon peripherally in many of his works, but here they are central. Both were written at a time when the inflammatory anti-Semitism of the turn of the century had already been victorious in Vienna under the leadership of Karl Lueger. The Dreyfus Affair had run its course.

As in France, in *Professor Bernhardi* a single event, falsified by anti-Semitic malice, becomes a political scandal that agitates broad segments of society, a medical institution, the church, the courts, the press, and government. The play depicts various types of Jews and Christians in their multiple, often convoluted relationships. There is the timid Jew, the militant Jew, baptized Jews, and "half-Jews" born of mixed marriages, which were a frequent occurrence in Vienna. Among the non-Jews there is the anti-Semite who practices "tokenism"; the German nationalist who uses the anti-Semitic currents to gain personal power; a malevolent intriguer who can only be classified as "pre-fascist," a feat of divinatory prescience on the part of the playwright; a liberal forty-eighter who still believes in the "healthy instincts of the populace"; a state minister, a completely new ilk of orator in the age of mass politics; a Catholic priest torn between the duties to his religion and to his church; and a plethora of other characters representing nuances of behavior or ideology—in short, a remarkable panorama of society in the first decade of the twentieth century.

But whereas anti-Semitism is crucial to the dynamics of the play, Schnitzler seemed to be probing more deeply than into the mere relationship between Jews and Christians at a particular moment in history. The fundamental question the play raises is how an ethical life is still possible in a totally fragmented society in whose midst a vacuum of values gapes threateningly, where anything private that touches the public sphere is transformed into a grotesque lie. No binding answers are given. In an exciting confrontation between the freethinker, physician, and scientist Bernhardi and the priest, who clings to his religious traditions, the hopeless relativism of their values becomes apparent. All they can do is shake hands across the abyss. Bernhardi's resolution to act according to his conviction but without rigid principles in a "special case"—in other words to establish a "casuistic ethics"—turns out to be a desperate attempt to hold fast to one of the central elements of enlightened liberalism: the autonomous self that has entered into a crisis during the fin de siècle. Bernhardi fails, a modern Don Quixote in a cynical world, a mixture of heroism and ridicule. It is no doubt because of his failure and the frailty of all human institutions, in the sense of a *comédie humaine,* that the author dared subtitle this drama of frustrations "a comedy."

Schnitzler predicted correctly that some day posterity would be able to reconstruct the social fabric of his time from *Der Weg ins Freie.* Though anti-Semitism pops up again and again in this novel, the rise of the Christian Social Party has been symbolically compressed into the character of a petty bourgeois ne'er-do-well and his cronies

in the newspaper and a cycling club. But Schnitzler uses perhaps an even more effective method to illustrate the homelessness of the Jews in their homeland, for the reader sees them largely from the perspective of the musician and aristocrat Georg von Wergenthin, the non-Jewish central character. Even though he moves almost exclusively in Jewish circles and conducts his extensive conversations about art with the Jewish writer Heinrich Bermann, a somewhat gloomy self-portrait of the author, he basically remains a stranger to the Jews; indeed, he is alienated from them by the bizarre, almost exotic psyche of most of them. "Again one," he thinks to himself, "who has been insulted! It was absolutely impossible to associate innocently with these people." On another occasion he feels "enervated": his interlocutor needed not have "notified him officially of his membership in the Jewish race. . . . He knew it, and he didn't hold it against him; but why did they always start talking about it themselves? Wherever he went, he only met Jews who were ashamed of being Jews or others who were proud of it and were afraid people might think they were ashamed." Georg is the liberal, refined Viennese, open-minded, willing, and even eager to experience new or strange phenomena. If *he* is incapable of overcoming a certain reservation that sometimes borders on irritation vis-à-vis the Jews, then their chances for acceptance are slim indeed.

Added to this difficulty is another: Georg von Wergenthin has little inner strength. He cannot sustain his support for anyone or anything, and in this he is a faithful reflection of his home town. The entire culture of Vienna, despite its richness and brilliance, seems to have been beset by such a lack of willpower that it is unable to offer anyone a firm foothold. It is the secret and perhaps the most essential message of the novel that its scenery is one of farewell, a lingering "still." The brothers Wergenthin still live in style in the imperial capital; they are still popular, admired wherever they go. But the days of elegant idleness are drawing to an end. The reader reaches with them the point when their finances force them to dissolve their Viennese household and find employment abroad.

This "still" also hovers over the Jews. They are

still not persecuted in an active way, not deprived of their possessions, not driven out. They have become insecure; with the anti-Semitic air they constantly breathe in a menacing element. Again Schnitzler has offered a great variety of Jewish types, each representing a realistic possibility in this particular milieu. Almost all of them, though, especially the younger ones who did not grow up in the liberal era and no longer feel protected by liberal values, have become vulnerable. Whether they turn to the Social Democrats under the pressure of circumstances, try to assimilate more consciously, or embrace their outsider status in a gesture of defiance, inwardly they have all been affected: they are torn asunder, get into conflicts, and become cynical or aggressive. Above all, they are thin-skinned and sensitive to an almost pathological degree.

A particularly characteristic case is that of Oskar Ehrenberg. His mother and sister have social ambitions: they maintain an open house, a "salon" frequented by an upper-class and artistic public. The father is an arms manufacturer, a self-made man who rose from humble circumstances and, to the chagrin of his family, makes a show of his Jewishness. Oskar plays at being a "Lord" even at the age of fifteen, he "dresses like a dandy," he "wears a monocle in an eye." His propensity toward the nobility and aristocratic paraphernalia only increases with the years. The fear of disinheritance is all that keeps him from converting to the Catholicism of the ruling circles. But the old Ehrenberg hates the "feudal gang." The tensions between son and father become insurmountable and finally explode in a public scandal that is reported to Georg: "Yesterday at noontime Oskar passes St. Michael's Church raising his hat. You know that at the moment nothing is regarded as being more elegant than piety. Heaven knows how often he had been guilty of such hypocrisy before. But yesterday misfortune had it that the old Ehrenberg came along at that precise moment. He sees Oskar taking his hat off in front of the church and, seized by an uncontrollable wrath, takes a swing at his son and slaps his face. A slap in the face! Oskar, the lieutenant in the Reserves! Downtown in the middle of the day!"

The system of values in which Oskar lives demands drastic measures to restore his "honor." He puts a bullet through his head, though he loses only an eye. With the Prince of Guastalla, a nonconformist and outsider in *his* group, he takes up traveling. They become another pair for whom Vienna is no longer a safe haven.

But despite the many different Jewish types Schnitzler characterizes, basically the dilemma in which the entire ethnic group finds itself boils down to one fundamental dichotomy: the point of view of the Zionist whose moment in history has definitely come and who advocates the return of the Jews to their ancient homeland in Palestine against that of Heinrich Bermann, Schnitzler's counterpart, the skeptical individualist who accepts his existential isolation as a Jew and a loner but is adamantly resolved to stay in Vienna, the only home he has known. Even though Schnitzler shares the latter's position, he lends Heinrich's opponent much of his own rhetorical force in one of the central arguments of the book.

It is not a question, the Zionist expounds, "of the few Jewish bureaucrats who are not promoted, the Jewish lecturers who are made professors too late or not at all—these are secondary inconveniences so to speak. The question here is of entirely different people . . . about whom, my dear Heinrich, you haven't thought enough despite the obligation you had of doing so." And then he tells Heinrich about the Zionist congress that he attended in Basel, about "the nostalgia for Palestine . . . a deep, never extinguished feeling that is now inflamed by necessity." He tells him of "old men, not at all uneducated, nay, learned, wise men" whom he "saw crying for fear that, even if the most ambitious Zionist plans came true, they would be unable to set foot on the land of their fathers."

Heinrich's reply is no less eloquent. He regards "Zionism as the worst affliction ever visited upon the Jews." Nationalism and religion had always been words that infuriated him in their superficial and insidious ambiguity. Fatherland was a fiction—a political concept that was indeterminate, changeable, not to be pinned down. Only one's homeland had reality, and therefore the feeling for a homeland was tantamount to the right to that homeland. Furthermore, he had no sense of community with anyone on earth; with the crying Jews in Basel no more than with the howling pan-Germans in the Austrian parliament; with Jewish usurers as little as with the robber barons of the high aristocracy; neither with a Jewish tavern owner nor a Christian Social grocer. Least of all could he feel a connection with people, from whom he was separated by an inner distance only because of having suffered the same persecution and of being subjected to the same hatred. He would be willing to accept Zionism as a moral principle and a humanitarian idea provided that it honestly identified itself as such; but the idea of erecting a Jewish state on a religious and national basis seemed to him like a senseless rebellion against the spirit of all historical evolution.

These passages culminate in Georg's train of thought, with which the author also identifies to a significant degree: "An inkling overcame him of the mysterious fate of this people which seemed to be embodied in every one of its members; in those who tried to escape from their origin as if it were a disgrace, a pain or a fairy tale that had nothing to do with them as well as in those who stubbornly kept harping on it as if it were a destiny, an honor or an ineluctable fact of history."

In summary, Schnitzler was a thoroughly assimilated Viennese citizen, outwardly indistinguishable from the Austrian upper bourgeoisie. As a result of the rekindled anti-Semitism, however, he was treated more and more as an outsider, often a disgusting intruder, despite the undeniable successes he also had. As a scientifically trained liberal, he was a rationalist, an individualist, and an agnostic. Zionism he regarded as one of the eccentricities into which the Jews were pushed, and he believed sycophancy and baptism to be indignities. This did not leave much leeway. His great contribution was that he observed the Jewish Question in all its intricacy with the diagnostic skills of the trained physician that he was and the psychological acumen that became his trademark as a writer. His works in which he illuminates these complex relationships merit great attention both as documents and as artistic masterpieces. As a human being with a poetic nature, he suffered from the *malheur d'être juif* (the misfortune of being Jewish), not only outwardly because of the incessant vilifications and the obstacles that were piled in the path of his artistic progress, but also because of the inner damage that was inflicted on his most intimate creative impulses. But he was spared the worst. He died in time. Only a few years later he would have been driven into exile or into the gas chambers by those whom he had seen through, regardless of his age or his deep-rootedness in the culture of his native city.

Bibliography

Klara Pomeranz Carmely, *Das Identitätsproblem jüdischer Schriftsteller im deutschen Sprachraum: Von der Jahrhundertwende bis zu Hitler* (Königstein / Taunus: Scriptor, 1981); Alfred Pfoser, Kristina Pfoser-Schewig, and Gerhard Renner, eds., *Schnitzlers "Reigen,"* vol. 1, *Der Skandal: Analysen und Dokumente*, vol. 2, *Die Prozesse: Analyse und Dokumente* (Frankfurt a. M.: Fischer Taschenbuch Verlag, 1993); Peter Pulzer, *The Rise of Political Anti-Semitism in Germany and Austria*, rev. ed. (Cambridge, Mass.: Harvard University Press, 1988); Arthur Schnitzler, *Freiwild* (Berlin: Fischer, 1902); Schnitzler, *Jugend in Wien* (Vienna: Molden, 1968); Schnitzler, *Professor Bernhardi* (Berlin: Fischer, 1912); Schnitzler, *Der Reigen* (Berlin: Fischer, 1900); Schnitzler, *Der Weg ins Freie* (Berlin: Fischer, 1908); Carl Schorske, *Fin-de-siècle Vienna: Politics and Culture* (New York: Knopf, 1980); Egon Schwarz, "Arthur Schnitzler und das Judentum," *Im Zeichen Hiobs: Jüdische Schriftsteller und deutsche Literatur im 20. Jahrhundert*, ed. Gunter E. Grimm and Hans-Peter Bayerdörfer (Königstein / Taunus: Athenäum, 1985); Schwarz, "Melting Pot or Witch's Cauldron? Jews and Antisemites in Vienna at the Turn of the Century," *Jews and Germans from 1860 to 1933: The Problematic Symbiosis*, ed. David Bronsen and Reihe Siegen (Heidelberg: Carl Winter, 1979); Reinhard Urbach, *Schnitzler-Kommentar: Zu den erzählenden Schriften und dramatischen Werken* (Munich: Winkler, 1974); and Robert S. Wistrich, *The Jews of Vienna in the Age of Franz Joseph* (New York: Oxford University Press, 1989).

EGON SCHWARZ

1922 *Milgroym,* a Yiddish magazine of arts and letters, is founded in Berlin by Mark Wischnitzer

The year 1922 marks the high point of Yiddish literary life in Berlin. For a few years, at the beginning of the 1920s, Berlin became a major literary center for Eastern European Jews. The Russian Revolution, followed by civil war, famine, and anti-Semitic pogroms in the Ukraine, caused a great number of Yiddish writers from the "Kiev group," such as Dovid Bergelson, Der Nister, Leyb Kvitko, Peretz Markish, and Dovid Hofshteyn, to expatriate themselves to Berlin, which was already a haven for Russian intelligentsia in exile. Biely, Gorki, Ehrenburg, Nabokov, and Tsvetaieva were in Berlin at the time, and the Russian presence was so significant that Charlottenburg, the area where most Russian émigrés settled, was commonly called "Charlottengrad." Also sojourning in Berlin were the Lithuanian-born writer Moyshe Kulbak, as well as a group of researchers, historians (such as Simon Dubnow and Elias Tsherikover), and linguists (for example, Max Weinreich and Nokhem Shtif). Berlin had also become a gathering point for Hebrew writers (like Bialik, Agnon, and Berdyczewski), and for Russian Jewish artists (such as Lissitzki, Tchaikov, and Rybak).

A number of Yiddish publishing houses were transferred from Russia to Berlin, or opened branches there to take advantage of the inexpensive and unrivaled printing facilities in Germany. The Folksfarlag (The people's publishing house) of Kiev, for example, was resuscitated in Berlin by its director, Wolf Latzki-Bertoldi, under the new name of Klal Farlag (The community's publishing house), with the financial support of Ullstein; it published over eighty Yiddish books during the year 1922 alone. Others were simply founded in Berlin, such as Wostok (East), Shveln (Thresholds), Funken (Sparks), and Yidisher literarisher Farlag (Yiddish literary publishing house); these became the mouthpieces for the major Soviet Yiddish writers in Berlin.

At the same time, more than twenty Yiddish periodicals sprouted, often of very high quality. The most lavishly presented, *Milgroym* (The pomegranate), was founded by the historian Mark Wischnitzer and coedited by the Yiddish writers Dovid Bergelson and Der Nister. The color illustration on the cover of the first issue, which represented a pomegranate painted in the style of naive popular art, and the flyleaf with a woodcut of Jerusalem, indicate a strong dedication to Jewish folklore and tradition. The journal, which had a Hebrew counterpart called *Rimon,* was multifarious, if not eclectic in all respects, and included a wide mix of European and Jewish or Yiddish arts and literature.

Other journals were no less interesting in their interdisciplinary and universalist, cross-cultural approach. For instance, *Der Onheyb* (The beginning), edited by Dovid Einhorn, Shmarya Gorelik, and Max Weinreich, published not only poetry by Berlin Yiddish writers such as Kulbak and Einhorn, translations of German-Jewish writers such as Else Lasker-Schüler and Max Brod, translations of European and world literature (for example, works by August Strindberg, Oscar Wilde, and Lao Tse), but also Max Weinreich's critical edition of an old Yiddish historical poem, *Megilas Vints* (The scroll of Vincent), and literary criticism by Shmarya Gorelik. The *Kunst-ring-almanakh* (Art circle almanac), edited by Kalman Zingman, gathered literary criticism by Bal-Makhshoves and Shmarya Gorelik, Expressionist poems by Moyshe Broderzon, and prints by Marc Chagall, El Lissitzki, and Joseph Tchaikov. Else Lasker-Schüler wrote a personal dedication to the journal *Albatros,* which was founded in Warsaw and whose third issue appeared in Berlin. Other journals with a significant belletristic section included the organ of the Jewish Socialist Labor Party, *Dos Fraye Vort* (The free word); the bimonthly of the Poale Zion *Unzer Bavegung* (Our movement); and the organ of the Verband der Ostjuden in Deutschland, *Der Mizrekh Yid* (The Eastern Jew).

This multitude of journals gives the impression of an extraordinary intellectual effervescence in the Yiddish world, of an opening up to world arts and literature, and of a particular interest in building bridges between German-Jewish and Yiddish culture. The only disturbing fact is that this lively culture was like a splendid but short-lived fireworks display. With the apparent lull during the New Economic Program (NEP) in the Soviet Union and the rise of nationalism in Germany, the Yiddish writers dispersed; most of them returned to the Soviet Union, others to Poland or America. The flood of periodicals ebbed after a few issues, and the publishing houses, which had turned Berlin into one of the most productive Yiddish publishing centers in the world, were dismantled. One can only wonder why this throbbing culture vanished almost overnight, why the links established with German Jews did not prove to be any more resilient.

A partial answer to this question resides in the fact that when the Yiddish writers came to Berlin, Yiddish culture had preceded long before; it had already been imported to Germany through a complex network of political discourse and cultural transfers. The early German Zionists had rediscovered their Eastern brethren, for whose plight they had conceived a political solution in Palestine. But they also needed to use the vibrant Jewish culture in the East to invigorate the acculturated German Jews in search of their identity and roots. German Jews had assimilated linguistically and culturally during the nineteenth century, and Yiddish had gone out of use in Germany. The Yiddish-speaking Jews of Poland and Russia thus appeared to German Jews as a living image of their lost cultural identity. Whereas the general public, as well as most liberal or German-national-minded Jews, despised the unassimilated Eastern European Jews, a small fraction of intellectuals became deeply fascinated with their culture. A few Zionists, along with Martin Buber and Berthold Feiwel, organized the Democratic Fraction in 1901 and demanded a commitment to Jewish cultural renewal within the World Zionist Organization. In the same year, Buber published his article "Jewish Renaissance," in which he called for a rebirth of Jewish culture based on a creative reconstruction of the past.

The first translations of Yiddish literature appeared in *Die Jüdische Moderne* and in the Zionist organ *Die Welt,* and these were often signed by Buber himself. Several other periodicals, often very different in outlook, made a point of introducing their German-Jewish readers to Eastern European culture and literature: these included the monthly *Ost und West,* edited by Leo Winz, and the Zionist *Die Jüdische Rundschau,* or *Die Freistatt,* edited by the independent-minded, Yiddishist-oriented Fritz Mordechai Kaufmann. Buber's translation of the Hasidic masters received general acclaim in Germany. A voluminous number of almanacs, anthologies, and collections devoted to Eastern European Jewish culture appeared, meant to enhance Jewish bourgeois living rooms. The German occupation of Poland gave many German Jews the opportunity to hear Yiddish, to visit Yiddish theaters, and to confront the culture directly. Alfred Döblin, Arnold Zweig, and Samy Gronemann wrote travel reports about their visits to the East. The defense of the German cultural and political imperialism in Poland increased the strategic interest in Yiddish, which was rediscovered as a "German dialect" Jews had faithfully kept since the Middle Ages.

Theater was one of the most interesting forums through which Yiddish culture was mediated. A number of Eastern European troupes toured Germany and were greeted with enthusiastic ovations, among them the Vilner troupe, which became the Jüdisches Künstlertheater Berlin, the Moscow Goset, which played under the name of Jüdisches akademisches Theater, and the Moscow-based Hebrew-language Habimah. Because the performances were not translated and were often based on songs and dances, they gave rise to strong unmediated emotions. According to Arnold Zweig, Habimah's staging of the *Dybbuk* immersed his contemporaries in "primordial worlds of exorcism," in which "Jews, coming right out of Chagall's pictures, painted like the dance masks of wild tribes, in costumes of South Seas' people . . . were jumping, walking, contorting themselves." The deep longing of German Jews for "age-old, raw paganism" (Julius Bab), meaning the return to primitive forms of society and community, and to ancient times when "theater and religious cult were one" (Max Krell), loom large in the recensions written about Yiddish theater in Germany at the time. Remaining unaware of the avant-gardistic endeavors of the Yiddish theater directors, German Jews primarily wanted to be spellbound, carried back into the archaic and magic world of the ghetto.

A number of individuals acted as mediators between both cultures. Among them, there were Jews from the border areas, such as Posen and Galicia, who had been themselves standing on the boundary between two cultures. Others had come from Eastern Europe to Germany to study at the beginning of the century and had remained there, earning their livelihood with the trade of selling their home culture to the acculturated German Jews. Among them were the first generation of Yiddish literary critics and researchers, including Isidor Elyashev (Bal-Makhshoves), Shmarya Gorelik, Abraham Coralnik, Max Weinreich, and Nokhem Shtif. The last two developed in Germany the fundaments of their academic research in Yiddish linguistics and literary history. They planned the foundation of the YIVO Institute for Yiddish Research while in Berlin in 1925, but returned to the East (Weinreich to Wilno, where

YIVO was established, and Shtif to the Kiev Institute for Proletarian Culture) to implement the task they had set for themselves. Others, who remained in Germany, such as Shmarya Gorelik, had to accommodate their production to the demands of the German-Jewish audience and often betrayed the culture they were supposed to mediate. This is mostly the case of the translators, of whom the most famous is Alexander Eliasberg. His translations were violently criticized by Gerhard Scholem and Fritz Mordechai Kaufmann for creating a "sentimental atmosphere" absent from the original texts. Most of what Germans were given to read in terms of Yiddish literature was mistranslated and misinterpreted according to schemata inherent not to the original, but to the target or host culture: a romanticized, nostalgic vision of the shtetel, which had never been present, either in the works of the classics, which had fought against the backwardness and the social injustice of the ghetto in the spirit of the Haskalah, or in the work of the avant-garde generation of the writers who were living in Berlin at the time.

And indeed, what were the young Yiddish writers living in Berlin writing about? Strangely, the effect of Berlin on their work was negligible. They continued to write about the East and for the East. Der Nister's collected tales, which appeared with the Yidisher literarisher Farlag in Berlin in 1922–23, were written in his very idiosyncratic allegorical style, which was influenced mainly by the Hasidic master Rabbi Nakhman of Braslav and by the Russian symbolists. Only after his return to the Soviet Union in 1926 did the intrusion of the city, the masses, and the economics of modernity, which eventually led him to renounce his allegorical symbolism, slowly penetrate his fantastical tales and turn them into Kafkaesque nightmares. Kvitko and Hofshteyn's lyrics, which were illustrated by Chagall, Lissitzki, and Rybak, dealt with the Petliura pogroms in the Ukraine. Kvitko also became a great master of children's literature for use in the Soviet school system.

Bergelson's collected works, published by Wostok in 1922, constitute his prerevolutionary prose. He depicted in a sophisticated impressionist manner, which was informed by an aesthetics of the void and the oblique, the slow decline of the petty bourgeoisie of the shtetel, who were left to idleness as the shtetel was bypassed by modernity. In Berlin, he wrote new stories on the background of the revolution, the civil war, and the pogroms in the Ukraine. A certain sympathy for the Communists, albeit distanced, cannot help but be overshadowed by a sense of doubt and weariness, and the strongest impression left by the stories is that of chaos and loss of perspective. Individual characters are swept along by history and left stranded by an open end.

Bergelson depicts paradigmatically the obsession of the Yiddish author with the tragic fate of Ukrainian Jews in the story "Among Emigrés." A deranged Jewish youth exiled in Berlin feels compelled to undertake the mission of assassinating the Ukrainian pogromist who lives incognito in the same shabby Berlin hostel. He approaches a Berlin Yiddish writer, asking him to provide him with a weapon, which is supposedly his duty since "the writer is the soul of the nation." But the writer turns him into a psychiatrist. This action is symptomatic of the ambivalence that characterized Yiddish writers in Berlin. They lived in the opulence of the West, wrote about Jewish fate in the East, but felt disconnected from the masses of their readers. As the critic Bal-Dimyen (the literary pseudonym of Nokhem Shtif) wrote in *Dos fraye vort,* they were "worshipping the golden calf," "celebrating the persecutions at their writing desk, silently longing for dollars, but really are good for nothing" (Bal-Dimyen 1923, 33).

Often, this disorientation is phrased in a modernist poetic aesthetics and linked with the general loss of orientation of the entire post–World War I generation. Bergelson emphasized in the first issue of *Milgroym* how disconnected his generation had become after the "great, ineluctable destruction" of the Great War, and he defined a new world where "there is no more law, no more space and order . . . a chaotic life lies within me . . . there is no unified meaning in my life" (Bergelson 1922, 43). This sense of fragmentation and of uprootedness is found again in Dovid Hofshteyn's "The Song of My Indifference," which was published simultaneously in *Milgroym*

and in *Shtrom,* the organ of the fellow travelers in Moscow:

And I, what should I do
When in front of my eyes
Continuously stand
Phosphor questions—lightenings
"Where?"
"Where to?"
I am tired now
Of hovering
Of dizzying
Of soaking in foreign waters
                                    (Hofshteyn 1922, 44).

These lines stand in sharp contrast with the views of the artistic editor of *Milgroym,* Rachel Wischnitzer-Bernstein, who claimed to recognize "a feeling of national unity" and of "appurtenance to the national organism" among the young generation of artists whom she calls "extatics" creating a "new religious art" (Wischnitzer-Bernstein 1922, 4). The tensions between her conservative, holistic approach, and the uprootedness and loss of transcendence and totality of the Yiddish avant-garde generation, caused the cooperation to break up after the first issue of the journal. Der Nister and Bergelson withdrew from the editorial board.

In fact, the first issue of *Milgroym* had been greeted by a wave of protest from the most famous Jewish critics and artists in the East. It was condemned for displaying "popular art from the British Museum" instead of looking for its authentic living forms in Eastern Europe. The painter Joseph Tchaikov attacked Rachel Wischnitzer for presenting Rybak as an artist who supposedly "aimed at following the national bigotry of the eternal unity of the Jewish people" (Tchaikov 1922, 78–79). The Warsaw poet Melekh Rawicz violently castigated the Berlin "traitors": "Somewhere in Berlin, in the smoky atmosphere of the 'Romanisches Café,' many among the best creators of Yiddish literature are hanging around, pretending to create a pseudo-Yiddish culture. But those who are sitting at the 'Romanisches Café' and are looking at us from afar, as we are pulling the carriage of our culture, are simply deserters." Peretz Markish, also in Warsaw at the time, accused the Berlin writers of "marketing a new Jewish people, a new Yiddish culture . . . a new territory for the Jewish spirit" (Markish 1922, 62) and of trying to turn Berlin into a new Jerusalem where they wanted to celebrate a sacrilegious new cult of Yiddish. From Moscow, the Communist critic Moyshe Litvakov rebuked the Berlin émigrés on political grounds. For him, there were only two options: "Moscow or Jerusalem, the future or the past, bourgeois bigotry or proletarian ascent" (Litvakov 1926, 28). From Moscow, too, the Berlin writers were accused of building a new Jerusalem in a place where Yiddish culture had no legitimacy. The story of *Milgroym,* usually hailed today as "the highlight of Yiddish publication in Germany" (Fuks 1988), only tells of the failed attempt of the exiled Yiddish writers to create a new branch of Yiddish culture.

Few Yiddish writers wrote directly about their Berlin experience and, if ever, could only do so many years later. After his emigration to the Soviet Union, Moyshe Kulbak published in 1933 a cycle of sixty-two twelve-verse poems under the title *The Disno Childe Harold,* a poetic mock-epic about his formative years in Berlin. He conjures up a fresco of Berlin types, from loud Moscow businessmen swamping the Kurfürstendam with "checkbooks and gold" to German petty bourgeois, among whom he discovers with gentle irony that "each worker is a Marxist and each grocer a Kantian" (Kulbak 1953, 232). His affected enthusiasm for the throbbing night life where "the jazz band shrieks with colonial screams / In black fires and Negro dances" (237) is tempered by the tribulations of new immigrant life: "The first half of the night in a cabaret / With jazz bands and condoms / The other half, he lies under the yoke of AEG / And Borsig's dark locomotives" (243).

But the German culture gradually disclosed by Kulbak's hero, the "man with the pipe," appears as a threatening hodgepodge of modernity and dormant nationalism, of which the European artistic avant-garde and its "sweet decadence" (Kulbak 1953, 239) is just another obscene symptom: "Expressionism screams with red

feet / Dada with its pants fallen down." Kulbak deplores the inability of his hero to compose a coherent whole out of his self-taught cultural patchwork ("a little Blok, a little Schopenhauer, Kabbalah, Peretz and Spinoza"), and the final result is: "uprootedness, and sadness, sadness, sadness" (252).

Similarly, David Einhorn casts in the form of an ominous enumeration of single words his impressions about Berlin culture and politics in his travel account *From Berlin to San Francisco* published in Wilno in 1930 (17–18):

State
Nation
Organization
Community
Duty.
Triangle
Ellipse
Cube
Cubism
Futurism
Expressionism
Abstract form
Primitivism
Einstein
Theory of relativity
Freud
Psycho-analysis
Soviet power
Communism
Dictature
Democracy
Republic.
Seven hundred thousand
Eight hundred thousand
Ten per line
Backs and napes
They were marching over an abstract line with
    rhythmic steps
One two three
One two three
Up to the horizon
Red flags
Black-white-red flags
Black-red-golden flags

Banners
Inscriptions
Slogans:
City
Reich
Nation
Class
Community
Duty
Categorical imperative
Kant Strasse.

Although Einhorn mixes the categories of political sociology, geometry, abstract art, political extremism, and the triad of German-Jewish thinkers Einstein, Freud, and Marx, his catalog conveys a sad and threatening image of Germany as a country where everybody, from Communists to right-wing nationalists, including intellectuals and artists, is united by a common sense of order and obedience that erases even the cultural achievements Weimar Germany is famous for. Whereas Kulbak drew a picture in which "the other Germany" of the Communists still represented a hope for the future, Einhorn's Germany is a cold and hopeless society ready for dictatorship.

In summary, Yiddish culture in Berlin remained a culture in exile that never put down roots in Germany. Its fate became a witness to the failed encounter between Eastern European Jews and their German brethren, and to their aborted attempt to build bridges between Yiddish and German-Jewish or European cultures. Although the interest in Yiddish culture enriched German-Jewish life, it dwindled because it was no longer useful for the purposes of either German politics in Poland or the Zionist movement, which gradually turned toward Hebrew and colonization work in Palestine. As Yiddish culture appeared to be threatened in Eastern Europe, its natural center, Yiddish cultural activists in Warsaw and Moscow took the Berlin émigrés to task and urged them to return to help strengthen the foundations of a modern Yiddish culture on its natural ground. Opening up to German or European cul-

ture was no longer a priority, and Yiddish writers were enjoined to go home.

Bibliography

Steven E. Aschheim, *Brothers and Strangers: The East European Jew in German and Jewish Consciousness, 1800–1923* (Madison: University of Wisconsin Press, 1982); Bal-Dimyen (pseud. of Nokhem Shtif), "Felyeton: Literatur (siluetn fun Romaisches Kafe)," *Das Fraye Vort* 5 (1923); Delphine Bechtel, "Babylone or Jerusalem: Berlin as Center of Yiddish Modernism in the 1920s," *Insiders and Outsiders: Jewish and Gentile Culture in Germany and Austria,* ed. Dagmar Lorenz and Gabriele Weinberger (Detroit: Wayne State University Press, 1994), 116–23; Bechtel, "Cultural Transfers Between *Ostjuden* and *Westjuden:* German-Jewish Intellectuals and Yiddish Culture, 1897–1930," *Leo Baeck Institute Year Book* 42 (1997); Bechtel, "'Primordial Worlds of Exorcism': Theater as Forum for Cultural Contacts Between *Ostjuden* and *Westjuden,*" *Proceedings of the Eleventh World Congress of Jewish Studies* (Jerusalem: World Congress of Jewish Studies, 1994), 39–46; Bechtel, "Les revues modernistes yiddish à Berlin et à Varsovie: La quête d'une nouvelle Jérusalem?" *Etudes Germaniques* 46 (Apr.–June 1991): 161–67; Dovid Bergelson, "Der gesheener oyfbrokh," *Milgroym* 1 (1922); David Einhorn, *Fun Berlin biz San Frantsisko* (Warsaw: Kulturlige, 1930); Leo and Renate Fuks, "Yiddish Publishing Activities in the Weimar Republic, 1920–1933," *Leo Baeck Institute Year Book* 33 (1988): 417–36; Sander L. Gilman, "The Rediscovery of the Eastern Jews: German Jews in the East, 1890–1918," *Jews and Germans from 1860 to 1933: The Problematic Symbiosis,* ed. David Bronsen (Heidelberg: Carl Winter, 1979): 338–65; Joachim Hemmerle, "Jiddisches Theater im Spiegel deutschsprachiger Kritik: Von der Jahrhundertwende bis 1928," *Beter und Rebellen: Aus 1000 Jahren Judentum im Polen,* ed. Michael Brocke (Frankfurt a. M.: Koordinierungsrat der Gesellschaften für Christlich-Jüdische Zusammenarbeit, 1983), 277–312; Dovid Hofshteyn, "Di lid fun mayn glaykhgilt," *Milgroym* 1 (1922); Moyshe Kulbak, *Disner Tshayld Harold,* quoted from *Geklibene verk* (New York: Tsiko Bikher-farlag, 1953); Moyshe Litvakov, "Yerushe un hegemonye," in *In umru,* vol. 2 (Moscow: Farlag shul un bukh, 1926); Peretz Markish, "Biznes: Moskve—Berlin," *Khalyastre* 1 (1922); Trude Maurer, *Ostjuden in Deutschland, 1918–1933* (Hamburg: Hans Christian Verlag, 1986); Melekh Rawicz, "Di dezertern funem yidishn emes,"

Di vog 2 (1922); Zosa Szajkowski, "The Struggle for Yiddish During World War I: The Attitude of German Jewry," *Leo Baeck Institute Year Book* 9 (1964): 131–58; Joseph Tchaikov, "Milgroym," *Shtrom* 3 (1922); and Rachel Wischnitzer-Bernstein, "Di raye kunst un mir," *Milgroym* 1 (1922).

DELPHINE BECHTEL

1923 Kafka goes to camp

In July of 1923, the tubercular and feverish Franz Kafka found himself in the vacation town of Müritz, observing a group of "Eastern European Jews whom West European Jews are rescuing from the dangers of Berlin. Half the days and nights the house, the woods, and the beach are filled with singing. I am not happy when I'm among them, but on the threshold of happiness" (Kafka 1977, 373). This summer camp had been created by Siegfried Lehmann, one of the leaders of Jewish education in Berlin, to bring inner city Eastern European Jewish children from the *Scheunenviertel,* the Jewish immigrant neighborhood in the middle of the city, out into the healthy countryside. Such "preventoria" were intended to decrease the number of cases of tuberculosis in the inner city. The children Kafka saw there were "healthy, cheerful, blue-eyed children," according to a letter to Max Brod (372), but they were also "Hebrew-speaking, healthy, and cheerful," according to a simultaneous letter to Robert Klopstock (372). Kafka reached the threshold of happiness observing this summer camp.

The countryside is the antithesis of the city. In the dark, cold cities of Berlin, Vienna, and Prague, Jews "to the European have the same Negro face" (Kafka 1990, 136). In the country, all the Jewish children from the East are suddenly transformed into beautiful, healthy little "blue-eyed" Germans. These healthy children were the antithesis of the experience of the Western Jew in cities, the very Jews who were rescuing them! Berlin is for Kafka a place in which "when I get out down there, at the Zoo, say, I have trouble with my breathing, start to cough, become more anxious than I ordinarily am, see all the dangers of this city uniting against me" (Kafka 1977, 383). Berlin is the locus of illness and corruption, but in the country all of the Jews, at least all of the Eastern Jews, breathe well.

These Yiddish-speaking children, who were learning Hebrew at camp, provided Kafka with an indirect introduction to one of their counselors, the nineteen-year-old Dora Dymant. From Galicia, she had been raised in the penumbra of the court of the Gerer rebbe. As a result, she spoke Yiddish, her mother tongue, but she also knew Hebrew well. As a young woman she came to Breslau, where she became involved with the secular world. In the summer of 1923, she was employed by Siegfried Lehmann's Jewish People's Home in Berlin as a counselor. By the beginning of August the intensity of her relationship with Kafka was such that the two imagined a future life that would eventually move from an interim stop in Berlin to Palestine. Dymant was Kafka's last great love, but she too was part of the world of disease that formed Kafka's experience.

Kafka's Jewish experience is caught in the web of words that surrounded his life— words in Yiddish, German, Czech, and Hebrew. These words were connected intimately to conceptions of nationhood and were part of the national project to define the health or illness of its inhabitants. Kafka's world was one of people reduced to words:

even his experience of the summer camp was one tied to the language(s) spoken by the "blue-eyed" healthy children. At that moment at the shore, Kafka looked and saw children playing—children brought to the West to help them recuperate or to help them build their bodies to resist the "Jewish" illnesses of the Pale and the city. And part of that recuperation was the Zionist dream of a Hebrew-speaking Jewry ready to recapture its nationalistic role in the Holy Land. Yet the positive isolation of the camp, its goal of strengthening the body, and its transformation (in Kafka's view) of Jews into "blue-eyed" Germans, all reflect a complex relationship to the idea of a special place where healing could take place. And for Kafka, part of that healing came to be an understanding of his masculinity, the masculinity of the tubercular, in his relationship with Dora Dymant.

For Franz Kafka, the final moment in the meaning of tuberculosis came in a double reading of therapeutic space as an answer to the anxiety about confinement and punishment that is intimately associated with the image of tuberculosis at the turn of the century. This anxiety takes on a very different meaning when read from a Jewish perspective as a commentary on the Jewish body. Here it is not Alfred Dreyfus's body—the Jewish body that denies its Jewishness—but rather the body of the person with disease, with tuberculosis, who cannot be Jewish because Jews, according to the myth, have a magical immunity from tuberculosis. Yet Dreyfus's exile is to a space where one had earlier isolated lepers: "auf dem man früher die Aussätzigen interniert hatte" (Dreyfus 1901). These are the original inhabitants of "Devil's Island," now replaced by *male* convicts. These contradictions in the space associated with specific illnesses enables Kafka's tale of the "Penal Colony" to be both about Jews and inherently not about Jews; he drew on discourses that are heavily coded as Jewish but that self-consciously distance this labeling. Indeed, the focus on masculinity in that story (women are reduced to observers of male-male interaction) is one byproduct of the image of Devil's Island as a space of illness. One might add that this tradition of associating Jews with infectious disease be-

comes part of the rationale for French anti-Semites in the 1930s. Under Pétain, the French "special police" in charge of rounding up Jews promised to obey a charter of twenty-one points, one of which was "for French purity and against Jewish leprosy."

Walter Müller-Seidel has brilliantly illustrated how very important the notion of deportation was in the legal culture of the turn of the century. But banishment is also a set trope in the discourse of illness at the turn of the century—one was banished from society whether one went into the hospital voluntarily or not. Indeed, Peter Detweiler's idea of the "fresh air" cure for tuberculosis was tied to a controlling medical regime and the de facto isolation of the patient from the world. By the 1890s, at Davos, the site of Thomas Mann's *Magic Mountain* (1924), the idea of Detweiler's sanatorium had reached a peak of efficiency in Karl Turban's closed and controlled environment, as much a "total institution," in Foucault's sense, as the prison-island. One could be indefinitely banished to this space of healing. As Thomas Mann observes in *The Magic Mountain,* the degree of one's infection "infallibly reflected the chances of recovery with which the patient had to reckon; the number of months or years he must still remain could with ease be deduced from it, beginning with the six months that Hofrat Behrens calls a 'week-end,' and ending with the 'life sentence,' which taken literally, often enough meant very little indeed" (Mann 1982, 345). The use of a prison vocabulary to register the sense of isolation felt in sanatoria parallels the stigmatization of illnesses such as tuberculosis. For becoming ill was much like having committed a crime—both were evidence of degeneration, or a regression to the real degeneration that one had until then concealed.

According to the French physician Jules Héricourt, tuberculosis was a "social disease," like syphilis. The stigma of disease was associated with the visible stigmata of disease written on the body. But these stigmata only revealed the innate nature of the body. Tuberculosis is the result of "the privations and the fatigue undergone by men of weak constitution [that] end by reawakening attenuated or torpid cases of tuberculosis" (Héricourt 1920, viii). The result of contracting this disease that one was predetermined to contract was the need to be notified and isolated in a sanatorium: "It has been objected that it would be cruel to inform patients that they are tuberculous, and would result in many tragedies of despair. It does not seem to us that this argument is valid: the consumptive, whose treatment is a matter of general hygiene rather than of medical therapeutics, has every reason for requiring to know what ails him if he wishes to recover, for he must in that case adopt a mode of life to which he would never constrain himself if he did not know himself to be seriously threatened" (47). The patient must become his own jailer; he must acknowledge his own danger to the body politic through his own body.

Héricourt's British translator, Bernard Miall, provided the ultimate rationale for the compulsory reporting and hospitalization of the tuberculous patient—the need for a eugenics that would separate the healthy from the sick, the beautiful from the ugly:

We need a religion of beauty, of perfection. It would be a simple matter to teach children to worship perfection rather than hate it because it reveals their own imperfection. For we cannot teach what beauty is without making plain the hideousness of egoism. Beauty is the outward and visible sign of health-perfection-virtue. Pleasure is the perception of beauty, or some of its elements. What makes for the fullness and perfection of life, for beauty and happiness, is good; what makes for death, disease, imperfection, suffering, is bad. These things are capable of proof, and a child may understand them. Sin is ugly and painful. Perfection is beautiful and gives us joy. We have appealed to the Hebraic conscience for two thousand years in vain. Let us appeal to the love of life and beauty which is innate in all of us. A beauty-loving people could not desire to multiply a diseased or degenerate strain, or hate men and women because they were strong and comely and able. The balance of the races is overset, and only the abandonment of voluntary sterility by the fit, and its adoption by the unfit—which is eugenics—can save us. (Héricourt 1920, 244–45)

The ugliness of the "habitus phthisicus," the tubercular body type, was considered a sign of its inward flaws, flaws of character in addition to the infection itself. The only thing to do with such degenerate types, according to Miall, was to isolate them, to deport them to hospitals, where, in spite of their intense sexual drive, the public could be assured that they would not reproduce any further.

Unsuspected by Müller-Seidel, however, deportation had a broader meaning during this period when it came to disease. Hans Gross's views on deportation were closely connected to conjectures about degenerative illness and disease, and paralleled the views of his hygienist colleague Ferdinand Hueppe. Gross was one of Kafka's professors of law, whose views played a large role in Müller-Seidel's discussion of deportation because of the importance of his son, the radical psychoanalyst Otto Gross, in the Prague of Kafka's time. During this era, one exiled degenerates from society and put them into penal colonies. But degeneration was not manifested simply in crime, although the literature of the period insists that those predisposed to tuberculosis also manifested a higher rate of sociopathic acts. Degeneration was more than the "morbid deviation from the type," to use the classic definition of the mid-nineteenth century. By the close of the nineteenth century, it also meant the inheritance of negative acquired characteristics. In sheltering them, society spared these individuals the struggle for life, enabling them to develop and grow. Then they would merely degenerate and commit sociopathic acts. The degenerate criminal should be permanently exiled, recommended Gross, because he can no more be "cured" of his criminality than an amputee can be cured of a missing limb. The period from 1890 to 1920 was the age of the great debate about the required reporting of tuberculosis and the resultant social status of those officially labeled as ill. This debate paralleled the growth of the sanatorium movement, especially the debates in Germany and Austria about the construction of state-supported sanatoria.

The history of this question in Austria is not unimportant. Up to 1882 the pattern for the control of infectious diseases in Austria was set:

where multiple cases of a disease such as cholera appeared, the local authorities had to turn to provincial (*Kreisamt*) doctors, who declared an emergency. The ill were quarantined in their homes, and the authorities had to ensure the "necessary isolation, hygiene and ventilation of the room" (Uffelmann 1878; 83). Only in exceptional cases could the health commission declare that an individual could be removed from the home by the police.

Tuberculosis was neither reportable nor quarantinable, as it rarely was seen as occurring in the appropriate number of cases (4–10) in one place at one time. With Robert Koch's discovery of the tuberculosis bacillus in 1882 came a greater interest in tuberculosis as a social and hygienic problem. But in 1888, when a requirement to report all infectious diseases was introduced in Austria, tuberculosis was excepted. By 1892 a form was prepared by the medical bureaucracy that listed all infectious diseases (such as measles), but not tuberculosis. The rationale was that there is no sense in requiring notification for a disease "unless the sanitary authorities were able to deal effectively with [it]" (Fornet 1911, 314). Even the simple question of how many death notifications from the disease were issued was impossible to compile because of a lack of uniform reporting in Austria. But lurking behind this seeming inability was a high degree of awareness of the stigmatizing nature of tuberculosis. Indeed, reading the death statistics for the turn of the century in Austria is complicated by this stigmatization. In 1895, the standard death from lung disease came to be labeled "pneumonia" because of the unpleasant connotations of the label "tuberculosis."

Although hospitals dedicated to tuberculosis had existed in Austria as early as 1844, the first modern tuberculosis sanatorium was built in Austria only in 1898, and by 1911 there were only three large sanatoria and "three small sanatoria for Jews, all of which are charitable institutions erected by private initiative" (Sutherland 1911, 320). In 1903, the first organization to aid those suffering from tuberculosis (the Hilfsverein) was founded in Austria, followed in 1911 by the founding of the Austrian Central Committee to Counter Tuberculosis. Only in 1914, with the beginning of the war and the explosion of tuberculosis throughout the empire, were guidelines developed to deal with tuberculosis as an infectious disease. In 1915 the first quarantine laws for tuberculosis were promulgated in Austria. This was followed in 1916 by a law depriving patients with tuberculosis of their civil rights and making them wards of the state. The debate still raged until 1917 whether the hospitals should be private or state-run, but that every person with tuberculosis should be hospitalized was no longer in doubt. In 1919, at the close of the war, Julius Tandler, now the minister of health of the new Republic of Austria, introduced the requirement of notification for pulmonary and laryngeal tuberculosis. And it was only in 1919 that the Masaryk League Against Tuberculosis was founded in Prague. After his death, Kafka's colleagues at the state-run insurance company where he worked contributed 330 crowns in his memory on June 25, 1924, toward the eradication of tuberculosis in Prague.

All of these changes were preceded by intense public debate of which Kafka would have been well aware. Tuberculosis was thus understood as threatening isolation from society, either voluntary isolation (with the rise of the sanatorium movement) or compulsory isolation. Thomas Mann's *Magic Mountain* (in which Kafka appears as an exemplary tubercular) captured the anxiety about the former. Franz Kafka's work, especially *The Castle* (1914–15), captured the anxiety about the latter. The isolation of *The Castle,* and K.'s impossible struggle to attain access to it, is a simple reversal of the anxiety and attraction of the sanatorium. Kafka, who spent every possible vacation as an adult visiting health spas, knew of the attraction of being treated as a patient even when one's illnesses were psychosomatic. The placebo effect of living as a voluntary patient carried with it a frisson of being ill while not being ill. How different it was when one was truly ill, when the choice of coming and going was no longer one's own. It is important to understand that compulsory notification and compulsory treatment came to be a reality in Austria and Czechoslovakia only at the very moment when Kafka himself became ill. *The Castle* represents a world with heightened and focused sexuality. It is a world framed by a sense of the impossibility of entrance (escape) but the focused desire to access (escape) the confines of the castle. Indeed, the very physical presence of the castle looming on the hill overlooking the inn and the village suggests the isolation of the sanatorium. At the very time Kafka was writing the novel, there was a parallel anxiety about being confined to a "criminal lunatic asylum (for hysterics or epileptics), or transportation for an indefinite period, with supervision from 5 to 10 years" (Ferri 1899). The crime to be so punished was "malicious injury or disfigurement; mutilation; rape or outrage with violence; restraint on personal liberty." Being put into an asylum if one were hysterical or into a sanatorium, if one's hysteria came to be written on one's body as a somatic illness, became the same thing for Kafka.

During the war, the anxiety concerning the meaning of tuberculosis for Kafka became most acute. His understanding of his illness in 1917 fell very much in line with the increased number of cases of tuberculosis assumed to have occurred during the war. No longer did the possibility exist of some type of acquired or racial immunity to tuberculosis, or the illusion that "lifestyle choices," such as exercises, nude bathing, or Fletcherism, would protect an individual from contagious illness. Indeed, Vera Pohland has argued quite convincingly that by 1917, when K. E. Ranke proposed a three-stage theory of tuberculosis on the model of syphilis, whatever "positive," aestheticizing features had been associated with tuberculosis in the nineteenth century had been completely abandoned. By 1917 tuberculosis in Central Europe was a completely and negatively stigmatizing illness. The seemingly attractive fantasy of the female tubercular in Dumas's *Lady of the Camellias* (set to music in Verdi's *Traviata*) or Murget's Mimi (set to music in Puccini's and Leoncavallo's *Bohème*) in the late nineteenth century was impossible. This alteration coincided, significantly, with the great tuberculosis epidemic associated with World War I, and with the final "proof" that Jews, wherever they lived, were just as likely to contract this illness as their non-Jewish neighbors.

All about him Kafka saw individuals whose immunity was greater than most contracting this "social" illness that put them on the wrong side of the debates about compulsory notification and hospitalization. When Kafka internalized his sense of his own illness, when he came to understand that self-cure is impossible and that he was becoming what he was fated to become, then the model of the unattainable castle (from which one is excluded) transforms itself into the sealed world of the late tale "The Burrow" (Kafka 1971, 24). The burrow of the nameless animal is a haven, fashioned with the animal's blood: "I was glad when the blood came, for that was proof that the walls were beginning to harden; and in that way, as everybody must admit, I richly paid for my Castle Keep" (328). The inhabitant of this blood-soaked castle can sleep only "beneath the moss on the top of my bloodstained spoil" (341). Even its own death would not be pointless in this protected warren, "even in my enemy's mortal stroke at the final hour, for my blood will ebb away here in my own soil and not be lost" (340). Blood as a sign of purification, as in the ritual of *shohitah,* mixes with its perversion and misreading in the debates about ritual murder and ritual slaughter and with the blood of Kafka's own experience of tuberculosis to provide a frame for this reversal of the "Castle" into the "Castle Keep."

"The Burrow" was one of the unpublished tales that was not included in *A Hunger Artist*. At the time of Kafka's death in 1924, he was reading the proofs of this small volume of four tales. "A Hunger Artist," the title story, reproduces much of the anxiety about confinement, exposure, the spectacle and emaciation of the body, and becoming what one was fated to become by projecting it onto the social reality of the hunger artists who actually functioned as carnival geeks at the turn of the century. The anxiety becomes a positive quality that suffuses the entire narrative, and yet one can read in this reversal all of the anxiety that Kafka repressed. For Kafka's geek turns out in the end to have been a freak—he has no real control over his actions, he must become what he is fated to become, a hunger artist. "I have to fast, I can't help it—I couldn't find the food I liked. If I had found it, believe me, I should have made no fuss and stuffed myself like you and anyone else" (Kafka 1971, 277). Here Kafka evokes a ritual of starvation not through the agency of the artist but because of a programmed capacity of the artist's body over which he has no control. It is a specific form of anorexia nervosa from which this figure suffers, fashioned by the dictates of his body and his mind as understood by the culture in which he lived. His body manifests the predisposition of the Jewish or tubercular body for disease. It is also evident that this skeletal body, in the discourse of the time, was understood as a feminized body. The claustrophobic sense of inevitability is heightened by its ending. The death of the protagonist and his replacement by a panther evokes more than Rilke's poem. We have in it a mindless, nonreflective, but aesthetically pleasing—in other words, healthy—body replacing the deformed and acutely self-reflexive hunger artist. This volume also includes "A Little Woman" and "Josephine, the Singer," each of which raises issues about illness, masculinity, and Jewish identity. These are never the sole focus of each tale but are certainly indispensable components.

If we now turn to the final medical accounts of Kafka's body at the end of his life, we can see how anxiety of becoming what one was fated to become has inscribed itself on Kafka's body as well as on his psyche. Kafka's physicians, beginning in 1918, saw him as an extension of his lung. And they also began to use euphemisms. Kafka commented to his sister Ottla that Dr. Mühlstein said it was "a catarrh of the apex of the lung (that's the phrase, the way people say piglet when they mean swine)" (Kafka 1982, 19). In their medical records they are quite a bit more direct. (I am struck by the similarity of the doctor's comments in Thomas Mann's sanatorium novella "Tristan" [1903]: "It was, as we have heard, an affection of the trachea—a word that in Dr. Hinzpeter's mouth sounded so soothing, so consoling, so reassuring, that it raised their spirits to a surprising degree" [Mann 1936].) Dr. J. Kodym documented the pulmonary tuberculosis on November 20, 1918, and Dr. Ernst Fröhlich attested to his illness on February 28, 1919. Each report reflects on the gradual disappearance of Franz Kafka in the eyes of his physicians and employer,

and his replacement with Franz Kafka's lung. Thus the pulmonary specialist Dr. Leopold Strelinger documented Kafka's illness at the Slovakian sanatorium at Tatranské Matliary on March 2, 1921, concentrating only on the state of the various lobes of the lung. On May 5, 1921, he reported again to Kafka's employer about the state of his lungs, requesting a further five-month stay for Kafka. On April 10, 1924, in the final year of his life, Kafka was admitted to the clinic of the Jewish laryngologist Markus Hajek. Hajek's records focus on the profound destruction that the infection had caused within the body. Here the importance of the relationship between the ill body and the ill mind, whether psychosomatic or inherited, whether predisposition of the habitus phthisicus or the immunity of the Jew, vanish. What is left is the decaying lung and the heightened certainty of early death following chronic illness.

Franz Kafka reflected at the end of his life on his society's view of a sick male Jew. His own explanations of his tuberculosis reflect its relationship to his self-diagnosed madness. Yet the working out of this "madness" with his letters and accounts of his illness had its own literary dimension. There is a constant inscription and reinscription, moving further from the notion of an illness predisposed because of his family's history and toward one inscribed in his lived experience. With all of the twisting and turning, there are still bits and pieces of the discourses about illness, masculinity, and Judaism that remain accessible in Kafka's texts. In order to overcome his fundamental inability to control the cultural language of his time, Kafka provided a new literary discourse laced with irony in which these hanks of hair and bits of bone are contained. Thus the reader can return to the world of the literary text for a final rereading of Kafka's own sense of his body that remains as tentative and bounded as his text.

Bibliography

Mark Anderson, ed., *Reading Kafka: Prague, Politics, and the Fin de Siècle* (New York: Schocken, 1989); Giuliano Baioni, *Kafka: Letteratura ed ebraismo* (Turin: Giulio

Einaudi, 1984); Harold Bloom, *The Strong Light of the Canonical: Kafka, Freud and Scholem as Revisionists of Jewish Culture and Thought* (New York: City College of New York, 1987); Iris Bruce, "A Life of Metamorphosis: Franz Kafka and the Jewish Tradition," Ph.D. diss., University of Toronto, 1991; Marina Cavarocchi, *La certezza che toglia la speranza: Contributi per l'approfondimento dell'aspetto ebraico in Kafka* (Florence: La Giuntina, 1988); Laurent Cohen, *Variations autour de K.: Pour une lecture juive de Franz Kafka* (Paris: Intertextes éditeur, 1991); Alfred Dreyfus, *Cinq années de ma vie* (Paris: Fasquelle, 1901), 104; Enrico Ferri, *Criminal Sociology* (New York: Appleton, 1899), 204; W. Forner, "The Movement in Germany, Austria, and Hungary," *The Control and Eradication of Tuberculosis*, ed. Halliday G. Sutherland (Edinburgh: Green, 1911), 314–30; Sander L. Gilman, *Franz Kafka: The Jewish Patient* (New York: Routledge, 1995); Grözinger, *Kafka und die Kabbala: Das Jüdische im Werk und Denken von Franz Kafka* (Frankfurt a. M.: Eichborn, 1992); Hans Gross, *Kriminal-Psychologie* (Leipzig: Vogel, 1905); Karl Erich Grözinger, Stéphane Moses, and Hans Dieter Zimmermann, eds., *Kafka und das Judentum* (Frankfurt a. M.: Jüdischer Verlag / Athenäum, 1987); Rotraut Hackermuller, *Das Leben, das mich stört: Eine Dokumentation zu Kafkas letzten Jahren 1917–1924* (Vienna: Medusa, 1984); Jules Héricourt, *The Social Diseases: Tuberculosis, Syphilis, Alcoholism, Sterility*, trans. with a final chapter by Bernard Miall (London: Routledge, 1920); Jean Jofen, *The Jewish Mystic in Kafka* (New York: Peter Lang, 1987); Franz Kafka, *The Castle*, trans. Willa Muir and Edwin Muir (New York: Knopf, 1992); Kafka, *The Complete Stories*, ed. Nahum N. Glatzer (New York: Schocken, 1971); Kafka, *Letters to Friends, Family, and Editors*, ed. Max Brod, trans. Richard Winston and Clara Winston (New York: Schocken, 1977); Kafka, *Letters to Milena*, trans. Philip Boehm (New York: Schocken, 1990); Kafka, *Letters to Ottla and the Family*, trans. Richard Winston and Clara Winston,

ed. N. N. Glatzer (New York: Schocken, 1982); Kafka, *The Trial*, trans. Willa Muir and Edwin Muir (New York: Schocken, 1984); Thomas Mann, *Death in Venice and Other Stories*, trans. H. T. Lowe-Porter (New York: Vintage, 1936), 325; Mann, *The Magic Mountain* [1924], trans. H. T. Lowe-Porter (New York: Knopf, 1982); Ernst Pawel, "The Judaism of Franz Kafka," *Journal of the Kafka Society of America* 10 (1986): 80–82; Heinz Politzer, *Franz Kafka: Parable and Paradox*, rev. ed. (Ithaca, N.Y.: Cornell University Press, 1966); Jill Robbins, *Prodigal Son / Elder Brother: Interpretation and Alterity in Augustine, Petrarch, Kafka, Levinas* (Chicago: University of Chicago Press, 1991); Ritchie Robertson, *Kafka: Judaism, Politics, and Literature* (Oxford, Eng.: Clarendon, 1985); Ernestine Schlant, "Franz Kafka's Historical Consciousness," *Newsletter of the Kafka Society of America* 4 (1980): 15–20; Bernhard Siegert, "Kartographien der Zerstreuung: *Jargon* und die Schrift der jüdischen Tradierungsbewegung bei Kafka," *Franz Kafka, Schriftverkehr*, ed. Wolf Kittler and Gerhard Neumann (Freiburg: Rombach, 1990), 222–47; Mitchell Silver, "The Roots of Anti-Semitism: A Kafka Tale and a Sartrean Commentary," *Judaism* 30 (1981): 263–68; Paul Slezak, *Geschichte der österreichischen Sanitätsverwaltung* (Vienna: Urban und Schwarzenberg, 1956), 42–47; Halliday G. Sutherland, ed., *The Control and Eradication of Tuberculosis* (Edinburgh: Green, 1911). Enzo Traverso, "Rationalité et barbarie: Relire Weber, Benjamin et Kafka après Auschwitz," *Les Temps Modernes* 568 (Nov. 1993): 7–29; Julius Uffelmann, *Darstellung des auf dem Gebiete der öffentliche Gesundheitspflege in ausser-deutschen Ländern bis jetzt Geleisteten* (Berlin: G. Reimar, 1878), 83–102 and 448–67; Lovis M. Wambach, *Ahaser und Kafka: Zur Bedeutung der Judenfeindschaft in dessen Leben und Work* (Heidelberg: Carl Winter, 1993); and Melvin Wilk, *Jewish Presence in T. S. Eliot and Franz Kafka* (Atlanta: Scholars Press, 1986).

SANDER L. GILMAN

1925 *Jud Süss* by Lion Feuchtwanger is published

Lion Feuchtwanger's 1925 novel *Jud Süss* dealt with the issue of Jewish identity in a way unlike most previous German works. It broke new ground for the historical novel as a genre, opened up possibilities for addressing the problem of ethnic and national identity, and positioned itself critically within a discourse of anti-Semitism that was to reach a pinnacle in Nazi representations of the Jew in the 1940s. The extraordinary popularity of this work resulted as much from the topicality of the subject matter as from Feuchtwanger's mastery of the historical novel. The story of Jud Süss, which originated at a time of religious *Kulturkampf* in Lessing's Germany of the eighteenth century, was deemed by Feuchtwanger to be relevant to the rise of anti-Semitism in Europe immediately following World War I.

Joseph Süss Oppenheimer was born in Heidelberg in 1692, the offspring of a liaison between Freiherr von Heyersdorff and the daughter of a Jewish cantor in Frankfurt am Main. His mother's eventual husband, who became his legal father, was the Jewish director of a troupe of strolling players. Reared as a Jew, Süss was by heredity half-Jewish, because his natural father, von Heyersdorff, was a gentile.

As a young man, Süss went to Frankfurt, where he rapidly became a power in the financial world, one of the few areas open to Jews at the time. He also developed a considerable reputation because of his relations with the women of the land. He was serving as the Palatinate's lord high steward and war adviser when in 1732 he became acquainted with Prince Karl Alexander of Württemberg, who in October 1733 became Duke of Württemberg. Süss Oppenheimer was made his financial adviser with the task of procuring money to pay off the national debt. In return, he was given financial control of the duchy, with authority to collect taxes and tolls.

Süss's financial measures were resisted by the Protestants of the Württemberg diet, who turned to the duke with an appeal to intervene. Karl Alexander refused and, through the instigation of the Jesuits, eventually turned against the diet. The duke's political conflict with the diet (in which Süss did not become involved) centered on his proposal to impose a military regime in a Protestant country, which would have invalidated the constitution and forced the people to turn Catholic. A coup was planned, but on the day it was to take place the duke threw a fit of rage over the demands put forth by the diet, suffered a stroke, and died. Süss Oppenheimer was arrested and after a lengthy trial was condemned to death by hanging because he had "mixed carnally with Christian flesh." He was executed on February 4, 1738.

Lion Feuchtwanger became aware of the historical tale of Jud Süss Oppenheimer at an early point in his prolific career, and he drew on this material for two separate fictional works. In 1917 he published a drama entitled *Jud Süss,* which premiered in Munich at the Schauspielhaus in October of the same year. Between 1920 and 1922, the author went on to write his historical novel, which was first turned down by all of the major publishing houses in Germany and finally published by the tiny Müller Verlag in 1925. By the early 1930s it had already become a national and international bestseller: some 200,000 German copies had been published and, translated into over fifteen languages, it reached a total foreign publication figure of 640,000. The novel appeared in the United States under the title *Power* in October 1926, and a month later in England as *Jew Süss,* where it went through twenty-eight reprintings in a year and a half. "There is an unmistakable quality of greatness in the work," wrote the *Times Literary Supplement* in 1927, "It is one of the most remarkable historical novels of recent years."

Lion Feuchtwanger was not the first or only artist to render the story of Jud Süss in a fictional mode. Starting even before Süss's execution, the extraordinary events surrounding the life and demise of the gallant court Jew became the stuff of song and verse, written and performative representation. The romantic writer Wilhelm Hauff's mildly anti-Semitic version of the story, serialized as a novella in 1827, went through numerous reprintings and served as the model for a tragedy by A. F. Dulk in 1848, as well as for Eugen Ortner's 1930 *Volksstück* and Veit Harlan's viciously racist Nazi feature film of 1940. Other, more sympathetic depictions to appear in the nineteenth century included Rabbi Markus Lehmann's serialized novel for the *Israelit* in 1872 and a chaste, indeed even edifying, portrayal of Süss by the popular Jewish writer Salomon Kohn in 1887.

It is significant that in writing both his play and the novel, Lion Feuchtwanger returned to historical records. In so doing, he did not seek to claim absolute historical accuracy in the depiction of Süss's biography, but rather employed history in order to create an "epic" framework that would do justice to the thoroughly contradictory nature of both the extraordinary central figure and the context in which he lived.

But for Feuchtwanger this was also a book for and about the present—about the postwar Germany of the 1920s. The author's difficulty in getting the novel published most likely had to do with the fact that, as he himself somewhat euphe-

mistically put it, many publishers feared the public would be "offended by its controversial material, the questionable rise of a German Jew from out of the ghetto, and his subsequent fall" (Feuchtwanger 1976, 523). Yet for Feuchtwanger this was, paradoxically, one of the reasons for the book's considerable success: "As a result of their defeat in World War I, the German people suffered from a strong inferiority complex, which found its expression in anti-Semitic rumblings that were later to erupt in horrible explosions of violence. All of that was anticipated and graphically portrayed in the novel. It touched the nerve of the people" (524).

Feuchtwanger's own writings on the historical novel as a generic form suggest a number of elements that help explain the manner in which history was to function within his works. As is clear from the above, the story of Jud Süss as material from the past for fictionalization takes on its importance—indeed, finds its very starting point—in the author's own experience (*Erlebnis*) and as something that is necessarily rooted in the present. In Feuchtwanger's view this does not mean that the historical serves as a "neutral ground" to be totally transformed into the "eternal same." Nor does history figure simply as "inspiration" in order to incite the writer to flights of fancy. Rather, for Feuchtwanger, a historical novel has the potential to mobilize perception in a present crisis by bringing a similar set of circumstances from the past into focus. Thus, what happened to Jud Süss in the 1730s is activated by a German-Jewish writer two hundred years later as a familiar but also distanced moment of the then present crisis of twentieth-century Jewry.

Understanding Feuchtwanger's use of history in turn helps us to see how this work took on the important role it played vis-à-vis the evolving fictionalizations of Jud Süss Oppenheimer. Inserted against the grain of existing literary depictions of the legendary Süss, Feuchtwanger's novel successfully mediates, as a critical historicization in the Brechtian sense, between the caricature of the scheming and profligate court Jew, on the one hand, and the hagiographies of him as an innocent victim of vicious anti-Semitism, on the other. Yet as Feuchtwanger later comes to understand, the novel also serves presciently as a countertext to the likes of Veit Harlan and Joseph Goebbels, who would later bend the Jud Süss story to serve the policy needs of mass extermination. Any discussion of Feuchtwanger's classic of anti-anti-Semitism must take into consideration its inner textual tensions as well as the remarkable history of its reception over the years.

The genesis of Lion Feuchtwanger's *Jud Süss* is best read within the interface of three textual fields: the historical sources, the 1917 play, and the novel. Important for Feuchtwanger as a starting point was his discovery of Manfred Zimmermann's biography entitled *Josef Süss Oppenheimer, ein Finanzmann des 18. Jahrhunderts,* which was written in 1874 and focused on the economic role of the Jew in the early growth and expansion of capitalism in Germany at the outset of modernization. In addition to Zimmermann's biography, Feuchtwanger was also known to have consulted documentary materials from the earlier period, including the numerous brochures, political tracts, and historical records that appeared surrounding and subsequent to the trial and execution of Süss in 1738. In working through these materials, two important emphases emerged in Feuchtwanger's account that were to alter the fictional configuration of the Jud Süss myth in fundamental ways.

The first emphasis concerns Süss's relation to Duke Alexander and the conflicts with the Protestant estates. Whereas many of the earlier fictional treatments (Hauff 1828) placed Süss at the center of intrigue as someone who manipulated the duke into a brutal showdown and who almost single-handedly terrorized the Protestant estates, Feuchtwanger shifted the emphasis from Süss as the single agent of machination to a depiction of a man who became a scapegoat due to his own rise to fame and power. This portrayal was not intended to exonerate the court Jew by making him a mere victim of circumstance. Süss was clearly conceived as someone who ruthlessly schemes to bring about the economic and political reordering of the Duchy of Württemberg, and whose enormous skills at extorting capital from the land provided within two years the financial means by which Duke Alexander, with support of the Cath-

olics, would be able to wage his unrelenting war against the Protestant estates. Although not minimizing in any way Süss's responsibility in these economic measures, Feuchtwanger's depiction of Süss nevertheless contextualizes him within the larger socioeconomic transformations of the nation-state during the emergence of eighteenth-century nationalism. More important, it is the intrigue of the Catholics in their conflict with the Protestants, not the scheming of the Jewish courtier, that ultimately becomes the driving political force behind Alexander's efforts to seize power.

Feuchtwanger's literary reconfiguration of Jud Süss from a stereotype of one-dimensional Jewish profligacy and consummate evil into a prototypical eighteenth-century "finance man" in an age of political transition provided the initiating concept for his play of 1917. Because the author had for a long time been concerned about the inadequate representations of the Jew in world literature (he himself wrote a dissertation on Heinrich Heine's *The Rabbi of Bacharach* in 1911), he was gratified to find in Zimmermann's historically differentiated depiction of Süss the material with which to counter a stereotype. But this same material also presented Feuchtwanger with a major problem, namely, how to confer upon his central figure the inner qualities necessary for fundamental insight and spiritual change—how to lend to this sociological representation the quality of characterological agency so necessary for dramatic peripetia and the unraveling of the denouement. How, in short, was the financier Süss to become a tragic figure worthy of the generic medium?

Feuchtwanger's efforts to resolve the problem of dramatic contingency resulted in his creating a number of new characters not found in the historical records, figures who in turn served to open up another dimension of Süss's identity. Key in this regard was his attributing to Süss the existence of an illegitimate daughter named Tamara, who lives deep in the woods in a magic castle under the guardianship of her great uncle, the kabbalist Magus. Hidden away from the rest of the world, Tamara, her mystical Magus, and their precious, secreted abode clearly come to represent all that is the opposite of Süss's life at the decadent court. Tamara, in turn, also serves a double function for the Jud Süss drama. At the level of narrative, it is the discovery and attempted seduction of Tamara by Duke Alexander, resulting in her accidental death, that compels a raging Süss to avenge his daughter by driving the duke into a state of apoplexy and to his death, which in turn leads to Süss's own demise at the hands of an equally vengeful Protestant populace.

But more important than its narrative function is what Tamara and the Magus come to *mean* as an alternative identity to Süss the conniving, courtly Jew. "What is my true self?" ("Welches ist mein wahres Ich?"), Süss asks at the beginning of act two, and the postulated alternatives represent a set of binary choices that are central to the way in which the author wrestles with the question of Jewish identity from that point forward: in Feuchtwanger's drama Süss becomes a lover of sensual pleasure, worldly goods, and outer appearances, as well as a pursuer of knowledge and the inwardness of the soul. Feuchtwanger's fight against the stereotype of the Jew Süss as sexual marauder and capitalist conniver thus entailed a remapping of Süss's spiritual struggles across the landscape of eighteenth-century idealism. For central to this juxtaposition, at the level of *Weltanschauung* as well as of literary trope, was the notion of the Jew as a cipher for the conflicting forces of societal modernization. Like the Christian pietism represented by characters such as Magdalene Weissensee, Jewish mysticism was to provide a critique of all those instrumental rationalists "for whom people are nothing more than numbers." Thus already in the dramatic figure of Feuchtwanger's Süss we find the philosophical struggle between being and appearance, body and soul, the material and the spiritual, which will be so central to the novel as well.

Despite the extraordinary success of the drama *Jud Süss* in Munich, Feuchtwanger was not satisfied with his representation of the Jew. And the problem was once more a generic one. If the introduction of mysticism lent to the central character a philosophical and dramaturgical complexity that was vital to Feuchtwanger's enlarged concept of this character, it was precisely the dramatic structure itself that curtailed his effort to place the story of Jud Süss Oppenheimer within a broader, multilayered network of sociohistorical experience.

Thus Lion Feuchtwanger decided to write a novel that would permit him to unravel the story of Jud Süss within a larger epic panorama of Jewish cultural history. Although the daughter (now named Naemi) and the Magus (here Rabbi Gabriel, the wandering Jew) were to remain central components of the narrative, they were joined by other Jewish characters, one of the most important of whom was the businessman Isaac Landauer.

Landauer represents an expression of Jewish economic power in European society that was wielded in a manner radically at odds with that of Süss. Contrary to the younger, more impetuous courtier, Landauer disdains the pomp and material trappings of wealth. Furthermore, he makes no attempt to assimilate his Judaic manner of dress (caftan, temple curls, and beard) and speech (addressing associates as "Reb") to the customs and fashions of the time. A paragon of modesty and reserve, Landauer is careful never to antagonize his superiors lest they discover the extent of his power over them and find grounds for his dismissal. The sources of his satisfaction are inner and savored in private. Süss, on the other hand, is depicted as having an insatiable appetite for people and fame, and his excessive daring proves to be his downfall. Thus the courtier shows himself to be lacking in the very circumspection that Landauer knows is so crucial to the survival of an oppressed minority such as the Jews of this period and locality.

By presenting an epic panorama of the Jewish experience, Feuchtwanger shows that the fate of Jud Süss was in part of his own making. Süss's confrontation with the issue of identity and choice, in fact, serves as a central turning point for the novel itself. Having been unjustly accused of crimes beyond his control on the basis of his identity as a Jew, Süss discovers that his father was a gentile and that by making that public he can avoid his execution. His subsequent refusal to do so becomes an affirmation of his own Jewishness, an assertion against the false values under which

he has been laboring. What is important, however, is that this "Jewish" self is linked as much to
the worldly Reb Landauer as it is to the otherworldly Rabbi Gabriel. Thus Feuchtwanger's final assertion of Jewish identity is not a flight into
spiritual transcendence (as was the case in the
drama), but rather an affirmation of the historical
contradictions that are a part of *any* formation of
self. Süss's "identity" is put together from the
many pieces of his own experience and those
around him: the world of his daughter, the
preachings of Rabbi Gabriel, the interactions
with the pragmatic Landauer, and even his thoroughly symbiotic relationship with Duke Alexander.

The question of Jewish identity was to remain
central in subsequent representations of the Jud
Süss story, in particular the two major films to
appear during the reign of European fascism. The
first was a British production of 1934 entitled *Jew
Süss* under the direction of Lothar Mendes and
based for the most part on Feuchtwanger's novel.
The political position of this film is announced in
its opening lines. As was the case in Feuchtwanger's novel, there is a clear effort to link the
historical Jud Süss to the present political situation, in this case the growing anti-Semitism in
Nazi Germany: "In 1730, Württemberg—now a
part of Germany—was an independent duchy.
Then, as now, the Jews were judged differently
from other men." This historical perspective is
further underlined in the film's prologue, where
we are shown the ghettos in which the Jews have
been held captive and out of which they will
attempt to break in the years that follow. It is
described as a place where "official regulation
confined them to ridiculous and shameful garb,
pressed them into narrow quarters, and barred the
gates of the ghettos guarding their going in and
their coming out." In Lothar Mendes's *Jew Süss,*
the central character is situated within the context of Jewish assimilation of the eighteenth century, and his later hanging by the Protestant estates is presented as the result of the failure of
assimilation and the growing anti-Semitism in
the Germany of that time.

In Veit Harlan's Nazi version of the Jud Süss
story, the emphasis is clearly one in which the Jew
is perpetrator, not victim, and his brutal execution a "horrible example" of what should and
must be done to all Jews who violate the codes of
biological, as well as cultural, assimilation. Here
Harlan turned back to the tradition of Wilhelm
Hauff and German romanticism to create a Jewish monster who, with the help of his ruthless
sidekick Levy, was to terrorize the populace under
a helpless and profligate Duke Alexander, and
whose execution at the end of the film is accompanied by the invocation of a Jewish prohibition
(*Judenbann*) with clear reference to the contemporary situation in Nazi Germany: "May our descendants hold firm to this law, so that they can
be spared much suffering for their lives and property and for the blood of their children and their
children's children."

In Harlan's rendition of the Süss story, the
message of racial identity is clear and dominant
throughout. The financier Süss is hated for his
economic exploitation of the simple Protestant
folk, his straightening of the roads and leveling of
tolls. In addition, his religious brethren are presented as bizarre and cacophonous, in contrast to
the purity of heart and tonal harmony of the children of Christ. But Süss's rape of the innocent
Dorothea, situated structurally as the dramatic
turning point of the film, becomes the consummate signifier of Jewish barbarism and singularity of tribal intention. Where Feuchtwanger
had opened up Jewish identity to the historical
complexities of an entire age, Harlan's 1940 *Terra*
film creates in the Jew a cipher of biological es-
sentialism, the metonymic counter to Aryan supremacy: Süss is confined visually to a stereotype
of the Eastern European Jew who will disguise
himself as a courtier for purposes of Aryan assimilation; depicted narratively as having one insatiable desire—to violate the purity of German
blood; reduced morally to the evil Other of middle-class German propriety and well-being.

Viewed within the context of Nazi *Kulturpolitik* of the early 1940s, it should come as no
surprise that the minister of propaganda Joseph
Goebbels was involved in shaping this film from
beginning to end: he was a part of choosing the
director, casting the actors, writing the script,
and even reshooting the final scene (he had found

the original version to be too sympathetic toward the central character). For *Jud Süss* was but one of three anti-Semitic films to be premiered in 1940 (*The Eternal Jew* and *The Rothschilds* were the two others) as part of an orchestrated preparation for the Final Solution. In each of these films, the political task at hand was to perform an unveiling process; to reveal behind the Jewish masks of falsely constructed national identities the larger biological truth of their one irrevocable self; to educate an audience, finally, in the fine points of reading the Jewish physiognomy. In *The Eternal Jew*, for instance, the central sequences consist of a series of close-up dissolves in which the bearded, long-haired, swarthy faces of supposedly Polish ghetto Jews dissolve into the clean-shaven, "modern" looking physiognomies of the assimilated. The message is a simple and straightforward one. Behind every seemingly Westernized Jew of the major metropolitan cities lies the lurking, sinister *Ostjude*.

Harlan's *Jud Süss* takes the strategy of anti-Semitic visual literacy as a form of Nazi identity politics to yet another level. For here the Jewish mask of polished Jud Süss is juxtaposed by the chameleon-like activities of several different Jewish-looking Jews, all represented by the same actor. The story goes that the famous actor Werner Krauss attempted to get out of playing the Rabbi Loew in the film by informing Goebbels that he would play Loew only if he could do every Jewish part in the film with the exception of the lead. Goebbels's unexpected acceptance of the offer not only forced Krauss's hand, but influenced as well the interpretive direction of the film as a whole. Krauss's performance of all seven of the minor Jewish roles clearly underscores the central message of this cinematic *Jud Süss:* underneath the mask of difference, it would want to say, every Jew looks and is the same. The performance of Jewish posturing cannot and will not hide the deeper truth of this sameness if only the German populace remain vigilant as active observers.

A few months after the premiere of *Jud Süss* in Berlin and Venice, Lion Feuchtwanger wrote an open letter to Veit Harlan and several of the major actors in the film in which he accused them of turning his novel "with the help of a little Tosca into a vicious anti-Semitic hate film in the spirit of Julius Streicher and his journal *Der Stürmer*." Particularly painful for Feuchtwanger must have been the fact that Eugen Klöpfer, the actor who portrayed the Protestant leader Sturm, the chief antagonist to Süss in the film, had himself played the lead in the author's 1917 production of the play. But Feuchtwanger was mistaken in one important respect. Not having seen the film, he could not know that Harlan based his screenplay not on the Feuchtwanger novel but rather on Hauff's serialized novella of the late 1820s. For had Feuchtwanger seen the film, it would have been clear to him just how incompatible the two indeed were, not only at the level of story, but in the very construction of Jewish identity. Lion Feuchtwanger's *Jud Süss* has remained a classic of anti-anti-Semitism, as much for the brilliance of its storytelling as for the refusal to compromise in its fictional construction of the central character.

Bibliography

Lion Feuchtwanger, *Jud Süss: Schauspiel* (Munich: Müller Verlag, 1917); Feuchtwanger, *Jud Süss* (Frankfurt a. M.: Fischer Taschenbuch, 1976); Regine Mihal Friedman, *L'image et son juif: Le juif dans le cinema nazi* (Paris: Payot, 1983); Wilhelm Hauff, *Jud Süss* (1827), in *Novellen von Wilhelm Hauff* (Stuttgart: Franckh, 1828); Friedrich Knilli and Siegfried Zielinski, "Lion Feuchtwangers *Jud Süss* und die gleichnamigen Filme von Lothar Mendes (1934) und Veit Harlan (1940)," *Text und Kritik* 79–80 (Oct. 1983): 99–121; and John Spalek, *Lion Feuchtwanger: The Man, His Ideas and His Work* (Los Angeles: Hennessey & Ingalls, 1972).

DAVID BATHRICK

1925 Hugo Bettauer's assassination by Otto Rothstock in Vienna marks the first political murder by the Nazis in Austria

The Jews are afraid in Vienna. They have always been afraid and they will always be. One cannot take fear away from the Jews. No one can take it from them.

—Thomas Bernhard, 1989

On March 10, 1925, Otto Rothstock, a twenty-year-old unemployed dental technician, followed Hugo Bettauer (1872–1925), the converted Jewish writer and journalist, into his editorial offices in Vienna. Pushing himself before the half-dozen who were already waiting to consult with Bettauer, Rothstock shot him at point-blank range five times with a Bulldog six millimeter, fatally wounding the man known for his best-selling novel, *Die Stadt ohne Juden* (The city without Jews), and as the father of the sexual revolution in Vienna. Bettauer's assassination, the first Nazi-organized murder in Austria, conflated two increasingly prevalent trends of the 1920s: the fear of sexuality and the hatred of Jews.

Little is known about the early life of the enigmatic and controversial Bettauer, one of the most provocative figures of his day. Born in Vienna, at the age of eighteen he converted from Judaism to the Protestant Church, a denomination chosen by many Jews who wanted to rid themselves of the religious stigma of being Jewish, but who felt uncomfortable making the "giant step" to Catholicism. In the late 1890s, Bettauer left on the first of two trips to New York, where he worked for various German-language newspapers and began to write serialized novels.

Returning to Vienna in 1908, Bettauer continued to write for the journals for which he served as a correspondent in America as well as for *Die Zeit,* a left-liberal paper, and the imperial war-propaganda publication *Donauland* (such authors as Hugo von Hofmannsthal and Stefan Zweig contributed to *Donauland* as well). For four years, he was the "salon" editor of the great liberal daily *Die Neue Freie Presse,* where he also served in 1918 as a war correspondent from the front in Lemberg. This work established Bettauer's reputation with the press, as can be seen in his unanimous reelection in 1913 to the executive committee of Concordia, the Austrian writers' and journalists' association. After the war, Bettauer was a press correspondent for the American Relief Committee for Sufferers in Austria, which provided economic aid to the poor in the new republic. He published numerous articles in the liberal papers *Der Wiener Morgen, Der Tag,* and *Die Stunde.*

In the early 1920s Bettauer wrote twenty-three "Wiener Romane." These were simple stories, entertaining *Trivialliteratur,* not great literature, but incisive portrayals of the lives of ordinary people with emphasis on the exploitation of women and the poor. Nine of his works were made into films, including the 1925 G. W. Pabst picture *Die Freudlose Gasse,* which starred the neophyte Swedish actress Greta Garbo.

In 1924, in collaboration with silent partner Rudolf Olden (1885–1940), who subsequently became a professor at Oxford and president of the Austrian PEN club in exile, Bettauer published the first of his very successful newspapers, *Er und Sie: Zeitschrift für Lebenskultur und Erotik* (He and she: A magazine for lifestyles and eroticism), followed that same year by *Bettauers Wochenschrift* (Bettauer's weekly) and *Bettauers Almanach*. The first issue of *Er und Sie* reached 60,000 readers, and the magazine had 200,000 readers within five weeks. The sixteen-page publication dealt with sexual emancipation and contained advice to the lovelorn as well as "personals" and serialized fiction. For all their popularity, however, the criticism in these periodicals of the political conservatism of the era deeply offended the political parties and provoked a flood of opprobrium in their press publications.

Like his newspapers, *Die Stadt ohne Juden* (1922) was a huge success, attesting to its accurate and biting portrayal of the anti-Semitic climate of the time. As a result of the political, economic, social, and even sexual transformations after the war, there was a pervasive spread of anti-Semitism in Austria that Bettauer elevated to the central theme of the novel. The satirical work sold a phenomenal 250,000 copies, was translated into several languages, and was made into both a play and a movie. The English edition (1926) appeared to rave reviews: "Bettauer is first and last a realist, an accurate and astute observer," wrote the *New York Evening Post* on the flyleaf to the *Stadt ohne Juden*. The publicist, Hans Habe, declared it a "document of its time of lasting worth" (Habe 1954, 111). In 1983, *Vienne sans ses Juifs* appeared again in Paris. In 1991, the rediscovered, restored film of Bettauer's work was broadcast on Austrian television and shown under the auspices of the Vienna film festival. The book, in contrast to the Bresslauer film, sets the scene unmistakably in Austria.

Despite its frighteningly accurate forecast of the 1930s, sadly *Die Stadt ohne Juden* reflected the already multifaceted expressions of anti-Semitism of 1922. In the postwar period, when a lack of consensual democracy or trust among the political parties dominated, anti-Semitism became useful as a technique of political integration despite the decrease in the percentage of Jews in the population. It infected popular political slogans. It acted as the catchall that held together the otherwise disparate constituencies of the Christian Social and German Nationalist parties in an era of great political tension and economic crisis. The political parties also used anti-Semitism to undermine one another: the Social Democrats accused the Christian Socials of pandering to Jewish capital, whereas the latter decried the internationalist conspiracy of Jews with the Socialists.

Primarily for this book, Bettauer was included among the *entartet* or "degenerate" writers of the 1938 *Der Ewige Jude* exhibition in Munich. Without a doubt the novel, published thirteen years before the Nuremberg Laws—and peopled by a mustachioed, fanatical leader, a populace where people greet each other with "Heil!" and Jews that are deported from Vienna on trains—augured ominously and uncannily for the tragic future of the Jews.

The story, made up of a basic framing plot with a series of loosely connected vignettes, concerns the growing unrest in Vienna brought on by true-to-life and terrible economic deprivation, run-away inflation, and the devaluation of the Krone. What Bettauer's novels lacked in sophistication and textuality they made up for in immediacy and the popular but blunt portrayal of disturbing problems drawn from the political reality. To secure the legitimacy of his government, fictional chancellor Karl Schwertfeger, a composite cameo of contemporary politicians Karl Lueger, Michael Mayr, and Ignaz Seipel, harnesses the cross-class rhetoric of anti-Semitism to push an "Anti-Jewish-Law" through the parliament. The law requires that before the new year all Jews—including baptized converts and the children of mixed marriages—must leave Austria.

As the Jews roll out of Vienna on special trains, people celebrate their liberation from the upper-middle-class mercenary usurpers, who they believe to be controllers of press and politics, and from the conspicuously caftaned, poor Galician Jews. After a brief period of jubilation, when Aryans rejoice over the removal of the Jewish racial parasite who leeches on the blood and society of simple, good Christian folk and the non-Jews take over all the businesses of the Jews, the economy still does not improve. On the contrary, with Jews abroad influencing the financial community to halt all loans and investment in Austria, things grow worse. Gradually Vienna, once the great cultural metropolis, becomes little more than a village without its Jewish playwrights, poets, and patrons of the arts. Politics becomes bland without the pepper of anti-Semitic rhetoric. The Nazi party has to fold for lack of a scapegoat. Without Jews to hate, Vienna loses its "motor energy" (62), and things grind to a halt.

Concurrent to the political satire, Bettauer weaves in a love story between Lotte Spineder, the Christian daughter of a civil servant, and Leo Strakosch, a Jewish artist forced into exile in France. The human dimension emphasizes both the ludicrousness and tragedy of the expulsion of the Jews. Out of love for Lotte, Leo smuggles himself in disguise back into Austria, where he incites the people against the government, helps in the founding of a new liberal, bourgeois party that demands the repeal of the *Antijudengesetz,* and sabotages the vote in the parliament to assure the success of the repeal of the law and the return of the Jews to Austria.

The driving force behind the law is Schwertfeger, who feels he has found the resolution to Austria's economic ills and its crisis of political legitimacy. "Hinaus mit den Juden aus Österreich!" (Expel the Jews from Austria!) is sure to guarantee the country's renewal and, in contrast to the *Anschluß* (annexation) solution, his own political power and immortality as well. In a maniacal and inspired speech before parliament, Schwertfeger justifies the expulsion of the Jews with the most perversely twisted but benign rhetoric of racial and political anti-Semitism. Through his words, Bettauer mordantly captures the language of hatred already so prevalent in 1922.

"Yes, ladies and gentlemen, I value the Jews. I had Jewish friends even before I sat in the hot seat of politics. . . . I am prepared at anytime to recognize, yes even to admire the traditional Jewish virtues, the extraordinary intelligence, their up-

ward mobility, their exemplary sense of family, their internationalism, their ability to adapt to any milieu" (11). In this echo of Mayor Karl Lueger's infamous "Wer Jude ist, bestimme ich" (I am the one who determines whoever is a Jew), the character cynically damns the Jews with his praise of their typical Enlightenment qualities. Expressing the nationalist, romantic ideal of simplicity and irrationality, when speaking of Aryans as "a naive honest people, dreamy, playful, clinging to unproductive ideals" (11), such anti-Semites articulated their critique of the values of modernity and liberalism in racial terminology (or couched their racism behind a critique of modernity).

"Despite, no because of this, the conviction grew stronger in me over the years that we non-Jews can no longer live with and next to the Jews. It means either bend or break, that either we must give up our Christian way, our presence and being or the Jews must" (11). This concept of the Jew as "other," as foreign to some sort of innate Christian character and blood, gained prominence through the rabid, nineteenth-century nationalist Georg von Schönerer, but emerged in the 1920s in mainstream political platforms like the Salzburg Program of the Großdeutsche Partei, which stated that the Jew is a "Fremdkörper" (foreign body). The center Christlichsozialen in their party program of 1919 more subtly called for the "State protection of the Christian family."

These biological metaphors, popularized in the nineteenth century (for example, by Nordau), gained prominence particularly after the war when war profiteers, financiers, and all those with money were perceived as leeches who profited from the physical and economic enslavement of the lower middle and working classes. The frequent use of perverted metaphors of Social Darwinism—parasitism, infection, physicality, and so forth resonate with a double, violent meaning. They turn the Aryan into the victim of the small pest's lasciviousness and, therefore, justify his attempts to eradicate the nuisance.

By the early part of the twentieth century, anti-Semitism had experienced a telling transformation. Although on the one hand, it had become more "tamed" and "civilized," as witnessed by the disappearance of the explicitly anti-Semitic one-issue parties of the latter part of the nineteenth century (such as Schönerer's Alldeutsche Partei), it had also attained a greater degree of normalcy; anti-Semitic talk—if not action—became de rigueur in Austrian politics.

Die Stadt ohne Juden concedes the stereotype that "hook-nosed" Jews often *did* frequent the best restaurants and coffee houses. Bettauer, however, humorously tried to show that their patronage of Austrian culture and influence over its economy were not a burden but a necessity for the country's survival and flourishing. Even at the end, when the Jews are welcomed back, they are still reviled as Jews and thought of as a foreign element; only now the nation realizes that their presence is integral to the functioning of society. Hence, he even justified to some extent the claims of the anti-Semites without legitimizing their consequences. The existence of anti-Semitism is decried not as an affront to liberal values but as harmful to the otherwise symbiotic economic relationship of Jews and Aryans.

Highly assimilated and even religious Catholic families are torn apart because one relative or another has a Jewish parent. "Our best Christian citizens are soaked through with Judaism," wrote Bettauer (28). This characterization mirrored the close intermingling and coexistence of anti-Semites and Jews that we can hardly imagine today, but which was integral to Vienna at the time. Some Jews in the book complain that they couldn't stand to go to Palestine and be only among Jews, and one sensitive young poet commits suicide because he cannot feel inspired without the landscape of his homeland. Tongue-in-cheek, Bettauer describes how even the prostitutes lament the loss of their best clients through the law. Some of them even convert to Judaism to follow their business abroad.

The populace, however, rejoices at the loss of the Jew. People are, at first, more friendly on the streetcars. Apartments and jobs can be easily found due to the precipitous drop in the population from the departure of the Jews and all their close relatives and friends. People greet one another on the street with "Heil!" (63). A cult develops around the unmarried Dr. Schwertfeger, in which women throw themselves at his carriage in the hope of touching him. From the very beginning, Bettauer hints to his readers that this leader of the Christian Social Party is also a psychologically unstable megalomaniac.

Lotte relates to Leo how the opera houses are empty and the theaters, where Jewish works may no longer be performed, have gone bankrupt. The *Kaffeehäuser* have become beer halls. The department stores, now taken over by Christians, cannot move the fashionable, expensive merchandise they once sold. When the Jewesses were finely and elegantly dressed, the Christian society women did not want to take second place, explains a clerk to the owner of a fancy shop on the Kärntnerstraße. Since then only loden, cotton, and flannel remain on display, advertised as the latest Paris fashion!

In a barely fictional excursus in *Die Stadt ohne Juden,* Bettauer summarizes the Zeitgeist:

In those years which followed the end of the war and the coup, Vienna had developed more and more into the center of a central European luxury and the life of certain classes had acquired a voluptuousness which was considered unparalleled. But the vast majority of the Viennese population, not just the workers but also the middle class had seen with gritted teeth how the foreign elements, above all the Jews from Galicia, Rumania and Hungary, played the lords of Vienna, threw about the almost worthless Austrian money; drank champagne when the little man could hardly afford a glass of beer, bedecked their women with pearls and furs, while the really good society had to sell the old family jewels piecemeal. They raced through the streets in magnificent luxury cars, took the apartments away from the native Viennese and filled the old cultivated city with their noisy, vulgar affected behavior. When the Jews were chased out all that changed thoroughly from day to day. The beguiling luxury disappeared, the sale of Vienna stopped, one no longer had to get on line to get hold of a place at the Opera. Life became calmer, more stable, simple. Until it was revealed that a city like Vienna cannot live without luxury (57).

Both in the book and in real life, it was a small

step from the biological metaphors of the late nineteenth century to the outright sexual language of the anti-Semitism of the early twentieth. In the history of anti-Semitic propaganda, Jews have generally been associated with sexual potency. In *Die Stadt ohne Juden,* the chancellor claims that Vienna's Christian people are "dominated, oppressed and *raped*" by the Jewish minority. It is not an exaggeration to say that, in addition to other material causes, a fear of sexuality also engendered anti-Semitism in the same way that it has led in other cultures to anti-Black prejudice. Especially in the Bettauer case, where the objection to his religion was directly linked to his sexual agenda, the so-called sexual demonology of the Jew, later to be exploited by the Nazis, became very important. The Austria of the 1920s exhibited similar trends to the Paris of the 1890s described by Stephen Wilson in his book, *Ideology and Experience: Anti-Semitism in France at the Time of the Dreyfus Affair* (1982). He wrote: "Sexual promiscuity symbolized modernity, the abandonment of hierarchy, the confusion of traditional categories" (587).

Such a definition of anti-Semitism assumes a Freudian belief in the externalization and projection of repressed sexuality—that is, in attributing sexual characteristics to one's enemy. The Austrian projected his fears and insecurities onto the Jew; he saw in the Jew what he himself no longer was: the all-powerful hegemon of an empire and unchallenged leader of an exclusively patriarchal world. For Vienna of the early twentieth century, where women could vote and the war had redefined gender roles, such notions hardly seem farfetched. Sexuality in Austria, as in other countries, had been institutionally suppressed by invasive Catholic politics and Victorian moral codes. But the breakdown of the gender hierarchy meant the "return of the repressed," or the reappearance of unconfronted but never abolished desires and fears.

In anti-Semitic imagery, men represented the circumcised and the circumcisers. Not only rational and mercenary, the Jew was said to possess a predatory sexual nature. Their image, interestingly like that of the father figure, represented aggression, castration, and dangerous sexuality.

The supposed sexual potency of the Jewish male rendered him unequivocally an object of hatred and fear. He deflowered Christian girls. Sexuality for these girls was akin to destruction, not just of the individual, but of the bloodline of her race.

The image of females was more ambiguous and hence extremely powerful. It was a bifurcated vision of the Jewess as corrupted and as an object of desire. She was the erotic seductress, enchantress, prostitute, and witch. She gave pleasure but spread disease. She transmitted sexual energy and, at the same time, robbed her lover of his strength, deterring him from his purpose. The other side of this dark psychological puzzle of anti-Semitic hatreds, wrote Jean-Paul Sartre, was "a profound and sexual attraction to the Jews" (Wilson 1982, 585). Wilson pointed out the similarity of the Jewess and the emancipated woman, which helps to explain the appeal of anti-Semitism among, in particular, those groups who also opposed emancipation.

Such Freudian interpretations cannot stand alone. The sexual dimension, however, is vital to understanding not just the text of *Die Stadt ohne Juden* but the real anti-Semitism that it depicted and, more specifically, the hostile reaction to Hugo Bettauer. The publication of *Die Stadt ohne Juden* came shortly after the censorship of Arthur Schnitzler's *Der Reigen* in 1921—a prohibition that provides another example of the fear and unease aroused by a Jewish author promoting sexual freedoms in a fictional work.

At first Bettauer made light of this trend: "To have a Jew as a lover meant to be taken to the theater and to the finer cafés, to be well treated and generously received" (58). But then he went on to identify the fundamentally *sexual* rather than the *economic* threat that Jews seemed to pose to others: "When the sweet girls were among themselves and on good terms, when they traded stories of their erotic experiences then they told of the sensuality of Jews and the variety of their erotic inclinations in contrast to their good and upright, but far less amusing, Christian friends" (59). Only half-jokingly did he uncover the fear of Jewish virility, which he quite seriously believed lay at the root of much of the racism of his day.

Bettauer continued: "Possibly, quite likely,

. . . the anti-Semitism among the male population of Vienna became so strong, so fanatic, in the course of the decade because the young man with the swastika saw and could not get over how the Jewish competition snatched away the pretty girls" (59). Although not particularly remarkable at first, this is probably the most noteworthy paragraph of the whole novel. Here Bettauer reveals the sexual anti-Semitism behind the "acceptable" political variant of the postwar period. After Klaus Theweleit and Erich Fromm, perhaps such a reading might seem reductionist, but this interpretation resonated then with a profound and simple truth.

The distrust of sexuality had another, related consequence: the concomitant fear of psychoanalysis, the so-called Jewish science. Not surprisingly, given his belief in the sexual cause of social problems such as anti-Semitism, Hugo Bettauer had a major effect on the development and institutionalization of psychoanalysis in Vienna at a time when the movement was still controversial and esoteric.

The need for attention to the psychic wellbeing of men and women was, at best, of no interest to the Christian Socialists. In reality, psychoanalysis represented the anathema of the Christian viewpoint on education and a threat to the Church doctrine. Critique of the "pansexualism" of psychoanalysis and its "denial of the divine" characterized the vocabulary used by Catholic thinkers to dismiss its influence and identification of sex at the root of all neuroses. The importance of psychology, however, was not denied by the founders of "Red Vienna," though its leaders, too, were not keen on Freudian psychoanalysis. The Socialists were quite concerned with the nature of child-rearing and character development to the extent of inculcating an appropriate class consciousness. A better part of the Austro-Marxists, however, tended toward the school of individual psychology as described by Alfred Adler.

Little about psychoanalysis ever appeared in the papers. In the Bettauer publications, however, the subject surfaced weekly, both directly and indirectly. As one medical doctor wrote to Bettauer: "Just as we doctors take on the physi-

cally ill, striving to advise and help, so are you the doctor of the psychically ill" (*Er und Sie,* Mar. 13, 1924). The "Probleme des Lebens" column unreservedly and repeatedly recommended psychoanalytic therapy to its troubled readers. One humorous example taken from *Bettauers Wochenschrift* (Nov. 6, 1924): "Lonesome: You are 29 years old, intelligent, educated, with a good job and longing for a companion who would share with you your sorrow and joy. But your emotional life has a unique twist: you believe that you can only live with a girl who has lost one foot. I advise you unconditionally to fight against this abnormal predisposition. This doubtless concerns a case which necessitates psychoanalytic treatment. Consult the Psychoanalytic Ambulatorium." (The Ambulatorium, opened in 1922 amidst great controversy, was the clinic and teaching institution of the Vienna Psychoanalytic Association. Freud was its honorary chairman.)

The psychoanalyst Dr. Richard Sterba recorded Bettauer's influence in his memoirs, *Erinnerungen eines Wiener Psychoanalytikers* (Remembrances of a Vienna psychiatrist):

An unexpected and independent source of propaganda for analysis came in the mid-twenties from a weekly tabloid by the name of *Bettauers Wochenschrift*. The editor, Josef [Hugo] Bettauer, was a Viennese, who had spent several years as a journalist in New York and published numerous popular novels. In his weekly, which had a wide circulation among the masses, sexual themes were handled with then unheard of openness for which Bettauer faced judicial proceedings from which he was acquitted. One rubric of his paper was reserved for the queries of readers regarding sexual matters. In his answers Josef [Hugo] Bettauer often directed questioners, who seemed to have suffered from sexual problems and perversions, to the Psychoanalytic Ambulatorium. This brought more people seeking help to the clinic than could be accommodated with spots for therapy. In any event, a selection of the best-suited cases for psychoanalytic therapy could be found which was very advantageous for the teaching candidates. In the year 1926 [1924] Bettauer was shot by a fanatical National Socialist. The influence of his paper was noticeable even several years thereafter from the increase in those seeking help at the Ambulatorium. Most people who came to the Ambulatorium via *Bettauers Wochenschrift* were ill-educated and had heard hardly anything of psychoanalysis. In this respect, they were particularly advantageous cases for beginners as they, in contrast to those with superficial knowledge, could not use misunderstood analytical concepts such as intellectual resistance (35).

In addition to Sterba's words, we have the figures of Dr. Eduard Hitschmann's *Ten Year Anniversary Report of the Ambulatorium* published in the *Internationale Zeitschrift für Psychoanalyse* in 1932. Although 159 patients came in 1922–23, 354 turned up in 1923–24 and 305 in 1924–25. "The high point around 1924 was achieved with the help of a Viennese paper which reported on the activities of the Ambulatorium and recommended consultation." Between 1923 and 1925 the number of women seeking help trebled. Statistics from the municipal Socialist marriage counseling center also indicate a dramatic increase in inquiries after 1923. One doctor reported that of 2,000 clients seen during a three-year period, one-third suffered from sexual problems.

Just as psychoanalysis aroused tremendous acrimony from politicians, clerics, and the medical establishment, the sexually charged *Stadt ohne Juden,* despite its overwhelming commercial popularity, vexed the elites. It is not hard to find in Pan-German and National Socialist literature endless tirades against "jüdische Volksvergiftung" (the Jewish poisoning of the people) and "jüdische Parasiten" (Jewish parasites). The reaction of the Austrian Nazis, for whom anti-Semitism represented the central political tenet, protested against Bettauer's literary success. One critic, Robert Körber, wrote: "Hardly any other product by a Jew exudes a more filthy spirit of Jewish degeneracy and depravity than this pornography in which the German people of Vienna are degraded into prostitutes—the Helots of the Jews" (Rütgen 1989, 215). Robert Musil recorded in his diaries that they regarded the novels not as social realist literature but as *Bettsauereien* (bed-wetting).

The Christian Socialists took up much the same refrain. They saw in Bettauer the epitome of anti-Christian morality. "We will not allow the Mayor [Seitz]," said Anton Orel, Christian Socialist member of Parliament and editor of *Die Volksturm,* "to impose this Jew, Bettauer, on us to defile our children with Jewish poison and smut" (*Arbeiterzeitung,* Mar. 22, 1924). Bettauer's mockery of the Christian Socialists in *Die Stadt ohne Juden* only reinforced their resentment of his popularity. Although the book was as much a stereotype of Jews, the defensive Christian Socialists, who felt threatened by their exclusion from power in Vienna, saw it as the dissemination of Jewish propaganda and a further attempt to undermine their theistic ideology. "As if it is not enough," declared the *Reichspost,* party organ of the Christian Socialists, after Bettauer's death, "in his novel, *Die Stadt ohne Juden,* he screams his nonsense daily in the ears of the Viennese, openly mocking the Christian people, saying that they should be happy to have Jews who pay well for the virginity of Christian girls" (Hall 1978, 25).

The Christian Socialists, like the Pan-Germans, turned this anti-Semitism into a weapon against the Social Democrats, many of whose founders were Jewish. The necessity of having to defend the rights of unpopular minorities put the Social Democrats in a difficult political position with regard to Hugo Bettauer. The desire to promote an author who so sharply criticized their political enemies clashed with the Social Democrats' instinct to distance themselves from the source of attack. In *Die Stadt ohne Juden,* Bettauer also criticized them. Hence, the Socialists' initial position of active support for Bettauer wavered and gradually evolved into silent abandonment. In *Die Stadt ohne Juden,* the Socialist deputies do not fight back; they merely leave in protest, guilty of passive complicity.

The hostility and venom with which Bettauer's liberal program as well as his cult popularity were regarded became evident after September 1924, when his acquittal for violation of the morality codes began a crescendo of unabated hatred in the press. The unanimous reaction against him reflected that the political camps, commonly thought of as diametrically opposed, were not always at odds but felt a sense of common threat on several levels. To a great extent, they agreed about Bettauer and the danger his sexual liberalism posed to the preservation of a bourgeois culture already weakened by the war and the changing role of women. Furthermore, the anti-Semitism elicited by Hugo Bettauer's agenda of tolerance was so extreme as to make religion not a byproduct but a cause of the elites' growing insecurity. The Social Democrats and the Nazis—despite enormous ideological differences—shared this clinging to a thoroughly conservative, patriarchal, bourgeois, even Victorian morality during an era of upheaval and uncertainty.

Hugo Bettauer was a lightning rod that, alas, channeled the defensive tendencies of the mid-1920s. He was popular and yet apolitical; he was a liberal in a nonliberal age; he was a feminist in a patriarchal, clerical society; and he wrote about sexuality, a formerly taboo subject, in the mass press, the shaper of public opinion. Bettauer's "racial" and religious *otherness* (despite his conversion) emphasized the danger he posed to Christian values and prevailing morality. Ironically, the dramatic events of his life received more attention from his contemporaries than the revolutionary content of his work. The effective condoning of his murder in 1925 signaled the impending breakdown of those liberal values that undergird democracy. Fascism had already infiltrated Austria, manifesting itself in the cultural arena long before it became expressly political.

In 1938 the *Völkischer Beobachter* called Bettauer a "clueless angel" for having presented the Nazis with the gift of the "Jewish solution" in the form of *Die Stadt ohne Juden*. Whatever the humor in the prescient *Stadt ohne Juden*, the ending was not a happy one for Hugo Bettauer or for the Jews of Vienna, who never were invited back from Auschwitz, Mauthausen, or Theresienstadt.

Bibliography

Hugo Bettauer, *The City Without Jews,* trans. Salomea Neumark Brainin (New York: Bloch, 1926); Bettauer, *Die Stadt ohne Juden* (Frankfurt a. M.: Ullstein, 1988); Leon Botstein, *Judentum und Modernität* (Vienna: Böhlau Verlag, 1991); Karl Fallend, *Wilhelm Reich in Wien: Psychoanalyse und Politik* (Vienna: Geyer-Edition, 1988); Helmut Gruber, *Red Vienna* (New York: Oxford University Press, 1992); Hans Habe, *Ich Stelle Mich* (Vienna: Kurt Desch Verlag, 1954); Murray Hall, *Der Fall Bettauer* (Vienna: Löcker Verlag, 1978); Anton Kuh, "Bettauer," *Luftlinien: Feuilletons, Essays und Publizistik,* ed. Ruth Greiner (Vienna: Löcker Verlag, 1981); Ivar Oxaal, Michael Pollak, and Gerhard Botz, eds., *Jews, Antisemitism and Culture in Vienna* (New York: Routledge, 1987); Bruce Pauley, *From Prejudice to Persecution: A History of Austrian Anti-Semitism* (Chapel Hill: University of North Carolina Press, 1992); Pauley, *Hitler and the Forgotten Nazis* (Chapel Hill: University of North Carolina Press, 1981); P. G. J. Pulzer, *The Rise of Political Anti-Semitism in Germany and Austria* (London: P. Halban, 1988); Herbert Rütgen, "Anti-semitismus in allen Lagern: Publizistische Dokumente zur ersten Republik Österreich 1918–1938," Ph.D. diss., Karl-Franzens Universität Graz, 1989; Richard Sterba, *Erinnerungen eines Wiener Psychoanalytikers* (Frankfurt: Fischer Verlag, 1985); Stephen Wilson, *Ideology and Experience: Anti-Semitism in France at the Time of the Dreyfus Affair* (Rutherford, N.J.: Fairleigh Dickinson University Press, 1982); and Robert S. Wistrich, *Hitler's Apocalypse* (London: Weidenfeld and Nicolson, 1985).

BETH SIMONE NOVECK

1926   Georg Hermann writes a pamphlet attacking the special issue of Martin Buber's *Der Jude* devoted to the topic of anti-Semitism and Jewish national characteristics

By all accounts, the middle years of the Weimar Republic were relatively stable, allowing at least for a modicum of hope. The horrendous inflation was under control, Hitler's Beer Hall Putsch had been thwarted, and the "spirit of Locarno" guided European diplomacy. In June of 1926 Stresemann, the centrist foreign minister, had concluded a treaty with the Soviet Union, and a few months later Germany entered the League of Nations. All of these achievements, however, were denounced by the nationalist and revanchist right-wing parties, which were set from the end of World War I against all attempts to institute a Western-style democracy in Germany.

Even supporters of the young Weimar Republic subscribed to the pervasive notion that there must be a uniquely German way to regain self-respect and international status after the fiasco of the war and the humiliating and costly stipulations of the Versailles treaty. Fairly liberal intellectuals bought into this myth, turned to their Germanic roots, and promoted a national consciousness that became increasingly anti-Semitic. Alarmed by this development, Martin Buber's monthly *Der Jude* (The Jew) published a special issue in late 1925 under the title *Antisemitismus und jüdisches Volkstum* (Anti-Semitism and Jewish national characteristics) and invited several non-Jewish writers to express their views on that subject.

Georg Hermann, author of the best-seller *Jettchen Gebert,* who proudly called himself "the Jewish Fontane," was appalled when he read this special issue. In a booklet entitled *Der doppelte Spiegel* (The double mirror; 1926), he responded to it with righteous indignation and with almost prophetic insight. Bemoaning the transvaluation of all values since the outbreak of the war, Hermann confessed to be at a loss not only vis-à-vis all ethical and aesthetic questions of the day, but also with regard to religious and political matters (Hermann 1926, 3f.). Until 1914, he had considered himself lucky to be born in 1871 in Berlin, right after the founding of a united Germany. There he was in the heart of the new country and yet, as a Jew, apt to step back and keep some distance. In those days, one was wont to speak of Jews and Christians, rather than of Jews and Germans, as people do nowadays, Hermann continued. When he grew up, Jews accepted the fact that a number of higher military and civil service careers were taboo for them. The exclusion from scientific careers was more painful—a loss not so much for the Jews as for science, which was supposed to be international, to transcend arbitrary borders (7f.). Of course, he had been aware of a wave of anti-Semitism at the turn of the century. It had been an irritant, but Jews did not take it too seriously, because intellectual circles, with whom they shared a faith in liberal education and in the progress of mankind, did not catch the infection (10f.). Hermann stated that until 1914, he knew his way around and held quite definite opinions and an idealized view of "the German," which he carried from his reading of German literature into everyday life (20).

All of this changed with the war, which unlike most other German writers (including Thomas Mann), Georg Hermann never supported. After the collapse, a new and virulent anti-Semitism sprang up, originating among frustrated army officers and Munich right-wingers (Hermann 1926, 28f.). Jews were made scapegoats in order to divert the disgruntled masses, Hermann wrote. Hostile graffiti appeared, as well as pamphlets illuminated with skulls and swastikas. Published by secret organizations, these broadsides contained ordinances against the Jews that were to be enforced should those organizations ever come to power (35f.). Yet the Jews were completely acculturated in Germany and in many ways indistinguishable from their non-Jewish neighbors (37f.), except for being more infatuated with German art and culture than other Germans, Hermann mused (43). His assessment of 1926 is corroborated in George L. Mosse's 1983 lectures, *German Jews Beyond Judaism*, although Mosse mentions the author of *Jettchen Gebert* only in passing. The latter ends the introductory part of *Der doppelte Spiegel* with the bitter observation that for many Jewish intellectuals, "the German was the most formidable disappointment of his life" (51).

In the second part of this slim booklet, Hermann concentrates mainly on four of the non-Jewish contributors to the special 1925 issue of *Der Jude* mentioned above—namely, Oscar Schmitz, Otto Flake, Wilhelm Michel, and Wolfgang Schumann. All of these men were known as philo-Semites who were full of good intentions, "and, yet, what misconceptions of the German Jew, of his mentality, his tradition, his religion, and above all of [his] guaranteed and self-evident rights . . . in Germany!" If these opinions had nestled themselves in the minds of intelligent, progressive German writers, "whose humaneness is beyond any doubt," Hermann shuddered to think what might go on in other people's heads. He knew these colleagues personally and he was sure that had he been able to show them back in 1912 what they were writing dur-

ing this period, they would have considered it a bad joke at their expense. These then, wrote Hermann, were the bitter results of a "ruthless and ingenious Seven Years Propaganda War" (Hermann 1926, 53f.). Subsequently he selected a number of assertions made by these four gentlemen and refuted them one by one in a most astute manner (59–79).

Nor did Hermann allow the Jewish contributors to the special anti-Semitism issue of *Der Jude* to get off scot-free. Although most of them took refuge in Zionism and / or a new affirmation of their Jewish faith—two trends to which Hermann does not subscribe (Hermann 1926, 12)—all failed to rebut the many preposterous contentions made by their guest contributors, and they neglected to point out that present-day German anti-Semitism was first and foremost an indictment of the better educated classes (55f.). In his brief epilogue, Hermann expressed gratitude to the contributing non-Jewish intellectuals for disclosing so openly the confusion that reigned in German minds regarding their Jewish fellow-Germans. "What is at stake," he writes in closing, "is nothing less than the well being of 600,000 German brethren and the spiritual recovery of 60,000,000 German brethren" (92f.), emphasizing by this choice of words that he thinks in terms of Jewish Germans rather than of German Jews.

Yet, Hermann, well-read and an art critic in his own right, did not focus exclusively on Germany. Also in 1926—a crucial year because of the death of his young second wife, Lotte Samter-Hermann—he revisited the Netherlands. In his essay "Amsterdam," written in March 1926 (three months before *Der doppelte Spiegel*) and dedicated to Lotte's memory, he professes his love for the tidy, sparkling clean, and democratic neighbor country, exclaiming that over the years as tensions grew worse in Germany, they had frequently "played with the idea of moving to Holland," where they had "almost more friends than in Germany" (Hermann, *Holland* 1926, 91–96). By 1926, at least half a dozen of Hermann's novels had been translated into Dutch. Moreover, for almost five years, he had been a literary correspondent for the *Algemeen Handelsblad*, a prominent Dutch newspaper. His "Letters about German Literature" had appeared weekly in the Saturday night edition, and as a mediator between the German and Dutch cultures, he had been a frequent guest of honor of the Dutch PEN club as well as a well-liked lecturer in several Dutch towns. The first chairman of the German Writers' Union, Hermann could speak with considerable authority. In his *Randbemerkungen* (Marginalia; 1919) and throughout his work, he had proven himself a Western European in outlook and a pacifist of Socialist leanings. Moreover, he remained a keen and critical observer of the sociopolitical upheavals during the Weimar Republic. But as a writer in his mid-fifties, he was language-bound, and so, despite his serious misgivings, he left Germany for Holland only after Hitler had come to power. Until then, he continued writing essays on literary, art-historical, and sociopolitical subjects mainly for the *Vossische Zeitung*. Many of these were collected in *Die Zeitlupe* (Slow motion; 1928) and in *Vorschläge eines Schriftstellers* (A writer's suggestions; 1929).

Until 1930, Hermann also kept publishing novels, most notably *Tränen um Modesta Zamboni* (Tears for Modesta Zamboni; 1927), a romantic fantasy set in fascist Italy, and *Grenadier Wordelmann* (1930), a sympathetic chronicle of a rifleman's futile struggle for justice during the time of Frederick the Great. Part of the action of the latter book takes place in Potsdam, a historic venue dear to Hermann's heart. He devoted his charming *Spaziergang in Potsdam* (Stroll through Potsdam; 1929) to it. Similarly, sixteen years earlier, he had published *Das Biedermeier im Spiegel seiner Zeit* (The Biedermeier reflected in documents of its time; 1923), which contained interesting first-hand materials he had gathered as background information for his most famous two-volume sequel, the fateful tale of *Jettchen Gebert / Henriette Jacoby* (1907–8), mentioned above. These two novels, set in Berlin, in an acculturated Jewish milieu of the late 1830s, show Hermann's fine characterization, his warm sense of humor, and his love for detail. An avid collector, he had surrounded himself with many period figurines, chandeliers, bell pulls, and other knickknacks, which function as leitmotifs in his narration. The novels tell the story of a charming and

intelligent young Jewish orphan who fled from her wedding dinner because she could not abide the thought of being married to an unloved husband and who—caught between a long-standing affection for her mentor uncle and her infatuation with a much younger non-Jewish writer—eventually took her own life. According to Hermann's Dutch biographer, C. G. Van Liere, 166,000 copies of *Jettchen Gebert* had been printed by 1933. The sequel appeared in nine languages, including an American edition entitled *Hetty Geybert*. A play adaptation of 1913 saw countless performances. The story was rendered into a film as early as 1918 and turned into a most successful musical in 1928 (Van Liere 1974, 216, 68, 77ff.).

When Georg Hermann made his breakthrough with *Jettchen Gebert,* he was a married man of thirty-five and the father of three daughters. In contrast to his two older brothers—Ludwig Borchardt, who was on his way to fame as an Egyptologist, and Heinrich Borchardt, who was soon to be acknowledged as the architect of several German department stores—Georg, who eventually took his father's first name, Hermann, as his pseudonym, had so far not been successful. As the youngest of the six Borchardt children, he had suffered most under his father's bankruptcy in 1875. He did not finish his gymnasium education, tried in vain to become a businessman, started to write, and, after his military service, lived again with his widowed mother, who came from a prominent Jewish family. She had a strong personality and Georg both admired and loved her deeply. He took some odd jobs and subsequently studied art history, literature, and philosophy while occasionally publishing short pieces in periodicals (Van Liere 1974, 17ff., 71). His first novel, *Spielkinder* (Dilettantes; 1897), contained so many autobiographical elements that it upset his family (Van Liere 1974, 20). According to Georg Hermann's own preface in the 1922 edition of his collected works, this first outpouring was at best a moderate success. That, however, did not prevent him from writing a pentalogy of autobiographical novels later in life.

Soon after the *Jettchen Gebert* books, Hermann published *Kubinke* (1910), the tragic story of a journeyman barber, set in a brand new middle-class neighborhood of contemporary Berlin. Young, innocent Kubinke has come from the countryside to the rapidly expanding capital, hoping to work himself up from his marginal existence. While making house calls to shave his relatively affluent clientele, he meets three house-maids and promptly falls in love with each. Kubinke's plans to marry the coyest one of them progress nicely, until the other two claim that he has made them pregnant. They sue him for child support and Kubinke, driven to despair, hangs himself in the tiny attic room he shares with another journeyman barber. This tragic-comic novel found many readers. It reached an edition of 17,000 by 1913 and was made into a film in 1926 (Van Liere 1974, 216, 77). *Kubinke* is not set in a Jewish milieu. Although its subject matter is rather typical for the naturalistic period in German literature, the novel stands out for Hermann's warm and delicate sense of humor, the gentle irony with which he portrays his characters and their ambiance, and his loving and detailed description of the seasonal changes even in a big city.

Of his subsequent novels, *Heinrich Schön Jr.* (1915), with its Schillerian *Don Carlos*-motif, is set in Biedermeier Potsdam, whereas the *Doktor Herzfeld* sequel *Die Nacht des Doktor Herzfeld* (The night of Dr. Herzfeld; 1912) and *Schnee* (Snow; 1921) unfold in contemporary Berlin. Dr. Herzfeld is a Jewish intellectual: unorthodox, progressive, and a collector of books and fine art objects—preferably of Far Eastern origin—much like Georg Hermann himself in those days. Of course, Dr. Herzfeld rejects jingoism and the barbarity of war. He shares Hermann's awareness, his contemplative, highly sensitive but somewhat self-indulgent nature. In addition, like his creator, he sees himself at the mercy of women. The *Doktor Herzfeld* books, as well as the vast majority of Hermann's novels, are imbued with a fateful sense of inevitability, foreshadowing the chief protagonist's death.

Shortly after the beginning of the Great War, the Georg Hermann-Borchardt family moved to Neckargemünd near Heidelberg. Here, besides short stories and critical essays, Hermann wrote the first volume of his fairly autobiographical

string of novels, *Die Kette* (The chain), in which he interweaves the portrayal of a moment in history with a fictionalized version of his own life story. Fritz Eisner stands for the author and Ännchen for his first wife, the pianist Martha Heynemann. In *Einen Sommer lang* (For one summer; 1917), Hermann tells of a summer's courtship, paralleling their own in the year 1900. But at the time of writing, their marriage had long since been on the rocks. Shortly after the novel was published by Ullstein, the couple went through an acrimonious divorce, and Georg Hermann married a young editor of his publishing house, the aforementioned Lotte Samter, who bore him another daughter (Van Liere 1974, 44). She also helped him with the preparation of his collected works in five volumes (1922). The last volume contains short prose, both fictional and nonfictional, which so far has been mentioned only in passing in this overview. Meanwhile, the new family settled near Neckargemünd, so that Georg Hermann could stay in close touch with his three teenage daughters from his first marriage. To them he dedicates the second volume of his autobiographical pentalogy, *Der kleine Gast* (The little guest), which was written in the early 1920s and typed and edited by Lotte (37f.). Analogous but not identical to a similar occurrence in Georg Hermann's life, the book deals with the trauma of an infant's death early in Fritz Eisner's first marriage, which is then already clearly deteriorating. DVA published the book in 1925 just before Lotte's death early the next year.

In the third installment of his autobiographical sequel, *November achtzehn* (November eighteen; 1930), one of his last publications in pre-Hitler Germany, Hermann described the heady revolutionary days in Berlin, from just before until just after the armistice of 1918. As the German Empire collapses, Fritz Eisner and his liberal and Socialist friends, all members of the enlightened Jewish bourgeoisie, expect a better future, even though Eisner's participation in the action is limited to that of a sympathetic observer. These were also hopeful days in the private life of Fritz Eisner and Ruth Bloch (the Lotte Samter figure in the last three volumes of the pentalogy), because Eisner's first wife will no longer obstruct a divorce. Again the parallels with Georg Hermann's history are obvious, although Fritz Eisner is not identical with his creator, because he represents only the latter's more passive and contemplative side. Georg Hermann, after all, inserted himself vociferously in the debate of the day, as evidenced by *Der doppelte Spiegel,* and by his complaint, once in exile, to his "Danish" daughter, Hilde, that DVA had shortened his *November achtzehn* by some sixty pages and had thereby deprived the story of its original sharp edges (July 5, 1933).

It is precisely because Georg Hermann had spoken out many times and in no uncertain terms that he received death threats from 1931 onward. Having been tipped off that there had been a house check in early March 1933, he fled to the Netherlands, where his Dutch publisher, Querido, first put him up in Laren and then helped him get settled nearby. But it is one thing to be an honored guest of the PEN club and another to be a refugee, a widower in his sixties who had to see a thirteen-year-old daughter from his second marriage through school. In a letter to his older daughter in Denmark, Hermann was confident that he would be able to pick up in Laren where he left off in Germany, fully expecting that Ullstein would continue to print his works and that Querido would eagerly follow suit with Dutch translations (Mar. 13, 1933). He was soon to be disabused of this notion. Ullstein did not publish the last two volumes of *The Chain* sequel, and in the Netherlands, conditions had taken a turn for the worse in the wake of the Great Depression. Neither Hermann's *Wordelmann* nor *November* had been translated into Dutch. Furthermore, over the following years, refugees from Hitler's Germany would be less and less welcome by a conservative Dutch administration.

Nonetheless, the Dutch publishing houses of Allert de Lange and Querido soon opened German-language branches to disseminate work by writers who could no longer publish in Germany. In 1934, *Ruths schwere Stunde* (Ruth's difficult hour), volume four of Hermann's pentalogy, was one of the first books published by Allert de Lange. The setting of this novel is Munich after the failed revolution, where in the summer of 1919 Ruth has her child under less than optimal

conditions. Gone is the hopeful mood of November 1918. Fritz Eisner and his friends notice the first signs of a virulent anti-Semitism, and some of their reflections parallel Hermann's caustic pronouncements in *Der doppelte Spiegel.*

The last volume of the pentalogy was published almost concurrently with *Ruths schwere Stunde* by a Jewish book club (Jüdische Buch-Vereinigung) in Berlin. It bears the telling title *Eine Zeit stirbt* (The death of an epoch; 1934). Set in Berlin during the height of the inflation, the author shows that it is not only the currency that has lost its value: the ideals and the raison d'être of writers like Fritz Eisner and many Jewish intellectuals of his generation have also been devaluated. Again, Hermann interweaves the general malaise with Eisner's personal despair. Disgust drives his good friend the Communist banker Paul Gumpert and Gumpert's much younger spouse to commit suicide, and shortly afterward, Eisner's own young wife, Ruth, dies from a kidney disorder. All Eisner can hope for is that his daughters will be able to cope better than his own generation because they are not burdened with the memories and aspirations of an enlightened bourgeoisie, whose time has gone forever.

In the mid-1930s, when these two last volumes of *The Chain* appeared, Georg Hermann's readership was scattering all over the globe and people were too preoccupied with the hectic task of coping on a day-to-day basis to savor this writer's detailed and finely nuanced prose. Neither book was translated into Dutch or into any other language. The once famous and highly respected author had become just one more Jewish refugee writer, whom nobody needed or wanted. In his isolation in Laren he wrote *Rosenemil,* a warm and humorous description of the Berlin demi-monde at the turn of the century. This work is terser than its predecessors, and it provides more action and suspense. Yet it could appeal only to the nostalgic and the homesick, and who would that be in 1935, when Allert de Lange published it? Despite positive reviews, Hermann's strenuous efforts to have *Rosenemil* translated into Dutch, English, or Danish were in vain.

Yet curiously enough, a *Rosenemil* film was one of the first postunification products of East-West

German cooperation: it was shot by DEFA and GALLA in Berlin and Bucharest in December 1991. Decades after his mostly miserable years in Dutch exile, which ended in November 1943 when the door of one of the infamous cattle cars slammed shut behind the seventy-two-year-old writer, there have been signs of a Georg Hermann renaissance. It began in the mid-1960s, with an East German publication of Georg Hermann's selected works in large single editions under the editorship of Bernhard Kaufmann. Between 1964 and 1984, eight volumes appeared, excluding *The Chain* pentalogy, but including (as volume seven) a selection of Hermann's shorter prose—his stories, sketches, autobiographical essays, and politically astute introduction to *Das Biedermeier im Spiegel seiner Zeit*. An annotated and handsomely illustrated edition of *Spaziergang in Potsdam* was added in 1985. Meanwhile, in the western part of Germany, there has been no systematic effort to republish Georg Hermann's works, but the 1960s and 1970s saw new editions of *Jettchen Gebert* and *Kubinke*, an edition of a shortened version of *Rosenemil*, and new printings of *Das Biedermeier im Spiegel seiner Zeit* and *November achtzehn*. In 1974, the extremely useful dissertation by C. G. Van Liere, *Georg Hermann: Materialien zur Kenntnis seines Lebens und seines Werkes* (Georg Hermann: Materials concerning his life and works) came out in book form. It provided much of the biographical and bibliographical information for the present contribution. In 1987 a number of German-language articles about Georg Hermann appeared in scholarly publications, including one by Hans-Otto Horch in the *Bulletin of the Leo Baeck Institute*, one by Hanne and Hans-Peter Bayerdörfer in a *Festschrift für Egon Schwarz*, and one each in *Neophilologus* and *Exilforschung*, five by the present author. There have been no new editions of Georg Hermann's work in translation, but Gordon Craig devoted several columns to *Jettchen Gebert* in the *New York Review of Books* 35, no. 8 (May 1988). Three years before, the Leo Baeck Institute and the Berlinische Galerie organized an exhibition in Berlin on "The Contribution of German Jewry to German Culture from the Eighteenth to the Twentieth Century." It was presented with the title *Jettchen Geberts Kinder* (Jettchen Gebert's children), proving that the name of Georg Hermann's early heroine still stands for cultivated German Jews.

Meanwhile, Georg Hermann's writings during his exile years have gone largely unnoticed. His many essays and commentaries on the events of the day—for example, on the disastrous Evian Conference of 1938, where Western nations decided not to admit more Jewish refugees—were never printed. The manuscripts are stored and catalogued in the archives of the Leo Baeck Institute in New York under the number AR 7074. The Georg Hermann holdings in the library of this institute are probably the most complete in the United States.

As a refugee, Hermann completed two more novels, *B. M.: Der unbekannte Fußgänger* (B. M.: The unknown pedestrian; 1935) and *Der etruskische Spiegel* (The Etruscan mirror; 1936). Each was published in Amsterdam by Menno Hertzberger in small editions, full of printing errors. Both novels deal with the uprootedness and disorientation of a fleeing German writer past his prime, who comes to realize after Hitler's takeover that, from now on, he is first and foremost a Jew. Both Benno Meyer in Paris and Harry Frank in Rome experience a last and passionate infatuation, and both novels, predictably, end with their anti-hero's death. Hermann had expected that at least *Der etruskische Spiegel*, with its beautiful descriptions of the Roman ambience, would be translated and sold in England, and for this reason, he probably downplayed the refugee aspect in this work. His hopes were again disappointed. For a discussion of the problems of assimilation hidden in this last completed novel, see my German essay in *Conditio Judaica* 5 (1993).

Hermann's letters from exile to his daughter Hilde chronicle his valiant efforts to make a living for himself and his youngest daughter. There was some reprieve when in 1936–37 Fritz Hirsch revived the *Jettchen Gebert* musical under the title *Wenn der weiße Flieder wieder blüht* (When the white lilac is again in bloom) and staged many successful performances all over the Netherlands. A new Dutch edition of *Jettchen Gebert* 1 and 2 in a single volume, appearing in 1938, also gave him some hope. Yet Hermann made very little money on both ventures and eventually the once famous writer had to ask for charitable support. His treatise "Weltabschied" (A farewell to the world), written for his children in 1935, is on the one hand the leave-taking of an elderly, ill, and presumably superfluous person, while on the other it stands in the tradition of several of his earlier self-reflections from 1914 onward, in which he would periodically draw up a balance sheet of his life (for example, the "Weltabschied" in *Der doppelte Spiegel*). Hermann still affirms life and human potential, but he condemns nation states and their militaristic propaganda machines. Why should nations be allowed to murder, steal, lie, and cheat with impunity? Why may they engage in behavior for which an individual would be punished? He maintains that he still believes in progress, even though his country, Germany, had for the last twenty-one years turned his hopes and those of his fellow Jews into despair. Until 1914 one was hardly aware of being a Jew, Hermann continues. His Judaism had been like a vest under his jacket. It felt nice and comfortable, but he would never have worn it over the jacket of a decent European, as so many Jews presently tend to do. Even now, his Judaism is not nearly as important to him as his participation in progressive European culture. But many of the Jews he knew were of the highest moral caliber—they were people capable of helping mankind improve, individuals bent on taking their social responsibilities seriously. It makes him proud to count himself among them. He would, however, have been more productive had he not been born in Germany, where his life as a future-oriented author had been a continuous battle from 1914 on. All in all, though, Hermann feels, he has been better off than millions of others, and if he has to part from this world with many stories untold, he will take comfort in the fact that he is leaving numerous written pages behind, for his children and other interested parties to peruse. This farewell essay and a selection of Georg Hermann's letters written to his daughter in Denmark from 1933 to 1941 which I edited appear under the title *Unvorhanden und stumm, doch zu Menschen noch reden* (Unavailable and mute, but still talking to people; 1991).

Sadly, there exists next to nothing by or on Georg Hermann in the English language. An anthology of some of his writings, especially of his shorter prose pieces, would make excellent and informative reading.

Bibliography

Georg Hermann, *Ausgewählte Werke in Einzelbänden*, 8 vols. (Berlin: Das Neue Deutschland, 1964–84); Hermann, *Das Biedermeier im Spiegel seiner Zeit* (Oldenburg: Stalling, 1965); Hermann, *Der doppelte Spiegel* (Berlin: Alweiss, 1926); Hermann, *Gesammelte Werke*, 5 vols. (Stuttgart: DVA, 1922); Hermann, *Hetty Geybert*, trans. Anna Darwell (New York: G. H. Doran, 1924); Hermann, *Holland, Rembrandt und Amsterdam* (Heidelberg: Merlin, 1926); Hermann, *November achtzehn* (Königstein / Taunus: Scriptor, 1980); Hermann, *Randbemerkungen, 1914–17* (Berlin: Fleischel, 1919); Hermann, *Unvorhanden und stumm, doch zu Menschen noch reden: Briefe aus dem Exil 1933–1941 an seine Tochter Hilde. Weltabschied, ein Essay* (Mannheim: Persona, 1991); Hermann, *Vorschläge eines Schriftstellers* (Baden-Baden: Merlin, 1929); Hermann, *Die Zeitlupe und andere Betrachtungen über Menschen und Dinge* (Stuttgart: DVA, 1928); Leo Baeck Institute, *Jettchen Geberts Kinder / Jettchen Gebert's Children: The Contribution of German Jewry to German Culture from the Eighteenth to the Twentieth Century, Exemplified on the Leo Baeck Institute Art Collection, New York*, illus., bilingual catalogue (Berlin: Publica, 1985); George L. Mosse, *German Jews Beyond Judaism* (Bloomington: Indiana University Press, 1985); Laureen Nussbaum, "'Das Kleidungsstück der europäischen Geistigkeit ist einem besudelt worden . . .' Georg Hermann-Jettchen Geberts Vater-im-Exil," *Fluchtpunkte des Exils und andere Themen: Exilforschung, Ein internationales Jahrbuch,* ed. Thomas Koebner (Munich: Text & Kritik, 1987), 224–40; Christian Rehse, "Ein Stück vom seltsamen Zauber der garstigen Stadt: Literaturort Berlin (27): Georg Hermann, Autor von *Jettchen Gebert* und die Lust am 'Milljöh,'" *Der Tagesspiegel* 14, no. 742 (Nov. 20, 1993): 15; Gheorghe Stanomir, "Georg Hermann und das Haus Poststraße 2," *Neckargemünder Jahrbuch 1993,* ed. Wolf-Peter Haasemann (Neckargemünd: Heidelberger Verlagsanstalt, 1993): 85–105; and Cornelis G. Van Liere, *Georg Hermann: Materialien zur Kenntnis seines Lebens und seines Werkes* (Amsterdam: Rodopi, 1974).

LAUREEN NUSSBAUM

February 18, 1926   Playwrights and theater critics in the Weimar Republic assume the role of advocates for justice

Throughout the course of the Weimar Republic, the judiciary was the subject of vigorous and sometimes acrimonious debate. It was frequently argued that this controversy would ultimately undermine the authority of the courts. Paul Levi, an outstanding lawyer and member of the Reichstag, commented on this opinion in an address to the house on February 18, 1926: "I object: We know a different authority which in our eyes is higher than the authority of the courts and that is the authority of law and justice." Walter Jens wrote a play in honor of Paul Levi, one of the Jewish martyrs of the Weimar Republic who committed suicide in 1930, that is entitled *Ein Jud aus Hechingen* and was produced in 1992. Levi's comment of 1926 sheds light on the debate over fundamental principles of jurisprudence and the relationship of law and politics. The position of legal positivism, which regards law as ultimately instrumental in preserving the power of the state, is opposed by the Enlightenment idea of natural law, according to which universal human rights represent a higher good vis-à-vis the state and must therefore be protected against state power. Some years later, in 1929, Arnold Zweig dealt with this conflict in his novel *Der Streit um den Sergeanten Grischa* (The controversy about Sergeant Grischa), in which the historical background of the controversy is presented: the authoritarianism of Wilhelmine Germany. He shows that the judiciary standards and the constitutional ideal of the young democratic republic were constantly undermined by the courts, who still favored authoritarian, monarchist state rule and whose legal positivism had been shaped under the influence of the "power interests of the Bismarckian state towards the end of the nineteenth century" (Petersen 1988, 56–78). In the many cases of political crimes, the sentences pronounced by these courts proved to be one-sided, strongly in favor of offenders from the right. As early as 1921–22 Emil Julius Gumbel gave a detailed account of this in his book *Vier Jahre politischer Mord* (Four years of political murder), and even the minister of justice Gustav Radbruch, who was a member of the Social Democratic Party, admitted that the public sense of justice was being constantly challenged by the way in which law and justice were handled by the courts (39).

It was certainly not by chance that German-Jewish intellectuals like Levi and Zweig took such an active stand in the general debate about the judiciary. From the very beginning, they advocated maintaining the legal and constitutional form of the Weimar Republic. In 1926, Theodor Heuss, who was later to become the first president of the Federal Republic, published a book entitled *Staat, Recht und Freiheit* (Republic, law, and liberty), which contained the collected writings of Hugo Preuss. A prominent professor of constitutional law since 1889, Preuss was commissioned by the first republic (which was governing in 1918) to draft a constitution for the German Republic. This draft was later accepted by the national assembly in Weimar in July 1919 and ratified by the president of the republic in August of the same year. Preuss had coined the term *Obrigkeitsstaat* (authoritarian state) to characterize the Wilhelmine monarchy and had taken great care "to limit state power by the institutions of formal law," to place "basic rights on the highest level and to abolish all legal privileges or disadvantages, formerly connected with birth and class" (Petersen 1988, 18–19). As a politician, Preuss was a founding member of the German Democratic Party (Deutsche Demokratische Partei, DDP), which occupied a strong position in the liberal center of the political spectrum and proved to be one of the pillars of the republic. Exactly for that reason it was slandered as "the party of the Jews" by its right-wing opponents who did not hesitate to defame the Weimar state as the "Republic of the Jews."

The strong commitment to the Weimar Republic by Jewish intellectuals and lawyers, as well as by Jewish writers and journalists, did not happen by chance. It mirrored the experiences of their generation. In August 1914, the majority of German Jews had shared the belief that complete assimilation and civil equality could be achieved by uncompromising support of the nationalist mood of war and the official war aims of German chauvinism. Yet during the war years, the registration of Jews in the army (*Judenzählung im Heer*), which was ordered by the Prussian military staff, indicated that Jews were not regarded as being on the same level as German citizens. The registration insinuated that Jews were less active in the front line of war than others and that they could be regarded as scapegoats in the years when it seemed hopeless to dream of a German victory.

Anti-Semitic propaganda proved to be successful in this case when blame had to be allocated for the general situation. Arnold Zweig gave literary expression to this incident in his novel *Erziehung vor Verdun* (Education before Verdun; 1935). After the defeat and capitulation in 1918, there were different forms of the "stab-in-the-back legend," and Jews were labeled unpatriotic, and active mainly behind the lines. In addition, Jews were accused of being enemy agents, supporters of capitulation and retreat in 1918, and, last but not least, of being the manipulators behind the scenes at Versailles, acting at the behest of the international Jewish financial aristocracy whose alleged aim was total world domination. Facing anti-Semitic discrimination in various forms, the younger generation of German-Jewish intellectuals no longer regarded national solidarity with the Germans as sufficient for securing their own existence and identity within the German predicament. A new basis was required, either by transforming the German revolution of 1918 into a universal revolution of humankind—and many German-Jewish intellectuals supported the utopian concepts of that sort in the years from 1918 to 1920—or by striving for realistic consolidation of those political and legal conditions that had been proclaimed in the revolution and by the Weimar Republic itself.

German-Jewish intellectuals' commitment to the republic was based on diverse political opinions and revealed different degrees of political effectiveness. In support of the notion of a "literature for the Republic" was the "theater for the Republic" or the "cabaret for the Republic," both of which were geared toward political effect. The fact that the stage was accorded a special significance in terms of its public influence is not surprising in those decades, considering that modern mass media had not yet been firmly established. There was, however, also a historical precedent for this privileged status, because the German theater was traditionally regarded as the predominant forum of national education. Indeed, it was expected that German theater would be instrumental in shaping the public and intellectual life of the new democratic state. The first years after 1918 were marked by this idealism, the result of a lack of experience with antidemocratic segments of the population and with authorities still loyal to the old monarchy and its system of values based on nationalist ideology. The hope for a basic renewal of society was still so strong that the forces opposed to the new republic were not taken seriously enough. The army, for example, despite all restrictions, tried to maintain itself as a state within the state; similarly, the civil service attempted to preserve continuity with the Wilhelmine state; and the judiciary and educational system, including the universities, revealed a slavish dependency on Wilhelmine chauvinism.

Certainly, on the whole, the difficulties resulting from the German mentality, shaped in the nineteenth century, were underestimated by intellectuals. Their main ideological impulse in 1917–18 had been general pacifism and antinationalism. These tenets formed the core of the idealistic message of the Expressionist playwrights, as was the case with Walter Hasenclever's dramas. Two years before the end of the war, he proclaimed universal human renewal through peace and an end to the nationalist state—a program that he incorporated in his adaptation of Sophocles' *Antigone*. Antigone's voice, coming from beyond the grave, preaches the gospel of the new man while the dictator of the old regime, Creon, abdicates. In the year of the revolution, 1918, Ernst Toller proclaimed the necessity of complete inner renewal in his play *Die Wandlung* (The transfiguration) and developed an example of such renewal in the German-Jewish artist himself. Friedrich, the protagonist, can be regarded as a model for a whole generation. His feeling of "not-belonging" motivates him to identify completely with German war patriotism. As a soldier, he volunteers for suicidal missions, and as an artist and sculptor, he dedicates his life to carving a statue with the title "Victory of the Fatherland." The real experience of war, however, leads Friedrich to a fundamental conversion: experiencing misery, exclusion, and destruction as the universal destiny of humankind, he undergoes a complete change. After having destroyed the statue-idol, he gains a new identity as a prophet of change in the name of humankind and as a charismatic new leader of a "revolution" on a worldwide scale.

Idealistic utopianism of that sort could not content itself with the political and social change that had taken place in 1918. Among the ranks of the dissatisfied were Ernst Toller and Ludwig Rubiner, as well as the other intellectuals who supported the Munich Soviet Republic in 1919. This group included Gustav Landauer, whose idealistic socialism manifested itself equally in his social and political writings, as well as in his studies of literary history and theory, and Erich Mühsam, the playwright and poet who represented the anarchistic wing of the Munich intellectual elite of those months.

In contrast to the younger playwrights like Toller and Mühsam, the elder generation of German-Jewish artists, writers, and critics in the theater attempted after 1919 and even more so after 1921 to find security within the framework of the republic and its legal guarantees as a basis for securing German-Jewish existence in its private, professional, and public aspects. Not the least of these guarantees was the elimination of the censorship restrictions of the preceding era. Artistic freedom was, so to speak, the test case for the freedom of republican life. In the Weimar Constitution, censorship was generally abolished, and freedom of art and freedom of speech were firmly anchored among the basic human rights (articles 142 and 118) (Petersen 1988, 82). Under these conditions, German-Jewish playwrights and critics felt challenged to assume the role of the "advocate" who comes to the assistance of justice and constitutional rights of the republic whenever they seem to be endangered by the old authoritarian forces. On the stage and in the press, a "struggle for rights" was carried out, to cite Karl Emil Franzos, the Jewish liberal authority until that time on assimilation and acculturation.

The most important demonstration of a "Theater for the Republic" was provided by Leopold Jessner, who, as a Social Democrat and convinced supporter of a democratic state, took over the direction of the Prussian State Theater, the former court theater. It became the leading stage of the Weimar Republic, in both political and artistic terms. Jessner opened the new theater with a production of Friedrich Schiller's *Wilhelm Tell*, a play that had degenerated in the Wilhelminian theatrical tradition into a chauvinistic spectacle. In Jessner's treatment, it became a signal for revolutionary change and at the same time a model for a radically modern, abstract theatrical style, in which the previous twenty years of theater reform were distilled into a new shape. Jessner ratified the new Weimar Constitution, as it were, for the stage by installing the classical Weimar of Goethe as a theater of ideas and reflection. Many directors followed in his footsteps, from Karlheinz Martin to Bertold Viertel, from Jürgen Fehling to Erwin Piscator. Jessner himself, who for a decade was subjected to intrigues and attacks from the Right, provided in 1926 yet another demonstration of his standpoint with a production of Shakespeare's *Hamlet*. Under the motto "Something is rotten in the state of Denmark," he contrasted the old Wilhelmine order represented by the court with the new republic in the figure of Hamlet, played by Fritz Kortner. In the mousetrap scene in act 3, the royal box of the former court theater was reproduced on stage, from which Claudius and Gertrude observe the play within a play, dressed in Wilhelmine costumes. The new republican theater and its audience watched its Wilhelmine past reflected back from the stage.

The republic received equally vigorous support from the new political cabaret, which, after initial inspiration from Max Reinhardt, emanated from Berlin. Through writers such as Kurt Tucholsky and Walter Mehring, it had direct connections with the political satire and journalism of the Weimar Republic, especially with *Die Weltbühne* (formerly *Die Schaubühne*), whose theater critic Siegfried Jacobsohn was the first important journalistic supporter of the political cabaret (he was followed later by Carl von Ossietzky). With *chanteuses* and *compères* such as Rosa Valetti, Trude Hesterberg, Valeska Gert, Marlene Dietrich, and Fritz Grünbaum, cabaret prepared the way for the development of epic theater.

The high profile and public effect of the Theater for the Republic provoked countermeasures from its opponents within its first years. Because theater censorship was legally abolished, such groups sought to exert indirect censorship by laying charges of "indecency," "obscenity," or "blasphemy." A particularly spectacular case, which demonstrates the possibilities of such legal action, was a production of Arthur Schnitzler's *Reigen*—a play that until 1918 had been banned from the stage in Germany and Austria—produced by the Reinhardt actress, Gertrud Eysoldt, artistic director of Berlin's Kleines Theater. When the theater

was faced with a charge of "indecency," Berlin's theater critics, in the person of Alfred Kerr, came to its aid by praising the extremely decent production and asked as a matter of principle: "May one ban plays? No, not even badly written and badly acted ones" (*Berliner Tageblatt,* Dec. 23, 1920, cited in Rühle 1988, 279). When the case actually came to trial, Alfred Kerr testified once again at the court's request as an expert witness; it was his performance as Advocatus that moved the court to reject the charges against the artistic director. In this trial, the Weimar Constitution emerged victorious. The anti-republican forces, however, revealed themselves in a tell-tale coming out. The *Reigen* trial demonstrated how literature and theater could be put under public pressure by means of legal action and large-scale press campaigns with spectacular results. Numerous performances in Berlin, Munich, and Vienna were disrupted, and anti-Semitic attacks on the author made the headlines. In collaboration with like-minded groups in Vienna, where these events even resulted in questions being asked in parliament, the right-wing forces actually triumphed over the republics, for Arthur Schnitzler felt constrained by events to ban all performances of the play.

From this point on, however, Jewish dramatists, together with the leading Berlin and Viennese theater and literature critics, were prepared. Names such as Julius Bab, Arthur Eloesser, Fritz Engel, Monty Jacobs, Siegfried Jacobsohn—and, for a time, Alfred Polgar—made up the critical phalanx in Berlin.

A few years later, in 1928, Ferdinand Bruckner had a character in his play *Die Verbrecher* (The criminals), the cook Ernestine, utter the sentence: "The lawyers are all Jews" (in Rühle 1988, 316). She abuses the lawyer of her lover, whom she has murdered out of jealousy. She is now trying to indict the lawyer for the crime by manipulating evidence. Because the court is biased in her favor, her strategy has been successful. Her sentence is certainly intended in a malicious, anti-Semitic way. Although there was still a vague religious motivation behind it, this aspect of anti-Semitism, although still important for the general mentality, had been overlaid by secular elements. The remnants of such clichés, however, could be all the more easily reactivated for secular purposes when the original religious preconditions had largely disappeared. The cook was nevertheless correct, albeit in another sense than the one of which she was conscious: seen from a social historical perspective, it was a fact that in Wilhelmine Germany, Jewish academics were forced into private legal professions because state positions in courts or as state prosecutors were closed to them. This resulted in the situation that, even in the Weimar Republic, a large number of Jewish lawyers were confronted by courts and state prosecutors where Jews were almost entirely absent. The one side represented the law in its dynamic function as representing the accused, the other, the old authoritarian structures. In this sense, the play *Die Verbrecher* reflects Paul Levi's statement of 1926, which privileged the higher authority of law over the authority of the courts. It is then small wonder that the Munich production of the play, with Therese Giehse as the cook, was only permitted as a "private performance," because an open public performance would have been perceived as undermining the standing of the judiciary.

The particular dialectic of the play *Die Verbrecher* lies in the fact that the courts themselves, "the ill-judged judges," as Toller had put it in *The Transfiguration,* are on trial. The German-Jewish theater critics Kurt Pinthus, Monty Jacobs, and Fritz Engel (all on October 24, 1928) stressed this without exception, and they expressly pointed out a connection to the murder case of the Polish farm laborer Jakobowsky as a historical precedent for the play's conception. Those on trial in Bruckner's play are the "criminals of social deprivation," or those who, cognizant of the procedures and conditions of the existing courts, knew how to manipulate them and even how to use legal regulations (such as §175, prohibiting homosexuality) to blackmail others. But the real crimes, which were not litigable and certainly not before existing courts, were those of the judicial institutions themselves. These crimes included even judicial murder, because they were subject to an outdated, Wilhelmine mentality, moral code, and nationalism that could not be adapted to the new political situation of the re-

public. These courts suppressed the finding of truth by means of prejudiced evaluation and strategies of investigation. The dynamics of social and political development in the republic were irreconcilable with the conditions of the judiciary. In the dialogue between two unbiased judges who pose in the play the question of the "essence of law," the conflict between a positivistic, state-centered notion of the authority of law and an enlightened, natural, and dynamically understood development of human and social rights was shown to be unresolvable. (Bruckner was by no means strictly supportive of the younger generation. In his play *Krankheit der Jugend* [Sickness of youth; 1925], he had already depicted their being endangered by the crisis in values of the postwar period, their lack of orientation, and their attraction to "strong ideologies." He later placed *Die Verbrecher* as the second of a trilogy of plays under the heading *Youth between the World Wars.* The last of the trilogy, *Die Rassen* [The races], demonstrated the susceptibility of this generation of youth for the chauvinistic and National Socialist ideologies of the year 1933.)

Bruckner's plays made up the most comprehensive articulation of the legal and judicial dilemma by a German-Jewish dramatist. They also provided the most important contribution to the dramaturgical form of the documentary justice play by featuring trial scenes as the dominant dramatic pattern, and by using the New Objectivity techniques of simultaneity and collage. *Die Verbrecher* thus became the epitome of drama of the late 1920s, which was critical of ideology and power. (Karl Kraus, the father not only of the language documentation techniques of the New Objectivity but also of judicial critique, presented in his World War I drama *The Last Days of Mankind* model scenes of a satirical representation of the language of trials and justice in the case of military tribunals at the front in World War I.)

The spectacular focal point of Bruckner's play was the twin problems of capital punishment and judicial murder, and on this level a number of other plays followed a similar path—for example, Erich Mühsam's play *Sacco and Vanzetti,* which dealt with the trial of American anarchists, or

Alfred Wolfenstein's drama *Die Nacht vor dem Beil* (The night before the guillotine). But apart from this theme dealing with fundamental questions of law and punishment, justice plays between 1926 and 1933 took up a number of other publicly debated issues, such as the question of abortion and the crimes of concealment, blackmail, and the economic side-effects resulting from its illegal status. These issues are considered in Friedrich Wolf's *Cyankali* (Cyanide; 1929), by Carl Credé in *Paragraph 218,* and by Hans José Rehfisch in *Der Frauenarzt* (The gynecologist; both 1928). They received support from theater critics once again, for example from Kurt Pinthus (*Acht-Uhr-Abendblatt Berlin,* Sept. 7, 1929, on the premiere of *Cyankali*), who took up and popularized the demand for a plebiscite on the question of abortion (Rühle 1988, 888–89, 902). Just as controversial were the issues of homosexuality, penal reform, juvenile correctional facilities, and youth welfare education, all of which were intensely debated throughout the Weimar Republic. Peter Martin Lampel's drama *Revolte im Erziehungshaus* (Borstal revolt) was one of the most frequently performed plays of the 1928 season.

No less controversial than these issues concerning social life in general were the explicitly political issues brought to public attention by the theater and its critics. The assassination of Walter Rathenau in 1922 resulted in the Reichstag passing a law in "Protection of the Republic." The trial Fechenbach versus the Jewish former secretary of Kurt Eisner, the Bavarian minister president murdered by right-wing extremists, revealed a right-wing "Judiciary of Vengeance" directed against the alleged November criminals, and it contributed among other things to the founding of a republican judges' association. Its members included the former federal minister of justice Gustav Radbruch, the constitutional lawyer Max Alsberg, the member of parliament Otto Landsberg, the industrial lawyer Hugo Sinzheimer, and other prominent Jewish representatives of a critical judiciary in the Weimar Republic. Their connections with the *Weltbühne,* the leading organ critical of the judiciary (Rühle 1988, 958), were striking, as were their affilia-

tions to the German League of Human Rights, whose political advisory council included Ernst Toller, Manfred Georg, Leo Lanja, Erich Mühsam, and Erich Weinert. Walter Hasenclever and Peter Martin Lampel belonged to the league's circle of consultants; Lion Feuchtwanger, Emil Ludwig, and Thomas Mann belonged to the sub-organization, the Jakubowski Foundation, which was devoted to shedding light on judicial murders (Petersen 1988, 112). There also existed affiliations to the Group 1925, in which artists and writers joined forces to oppose judicial interference in the spheres of literature and theater. Paul Levi belonged to the wider circle of this group, as did a number of other prominent writers such as Alfred Döblin, Piscator, Brecht, and others.

After 1928, the judicial question was treated in drama and theater in an even more radical fashion. During these years, highly publicized trials took place dealing with the lynch-law murders committed by anti-republican right-wing extremists after 1920. Walter Mehring wrote *Der Kaufmann von Berlin* (The merchant of Berlin) for the Piscator production, in which the focal point was a so-called lynch court from the inflation year 1923, which was convened by the Wilhelmine military as part of their preparations for a coup d'état against the republic. In these "court proceedings," political anti-Semitism appeared in the form of the Wise Men of Zion, who embodied the ideological delusion of the supposed Jewish plan for domination of the world. The scene also represented a full-scale assault on the democratic republic, for the death sentence passed was directed against the "Saddler of Heidelberg," that is, President Friedrich Ebert. The other *menetekel* that the play cast on the stage wall was the pogrom that broke out in Berlin in 1923 against the enclave of Eastern European Jews situated in the so-called Scheunenviertel near Alexanderplatz. It is given the main emphasis in Mehring's play. (In Piscator's production, it was deemphasized in favor of demonstrating the class structure of the conditions of power in accordance with Marxist classificatory patterns.) The fact that Mehring's political critique also included a particular interest in Berlin's Eastern European Jewish minority's culture and language—for which Piscator specially employed a Yiddish-speaking actor, Paul Baratow, from New York—received less attention than it deserved from the German-Jewish theater critics. The German-Jewish relationship was for these critics the central issue, not the "inner-Jewish" relations between German and Eastern European Jews, who as the result of, among other things, their Yiddish language, the so-called *Jargon,* were not regarded as culturally equal. This view of Eastern European Jewish culture did change after 1917–18, above all in the area of literature and theater, as a result of direct contact with the culture and the influence of cultural Zionism. The prevailing attitude of German Jews, however, remained largely unchanged.

In the same year, Hans José Rehfisch and Wilhelm Herzog wrote their justice play *The Dreyfus Affair,* a work of considerable historical and documentary accuracy and a brilliant handling of the trial dramaturgy. The play attempted on the basis of the historical trial of 1898—that is, the trial against Emile Zola that provided the turning point in the Dreyfus Affair and led to the revoking of the conviction—to create a dramatic parallel with the present. The main points of comparison are the power of the military, which is nondemocratic but still influential in the French Republic; its monarchist ideology; and the abrogation of a judicial status beyond the control of public justice. Such parallels provided the link between 1898 and 1929–30. The unmasking of the authoritarian ideology of the military and a judiciary biased toward it was carried by the hero of republicanism and avant-gardistic spokesman of literature, Emile Zola. The *coup de théâtre,* the turning point in the third act, shows Zola as the public and moral advocate of the French Republic who succeeds in provoking a retrial in civil courts. His letter "J'accuse," published in the journal *L'Aurore,* accomplished this goal by having its author offer himself as a kind of pawn of democracy. The writer as advocate for the republic thus occupied the central position in the play. That the public trial initially goes against Zola and forces him into exile in England is no longer of great importance, for the public hearing has forced the military hierarchy to reveal its un-

just handling of the initial trial, an admission that resulted in its complete discrediting. So the play generated hope beyond the fifth act: the moment of truth was nigh, even if it had not yet come. The spectator's historical knowledge drew a parallel between Dreyfus's subsequent rehabilitation and the victory of the French Republic over the monarchist military. This was the main political point of the play: all analogies to Germany of 1929 had as their maxim that, owing to the advocatory brilliance of the writers and artists of the theater, the moment of truth would also come for the German Republic and the reactionary forces would be vanquished.

Once again Jewish theater critics were enthusiastic about the play. Monty Jacobs, for instance, in the *Vossische Zeitung* of November 26, 1929, saw in it "the unmediated breakthrough of historical truth"; and Alfred Kerr, who in the *Berliner Tageblatt* of the same day spoke of the struggle against the "flag fetish," that is, against German militarism, recognized the significance of the play in its metaphorical importance in the struggle against the momentary "sea-sickness in Germany"—against the tide of nationalism and anti-Semitism.

The role of the writer was subject to an apotheosis: as the conscience of the nation and advocate of the law against the courts, Zola became an idol. It is significant that one of the authors of the play, Rehfisch, belonged to that generation of Jewish lawyers who were permitted access to the judicial professions in the Weimar Republic, in his case as state prosecutor. The role of wearing the gown of public prosecutor by no means satisfied him. In collaboration with Erwin Piscator he sought from 1923–24 onward the public and judicial arena of the stage. In so doing he assumed the same role of public prosecutor that Friedrich Wolf was to declare four years later in his pamphlet "Art Is a Weapon: A Conclusion" (1928), with reference to Zola's manifesto "J'accuse" and other international authors, to be the central line for writers (Wolf 1957, 147). Wolf's phrase of the "poet as conscience of his time" is a direct allusion to Anatole France's eulogy over Zola's grave: "For one moment he embodied the conscience of humanity." The fact that this was used as ammunition against the ever increasing chauvinistic anti-Semitism illuminates a fatal situation: German-Jewish dramatists and critics, as advocates of the republic, were being forced increasingly to enter the public arena as advocates for themselves. Alfred Kerr, who carried out the most vociferous feuds for the republic and against a biased judiciary, once again entered the arena in these years, taking sides in 1930 for Arthur Schnitzler's *Professor Bernhardi,* a play in which he saw a more effective "model for the present" than in all the topical documentary dramas of the past four years. With a subtle psychological characterization devoid of all directly provocative black-and-white polemicism, the play seemed to him to adhere to the appropriate dramatic pattern (Kerr 1985, 498–500). Kerr's commentary differed sharply from that of many other observers, such as Paul Levi, who believed that an improvement in the German judicial system was becoming apparent; Levi and others failed to anticipate the scale of the problems the Great Depression would bring in destabilizing the republic (Petersen 1988, 41). In my view, the advocate takes sides; he is mistaken in his political assessment of the present situation like the majority of his Jewish and non-Jewish colleagues. He severely underestimates the danger, but this cannot be held against him or his ethical and political commitment. It is in this sense that Ludwig Marcuse praised the critic Alfred Kerr as one of the great republicans of the Weimar period: "His political activism was unique in the Weimar Republic" (Kerr 498).

What can one finally deduce from this permanent, often brilliant, and sometimes dogged struggle for law and justice that German-Jewish dramatists and critics conducted? Perhaps it has to do with the fact that being Jewish, even in the situation of near total acculturation that characterized the intellectuals of the Weimar Republic, is linked to a notion of identity created by an act of law. Law is the basis of justice, the just person, the foundation of the world. In the same year that Paul Levi made his impassioned statement on law and justice before parliament, a comedy by Hans José Rehfisch was staged simultaneously at twelve German-speaking theaters. It dealt with

the judicial crisis of the Weimar Republic as reflected in the understanding of law and justice of the man on the street. Nickel, the hero of the play, is one of the those rogues and alcoholics who, like Johann Nestroy's Knieriem in *Lumpazivagabundus,* distinguish themselves from their drab fellows through their delight in metaphysical speculation. Nickel has been shot during a break-in he attempted with a friend. Racked with fever and fear of death, he is very susceptible to the overtures of the Jewish Dr. Gnadenfeld, who tells him the story of the thirty-six just men, for whose sake the world is spared from divine judgment. The comic point of the play is that Nickel tries to follow in the footsteps of the just men, although he is by no means fit to do so. But by admitting to his earlier misdeeds he does a good (lawful) deed that might at best qualify him to apply for the status of a just man. The author seems to be saying in a comic way that the government of the world is not in such bad shape after all, if at least the consciousness of law and justice is present, even if it is not actually realized.

Walter Mehring also referred to the legend of the thirty-six just men in his description of the Berlin Scheunenviertel in *Der Kaufmann von Berlin,* part 1. The background to the story here, however, is the pogrom that the author cites as a reminder and a dangerous menetekel for the late 1920s. The warnings of the city meshuggene are not taken seriously, neither by the characters around him nor by the critics of the premiere. Only Alfred Kerr recognized in the work as a whole the character of the "unpleasant play," which for him meant an "honest work" (Kerr 1985, 466).

One cannot but help get the impression that from time to time German-Jewish dramatists and theater critics saw themselves as messengers of the law in the sense of the old legend. They tried to make their heritage of Jewish law have an effect on the republic of the nation that they felt or wanted to feel a part of, in the hope that the strengthening of law and justice in the Weimar Republic would lead to a reinforcement of their own legal and civil status. The German theater offered itself as a moral or moral-judicial institution. Not only did it offer the trial format as a stage form but also, as Schiller put it in his speech about the stage as a moral institution, it hunted out right and wrong in those hidden folds of the soul that were beyond the reach of worldly justice. Schiller was the model not only for Jessner and his Theater for the Republic, but also for Wolf and Rehfisch. As the consciences of the Weimar Republic, they used the stage as a forum in which they assumed the role of advocate against the perversion of justice enacted by courts still rooted in the Wilhelmine state and sitting in judgment over the Republic, and with Zolaesque verve they took up the "J'accuse" of the Dreyfus period and formulated it anew for the Weimar years.

Bibliography

Thomas Anz and M. Stark, eds., *Expressionismus: Manifeste und Dokumente zur deutschen Literatur, 1910–1920* (Stuttgart: Metzler, 1982); Hans-Peter Bayerdörfer, "Schrittmacher der Moderne? Der Beitrag des Judentums zum deutschen Theater zwischen 1848 und 1933," *Schriften des Historischen Kollegs* (Kolloquien 25), ed. Shulamit Volkov (Munich: 1994): 39–56; Walter Hinck, *Das moderne Drama in Deutschland* (Göttingen: 1973); Anton Kaes, ed., *Weimarer Republik: Manifeste und Dokumente zur deutschen Literatur, 1918–1933* (Stuttgart: Metzler, 1983); Alfred Kerr, *Mit Schleuder und Harfe: Theaterkritiken aus drei Jahrzehnten,* ed. Hugo Fetting (Munich: dtv, 1985); Friedrich W. Knellessen, *Agitation auf der Bühne: Das politische Theater der Weimarer Republik* (Emsdetten: Verlag Lechte, 1970); Thomas Koebner, "Das Drama der neuen Sachlichkeit und die Krise des Liberalismus," *Die deutsche Literatur in der Weimarer Republik,* ed. Wolfgang Rothe (Stuttgart: 1974): 19–46; Koebner, "Das Drama der Weimarer Republik," *Handbuch des deutschen Dramas,* ed. W. Hinck (Düsseldorf: Bagel, 1980): 401–17; Walter Laqueur, *Weimar: Die Kultur der Weimarer Republik* (Frankfurt a. M.: Peter Lang, 1970); Klaus Petersen, *Literatur und Justiz in der Weimarer Republik* (Stuttgart: Metzler, 1988); Irmgard Pflüger, *Theaterkritik in der Weimarer Republik* (Frankfurt a. M.: Peter Lang, 1981); Günter Rühle, *Theater für die Republik: Im Spiegel der Kritik, 1917–1933* [1967], 2 vols. (Frankfurt a. M.: Fischer, 1988); Rühle, *Theater in unserer Zeit* [1976] (Frankfurt a. M.: Suhrkamp, 1980); Rühle, *Zeit und Theater,* 3 vols. (Frankfurt a. M.: Propyläen Verlag, 1972–73); Heinrich August Winkler, "Die deutsche Gesellschaft der Weimarer Republik und der Antisemitismus," *Die Juden als Minderheit in der Geschichte,* ed. Bernd Martin and Ernst Schulin (Munich: dtv, 1981): 271–89; and Friedrich Wolf, *Aufsätze über Theater* (Berlin: Aufbau, 1957).

HANS-PETER BAYERDÖRFER

July 15, 1927   The Vienna Palace of Justice is burned in a mass uprising of Viennese workers, a central experience in the life and work of Elias Canetti

I can still feel the indignation that came over me when I picked up the *Reichspost*; its huge headline read, "A Just Verdict." There had been shooting in Burgenland [the region of Eastern Austria bordering Hungary], workers had been killed. The court had let the murderers go free. Now the governing party's newspaper called this exoneration a "just" decision, as the headline trumpeted. . . . From every quarter of Vienna the workers marched in dense processions to the Palace of Justice, whose very name embodied injustice in their eyes. It was an entirely spontaneous reaction, I felt by my own actions just how spontaneous. I rode into the city on my bicycle and joined one of the trains of protesters.

The workers, who were otherwise well-disciplined, who trusted their Social Democratic leaders and were satisfied that those leaders ran the City of Vienna in an exemplary fashion, acted on this day *without* their leaders. When they set the Palace of Justice on fire, Mayor Seitz stood in their way on a fire truck, his right fist raised on high. His gesture was ineffectual: the Palace of Justice *burned*. The police were told to shoot; there were ninety dead.

Elias Canetti's autobiographical account of this mass uprising of Viennese workers, and his own minor role in it, written some fifty years after the event, still breathes with the outrage and excitement of the young Canetti's Communist sympathies. But far from leading to revolution and a more just society, the historical events he described had sinister implications for Austrian history and the fate of Austria's Jews. The "workers" who had been killed on January 30, 1927, were demonstrators for the Austrian Social Democratic Party (SDAPÖ); their attackers were members of the local *Frontkämpfer* organization (right-wing World War I veterans); Walter Riehl, the lawyer who successfully pleaded that the murderers acted in self-defense, was a Nazi. Although Canetti interprets the largely spontaneous protest against this verdict positively, the ensuing reaction from the political Right, and even from the more conservative Social Democrats (Karl Renner and Julius Deutsch), was not so sanguine: the "crimes" of the horde (foremost among them the destruction of property) were widely attributed to the Social Democrats' failure to educate their followers in proper party discipline, and some of the Social Democratic leaders admitted as much. Predictably, the nascent Austrian Nazi Party blamed the uprising on a "Jewish conspiracy" by the Social Democratic leadership to corrupt their loyal German followers, a ridiculous and untenable argument that would become ever more familiar in this "accelerated time" (Canetti's words). Chancellor Ignaz Seipel, a Catholic priest and political arch-conservative, seized the opportunity to call for a rollback of recently established republican rights, including the right to trial by jury and freedom of the press. The Social Democrats, unsettled, were placed on the defensive; the republic and its liberal constitution of 1920 were called into question.

Thus these events were one of the first clear signs of the end of Austria's First Republic and the coming of fascism. For that reason alone, they might be seen as central to the life of an Austrian-Jewish writer like Canetti, who would emigrate from Austria at the last possible minute (1938), never to return. For Canetti's individual, intellectual development, however, his experience of July 15 has another, though related, dimension. Canetti's central concern is the crowd, a topic to which he would devote over thirty years of study, culminating in the 1960 publication of his idiosyncratic anthropological study, *Crowds and Power*. The 1927 experience was not Canetti's first encounter with the mass, but Canetti calls this day "perhaps the most decisive day of my life since the death of my father." For it was on that day that he "realized that the crowd does not need a *leader* (*Führer*), all previous theories notwithstanding." With this seemingly simple statement, Canetti challenges not only the führer phenomenon, but also the strong-arm political conservatism that was urged by the Right in response to July 15. Not least, Canetti's claim contradicts the best-known "mass psychologist" of the day, Sigmund Freud, whose *Group Psychology and Ego Analysis* Canetti had read and rejected in 1925. So basic is the experience of the mass to Canetti that he posited a "mass drive," which he placed "next to the sex drive as its equal." Canetti objects to the reductionism inherent in Freud's theory, claiming that Freud acknowledges neither the phenomenon nor the power of crowd experiences.

Canetti's plea for the irreducibility of experience (and of art) is both his boldest contribution to twentieth-century thought and the most problematic aspect of *Crowds and Power*. In his desire not to reduce the phenomenon, Canetti often reduces his own thought to description without explanatory or methodological potential. His work is nonetheless an original and independent challenge to the truisms of twentieth-century intellectual life. Four concepts are both central and original to this study: the command and its "sting" (*Befehlsstachel*), transformation (*Verwandlung*), the survivor (*der Überlebende*), and especially his diagnosis of the structure of power. The command, according to Canetti, bears an almost physical sting that lodges itself in the person who carries out the command and remains there unchanged until he or she can discharge it by passing on an identical command to another person. Canetti's description applies especially well to hierarchical structures (such as the military) and to the parent-child relationship (Canetti shows overwhelming sympathy for the child, who receives more commands than any other member of society). Psychologists might call this operation "identification with the oppressor"; Canetti, however, resists psychologizing in favor of the mechanistic metaphor of the sting.

Much of Canetti's research for *Crowds and Power* consisted of readings in the mythology and practice of world religions, from the mightiest to the most obscure. Canetti sees transformation (or metamorphosis) as a basic element of both literature and religion, and as one of humanity's best hopes. As long as a religion allows and even enables its constituents to transform themselves, Canetti approves; this happens especially in totemistic and animistic religions in which identification with a particular animal, consultation of the animal as an oracle, and even ritual transformation into the animal are holy acts. (An ecological impulse in Canetti's work can be traced to his belief in the central role animals play in preserving the human capacity for transformation.) Once a religion has become too large, however, and ossified in its structures, it tends to regularize and limit the formation of crowds (for example, by encouraging worship together only at certain times), as well as the possibilities for transformation; here Canetti has a sharp eye for pointing out religion's complicity with power. His diagnosis is most biting when applied to the Catholic Church, whose political representatives were the leading voice against the crowd on July 15: "There has never been a state on earth capable of defending itself in so many ways against the crowd. Compared with the Church all other rulers seem poor amateurs" (Canetti 1960, 155). Canetti sees the Church's function as postponing the experience of the "open crowd" indefinitely (that is, until the afterlife); the Church, like the Social Democratic Party in 1927, is to discipline the people and keep them from discovering one another in a revolutionary crowd capable of transforming itself and the world.

Canetti affirms the "open crowd," the free and anarchical gathering of people that enables their experience of one another and their transformation. The opposite is true of the holder of power, who regiments the masses, separates himself from them, and opposes them, making of them a collection of dead or at least immobile bodies in order to bolster his own feelings of power. This kind of control of the crowd is the opposite of transformation, and death itself is the ultimate enemy of transformation. In "The Survivor" (a section of *Crowds and Power* also published separately), Canetti amasses examples from world history to demonstrate the deep need of the powerful to pile up ever more corpses in order to "win" and see themselves as the sole survivor. The applicability of these ideas to the aesthetics of fascism and to the Holocaust is apparent.

Crowds and Power ends with a discussion of the similarities between the holder of power and the paranoiac (a reading of the Schreber case without Freud) and with an impassioned complaint against the survivor, the command, death, and the power it serves. But because no methodology is developed that could even pretend to offer solutions to concrete problems (as do Freud's dream analysis and his "talking cure"), the book has not had the influence Canetti might have wished for it. Social scientists view it as a literary work, whereas literary scholars at most apply its insights to Canetti's own works. Although the insights of *Crowds and Power* might fruitfully be connected to the work of Foucault, Freud, Adorno, Reich, and others, Canetti strongly resisted such comparisons. The sui generis nature of *Crowds and Power*, combined with the fact that the author held a position defiantly outside of any discipline or professional organization that might promote it, has hindered its reception.

Canetti's lasting literary reputation, sealed by his receipt of the Nobel Prize for literature in 1981, is founded on his first novel, *Die Blendung*, which was completed in 1932 and published in 1936. Translated as *Auto-da-Fé*, its title literally means "the blinding." Canetti has pointed to the relationship between his only novel and the 1927 fire by calling the novel a "fruit of the fire." Here, Canetti's central notion of the crowd overlaps with anti-Semitism and misogyny. The protagonist (really an anti-hero), Peter Kien, seems to stand apart from the crowd: an individualist and intellectual, his very name (Peter means "rock") signifies the opposite of the transformation Canetti glorifies. The character's original name, Kant, makes it clear that he stands for the Enlightenment ideal of autonomy. But his lonely scholarly aerie—a self-contained, four-room library at the top of an apartment building—is threatened by a woman and a Jew. First his housekeeper, Therese, swindles him into marriage. This in itself signifies the breakdown of his isolation, but the woman is further associated with the proletarian mass by her rudeness and lack of education, and with the symbolic idea of the mass through the metonymy of water: she wears a blue skirt and at one point "dissolves" into a stream of tears. The "rock" is always worn down by the persistence of water, and Kien is no exception: his new wife throws him out of their apartment after a bitter struggle, and he enters the real space of the mob, the street.

In a cellar bar frequented by denizens of the demimonde, Peter Kien is thrown on the mercy of a Jewish pimp and swindler, Siegfried Fischerle, who gradually acquires most of Kien's money. Fischerle is a brutal caricature of the would-be assimilated Jew: although his first name tries to signify Germanness, his hump is the physical reminder of the Jewish "nature" he cannot shed. A pseudo-intellectual who fancies that he would be a chess champion if he only had the financial backing, Fischerle gradually draws the reader into his plot to bilk Kien and flee to America. Though Fischerle spends Kien's money on a flatteringly tailored suit designed to hide the hump, it is only his brutal murder that "frees" him from the hump once and for all. Fischerle is captured by one of his "wife's" customers and slaughtered like a beast; the attacker carves off his hump, throws it in a corner, and proceeds to make love to the murdered man's wife "all night long." The connections among Jewishness, women, and prostitution all recall the misogynistic and (self-hating) anti-Semitic theory of Otto Weininger. Although Canetti clearly and prophetically saw the impossibility of Jews being accepted—with or without the "hump" of Jewishness—in mainstream Austrian society, it is less clear to what extent he himself had internalized the negativity he purges in this novel.

Peter Kien, who appears to represent the privileged sons of the haute bourgeoisie (both Karl Kraus and Canetti himself have been suggested as models), is ultimately destroyed, not by women or Jews, but by forces within himself. In a paranoiac panic, he sets fire to his own library and goes up in flames along with his priceless collection of books. Kien projects onto the external world a threat that is no longer present (Fischerle is dead, Therese safely remarried) and commits suicide to escape. The lonely scholar who—like Vienna's conservative leaders—believed himself above the plebeian mass, finally succumbs to its pull within himself. Kien's final self-immolation has also been read as an instance of homosexual panic strongly influenced by Kien's virulent misogyny, a reading supported by his lengthy Weiningerian diatribe against women in the book's penultimate chapter. Whether Kien hates the mass in himself, the woman in himself, or possibly even the Jew in himself (either of which would also symbolize the mass), the mechanism and the result are the same; both rely heavily on the Freudian concept of repression, though Canetti would certainly have preferred a different terminology.

The reception of *Auto-da-Fé* was cut short by Nazism, the annexation of Austria, Canetti's own flight to England in 1938, and World War II. A second edition, appearing in 1947, also found little response; it was not until the book's third appearance in 1963 that it enjoyed extended critical reception. Canetti's two plays from his Viennese period—*The Wedding* (1932) and *Comedy of Vanity* (1934)—suffered a similar fate; both were first premiered in 1965, more than thirty years after they were written. Both plays experiment with turning the crowd into a stage character, and both are deeply pessimistic, even apocalyptic: the first ends in mass death, the second in an eruption of mass narcissism.

With a decidedly Marxist bent, *The Wedding* portrays a petty bourgeoisie that strives only for property (in the form of real estate and sexual "ownership"). The biblical story of Samson's destruction of the temple forms the play's narrative kernel; the dramatic realization relies on Canetti's theory of the acoustic mask, a technique also used in *Auto-da-Fé*. In its most extreme form, each person's acoustic mask is an immutable and limited characteristic set of words, expressions, and intonations that both reveal and mask the individual's character but do not foster communication. In this play, a parrot's obsessive repetition of the word "House" offers such an extreme version; the bird is not capable of linguistic communication, but nonetheless wears an acoustic mask that mirrors the materialism of its human surroundings.

The central premise of *Comedy of Vanity* is a government edict banning mirrors, photographs, or any other human likeness that might promote vanity. Although the content of the edict seems like an extreme interpretation of the biblical first commandment, the form in which it is carried out (a huge bonfire) reflects the book burnings in Nazi Germany shortly after Hitler's seizure of power. It is unfortunate that, like *Auto-da-Fé*, these early works were denied the full effect they might have had in their own time. (Canetti was, literally, not alone in having his literary career fatefully altered by the war. His wife, the former Veza Taubner-Calderon, whom he married in 1934, was at the time of their marriage a more successful author than her husband, having published several short stories in Vienna's *Arbeiter-Zeitung* and elsewhere, whereas Canetti had published nothing. Veza's creativity was disrupted by the flight to England, however, and she did not publish for the remainder of her life. Three of her books are now available under the name Veza Canetti.)

Canetti's third play, *The Numbered* (1952; also translated as *Life-Terms*, 1982), dramatizes Canetti's most radical philosophical position: his opposition to death. Instead of names, the characters in this play have numbers assigned by a government bureaucrat that signify the age at which they will die. Government regulation and control of death, although they do away with murder and aggression (both pointless, because death is pre-ordained), lead to other undesirable social by-products such as the devaluation of those "destined" to die young. It is taboo to reveal one's birth date, which is engraved in a locket that holds the key to both age and life expectancy; but one citizen becomes skeptical of the entire system, breaks his locket, and discovers that it is empty, a fraud. Perhaps one may read into this taboo—breaking Canetti's wish that death itself may one day be revealed as a fraud.

The tortured history of the reception of Canetti's early works deserves further, biographically based comment, for Canetti's life story both underscores and radically questions his multiple identities as an Austrian, a bearer of German culture, a pan-European citizen, a Jew, and even a literary artist or *Dichter*. Canetti was born in Ruschuk, Bulgaria, in 1905, to Sephardic Jewish parents who had fallen in love in Vienna after being drawn together by their common love for that city's Burgtheater. Because German was the "secret language" that united his parents in love and literature, the child Elias was attracted to this language and to Vienna long before he himself experienced either. Early in his autobiography, Canetti notes that most of the Sephardic Jews he knew were still Turkish citizens and that the Ottoman Empire had treated them better than it treated Christians. Thus Canetti's earliest identity spans not only Eastern and Western Europe, but also the traditional enemy of a Europe conceived as Christian, the great Muslim empire. The Canetti family moved to Manchester, England, when Elias was five; here, he added French and English to his Spanish (Ladino), Bulgarian, Hebrew, and snippets of Turkish. Canetti did not learn German until age eight, and then under traumatic circumstances: his father's sudden and unexpected death prompted Canetti's mother to take him and his two younger brothers "back" to Vienna, where she forcibly taught him German in a period of three months. It seems likely that this powerful personal legacy played as strong a role as any cultural or literary considerations in Canetti's later unwavering loyalty to the German language while in exile.

These events are related in Canetti's three-volume autobiography, which some critics such as Sander Gilman and Dagmar Barnouw consider his finest work; this appeal seems due in equal measure to the international odyssey of the life itself and to the vivid engagement with which it is told. The three volumes—*The Tongue Set Free, The Torch in My Ear,* and *The Play of the Eyes*—offer a highly readable, but also very subjective, account of European intellectual and cultural life from 1905 to 1938. Canetti's early travels across Europe not only gave him a core identity as a pan-European, but also mirrored the cosmopolitan nature of what was Habsburg Austria, which prided itself on being a *Vielvölkerstaat,* or state of many nations. Within this "multicultural" context, however, it was always clear that German language and culture had the upper hand. It is therefore no coincidence that Canetti's mother, a member of the Jewish middle class concerned with economic and social status, would take her sons to the capital and teach them German, rather than returning to the backwater of Ruschuk. Whatever emotional considerations played a role in her decision, they were supported by strong practical incentives.

The "class distinction" between the lowly Eastern Jews and the assimilated German Jews is made palpable in numerous ways in Canetti's autobiography. The beginning of *The Tongue Set Free* fairly bursts with the child's excitement at the varied experiences his village provides him. He is proud to recite the child's question at Passover (but oddly "translates" the holiday for his readers as "Easter"). Already as a child, however, he is ashamed of a grandfather who claims he speaks seventeen languages, including some Western ones, although he has never left the Balkans. On his only visit back to his extended family in Bulgaria as an adult, Canetti experiences the East as a backward place where individuality is squelched by the demands of family, and he vents his own feelings of oppression in a misogynistic tirade against a female cousin.

Canetti's ambivalence toward his Jewish origins can be seen clearly in his relationships with two father figures who embody different aspects of Jewish heritage and identity. During the early 1930s, Canetti made a daily pilgrimage to the coffeehouse table of a man he called "Dr. Sonne" (Dr. Sun). This solitary scholar was himself an Eastern Jew whose family had lived in Przemysl, and who had published Hebrew poetry under the name Abraham ben Yitzchak. From him, Canetti learned to appreciate the riches of the Sephardic poetic tradition and above all the Hebrew Bible. Discussing Martin Buber's new translation with Dr. Sonne was, Canetti (1980) writes, "my opportunity to learn the wording [of the Prophets] in the original language. Until then, I had avoided such knowledge; it would have made me feel trapped to learn more about things so close to my roots." Whether Canetti's avoidance of things Jewish was assimilationism, self-hatred, or merely a young adult's rebellion against the limitations of tradition and provenance, it was in some measure shared by Dr. Sonne himself, who participated in a dance of denial: "He never used the word 'Jew' to refer to either me or himself" (Canetti 1980).

Another father figure, closer to the Jewish religion but far more removed from Canetti, provokes feelings of shame in the author at his loss of Jewish heritage. In *The Voices of Marrakesh*, Canetti records his impressions of a trip to Morocco in 1954. He is fascinated by the Mellah, the slum-like Jewish quarter; there, Canetti is overcome by "boundless love" for an acquaintance's father, a scholar of scripture who reads all night. Their meeting takes place in silence, because they have no language in common, and Canetti avoids a second meeting by turning down an invitation to celebrate Purim with the family: "I imagined his father's disappointment at my ignorance of the old customs. I would have done everything wrong, and I could only have said the prayers like someone who never prays. I was ashamed in the face of the old man, whom I loved." Love and distance, secret communication and silence, reverence and rejection characterize Canetti's paradoxical relationship to things Jewish and non-Western.

It is possible that the sense of shame in the above passage feeds from the guilt of a Holocaust survivor who did not take the Holocaust as an occasion to return to the beliefs and traditions of Judaism, or even to involve himself in the politics of the newly formed state of Israel. Nonetheless, Canetti's moral seriousness gains its full impetus and effect from the Holocaust. His immediate reaction to the war was a form of artistic asceticism: he abandoned his projected "Human Comedy of Madmen," which would have comprised seven novels in addition to the first, and forbade himself all literary activity until *Crowds and Power* was completed. He broke the taboo only once, for his third play. As a counterbalance to this work, in 1942 he began to keep an intellectual diary of "jottings" (*Aufzeichnungen*); these have been published in three volumes spanning fifty years. The jottings are Canetti's most spontaneous, unguarded self-revelation, because they are not structured with an eye to personal mythology as is the autobiography; this has led one scholar (Eigler) to view them as a Derridean "supplement" to the autobiography, a sort of autobiographical repressed. At the same time, the jottings are pruned into aphorisms that are carefully selected and cryptically encoded; many entries of a seemingly personal nature are phrased in the third person so that the reader never knows whether Canetti is revealing something of himself, recording the attitudes of a friend, or making a general observation about human nature.

Aside from the immediate outrage expressed in his entries from the war years, Canetti's first extended reckoning with the war occurs in two essays from 1971, published in *The Conscience of Words*. "Hitler According to Speer," Canetti's response to Speer's diaries containing his monumental architectural plans for Berlin, would have become a discussion of fascist aesthetics in the hands of any other writer. But Canetti is interested in the content of this aesthetic, particularly as it concords with his findings in *Crowds and Power*. The virtuosity with which he applies his own terminology to Speer's and Hitler's plans suggests that *Crowds and Power*, however early it may have been conceived, was in its execution always guided by the phenomenon of Hitler. Speer's plans are emblems of Hitler's power, not only because of their size, but also because of their intended use in forming and maintaining the crowds on which Hitler depended. Hitler's truest subjects, however, are the masses of dead: the dead of World War I, those he had assassinated, the soldiers who would fall in his own war, and those he gassed. Canetti compares Hitler's paranoiac nature with his own discussion of the Schreber case, the conclusion of *Crowds and Power,* once more strengthening the impression that the longer work is a response to Hitler.

In the second essay, "Dr. Hachiya's Hiroshima Diary," Canetti turns to the "other" holocaust. Although he elsewhere makes the threat of nuclear war the most important issue confronting the human race (in *The Sundered Future*), here Canetti is concerned with the morality of surviving a catastrophe. Canetti repeatedly distances himself culturally from the Japanese doctor, who is a Buddhist and a believer in the emperor, yet he also confesses that he has understood the Japanese better through this piece of writing than any other. No wonder, because Canetti is in the same survivor position as this doctor, who must try to cure the victims of a disease he does not understand. When the doctor pays his respects to the dead by praying for each one of them at the site of their death, the religiously skeptical Canetti seems to concur that such piety is the only way to survive with one's own dignity intact and without succumbing to the crass position of power inherent in survival. It is typical of Canetti that he does not address the question of his own survivorship directly, but displaces it onto a cultural "other."

In Canetti's penultimate volume of jottings, *Die Fliegenpein* (The agony of flies; 1992), he makes a rare first-person confession that summarizes his difficult position as a secular humanist Jewish writer: "My stubborn resistance to the Bible, which kept me away from it for decades, has to do with the fact that I never wanted to give in to my origin. . . . I didn't want to lead an intellectual life that was predetermined from the outset, I didn't want a *prescribed* intellectual life. I wanted to be surprised and overpowered again and again, and thereby gradually become a friend and connoisseur of all that is human. I could not simply accept the preponderance of the Biblical that has marked the world for so long."

Referring only obliquely to his Jewishness, Canetti seems to include the worldwide influence of Christianity under colonialism in his rejection of the biblical. He thus both claims and rejects not only Hebrew Scripture, but also the New Testament as part of his origin, and he opposes both of these narrowly scriptural traditions to a post-Enlightenment notion of humanity that Canetti always aspired to know in its entirety.

Bibliography

Elias Canetti, *Das Augenspiel: Lebensgeschichte, 1931–1937* (Munich: Hanser, 1985); Canetti, *Die Blendung* (Munich: Hanser, 1963); Canetti, *Dramen* (Munich: Hanser, 1964); Canetti, *Die Fackel im Öhr: Lebensgeschichte, 1921–1931* (Munich: Hanser, 1980); Canetti, *Die Fliegenpein: Aufzeichnungen* (Munich: Hanser, 1992); Canetti, *Das Geheimherz der Uhr: Aufzeichnungen, 1973–1985* (Munich: Hanser, 1987); Canetti, *Die gerettete Zunge: Geschichte einer Jugend* (Munich: Hanser, 1977); Canetti, *Die gespaltene Zukunft: Aufsätze und Gespräche* (Munich: Hanser, 1972); Canetti, *Das Gewissen der Worte: Essays* (Munich: Hanser, 1975); Canetti, *Masse und Macht* (Hamburg: Claassen, 1960); Canetti, *Die Provinz des Menschen: Aufzeichnungen, 1942–1972* (Munich: Hanser, 1973); Canetti, *Die Stimmen von Marrakesch* (Munich: Hanser, 1978); Veza Canetti, *Die gelbe Straße* (Munich: Hanser, 1990); V. Canetti, *Geduld bringt Rosen* (Munich: Hanser, 1992); Friederike Eigler, *Das autobiographische Werk von Elias Canetti* (Tübingen: Stauffenberg, 1988); Eigler, *Essays in Honor of Elias Canetti,* trans. Michael Hulse (New York: Farrar, Straus, Giroux, 1987); Kristie A. Foell, *Blind Reflections: Gender in Elias Canetti's "Die Blendung"* (Riverside, Calif.: Ariadne Press, 1994); Richard H. Lawson, *Understanding Elias Canetti* (Columbia: University of South Carolina Press, 1991); Barbara Meili, *Erinnerung und Vision: Der lebensgeschichtliche Hintergrund von Elias Canetti's Roman "Die Blendung"* (Bonn: Bouvier, 1985); and Gerald Stieg, *Frucht des Feuers: Canetti, Doderer, Kraus und der Justizpalastbrand* (Vienna: Edition Falter im Österreichischen Bundesverlag, 1990).

KRISTIE A. FOELL

1928 Jakob Wassermann's novel *Der Fall Maurizius* presents the final expression of his views on the relationship of Germans and Jews

When Jakob Wassermann completed *Der Fall Maurizius* (The Maurizius case) in 1928, the novel stood, he said, as the culmination of all his previous efforts. He now understood everything that he had achieved before as a preparatory stage on the way to this work. Although the qualities in its construction and execution lift it far above all of Wassermann's other fiction and justify his sense that this was a momentous point in his career as a writer, that point of preeminence only intensifies the book's most ominous undertone. Since the early years of his literary success, Wassermann had established himself as a Jewish voice speaking from a representative position well within the mainstream of German values. His attempts throughout his career to formulate assured expressions of those values and represent them in a plausibly portrayed contemporary world reflect the level of strength and confidence in that body of opinion. Despite the vigor of his talent in this endeavor, what he actually achieved in *Der Fall Maurizius* set the scene for a defeat of his own ideals.

The rigor and consistency of Wassermann's exposition does not approach the condition of Germany as a sphere of social relationships, but follows the lines of force generated by the fundamental concepts of the nation's identity. The individual fates he describes all take their measure from their place within that balance or imbalance of forces. The conclusion imposed on him by his own creation evidently disturbed and dissatisfied him. In his last lines, he denies his own concluding moment by explicitly promising the reader a future continuation of the story. *Der Fall Maurizius* attempts to draw together a series of themes expressing the existence of a Germany divided between a past before World War I and the present in the Weimar Republic, and between its ideal conceptions of itself and the frailties jeopardizing its precarious reality.

Wassermann's storytelling weaves many axes of tension together here: the claims of youth, obligations to the state, the rights of sexuality and love, the place of talent and ambition, the ties of loyalty in friendship and family, and the choices open to a Jew in Germany. All require reconciliation within a sphere of justice, but the image of justice first falters and then collapses into a grotesque distortion of itself. Neither of the two books that fulfill the promise to further explore the story, *Etzel Andergast* (1931) and *Joseph Kerkhovens dritte Existenz* (Joseph Kerkhoven's third existence; 1934), succeed in reaffirming an unambiguous substance for that value. And there can be no doubt that the narrative's failure to find closure in a clear judgment reflects the author's inability to realize his pedagogical intention, not his pursuit of a modernist aesthetics. Despite his own intentions to speak hopefully and helpfully for a better future, Wassermann appears to have focused the language of his own world in that historical moment only to articulate the last gasp of the past for which he had indeed established himself as spokesman.

We can only understand the full significance of this book in terms of the meaning of this moment in the existence of a quite particular public for whom and to whom he spoke. The connection between Wassermann and his readership determined the success of his standing at its peak, and the limitations of his achievement similarly reflect restrictions in the idiom through which he addressed that public. Even though the situation from which Wassermann wrote as a German and a Jew always gave him his specific material, his line of approach to that situation clearly touched a familiar chord in the experience of readers beyond the enclosure of one nation or one language. In his foreword to a volume on Wassermann's work published in 1935, two years after the author's death, Thomas Mann described Wassermann's career as having made him a "world star of novel writing" (Karlweis 1935).

As always, Mann chose his term precisely. A star's significance derives from his or her power to focus a certain form of attention, but such a relationship to the public need not indicate a major event in the development of a literary medium that future generations will recognize in the same way. Mann acknowledged a talent, but raised a query at the same time. That query has two sides because the success to which Mann alludes has two aspects. Wassermann's preeminence as a writer in Germany indicates his capacity to reflect the world of his German readers, but his preeminence as a German writer on the world stage reflects that aspect of German experience that articulated an international element in the self-consciousness of a reading public. Therefore although we may read the significance of his strengths and shortcomings in the German context as an indication of contradictory forces in the history of German culture, Wassermann's emergence as a world figure also gives us a measure of Germany's new role in international literary relations. It was not self-evident to Mann that Germany should produce a "world star" at all, nor that this particular writer should be elevated to that prominence.

Wassermann had certainly been remarkably productive. His novels and stories, his essays and biographies together amounted to over fifty titles, but his ability to reach a wide readership now seems even more remarkable. Printings of the novel *Das Gänsemännchen* (The little goose man; 1915) had reportedly risen to a total of 291,000 copies by 1933. Lion Feuchtwanger's commentary on *Das Gänsemännchen* in *Die Schaubühne* (Jan. 6, 1916) gives a good indication of how it was received, and may stand as a more general judgment of Wassermann's talent. Feuchtwanger remarked that two features struck the reader right away. First, the book showed a naive, stubborn lack of concern for the inadequacies of its artistic and technical form, but this was accompanied by an "implacable, raging, divine fire of pathos" (13) that lifted it far above the novels of the previous few years. Such pathos clearly marks the point of engagement with the times; that engagement drew all of Wassermann's interest and left him indifferent to any aesthetic consideration beyond communicating a response to the most intensely visible issues of the day.

The equivocal status of star to which Mann adverts even in that delicate and endangered moment at the end of Wassermann's career presents a still more complex question now. If we look at the record of his achievements in his lifetime and compare such an impressive career with his reputation today, the contrast would seem to confirm the most negative implication of Mann's phrase. This once bright fame has now sunk close to the horizon of oblivion. Yet Wassermann's work cannot simply be relegated to the list of popular successes whose approval by a large and undiscriminating public betokens too great a kinship with a passing taste for insubstantial writing. Mann himself had also long taken Wassermann's work seriously and discussed it as a solid contribution to the culture of his time—in his "Tischrede auf Jakob Wassermann," which first appeared on April 10, 1929, in the *Berliner Tageblatt,* he speaks as a genuinely appreciative reader. Hugo von Hofmannsthal counted himself a friend and admirer from early on, as did Arthur Schnitzler, and the breadth of appreciation Wassermann had earned among his peers by the end of his life is left in no doubt by the warm expressions of goodwill Heinrich Mann collected for the issue of *Die Neue Rundschau,* which celebrated Wassermann's sixtieth birthday in 1933.

The criticism that today relegates Wassermann to this reduced standing does not see something different in his work: it simply fails to find the same value in what it sees. The most common objections note Wassermann's failure to construct plausible characters and his propensity to deploy his figures as embodiments of ideas. The abstract quality of these figures may strike us as false today, but not because our preferred literary forms are free of abstraction. A fictional narrative always achieves its intelligible form by generalizing the view of a situation, or by developing a comprehensible and recognizable type. The difference in a case like Wassermann's writing lies in the sphere for which he has devised his representative personae. The essence of human existence for him is not to be discovered in the psychology of different temperaments, nor in the defining functions of class and role in a social structure. Only ideas identify the dynamic focal points through which human destinies articulate themselves in their full gravity for the reader. Therefore the process by which Wassermann creates his figures does not strive toward a social or psychological typology, and does not result in a recognizable person representing a generality of existences. He instead constructs a typology of discourses in which each figure speaks for a nodal point in the web of ideas with which the shape of a community is described.

Those of Wassermann's contemporaries who have survived with canonical status did so because they were more gifted in the art of integrating ideas into individual representations. Yet even so, their respect for Wassermann in their own time indicates a similar engagement with a preeminent texture of ideas, as indeed their work demonstrates. Wassermann's success as a German author illustrates the state of a culture that endeavored to understand itself through such constellations of ideas rather than in terms derived from more immediately visible aspects of social and individual life. His success as a world author demonstrates the extent to which German culture had established its authoritative place in the international arena through this characteristic texture of meanings. The subsequent decline of his reputation, and the weaknesses in his position that emerge with such paradoxical clarity in his best work, also demonstrate how profoundly inadequate that entire body of ideas had grown when engaged at the levels of concrete human needs, to which he had undertaken to give voice with such unequivocal passion.

The fate of oblivion does not necessarily dishonor the forgotten, and the mortality of human efforts can scarcely be used as an argument against their nobility. One can see as clearly in Wassermann's fiction, as in his programmatic writings, that he never attempted to sublimate his material into a purely aesthetic register. Here flows the direct source of the pathos to which Feuchtwanger refers. The classical separation pronounced by Schiller between a serene independent domain of art and the earnestness of life had no defining power for Wassermann. His notion of what an artist is, and what an artist does, accepted precisely the same burden of moral obligations in completely unmediated form as that which he assumed as a member of his community. The close tie with his contemporary readership that this brought him presents an almost insurmountable obstacle to readers today. The relationship between his personal existence, his historical circumstances, and his writing, moreover, reflects how he understood the necessities imposed on a Jewish writer. His work accepts no substantial break at any point between his self-consciousness as a German and a Jew and his task as literary artist.

Born in 1873, Wassermann experienced a period in which many of the civil disabilities afflicting Jews had given way before the modernity of the newly unified German empire. But born into poor and troubled family circumstances, he quickly discovered how vulnerable he remained to the never-ending history of anti-Semitism. He grew up knowing that the Jewish community in the place of his birth, Fürth, probably originated in the ninth century and that his family roots

reached back through four centuries in that locality. Yet although he drew on this knowledge as
the foundation for an innate tie of blood to the
German landscape and an unshakable claim to a
German identity, the autobiographical work
Mein Weg als Deutscher und Jude (My way as a
German and a Jew; 1921), recalls his pain and
disappointment on finding that it counted for
nothing to many Christian Germans.

Wassermann responded in a way that situates
him distinctively within this conflict between
German and Jewish identities, because he agrees
with one part of the reasoning turned against
him. He does agree that a Jew after any number of
centuries in Germany has still become no less a
Jew, and remains entirely distinct. The reader of
Mein Weg als Deutscher und Jude will be startled to
find how intently Wassermann insists that his
Jewish character does indeed remain unalterably
"Oriental" by virtue of his blood. This Oriental
identity is not a vague historical association, but a
living part of his nature: this "Oriental impulse in
my blood," he claims, accounts for a particular
relationship to the activity of storytelling (49).
He even repeats this idea of the Jew's Oriental
character as late as 1928 in an essay entitled "Die
psychologische Situation des Judentums" (The
psychological situation of Jewry), despite his
awareness of the misuse it invited (Wassermann
1984, 147).

At the same time, Wassermann continued to
insist that no man or woman with his background
should concede any restriction on their full place
in Germany as a German. Though he offended
many Jews by saying so, he experienced his Oriental identity as a special case of a German identity, not as a mode of kinship with Jews of other
national origins. In *Mein Weg als Deutscher und
Jude* he notes that he found no trace of a common
bond by which he might understand the essence
of a Polish or Galician Jew beyond what any individual owes another individual case (115). The
emphasis on individual value that he repeats in
this context qualifies what otherwise might
wrongly be taken to imply a leaning toward the
German side of his condition as a choice or preference giving priority over the Jewish side.

The either / or of national mythologies and
exclusive solidarities that ravaged his contemporary world, as it ravages ours, produced no such
leanings in his sensibility. He cites the example of
his distance from foreign Jewry in order to illustrate a fundamental turn of his character, not to
provide evidence for his Germanness. He has, he
writes, no proclivity to feel special love for anyone
because of the collectivity that encloses them
both. Honor, respect, and love, he states plainly,
are earned by individuals. He found himself incapable of transferring such judgments or feelings
from those values of personal merit, where they
are truly in place, to any idea that merely constitutes a group by arbitrary definition and does not
name the genuine presence of a shared human
quality.

It might seem a paradox that Wassermann
should also preserve the significance of blood in
his understanding of who he was, but here, too, he
shows his characteristic unwillingness to exclude
or choose one thing in preference to another. One
element of the distance that now frustrates a subsequent generation of readers emerges in the peculiar medium of his thought, which does not
seek to engage ideas through the clarity and autonomy of analysis, but accepts them as they figure in a peculiar idiom of his times. This medium
of thought does not isolate concepts in their purity, where they oppose or contradict one another,
but gathers them up within the tributaries of an
expansive, progressing stream of experience that
displaces the function of historical consciousness.
Though the closing statement of *Mein Weg als
Deutscher und Jude* describes the role of a Jew and
German in his situation as a contribution to a
future synthesis that will assimilate all things, we
only fall into yet another misconception if we
attempt to find the philosophy of history that
corresponded with his view. The naive indifference to artistic form in his fiction is accompanied by an equally stubborn neglect of philosophical discrimination. His ideology, too, is
sustained by pathos rather than by any structured
position. The scholarly literature on Wassermann
often gestures vaguely toward Nietzsche as a
philosophical influence, just as it commonly in-

vokes Dostoevsky and Tolstoy as literary antecedents. The manner of his engagement with all the
currents of his times makes such specific points of
connection misleading.

In this pathos, however, Wassermann not only
foregrounds his experience as a Jew more than
does any other comparable figure, but also draws
from a level of the circumambient culture that
few Jews of literary talent accepted as the natural
idiom of thought. He began to write early, and
although he was largely self-educated and had to
endure the most unfavorable material circumstances, by 1897 he had established a significant
reputation with the novel *Die Juden von Zirndorf*
(The Jews of Zirndorf). The reader today will see
this text at once as the paradoxical product of a
considerable individual power at work within a
strangely enclosed intellectual horizon. This is
not the enclosure of a perspective restricted to the
limits of a Jewish world, nor is it parochial in any
regional sense. The responses that engage one another in this book reflect a world that has absorbed many strands of thought from its own past
and present through clumsy processes of mediation in which the narrator is himself inextricably
entwined. This is the world of an imperfectly
educated German population at the social level to
which the light of its most articulate critical tradition can only penetrate in attenuated form.

The book consists of two parts, the first of
which gives an account of how the community of
Zirndorf (from Ziondorf), to which Wassermann
had family ties through his father, was founded
by Jews from Fürth after their plan to follow
Sabbatai Zevi to the Holy Land collapsed. The
main body of the narrative depicts life in that
community after more than two hundred years, in
the late nineteenth century. Beyond the tensions
between Jews and Christians in this context,
Wassermann portrays a larger domain of loss that
links the two groups. Just as the Jews have suffered a history that deprived them of their own
kingdom and homeland, so too do Germans exist
in a fragmented national world. Wassermann also
makes the point in *Mein Weg als Deutscher und Jude*
that Germans lack the historical continuity or the
stable center for a basis equivalent to that on

which the French or English have established the
fully articulated relationships of their national
literature. This fundamental notion stands at the
heart of how Wassermann defines Jewishness,
Germanness, and the place of the writer. It also
stands at the heart of prescriptions he first suggests in *Die Juden von Zirndorf* and subsequently
develops in all aspects of his writing for a salvation that joins all three.

The false path that tempts Jews, he maintains
repeatedly, turns the sharpened view of an ostracized existence to advantage by spying out the
weaknesses of the oppressor and exploiting them.
The ever-present political error of Jews has drawn
them too eagerly to take the shortsighted step
from their tenuous place at the margin of national
life to leadership at the forefront of radical
change. In Wassermann's view, the final dissolution of traditional ties will not emancipate them
in the resulting state of universal disinherited-
ness. The correct path begins with the proud affirmation of an Oriental heritage, and, through the
strength of this experience, finds its way to a
deeper connection with an essential vitality in
the passions and the sufferings of the people. The
same affirmation of a living connection with the
thoughts of ordinary people promises a restoration of German experience for Christians, and
may help release Germans from their fear of the
unsettling difference in their Jewish compatriots.

In *Mein Weg als Deutscher und Jude*, Wassermann takes Heine as the prime example of the
Jew whose embrace of change and contempt for
tradition proceeds in step with his denial of his
own identity in a Jewish past. But in *Die Juden von
Zirndorf* Wassermann had already extended this
notion of "Jewishness" to include the false position of cynical wit and empty intellectuality of
the non-Jewish "Literat," or writer who lacks full
creative depth specifically because he separates
himself from ordinary people and denies his
proper share in their thoughts and feelings. The
character of Gudstikker, a writer who is not Jewish, receives this designation of "Jewishness" because of the shallow arrogance of his writing, and
receives it from Agathon, the Jewish character in
whom a true tie to the Jewish past survives in its

greatest fulfillment. That point perhaps appears most explicitly in the short piece entitled "Der Jude als Orientale" (The Jew as Oriental), which was written in 1913 in the form of a letter to Martin Buber. But Wassermann always maintained that only the Jew who preserved his Jewish identity, and only the writer who preserved his identity with the inheritance of tradition, could sustain the quality of the "schöpferischer Mensch," or creative person (Wassermann 1984, 30).

Wassermann voiced unrelenting criticism of the way German society excluded its Jewish citizens from full membership in national life. Indeed, he was provocative without hesitation, fear, or restraint about the injustice and hypocrisy of that society. And yet, because he did not attempt to overcome the injustice inflicted on him by rejecting the community from which that rejection came, both Jewish and non-Jewish commentators have situated him according to quite inappropriately simplistic categories of Jewish experience. On the one hand, he sometimes appears as a "self-hating Jew." Theodor Lessing names him in *Der Jüdische Selbsthaß* (Jewish self-hatred; 1930), together with the grand literary talents of Hugo von Hofmannsthal, Franz Werfel, and Karl Kraus, as a writer haunted by the will to escape his Jewish identity. Without endorsing that judgment for the others named, one can certainly say Wassermann has as little in common with these other authors in his relationship to his Jewish origins as their conception of their role as *Literaten* has to his understanding of himself in the role of a creative person.

The other side of this misconstrued relationship with Wassermann's circumstances appears in the ideologically milder idea of the Jew's unrequited love for Germanness. This widely established conventional formulation not only substitutes love for the other as less disturbing than hatred for oneself, but also soothes the tensions that might be aroused by dwelling on his harsh criticisms of German attitudes to Jews. Those who were closest to the target of Wassermann's harshest words, of course, found it natural to find him sunk in hatred of Germans. The notion of an unrequited Jewish love for Germany does appear as a rhetorical question posed in a rhetorically overheated passage of *Mein Weg als Deutscher und Jude* (129). Yet the interpretation of that figure must surely be ascertained by his general determination that he finds himself temperamentally incapable of any such attachment to arbitrary collective concepts. One must nonetheless consider carefully how and why that notion of unrequited love should be so widely foregrounded.

To the extent that it does not simply spring from the need to render him harmless, such an emphasis may be attributed in part to its appearance in the confessions of the most arresting character in his most substantial novel, Gregor Waremme in *Der Fall Maurizius*. Yet Waremme illustrates all the elements of a Jewish fate in its inward effects that Wassermann himself had managed to avoid. By dint of apostasy and suppressing the name with which he was born, Waremme pursues expression for his intellectual talents among the most reactionary elements of German nationalism. The ever greater demands of performing a public role that denies his real identity cause the catastrophe on which the novel turns, because the persona Waremme has invented to dazzle the world has been spun from uncontrollable excesses of both love and hatred.

Unlike Waremme, Wassermann succeeded in finding a path, even though his path, too, never resolved the loneliness and exclusion of being a Jew in Germany. And though he articulates admiration and resentment in the most forthright terms, Wassermann's concern is always to preserve measured judgment and clear vision. The significant parallel between Wassermann's own position and that of his narrative creation lies in the lack of resolution each demonstrates, not in the simplifying passions of any love or hatred to be found in or imputed to one or the other. Speaking for his own experience in 1921, Wassermann concludes that because the origins of the problem lie in Germans and not Jews, the solution lies there, too, rather than in any decision, insight, response, or action that Jews might undertake. The character he creates in 1928 illustrates the appalling effects the German failure to change the situation has produced in a Jew. Waremme is a monster incapable of realizing the fundamental virtues of a human existence in himself. Yet that failure and its effects lead to no clear judgment because Waremme's fate shows only how he has been denied an existence for which he might be held accountable.

This placing of a Jewish fate beyond the point of judgment defeats the effort undertaken to bring the concept of justice into this novel's very ambitious narrative. The character Waremme is the focal point of conflicting abstract or exterior forces, but even though the novel gathers them together in one function, they do not appear in the form of an interior experience that might define an aesthetically coherent motivation of the story. The Jewish existence Wassermann unfolds in his autobiographical writings and describes in his essays presents the task of avoiding the catastrophic temptations of inappropriate love and hate, both of which are blinding—even in their most dazzling brilliance. The general failure of an aesthetically satisfying coherence in Wassermann's fiction parallels and reflects this negative way of proceeding in his ideological critiques. Though he wrote in the earliest hope that some mediating idea must ultimately reconcile all conflicts, he never accepted the restriction imposed by any one specific idea or constellation of ideas in a single illuminating perspective.

To the counterperspective that he brought to bear on each narrow basis of opinion, all illuminations were blindness unless their light reached all eyes equally. The hope that establishing a Jewish state would put an end to the hatred of Jews as an anomalous nation struck him as baseless, just as did the idea that Jews could escape that hatred by surrendering their identity and assimilating. He dismissed all the Jewish options over which his contemporaries squabbled—from religious separatism to assimilation, or Zionism—just as he dismissed the promise of any and every political utopia. Movement toward a better future depended for him on the pride and courage that keeps individuals from being seduced by falsely utopian ideas and myths.

By 1928, however, this faith and hope are shown to be illusory. The narrative form imposed by the themes of *Der Fall Maurizius* defeats his faith that humankind has the capacity to resist such seductive powers. This novel, for whose birth all of Wassermann's previous work had seemed to him only preparatory labor, signals the end of that last attenuated concept of progress and hope for the human condition. Not only does Waremme simply exceed the capacity of judgment because the thread of injustice has wound itself too deeply into his fate, but the figure of Etzel too, portrayed in all innocence as the soul of justice, emerges as a seducer, a betrayer, and a destroyer as well. This sixteen-year-old boy, whose name is a German variant of Attila, leaves a trail of destruction behind him because the world cannot assimilate the demand for justice. And Wassermann lets the gentlest voice that speaks from the humblest life in his novel, the old prison guard Klakusch, pronounce his judgment of all judgments in this world. If humanity has based its entire existence on an order that is not only unjust, but can never aspire to achieve justice, then we must do away with this humanity and create another in its place, he says.

History and oeuvre run together, and falter together at this point, 1928. The life of Weimar Germany had five more years to run, as did Wassermann's career, but the way forward into the future was already darkening for both. The belief in humane values and the individual within a liberal bourgeois tradition was now gone—those who endeavored to look for their own salvation along the path Wassermann had explored as a German and a Jew would soon lose their way and vanish into night and fog. Enfeebled by rejections of its own internal essence, Germany, with its inadequate past, would indeed abolish its own humanity in order to create another Germany in its place, but that would be a Germany without Jews.

Bibliography

Marta Karlweis, *Jakob Wasserman: Bild, Kampf und Werk. Geleitwort von Thomas Mann* (Amsterdam: Querido, 1935); Henry Miller, *Reflections on the Maurizius Case* (Santa Barbara, Calif.: Capra, 1974); Dierk

Rodewald, ed., *Jakob Wassermann, 1873–1934: Ein Weg als Deutscher und Jude* (Bonn: Bouvier, 1984); Kaspar Schnetzler, *"Der Fall Maurizius": Jakob Wassermanns Kunst des Erzählens* (Bern: Herbert Lang, 1968); Jacob Wassermann, *Der Fall Maurizius* [1928]; (Munich: Langen Müller, 1985); Wassermann, *Die Juden von Zirndorf* (Berlin: Fischer, 1918); Wassermann, *Mein Weg als Deutscher und Jude* [1921], in *Jakob Wassermann: Deutscher und Jude. Reden und Schriften 1904–1933,* ed. Dierk Rodewald (Heidelberg: Lambert Schneider, 1984); and Rudolf Wolf, ed., *Jakob Wassermann—Werk und Wirkung* (Bonn: Bouvier, 1987).

MARCUS BULLOCK

1928   Erich Fromm joins the Institute for Social Research and begins a ten-year affiliation with the Frankfurt school

The Frankfurt school had a highly ambivalent relation to Judaism. On one hand, its members were part of that Enlightenment tradition that opposed authority, tradition, and all institutions of the past—including religion. They were also, for the most part, secular Jews who did not support any organized religion or practice religious or cultural Judaism. In this sense, they followed the tradition of Heine, Marx, and Freud, for whom Judaism was neither a constitutive feature of their life or work nor a significant aspect of their self-image and identity.

And yet the Frankfurt school's relation to Judaism was varied. Several key members had Orthodox Jewish upbringings, or at least studied and practiced some elements of Judaism. Moreover, for some of the members, Judaism played an important role in their life and work. The Judaic heritage of Walter Benjamin and Erich Fromm figured importantly in key stages of their lives and works. Judaism was of some but arguably not major significance for Leo Lowenthal and Max Horkheimer at different stages of their lives; and Judaism appears not to have been particularly important for Herbert Marcuse and Theodor Adorno.

Yet all Jews were outsiders in Weimar Germany, and all of the Frankfurt school were forced into exile because of their Jewish background after the rise of fascism in 1933. One could argue that the members of the Frankfurt school were also to some extent outsiders in the United States, where they found exile, in part at least because of their Jewishness. At this time, members of the Frankfurt school made anti-Semitism, prejudice, and the situation of the Jews a major thematic focus of their work.

During the years in Weimar prior to the members' emigration in 1934, however, the Frankfurt school did not thematize the issue of the situation of the Jews in their major works, and in a 1938 article the director of the Institute for Social Research, Max Horkheimer, wrote an article entitled "The Jews in Europe," in which anti-Semitism was explained as a mere reflex of the vicissitudes of monopoly capitalism in the end of its liberal phase. During World War II, however, the group began serious studies of anti-Semitism and published some brilliant "Theses on Anti-Semitism" in the seminal text by Horkheimer and Adorno, *Dialectic of Enlightenment* (with Leo Lowenthal adding some material to the "Theses"). In addition, the Frankfurt school published a series of books, *Studies on Prejudice,* which focused on anti-Semitism and which were funded in part by American Jewish groups.

In this entry, I will discuss the ways that Judaism, psychoanalysis, and Marxism intersected in the work of Erich Fromm, constituting a distinctive mode of Jewish writing that combined religion and Enlightenment conceptions. I argue that Fromm was at once traditionally Jewish and radically secular and that his early immersion in Jewish religion and culture came to shape his distinctive views and work.

The Frankfurt school was one of the first groups to bring Freud and psychoanalysis into its social theory. Erich Fromm (1900–1980) was one of the first to carry through a synthesis of Marx and Freud and to develop a Marxian social psychology. Born in Frankfurt in 1900, Fromm was affiliated with the Institute for Social Research from 1928 to 1938. Drawing on his training in psychoanalysis, Fromm combined Freudian psychology with Marxian social theory. Yet Fromm was also deeply immersed in Judaism and later indicated the ways in which he was influenced by the messianic themes in Jewish thought: "More than anything else, I was moved by the prophetic writings, by Isaiah, Amos, Hosea; not so much by their warnings and their announcement of disaster, but by their promise of the 'end of days.' . . . The vision of universal peace and harmony between nations touched me deeply when I was twelve and thirteen years old" (Fromm 1963, 5).

Fromm told the story of how his great-grandfather, Seligmann Fromm, sat all day in his little shop and studied the Talmud. When a customer came in, he would look up and, impatient because of the interruption, might even tell the customer to go to another store. Fromm himself was born into an Orthodox Jewish family, and both of his parents came from families of rabbis. He was deeply influenced by the serious scholarship of his ancestors and was himself a very dedicated scholar who was also strongly animated by a sense of moral values and a passionate desire for justice—motifs influenced by his Jewish upbringing.

Throughout his youth, Fromm was deeply involved in the study of the Talmud. With his friend Leo Lowenthal, who was later an important member of the Frankfurt school, he joined the circle around the eminent Rabbi Nehemiah Nobel, the rabbi of the largest Frankfurt synagogue. Moreover, as Martin Jay documents in another entry in this volume, Fromm was involved in the formation of the Freies Jüdisches Lehrhaus (Free Jewish School) in Frankfurt in the 1920s with Franz Rosenzweig, Martin Buber, and other prominent Jewish intellectuals. It was "free" because there were no restrictions on admission, and it was wholly administered by the teachers and students themselves.

After studying in Frankfurt for two semesters, Fromm went to Heidelberg in 1919, where he studied sociology, psychoanalysis, and philosophy and completed a doctorate in sociology: his dissertation, "Jewish Law: A Contribution to the Sociology of the Jewish Diaspora," was directed by Alfred Weber. While studying in Heidelberg, Fromm became acquainted with Habad Hasidism via Rabbi Salman Rabinkow, who also imbued Fromm with a messianic version of Socialism. Fromm was impressed by the Hasidic emphasis on the importance of the rituals of both everyday life and moral values, as opposed to the intellectualistic rationalism of some forms of Judaic theology.

Fromm's dissertation carried out sociological investigations of three Jewish communities—the Karaites, the Hasidim, and Reform Jewry. Fromm concluded his dissertation by arguing that Hasidism "does not seek to change religion for the sake of the economy but to overcome need through the power of religion. . . . Karaism and Reform lack new religious ideas, they dogmatize religion. Hasidism, in contrast, integrates its specific religious life in the sociological structure of Judaism, avoids dogma, and retains the objective validity of the law. Reform Judaism is the noncreative, ideological way out that takes the place of mass baptism. Hasidism is the creative, religious way out that overcomes pseudo-messianism."

Throughout his life, Fromm distanced himself from dogmas and affirmed more creative and open solutions to the problems of human existence. Although he later moved away from Judaism, it is reported that Fromm never tired of singing Hasidic songs or studying Scripture. In an unpublished memoir on Rabbi Rabinkow summarized in Rainer Funk's book on Fromm, Fromm praises his teacher's synthesis of the politics of protest with traditional Jewish religiosity, as mediated by the spirit of radical humanism.

In the 1920s, Fromm was active in several groups that promoted Jewish religion and culture. He also, as mentioned, helped found the Freies

Jüdisches Lehrhaus, at which he taught for some years. The return to Jewish tradition in Weimar was partly influenced by the extremely precarious economic and political situation, which included outbursts of anti-Semitism. Fromm was deeply involved in the cultural life of Weimar: he became editor of a small Jewish newspaper at age twenty-three and participated in attempts to form a revitalized Jewish community.

In the middle of the 1920s, Fromm was introduced to psychoanalysis via the Jewish psychoanalyst Frieda Reichmann, who later became his wife. Reichmann ran a private psychoanalytic institution in Heidelberg, and because it practiced Jewish traditions, the institute earned the nickname "Torah-peutic Clinic." Fromm himself trained as a psychoanalyst, opened his own practice in 1927, and married Reichmann.

Fromm's first published essay was "The Sabbath." Drawing on psychoanalysis, he argued that "the Sabbath originally served as a reminder of the killing of the father and the winning of the mother; the commandment not to work served as a penance for original sin and for its repetition through regression to the pre-genital stage" (Fromm 1927, 9). Later, Fromm was more sympathetic to the Sabbath; he related it and other religious holy days to the human desire for transcendence, for stepping out of mundane routine, and for consecrating individuals for spiritual goals above and beyond commerce and worldly matters.

Fromm's critical position toward Judaism and bourgeois society at the time was no doubt influenced by his move toward a Socialist humanism that would lead him to attempt to combine Marx, Freud, and, I would argue, a version of a humanism animated by concern with morality and justice that was shaped by his early immersion in Judaism. During the late 1920s, Fromm became a prominent member of the Frankfurt Institute of Psychoanalysis (the second such institute to be formed in Germany, after one in Berlin). He also began lecturing at the Institute for Social Research in Frankfurt and affiliated himself as well with this institute, becoming one of its most influential members during his 1928–38 tenure.

In his essays of the late 1920s and 1930s, Fromm elucidated the common dialectical and materialist elements in Marx and Freud and applied his Marxian social psychology to interpret such phenomena as religion, the sadomasochistic roots of the authoritarian personality, and the dominant bourgeois character types. One of his first major essays was "The Dogma of Christ" (1930; reprinted 1963), and in this work, Fromm argued against the interpretation of the origins of Christianity developed by another psychoanalyst, Theodor Reik. Whereas Reik saw the doctrine in which the Son was of the same single substance as God the Father as a victory for the Oedipal drive to displace the primacy of the father (and thus considered the doctrine analogous to individual compulsive neurotic symptoms), Fromm saw the concept as the result of a long social process in which early Christian radicals matured and accepted equality with the father. Fromm thus rejected both Reik's tendency to see religious phenomena as merely neurotic symptoms and argued for the primacy of sociological developments in explaining religious and other phenomena.

Fromm also presented a quasi positive view of Protestantism, suggesting that its individualism and stress on the activity and belief of the individual indicated a modern era in which it was possible for the masses to play an active role in social life and thought, "as opposed to the infantile-passive attitude of the Middle Ages." In the medieval era, by contrast, Catholicism, with its "veiled regression to the religion of the Great Mother," offered the infantilized masses the fantasy-gratification of being a child loved and cared for by its mother.

In the following years, Fromm would always insist that sociology and psychology must be combined in the study of religious and all other sociocultural phenomena. Fromm sketched the basic outline of his project in his article "The Method and Function of an Analytic Social Psychology," which he subtitled "Notes on Psychoanalysis and Historical Materialism." He argued that Freud's theory, properly interpreted and reconstructed, is compatible with historical materialism. For Fromm, psychoanalysis is a materialist psychology that analyzes instinctual drives and needs as the motive forces for human behavior. It carries out an inventory of the basic instincts and dissects the unconscious forces and mechanisms that sometimes control human behavior. Psychoanalysis also analyzes the influence of specific life experiences on the inherited instinctual constitution. Thus, in Fromm's view, Freud's theory is "exquisitely historical: *it seeks to understand the drive structure through the understanding of life history*" (Fromm 1970, 137–62).

Fromm thus believed that both Freudian and Marxian theory were deeply historical. Perhaps the Judaic emphasis on redemption in historical time, on breaks and ruptures in history, led Fromm to historicist views. In any case, his appropriation of Freud and Marx was always mediated by a strong concern for morality, justice, and the well-being of the individual—motifs that were part of his assimilation of his Jewish heritage.

Yet in the late 1920s Fromm gradually became more critical of organized religion. The key conception of psychoanalysis for Fromm was the "active and passive adaptation of the biological apparatus, the instincts, to social reality." Psychoanalysis is especially valuable for social psychology in that it seeks "to discover the hidden sources of the obviously irrational behavior patterns in societal life—in religion, custom, politics, and education" (Fromm 1970, 141). Fromm thus began to see all organized religion as forms of irrational behavior that manipulated human needs—a conception that was also advanced by Freud in *Future of an Illusion*. In this way, Fromm was definitely distancing himself from Orthodox Judaism.

Moreover, Fromm's position was strongly secular; it identified with the secular ethos of modernity. He believed that an "analytical social psychology" is thoroughly compatible with historical materialism because both are materialist sciences that "do not start from 'ideas' but from earthly life and needs. They are particularly close in their appraisal of consciousness, which is seen by both as less the driving force behind human behavior than the reflection of other hidden forces" (Fromm 1970, 142). Fromm thus came to

reject spirituality as a guiding force in human life and instead saw all intellectual responses as derivative of material needs and social experience.

Yet Fromm never subscribed completely to a reductionist version of either Freudian or Marxian theory. Although historical materialism tends to assume the primacy of economic forces and interests in individual and social life, whereas the psychoanalytic focus is on instinctual and psychological forces, Fromm believed that they could be fruitfully synthesized. In particular, he believed that an analytical social psychology could study the ways that socioeconomic structure influences and shapes the instinctual apparatus of both individuals and groups.

For instance, in Fromm's view, the psychoanalytic emphasis on the primacy of the family in human development could also be given a historical materialist twist. Because "the family is the medium through which the society or the social class stamps its specific structure on the child" (Fromm 1970, 145), analysis of the family and socialization processes can indicate how society reproduces its class structure and imposes its ideologies and practices on individuals. Psychoanalytic theories, Fromm suggested, which abstract their tenets from studies of the ways that a given society socializes its members into accepting and reproducing a specific social structure, tend to take bourgeois society as a norm and to illicitly universalize their findings. Historical materialism corrects these errors by stressing the intrinsically historical nature of all social formations, institutions, practices, and human life.

For Fromm, natural instincts are part of the base (*Unterbau*) of society, and he believed that our understanding of human behavior and social processes would be enriched by reciprocal knowledge of how society molds and adapts instincts to its structures, and how human beings shape and change their environments to meet their needs. "In certain fundamental respects, the instinctual apparatus itself is a biological given; but it is highly modifiable. The role of primary formative factors goes to the economic conditions. The family is the essential medium through which the economic situation exerts its formative influence on the individual's psyche. The task of social psychology is to explain the shared, socially relevant, psychic attitudes and ideologies—and their unconscious roots in particular—in terms of the influence of economic conditions on libido strivings" (Fromm 1970, 149).

Fromm's belief in a core of human nature that is shaped by society, yet possesses its own dynamic structure, combined the instinct theory of Freud and the humanism of Martin Buber, who also stressed the primacy of social relations in shaping human beings (though Buber's focus was more ethical than instinctual). Later, Fromm would attempt to define what he considered basic human needs, some derived from human biology (for example, needs for food and sex); others from an individual's societal perspective (such as the need for relatedness); and still others from human spirituality (for instance, the need for meaning and transcendence).

Following Marx, Fromm believed that ideologies played a key role in shaping human thought and behavior and that psychoanalysis could help explain how socioeconomic interests and structures are transformed into ideologies, as well as how ideologies shape and influence human thought and behavior. Such a merger of Marx and Freud would, in Fromm's view, immeasurably enrich materialist social theory by providing an analysis of the mediations through which psyche and society interact and reciprocally shape each other. Every society, he claimed, has its own libidinal structure and processes whereby authority is reproduced in human thought and behavior. An analytical social psychology must thus be deeply empirical to explain how domination and submission take place in specific societies, in order to provide understanding of how social and psychological change is possible.

For the next several decades, Fromm was an important force in advocating a Marxian humanism that would be concerned with both the full development of the individual and the creation of a just and egalitarian society. Such a project was obviously thwarted by the rise of fascism, and Fromm and his fellow members of the Institute for Social Research, in exile in the United States after 1934, dedicated much effort to clarifying this strange phenomenon of an aggressively anti-

modern doctrine appearing in the midst of modernity and utilizing modern techniques of communication and manipulation to control the masses, as well as modern technology to carry out an imperialist war and a war against the Jews.

Forced to flee from Nazi Germany in 1933, Fromm settled in the United States and lectured at the New School for Social Research, Columbia, Yale, and Bennington. In the late 1930s, Fromm broke with the Institute for Social Research, and with *Escape from Freedom* (1941), he began publishing a series of books that would win him a large audience in the United States and eventually throughout the world.

Escape from Freedom argued that alienation from soil and community in the transition from feudalism to capitalism increased insecurity and fear. Documenting some of the strains and crises of individualism, Fromm attempted to explain how alienated individuals seek gratification and security from social orders such as fascism. Protestantism, with its emphasis on individual salvation and damnation, increased individuals' fear and made them susceptible, he argued, to social powers. Moreover, capitalism, with its emphasis on individual gain and its harsh market that mediated success and failure, also contributed to feelings of insecurity. Migrations from country to towns and factories, central to industrial modernity, created a new urban civilization that increased individuals' feelings of rootlessness.

In the late 1930s, Fromm broke with the Frankfurt school, in part over his interpretation of Freud and in part over personality conflicts with key members such as Adorno and Marcuse. Henceforth, Fromm would go his own way. He often appeared as a prophet in the desert of American affluence and consumerism as he attacked the "marketing orientation," the bourgeois proclivity to privilege, having over being, and indeed the entire American system of institutions and values.

Fromm's post–World War II books, *Man for Himself* (1947) and *The Sane Society* (1955), applied his Freudian-Marxian perspectives to sharp critiques of contemporary capitalism. Fromm popularized the neo-Marxian critiques of the media and consumer society, and he promoted democratic Socialist perspectives during an era when social repression made it difficult and dangerous to advocate radical positions. Although his social critique was similar in many ways to that of his former colleague Herbert Marcuse, the two thinkers engaged in sharp polemics from the mid-1950s into the 1970s. Marcuse began the argument by attacking Fromm as a neo-Freudian revisionist, and Fromm retaliated by calling Marcuse a "nihilist" and "utopian." Marcuse claimed that Fromm's emphasis on the "productive character" simply reproduced the "productivism" intrinsic to capitalism, and that his celebration of the values of love, in books like *The Art of Loving* (1957), and religious values simply reproduced dominant idealist ideologies.

Part of the split between Fromm and Marcuse might have resulted from their various responses to Judaism. Although Fromm distanced himself in the 1920s from organized Jewish religion, Jewish motifs and values continued to animate his work. Marcuse, meanwhile, committed himself to more secular goals—notably to the happiness and gratification of the individual—as well as to a revolutionary overthrow of existing society. Like Marcuse, Fromm maintained staunch Socialist and anticapitalist perspectives, but he was more committed than Marcuse to Enlightenment values and a version of moral humanism. Perhaps Fromm's radicalism—and that of the Frankfurt school—derived in part from his outsider status as a Jew forced into exile. But in Fromm's case, it was the Jewish commitment to values, justice, and community that shaped his particular set of values, his critical position, and his commitment to Marxian Socialism and humanism.

Fromm's aversion to the horrors of the world wars made him suspicious of nationalism, and although he was briefly a Zionist in the 1920s, he was critical of Israel's policy toward Arabs and of Jews who supported their oppression. Rather, Fromm's humanism was broad and ecumenical and his desire for justice universal. In 1966, he published a book on the Old Testament, *You Shall Be as Gods,* in which he developed "a radical interpretation of the Old Testament and its Tradition."

Fromm continued to be a prolific writer until his death in 1980. He published a series of books promoting and developing his unique synthesis of Marxian, Freudian, and Judaic inspired or inflected ideas. He was also politically active: he helped organize the Society for an Anti-Nuclear Environment (SANE), engaged in early "Ban the Bomb" campaigns, and participated in the antiwar movement of the 1960s. Fromm continued to argue for a humanistic and democratic Socialist position and claimed that such elements were intrinsic in Marxism. His many books and articles had some influence on the New Left and a broad public, and they continue to be widely read and discussed today.

Fromm thus represents a unique blend of secular and religious writing, influenced at once by Judaism, the Enlightenment, Marxism, Freud, and other forms of humanist and radical thought. He represents a form of thought that is radically secular and yet attempts to preserve elements of Jewish culture that he deems valuable. At times, Fromm himself adopted a prophetic style and always fought for justice and a more humane social organization.

Bibliography

Daniel Burston, *The Legacy of Erich Fromm* (Cambridge, Mass.: Harvard University Press, 1991); Erich Fromm, *The Art of Loving* (New York: Bantam, 1956); Fromm, *Beyond the Chains of Illusion* (New York: Pocket Books, 1965); Fromm, *The Crisis of Psychoanalysis* (Greenwich, Conn.: Fawcett Premier, 1970); Fromm, "The Dogma of Christ" (New York: Holt, Rinehart and Winston, 1963); Fromm, *Escape from Freedom* (New York: Holt, Rinehart and Winston, 1941); Fromm, "Das jüdische Gesetz: Ein Beitrag zur Soziologie des Diasporajudentums," Ph.D. diss., University of Heidelberg, 1922; Fromm, *Man for Himself* (New York: Holt, Rinehart and Winston, 1947); Fromm, "Der Sabbath," *Imago* (Vienna: Internationaler Psychoanalytischer Verlag, 1927); Fromm, *The Sane Society* (New York: Holt, Rinehart and Winston, 1955); Fromm, *Ye Shall Be as Gods* (Greenwich, Conn.: Fawcett Premier, 1966); Rainer Funk, *Erich Fromm: The Courage to Be Human* (New York: Continuum, 1982); Douglas Kellner, *Critical Theory, Marxism, and Modernity* (Baltimore, Md.: Johns Hopkins University Press, 1989); and Rolf Wiggershaus, *The Frankfurt School: Its History, Theories and Political Significance* (London: Polity Press, 1993).

DOUGLAS KELLNER

1928   The first issue of the *Jewish Children's Calendar,* edited by Emil Bernhard Cohn, is published in cooperation with the Commission on Literary Works for Youth of the Grand Lodge for Germany of the Independent Order of B'nai B'rith

Various aspects of the historical development of German-Jewish literature for children and young adults are intertwined in the *Jewish Children's Calendar,* which critics have celebrated as exemplary. The work appeared during a period of intensive publication in this branch of literature, whose history reflects many facets of German-Jewish cultural relations. Moreover, the *Calendar's* content points to a change in function that is significant for the further development of Jewish children's and young adult literature after 1933.

The *Calendar* shows that this genre—which was accorded a high rank in Jewish pedagogy—was not the least important area in which the transfer of German-Jewish culture took place. On the one hand, the great significance traditionally placed on knowledge and education by Jewish culture contributed to this view; on the other, the general character of children's and young adult literature as a means of enculturation led to this high level of respect.

Cohn's children's calendar was brought out in cooperation with the Independent Order of B'nai B'rith's (IOBB) Commission on Literary Works for Youth (Jugendschriftenkommission), which had been founded in 1904 in connection with the youth literature movement. Directed at first toward children and later increasingly toward Jewish youth, the *Calendar* is an anthology that appeared between 1928 and 1936. Addressing his readers in the guise of the comical figure "Uncle Josua Witzmacher (Joke-maker)," chief editor Cohn asserts that there is "only one undivided Jewish youth," regardless of whether it "speaks German, Hebrew or Yiddish, whether it is western or eastern, whether it wants to go to Erez Israel or to remain in Germany" (3:124). The volumes' contents are arranged according to an entertaining principle of alternation, and the variety of texts they contain testifies to the literary pluralism characteristic of the 1920s. Included are poetry, short stories, and shadow games using puppets, as well as many riddles, plays for children's theater, Hanukkah fairy tales, directions for arts and crafts projects, songs, biographical stories of exemplary Jews, picture stories, legends and comical tales, dice games, reports from the Jewish sports movement, and Zionist news about Palestine.

The *Calendar* was innovative in a variety of ways. The distinctly humorous basis was a novelty for Jewish children's literature, a gain whose significance for the genre's production in the 1920s lies in the vast increase in entertainment value for its audience. And the many illustrations exhibited a new level of quality for Jewish young adult literature (the calendar of religious holidays for the first issue created by Nina Brodsky, for example, reveals a great affinity for modern Russian painters such as Chagall). A further noteworthy aspect is the modernity of the overall conception of the *Calendar,* which ranges from the idea of reader participation in the production of texts to the selection of contents and linguistic form. The *Calendar*'s modern understanding of childhood is especially advanced in outlook, and with this work, Jewish children's literature found itself in the vanguard.

The main intention of the edition is to inculcate its young readers with a self-consciousness that is equally balanced between German and Jewish cultures. Because of the overwhelming influence of the German culture, the *Calendar* strove to communicate to young Jews of all backgrounds a feeling of belonging to a common Jewish culture. Thus, for example, Jewish inventors are portrayed in order to emphasize the contribution of Jews to European cultural history. In addition, the work's highly diverse contributions display their shared concern in the deliberate affirmation of Jewish identity.

In tune with the tenor of the times, anti-Semitism and the intensifying persecution of the Jews in Germany are seismographically reproduced in the *Calendar:* from the beginning, readers are emphatically encouraged to defend themselves against anti-Jewish behavior in their daily surroundings. Even in the first issue of 1928, for example, a shadow game describes how an omen—the Menetekel—appears to Belsazar in the form of a swastika; the children are openly warned: "Be afraid of this kind of cross, / For it portends a terrible loss" (1:120). After 1933 the call for resistance against anti-Semitism was accompanied more and more by barely veiled exhortations to emigrate. The focus in the 1934 issue was the fate of the Marranos—a historical tale that serves as an anticipatory warning of the expulsion and destruction of the German Jewry—and the appeal of a Zionist reorientation toward life in Palestine, which was amplified with factual reports. This literarily demanding *Calendar,* which was first published to strengthen Jewish self-consciousness as an integral part of German culture, ended in 1936 with an awareness of renewed separation, a warning of threatened destruction, and implicit calls to emigration.

As a whole, Cohn's *Calendar* contains a mixture of the most important pedagogical ideas concerning Jewish children's literature in the Weimar Republic. In general, the German-Jewish young adult literature of this period reveals both traditional and modern influences, as older pedagogical theories concerning literature and its function—which only began to undergo experimental revision to any great degree in the 1920s—were adopted partly unchanged and partly in modified form.

A striking conscious promotion of a specifically Jewish children's and young adult literature, written in German and presented in a way appropriate to its audience, had been developed since the Haskalah. With regard to the process of acculturation, which was supported by both reformist pedagogy and the neo-Orthodoxy, this literature had since filled the complementary function of fostering both emancipatory deghettoization and the protection of Jewish self-determination. Until 1933, pedagogues for the most part were agreed with this view of literature. Their concordance was not adversely affected by the organization of the German Jewry into various groups because this view allowed for distinctions and internal divisions associated with diversity.

Although its fundamental basis remained unchanged, this conception of literature underwent a characteristic change of accent in the 1920s as many texts began to self-consciously emphasize the independence and equal worth of the Jewish culture (no longer especially distinguished by religion). In this regard, the Jewish youth literature movement at the turn of the century was pathbreaking: in fact, in its debate, which concentrated on biography and the fairy tale (conducted in, among other places, Spanier's *Wegweiser* [Signpost]), an altered consciousness can already be discerned. The initial affirmative reception of Heinrich Wolgast's work, for example, gave way to a modification of his theses according to how Jews of this era measured their identity and cultural independence. The development of this pedagogical theory of literature had aftereffects well into the 1920s—the debate returned at the end of the decade and continued on into the 1930s—and it led to a creative flood of literary publications that put the theory into practice. As if in answer to the theoretical demands for the rejection of anti-Semitic writings and for the development of a modern Jewish young adult literature appropriate to the changed circumstances of the times, a shift toward innovation and aestheticism occurred in the 1920s, especially in the area of children's and young adult belles lettres.

The complaint concerning the lack of suitable works of Jewish young adult literature had set the tone of the public debate since the end of the empire. From that time on, with growing success, a threefold strategy was used in an attempt to remedy this deficiency: anti-Semitic tendencies were to be avoided, adult German-Jewish literature was to be included to a greater degree (so that the canon of works for youth could be significantly enlarged), and the Jewish literature that was expressly intended for children and young adults was to be modified. What began as a mostly defensive and support-seeking publication emerged as an aggressive contribution to Jewish young adult belles lettres. The introduction of specific series of children's and young adult literature—for example, the Bar Kochba Jugendbücherei (Bar Kochba youth library; 1920)—was a part of the last-named approach. A simpler solution for publishers was found in anthologies thematically related to Jewish culture, an example of which is the three-volume collection *Für unsere Jugend* (For our youth; 1911–26), edited by Elias Gut. With such literature stamped by Jewishness, decidedly "Jewish" reading materials for young people were to be made available and the reading habits of young Jews, which were in no way limited to Jewish topics, were to be influenced in a culturally specific way.

The young adult literature of the Weimar Republic acquired a developmentally new impulse with Zionism; not until 1918 was an appreciable portion of the spectrum of young adult literary texts for the first time markedly Zionist. Remarkably, the influence of Zionism on the Jewish pedagogy of literature was noticeably slow in exerting its force. An intensive Zionist production

of young adult literature began to develop in Germany only after World War I, and it was revived with great consequence in the completely changed political climate after 1933.

One reason for this lag was that the German Zionist movement, which had been intensified by the Balfour Declaration in 1917, was primarily supported by the underclass of Eastern European Jewish immigrants, whereas the bourgeois majority of the Jewish population in Germany had long distanced themselves from Zionism because they regarded it as endangering their integration as German citizens. Because of these reservations, a Zionist pedagogy and Zionist children's and young adult literature first became visible in Germany in the 1920s. A comparatively early example is the eight-volume *Schriften des Ausschusses für jüdische Kulturarbeit: Jüdische Jugendbücher* (Writings for the committee for Jewish cultural work: Jewish young adult books; 1920). This series, attributable to the initiative of Salman Schocken, included only newly composed texts related to Jewish themes—some of which were Zionist—that were thus of great current interest.

Zionism contributed significantly to a secularization and politicization of Jewish children's and young adult literature during the course of the 1920s. Above all, this remolding transpired in connection with the Jewish youth movement, a process that can be particularly clearly traced in the quickly disseminated political pamphlets and magazines of youth organizations such as Blau Weiß, Hechaluz, Kadima, or Haschomer Hazair, among others. Martin Buber's writings were especially influential in the Zionist youth movement; Siegfried Bernfeld was another programmatic theoretician, whose foundational work *Das jüdische Volk und seine Jugend* (The Jewish people and their youth; 1919) outlined a Zionist educational utopia. On the whole, agreement between the liberal Jewry and Zionism can be stated too. In the area of literature, this concerned, among other things, the discovery of Eastern European Jewish literature in the 1890s and beyond. Moreover, the Zionist production of young adult literature supported the movement toward learning Hebrew. Sharing in equal measure a retrospective sensibility for Jewish culture, both liberal Jews and Zionists supported the movement to publish young adult literature.

The emphasis on the inner worth of Jewish culture that was so fruitful for the development of children's and young adult literature had other causes in additon to Zionism. A socioeconomic precondition for the pluralism then developing in this literature was the expansion of Jewish publishing facilities. Another reason was the disappointment of the German Jews' hopes of integration, which had already been connected with imperial nationalism before receiving a boost from the intensified patriotism during World War I. Despite German Jews' official equality in the Weimar Republic, increasing anti-Semitism, in combination with economic depression, significantly helped to perpetuate their position as a separate social group. Relevant here was a turning point that was reached in 1916: the census of Jews in the German military conducted that year in the interests of anti-Semitism had a distinctly sobering effect on the expectations of emancipation. The shock was registered in young adult literature and can be discerned, for example, in Jakob Loewenberg's *Kriegstagebuch einer Mädchenschule* (War diary of a girl's school; 1916). An attack upon the anti-Semitic segregation of Jews, this text is a demonstration of the patriotism of the German Jewry.

The swift increase in the criticism of assimilation—no longer practiced solely in orthodox texts of young adult literature—is symptomatic of this disillusionment, and the Jewish reaction not only consisted of resistance to anti-Semitism (following the example of the Centralverein deutscher Staatsbürger jüdischen Glaubens [Association of German Citizens of the Jewish Faith]) but also was characterized by a new appreciation for the inner worth of Jewish culture.

To sum up, Jewish children's and young adult literature remained tied to available texts and older pedagogical ideas until the rise in production of the middle 1920s led to an immense expansion of the literary market. With increasing speed, the development of new literary forms—ranging from broad differentiation of styles to an experimental pluralism of presentation—followed upon the heels of a sluggish early phase.

Such pluralism was the chief characteristic of the Jewish children's and young adult literature during the Weimar era.

Blossoming until 1938 in an unprecedented variety of forms, the Jewish children's fairy tale offers the most impressive example of this development. Literary critical recognition of fantasy within Jewish pedagogy was slow to be awarded. Having long been regarded as a potential source of irrationality and as an attack upon reason and monotheism, fantasy had been rejected by critics, who relied on both enlightened and neo-Orthodox positions. Such reservations were shared entirely by the general contemporary theory of children's literature, and it was only with the psychoanalytically oriented criticism of the 1920s and 1930s that the fairy tale was judged to have special value as a forum for the articulation of the unconscious. In the field of Jewish children's literature, Tom Seidmann-Freud created artistically unique picture books whose illustrations were stylistically related to New Objectivity and whose contents were markedly psychological. For example, *Die Fischreise* (The fish journey; 1923), translates a childlike inner world into images reminiscent of a dream.

The significant potential for innovation represented by the diversity of fairy tales created in the 1920s can be appreciated if we remember that no artistic fairy tales written for Jewish children had been available until the turn of the century. With the newly discovered realm of the fairy tale, Jewish authors consequently created for themselves a free space for improvisation that was unencumbered by the weight of tradition, and they advanced into this area of belles lettres with increased intensity from 1918 until the end of the 1930s. Thus, the Jewish children's fairy tale quickly displayed a great richness of variation: Max Nordau became known as a writer of nature fairy tales; Babette Fried and Frieda Weissmann filled the demand for religiously orthodox pedagogical fables; Heinrich Loewe, Siegfried Abeles, and Simon Neumann created Zionist children's fairy tales; religious and moralistic parables serving the education of childlike consciences were brought out by Heinrich Reuß, Hermann Schwab, and Else Ury; Lina Wagner-

Tauber wrote fairy tales in the style of the Torah or Midrashim writings; and Irma Mirjam Berkowitz, Siegfried Abeles, and Ilse Weber produced belletristically oriented children's fairy tales. In 1928, this blossoming of artistic fairy tales created for Jewish children was narratively described by Ilse Herlinger (in a post-romantic imitation of W. Hauff) in her *Märchen vom Märchen* (A fairy tale of the fairy tale).

After an earlier period dominated by religious pedagogical literature and borrowings from adult readings, the Weimar years can be characterized as the first flowering of belletristic Jewish children's and young adult literature. Although fairy tales came to dominate the realm of children's literature, the young adult story (in a broadly diverse spectrum) and the adolescent novel became the chief narrative forms available to young adult readers. Both quantitatively and qualitatively, the 1920s produced a German Jewish literature of superior value; distinguished by its push toward modernization, its chief characteristic was its openness to innovation and variety. In illustration of the breadth of literary offerings that was attained, the listing here of a few genres and leading authors will have to suffice: anthologies related to the Talmud and Midrash as well as to contemporary literature (Steinhardt); journals (Klötzel); comical puppet games (Baerwald, Baer, and Baer-Freyer); picture books (Seidmann-Freud); young adult stories (Abeles, Flanter); religious pedagogical stories, for instance, about exemplary biblical figures (Einstädter, Prinz); fairy tales, poetry (Loewenberg); folkloristic Hasidic tales (Bloch, Buber); holiday stories (Ehrmann, Flanter, Ludwig); girls' books (Samson); Zionist adventure stories directed to male youths (Böhm, Gelbart, Simon, Smolly); and adolescent novels (Winder, Thomas).

The main tenet of these texts was German-Jewish self-determination, which was represented as a goal that was attainable but would have to be struggled for. Along these lines, H. Freudenberger's anthology for young adults is entitled *Im Kampf um die Menschenrechte* (In the struggle for human rights; 1927). The contemporary young adult literature, however, offers counterexamples that articulate the shadows of this double-sided, finely balanced self-determination and that, in regard to the conflicts of acculturation, warn the Jewish minority about possible failure. It is primarily these texts—those that highlight the dark side of the idea of German-Jewish cultural symbiosis—that, to an unprecedented degree, introduce modern elements into Jewish children's and, above all, young adult literature.

Cheskel Zwi Klötzel, for example, contributed significantly to bringing objectivity and currency into Jewish young adult narrative literature (to that extent he is comparable to Erich Kästner). Not only with its title figure did Klötzel's youth magazine *Bar Kochba* (1919–21) shift the focal point to a commitment to a powerful Jewry. The magazine published Klötzel's story *Moses Pipenbrinks Abenteuer* (Moses Pipenbrink's adventure; book ed. 1920), which contains an adaptation of the tale of the biblical Moses. Depicting a childhood preoccupied with finding a Jewish home and identity, the story relates a childlike search for a homeland that reflects the Jewish people's experience of exile. For Moses, the familiar dwelling place amidst non-Jewish culture is by itself insufficient and remains a temporary refuge. What is remarkable here is that the portrayal of Moses' path through life already reflects the modern understanding of such a journey as a search that can never be concluded.

In Edmond Fleg's *Ein kleiner Prophet* (A little prophet; 1927), the degree to which a boy with religious and cultural self-determination as a Jew must orient himself toward resistance and negative experiences is brought to narrative expression. The leitmotif of this childhood, shown from an inner view of psychological development, is a securing of Jewish identity that is in the end successful, although it is marked by a succession of crises.

From the area of adult literature, Jakob Wassermann's autobiography *Mein Weg als Deutscher und Jude* (My path as German and Jew; 1921) was taken over as young adult reading matter. It is an account that is written out of a sense of self-worth that mediates between "German" and "Jewish." Because this theme was controversial for the whole of German-Jewish literature, this book, which placed its main focus on the problematic of German-Jewish self-determination and articulated it sharply for the first time, became a seminal work with which the German Jewry could identify. Although the genre of biography had up to that point been more inclined toward harmony, it here incorporated the omens of disharmony and contradiction that were symptomatic of the situation of German Jews.

A short time later, Felix Salten brought out his famous animal novel *Bambi* (1923), a multi-layered text that thematizes the psychological development of the basic conflict between childhood and adolescence. Salten's depiction of nature serves, among other things, to convey the idea of a basic equality of all creatures over and above the affirmation of their diversity, a message that can be heard on the level of cultural differences and criticism of assimilation. Jewish readers could abstract his call for respect for the natural differences among the creatures and apply it to yet another aspect of cultural difference; according to this reading, the novel contains a skeptical warning against a Jewish readiness to assimilate that was going too far, that would lead to the loss of identity and that was a threat to the Jews' very existence. To this extent, Salten's novel can also be read as a literary problemitizing of human and cultural bonds prudently placed on another level; it reflects the necessity—if they were to survive—for the German Jews to recognize and accept a cultural self-determination that had to be carried out (at least) twice.

From the area of forbidden young adult readings, a further example is Ludwig Winder's adolescent novel *Hugo: Tragödie eines Knaben* (Hugo: A boy's tragedy: 1924), which portrays the awakening of youthful sexuality as a problematic experience. Hugo's sexual self-acceptance fails; his "search for happiness" ends in pain, in being "crippled" (231), and in "being shut out from the beginning on" (139). In the end, Hugo's life ends tragically after an ambivalent physical advance that is probably meant as a gesture of affection but which he perceives as a threat. This depiction of youth closes with a death scene of failed communication that can be transposed to the German-Jewish "dialogue." On account of its

thematic openness, critical clarity, and psychological truthfulness, this novel is conspicuous in the spectrum of German-Jewish young adult literature. Decisive here is the new dominance of the portrayal of the Jewish youth's despair over his status as outsider and his sense of rupture.

Although the 1920s had already brought warnings, which were mostly beneath the surface and more subtle than in Cohn's Menetekel scene, the National Socialists' takeover of power in 1933 precipitated a clear breach of Jewish rights. The Jewish literary community responded by radically changing the function assigned to Jewish children's and young adult literature. In view of the changed political portents of racist-motivated persecution and destruction, writings for Jewish children and young adults in Germany were transformed into a literature of resistance, exile, and self-assertion. With Zionism now markedly predominant, this literature encouraged Jewish children to transfer their concept of homeland from Germany to Palestine—and thus abandoned the function of fostering a German-Jewish identity that it had been charged with since the Haskalah. Characteristic from this point on is the division of attention between the old homeland and the new, as, for example, in Strauß's *Zauberdrachenschnur* (Magic kite string; 1936). Equally symptomatic was Berkowitz's titling of a children's book *Benni fliegt ins gelobte Land* (Benni flies to the promised land; 1936); in the guise of literary fantasy, this story anticipates segregation and banishment.

The ghettoization brought about by the National Socialists' policy of deassimilation caused a tremendous intensification in young adult literature. However, in contrast to the earlier period of belletristic blossoming in the 1920s, this second flowering of belles lettres for Jewish children and young adults signaled the end of the German Jewry's efforts toward acculturation and emancipation. The significance of Palestine as a homeland is urgently emphasized in these texts, as Zionism now disclosed the most important perspective on the future. Connected with this demand for emigration was the expectation of sloughing off the role of outsider that was bound up with existence in the Diaspora—in this sense, the stakes were raised from a mere future hope to a strategy for survival. This situation quickly found expression on the textual level in a Jewish young adult literature that was from this point on dominated by Zionism and that helped Jewish youth prepare mentally for emigration.

Even though the existential threat could mostly only be hinted at in young adult books because of the conditions of censorship after 1933, and despite the many illusory hopes that this literature expressed, as a whole it nevertheless contains remarkably little escapism. In the narratives brought out until the liquidation of the Jewish publishing facilities in 1938, Jewish childhood and adolescence stand in the center of literary attention, illuminated by a modern pedagogy oriented toward political resistance. In a quick reaction, the ideals conveyed to youth were adjusted to reflect a powerful Jewry, and the warning calls for emigration are by no means contained only in Zionist writings. In addition, a not-to-be underestimated potential for resistance lies in the unofficial subtexts of this literature. For example, Hirsch's *Gespräch im Nebel* (Conversation in the mist; 1935) contains a cloaked but urgent reminder of the need for political responsibility and renunciation of the National Socialists' policy of deassimilation.

After a current of discontent, contradiction, and crisis had been articulated in the diversity characteristic of the children's and young adult literature of the 1920s, the accent in this literature during the 1930s was in the end placed upon deep skepticism and disillusionment. Having traced the political and ideological circumstances that had become existence-threatening for Jewish youth in National Socialist Germany, this literature issued a clear warning against acculturation.

Bibliography

Werner T. Angress, *Between Fear and Hope: Jewish Youth in the Third Reich* (New York: Columbia University Press, 1988); Wolfgang Benz, ed., *Die Juden in Deutschland, 1933–1945* (Munich: Beck, 1988). Reiner Bernstein, "Zwischen Emanzipation und Antisemitismus: Die Publizistik der deutschen Juden am Beispiel der 'C.V.-Zeitung,' Organ des Centralvereins deutscher Staatsbürger jüdischen Glaubens, 1924–1933," Ph.D. diss., University of Berlin, 1969; Emil Bernhard Cohn, ed., *Jüdischer Kinderkalender / Jüdischer Jugendkalender / Jüdisches Jugendbuch*, vols. 1–6 (Berlin: Jüdischer Verlag, 1928 / 29–1936); Volker Dahm, *Das jüdische Buch im Dritten Reich*, rev. ed. (Munich: Beck, 1993); Harald Flasdick, "Literaturkritik in jüdischen Periodika der Weimarer Republik," Ph.D. diss., University of Wuppertal, 1988; Thomas S. Hansen, "Emil and the Emigrés: German Children's Literature in Exile, 1933–1945," *Phaedrus* 11 (1985): 6–12; Jutta Hetkamp, "Die jüdische Jugendbewegung von 1913–1933," Ph.D. diss., University of Essen, 1991; Hans Otto Horch, "Admonitio Judaica: Jüdische Debatten über Kinder- und Jugendliteratur im 19. und beginnenden 20. Jahrhundert," *Das Bild des Juden in der Volks- und Jugendliteratur vom 18. Jahrhundert bis 1945*, ed. Heinrich Pleticha (Würzburg: Königshausen & Neumann, 1985), 85–102, 179–228; Horch, *Auf der Suche nach der jüdischen Erzählliteratur: Die Literaturkritik der "Allgemeinen Zeitung des Judentums" (1837–1922)* (Frankfurt a. M.: Peter Lang, 1985); Dirk Krüger, *Die deutsch-jüdische Kinder- und Jugendbuchautorin Ruth Rewald und die Kinder- und Jugendliteratur im Exil* (Frankfurt a. M.: dipa, 1990); Zwi Erich Kurzweil, *Hauptströmungen jüdischer Pädagogik in Deutschland von der Aufklärung bis zum Nationalsozialismus* (Frankfurt a. M.: Diesterweg, 1987), 83–112; Hans Lamm, "Jüdische Kinder- und Jugendliteratur in Deutschland vor und nach 1933: Antijüdische Kinderbücher nach 1933," *Das Bild des Juden in der Volks- und Jugendliteratur vom 18. Jahrhundert bis 1945*, ed. Heinrich Pleticha (Würzburg: Königshausen & Neumann, 1985), 103–6, 229–40; Hans Jochen Markmann, "Jüdische Jugendbucher zwischen Machtergreifung und Novemberpogrom," *Fundevogel* 68 (1989): 8–12, and *Fundevogel* 69 (1989): 4–8; Glenn Richard Sharfman, *The Jewish Youth Movement in Germany, 1900–1936: A Study in Ideology and Organization* (Chapel Hill: University of North Carolina Press, 1989); Zohar Shavit et al., *Deutsch-jüdische Kinder- und Jugendliteratur: Von der Haskala bis 1945. Die deutsch- und hebräischsprachigen Schriften des deutschsprachigen Raums. Ein bibliographisches Handbuch* (Stuttgart: Metzler, 1995); Joseph Walk, *Jüdische Schule und Erziehung im Dritten Reich* (Frankfurt a. M.: Hain, 1991); Ludwig Winder, *Hugo: Tragödie eines Knaben* (Vienna: Rikoli, 1924); and Heinrich Wolgast, *Das Elend unserer Jugendliteratur: Ein Beitrag zur künstlerischen Erziehung der Jugend* (Hamburg: Selbstverlag, 1899).

ANNEGRET VÖLPEL

1932 Gertrud Kolmar completes her poetry cycle
Weibliches Bildnis and thus reshapes her identity
as a Jewish woman poet

In 1932, Gertrud Kolmar finished more than fifty poems of the cycle *Weibliches Bildnis*, which focuses on the lives of different women, from wanderers, witches, dancers, and gardeners to mothers and daughters. Most of the poems are written in the first person, giving a lyrical cohesion and thematic unity to them; but in many ways, all of the poems revolve around one poem in the cycle, "Die Jüdin." In "Die Jüdin," Kolmar undertakes the dual project of reviving Jewish traditions while at the same time creating spaces within German and Jewish literary traditions for the enunciation of a female voice. Her desire to base a new identity in sacred history and the most sacred of Jewish texts, the Bible, was intricately bound with her sense of the textual traditions of Judaism and her awareness of her exclusion from those traditions because she was a woman. The marginalization and alienation experienced by the women personae in *Weibliches Bildnis* all reflect Kolmar's experience as a Jewish woman living in Germany in the 1920s and 1930s. Each of the poems in this cycle represents an aspect of German-Jewish identity that Kolmar struggled with—from misogynistic and anti-Semitic stereotypes of Jewish female sexuality as vampiric in "Verwandlung" to feelings of being outcast and homeless in "Die Landstreicherin" to a bitter awareness of her exclusion from male literary traditions in "Die Dichterin."

Kolmar felt excluded not only as a woman poet but also as a Jewish poet. She tried to get *Weibliches Bildnis* published from 1932 through 1933, and even found an advocate for the poems in Ina Seidel, who helped publish four of Kolmar's poems—three from *Weibliches Bildnis*—in the 1933 collection of German women's writing, *Herz zum Hafen*. But on February 15, 1933, the cycle was rejected by the publisher Seidel had lined up for her. The timing of the rejection was not lost upon Kolmar, who, according to Karl Josef Keller, complained that she felt that her "Aryan" acquaintances and contacts had suddenly abandoned her after Hitler's rise to power (Woltmann 1993, 79).

Jewish and female identities were inextricably bound for Kolmar, and what becomes apparent in her poetry is that Kolmar's work derives much of its power from its situation at the juncture of the women's and Zionist movements. Although she was not an "active" participant in either of these movements, her works are marked throughout by a conscious engagement with discourses of the "modern woman" in general, and of modern Jewish women in particular. Kolmar's sister, Hilde Wenzel, claims in her afterword to the 1980 collection of Kolmar's poems, also entitled *Weibliches Bildnis*, that Kolmar's interest in Zionism and revolutionary politics began at an early age: "The only one out of the whole family, she was already as a young girl open to Zionist thinking, and consciously rejected the influence of the Wilhelminian era even though her father was under its sway, in spite of his commitment to Judaism" (772). But

Kolmar, like her cousin Walter Benjamin, was never an ardent Zionist, in spite of the movement's effect on her work and thinking.

Kolmar's response to the discourses of modern Jewish nationalism was mediated by her awareness of the marginalization of Jewish women in these discourses. Her elder contemporary, Else Lasker-Schüler, considered her poetry to be a contribution to Zionism, but felt that this contribution was underappreciated. In her 1937 travel memoir *Das Hebräerland* she asserts: "I participated in the building of Palestine through the writing of my Hebrew Ballads; I've not been idle with regards to God's work." In her wonderfully ironic way, she continues: "And, credulous as I am sometimes, it makes me happy that the woman poet counts for something in the fatherland. (Lasker-Schüler 1986, 31). Lasker-Schüler's wry acknowledgment that the work of a woman poet was not necessarily valued in the "fatherland," whether it was Palestine or Germany, indicates the sort of resistance that even the most famous Jewish women writers faced. (The fact that her work *did* play some role, at least in the German Zionist movement, is alluded to by Gershom Scholem, who testifies in his autobiography *From Berlin to Jerusalem* [1980, 45] that Lasker-Schüler's "Hebrew Ballads" were read at German Zionist meetings in the 1910s.) This is the same dilemma Kolmar faced as she sought to reconstruct and expand notions of Jewish identity to include expressions of modern German-Jewish women's identities. Her project as a writer was intricately bound with her sense of the textual traditions of Judaism and modern Jewish nationalism, as well as her awareness of her marginality as a Jewish woman. Although "Die Jüdin" expresses Kolmar's consciousness of her marginalized position as Jew and woman in German society, it reaffirms her desire to rewrite traditionally male-centered discourses of Jewishness.

In her search for new configurations of Jewish identity, Kolmar, like many of her contemporaries, turned to the East. Through their encounters with Jews and Jewish traditions from the East and through the works of Martin Buber (especially his popularizations of Hasidic legends, which began to appear in 1906), German Jews began to reevaluate the spiritual importance of Judaism in their lives. Kolmar's relationship to the East, Eastern Jews, Russia, and Palestine occurred within the context of a nuanced German-Jewish "Orientalism"—that is, the "Orientalism" of Jews who themselves were continually represented as being from the East, even if they had been living in the West for generations. Although anti-Semitic discourses of the 1920s and 1930s represented Jews as being both "foreign" and "Eastern," for European Jews at the beginning of this century the East began to symbolize not only Eastern Europe and Russia, but also the ancient and nascent homeland developing in Palestine. In their search for both cultural and political rootedness, the East—encompassing both the Diaspora experience in Russia and the developing state of Israel—began to emerge as a haven in the German-Jewish imagination at the same time that it represented a threat in the non-Jewish German imagination.

Kolmar alludes to her search for inspiration from an undifferentiated East in a letter to her sister, Hilde (dated May 13, 1939), in which she rejects the possibility of emigration to America or England (referred to circumspectly—because of the censors—as "the way to the West") because, "I once turned my face—as in our prayer—towards the East, and you know that this is not just 'the latest fashion' with me" (Kolmar 1970, 25). She then recalls meeting (at age nine) a girl from a family she calls "very Asiatic Russians," which occasions her to remark, "I, too, may well be a kind of 'hindered Asian'—and I would be happy if the hindrance could be laid aside; as a European the path to the West might have come to me more easily" (25). Kolmar's affinity for the East, as well as her consciousness of her problematic relationship to the "East" as a "European," leads her to perceive herself as a "hindered Asian" caught between her life in a Western, highly assimilated Jewry and her yearning to be part of an "Eastern" Jewry, one whose location—both cultural and geographic—lay uncertainly between Palestine and Russia. Her description of herself as a "hindered Asian" highlights the ambivalence with which German Jews approached the East; when they tried to establish stronger links to their often romanticized notions of their Eastern heritages—as well as maintain their sense of German identity—they were "orientalized" and "othered" in mainstream German discourses.

"Die Jüdin" begins with the jarring assertion: "Ich bin fremd," which can be translated "I am strange" or "foreign" (Kolmar 1987, 34). This three-word sentence stands alone in its own stanza and demonstrates from the start Kolmar's consciousness of her "foreignness" and marginal status in German society. It is also possible to read the opening line as an affirmation of her difference, the opening act of displacement in a poem that seeks to redefine the meanings of "Jewishness" for a modern German-Jewish woman. But this opening additionally affirms her difference and independence from the constructs of Jewishness and womanhood offered her by German and German-Jewish societies. (Even the word "Jüdin" marks her off from the rest of society insofar as it signifies both ethnic and gender identities marginalized from mainstream German and German-Jewish cultures.)

"Die Jüdin" both embraces and feels ambivalence toward her marginality, as is apparent in the first stanzas of the poem (Kolmar 1987, 34):

Since no one dares approach me
I want to be girded with towers
That wear their steep, stone-gray caps
Aloft in the clouds.
You will not find the bronze key
To the musty stairs. They spiral skyward
Like a serpent lifting its scaly head
Into the light.
Ach, this wall crumbles already like cliffs
That have been washed by thousand-year-long
    streams.

Paradoxically, she responds to her marginality with the desire to be "girded with towers." This phrase, and many other similar examples throughout her work, indicate the sometimes ambivalent attitude Kolmar had toward taking refuge in a patriarchal tradition while striving to go beyond the constraints of that tradition. And for Kolmar, tradition and identity are ineluctably bound to language; the trope of the tower in her work is also tied to language by the story of the Tower of Babel, where the people decide: "Come, let us build ourselves a city, and a tower with its top in the heavens, and let us make a name for ourselves" (Gen. 11:4). Likewise, "Die Jüdin" wishes to construct towers whose "stone-gray caps" reach to the heavens through the architecture of language. It is precisely Kolmar's relationship to language and textuality that mediated her relationship to the divine and informed her understanding of her position as a German Jew, a woman, and a poet.

The first three stanzas also explore a complex allusion to a passage in the Song of Songs (8:8–9) that represents the female body as a city protected by walls and towers:

We have a little sister,
Whose breasts are not yet formed.
What shall we do for our sister
When she is spoken for?
If she be a wall,
We will build upon it a silver battlement;
If she be a door,
We will panel it in cedar.

The tower / wall trope is frequently associated with the female body as well as the literal, figurative, and divine defenses of Israel in the Hebrew Bible (see, for example, Ps. 48:13 and 2 Sam. 22:51). But the female character in the Song also resists this appropriation: "I am a wall, / My breasts are like towers. / So I became in his eyes / As one who finds favor" (8:10) and "My vineyard, my very own, is for myself" (8:12). Although the trope of towers represents women and their bodies as in need of patriarchal protection, they also embody the principles of power, defense, closeness to God, and a powerful female sexuality: "Your neck is like the tower of David, built for an arsenal" (4:4) and "Your neck is like an ivory tower, / Your eyes are pools in Heshbon, by the gate of Bath-rabbim. / Your nose is like a tower of Lebanon overlooking Damascus" (7:4). Indeed, the Songs of Songs contains the only affirmation of female sexuality (outside of motherhood) in the Bible, and as biblical scholar Renita Weems points out, "The protagonist in the Song is the only unmediated [first person] female voice in scripture" (Weems 1992, 156). (On the basis of thematic elements and our knowledge of priestess-poets in the ancient Near East, Weems and other scholars consider it likely that the Song of Songs was written by a woman.)

The slippage between the "towers" as metaphors for patriarchal defenses and as a representation of the cultural meanings and appropriations of the female body becomes clearer in Kolmar's "Die gelbe Schlange" (The yellow snake; 1938) which begins:

I was also a girl in the dream.
And my breasts lay, shining islands,
On each one a small brown city
With a pointed tower
And red, secret currents of underground
    streams.

In this poem, Kolmar literalizes and reappropriates the metaphor of "breasts like towers" by connecting them with a subversive and independent women's tradition—one that finds its roots in ancient Near Eastern traditions connecting women, snakes, and goddesses to wisdom. Of course, the color yellow is also a symbolic marker of outlawed Jewishness, as in "Die gelbe Rose" (August 1933) from the cycle *Das Wort der Stummen* (1933), which ends with the lines: "The Norseman extols himself as better than the Jew and Hottentot / And the priest creates for him in a narrow a new God— / I still wait upon them all with the shovel full of earth" (Kolmar 1987, 738). In "Lied der Schlange," also from *Das Wort der Stummen,* Kolmar alludes to the Ophites, an early Christian Gnostic group that worshiped the snake in the Garden of Eden as a bringer of wisdom. (Medieval representations show the serpent in the Tree of Knowledge of Good and Evil as being a woman—possibly Adam's rebellious first wife, Lilith—from the waist up.) Gabriele von Natzmer Cooper documents the positive associations snakes have in German, biblical, and ancient Near Eastern traditions in her article on Gnosticism and resistance in "Lied der Schlange." The metaphorical transformation of the towers into a serpent in "Die Jüdin" also points to her

defiant alliance of her identity with a traditional figure of evil, one clearly associated with women and women's quest for knowledge and the expression of female sexuality.

It can be argued that "Die Jüdin" remakes herself as a tower for her own defense, as well as that of the Jewish people. This desire is also apparent in the poem "Wir Juden" (dated September 15, 1933), where Kolmar likens herself unto a victory arch through which her people will some day march: "You! When the bitter hour calls, I will rise up, here and now, / And I will be your arch of triumph, through which the tortures march!" (Kolmar 1987, 751). The poem's allusion to the Nazi torch march through the Brandenburg Gate on January 30, 1933, is unmistakable: "O, if I could lift my voice like a blazing torch in the dark wasteland of the world / Crying, Justice! Justice! Justice!" (751). Kolmar wrote many explicitly anti-Nazi political poems during 1933 (such as the bitterly sarcastic "Anno Domini 1933," "Eternal Jew," and, even so early, "For the Prisoners"). These are not to be seen strictly as anti-Nazi poems, however; rather, they also fit into an aesthetics of modern Jewish identity that Kolmar was developing before the Nazi ascendancy to power.

In "Die Jüdin," Kolmar treasures biblical narratives of deciding events in Jewish history, such as Abraham's departure from the city of Ur (Gen. 12), or ancient Hebrew victories such as the conquest of Jericho (Josh. 6), the victory of the Judge Deborah over the Canaanites (Judg. 4–5), and Samson's pulling down of the temple of Dagon (Judg. 16:23–30). As she finds the trumpet of Jericho, she recalls the inspiration to be drawn from the ancient traditions even though they lay in ruins: "What blew apart the haughty walls, / Grows black in the ground, wasted, hidden; / Yet once I drew breath to sound its note" (34). The biblical figure of most importance to the poem, however, is certainly Deborah.

It is no coincidence that in composing her own song about Jewish female identity Kolmar wishes to merge with the only known female leader of the ancient Israelites. What is perhaps more coincidental is that the Song of Deborah is considered by contemporary biblical scholars to be one of the two most ancient texts in the Bible—the other is the Song of Miriam (Exod. 15:21). (Modern biblical scholarship has amply documented the importance of ritual songs that were performed by women in ancient Israel, and now considers it likely that the Song of Deborah was written by a woman.) In composing her own "song" about the Jewish people, Kolmar goes back to one of the rarest and most precious of all biblical texts: one ascribed to a female author. In Deborah, "Die Jüdin" finds her most valued and important textual and spiritual ancestor: a woman poet who stood out in a male-dominated tradition and roused her people to resistance.

Kolmar (1987, 34) finds herself transformed during a "research trip" she wishes to undertake to find the roots of her identity in the Near East:

I wish to mobilize a research trip
To my own ancient land.
Perhaps I can still discover
The buried Ur of the Chaldeans somewhere
The idol Dagon, the tent of the Hebrews,
The trumpet of Jericho.

The fact that she would cast what is, in some ways, the most important of her poems in terms of a "research trip" bespeaks the importance of Near Eastern mythology and biblical scholarship in her work. German-Jewish interest in the Near East was sparked not only by the Zionist movement, but also through renewed interest in the history and mythology of the Near East through the sensationalization of archeological discoveries such as King Tut's tomb in 1922, and in Palestine, the excavations at sites of major biblical cities such as Jerusalem, Jericho, and Megiddo from the 1920s through the 1930s. From the 1910s through the 1930s, biblical archeologists sought to establish a historical basis for Scripture, and thus to call into question the work of nineteenth-century biblical scholarship, which tended to view the Bible more as mythology than history. The new understanding of biblical history created by such discoveries obviously had a profound influence upon European Jews, for whom this understanding of biblical history

played a key role in forming the modern Jewish identity.

On her research trip through tradition and imagination, Kolmar finds a trunk containing beautiful, ancient garments—texts and textiles—within which she clothes herself and finds protection (Kolmar 1987, 35):

Amazed I clothe myself. Although I am small
And far from ages glorious and strong.
All about me tower the shining expanses
Like shelter, and I grow into them.
Now I seem strange, and can no longer
    recognize myself,
Since I was there before Rome and Carthage,
And suddenly the altar fires of the judge and
    her tribe.
Burn in me,
And from the hidden golden bowl
A painful glistening runs through my blood,
And a song will call me by a name
That suits me once again.

And yet she also finds herself "strange" when she clothes herself in the Jewish tradition, a discovery that indicates not only a recognition of the stranger she and other Jews had become to their heritage through assimilation into German society, but also, on another level, the stranger she remained, as a woman, to a patriarchal Judaism.

In spite of the affirmation of Jewish female subjectivity found throughout Kolmar's works, there is a persistent and harrowing consciousness of ambient misogyny and anti-Semitism that pervades even her most beautiful visions. Her poem "Asien" (1937), a paean to a legendary, feminine, maternal East ("Mother, / That you were to me even before I was born, / I am coming home"), ends with the image of vultures circling the "Towers of death, / Towers of silence," remembering not only the so-called "towers of silence" where Parsis leave their dead to be excarnated by vultures, but also presaging the slaughter of six million Jews during the Holocaust (Kolmar 1987, 534–36). "Türme" (1937) suggests that the defenses built by "Die Jüdin," although they provide her with a "spiritual" protection against Nazi German society, cannot prevent her further isolation, persecution, and silencing within that society "on the shores of a northern sea" (517). The trope of the tower in this poem, written in the late 1930s, expresses a much greater pessimism (517):

Where on craggy cliffs, churning ice-green
    waves noisily crash,
Smashing, spraying,
Stands the tower.
Hard, dark, oppressed, silent in the gray
    desolation.
Extinct.
Without mouth.
No door, no gate: locked.

In spite of her written scream of protest, she still finds herself "silent," "dark," "oppressed," and "without mouth"; the Nazi reign renders her gifts of language and tradition useless and her dreams of a new German-Jewish identity futile.

But "Türme" (Kolmar 1987, 519) ends with the stirrings of desire for a new faith, and for possible escape:

Perhaps my soul forgot me in my dream.
And sank, wings spread towards morning,
    where the tower
stood to meet its wandering flight,
And roved through hot, enchanted, lifeless
    rooms,
In search of ancestors,
And touched the hovering strings that still
    resound.

In spite of the risk of losing herself and her identity, Kolmar still finds meaning in texts—the German word *Saiten* (strings) is a homonym with the word *Seiten* (pages)—texts that still resonate with her personal and historical dilemmas as a German-Jewish woman.

The ending of "Die Jüdin" also confronts the vicissitudes of Jewish history and the difficulties presented to Jewish women seeking support within a patriarchal tradition. Although tradition is seen to foster the strength of "Die Jüdin," God batters the "towers," allowing them to both stand and fall in the storms of history: "Enormous, crumbling towers of wind, / As green as

nephrite, red as coral, / Blow across the towers. God lets them fall in ruin, / And yet still stand for ages more" (Kolmar 1987, 35). Indeed, the "columns of wind" that destroy Kolmar's "towers" seem malevolent avatars of the "pillars of cloud and fire" through which the Lord led the ancient Israelites through the wilderness to the Promised Land (see Exod. 13:21). They also sound remarkably like the winds blowing her cousin Walter Benjamin's "angel of history" backward into the future: "His face is turned towards the past. Where we perceive a chain of events, he sees one single catastrophe which keeps piling wreckage upon wreckage and hurls it in front of his feet. The angel would like to stay, awaken the dead, and make whole what has been smashed. But a storm is blowing from Paradise; it has got caught in his wings with such violence that the angel can no longer close them" (Benjamin 1968, 257–58). The ruins that permeate Kolmar's texts—ruins of patriarchy, ruins of tradition—suggest that Kolmar perceived God and men as being indifferent to the fate of her poetry. Insofar as Kolmar uses "breasts like towers" as a metaphor for the female body, divine opposition can be read as alternating patriarchal indifference and hostility toward Jewish women and their works. But Kolmar also sought to reappropriate the Bible and Judaism for Jewish women. She wanted her work to constitute a kind of modern Midrash, yet one which was threatened by, and threatening to, traditional Judaism.

Kolmar's struggles with tradition, modernity, and Jewish female identity never got a full hearing during her lifetime. Although *Weibliches Bildnis* was finally published in the volume *Die Frau und die Tiere* in 1938 by the Jüdischen Buchverlag Erwin Löwe, most copies of the book were destroyed by the Nazis during the November pogrom. Though she apparently had hopes of emigrating from Germany in the early 1930s, Kolmar stayed in Berlin to take care of her aging father after her other siblings left the country. In this way, her fate mirrored that of thousands of Jewish women who were compelled to remain in Germany to take care of aging parents (see Kaplan 1990). Kolmar lived with her father in the

Berlin suburb of Finkenkrug until they were forced under Nazi law to sell their possessions and property and move into tenement housing in 1938. In 1940, she was sentenced to forced labor in a munitions factory in Berlin. In 1941, her eighty-year-old father was sent to the concentration camp Theresienstadt. In February of 1943, the workers in the factory where Kolmar labored were rounded up and sent to Auschwitz, where she perished among the "Towers of silence, / Towers of death."

Bibliography

Walter Benjamin, "Theses on the Philosophy of History," *Illuminations,* ed. Hannah Arendt (New York: Schocken, 1968), 253–64; Marion Kaplan, "Jewish Women in Nazi Germany: Daily Life, Daily Struggles, 1933–1939," *Feminist Studies* 16 (fall 1990): 579–606; Gertrud Kolmar, *Briefe an die Schwester Hilde (1938–1943),* ed. Johanna Zeitler (Munich: Kösel Verlag, 1970); Kolmar, *Weibliches Bildnis: Sämtliche Gedichte* (Munich: Deutscher Taschenbuch Verlag, 1987); Elisabeth Langgässer with Ina Seidel, *Herz zum Hafen: Frauengedichte der Gegenwart* (Leipzig: R. Voigtländers Verlag, 1933); Else Lasker-Schüler, *Das Hebräerland* (1937; Munich: Deutscher Taschenbuch Verlag, 1986); Gabriele von Natzmer Cooper, "Das süßere Obst der Erkenntnis: Gnosis und Widerstand in Gertrud Kolmars apokalyptischen 'Lied der Schlange,'" *Seminar* 29 (May 1993): 138–51; Gershom Scholem, *From Berlin to Jerusalem* (New York: Schocken, 1980); Scholem, *Major Trends in Jewish Mysticism* (New York: Schocken, 1974); Renita J. Weems, "The Song of Songs," *The Women's Bible Commentary,* ed. Carol A. Newsom and Sharon H. Ringe (Louisville: John Knox Press, 1992), 156–60; Hilde Wenzel, "Nachwort," in Gertrud Kolmar *Weibliches Bildnis* (Munich: Kösel Verlag, 1960), 771–83; and Johanna Woltmann, ed., *Marbacher Magazin* 63 (1993).

JOHN BORMANIS

February 28, 1933 Karl Wolfskehl, member of the George Circle, carrying several books he loves too much to sell, boards a train for Basel and leaves Germany forever

The Jewish members of the group known as the George Circle were the quintessential embodiments of the German Jews' dream to participate fully in German society. Celebrated and honored between 1892 and 1933, they devoted their lives to advancing Germany's literary scholarship; then, tragically, the country they adored repudiated them and all they had to offer.

Stefan George, German poet, visionary, and peripatetic eccentric, created the George Circle. George saw himself as a modern-day Socratic master who guided and inspired intellectually gifted young writers. Taking Nietzsche's cult of the "superman" and transforming it into a reverence for "ideal" men, George hoped, through his poetry, to counter what he considered the degrading influences of the modern materialistic age.

Beginning in the 1890s, Stefan George drew an elite circle of disciples from contributors to his poetry journal, *Blätter für die Kunst* (Leaves or pages for the arts). Only the most promising talents from a wide variety of literary fields became part of his select group. These men, in turn, brought new prospects to the master's attention.

Members of the inner circle called *George Meister* (master) and were permitted to address him in the familiar *du* (you) form. Scores of young men, including friends and colleagues of inner circle members, failed to meet the Meister's exacting standards and thus remained in the outer rings. Many others, attracted to the elite status of George and his group, proclaimed themselves to be part of the circle without actually being members.

Almost half of George Circle members were Jewish, of Jewish background, or had at least one Jewish grandparent. For the purposes of this essay, however, "Jewish" members of Stefan George's inner circle will be defined as men and women with two Jewish parents who were neither reared as Christians nor converted to Christianity later in life. This group included five men and one woman: Karl Wolfskehl, Friedrich Gundolf, Erich Kahler, Gertrud Kantorowicz, Ernst Morwitz, and Ernst Kantorowicz. At least a dozen other Jews were on the circle's periphery or were close friends of circle members. In addition, three other circle members were Christians of part-Jewish ancestry. Hugo von Hofmannsthal, the revered Austrian poet, was the most prominent of this latter group, although he remained under George's intellectual wardship for only a short time.

With the exception of Wolfskehl, the Jews of the George Circle led highly assimilated, secularly oriented lives. Most came from well-to-do families and were able to pursue academic and / or writing careers without worrying about making a living. All six considered themselves part of the German nation and culture, yet each experienced anti-Jewish discrimination, often in the form of exclusion from campus student organizations. They were outsiders not by choice, but because the German people as a whole did not accept Jews as fellow Germans.

For these intelligent, ambitious, and talented young people, membership in the George Circle offered opportunities unobtainable elsewhere. The most obvious benefit was the chance to interact with a unique group of scholars and intellects. Perhaps even more important, the George Circle provided a setting free of prejudice and discrimination. Stefan George sought genius and talent; he valued his disciples for what they could contribute regardless of their religious backgrounds. By becoming George's protégés, Wolfskehl, Gundolf, and the others believed that Germany accepted them as true insiders—members of a high profile, high status literary coterie.

Karl Wolfskehl, the first Jew to become a member of the George Circle, was born on September 17, 1869, in Darmstadt. He came from a prominent Jewish family whose ancestors, the aristocratic Kalonymus clan, had lived in Germany for almost a millennium. Wolfskehl's early years coincided with a time of momentous change for Germany and its Jews. Two months before his birth, the Prussian-formed North German Confederation emancipated its Jews and granted them broad, but not complete, civil rights. The newly enfranchised Jewry had been freed from the ghettos barely fifty years earlier. In 1871, a united Germany extended civil rights to all the Jews in the empire.

Protest against Jewish participation in German life and society did not take long to appear. When Wolfskehl was ten, Wilhelm Marr published the anti-Semitic tract *Der Sieg des Judenthums über das Germanenthum* (The victory of Judaism over Germandom; 1879) and formed the politically oriented Anti-Semitic League. While Wolfskehl was a gymnasium student, Heinrich von Treitschke coined the slogan "Die Juden sind unser Unglück" (The Jews are our misfortune), which later became a popular Nazi catch-phrase. At the same time anti-Semitic movements in German and Austrian universities, which had recently begun to admit Jewish students, purged Jews from fraternal eating societies and other student organizations. Anti-Jewish riots broke out

on some campuses. Most German and Austrian Jews clung to the belief that anti-Semitism was a *temporary* mania of the politically manipulated lower middle classes, and thus they ignored or downplayed the problem.

Because of his family's thousand-year-long history in Germany, Karl Wolfskehl believed that he could be both a committed Jew and an equal and contributing member of German society. He enrolled at the University of Giessen, where he worked on a Ph.D. in German literature and quickly built a reputation as a gifted literary historian. Wolfskehl met Stefan George in 1892, and the encounter with the charismatic poet changed the direction of Wolfskehl's professional life. Poetry became his main interest and George his close friend, guiding light, and mentor.

The same year that Houston Stewart Chamberlain published his ringing declaration of Teutonic superiority, *Grundlagen des Neunzehnten Jahrhunderts* (Foundations of the nineteenth century; 1898), Wolfskehl married and settled in Munich. He devoted himself to translating and transcribing old Germanic poetry and to writing his own verses. The Wolfskehls moved to a large, comfortable flat on Leopoldstrasse in the Schwabing artists' quarter of the city, and their home became a favorite gathering place for Munich's writers and intellectuals. Whenever Stefan George's wanderings brought him to Munich, the Meister stayed with the Wolfskehls in a room reserved exclusively for his use.

At the beginning of the new century, Wolfskehl joined with two of George's other friends, irrationalist philosophers Ludwig Klages and Alfred Schuler, to form a Munich branch of the George Circle known as the *Kosmikers* (cosmics). In frequent, lively discussions, the three men explored their common interest in pre-Christian mythology, but Klages and Schuler soon declared themselves Aryans and anti-Semites. They demanded that Stefan George turn his back on Wolfskehl. Instead, George broke with Klages and Schuler and, in 1904, excommunicated them from the circle.

Perhaps his erstwhile friends' growing anti-Semitism spurred Wolfskehl to consider the necessity of a Jewish homeland, safe from prejudice and persecution. The man who had seen no di-chotomy between his German and Jewish selves traveled to Basel in 1903 as a delegate to the Sixth Zionist Congress. But whether owing to a disgust over the friction caused by the Uganda Plan or simply to a rush of more pressing personal mat-ters, Wolfskehl did not participate in any subse-quent congresses.

From 1904 to 1919, Wolfskehl delighted in his continued association with the George Circle and wrote on a wide range of topics from serious analyses of art, drama, and music to lighthearted verses on the joys of pipe smoking. Above all, he adored books and eventually accumulated a li-brary of more than 30,000 rare volumes. When Wolfskehl and his wife separated in 1919, he moved to a small flat and left his beloved library temporarily in his wife's and daughters' care.

Throughout the Great War, Wolfskehl re-mained detached from partisan passions, but the troubled Weimar era's growing anti-Semitism distressed him deeply. Through his writings, he tried to convince his countrymen that Germans and Jews were inextricably linked by centuries of common history and culture. As the decades passed, Germans' increasing hatred of Jews drove a mental wedge between his German and Jewish identities. In the end, the Nazis robbed him of his German half. He could only mourn its loss.

In 1899, Karl Wolfskehl had introduced Stefan George to a brilliant young Jewish scholar named Friedrich Gundelfinger. George and Gundelfinger discovered that they shared a deep interest in behavioral and moral guidelines pro-vided by the great men of the past. George pub-lished Gundelfinger's early writing in the *Blätter für die Kunst* and encouraged his young colleague to change his last name to the more Aryan-sound-ing "Gundolf." In large part due to George's guidance, the young man became a brilliant and innovative literary historian.

Gundolf received his Ph.D. and became a lec-turer at the University of Heidelberg in 1911. From 1908 to 1918, he edited a ten-volume Ger-man translation of Shakespeare's works. The year he began teaching he published *Shakespeare und der deutsche Geist* (Shakespeare and the German spirit), a discussion of the English bard's effect on German literature. The book was extremely well received, and its content and style set an example for future literary historians. Other major works on Goethe, Kleist, and Caesar followed, all popu-larizing Stefan George's views. Gundolf also served George by introducing the Meister's poems to the German reading public. At the same time, Gundolf formed a Heidelberg branch of the George Circle and peopled it with a new genera-tion of gifted students devoted to George's prin-ciples.

Although Gundolf's devotion to George bor-dered on adoration, the two men had their differ-ences. When Gundolf accepted a professorship in 1916 and later married, Stefan George felt re-buffed and betrayed. Although the Meister even-tually broke off the friendship, Gundolf remained fiercely loyal to George and retained his friend-ships with other circle members.

Elected to the Heidelberg Academy of Sci-ences in 1929, Gundolf also won the prestigious Hamburg Lessing Prize the following year. In 1931, at the pinnacle of his career, the fifty-year-old Gundolf fell ill. He died on July 12, Stefan George's sixty-third birthday. So great was Gun-dolf's literary renown that newspapers through-out the country gave his obituary front-page coverage. Germany mourned, but growing anti-Semitic agitation would soon prove that even Gundolf's great fame could not survive Nazi racism.

Erich Kahler, another young Jewish scholar and soon-to-be philosophical and literary histo-rian, received his introduction to Stefan George via Gundolf and Wolfskehl. George and the circle impressed the importance of classical moral values upon the young man and encouraged his interest in interpreting the past, especially the historical development of the human conscious-ness, through an anthropological perspective.

Kahler moved to Munich, where George Cir-cle members continued to support and guide his work. In 1919 he published *Das Geschlecht Habs-burg* (Dynasty of the Habsburgs) and followed it the next year with *Der Beruf der Wissenschaft* (Knowledge, a vocation). Critics acclaimed his works, and their praise established his reputation as an important German historical philosopher and moralist. Kahler remained in Munich, where he began two further studies, *Israel unter den Völkern* (Israel among the nations) and *Der deutsche Charakter in der Geschichte Europas* (The German character in the history of Europe).

Only one woman saw her writing printed in George's *Blätter für die Kunst*. Gertrud Kantorowicz's inclusion in his journal was remarkable, considering that the George Circle was a male outpost formed to celebrate the cult of the perfect man. Moreover, Stefan George considered females to be superfluous distractions to the artistic life. He accepted her help in preparing the journal, nevertheless, and printed one of her poems in the 1899 issue. Even so, it appeared under the male-sounding name "Gert. Pauly."

Gertrud Kantorowicz was an unusual woman in many ways. She came from a highly assimilated, wealthy Jewish merchant family in Posen, a Prussian city originally part of Poland. Intelligent and ambitious, she enrolled at the University of Berlin, not to dabble in a variety of courses, as did the few university women of her time, but to seriously pursue academics. She concentrated on art history and architecture. A rebel against the feminine social conventions of her time, she carried on a long-term affair with her professor, the well-known Georg Simmel, and gave birth to a daughter in the late 1890s. Because she refused to marry or be tied down by traditional motherhood, Simmel took major responsibility for their child's care.

Kantorowicz spent the opening years of the new century writing poetry and translating foreign works into German. She supported and guided Simmel's career and introduced a collection of his writings. Her main intellectual interests, no doubt due in some part to Stefan George's influence, were Greek architecture and Italian Renaissance art.

Some time before 1914, Kantorowicz also trained as a nurse. During World War I, she registered as a Red Cross nurse and served in a German military hospital in Constantinople. Whether she was drawn to service by patriotic duty, the desire for adventure, or both, her years as a war nurse left little time for research and literary composition. After Germany's defeat, Kantorowicz returned to Berlin and her writing. Between 1919 and 1933 she completed all but the final chapter of *Vom Wesen der griechischen Kunst* (The inner nature of Greek art). She never finished the book: its conclusion forever eluded her.

Ernst Kantorowicz, Gertrud Kantorowicz's first cousin, also became a member of the George Circle. Even as a student, he had prided himself on being a right-wing German patriot. In 1914, he curtailed his studies at the University of Berlin to enlist in his hometown's field artillery regiment. Shipped to the Western Front in France, Kantorowicz was wounded during the Battle of Verdun. After Germany's defeat in 1918, he joined the *Freikorps,* a paramilitary organization composed of ex-officers, drifters, and adventurers. He opposed the democratic "mediocrity" of the Weimar Republic, and, while visiting Munich, he took up arms to prevent a feared Marxist "takeover" of the city.

While studying for his doctorate at the University of Heidelberg, Kantorowicz met Friedrich Gundolf, who introduced him to the Heidelberg contingent of the George Circle. The circle, with its belief that "great men make great ages," enormously affected the style and content of Kantorowicz's writing. He published *Kaiser Friedrich der Zweite* (Holy Roman Emperor Frederick II) in 1927. The German reading public was hungry for information about Germanic heroes, and the book's heavy doses of Teutonic mythology mixed with medieval legend appealed to their national pride. The book was an immediate success. Academia, however, denounced it as a glorification of myth, rather than a factual, unbiased history. Kantorowicz came back with a written rebuttal that defended his historical style and proved his scholarly merit. The brilliant biography and its defense won him a coveted professorship at the University of Frankfurt.

Kantorowicz began teaching medieval history in 1930 and was appointed a full professor in 1932. His promotion was, in large part, made possible by the very Weimar regime he hated, for only after 1918 could Jews be promoted to full professorships within the German university system. In spite of his political conservatism, his military record during the Great War, and his lack of identification with the Jewish people, the growing Nazi movement on university campuses in the early 1930s made Kantorowicz's professional life extremely difficult. The atmosphere became so bitter that he accepted an invitation to teach at Oxford New College in Great Britain for the 1933 academic year.

Like Kantorowicz, Stefan George had long been a critic of the "bourgeois" and "mediocre" Weimar government. In a 1928 volume entitled *Das Neue Reich* (The new reich), George called for an ideal German state headed by an ideal leader. This "cult of the super-leader," equally influenced by Plato's *Republic* and Nietzsche's various works, had been the cornerstone of George's poetic visions for more than thirty years. His circle spread the concept to an entire generation of impressionable youth, planting, as several later critics claimed, a seed of leader-worship that would be harvested later with horrifying results by Hitler and the National Socialist movement.

Upon Hitler's ascension to power on January 30, 1933, the Nazis, whose membership included such George admirers as architect Albert Speer and propagandist Joseph Goebbels, praised Stefan George as the *Künder des Reichs* (Prophet of the Reich). Nazi leaders wooed Stefan George, but he consistently ignored their adoration. In fact, he held the Nazis in contempt, but he refused to descend from his self-imposed intellectual separation to speak openly against them. Finally, he removed himself from his Nazi admirers by voluntarily embracing exile in Switzerland.

Still the Nazis persisted. They offered him the presidency of Germany's Dichterakademie—the equivalent of naming him poet laureate. George scoffed at the offer by sending a Jewish member of the circle, Ernst Morwitz, back to Germany with his official refusal. Sending Morwitz suggests that George condemned Nazi racial attitudes. Yet in spite of his close, amicable relationships with Jews, George took little interest in the Jews' fate under Nazism. "In politics things go awry," he declared. "It's the Jews' business and not so important to me" (Evans 1970, 198). But Nazi racism was very important to George's Jewish disciples. Their lives hung in the balance as a result of the National Socialist takeover.

Just after Hitler became chancellor, Karl Wolfskehl sold his rare book library to Salman Schocken, the Jerusalem publisher. In turn, Schocken pledged Wolfskehl a permanent yearly stipend. With this small but continuing source of money, Wolfskehl awaited the Nazis' next move. He didn't wait long. On the last Monday in February, Nazi vandals burned the German parliament building, the Reichstag. Blaming the Socialists, the Nazis used the Reichstag fire as an excuse to begin their bloody reign of terror against a panoply of perceived enemies.

The next day, February 28, 1933, Karl Wolfskehl boarded an express train for Basel, Switzerland. Carrying a small amount of clothing, some personal items, and a few books he loved too much to sell, he left Germany forever. Grieving, the man who had steadfastly clung to both his German and Jewish heritages later wrote: "I have lost *everything*. I have lost my native land; do you know what that means to a poet?" (Grunfeld 1979, 77).

In May 1933, while wandering from one Italian city to another, Wolfskehl met a young university student named Margot Ruben. He was sixty-four at the time and nearly blind. She became his companion, guide, assistant, and transcriber, writing down his verses as he composed them in his mind. In one of his most poignant poems, the lament "An den Deutschen" (To the Germans), the haunted Wolfskehl wrote of his deep love for Germany, its culture, and its people.

His profound sense of loss drove Wolfskehl to abandon Europe to its irrational hatreds. He set sail with Ruben for New Zealand in May 1938 and remained there throughout the war years. After Hitler's defeat, Wolfskehl refused an invitation to return to Germany. "My native land," wrote the traumatized exile, "has completely forgotten that a German poet named Karl Wolfskehl still exists" (Grunfeld 1979, 78). Wolfskehl died in 1948, a national poet without a nation to honor him.

The Nazis even attacked Wolfskehl's deceased friend, Friedrich Gundolf. In 1933, Joseph Goebbels's anti-Semitic propaganda sheet, the *Völkischer Beobachter*, declared that Gundolf's once renowned works were simply "a typical case of Jewish intellectualism." (Decades before, while a student at the University of Heidelberg, Goebbels had tried to attach himself to Professor Gundolf in hopes of establishing a connection to Stefan George. The future Nazi propaganda minister had recoiled in horror upon discovering that Gundolf was a Jew.) Soon after Hitler's takeover, the Nazis removed Gundolf's books from the bookstores and prohibited any further printing of his works. Furious at the assault on her husband's memory, Gundolf's widow, Elizabeth, left Germany with his manuscripts and papers and helped establish the Gundolf Archives in London.

Early in 1933 the Gestapo searched Erich Kahler's residence in Munich looking for his about-to-be published *Der deutsche Charakter in der Geschichte Europas.* The Kahlers, away during the raid, hastily escaped to Switzerland. With the encouragement of his friend in exile Thomas Mann, Kahler and his wife emigrated to the United States in 1938, where Kahler joined the stellar group of émigré intellectuals in Princeton, New Jersey, that included physicist Albert Einstein.

Erich Kahler taught at the New School for Social Research, was a visiting member of the Institute for Advanced Studies in Princeton, and served as professor of German Literature at Cornell, Princeton, and several other universities. He published *Man the Measure: A New Approach to History* (1943) and the following year joined with Albert Einstein in a vigorous defense of the Jewish homeland entitled "The Arabs and Palestine." Three years before his death, Kahler published *The Jews Among the Nations* (1967), an English-language version of his 1936 German original. *The Germans,* a translation of the manuscript the Gestapo had tried to confiscate in 1933, was published posthumously in 1974.

Unlike Wolfskehl and Kahler, Gertrud Kantorowicz remained in Germany after 1933. Although she possessed an immigration permit for Great Britain, she stayed in Berlin as an act of defiance. Kantorowicz all but abandoned her writing and joined a small resistance group in order to rescue other Jews in imminent danger of roundup and deportation. In keeping with her independent and rebellious nature, she rarely considered her own danger and continued to behave as if she were immune from arrest.

At last, in 1942, Kantorowicz agreed to leave Germany, not to save herself but to guide three older Jewish women to safety. As they neared the Swiss border, a German patrol discovered them. The Germans killed one of the women and captured Kantorowicz and the third woman. The fourth would-be refugee escaped. Kantorowicz was sent to Theresienstadt, where she worked as a nurse in the "model" concentration camp's primitive hospital. The muse within her was reborn during her captivity, called to life in order to record the suffering she witnessed. One of the most moving of her poems was "Daughter of the Day," a tribute to a revered old woman whose death was both a release from sorrowful captivity and a transformation into what lay beyond life itself.

Early in 1945, Kantorowicz fell desperately ill. She died on April 19, 1945, within days of Theresienstadt's liberation by the Allies. Long after her death, others completed and published her life's work, *The Inner Nature of Greek Art* (1992).

Ernst Kantorowicz was teaching at Oxford New College when the Hitlerian regime came to power. Returning to the University of Frankfurt after completing his year at Oxford, he discovered that new rules required all faculty members to swear an oath of allegiance to the Führer. This Kantorowicz could not do, and he resigned his post in October 1934. A few months later, the Nuremberg Laws made it illegal for any Jew to teach in German schools.

Like Gertrud Kantorowicz, Ernst stubbornly refused to abandon his country, but Kristallnacht (November 9–10, 1938) finally convinced him that the situation for Jews in Germany was beyond hope. With the help of Christian friends, Kantorowicz escaped to Holland. The Emergency Committee for Displaced Scholars brought him to the United States, where he accepted a position at the University of California, Berkeley, in 1939.

Eleven years later, in what surely resurrected a specter from his past, Kantorowicz refused to take the new loyalty oath the University of California Regents required of all teaching staff. He moved to Princeton, where he joined Kahler and Einstein at the Institute for Advanced Study. He taught German medieval history and wrote several books on the subject that pioneered the study of the interrelationship between theology and monarchy. Kantorowicz remained in Princeton until his death in 1963.

Ernst Morwitz, the Jewish man Stefan George had sent to deliver his refusal of Nazi honors, spent the decades after George's death publishing the Meister's works and translating them into English. Morwitz died in 1971, the last and, perhaps, the most devoted of the original Jewish members of the George Circle.

The Jews in the George Circle achieved insider status among Germany's literati and became objects of respect, if not awe, via their close association with Stefan George. This achievement, however, plus their desire to be accepted as "authentic" Germans—a desire shared by the great majority of Germany's Jews—blinded them to the depth of German prejudice. With the rise of anti-Semitism as Nazi state policy, George Circle Jews again became outsiders who were denigrated, shunned, and persecuted in the land of their birth.

In retrospect, the world gained by Germany's literary loss. Karl Wolfskehl, Erich Kahler, Ernst Kantorowicz, and Ernst Morwitz, ably aided by a group of mainly Jewish circle associates in Holland known as Castrum Peregrini, have spread Stefan George's poetry and ideas far beyond Germany's borders. Even more important, Jews, both inner circle and affiliate, brought their talents with them into exile, transplanted them into fertile soil, and brought forth new literary creations to enrich the cultures of their adopted homelands.

Bibliography

Arthur R. Evans, Jr., ed., *On Four Humanists: Hofmannsthal, Gundolf, Curtius, Kantorowicz* (Princeton, N.J.: Princeton University Press, 1970); Peter Gay, *Weimar Culture: The Outsider as Insider* (New York: Harper & Row, 1968); Frederic V. Grunfeld, *Prophets Without Honor: A Background to Freud, Kafka, Einstein and the World* (New York: Rinehart and Winston, 1979); Erich Kahler, *Man the Measure: A New Approach to History* (Boulder, Colo.: Westview Press, 1956); Kahler, *The Jews Among the Nations* (New York: Frederick Ungar, 1967); Gertrud Kantorowicz, *The Inner Nature of Greek Art,* trans. J. L. Benson (New Rochelle, N.Y.: Aristide D. Caratzas, 1992); Georg Peter Landmann, *Stefan George und sein Kreis: Eine Bibliographie* (Hamburg: Hauswedell, 1960); Paul Mendes-Flohr, *Divided Passions: Jewish Intellectuals and the Experience of Modernity* (Detroit: Wayne State University Press, 1991); Jehuda Reinharz and Walter Schatzberg, *The Jewish Response to German Culture* (Hanover, N.H.: University Press of New England, 1985); Carol North Valhope (Olga Marx) and Ernst Morwitz, *Stefan George: Poems* (New York: Pantheon, 1943); Richard and Clara Winston, trans., *An Exceptional Friendship: The Correspondence of Thomas Mann and Erich Kahler* (Ithaca, N.Y.: Cornell University Press, 1975); and Karl Wolfskehl, *Gesammelte Werke,* 2 vols. (Hamburg: Claassen, 1960).

ALEXIS P. RUBIN

1933   The Cultural League is formed to concentrate all "Jewish" cultural life in one central organization under Nazi supervision

On April 1, 1933, two months after the Nazi takeover, Jewish businesses throughout Germany were boycotted, civil servants dismissed, doctors and lawyers threatened, and artists barred from performing. About 8,000 Jewish actors, musicians, singers, directors, and stage and concert technical personnel were suddenly thrown out of work.

Three years later a high official of the ministry of propaganda looked back upon the initial difficulties of the new regime: "Considering the unbelievable extent to which Germany's theaters were overrun by Jews, one can realize that a vast number of Jewish performing artists were forced to look for some other means of livelihood," wrote Reichskulturwart (cultural guardian of the Reich) Hans Hinkel. "It is not surprising that, having achieved the takeover of power and having begun the de-Judaization of the arts and our entire German cultural life, we were faced with the question of what was to become of all the many Jewish performers" (Hinkel 1936). His interim program in the autumn of 1936 bore the title "The Policy of Cleansing Our Theaters of Jews."

At the beginning, the Nazis had no clear idea of what to do with the thousands of dismissed Jews. They had not yet developed the tightly meshed institutional machinery that later became typical of National Socialist rule, under which the victims created by departments of government were put under the administrative custodianship of new agencies instituted for that special purpose. The Nazis saw clearly, however, that their reputation abroad could suffer if mass Jewish unemployment were to become an international scandal. At this time, still concerned about their image in the world community, they were eager to agree to a Jewish self-help project that would bear the economic and social costs of the exclusion of Jews from cultural life. In this way they could carry out their plan to force Jews off the stages and out of the concert halls without the unemployed artists and personnel becoming a burden to the state. In the summer of 1933, the authorities, who had not reckoned with such a convenient solution, approved the foundation of a "Kulturbund Deutscher Juden" (henceforth, Cultural League).

The founder and director of the project until the November pogrom in 1938 was the Berlin neurologist, musicologist, and conductor Kurt Singer. Among the persons who supported him in creating a Jewish theater, opera, and concert company were the former Ullstein journalist Werner Levie, the writer and theater scholar Julius Bab, the directors Fritz Jessner and Fritz Wisten (the latter also the dominant actor of the troupe), and the former stage decorator of the Berlin City Opera, Heinz Condell. They were joined by a number of conductors who later achieved international renown, such as Joseph Rosenstock, Wilhelm Steinberg, and Rudolf Schwarz. Many prominent representatives of German Jewry, such as the painter Max Liebermann or the writers Jakob Wassermann and Georg Hermann, took honorary posts in the Cultural League; others took active roles as functionaries. The driving force in building and expanding the enterprise, however, was Kurt Singer. After his dismissal as deputy director of the City Opera of Berlin, he considered the Cultural League his "life work." He personified the founding spirit of the organization by exalting the Cultural League beyond the status of an emergency aid project. The declared intention of the organization was to convince the Germans that Jews were not only human beings but cultivated people as well. Singer transparently reflected this thinking; at times in a comical, usually in a grotesque, and finally in a tragic way. As we know today, this attempt to educate the Nazified populace was completely unsuccessful, except for one possible aftereffect: the frequent postwar German demand that Jews should always be morally superior human beings who behave in an exemplary manner.

Julius Bab also believed in the power of a good example. Although he spoke of "disgusting" negotiations with the Nazi authorities and was one of the few who recognized the ghetto character of the envisioned Jewish cultural activity, he too hoped that the Cultural League could become a moral institution for Germans. In a letter written in July 1933, he wrote: "It remains a bitter matter—a ghetto enterprise, which, however, we want to operate so well that the Germans will be put to shame" (Bab 1933). In other words, he hoped that of all projects a Jewish theater could succeed where others, including his own movement for a popular theater (*Volksbühnenbewegung*), had failed in the preceding decades.

But Bab's point of view was far more sober than that of other artists, intellectuals, and functionaries involved in the debate accompanying the founding of the association. Moritz Goldstein, for example, a prominent Berlin author who had coined the incredible phrase about the Jews being "the trustees of German culture," declared in the *Jüdische Rundschau* at the end of 1933: "Continue! Even if we are confronted with the repeal of civil equality for Jews: the world-historical fact of their entry into the European cultural community cannot be repealed. . . . May that which is forced upon us be meant as a ghetto:

mind and spirit will rule within. That alone is significant. All else is external."

Those readers with a knowledge of contemporary poetry must have noticed the resemblance to the lyrical consolation "poverty is a quiet glow from within," with which Rilke had once sought to glorify the condition of the have-nots. In a letter to Thomas Mann, the writer René Schickele heaped scorn upon such attempts to cast the ghetto in a good light: "According to newspaper reports, Wassermann belongs to the executive committee of the newly founded Berlin ghetto. . . . The whipping boys are organizing themselves under the supervision of the storm troopers—a splendid sight."

A former actor in state-run theaters, Fritz Wisten, who had just been thrown out of the "cultural community" of Goldstein's rhetoric, bubbled over with enthusiasm for the enterprise. "It is becoming increasingly clear to me," he wrote to Julius Bab in Berlin, "that a project is taking shape which promises to become the ideal theater in every respect: a cast, forced by the totality of outward circumstances to perform theater with a heroic obsession which has not been seen on the stage for a long time."

Tucholsky, in exile in Sweden, had no knowledge of this letter, but had received word of similar high-spirited testimonies. To him, the undertaking was a real-life satire, like the ghastly final form of conditions caricatured in his writings. In his famous last letter to the writer Arnold Zweig, he revealed contempt for those he was criticizing. "There one sees," he wrote about the Cultural League, "that the same people who played first fiddle in many areas now accept the ghetto—the idea of the ghetto and its realization. . . . They are locked away; they are put into a Jewish Theater with four yellow splotches in the front and back, and they have . . . only one ambition, 'Now we will show them that we have the better theater.'"

Max Reinhardt, from his London exile, had laconically informed the authorities that he had no intention of continuing his work as Germany's most famous stage director, because in his view bare toleration stifled the atmosphere necessary for good theater. The theater of the Cultural

League was not only tolerated but, as would be seen, systematically promoted. On the outskirts of the Berlin theater district a theater was rented with the approval of the Nazi authorities, where, in the following years, arts that had generally been performed in separate places were brought under one roof: drama, musical theater, concerts, cabaret, films, and recitals. On October 1, 1933, the Cultural League of German Jews was ceremoniously inaugurated with Lessing's *Nathan the Wise,* a sort of credo of the Jewish liberal middle class. "The evening was one of the great experiences of Berliner Jewry in those years," wrote the chronicler of the Jewish theater in Nazi Germany, Herbert Freeden. "The beginning pauperization had not yet taken on outwardly visible forms. The picture presented by the galleries was strongly reminiscent of the Reinhardt years" (Freeden 1985). On stage, aphoristic statements of noble sentiments were declaimed, such as "I know the thinking of the good, know / That the good are spread throughout all lands." The actor Kurt Katsch, who was writing his memoirs with the title *From Ghetto to Ghetto,* addressed the premiere audience as Nathan: "May everyone strive zealously / In his unbiased love!"

The program brochure directed a completely different injunction at the viewers of Lessing's plea for enlightenment and tolerance: "For technical reasons, parking in front of the theater is not permitted. We request our members to remember that we are representatives of a community in need, and for all to dress and behave accordingly. We wish to give no cause for complaint to anyone. We request that our members refrain from political discussions of any kind at this presentation."

This was the only performance of *Nathan the Wise* in Nazi Germany; a musical pendant to it were the four performances of Beethoven's *Eroica* by the Cultural League's orchestra in August 1934, in honor of the deceased *Reichspräsident* von Hindenburg. The excluded went to exclusive performances. No public mention of programs and playing schedules was allowed, except in the Jewish press. The public sale of tickets was forbidden. Those attending the performances had to legitimate themselves with a special identity card.

Until 1938, the "Hinkel Office" in the ministry of propaganda kept the musical and theatrical productions relatively free of harassment by local party officials and prevented the interference of competing government agencies. True, no performance was permitted without the approval of the *Reichskulturwart* Hinkel, and all texts had to be presented to the censors; true, the league was gradually prohibited from performing all German authors and "Aryan" composers; nonetheless, the functionaries of the Cultural League continued to regard the systematic narrowing of their maneuvering space as a series of temporary restrictions or as the gradual establishment of a stable arrangement. The combination of culture and coercion made many leading members succumb to the illusion that there could be a lasting coexistence between a minority stripped of all rights and the Nazis. This thinking was most strongly evident in the concept of a "Jewish State Theater in the Third Reich." This was to be an institution in which "Jewish culture," as opposed to "German culture," would not only flourish but would be created anew. In this bizarre final stage of the German-Jewish symbiosis, the Jewish cultural functionaries tried to make a virtue of every necessity: censorship and prohibitions were perceived, on the one hand, as massive restrictions, but also as an opportunity to recover Jewish traditions. At the beginning, Goethe and *Figaro* were approved for performance, but gradually the league was barred from presenting works of the classical and romantic periods. It was forbidden to present Beethoven in 1937; after the annexation of Austria, Mozart became taboo. The growing gaps in the repertory had to be filled with the works of Jewish authors and Jewish composers. But with the exception of the devoutly Christian music of Mendelssohn or the modern secular music of Mahler, both of which were banned outside of the league, nearly all so-called Jewish presentations turned out to be flops. The audiences stayed away, not because the repertory was not Jewish enough but, on the contrary, because they were not at all interested in a separate Jewish culture. The most successful play on the stage of the League in 1936 was *A Midsummer Night's Dream* by Shakespeare.

The ban on performing "German" works developed into the command to present a "Jewish repertory" under the meticulous scrutiny of the censors. The overwhelming majority of Jewish theatergoers, however, were not responsive. They showed little interest in plays devoted to specifically Jewish themes, or in translations and adaptations of Yiddish authors such as Sholem Aleichem or Mendele Moicher Sforim. Neither plays written especially for the league on commission nor even a composer competition roused any enthusiasm among Jewish audiences. Rather than attending "hours of dedication" or listening to specially commissioned inspirational ethnic music, the audiences preferred to risk visiting public theaters—in spite of humiliating experiences— or to be entertained by *Countess Maritza*, the last popular production of the cultural ghetto. The *Manchester Guardian* commented ironically in 1935 on the paradoxical fact that the result of the project was something completely undesired by the Nazis: German, and not Jewish culture. "The fact that the Jews have created an atmosphere of the purest German culture is a thorn in the flesh of the German authorities; this development took them by surprise, to say the least."

Up to the demise of the Cultural League, all attempts to enrich the program with Eastern European Jewish popular theater or with liturgical and Hasidically influenced music met with skepticism, uninterest, or even outright rejection by the audiences. "Jewish art" neither was created, nor could strike roots. Even those in power recognized this from time to time. In 1935, the Nazi ideologue Alfred Rosenberg complained that the Cultural League had not done its homework: "The Cultural League, by staging a series of plays that have practically nothing to do with Jewish affairs, has accomplished as little as in its ever so elevating and highly artistic concerts, in which indeed Jews perform for Jews, but without conveying anything Jewish to them" (Künste 1992, 64).

Following the Berlin example, regional and local cultural leagues were founded throughout the territory of the German Reich. In 1938 there were seventy-six cultural leagues in one hundred cities. Like Berlin, Hamburg and Cologne had their own theater companies, and the Cultural League of Rhein-Main had its own symphony or-

chestra. The Berlin league, with around 18,000 subscribing members enrolled in 1937, had the largest membership; the smallest affiliation was that in Köstrin, which had only twenty-four members. In 1935 the Cultural League of German Jews was required to change its name to the Jewish Cultural League. The Gestapo had objected to the registration of the organization under the original name "for reasons of state interest": there were not supposed to be "German Jews" anymore. Instead, the term "Autonomy of Jewish Cultural Life" was introduced, a forerunner of the "Self-Management" that was later practiced in concentration camps such as Theresienstadt. This propaganda ploy, which was construed to deceive the victims as well as to dupe the outside world, disguised the systematic exclusion of Jewish artists and audiences behind an allegedly benevolent policy of sponsorship. The main purpose hidden behind the swindle was the intention of ghettoizing the Jews by degree. As a kind of cultural supplement to the notorious Nuremberg Laws, the ministry of propaganda and the Gestapo decreed the fusion of all cultural leagues into a central Reichsverband Judischer Kulturbünde. Both Nazi bureaucracies, jealously competing for jurisdiction in the Jewish Question, credited themselves with having merged all Jewish cultural leagues and thereby facilitating comprehensive registration and centralized surveillance.

In 1937 exactly 1,425 artists were "comprehensively registered" to ease their "centralized surveillance": there were 111 actors, 81 actresses, 78 male opera singers, 119 female opera singers, 100 male concert singers, 148 female concert singers, 174 instrumentalists, 154 musical entertainers, 32 reciters, 54 lecturers, 49 male cabaret artists, 22 female cabaret artists, 25 male acrobats, 61 female dancers and acrobats, 171 painters, 225 sculptors, and 21 illustrators. The Reichsverband had a total of about 50,000 subscribers in 1936 and 1937, only a little more than 10 percent of the Jewish population still living in Germany. The superintendent, Kurt Singer, complained at the time about the lack of interest, particularly among Berlin's Jewry. In the capital there were 12,000 families without any member in the Cultural League. In a letter to members on April 6, 1937, Singer expressed his disapproval: "It is well-known that a large part of Berlin's Jewry steers clear of the Jewish Cultural League as a matter of principle. These people attach more importance to setting foot in other theaters; they reject being 'ghettoized' or having any ties whatsoever" (Singer 1937). The "Hinkel Office" in the Ministry of Propaganda also criticized Jewish unwillingness to join the Cultural League, because this endangered its registration policy. Always in the perfidious pose of an advocate of the Jewish cause, Hinkel remonstrated: "The Jewish artists, too, would be even better off, they could be paid even more and be given even more opportunities to perform, if all members of the Jewish race would attend the Jewish programs. Only 18,000 Jews in Berlin, from a population which far exceeds 160,000, are members of the Cultural League; that is a sign of insufficient Jewish racial consciousness."

Certainly, a cardinal reason for the stagnating or declining membership of the Cultural League was the loss of many members through death, impoverishment, and, above all, emigration. One of the paradoxes of the project was that every emigrant meant one fewer member. All who fled to a foreign country left the Cultural League behind them. With the rising number of emigrants came the shrinking size of audiences and reduced proceeds from membership dues. Until 1938 the executives of the Cultural League responded testily whenever an actor, singer, dancer, or musician emigrated. The Cultural League did not want to lose its artistic elite and considered the fledgling Palestine Orchestra, for example, to be an unwelcome competitor.

Musicians, both instrumentalists and singers, had more opportunities in foreign countries than did those in the acting profession. Many virtuosos found positions in the greatest orchestras of the free world—as long as it was still possible to get out of Germany. Only a few emigrated actors remained in their profession, such as Kurt Katsch, the Nathan of the Cultural League premiere. He was among those actors who, because of their German accents, were soon being sought in Hollywood to portray Nazis. In Katsch's case this second career as an "accent clown" had a

bizarre aftermath. After the war, when the actor wished to return to Frankfurt, he was informed by the superintendent of the theater, Harry Buckwitz, that his typecasting was not in demand. In other words, the same theater that had thrown him out in 1933 penalized him after 1945 for emigrating and playing in anti-Nazi films.

In November 1938, the masquerade of "cultural autonomy," which the Nazis had been careful to maintain, was brutally obliterated. Leading officials of the Jewish Cultural League had held on to this illusion to the last: they had even begun to sell shares to purchase the theater that had been leased until that time. In November of 1938, this building was one of the few Jewish institutions that was neither demolished nor burned down. The Jewish Cultural League was the only remaining Jewish organization that was permitted to operate in Nazi Germany after Kristallnacht. In fact, on Hinkel's order, the theater was forced to perform a light comedy of student life. "The opening night of Merton Hodge's 'Rain and Wind' is unparalleled, even in the turbulent annals of theater history," wrote Herbert Freeden (1985) about the days following the pogrom. "The portals of the theater on Kommandantenstraße were wide open. The semi-circle of galleries glowed in their old luster. The chandeliers on the ceiling shone brightly, as ushers in elegant uniforms stood in the lobby and on the red carpets leading to the lodges. At home, women waited for news of their missing husbands and sons who had been rounded up; at home, people sat among the rubble of their ruined livelihoods and here in the theater the lights went on by command."

After 1938, the entire project shrank to a small and grotesque illusory world, finally becoming in detail the forerunner of the cultural program of the concentration camps. This was a time of farewell performances; the founders of the Cultural League emigrated, and many stars of the Cultural League stage, opera, orchestra, and cabaret departed to find safe havens—often only temporarily. As the membership sank rapidly, the organization's income dwindled accordingly. The repertory became thinner and thinner, until only royalty-free translations of foreign comedies and farces were performed. In Berlin the Cultural

League had to move out of its theater building and continue in a neighboring hall, where a small company could put on scaled-down, inexpensive productions.

In the Cultural League throughout the Reich, programs virtually ceased except for occasional "Variety Evenings" and "Musical Afternoons." The last tour of the Berlin Theater, a production of Molière's *The Imaginary Invalid* that resembled a grisly parody of a deadly reality, took place in 1940. The director Fritz Wisten, artistic general director of the shrunken organization after the departure of all founding members, listed the Cultural League programs that took place outside of Berlin as "living programs." As if to emphasize that in organized culture (for which the Nazis coined the still common term *Freizeitgestaltung,* free time formation) terror and coziness (*Gemütlichkeit*) can peacefully coexist, the program planners were permitted to present to their thinned audiences, who were now barred from all other public events, popular plays such as *Masquerade, The Postmaster,* or *How Could You, Veronika?* Ferenc Molnar's *Play in the Palace,* which was successfully produced for two seasons running, became the last production of the Cultural League stage. The director of the performance in the late summer of 1941 was the actor Ben Spanier, for whom this last production became a grotesque dress rehearsal. After being deported to Theresienstadt, he produced this social comedy on the concentration camp stage before he was sent on to Auschwitz.

On September 11, 1941, a few days before the introduction of the yellow star and a few months before the deportations began, the Cultural League was dissolved by order of the Gestapo. Jews were now to gather together at collecting points instead of in the theater. The Cultural League was dismantled; movable valuables such as costumes, equipment, and the leftover editions of Jewish books were confiscated. The remaining actors, musicians, and employees who could not emigrate or flee were required to perform forced labor or to serve as lackeys in the bureaucracy of the Reichsvereinigung der Juden until they were finally forced to place themselves on deportation lists.

Several months after the end of the Cultural League, cofounder Julius Bab, who had escaped to America by way of Paris, wrote in the New York–based German-language Jewish newspaper *Aufbau:* "Certainly it is a good thing that the end has come to the Nazis' devilish game of telling the world that the Jews in Germany could even afford a theater and an organization of the arts. From its inauguration, this was the only purpose of the Cultural League; the reason why it was not only tolerated, but ordered into existence. . . . It is good that the lie has come to an end."

Unfortunately, Bab was mistaken. The closure was only the beginning of the end. An end had only come to the long rehearsals for a short, grisly horror in Westerbork, Theresienstadt, Auschwitz, and other places of destruction.

Bibliography

Akademie der Künste, ed., *Geschlossene Vorstellung: Der Jüdische Kulturbund in Deutschland 1933–1941* (Berlin: Edition Hentrich, 1992); Julius Bab, "Julius Bab an Fritz Wisten," letter dated May 19, 1933, in the Fritz-Wisten-Archiv of the Akademie der Künste (Berlin), FWA 74 / 86 / 996; Yehoyakim Cochavi, *Jewish Spiritual Survival in Nazi Germany* [Hebrew] (Tel Aviv: Ghetto Fighters' House, 1988); Volker Dahm, "Kulturelles und geistiges Leben," *Die Juden in Deutschland, 1933–1945: Leben unter nationalsozialistischer Herrschaft,* ed. Wolfgang Benz (Munich: Beck, 1988), 55–267; Etty, *De nagelaten geschriften van Etty Hillesum, 1941–1943* (Amsterdam: Uitgeverij Balans, 1991); Herbert Freeden, *Jüdisches Theater in Nazideutschland* (Berlin: Ullstein, 1985); Glen W. Gadberry, "Nazi Germany's Jewish Theater," *Theater Survey* 21 (May 1980): 15–32; Eike Geisel and Henryk M. Broder, *Premiere und Pogrom* (Berlin: Siedler, 1992); Hans Hinkel, *Handbuch der Reichskulturkammern* (Berlin: Deutscher Verlag für Politik und Wirtschaft, 1937); Hinkel, "Judenreine Theaterpolitik," *Göttingen Tageblatt* (Aug. 9, 1936); Philip Mechanicus, *In Depot: Dagboek uit Westerbork* (Amsterdam: Van Gennep, 1989); and Kurt Singer, "Der Jüdische Kulturbund wirbt," letter dated Apr. 6, 1937, in the Fritz-Wisten-Archiv of the Akademie der Künste (Berlin), box 76, file 86, folder 5032.

EIKE GEISEL

TRANSLATED BY
STEVEN K. LANGE

September 15, 1935   Passage of the Reich Citizenship Act
and the Law for the Protection of German Blood and
German Honor in Nazi Germany forces the children's book
author Mira Lobe to emigrate to Palestine

Mira Lobe, born on September 17, 1913, in Görlitz (today Gorlice, Poland), was commonly regarded as one of the best writers of books for children and young people in Austria. The list of her published work comprises around a hundred books as well as numerous contributions in verse and prose to various anthologies. The following statistics should give an idea of her recent standing. More than 300,000 copies of each of her two best-known children's books, *Die Omama im Apfelbaum* (The Omama in the apple tree; 1965) and *Das kleine Ich bin ich* (The little I is me; 1972), have been printed in Austria. Some three hundred German-language publishing houses have been involved in the publication of her work; her books have been translated into more than thirty languages; and there have been film versions, television series, dramatizations, musicals, radio plays, and musical settings of a number of her works in Austria, Germany, England, and Japan. Numerous prizes and awards since the 1950s testify to the high regard in which she is held, not only in the German-speaking world. In 1980 she received the Austrian Award of Merit for Children's and Young People's Literature.

In 1936, after a long wait, she obtained an entry visa for Palestine, but not before having learned Hebrew with a group of young Zionists in Berlin as well as acquiring proficiency in a trade. After fourteen years in Palestine / Israel, she came back to Austria in 1950 with her husband, the actor and theater director Friedrich Lobe, who had received an appointment at the New Theater at the Scala (which was open from 1948 to 1956). Friedrich Lobe had acted in various important theaters in Germany in the 1920s and had even for a short time been manager and director of the avant-garde Berlin theater the Tribune. Mira Lobe met him in Palestine while working with the workers' theater Ohel. Back from Palestine in 1950, she brought with her a novel, *Insu-Pu, die Insel der verlorenen Kinder,* which had appeared in Tel Aviv in Hebrew and now came out in Vienna (1951) in German. She wrote of her publication, "I shall never forget how it felt to see myself in print in my own language" (Bamberger 1980, 105). For the Scala Theater in Vienna, soon to be denounced, in the spirit of the Cold War, as a Communist, Mira Lobe produced a social-critical play for the young on the subject of unemployment. It was called *Herr Hecht und der Geheimverein* and had its first performance in March 1953 with Otto Tausig as director. For what turned out to be a brief spell, the Lobes moved, after the closure of the Scala in 1956, to East Germany, and made their home in East Berlin. As early as 1958 they were back in Vienna; Mira Lobe remained in Austria.

As the daughter of a middle-class family in Görlitz, Lobe had had what she called a "thoroughly normal childhood." Her father, a businessman by the name of Rosenthal, was also musical; he conducted the synagogue choir and played the organ in the Protestant church. He was a socially conscious man; he gave Mira Lobe her first object lessons in the social divide by taking her with him into the slum quarter of the city. Mira's mother was "a member of the Literary Society and the Arts Association, social-democratic and 'idealistic,'" according to Wolf Harranth, author of the first (short) biography of Mira Lobe. As a fifth-grader Mira joined the Social Democratic Working Class Youth movement, "secretly," as she once said.

It may well be that memories of punishment methods in school belonged equally with her first experiences of class distinctions and status to "a thoroughly normal childhood" in Germany. After the war she recalled: "I sobbed inconsolably not because [the caning] hurt but because I had been humiliated. The lasting impression was of the inviolable dignity of man—even at the tender age of eight." She also remembered from this time: "Strangely enough, it was not disgust that seized me [at the spectacle of a lice-infested working-class child] but a choking feeling that I later identified as a social conscience" (Bamberger 1980, 105). Some time later, when a German teacher had dismissed an essay of hers on Heinrich Heine as "the voice of the blood," she being the only Jewish girl in the class, it became clear to her "that I would not remain in Germany." After the enactment of the Nuremberg Laws (1935), there could be no question of her studying German literature and art history at a German university as she had planned; "no question either of remaining in the fatherland, so-called, which had suddenly ceased to be one" (105).

Such were the private circumstances and public experiences that set their mark on Mira Lobe and became the constituent factors of her literary work. Racism and loss of the fatherland strengthened and refined the sensitivity she had already developed for the plight of the outsider—minorities, the individual threatened and enslaved, the excluded. When Mira Lobe spoke of the bases of her particular critical-emancipatory perspective, she liked to quote Sigmund Freud, who ascribed his unprejudiced vision to his Jewishness: "I found that I was free from many prejudices which

inhibited others in the exercise of their intellects. I had been prepared for the role of opposition and could dispense with a harmonious agreement with the compact majority" (Leiter 1980, 4). This ability to dispense with general agreement and this view of the whole from the edges was formulated anew by the eighty-year-old author when in 1993 she sketched an oval on the coffeehouse table, tapped the outline with her finger, and said, "Do you know, I too always feel as if I were out here somewhere on the edge" (Freund 1992, 2).

"If there is something I can't stand it's when someone says: 'That's the way it is.' It makes me feel constricted, as if I were confined in a cage. . . . I felt a stranger, I wanted to get away somewhere far, far away. I had a longing to be myself." These are the words, and the thoughts, that Mira Lobe gave the youthful heroine of her novel *Die Räuberbraut* (1974). The girl gives expression here to an attitude and a state of feeling, to commitment and resistance, but also to impotence and alienation in a society that out of its own satiety and indifference allows political criminality free rein and ignores human want and misery. The words apply equally to Mira Lobe's experience of life and her own perception of herself, and they relate also to an essential aspect of her work as a writer of books for children and the young. What is it that has raised her writings above the general run of literature written in this field? What is it that makes so many of her books suitable for grown-ups—what makes them parables and allegories of human life, even though they are customarily categorized as literature for the young? What are the experiences that nourished her creativity with its urge to spread enlightenment, encourage practical humanity, tolerance, and democracy? In what form is the Jewish experience present and palpable in her oeuvre?

This specific quality of Mira Lobe's work is best understood by keeping in mind the view expressed in Marcel Reich-Ranicki's book, *Über Ruhestörer: Juden in der deutschen Literatur* (1989):

I take exception . . . above all to the view that literature produced by Jews is different because

Jews have a different mentality, a different heritage. In the last hundred years Jews have played their part in all the various trends of German literature. . . . There is no earthly way by which, looking at a poem or a piece of prose, one could say the style suggests a Jewish author. Not in a single instance. There is no such thing as a Jewish style unless it be that a given Jew writes bad German. But the influence is enormous. Not the influence of the Jewish heritage or any Jewish disposition, but the influence of the biography of the Jew: the Jew within a non-Jewish society. . . . That belonging to an oppressed minority strengthens and intensifies certain human characteristics of the oppressed individual, can, indeed, in a high degree, distinctively shape the structure of his psyche, cannot be disputed. (201)

There are, with few exceptions, no Jewish figures in the work of Mira Lobe. In one story only (the more darkly powerful, perhaps, for its singularity) does she openly and directly deal with the problem of the Jewish experience or, more specifically, the Jewish female experience: the short story "Die Lüge" (The lie) in the anthology *Der Eisstoß* (1972) edited by Oskar Jan Tauschinski. In this little work—which was written, it should be noted, not for children but for adults—her central preoccupations come together within a single focus. The story is of a young Romanian Jewess named Mína who manages to escape from her persecutors and find refuge in Palestine. The story's background of fact is provided by the incredibly brutal pogroms against the Jews, which came about after the reconquest of the Bukovina in July 1941 by Romanian and SS troops. The Bukovina had been occupied by Red Army troops in June 1940 as a consequence of the Hitler-Stalin Pact. According to the latest estimates, more than half of Romania's 800,000 Jews fell victim to the campaign of persecution and extermination instituted by the Germans and the Antonescu regime.

The main interest of the author lay not in the physical extermination but in the spiritual destruction of a young woman, expressed in what the narrator calls the "myth of the heroic daughter." The story reveals that the young woman does not—indeed, cannot—tell the whole truth about the terrible events surrounding the deportation of her family and the murder of a neighbor. She cannot speak out because that would include the monstrous and self-annihilating recollection of her own shameful enslavement in a brothel called "For Officers Only." This Mína edits out of her account of events: instead, she presents herself as the heroic daughter who, gravely wounded, still attempts to save her father's life. We discover that she incurred the injury to her knee while trying to escape from the brothel. But this must be repressed, because nothing is allowed to remind her of the brothel. "To whom could she have spoken of it? How could she tell her story when it began: I was a whore in a brothel for soldiers . . . ?" The destruction her degradation brings about is so complete that she is left at a point where, in the words of the narrator, "her last meager right [is denied her]: that of speaking the truth." The "heroic myth," which Mína believes herself, is a concrete necessity for her simple physical survival, but in the face of such a traumatic experience she becomes unable either to give or to receive love. Mína, according to the narrator, is reduced to a "person" lacking a warm human identity. To her uncle she appears, as a result, "full of hate and rebellion."

The narrator gives us at first a "conventional" victim story, the like of which is frequently told by Jewish men and women; a story that can serve the function of collective communal dialogue. By being borne in community the suffering can be made bearable and, to all appearances, mastered. But the narrator does not restrict herself to this particular function; she illuminates another dimension, within which the young woman is not allowed to find sympathy and support even within the Jewish community of victims because she cannot break the taboo that forbids her to speak of her enslavement and degradation as a woman. No safety net is spread for her with her specifically female experience; as a Jewish woman she remains, in this regard, solitary. Even the narrator, herself a member of the Jewish community of victims, fails in the task of helping; she recognizes her failure but soothes her conscience with her helplessness: "For a few days I wondered if I ought to visit her in the home. But I did not; I was too cowardly. She would tell me again of her father, the myth of the heroic daughter who threw herself upon his dead body." Cowardice, in the work of Mira Lobe, is a key word.

Mira Lobe's short story is more than a one-dimensional study of the catastrophic psychological consequences of the violence that breaks the will of women; this element is placed in indissoluble association with the fate of the Jews in the twentieth century.

The story "Die Lüge" offers a tragic working out of the preoccupations that recur in the writer's books for children and the young, which transform these themes into bright and optimistic forms. But the potentially tragic dimension always lurks in the background. Mira Lobe turns the prophylactic force of her writing, in a world made perilous and menacing, toward mastering and warding off all those things that in "Die Lüge" become catastrophic reality. Her endeavor seems to me to be nourished by her particular experience as a Jewish emigrant, committed to the values of the Enlightenment.

Her world is an uncertain and dangerous place, threatened by the divisions of class and rank and by gender-specific injustice—a world that has exchanged solidarity for success fetishism. A particularly impressive story is "Keine Schule für Sara" (No school for Sara), which was published in the anthology *Ich verstehe die Trommeln nicht mehr: Erzählungen aus Afrika* (1979), edited by Renate Welsh. Here the author shows how racist exploitation compels a black family to break off the education of their daughter Sara. Her father, once an idealistic revolutionary, is a broken man. He removes his daughter from the hostel. The teacher sums it up bitterly: "Stealing bread is forbidden. Anyone who steals bread is punished. But these white gentlemen steal our children!"

Liberty, equality, and solidarity must be continually reachieved. Over and over again the stories of Mira Lobe portray a world characterized by arbitrary power and dictatorial aspirations; they make explicit the causes and consequences of physical and mental violence; they exhibit the distortion of reality that results from the habit of glossing over things; and they emphasize the power of the imagination to soothe suffering and master life. They have nothing to do, however, with bland daydreaming or simple adventure.

Lobe's books are critical of authority. The most recent example is the book for small children, *Die Yayas in der Wüste* (The yayas in the desert; 1986). A male yaya rises to the position of "great guru" and, acting completely alone, makes decisions that are counter to all reason and that are very nearly fatal to the entire animal population of the desert. In the end, however, the great guru is willing to learn and to change his ways.

Lobe's books question the justification and utility of traditional modes of thought and action and explore the practical possibilities and risks of change. A good example is *Denk mal, Blümlein* (1971). Herr Blümlein, a gardener who is fond of children and is an antimilitarist, helps some children to convert an equestrian monument into a useful rocking horse for the park. Herr Blümlein is dismissed, but the children turn the statue of the heroic warrior—who, after heavy rains, falls off his horse into the grass and gets his nose out of joint in the process—into a memorial for the dismissed gardener.

Mira Lobe also turned her attention to the lie of language. Her works show a high degree of critical consciousness with regard to language: they reveal empty phrases and mere *façons de parler* for what they are. Moral conceptions customarily invoked in the educational process are also critically illuminated. She takes her readers behind the scenes to show them hypocrisy and dishonesty; she turns the spotlight on prejudices. In her book *Die Geggis* (1985), she presents the traditional education in prejudice as the expression of collective fears. At the end, however, we have the liberating recognition: "If I did not know that I am I and you are you, I would believe that I am you and you are me."

Mira Lobe explored the room for maneuver between the necessity of "civil courage" and the dangers of blind, collective action. In the book *Dobbi Dingsda fängt ein Monster* (1993), the supposedly weak Dingsdas (Thingummies) are menaced by a monster "from right down and right inside" the earth. Their first impulse is flight. But Dobbi organizes the peaceful and tender Dingsdas into a resisting force. When the monster is caught, he turns out to be a "poor Who-knows-what," without a home of his own and full of grief. The victors, nevertheless, want to drag him out into a lonely and desolate region and leave him there to starve. But Dobbi prevents the act of collective vengeance.

The writer never openly or directly made anti-Semitism, the persecution of the Jews, or Jewish life after 1945 a central issue of her work. From the 1960s, nevertheless, these themes increasingly found a place even in her literature produced for young people. But, interestingly, it was not the Jewish emigrant writer Mira Lobe who intrepidly attacked such themes; rather, it was a few of her non-Jewish Austrian colleagues: Winfried Bruckner (*Die toten Engel,* 1963; *Damals war ich vierzehn: Leben unter dem Hakenkreuz,* 1978); Käthe Recheis (*Das Schattennetz,* 1964); Renate Welsh (*In die Waagschale geworfen,* 1988); and Peter Sichrovsky (*Mein Freund David,* 1990).

Mira Lobe's message is more carefully concealed, more coded, than those expressed by these writers. In particular, her books for the very young are often sharply fundamental parabolic constructions. In two early works, *Insu-Pu, die Insel der verlorenen Kinder* (Hebrew, 1948; German, 1951) and *Der Tiergarten reißt aus!* (1953–54), the reader with an awareness of what to look for discovers, in contrast to the later books, the most unambiguous allusions the author ever made to the Jewish plight, even though it does look as if she was at pains to eradicate even these meager traces. There is, for instance, in *Insu-Pu* an account of a dangerous undertaking involving the transportation of children from war-torn Urbia to Terrania. The journey to the strange and distant land is so described that it can be read as an account of a forced emigration. The whole, however, is so completely coded that the young post-1945 Austrian readership is not compelled to face the realities of emigration and exile but is given the chance, instead, to relate it to the Austrian experience of the allied bombing of German lands.

As for *Der Tiergarten reißt aus!* all the summaries of its contents tell us that it narrates the story of a zoo attendant's two children who try to restore the animals to their natural living conditions. What they do not record are the revealing details of Trude's dream of the liberation of the animals. After the liberation, for instance, we have "touching scenes of reunion" between certain animals; after they have been "collected together and sent away," the lion rejects the imputation that "we are lazy or even given to thieving." At the same time, however, the lion must stomach the reproach of "surpassing human beings" in arrogance. Finally, the animals are graciously allowed to stay "if they behave like good and decent citizens," although first the plan by a superintendent of police simply to shoot the "beasts" must be, with difficulty, warded off. This plan wakes in the lion "memories of days in the desert long past . . . and not pleasant ones either: . . . an uncle of his had been shot [by the hunters]; a cold shiver passed through the lion when he recalled it." After the failure of his extermination plan, the superintendent "washes his hands in innocence," and a few of the animals try out for the first time in freedom "the grave, majestic walk of the desert: . . . The difference a few hours of liberty makes."

Three motifs are clearly manifest in the work of Mira Lobe. These, it is true, could be regarded as constituent elements of the genre of critical fiction for children and the young generally, but in the case of Lobe it is more than likely that they have a basis in an experience of life. First, her fictions incline to situations in which some person or creature is suddenly made to feel *different, other* (and alone), because he, she, or it, in behavior or appearance, diverges from what is usual or feels somehow obliged to act in a manner that is regarded as extraordinary. These characters often come to be branded as aliens or even enemies. Figures in Lobe's stories lose the safety and security they have taken for granted, or are outcasts right from the start.

A second recurrent element is the sudden *catastrophe,* the imminent overthrow of order, which requires one to prove one's mettle, to master or prevent it, to overcome and thus survive. Lobe's survival stories that particularly call for solidarity include: *Bimbulli* (1964), *Dobbi Dingsda fängt ein Monster* (1993), *Komm, sagte die Katze* (1974), and *Willi Millimandl und der Riese Bumbum* (1973). *Komm, sagte die Katze* is remarkable for its theme of a flood compelling a sense of community that ignores distinctions of every kind until, with the return to normal conditions, the usual modes of behavior reassert themselves. Practical bravery; the courage to uphold one's convictions; the capacity for resistance, guile, and imagination; and the will to unified group action in the interest of survival: these are presented as the forces that help people to overcome peril. Young children and older ones, and even adults, appear who act from a sense of duty toward the human conscience and its continued watchfulness. They stand up and face the menace of reality without hushing it up or glossing it over. Slinking away from moral obligation or responsibility must not, in the world of Mira Lobe, be given the slightest chance.

Not least among the writer's aims was the development of the capacity for empathic experience. As a motto for the novel *Die Sache mit dem Heinrich* (1989), which she wrote for older children, she chose a passage from the farewell letter of Che Guevara: "Above all I wish for all of you that you will always be able to feel every injustice done to anybody else in any part of the world deep in your inmost being."

Third, the basis of all successful striving to overcome exclusion, authoritarian usurpation, and catastrophe in Lobe's view is a strong, calm self-confidence. It is the precondition for having both the energy required for principled resistance and the courage to be different where difference entails conflict. Mira Lobe allows many of her characters to make a first discovery of themselves, and this is always an experience that liberates and strengthens.

The best-known and perhaps also poetically the most successful realization of the fundamentals of the Lobe world is to be found in the writer's work of the 1970s, preeminently in *Das kleine Ich bin ich* (1972), which won many awards, and in *Dann rufen alle Hoppelpopp* (1977). In both of these books, written for the very young, the theme of personal insignificance (once in particularly impressive rhymed trochaic tetrameters, once in

prose) is developed to the point of the near annihilation of identity. Of "the somewhat different animal" we are told:

Through the town and through the streets
the colorful animal goes his way
goes and wonders to himself
Is it true that I am nothing at all?
Everyone says I am Nobody
Just a little
Nobody Special . . .
What if I don't exist at all?
[. . .] And the little colorful animal
quite unable to help himself
very nearly starts to weep.
But then . . .

In another passage, where five rabbits have allowed themselves to be persuaded by a stranger that they could only achieve individual identity by surpassing each other in swiftness, strength, cunning, and courage (although one of them is in danger of ending up a casualty of the process), we have the following. "'And what am I?' asked Kunikl. 'You? You are nothing at all!' answered the industrious bunny rabbits. Kunikl sat on the meadow and wept."

In both cases there is, of course, a happy ending. The colorful animal, with sudden insight, ceases to let himself be defined by the others and condemned to alien nonbeing; he achieves the freedom of "I am I." And the supposedly insignificant rabbit is the first to recognize a threat to all of them and to form them into a unitary group for survival. In both these of books, Mira Lobe introduced notions of experienced insignificance and powerlessness, which are probably not unknown to children, but which take them to no extreme conclusion. The bunnies find a place of safe refuge within themselves that helps them to achieve integration. To Mína in "Die Lüge" this is denied. How would the writer's novels for a grown-up readership have been received if ever she had been encouraged to produce them?

Mira Lobe's books communicate the Jewish communal experience of the twentieth century but not unmediated, not openly. This may have something to do with the fact that she perceived herself as an antifascist agnostic living in postwar

Austria. From the 1960s on, she was one of the most important and highly regarded Austrian writers for children. Jewish identity had its place only in the background of her creativity. To this extent her work was part of a tradition identified by Ruth Beckermann in her book *Unzugehörig* (1989), although she referred to people younger than Mira Lobe by a generation. What Beckermann writes is, nevertheless, equally true of the Lobe generation: "Some had integrated themselves, full of *élan* and enthusiasm, in [postwar] Austrian society. The period around 1968 was favorable to the most various illusions. The alliance with the New Left seemed viable; it was, after all, based on a common anti-fascism. In an act, the violence and rigor of which impressed us, our new friends broke with their Nazi parents, while we, with considerable naïveté, were prepared to feel ourselves accepted and at home. We didn't realize that once again, and for a long time before we sensed it, we had cut off a part of ourselves. We didn't hide the fact that we were Jews; we only never mentioned it."

Considered in the light of this, the attacks on the novel *Die Räuberbraut* (1974), made in the course of the antiterrorism debate of the 1970s, take on a new and disturbing dimension. At the time a well-known Austrian journalist discovered in Mira Lobe's work "Marxist-Anarchist turns of phrase" and denounced her as the "mother of terrorism"—Mira Lobe, of all people.

Lobe's work leads, often in parabolic fashion, to fundamental issues—for example, the questioning of the possibility of survival—and then breaks off at this point or supplies positive solutions. She would have nothing to do, she said, with books "infatuated with death." It may be that anything that is not courageous and life-affirming is not, from her point of view, an option to be offered to children and adolescents. That there is the potential in the author for a more far-reaching exploration is obvious from the quality of such stories as "Die Lüge" or "Keine Schule für Sara." It is impossible to tell how far Mira Lobe allowed herself to be influenced or overruled by the needs and strategies of publishing houses and of the institutions that foster children's literature in Austria.

Lobe's work aims at smuggling the spirit of a humanistic enlightenment into the hearts and minds of her readership. She found for herself a sort of "middle" literary form, one midway between complete exclusion and open confrontation and still capable of a critical engagement with the more disturbing aspects of human or historical experience. Her literary process, especially in the Austria of the postwar years, proved (the emphasis must be on the past) to be a thoroughly effective way of winning over children, young people, and, not least, adults, to an affirmation of beliefs close to her own heart.

When I looked her up in 1994 to inform her of my intention of writing a short account of her work under the heading "Lobe, Literature, and Jewishness," she was amazed: "Well! my dear," she exclaimed, "But I have nothing to do with any of that!" Mira Lobe died on February 6, 1995, in Vienna.

Bibliography

Richard Bamberger, ed., "Mira Lobe: Autobiographische Notiz," *Jugendschriftsteller deutscher Sprache: BRD, Österreich, Schweiz* (Vienna: Leinmüller, 1980); Ruth Beckermann, *Unzugehörig: Österreicher und Juden nach 1945* (Vienna: Loecker, 1989); Michael Freund, "Freiheit ist besser als Speck," *Der Standard* (May 1, 1992): 2; Wolf Harranth, "Das könnte ich können: Ansätze zu einer Biographie," *Freiheit ist besser als Speck: Texte für Mira Lobe* (Vienna: Jugend & Volk, 1993), 7–19; Helmut Leiter, "Mira Lobe," manuscript of speech given in honor of Lobe upon her being awarded the Austrian "Fördigungspreis" for children's literature, 1980; Mira Lobe, *Bimbulli* (Vienna: Jungbrunnen, 1964); Lobe, *Dann rufen alle Hoppelpopp* (Vienna: Jugend & Volk, 1977); Lobe, *Denk mal Blümlein* (Vienna: Jungbrunnen, 1971); Lobe, *Dobbi Dingsda fängt ein Monster* (Vienna: Jungbrunnen, 1993); Lobe, *Die Geggis* (Vienna: Jungbrunnen, 1985); Lobe, *Insu-Pu, die Insel der verlorenen Kinder* (Vienna: Waldheim-Eberle, 1951); Lobe, "Keine Schule für Sara," *Ich verstehe die Trommeln nicht mehr: Erzählungen aus Afrika*, ed. Renate Welsh (Vienna: Jungbrunnen, 1979); Lobe, *Das kleine Ich bin ich* (Vienna: Jungbrunnen, 1972); Lobe, *Komm, sagte die Katze* (Vienna: Jugend & Volk, 1974); Lobe, "Die Lüge," *Der Eisstoß*, ed. Oskar Jan Tauschinski (Vienna: Jungbrunnen, 1972); Lobe, *Die Omama im Apfelbaum*

(Vienna: Jungbrunnen, 1965); Lobe, *Die Räuberbraut* (Vienna: Jugend & Volk, 1974); Lobe, *Der Tiergarten reißt aus!* (Vienna: Schönbrunn, 1953); Lobe, *Willi Millimandl und der Riese Bumbum* (Vienna: Jungbrunnen, 1973); Lobe, *Die Yayas in der Wüste* (Vienna: Jugend & Volk, 1986); and Marcel Reich-Ranicki, *Über Ruhestörer: Juden in der deutschen Literatur* (Munich: dtv, 1989).

KARL MÜLLER

1935 At the International Writers Congress in Paris, the exiled German authors lay down the foundation of their opposition to the Nazis: the defense of the "Ideas of 1789"

By 1930, years of political, social, and economic crisis had polarized the German intelligentsia into Left and Right and had further split the workers' movement. It was still an open question as to whether it would come down to a war of revolution—and if it did, it was not clear whether it would be a socialist or a nationalist revolution. Three years later the Nazis came "legally" to power. For the first time a counterrevolution presented itself as a revolution.

For the opposition authors, the burning of the Reichstag in February 1933 served as a beacon. The book burnings followed a few weeks later. Open opposition was from this point possible only from exile. For over 2,000 writers and journalists, as well as many musicians and painters, emigration was the only option. The cultural coalition that had formed in the Weimar Republic—as inconsistent as it had been—was destroyed.

The most important center for the German—and predominantly Jewish—émigrés (and the place where they arrived in the greatest numbers) was Paris, right up until its "fall" in 1940. France had had a reputation as the land of asylum for German intellectuals since Heine's time. As a literary metropolis, its capital was very attractive. It seemed to the émigrés to be a particularly advantageous point from which to observe the events in Germany; one remained nearby, able to return after (as the widespread illusion had it) the brief Right-radical interlude of the Nazis had come to a quick end.

Even the most pessimistic did not foresee the twelve-year reign of National Socialism. Nor did they imagine that the epoch would divide itself into two nearly equal parts: six years of preparation for war (1933–39) and six years of war (1939–45). Only this mindset explains how, despite everything, they fought with astounding spirit, courage, and cunning in the attempt, right up to the outbreak of the war, to battle fascism and its above all anti-Semitic propaganda with "the weapon of words." Part of this battle involved enlightening—and, looking ahead, warning—their host country, and thereby continually risking their own credibility. To risk one's own reputation abroad by taking up the role of Cassandra—even this required the strength to resist.

Arnold Zweig, the leftist novelist and Freudian whose psychoanalytic study of anti-Semitism in the Weimar Republic, *Caliban,* had been published in 1927, continued to react after the events of 1933. In exile in the south of France, where he had contact with Heinrich Mann and Lion Feuchtwanger, he struck a "balance of German Jewry," laid out in social-historical and intellectual-historical terms. Liberalism, which for many was synonymous with the principles of the French Revolution, had stood in "the Middle of Europe" for Western Civilization. On the one hand, "the cause of human equality . . . the cause of human rights" was "identical with the cause of the Jews"; on the other hand, the Workers' Party had always known "that they were the heirs to and managers of the Great Revolution." Most Jews failed to recognize "that, if one were to strip away their equal rights, they did not possess the means to fight to keep them." Now we were experiencing the situation in which a great Central European power (the Third Reich) was repealing the "Blessings of 1789." Insofar as both the Left and the Jews were deprived of "equality in human rights," there appeared to be a natural alliance of "Jewish intellectuals with the Workers' Parties." It was also apparent, however (now that it was too late), that the majority of Jews in Germany had assimilated into the wrong class, the bourgeoisie; for, taking their real "social situation" into account, they are "not bourgeois, but proletariats. They are proletariats with comfort and in ten-room apartments, with high levels of education and in intellectual jobs, but . . . they are not able to secure their present and their future with their own power, since they neither have political guarantees for their right to vote nor do they own the means of production" (Zweig 1961). They had deluded themselves with illusions about the potential for the repeal of constitutions. Nevertheless, enlightenment remained the necessary goal of a humane Socialism, and it was the role of the Jews, everywhere in the world, to be the bearers of *ratio,* of "reason."

Zweig, who declared the "repeal" of the German-Jewish intellectual symbiosis, traced the roots of this relationship—so fruitful in the past, but always in danger—back a century and a half to the symbol of reason and Enlightenment: the friendship between Lessing and Moses Mendelssohn.

Sanary-sur-Mer, where Zweig's "balance" appeared in 1933, was the second center of German writers in French exile. Along with Feuchtwanger, Arnold Zweig, Ludwig Marcuse, and Ernst Toller, Hermann Kesten and others lived here at least on occasion. The main site was of course Paris, where there was a concentration of publishing organs—book publishers, magazines, and newspapers. It was there that an organiza-

tional infrastructure was built. The aid committees also had their offices in the capital.

By autumn there was a newly founded *Schriftstellerverband* (Association of writers) headed by the former expressionist Rudolf Leonhard; in addition to him were Anna Seghers, Alfred Kantorowicz, and Ludwig Marcuse. Heinrich Mann served as honorary chairman. In the same autumn, Max Horkheimer and Friedrich Pollock moved the *Magazine for Social Research,* the organ of the Frankfurt school, to Paris, where it was published by Félix Alcan until 1940. Willi Münzenberg, who had led an entire media network for the German Communist Party (KPD) in Berlin, had also moved to Paris and prepared with his colleagues—including Arthur Koestler and Alfred Kantorowicz—the "Brownbook on the Reichstag Fire and the Hitler Terror"; its appearance had an international effect.

One year after the book burnings of May 1933, the German Freedom Library in Paris was opened, with Kantorowicz serving as general secretary. The library collected exile literature from the nineteenth century until the present day. One more date: the Institute for the Study of Fascism (INFA) was founded in June 1934. This institute was a sort of documentation center for education about Nazi Germany under the ideological leadership of Manès Sperber.

What resonance did German-language literature have in France? In hindsight, the period of the beginning of the crisis in France appears to have been simultaneously advantageous and disadvantageous. The émigrés were indeed especially affected by the limitations and complications that crisis brings; the added pressure brought by the spread of fascism, however, also awakened understanding and sympathy for the plight of the German writers and journalists in the progressive wing of the French intelligentsia, who responded by greatly easing access to publication—a concrete expression of solidarity.

Through the efforts of the French Left to build a common front through various antifascist committees—the preliminary efforts that led to the People's Front in 1935—those writers exiled from their increasingly dangerous neighboring country, whose problems threatened to spread over the borders, were accepted as fellow fighters and were given the opportunity to issue an authentic warning. It is in light of this development that the outstanding success of the "first anti-Nazi play" in the Paris Theater—Ferdinand Bruckner's *Die Rassen*—must be seen. With over one hundred performances, it became the most successful play written by an emigrant playwright. Its success is also noteworthy because the genres of drama and poetry rarely find much favor abroad because they are more difficult to translate. Novels and essays are generally better received: they become the representative forms of exile literature. The common fight achieved an international character, with German and French writers occasionally publishing on the pages of the same magazines.

Among the three hundred books and 1,300 articles published by German-speaking writers in exile in France between 1933 and 1940, one can discern what could be published in French translation, by whom these pieces were being written, and where they were appearing. What were the interests of the host country's readers and publishing houses, and what expectations did the German-speaking writers seek to meet?

It is readily apparent that the book market was more traditional and more commercial than the magazine market. The smaller size of the book market, the longer time needed for book production, the prohibitive costs of translation, and the greater risk of investments after the crisis—all of these factors contributed to the tendency to focus on current trends and fashions. What was fashionable in the literature of these years—in France and abroad—was primarily the biographical and historical contemporary novel. It is hardly surprising, therefore, to find among the top producers three writers of glorified popular fiction: Stefan Zweig, Emil Ludwig, and Vicki Baum. With seventeen, fifteen, and fourteen translations, respectively, they maintained their positions at the top of the best-seller lists that they had occupied in the 1920s.

At the next level were Thomas Mann (with nine translations), Heinrich Mann (with five), Jakob Wassermann (six), and Ernst Erich Noth (seven). After them came Gina Kraus (four), Jo-

seph Roth (three), Lion Feuchtwanger (three), Irmgard Keun (three), and Adrienne Thomas (three). With two translations apiece were Alfred Döblin, Arnold Zweig, Siegfried Kracauer, Gustav Regler, Ödön von Horváth, Arthur Koestler, Alfred Neumann, and Ernst Glaeser. Rounding out the list with one translated book to their credit were René Schickele, Annette Kolb, Bernard von Brentano, and Anna Seghers.

A quick glance at this list of names shows no members of the avant-garde (with the exception of Döblin): neither Bertolt Brecht nor Walter Benjamin, neither Ernst Bloch nor Hermann Broch nor Elias Canetti was well enough known in the French publishing houses at the time to have their works published. Paris had almost no acquaintance with the new literary-political forms of 1920s Berlin, because they conflicted so openly (especially in their collective tendencies, like Brecht's *Lehrstücke*) with the still individualistic psychologically oriented *goût littéraire*. It was not until after the war that these authors got their first real French reception, which continues to the present day. During the few years of 1933–36, several changes are noticeable. When one compares the publications of 1933—when the literary marketplace, with few exceptions, had not yet reacted to the upheaval in Germany—with those of the following years, two movements emerge. The first was the overtaking of the historical novel by the contemporary novel (*Zeitroman*) in the first years of the exile. Many German-speaking writers were reacting to current developments or were simply trying to add to earlier successes. The slowing of this development after 1936 can be attributed to the oversaturation of the French market.

The second movement of these years draws on the boom in political books after 1934: the demand for information about the "new" Germany led to a veritable flood of representations, reports, and documentations about the fall of the Weimar Republic, the crisis that prepared the way for the rise of National Socialism, the tenets of National Socialism, the persecution of the opposition, and the concentration camps. With an average of fifteen translations each year, this field of literature was a match for the only slightly larger domain of belles lettres. Between the two movements stood the solid field of handbooks (of history, music, economics, and so forth).

After November 1934, writers of both East and West were preparing for the International Writers Congress, whose catchword—"the defense of culture"—had been coined by Paul Vaillant-Couturier. In the summer of 1934, the First United Congress of Soviet Writers took place, and numerous western authors attending also participated in the Paris congress—Johannes R. Becher, Klaus Mann, and André Malraux. The most important figure joining the two congresses was Ilya Ehrenburg, a Russian writer and journalist who was well acquainted with the earlier Berlin and the contemporary Paris scenes.

It was not readily apparent that the interests of the Comintern also played a role at the Paris congress in recruiting nonfascist intellectuals into active opposition against Nazi Germany. There was widespread consensus for the need for a cultural resistance against the apparently unstoppable rise of fascism in Europe. In other words: the goal of the congress organizers was to spread the political anti-fascist movement as far into the cultural sphere as possible. The congress, held June 21–25, 1935, became a big story in the media that 250 writers from thirty-eight countries gathered together. To build an alliance meant above all to put disagreements in the background in the interest of achieving a united front against the "totalitarian states," by which the Third Reich and Mussolini's Italy were meant, but not the Soviet Union. The defense of culture amounted to a defense of the Ideas of 1789. The dominant ideas were freedom, nationalism, individualism, and humanism. The protection and conservation of human rights were discussed much more than were social changes. Aesthetically, different forms of realism prevailed over avant-garde techniques. Intellectual oppositions like "reaction and progress" or "culture and barbarism" had wide currency; leftist vocabulary clearly dominated the conference.

The general consensus that the Revolution of 1789 was not yet "completed" allowed, on the one hand, for a declaration of commitment to the future realization of the revolution. On the other hand, it relativized the relationship to a twenty-year-old event—the Russian Revolution—in a way that disturbed many hoped-for allies.

The majority of the German-speaking participants were of Jewish descent. Egon Erwin Kisch, Alfred Kerr, Max Brod, and Klaus Mann all spoke on the first two days. They were followed by Alfred Kantorowicz, Rudolf Leonhard, Anna Seghers, Lion Feuchtwanger, and Ernst Bloch. Ernst Toller and Ludwig Marcuse sent greetings. Among the prominent French writers were André Gide and André Malraux; English-speaking writers were represented by Aldous Huxley and Michael Gold.

The selection of the main themes of the congress signaled an ecumenical line: "the cultural legacy," "nation and culture," "humanism," and "the individual" (see Klein 1982). Although the French writers above all debated how their amorphous "individualism" could be reconciled with a new mass collective community, Becher proclaimed humanism to be the bridge between the bourgeois writers (the "protectors") and the workers (the "fighters"). The same was the case with the "freeing of the legacy from the hands of those who illegally appropriated it" (those in the Third Reich, for example) and the "purification of our relationship to the Fatherland." The nation as a positive entity stood also in the center of Anna Seghers's speech "Love of the Fatherland": "The masses react inexorably to every mistake in the estimation of the national question." Seghers insisted on appealing to the longings of the young people in Nazi Germany, of taking the subjective factor more seriously. Klaus Mann argued along similar lines: in his view, the Left had not taken the "irrational" needs of the youth into account and had argued too narrowly and economically. "Socialist humanism" was instead "the complete and utter opposite of fascism."

The ideas of Enlightenment guided the language of Heinrich Mann (who described "knowledge" and "freedom to think" against "barbarism") and of Feuchtwanger, who declared his historical novels to be written "for reason and against stupidity." Brecht questioned the "puz-

zle" of fascist evil in his own way; instead of lash-
ing out against the appearance of barbarism, he
sought to expose its roots: the "maintenance . . .
[of bourgeois] property relations."

It remains to be noted that many of the famous
writers who emigrated from Berlin to Paris did
not take part in the congress, including such
unique authors as Alfred Döblin, Siegfried Kracauer, and Walter Benjamin. Nor did Joseph
Roth participate, although he had left his native
Austria and gone into French exile five years before the *Anschluß*.

The political activities of the exiled writers
after the congress of 1935 get only a brief mention: the (failed) attempt to form a German
People's Front and the participation in or public
support of the Spanish Civil War.

Shortly before the outbreak of World War II,
the antifascist movement, which was splitting
apart in the late 1930s, found a historical event
that provided the chance to take stock of itself:
the sesquicentennial celebration of the French
Revolution in July 1939. Many exiled writers
were invited to contribute to the numerous special memorial editions of Parisian newspapers and
magazines.

Walter Benjamin's contribution to the sesquicentennial celebration, published in the Paris-
based magazine *Europe,* consisted of commentaries
to letters collected under the title "Allemands de
Quatre-vingt-neuf." Benjamin sought to present
the effects of the revolution on contemporary
writers such as Herder, Forster, Hölderlin, and
others to the French public in such a way that—in
the reflection of German witnesses—some of the
problems of 1789 would be made visible again,
having maintained their power through historical
metamorphoses. To him, the most important
problem seemed to be nationalism. Those French
revolutionary armies could have claimed a historical right for themselves: "Mars français, protec-
teur de la liberté du monde." But the "seeds of
degeneration" in this same land, the connection of
the cult of "Virtue" with the "Terror," were also
planted. The storm clouds on the horizon of the
history of the bourgeoisie broke out "in contemporary Germany in the form of the most frightening storm. . . . The equation of the national ideal

with virtue, as Robespierre had in mind, became
with Hitler the equation of the national ideal with
race, which shows the difference between the
bourgeois leaders of the heroic age" and those of
the downfall.

In the heroic beginning of the epoch of 1789
stood the optimistic belief in progress, which in
France proceeded from the prevalence of reason
(with also the violence that was considered legitimate) and the confidence that natural conditions
could be overcome: in short, they believed in applied Enlightenment as a progressively conceived
process of humanization. At the end of the 150-
year period, according to Benjamin, the rebarbar-
ization of bourgeois society had begun, which—
most radically in Germany—brought about fascism in order to prolong its position in ruling and
production. Benjamin warned—only a few weeks
before the outbreak of the war—that the destruction of the Workers' Movement could also pose a
threat to other countries. Benjamin's critique, the
result of his experiences with the People's Front
and discussions in exile, was directed at the stubborn retention of formerly progressive concepts,
such as historicism and the faith in progress,
which had become antienlightened.

The ground for the differing views of the
writers in exile becomes visible here: the French
Revolution is not a united inheritance; it was not
the same for everyone. Whereas the liberals ral-
lied around 1789, the Jacobins saw their source in
1793. From the philosophy of the Enlightenment, liberal democracy could diverge (human
rights, the establishment of democratic institutions, individual freedom—with the societal correlative of capitalism), as could Jacobean-messi-
anic democracy, which proceeds in part from the
assumption that a true community cannot tolerate private ownership of the means of production.
Genealogically, one can speak here of the lineage
of Rousseau to Robespierre to Babeuf to Blan-
quito Lenin. Brecht and Benjamin stand in this
family line, whereas Feuchtwanger, contrary to
his own belief, was the embodiment of liberalism.
Heinrich Mann occupied a middle position, in
which he had a deluded propensity to see both
tendencies joined together, as contradictions out-
maneuvered the mutually exclusive conceptions.

Because 1789 meant the point of national consensus, whereas 1793 had divided the people, the bourgeois-liberal postulates held the upper hand in the aspiring German People's Front in exile. All, even the Communists, were outspoken in their acceptance of the front. Feuchtwanger and Heinrich Mann were not in a position to know that the Comintern sought to steer the Western People's Front to the realpolitical interests of the Soviet Union, to the point of sacrificing Socialist ideas if necessary. Their faith in the power of ideas, which the course of history finally decided, allowed them to imagine and hope for a combination of 1789 and 1917. The first, the liberal line, had planted itself in France; the second, the Jacobean line, planted itself in Russia. A coming together of the two strands on the European continent did not appear unthinkable.

For the writers in exile, the year 1940 showed signs of the apocalypse. If they did not decide to take their own lives in desperation—like Benjamin, Carl Einstein, Ernst Weiss, and Walter Hasenclever—there remained only flight, if possible to the United States, where they anticipated finding what was promised in Berlin as the "New European Order." While still in Finland, Brecht noted with grim cynicism in his diary: "The last performances of the *Marseillaise* will be silenced forever by the German bombers." Thomas Mann, who followed the developments in France in the newspapers from his home in California, quoted the press of the Third Reich on the occasion of the forthcoming Bastille Day celebration: "The conquered country must atone for its 'mistakes and crimes.' . . . Bastille day has to become a day of mourning, because it was the day on which everything bad began."

Every catastrophe seemed to be quickly followed by another. The most demoralizing of these for the émigrés had begun even before the outbreak of the war: the pact between Hitler and Stalin. In terms of foreign policy, the realization of the People's Front would have required an alliance of the Soviet Union with the western democracies against the fascist axis. But that would come only later.

Thus were the republican ideas carried through —deformed and detoured, with innumerable victims and for many much too late. If the price had not been so high, Lion Feuchtwanger and Arnold Zweig could have relaxed in their certainty that the ideas of 1789—which had human rights, individual freedom, and the sovereignty of the people at the center—would survive the dictatorial regimes.

Bibliography

Walter Benjamin, "Allemands de Quatre-vingt-neuf," *Gesammelte Schriften*, vol. 4 (Frankfurt a. M.: Suhrkamp, 1972); Albrecht Betz, *Exil und Engagement: Deutsche Schriftsteller im Frankreich der dreißiger Jahre* (Munich: Text & Kritik, 1986), Lion Feuchtwanger, *Centum opuscula* (Rudolstadt: Greifenverlag, 1956); Alfred Kantorowicz, *Exil in Frankreich* (Bremen: Schünemann, 1971); Wolfgang Klein, *Paris 1935: Erster Internat. Schriftstellerkongreß zur Verteidigung der Kultur* (Berlin: Akademie, 1982); Heinrich Mann, *Ein Zeitalter wird besichtigt* (Reinbek: Rowohlt, 1976); Klaus Mann, *Der Wendepunkt* (Berlin: Aufbau, 1974); Dieter Schiller et al., *Exil in Frankreich* (Leipzig: Reclam, 1981); Manès Sperber, *Bis man mir Scherben auf die Augen legt: All das Vergangene* (Vienna: Europaverlag, 1977); and Arnold Zweig, *Bilanz der deutschen Judenheit* [1933] (Cologne: Melzer, 1961).

ALBRECHT BETZ

TRANSLATED BY TODD HERZOG
AND HILLARY HOPE HERZOG

1936   Abraham Joshua Heschel's first major scholarly work, *Die Prophetie,* is published in Cracow, Poland, and distributed by Erich Reiss Verlag in Berlin

In December 1932, at the Friedrich-Wilhelms-Universität in Berlin, a still youthful Eastern European Jew, Abraham Heschel (1907–72), submitted the typescript of his *Inaugural-Dissertation* to his cosponsors, Max Dessoir of the philosophical faculty and Alfred Bertholet of the theological faculty. On February 23, 1933, Heschel passed his oral examinations for the doctorate. Four days later the Reichstag was set on fire, allowing Hitler further to consolidate his tyranny. Heschel, who was required to submit 200 published copies of his dissertation but was unable to find a publisher in Germany, was finally accorded the doctorate on December 11, 1935, after submitting galley proofs of *Die Prophetie,* which was published the following year by the Polish Academy of Sciences and Letters in Cracow.

Unlike two other spiritually gifted Eastern European Orthodox Jews, Joseph Soloveitchik (1903–93) and Alexander Altmann (1906–87), who wrote their dissertations on Hermann Cohen and Max Scheler, respectively, Heschel chose a biblical subject—and the one closest to his heart: the immediacy of the Bible's "God of pathos," a personal divinity who reveals passionate judgments of human actions to the Hebrew prophets. Heschel's phenomenology of consciousness (his thesis was originally entitled "Das prophetische Bewußtsein") formulated categories that later helped him convey, in often resplendent English prose, a sense of "radical amazement," intuitions of God's presence, as he evoked the inner life of holiness and moral vigor. Heschel's thesis, composed in Nazi Germany, mapped out this unique contribution to the spiritual life of modern Jewry.

Heschel's absorption of German culture typifies, in many respects, the itinerary of many Eastern European Jews from towns in Russia and Galicia, who migrated West to acquire a consummate European education. Born in Warsaw to parents whose ancestors were among the first disciples of Baal Shem Tov, the founder of Hasidism, Heschel received a thorough religious training, mastering the Bible, Talmud, and Hasidic written and oral sources. His native language was Yiddish, but he of course mastered Hebrew, both biblical and modern, as well as Aramaic. He was guided into modernity by Fishl Schneersohn (1887–1958), a physician, psychiatrist, and literary author born in Kamenetz-Podolsk who had received his medical degree from the University of Berlin. Heschel left Warsaw to study at the secular, Yiddish-language Real-Gymnasium in Vilna, the city known as the Jerusalem of Lithuania. By then he had published two poems in Yiddish in Warsaw. With support from secular writers in his native city, he studied Polish and German in preparation for the university.

Arriving in Berlin in 1927, Heschel matriculated at both the university and the liberal rabbinical and research institute, the Hochschule für die Wissenschaft des Judentums, while maintaining contacts with people at the Orthodox Hildesheimer Seminary. Like many of his peers who were educated only in yeshivas or by rabbinic tutors, he was required to pass examinations for the Foreign Students Institute in German, literature, history, Latin, and mathematics in order to qualify for full university matriculation. He was a cultural immigrant who maintained his "mother tongue," Yiddish, while forming his mature identity within various German institutions, Jewish and secular.

In the end rejecting the ideologies of his two degree-granting institutions, Heschel found a spiritual and intellectual sanctuary in a discussion group led by David Koigen (1879–1933), a Russian-born social philosopher who in 1920 met Fishl Schneersohn at the University of Kiev. In fact, both men had entered modernity from a traditional Hasidic upbringing. Koigen formed his thinking at the universities of Vienna, Leipzig, Berne, Zurich, and Berlin, where he studied with Dilthey and Simmel and had first met Martin Buber. It was probably in Koigen's seminars that Heschel forged his commitment to revive an authentic Hasidic spirit among contemporary Jews. The background was defined in Koigen's vivid autobiography, *Apokalyptische Reiter* (Apocalyptic horsemen, 1925), which recounts his experience of the Russian revolutions, the ensuing civil wars, and his rediscovery of the naive faith of the simple Ukrainian Jews among whom he grew up. A year after Koigen's sudden death on March 7, 1933, Heschel published a memorial essay in the Zionist newspaper *Jüdische Rundschau,* in which he explained that his Berlin mentor represented "an ancient will, which, since the Bible, we find in Jewish thinking through the Aggadah, Kabbalah, and Hasidim" (Feb. 27, 1934). Heschel thus defined his own mission.

Neo-Kantian epistemology provided the paradigm against which Heschel formulated his theology of divine pathos. Early in his studies, he realized that his professors were not addressing the right questions: "To them, religion was a feeling. To me, religion included the insights of the Torah which is a vision from the point of view

of God" (Heschel 1954). Theocentrism was Heschel's model. God is the subject of which human beings are objects of concern.

In a dramatic autobiographical parable, Heschel summarized his cultural crisis. It begins: "I came with great hunger to the University of Berlin." He describes himself walking alone "through the magnificent streets of Berlin. I admired the solidity of its architecture," he continues, "the overwhelming drive and power of a dynamic civilization. There were concerts, theaters, and lectures by famous scholars about the latest theories and inventions, and I was pondering whether to go to the new Max Reinhardt play or to a lecture about the theory of relativity." But religious memory intervened. Heschel realized that the sun had set without his mandatory prayer, and the words of the Hebrew *Minha* service rang in his awareness; then the words of Goethe's famous poem "Über allen Gipfeln ist Ruh" (O'er all the hilltops is quiet) which he transformed into "O'er all the hilltops is the word of God." For Heschel, this was a drama of attentiveness, not a clash of doubt and faith. If there was a battle to be fought, he would "give the weaker rival a chance: to pray first, to fight later," Piety had wrestled with philosophy and won.

Heschel preserved his spirit while immersed in German culture. He continued to write poetry in Yiddish, and he published significant sequences in the New York periodical *Zukunft* and in a Yiddish periodical, *Berliner Bleter,* which he cofounded. Heschel collected these poems and added more to publish his first and most autobiographical book, *Der Shem Ham'forash: Mentsh* (Mankind: God's ineffable name; 1933).

At the same time, other German institutions sustained him. After completing his university examinations and his degree at the Hochschule (Heschel was ordained in June 1934), and while he was still seeking a publisher for his dissertation, Heschel deeply impressed Erich Reiss (1887–1951), a cultured German-Jewish publisher and friend of Gottfried Benn and Max Reinhardt. (The Erich Reiss Verlag, founded in 1908, specialized in German literature and translations, theater, the fine arts, and some Jewish subjects.) Reiss invited Heschel to establish a new series, "Judaism Past and Present," and to solicit manuscripts from Jewish authors excluded from "Aryan" firms. The series opened with the first book Heschel wrote in German for a wide readership, a biography of Moses Maimonides, whose eight-hundredth birth anniversary was celebrated throughout the world.

The dust jacket of Heschel's *Maimonides* (1935) announces several projects that, if realized, would have enhanced the recently awakened Jewish renaissance: a book by historian Mark Wischnitzer, husband of Rakhel Wischnitzer-Bernstein, an art historian who had contributed an essay to Heschel's ephemeral Yiddish journal; a biography of Philo of Alexandria by Edmund Stein, professor at the Warsaw Institute for Jewish Studies; a book on Rashi by Ismar Elbogen, one of his teachers at the Berlin Hochschule; and three anthologies: one each of beautiful Jewish poems, Jewish letters, and Jewish art history. Heschel also announced the belated publication of his dissertation with the provisional title *Die Propheten* (The prophets). But history disrupted this cultural flowering. Only Wischnitzer's *Jews of the World* and Heschel's two books actually appeared.

As an editor, however, Heschel made another significant contribution to the spiritual resistance of German-speaking Jewry. He helped publish *Der Sohn des verlorenen Sohnes* (The son of the lost son; 1935), the first novel of Soma Morgenstern (1896–1976), who was a journalist from Vienna and friend of Walter Benjamin. Morgenstern's autobiographical story of the son of an apostate Jewish doctor living in Vienna who returns to his Hasidic roots in the Ukraine appealed both to nonobservant Jews and the Orthodox. Morgenstern's recognition of the rifts within contemporary European Jewry struck deeply.

Heschel participated fully in the spiritual resistance to the Nazis. In 1935, he taught at the Berlin Lehrhaus, a gathering place for Jewish thinkers of all kinds. That year he completed his spiritual and intellectual biography of the Rambam (as Maimonides was also known), which emphasized both the sage's preoccupation with prophetic inspiration and his activist final years as healer of bodies. Heschel had found his genre: he combined portrayals of the inner life with an ethical engagement with history. His series of brief essays on talmudic sages, meant to inform assimilated German Jews how classical Judaism was created in times of persecution and exile, appeared in the Berlin *Jüdisches Gemeindeblatt* from February to August 1936. Heschel's biographical essay on Don Isaac Abravanel, the Spanish-Portuguese scholar and statesman, was the last book published by the Erich Reiss Verlag in 1937 before it was liquidated by the Nazis. He concludes wryly by explaining that because the "desperate Jews of 1492" were expelled from the Iberian peninsula, they could not share responsibility for mass murders perpetrated in the New World by the Conquistadors. A strange consolation indeed for loyal German Jews soon to be driven from their homeland.

Meanwhile, Heschel had met Martin Buber (1878–1965), the acknowledged leader, with Leo Baeck (another of Heschel's professors at the Hochschule), of Jewish renewal and resistance. Their subsequent involvement was mediated, perhaps, by another distinguished German-Jewish institution, the intellectual periodical *Der Morgen,* which was founded in 1925, and among whose contributors we find Alexander Altmann, Leo Baeck, Hugo Bergmann, Martin Buber, Joseph Carlebach, Ernst Cassirer, Ludwig and Lion Feuchtwanger, Franz Rosenzweig, Ernst Simon, and many more. Heschel was introduced into this community by the multitalented Leo Hirsch (1903–43), a poet, playwright, essayist, and journalist—and an observant Eastern European Jew who wrote books in German on Judaism, ritual, and cultural history and taught courses on Yiddish literature at the Berlin Lehrhaus. Hoping, perhaps, that Heschel's Yiddish poetry might help remedy Jewish alienation—what Hirsch called the *seelisher Luftmensch* (a spiritually empty person)—a reviewer at *Der Morgen* praised Heschel's collection as "modern poems from a Polish Jew" whose Western scholarly training lent credence to his "innate Jewish force" (Aronstein 1935). In June 1935, Leo Hirsch published his German translation of Heschel's emblematic poem "I and Thou," which had already been published twice in Yiddish.

That same month, Heschel began a substantive correspondence with the author of the original "I and Thou" (1923).

As an event of intellectual history, Heschel's "dialogue" with Buber fortifies prophetic faith derived from divine revelation against religion interpreted by social philosophy—the two prominent conceptions of Judaism in the twentieth century. Heschel first wrote Buber in June 1935, soon after his "I and Thou" poem appeared in *Der Morgen.* Buber answered immediately, enclosing a recent offprint of his own, "Sinnbildische und sakramentale Existenz in Judentum" (Symbolic and sacramental existence in Judaism), a contribution to the previous year's Eranos Conference.

Heschel's response, dated July 24, 1935, defines his position as a modern religious thinker: "I must confess that I would not endure it to experience the event [of prophetic inspiration] as a mere illustration,—to have no meaning [in itself], to be just a *sign* of meaning [*Sinnbild*]" (Kaplan 1996, chap. 6). Such was the thrust of Heschel's dissertation: to refute anthropological or psychological accounts of divine revelation. Alarmed at what he considered to be—at least potentially—Buber's subversive message, Heschel asserted the transcendent source of the Sinai revelation.

Heschel's confrontation with Buber had completed his battle with neo-Kantianism. Buber's historical interpretations, despite Buber's recognition of God's initiative as the "Eternal Thou," might lead to a secularized religion. For Heschel, nothing less than the living God could make Judaism survive in the contemporary world.

Of more immediate consequence than their philosophical differences, however, was the fact that, as director of the Frankfurt Freie Jüdische Lehrhaus and chairman of Mittelstelle für Jüdische Erwachsenenbildung (Center for Adult Education), Buber might help Heschel find a paying position. Frankfurt am Main, where Buber had reopened Rosenzweig's *Lehrhaus* in 1933, was the final stage of Heschel's journey from Hasidism into modernity. Appreciating Heschel's knowledge of classical Jewish sources, his training in European philosophy, and his authentic Hasidic spirit, Buber invited him to Frankfurt to be co-director with the jurist Ernst Kantorowicz

(1892–1942), who did not have adequate Jewish knowledge. On March 1, 1937, Heschel, at age thirty, arrived in Frankfurt to begin his work on adult education by drafting guidelines on the prayerbook and other Jewish sources. He lectured in Frankfurt and traveled by train to neighboring towns, teaching the rudiments of Bible study, Jewish philosophy, and more.

During the nineteen months that he lived in Frankfurt, Heschel became the prophetic witness he would remain. His intellectual life flourished even though his civil status was increasingly at risk. He completed projects begun in Berlin: he distributed his books—on the prophets, on Maimonides, on Abravanel—and he began to redact monographs on the medieval metaphysician Solomon Ibn Gabirol. Heschel carefully placed these purely technical studies (all written in German) in publications associated with German Liberal, Orthodox, and American Reform institutions. Closer to his heart, however, was a new project: essays on prayer that might lead to a more personal book on religious consciousness.

In February 1938, Heschel was called upon to expound his understanding of the impending war. Buber had been invited to address a group of Quaker leaders by his friend, Rudolf Schlosser (1880–1944), a German Quaker and pacifist. But that evening Buber was overcome by influenza, and he designated Heschel to take his place. Among those present were Rudolf and Amalie Schlosser and the widow of Franz Rosenzweig. "Buber's assistant"—as Heschel was known—interpreted the historical moment in theological terms. Entitled "Versuch einer Deutung" (Seeking a meaning), his speech opened dramatically with a symbolic scene: "Carried over the gates of the world in which we live is the escutcheon of the demons. In our time it is happening that the peoples are forging their sickles into swords and their scythes into spears. And by inverting the prophetic words entirely, the peoples turn away from the words that come from Zion." (Heschel published a revised translation of this speech in the *Hebrew Union College Bulletin,* Mar. 1943.)

Heschel's judgments were bold. His audience—Jews, and Quakers who heroically saved Jews and others from the ravages of disease, poverty, and persecution—would have understood that religious people are particularly sensitive to the emergency's true meaning. Heschel judged contemporary civilization as a whole, especially institutional religion, for the trivialization of belief and diminished moral courage. People had lost contact with ultimate truth and replaced "God's Name" with idols. In addition, Heschel's historical assessment was realistic: Jews must leave Germany. His distinctive blend of intimacy with God and ethical urgency, however, pointed to a theological confidence even at the brink of despair: "The Jewish teachers tell us: Wherever Israel had to go into exile, the Eternal went with them. The divine consequence of human fate is for us a warning and a hope."

Then one horrifying week shattered any hint of security that Heschel, or any other Jew in Germany, might have preserved. On March 12 the Germans invaded Austria, and the *Anchluß* (annexation) was completed the very next day. That same day, as well, Martin Buber and his wife left Frankfurt for Jerusalem. Heschel's family in Vienna endured persecution, while in Warsaw his mother and sister remained helpless. He and Buber continued to exchange letters quite regularly, and on April 25, 1938, Buber was installed at the Hebrew University in Jerusalem as professor of social philosophy. Heschel, himself without a visa, had no choice but to remain in Frankfurt and continue his research and pedagogical activities. But on October 28, Heschel was one among thousands of other Jews with Polish passports crammed onto sealed and guarded trains and driven to the border between Germany and Poland.

Contacts in Warsaw helped Heschel return home by the first week of November 1938. He found temporary refuge with his mother and sisters, near the neighborhood where he had grown into adolescence. Heschel was fortunate to have been deported, for Hitler's police had carried out an expulsion that inaugurated the destruction of European Jewry. The following week, during the night of November 9–10—called "Bloody Thursday" at the time—synagogues and Jewish stores were burned, Jews were beaten and sent to concentration camps, and many Jews committed

suicide. Four days later, Heschel's friend and benefactor Erich Reiss was arrested in Berlin and sent to the Oranienburg concentration camp. At the time, who could have imagined the aftermath?

Three weeks after his return to Warsaw, Heschel was invited to join the faculty of the Warsaw Institute for Jewish Science (Instytut Nauk Judaistycznych), a modern academic institution established in 1928. Replacing the eminent historian Moses Schorr (1874–1941), Heschel taught Bible and Jewish philosophy. By then Heschel was constructing the "systematology" of Judaism (as he explained in a letter to Buber) that he would elaborate during his first decade in the United States. Heschel had established a definitive direction for his writings.

Heschel advanced the possibility of a faculty position at a Reform rabbinical seminary, Hebrew Union College in Cincinnati. For several years already, its president, Julian Morgenstern, had dedicated himself to saving a group of European Jewish scholars he called his "College in Exile." Heschel went on a transit visa to London, where he remained for nine months. After finally obtaining a nonquota visa, Heschel embarked for New York, and on March 12, 1940, he reached safe haven.

Heschel had absorbed the cultures of several European cities—Hasidic and modern Warsaw; secular Vilna; cosmopolitan Berlin; and Frankfurt. In 1939 his two essays on prayer asserted the power of human piety to touch God's consciousness and join two modern Jewish institutions: "'Al Malhut ha-Teffila" (On the essence of prayer) was intended for the Mayer Balaban Festschrift in Warsaw, but the volume was confiscated and destroyed by the Nazis; "Das Gebet als Äusserung und Einfühlung" (Prayer as expression and empathy) was published in the 1939, swan song issue of the *Monatsschrift für die Geschichte und Wissenschaft des Judentums*. This issue was also confiscated, but a few copies survived.

In the United States, where he was mastering still another language, Abraham Joshua Heschel transplanted his religious insight to new soil: "By penetrating the consciousness of the pious man, we may conceive the reality behind it" (*God in*

Search of Man, p. 8). In Hitler's Germany, Heschel had become a translator of Hasidic holiness; as an immigrant he would repeatedly renew the task.

Bibliography

Fritz Aronstein, review of *Der Schem-Hammeforasch-Mensch* in *Der Morgen* 10 (Mar. 1935): 570–71; Alexander Altmann, *The Meaning of Jewish Existence: Theological Essays, 1930–1939,* ed. Alfred Ivry, introd. by Paul Mendes-Flohr (Hanover, N.H.: University Press of New England, 1991); Martin Buber, "Sinnbildische und sakramentale Existenz in Judentum," *Eranos-Jahrbuch* 2 (1934): 339–67; Buber, *The Origin and Meaning of Hasidism,* trans. Maurice Friedman (New York: Horizon Press, 1958), 152–81; Abraham Heschel, *Die Prophetie* (Cracow: Polish Academy of Sciences, 1936), expanded trans., *The Prophets* (New York: Harper and Row, 1962); Heschel, *Don Jizhak Abravanel* (Berlin: Erich Reiss Verlag, 1937); Heschel, *God in Search of Man: A Philosophy of Judaism* (New York: Farrar, Straus & Cudahy, 1955); Heschel, *Maimonides: Eine Biographie* (Berlin: Erich Reiss Verlag, 1935); Heschel, *Moral Grandeur and Spiritual Audacity: Essays,* ed. Susannah Heschel (New York: Farrar, Straus & Giroux, 1996); Heschel, "Versuch einer Deutung," *Begegnung mit dem Judentum: Ein Gedenkbuch,* ed. Margarethe Lackmund (Bad Pyrmont: Stimme der Freunde, 1962), 11–13, rev. and trans. Heschel, "The Meaning of This War," *Hebrew Union College Bulletin* (Mar. 1943); Edward K. Kaplan, *Holiness in Words: Abraham Joshua Heschel's Poetics of Piety* (Albany: State University of New York Press, 1996); David Koigen, *Apokalyptische Reiter: Aufzeichnungen aus der jüngsten Geschichte* (Berlin: Erich Reiss Verlag, 1925); Koigen, *Das Haus Israel,* ed. Ernst Hoffmann (Berlin: Schocken Verlag, 1934); and Soma Morgenstern, *Der Sohn des verlorenen Sohnes* (Berlin: Erich Reiss Verlag, 1935), trans. Joseph Leftwich and Peter Gross, *The Son of the Lost Son* (Philadelphia: The Jewish Publication Society of America, 1946).

EDWARD K. KAPLAN

1936   Philo Press publications mark a turning point in the Centralverein's practice and ideology, from ambivalence about Jewish "reemancipation" to an endorsement of the settling of Palestine

In the summer of 1936, two series of articles were published in the periodical of the Central Organization of German Citizens of the Jewish Faith (Centralverein deutscher Staatsbürger jüdischen Glaubens), the *C. V.-Zeitung:* "Jüdische Jugend im Alltag Palästina" (Jewish youth in everyday Palestine) by Heinz Warschauer, and "Das Knabenschiff" (The boys' ship) by Fritz Rothgießer. That same year, both series were published by Philo Press as books aimed at Jewish youth. In the transformation from newspaper series to book, "Jüdische Jugend im Alltag Palästina" was retitled *Jüdische Jugend baut auf: Vom Kibbuz in Palästina* (Jewish youth is building: From a kibbutz in Palestine). The account of a young man's impressions upon visiting Palestine focuses on the lifestyle of Kwuzat Habacharut, a group consisting mainly of young Jewish immigrants from Germany. Each short chapter relates a different aspect of the collective's activities: its interactions with the Arabs, its work, leisure, bathing, and so forth.

The second book is a novel set during the expulsion of Spanish Jewry. The Sedano Jewish community finds temporary refuge near Arsila in Morocco. Pirates spirit away the Jewish boys to sell them into slavery; after a failed rebellion, they are rescued by Venetian sailors who, together with the boys, sink the pirates' vessel. After landing safely in Venice, the boys are joined by their families, all of whom are adopted by the local Jewish community. These two books allegorically suggest options for dealing with the plight of Jews in Nazi Germany. Yet despite their almost simultaneous publication by the same Jewish organization, their implicit recommendations are quite dissimilar.

Between the Nazi rise to power in 1933 and the banning of the Centralverein at the end of 1938, the organization underwent a variety of ideological permutations. The rapidly deteriorating situation of German Jewry prompted the Centralverein to reassess certain entrenched principles and policies. The appearance of the abovementioned books reflected a transitional stage in the organization's attitude toward Jewish nationalism and Palestine: *Das Knabenschiff* recycled ideas inherited from the Centralverein's ideology during the first years of the Third Reich, whereas *Jüdische Jugend baut auf* signified a new direction in the Centralverein's thinking. The publisher of the books, Philo Press, which was founded in 1919 as the Gabriel Rieser Press, had long been associated with the Centralverein. The Centralverein's outreach to youngsters via the Philo Press had begun in the Weimar era but increased dramatically after the onset of Nazi rule. Though not expressly a children's press, it published eleven books for young readers between 1933 and 1938. Four had been newspaper serials in the *C. V.-Zeitung,* and five were part of the "Philo-Bücherei" (Philo library) literary collection, which was Philo Press's response to the popular "Schocken-Bücherei" (Schocken library). The publisher's efforts were part of the overall intensification of educational and cultural activity in the German-Jewish community between 1933 and 1938, as the leadership of the community came to fear for the preservation of Jewish identity among members of the next generation.

Literature addressed to children became a key tool in this educational effort, and youth movements, various communal organizations, adult publishing houses, and journalistic bodies all participated in the production of such works. Each ideological trend within German Jewry turned out a ramified children's literature of its own. Many organizationally and ideologically nonaffiliated publications took part in this effort as well. Although the main purpose of these works was to reinforce Jewish identity in the face of the officially sponsored assault against it—to create a "mobilized" literature that would offset government measures threatening Jewish cohesiveness—they had other aims as well. These works helped fill the breach created when Jewish youngsters who had been expelled from the gentile environment and shunned by their friends found themselves with a lot of time on their hands. Such literature offered a psychological haven from the hostile environment outside.

Consequently, *Jüdische Jugend baut auf* and *Das Knabenschiff* share certain characteristics common to all of this "mobilized" literature. First, their settings are physically and chronologically remote from contemporary Germany. In fact, practically the only literature for children written after 1933 that referred to the German present was children's supplements to newspapers and some youth movement publications. Books with plots set in Nazi Germany, like *Einer wie Du und Ich: Eine Jugenderzählung aus unseren Tagen* by Hans-Martin Schwarz (published by Alter in 1937) or *Spatz macht sich* by Meta Samson (published by Philo in 1938), are rare. Of course, many works treated the present indirectly. *Das Knabenschiff* is set in the western Mediterranean of the fifteenth century, whereas the plot of *Jüdische Jugend baut auf* takes place in Palestine, which is portrayed as the district of the future. Both, however, manifestly concern events in Germany during the 1930s.

A second feature running through most German-Jewish children's literature of the era is the protagonist's mastery over his own destiny. Often, the active position taken by the protagonist is aimed toward his destiny as a Jew, and in this sense he is a creative subject of his Jewish self-history. It is not surprising, then, that many of the protagonists are borrowed from the pantheon of traditional Jewish heroes and role models that succeeded in influencing Jewish history: the Maccabees, Maimonides, Prager Rabbi Löw, and so forth.

Points of convergence shared by *Das Knabenschiff* and *Jüdische Jugend baut auf* end there, however, for each was informed by its own ideological agenda and proposal for German-Jewish salvation. *Das Knabenschiff* relates a veritable odyssey during which the kidnapped boys affirm their religious identity. They probe metaphysical matters such as fate versus chance, meaning in human existence, and questions of theodicy. Such meditations are prompted by the text's primary concern—namely, the existential straits in which Spanish exiles found themselves. The analogy to refugees of the Inquisition must have seemed very attractive to German-Jewish authors, for Hermann Sinsheimer's popular *Maria Nunnez* (published by Philo in 1934) introduced it two years earlier. Persecution in both countries began after an epoch of coexistence and cultural cross-pollination. Still, there was a difference in the types of persecution faced by the two communities: Spanish Jews had the choice of flight or conversion, and opting to flee was simultaneously an affirmation of Jewish identity. German Jews, however, had no recourse to conversion. Yet the model of coreligionists taking the extreme measure of voluntarily uprooting themselves in order to persevere as Jews certainly ameliorated the painful prospect of an involuntary extirpation. For German Jews not yet thinking in terms of abandoning the country of their birth, the Spanish precedent served as an example of a Jewish community weathering a crisis by finding succor in its faith.

This faith, as seen in *Das Knabenschiff,* does not necessarily mean cult, prayer, or asceticism, but the belief in a metaphysical meaning of fate, in

God's supervision being everywhere and in the human ability to reach greatness. This assertion implies that a steadfast conviction in one's religious identity can see one safely through tribulations. The stories of the community who chose to leave behind the comforts of home rather than convert, of the triumph of the Spanish boys over the pirates, and finally the narration of their arrival in Venice were to inspire inner freedom as a shield against external oppression and to promote the belief that one's civic fate was not fully beyond the community's control. Only the determination in favor of Judaism, which in this context signifies inner freedom, could lead to a collective and civil freedom, as it is symbolized by the community's deliverance in Venice—"the state which . . . for all Spanish Jews embodied tolerance and security" (21).

The book's accent on themes of inner renewal and religious rededication nearly overshadows the fact that the precondition of the Sedano community's survival as a Jewish community is its emigration. German Jewry associated with the Centralverein in the early years of the Reich preferred to believe that the lapse of civil emancipation would be remedied shortly by a "second emancipation," and this belief was the ideological backdrop to the optimistic emphasis in *Das Knabenschiff*. As Margaliot has shown (1971, 167–79), the notion of "second emancipation" was often coupled with an insistence on "inner emancipation," by which a return to *Judentum* would give Jews the fortitude to ride out the storm and enable their eventual return to *Deutschtum*. Writing in *Der Morgen* in August 1933, Heinz Kellerman opined that in order "to preserve Germanness . . . [we must] acquire Jewishness," and to this end, "our Jewishness cannot be determined by the pressure of outside coercion, but rather by an consciousness of freedom."

Another indication that the plot line concerning emigration is happenstantial and not reflective of any recommendation on Rothgießer's part is the total absence of any reference in the book to Jewish nationality or nationalism. For instance, the Venetian Jews who welcome the refugee Sephardics are called "Glaubensgenossen" (core-

ligionists). *Das Knabenschiff*'s religiocultural delimitation of Judaism implicitly encouraged German Jewry's ironic penchant to see Jewishness as a means toward reemancipation and reacceptance as part of German culture, and it stands in sharp contrast to the portrayal of Judaism in *Jüdische Jugend baut auf*, which marks a critical turning point in the Centralverein's thinking toward Zionism and the settling of Palestine.

It seems that *Jüdische Jugend baut auf* is not a part of "immigration literature," which was common in the period and meant to supply information about potential destinations for relocation, although it could have served for this purpose and probably did for many. An available source for the details of this book was documentary literature relating impressions of Palestine (*Reiseberichte*), which were published as books or as newspaper reports. Zionist literature that focused on problems and questions from pioneers' lives in Palestine was popular as well, especially among Zionist circles. Publication of that literature dealing with the Hechaluz movement and its submovement Habonim Noar Chaluzi increased. These movements, which were socialistic and pioneer oriented, had published dozens of booklets that dealt mainly with the Labor Movement's activities in Palestine. Within this scope, booklets were dedicated to the second wave of Zionist immigration (for example, *Anfänge: Aus den ersten Tagen der zweiten Alija. Eine Sammelschrift,* 1934), panegyrics were published on the egalitarian kibbutz way of life (for instance, *Kibbuz: Kultur und Wirtschaft. Aus der Tagung des Kibbuz Hameuchad in Jagur, Juli 1933,* 1933), doctrinal apologetics were developed concerning the conflict with the Arabs (see *Zum jüdisch-arabischen Problem. Ein Sammelbuch,* 1933), and paeans were written to "Awoda Iwrit" (such as *Kfar: Im Kampf um Jüdische Arbeit,* 1934). These booklets were aimed at the members of the movements and not necessarily at the general public. In most cases they consisted of essays written by key people in the Labor Movement in Palestine, or they were descriptions and memoirs written by pioneers. Although the author of *Jüdische Jugend baut auf* sympathizes with the project of settling Palestine, his attitude is quite different from the one found in Zionist literature of the era generally and from that of *Hechaluz* in particular.

One of the most striking features of this book is the author's reluctance to use the word "Zionism" or any version of it in the text, almost as if he had reached the junction at which the unlikelihood of a "second emancipation" had been acknowledged, but any mention of the alternative by name was still taboo. Nevertheless, he is compelled in his descriptions of everyday life to resort to Zionist terminology, such as "Conquest of the soil," "Hebrew Labor," or "the vanguard of Hebrew labor," and to salient Zionist events and personalities such as the battle of Tel-Chai and Chaim Arlosorov.

Occasionally, Warschauer goes so far as to meditate on basic Zionist principles, without explicitly elaborating on their parent ideology: "One must be able to place oneself in the soul of people who have led unproductive lives in Exile or were torn away from their productive ones and now attempt with all their might and spirit to fundamentally reform the Jewish situation of the last nineteen hundred years. That this is a splendid undertaking, that a future for Jews as Jews can be ensured, that 'pioneering' ['Chaluziut'] is the sole trump card that we in our present sorry predicament have to show, can only be understood by someone who himself is a bit moved by this spirit" (99–100).

Similarly, when relating the concept of "Awoda Iwrit" (Hebrew labor), the author explains the rationale behind it while managing not to utter the unspeakable name of the ideology to which it belongs: "In Palestine, Jews will do all the work themselves for which they have been trained, and will not leave Arabs to do work in which Jews are competent just because perhaps it pays badly" (58). Warschauer attributes this thinking to "nationalen Gedanken" (national ideas) and offers his own nonideological explanation for this policy, speculating that the creation of positions for Jews in any and every type of employment is a way of maximizing the number of immigration certificates. For instance, in *Kfar Saba: Im Kampf um Jüdische Arbeit,* a booklet dealing with the same subject, the enumeration of pragmatic and material advantages of "Hebrew labor" takes a back seat to the grandiloquent presentation of its ideological import.

In *Jüdische Jugend baut auf* a young Jewish German enthusiastically describes his experiences among an idealistic band of German immigrants to Palestine. This work downplays the ideological dimension of the construction of Jewish independence in Palestine wherever it can, preferring simple, nontheoretical, and nonideological descriptions of daily life. Events are often narrated through a rather bourgeois lens; items on the *kwuza* menu and their caloric value, property belonging to the kwuza, aspects of the kwuza budget, and aspirations of kwuza members for creature comforts are all described at length. Warschauer may have believed that such a narrative strategy would help his German-Jewish readers to a greater comprehension of kibbutz life in Palestine. On the other hand, he may have been simply expressing a typical distaste of particular circles of German Jews for the Zionist option, with its connotations of Jewish national allegiance and Socialist policy.

The text's sympathetic rendering of settlement in Palestine, its semantic coyness aside, indicates a shift in the Centralverein's general opposition to emigration from Germany and into Palestine in particular. Insofar as one can gauge the evolution of the Centralverein's orientation by the books it approved for publication by the Philo Press, it would seem that it sanctioned more than merely Palestine qua haven, for the text cites the imperative of righting the inverted pyramid of Jewish occupational patterns in the Diaspora, and of manufacturing the idealized Sabra pioneer to supplant the spoiled, fragile, and emotionally stunted German "Yecke."

The Centralverein's shift was complex and not unequivocal. In its hailing of the new Palestinian super-Jew and supporting the critique of unproductive Jewish life in the Diaspora, echoes of anti-Semitic perspectives on German Jewry resonate distressingly. But other elements figure prominently as well, such as a valorization of the basic Zionist aim—namely, the survival of Jews as Jews—even if this meant conceding to the Zionists the expanded definition of Jews from a religiocultural population to a nation and forfeiting the dream of a second emancipation. Furthermore, the text's descriptions of Palestinian life in bourgeois terms implied that German Jews ideologically associated with the Centralverein would continue to reject many aspects of Zionist settlement but that their practical need for refuge took precedence: they would venture forth into a Palestine whose reality they had deliberately misrecognized in order to make it more palatable. In other words, throughout the book there is a tension between a pragmatic acceptance of Zionism and an effort, expressed mainly in the text's semantics, to deny the national Zionist aspect of the Pioneer enterprise in Palestine. This duality characterizes the ideology of the Centralverein during the last years of its existence.

This ambivalent approach to settlement in Palestine combined the influences of anti-Semitic propaganda, agreement with certain bedrock aims of Zionism, reservations about others, but most of all the acute awareness that German Jewry would be well advised to make a virtue out of the probable necessity of acting on the Zionist option. This uneasy mix of considerations characterized the Centralverein's reluctantly favorable attitude toward Zionism from 1936 until its operations were forcibly suspended in 1938. *Das Knabenschiff* represents the efforts to convince German-Jewish children and youth that a reinvigorated sense of Jewish self was an adequate response to Nazi barbarity; *Jüdische Jugend baut auf,* despite its hesitations and even inconsistencies, signaled the end of the Centralverein's attempts to emotionally empower German-Jewish youth for the task of determining their own fate on German soil. Henceforth, the youth would be instructed to ready themselves to build their future elsewhere, notably in Palestine. Yet it seems that in summer 1936 these two orientations still were valid. Therefore, one might say that in the

Third Reich books for Jewish children and youth functioned both as terminators of familiar stands and as pronouncers and creators of new opinions that signified the beginning of the change and designated it.

Bibliography

Anfänge: Aus den ersten Tagen der zweiten Alija. Eine Sammelschrift (Berlin: Hechaluz, 1934); Ingrid Belke, "In den Katakomben—Jüdische Verlage in Deutschland 1933–1938," *Marbacher Magazine* 25 (1983): 1–18; Yahoyakim Cohavi, "Cultural and Educational Activities of the German Jews, 1933–1941, as a Response to the Challenge of the Nazi Regime" [Hebrew], Ph.D. diss., University of Jerusalem, 1986; Volker Dahm, *Das Jüdische Buch im Dritten Reich* (Munich: Beck, 1993); Herbert Freeden, *The Jewish Press in the Third Reich,* trans. William Templer (Providence, R.I.: Berg, 1993); *Kibbuz: Kultur und Wirtschaft. Aus der Tagung des Kibbuz Hameuchad in Jagur, Juli 1933* (Berlin: Hechaluz, 1933); *Kfar Saba: Im Kampf um Jüdische Arbeit* (Berlin: Hechaluz, 1934); Abraham Margaliot, *Between Rescue and Annihilation: Studies in the History of German Jewry, 1932–1938* [Hebrew] (Jerusalem: Jad waShem; The Institute of Contemporary Jewry, 1990); Margaliot, "The Political Reaction of German Jewish Organizations and Institutions to the Anti-Jewish Policy of the National Socialists, 1932–1935" [Hebrew], Ph.D. diss., University of Jerusalem, 1971; Fritz Rothgießer, *Das Knabenschiff: Eine Erzählung* (Berlin: Philo, 1936); Meta Samson, *Spatz macht sich* (Berlin: Philo, 1938); Hans-Martin Schwarz, *Einer wie Du und Ich: Eine Jugenderzählung aus unseren Tagen* (Berlin: Jüdischer Buch- u. Zeitschriften Verlag Robert Alter, 1937); Hermann Sinsheimer, *Maria Nunnez: Eine jüdische Überlieferung, Frei erzählt* (Berlin: Philo, 1934); Heinz Warschauer, *Jüdische Jugend baut auf: Vom Kibbuz in Palästina* (Berlin: Philo, 1936); and *Zum jüdisch-arabischen Problem: Ein Sammelbuch* (Berlin: Hechaluz, 1933).

RIMA SHICHMANTER

1937 Hermann Broch writes a narrative entitled *The Return of Virgil,* thus beginning an eight-year project that culminates in the novel *The Death of Virgil*

In the spring of 1950, roughly a year before Broch's death, his son wrote him from Vienna that Broch was still an "unknown quantity" in Europe, alluding to the title of Broch's second novel. Broch was never widely received during any phase of his work; his fictional writings were probably too theoretical and his nonliterary texts too difficult and abstract. At the core of his work is the idea of the "disintegration of values," and this complex idealistic philosophy, which encompasses the areas of theory of history and epistemology, does not easily lend itself to relaxed, recreational reading. Broch noticed a decline of European culture, evidenced particularly in the dissolution of a central value system into increasingly smaller subsystems. This process was making communication between social groups and ultimately between individuals (the last and smallest unit) more and more difficult. Broch believed that he was living at a time when the dissolution of values had reached its nadir. According to historical dialectics, as he understood it, this nadir also marked the beginning of an opposite process that would culminate in the establishment of a new central value system. In his fictional work, Broch attempted to show the process of disintegration, to illustrate the great European cultural crisis, whereas with his theoretical works he sought to provide a "building block," as he called it, that would aid in the construction of a new value system. Even if one cannot relate each and every word of Broch's work to his theory of the disintegration of values, nevertheless this philosophy is undoubtedly at the core of his writings.

When Broch was born in Vienna on November 1, 1886, his father had already planned out his life: the firstborn of the Jewish textile merchant Josef Broch and his wife Johanna was to follow in his father's footsteps—learn the textile trade, take over the firm, and expand it. Josef Broch, who had his beginnings in the *Gründerzeit* and rose from errand boy to respected businessman in the Vienna textile industry, held to this plan for decades. Following his own inclinations, the son wished to attend a humanities high school, but his father enrolled him in the *Realschule,* a non-classical secondary school. After graduation in 1904, Hermann Broch would have preferred to study philosophy at the university, but his father insisted that he study engineering. Broch concluded these studies in 1907. He then became assistant director at the "Spinning-Mill Teesdorf" in Teesdorf near Vienna, which his father had bought for him and his brother Fritz, who was three years younger. In 1909, when Broch married Franziska von Rothermann, the daughter of a Hungarian sugar merchant of German descent, he appeared indistinguishable from numerous other young businessmen consumed exclusively by thoughts of business, money, and merchandise.

It only seemed that Broch had given in to his father's wishes, however; in fact, he continued to pursue his philosophical and literary interests. As early as 1909 he documented his cultural pessimism—influenced by Karl Kraus—in his notes *Kultur 1908 / 1909*. In 1913 he was writing short contributions on Thomas Mann, Karl Kraus, and Immanuel Kant for the *Brenner* magazine in Innsbruck. During World War I, Franz Blei discovered Broch's critical talent in the Café Central; subsequent to this point in 1917–18, Broch wrote contributions to Blei's periodical *Summa*. In the meantime, Broch had taken up a thorough autodidactic study of philosophy, concentrating on Schopenhauer, Nietzsche, and Kant. After 1916 he became an outspoken follower of the neo-Kantians and was particularly influenced by the writings of Heinrich Rickert. Among his coffeehouse friends at that time were Milena Jesenska and Eva von Allesch. The latter became his companion for a decade (1918–28). In 1923 he divorced his wife.

In 1925 Broch was able to fulfill his longtime wish to sell the factory and begin regular studies of philosophy and mathematics at the university. The sale was concluded in 1927, and for a while Broch enjoyed the life of a student, following only his personal intellectual pursuits. He was especially interested in the neo-positivism of the Vienna Circle. But in 1928 he was already overcome by what nowadays one would call a midlife crisis. It was obvious that the money from the sale of the factory would support him for only a few years; he lacked ambition for an academic career; and a return to business life was out of the question for him. Broch did what was common in his circles during the 1920s in Vienna—that is, he lay on a couch to be analyzed by Freud or one of his disciples. A follower of Freud took pity on him. She dissected his obvious feelings of duty and carefully exposed her patient's love of life and pleasure, as well as his literary creativity and productivity. Broch, who as early as 1917 and 1919 had written experimental-modernistic novels (*Eine methodologische Novelle* was published in 1917 in *Summa; Ophelia* remained unpublished), rediscovered his love of writing, all the more so because this passion could be combined with the idea of a profession: that of the independent, money-earning writer.

With a creative fervor that he had never before experienced and never would again, Broch developed the plan for a novel that eventually grew into the voluminous trilogy *The Sleepwalkers* (*Die Schlafwandler*). In 1930 he found in Daniel Brody, director of Rhein Publishing in Zurich and owner of the German rights to the books of James Joyce, a sympathetic and cooperative publisher who published the trilogy in the two years following. In no other fictional work is Broch's theoretical concept as evident as here. By including a series of essays entitled *The Disintegration of Values* (*Zerfall der Werte*) in the third volume of his trilogy, Broch even managed to incorporate a short version of a long-planned philosophical book. This was an unusual experiment for which his readers did not thank him. According to Broch, the titles of the novel's sections, "1888: Pasenow or The Romantic" ("1888: Pasenow oder die Romantik"), "1903: Esch or Anarchist" ("1903: Esch oder die Anarchie"), "1918: Hugenau or the Realist" ("1918: Hugenau oder die Sachlichkeit") marked the stations of the process of cultural decline. Whereas Robert Musil had exemplified the disintegration of the old values by portraying the conditions in Vienna, Broch illustrated this process through figures from the Wilhelminian era because he perceived the evidence of Europe's decline of values most strongly in Germany.

The external design of the book may have been influenced by Heinrich Mann's *Kaiserreich-Trilogie*, to which there are several obvious parallels. Broch's style, however, was influenced by that of avant-garde novelists like André Gide, John Dos Passos, Alfred Döblin, and above all James Joyce. On Joyce's fiftieth birthday (in the spring of 1932) Broch delivered the speech "James Joyce and the Present Age" ("James Joyce und die Gegenwart"), a testimonial to modernism that, however, also maintained that Goethe was the forerunner of the modern novel with his work *Wilhelm Meisters Wanderjahre*. Like other new novels of the 1920s, the narrative technique in *The Sleepwalkers* employed innovative methods such as interior monologue, stream of consciousness, montage, collage, and the mixing of genres. The style of each novel is suited to the era with which it deals—that is, with romanticism, anarchy, and new objectivity as Broch pictured them.

As the work unfolds, the decline of values is illustrated, culminating in the crisis of 1918; the epilogue of the work expresses the hope for the birth of a new central value system that, however, is not defined within the book. Broch's value theory was—in accordance with the Kantian heritage—formal and (in contrast to Max Scheler's value philosophy, for example) not determined by material means.

After the completion of his monumental work, Broch produced several smaller ones: lectures and essays on such topics as the modernistic novel, kitsch, and myth. He also wrote the drama *The Atonement* (*Die Entsühnung;* first performed in spring 1934 in Zurich), the short novel *The Unknown Quantity* (*Die Unbekannte Größe*), and a number of largely unpublished poems. In his drama—which was once again a variation on the topic of declining values—he provided a cross-section of German society at the time of the world economic crisis of 1930. Broch realistically portrayed the arguments between factory owners and unions, as well as the relationship between politics and capitalism. The work effectively criticized contemporary society. In addition, with the inclusion of a woman's death lament, it indicated a radical denial of a male-oriented society. In the novel *The Unknown Quantity* (1933), Broch was more concerned with the areas of psychology and knowledge. The book's protagonist, an assistant in the university's mathematics department, finds himself in emotional turmoil when he attempts to combine love and the pure striving for knowledge. This was probably Broch's weakest book; at least Broch himself saw it that way.

Broch had hardly made a name for himself as a writer when his career as an author was endangered by Hitler's coming to power in 1933. As a Jewish writer in Germany, he lost his newly acquired audience. The response in the press to *The Sleepwalkers* had been great and on the whole positive, although the book did not become a bestseller. Now his reading audience would be limited to Austria and Switzerland. An intuitive man, Broch knew from the beginning—a well-documented fact—that Hitler's anti-Semitic regime would end in a police state, in racial suppression, and eventually in the great European war. Like many antifascist writers, Broch wanted to contribute to the fight against National Socialism with his own work, and between 1934 and 1936 he wrote the novel *The Spell* (*Die Verzauberung*). Although this book deals with other topics as well, it is above all anti-Hitler. It is a literary parable about mass delusion and about the masses in bondage to a dictator. The action takes place in an Alpine village around 1930. The Hitler figure, Marius Ratti, is antithetically juxtaposed to the figure of the healer, Mother Gisson, who is the personification of humanity. The book's narrator, an aging country doctor, temporarily vacillates between the two positions of Ratti and Mother Gisson, but in the end he decides against Ratti's party.

Broch's main concern was to demonstrate the process of emotional change and spiritual recognition in the narrator. Ideally, the reader was to take part in this development and to reach similar insights. Here too, as in the drama *The Atonement,* the contrast between male and female is important, and again women are the bearers of hope. Mother Gisson possesses traits of the Greek goddess Demeter and of the "Great Mother." Broch, who in the mid-1930s speculated in several essays—most notably in 1934 in the essay "Geist und Zeitgeist"—about a future mythical novel, a new, Homerically naive narration, attempted to approach this ideal with his novel *The Spell*. The first version was finished in early 1936. He began the second version the same year; it remained a fragment, however, and in early 1951 he started on a third version. This, too, remained unfinished—he died while he was working on it.

In 1936 Broch fell into a deep existential crisis. He questioned whether it was still ethical to write novels in view of Hitler's politics. Literature seemed to him less and less useful as a means of fighting National Socialism. In 1934 Karl Kraus had stated that it was senseless to confront Hitler "under the protection of the metaphor," and Broch began to share this opinion. The arguments against writing during a fascist era, which he expressed mostly in his letters, amount to a "negative aesthetics" in which the failure of literature in the political fight is exposed. Although in subsequent years Broch did not give up his existence as a writer, his later works concentrated largely on political theory, publicity, and activity. The first result of this new orientation was the voluminous *Völkerbund-Resolution* (League of nations resolution) of 1936–37. Here Broch attacked forced emigration, the violation of human rights, and the warmongering of the fascist countries. He expected the League of Nations to take measures to stem the tide of aggression in these countries, above all in the Germany of Hitler. He discussed this matter in his correspondence with numerous intellectuals, from Thomas Mann to Jacques Maritain. With their help he attempted to recruit the most important international peace organizations to sign the resolution. But not only was Broch inexperienced in the practical side of politics, he also recognized more and more clearly that the Geneva organization would be ineffective against the fascist states. Toward the end of 1937, he abandoned his campaign.

As soon as Broch recognized the futility of his efforts as far as the *League of Nations Resolution* was concerned, he returned to writing. In 1937 he wrote a narrative entitled *The Return of Virgil* (*Die Heimkehr des Vergil*). During the following eight years this short piece of prose grew into the novel *The Death of Virgil* (*Der Tod des Vergil*), Broch's second literary masterpiece. In this book Broch attempted something unique in literary history, a kind of a paradox: Broch wrote a novel from the viewpoint of "negative aesthetics"—that is, he wrote against writing. Here the ethical reservations against novel writing and against an aesthetic existence, which can be found in virtually all his letters during those years, resurfaced in the context of the novel's action. Virgil reproaches himself with comments such as "Aye, this would be the outcome: the one lacking perception would bring perception to those unwilling for it, the word-maker would be calling out speech from the mute, the derelict would impose duty on those ignorant of duty, the lame would guide the halt" (Broch 1945, 144). The impetus for taking up the Virgil topic had come from the legend of Antiquity, which reported that the dying Roman author had given the order to destroy the unfinished *Aeneid*. Broch projected his "negative aesthetics" onto the work and onto Virgil's inten-

tion, seeing in him a kindred soul who had turned against writing with his ethical arguments.

Furthermore, Broch saw a parallel between his own era and that of Virgil. Medieval reception of Virgil's works had elevated the Roman author to a Christian prophet on the basis of his presumed announcement of the coming of Jesus in his fourth eclogue. The main figure in Virgil's *Eclogues* is the boy whose birth is announced as the imminent moment of salvation. This birth marks the moment of global change: the present, filled with poverty, fear, and discord, turns into a future that is the exact opposite, a time of salvation with all the earmarks of a golden past—a time of abundance, happiness, and above all, peace. The coming of this new salvation is promised in the smile with which the boy greets his mother after his birth. Broch recognized correctly that Virgil's work is grounded on the idea of polarity between the worlds and the turn from the bad to the good. This insight fit Broch's scheme of the "disintegration of values" in the present and of hope for a new cultural beginning after the nadir had been reached. The inferno of the turnover takes place in Virgil's psyche: in his dying moments he recognizes the futility of his poetic efforts to prevent the crisis of the millennium. Broch retained the images and metaphors of the bearers of hope such as the child and Plotia, which signal his own positive hopes for the future.

In the narrative *The Return of Virgil* (1937) the basic concept of the great novel *The Death of Virgil,* first published in 1945, is already recognizable. Work on this book was continually interrupted, however, particularly by Broch's emigration in July 1938 to England and again in October of the same year to the United States. Although from 1933 to 1938 Broch had remained without public support and acclaim in Austria, he had nevertheless been able to maintain a sphere where such works as *The Spell,* the *League of Nations Resolution,* and his Virgil project could blossom. On the day of Austria's *Anschluß,* Broch was taken into custody by National Socialists in Alt Aussee in Styria. Since 1933 the author had increasingly retreated to the mountains: *The Spell* was written in 1935 in Mösern in the Tyrol, the *Resolution* in Alt Aussee. After a three-week incarceration in Bad Aussee, Broch, who had been arrested as a suspected Communist, was released. No one in the village knew that he was Jewish. On his passport "Roman Catholic" was listed as his religion; Broch had converted to Catholicism in 1909. After seemingly interminable efforts, he succeeded in obtaining in Vienna a visa for England (James Joyce assisted him in this matter). For two months Broch lived with the writers Edwin and Willa Muir, who had translated *The Sleepwalkers* into English. Under the sponsorship of Albert Einstein and Thomas Mann, Broch was able to obtain a visa for the United States. From this time on, he invested most of his effort in his political, antifascist, and democratic-theoretical projects.

In 1939 Broch joined a group of American East Coast intellectuals and European writers in exile who, under the guidance of Giuseppe Borgese, collaborated on a book entitled *The City of Man,* which was published in 1940. While working on this project Broch became Borgese's closest collaborator, and he contributed important ideas to the book. The publication's purpose was to combat global suppression, enslavement, and warmongering by Hitler and the other fascist dictators with a vision of a world democracy that was based on human rights and the concept of peace. During this process, Broch conceived important ideas for his continued politological, legal, educational, and mass-psychological studies during the 1940s. In view of the founding of the United Nations Organization he was working on a theory of international human rights; for the postwar period he wrote an extensive book entitled *Theory of Mass Hysteria* (*Massenwahntheorie*), which deals with the return of the (formerly) fascist countries to democracy (thus the work also contains a theory of democracy); for the United Nations Educational, Scientific, and Cultural Organization (UNESCO) Broch compiled a memorandum on the education of youth in internationalism and humanity; and for postwar Germany he wrote a resolution on the topic of reeducation. At that time interdisciplinary works did not yet carry today's import; consequently Broch, who was known only as a writer, found it difficult to be taken seriously by scholars in other disciplines such as

political science, law, psychology, and education. His nonliterary works failed to attract an audience, and the theory of mass hysteria was abandoned as an unpublished fragment.

Broch would have much preferred to put all his efforts into the fight against Hitler and for democracy, as he had stressed in numerous letters, but it was imperative for his survival that he not give up his existence as a writer. His writings on the theory of mass hysteria were supported between 1940 and 1947 by such renowned American foundations as Guggenheim, Rockefeller, and Bollingen.

When this support ceased, Broch returned to previous, prewar projects with essays and lectures on kitsch and myth, and with fictional works such as *The Guiltless* (*Die Schuldlosen*). A new project was the extensive cultural-historical study *Hofmannsthal and His Time* (*Hofmannsthal und seine Zeit*), which he began in 1947. Initially Broch was to provide only a short essay on Hofmannsthal's prose works as the introduction to an English-language edition of the American Bollingen series. Broch did not deliver this foreword, entitled "Hugo von Hofmannsthal's Prose Writings" ("Hugo von Hofmannsthal und seine Prosaschriften") until years later, in early 1950.

In the meantime Broch was working on a book for which he had no contract but whose topic occupied him to such an extent that he dismissed all economic considerations. All his life Broch had been hesitant to write his autobiography. In the book on Hofmannsthal he saw an opportunity to portray his own youth and fin-de-siècle Vienna; thus the work embodies autobiographical traits and is a strongly subjective evaluation of that era. One of the striking aspects of this study is a reprise of the interdisciplinary approach, the synthetic view with which history, sociology, art, and literature are grasped. *Hofmannsthal and His Time* is by no means a complete picture of the situation of art and society at the turn of the century. In sketching the European panorama, Broch portrayed largely that social class with which he was best acquainted by virtue of his origin—that is, the middle class. Of the arts, Broch analyzed extensively only opera in music (Wagner), symbolism in literature (Baudelaire), and impressionism in painting (Cézanne). This selection made sense, however, because it contributed important insights and made it possible to proceed to address the central problems of the era. Already in the first few sentences Broch clearly expressed his aversion to and critical distance from the middle class and its culture: "The period of Hofmannsthal's birth . . . [was] certainly one of the most wretched in world history. This was the period of eclecticism, of false Baroque, false Renaissance, false Gothic. Wherever in that era Western man determined the style of life, that style tended toward bourgeois constriction and bourgeois pomp, to a solidity that signified suffocation just as much as security. If ever poverty was masked by wealth, it was here" (33).

In retrospect, fin-de-siècle Vienna appeared to Broch to be the time of the "gay apocalypse," and this term was quickly accepted into the idiom of international cultural history writing. In this work Broch was also mindful of the categories of his philosophy of values, and Vienna—here representative of Europe—seemed to him the incarnation of the "value vacuum of the epoch."

In 1933 Broch had published several short stories; best known among them were "The Return" and "A Slight Disappointment" ("Eine leichte Enttäuschung"). Even then he was preoccupied with the idea of turning the half-dozen stories into a novel, but, unable to find a publisher, he gave up his plan. In the spring of 1949, the Munich publisher Willi Weismann expressed an interest in publishing the old short stories, and Broch decided to take up once again the long forgotten project. The result, within a year, was the novel *The Guiltless,* in which the old short stories were revised and integrated. The title was intended to be ironic. Disappointed with the developments in postwar Germany, in which he saw an absence of contemplation, change, and atonement, Broch wanted to provide the Germans with a mirror. In a commentary he wrote of the intent of his book: "The novel deals with conditions and types prevalent in the pre-Hitler period. The figures chosen are thoroughly 'apolitical'; what political ideas they have are vague and nebulous. None of them is directly 'guilty' of the Hitler catastrophe. That is why the book is entitled *The*

Guiltless. Nevertheless it is precisely from such a state of mind and soul that Nazism derived its energies. For political indifference is ethical indifference, hence closely related to ethical perversity. In short, most of the politically guiltless bear a considerable share of ethical guilt" (Broch 1974, 289).

Broch wrote *The Guiltless* in New Haven, Connecticut. He had moved there in the spring of 1949, having lived since 1942 in Princeton in the home of a friend, the philosopher and cultural historian Erich von Kahler. Yale University had named him lecturer in German literature (albeit without any compensation). Toward the end of 1949 he married again, this time the graphic artist Annemarie Meier-Graefe. Very weakened by a ten-month hospital stay, Broch died of heart failure in New Haven at age sixty-four on May 30, 1951.

In Germany the reception of Broch's work after the war's end took quite a different turn from that in the United States. Although in America *The Death of Virgil* was highly acclaimed (it appeared in the excellent translation by Jean Starr Untermeyer at the same time as the German edition), the novel found no resonance in Germany. Nor did *The Guiltless* meet with more success when it appeared in 1950. On the other hand, although the political theoretician Broch was hardly acknowledged in the United States, he was noticed in Germany in 1950 when his essay "In Spite of It: Humane Politics. Realization of a Utopia" ("Trotzdem: Humane Politik. Verwirklichung einer Utopie") appeared at the beginning of the year. Here Broch had summarized his democratic-theoretical and his human rights ideas. The essay earned him an invitation to the much publicized Congress for Cultural Freedom, which took place in Berlin in mid-1950. Although Broch was not able to accept the invitation, he sent an address entitled "The Intellectuals and the Fight for Human Rights" ("Die Intellektuellen und der Kampf um die Menschenrechte"), in which he outlined the task of the intellectual who is critically engaged in the issue of human rights and who is not bound to a political party.

Broch did not become known until after his

death—specifically, not until the 1950s and 1960s, when the Rhein-Verlag in Zurich published a ten-volume selected edition of his works. Broch's books, however, never achieved real popularity. Nor did this change with the publication of the complete and annotated edition of the author's works between 1974 and 1981. Because of Broch's subtlety and his multidimensionality, the reader can gain insights from his work only by not shirking the efforts of a continuous intellectual hermeneutic involvement.

Bibliography

Hermann Broch's papers are at the Beinecke Rare Book Library, Yale University, New Haven, Connecticut. See Christa Sammons, "Hermann Broch Archive, Yale University Library," *Modern Austrian Literature* 5 (1972): 18–69. A part of Broch's correspondence—including the one with his publisher, Daniel Brody—is in the Deutsches Literaturarchiv, Marbach, Germany. Broch's philosophical library can be found at the library of Universität Klagenfurt in Klagenfurt, Austria. See Klaus Amann and Helmut Grote, *Die Wiener Bibliothek Hermann Brochs: Kommentiertes Verzeichnis des rekonstruierten Bestandes* (Vienna: Böhlau, 1990).

Hermann Broch, *The Atonement*, trans. George E. Wellwarth and H. F. Broch de Rothermann, *German Drama Between the Wars: An Anthology of Plays*, ed. George E. Wellwarth (New York: E. P. Dutton, 1972), 19–106; Broch, *The Death of Virgil*, trans. Jean Starr Untermeyer (New York: Pantheon, 1945); Broch, *The Guiltless*, trans. Ralph Manheim (Boston: Little, Brown, 1974);

Broch, *Hugo von Hofmannsthal and His Time: The European Imagination, 1860–1920*, trans. Michael P. Steinberg (Chicago: University of Chicago Press, 1984); Broch, *Kommentierte Werkausgabe*, ed. Paul Michael Lützeler, 13 vols. (Frankfurt a. M.: Suhrkamp, 1974–81); Broch, *The Sleepwalkers*, trans. Edwin and Willa Muir (New York: Little, Brown, 1932); Broch, *The Spell*, trans. H. F. Broch de Rothermann (New York: Farrar, Straus and Giroux, 1987); Broch, *The Unknown Quantity*, trans. Willa and Edwin Muir (New York: Viking, 1935); Stephen D. Dowden, ed., *Hermann Broch: Literature, Philosophy, Politics: The Yale Broch Symposium* (Columbia, S.C.: Camden House, 1988); Thomas Eicher, *Erzählte Visualität: Studien zum Verhältnis von Text und Bild in Hermann Brochs Romantrilogie "Die Schlafwandler"* (Frankfurt a. M.: Peter Lang, 1993); Michael Kessler and Paul Michael Lützeler, eds., *Hermann Broch: Das dichterische Werk* (Tübingen: Stauffenburg, 1987); Paul Michael Lützeler, *Brochs theoretisches Werk* (Frankfurt a. M.: Suhrkamp, 1988); Lützeler, ed., *Hermann Broch* (Frankfurt a. M.: Suhrkamp, 1986); Lützeler, *Hermann Broch: A Biography*, trans. Janice Furness (London: Quartet Books, 1987); Lützeler, *Hermann Broch: Eine Biographie* (Frankfurt a. M.: Suhrkamp, 1985); Lützeler, *Hermann Broch—Ethik und Politik: Studien zum Frühwerk und zur Romantrilogie "Die Schlafwandler"* (Munich: Winkler, 1973); Monika Ritzer, *Hermann Broch und die Kulturkrise im frühen 20. Jahrhundert* (Stuttgart: Metzler, 1988); Friedrich Vollhardt, *Hermann Brochs geschichtliche Stellung: Studien zum philosophischen Frühwerk und zur Romantrilogie "Die Schlafwandler" (1914–1932)* (Munich: Niemeyer, 1986).

PAUL MICHAEL LÜTZELER

March 11, 1938　After German troops march into Austria, many Austrian- and German-Jewish writers flee

In 1938 Hitler's war on Germany's Jews reached its first calamitous apogee, soon to be surpassed by the ultimate horrors of the Holocaust. Having eliminated virtually all political foes—union leaders, Social Democrats, pacifists, Communists, and some army generals, as well as intellectuals and religious and artistic nonconformists—and having settled hundreds of personal scores, Hitler and his henchmen turned the full powers of a coldly efficient police state and a dictatorship upon the Jews, the declared "arch enemies." Under the pretext of avenging the assassination of a minor Paris-based foreign service official, the individual act of a young Polish Jew, the Nazis pillaged and burned nearly every synagogue in Germany; arrested, maimed, and killed thousands of Jews; expropriated Jewish property; fined each Jewish citizen; and throttled, if not eliminated, the last emanation of German-Jewish intellectual life. As Nazi domination spread across Europe through Hitler's wars—but also through the passivity of the European democracies and the connivance of a sympathizing population—these inhuman acts followed each aggrandization. What had been a gradual strangulation of Jewish life in Germany through book burnings, racial laws, arrests, and violence over the years since 1933 was telescoped into weeks or months in the Nazi-occupied territories.

There followed a general attempt at flight by Jews—flight was often thwarted—and a mass exodus of Jewish intellectuals and writers, a "brain drain" unprecedented in modern history. These intellectual elites joined now previously exiled or self-exiled political opponents of the regime—many Jews among them—or those more prescient and or more fortunate in obtaining immigration permits. After 1938 German-speaking Jewry scattered across the globe. Seeking refuge at first in countries adjacent to their homeland, the refugee writers ultimately found new homes, often in unsettling circumstances, in predominantly the larger cultural hubs of the world. The exodus was so all-encompassing that it caused Rabbi Leo Baeck, one of the religious leaders of German Jewry, to quote a despairing aphorism: "God is a refugee." The poet Mascha Kaléko, fleeing Germany for New York, expressed a similar thought in her poem *Überfahrt* (Crossings; 1938): "Wir haben keinen Freund auf dieser Welt. / Nur Gott. Den haben sie mit uns vertrieben." (We have no friend upon this earth. / Except God. They banished him with us.) The flight of the intellectuals signified, for all practical purposes, the end of the perceived century-old blending of German-Christian and German-Jewish culture, a "symbiosis" that other observers, for example the pre-Hitler immigrant Gershom Scholem, derided as a "one-sided declaration of love [on the part of the Jews]" (Scholem 1970, 7).

Real or illusionary as such a symbiosis may have been, the shattered belief in such a mutuality is one of the recurring and unifying motifs of German-speaking Jewish exile writing that distinguished it from the literary works of most of their Christian fellow refugees. In many other respects, their religious affiliation did not set the exiles apart from one another, nor did, for the most part, political convictions—except for those of the Communists. As for the latter, the "fronts" perceived by some literary historians were fluid. Alfred Neumann, primarily an author of historical novels, wrote *Es waren ihrer sechs* (Six of them; 1944), a fictionalized account of resistance against Hitler inside Germany. Klaus Mann, a redoubtable polemicist and the author of two politically charged antifascist novels, *Mephisto* (1936) and *Der Vulkan* (The volcano; 1939), temporarily abandoned politics for an artist novel, *Symphonie* (Pathetic symphony; 1935), which was based on the life of Tchaikovsky. Neumann was Jewish; Klaus Mann the child of a mixed marriage. But both alternated between texts with a political message and apolitical works.

Common to all exiles were the exhausting and demeaning struggles for daily existence and the concomitant search for jobs, however lowly. When even this search failed, they were forced to appeal to Jewish charities. The stresses and strains of exile caused some writers, such as the expressionist Alfred Ehrenstein, to fall silent. But even those who continued to write could rarely support themselves exclusively by their pen. Many among them, such as the Jewish writers Heinz Politzer and Ernst Waldinger, vied for the few jobs available as German teachers in high schools or colleges. Others had to rely on the income of wives or women friends, a humiliating dependency to most European men. Many exiles experienced the sudden fall from prominence to obscurity that only the most established, globally renowned writers or the successful authors of mass market entertainment escaped. The non-Jew Thomas Mann and the Jewish Lion Feuchtwanger and Franz Werfel constitute examples of the former; the non-Jew Erich Maria Remarque and the Jewish writers Vicky Baum and Hans Habe illustrate the success of the writers of popular fiction.

Common to both groups, again with the stated exceptions, was the eroding value of their literary language. It was a devaluation in a double sense; German literary works were only marginally marketable beyond the precluded (barred) outlets in Germany and, after 1939, in Austria and Czechoslovakia. The few and often feeble publishing houses that published exiled writers —in Holland (until the German invasion), Sweden, the Soviet Union, Switzerland, the United States, Latin America, and Australia—were no surrogate. Also, some writers felt an aversion to writing in the "language of the Barbarians," understandably felt even more intensely by Jewish writers and their Jewish public. Conversely, other writers saw their mission as preserving the German language so that it would remain undefiled by Nazi jargon. For example, in essays and creative works the gentile—and Communist— Johannes R. Becher and the Rumanian-born Jew Elias Canetti (later a Nobel Prize winner), dedicated themselves to such a mission. But no matter what their attitude to the German language, and it was frequently a love-hate relationship, they usually commanded over no other tool; they literally had "to watch their language" against an intrusion by the defiled Nazi-style German prevailing in their home country or against calcification caused by their absence from their linguistic roots. Very few had the means to employ top-notch translators or to have such a service provided by a publishing house; fewer still succeeded in the leap from their native German into the language of their country of asylum. Among the Jewish writers who managed to do so were Paul Engel as Diego Viga into Spanish; Vicky Baum, Hertha Pauli, and Robert Neumann into English; and Ernst Erich Noth into French. Obviously those writers who had grown up bilingually, such as the Alsatian Jews Yvan and Clair Goll and Ferdinand Lion, could switch more readily, even if German had been their predominant language.

The literary texts of the exiles—and certainly those of the Jews among them—reflected all such travails and tragedies. They found expression in every genre of literature, though, of course, the structural conversion of this frequently autobiographical raw material varied from author to author. Heinz Liepmann, in his novel *Wird mit dem Tode bestraft* (Will be punished by death; 1935) chronicled the emergence of the Nazi dictatorship; Friedrich Wolf, in his drama *Professor Mamlock* (1935), excoriated the removal of Jewish professionals from their jobs; Gabriele Tergit, in her novel *Effingers* (Family Effinger; 1951) documented the persecution of the Jews in Germany; and Bruno Frank, in his novels *Der Reisepaß* (The passport; 1937) and *Die Tochter* (The daughter; 1943), painted the obstacle course facing Jewish and non-Jewish immigrants. Franz Werfel's comic drama of survival, *Jacobowsky und der Oberst* (Jacobowsky and the colonel; 1944), was a success both on Broadway and in postwar Germany. Anna Seghers, in her canonized novel *Transit* (written 1940–44; published in 1948), and Salamon Dembitzer, in his subliterary novel *Visas for America* (1952), produced texts dealing with the travails of flight and immigration. Joseph Roth, in his novel *Legende vom heiligen Trinker* (Legend of the saintly drunkard; 1939), chronicled the despair and self-destruction of an outcast like himself. Theodor Kramer's poems express the longing for loved ones and a beloved country left behind; Else Lasker-Schüler mourns the loss of a communal language; the poems of Ilse Blumenthal-Weiss and of the Nobel laureate Nelly Sachs are dirges to the victims of the Holocaust. Events from the history of those times, such as the rape of Czechoslovakia or the betrayal of the Jews at the Evian Conference, supply the plots for, respectively, Stefan Heym's novel *Hostages* (1943), first published in English, and Hans Habe's fiction *Die Mission* (The mission; 1965). Finally, life in exile, but mostly its debilitating frustrations, accompany the poems of Rose Ausländer and the novel *In Lisas Zimmer* (In Lisa's room; 1965) of Hilde Spiel and of Lion Feuchtwanger's novel *Exil* (1939). Not only the despair of the exile but also his or her undiminished pride and acceptance of fate resonate in Karl Wolfskehl's magnificent poem *Glocke am Strand* (Bell at the shore; 1941). All of the above authors in this selective enumeration were Jews, but their worldviews ranged from Communism (for example, Wolf and Seghers) to traditional Enlightenment thought (for instance, Bruno Frank and Hilde Spiel) and from leftist anti-capitalism and anti-Americanism (such as Dembitzer) to Hertha Pauli's salute to America, expressed through her sensitive and felicitous translation of Emma Lazarus's poem *Liberty Enlightening the World* (1951), or by Julius Bab's equally impressive translations of Walt Whitman.

Like their non-Jewish contemporaries, the Jewish authors dealt in various forms with the subject of exile itself. Hans Sahl's novel *Die Wenigen und die Vielen* (The few and the many; 1959) deplores the factionalism among the exiles and the selfishness of many. Hilde Domin's early poetry and novel of return *Das zweite Paradies* (The second paradise; 1968) dissect the strains upon a married couple imposed by the stresses of exile. Lion Feuchtwanger's novel *Exil* shows both the "glory and the misery" of exile—to borrow a phrase from an essay title of the same period. The novel also exposes the Nazi machinations in neighboring countries. Poems by Rose Ausländer, Vera Lachmann, and Walter Mehring conjure up the dual peril of being both a Jew and an exile. This "double jeopardy" is intensified by the metaphors or other tropes that the Jewish exiles created. Although they, together with non-Jewish refugees, drew on world literature (by, for example, Homer, Dante, Ovid, and Victor Hugo), they invoked at least as frequently Jewish exilic experiences. Robert Neumann's novel *An den Wassern von Babylon* (By the waters of Babylon; 1939) links the persecution of the Jews in twelve different nations by having representatives from each become the victims, on their way to Palestine, of a bus accident. Emil Bernhard Cohn recalls the Cossacks' persecution of the Jews with the metaphor of *Die Jagd Gottes* (God's pursuit; 1936). Karl Wolfskehl, in his poem *Am Seder zu sagen* (A poem to be recited during Seder; 1934, Eng. trans. 1934) uses the enslavement of the Children of Israel and their flight from Egypt as a metaphor for persecution and flight throughout the ages:

Immer wieder, wenn vom Wanderstaube
Müde wir geruht in Anderer Laube
Riß der Andern Faust auf uns voll Droh'n . . .
Immer wieder.

(Again, again, when we, covered with the

journey's dust, / rested, tired in a stranger's bower, / the others roughly lifted us and threatened . . . / Again and again.)

The styles differ as widely. They range from the naturalistic-historicizing novels of Feuchtwanger, which sometimes blended fact and fiction, to the expressionism of Lasker-Schüler, to the symbolism of Wolfskehl, Werfel, and Ausländer, to the mysticism of Nelly Sachs. Less easily classifiable are the numerous works, not previously mentioned, that addressed the same problems quasi historically—that is, works alienated from the here and now via past parallels. Alfred Neumann's *Der Pakt* (Strange conquest; 1950) and Hermann Broch's *Der Tod des Vergil* (Death of Virgil; 1945) depict authoritarianism in nineteenth-century America and in ancient Rome as analogous to the political tenor of the present.

Setting the exiled writers apart from their contemporaries who remained in Nazi-occupied Europe is easy. The quality of their texts simply far outstrips that of the works written under the jackboot. But, as indicated by the occasional earlier pairing of gentile and Jewish immigrant authors, the divide between those who left Germany is often nonexistent or nearly invisible. Heinrich Mann also wrote protohistorical novels, and Bertolt Brecht fictionalized the rise of the Nazi regime and ideology. A particularly telling example of congruent interests is provided by the gentile author Brecht and the Jewish writer Feuchtwanger. They collaborated on *Die Gesichter der Simone Machard* (The visions of Simone Machard; 1948), a drama about occupied France that employs the story of Joan of Arc as intertext. In one genre of literature, however, the Jewish exiles predominated. They daringly chronicled a tragic era from beginning to end through texts replete with satiric, ironic, and humorous passages, much in the tradition of Jewish gallows humor. As early as 1934 Salomon Friedländer (Mynona) published from his exile in France a collection of grotesque vignettes entitled *Der lachende Hiob* (The laughing Job). Werfel, quite appropriately, gave his drama *Jacobowsky and the Colonel* the subtitle "Comedy of a Tragedy." When writing his futuristic novel *Stern der Ungeborenen* (Star of the unborn; 1947) he poured irony on the follies of the Nazi era. With witty aphorisms the Viennese Alfred Polgar exposed Nazi pretensions, as had his countryman Karl Kraus in *Die dritte Walpurgisnacht* (The third Walpurgisnight; 1935), which was written before Hitler's march into Austria and which Kraus did not live to see.

The coupling of wit and despair continued in postwar exile literature. Jakov Lind, who camouflaged his Jewish identity in occupied Holland, heightened the horror of his surrealistic narrative *Eine Seele aus Holz* (Soul of wood; 1962) by clothing barbarism in humor. Edgar Hilsenrath's *Der Nazi und der Friseur* (The Nazi and the barber; 1977) is full of grim, satiric humor. Of course there were experiences—historical and psychological—that were felt almost exclusively or more intensely by Jewish exile writers and hence were echoed in their literary works. The persecution and discrimination by the Nazis—or simply the subtle withdrawal by neighbors, acquaintances, and friends—forced upon many German-speaking Jews a reexamination of their Jewishness, an affiliation that in the past had been sometimes perceived only dimly or even denied. For some the renewed and virulent persecution came as no surprise. The best-selling novelist Jakob Wassermann found in the Nazi takeover confirmation of the disillusionment he had expressed in the essay *Mein Weg als Deutscher und Jude* (My path as a German and Jew; 1922). In his essay *Selbstbetrachtungen* (Self-reflections; 1933) the last shreds of hope were removed.

Three other reactions to the total persecutions surfaced, some of them reminiscent of reactions to the pogroms throughout the ages. With their true reasons for doing so often hidden by rationalizations, several exiled authors, including Kurt Tucholsky, Martin Carl Einstein, and Karl Jacob Hirsch, divested themselves of the burdensome and endangering faith. Alfred Döblin, who had previously left Judaism, became a Catholic during his exile. Their autobiographies, interestingly enough, were often apologies for their defection. A century previous the poet Heinrich Heine had found the perfect metaphor for his conversion. Developing an attack of vertigo while standing near a precipice, he clings in desperation to a memorial crucifix near him. "Surely," he writes, "nobody will resent the fact that I embraced the cross during such a miserable situation" (Heine 1890, 74). But just as Heine found it impossible to amputate his Jewishness, so too did his twentieth-century successor Kurt Tucholsky realize—despite his occasional descent into Jewish self-hatred—the impossibility of such a severance: "I have left the Jewish religion, but I know that one really can't" (Tucholsky 1969, 117). Hermann Kersten's novel *Die fremden Götter* (Alien gods; 1949) thematizes the riving of a Jewish family when the daughter converts to the faith of her Catholic rescuers.

Other Jewish authors found an answer to physical and spiritual suppression in *aliyah*—that is, immigration to Palestine—often as the consummation of long-held Zionist ideals. In fact some spurned the designation "exile" because they viewed resettlement in Palestine as a return to the true Jewish homeland. Max Brod's works, written in Palestine, reflect his hopes and aspiration for a Jewish homeland as well as his meditations on its historical past. His novel *Der Meister* (The teacher; 1952) paints an admiring picture of Jesus—not as the Messiah, but rather as a gifted rabbi and Jewish prophet.

Although Brod's Zionism was strengthened in Palestine, that of Arnold Zweig all but vanished. Disillusioned by the conflict of Arabs and Jews and by a perceived Jewish nationalism, and envisioning Socialism as the only promise for the future, he poured his disappointment into his *Der Traum ist teuer* (The dream is expensive; 1962). He, like his fellow Socialist Louis Furnberg, returned to Germany (that is, to the German Democratic Republic after the war). Other Jewish writers, such as Fritz Kortner, Wolfgang Hildesheimer, and Jakov Lind, went to Palestine or Israel only for a brief visit. Still others, such as the incomparable lyricist Else Lasker-Schüler and the dramatist Max Zweig, could not, despite their affinity for their new homeland, overcome the dual obstacles of minute outlets for their works in German and their inability to master Hebrew. Their ambivalence was once expressed by Max Zweig: "I now feel that Israel is my homeland, but Austria is my fatherland now as before"

(Zweig 1991, 59). Conversely, the most recent immigrants to Israel, voluntarily exiles from Germany such as Jenny Aloni and Lea Fleischmann, appear to have grown roots there. The short-story collection *Abrahams Rückkehr* (Abraham's return; 1989) by Lea Fleischmann, though written in German, is suffused with an attachment to Israel and its Jewish tradition.

Judging from their works, the most common reaction of Jewish authors in exile to persecution was a closer adherence to the faith of their fathers. The text that typifies this reaction is Soma Morgenstern's *Der Sohn der verlorenen Sohnes* (The son of the lost son; 1935), which was published in Germany. Contrary to Kesten's novel, Morgenstern depicts the return to, rather than the apostasy from, Judaism. Nelly Sachs, only loosely tied to Judaism in her youth, immersed herself in the mysticism of the Kabbalah and Gershom Scholem's commentaries. Her poetry, written during her Swedish exile, reflected her nearly discovered intellectual world by presenting a Judaism close to her mystical sources. Friedrich Torberg, a liberal Austrian novelist, describes in his fictionalized biography *Süsskind von Trimberg* (1972) the tragedy of failed emancipation. His title hero, a medieval minstrel and the first German-Jewish author of record, is cast between the two cultures and ends up as an outcast from both. Torberg himself, whose early fame rested on a thoroughly Austrian social narrative of a high-school tragedy, became a best-selling author toward the end of his life by writing humorous tales of Jewish life—for example, *Die Tante Jolesch* (Aunt Jolesch; 1975)—and by translating into German the works of Israeli humorist Ephraim Kishon. He signaled by both his tragic narratives and his humor his closer identification with his Jewish heritage.

The reassertion of a Jewish identity after the crucible year of 1938 took many forms and expressed itself in many literary genres. Examples range from the historical drama *The Marranos* (1948; first published in English), about the Spanish Inquisition, by Emil Bernhard Cohn, to Jewish narratives for children by the exiled writer Wilhelm Speyer and *Bambis Kinder* (Bambi's children; 1940) by Felix Salten.

The bond of communal suffering if not of a common religion is noticeable even in areligious and Communist authors. The Socialist writer Anna Seghers movingly evoked a common German-Jewish past and its extirpation in an episode within her novel *Ausflug der toten Mädchen* (The school excursion of the dead girls; 1946). Coupled with the rediscovery of Jewish roots is the occasional tearing away from the German matrix. Few went as far as the composer Kurt Weill, who all but banished German from his language. More frequently and symptomatically the Jewish exiles divested their characters and themselves of names with German origins. In Palestine, where such a practice was common, the writer Fritz Rosenfeld adopted the name Shalom-Ben Chorin. In America the essayist and translator Erich Basch became E. B. Ashton and the aphorist Kurt Bauchwitz became Roy C. Bates; in France Johannes Meyer became Jean Améry; in England the novelist H. G. Adler curtailed his first name to initials, because his given name coincided with that of the infamous SS leader Heinrich Himmler. The Alsatian-German author Yvan Goll retained his name, but the personae in his poetry now frequently assumed the French designation Jean-sans-Terre.

But in their search for literary means to express their newly defined identity, the exiles most often borrowed symbols and analogues from the Old Testament and from postbiblical texts. The *sefer*, the Book of Books, furnished both parallels of past Jewish suffering as well as the implicit hope of survival. The story of Job, for example, the servant and touchstone of God, became an intertext for poems by Wolfskehl, Yvan Goll, Sachs, Ilse Blumenthal-Weiss, and numerous others. None of these, of course, promised Job or his modern successors full restoration at the end of God's grim tests.

Walter Hasenclever, in his drama *Konflikt in Assyrien* (Conflict in Assyria; 1937) revived the Purim legend in a drama with a happy end unwarranted by the circumstances. Franz Werfel, wavering all his life between Catholicism and Judaism, wrote a pageant-like biblical music drama, *Weg der Verheißung* (The eternal road; 1937, first published in English), in collaboration

with two Jewish exiles—Kurt Weill and the theater director Max Reinhardt. The spectacular work shows a threatened Jewish community drawing renewed fortitude from reenacted episodes from the Bible. Walter Mehring, in his lyric cycle *Briefe aus der Mitternacht* (Letters written at midnight; 1937–41), derives metaphors from both Jewish and Christian lore. His poems, accompanying his flight, incarceration in France, and deliverance, draw on the myths of the flood, Job, Ahasverus, and the Three Kings.

Of course Jewish authors had no monopoly on drawing their material from the Bible. Thomas Mann in his Joseph tetralogy (1933–43) fleshed out the sparse Joseph legend with Hebrew and Egyptian myths and ethnology. Similarly the postbiblical history of the Jewish people served as a further reforged link to the Jewish past. Lion Feuchtwanger, in his Josephus trilogy (1932–45), painted the lives of the Jews under Roman dominance from the vantage point of the historian Josephus, an early convert to Christianity. Efraim Frisch, the editor and *spiritus rector* of the pre-Hitler magazine *Der Neue Merkur*, evoked the precarious life of the Polish shtetl and of a Jewish soldier caught up in World War II in his unfinished novel *Gog und Magog*.

Occasionally the rapprochement to Judaism took the form of an evocation of the most recent (and often idealized) Jewish life in Germany and Austria. Rudolf Frank's *Ahnen und Enkel* (Forefathers and grandchildren; 1936), still published by a Jewish publishing house in Germany, was one of the last fictional asseverations of a former German-Jewish symbiosis. Also, in the autobiographies of Ernst Toller, *Eine Jugend in Deutschland* (Young years in Germany; 1933), Elias Canetti, *Die gerettete Zunge* (The tongue set free; 1977), Margarete Susmann, *Ich habe viele Leben gelebt* (I lived many lives; 1964), and Stefan Zweig, *Die Welt von Gestern* (Yesterday's world; 1944) there are references or longer passages to Jewish life in the early decades of the century. Max Tau's nostalgic memoir *Das Land das ich verlassen mußte* (The land I had to leave behind; 1961) earned him the peace prize of the German book trade after the war.

After 1939 the utopian depictions of German-

Jewish life were increasingly overshadowed by poetry, drama, and fiction of the Shoah. It is only a slight exaggeration to speak of a collective dirge by the Jewish exiles (but not by them only) to the victims of the Holocaust. The first volume of Nelly Sachs's collected poetry *In den Wohnungen des Todes* (In the dwellings of death; 1944–45), as well as her *Mysterienspiel Eli* (1962) and many other poems and plays, return in prophetic language to the theme. Paul Celan's *Todesfuge* (Fugue of death; 1952), perhaps the most enduring and most powerful poem of modern German lyrics, commemorates the dead and pillories the perpetrators. H. G. Adler's autobiographical concentration camp novel *Panorama* (1968) and Max Brusto's collection of short stories *Visum oder Tod* (Visa or death; 1981) chronicle Jewish suffering. Although the persecution of political concentration camp inmates overshadows the suffering of Jewish prisoners, Peter Weiss's documentary drama *Die Ermittlung* (The investigation; 1965) captures the horror of Auschwitz and the judicial callousness during the trial by stitching together excerpts from the transcript. By bearing witness to the Shoah, the exiled Jewish writers, together with the eloquent testimony by many of the survivors, helped bestir the world's conscience.

In addition, by strengthening their links to Jewish heritage without relinquishing their German legacy, many of the Jewish exiles helped keep the German-Jewish tradition alive. The evocation of this tradition continues. The works of some of the younger immigrants still transmit that tradition to the readers of their host countries, because the successor generations of exiles have in the meantime mastered the language of their country of asylum. Silvia Tennenbaum's generational novel *Yesterday's Street* (1981) and Frederic Morton's *Crosstown Sabbath* (1987) join earlier texts such as Henry William Katzy's novel *Die Fischmanns* (The Fischmanns; 1938) as a testimony to a vibrant culture that once was.

Bibliography

Werner Berthold, ed., *Deutsche Intellektuelle im Exil: Ihre Akademie und die "American Guild for German Cultural Freedom"* (Munich: Saur, 1993); Wolfgang Benz and Marion Neiss, eds., *Deutsch-jüdisches Exil: Das Ende der Assimilation?* (Berlin: Metropol Verlag, 1994); Angela Graf and Hans-Dieter Kübler, eds., *Verbrannte Bücher Verbrannte Ideen Verbrannte, Zum 60. Jahrestag eines Fanals* (Hamburg: Buchverlag Otto Heineretter, 1993); Kurt R. Grossmann and Arich Tartakower, *The Jewish Refugee* (New York: Institute of Jewish Affairs, 1944); Heinrich Heine, *Die Harzreise* in *Sämtliche Werke,* ed. Ernst Elser, vol. 3 (Leipzig: Bibliographisches Institut, 1890); Renate Heuer, ed., *Lexikon deutsch-jüdischer Autoren* (Munich: K. G. Saur, 1992); Hans Otto Horch, *Judentum, Antisemitismus und europäische Kultur* (Tübingen: Francke, 1988); Lothar Kahn, *Between Two Worlds* (Ames: Iowa State University Press, 1993); Harro Kieser, Susanne Mittag, and Klaus Körner, eds., *Literatur und literarisches Leben in Deutschland, 1945–1949* (Frankfurt a. M.: Arbeitskreis selbstständiger Kultur Institute e.V., Deutsche Bibliothek, 1989); Helmut Koopmann, *Thomas Mann Handbuch* (Regensburg: Kröner Verlag, 1990); Helmut F. Pfanner, *Exile in New York: German and Austrian Writers After 1933* (Detroit: Wayne State University Press, 1983); Gershom Scholem, "Vom Mythos deutsch-jüdischer Symbiose," *Judaica 2* (Frankfurt a. M.: Suhrkamp, 1970); Hans Schütz, *Juden in der deutschen Literatur* (Munich: Piper, 1992); John Spalek and Joseph Strelka, eds., *Deutsche Exilliteratur seit 1933,* 2 vols., vol. 1: *Kalifornien* (Bern: Francke, 1976); Spalek and Strelka, *Deutsche Exilliteratur seit 1933,* 2 vols., vol. 2: *New York* (Bern: Francke, 1989); Guy Stern, *Literatur im Exil: Gesammelte Aufsätze, 1959–1989* (Munich: Max Hueber, 1989); Kurt Tucholsky, *Politische Briefe,* ed. Fritz J. Raddatz (Reinbek: Rowohlt, 1969); Eveline Valtink, ed., *Jüdische Identität im Spiegel der Literatur vor und nach Auschwitz* (Hofgeismar: Evangelische Akademie Hofgeismar, 1988); Hans-Albert Walter, *Deutsche Exilliteratur, 1933–1950: Bedrohung und Verfolgung bis 1933,* vol. 1 (Darmstadt: Luchterhand, 1973); Joseph Walk, ed., *Kurzbiographien zur Geschichte der Juden* (Munich: K. G. Saur, 1988); Renate Wall, ed., *Verbrannt, Verboten, Vergessen: Lexikon verfolgter deutschsprachiger Schriftstellerinnen 1933 bis 1945* (Cologne: Papy Rossa Verlag, 1994); Elsbeth Wolffheim, *Dem Schlächter zuvorgekommen: Freitod deutscher Autoren im Exil, 1933–45* (Bremen: Radio Bremen, Jan. 24, 1979); and Max Zweig, *Religion und Konfession: Bruchstücke eines Bekenntnisses* (Klagenfurt: Mnemosyne, 1991).

GUY STERN

1938 During the Austrian *Anschluß* to the Third Reich, Friedrich Torberg escapes from Prague, first to Zurich and then to Paris

The relationship of Jews to Austria has always been special. It is well known that Theodor Herzl reveled for a time in the vision of Vienna as a new Jerusalem. Many German-language authors—Arthur Schnitzler, Peter Altenberg, Hermann Broch, Joseph Roth, Franz Kafka, and many others—whether in the capital or the remote corners of the multiethnic empire, felt a self-evident bond to the "Austrian House" and at the same time experienced an existential uncertainty in the *Heimat*. In his book *Unheimliche Heimat*, W. G. Sebald described this condition as follows: "The discussion of this set of problems in the German-language ghetto stories of the nineteenth century is full of ambivalence, and the literature of the fin de siècle also offers no solution. What emerges more and more from Schnitzler and Altenberg to Broch and Joseph Roth is a complex illusionism which is conscious of its own untenability and which, in that it is still working with the conception of a homeland, also conceives of itself as a training in exile" (Sebald 1976, 3).

Friedrich Torberg is a descendant of this generation of writers. He experienced the great rupture of the expulsion and extermination of Austrian Jews as a thirty-year-old man, in the early stages of his creativity. For this reason, the path of Torberg's life and work can be read as exemplary of Austrian-Jewish identity during the prewar, wartime, and postwar periods. His correspondence of the emigration period contains a particularly extensive treatment of the various Jewish models for existence: assimilation, conversion, communism, and Zionism. And naturally his thoughts revolved around Nazism and the participation of the Austrian people in its realization. Although he was able to reach clear judgments of his then fellow citizens, there was always an echo of a retrospectively transfigured way of life and later, after his return to Vienna (1951), the attempt at sentimental adaptation to the living conditions in the current "state without Jews."

"I belong," Torberg wrote in 1946 from New York to his friend Milan Dubrovic in Vienna, "neither to those Jews who first needed Hitler to discover the fact that they were Jews nor to those who would not allow Hitler to 'prescribe' it. Rather, for me it is, now as before, self-evident" (Torberg 1982, 108). Friedrich Torberg—born in 1908 as Friedrich Ephraim Kantor in Vienna—was a conscious Jew throughout his life. It was in this vein that he joined the athletic club Hakoah as a twelve-year-old, where he became a successful water polo player. He was, in fact, not only an enthusiastic athlete, he also wanted "to contradict *via facti* the vulgar anti-Semitic cliché of the Jews as physically inferior, cowardly, afraid of the water, and presenting a figure thoroughly unsuited to physical activity" (Torberg 1978, 162). As a self-conscious Jew, he debated in the famous café of the literati, Literatencafé Herrenhof, and wrote for the Prague

Zionist weekly *Selbstwehr*. During the Austrian *Anschluß* to the Third Reich, Torberg happened to be in Prague, and he fled from there first to Zurich, then Paris. Supported by the American Jewish emergency committee JOINT and placed on the American PEN organization's list "Ten Outstanding German Anti-Nazi Writers" (along with, among others, Alfred Polgar, Heinrich Mann, and Franz Werfel), he received a visa for the United States and arrived in New York on October 18, 1940. With a one-year contract with Warner Brothers in his pocket, he pressed on to Los Angeles.

And yet he felt out of sorts in the "certain celluloid-wrapped detachment from the world" in California, whose center another Viennese émigré, the actress Gisela Werbezirk, characterized as "Purkersdorf with trees" (Purkersdorf is a Viennese suburb) (Torberg 1994, 27). Torberg did, however, manage to accomplish the unusual: a film for which he wrote the screenplay became successful. The film *Voice in the Wind* by Arthur Ripley (with Francis Lederer in the lead and Gisela Werbezirk and Alexander Granach in supporting roles) told the story of a pianist from Prague who performs at a concert one of the compositions forbidden by the Nazis, gets arrested, is able to flee, and awaits passage to America. *Voice in the Wind,* filmed as an independent production, was bought by United Artists and brought Torberg new film offers, which he declined. He was happy that the money he had earned enabled him to move to New York in 1944. There he worked with Alfred Polgar, under the direction of Willi Schlamm, on the project of a German-language edition of *Time;* this, however, did not appear in 1945. After this, Torberg became a consultant to the exiled Bermann-Fischer publishing house.

Torberg finally returned to Vienna in 1951 with serious misgivings and lived there for almost three decades, until his death in 1979. As a multifaceted *homme de lettres,* he wrote his last novel, *Süßkind von Trimberg,* with the same passion with which he composed feuilletons and reviews and exercised his capacity as editor of the journal *FORUM: Österreichische Monatshefte für kulturelle Freiheit* (1954–65), which polemicized against Brecht's political message and against the

aesthetics of the literary avant-garde. At the same time, he was editor of the works of Fritz von Herzmanovsky-Orlando and the translator— more accurately, the manager—of Ephraim Kishon in German-speaking countries.

"I am," he wrote in 1955 in a letter to Max Brod, "a German-Jewish [*sic*] writer, that is, a Jew writing in the German language; I have known from the first that I am one, and this knowledge has since then at the most been increased to include the likelihood that I will be the last" (Torberg 1988b, 75). Fortunately, Torberg was wrong in this assumption, but his statement does describe the state of mind of the returnee who suddenly gets a hearing and is honored principally because of his Jewishness. Or, as Torberg himself usually expressed it, he was assigned the role of "Jew of the day" (*Jud vom Dienst*). This astonishment over the peculiar chosenness of the Jews, the shock over the apparently normal relationships with "host peoples" (*Gastvölkern*) who could suddenly reverse their positions, runs through Torberg's life and writing after the shock of the expulsion and annihilation.

In contrast, during the interwar period, Jewishness, including the corresponding anti-Semitism, was so self-evident that Torberg could write his first novel without even referring to this topic. As a twenty-two-year-old in 1930, he achieved a striking success with the novel *Der Schüler Gerber hat absolviert* (The student Gerber received his diploma). This story of a schoolboy who is driven to suicide by the unfair treatment of the school system was translated into many languages, and it offered Torberg, who had failed to graduate high school, an entry into the Viennese literary coffeehouse society.

The coffeehouse, or rather, the loss of the coffeehouse, became for Torberg, after the Austrian *Anschluß* on March 11, 1938, a metaphor to which he repeatedly returned in order to depict the decline of a way of life. For Torberg, Nazism did not mean the discovery of his Jewishness or the adoption of the role of the Jewish pariah (as it had for Zweig, who believed in assimilation, and Werfel)—he had always been a nationally engaged Jew, a Zionist. Rather, it meant the final loss of the third component of his identity, alongside the German language and a Jewish consciousness: the unparalleled combination of the Old Austrian city cultures. Although the Habsburg monarchy broke apart in 1918, one could still take the trolley from Vienna to Bratislava and back; in the coffeehouses of Prague, Budapest, Vienna, and Czernovitz, the *Prager Tagblatt* and the *Pester Lloyd* still lay next to the *Neue Freie Presse*. Not until 1938 was this world definitively destroyed.

The destruction of this multinational world by the German "master race" occupied Torberg in many of his letters during his emigration period. To his friend Peter Heller he wrote: "And one day we will stand before the doors of all of the coffeehouses that constitute our lives, and they will all be closed. That is the end of these times" (Torberg 1982, 41). (Later Torberg illuminated this lost world in his collections of anecdotes, *Die Tante Jolesch* [Aunt Jolesch] and *Die Erben der Tante Jolesch* [The heirs of Aunt Jolesch].) In New York, he was able to find the occasional ersatz coffeehouse. Arthur Koestler describes how Torberg selected the Oak Room as his habitual haunt: "He seemed to have personally brought the bar and the musicians and the atmosphere along from Vienna. I suppose he had a magic carpet, and wherever he landed he was Viennized." The coffeehouse, as a place for the expression of individual spirit and wit, represented for Torberg the humanistic counterpoint to National Socialism and Communism, and thus was the usual site of his basic theme of the effects of totalitarianism, be it of an Eastern or Western stamp, on the individual.

In the United States, far from the Viennese coffeehouses in which energy was not only generated but also fizzled out, Torberg wrote both of his most significant works: the novella *Mein ist die Rache* (Revenge is mine) and the novel *Hier bin ich, mein Vater* (Here I am, father). *Mein ist die Rache,* written in 1942, was published first by Pazifische Presse (1943) and then by Bermann-Fischer Verlag in Stockholm. It tells the story of a man who appears to be waiting for someone to arrive on the ships from Europe at New York harbor. One day the man recounts to the author the tale of the rabbinical candidate Joseph Aschkenasy, who

has been able to escape from the Heidenburg concentration camp after shooting the camp commander Wagenseil. He has even managed to flee to the United States. Since then, he has been waiting for one of the seventy-five inmates of the Jewish barracks to arrive, so that he knows that he saved at least one person besides himself with his act. At the center of the novella lies the question of whether the victim, measured by Jewish conceptions of morality, has the right to vengeance or whether this is a matter only for God. Thus the prisoner defies Wagenseil's command to commit suicide. He also dismisses the idea of killing the Nazi and dies under torture. "It is good that he didn't do that," Aschkenasy says after Landauer's death. "It is good that his sacrifice remains pure before the Lord. Mine is vengeance and retribution, says the Lord." In this novella, the issue is Jewish nonresistance, which Hermann Broch, Torberg's literary model and a sharp critic of his persistence in "Geschichtl-Erzählen," discusses in a letter to the author: "That you have emphasized the silent agreement of the Jews to nonresistance, this most uncanny of their unwritten tradition of law, by which all Jews, wherever they came from, irrespective of whether they are brave or cowardly, must comply and do comply, you cannot appreciate that enough; here lies what is specifically not pagan in the Jewish destiny, from here it points to the future" (Torberg 1988b, 23). How should the Jews react to the Nazi will to extermination? Should they use their room to maneuver and in so doing make themselves "impure"? Is there such a thing as the purity of the victim? And does it affect the guilt of the perpetrator if the victim does not remain absolutely innocent? These are questions that continually arise even today in the discussions about victim and perpetrator and that only a very few surviving victims, such as Primo Levi, have attempted to answer. In German-speaking countries in particular, a rug is anxiously thrown over the conditions of survival, just as if their uncovering would make the perpetrator less guilty.

The novel *Hier bin ich, mein Vater,* written in the years 1943–46, was first released by Bermann-Fischer in Stockholm. It describes the tragedy of the young Viennese Jew Otto Maier, who is recruited by his former schoolmate, the classic anti-Semite Franz Macholdt, as a Nazi informer, after he is promised that his father will be released from the concentration camp at Dachau. Maier betrays friends and colleagues; he carries on although his request for his father's release is put off again and again, and even after he learns from a friend of his father's death and reads for himself the directive of the camp authorities pertaining to his father's death. When Macholdt later sends him to Paris on a special mission and promises that his father will be released as soon as it is completed, Maier resolves to offer his services to the French secret service, which, however, shows no particular interest in him.

One of the strengths of the novel lies in its exposure of internalized anti-Semitic stereotypes. Maier recognizes in the end that he always aspired to be treated by non-Jews as one of their own, "Namely: as, according to their standards, a normal person. That was the somewhat faulty reasoning that came over me then: that I always governed myself according to *their* standards. It never occurred to me that there might be something wrong with these standards. I always accepted my Jewishness as a defect and saw those who made me feel this way as accusers. I never dared to suppose that perhaps the accusers themselves suffered from a defect."

Another strong point lies in the discussion at the end of the novel, as Maier encounters his former religion teacher Jonas Bloch in Paris and they debate the issue of why a different standard of values should apply to the Jews than to other peoples. Other peoples may conquer and oppress nations; a Frenchman or an Englishman may become a spy—why not a Jew? "That precisely we Jews—the weakest of all—we, who are persecuted and stepped on by all—that precisely we Jews should always be bound to a higher morality. I resist this obligation." "I hope you resist in vain," Bloch answers him. "Don't you see that one who defends oneself against such a moral challenge acknowledges it precisely in this act?" And further: "We defend ourselves exactly with our morality. Exactly with our belief that one day morality will come before force. That one day— and hopefully this doesn't sound too solemn to

you—good will triumph over evil. Or if not triumph—because good is not intent on victory— then nevertheless gain the upper hand. Maybe, you know, maybe one day the others will have our morality. That is possible. But that we would one day have their power is impossible. God has taken care of that for all time. We will return home to Zion, we will build the temple—and will not have their power, but rather always our morality" (Torberg 1948, 325).

Torberg did not content himself with the description of the then hardly known atrocities of the Nazis and the suffering of the Jews. He was not interested in the deeds of the Nazis, but in undertaking an unsparing analysis of the individual reactions of Jews. For he can understand the Jews, but those who hate them never cease to astonish him—the hatred of "all" Jews in Scholem's sense. "One does not hate us for what we do, but for what we are," Torberg states in *Mein ist die Rache*. And many years later in the novel about the Jewish *Minnesänger, Süßkind von Trimberg,* Torberg writes that "it cost *them* no great effort to accept them as one of their own— and in the next minute as a leper and refuse."

The Jews he could understand and criticize. With the greatest vehemence he turned against those surviving Jews who, as he wrote to Max Brod in 1945, "exactly and explicitly *with Jewish motivations* threw themselves into the arms of their supposed liberator and bestower of blessings, Stalin. This Jewish motivation let them appear to themselves as being strong in character and convictions in the bargain, although in the *best* case, it's a matter of stupidity, opportunism, and shortsightedness: Stalin has nothing against the Jews, therefore, I'm for him. With this, Buchenwald becomes the standard for our claims and the Nuremberg Laws the barometer of our rights" (Torberg 1988b, 56).

Torberg vehemently upheld the identification of Nazism and Communism, not despite, but because he was a Jew. In 1947, he wrote to Brod:

Namely, I do that directly from *two* Jewish motives: first, from one related to Jewry: in that great final aim of Communism, which if, God forbid, it should be achieved, would preclude the survival of that Jewry no less radically than Nazism; and secondly, from a motive related to the environment: in that namely every well-meaning non-Jew could otherwise reproach me that I had nothing to object to in Hitler but his anti-Semitism. . . . If I decline to identify a brutal, pan-Slavic dictatorship for what it is, and appeal to a "final aim" long since betrayed, sold out, and profaned through its means, the suspicion would arise that I am nothing but a shabby opportunist, who is content that this dictatorship doesn't kill me, like that one, because of my crooked nose, but rather as a counter-revolutionary or for some other pretext that just suits it (for example, that I am learning Hebrew and want to go to Palestine). And as far as the messianic component is concerned, I leave this *more than ever* willingly to the clan [Jewry], to which I have the unearned distinction of belonging; and if this clan cannot lure me away from the second coming of Christ, they surely won't be able to with the second coming of Lenin. (Torberg 1988b, 71–72)

In spite of this, Torberg, who characterized himself as a "Socialist not of a Marxist stamp," respected the *Haschomer-Hazair-Kibbutznikim* in Palestine and compared them with the social revolutionary students in czarist Russia. Each in turn was necessary for the improvement of society. "But God (and I mean God) have mercy on us if they come to power" (Torberg 1988b, 72).

Compared to Communism, which for Torberg held great dangers, conversion to Christianity and the assimilation of Jews in the United States seemed harmless. In 1947, he viewed the meddling of American Jews in the problems of the yeshiva as empty grandstanding to strengthen their own self-confidence, because not even a quarter million American Jews would give up their American citizenship in favor of Palestine.

Torberg himself, as he wrote to Heinz Politzer in 1945, stood alone among émigré writers, because he wanted neither to Stalinize nor Americanize. Nor did he let himself be taken in by the "vulgar Zionists." As he was told of a kibbutz discussion of *Mein ist die Rache* in which all agreed that it was self-evident that Aschkenasy had to shoot the camp commander and no one could

understand why this was a problem, he replied: "We already have enough farmers, bomber pilots, and world-champion boxers; it's high time that we occupy ourselves again a little with books. And I am thoroughly of the opinion (which I also tried to make clear to them over there), that we became Zionist in those days mainly because the order of our parents and responsible guardians to limit ourselves to 'the Mosaic religious creed' struck us as wrong, cowardly, horrible, and dangerous; but it is just as dangerous to want to turn Judaism into 'just a nation,' as it was once 'just a religion'" (Torberg 1988b, 295).

In 1946 Torberg wrote to Politzer, who did not feel at all comfortable in humorless, rustic Palestine, that he held Palestine to be the only position in the world that the Jews could occupy, "not the *best,* but the only one": "That is *not* to say that all Jews should go to Palestine. That is *not* to say that the Galut does not have as vital a function as the yeshuv. And accordingly, that is not to say that I would have the smallest quarrel with you because the Palestinian reality does not agree with you as a basis for life. One must not be in Palestine. But one must, I believe, be *for* Palestine" (Torberg 1988b, 303).

Torberg did not go to Palestine but returned to Vienna. What was the Vienna to which he returned in 1951? Since the expulsion of the largely Jewish intelligentsia, intellectual life in Austria has been lacking, and is even today. The second republic of Austria, liberated from the Nazis in 1945, has not hurried to call back the artists and scientists who had been driven out, let alone the anonymous surviving Jews. After all, the Viennese had settled into the 70,000 vacated apartments just as the second order of the talented had, after the elimination of the Jewish competition, established themselves in the music world, newspaper editorships, and teaching positions. Even the express wish of Arnold Schönberg to return to Vienna (he had settled in Los Angeles) was frustrated by officials.

The authors Hermann Broch, Elias Canetti, Erich Fried, Johannes Urzidil, and others did not return from England or the United States. What an opportunity for the mediocre, those who stayed behind, to attain honor and glory. Writers such as Alexander Lernet-Holenia and Rudolf Henz, both former members of the National Socialist Imperial Board of Literature; Nazi sympathizers like Gertrud Fussenegger, Bruno Brehm, and Mirko Jelusisch; and Nazi poets such as Max Mell published book after book and graced Austrian schoolbooks into the 1980s. A nostalgic conception of the Austrian character that harked back to the ostensibly intact world of the monarchy or to the eternal values of nature and the peasantry was to soothe the shock of the collapse of the National Socialist value system. A conservative literary enterprise was established, and no one upset the tranquillity of the country as Group 47 did, for instance, in the Federal Republic. It was not until the late 1950s that the Wiener Gruppe (Gerhard Rühm, Ossi Wiener, and Konrad Bayer) upset the stifling climate of postwar Austria. In the literary world, there were only isolated Jewish returnees, such as the cultural journalist Hilde Spiel, the lyric poet Hermann Hakel, the cabarettist Karl Farkas, and two authors significant in Viennese cultural life of the 1950s and 1960s, Hans Weigel and Friedrich Torberg.

Torberg returned to a postwar Vienna that again imposed conditions on Jews—namely, the repression of their own story. The Viennese considered the score settled, that they started at zero. And they acted as though that were possible. Torberg, the great letter writer, shared his reservations regarding his return to Austria with his friends. In his letters, he viewed the problem from all sides, entertained no false hopes of retrieving *his* Vienna, and saw with unsparing clarity how sad and provincial the city had become since the expulsion of the Jews. With loden coats and Styrian hats, the Austrians, who had again arrived at their own state, showed just how much they would differentiate themselves from the Germans.

In 1946 Torberg wrote from New York to his friend Hans Weigel, who, as a Jew, had been driven out of Vienna but, as an Austrian-Jewish anti-Semite, had immediately hurried back at the end of the war in order to take part with great success in the denial of anti-Semitism. Torberg believed it would be difficult for him to declare

the score with the Austrians settled. And assuming he was prepared to do so, his partners in this settlement, who in his eyes would incur heavy losses, would not thank him for it but further insult him and put him in the position of deciding when they are even: "Or he says: 'yes, okay, we're even'—but of course you have not returned as a Jew, but as an Austrian. In short: he sets conditions. He sets conditions! Speaking like a Jew is desirable. . . . And if I don't want to meet them, he will make very plain to me that he was not the one who had called me. I find, however,—and hopefully I don't have to guard against any sort of verbal misunderstanding—I find, however: he ought to call me. If he does not do this, then he gives his belated approval to my forced departure in those days (which was ostensibly forced upon him just as on me), and as far as he is concerned I can go right ahead and stay where I am. If I choose nonetheless to come back, that's my concern, and he sees it as a concession that he doesn't hinder me in doing so. And that is not at all what I conceive of as a settled score" (Torberg 1988b, 411–12).

To return to his personal motive, Torberg wrote on principle in a long letter to his friend Fritz Thorn on July 7, 1947: "In an inquiry secretly conducted in those days by the Czechs, into whether in a reestablished Czechoslovakia there ought to be German newspapers and German theater, I answered no. To the question as to whether Jews should be part of (at least German-language) Austrian newspaper and theater organizations, I would honestly answer yes, because I cannot and do not wish to imagine my own life without Austrian theater and Austrian newspapers."

Nonetheless, why did Torberg return? Manès Sperber remembers a meeting with Torberg, who was on the return trip from New York to Vienna, in a café across from the Jardin de Luxembourg in Paris. "We talked about a lot of things and were scarcely surprised that we agreed on almost everything. At one point I asked him for the reason that could make him to determine to return to Vienna. He gave me several answers, which were clever, but not convincing enough, not compelling for the author of *Hier bin ich, mein Vater*"

(Strelka 1978, 227). Perhaps one could maintain a clear vision only as long as one kept a distance. Whoever returns must build himself a more or less solid structure out of illusions.

Torberg returned, and after a short time took an important position in cultural life. He took ironic pleasure in his role as cultural pope, representative Jew, and friend of Israel. His every wish was met by the small Jewish community, who were proud of their prominent member. Spoiled by official Austria, he took part in the Austrian version of mastering the past (*Vergangenheitsbewältigung*): according to this style, one spoke with wistful nostalgia of well-known or particularly witty Jews without discussing the enthusiasm and active participation of the populace in their expulsion and extermination in the recent past.

Torberg held to tradition and saw himself as the last in a line of German-Jewish writers. For this reason, he concerned himself for decades with the fate of allegedly the first Jew to write in the German language: Süßkind von Trimberg, "a Jew," as Torberg said, "who felt through and through that he was a Jew, but who could express his feelings only in German." In Torberg's identification with Süßkind lies one reason for his returning to Vienna while at the same time maintaining an untiring engagement with all things Jewish. Only in returning to the German language could Torberg express his feelings. Torberg allowed his ideal, projected back into the past, of a Jewish-Austrian symbiosis to reemerge in a collection of anecdotes about cranks and true originals, at the center of which stood *Tante Jolesch*—but remained all the while fully conscious that the wellspring out of which he created was irretrievably dried up. "This is," he wrote in the foreword to *Tante Jolesch,* "a book of melancholy. Perhaps I should have written a book of mourning, but this I would rather do by myself. Melan-

choly can smile, grief cannot. And smiling is the lot of my tribe."

Bibliography

David Axmann, ed., *Und Lächeln ist das Erbteil meines Stammes: Erinnerung an Friedrich Torberg* (Vienna: Edition Atelier, 1988); Franz-Heinrich Hackel, *Zur Sprachkunst Friedrich Torbergs, Parodie, Witz, Anekdote: Mit einem Anhang unbekannter Arbeiten aus der Frühzeit Torbergs* (Frankfurt a. M.: Peter Lang, 1984); Winfried Georg Sebald, *Unheimliche Heimat: Essays zur österreichischen Literatur* (Salzburg: Residenz, 1976); Josef Strelka, ed., *Der Weg war schon das Ziel: Festschrift für Friedrich Torberg zum 70. Geburtstag* (Munich: Lange Muller, 1978); Frank Tichy, *Torberg: Ein Leben in Widersprüchen* (Salzburg: Otto Müller, 1995); Friedrich Torberg, *Auch das war Wien,* in *Gesammelte Werke,* ed. David Axmann and Marietta Torberg, vol. 15 (Vienna: Langen Müller, 1988); Torberg, "Briefwechsel mit Paul Rohner," *Filmexil* 4 (1994): 27; Torberg, *Die Erben der Tante Jolesch* (Vienna: Langen Müller, 1978); Torberg, *Hier bin ich, mein Vater* (Stockholm: Bermann-Fischer Verlag, 1948); Torberg *In diesem Sinne . . . Briefe an Freunde und Zeitgenossen* (Frankfurt a. M.: Ullstein, 1988b); Torberg, *Kaffeehaus war überall: Briefwechsel mit Käuzen und Originalen* (Vienna: Langen Müller, 1982); Torberg, *Mein ist die Rache* (Los Angeles: Pazifische Press, 1943); Torberg, *Der Schüler Gerber hat absolviert* (Berlin: Paul Zsolnay Verlag, 1930); Torberg, *Süßkind von Trimberg* (Frankfurt a. M.: Fischer, 1972); Torberg, *Die Tante Jolesch oder Der Untergang des Abendlandes in Anekdoten* (Vienna: Langen Müller, 1978); Torberg, *Eine tolle, tolle Zeit: Briefe und Dokumente aus den Jahren der Flucht, 1938–1941,* in *Gesammelte Werke,* vol. 18 (Vienna: Langen Müller, 1988a); and Torberg, *Voreingenommen wie ich bin: Von Dichtern, Denkern und Autoren,* in *Gesammelte Werke,* vol. 19 (Vienna: Langen Müller, 1991).

RUTH BECKERMANN

TRANSLATED BY
HILLARY HOPE HERZOG
AND TODD HERZOG

1938 Sigmund Freud's departure from Vienna for exile in England marks a symbolic end to the wave of emigration of German-speaking Jewish psychotherapists and psychoanalysts in Germany and Austria

When Sigmund Freud arrived in Britain in June 1938, his settling there was not the beginning of the exodus of anti-Hitlerian, mainly Jewish psychoanalysts and psychiatrists from Germany but marked more or less its symbolic end. Anna Freud, in a personal communication, was of the opinion that the further development of psychoanalysis would have been the same had psychoanalysis had the chance of remaining in (a non-Nazi) Germany. But this speculation seems to have little importance in comparison with the symbolic value of Freud's exile: the fact that he had to share the fate of so many other German Jews. With his emigration, the language of psychoanalysis switched from German to English. The real success of psychoanalysis was still to come and was partly a consequence of the exodus. In this way psychoanalysis remained impervious to the harm the exodus did to virtually all the German-Jewish exiles.

It was not Britain that would become the new home of psychoanalysis, but America. Even most of those psychoanalysts who accompanied Freud to Britain sooner or later continued on to the United States, for example, Ernst and Marianne Kris, and Max Schur. Even the departure of Freud from Vienna was not without symbolism. The only witness of Freud's departure was the twenty-five-year-old Heinz Kohut. In 1938 Kohut was not a member of the Viennese psychoanalytic society (all of the members had left Vienna without difficulty before Freud), but at the time of Freud's departure he was in analysis with August Aichhorn, who had rejected emigration and survived the war in Vienna. Aichhorn had received the information about Freud's departure by train from the Freud family, probably from his close friend Anna Freud, and told Kohut that the last chance to ever see Freud was at the Vienna station. Kohut left immediately for the station, and Aichhorn's prediction proved correct, for Freud was never to return to Vienna. Kohut, however, later became president of the American Psychoanalytic Association and thereafter created his own theory of psychoanalysis, which in the opinion of the Freudians partly contradicted central psychoanalytic assumptions.

The emigration of German-speaking psychiatrists and psychoanalysts from 1933 to 1938 was indeed the most extended emigration movement in the history of psychiatry. Out of the approximately 3,000 psychiatrists in Prussia-Germany and Austria, about six hundred emigrated. Not all, but most of these émigrés were Jewish. They went to a hundred countries around the globe, but most went to the United States. Psychoanalysis emigrated almost in its entirety.

Psychoanalysis was not the first psychodynamic movement in which German Jews were creative and influential. The earlier movement, however, has escaped the attention of historians, partly because the psychoanalysts themselves at best saw in these earlier therapists only forerunners and at worst ignored them completely. Ellenberger's otherwise brilliant book *Discovery of the Unconscious* (1970) does not mention German Jews at all, though they not only produced a huge literature but were also very influential politically.

Among them, for example, was the famous Berlin professor Marcus Herz (1747–1803), the husband of the even more famous Henriette Herz (1764–1847), whose salon in their home was the most important center of Berlin's intellectual life during the romantic period. Marcus Herz, the son of a Torah scribe, was a close friend of Immanuel Kant and Moses Mendelssohn, and taught medicine to the writer Ludwig Börne. Herz was the psychotherapist of King Frederic William III, who bestowed upon him in 1787, at age forty, the title of professor and a lifelong pension. He was also was the psychotherapist of Karl Philipp Moritz (1756–93), the editor of the world's first journal of psychiatry (*Gnothi Sauton oder Magazin für Erfahrungsseelenkunde als ein Lesebuch für Gelehrte und Ungelehrte*). Marcus Herz published this treatment in detail in a paper entitled "Etwas Psychologisch-Medizinisches: Moritz's Krankengeschichte."

Another very influential Jewish psychotherapist and prolific writer was Adalbert Friedrich Marcus (1753–1816), who was professor at the then leading German university of Bamberg, as well as the personal physician and counselor of Franz Ludwig von Erthal, the prince-bishop of Bamberg and Württemberg. Marcus was also the founder and first director of the General Hospital of Bamberg, and a close friend of the writer E. T. A. Hoffmann, who was then opera director at Bamberg and who painted himself and Marcus as characters on the stage. Marcus wrote an expert opinion concerning the possible insanity of the murderer J. C. Woyzeck, the model of Georg Büchner's play and Alban Berg's opera. He declared Woyzeck to be psychologically unfit and thus not responsible for his actions, but Woyzeck was nevertheless beheaded after other psychiatrists declared him responsible. The question was much discussed in public, because Marcus was a prominent public figure. On New Year's Eve, 1807, for example, he gave a party for fifty people and counted among his famous guests the philosopher Hegel and E. T. A. Hoffmann. The venue for the party was Europe's first modern mental hospital, St. Getreu in the Benedictine Abbey of Bamberg, Michaelsberg, which Marcus had founded in 1803.

A third influential Jewish psychotherapist was Johann Ferdinand Koreff (1783–1851), a professor at the Berlin university and also a close friend of E. T. A. Hoffmann. Koreff was the personal physician and psychotherapist of the Prussian state chancellor Duke Carl von Hardenberg, who was an uncle of the poet Novalis. Koreff became one of the most influential persons in the kingdom of Prussia and the chief reformer of the mental hospital system. Although Koreff was immensely gifted, he did not publish his medical writings extensively; instead he produced literary works, including many poems and a libretto. It has been said that there was hardly a crowned head in continental Europe who had not been his patient. Like the physicians mentioned above, he was an enthusiastic therapist. Koreff later lived in Paris, where he became the physician of Heinrich Heine and of Mme. Duplessis, the model for Dumas's *Lady of the Camellias*. Koreff was always controversial, and he became a frequent topic of literature. The Bibliothèque Nationale in Paris has the following controversial notes in its archive, written by an unknown hand and not without an element of anti-Semitism: "Il possède toutes les lumières de la science" (He possesses all the knowledge of science) and "sa médicamentation composée n'est qu'un assemblage de tours de gibecière. Il est comme les journalistes, qui servent à leurs abonnés les opinions qui leur plaisent, sans qu'ils y aient foi" (his medication is composed only of a bag of tricks. He is like the journalists who serve their subscribers opinions that please them [the subscribers], without believing in these opinions).

These figures represent only a small section of the psychodynamic school and of successful therapeutic treatment, which had developed in Germany since the beginning of the eighteenth century and which after 150 years came to a preliminary end in the middle of the nineteenth century. There was no parallel movement in the other European countries. As far as it is known, none of its members emigrated to the United States. Obviously none of them belonged to the "forty-eighters"—those approximately one million German inhabitants who came to the New World around the year 1848.

The intellectual situation for the psychoanalytic immigrants, who came to the United States from Germany between 1933 and 1945, was very different. The psychodynamic school discussed above had come out of the German philosophy of the Enlightenment and was closely connected, both personally and philosophically, with its idealistic branch. Psychoanalysis had the same roots but drew additionally from other philosophies of the second half of the century, such as Darwinism. It is still not quite clear why psychoanalysis was so successful in the United States. Freud's well-known skepticism regarding the chances of psychoanalysis in America seemed more justified.

Among the reasons for the surprising acceptance was perhaps the fact that the émigré psychoanalysts wrote in part about their personal problems, which at the same time resonated within the American intellectual population. One example was Erik Erikson and his book *Young Man Luther*. Erikson demonstrated how Luther could solve his own identity crisis only by formulating a new doctrine, which provided the Zeitgeist with a new identification and hence inaugurated a new historical phase. In Erikson's teaching on the progress of human growth, one identification follows the other, and the history of mankind is ruled by the same process. In a desperate effort, Luther moved his own "patienthood" to the higher level of a general patienthood of human society and attempted on this level to solve for his fellow human beings what he could not solve for himself. The title of *Young Man Luther* is a quotation from Freud's *Moses and Monotheism,* of which the final essay was the only essentially new writing that Freud was able to accomplish in his London exile. The German title *Der Mann Moses und die monotheistische Religion* makes Freud's influence even more evident. The parallels are obvious. Moses was the founder of the Jewish religion, and Luther was the founder of an evangelical, German religion. By translating the Holy Bible into the German language, Luther gave a new cultural and linguistic identity to the Germans, an identity that has remained essentially unchanged to the present day. For both Luther and Erikson, the central question revolved around the identity of the person and the culture, and of the identification of the person with a given culture. This problem was typical of Americans and Jews, or at least it was perceived as such.

Erik Homburger Erikson was born in 1902 near Frankfurt, Germany, the child of Danish parents. His parents, however, separated before his birth, and his mother, Karla Abrahamsen, first educated him at Karlsruhe, Germany, without initially explaining to Erik his identity. Later she married the German-Jewish pediatrician Theodor Homburger, who adopted Erik but never accepted him fully, because Erik developed an inclination toward the arts and artists, whereas his adoptive father had wished him to become a good doctor—of physics. From his adoption, Erik took on as his family name Homburger Erikson, the names of both of his fathers, which seriously fractured his identity. For a time, the solution to this problem seemed to be psychoanalysis, a close relationship with Anna Freud in Vienna, and taking a job as the teacher of American children. But then emigration became necessary. Erik first went to Denmark, the homeland of both his biological mother and father. But there, because he had been adopted, he was considered to be a German (and Jewish?) foreigner. In 1940 he finally went to America, the country of his wife Joan Serson, whom he had met at the carnival in Laxenburg, Austria. Beginning in 1940, Erikson's writings did speak of ego-identity; without going into the details of Erikson's biography *Young Man Luther,* it may be said that it is highly autobiographical book.

Identity was the general problem of the highly educated Jewish emigrants who were suddenly forced out of the German language and culture that had been the unquestioned source of their identity. Heinz Kohut, in an interview with Susan Quinn, expressed the problem in a striking way:

I had the feeling of a crumbling universe, not just because of Freud [who had just left Vienna], but because this was a symbol of everything that I had lived for. I was passionately involved with German and Austrian culture, this was the peak of humanity to me—Goethe and the great German philosophers and writers and the German musicians and the whole refined Viennese culture, and I was sitting up in coffeehouses until three in the morning, discussing each night another sonnet of Rilke. You know, this was life for me. And then all of a sudden these bullies came along who claimed they were the real Germans, you see, and I was all of a sudden a foreigner and didn't belong. It was the end of a world, it was the end of an era. And I had the feeling it was the end of my life, not in terms of necessarily danger to my own life, but in terms of the continuity of my cultural existence. And this is something very difficult to explain to people, and I generally don't try to.

Thus despite anti-Semitism and the problems surrounding Jewishness, the identity of the intellectuals centered on German philosophy (Kohut mentioned previously in the interview that he had studied Schopenhauer, Nietzsche, and Kant thoroughly), literature, and music. In the United States, in spite of the fact that 20 percent of the population had a German background, this German culture had almost no tradition and therefore was not understood. Since then, this lack of understanding has certainly changed to a considerable degree, but the change has occurred as a direct result of the intellectual immigration.

In some respects, the psychoanalytic émigrés were familiar with the American tradition of spiritualism, and in psychiatry, with the so-called life charts of Adolf Meyerian psychiatry. They were perhaps also fairly well acquainted with the Quaker tradition of caring for the insane and others, regardless of the cause of their need—a tradition represented by the American psychiatrist Pliny Earle, who had visited many of the European, and in 1849, German psychiatric hospitals.

Yet the English translations of the writings of Freud, which were available when the psychoanalysts arrived in the United States, did not meet Americans' needs. It is well known that the translations by James Strachey and others stressed a more technical use of the writings, which was obviously better suited to the English and American tradition of a commonsense philosophy. It is striking to see in the published correspondence of Alix and James Strachey that whenever translation problems are mentioned it is in relation to the technique and not in relations to the philosophical and cultural background of the work. Paradoxically, this tendency to more technical viewpoints might well have been one of the major causes of the success of the writings of Freud in English, because most of the psychoanalytical practitioners were more interested in how to carry out psychoanalytic therapy than in its cultural background. But the psychoanalytical émigrés had other things in mind. Most of them shared with Freud the humanistic classical education of eight years of training in Latin and six years in classical Greek. In Freud's writings there are countless allusions to and quotations of Greek and Latin writers and, above all, quotations of Goethe's writings, without mentioning the source. Freud owned and obviously read all 62,000 pages of the Sophia edition of Goethe's writings (1885–1919). At least in the case of Thedor Reik, it is known that he read not only all 143 volumes but also everything written on Goethe that he could find in Viennese libraries. Even some more modern and very successful psychoanalysts like Otto Kernberg, who as an eleven-year-old was forced into emigration with his parents, share this intellectual background with the early psychoanalysts and have increasingly come to feel the necessity of re-reading about the origins of psychoanalytic thinking.

When writing, Freud obviously did not think of the reader of the English translation but of his fellow classical German intellectuals; it was not necessary to quote or mention the source, because his readers knew what was meant. Translators, however, had to be familiar with this background and be able to explain it to the English reader. Richard Sterba showed me his own copy of Freud's translated writings and pointed to his countless handwritten corrections, which he used when teaching psychoanalysis. It is quite disturbing that up to the present day there is no really satisfying English translation of Freud, whereas the situation for the Italian, Spanish, and even French translations is much better.

It is, however, easier to understand why after one or two decades of psychoanalytic dominance in American psychiatry, American medicine finally more or less gave up psychoanalysis. The argument was that the success of psychoanalysis in treating or healing symptoms or disturbances did not seem to be superior to the success of other forms of medical treatment, including medication. Implicit in this sort of statement (it is not necessary to go into the details of statistics here) is the notion that psychoanalysis is based on fundamentally false assumptions. One such view was forwarded by Max Isserlin (1879–1941), a scientific critic of psychoanalysis. In the psychoanalytic literature, Isserlin generally is referred to as an enemy of psychoanalysis. He, like Freud, was Jewish and therefore forced into exile. He went to Britain, where he died. In 1910 and 1912, Isserlin had published two papers, which on the one hand demonstrated that he had read all the psychoanalytic literature that had been published up to that time. On the other hand, he criticized Freud as well as C. G. Jung from a scientific viewpoint, arguing that the psychoanalytic assumptions were yet to be proven scientifically, that psychoanalytic interpretations were based on unscientific methods, and that the efficacy of psychoanalysis as a treatment had yet to be demonstrated. Obviously, this critique persists today. I do not want to respond to it here, because psychoanalysis is treated here as a cultural and historical fact independent of its character as a possible natural science.

There are some remarkable points about Isserlin that make his case more important than it at first appears to be. First is the "Isserlin affaire," as C. G. Jung called it in his letters to Freud. Isserlin wanted to attend the psychoanalytic congress at Nuremberg in 1910, but Jung wrote to Freud "I don't want this dirty guy," which sounded very

much like "I don't want this dirty Jew." Consequently, Isserlin could not attend the meeting, even when he promised only to listen and not to speak there. Isserlin, however, was the psychotherapist at Kraepelin's psychiatric outpatient department in Munich, where he practiced psychotherapeutic, if nonpsychoanalytic, treatment and taught his views to medical students. Later, in 1926, Isserlin published a textbook of psychotherapy that even from today's viewpoint is not bad. In 1910, when Eugen Bleuler was writing his schizophrenia book, Kraepelin visited him in Zürich, and, according to Jung's report to Freud, the two men talked about the Isserlin case. Bleuler was so upset—he considered Jung's behavior to be a symptom of the sectarian, nonscientific ideology of the psychoanalytic movement—that he cut his ties and those of his followers in Zürich to the psychoanalytic organization. We do not want to discuss the fact that Freud publicly gave another, entirely psychoanalytic interpretation of Bleuler's decision. Emigration obviously did not extinguish older problems but added new ones.

Bibliography

Harry Ellenberger, *The Discovery of the Unconscious: The History and Evolution of Dynamic Psychiatry* (New York: Basic Books, 1970); Marcus Herz, *Grundriß der medizinischen Wissenschaften* (Berlin: n.p., 1782); Max Isserlin, *Psychotherapie: Ein Lehrbuch für Studierende und Ärzte* (Berlin: J. Springer, 1926); Adalbert Friedrich Marcus, *Entwurf einer speziellen Therapie* (Nuremberg: 1805–12); William McGuire and Wolfgang Sauerländer, eds., *Sigmund Freud / C. G. Jung Briefwechsel* (Frankfurt a. M.: S. Fischer, 1974); Uwe Henrik Peters, *Anna Freud: A Life Dedicated to Children* (New York: Schocken, 1985); and Peters, *Psychiatrie im Exil: Die Emigration der dynamischen Psychiatrie aus Deutschland, 1933–1939* (Düsseldorf: Kupka-Verlag, 1992).

UWE HENRIK PETERS

1939 Else Lasker-Schüler becomes permanently exiled in Jerusalem when Swiss immigration authorities deny her reentry to Switzerland

The work of Else Lasker-Schüler represents the zenith and final point of pre-Holocaust poetry by German Jewish women. In Berlin the poet had cast herself in the role of the exotic stranger destined for the company of the princes and princesses of the *Arabian Nights*, a Jewish woman poet in the German diaspora. She wrote in German but maintained that Hebrew was the language of her soul. Her self-created synthetic identity allowed her to blend her post-emancipation German-Jewish background with fanciful notions of a faraway homeland.

Heartbroken by her life in exile since 1933, the transformation artist Lasker-Schüler surrendered her last masks in 1939 when a letter from her lawyer Emil Raas informed her that the Swiss immigration authorities denied her reentry to Switzerland. In 1934 she had visited Jerusalem for the first time. Her exuberant account *Das Hebräerland* (The land of the Hebrews), written after her return to Europe, reveals how deeply the encounter with the Middle East had affected her. In 1937 she returned to Jerusalem in the course of a lecture and study tour; she undertook a third trip to Palestine in 1939.

Lasker-Schüler had already booked her return trip to Switzerland via Egypt and was preparing to leave when she was suddenly cut off from the German-speaking sphere (Bauschinger 1980, 266). Subsequently all direct interaction between Lasker-Schüler and the German-speaking public ceased, and she had to abandon her hopes for a wider reception of her works, particularly her plays. She had already been sick and overwrought upon her arrival in Jerusalem. Now she went into a deep depression and an existential crisis.

In Switzerland, Lasker-Schüler had been exposed to dire circumstances as an undesirable alien. Jerusalem, however, was the place of her ultimate disillusionment; she was homesick for Germany, to which she never returned. Although her economic situation improved somewhat, it was here that her dream world shattered—in a letter to Leo and Margarete Kestenberg she coined the sarcastic term "Misrael" to vent her frustration (Lasker-Schüler 1969, 197).

Numerous poems in her anthology *Mein blaues Klavier* (My blue piano; 1943) convey alienation from the here-and-now and nostalgia for the world of her past. Often her speakers express a desire to return to their mother's womb. *Weltflucht* (withdrawal), anxiety, and fragmentation reveal the trauma of separation that Lasker-Schüler underwent in 1939. She never regained the playful poise that had made her famous. Many of her friends dismissed her oppressive fears as paranoia, but history proved her right: she did live in a hostile world that persecuted her beyond her death in 1945. Her tomb at the Jewish cemetery on the Mount of Olives was vandalized by Arabs and rediscovered only in 1967.

Immediately after the Nazi takeover in 1933, Lasker-Schüler escaped to Switzerland, but her name did not appear on "denaturalization lists" before September 1938. Bauschinger maintains that the official act of robbing her of her German citizenship brought home to the poet the loss of her hitherto unacknowledged and often unappreciated home, Berlin, with the Romanisches Café as its center (Bauschinger 1980, 264–65). Before traveling to the "Orient," Lasker-Schüler asserted that Palestine was her true home. After she settled in Jerusalem it became obvious that her claim was based on illusion. She was no romantic stranger as a Jew among Jews but had to confront the city of her dreams and her German-Jewish identity without disguise and role-playing. The destruction of Germany as she knew it caused the breakdown of her inner reality. There was no substitute in Palestine for what she had lost. The everyday reality of the war-torn country foiled her fantasies and her creativity. In addition, she encountered communication barriers that undermined her self-confidence as a poet. She never became fluent in modern Hebrew, which she loved as the language of the liberated Jewish nation, and she continued to despise Yiddish as the ghetto language of the Diaspora.

Lasker-Schüler shared her alienation with many other German-Jewish authors in exile who had eluded Nazi persecution. They had saved their lives but did not escape the odium of their native culture. The German language, which Lasker-Schüler had finetuned into a unique literary medium, was associated with anti-Semitism and the Nazi state. After 1939 it was stigmatized as the language of warmongers, and in the 1940s German culture became identified with genocide. Zionists discouraged the use of German altogether. During this era Lasker-Schüler's inclusionary, almost cosmic concept of herself and the world met with indifference or rejection. Although she embraced the internal and external "other"—her female and her male self; her male and female friends; Jews and Christians; Jews and Arabs; rich and poor—her contemporaries drew

ever narrower racial, national, and cultural boundaries. Having escaped European anti-Semitism, she now witnessed the Jewish-Arab conflict in Palestine, which filled her with bitterness. Ultimately, her lifelong struggle for personal deliverance and peace ended in a blind alley.

Lasker-Schüler's literary works, particularly her poetry, reflect her personal and professional plight. During the 1930s her childlike exuberance gradually gave way to despair as all avenues of freedom and progress closed and Jews and women were stripped of their barely acquired rights. At the beginning and at the height of her career, Lasker-Schüler gloried in the choices modernity had bestowed upon her as a Jewish woman. The images she used to describe herself and her creative process epitomized the fluidity of gender roles and identity made possible by the industrial revolution. In defiance of traditional class and gender roles, she assumed imaginary male and female personae such as Princess Tino of Baghdad and Prince Jussuf of Thebes.

In Jerusalem Lasker-Schüler was defined by her age, her German origin, and her status as a refugee and exile, whereas in Berlin she had been known by such epithets as "Black Swan of Israel" (Bänsch 1971, 52ff). Her emphatic statement to Ludwig von Ficker, "Thank God I'm a Jew" in the masculine rather than the feminine expresses her iconoclastic proclivities in a nutshell (Lasker-Schüler 1969, 112). Her biography formed an integral part of her creativity. A passionate moviegoer, she applied the make-believe of cinema to her own life. She changed her birth date, invented a spectacular family background, and bestowed fanciful names and titles upon herself and her friends to adorn and poeticize her world.

These efforts are the literary equivalent of the aspirations of turn-of-the-century painters and designers such as Gustav Klimt and Otto Wagner to aestheticize everyday life. The stylized nature imagery and the exotic figures of Lasker-Schüler's early poetry and sketches—for example, *Styx* (1902) and *Der siebte Tag* (The seventh day; 1905)—evoke sensuous and rarefied *Jugendstil* atmospheres. Also the prose of *Das Peter Hille-Buch* (The Peter Hille book; 1906) and the poems and prose in *Die Nächte Tino von Bagdads*

(The nights of Tino of Baghdad; 1907) reveal her predilection for exquisite ambiances.

The role of the great lover and vagabond that Lasker-Schüler had played in Berlin enabled her to face poverty, the general lot of women under patriarchy, with relative ease. As a twice-divorced Jewish woman without a regular income, she faced inordinate material hardship. She lacked practical talent and was notorious for her money problems. Her pamphlet *Ich räume auf! Meine Anklage gegen meine Verleger* (Making a clean slate! My accusations against my publishers; 1925, Eng. trans. 1925) and her letters document her plight, which surprisingly did not affect her poetry. Her appreciation for luxury was untainted with greed and her love was free of selfishness. She bore few grudges. Consumed with a passion for humankind, she was unforgiving only toward fanatics: anti-Semites, militarists, racists, and misogynists.

Lasker-Schüler's love of Judaism was cosmopolitan, and so was her attachment to Germany. Her regionalism, evident in the drama *Die Wupper* (The wupper; 1919), did not preclude an admiration for the exotic, nor did her Jewishness prevent her from appreciating Christian piety. From her passion for life, physical beauty, and sexuality sprang an unparalleled language of rapture and ecstasy. Lasker-Schüler expressed her motherly love for her son Paul as well as her erotic desires with an abandon that rendered the response of the beloved irrelevant. Like Rahel Levin and Pauline Wiesel, her historical predecessors, she was unconcerned with the pains of rejection. She affirmed her femininity and her Jewish identity without compromising any part of herself—either her individuality or her independence.

Lasker-Schüler was born in 1869 in Elberfeld, a suburb of Wuppertal. After her divorce from the dermatologist Lasker, she moved to the German capital during the exuberant anarchism of the pre–World War I era. This experience marked her clearly as a member of a different generation than Gertrud Kolmar and Nelly Sachs, with whom she is frequently compared. Her work, like theirs, grew out of the multicultural Berlin *bohème*, where many Jewish women overcame their double marginalization

and rose to prominence. The metropolis offered her the necessary space to test her limits apart from bourgeois and gentile norms. She lodged in boarding houses or cheap hotels and used coffeehouses as her salon and study. In this milieu where the intellectual establishment and the avant-garde of gentile and Jewish society met, she blossomed as the friend of intellectuals and artists of all walks of life, philosophies, and backgrounds.

Leaving her middle-class existence had deprived Lasker-Schüler of the protection traditionally enjoyed by a woman of her background. She stood out as a target for Nazi hoodlums and tried in vain to escape her increasingly fascist and technocratic society by retreating into imaginary anti-worlds. After she fled from Nazi Germany, her works were accessible only to the *Kultusgemeinde,* the official Jewish community, whose activities were terminated after the Kristallnacht. Then they were outlawed, forgotten, and slowly rediscovered in postwar Germany. Bauschinger (1980, 332) notes that most early critical studies about Lasker-Schüler were biased and full of factual errors. Even her former friends repudiated the poet as a mental case or a nymphomaniac and interpreted her defiance of convention as mental instability.

Early in her career Lasker-Schüler had problematized social norms, gender, and Jewish identity, but rarely nationality and individual rights. The radicalization of the public sphere at the end of the Weimar Republic led her to a heightened awareness of her individualism and her attachment to both Germany and the German language. The latter in particular made her vulnerable to the anti-Semitic policies of the Nazis. Unlike polyglots like Claire Goll, Lasker-Schüler wrote exclusively in German. Her sense of spiritual or national Judaism was not strong enough to counterbalance the loss of her German existence. She had reached the end of her resources when she settled in *Eretz* Israel, a sick, uprooted woman, advanced in age, who failed to integrate herself into her new society.

The collective experience of persecution was an important aspect of Lasker-Schüler's Jewish identity. Her attachment to the Jewish people and the Hebrew language was intuitive, based on her ancestry and her spontaneous love of Judaism. Central to her ahistorical concept was the idea of an innate proclivity, reminiscent of Goethe's *entelechia*. In his description of the Schüler family's admiration for German literature, particularly Goethe, Jakob Hessing suggests that classical and romantic authors had shaped the poet's view of the world (Hessing 1985, 28).

On the other hand, Lasker-Schüler's ignorance of Jewish tradition and halakhahic law is evinced by her erroneous accounts of Jewish customs and her romanticized notions of Jewish spirituality in *Hebräische Balladen* (Hebrew ballads; 1913). It would be incorrect, however, to blame the deficiencies on assimilation. Rahel Levin's and Fanny Lewald's complaints several generations earlier suggest that Jewish educational practices were the reason why women remained ignorant of religious matters. Barred from the study of Scripture, they attended Christian schools and engaged in secular pursuits—religious erudition could not possibly become the cornerstone of their identity. Not surprisingly, Lasker-Schüler's stirring poem "Mein Volk" (Lasker-Schüler 1959, 137, 292) and *Hebräische Balladen* (291–311), which constructed Jewish identity from ethnicity and a common history, struck a chord with numerous Jewish women writers.

In more ways than one the poet had already been a marginal figure in Berlin. Even when she did not focus on Jewish topics her perspective differed from that of the literary mainstream. For example, in *Die Wupper,* which is set in the familiar landscape of her childhood, the dominant perspective is that of an outsider looking in. Thus Germany's western industrial region is transformed into a magical but cruel soul scape. The self-portrait of the poet as the Prince of Thebes on the book cover, a Mediterranean-looking woman's head with short black hair, suggests alienation on another level. The image represents the poet's inner self, the harsh reality of the *Galuth,* the Diaspora.

The rural working class environment of *Die Wupper* is reminiscent of Georg Büchner's *Woyzek*. Regional dialect, fairy-tale motifs, and stock characters such as a lecherous grandfather, the witch-like Mother Pius, a precocious girl, and her bourgeois seducer Heinrich (named after Goethe's Faust), place the work in the tradition of popular drama that empowers the oppressed. The social issues addressed in *Die Wupper* have inspired productions in the Bauhaus style, whereas the play's charismatic aspects have prompted lyrical expressionist performances.

As one living on the verge of homelessness, Lasker-Schüler was uniquely qualified to portray the misery as well as the grandeur of vagrant life. She shared the *bohème*'s admiration for vagabonds such as her first mentor Peter Hille, Waldemar Bonsels, and Hugo Sonnenschein. The vagrants in *Die Wupper,* three men equally as pathetic as poetic, possess the demonic qualities of witches and the magic of the miracle rabbis of Hasidic culture. They are not intended to denounce social ills or advocate social rehabilitation but are portrayed without moral indignation, suggesting that the compulsion of the exhibitionist Pendelfredderech may be his individual path to glory. In the same vein the poet assigns to the senile grandfather wisdom and dignity. His nonsense words "Tum Tingeling" (Lasker-Schüler 1962, 980, 989ff.) are a magic formula in the midst of chaos. Lasker-Schüler, clearly familiar with Socialist literature, also uncovers class-specific interests, but *Die Wupper* does not follow Marxist theory. The oppressed are shown to possess a power independent of money and status, one that is based on the sexual and emotional needs of the privileged. Animal instincts and drives form a connecting bond between all characters—there are no outsiders to the human condition, not even the exponents of modern bureaucracy, the gentlemen with top hats.

The ultimate power resides with the card reader, faith healer, and procuress Grandmother Pius, a multivalent figure like Elias Canetti's Therese in *Die Blendung* (Auto-da-fé) and Hermann Broch's Mother Gisson in *Bergroman* (Mountain novel), who is in part a witch, in part a Great Mother figure. None of the "moderns" are a match for this archetypal character manipulating their desires. By suggesting that the forces governing human life are separate from the social and economic hierarchy, *Die Wupper* questions the surface structures of patriarchy.

Die Wupper is epic theater, but in contrast to Brecht, Lasker-Schüler avoids didacticism. Her drama's aloofness reflects the poet's own situation: as a Jewish woman she was affected by the conditions she portrayed, but she was even more marginal than proletarian men. Hence her detachment, which has been an attribute of German-Jewish writing since Heine. The very marginalization that caused the alienation of Jewish authors prevented them from taking the issues of the dominant culture seriously. Particularly the most "German" of German dramas, *Faust,* has often been the target of their satire, as is the case in *Die Wupper,* where the central scene is the seduction of a girl by a privileged man. Whereas *Faust*'s Gretchen is elevated to become the paragon of German womanhood despite her transgressions, Lasker-Schüler's Lieschen remains a nobody. What could be a lofty romance is reduced to a deadly post–World War I farce.

Else Lasker-Schüler's rebellion against traditional gender roles began in the Wilhelminian era and continued through the Weimar Republic. In her erotic poetry she cast herself in the role of a troubadoura courting and showering her beloved with compliments and imaginary gifts as a minstrel would his lady. Her early work is a passionate outcry against the efficiency, barrenness, and atrophy of the industrial age and exalts the spontaneity of children and poets. Lasker-Schüler based her ideal of personal autonomy on her experience of love and suffering, which she felt with almost mystical intensity. Her passionate androgynous creativity was anathema to the petty bourgeois mentality and heterosexual prudery of the National Socialists.

Long before National Socialism, Lasker-Schüler explored alternatives to an exclusively German identity by trying to reconstruct her own Jewish identity. Such an undertaking required considerable resourcefulness on the part of an emancipated, German-identified woman. Despite her general disinterest in Eastern European Jewish culture, Lasker-Schüler was fascinated with its mysticism and oral tradition as described by Martin Buber. She looked to the Middle East, Egypt, Iraq, and Palestine for inspiration. Her ideal was a Jewish-Christian synthesis to keep both religions intact and to end the Jewish Question.

As the situation in Germany worsened, matters of content became Lasker-Schüler's priority, and she turned to drama and prose as her major genres—for example, the essays in *Konzert* (Concert; 1932) and the narrative and drama *Arthur Aronymus* (1932). Her creativity was increasingly affected by her distress; this aspect is shown in the extremely fragmentary journal of her Middle East travels, *Das Hebräerland,* whose narrative voice vacillates between hope and despondency. These texts still contain a ray of hope, however, in contrast to *Mein blaues Klavier* and the drama *Ichundich* (I and I; 1961), which was written during her last years in Jerusalem and considered unfit for performance until recently.

It is obvious from *Arthur Aronymus,* which is set in the era of emancipation and early anti-Semitism, that Lasker-Schüler assessed the situation in 1933 realistically. Against her idealized family background she explored the viability of a German-Jewish synthesis. On the surface the play seems innocuous, but the discrepancies of content and style suggest an abyss beneath the fairy tale of a Jewish-Christian spirituality. Visions of sweetness and light clash with brutality, revealing that the golden age of Arthur Aronymus's childhood, if it ever existed, was an era of false confidence. On the eve of the Nazi victory, Lasker-Schüler, a victim of the illusionary German-Jewish symbiosis, faces up to the fact that after the Dreyfus Affair, the Russian pogroms, and the political anti-Semitic campaigns in Germany, there was little hope to achieve intercultural harmony.

Arthur Aronymus shows that anti-Judaism had poisoned the minds of young people long before these crises. A sense of danger dominates the work despite the conciliatory laughter of the adults who have barely overcome their own bigotry. It is suggested that German culture failed the Jews by luring them from the ghettos only to destroy them. As in Heinrich Heine's *Rabbi von*

Bacharach (The rabbi of Bacharach), in *Arthur Aronymus* the romantic form clashes with the story of a pogrom told in the tone of a fairy tale. Lasker-Schüler recounts how on Christmas Eve during the pogrom of Gesecke Jewish children were hanged like candy (*Konfekt*) in the great hall of the school (Lasker-Schüler 1962, 560). In the character of Dorchen, the poet transformed her own recollection of anti-Semitic harassment into the story of a girl suspected of witchcraft because she suffers from Chorea Minor, a condition with which Else Lasker-Schüler had been afflicted as a young girl. Ironically, Arthur Aronymus formulates his religious ideal during these troubled times, and the marriage between a Jew and a Christian unites the bishop and the Schülers as one family. During the feast Easter and Passover foods are served.

The happy ending reveals the poet's desire for harmony, but it does not obliterate the earlier tensions. The behavior of the younger generation suggests that peace will not last. The adults may celebrate their newly established friendship, but the children are playing witch-hunt. Under the leadership of the bishop's nephew, they proceed to burn Arthur, the most peace-loving Jew, whose jump over the fence prefigures Lasker-Schüler's escape to Switzerland.

Arthur's costume suggests a connection between anti-Semitism and misogyny, pogroms and witch-hunts. The children enjoy the game of persecution more than any other diversion. They experience the same sadistic pleasure that propelled the Nazi actions and tortures, as well as the burning of women centuries before. Lasker-Schüler's image of a Jewish boy dressed up as a witch who is led to the stake by a cheering mob is foreboding, and for the year 1932, fitting.

In terms of style, the poetry cycle *Mein blaues Klavier,* the major publication of Lasker-Schüler's Jerusalem years, is more indirect than her earlier works (see Lasker-Schüler 1959). Austere forms and emotional detachment, almost numbness, indicate a strikingly new relationship to reality. The poet now uses adjectives and epithets sparingly. Her subjectivism has given way to a search for universal values. *Mein blaues Klavier* reflects the disenchantment and anxiety that were her companions in exile. Lasker-Schüler mourned her dead, particularly her son Paul and her mother, and the times and places of her youth to which she could not return. Old age and infirmity overpowered her, but most importantly, she lost her lifelong hope for world peace.

Thus the great lover was slowly transformed into a great mourner, who longed for an end to her suffering. Yet even in her despondency she retained the transcendental hope of returning to the naïveté of childhood in some other world, as is suggested in the poem "Mein blaues Klavier" (My blue piano; Lasker-Schüler 1959, 337). Before letting resignation take hold, Lasker-Schüler tested one last time her proven methods of transforming reality: myth-making, eroticism, and poetic subjectivity. They prove futile against the terror spread by Nazi Germany's invasion of the countries for which the poet had an affinity. She felt cornered, outnumbered. In the context of *Mein blaues Klavier,* even previously published poems such as "An meine Freunde" (To my friends; 331–32) assume a new, sinister meaning. In the new environment the text reads like a passionate declaration of loyalty with the Nazi victims, whereas "Ich liege am Wegrand" (I lie at the roadside; 346) and "Die Verscheuchte" (The expelled woman; 347) lament the refugee's dilemma: those who escaped death feel like garbage ("Kehrricht"), unworthy of living after so many have perished. There is no escape from devastation, neither by remembrance as in "Meine Mutter" (My mother; 333) and prayer as in "Gebet" (Prayer; 338), nor by love and sensuality as in "Über glitzernden Kies" (Across glittering gravel; 339). As the imagery of the last poem unfolds, it evokes the terror of the Kristallnacht, which the poet can only imagine. Overall, the anthology conveys the suffering of a refugee unable to shake off the trauma of persecution and survivor's guilt. Only in a few poems does an androgynous speaker emerge, who overcomes suffering by endurance. Faith and acceptance provide the ultimate hope promising triumph over agony. This spiritual posture enabled Lasker-Schüler to confront Jerusalem, the temporal and the holy city.

In her last drama, *Ichundich* (Lasker-Schüler

1961, 85–103), a vision of the doomed concentration camp world, Lasker-Schüler combined political satire with a style and language reminiscent of Goethe's *Faust II*. The inclusion of English and Hebrew vocabulary intimates that the inferno created by Germany caused a worldwide "Babylonic" confusion. Lasker-Schüler's choice of genre associates her with the antifascist *littérature engagée* of, for example, Heinrich Mann's satire *Lidice* (1943). *Ichundich* is *Welttheater,* universal theater, with a theater in hell, Jerusalem, the Hinnon Valley, the Tower of David, and a garden close to the old city wall as its scenery. Despite its geographical setting it is first and foremost a German drama, rich with allusions to *Faust*. The Sturm und Drang dramaturgy encompasses multiple time frames and levels of reality. The characters include literary and historical figures such as Faust, Mephisto, Nazi leaders, Lasker-Schüler's friends, and the poet herself. Through the confusion of aesthetic and ethical values, Lasker-Schüler expresses her critical attitude toward authors like Karl Kraus and Klaus Mann, who only targeted Nazi aesthetics—whereas the issue at hand was not the Nazis' bad taste, but their crimes. There is no indication that Lasker-Schüler endorsed a specific resistance movement. Her text rather suggests that Nazi Germany eludes her literary system of reference, a phenomenon with which she and the people of her background fail to come to terms because they lack the necessary tools.

In the dialogue between Faust and Goebbels, Faust is shocked by the brutality with which the Nazis treat Herschel Grynszpan, whose attack on the secretary of the German embassy in Paris served the Nazis as a rationalization for the Kristallnacht pogrom. Although Faust caused the demise of Gretchen and many other innocent people by following his sexual urges, greed, and lust for power, he subscribes to traditional values. His ideals of valor and bravery fall on deaf ears with the Nazis. Compared to their barbarism—expressed by drunkenness, offensive language, and the unexpected use of street jargon by even pretentious Nazi characters—Mephisto's and Faust's transgressions appear innocuous, almost civilized. Lasker-Schüler resumes the witch motif

from *Arthur Aronymus* to show that in Nazi Germany guilt lies not with the accused, but with their accusers. Ultimately, however, the poet seems cognizant of the fact that her drama's chaotic action does not even come close to depicting the upheavals of World War II. All she has to offer are religious and cultural fragments. Her approach is appropriate to her topic: the breakdown of traditional poetic discourse as a result of the collapse of Western civilization. At the same time, the words of poetry fail to describe the global catastrophe.

If the existence of men such as Hitler, Goebbels, and Himmler negates the validity of the German cultural heritage, the poet has to admit that her life's work has become an anachronism. This realization pervades *Ichundich*. Lasker-Schüler demolishes the discourse of the educated middle class to pronounce her condemnation of an intellectual tradition so easily co-opted by totalitarianism, and an intellectual caste who so willingly followed the Nazis.

Ichundich traces the breakdown of language and symbols in the face of the unprecedented global catastrophe, but it does not offer any solution or consolation beyond the verdict that civilization as the author knew it has collapsed. In *Ichundich,* Lasker-Schüler, whose focal point was not Zionism, religion, or a future Jewish state, mourns her lost youth, her German culture, and the broken promise of a union between Germans and Jews. As the final lines of her last play suggest, the answer to her problems must be sought in religion and poetry. For this reason, she adheres to the themes and tools of classical German literature, the apex of her lost culture, and formulates her ultimate concern as Faust's famous *Gretchenfrage:* "Do you believe in God?" On the plane of visionaries and believers to which Lasker-Schüler relegates the dramatic character of the poet, a positive answer is still possible: "I am so glad: God is 'here'" (Lasker-Schüler 1961, 103).

In her years of exile, Lasker-Schüler remained one of the guardians of Germany's legitimate literary tradition and one of the messengers of its demise. Her identification with Germany, her age, and her failing health left her no energy to explore new directions, but she did disclose the tragedy of German Jewry and of European culture at large. It seems no coincidence that she died in the year of the Allied victory over Germany, having completed *Ichundich* as her requiem to the German-Jewish symbiosis. She was spared complete knowledge of the Shoah and did not live to see the state of Israel, a new beginning for which she was not prepared.

Bibliography

Dieter Bänsch, *Else Lasker-Schüler: Zur Kritik eines etablierten Bildes* (Stuttgart: Metzler, 1971); Sigrid Bauschinger, *Else Lasker-Schüler, ihr Werk und ihre Zeit* (Heidelberg, Stiehm, 1980); Bauschinger, "'Ich bin ein Jude: Gott sei Dank': Else Lasker-Schüler," *Im Zeichen Hiobs: Jüdische Schriftsteller und deutsche Literatur im 20. Jahrhundert,* ed. Günter Grimm and Hans-Peter Bayerdörfer (Königstein: Athenäum, 1985), 84–123; Meike Fassmann, *Spielfiguren: Die Ich-Figuration Else Lasker-Schülers als Spiel mit der Autorenrolle* (Stuttgart: M & P, 1992); Sonja M. Hedgepeth, *Überall blicke ich nach einem heimatlichen Boden aus: Exil im Werk Else Lasker-Schüler* (New York: Lang, 1994); Jakob Hessing, *Else Lasker-Schüler: Biographie einer deutsch-jüdischen Dichterin* (Karlsruhe: Von Loeper, 1985); Hessing, *Die Heimkehr einer jüdischen Emigrantin: Else Lasker-Schülers Rezeption 1945 bis 1971* (Tübingen: Niemeyer, 1993); Erika Klusener, *Else Lasker-Schüler mit Selbstzeugnissen und Bilddokumenten* (Reinbek bei Hamburg: Rowohlt, 1980); Else Lasker-Schüler, *Gedichte, 1902–1943,* in *Gesammelte Werke,* ed. Friedhelm Kemp, vol. 1 (Munich: Kösel, 1959); Lasker-Schüler, *Lieber gestreifter Tiger,* in *Briefe von Else Lasker-Schüler,* ed. Margarete Kupper, vol. 1 (Munich: Kösel, 1969); Lasker-Schüler, *Prosa und Schauspiele* in *Gesammelte Werke,* ed. Friedhelm Kemp, vol. 2 (Munich: Kösel, 1962); Lasker-Schüler, *Verse und Prosa aus dem Nachlaß,* in *Gesammelte Werke,* ed. Werner Kraft, vol. 3 (Munich: Kösel, 1961); Lasker-Schüler, *Wo ist unser buntes Theben,* in *Briefe von Else Lasker-Schüler,* ed. Margarete Kupper, vol. 2 (Munich: Kösel, 1969); Anne Overlack, *Was geschieht im Brief? Strukturen der Brief-Kommunikation bei Else Lasker-Schüler und Hugo von Hofmannsthal* (Tübingen: Stauffenburg, 1993); Andrea Parr, *Drama als 'schreitende Lyrik': Die Dramatikerin Else Lasker-Schüler* (Frankfurt a. M.: Peter Lang, 1988); Michel Rachline, *La muse de Berlin: Le roman d'Else Lasker-Schüler* (Paris: O. Orban, 1987); Ruth Schwertfeger, *Else Lasker-Schüler: Expressionist, Woman, Jew, and Exile* (New York: St. Martin's, 1991); and Leon I. Yudkin, *Else Lasker-Schüler: A Study in German Jewish Literature* (Northwood: Science Review Ltd., 1991).

DAGMAR C. G. LORENZ

1939 Max Horkheimer's "Die Juden und Europa" appears

During World War II, the writers associated with the Institute for Social Research (who have subsequently come to be known as the Frankfurt school) devoted sustained attention to the study of anti-Semitism. The institute's studies of anti-Semitism and the image of the Jew, moreover, were intimately intertwined with the philosophical work of the Frankfurt school's leading figures and had an effect on the overall development of critical theory.

The overwhelming majority of those associated with the institute in the first two decades of its existence—including Theodor W. Adorno, Walter Benjamin, Erich Fromm, Henryk Grossmann, Arkady Gurland, Max Horkheimer, Otto Kirchheimer, Leo Lowenthal, Herbert Marcuse, Franz Neumann, Friedrich Pollock, and Felix Weil—were (wholly or in part) of Jewish origin. Fromm, Grossmann, and Lowenthal were directly involved in Jewish life early in their careers. The institute, however, which initially had a Marxist orientation, did not, in the period immediately following its creation in 1923, devote its resources to the study of anti-Semitism. To be sure, anti-Semitism was considered by those who created the institute as an example of the kind of question that demonstrated the need for an entity devoted to social research, and the founders used this argument when they conducted their initial negotiations with Hermann Weil (who provided the institute's endowment) and with the University of Frankfurt (with which the institute was formally affiliated before the Nazi era). These allusions to the need for studies of anti-Semitism, however, seem to have been lures rather than actual indications of the core interests of the institute's affiliates in the 1920s.

This situation began to change when Max Horkheimer became director of the institute in 1930. It is obviously true that neither Horkheimer nor those closest to him in the institute wrote extensively on anti-Semitism in the years leading up to World War II. The Frankfurt school seems to have deliberately avoided public discussion of the Jewish Question as such in Weimar Germany (Jay 1973, 133). The subject of anti-Semitism, moreover, is glaringly absent from the institute's major collective work of the 1930s, *Studien über Autorität und Familie,* which was published in Paris after the core group of the Frankfurt school had already left Germany. Toward the end of his career, however, Lowenthal, for one, came to believe that the Jewish origins of the Frankfurt school's members had in fact had a significant effect on their work: "However much I once tried to convince Martin Jay that there were no Jewish motifs among us at the institute, now, years later and after mature consideration, I must admit to a certain influence of Jewish tradition, which was codeterminative" (Lowenthal 1987, 112). Horkheimer, moreover, claimed that he had been quite concerned with the growth of anti-Semitism in Germany. "As early as 1930 when I still was in Frankfurt," Horkheimer wrote in 1944, "I became aware of the gravity of the problem of anti-

Semitism, which even then was a real menace in Germany and in the rest of the world. At that time, I tried to convince outstanding leaders of community life in Germany, in France, and in other countries of its seriousness" (Horkheimer 1946, 1). Though Horkheimer did not make such a link, his prescient recognition of the threat posed by anti-Semitism may help to explain the institute's decision to go into exile at an early date.

Whatever the actual record of his early publications and activities may be, Horkheimer's interest in anti-Semitism clearly manifested itself after the institute succeeded in reestablishing itself in the United States. In 1939, for example, Horkheimer published a seminal article, "Die Juden und Europa," in which he attempted to explain the links between contemporary anti-Semitism, capitalism, and liberalism. "The new anti-Semitism is the emissary of the totalitarian order, which has developed from the liberal one. . . . The order which set out as the progressive one in 1789 carried the germs of National Socialism from the beginning," Horkheimer proclaimed (77, 89). According to Horkheimer, the anti-Semitism of the totalitarian order is rooted in fascism's ascendant phase. Though the Nazis continued to make use of anti-Semitism after that phase, "anti-Semitic propaganda is addressed to foreign countries," and in these countries, "reserve armies of the unemployed and the petty bourgeoisie love Hitler . . . for his anti-Semitism, and the core of the ruling class agrees with that love" (92).

In the same year in which Horkheimer released this article, he and his associates began to discuss the possibility of conducting a full-scale research project on anti-Semitism. The institute's proposed project (an early version of which was drafted by Adorno) hypothesized that "anti-Semitism is one of the dangers inherent in all more recent culture" (Institute for Social Research 1941). Far from accenting the German roots of Nazi anti-Semitism, the institute's members tended to believe that totalitarian anti-Semitism might encounter less resistance in the United States than it had in Europe, and that the anti-Semitism already present in America would be

likely to gain momentum when World War II ended (Institute for Social Research, Dec. 15, 1942). In 1942 the institute's members proclaimed that "we are convinced that at present there is very little anti-Semitism in Western Europe, and even in Germany" (Institute for Social Research, Dec. 30, 1942). Lowenthal may be taken as speaking for his friends as well as for himself when he reports that it was not until they came to the United States that they "suddenly discovered that something like a real everyday anti-Semitism did exist here. . . . That hotels and clubs, even whole professions, were simply closed to Jews—that didn't yet exist in Germany to such an extent" during the formative years of the institute's members (Lowenthal 1987, 30–31).

As had Horkheimer's article on the Jews and Europe, the institute's project proposal on anti-Semitism also contended that "the foreign rather than the German masses are the spectators for whom German pogroms are arranged" and suggested that "National Socialism has more in common with the French Revolution than is generally assumed" (Institute for Social Research, Dec. 30, 1942, 124, 129). Through the use of experimental films and other techniques, the institute proposed both to measure anti-Semitism in various strata of the American population and to develop a typology of anti-Semites. The proposed empirical anti-Semitism project, in sum, echoed the theoretical ideas outlined by Horkheimer in "Die Juden und Europa" and was designed to complement the philosophical work of the institute's director.

The members of the Frankfurt school vigorously pursued funding for their proposed study of anti-Semitism for several years—primarily, it ought to be stressed, because the financial plight of the institute made it desirable for it to find new sources of income. Current events and a growing understanding of the significance of anti-Semitism, however, contributed to the sustained interest that key institute members displayed toward the issue of anti-Semitism during the early 1940s. "I cannot stop thinking about the fate of the Jews any more," Adorno wrote to Horkheimer in August of 1940. "It often seems to me that everything that we used to see from the point of view of the proletariat has been concentrated today with frightful force upon the Jews. No matter what happens to the project, I ask myself whether we should not say what we really want to say in connection with the Jews, who are now at the opposite pole to the concentration of power" (Wiggershaus 1986, 275). Horkheimer concurred, for he believed, as he wrote in a letter to Harold Laski, that "society itself can be properly understood only through anti-Semitism" (690). From Horkheimer's perspective, writing on anti-Semitism would enable him both to describe his philosophical ideas in a way that would be of interest to a broader public, and to provide him with "an opportunity to develop some of those ideas in a more concrete material" (Horkheimer to Marcuse, Apr. 3, 1943, MHA). In 1941 and early 1942, therefore, Horkheimer and Adorno resolved that the major philosophical book that they intended to write would crystallize around anti-Semitism.

When in March 1943 the institute finally received a grant from the American Jewish Committee (AJC) to support its proposed anti-Semitism project (which had been reworked largely by Neumann and Marcuse), Horkheimer, Adorno, Lowenthal, and other key members of the institute began to devote substantial blocks of time to actualizing the plans sketched out in the project proposals. Horkheimer was worried that the empirical work that the institute had pledged to conduct would distract him from the theoretical work he longed to do. Nevertheless, he believed both kinds of projects to be necessary: "I have always felt," Horkheimer wrote in 1942 to Neumann (with whom, to be sure, Horkheimer was not very open at that time), "that the project on anti-Semitism was one through which we could combine the practical with the theoretical point of view. I am therefore eager to take a real part in this work" (Horkheimer to Neumann, Oct. 24, 1942, MHA).

Shortly thereafter, the school's philosophers began committing to paper the theoretical underpinnings for their approach. Major portions of the "Elements of Anti-Semitism," which were eventually published after World War II in *Dia-*

lectic of Enlightenment, were first drafted by Horkheimer and Adorno with the aid of Lowenthal in the summer of 1943. "Anti-Semitism is a deeply imprinted schema," the critical theorists noted in this work, "a ritual of civilization; the pogroms are the true ritual murders" (Horkheimer and Adorno 1990, 171). The "Elements of Anti-Semitism" attempts to shed light on its subject through a series of interconnected theses, each of which focuses on one aspect of the problem but all of which are meant to permeate each other.

One of the theses is designed to explain the "objective" roots of anti-Semitism from a Marxist perspective: "Bourgeois anti-Semitism has a specific economic reason: the concealment of domination in production" (Horkheimer and Adorno 1990, 173). A second component explores the religious origins of anti-Semitism and indicates that Christians, "who support the religion of the Son," have hated Jews—"the adherents of the religion of the Father"—as "those who know better" (179). A further thesis, which dates from April 1944, is devoted to the notion that anti-Semitism is based on false projection. "No matter what the Jews as such may be like, their image, as that of the defeated people, has the features to which totalitarian domination must be completely hostile: happiness without power, wages without work, a home without frontiers, religion without myth. These characteristics are hated by the rulers because the ruled secretly long to possess them. The rulers are only safe as long as the people they rule turn their longed-for goals into hated forms of evil. This they manage to do by pathological projection" (199).

It is precisely this portion of Horkheimer and Adorno's explanation of anti-Semitism that they and their associates attempted to corroborate in the initial studies undertaken by the institute with the material support of the AJC. Horkheimer insisted that his own ideas on anti-Semitism put greater stress on economic and social factors than on psychology, and that he had an aversion to psychology as practiced in his day—because, for one thing, it tended to accept as given presently existing society. Horkheimer and his associates, however, studied anti-Semitism from what

Horkheimer preferred to call the vantage point of cultural anthropology, and, making use of psychoanalytic insights, they presumed that anti-Semitism "rests on personal insecurity of the anti-Semite." The portion of the project with which Horkheimer was most closely associated hypothesized that "this insecurity is often a result of frustration—and [that] anti-Semitism is its compensatory aggression . . . the anti-Semite projects his psychology on his victim, and succeeds in representing him as the aggressor" (Institute for Social Research, Aug. 10, 1944).

A second part of the work conducted by associates of the institute with the support of the AJC in 1943 and 1944 revolved around both the cultural characteristics of modern anti-Semitism and the image of the Jew in Western culture. "Anti-Semitism," the institute's members wrote in the report summarizing their work, "appears as an expression of hostility which is an inherent trait of our particular civilization. Hostility aims at the 'stranger,' the 'alien'—and it is an elementary lesson of history that the Jew was considered an 'alien' in all societies in which he has lived under the Diaspora" (Institute for Social Research, Aug. 10, 1944, 24). The institute's report stressed that "[t]he image of the Jew in contemporary society—still an image of 'otherness' and 'foreignness'—has evolved from the Jewish group's peculiar proximity to and rivalry with the non-Jewish middle classes. It is connected—through psychological projection mechanisms—with the social and economic functions which the Jews performed in the development of capitalism. . . . The psychological study of this 'image of the Jew' is thus intimately interconnected with the analysis of the specific position of the Jewish group in modern society" (25–26).

One of the major factors creating vulnerability, the report continued, revolved around changes in the economic role that Jews played in capitalist societies. The economic changes in Europe that had battered the middle classes had made the Jews "economically more vulnerable and increasingly isolated from the economic trend of the times. As marginal fields of enterprise disappeared, the Jews were left without any new areas of retreat. As a group they were both

weaker and more exposed" (Institute for Social Research, Aug. 10, 1944, 30). By means of a psychological projection mechanism, in turn, the non-Jewish middle classes blamed their economic defeat on the Jews. Thus the "frustrations of the subjugated were turned by a process of projection from the real forces of oppression to the Jews" (31). In concluding this portion of their study, the institute's members warned that "study of the American scene suggests that traits peculiar to the set-up of the United States—its multi-national composition, certain religious connotations of its political tradition, its relative political and economic independence from the rest of the world, the carryover of force and violence from the pioneering era, etc.—make for a situation that lends itself as well as it did in Germany, to the use of Jews as the Fascist 'enemy'" (35).

The institute's work on anti-Semitism in 1944 was furthered by an additional grant from the New York–based Jewish Labor Committee in the middle of that year. Horkheimer had been highly skeptical of the notion of conducting a research project devoted to labor anti-Semitism, and he had at one point described Neumann's advocacy of such a project as "idiotic" (Horkheimer to Pollock, Dec. 11, 1942, MHA). As soon as funds for the project were in hand, however, Horkheimer cooperated with those members of the institute who were directly involved with the study.

The labor project was carried out primarily by a group of 270 non-Jewish factory workers, who agreed to engage in "guided conversations" with fellow workers intended "to elucidate the nature, intensity and extent of anti-Semitic feeling among specific groups of workers" (Institute for Social Research, Feb. 29, 1944). Long-term affiliates of the institute, including Gurland, Lowenthal, Paul Massing, and Pollock, were responsible for analyzing the data gathered by the field workers and were regularly given advice and guidance by Adorno. Even before it had begun its project on labor anti-Semitism, however, the institute explicitly explained to the Jewish Labor Committee that it understood contemporary anti-Semitism as a "rationally manipulated, cold, planned . . . scheme," in which "even the followers do not quite believe in their own prejudice"—a point, it ought to be noted, that Horkheimer and Adorno spelled out in their final thesis on anti-Semitism, which they added to "Elements of Anti-Semitism" at some point between 1944 and 1947 (Horkheimer and Adorno, Jan. 20, 1944).

The institute's research team for the project on labor anti-Semitism ultimately wrote (but never published) a 1,449-page study. In describing the study's findings, Lowenthal stressed that though the study was primarily concerned with the nature and not with the extent of anti-Semitism, the study had found that anti-Semitism was widespread among those who had been surveyed. Massing, whose work for the project centered on the impact of fascism and World War II on anti-Semitic attitudes, emphasized that the fact that the Nazis had succeeded in murdering millions of Jews had itself contributed to stereotypical anti-Semitic attitudes (by reinforcing preexisting attitudes toward Jews) and also suggested that "the worker forms a good deal of his opinion and prejudice as a result of his consumer interests rather than his shop interests" (Adolph Held to H[orace] M. Kallen, Sept. 19, 1945). Gurland, finally, who addressed the issues of the social and economic motivations of anti-Semitism, asserted that "the Jew, in the eyes of the worker, has become a substitute for social conditions that he does not like . . . that cause him suffering and hardship," and indicated that this substitution could make the average American worker an easy target of fascist propaganda (Gurland 1945).

Horkheimer summarized his understanding of the significance of anti-Semitism during this period in a letter to an American-Jewish periodical drafted by Adorno in August of 1944:

[R]acial discrimination in general and anti-Semitism in particular, are truly a mere spearhead of the forces making for the destruction of democracy altogether. Modern anti-Semitism is a political weapon in the hands of those who wish to transform our industrial culture into a system of fascist oppression. Whoever accuses the Jews today aims straight at humanity itself. The anti-Semites have invested the Jews with the reality of that democracy which they wish to destroy. Wittingly or unwittingly, the Jews have become the martyrs of civilization. To protect them is no longer an issue involving any particular group interests. To protect the Jews has come to be a symbol of everything mankind stands for. Anti-Semitic persecution is the stigma of the present world whose injustice centers all its weight upon the Jews. Thus, the Jews have been made what the Nazis always pretended that they were—the focal point of world history. Their survival is inseparable from the survival of culture itself. (Horkheimer to Rosengarten, Sept. 12, 1944)

By the end of 1944, in sum, members of the institute had already devoted sustained and considerable energy to the questions of anti-Semitism and the image of the Jew, and they had deliberately linked the theoretical work done by Horkheimer, Adorno, and Lowenthal with the empirical work undertaken by other members of the institute. Horkheimer's appointment as director of the newly created Scientific Department of the American Jewish Committee, which began in October 1944, marked the beginning of a new phase in the work conducted by institute members on anti-Semitism and made it possible to initiate a broad range of projects related to anti-Semitism. These projects were built in large part on the years of relevant work that had already been conducted by the Frankfurt school in the years leading up to that date.

Bibliography

Theodor W. Adorno, "Anti-Semitism and Fascist Propaganda," *Anti-Semitism: A Social Disease,* ed. Ernst Simmel (New York: International Universities Press, 1946), 125–37; Adorno, "Scientific Experiences of a European Scholar in America," *The Intellectual Migration: Europe and America, 1930–1960,* ed. Donald Fleming and Bernard Bailyn (Cambridge, Mass.: Harvard University Press, 1969), 338–70; Ehrhard Bahr, "The Anti-Semitism Studies of the Frankfurt School: The Failure of Critical Theory," *Foundations of the Frankfurt School of Social Research,* ed. Judith Marcus and Zoltan Tarr (New Brunswick, N.J.: Transaction Books, 1984), 311–21; Dan Diner, "Reason and the 'Other': Horkheimer's Reflections on Anti-Semitism and Mass Anni-hilation," *On Max Horkheimer: New Perspectives,* ed. Seyla Benhabib, Wolfgang Bonß, and John McCole (Cambridge, Mass: MIT Press, 1993), 335–63; Arkady Gurland, "Stenographic Report to the National Executive Committee of the Jewish Labor Committee on the Susceptibility of American Labor to Anti-Semitic Propaganda Presented by the Institute for Social Research on March 10, 1945, at Hotel Pennsylvania, New York City," 66, 68, Jewish Labor Committee Collection, Wagner Archives, Tamiment Institute, New York (hereafter JLC Collection); Adolph Held to H[orace] M. Kallen, Sept. 19, 1945, Horace Kallen Collection, file 942, item 46282, YIVO Institute for Jewish Research, New York; Max Horkheimer, "Die Juden und Europa," *Studies in Philosophy and Social Science* 8 (1939): 115–37; Horkheimer, "The Jews and Europe," *Critical Theory and Society: A Reader,* ed. Stephen Eric Bronner and Douglas MacKay Kellner (New York: Routledge, 1989), 77–94; Horkheimer, "Sociological Background of the Psychoanalytic Approach," *Anti-Semitism: A Social Disease,* ed. Ernst Simmel (New York: International Universities Press, 1946), 1–10; Horkheimer and Theodor W. Adorno, "A[d]dress to a meeting of the Jewish Labor Committee," Jan. 20, 1944, Max Horkheimer Archiv (MHA), Stadt- und Universitätsbibliothek, Frankfurt a. M.; Horkheimer and Adorno, *Dialectic of Enlightenment,* trans. John Cumming (New York: Continuum, 1990); Horkheimer and Adorno, *Dialektik der Aufklärung* in *Horkheimer, Gesammelte Schriften,* ed. Gunzelin Schmid Noerr, vol. 5 (Frankfurt a. M.: Fischer Taschenbuch, 1987), 13–290; Horkheimer to Jacob [*sic*] Rosengarten, Sept. 12, 1944, MHA; Institute for Social Research, "Memorandum on the Project on Anti-Semitism," Dec. 30, 1942, MHA; Institute for Social Research, "The Political Function of Anti-Semitism: Supplementary Statement to the Research Project on Anti-Semitism," Dec. 15, 1942, MHA; Institute for Social Research, "Project on Anti-Semitism and American Labor," Feb. 29, 1944, MHA; Institute for Social Research, "Research Project on Anti-Semitism," *Studies in Philosophy and Social Science* 9 (1941): 24; Institute for Social Research, "Studies in Anti-Semitism: A Report on the Cooperative Project of Anti-Semitism for the Year Ending March 15, 1944," Aug. 1944, MHA; Martin Jay, *The Dialectical Imagination: A History of the Frankfurt School and the Institute of Social Research, 1923–1950* (Boston: Little, Brown, 1973); Jay, "The Jews and the Frankfurt School: Critical Theory's Analysis of Anti-Semitism," *Permanent Exiles: Essays on the Intellectual Migration from Germany to America* (New York: Columbia University Press, 1986), 90–100; Leo Lowenthal, *Critical Theory and Frankfurt Theorists: Lectures—Correspondence—Conversations* (New Brunswick, N.J.: Transaction, 1989); Lowenthal, *An Unmastered Past: The Autobiographical Reflections of Leo Lowenthal,* ed. Martin Jay (Berkeley: University of California Press, 1987); Lowenthal, "Vorurteilsbilder. Antisemitismus unter amerikanischen Arbeitern," *Schriften,* ed. Helmut Dubiel, vol. 3 (Frankfurt a. M.: Suhrkamp, 1982), 175–237; Joseph Maier, "Jüdisches Erbe aus deutschem Geist," *Max Horkheimer heute: Werk und Wirkung,* ed. Alfred Schmidt and Norbert Altwicker (Frankfurt a. M.: Fischer Taschenbuch, 1986), 146–62; Judith Marcus and Zoltan Tarr, "The Judaic Elements in the Teachings of the Frankfurt School," *Leo Baeck Institute Year Book* 31 (1986): 339–53; Eva G. Reichmann, "Max Horkheimer the Jew: Critical Theory and Beyond," *Leo Baeck Institute Year Book* 19 (1974): 181–95; Zoltan Tarr and Judith Marcus, "Erich Fromm und das Judentum," *Erich Fromm und die Frankfurter Schule,* ed. Michael Kessler and Rainer Funk (Tübingen: Francke, 1992), 211–20; and Rolf Wiggershaus, *Die Frankfurter Schule: Geschichte. Theoretische Entwicklung, Politische Bedeutung* (Munich: Carl Hanser, 1986).

JACK JACOBS

1940   In the year of the Hitler-Stalin pact, Walter Benjamin dictates his *Theses on the Philosophy of History* and, attempting to escape from Nazi-occupied France, kills himself at the Franco-Spanish border

To write history is to give dates their physiognomy.

—Walter Benjamin

Born in Berlin in 1892, Walter Benjamin grew up in an assimilated upper-middle-class "ghetto," the "prisoner" of a "clan" whose "attitude of stubbornness mingled with self-confidence" seemed calculated to placate a lurking malaise: a case study, this, in Freud's *Unbehagen in der Kultur.* After finding kindred spirits at the "free school" at Wickersdorf, he studied philosophy at the universities of Freiburg, Munich, and Berlin, where he became active in what he would later call "the last true élite of bourgeois Berlin," a small offshoot of the *Jugendbewegung,* the first student movement of the century. The outbreak of World War I, which provoked a double suicide among his closest friends, abruptly ended this youthful period of revolt, which he would later criticize for its ill-directed sectarian idealism. When Gustav Wyneken, his first and only mentor, called upon the young to serve the fatherland, Benjamin denounced their erstwhile führer's "wresting" from him the legacy he had "betrayed": the idea of youth. Like his younger friend Gershom Scholem, Benjamin was immune to the nationalist euphoria in which others saw an opportunity for all-German symbiosis. *His* war was with the world whose war it was. In one of his very last letters, written in May 1940, he would relate Proust's sense that "this isn't it" to the precarious structure of French-Jewish assimilation (Benjamin 1994, 631–32). This "basic experience" was also his.

It was in a series of exchanges with Ludwig Strauss, an essayist and poet who tried to win him over to Zionism, that Benjamin first felt the need to come to terms with his German-Jewish origins. "As I hardly need tell you," he wrote to Strauss in 1912, "I received a liberal upbringing. I had my decisive intellectual experience [Wickersdorf] before Judaism ever became an important or problematic issue for me. All I knew of it was really only anti-Semitism and a vague sense of piety. It was remote as a religion, and unknown to me as a national aspiration" (Benjamin 1972–89, vol. 2, no. 3, 86). As a lived experience, *das Jüdische* was, however, sufficiently "self-evident" to him to spare him all the identity crises, self-denials, and self-celebrations so characteristic of his and later generations of assimilated Jews.

Refusing to be tied down either to religious Judaism or to nationalist Zionism, Benjamin nevertheless shared their singlemindedness. "Only one [body of belief] can predominate," he claimed; "all others have to prove themselves, the Jewish included" (Benjamin 1972–89, vol. 2, no. 3, 87). The best Western European Jews were no longer free as Jews. Their freedom lay rather in a "religiosity" divorced from all religious belief.

Such lingering echoes of Jewish monotheism were a far cry from the "polytheism"—the separation of the good, the true, and the beautiful that Max Weber would describe as inherent to the modern condition. But it was equally far from Martin Buber's cult of "the Jewish experience" (*das jüdische Erlebnis*), which (like Ernst Jünger's subsequent fetishization of the "war *Erlebnis*") Benjamin recognized as the reactive byproduct of an all-too-German vitalism (*Lebensphilosophie*). A pseudo-romantic cult of Jewishness was the false solution to the dual malaise prompted by the disenchanted world and the problematic situation of the assimilated Jew.

Already at Wickersdorf, Benjamin had discovered his Jewishness "not through speculation or pure emotion, but from inner and outer experience (*Erfahrung*)." The "idea" of youth could not but exert a strong intuitive appeal over minds that were obscurely struggling to find their way beyond two equally unacceptable alternatives: a return to religious orthodoxy or assimilation to a society that oppressed the young and only half-accepted the emancipation of the Jews.

This was the dilemma described in Kafka's "Letter to the Father" (1919): that of a generation whose fathers had failed either to pass on *their* fathers' faith or to break with it. Kafka, Scholem, and Benjamin, who all broke with the bad faith of their assimilated fathers, would all come to comparably radical terms with this failed transmission. "If Zionism hadn't got in the way," Kafka wrote, German-Jewish letters "could easily have turned into a new secret doctrine, a Kabbala." For Scholem, on the other hand, the Kabbalah *was* the secret doctrine of a properly conceived Zionism. In Benjamin's case, something did indeed get in the way, but it was historical materialism, not Zionism. This would not, however, prevent Scholem, who always regretted Benjamin's turn to Marxism, from describing him as a "talmudic scholar marooned in the profane" (Scholem 1978, 187). Both would in turn exchange subtly differing appreciations of Kafka's literary efforts to catch the dying fall of an "imperial message" almost lost in transit.

In his exchange with Strauss, Benjamin largely shared the Zionist diagnosis of the German-Jewish dilemma and partially supported Zionist solutions, but he nevertheless sought "another way." The third way would indeed always be the one he chose. If "Palestinian" Zionism was a "natural necessity," above all for Eastern European Jews fleeing persecution, "German" Zionism amounted, in his eyes, to a grotesque cultural hybrid. The only firm ground on which Western European Jewry could stand was a "cultural" Zionism that "sees Jewish values *everywhere* and works for them" (Benjamin 1972–89, vol. 2, no. 3, 838). Its first priority was to provide itself with a journal of its own that was committed only to the values of "the literary movement" and to an "internationalism" incompatible with any nationalist agenda. The ground on which he had chosen to stand was not, however, as firm as he had claimed. A Zionism of the spirit was, he conceded, an "inverted tower of Babel" that would never reach the ground (2:3, 843). The journal that Benjamin himself tried and failed to found several years later—*Angelus Novus*—would likewise never get beyond its own Messianic "announcement" (*Ankündigung*).

Benjamin's version of cultural Zionism proved to be far removed from Scholem's. From 1915 till 1940, at first in Berlin and Bern—and after 1923, between Berlin, Paris, and Jerusalem—these "foreign friends" (to quote a formula coined by the young Benjamin) would nevertheless engage in an exemplary German-Jewish dialogue that immeasurably widened and deepened Benjamin's earlier exchange with Strauss. From analogously unorthodox positions at the margins of their respective camps, each saw his "idea" lose out to realpolitik without ever retracting his original, irrevocable commitment to it. An exact accounting of their mutual indebtedness is a difficult and intricate matter. Thus, although Benjamin learned almost everything he knew about Jewish mysticism from Scholem, the first paragraph of *Das Leben der Studenten*—an address that predates their first meeting by a year—already contains in a nutshell the messianic philosophy of history that underlies all his subsequent thinking. And although Scholem's "esoteric" Zionism largely developed out of a visceral rejection of German-Jewish assimilation combined with a subsequent immersion in Jewish mysticism, it also seems to bear the traces of his early exchanges with Benjamin, whose "Zionism of the spirit" was itself, by his own admission, a "thoroughly esoteric" idea (Benjamin 1972–89, vol. 2, no. 3, 842). Like Benjamin's Marxism, which aimed to recast this theological heritage in a materialist mold, Scholem's Zionism rested, that much less deviously, on a kabbalistic philosophy of language. To this extent, the "fiery disputations" provoked by Benjamin's turn to Marxism were fought out on the basis of shared convictions. As early as 1930, Scholem recognized that in an enlightened age Jewish theology was obliged to seek refuge in art, Marxism, or psychoanalysis. He thereby anticipated by ten years the first of Benjamin's *Theses on the Philosophy of History.* He would, however, proceed to read into that thesis a final rallying to his own position, just as he had always seen in Benjamin's Marxism a betrayal of his Jewish calling that was no less deluded about its Soviet partners than was the unrequited love of assimilationist Jews for their German hosts. Benjamin's invariable response to anti-Communist Jews and anti-Jewish Communists was to refuse sterile alternatives: radical politics that are "just" and for that reason seek precisely to be nothing but politics, will always be active on behalf of Judaism and, far more importantly, will always find Judaism active on their behalf (Benjamin 1994, 301). Neither Communism nor Judaism could with impunity exclude the other. However ambivalent the emancipation of European Jewry had proved to be, it was the consummation of the enlightenment, not a retreat from it, that was devoutly to be wished. This lifelong conviction would find its final formulation in the Judeo-Marxist partnership invoked in the *Theses.*

Benjamin was, like most of his generation, a disinherited Jew. Through what channels of transmission he nevertheless managed to pick up what he needed from theology remains as mysterious as the comings and goings of the little hunchback that he finally chose to be its emblem. In his writings, theology and historical materialism wax and wane in inverse proportions. Three moments may be schematically distinguished: a prematerialist, quasi-theological revolt against a compromised enlightenment, a materialist gamble on the Soviet Union, and a theologico-materialist retreat from it. "We need history," Benjamin cites the author of *The Use and Abuse of History for Life* as saying, "but not the way a spoiled idler in the garden of knowledge needs it." In the face of their parents' halfhearted assimilation to a lifeless, bourgeois world of unenlightened enlightenment, Benjamin and Scholem felt a vital, present need for those dimensions of history and theology on which "enlightened" Judaism had turned its back. Scholem accordingly set out to reclaim the "secret treasures" of Jewish mysticism from a hitherto assimilationist Wissenschaft des Judentums by harnessing that science to Zionist ends. Forging a German-Jewish partnership of his own, he sought to extend the national aims and scholarly methods of German romantic philology to the needs of the Jewish people—in effect, to foster a cultural renaissance in an *Altneuland.*

To construct an entirely new society with the old theological materials was, in a quite different sense, Benjamin's materialist hope. There was, in his eyes, no restoring the old calendar out of which the modern world had fallen into "empty, homogeneous time" (Benjamin 1968, 263). Rather, the old heirlooms would have to be deposited at the pawn shop in return for the "small change" of the new (Benjamin 1972–89, vol. 2, no. 1, 219). Although he admitted to himself, in a late note, that his thinking was as saturated by theology as blotting paper by ink, Benjamin immediately added that if the blotter had its way it would blot out the last vestiges of holy writ (vol. 5, no. 1, 588). It was this latter impulse that Scholem, for all his fascination with the "frontier between religion and nihilism," was never able to accept. The promised land was, in Benjamin's perspective, a truly disenchanted, truly enlightened enlightenment—an alternative both to Max Weber's version of the disenchanted world and to any reenchanted return to a religion that was itself a world-historical model of *Entzauberung.* It was, in short, the birth of (a certain) Communism from (a certain) Jewish theology. Official hostilities were to be superseded by an alliance between two equally unorthodox and nonsectarian partners. Whether such a program amounted to a "secularized" form of Jewish messianism, in the parasitic sense that Scholem attached to that term, is questionable. For secularization, as Benjamin conceived it, was as open and unfinished a project as Zionism was for Scholem.

It was nonetheless Scholem who best defined the Judaism of a Benjamin, a Kafka, and a Freud when he called them *Männer aus der Fremde:* no simple "foreigners" but rather men from "the foreign"—a land that could not be settled, either as Zion or, and least of all, as the noncolonizable "other." Entirely but never exclusively Jewish, they were Jews both within and toward Judaism "itself." Benjamin, who denounced the "intolerable gesture of the theological professional," was never tempted to play the professional Jew, or indeed a professional of any kind. *Das Jüdische* was "self-evident" to him. What it entailed was, however, a dwindling of self-evidence. Like *die Fremde,* the word itself is neither quite a noun nor quite an adjective, but rather a strange cross between the two. "The closer you look at a word, the more distantly it looks back."

This paradox is best described in two essays written by two other assimilated German-Jewish thinkers: George Simmel's "Appendix on the Stranger" and Sigmund Freud's "The Uncanny" (*Das Unheimliche*). All three—the (German) Jew, the stranger, and the uncanny—emerge as inalienable aliens, inside and outside, homeless and yet uncomfortably close to home. Not for nothing does Hannah Arendt identify Benjamin's hapless existence with another intimate stranger, the "little hunchback" who recurs throughout his writings. Half subject, half "it," this figure is also an image of the German-Jewish stranger, and likewise enacts the intimate duality of knowing and unknowing, canny and uncanny, that defines *das Unheimliche.*

Freud's conception of the uncanny as the "return of the repressed" also applies particularly well in this context to the persistence of a certain Judaism across several generations of denial. His own scattered remarks on the mysterious and powerful forces that bind him to Judaism intimate that it would have taken *another* Freud to

analyze them. Scholem, for his part, explicitly resorts to the word *unheimlich* to describe the strenuous efforts made both by assimilated German Jewry to exorcize its origins and by rationalist Jewish scholarship to deny any value to the Kabbalah. A far-reaching parallel is observable here between Freud's, Scholem's, and Benjamin's respective projects. All are engaged in securing recognition for various unassimilable strangers who are so many "foreign friends"—among them Jewish mysticism, the German baroque, and the human unconscious—and thereby act as the foreign correspondent of their own situation.

If, as Scholem insists, Benjamin's Marxism, like Kafka's writings, obscurely harks back to the lost, esoteric, and thus doubly secret lore of a Jewish mysticism that can nevertheless still break out today "in you or in me," it also partakes of secular Jewish traditions marked by secrecy of a rather different order. Hannah Arendt has written of the "hidden tradition" of the Jewish "pariah," which extends from Heine to Bernard Lazare, Kafka, and Charlie Chaplin. Isaac Deutscher has in turn traced the emergence of the "non-Jewish Jew" back to Spinoza, including in this secular image such figures as Heine, Marx, Freud, and Trotsky, and placing it under the patronage of *Akher,* the "stranger" or "other" who, according to the Midrash, left the Jewish fold never to return. These overlapping genealogies constitute the family of all those Jews who might have taken as their motto Kafka's wry phrase, "My people, provided I have one . . ." (Benjamin 1968, 258). Benjamin, too, would be in many respects a voluntary and involuntary "pariah," an extraterritorial (though not a "non-Jewish") Jew who stood at the intersection between several underground traditions. Unlike those who "empathize" with the "powers that be" (Benjamin 1968, 258) and survey the great tradition like a general taking the salute, the materialist historian, as Benjamin conceives him, like the psychoanalyst according to Freud, attends to the tradition of the oppressed.

After avoiding conscription, Benjamin emigrated for the rest of World War I to Switzerland, where he wrote his dissertation for the University of Bern on the concept of criticism (*Kunstkritik*) developed by the early German romantics. He thereby laid the philosophical groundwork for his own subsequent redefinition of the critic's task. Not for the last time would he be reduced to preserving a "critical" German past for the German present from across the German border. When a decade later the charge of "destructive criticism" (*zersetzende Kritik*) became an anti-Semitic stereotype, and "creative" (*schaffend*) German capital came to be opposed to its "extortionist" (*raffend*) Jewish counterpart, he would sketch the portrait of a "destructive character" who avoids "only creative work."

Benjamin's sense of his vocation found expression in a messianic philosophy of language and history, which he expounded in his early essays "On Language as Such and on the Language of Man" and "The Task of the Translator." The Fall, as there conceived, is that of language: the disintegration of Adamic names into the Babel of arbitrary signs. The resulting task is to translate the many fallen languages back toward the one "pure language." Such translation is not a matter of assimilating the foreign language to one's own, but of alienating both from their present estrangement, this in the name of an ultimate, messianic reconciliation of all languages. So "near" to that consummation, and "yet infinitely remote," languages are thus not, in the last instance, "foreign" to one another: a "hidden relation" obtains between them (Benjamin 1968, 72). Any premature bid to reconcile them can, however, result only in Esperanto—the travesty of a universal language that is still struggling to be born. Here too, "assimilation" is forbidden, under pain of betraying the Messianic promise. Like Kafka's letter on the fourfold impossibility of being a German-Jewish writer and Celan's later lecture *Der Meridian,* Benjamin's messianic theory of translation, with its implicit poetics of modernist "estrangement" and quasi-Mallarméan purity, distantly echoed by his later partisanship for Brecht's theater of "alienation," is that of a stranger foreign to all home- and fatherlands, a writer who belongs, if at all, to language. Here, too, however, the foreign persists. Nothing is as inalienable as one's own language. At the same time, in Benjamin's theory, the mother language points symbolically to its matrix, the "pure language" that is so near and yet so far.

A similar logic governed Benjamin's analysis of German-Jewish relations. "Three times mistrust of all reconciliation: between classes, between nations, between individuals," he wrote in 1929. He eyed all talk of a "German-Jewish symbiosis" with equal suspicion. "German and Jew," he wrote to Scholem in 1917, are "related extremes" but are unlikely to form any true "community." Here too it was a question of "foreign friends" and a hidden tradition. Benjamin was convinced that the only viable relations between Germans and Jews would have, for the foreseeable future, to shun the public eye. Hence his decision not to sign *Die deutsche Bauhütte,* a political manifesto circulated in 1923 by a close but distant friend, Florens Christian Rang, who in Benjamin's eyes embodied the best of German-Protestant culture. Benjamin's letter of explanation says much about the state of German-Jewish relations between the wars. It begins by stressing the depth of his ties to Germany, especially to its language and literature. Not for nothing, Benjamin goes on, is he presently engaged in a critical revaluation—literally, a redemption (*Rettung*)— of German baroque literature. As if to refute the cliché of the rootless cosmopolitan Jew, he proceeds to question all claims to a Europeanness detached from limited, national origins. But only those who belong "in an eminent sense" to their country are entitled speak in its name. The Jew should "certainly not speak out [*reden*]." It is questionable whether he may have "any say at all" (*mitreden*).

Therein lay the dilemma of the German Jew: he belonged without belonging. "We Jews administer the intellectual property of a people," Moritz Goldstein had stated in the much-discussed article "German-Jewish Parnassus" in 1912, "which denies us the right and the ability to do so." Eleven years later, Benjamin added, "The Jew who today *publicly* supports even the best German cause betrays it, because any public German statement on his part is (in a deep sense) necessarily venal" (Benjamin 1994, 215). The Jew may, moreover, have to pay the consequences for his venality in a quite different coin. The murder of Walter Rathenau—a Jew who as foreign minister negotiated war reparations on behalf of the nation—was not, in Benjamin's eyes, without a certain "necessity." *Another* assassination, however, weighed much more heavily on the national conscience—that of Gustav Landauer, the revolutionary anarchist who "screamed" against the nation instead of "speaking" in its name.

Benjamin's conclusion is unambiguous. Given the unequal status of Germans and Jews, the only legitimate form of exchange lies in the secret relations (*geheime Beziehungen*) that might develop between their "nobler representatives." Eight years later, Scholem will condemn Zionist realpolitik for its betrayal of the secret inner-Jewish relations that exist between Zionism and the Kabbalah; and forty-three years later, he too will conclude, at the end of his celebrated essay "Jews and Germans," that fruitful relations between Germans and Jews can, in the aftermath of the Shoah, "only be prepared away from the limelight" (Scholem 1978, 91).

For Jews of Benjamin's generation, secrecy came to have a more pressing meaning: the need—in Brecht's phrase—to "efface the traces" in the face of increasing Nazi persecution. "Agesilaus Santander"—an esoteric autobiographical fantasy written on Ibiza the year that Hitler came to power—plays elaborate variations on this theme (Benjamin 1972–89, vol. 6, 520–22). These two exotic middle names were (the writer claims) intended by his parents as the non-Jewish alibi in the event that their son should one day want to become a writer. No parents could at the time, he adds, have been more prescient. But when he indeed chose that vocation, he decided not to publish under his nom de plume. Instead of making his middle names public, the better to hide behind them, he chose to hide them within himself, thereby converting them into the secret name that Jews traditionally give their children. In his commentary on this text, Scholem notes that the (Hebrew) name in question is "secret" only because assimilated Jews generally make no use of it. Wittingly or not, the author of "Agesilaus Santander" may be confusing two very different forms of secrecy. More significantly, he has thereby put an assimilated Jew's ignorance of Jewish lore to anti-assimilationist use. He has, moreover, done so in quasi-accordance with the "talmudic doctrine" (to which he elsewhere refers) of the "forty-nine levels of meaning contained in every passage of the Torah."

"Agesilaus Santander" contains several such layers, one more "secret" than the other. In the first place, the author has replaced the middle names his parents actually gave him (Benedix Schönfliess) by entirely apocryphal pen names. By allegedly proceeding to dissimulate these alleged middle names in mock-accordance with Jewish custom, he appears to have "dissimilated" them. In so doing, he has effectively corrected his parents' misguided foresight. By first changing and then hiding his middle names, he has converted the assimilationist alibi with which they supplied him into the secret names that they *failed* to give him. Thereby he is perhaps protesting, albeit less directly than Kafka in his "Letter to the Father," against their failure to pass on their fathers'—the Father's—name. What he is, however, simultaneously suggesting is the literary, even arbitrary, nature of his own dissimilationist gesture, which is far removed from any actual reimmersion in the tradition of his fathers. His self-invented middle names are, in effect, no more Jewish than his given ones. They are, indeed, so outlandish as to suggest a further level of secrecy. It was Scholem, the practiced Kabbalah scholar, who cracked the code, deciphering "Agesilaus Santander" as the almost perfect anagram—we might even say: the quasi-kabbalistic recombination—of "Der Angelus Satanas." Thus, as in certain Jewish jokes where all efforts to efface a Jewish name merely provoke a return of the repressed, the secret names that were designed to conceal the author's Jewish origins contain others which—in accordance with Benjamin's biblically inspired theory of the name—hold the key to their bearer's destiny. These hidden names are, however, pure blasphemy and pure invention. The truth that they contain is authenticated only by the author's own, far from biblical word, and marks a willful violation of religious tradition.

The oxymoronic "angel of Satan" is as Janus-faced as the little hunchback, the trickster who alternately figures in Benjamin's writings as the *adversary* of the Messiah and—"slightly displaced," like an almost perfect anagram—his *secret agent.* One layer of displacement thus conceals another. Two or three levels down lies not some Jewish bedrock—there is nothing particularly Jewish about hell's angels—but another manifestation of the uncanny.

At this point, Benjamin proceeded to give a similar twist to the talmudic legend of the "new angels" who sing their ephemeral hymn of praise to God before disappearing into thin air. *His* angel was, he claims, interrupted in mid-song. Here too the little hunchback has evidently been at work. Not content with outwitting the assimilationist strategy of Benjamin's parents, the "denizen of the displaced [*entstellt*] life" has also truncated his angel's message.

And yet something identifiably (though not exclusively) Jewish has survived in and through these cumulative displacements and interruptions of Jewish tradition. It has been transplanted from the medium of the creative Word—the "secret password" of Creation, as Benjamin's early essay on language calls it—to that of the literary word, which has secret passwords of its own. Perhaps, as Benjamin and Scholem both suspected, Jewish tradition best survives *by way of* such displacement. Perhaps, as Kafka wrote to his father, there is more piety in saying good riddance to tradition than in paying lip-service to it. Only then, perhaps, is a "new Kabbala" possible. Liberated from all liturgical forms, the surviving letters of tradition can now recombine in unprecedented ways. In reinscribing his name within and against the tradition of the Name, the author of "Agesilaus Santander" has rewritten his genealogy and thereby written himself out of the blocked alternative between assimilation and a return to the fold. His parents' son has indeed become a writer, but not the one they had in mind—a "man of letters" in a free sense.

Benjamin had already discovered that the Jewish establishment was no more favorable than the surrounding culture to the unprejudiced study of German-Jewish relations. An "edifying and self-

justifying *Judaistik*" stood in the way. The article that he was commissioned to write in 1930 for the German *Encyclopedia Judaica* on "Jews in German cultural life" fared little better than the one he wrote on Goethe a few years later for the *Great Soviet Encyclopaedia.* Rewritten and abridged by the editors, it was, in Benjamin's words, "purged of everything essential." "Religion especially," he had written eight years earlier, is something that "only free spirits" should address.

Benjamin did not deny either part of his German-Jewish make-up. Instead, he made the tension between them the medium of his thinking. He considered German culture from the position of a Jew; but he articulated his Jewishness from a similarly oblique angle. Having originally measured Judaism against the "Wickersdorf idea," he wrote to Scholem in 1928 that the Jewish world, intrinsic though it was to his thinking, could emerge only from behind the "enclosure" of his engagement with German and French literature. If he is here referring to the ancient religious injunction to "make a fence around the Torah," the shift of focus is all the more significant. The metaphor of enclosure points, moreover, to something like an incest taboo. Another foreign ground is needed to guard against an excessively endogamous relation to Judaism. Here too the task is to estrange one's "own" from itself. "Pure language," as conceived in "The Task of the Translator," is not Hebrew, as it was for certain kabbalists: it is the matrix of all languages. Hence, perhaps, Benjamin's repeated postponement of his plans to visit Palestine: the promised land was not the promised land. "Method," he wrote, "is detour." It is as if his delays and detours constituted the necessary condition for what Scholem termed his "asymptotic" relation to Judaism; as if, for Benjamin, "secret relations" characterized not merely German-Jewish but also inner-Jewish affairs.

According to the "Theses," a fleeting "constellation" obtains between the historian's "endangered" present and a no less "oppressed," no less "particular" past. In "Agesilaus Santander" Benjamin claimed, for his part, to have been "born under Saturn—the planet of slow revolution, the star of hesitation and delay"—a planet whose influence would pale only before that other revolution that Benjamin would still call in 1940 "the rising sun in the sky of history" (Benjamin 1968, 257). This fluctuating configuration of melancholy and revolution was at once individual, world-historical, and German-Jewish.

Like everything else that Benjamin wrote, his major critical work, a pioneering study of the German Baroque *Trauerspiel* written in the mid-1920s, represents such a "secret rendezvous" between past and present (Benjamin 1968, 256). It also marks a secret relation between Germans and Jews. Not for nothing does it dwell on the collective prejudice that has, from Goethe onward, devalued allegory and *Trauerspiel* in the name of symbol and tragedy. A peculiar constellation emerges here between the marginal position assigned, in the wake of German Romanticism, to the German Baroque within the academic-literary pantheon and that of the Jew in modern European society. But Benjamin's anatomy of melancholy also opens up further, overlapping constellations. Not merely does the seventeenth-century German Protestant "play of mourning" here join an age-old Jewish literature of "lament"—a lament that, in Benjamin's account of nature's mute complaint at being named, becomes the silent, plaintive "unhomely" wail of the "stranger," of Jewish theology's own inner "Jew," at the divine order of things. It also gives form to the developing historico-religious crisis that finds expression two centuries later in Baudelaire's allegorical poetry. The constellation that presides over Benjamin's subsequent work on Baudelaire, which he pursued in the middle to late thirties, is a three-point constellation between the historical present, its nineteenth-century origins, and their seventeenth-century antecedents. Where Max Weber correlates the Protestant ethic with the spirit of capitalism, and Werner Sombart, in Marx's wake, singles out the role of Jews in the emergence of the capitalist economy, Benjamin's dovetailing of Protestant and Jewish eschatology dwells, for its part, on the underside of the same process. The world may be "disenchanted," but it is not "redeemed." Unlike tragedy, unlike Freud's "work of mourning" (*Trauerarbeit*), both of which bring cathartic reso-

lution, the *Trauerspiel* is a potentially interminable "play of mourning," an endless process of "mourning and melancholia, a "trial" (*Prozeß*) that, in Benjamin's reading of Kafka, finally puts the court itself on trial.

If it took a German Jew to save the German Baroque from the prevailing system of aesthetic values, such rehabilitation of one "stranger" by another was hardly calculated to gain him a *Habilitation* at a German university. Benjamin's study of Baroque *Trauerspiel* was an idiosyncratic German-Jewish venture thinly disguised in mock-academic robes. As such, it was itself much too "baroque" to win acceptance. But its *chutzpah,* as he called it, was an answer to a much deeper insolence—that of a Werner Sombart, the German professor who had in a much-discussed article published in 1912 advised the Jews not to apply for the higher positions to which they were now entitled. The Jews had originally considered emancipation their "entry-ticket" into European civilization. Two years after refusing to sign a political petition on the grounds that the sociopolitical situation of German Jews made any such gesture look "venal," Benjamin's devious bid for entry into the academy—which was, like Baudelaire's candidacy for the Académie Française, a "sociological experiment"—was intended to test the limits of *another* academic politics. "Intellect [*Geist*] cannot be tenured," a German professor would comment decades later. Decades before, Ludwig Klages had in an influential work denounced "intellect" as the adversary of the "soul."

Already before World War I, Benjamin had not hesitated to identify himself as a literary intellectual (*Literat*) dedicated to the life of the mind (*Geist*)—terms that were soon to carry anti-Semitic overtones. After his calculated failure to enter the university, he lived by his pen, publishing notably a dazzling montage of short politico-literary texts entitled *One-Way Street* (1928)— French surrealism as practiced by a newly Marxist German-Jewish *flâneur*—until, in the early thirties, no longer able to publish in Germany, he joined the growing exodus of German Jews (and with them most of German culture) from Germany. As early as 1923, he had briefly envisaged emigration as a possible solution to his material and cultural dilemma. He successively considered Capri (and later stayed on Ibiza), where life was sun-drenched and cheap, Jerusalem, where he might undertake the commentary of *holy* texts, and Moscow, which held out to the isolated intellectual the promise of a meaningful collective framework. In 1932, he finally emigrated to Paris, where he would eke out a meager existence, largely on the basis of the small stipend he received as a regular contributor to the émigré *Zeitschrift für Sozialforschung*.

Shortly after leaving Germany, Benjamin wrote a series of pieces entitled *A Berlin Childhood around Nineteen Hundred* as an antidote to the homesickness that he anticipated now that he was separated, perhaps permanently, from his native city. These complex vignettes make an instructive contrast with Stefan Zweig's *World of Yesterday*, which places nostalgic memories of a pre-war childhood lived out in the gilt-edged security of the Habsburg Empire within the massive, immovable frame of a "golden age." There was, Benjamin knew, no such thing as "life as it actually was" (Ranke's *wie es eigentlich gewesen*). Like history at large, autobiography was, as Proust's *A la recherche du temps perdu* had shown, a shifting constellation between past and present. Benjamin's memoir was, however, also intended as an antidote to its addictive Proustian model. In the dark room of the intervening years, the Proustian "involuntary memories" of his protected childhood had, like photographic negatives developed into images which revealed within the world of yesterday so many premonitory "memories of the future." The closing section identifies the hidden photographer who took away the pictures when he wasn't looking as the elusive little hunchback of German folklore. As the master of the past, of oblivion and memory, his (un)familiar spirit has become the caring coauthor, or ghostwriter, of his own memoir.

What *A Berlin Childhood* did for his own past, the so-called Arcades Project (*Passagenwerk*) sketched out in the prospectus *Paris, Capital of the Nineteenth Century* was to attempt for the prehistory (*Urgeschichte*), at once archaic and recent, of the world-historical present. Here too the past contained memories of the future. At a time when many others were seeking to *mediate* between historical materialism and psychoanalysis, Benjamin conceived the materialist historian as a *medium* who interprets the "phantasmagorias" of the nineteenth century, its collective dreams and nightmares, the better to awaken (in his and Stephen Daedalus's phrase) with the former and from the latter before it was too late. Throughout the thirties, Benjamin worked at the Bibliothèque Nationale on this huge, never-completed venture, which dangerously delayed his departure from Paris. Only the studies on Baudelaire achieved partial completion. They mark another secret rendez-vous between two untimely contemporaries—the *poète maudit* who, abhorring "progress" and the "avant-garde," *thereby* inaugurates literary modernity, and the Jewish refugee who, as a still more representative casualty of progress, is, as Arendt will observe in 1943, the vanguard of the future.

During his early years of exile, one of Benjamin's most cherished projects was to bring out in Germany a small volume of selected letters that he had, under cover of anonymity, managed to publish one by one, complete with brief accompanying commentaries, between 1931 and 1932 in the *Frankfurter Zeitung*. The project was, like the *Habilitation*, a contraband operation, and it too failed to reach its destination until long after everything was over. Under the simple but telling title *Deutsche Menschen* and the editorial pseudonym Detlev Holz, a relatively complete but practically unnoticed edition of the letters came out only in Switzerland—further confirmation of Benjamin's earlier claim that a genuine German-Jewish dialogue was effectively excluded from the public sphere. Enforced secrecy was, moreover, not merely the volume's fate, but its underlying theme. In an unpublished introduction, Benjamin writes that its intention is to show that "the face of that 'secret Germany' that one likes to look for nowadays behind shrouds of murky fog. For there is indeed a secret Germany. But its secrecy is . . . the work of noisy, brutal forces which, in refusing it public efficacy, condemn it to efficacy of a secret kind" (Benjamin 1972–89, vol. 4, no. 2, 945). What was *unheimlich* about this situation is that one version of *das geheime Deutschland* had usurped the legitimacy of the other and was in league with the very forces that had always reduced the other, better Germany to a secret, underground existence. This was Germany's (and Benjamin's) "hidden tradition"—the tradition of German enlightenment exemplified by such impoverished, exiled figures as Forster, Büchner, and Hölderlin. Written between 1783 and 1883, the letters from this banished past span the rise and decline of German bourgeois humanism, opening onto an age when the bourgeoisie can maintain "only its positions, no longer the spirit in which it had conquered them" (Benjamin 1972–89, vol. 4, no. 1, 151). They are to hold up to present-day Germans as human beings (*Menschen*) of a quite different mettle—burghers who, from within their crabbed style and provincial confines, belonged to humanity at large. Nowhere is the configuration between an oppressed past and an endangered, and endangering, present more evident than here.

"It is a harsh light," writes Benjamin, "that falls from such letters on the long procession of German poets and thinkers who, shackled to a common plight, shuffle past the foot of that Weimarian Parnassus on which professors have resumed their botanical excursions" (Benjamin 1972–89, vol. 4, no. 1, 213). This sentence—which reads even more ominously today now that the shadow of Buchenwald hangs over Weimar—sums up Benjamin's entire critical program. The German-Jewish experience of the "stranger" converges here with the Marxian axiom that it is the view from below that is, at least potentially, the truest, the only universal vantage point. It is in this sense that Benjamin defines the critic as a "strategist in the struggle for literature," one who, in writing "on his own behalf," writes on behalf of all. To become "le premier critique de la littérature allemande," as Benjamin intended before being forced to emigrate, meant nothing less than "recreating criticism as a genre." Taking his cue from Goldstein's "German-Jewish Parnassus," he proceeded to consider the "Weimarian Parnassus" from a German-Jewish angle, notably in his study of *Die Wahlverwandtschaften* (1924), which replaces the idolatrous hero-worship surrounding Goethe, especially the myth of a life

lived as its author's greatest work of art, by a critique of the "mythical" forces at work in it.

In this connection, Benjamin launched a thunderbolt at Gundolf's Goethe, the "monumental" work of an assimilated Jew (Gundelfinger) whose cult of Goethe, combined with that of Stefan George, is couched in prose turgid enough to provide a smokescreen behind which Mount Parnassus can, as Benjamin put it in 1931, serve as a "bridgehead in the civil war." It is from the same angle that the author of *Deutsche Menschen* considers Hölderlin hymns to Greece and Germany. One or two years before so many young Germans had gone to war on behalf of the state with Hölderlin in their knapsacks, Benjamin had been among those students who had, still more idealistically, fought their battle against the older generation—and then their war—with youth, George, and Hölderlin as their only ammunition. Now that German professors were again extracting disquietingly missionary visions of national destiny from Hölderlin's hymns, Benjamin interpreted these hymns in terms of a "community of suffering" between Greece and Germany not unrelated to the "secret relations" he himself had postulated between Germans and Jews. The cultivation of a Greco-German Parnassus was, in effect, an insidious way of evacuating the Greco-Jewish and German-Jewish heritages from the national pantheon.

"An ark built according to the Jewish model" when the "fascist flood began to rise," *Deutsche Menschen* was intended to save some samples of German humanity from antediluvian times. The title would be half-echoed by Arendt's postwar *Menschen in finsterer Zeit* (Men in dark times), a heterogeneous company ranging from Lessing to Pope John XXII, among them Benjamin, Rosa Luxemburg, and Brecht. The author of *Deutsche Menschen* would not, however, have entirely subscribed to the Heideggerian dictum that Arendt liked to cite: "The light of the public sphere [*Öffentlichkeit*] darkens everything." In Benjamin's view, not *all* reason and enlightenment darkened; their present twilight did; and what it obscured was, among other things, the best traditions of the Enlightenment.

This claim would also be the burden of Benjamin's intellectual testament, written in the darkest hour. The *Theses on the Philosophy of History* open with the allegorical description of a chess automat at which sits "historical materialism," in the guise of a Turkish puppet (Benjamin 1968, 255). He can take on all comers, however, only because the apparatus conceals a system of mirrors designed to give the illusion of transparency and in fact hides "theology," in the guise of a "little hunchback" who secretly pulls the strings. Unaided, the so-called forces of progress are evidently no match for fascism. Unable to do without the foreign friend that it persists in considering its enemy, the Enlightenment still needs the leading-strings from which Kant had thought to emancipate it. Theology, "which today, as we know, is small and ugly and has to keep out of sight," thereby finds itself in much the same position as the authentic Enlightenment, the "secret Germany" to which Benjamin had urgently appealed. It thereby enjoys a decisive positional advantage from which it can, as Benjamin had said of the hidden tradition of German Enlightenment, deploy an "efficacy of a secret kind." The Turk, whom Benjamin in a comparable parable calls Ali Dei, can serve as an alias, a Communist front organization. Thanks in part to the delusions of transparency that modern reason entertains about itself, theology can hide inside historical materialism and act as a *deus in machina*. This ingenious neo-Pascalian gamble on a hidden god makes for considerable irony at the expense of the Enlightenment—but it is, in every sense, irony *from within*.

This secret alliance between theology and historical materialism is generally assumed to have been Benjamin's answer, in 1940, to another equally disconcerting but far less fanciful one that had thrown the antifascist forces into disarray: the Hitler-Stalin pact. The question at issue, he had written on his return from a visit to Moscow in 1927, is "not which reality is better" but "which reality is inwardly convergent with truth." The Hitler-Stalin pact clearly marked the final divergence of Soviet reality from Communist truth—the culmination, as Benjamin now saw it, of a historical process in which Soviet Marxism had turned into a modern version of Oriental despotism. The image of an automat suggests progress of the kind that Benjamin likens in the ninth thesis to a storm—elsewhere called the "storm of oblivion"—and, in his notes, to a runaway train. That of a hookah-smoking Turkish puppet even intimates that Communism itself has, as an all-too-bourgeois religion of progress, now become the new "dogmatic slumber" of reason, the new "opium of the people." Against such massive historical perversions, Benjamin ventures some inversions of his own. Only actual theology—theology, that is, in its actual, reduced form—can, he implies, destroy the new idolatry. Almost a century after Marx's announcement of the "specter" of the coming revolution, Benjamin tacitly announces that historical materialism needs to be reanimated by the active presence in *its* "substructure" of a specter from the *past*. An irrational rationalism, be it Marxist or bourgeois, tries at its peril to exorcize that ghost. "Enlightenment," Adorno and Horkheimer will reiterate, "is totalitarian." The little hunchback is to do for Marxism what *its* "old mole" was to do to bourgeois society.

By a related irony, the little bogey-man of childhood mythology functions here as a parody of the *ideological* bogey-men who were being brandished at the time by both partners of the Hitler-Stalin pact. He resembles both those "crooked" Jews who were allegedly pulling the strings of a Bolshevik world conspiracy and the "outside agitators" who were purportedly infiltrating the party apparatus as part of a Jewish-Trotskyite plot. Just as a secret Germany does indeed exist, but not the one that goes under that name, so too there is indeed something like a Jewish-Communist conspiracy. In caricaturing such caricature, Benjamin's First Thesis amounts —pace Nietzsche—to a transvaluation of all *anti-Semitic* values.

But the secret alliance between theology and historical materialism can apparently work only under two highly paradoxical conditions. In the first place, it may even have to be kept secret from one of the partners—the younger, the more doctrinaire of the two. For while historical materialism is supposed to "enlist the services" of theology, the hunchback seems to be operating behind the puppet's back. Secondly, it could just be that (as a letter that Benjamin had written to Scholem on Kafka two years earlier also seems to suggest) the very damage inflicted on Jewish theology by the so-called Enlightenment has, in reducing it to the shrunken, disfigured proportions of a dwarf, thereby released its saving powers into the historical world.

In extremis, help thus lies, if at all, in the implausible partnership between two far-flung traditions, each of which has been driven underground by the cumulative tyrannies of the day— bourgeois, Soviet, Nazi. Theology—notably Jewish mysticism, an occult tradition of illumination that has today become doubly secret— has had to take refuge from the cold, bright light of modern reason. And although the words "automat" and "apparatus" seem to point to the real, existing institutions that have given material force to Marx's ideas, the figure of the "historical materialist" invoked in the *Theses* occupies a position that now stands entirely alone amidst the warring camps. The "idea" has once again become as "esoteric" in 1940 as it was in 1913. But it still remains oriented, as if by a "secret heliotropism," toward the coming revolution. All esoteric secrecy is, for Benjamin as for much Jewish mysticism, ultimately destined to be consumed by its exoteric consummation. Indeed, theology, as Benjamin comes to conceive it, perhaps wishes for nothing better than to be properly blotted out. Who knows? One day, when the apparatus is more genuinely transparent, the little hunchback may disappear without trace into the tabula rasa of a messianic, no longer messianic Enlightenment.

This providential interplay between two hidden traditions recalls the "noble complicity" that, according to Benjamin, unites the best of German and Jewish culture. That *Jewish* theology should in 1940 find its cryptic embodiment in a semipagan goblin drawn from *German* folklore, and should then reenter the "scientific socialism" invented by another German Jew, marks a secret rendez-vous between several secret German-Jewish relations.

"Did we not grow up with German fairy-tales?" Moritz Goldstein had asked in his "Ger-

man-Jewish Parnassus": "Did we not play Red Riding Hood and Sleeping Beauty ? . . . Was not the German forest also there for us? May not we, too, lay eyes on its elves and gnomes?" Benjamin, too, grew up with German folklore. He gave pride of place, however, to the less canonic figure of the little hunchback, whom he first encountered in his *Deutsches Kinderbuch.* Like Grimms' fairy tales, with which Benjamin associates him, the folk song about the *bucklicht Männlein,* the little mischief-maker who catches us napping, belongs to the popular lore rediscovered by German romanticism; it was first transcribed by Clemens Brentano for *Des Knaben Wunderhorn* (1802), the same anthology that was to inspire certain of Gustav Mahler's Lieder: "O dear child, I beg of you / Pray for the little hunchback too" (*Liebes Kindlein, ach ich bitt / Bet fürs bucklicht Männlein mit*). What Benjamin could not know is that it was Clemens Brentano who had added this final couplet, thereby domesticating the lawless force of the original trickster. Read through Benjamin's life and work, this romantic-Christian plea acquires German-Jewish undertones. The scapegoat—the "Jew"—on whom we like to blame our mishaps is pleading here for inclusion in the child's prayers. He thereby echoes the mute lament of Nature who (in Benjamin's early essay on language and again in the *Trauerspiel* book) awaits redemption from a language which, in naming it, brings it a bliss tinged with an irremediable sadness. The hunchback's plea (*ach ich bitt*) for representation (*Bet . . . mit*) also distantly recalls the question that Benjamin had raised with Florens Christian Rang: may the German Jew, who is not entitled to speak out (*reden*) on national affairs, even speak up (*mitreden*)? Nature, the hunchback, and the German Jew are all, in different ways, the inner strangers of the Word.

"So ends the folksong," writes Benjamin in his Kafka essay. "In its depth Kafka touches . . . the ground of folk tradition . . . , the German as well as the Jewish." It was hardly self-evident in 1934 for an exiled German Jew to be reclaiming *Volkstum* as the ground on which Germans and Jews could meet. The Nazis were driving the Jews from German soil in the name of the German people. Scholem was reclaiming Kafka from German literature on behalf of the Jewish people. Benjamin, for his part, was staking out a ground where secret relations between traditions could take place at several removes from the national mythologies broadcast in the public sphere. Foreign languages, cultures, and friends had most in common, he was persuaded, where they could be most idiomatically themselves. Therein lay the answer both to the fond illusion of a "German-Jewish symbiosis" *and* to any nationalist separatism that denied the reality of a shared, divided history. One "prototype of distortion" thereby corrected another. Against the degeneration of authentic *Volkstum* into the rabble-rousing sentiments whipped up by the Nazi press, the stunted hunchback stood, paradoxically, for the only wholesome interplay between the German and Jewish peoples. Even Nietzsche's Zarathustra, who resists all Judeo-Christian pity for the lame and the halt, was not above an ironical exchange with the hunchback (*der Bucklichte*) who speaks in their name.

Irony is, according to Kierkegaard, a "minute, invisible personage," not unlike an "elf wearing a *Tarnkappe*." The parable of the dwarf in the automat, which recalls not merely Poe's story *Maelzel's Chess-Player* but also his "imp of the perverse," is sufficiently ironical and elusive to resist the "enthusiastic misunderstanding" to which, Benjamin feared, his *Theses* would be exposed. Popular German, German-Christian, and German-Jewish by turn, the little hunchback is neither racially, religiously, nor ideologically pure.

There is no need, therefore, to decide whether he stands for theology in general (in an "enlightened" epoch that relegates to an underground existence everything that it cannot remake in its own image) or, more specifically, for *Jewish* theology (in a fascist era that forces even errant Jews to assume their common particularity). It is true that the theological motifs scattered throughout the *Theses* belong mostly to that apocalyptic tradition of Jewish Messianism which Scholem once likened to an "anarchic breeze" blowing through the "well-ordered house" of orthodox Jewish observance; and that in Benjamin's writings the little hunchback disturbs the bourgeois and Marxist order of things in similarly anarchic fash-

ion. Even in his final guise, however, he is too multiple and stratified to stand for an *exclusively* Jewish theology—not even those heretical elements rehabilitated by Scholem. Not for nothing does Benjamin associate his final plea to the child with the saints who "include all creatures in their prayers," with Malebranche's notion of attentiveness as the "natural prayer of the soul," and with Origen's heretical doctrine of *apokatastasis*—the entry of all souls into heaven. Such all-inclusiveness is, however, as far removed from ecumenical eclecticism as the messianic idea of a universal language is from Esperanto. Apokatastasis no more precludes partisanship than irony excludes commitment. Unlike his Kierkegaardian counterpart, the little hunchback is not "sublated" as a "mastered moment" in the name of some higher seriousness. By a masterly but risky stroke, the unmasterable other is himself enlisted as the "master" in a deadly serious game of chess. Benjamin's last card—his joker—is a theology of the uncanny that assigns to anarchy the role of organizer.

Who else, in effect, but a fairy-tale will o' the wisp could hope to realize the program that the "Theses" implicitly set themselves—that of reuniting the divided left, or, in kabbalistic parlance, of "raising the sparks" of a scattered truth? The "Theses" hoped to do so by marshaling bits and pieces of Marx, Hegel, Fourier, Blanqui, Brecht, Nietzsche, Kraus, Klee, and Scholem, to mention only a few, into a single coherent strategy—a montage that held out the promise of a common language yet to come. In the end, only hope against hope, only a trick could do the trick. Benjamin observes that Kafka built such "tricks" into his stories in the absurd hope that, as Kafka put it, "inadequate, even childish measures may also serve to rescue us."

The times are out of joint. Seen in terms of the *Trauerspiel* study, the hunchback's anatomy is a melancholy allegory of everything "untimely, sorrowful, unsuccessful"—that is, unredeemed. The allegorical intent, however, as there conceived, "does not faithfully remain before the spectacle of the bones, but faithlessly leaps over to resurrection." So, too, does the little hunchback. The trickster's final trick is to convert: to convert his potentially sinister mischief into a Hegelian "cunning of reason." Interweaving the warp of forgetting with the weft of remembering, the hunchback alternately represents, in Benjamin's thinking, the distorting forces that the Messiah will one day overcome *and* the hidden messianic energies that may even nowadays save the day. But the difference between these roles is, in Benjamin's account, as imperceptible as that between forgetting and remembering, between the uncanny and the canny, as slight as the nudge that will one day, according to "a famous rabbi" (alias Scholem), enable the displaced world to fall into place. If, at the end of *Berlin Childhood,* his "work is"—in Benjamin's playful phrase—"behind him," this is because the text has itself been woven and warped by the little hunchback. Likewise, the hunchback of the "Theses" pulls the strings, plots, indeed writes the winning strategy. Theology plays much the same role in this *materialist* apparatus as does the unconscious in Freud's model of the *psychic* apparatus—each being the intimate stranger at reason's back, its "hunch," its cache of forgotten memories and family secrets. This is true to the extent that the analogy drawn by Freud between the psychic apparatus and a "magic writing-pad" has an exact counterpart in the intricate construction of Benjamin's chess automat. Like that contraption, the psychic apparatus, as Freud conceives it, is a partnership between two distinct but interdependent agencies—memory and consciousness. *This,* then, is the winning combination that Benjamin pits against fascism: the psychic apparatus writ large, with theology in the role of memory and historical materialism in the role of consciousness, the whole forming the "little writing-factory" that was, Benjamin knew, the only "productive force" he had at his disposal.

But the stark fact is that the German-Jewish culture emblematized, in suitably fairy-tale fashion, by Benjamin's little hunchback would be irrevocably destroyed and is now an object of his-torical study or, worse, the historicist "empathy" that Benjamin abhorred. All attempts to revive it today risk transforming the hunchback into a souvenir, a ghost of his former, already ghostly self, a mascot, a *Gartenzwerg.*

Bibliography

Theodor W. Adorno, "A Portrait of Walter Benjamin," *Prisms,* trans. Samuel and Shierry Weber (Cambridge, Mass.: MIT Press, 1983); Hannah Arendt, introduction to Walter Benjamin, *The Correspondence of Walter Benjamin,* trans. Manfred R. Jacobson and Evelyn M. Jacobson (Chicago: University of Chicago Press, 1994); Benjamin, *Gesammelte Schriften,* ed. Rolf Tiedemann and Hermann Schweppenhäuser, 8 vols. (Frankfurt a. M.: 1972–89); Benjamin, *Illuminations,* trans. Harry Zohn (New York: Schocken, 1968); Arendt, *The Jew as Pariah* (New York: Grove, 1978); Moritz Goldstein, "Deutsch-jüdischer Parnass," *Der Kunstwart* 11 (1912); Frederic Grunfeld, *Prophets Without Honor: A Background to Kafka, Einstein and Their World* (New York: McGraw Hill, 1979); Max Horkheimer and Theodor W. Adorno, *Dialectic of Enlightenment,* trans. John Cumming (New York: Herder and Herder, 1972); Hans Puttnies and Gary Smith, *Benjaminiana* (Giessen: Anabas-Verlag, 1991); Anson Rabinbach, "Between Enlightenment and Apocalypse: Benjamin, Bloch and Modern German Jewish Messianism," *New German Critique* 34 (1985): 78–124; Gershom Scholem, *Walter Benjamin—The Story of a Friendship,* trans. Harry Zohn (Philadelphia: Jewish Publication Society of America, 1981); Scholem, *On Jews and Judaism in Crisis* (New York: Schocken, 1978); Gary Smith, "'Das Jüdische versteht sich von selbst': Walter Benjamins frühe Auseinandersetzung mit dem Judentum," *Deutsche Vierteljahresschrift* (1991): 318–34; Irving Wohlfarth, "Geheime Beziehungen: Zur deutsch-jüdischen Spannung bei Walter Benjamin," *Studi Germanici* 28 (1990): 251–301; and Wohlfarth, "'Märchen für Dialektiker': Walter Benjamin und sein bucklicht Männlein," *Walter Benjamin und die Kinderliteratur,* ed. Klaus Doderer (Weinheim: Juventa, 1988), 121–76.

IRVING WOHLFARTH

1941 A four-year debate on child psychoanalysis begins between Anna Freud and Melanie Klein within the British Psychoanalytical Society

In the early 1920s the psychoanalytic method developed by Sigmund Freud for the treatment of neurotic patients began to be adapted to therapeutic work with children. This pioneering endeavor was carried out by two strong-minded women: Freud's daughter Anna and the slightly older Vienna-born Melanie Klein. The method developed through their efforts led to the establishment of a new profession, child psychoanalysis, and in addition, to a worldwide dissemination of psychoanalytic knowledge in the field of child mental health. The awareness created by psychoanalysis now influences a broad range of professionals involved with children, including teachers, youth workers, career counselors, social workers, speech therapists, nursery nurses, and health visitors.

Anna Freud and Melanie Klein obviously had much in common. Their similar cultural backgrounds, interest in psychoanalysis, and dedication to child mental health should have naturally brought them into some form of professional association. Both women also had to contend with issues that emerged from belonging to a minority group twice over, ethnic and professional. Yet far from joining forces, the two could agree on very little, and, what is more, became lifelong professional antagonists.

It is thus that the technique of child analysis developed through disputes and conflict, leading finally to an open confrontation, popularly referred to as the "controversial discussions" (King and Steiner 1991). These discussions took place between 1941 and 1945 in London, to which both Melanie Klein and Anna Freud had, by this time, emigrated. The discussions took the form of a series of presentations that were debated in the British Psychoanalytical Society. They were also remarkable in that they drew in not only the two protagonists and their small circle of adherents, but the entire society.

By the time of the discussions, both Anna Freud and Melanie Klein had achieved a great deal in their own right. On the basis of their observations and work with children they made significant contributions to psychoanalytic theory. Their insights had immediate relevance to psychoanalysis in general, inasmuch as they were derived directly from data that held clues to the earliest and most formative experiences in life. It was for this reason that by the time Anna Freud and Melanie Klein confronted each other in 1941, they did so not specifically as child psychoanalysts, but as representatives of two opposing streams within the British psychoanalytical establishment.

The content of the controversial discussions remains a rich contribution to the history of ideas, but a consensus on key issues could not be reached, either by the two women or by the society itself. Melanie Klein believed that the infant is born with a readiness for social interactions and is immediately capable of forming "object relations," even though these are rudimentary and incomplete. The infant, Melanie Klein suggested, apprehends only "parts and portions of the real world" (Klein 1935). But it does respond to maternal nurturing and becomes attached to a part of the mother that carries immediate significance for it—her breast. The latter represents not only food, but by virtue of offering also comfort and pleasure acquires the significance of "good." The maternal breast can also be missed, however, and when deprived of it the infant can react with frustrated aggression and experience it as "bad."

To Anna Freud such advanced differentiating capacities in the infant were hardly credible. Their postulation also threatened her father's model of development, according to which the infant is initially sheltered in a fetal-like "primary narcissism." Freud had envisaged the young infant as noticing very little of the outside world: he believed that its existence is governed by the "pleasure principle" and that its primitive mind drifts into dreamlike, hallucinatory states that hinder the full apprehension of worldly frustrations. Only gradually does the infantile mind accommodate the "reality principle," and only then are object relations tenable.

Such a difference of opinion may seem insufficient to have caused a fundamental rift between the two women. On the basis of her beliefs, however, Melanie Klein proceeded to hypothesize a rudimentary psychical activity that exists from birth and that she termed "phantasy." It is early phantasy, she felt, that both gives form to infantile instinctual life and also elaborates and represents worldly events internally, gradually enabling the emergence of clearer cognitive capacities in the infant.

Klein envisaged a complex content to early phantasy, suggesting that it could also be used by the infant for defensive purposes. Accordingly, overwhelming disturbance and anxiety in the infant trigger phantasies that reinforce a primitive mental mechanism of "splitting." Klein felt that this helps to explain the mechanisms at work in adult psychiatric conditions, including schizophrenia, manic-depression, and obsessional disorders. According to this view, all the important mental ingredients of adult psychotic illness are genetically present in early psychical life and are only gradually rendered harmless through healthy development.

Clearly this model indicated a radically different approach to analytic interpretations from the one favored by Anna Freud, who continued to attribute complex processes and pathologies only to much later stages of development. Because the disagreement could not be resolved, the situation was settled through a compromise that created three schools of thought within the British Psychoanalytical Society, the third one remaining "independent." This has influenced the training program and outlook of the society to this day.

To many adult psychoanalysts the significance of the discussions extends no further than their implications for the structure of the society, and they might therefore appear regrettable and divisive. From the angle of child psychoanalysis, however, they might be regarded differently. The fact that the nature of children's mental life was passionately debated, and that each of the pioneering women was subjected to a fierce critique from the other, represents a gain at least in one respect. Between them, Anna Freud and Melanie Klein articulated different but crucial issues in child mental health, and it is the contributions of both that add up to a rounded definition of child mental health needs. Perhaps the different viewpoints that they each brought to bear on the subject emerged from their almost opposite personalities and lifestyles.

Anna Freud, who never married, devoted her life singlemindedly to the cause of psychoanalysis, and later also to the care of her ailing father. She was by nature traditional and orderly, and so she was inclined to follow in her father's footsteps. His influence on her thinking was increased by the fact that she had also been his analysand for a period.

The main thrust of Anna Freud's efforts initially consisted in adapting her father's existing psychoanalytical method as faithfully as possible. This continuity that she sought with his thinking was not merely a question of an uncritical devotion to him. She actually favored an approach to her work that tended to be more "scientific," in the sense that she saw it as her task to study existing models, proceed logically in applying these, and systematically collect data to verify their value. In such tasks her orderliness and industry were obvious assets. These virtues appear also to have been a feature of the Freud household more generally. Like Sigmund Freud, Anna spent hours writing, corresponding, and systematically ordering her documents and reports. Her mother, equally well organized, seems to have derived confidence not only from an efficient household, but also from a belief that integrity and correctness reigned in the rest of society.

Two telling incidents highlight these inclinations both in Anna Freud and in the Freud household more generally, particularly as they put the family to a severe test. The incidents in question occurred in March 1938 in Vienna on the day when the Nazis invaded the Freud apartment. They were later recalled by Freud's son Martin: "The first was the view I had from the window of Anna being driven off in an open car escorted by four heavily armed SS men. Her situation was perilous; but far from showing fear, or even much interest, she sat in the car as a woman might sit in a taxi on her way to enjoy a shopping expedition" (Young-Bruehl 1988).

This self-possessed, courageous behavior fits in well with Martin's second memory from the same day: "The second scene . . . is of mother, highly indignant with an SS man who, on his way through a passage, paused at a large cupboard, pulled open its doors and began roughly dragging out her piles of beautifully laundered linen, all efficiently arranged in the way dear to her housewifely heart, each package held together by colored ribbons. . . . Without showing the slightest fear, mother joined the fellow and told him precisely what she thought of his shocking behavior in a lady's house" (Young-Bruehl 1988).

Years later, at the child analysis clinic that Anna Freud founded in Hampstead, she was to leave all her documents divided and tied with string in the same careful fashion that her own mother had kept linen: "At the end of each year, all the papers for the year were punched with two holes in their left margins and tied up with a string into six-inch-thick book-like parcels. . . .

there were exactly five parcels for each year. The system never varied" (Young-Bruehl 1988).

Indeed, this exactitude characterized Anna Freud's handling of her entire estate: "Anna Freud's own literary estate resembled an archaeological site, keyed precisely to the day-by-day, year-by-year living of her life. She filed away every piece of paper that came her way at 20 Maresfield Gardens from the end of the Second World War to 1982, and she kept carbon copies of every typewritten communication that left the house" (Young-Bruehl 1988).

An orderly approach extended also to Anna Freud's clear written style, as well as to the mode of training and research that she favored. Within the Hampstead Clinic, she developed a comprehensive indexing system that was taught to all the staff and used for the collection of an impressive archive of data. She also designed a profiling system that enabled a consistent, detailed approach to the diagnosis of children.

By comparison with Anna Freud's lifestyle, Melanie Klein's life appears turbulent and unconventional. In an act that was rather unusual for the period, Melanie Klein divorced her husband early. She later had a stormy battle with her daughter when the latter grew up and also became a psychoanalyst. Tragically, she also lost her son when he had a climbing accident. Over the years Melanie Klein "appeared to many to be fanatical in her total absorption in her 'work'" (Grosskurth 1985), while being "hopeless about household details." Her housekeeper arrived home one afternoon to find the kitchen "smeared from end to end with a red substance. Fearing that her employer had injured herself, she rushed into Mrs. Klein's bedroom, only to find her calmly reading in bed. It appeared that she had spilled a jar of beets" (Grosskurth 1985).

This impatience with mundane tasks was consistent with a personality that was passionate, spontaneous, and imaginative, but also at times capable of assuming a stubborn, uncompromising stance. In the early days Melanie Klein's liveliness and flamboyance were noted by Alix Strachey, a devotee and fellow trainee who was instrumental in encouraging her efforts. Strachey arranged for Klein's lectures to be translated into

English and read to the British Psychoanalytical Society in 1925. Yet on the day of the reading Strachey could hardly suppress her amazement at the extraordinary hat that Klein had chosen for the occasion: "a vasty voluminous affair in bright yellow with a huge brim and a cluster, a whole garden, of mixed flowers somewhere up the back, side or front—the total effect is that of an over-blown tea-rose" (Strachey 1986).

In reaction to this Strachey concluded, "She's a dotty woman. But there's no doubt whatever that her mind is stored with things of thrilling interest. And she's a nice character." Melanie Klein's mind, thus described, was felt by others as well to be highly original but anarchic, and Ernest Jones, founder of the British Psychoanalytical Society, noted that it was "neither scientific nor orderly." Indeed the approach that characterized Klein's work could be described more as "artistic" than scientific: she proceeded through intuition and emotion, exploring the depths of primitive phantasy life and favoring evocative description as a main explanatory tool. In line with this approach, Klein developed no systematic indexing or recording methods. She left behind only a handful of papers that expound her basic concepts, and these are intricate, dense, and repetitive. Yet each of her papers contains highly original contributions and brilliant insights, with a scope that is both sweeping and imaginative and covers everything from the earliest mental experiences to mechanisms that underlie major psychiatric afflictions.

The fundamental differences between the personalities and lives of Melanie Klein and Anna Freud affected the theoretical heritage they have left behind in other important ways. It is perhaps not surprising that Anna Freud, who approached the profession conventionally, began with the logical first step of training as a teacher and gaining experience with children. This left a lasting mark on her future work, which could never be confined entirely to a private consulting room. She continued to cultivate community-based work, extending her expertise to children who were deprived, orphaned, handicapped, poor, delinquent, and, for one reason or another, a concern of the state.

During the war years Anna Freud was able to secure a grant from the American Foster Parents Plan for War Children, to open the Hampstead War Nursery. Children were sent to her by the Hampstead Billeting Authorities, by hospitals from poor parts of London, and by psychiatric social workers from the East End Rest Centres. The Hampstead War Nursery offered places to children from bombed houses, "Tube sleepers" who had spent their nights on noisy platforms in the London Underground and developed sleep difficulties, children who had been sent back from evacuation after failing to settle down, children whose fathers had joined the armed services and whose mothers were at work, and other similar cases (A. Freud 1974).

Anna Freud not only organized expert care for those children but also trained the staff engaged with them to observe and record all the important psychological details that emerged. This project typifies Anna Freud's vision of the ideal child mental health provision: it combined a humane public service with a rigorous scientific research program.

Melanie Klein's initial approach to the profession equally left its mark on her long-term work, but it differed considerably from Anna Freud's. Klein did not train to work with children, nor did she follow any other conventional career path. Around 1914 she sought analysis for her own difficulties, and whilst engaged in this began also to observe her own children and discuss them with her first psychoanalyst, Sandor Ferenczi. She finally tried out some rudimentary analytical work with her son, which she wrote up and presented to the Hungarian psychoanalytical society as a prelude to joining it. Her work afterward focused on the private treatment of children in her own consulting room.

Anna Freud's first observations of children had been professional and slightly more distanced. Melanie Klein's personal involvement in the first observations of children led to a closer and more detailed look at their inner lives. Her observations were domestic, intimate, and close to the source. In the privacy of her own consulting room, she was able to respond naturally and intuitively to the children she saw, and so develop the crucially important psychoanalytic play technique.

Although Anna Freud continued to underscore the importance of work with children who are a concern of the state and a responsibility for society as a whole, it was paradoxically the work of Melanie Klein that put on the agenda for the first time the right of the child to a separate analytic space. Unlike Freud, Klein felt free to challenge accepted psychoanalytic givens. Feeling less encumbered by dogmas, Klein boldly asserted a much earlier onset of human relations than had hitherto been imagined. As suggested, her observations of infants convinced her that they were capable of a rudimentary recognition of their mothers from the very beginning of life. This ability to relate to separate others developed very fast, so that even within the first year of life the infant could come to a fuller recognition of the mother and other significant adults. This, in turn, implied that even a young child patient was able to perceive the analyst as a separate adult who was not emotionally confused with the parent. A child could thus engage with an analyst much as it did with nursery teachers and other helpful adults. Like the adult patient, the child patient could form a "transference" toward its analyst, transferring its typical patterns of relating to the arena of the analytic session.

Anna Freud objected to this notion. Although she agreed that "the child indeed enters into the liveliest relations with the analyst" (A. Freud 1946), she nonetheless concluded that "it forms no Transference neurosis." In her view, "The child is not, like the adult, ready to produce a new edition of its love-relationships, because, as one might say, the old edition is not yet exhausted." This, Anna Freud reflected, is due to the fact that "[the child's] original objects, the parents, are still real and present love-objects, not only in phantasy as with the adult neurotic; between them and the child exist all the relations of everyday life, and all its gratifications and disappointments still in reality depend on them. The analyst enters this situation as a new person . . . but there is no necessity for the child to exchange the parents for him, since compared with them he has not the advantages which the adult finds when he can exchange his phantasy-objects for a real person" (A. Freud 1946).

As far as Melanie Klein was concerned, an "old edition" of love-relationships already existed for the child, and this was the archaic, rudimentary one of earliest infancy. This "edition" had already been internalized and integrated into the child's view of reality, and colored its relationships with all the adults in its life, including the parents. The child's perception of ordinary parental behavior was, therefore, tinged with primitive elements that exaggerated its different facets; parental affection seemed more ideal to the young child than it was in reality, and by the same token, parental disapproval could be heard by the child as more persecutory and threatening than it actually was.

Klein held that the young infant gradually creates primitive mental representations of the good and bad aspect of its first relationship with the mother. These representations, or "internal objects" already integrated into the ego of the young child, were revived in the analytic relationship, endowing the child analyst with malevolent or ideal qualities much as if the analyst came to bear the mark of archaic features of the child-patient's earliest environment.

With this depiction of the mental capacities of young children, Melanie Klein challenged the very foundations on which Anna Freud based her thinking. As suggested, their debate increasingly assumed the significance of a battle for professional survival, and because their lives revolved around their psychoanalytic work, they had a growing personal investment in the outcome of what should have remained a strictly professional issue. The likelihood of discovering common ground either within or outside the realm of their psychoanalytic activities was thus remote.

This does not mean, however, that common ground did not exist. The lives of Anna Freud and Melanie Klein followed a pattern that owed much to a shared cultural and ethnic identity in a particular historical context. Paradoxically, they were not particularly conscious of the significance of their Jewish background. If anything, they lived as what Isaac Deutscher had labeled non-Jewish Jews and belonged to a familiar genre of

Jewish thinker who was concerned with universal issues and addressed the whole of society rather than the Jewish community. Among such thinkers were radical women who had been taking up struggles for causes outside Jewish society since the late nineteenth century (Shepherd 1993). Although Anna Freud and Melanie Klein did not think of themselves as rebels or radicals, they both poured their considerable energies into a universal cause—revolutionizing the understanding of infancy and childhood through psychoanalytic knowledge.

But although they could both retain an enthusiastic belief in the universal value of their findings before World War II, the Holocaust necessarily complicated such certainty. As psychoanalysts engaged in the study of human nature, they faced the difficulty of trying to retain a scientific objectivity in the face of what had been revealed about it. Their Jewishness appeared to threaten this scientific stance, but their discipline, psychoanalysis, demanded a transcendence of the subjective and the personal.

The conflict between a scientific / objective and a Jewish / subjective self was evident in Anna Freud's only Jewish project out of her prodigious output, which was a single paper that she devoted to the study of six young concentration camp survivors. These children, all of German-Jewish origin, had been orphaned in infancy when their parents were deported to Poland and killed in the gas chambers. The children were sent to Theresienstadt where, at under a year old, they became inmates of the "Ward for Motherless Children" (A. Freud 1951). In the ward they were cared for by adult inmates of the camp who were themselves exhausted and malnourished. Because Theresienstadt was a transit camp with frequent deportations, the children grew up in an atmosphere of terror, in addition to suffering appalling daily hardship.

Upon arrival in Britain in 1945, the young survivors were between three and four years old. They spent an initial two months at a reception camp run by a former superintendent of the Hampstead Nurseries, Alice Goldberger. This Hampstead connection proved useful when a prominent friend of the former Hampstead Nurseries, the wife of a member of parliament, offered the children accommodation in "Bulldogs Bank," a peaceful country house. Two former head nurses from the Hampstead Nurseries, Sophie and Gertrude Dann, took charge of the home.

After keeping index cards on the children according to Anna Freud's Hampstead method, Sophie Dann prepared a rough draft in consultation with Alice Goldberger, and on the basis of this Anna Freud published "An Experiment in Group Upbringing" in 1951 (Young-Bruehl 1988). The nature of the whole project exemplifies Anna Freud's attempt to negotiate an appropriate scientific relationship with an enterprise that threatened to become all too personal. All the staff and personnel that were central to the project had been trained in, or influenced by, her Hampstead program. Her life's work thus made a major contribution to the rehabilitation of young survivors. Yet Anna Freud had no direct involvement with the work and published a conclusion only on the basis of what others had observed and recorded.

This attempt to retain a distance from the project is evident also in the authorial stance that she adopts in "An Experiment in Group Upbringing." The title, resonating with all the recent horror that the term "experiment" had acquired in the camps, seems ironically chosen at first. Yet it is not openly explained by her and so remains ambiguous. Instead, Anna Freud proceeds to examine the results of this "experiment" with apparent scientific neutrality. For example, she does not focus on the children's explicit emotional responses toward the catastrophe that they had endured. Instead, she gives a dispassionate account of every aspect of their lives in Bulldogs Bank: their eating habits, indoor and outdoor activities, language development, relationships with adults and with each other, and the like.

Freud did include the topic of fears and anxieties in the paper, but she gave it no priority, either in the sequencing of her general account, where it is the fourteenth topic to be addressed, or in its unexceptional length. Her account of "Fears Based on Memories" (such as the children's highly revealing fear of dogs and of railroad cars) lasts a mere four paragraphs and elicits no reflections from her (A. Freud 1951, 216).

In the conclusion to her paper, Anna Freud noted: "Experiments of this kind, which are provided by fate, lack the satisfying neatness and circumspection of an artificial setup. It is difficult, or impossible, to distinguish the action of the variables from each other, as is demonstrated in our case by the intermingled effects of three main factors: the absence of a mother or parent relationship; the abundance of community influence; and the reduced amount of gratification of all needs, from the oral stage onwards. It is, of course, impossible to vary the experiment" (224).

Yet in spite of such measured language, Anna Freud's ability to remain scientifically calm in the face of the survivor project is only apparent, and the text conveys the pressures of conflicting voices within her. This becomes clearer when it is compared with another text, Sigmund Freud's "Moses and Monotheism," that Anna Freud read on behalf of her father at the 1938 International Psychoanalytic Congress. It is in this paper that Anna Freud would have come across her father's psychoanalytic approach to Jewish issues, and the scientific neutrality with which he tried to investigate the "special character of the Jewish people": "We found that the man Moses impressed this character on them by giving them a religion which increased their self esteem so much that they thought themselves superior to all other people" (S. Freud 1939, 123).

Anna Freud would have noted that throughout the paper the reader, invited to share her father's reflective process, is addressed with an inclusive first person "we," whereas the subject of contemplation, the Jewish people, is kept at a third person distance of "them." Some of the descriptions of the Jewish people are delivered in the language of an unbiased expert examining a curious artifact that has survived the ravages of time: "Trustworthy reports tell us that they behaved in Hellenistic times just as they do today, so that the complete Jew was already there" (S. Freud 1939, 106).

Yet this objective stance extends no further

than the language. The Jewish people in Freud's vision, having survived intact, became to him a precious specimen, much like the antiquities that he collected so enthusiastically throughout his life. Freud hypothesized that the Jewish people of his day not only revealed information about their own origin, but something about the universal mental structure that has evolved in civilized man. The relationship between Moses and the Jewish people was thus held up by Freud as an ancestral prototype of his structural theory of the mind, so that it falls into the category of papers like "Totem and Taboo" (1913) that envisage actual historical scenarios as the basis of internalized mental structure.

Freud argued that Moses instilled a value system in the Jewish people in the same way that the ego-ideal imposes morality on the ego in individual mental development—by raising their self-esteem until it became a substantial counterforce to the imperatives of instinctual desires. In individual psychic development, the ego similarly learns to renounce immediate gratifications through creating an internal ideal and, in trying to measure up to it, gains self esteem.

This example is cited here to demonstrate Freud's inability to contemplate the Jewish people with the kind of pure objective distance that his style attempts. Thus, the Jewish voice that is initially stifled in the paper in the service of a universally valid theory ultimately subverts the notion that theory-making can remain free of cultural influences, or indeed be useful without their effect. Freud's own concept of the "return of the repressed" aptly captures the way in which his Jewish aspect returns to take up a central position in his vision of mental life. His Jewish people thus emerge as admirable in spite of their "chosen people" superiority. In fact, such superiority is felt by him to be the necessary compensation for renouncing instinctual gratifications, and it therefore paves the way for an intellectual and spiritual, rather than a merely sensual, approach to living.

Anna Freud's paper on the child survivors seems far removed from the speculative reaches of "Moses and Monotheism," but it comes close to its essential sentiments on Jewish experience and extends a particular line of thinking within it. Just as Freud ultimately tolerated an aggressive, superior streak in the Jewish people, so too did Anna Freud conclude that her six survivors must be allowed to express normal aggression for the sake of recovering their mental health. The initial absence of such aggression, which she details in her paper, makes for an alarming catalogue of mental fragility. The children, having had their self-assertive impulses mutilated, were unable to express rivalry, envy, selfishness, and other forms of normal childish aggression. Her apparently neutral account of their peaceful daily lives in Britain is a growing testimony of the damage that had been inflicted on them, as Anna Freud heaps detail upon detail of their catastrophically meek "goodness." The notion that the Jewish people and Jewish children are entitled to self-esteem and self-assertive capacities is the sensitive issue at the heart of both works. It also shares something with Zionist ideals, endorsing healthy assertiveness in the service of self-"defemination."

Unlike Anna Freud, Melanie Klein had no Jewish projects. Her own response to the events of the war was a startling silence. In 1946 she published her paper "Notes on Some Schizoid Mechanisms," in which she explored the way in which emotion can be split off and deadened in all individuals. She suggested that this destructive mechanism is a universal part of the normal psyche, and that it exists in infancy. Yet while exploring such a destructive defense in the human psyche, she failed to refer to the scale of destruction just witnessed by the world. Perhaps this was her way of insisting on the objective, rather than specifically Jewish, roots of her ideas.

An explicit reference to Jewish issues and influences is not the most useful criterion by which to measure the Jewish dimension of the contributions of Melanie Klein and Anna Freud, however. Instead it seems more appropriate to look at the emotional experiences that both women explored in their works. Anna Freud was thinking about defense mechanisms when Freud contemplated the issue of the nature of Jewish strength in *Moses and Monotheism* (Young-Bruehl 1988). She quietly explored the means of the childish psyche for

survival. Her conclusion in her chapter on the young Holocaust survivors was that their excessive altruism was unnatural. Anna Freud thus demonstrated that too much compliance and altruism in children is unhealthy. It is already well known how such views changed the world's knowledge of upbringing.

Klein for her part explored the more aggressive reactions to loss and grief. In her 1940 work on mourning, she analyzed the triumphalism that can manifest in the individual who has outlived a deceased relative, and thus became the first to point out the phenomenon of survivor's guilt. Both this concept, and Anna Freud's work on the mechanism of identification with the aggressor, proved crucial for later attempts to understand the full scale of Jewish trauma. In their understanding of suffering and the human attempt to survive it, Anna Freud and Melanie Klein spoke with a Jewish sensibility, but they were thereby well placed to address the plight of a universal psyche.

Bibliography

Anna Freud, *The Psycho-Analytical Treatment of Children* (London: Inigo, 1946); A. Freud, *Infants Without Families (1939–1945)* (London: Hogarth, 1974); A. Freud, "An Experiment in Group Upbringing," *Indications for Child Analysis, 1945–1956* (London: Hogarth, 1951); Sigmund Freud, *Moses and Monotheism* (1939), in *The Standard Edition of the Complete Psychological Works of Sigmund Freud,* ed. James Strachey, vol. 23 (London: Hogarth, 1953–74); S. Freud, *Totem and Taboo* (1913) in *Standard Edition,* vol. 13; Phyllis Grosskurth, *Melanie Klein* (London: Maresfield Library, 1985); Pearl King and Riccardo Steiner, eds., *The Freud-Klein Controversies, 1941–1945* (London: Routledge, 1991); Melanie Klein, "The Psychogenesis of Manic-Depressive States" (1935), in Klein, *Love Guild and Reparation* (London: Hogarth, 1975a), 262–90; Klein, "Notes on Some Schizoid Mechanisms," in Klein, *Envy and Gratitude* (London: Hogarth, 1975b), 1–24; Naomi Shepherd, *A Price Below Rubies: Jewish Women as Rebels and Radicals* (London: Weidenfeld & Nicholson, 1993); Alix Strachey, *Bloomsbury / Freud: The Letters of James and Alix Strachey, 1924–1925* (London: Chatto & Windus, 1986); and Elisabeth Young-Bruehl, *Anna Freud* (London: Macmillan, 1988).

MEIRA LIKIERMAN

February 8, 1942 H. G. Adler is deported to Theresienstadt and begins his life's work of writing a scholarly testimony to his experience

H. G. Adler was one of the last exponents of the Prague school of German literature, which brought forth Rilke and Kafka. As a novelist, he wrote in the modernist tradition of Musil and Broch; and though he saw himself primarily as a poet, he also published, inter alia, on literature, sociology, religion, and philosophy. Yet it is as a witness and analyst of the Shoah that he is best known, and for this he belongs, according to Peter Demetz, in the company of Primo Levi and Elie Wiesel (Adler 1968, 582). This encyclopedic variety, to some extent imposed on his work by his life, condemned H. G. Adler to extreme isolation. As he said in an interview with Friedrich Danielis, "The experiences of a German writer of the Jewish nation who comes from Czechoslovakia, belongs to the Austrian cultural sphere, and is a loyal British citizen are not particularly pleasant. Someone like me does not belong anywhere. That is my fate" (Adler 1981b, 47).

Hans Günther Adler was born into an assimilated Jewish family in the Prague suburb of Karlin on July 2, 1910. His father, Emil Adler (1882–1942), was a bookbinder by trade, and his mother, Alice Fraenkel (1885–1942), a physical education instructor. As a first-grader at primary school, the young H. G. Adler did not even know whether he was Jewish or Christian, and later he owed a key religious awakening not to the Bible but to the *Bhagavad Gita*. By the time of the Shoah, however, he had already developed a Jewish consciousness and had created his own variety of ethical Judaism, "the orthodoxy of the heart," which was to remain the core of his belief.

Adler's mother developed an illness that cast a permanent shadow over his life and severely disrupted his education, isolated him from the family, and threw him onto his own resources. He was sent away from home to schools in various localities from 1920 to 1925, including the village school described in chapter 2 of his semiautobiographical novel, *Panorama,* and the Dresden "Kasten" of chapter three, which he called his "first concentration camp." Back in Prague, he left school and taught himself until he was able to matriculate externally at the normal age, in 1932. He entered the German University of Prague, majoring in musicology, minoring in literature, and studying philosophy and psychology as compulsory subjects. He completed his doctoral thesis on "Klopstock and Music" in 1935, but he was never able to practice the discipline in which he had been trained. While collecting source material at the Staatsbibliothek in Berlin in 1933, he had witnessed Hitler's seizure of power; from this point on, he realized the futility of his hopes for an academic career in Germany. Politically and domestically, he was experiencing the isolation that had already become a permanent feature of his life.

Voracious childhood reading in a community known for its cultural aspirations laid the foundations for Adler's *Bildung* (education). From the start, he aimed to be a poet and began writing in earnest in 1925: "My earliest creative literary endeavors were largely German, yes, even *reichsdeutsch* (imperial German) in orientation and tradition, and this became decisive for my whole life, even if that life did not let me be German for long, and the old Jewish heritage (*alte jüdische Geisteswelt*) gained supreme importance for me" (Adler 1981c, 242). At first, Adler knew little about modern literature, though he was adventurous in exploring the classics: he read Adalbert Stifter at fourteen, and Jean Paul, Kleist, and Goethe by the time he was sixteen. The Jewish mystical poet Alfred Mombert, together with Friedrich Hölderlin, became the formative influence on his early poetry. He read Musil and soon discovered Kafka, who occupied a central place in his literary imagination.

Despite his sense of isolation, Adler formed close ties, many of which survived the war. As a child he became friends with Franz Baermann Steiner (1909–52), who was himself to become a major poet and anthropologist, and together they founded a small literary circle that lasted until 1938. The slightly older Hermann Grab was another close literary friend.

Other constellations that had a decisive effect on Adler's development were the youth movement of the *Wandervögel,* the hiking group with whom he explored the Bohemian landscape, as is recalled in chapter 4 of *Panorama;* and a mystical circle around the Czech avant-garde photographer František Drtikol (1883–1961), which is remembered in chapter 5. The salon at the home of the Jewish doctor Emanuel Gross and his wife Bertha offered a haven for several young artists— and established ones, too, like the Czech painters Willi Nowak and Emil Filla. The young Günther Adler was a regular visitor, as was the Jewish sculptor from Czernowitz, Bernard Reder (1897– 1963), whose uncompromising ethics provided a model for Adler's attitude as an artist.

A different side of Adler's personality emerged in his relations to the Jewish philosophers, notably Erich Unger (1887–1950). Unger's *Philoso-phische Gruppe* (philosophical circle), founded in Berlin in 1927, made a strong impression on him, and Unger's belief in practice and in experimental philosophy—which also influenced Walter Benjamin—may have contributed to a project that occupied Adler for nearly the whole of his intellectual life. Begun around 1932, Adler's *Über Wirklichkeit und Sein* (On reality and being) eventually matured into his *Vorschule für eine Experimentaltheologie* (Introduction to an Experimental Theology; 1987). Long-term preoccupations like this enabled him to embed his experiences during the Shoah into a developing set of beliefs, by which he learned to transcend historical particularity.

Upon his graduation, Adler became a secretary at the Prague Urania, an institute for further education satirized in chapter 7 of *Panorama.* Here, Adler invited Canetti to give a public reading after the Czech translation of *Die Blendung* (Auto-da-fé; 1935) had appeared. Canetti remembers Adler in *Das Augenspiel* (The play of the eyes; 1985): "He was characterized by highly charged idealistic aspirations; he, the man who was soon to fall victim to that accursed age, appeared not to *belong* to the age at all. A person who was more influenced by the German literary tradition could hardly have been found anywhere in Germany" (Canetti 1985, 341).

At this point, Adler made plans to escape from Central Europe, but after spending six months in commercial training in Milan to prepare for his emigration to South America, he was refused a visa to Brazil in 1938 and found himself trapped in Prague. He married Gertrud Klepetar in November 1941, and they were deported together with her family on February 8, 1942. Adler always attributed his survival—insofar as any human agency was involved—to Gertrud. Later, he described the attitude that sustained him: "I said to myself: 'If I survive all of this, and I very much doubt it, then I will bear witness to everything that I experience, not, however, by a personal record, but in an objective, scholarly form. Apart from that, I will now give artistic expression to my experiences as best as I can.' It was this dual precept thanks to which I survived physically, and above all, morally for thirty-two months in

Theresienstadt and another six months in concentration camps" (Adler 1981a, 26).

Adler systematically set about collecting material for his *Theresienstadt* book and after six weeks began his first cycle of camp poems, "Theresienstädter Bilderbogen" (The Theresienstadt picture book), which he wrote in a vivid, almost expressionistic style. Poems like "The Arrival of the Old Men" and "The Hangman Helps" present images of "human cattle," "ragged hordes," and "a rotting woman on the hearse." Adler subsequently sought to transcend the minutiae of terror. Altogether, he wrote over a hundred poems in Theresienstadt. For Viktor Ullmann, composer of the Theresienstadt opera *Der Kaiser von Atlantis,* he wrote the cycle *Der Mensch und sein Tag.* Adler took refuge in complex verse forms like terza rima, handling them with innovative subtlety, as in the still unpublished cycle *Einsam in Banden* (Alone in bonds) of the winter of 1943. In poems like "Absage" (Refusal) and "Trost" (Comfort), he contrasted the "opaque matter of the shadow world" that he "must suffer" in all its "poison," "whippings," and "bloodstained rain" with the "salvation of unsullied purity" that "the old masters"—by which he means the mystics—discovered by "immersion into one's own breast." In Adler's work, the often violent imagery of traditional mysticism assumes new urgency amid the actual annihilation of the camps: "you go under, and yet you will survive." All of these poems, together with Adler's material for his *Theresienstadt* book, owe their preservation to Rabbi Leo Baeck, who looked after them when Adler was transported to the East.

On October 12, 1944, Adler was dispatched to Auschwitz together with Gertrud and her mother. On the "Ramp," Gertrud refused to desert her mother and chose to go to "the bad side." They were murdered on October 14, 1944. Adler himself was imprisoned for two weeks in the gypsy camp at Auschwitz-Birkenau. He presents the camp in chapter 9 of *Panorama:*

Forty bodies are lying heavily, they are not sleeping and not waking, they are simply lying, and there is no time among them, they are not alive and not dead either, but one can also say that many are alive and several of them are dead, you cannot tell in the dark who is dead and who is alive; and there is nothing here, only bodies, and the room is made of wood . . . ; there is a door which cannot be shut, it has no lock and no handle, this door is never open and never closed, it moves with every breath of air, it is hanging on unoiled hinges, it whistles when moved lightly and squeaks when moved heavily; . . . there is not a nail on the wall, no chair, no table, no bench, nothing, nothing, no beds, no straw sacks, there are only bodies here, these are the lost ones, they are wearing rags of every color, there are also a few blankets lying about, the bodies beneath them, then there are caps, scraps of cloth without a shape, a few tin pots, some spoons, perhaps some other possessions, picked out of the rubble and garbage, nothing else, but fear is here, pressed closely together, living fear in emasculated and bloated bodies, hate and despair, but even more fear, which does not wish to die, even when it is whipped, and there is a grinning here, and a hoping, which still moves among the decay, perhaps the hope does not succumb to the decay and does battle with fear. (465f.)

Adler's subsequent narration of Auschwitz does not spare the reader its details—the cynical use of a Red Cross van for carrying Zyklon B, the screams of the dying, and the bleeding noses of the dead are recalled as vividly as in any survivor's account—but he also seeks to commemorate the humanity by which some of the "lost ones" could withstand evil. It was in Auschwitz that Adler met Max Schiff, an Orthodox Jew from Slovakia, and there Schiff gave him instruction in the Talmud. These teachings are incorporated in *Panorama,* in which the figure of Mordechai cites the *Sayings of the Fathers* and talmudically responds to the intended degradation: "But why shouldn't we survive?" says Mordechai, and a smile spreads over his face "that they give us pieces of holy prayer shawls as rags for our feet, how foolish are they, but we fare well thereby, for it is said, thou shalt wrap thyself in these shawls when thou prayest" (Adler 1968, 490). This, I think, leads to the core of Adler's own experience of the Shoah,

the survival of human worth amid blackest evil—
this was the witness he bore.

At the same time, Auschwitz also laid the
foundations for Adler's political philosophy. "I
always had a very critical attitude towards the
state," he later observed. "In that respect, Theresienstadt simply taught me many lessons. That is
also true of the short time I spent in Auschwitz."
Here he does not elaborate those many lessons,
but explains: "Those two weeks [in Auschwitz]
were the most illuminating in my whole life, for I
saw how far power and government can go astray"
(*Jüdische Lebenswege,* 171). The mystical core of
Adler's thought in the camp coincided with the
political insight that he, as a naked human being,
physically experienced at the equally naked abuse
of power; these insights subsequently underpin
his theoretical attempts to grasp and validate the
character of human dignity, and to preserve it
from abuse.

Transported from Auschwitz to an outlying
camp of Buchenwald, Adler ended the war in an
underground factory at Langenstein near Hal-
berstadt. Another forty poems were written in
these camps. Their mood ranges from the proud
solidarity he expresses with a French resistance
fighter in "An Odic" (To Odic) to a yearning for
"desireless death" elsewhere. Joseph Strelka has
argued that such poems from the camps enter a
new spiritual territory, not just experientially,
but also aesthetically. There is something disarm-
ing about the simplicity of diction with which
the poems express a life in extremis. "This is the
end," Adler simply says in one of the very last
pieces, written in March 1945. "This is death, the
super-death / The death of deaths." Three weeks
later, he was liberated.

Adler returned to Prague in June 1945 to discover that his entire family had been wiped out.
He first worked in the orphanage opened by Pře-
mysl Pitter, where he taught the young painter
Jehuda Bacon, and then he spent sixteen months
at the Prague Jewish Museum. In February 1947,
to avoid the impending Communist takeover, he
fled to England, where he was granted political
asylum and, eventually, British citizenship. He
married the sculptress and pupil of Reder's, Bettina Gross, with whose mother, Bertha, he had

maintained his old friendship in Theresienstadt
before she, too, was deported to Auschwitz. Bettina provided him with a home in which, with
time, a living memory of prewar Prague was re-
created; family life enabled him to cope with exile
and poverty. In these years he renewed friendships with, for example, Franz Baermann Steiner,
Veza and Elias Canetti, and Leo Baeck, and he
formed new ones with writers like Erich Fried,
Ilse Aichinger, and other Prague exiles—notably
Franz Wurm and Grete Fischer. At first, Adler
planned to write in English, but in a repetition of
his fate of 1935, he was unable to find suitable
academic employment—this time as the result of
a lack of publications—and found himself
thrown into a life as a freelance writer and scholar
addressing a German-speaking audience. He
abandoned his first names, because Eichmann's
representative in the so-called Protectorate of Bohemia and Moravia was named Hans Günther,
and set about creating the life's work of
H. G. Adler.

In a frenzy of creativity that ran unabated for
ten years, Adler completed countless poems and
stories, as well as six novels (one of which he had
begun in the war) and the monumental *Theresienstadt, 1941–1945,* finished in 1948 but not
published until 1955. The book quickly established his reputation as the author of "the best
description and analysis of the National Socialist
persecution of the Jews" (*Die Zeit,* Oct. 18, 1974).
Yet the success of *Theresienstadt* did not end Adler's sense of alienation, because his whole postwar existence was characterized by the paradoxes
that the layering of his experiences induced. Besides, he distanced himself from every prevailing
school of thought, from Marxism to Freudianism.
In sociology, he was a follower of Simmel, and in
philosophy, a student of Schelling, at a time when
both were awaiting a revival that would take another thirty years; beyond this, he subscribed to
"the party of humanity," which is to say, he was a
follower of Mendelssohn and Lessing yet recognized the dangers attendant upon the Enlightenment. Adler's radical humanism did not allow
him to be placed easily within the main intellectual classifications of the time—not least because
he crossed the contemporary divide between poet

and scholar. Consequently, publication and money were a perpetual problem. *Theresienstadt* took seven years to find a publisher. The fiction and poetry fared much worse: *Eine Reise* needed ten years, *Panorama* twenty, and *Die Wand* thirty-five. Several novels still await their first printing, not to mention the majority of Adler's verse. With no institutional affiliation, his chief income in the years after 1955 came from broadcasting and lecturing. The one public function he took on simply set an official seal on his status as an outsider: he was president of the PEN Center of German Writers Abroad from 1973 to 1985.

Theresienstadt, 1941–1945 provides the analytic correlative to Adler's literary portrayals of the camps, though it is fueled by the same ethical concern. Among the earliest treatments of the Holocaust, and possibly still the most thorough study of any single camp, the book also won recognition for its general sociological character, comparable to *Middletown*. Three long chapters examine the history, sociology, and psychology of the "ghetto." Topics like the transports, administration, accommodation, diet, health, and culture are subjected to the same detailed scrutiny by a method that incorporates lengthy passages of source material and statistics, as well as philosophical and linguistic analysis, into a grand historical narrative. The conclusion (627–85) locates Theresienstadt in the context of history and ideology, and—in an argument that converged with that of contemporaries such as Adorno and Horkheimer—Adler scrutinizes there the contiguities of Nazism and modernity. Among other theories, Hermann Broch's concept of the "collapse of values," which had preoccupied Adler in Theresienstadt, is here transformed into an analysis of modern "mechanical materialism," which Adler sees as culminating in *Mein Kampf* and in the implementation of the Final Solution. Hitler's materialistic "dualism" is related to the ideology of a godless universe, in which naked power opposes "organic life" and treats human beings as masses; "administration becomes an end in itself" and destroys human individuality, so that "Germany and nearly the whole of Europe become the object of what almost amounted to an experiment." In this "sickness," the rulers and

their people attempted "to replace history"—hence their mad fictions of a thousand-year Reich—with a "paramythic" pseudoreligion, the credo of which was prejudice against Jewish alterity, and whose doctrine of salvation lay in the annihilation of otherness (632f.). The entire murderous but precarious structure is grounded in a nihilism that ensnares the destroyers more powerfully than their intended victims.

Whereas *Theresienstadt* employs the "internal" viewpoint of an inmate, *Der verwaltete Mensch* (Administered man; 1974) approaches its subject "externally" via the administrative mechanisms of the SS, to examine how deportation was possible, and thus how an institutionalized act of murder on an unprecedented scale could occur in a modern state. The book amounts to what Heinrich Böll, writing in *Der Spiegel,* called an "encyclopedia of the deportations." It examines the history of the Final Solution, the technique of deportation, and the Nazis' appropriation of Jewish property. Special features worthy of separate publication include the "Schicksale aus den Akten" (Human fates from the files; pp. 647–864), which consists largely of commentated documents that reveal the individuals trapped in the Nazis' bureaucratic labyrinth, and the theoretical conclusion (865–1038). The key idea, anticipated in the earlier book, lies in the central role Adler accords to "administration" in modernity, which he sees as more fundamental than the bureaucracy analyzed by Max Weber. According to Adler, there is a basic flaw in the modern theory of the state, typified in the American confusion of "Government" with "Administration," and traceable to Montesquieu's division of powers. Adler argues that not only must the three arms of power be divided, but all administration needs to be segregated from these organs to prevent other abuses of power like the Final Solution: administration should deal exclusively with *things,* government with *people.* Where this division does not obtain, the State—and Adler finds safeguards lacking in *every* modern State—commits the initial error that threatens to turn the Holocaust from an exception into a paradigm of modernity.

A series of essays, some of which are collected in *Die Freiheit des Menschen* (The freedom of man;

1976), elaborate on concepts in his major works, such as the masses, liberty, and society. Another thread running through his oeuvre—as Peter Staengle stresses—is a critique of language in the tradition of Karl Kraus. The sociological and the linguistic often merge, as in the Swiftian satire *Die Hausordnung* (The rules of the house; 1988).

Although literature was his chief pursuit— his sense of form and style also shaped his scholarship—Adler's literary achievement itself has yet to make its mark. His several novels differ radically in form but create a collective whole by transmuting different aspects of his life into fiction: *Panorama* leads from his childhood through Theresienstadt and Auschwitz to England in ten selected "pictures"; *Eine Reise* presents the period from deportation until liberation; the unpublished *Die Ansiedlung* treats a strange dwelling-place modeled on Theresienstadt; and *Die unsichtbare Wand* deals with the return to Prague and the problematic acculturation in England, against the background of some unspeakable disaster.

Modernistic techniques of cutting, blending, and montage are handled in classical German prose that, as Heinrich Böll observed in the case of *Eine Reise,* recalls the style of Stifter and Kafka (Böll 1966, 55). But the coherence and rhythmic character of the books reflect techniques of musical composition: Peter Demetz called *Panorama* "a score for ideas on the edge of music" (Adler 1968, 592). Each book is "through-composed." Phrases, sentences, and paragraphs build up into larger rhythmic blocks that, in the case of *Eine Reise* and *Die Wand,* are disconcertingly linked into a single uninterrupted flow of consciousness. One thinks, perhaps, of Bruckner's symphonic structures or Mahler's tragic beauty. The musically conducted narrative, however, can attain a powerful visual effect, and it also incorporates philosophical reflection in the tradition of the Viennese modernists.

Characteristically, the novels lead their figures into annihilation, from which a survivor emerges to attain a renewed acceptance of life. In *Eine Reise,* this key reversal is evoked in a "fairy-tale of nothingness" in which, through cognition of reality, the *will* reawakens, rehearsing "the first moment of creation," so that from "nothing" a "something" reenters the world (1–15ff.). *Die Wand* also employs the imagery of alienation— ice and fire—to conjoin the physical dereliction at the war's end with a metaphysical catastrophe: "A human survivor [*ein überlebter Mensch*] at a signpost in a deadly snowstorm, scorned by disaster; when the storm passed, his companions lay frozen to death, the sign-post was smashed, no destinations can be read on its splinters any more, even the paths have ceased to exist."

The hero reflects: "It was over. Over. Burned out. Ashes. Over. Nothing. And then I pulled myself together. I didn't want to get entangled again, I didn't want to martyr my knowledge with the daggers of deception. . . . I want to survive the truth, sacrifice myself to it, and if I may fulfill another task, I want to bear witness to the truth, however merciless it may be" (322f.). The conclusion of Canetti's response to the *Reise* is emblematic of Adler's achievement: "I would say that you have reintroduced *Hope* into modern literature" (Eckhart and Unger 1975, 73).

The many stories, three volumes of which have appeared, and the major body of verse, to which H. G. Adler devoted some of his best creative energy, have a range of reference that extends far beyond the Holocaust. Ironically, the poetry, which is perhaps his chief achievement, is the least known (because it is largely unpublished), though there has been recognition of its merits. Hermann Broch saw in it the (deeply unfashionable) attempt to maintain "an essentially lyrical" style, as exemplified in Hölderlin, and argued that it even "went beyond" its great model: "The dissolution of rationality in irrational symbols is perfectly . . . achieved" (Eckhart and Unger 1975, 112). Too experimental for the traditionalists, too lyrical for the modernists, and too naive in its expression of faith and pathos for either, the verse takes a route out of Hölderlin that bypasses Rilke and proves the very antithesis of Celan: in a voice that shifts disconcertingly from tenderness to satire—recalling the "lyrical irony" of *Eine Reise*—the mature poetry typically consists of highly articulated stanzaic structures that tumble in Pindaric cascades and bristle with references that range from the Psalms and folklore to contemporary events. A poem like "The Saints of the Tender Conscience," for example, pours scorn on the acquitted murderers in the postwar years, in terms that apply as much to the deportations as to other killing fields: "The strangled victims. The dismembered. Hunted / In hiding and combed from their rooms. / Children frozen to death by the wayside." As to the judgment on the perpetrators, Adler sardonically comments: "When in doubt: acquittal" (Adler 1975, 160).

Apart from one pause from around 1956–64, the stream of poetic inspiration continued unabated into Adler's final years. His style became increasingly vivid, condensed, and vatic; if anything, his despair deepened, yet his sense of an unending future intensified. Between these extremes, there also lay a stoic equanimity, which emerged in conversation and on the increasing number of occasions that journalists interviewed him as a witness. "I don't regret anything that I have experienced. Of course I regret that Auschwitz existed . . . but if it did exist, then I don't regret having been there" (*Jüdische Lebenswege,* 163f.). Despite his outrage at a history seemingly locked in a cycle of recurrence, his optimism led him to find a "creative" and "humane" approach to resolving human dilemmas via a "theology of the unknown." This was the subject of his last book, begun in 1932, the *Vorschule für eine Experimentaltheologie,* which expresses the philosophic sum of his experiences, and optimistically anticipates a postrational era of "intuition." It was for the future as for the past that he lived the present. On August 21, 1988, only a few months after the publication of this last book, H. G. Adler died in London, his life's work complete.

Bibliography

H. G. Adler, "Dichtung in der Gefangenschaft als inneres Exil," *Literatur des Exils,* ed. Bernt Engelmann (Munich: Goldmann, 1981a), 18–28; Adler, *Eine Reise: Erzählung* (Bonn: Bibliotheca Christiana, 1962); Adler, *Ereignisse: Kleine Erzählungen und Novellen* (Olten, Switz.: Walter, 1969); Adler, *Die Freiheit des Menschen: Aufsätze zur Soziologie und Geschichte* (Tübingen: Mohr, 1976); Adler, "Da gäbe es noch viel mehr zu berichten," Interview with Friedrich Danielis, *Das Pult* 14 (1981b): 47–58; Adler, *Hausordnung: Wortlaut und Auslegung* (Vienna: Atelier, 1988); Adler, *Die Juden in Deutschland von der Aufklärung bis zum Nationalsozialismus* (Munich: Kösel, 1960), trans. as *The Jews in Germany* (Cleveland, Ohio: Notre Dame University Press, 1969); Adler, *Panorama: Roman in zehn Bildern* (Olten, Switz.: Walter, 1968); Adler, *Stimme und Zuruf* (Hamburg: Knaus, 1980); Adler, *Theresienstadt, 1941–1945: Das Antlitz einer Zwangsgemeinschaft* (Tübingen: Mohr, 1955; 2d rev. exp. ed., 1960); Adler, *Die unsichtbare Wand: Roman* (Vienna: Zsolnay, 1989); Adler, *Der verwaltete Mensch: Studien zur Deportation der Juden aus Deutschland* (Tübingen: Mohr, 1974); Adler, *Viele Jahreszeiten: Gedichte* (Vienna: Dürer, 1975); Adler, *Vorschule für eine Experimentaltheologie: Betrachtungen über Wirklichkeit und Sein* (Stuttgart: Steiner, 1987); Adler, "Zu Hause im Exil," *Autoren im Exil,* ed. Karl Corino (Frankfurt a. M.: Fischer, 1981c), 242–53; Heinrich Böll, *Frankfurter Vorlesungen* (Cologne: Kiepenheuer and Witsch, 1966); Elias Canetti, *Das Augenspiel: Lebensgeschichte, 1931–1937* (Munich: Hanser, 1985); Peter Demetz, *After the Fires: Recent Writing in the Germanies, Austria, and Switzerland* (New York: Harcourt Brace Jovanovich, 1986); Willehad P. Eckhart and Wilhelm Unger, eds., *H. G. Adler: Buch der Freunde Stimmen über den Dichter und Gelehrten mit unveröffentlichter Lyrik* (Cologne: Wienand, 1975), including complete bibliography of 1945–75; Rüdiger Görner, "Überleben-Überwinden? Eine Betrachtung zum Werk H. G. Adlers," *Salzburger Jahrbuch für Philosophie* (1990): 75–88; Heinrich Hubmann and Alfred O. Lanz, eds., *Zu Hause im Exil: Zu Werk und Person H. G. Adlers* (Stuttgart: Steiner, 1987), including, on pp. 139–46, Alfred O. Lanz, "'Zu Hause im Exil': Biographische Skizze über H. G. Adler," based on authorized interviews; *Jüdische Lebenswege—Nahum Goldmann, Simon Wiesenthal, H. G. Adler* (Frankfurt a. M.: Fischer, 1987); Alfred Otto Lanz, "*Panorama*" *von H. G. Adler—ein "Moderner Roman," "Panorama" als Minusverfahren des Entwicklungsromans und Negation der Möglichkeit rationaler Welterkenntnis* (Bern: Peter Lang, 1984), including complete bibliography, 1945–83; and Jürgen Serke, "H. G. Adler: Der versteinerte Jüngling, der ein weiser Mann wurde," in Serke, *Böhmische Dörfer: Wanderungen durch eine verlassene literarische Landschaft* (Vienna: Zsolnay, 1987), 326–43.

JEREMY ADLER

1944   Hannah Arendt writes "The Jew as Pariah: A Hidden Tradition," in which she describes the forgotten tradition of Jewish "conscious pariahs"

Between April 1944, when Hannah Arendt's "The Jew as Pariah: A Hidden Tradition" appeared in the periodical *Jewish Social Studies,* and the publication of her essay "Zionism Reconsidered" in October 1945, Arendt witnessed the collapse of the Nazi regime that had made her a refugee, and of the political cause that absorbed her considerable energies in American exile. If the full revelation of the Nazi crimes proved just how doomed was the "project" of German-Jewish assimilation, the enthusiasm for Jewish statehood apparent at the American Zionist Convention in Atlantic City (October 1944), which Arendt attended, marked for her a "turning point" in the history of Zionism, the triumph of Jewish nationalism.

From 1938, when she completed her biography of the assimilated German Jewess Rahel Varnhagen, to the chapter on "The Jews and Society" in her monumental *The Origins of Totalitarianism* (1951, 1966), Arendt frequently returned to the conceptual pairing of the "parvenu" and the "pariah" to explain the peculiar history and fate of modern German Jewry. The parvenu, who aped the behavior of the wealthy and aspired to an exclusive world of commerce and culture, and the self-conscious pariah, who lived in the authentic awareness that only an outsider embodies the humanity that society otherwise denies, form a central motif in her thinking. Modern Jewish history, with its reverence for the court Jews, wealthy patrons of the arts and culture, and for its exceptional geniuses, was, she claimed, "apt to forget" about the countertradition of the pariahs: Heinrich Heine, Rahel Varnhagen, Sholem Aleichem, Bernard Lazare, Franz Kafka, and even Charlie Chaplin. Paradoxically, the parvenu, who desperately cast off all traces of Jewishness by becoming the exception, only affirmed the abnormal status of the Jew, whereas the rebellious pariah held to the "vaunted Jewish qualities" of "Jewish heart, humanity, humor, disinterested intelligence" and thereby embodied a far more universal attitude (Arendt 1978, 66).

Over three decades Arendt's emphasis shifted, however, from her sympathetic but unsparing psychological portrait of the brilliant and self-reflective woman who played hostess to Berlin's literary and political high society at the beginning of the nineteenth century, to the 1944 essay on the ambiguous "worldlessness" of the modern Jewish artistic and political pariahs. In the late 1930s Arendt could still measure the parvenu by the standard of the pariah, whereas by the 1940s it became clear to her that the very aloofness from civil struggle and political conflict that characterized the social pariah had assumed the mask of tragedy. If the pariah could once retreat into the freedom granted to the outcast, "today," she concluded, "the bottom has dropped out of the old ideology. The pariah Jew and the *parvenu* Jew are in the same boat" (Arendt 1978, 90).

The theme was further refined a decade later when she delivered the more equitable judgment that from the standpoint of the Jewish Question neither the parvenu nor the pariah was capable of more than an "artificial solidarity" with the victims of anti-Semitism: "Jews felt simultaneously the pariah's regret at not having become a parvenu, and the parvenu's bad conscience at having betrayed his people and exchanged equal rights for personal privileges" (Arendt 1966, 66, 67).

Arendt's biographer, Elisabeth Young-Bruehl, describes how her experiences in exile in Paris, where she worked briefly for the Baroness Germaine de Rothschild, produced astonishment at the failure of the wealthy and educated Jews "to think politically, to realize the necessity for Jewish solidarity in the European—the world—crisis" (Young-Bruehl 1982, 121). This peculiar incapacity to understand the political implications of their situation had disastrous consequences: "Had the Jews of western and central European countries displayed even a modicum of concern for the political realities of their times, they would have had reason enough not to feel secure" (Arendt 1978, 115). According to Leon Botstein, "Arendt's basic theoretical claim, the separation of the social from the political, and her call for a return, in modern times, to the primacy of the political originated in her understanding of the Jewish problem as decisively political rather than social in character" (Botstein 1983, 76).

Kurt Blumenfeld, one of the most effective leaders of German Zionism since before World War I and Arendt's friend and political mentor, first introduced her to the distinction between the rebel pariah and the unpolitical parvenu during the 1930s. Blumenfeld found it in the writings of Bernard Lazare, the Dreyfusard and "conscious pariah," who for Arendt always represented the counterimage of the official Zionist politics "from above," most strongly personified in the figure of Theodor Herzl. According to Arendt, "Lazare came to realize the real obstacle in the path of his people's emancipation was not anti-Semitism. It was 'the demoralization of a people made up of the poor and downtrodden, who live on the alms of their wealthy brethren, a people revolted only by persecution from without but

not by oppression from within, revolutionaries in the society of others but not in their own'" (Arendt 1978, 129).

The distinction between the parvenu and the pariah framed Arendt's biography of the German-Jewish salonnière Rahel Varnhagen (née Levin), which she had begun in 1929 and finished in exile in 1938 at the urging of Walter Benjamin (her cousin by marriage) and her future husband, Heinrich Blücher. The book was finally published in the United States in 1957 under the title *Rahel Varnhagen: The Life of a Jewish Woman*. Many years later Arendt recalled that what made Rahel "interesting" to her is how much "with utter naiveté and utterly unprejudiced, she stands right in the middle between pariah and parvenu" (Arendt 1992, 200). The central dilemma of German Jewry in the age of emancipation was refracted through the life of this extraordinary woman in whose salon gathered the greats of the romantic era, and who practically single-handedly invented the Goethe cult of post-Napoleonic Berlin (Arendt 1966, 59). In Rahel, Arendt found a kindred spirit, "my closest friend, though she has been dead for some one hundred years" (Young-Bruehl 1982, 56). Rahel's "original, unspoiled, and unconventional intelligence, combined with an absorbing interest in people and a truly passionate nature, made her the most brilliant and interesting of these Jewish women" (Arendt 1966, 59). But, as the final two chapters of the book written in Paris reveal, Arendt also saw a darker, more painful dimension of a life spent in the vain struggle to overcome her Jewishness, only to end up affirming its best qualities. Rahel displayed all of the infirmities enacted by German Jews of the romantic era: "Nineteenth-century Jews, if they wanted to play a part in society, had no choice but to become parvenus par excellence" (Arendt 1974, 201). If her effort to ingratiate herself with gentile society was an expression of her sincere desire to "have some rank, to become a normal person, to possess social equality" (202), she recognized that the Jewish pariah became a parvenu only by sacrificing, concealing, and abandoning truth. By her marriage to the much younger gentile Varnhagen (whose career she promoted), by her baptism, and by her taking the Christian name Antonie Fredericke von Ense, Rahel officially erased her existence as a Jew while, secretly, "altogether inwardly," she revolted against her condition.

Rahel's "misfortune and the secret of her remarkable vivacity," Arendt claimed, was her inability to fully become the parvenu, and to abandon her qualities as a "pariah." Rahel's biography illustrated the great paradox of German-Jewish experience. Unable to see her condition except as a defect or symptom, she could never escape from her Jewishness. Despite what she had officially achieved, she could never "extinguish a past which had passionately anticipated, pierced to the heart of, judged and rejected everything possible" (Arendt 1974, 205). Yet, in her private agony, Rahel became the paradigm of human virtue, of dignity and perceptual acuity—she became uniquely capable of seeing life as a "whole." To become a parvenu, she had to "purchase social existence by sacrificing nature" by giving up her most human qualities, "and this Rahel was not prepared to do" (205).

For Arendt, the German-Jewish tendency to regard one's status as a psychological condition, or worse, as a natural destiny, rather than as a religious or political identity, made German-Jews both vulnerable to and complicit in the anti-Semitism that threatened their existence. The problem of Jewish existence was insoluble as a personal problem and could be grasped only in the political sphere. Despite the notable exceptions—the parvenus—the Jews became social pariahs "wherever they had ceased to be political and civil outcasts" (Arendt 1966, 62). Arendt summed up the dilemma of German Jewry: "Being a Jew could develop from a politico-social circumstance into a personal individual problem only for persons who for whatever reason equivocally wanted 'to be Jews and at the same time not be Jews'" (Arendt 1974, 221). Arendt's book had made a "great impression" on one of its first readers, Gershom Scholem, who remarked to Benjamin that "it swims with powerful strokes against the current of edifying and apologetic Judaic studies" (Scholem 1989, 245). Her activities for the Jewish Agency on behalf of the swelling numbers of desperate Jewish refugees arriv-

ing daily in France, however, and the threatening posture of the French government after 1939, were not particularly conducive to scholarship. In May 1940 Arendt was interred as an "enemy alien," along with several thousand German Jewish women, in the notorious camp at Gurs. She secured her liberation and eventual emigration to American only during the chaos that accompanied the fall of France.

In the early 1950s, when Arendt once again contemplated publishing the book on Rahel, she admitted that it was "particularly alien to me now" (Arendt 1992, 197). To her mentor and close friend, the philosopher Karl Jaspers, she acknowledged that the concepts of pariah and parvenu could only peripherally account for anti-Semitism, and she feared that if she now belatedly published the book "people of goodwill will see a connection, which does not in fact exist, between these things and the eradication of the Jews. All this was capable of fostering social hatred of the Jews and did foster it, just as it fostered on the other side a specifically German breed of Zionism." Even more importantly, Arendt admitted that it had been "written from the perspective of a Zionist critique of assimilation, which I had adopted as my own and which I still consider basically justified today. But that critique was as politically naive as what it was criticizing" (197).

Though Arendt's conclusions more than once vindicate Rahel's status as a pariah, critics found her too impatient with her subject's irrepressible desire to be the parvenu, "applying an 'ought' that was too consistently informed by hindsight" (Barnouw 1990, 67). Jaspers too had reacted to her intemperate tone, accusing her of "moralizing about Rahel." He also commented on the autobiographical dimension of the work, noting that it "still seems to me to be your own working through of the basic questions of Jewish existence, and in it you use Rahel's reality as a guide to help you achieve clarity and liberation for yourself" (Arendt 1992, 192). Arendt responded by confessing that "what I meant to do was argue further with her, the way she argued with herself, and always with the categories that were available to her and she somehow accepted as valid. In other words, I tried to measure and correct the parvenu by constantly applying the standards of the pariah because I felt that was her own method of proceeding" (200).

Arendt returned to the theme of the pariah in the spring of 1944, this time devoting fuller treatment to those "bold spirits who tried to make of the emancipation of the Jews that which it really should have been—an admission of Jews *as Jews* to the ranks of humanity" (Arendt 1978, 68). These Jewish poets, writers, and artists transformed their lack of concrete spiritual and political influence among Jews into a feat of imagination and vision, evolving the concept of the pariah "as a human type." By mapping a tradition from Heinrich Heine (the schlemiel and lord of dreams), to Bernard Lazare (the conscious pariah), to Charlie Chaplin (the suspect), and finally to Franz Kafka's "poetic vision of the man of goodwill," Arendt drew attention to the common thread that linked these outcasts: "In their own position as social outcasts such men reflect the political status of their entire people" (68).

Yet even if their art exerted a powerful influence on the gentile world, these pariahs most keenly appreciated "just how ambiguous is the freedom which emancipation has ensured, and how treacherous the promise of equality which assimilation has held out" (Arendt 1978, 68). The "gay, insouciant impudence" of Heine's schlemiel shares the joys and sorrows of the common people, especially because what Rahel called "the true realities" has no place in the social and political world. But Heine's mockery of social conventions is also marked by aloofness and by a remoteness and distance from the world. The pariah's poetic clarity is the transformation of pariahdom into a vision of freedom that could ignore the facts of emancipation as they existed at the time. By contrast, Bernard Lazare, whom Arendt called the first Jew to perceive the "disastrous" connection between the hostility of his surrounding environment and the complicity of "his own highly-placed brethren," also failed because the social pariah refused to become a rebel and enter the arena of politics. Consequently, as Chaplin's comedy revealed, the Jew retained the sublime innocence of the schlemiel in an increasingly dangerous world, a world that Kafka described as

having eliminated the two Jewish modes of "escape," artistic detachment and political rebellion. For Kafka, whose Zionism was not incidental, the pariah discovers that the Jewish desire for normal existence is no longer possible in a society that is no longer human. Kafka's sense of entrapment expressed the truth that "neither the freedom of the schlemiel and poet nor the innocence of the suspect nor the escape into nature and art, but thinking is the new weapon—the only one with which, in Kafka's opinion, the pariah is endowed at birth in his vital struggle against society" (Arendt 1978, 83). It was not coincidental that her praise for the countertradition of the pariah occurred at the time of her deepest disappointment with Zionist politics. The pariah's social nonconformism, which she once called "the *sine qua non* of intellectual achievement," was still a source of inspiration.

During the mid 1940s Arendt came to regard modern Jewish history as framed by two movements, assimilationism and Zionism, each of which were products of anti-Semitism, and neither of which was capable of confronting it directly. Assimilation, she wrote in 1943, had a "'deep' philosophical meaning," it did not simply mean accommodation to a particular country, but rather an adjustment "in principle to everything and everybody" (Arendt 1978, 63). The purported harmony between Jews and their host nations had done little to erase their pariah qualities. Instead, "it performed an unprecedented feat: though proving all the time their non-Jewishness, they succeeded in remaining Jews all the same" (64). For Arendt, the price of this self-deception was political vulnerability, exposure to political caprice, and social discrimination: "It has been the mark of assimilated Jews," she argued, "to be unable to distinguish between friend and enemy, between compliment and insult, and to feel flattered when an anti-Semite assures them that he does not mean them, that they are exceptions—exceptional Jews" (Arendt 1992, 60).

Whereas assimilation proved a costly illusion, Zionism proposed no effective solution to the Jewish Question except to assert "the eternal anti-Semitism" of European humanity as an intractable problem that could be solved only by

recourse to a "one-sided interest in foreign politics." "Thus," Arendt concluded, "both sides relieved themselves of the arduous task of fighting
anti-Semitism on its own grounds, which were
political" (Arendt 1992, 142).

This assessment, which made the struggle of
the pariah against the parvenu paramount in Arendt's evaluation of political Zionism, also helps
account for her devotion to the cause of establishing a Jewish army composed of Jews of different
nations, to fight in "Jewish formations," and under a "Jewish flag." This campaign began in the
fall of 1941 and ended a year and a half later when
the idea was rejected by the Zionist leadership (in
favor of a Jewish brigade in the British Army).
The proposal that Jews be allowed to take up
arms against the Nazis as part of a supranational
military force was predicated on her conviction
that Jews would henceforth be responsible for
their own political powerlessness, that they had
to mount a political response to anti-Semitism,
and that only military participation would secure
the Jews a place in the peacetime order. Zionism
was important to her not because of its assertions
of Jewish nationhood, but because it asserted the
central fact that Jews could respond to anti-Semitism only as Jews, not as Germans or universal
citizens. The "Jewish people," she wrote, "is just
beginning to comprehend a truth heretofore unknown to it, that *one can only defend oneself as that
for which one has been attacked*" (Arendt 1989,
168). The fight to establish a Jewish army was
conceived by Arendt as an inner-Jewish campaign of the pariah people against its parvenu
leaders, whom she derisively referred to as "the
schnorrer and philanthropist International."

Arendt's disappointment with the Zionist
movement, her refusal to acquiesce in the formation of a Jewish state, and her insistence that as
the pariah people par excellence Jews bore a degree of responsibility for their collective destiny
confirmed her conviction that neither official Zionism, embodied in the ideas of Theodor Herzl
and the "practical" policies of Chaim Weizmann,
nor the cultural and social Zionists who "did succeed in creating a new type of Jew" were able to
offer "a single new slogan in the wide field of
Jewish politics" (Arendt 1992, 139). Through

Blumenfeld, Arendt had visited Palestine (1935)
as part of her work in Paris as director of the
Youth Aliyah. At the time, she was strongly impressed by Blumenfeld's vision of a "community
of peoples" built on tolerance and cooperation
between Jews and Arabs. When Blumenfeld supported David Ben-Gurion's endorsement of a
Jewish state under minority rule in 1942, Arendt
realized how much Zionist opinion had changed.
By calling for a Jewish state in Palestine, Jewish
leaders had, she believed, "abdicated" political
leadership to the Zionists and dealt a "deadly
blow" to those who desired "the necessity of an
understanding between the Arab and Jewish
peoples" (131).

In placing their hopes in the "Great Powers,"
Zionists forfeited all possibility of a political solution to reconciling Jewish and Arab demands.
Opting for a nationalist solution that solved the
"tragic conflict" by partition, Jewish leaders unwittingly provided anti-Semitism with a new
justification in regarding Jews as pulling the
strings of imperialist politics. This marked the
finale for Arendt's ideal of a Jewish nation—one
that existed within the framework of other nations but shared equal rights and equal status—a
vision that she thought could provide a model for
a political community that transcended the
bounds of the nation-state. After the Atlantic
City convention in October 1944, she broke
openly with what she regarded as the triumph of
the revisionist program.

Predictably, Blumenfeld reacted bitterly to
Arendt's critique of Zionism: he called her remarks a betrayal of the Jews in their hour of need.
From his perspective, her understanding of the
situation in Palestine as a "political-historical"
problem, as opposed to a "metaphysical-existen-
tial" problem, demonstrated that her judgments,
coming from abroad, were "totally indifferent"
and heartless" (Barnouw 1990, 112). Perhaps as a
response, and as a reminder that in the past
Blumenfeld had once considered the pariah perspective "useful, even essential" (119), Arendt
wrote her most substantive treatment of the concept during their painful rupture of relations.

Recently, social historians have reinterpreted
Arendt's negative picture of the Jewish entry into

German society as having been too starkly composed, too unchanging, and too one-sided. The concepts of parvenu and pariah, though providing an accurate snapshot of the conflicts that the Berlin Jews of Rahel's generation experienced, do not alone do justice to the economic and cultural successes of Jewish acculturation into the German bourgeoisie between 1800 and 1870. Arendt's judgment, colored by the "dark times" of the 1930s, was too hostile both to the Enlightenment and to the many dimensions of Jewish assimilation. She vastly underestimated the complex ways that German Jews, as Shulamit Volkov has shown, achieved full civil rights and became part of the educated bourgeoisie.

Arendt's focus on the parvenu also exaggerated the negative aspects of social climbing at the expense of *Bildung*, the German-Jewish path to acculturation made possible by the Enlightenment. Her viewpoint misses how much the eighteenth-century cult of friendship—including friendships between Jews and non-Jews, as George Mosse has shown—"was part of the ideal of *Bildung* itself" (Mosse 1985, 10). As Jaspers recognized, Arendt's depiction of the German Enlightenment "not only underplays it but also distorts it" (Arendt 1992, 193). The complex patterns of cultural absorption and religious distinction that different generations of German Jews negotiated are not discernible in what can be seen as a more specifically Jewish version of her teacher Martin Heidegger's famous distinction between inauthentic and authentic being.

In her 1944 essay, Arendt also acknowledged her debt to Max Weber's portrait of the Jews of the "scriptural age" as a pariah people. Though she did not choose to comment on the parallels, Weber's "story tellers, actors in a cultic masquerade, and gnostic intellectuals" in many ways prefigured Arendt's modern social pariah. In his *Ancient Judaism* (1917–19), Weber described how the Jews, after suffering the loss of their territory and exile, ultimately substituted confessional and ethical segregation for "political separation" as a guest people (*Gastvolk*). Unlike the Indian pariahs, whose existence was tied to a rigid caste system, the Jewish pariah was separated from the indigenous host peoples by certain "ritual barriers," either self-imposed or externally dictated. In this cultural and historical situation, the "ethos" of biblical Jewry combined social exclusion and otherworldliness with ethical absolutism and a rational orientation toward the daily affairs of the community. The status of the Jewish pariah was shaped by the experience of voluntary segregation, by strict observance of the Torah and its rituals, and by the prophetic "theodicy of Israel's suffering in the universal perspective of a wise and divine world government" (Weber 1952, 375).

The "otherworldliness" of the pariah was reinforced by social insularity and expressed in an exclusive theodicy that was profoundly indifferent to the surrounding gods and nations. Through the "the mighty pathos of eschatological threats and promises" (Weber 1952, 295), the Hebrew prophets secured the continued existence of the Jewish community in exile by giving "religious cohesion to a politically destroyed community." From Isaiah to Ezekiel, "prophetic politics" alternated between utopian expectation of future redemption and catastrophic foreboding, resulting in what Weber called a "tarrying mood," characterized by the "utopian world indifference of the prophets" (327).

Just three years after Arendt published "The Jew as Pariah," the philosopher Karl Jaspers published a small but powerful appeal to Germans to confront their responsibility for the crimes of the Nazi regime, entitled *Die Schuldfrage* (The question of German guilt). In this first and only publication of its kind in immediate postwar Germany, Jaspers too invoked the theme of the pariah. But this time, in an astonishing reversal, the Germans had become a people deprived of their national existence and excluded from the community of nations because of the enormous suffering they had inflicted on others—above all, the Jews. In a striking transposition of Arendt's image of the Jewish pariah coming to self-consciousness through social exclusion and alienation, the status of pariahdom became Jaspers's recipe for the Germans. As Weber and Arendt had demonstrated, social isolation was not without its benefits: exclusion from power was a powerful impulse to private humanity. With their state destroyed, their country under foreign rule, their leaders in flight or in custody, Germans now occupied a position not unlike the one occupied by the Jews—in an ironic twist, they had begun their own political diaspora. *Die Schuldfrage* is an attempt to provide a guide to the wanderings of the German spirit in this new incarnation as a stateless specter. As Weber admired the "tarrying endurance" of the Jews in exile as the path to inner purity and collective redemption, his student Jaspers conceived of the problem of moral self-education and "cleansing" as a "wager." If it fails, the pariah condition might become permanent; permanent loss of sovereignty and the exclusion of Germany from the world community. Jaspers warned of the consequence of not accomplishing this task: "This path is the only one which might protect our soul from a pariah existence" (Jaspers 1965, 10).

The specter of the pariah was again raised in the 1960s, during the storm of controversy that followed the publication Arendt's *Eichmann in Jerusalem: A Report on the Banality of Evil,* which first appeared in *The New Yorker* in 1963. Although Arendt's critics often focused on her "somewhat cavalier attitude with facts" (Laqueur in Arendt 1978, 255), at the center of the tempestuous dispute was her contemptuous attitude toward the role of the Israeli government in presenting the case, her portrait of Eichmann as a banal functionary, and above all, her assertion that Jews had been complicitous in their own destruction. According to her most persistent antagonist, Jacob Robinson, Arendt had now placed herself among the "enemies" of the Jews, a judgment echoed by Scholem as well. In his *New York Times* review, Michael Musmanno (who had been on the prosecution team at Nuremberg) wrote that her descriptions of the trial were so often at variance with the facts that "it can hardly be accepted as an authoritative historical work," and that her "scorn" for Prime Minister Ben-Gurion and Israel was evidence of "purely private prejudices" (1963).

As Botstein points out, those prejudices were made all the more egregious by Arendt's far more positive and appreciative views on American public life and its rejection of identity as the basis of citizenship: "By 1951 her increasing sense of comfort in America made her even more doubtful about Zionism. The implicit America-Israel contrast evident in *Eichmann in Jerusalem* culminated that process" (Botstein 1983, 92). Nonetheless, as Laqueur wrote in his somewhat more judicious review of the controversy, the outcry over her book was also caused by the fact that she had stumbled on the intricate and painful but nonetheless real problem—the complex spectrum of Jewish behavior from heroism and resistance to betrayal and collaboration in the Holocaust. The Eichmann affair made Arendt a pariah among the Jews. Not unlike the scandal provoked by Philip Roth's *Portnoy's Complaint,* published four years later, her openly critical attitude toward Jewish behavior was anathema to a still anxious minority. Ironically, the Eichmann affair and the debate over Roth's novel also may have marked the point when, as the civil rights movement was bringing the truly disenfranchised American minority into public consciousness, Jewish pariah status ceased to be publicly meaningful. Racism, not anti-Semitism, was the American issue, and American Jews, however much they might warn of the dangers of complacency, could consider themselves part of the majority. By 1966 Arendt's exchanges with her critics had diminished in intensity. As she wrote to Jaspers: "I think the war between me and the Jews is over" (Arendt 1992, 632).

Bibliography

Hannah Arendt, *Eichmann in Jerusalem: A Report on the Banality of Evil,* 2d ed. (New York: Viking Penguin, 1965); Arendt, *Essays in Understanding, 1930–1952,* ed. Jerome Kohn (New York: Harcourt Brace, 1994); Arendt, *Hannah Arendt–Karl Jaspers Correspondence, 1926–1969,* ed. Lotte Kohler and Hans Saner, trans. Robert and Rita Kimber (New York: Harcourt Brace Jovanovich, 1992); Arendt, *The Jew as Pariah: Jewish Identity and Politics in the Modern Age,* ed. Ron H. Feldman (New York: Grove Press, 1978); Arendt, *Die Krise des Zionismus: Essays & Kommentare,* ed. Eike Geisel and Klaus Bittermann (Berlin: Edition Tiamat, 1989); Arendt, *The Origins of Totalitarianism* (New York: Harcourt Brace Jovanovich, 1966); Arendt, *Rahel Varnhagen: The Life of a Jewish Woman,* trans. Richard and Clara Winston (New York: Harcourt Brace Jovanovich, 1974); Dagmar Barnouw, *Visible Spaces: Hannah Arendt and the German-Jewish Experience* (Baltimore, Md.: Johns Hopkins University Press, 1990); Seyla Benhabib, "Der Paria und sein Schatten: Über die Unsichtbarkeit der Frau in Hannah Arendts politischer Philosophie," *Babylon: Beiträge zur jüdischen Gegenwart* 9 (1991): 95–108; Leon Botstein, "Liberating the Pariah: Politics, the Jews, and Hannah Arendt," *Salmagundi* 60 (spring / summer 1983): 73–106; Margaret Canovan, *Hannah Arendt: A Reinterpretation of Her Political Thought* (Cambridge: Cambridge University Press, 1992); Karl Jaspers, *Die Schuldfrage* (Munich: Piper, 1965); Walter Z. Laqueur, "Footnotes to the Holocaust," *New York Review of Books* (Nov. 11, 1965), in *The Jew as Pariah,* 252–59; Bernard Lazare, *Job's Dungheap,* ed. Hannah Arendt (New York: Schocken, 1949); George L. Mosse, *German Jews Beyond Judaism* (Bloomington: Indiana University Press, 1985); Michael A. Musmanno, "Review of 'Eichmann in Jerusalem,'" *New York Times Book Review* (May 19, 1963); Gershom Scholem, ed., *The Correspondence of Walter Benjamin and Gershom Scholem, 1932–1940* (New York: Schocken, 1989); Shulamit Volkov, *Jüdisches Leben und Antisemitismus im 19. und 20. Jahrhundert* (Munich: C. H. Beck, 1990); Max Weber, *Ancient Judaism,* ed. and trans. Hans H. Gerth and Don Martindale (New York: Free Press, 1952); and Elisabeth Young-Bruehl, *Hannah Arendt: For Love of the World* (New Haven: Yale University Press, 1982).

ANSON RABINBACH

1944 Jewish writing in German continues in Theresienstadt and beyond

In the early summer of 1944, a poetry competition held as part of the officially sanctioned cultural activities attracted 3,000 entries of German verse from the more than 30,000 inmates of Terezin—or Theresienstadt, to use the revived Germanic name originally given the town by Joseph II in 1730 when it was founded. Klopstock had immortalized Joseph II in his "Song of Praise to the Emperor" with the words "You made the Jew a man." In November 1941, however, Jewish men were being made prisoners in Theresienstadt, initially men from the so-called Protectorate. Before the year was out, it became the destination also for Jewish women, and by the spring of 1942 German and Austrian Jews were arriving, many of them prominent leaders in the Jewish community—artists, industrialists, and decorated military veterans. They had been promised a safe retreat in the quiet garrison town; some had even made down-payments on apartments, requesting rooms with a southern exposure.

Despite the cultural activities that began to flourish in the spring of 1943, Jews faced two major adjustments in Theresienstadt beyond the obvious shock that this was not what had been promised: hard manual labor on a starvation diet with little sleep in overcrowded, lice-ridden barracks, and the threat of being transported elsewhere. Around 33,000 did not survive the first threat. Of those who did survive, 88,000 were transported from Theresienstadt to camps in the east, and of these people, only 3,500 survived. By 1944 Theresienstadt had been exposed for what it really was—the "ante-room to Auschwitz." This was the central anguish around which life (including cultural activities), revolved. Theresienstadt was more than a destination; it was a departure point. Two stanzas of Ilse Blumenthal-Weiß's poem "Bunter Abend" (Variety evening; translated in Schwertfeger 1989, 70) underscore the reality of the latter:

It's curtain time: Faces change to poses
Before an audience acting like it's home.
On stage they dance and sing and twirl
And kill the sadness with the theater's wings. . . .
The curtain falls: on empty floorboards
Vermin keeps on eating mind and limb.
To-morrow's dawn will bring another call
To stagger towards the slaughter-rail for
Transport.

Although "Variety Evening" is an accurate description of camp reality, this poem was written *after* the liberation of the camp (it was published in *Mahnmal* in 1960). The sources used in this essay are for the most part drawn from poetry and diaries written *in* the camps, in deference to the troubling preposition "in"—in the title's "Jewish writing in Theresienstadt." The issue has been addressed by Alvin Rosenfeld, among others, about the advisability of imposing a theory of aesthetic autonomy on camp literature. If it is hard to evaluate the writings "born of terror and silence" (as Ellen Fine calls them, quoted in Moll 1988, 38), the challenge to approach the work that predates and presages such writings is even more daunting. What was written in the camps has been largely marginalized by what was written after the camps—by writers like Paul Celan, Nelly Sachs, and Jean Améry—and assigned to a different kind of "Lebenstraum" than has any other body of writings in German literature.

"The year zero" (1945) may have defined new beginnings for German literary history, but it also elided the years, and especially the year that preceded it. Painful as it is, there is a modest body of camp writings—fragmentary, narrow in its themes, limited in genre—that were recorded in German by Jewish men and women, most of whom were not known as writers then—or after. Their work includes lyric poetry written in Auschwitz long before the painful struggle to define an aesthetic for Holocaust writings and certainly before the debate about the appropriateness of writing poetry after Auschwitz.

With the exception of two lyrical dramas written in Theresienstadt by Georg Kafka (a distant relative of Franz Kafka), the two genres that dominate all camp writings are the diary and the poem. The medical journals of Theresienstadt, compiled from the findings of hundreds of physicians interned there, constitute a special category of writings for which the term "medicina Theresiana" was coined by Professor Alfred Wolff-Eisner (Scheuer 1983, 53). Apart from these writings, there were also recipes and numerous jottings, including detailed descriptions (by Werner Weinberg in Bergen-Belsen) about transports and the size of barracks. Drama and fiction (like *The Terezin Requiem* by the Czech writer Josef Bor) would come later: like all postcamp literature, it underwent a painful birth.

Many of the poems composed in Theresienstadt were written for birthdays and other special occasions in relentlessly rhymed, stilted German that H. G. Adler called "rhyming sickness" (Adler 1960, 618). They are the literary equivalent of the art that depicted Theresienstadt as benign. The year 1944 is a culminating point around which to organize camp writings not because more (or less) was written then than in the other twelve years of the Third Reich but because what was written pulsates with the excruciating rawness of the Final Solution. Theresienstadt of 1944 is an appropriate *Ausgangspunkt* (starting point) not only in the literal sense but also as a stage on which the German-Jewish symbiosis was played out. Adler describes the German Jews of Theresienstadt as living in a false sense of their identity: "An advanced state of assimilation was taking bitter revenge on them. . . . The Germany of 1942 often seemed to these people to be that of 1900" (304). He also points out: "In Auschwitz sheer despair was supreme, and the reality of the situation was unambiguously recognized. . . . It was not that way in Theresienstadt, where almost anything could be repressed, where illusion ran rampant and hope, merely dampened by anxiety suffused everything that lay under thick fog" (82).

The most overt expression of what Adler perceived as "rampant illusion" was the daily rostrum of literary readings and cultural activities in the attics, at the end of what had become by 1944 a seventy-hour work week. Though long since expelled from German life, Jews did not jettison their cultural heritage in these deplorable camp conditions. There were lectures on Hegel, Kant, Hesse, and seminars on Faust by scholars in the sciences and in the humanities described by one woman—Alice Bloemendahl—as "guardians of the best of the European past, architects of a future that was fit for people to live in" (Bloemendahl n.d., 1). Even though lectures could not be titled "Jews in German literature" but only "German-speaking-Jews in literature," a German cultural heritage was invoked that was, in fact, more reminiscent of Germany at the turn of the century. For the German Jews of Theresienstadt, however, it was a bulwark against the stultifying daily life of the camp, which included the linguistic assault on the German language in the form of "Lagerdeutsch"—camp German that was rapidly evolving its own vocabulary.

Several diaries written "beyond Theresienstadt" suggest a German consciousness, but it is represented in terms more of erudition than of heritage. Quotations from prominent German writers—mostly non-Jewish—preface several diaries. (The most striking use of German writers in a diary is, of course, *Goethe in Dachau* by Nico Rost, the Dutch "Germanist," a political prisoner in Dachau.) Renate Laquer wrote her diary in Dutch in Bergen-Belsen and prefaces it with a quote from Goethe: "What I have, I see as if from afar and what disappeared has become reality." Ruth Klüger wrote about reciting ballads by Schiller to overcome the tedium of endless hours standing for roll call in Auschwitz. In 1944 Victor Frank quoted Nietzsche to his fellow prisoners and taught them that life has meaning. In Bergen-Belsen, a diary written in 1944 by a Frau Zielenziger is prefaced with a line from Rilke: "And courage has become so tired, and longing so great." There is, however, no equivalent in other camps for intellectuals (like Rabbi Leo Baeck) who were harnessed to hearses that were used as bread carts, and who discussed German philosophers as they pulled the carts through Theresienstadt.

Gershom Scholem perceives Freud, Kafka, and Benjamin as Jews who wrote with the full consciousness of the distance that separated them from their German readers; they knew they were German writers but that they were not Germans (Scholem 1986, 277). The Theresienstadt of 1944 not only crushed the German-Jewish identity; the problematic ambivalence was also crushed. There were 60,000 books in the library at Theresienstadt, confiscated from incoming transports, but by 1944 most of the librarians that had catalogued them had been sent to Auschwitz. The Red Cross visited in June; its representatives were restricted to areas of the town that had been beautified for the occasion. Several thousand elderly people, however, were transported to achieve the desired effect. A film was made that became known as "The Führer Gives the Gift of a City to the Jews," but the film producers were sent to Auschwitz after it had been made. The effect of this clash of illusion and reality is most clearly seen in the memoirs written after the liberation of the camp, which reveal a strong consciousness of alienation from a German-Jewish identity.

Diaries written in 1944 reveal an extraordinary mobility between ghettos, transit camps, work camps, and extermination sites, as Jews were systematically flushed from one level of expendability to another. The ability to do manual labor, mostly for the war industry, became the only reason to allow them to live—30 percent of the inmates did manual labor in Auschwitz (Kröhle 1989, 36). Experiences are documented that cover a geographical area that stretched from Les Milles in Provence to Auschwitz. One of the most cruel ironies is that Bergen-Belsen in 1944 was named an "Erholungslager" (recuperation camp) for those who were literally too ill to work; many died of thirst and starvation there. Of the 15,257 inmates at Bergen-Belsen in December 1944, around 8,000 of them were women and girls, among them Anne Frank, who died there in March 1945 (Kolb 1991, 37).

Auschwitz and its satellite camps were the epicenter of the German concentration camps, as Eugene Kogon later noted. Before it entered into symbolic language as a metaphor for unspeakable suffering, Auschwitz was a railway station. (There is a sense in which it has been frozen in that image.) At least, that is how an Austrian woman describes her first impressions when she arrived there in May 1944 from Drancy: "I press my nose against one of the cracks and read 'Auschwitz.' The name means nothing to me. A short time later we are at another little station and this time I read 'Birkenau.' We stop. The chains rattle. A crack opens" (Naor 1986, 31). Max Mannheimer remembers spending a vacation in Auschwitz as a teenager. The memory suddenly comes back when he is carting cement down the main street of the town: "I recognize the street again. As a sixteen year-old I spent a vacation there: . . . in an Auschwitz without barbed wire and gas chambers" (Mannheimer 1985, 113).

The word "Auschwitz" hangs like a huge shroud over camp memoirs, evoking a sense of terror that no other word can generate. Transports to the east were the dread of Theresienstadt, and by the autumn of 1944 not even the Jewish elders were spared. These transports began in the autumn of 1944—eleven of them between September 28 and October 28. Of a population of 11,804 men only 5,000 were left, and more and more women were pulled into the labor force. Trude Groag describes parting from her mother: "Then my mother's name was called. She walked with their head held high to the transport truck. She stood to the front when she got on. A thick, cold, damp mist enveloped everything. . . . In a few seconds a world of love had been swallowed up" (Groag n.d., 16). The first stanza of "Transport" (Schwertfeger 1989, 88), the poem Else Dormitzer wrote in Theresienstadt, reads:

Running, whispers, anxious questioning
In drab September days,
Here a querulous complaint, there quiet
   quavering,
A whole city is on its legs,
In every mouth a single expression stays;
Transport.

When Auschwitz is seen from the perspective of another camp—Dachau—the effect is even more alienating. Max Mannheimer was twenty-three when he arrived in Auschwitz in February 1943. He recorded his impressions in a diary he began to write later in Dachau: "It is the beginning of February without a coat. Without a hat. Without food. Without parents. Without siblings, wives. Without a home. Without help. Without hope" (Mannheimer 1985, 104). The same note of despair using a different word—*außerhalb* (outside)—is captured in the diary the Dutch lawyer Eberhard Kolb wrote in Bergen-Belsen: "It is now 1944 and there is still no end in sight. We stand outside of time, outside of life, outside of space" (Kolb 1991, 74). In the summer of 1944 Max Mannheimer was en route by foot to the west from Warsaw, before boarding a freight train in Kuvno with ninety prisoners: "We ask for water. A prisoner breaks off a gold filling from his tooth. He receives water for it. Gold for water" (125). In the train they are pushed and shoved together and beaten. "It does not help. The space does not get any bigger" (125). They finally arrive in Dachau and are renumbered: "Numbered three times and yet still alive" (125).

In Auschwitz Simha Naor wrote: "It is around Christmas time, 1944. Holidays are particularly loved by Mengele to make selections" (Naor 1986, 109). She is advised by the guard, a fellow-Austrian, that she must never show any emotion, never resist beatings, always give her age as younger, and destroy all personal documents. She further describes how she is tattooed with a red-hot needle dipped in blue ink (36). She sees the chimneys but does not want to believe that people are gassed there. Tea is described as "a dark grey, bitter-tasting, luke-warm liquid" (49).

Rosenfeld thinks it would be a misapplication of methods to search in ghetto and camp writings for "revealing patterns of imagery and symbolism, mythic analogies, or deep grammatical structures" (1980, 18). My observation is that there is no flatter prose landscape than that of camp writings, their chillingly laconic style broken only by even bleaker reminders of destruction, often captured in the word "Auschwitz." In Ravensbrück there was a little girl called Anna Horvath, motherless, her dad in Dachau. Women made up letters from her dad to comfort the child, who cried at night. Then comes the sentence: "Later she went with an annihilation transport to Auschwitz" (Buchmann 1959, 133). "September, 1944," writes Lisa Scheuer, "a really strange atmosphere hangs over this place." Scheuer writes about the stench, the smoke arising from the stacks, the brass bands, and the hum of the telegraph wires (35). Gerty Spies tells about the generosity of a woman called Heidi, who shared her very first food parcel with the twenty-five other women in her room, but then Spies adds (parenthetically) that Heidi later perished in Auschwitz.

Understatement and irony are also used, albeit unwittingly, and serve to underscore the total collapse of moral order. Simha Naor, employed as a physical therapist in Auschwitz, is assigned to the barracks that housed the criminals. She writes matter-of-factly: "I soon feel at home in this block among the criminals" (1986, 84). She records the pride expressed by her fellow inmates in their past crimes, which ranged from murdering a mother-in-law to burning down a friend's house. Justifying these crimes by standards practiced in the Reich they ask: "What's wrong with a little private murder?" When Naor points out that many are being murdered in Auschwitz by gas, she is promptly interrupted with "It's quite different here. Those are Jews, but after all, we are Aryans" (Naor 1986, 105). Another example in Naor's prose is her description of her first impressions of Bergen-Belsen. She writes: "Here people are dying of natural causes" (114). (In the last months thousands died of thirst.) Margarete Glass-Larsson did not write her memoir until the late 1970s, but there is one line that is as clear as the day it was said in Theresienstadt: "Carry me outside so that I can see the sky and a tree." The request was made by a terminally ill woman in the last moments of her life. The writer then adds: "So now there was one fewer in the cell" (Schwertfeger 1989, 55).

At times the grammatical structure of the camp diary evokes the tempo of the work being done. When that work is in a crematorium, the effect on the tone of the diary is shocking, as in the diary kept by Arnold Keller and Hans Horwitz in Bergen-Belsen between March 8 and April 16, 1944. They wrote: "After touching a corpse, immediately wash your hands. . . . Up with the coffin, lay the corpse on an iron bier and push it into the oven on two rollers; up it goes, doors open, push the corpse in, close the doors, wash your hands" (Keller and Horwitz 1944, 3).

Everything that was written in the camps bears the stamp of the fragmentary and the clandestine, whether written on scraps of paper and concealed in empty Zyklon B canisters in Auschwitz; smuggled from one barrack to the other in Quark (a kind of cottage cheese) in Bergen-Belsen; thrown from the train en route from Westerbork to Auschwitz (like the letter by Etty Hillesum); scribbled on toilet paper, as was the case for the Dutch Germanist Nico Rost in Dachau; or hidden, such as the work by Lisa Scheuer concealed in the hole dug for excrement behind the barracks of the Freiberg labor camp. Thomas Rahe sees the fragmentary aspect of camp writings as the formal correspondence to the reality that was being experienced; the diary was the best way to document for posterity lives that had been deprived of meaning (1994, 201). Diaries were written at great risk and enormous personal sacrifice, typically at the end of the day;

to borrow from Hopkins, they "bear man's smudge and wear man's toil." Malnutrition deprived inmates of energy and the ability to concentrate for long. Bread was frequently bartered in exchange for a pencil or a piece of paper.

By the early summer of 1944, rumors, called "bonkes" in Theresienstadt, were already infiltrating the camp that the Russians were at the door. The Bergen-Belsen inmates knew about the Normandy landings in June. There are tired, veiled references to the outside world in diary entries, a world that had been challenged to respond to the camps in the spring of 1944 by a detailed document with maps and diagrams of Auschwitz, prepared by two Slovakian Jews who had escaped (Rudolf Vrba and Fred Wetzlar). The document circulated in the highest quarters—including to Churchill, Roosevelt, and the pope—provided information on the mass extermination of Hungarian Jews.

Beyond news from the outside there are occasionally shafts of light and life that penetrate the camp writings, but they merely expose the darkness rather than mitigate it. Scheuer noted in her diary the beauty of the mountains surrounding Mauthausen. Resi Weglein wrote of hearing nightingales sing as she sat at an open window on the night shift. Little Pavel Friedmann's butterfly—"the last butterfly"—is a fragile reminder of life beyond Theresienstadt. He wrote, "It went away, I'm sure, because it wished to / kiss the world goodbye." Rising above Ilse Weber's heartbreaking letter-poem to the child she sent to safety in Sweden is the tentative arc of praise: "Yet I am glad that you are not here." The distinguished art historian Gertrud Kantorowicz wrote "Daughter of the Day" sometime before before she died in Theresienstadt in 1945. The first stanza reads: "And so you fade. The step of hours is halting. / No laughter gives its hem to our weeks gravenes's, / So you have learned to walk dark halls where / living light and flower can only flutter" (Schwertfeger 1989, 71).

We now know that Gertrud Kolmar died in Auschwitz, just as she had said in the poem "Nachruf" (Obituary) written between 1937 and 1940: "I shall die, like all the others / . . . And be dead, disappear completely, a nothing" (Schlösser 1960, 153). In another poem written around this time, she writes about the steps to her father's house being "dark, crooked, narrow and worndown." Else Lasker-Schüler in *Mein Blaues Klavier* (My blue piano) also mourns in her Jerusalem exile the collapse of aesthetic order—rats waltzing on the broken keyboard of a blue piano "near the cellar door." Twenty years after his internment in the camps Jean Améry wrote about the total collapse of an aesthetic idea of death. Grete Schmal-Wolf, dying in Theresienstadt, would have agreed. Two days before she died she wrote on a scrap of paper:

Dying means nothing here
In these sad and gloomy rooms.
One stretch and you are free from hunger,
Hate and hopes and dreams.
Nobody weeps. Nobody prays.
There is neither touching nor mourning.
Just like a leaf that falls from its branch
Death has here no meaning.
Neighbours look with quiet calm
On the corpse with its doll-like wrapping
Another death. So what?
And stolidly keep on eating.
They think Good for him. Keep slicing
In case they miss a crumb.
Then the stretcher comes. That's what dying
Means in these sad and gloomy rooms
                    (Schwertfeger 1989, 54).

As wretched a picture as this is of an impersonal death, it does not evoke the sheer awfulness of Ruth Klüger's "Der Kamin" (The chimney), the poem the thirteen-year-old composed in Auschwitz in 1944 and wrote down later in Christianstadt, one of the satellite camps of Groß Rosen. Her poem also serves to underscore the distance between Theresienstadt and Auschwitz, between the anteroom and hell. Truth for Klüger had been reduced to the chimney: "Everything, everything lies in its hand / Everything, everything will be burned." Nelly Sachs was to mourn the loss of Jewish life through those same chimneys in lines that overarch the literature of the Holocaust and have entered into the poetic language of the twentieth century. The diaries and poems of the camps have found no such entrée. Eli Wiesel has written that a story about Treblinka is either not a story or not a story about Treblinka. Survivors wrote about their past, about the time before the annihilation, but not about the annihilation. He writes: "You can't write about that— not if you are a writer" (Wiesel 1977, 25). But some (like Richard Glazar) did write, and they were not writers. Their writings occupy a peninsula-like territory—one attached and related to the mainland of German history and literature and approached by way of dark, crooked, narrow steps.

Bibliography

H. G. Adler, *Das Antlitz einer Zwangsgemeinschaft* (Tübingen: Mohr, 1960); Alice Bloemendahl, "Theresienstadt einmal anders," Yad Vashem Archives, Jerusalem, n.d., box 02, file 4542; Erika Buchmann, *Die Frauen von Ravensbrück* (Berlin: Kongress-Verlag, 1959); Richard Glazar, *Die Falle mit dem grünen Zaun* (Frankfurt a. M.: Fischer, 1992); Trude Groag, "Namen und Ortschaften in Erinnerungen der Frau Trude Groag," Yad Vashem Archives, Jerusalem, n.d., 03/3938; Dorothea Heiser, ed., *Mein Schatten in Dachau* (Munich: Pfeiffer, 1993); Miroslav Karny, Vojtech Blodig, and Margita Karna, eds., *Theresienstadt in der "Endlösung" der Judenfrage* (Prague: Panorama, 1992); Arnold Keller and Hans Horwitz, "Tagebuch aus dem Lager Bergen-Belsen," Bergen-Belsen Archives, 1944; Ruth Klüger, *Weiter lehen: Eine Jugend* (Göttingen: Wallstein, 1992); Eberhard Kolb, *Bergen-Belsen, 1943– 45* (Göttingen: Vandenhoek, 1991); Brigitte Kröhle, *Geschichte und Geschichten: Die literarische Verarbeitung von Auschwitz-Erlebnissen* (Bad Honnef: Bock & Herchen, 1989); Lawrence Langer, *The Holocaust and the Literary Imagination* (New Haven: Yale University Press, 1975); Hanna Levy-Haas, *Tagebuch aus dem KZ Bergen-Belsen, 1944–45* (Berlin: Rotbuch Verlag, 1979); Max Mannheimer, "Erinnerungen," *Dachauer Hefte* 50 (1985); Michael Moll, *Lyrik in einer Entmenschlichten Welt* (Frankfurt a. M.: Fischer, 1988); Simha Naor, *Krankengymnastin in Auschwitz* (Freiburg im Breisgau: Herder, 1986); Thomas Rahe, "Kultur im KZ: Musik, Literatur und Kunst in Bergen-Belsen," *Frauen im Konzentrationslagern: Bergen-Belsen, Ravensbrück,* ed. Claus Füllberg-Stolberg, Martina Jang, Renate Ribe, Martina Scheitenberger (Bremen: Temmen, 1994), 193–206; Alvin H. Rosenfeld, *A Double Dying: Reflections on Holocaust Literature* (Bloomington:

Indiana University Press, 1980); Lisa Scheuer, *Vom Tode, der nicht stattfand* (Hamburg: Rowohlt, 1983); Manfred Schlösser, ed., *An den Wind Geschrieben* (Darmstadt: Agora, 1960); Gershom Scholem, *Judaica 11* (Frankfurt a. M.: Suhrkamp, 1986); Ruth Schwertfeger, *Women of Theresienstadt* (Oxford: Berg, 1989); Resi Weglein, *Als Krankenschwester im KZ Theresienstadt* (Stuttgart: Silberburg, 1988); Elie Wiesel, "Art and Culture After the Holocaust," *Auschwitz: Beginning of a New Era?* ed. Eva Fleischner (New York: Ktav, ca. 1977); and Frau Zielenziger, "Tagebuch der Frau Zielenziger," Bergen-Belsen Archives, box 111, file 1118, pp. 1–2.

RUTH SCHWERTFEGER

1945 World War II ends, and eight-year-old Jurek Becker is freed from a concentration camp and begins to learn German

Jurek Becker's biography is unusual. When the Germans invaded Poland, the two-year-old was herded with his parents into the ghetto at Lodz, one of the waiting rooms for death. Without his parents, he was sent to the concentration camp at Ravensbrück and later to Sachsenhausen, from which he was freed by the Red Army. His entire family was killed, except for his father, who found him in 1945 and decided to settle, as Becker later mused, not in Brooklyn, Buenos Aires, or Tel Aviv but "the most exotic of all possibilities," East Berlin. At age eight, young Jurek forgot Polish and learned German with a survivor's fury, because his inability to speak it set him apart from the other children. His father, who was almost forty years older than his son, was an uncommunicative man who answered few of Jurek's questions. When asked why they had never returned to Poland, he reluctantly and succinctly answered: "Who lost the war, the Polish anti-Semites or the German ones?"

Growing up, Jurek joined the Free German Youth and in 1957 the Socialist Unity Party (SED). "I think I was what we used to call a good comrade," Becker told *Der Spiegel* in 1977. He was deeply disturbed by the participation of the German Democratic Republic (GDR) in suppressing the Czech uprising in 1968, and he had difficulties with his party on other occasions. When Wolf Biermann was deprived of his citizenship in 1976, Becker joined a number of other writers in protest and was expelled from the SED. In 1977 he left the Writers Union and was granted an unusual visa by his government that permitted him to live abroad but return to the GDR at any time. Becker moved to West Berlin without considering himself an exile, and his comments on the GDR and its political philosophy remained moderate.

Between 1962 and his death in 1997 Becker wrote eight novels, sixteen film scenarios, a number of short stories, and two immensely popular TV series. His biography and the fact that three of his novels deal with Jewish themes have persuaded some critics to include him among postwar German-Jewish writers, but Becker vehemently fought against such a classification. Chaim Shoham complains that Becker has "consciously and publicly distanced himself from his Jewishness. He is unwilling to define his identity according to his biological descent or the faith of his parents." Becker agreed. When asked about his origins, he answered, "My parents were Jewish." And if the questioner persisted in saying, "Then you are Jewish," he repeated the former statement. Under no circumstances was there "a feeling of belonging to a religious community." Such a membership, he felt, should rest on a voluntary act, which is ultimately an intellectual decision. Although the Jewish faith appeared to him more insightful and convincing than all others, it did not bring him a bit closer to the light. When it comes to religion, he considered himself an atheist. His Jewish critics saw his pronouncements as signs of a typical assimilationist tendency and pointed to a number of his writings as evidence that he was unable to cut himself off from his roots.

Becker was eight when he met his father and thirty-five when he lost him, and in between, the relationship was traumatic. In interviews, again and again he returned to the memory of the silence that prevailed between them. "Between us existed a condition of non-communication about the past, about war and persecution," he said (Hage 1986), and after his father's death in 1972 Becker had notebooks full of questions "which I did not ask and would not have asked even if he had lived to the age of two hundred." He blamed himself for the difficulty of a dialogue ("I was a monster") but imputed some of the blame to his father: "It must have been his education that made me dogmatic, that made me feel that the greatest happiness lay in winning a discussion, that I became a great quarreler. If I had a son like that, I would go crazy" (Hage 1986). He saw the relationship with his father not as a revolt but as the pathetic failure of two kindred souls to communicate.

It would seem obvious to connect Becker's first novel *Jakob der Lügner* (Jacob the liar; 1969) to the author's own ghetto experience. Becker said on a number of occasions, however, that his conscious memory began only at eight, when he moved to Berlin. This would seem to indicate an extraordinary repression, explained perhaps by the utter monotony of ghetto and camp life. Although Becker did extensive research on the conditions under which ghetto inhabitants lived, this does not indicate that he aspired to verisimilitude at any price. The question whether everything in the novel "could have happened" in the manner in which the author describes it is moot. On countless occasions the narrator, a relatively young, nameless man who lived in the same ghetto and survived the Holocaust, points to the fact that he was neither omnipresent nor omniscient and that he has filled in missing details as his reality-based imagination inspired him. His chief claim to authenticity is the story that Jacob told him, presumably during his ride to and stay in the death camp.

Jacob, a ghetto inhabitant in his fifties, is stopped one evening by a capricious German guard, who orders him to report to military headquarters for supposedly violating one of a myriad of rules. Fearful that he will never see the outside again, Jacob obeys and in the building overhears a radio news report that the Russians are only 150 miles away. After he is permitted to leave the post, he is eager to share the good news; knowing that nobody will believe his lucky escape, he makes his story credible by claiming that he owns a hidden radio. From then on Jacob is beleaguered by his fellow inmates who, turning from despair to clutch at a thin reed of hope, demand further news, which Jacob is forced to concoct. A power blackout relieves him only briefly. As spirits in the ghetto rise, suicides cease, and even plans for the future are made, Jacob recognizes his obligation and invents further good news. Meanwhile, the block-by-block deportations continue, and the novel ends when Jacob's own street is evacuated and he and others ride to their deaths.

Some critical readers have felt disturbed by the humor in the novel; the "entertaining ghetto" is the title of one article. In one lengthy scene, Jacob observes a soldier, carrying a newspaper as reading material, disappear into the outhouse that, of course, is reserved for Germans. Hoping for a fresh supply of news, Jacob enters the outhouse after it has been vacated and seizes the paper but discovers another soldier waiting impatiently outside. Another prisoner, feigning an accident, diverts the soldier's attention and shields Jacob's exit. In another scene Mischa, a young fellow worker, can persuade Rosa, his fiancée, to share his bed only by convincing her that his roommate who lives in the curtained-off other half of his lodging is a deaf mute. Such instances of often deft humor never conceal the fact that the ghetto inhabitants live on borrowed time, and these episodes are offset by such gruesome details as a stopped railroad car, from which the voices of incarcerated Jews emanate. Nor do the few instances of "good" Germans balance the overall brutality with which the Jews are treated.

Although Becker did not know the works of Sholem Aleichem or Isaac Bashevis Singer, the atmosphere of his fictitious ghetto bears some similarity to the shtetel, which they and many others described, especially in some of the anecdotes of less troubled days. There is solidarity and backbiting, generosity and greed, philosophizing and gossip, courage and cowardice, all on the very small and constricted scale of the Jewish community. Kowalski's barbershop, Jacob's ice cream and pancake parlor, and the offices of the tax collector and the money lender are all part of this prewar small-town atmosphere, which exudes a kind of *Gemütlichkeit* that has been destroyed by the invader and exists mainly in memory.

The biblical Jacob, son of Isaac and Rebecca, was also a liar who stole his brother's birthright and his father's blessing only to become the eponymous ancestor of the people of Israel. In his play "Jaákobs Traum" (Jacob's dream; 1918), the Jewish author Richard Beer-Hofmann suggests that Jacob had a strong feeling of being chosen by God for greatness, of playing a role for which he was destined. Though the Jacob of our novel has no such aspirations, he, too, is unwillingly thrust into a leadership role that he reluctantly assumes. Possession of a radio is punishable by death, and his daily affirmation of his lie for the sake of buoying up his fellow Jews' spirits is a heroic act. Acts of heroism, such as the uprisings in Warsaw or Buchenwald, were rare, but these tiny manifestations are the stuff of fiction.

Jacob stands out in a cast of colorful characters. There is Kowalski, who plies the barber's traditional trade of gossip mongering and who saves Jacob's life and commits suicide when Jacob confesses that the radio is an invention. Mischa and Rosa, whose impossible love blossoms in a desert, cling to each other even as they watch Rosa's parents being led away. Perhaps they are an indication of hope for a postwar Jewry. Rosa's father, the actor Frankfurter, revels in the roles that he played in his days of glory. The formerly world-famous heart specialist Kirschbaum and his sister maintain an air of upper-class gentility until the physician is requested to consult with the SS commander of the ghetto, who has had a heart attack. On the way to his last call he takes poison because either success or failure would be unbearable. The orphaned child Lina is being brought up by Jacob, who nourishes her not only with his own scant food ration but also with fairy tales and picture books that expand her horizons. An alien in this Eastern Jewish microcosm is Leonard Schmidt, aptly nicknamed "Assimilinski" by his fellow workers. A formerly prominent Berlin lawyer, Schmidt is lost in this world of totally different morals, in which he suddenly is reduced to being a penal worker.

The narrator's stance, too, is very much in the tradition of the Jewish storyteller. Though we learn almost nothing about his persona, we are aware of his presence on almost every page. Perhaps afflicted by survivor syndrome ("a thousand times I have tried to rid myself of this goddamned story, always in vain"), he seems to feel an obligation to tell Jacob's story as best he remembers it, without qualitative embellishments, but he takes the liberty of filling in details where facts are not known to him. He begins with a symbol of hope, a tree, which evokes both sweet and bitter memories. He fell from a tree and broke his hand at an early age, ending all prospects of becoming a violinist. Under a tree he made love for the first time; at a tree his wife was shot by the Germans. Trees, like all other growing things, are forbidden in the ghetto. Through an opening in the railroad car rolling toward the death camp, he sees trees that stand for freedom yet unrealized. The two outcomes of the story that the narrator offers us at the end of the novel—the true one and the desirable one—once more remind us that we are reading a story born of history. Both the author and the narrator are operating within the confines of an unchangeable reality. But just as a fictitious radio has created hope, an author and a storyteller can make us see historical events in a different light.

The central figure of Becker's next "Jewish" novel *Der Boxer* (The boxer; 1976) is not so much a victim as a survivor. Aron Blank's story begins in 1945, shortly after his discharge from a concentration camp where his wife and two of his three children were killed. He chooses to live in (East) Berlin and is assigned the apartment of a former Nazi. Through the aid of a Jewish agency, he manages to find his surviving son, Mark, who eventually is brought to Berlin to recover from his deprivations. A relationship with Paula, an employee of the Jewish agency, breaks up when her former fiancé returns from the war. After Mark comes to live with him, he begins another relationship of several years' duration with a nurse who had taken care of Mark, but when she insists on marriage he refuses, and the relationship ends. Aron, by occupation an accountant, reluctantly keeps the books of a successful black-market operator, and later works as an interpreter for the Russian occupation forces. Aron has few friends, and the loneliness and ennui of his life increasingly drive him to drink. The estrangement between father and son eventually leads to Mark's departure from home and from the GDR after he had begun studying mathematics at the university. Embittered by what he considers his son's desertion, Aron does not answer any of his many monthly letters from West Germany and many other countries over the next few years. Mark's last letter comes from Israel in May 1967, and it is assumed that he died in the Six-Day War.

Aron's story is told in 1973 by a fictitious narrator who has been interviewing him over the past two years. It never becomes quite clear why the rather uncommunicative Aron has submitted to this series of interrogations; possibly the seventy-three-year old man wishes to make some sense of a life that he regards as futile and to justify his role in the relationship with his son. When Aron was released from the concentration camp, he desperately strove for a new identity: he changed his first name from Aron to Arno, he wiped out the six war years by making himself six years younger, he altered his birthplace from Riga to Leipzig, and he refused to be considered a "victim of fascism" or to enjoy the benefits that could derive from such a status. He does not relish the company of other ex-camp inmates who gather in the back room of a bar, and when one of them tries to persuade him to emigrate with him to Palestine (in 1946), the idea is totally alien to him. Perhaps it is this frantic desire to suppress the past, which includes a refusal to ever speak to his son about it, that drives him to drink. In a rare reference to the past, he says to the narrator: "You mustn't think a camp like that is over from one day to the next. You see all that much too simply,

the camp follows you. The barracks pursue you, the hunger pursues you, the beatings pursue you, the fear pursues you. You're afraid that's the way insanity might start. And suddenly you realize that alcohol can help."

Aron is essentially a nonpolitical person whose relationship with Germany and Germans is noncommittal. He lives in East Germany in the belief that it is a firmly antifascist country. When Mark is beaten up in school, he mistakenly ascribes it to anti-Semitism and enrolls the boy in a boxing course, only to find that Mark enjoys the new skill and employs it to rough up other boys. He has forgotten his father's lesson: "A boxer, you see, is not one who forever boxes but one who knows how to. Unfortunately, however, boxers frequently box because they were boxers, and that's the trouble." A defensive skill turns into a weapon for aggression, symptomatic of Aron's failure as a father. Communication between father and son becomes more and more difficult, and when Mark strikes out to begin his new life, he leaves behind a Kafkaesque (Becker occasionally mentions Kafka as one of the influences on his writing; the other one is Max Frisch) long letter: "The origin of your loneliness, I am firmly convinced, lies within you. I have never known a human being who lives so separated from everything as you do, and one can't say that my presence has made a difference. . . . You can reproach me for never having talked about this while the opportunity existed. Then I reproach you for training me to be silent. . . . Why have we never talked about the important matters? It is not my fault that I can only guess at everything that goes on within your head but have never heard from you."

Among the matters never discussed is their Jewish background. No one could accuse him, Aron tells the narrator, of having made a Jew out of Mark. Being Jewish, he continues, is nothing but a declaration of faith, a choice of membership like the joining of a party. Just as a child of Catholic parents can decide when he comes of age whether he also wishes to be a Catholic, children of Jewish parents should have the same right. Being somewhat paranoid, Aron is sure that someone else, perhaps a girl, persuaded Mark to remain in Israel and join a kibbutz. Indeed, Becker does not give us many clues about Mark's motives, which renders dubious Chaim Shoham's thesis that the manner in which Mark lost his life is central to the novel.

The Boxer is a case study of a survivor whose survival is illusionary, because after his camp experience he has lost his *Lust auf Leben* (zest for life) and is unable to instill the desire to live in his sole remaining son. From the beginning of the novel Aron is a sick man, and his attempt to change his identity, his failures at love and friendship, his inability to find significant employment, his drinking, and his impotence as a father are stepping stones on his road to ruin. Only the decision to tell his story to the narrator with brutal honesty and self-effacement indicates a final reversal. Survivors can be victims, too.

Of the three novels under consideration here, *Bronsteins Kinder* (Bronstein's children; 1986) is the most entertaining, even though it deals with a death and its antecedents. It is told in the first person singular by a nineteen-year old German-Jewish boy who manages to inject a dry and sometimes black humor into an otherwise tragic story. The story takes place during a month in the spring of 1974, when the boy is living in East Berlin with a Jewish couple, Hugo and Rahel Lipschitz, and their daughter Martha (with whom he used to be in love). Hans Bronstein is about to study philosophy at Humboldt University, and because he finds his domestic atmosphere increasingly repressive, he is looking for a room. He reflects on the events during a two-week period in July and August of 1973 when he discovered that his father and two other concentration camp survivors had lured a former camp guard to a family cabin, where they held him prisoner and interrogated him, using frequent beatings to make him confess his criminal acts. The discovery led to considerable tension between Hans and his father. When Hans finally attempted to set the former camp guard free, he discovered his father's body: he had apparently died of a heart attack a short time earlier.

Once again the autobiographical elements are strong in this novel, and there are many similarities to *The Boxer*. But whereas Mark in that novel was a somewhat shadowy figure, the narrative viewpoint of Hans Bronstein is more clear in this novel. Here Becker deals with a new post-Holocaust generation that includes Elle Bronstein, his sister, and Martha Lipschitz. The three former inmates have little faith in the Germans' ability to deal with this case, even though they admit that the GDR is more likely to mete out some sort of justice than West Germany. Arno Bronstein finds Germany an inferior country, inhabited by an undignified mob that follows whatever leader happens to be in power. "They cannot try him out of conviction because they have none," he explains to his son. "They only know orders. Many of them imagine that the orders they are given correspond to their own opinions. But who can rely on that? Order them to eat dog turds, and if you are strong enough, they will soon consider dog turds a delicacy."

Hans, who has grown up in the GDR, takes his country for granted and has not encountered any anti-Semitism (Becker has said the same of himself). The closest he comes to it is an incident in the school shower room. A busy-body fellow student calls his attention to a sign that requires all bathers to remove their swimming trunks while showering. Irked by the fellow's self-importance, Hans hits him in the face, and the injured student complains to the teacher. The latter tries to mollify him by explaining to him that Hans may have wanted to cover up his "otherness." Hans is embarrassed, because he refuses to derive any advantages from his special status; similarly, a year later he declines to make use of the Victims of Fascism organization in getting a room. Without being in the least patriotic, he feels like a German among Germans. Becker originally planned to entitle the book (ironically) *How I Became a German*. Martha, too, has gained sufficient distance from the experience of her parents that she accepts the part of a young Jewess in a film about Nazi Germany, a part which she obtains, in part at least, because of her "Jewish looks." Hans's sister, Elle, is mentally imbalanced as the result of cruel treatment on the part of a German family who had taken money to look after her. But in some respects she seems a very wise woman (Hans frequently seeks her advice) who has taken refuge from a world that has destroyed her. In a very prosaic world, her poetic letters provide a dab of color that her brother misses in his own life.

Hans Bronstein is a German with a Jewish consciousness but not a Jewish identity. He is aware of his father's past, although his father, too (like Aron Blank), has omitted vital parts of his autobiography, and his knowledge of Yiddish surprises (and shocks) the son. Nor has Hans acquired a Jewish identity from his father, whose oft-repeated theory is that "Jews do not exist. Jews are an invention, maybe a good one and maybe a bad one, certainly a successful one. The inventors have disseminated their rumor with so much conviction and obstinacy that even the subjects and sufferers, the alleged Jews, have fallen victim to it and claimed to be Jews. This in turn made the invention so much more credible and lent it a certain reality. It was becoming more and more difficult to discover the beginnings of this mendacious matter, it was surrounded by a thick soup of history which one could no longer penetrate with arguments. The most confusing thing was that so many people had adjusted to their role as Jews and would fight to their last breath any attempt to take it away from them." Hans's views about the Holocaust, the German past, and Germans and Jews are those of many liberal and enlightened Germans of the 1970s. The thirty years of "normalcy" since 1945 have relativized his views, and his release of the camp guard is a symbolic act: "I could never hate him from the bottom of my heart, I just wanted to be totally separate from him."

Becker's early life and works were shaped by his life in the GDR and his Socialist convictions; although he resisted the rigidity of his government even before the Biermann affair, he did not lose faith in Socialism as an option. One often has the feeling that his "Jewishness" was thrust upon him and that he felt uncomfortable when reminded of the expectations and obligations that might derive from it. He was an inventive writer with a fine sense of humor, no stranger to the entertainment value of a good story—of a lifelike dialogue between credible persons in a timely situation drama. But his works lack the profundity of those by Christa Wolf or Volker Braun.

Abhorrent as it must seem to many Jews, Becker decided not to belong to the group into which he was born, even though he knew that "one is not only the person one imagines himself to be but for better or worse is also the one others consider him to be." In his essay "Mein Judentum" (My Jewishness; Schultz 1978, 18), he perhaps put it best when he concluded: "Why must I absolutely get to the bottom of such a riddle? Would I be smarter afterwards? I fear not. I fear I would only try in vain to clear up a mystery without which my life would be poorer."

Bibliography

Jurek Becker, *Begleitheft zur Ausstellung der Stadt- und Universitätsbibliothek Frankfurt am Main* (Frankfurt a. M.: Die Bibliothek, 1989); Becker, *Der Boxer* (Frankfurt a. M.: Suhrkamp, 1976); Becker, *Bronsteins Kinder* (Frankfurt a. M.: Suhrkamp, 1986); Becker, *Jakob der Lügner* (Neuwied: Luchterhand, 1970); Sander L. Gilman, "Jüdische Literaten und deutsche Literatur: Antisemitismus und die verborgene Sprache der Juden am Beispiel von Jurek Becker und Edgar Hilsenrath," *Zeitschrift für deutsche Philologie* (1988): 269–94; Volker Hage, "Wie ich ein Deutscher wurde: Eine Begegnung mit Jurek Becker in Berlin und Anmerkungen zu seinem Roman *Bronsteins Kinder*," *Die Zeit* 41 (Oct. 3, 1986); Irene Heidelberger-Leonhard, ed., *Jurek Becker* (Frankfurt a. M.: Suhrkamp, 1992); Susan M. Johnson, *The Works of Jurek Becker: A Thematic Analysis* (Frankfurt a. M.: Peter Lang, 1988); Hannes Krauss, "Jurek Becker—ein jüdischer Autor?" *Jüdische Intelligenz in Deutschland*, ed. Jost Hermand and Gert Mattenklott (Berlin: Argument, 1988); Sigrid Lüdke-Haertel and Martin Lüdke, "Jurek Becker," *Kritisches Lexikon zur deutschsprachigen Gegenwartsliteratur* (Munich: Text & Kritik, 1988); Hans Jürgen Schultz, ed., *Mein Judentum* (Stuttgart: Kreuz, 1978); and Chaim Shoham, "Jurek Becker ringt mit seinem Judentum: 'Der Boxer' und Assimilation nach Auschwitz," *Kontroversen, alte und neue*, ed. Albrecht Schöne, vol. 5 (Tübingen: Niemeyer, 1986).

FRANK D. HIRSCHBACH

1945 An official Soviet stamp permits the exportation of cultural documents, including a draft version of *Die Buche,* a never-published anthology of German-language Jewish poetry from the Bukowina found in the estate of Alfred Margul-Sperber

Throughout the 1930s, a group of Bukowina writers, among them Alfred Margul-Sperber, Rose Ausländer, Alfred Kittner, and Siegfried Laufer, collected and selected the poems of a number of Jewish German-language writers from the Bukowina. Their aim was to publish with a major German or Austrian press a definitive contemporary anthology that was representative of the region's cultural production. They insisted that the anthology should contain only poems of "authentic literary merit" and only the very best poems each of the selected writers had written. Very early in the process the anthology acquired its name, *Die Buche* (The beech tree), a title synonymous with the region and culture of the Bukowina, or "Buchenland."

The story of *Die Buche* is in many ways emblematic of the vicissitudes of Bukowina's Jewish culture. *Die Buche* was never published. By 1945, when the manuscript was exported from the newly Soviet territory Bukowina, the original purpose inspiring its creation had disappeared along with the very culture it was supposed to celebrate. In a speech given in Czernowitz in the early 1930s, during the rise of National Socialism in Germany, Margul-Sperber, a poet and an editor, had poignantly articulated the idea behind the anthology project. Margul-Sperber had challenged his audience to consider with him whether in the 1930s, more than a decade after the annexation of the Bukowina by Rumania in 1918 and a decade after the adoption of Rumanian as the official language in 1924, such a thing as a German-Jewish *poetry* of the Bukowina did indeed exist. Was there something that characterized the writing of the Bukowina as a literature identifiable amid the body of European writing, he asked, or was this only an example of a few individual texts, a few isolated Jewish writers writing in German?

In an attempt to answer this question, Margul-Sperber moved from textual to contextual concerns, insisting that the production of Bukowina's Jewish German-language poets was marked by a four-part tragedy: First, these writers were poets, and who, he asked, was buying and reading poetry during this period? Second, these poets were Jews, and thus the non-Jewish world wanted nothing to do with them, and the Jewish world was plagued by concerns other than poetry at the moment. Third, these Jewish poets wrote in German, a special tragedy at a time when even Jewish writers living in Germany were excluded from the right to their native language. And last, Margul-Sperber concluded, these poets lived in the Bukowina, where they had "neither echo nor audience," where there were no journals or presses, only daily newspapers with minimal cultural content. *Die Buche* was to provide a forum and a monument to a literature that had been composed within these tragic contradictions but that remained youthful, vital, and energetic nevertheless. Margul-Sperber concluded his presentation with poems from the projected anthology, exemplifying the vitality of what did, after all, form a literary tradition, however threatened and divided.

From its inception, the anthology project was plagued by fundamental difficulties. Who should be included? The selection was determined by the poets' cultural belonging, but some of the most important poets who were approached declined precisely on this basis. Victor Wittner, a poet living in Vienna since World War I, responded: "Unfortunately I cannot contribute to your collection out of principle. Writing I feel myself as a German poet and not as Rumanian, or Jewish poet, nor as a Rumanian Jew." Kamillo Lauer, also living in Vienna, pointed to the major psychic and cultural break caused by World War I and suggested that only younger poets who did not suffer this profound dislocation be included—thus he tactfully excluded himself. And the Viennese resident Erich Singer renounced all literary connection to his native Bukowina, which he had not visited since 1914; he insisted that his poetry emerged from the Western European cities in which he lived as an adult. If he was to be included, then it needed to be as someone from the pre–World War I imperial Bukowina, and not the newly Rumanian region. Joseph Kalmer also declined because, as someone supporting himself with his writing, he could not publicly declare himself a Jew. Each of these letters reflects the tremendous ambivalence of writers who were—and at the same time were not—identified with their native Bukowina and who seemed to spend their lives working through a cultural affiliation that informed their writing even as they tried, repeatedly, to sever themselves from it. Thus, in some of the final drafts of the anthology, the very poets who declined, like Wittner, are amply represented.

More vexing than the question of inclusion was the issue of publication. In 1936, satisfied with a working draft of the collection, Margul-

Sperber sent it to Schocken Press in Berlin. The editor, Moritz Spitzer, responded promptly that the Bukowina authors did not need to worry that Schocken would be prejudiced against Ostjuden (Eastern European Jews), as Margul-Sperber's initial letter of inquiry had anxiously suggested. Still, he added that "it is difficult to justify 'here' the publication of an anthology of German writings by Jews whose commonality lies in their belonging to a distant, non-German land." Spitzer sent another letter, a few months later, expressing both his appreciation of some of the poems and his continued ambivalence about publishing the book. But in December 1938, the decision was made by Hans Hinkel, the cultural director of the German Reich, who shut down the Schocken publishing company and forced them to return all outstanding manuscripts. Margul-Sperber's estate contains three handwritten and typed versions of the anthology, the third including poems written during and after the war as well. Not until 1991 was an anthology of Bukowina poetry to appear in Germany, though this one—Klaus Werner's *Fäden ins nichts gespannt: Deutschsprachige Literatur aus der Bukowina* (Threads stretched into the void: The German-language literature of the Bukowina)—was not at all based on the selections of *Die Buche*. Finally, in 1994, sixty years after the original project began, the long-forgotten anthology did in fact appear. Coedited and introduced by Amy Colin, a scholar whose parents are from the Bukowina, *Versunkene Dichtung der Bukowina* (Submerged poetry of the Bukowina) is dedicated to the memory of Alfred Margul-Sperber. The original manuscript has been significantly supplemented with selections by Alfred Kittner, who dedicated his postwar life to this project but died before its publication. Its appearance in 1990s Germany, however, conveys a very different meaning from its original intended one.

What Jewish culture was *Die Buche* intended to celebrate? Rose Ausländer describes Czernowitz—"a submerged city, a sunken world"—best in her reminiscences, which were published posthumously. Like others who evoke the Bukowina, Ausländer stresses the multicultural and multilingual character of this region and particularly of Czernowitz, its capital, where Rumanians, Ruthenians, Hungarians, Poles, Armenians, Hutsuls, Lipovanes, Germans, and Jews coexisted and interrelated through centuries of Russian, Ottoman, Austro-Hungarian, and eventually Rumanian rule. Jews first came to the Bukowina in the thirteenth century as traders and began to settle there in the fourteenth century, fleeing persecutions in Western Europe, particularly in German territories. Their presence increased steadily with the emancipation of Jews in the Austrian empire, and by 1918 the population of Czernowitz was 47 percent Jewish. Most of the Jewish population initially spoke Yiddish, and the Bukowina became an important Yiddish cultural center at the beginning of the twentieth century. The Bukowina hosted the first international conference on the Yiddish language, in 1908, and held the seat of the renowned Hasidic rabbi of Sadagura, who attracted thousands of followers from all over Eastern Europe. Czernowitz was also the home of Yiddish poets Elieser Steinbarg and Itzig Manger. Manger, who was raised speaking German and Rumanian, turned to Yiddish as his literary language in order to reverse the dominant impulse toward Jewish assimilation. This impulse was extremely strong in Czernowitz, which had opened its first German-language high school in 1808, housed an important German theater since 1839, and established the primarily German-language Franz-Joseph University in 1875, attracting professors from Austria. At the end of the nineteenth century, there were three Jewish daily newspapers published in German, as well as several magazines. The first collections of Bukowina's German-language (not exclusively Jewish) writing, "Die Buchenblätter," began to appear in the 1860s. Although the tradition of Jewish writing in the Bukowina dates back at least two hundred years, Karl-Emil Franzos (1848–1904), famous for his 1893 novel *Der Pojaz,* was the Bukowina's first internationally renowned and translated German-language Jewish writer. In an unpublished handwritten note, Franzos best characterizes the complicated cultural identity of most assimilated Bukowina Jews: "I wasn't yet three feet tall, when my father told me: 'Your nationality is neither Polish, nor Ruthenian, nor Jewish—you are German.' But equally often he said, even then: 'According to your faith, you are a Jew'" (Franzos 1920, 6). Set in the ghettos of Eastern Europe, *Der Pojaz* allows its protagonist to dream of a German literary and artistic education and to celebrate the religious and moral tolerance of the Austrian Reich. For Franzos, assimilation and modernization were imperative for Eastern European Jewry.

In the early years of this century and especially in the interwar period up to the early 1930s, Czernowitz and the Bukowina were symbols of Jewish emancipation; they were seen as truly exemplary. Culture and education by that time had become thoroughly modern: in his speech accepting the Georg Büchner Prize in Germany in 1958, Paul Celan recalled his homeland as "a region where people and books lived." The identification with German culture among Bukowina's Jews cannot be overestimated. Writing in 1937 about the relationship between Germans and Jews living in the Bukowina, Margul-Sperber begins with "words of thanks . . . that Bukowina Jews owe to the German people and to their culture." Before Jews encountered German civilization, Margul-Sperber continues, they found themselves in a cultural condition that was "unworthy of human existence." "Emancipated from the ghetto, Jewish youth sat at the feet of German teachers from the West and eagerly absorbed everything new, great and beautiful that Western culture and civilization could procure for them" (Wichner and Wiesner 1993, 110). Margul-Sperber's language may appear excessively self-deprecating, but he does convey quite accurately the unquestioned and deeply rooted German-Jewish symbiosis that developed in the Bukowina before World War I and that continued in the interwar period even under Rumanian rule. In the words of Amy Colin (1983, 756): "Despite the Rumanian rule, the growing nationalism, and the rise of fascism, the German Jewish component of Bukowinian culture reached its culmination precisely in the 1920s and 1930s." Rose Ausländer later recalled of the Rumanian period: "We remained Austrians, our capital was Vienna and not Bucharest" (Gottzmann 1991, 209).

The admiration for the Viennese writer Karl Kraus and for the Berlin mystic Jewish philosopher Constantin Bruner reached cult status. But students of philosophy also followed Spinoza, Nietzsche, Schopenhauer, Kant, Marx, and Freud, and students of literature avidly read Hölderlin, Rilke, George, Trakl, Mann, Hesse, Zweig, Morgenstern, Benn, and Brecht. Many, like Margul-Sperber himself, were educated abroad and became active cultural emissaries and translators, as well as interpreters of French, English, and American modernist literature.

Even as Bukowina writers like Margul-Sperber found their cosmopolitan identity in the West and in relation to a German culture with which they thoroughly identified, they continued to be nourished by the plurality of Bukowina's ethnic landscape. Many of the poets discussed here regularly translated Rumanian and Yiddish poetry into German, thus acknowledging the multiplicity of the Bukowina-Jewish cultural identity. German-Jewish culture in the Bukowina was clearly marked by the region's multicultural character, by the numerous languages spoken, and by the ethnic diversity of the region's inhabitants. At one point, for example, Karl Emil Franzos, a German-Jewish writer; Mihai Eminescu, one of Rumania's foremost poets; and the Ukrainian writer Fedkowicz were classmates. Eminescu's first poems were written in German in Czernowitz, and even after he switched to his native Rumanian, he continued to influence the German-language poets of subsequent generations.

The region's cultural diversity had a strong influence on the German language that was spoken in the Bukowina, especially during the interwar years when German ceased to be the official bureaucratic language and those continuing to speak it became more and more linguistically isolated. Many of the poets discussed here were born in what was already Rumania and were educated in Rumanian; they probably heard Russian and Ruthenian, and Yiddish, at the very least on a daily basis. In her retrospective poem "Bukowina" (1976), Rose Ausländer celebrates this multiplicity: "Viersprachig verbrüderte / Lieder / in entzweiter Zeit" (quadrilingual fraternizing songs / in a time asunder). But in the 1930s Ausländer deplores the effect of this "quadrilingual" life: "Through multiple linguistic influences, especially from the Yiddish . . . a jargon emerged from which those who were cultured and linguistically demanding—listening towards Vienna—distanced themselves" (Colin and Kittner 1994, 187).

Living on the margins of German culture, in, as is repeatedly emphasized, the easternmost outskirts of the former empire, the writers of the Bukowina had to assert their Germanness with every means available. Ausländer's affiliation with those who were "cultured and linguistically demanding" may explain the rigorously classical German and the traditional poetic form practiced by most of the poets of the interwar generation, the poets who like their contemporaries were would-be "Buko-wiener." Ausländer lost her admiration for Karl Kraus only when, in 1933, Kraus declared that the "phenomenon" of Hitler could only leave him silent. And Margul-Sperber asserted his affiliation with the ethnic Germans living in the Bukowina, deeply and sincerely deploring the "troglodyte" and "neanderthal" anti-Semitic press that began to gain ground in the 1930s. Nostalgic for three hundred years of peaceful cohabitation and cultural symbiosis, Margul-Sperber hoped, in 1937, that it was not too late, that the madness could still be stopped and the friendship regained.

These sentiments may begin to explain what appears to remain an unimpeachable relationship of Bukowina's Jewish writing to what the exhibit based on Margul-Sperber's estate calls "the language of the murderers." It has become virtually a commonplace among those critics writing on this literature that Bukowina's interwar poets were not linguistic or aesthetic innovators. Perhaps their traditional poetic form is to be attributed to the strong influence of Karl Kraus's aesthetic theories and his belief in aesthetic and ethical congruence, as Amy Colin suggests. Perhaps also, as Colin intimates as well, the echoes of Heine, Rilke, and George, even of Goethe and Eichendorff—the presence of romantic tropes, traditional fairy tale and folk tale motifs, and the adherence to rhyme, as well as the classical rhythms and syntax—reflect an attempt to posit and to celebrate a transhistorically pure German, immune to the influence of Hitler and a haven from persecution and destruction. For most of these writers, German appears to retain a purity that needed actively to be regained and thus to be thrown in the face of those who would appropriate their language and dispossess them of it. Ausländer shows this in her late poem "Mutterland" (Motherland), where motherland becomes synonymous with mother tongue and her German can survive the destruction and disappearance of her native fatherland:

Mein Vaterland ist tot
sie haben es begraben
im Feuer
Ich lebe
in meinem Mutterland
Wort.

(My fatherland is dead / they have buried
it / in fire / I live / in my motherland / the
word)

(Colin and Kittner 1994, 203).

Paul Celan is the only obvious exception to this neo-classicism; for him not only German but language and reason itself had become irrevocably tainted and his poetry became a struggle at once to reach and to avoid silence. But can Celan really be the only one to seriously fracture and to challenge the comfortable way in which Bukowina writers inhabited the German language?

Returning to the question Margul-Sperber posed in his 1932 speech about the literature of the Bukowina—of whether there is a distinctive *poetry* of the Bukowina, one that stands out against the background of European literary movements, styles, and regional definitions—it becomes apparent that distinctiveness lies precisely in constitutive and determining tensions and contradictions. These contradictions include the celebration of German as transhistorical, pure, and redemptive, on the one hand, and the consciousness of German as the language of the murderers, irredeemably sullied, on the other; the significance of the romantic thematics as evasion and denial, on the one hand, and as ironic commentary on a tragic historical circumstance, on the other; and the classical form as both a refuge from danger and fear and as a poignant counterpoint to an often crushing and despairing content. The Bukowinian poets' devastating testimonies to the ghetto and camp experiences challenge even the greatest efforts to retain the forms of tradition, and eventually they all in some ways break through any formal coherence and any uncomplicated connection to the German language.

Between the original drafts of the manuscript of *Die Buche* assembled in the late 1930s and their exportation from the Soviet Union in 1945, the poets who were or might have been included suffered exile (Alfred Margul-Sperber fled to Rumania, Victor Wittner to Switzerland, Erich Singer and Josef Kalmer to England); imprisonment in the Czernowitz ghetto (Rose Ausländer); deportation to the camps in Transnistria or to the German-occupied territory on the other side of the Bug river (Immanuel Weissglas, Alfred Kittner, Paul Celan, and Moses Rosenkranz); or death by disease, extermination, or suicide (Selma Meerbaum-Eisinger, Kubi Wohl, and Robert Flinker). In 1940, the Bukowina was occupied by the Red Army, and in June 1941 several thousand Jews were deported to Siberia. In July 1941, the German and Rumanian Nazis occupied the Bukowina. There were some initial mass murders of Jews; the Czernowitz ghetto was formed in October of the same year; and about two-thirds of the Jewish population was deported to the camps of Transnistria. The remaining Jewish population had to wear the yellow star and was compelled to do forced labor in Rumania. About 60 percent of the deportees to Transnistria perished there. In 1945, the Bukowina was annexed by the Soviet Union, and most of its remaining and returning Jewish population emigrated to Rumania. Many then went abroad.

By 1945, in the aftermath of such massive destruction and dislocation during the decade following Margul-Sperber's rhetorical question about whether there was a distinctive poetry of the Bukowina, the answer, in the form of these ever more pronounced contradictions, became poignantly clear. In the first part of his "Aus dem Schlaf gesungen" (Sung in my sleep), dated April 1945, Margul-Sperber, writing in rhymed couplets, reframes his question thus:

Wenn künftige Geschlechter einst erfahren
daß Kant und Hitler gleichen Stammes waren
sie fassen es nicht, und ihnen graust
vorm Volk des Faust, vorm Volk der
    Panzerfaust;
die Sprache die die beiden Wörter prägte
und die den Weisen wie den Würger hegte
birgt eine Frage, qualvoll und geheim:
Gibt es auf Mensch im Deutschen einen Reim?

(When future generations later learn / That
    Kant and Hitler come from the same
    stock / They won't believe it, and they will
    be spooked / by the people of Faust, of the
    people of fist / the language that formed
    both of these words / and that shelters the
    wise one and the murderer / contains one
    question, painful and secret / does German
    have a word that rhymes with *Mensch?*)
                    (Seydel 1968, 488).

For many poets, the German language itself is
similarly thematized and thus increasingly called
into question. Indeed, sometimes it was broken
down into its most basic components, as in Alfred
Kittner's 1945 "Die Schule des Todes" (The
school of death): "Als mich der Tod zur Tafel
ruft / Das A ist Grab, das U ist Gruft" (When
death calls me to the board / A is grave and O is
tomb) (Seydel 1968, 314). Kittner's regular meter and rhyme only make his point more devastating, his irony more biting. As Celan asks in his
1944 rhymed poem addressed to his mother,
a victim of the Transnistria camps, "Nähe der
Gräber": "Und duldest du, Mutter, wie einst,
ach, daheim, / den leisen, den deutschen, den
schmerzlichen Reim?" (And, mother, can you
still stand, as you once did at home, the soft, the
German, the painful rhyme?) (Seydel 1968, 456).

The knowledge confronted during the years of
persecution and genocide had the power to transform, ever so slightly, even the most traditional
lyrical texts. The traditional themes—nature,
love, home—came to be invoked in a spirit of
anger rather than celebration or nostalgia. Moses
Rosenkranz's 1947 "Heimatwind" is a good example: "Heimatwind mit Leichenodem / Streifte
diese Nacht im Garten / Meine Rosen, und zu

Boden / Sterbend sinken hin die Zarten" (Wind
from home with breath of corpses / Touched last
night in the garden / My roses, and to the
ground / The tender ones fell) (Werner 1991,
98). Unlike Rosenkranz, the young Selma
Meerbaum-Eisinger wrote her corpus of fifty-
seven love poems in the late 1930s and early
1940s; she died of typhus in Transnistria in 1941
at age eighteen. Read in relation to her tragic
story—her forcible separation from her boy-
friend, to whom the poems are dedicated, and her
premature death as well as his—the traditional
motifs of this love poetry come to acquire radically different meanings. Thus in the concluding
lines of her 1941 poem "Tränenhalsband" (Neck-
lace of tears): "Und der Wind singt uns beiden
den ewigen Sang von / Sehnen und Verzicht,
doch auch wenn es dir zum Sterben bang—du
rufst mich trotzdem nicht" (The wind sings for
both of us the eternal song of / longing and renunciation, but even if you are / frightened to
death—you don't call me, all the same) (Meerbaum-Eisinger 1984, 84). No poetry written "after such knowledge" could easily reclaim a lost
connection to an untainted past.

After 1945, Bukowina's culture became a culture of the Diaspora; its centers were Rumania,
where Margul-Sperber became a prize-winning
state poet; Israel, where there is still a German-
language Bukowina newspaper, *Die Stimme;* and
Germany—which counts Celan as perhaps its
major poet of the century, though he lived and
wrote in Bucharest, Vienna, and Paris until his
suicide in 1970, and which recognizes Rose Ausländer as a major German poet. Peter Stenberg
(1991) best assesses the significance of this dispersion and destruction: "There is perhaps no better indication of what German culture has lost
than the realization that Czernowitz—the easternmost urban outpost of that language and the
capital city of Bukovyna—must have produced
proportionately more major twentieth-century
writers whose native language was German, than
any other city. . . . [T]he fate of the Jews and
Germans of Czernowitz, and of the Yiddish and
German languages in that German-speaking city
of only half a century ago, serves as something of a

microcosm of what was about to happen throughout Eastern Europe."

Until the late 1980s, when regionalism and minority literatures became fashionable in Germany as in the United States, the literature of the Bukowina was largely ignored in anthologies, as well as by scholars and critics in the field of German studies. The one exception is an East German anthology edited by Heinz Seydel and published in 1968, *Welch Wort in die Kälte gerufen: Die Judenverfolgung des Dritten Reiches im deutschen Gedicht* (What word called into the cold: German poetry of Jewish persecution in the Third Reich), which does include a significant number of poems by Bukowina writers. Recently, the literature of the Bukowina has begun to experience a curious revival, on occasions such as the 1987 Graz conference entitled "Die deutschsprachige Literatur der Bukowina" and the 1991 anthology *Fäden in nichts gespannt*. Critics have begun to rise to the challenge of integrating this literature into the corpus of German literary production.

What is not yet clear is how the literature of the Bukowina might best be approached in contemporary study. Is it a particular example of a regional literature, the "fifth German literature" as some have said, counting it right after the other four: West and East German, Swiss, and Austrian? Is it a special example of German-Jewish symbiosis, extremely close and therefore specially problematic? Is it a distinctive form of Holocaust literature, one that poses the question of language in a quite radical sense? Is it to be studied as a continuing or as an arcane, a "sunken," tradition? Or is it a special form of diasporic expression, suffering from a double exile from the Austrian and then the Rumanian Bukowina?

In her late poem "Biographische Notiz" (Biographical sketch), Rose Ausländer identifies what has become of the writers and the writings of the Bukowina. The poem begins with the strong line "Ich rede" (I speak). After outlining what she speaks about—about the fire that put out the Pruth river, the weeping willows, the blood birches, the silenced song of the nightingales, the yellow star and its deaths, *not* about roses—Ausländer ends with an ontological reflection:

Fliegend
auf einer Luftschaukel
Europa Amerika Europa
ich wohne nicht
ich lebe

(Flying / on a swing in the air / Europe
   America Europe / I do not reside / I live)
                        (Ausländer 1984, 204).

Framed by these two verbs, "I speak" and "I live," her poem asserts a continuity of tradition that supersedes geography and residence. Written in German, it still finds its home there, inside the language that can articulate a diasporic imagination, and hovers above a world that may or may not remember the Bukowina as a place and a culture.

Bibliography

Rose Ausländer, *Gelassen atmet der Tag* (Frankfurt a. M.: Fischer, 1984); Amy Colin, *Paul Celan: Holograms of Darkness* (Bloomington: Indiana University Press, 1991); Colin, "An den Schnittpunkten der Traditionen—Deutsch in der Bukowina," *Neue deutsche Hefte* 30 (1983): 739–69; Colin and Alfred Kittner, eds., *Versunkene Dichtung der Bukowina* (Munich: Wilhelm Fink, 1994); Andrei Corbea and Michael Astner, eds., *Kulturlandschaft Bukowina: Studien zur deutschsprachigen Literatur des Buchenlandes nach 1918* (Iasi, Rom.: Editura Universitatii Alexandru Ion Cuza, 1990); Karl-Emil Franzos, *Der Pojaz: Eine Geschichte aus dem Osten* (Stuttgart: Cotta, 1920); Carola Gottzmann, ed., *Unerkannt und (un)bekannt: Deutsche Literatur in mittel- und Osteuropa* (Tübingen: Francke Verlag, 1991); Selma Meerbaum-Eisinger, *Ich bin in Sehnsucht eingehüllt* (Frankfurt a. M.: Fischer, 1984); Heinz Seydel, ed., *Welch Wort in die Kälte gerufen: Die Judenverfolgung des Dritten Reiches im deutschen Gedicht* (Berlin: Verlag der Nation, 1968); Peter Stenberg, *Journey to Oblivion: The End of Eastern European Yiddish and German Worlds in the Mirror of Literature* (Toronto: University of Toronto Press, 1991); Klaus Werner, ed., *Fäden ins Nichts gespannt: Deutschsprachige Literatur aus der Bukowina* (Frankfurt a. M.: Insel Verlag, 1991); and Ernest Wichner and Herbert Wiesner, eds., *In der Sprache der Mörder: Eine Literatur aus Czernowitz, Bukowina* (Berlin: Literaturhaus, 1993).

M A R I A N N E   H I R S C H

November 9, 1945   Alfred Döblin, one of the first German-Jewish writers to return to Germany, arrives in the French occupation zone

And when I returned—I didn't return.

With these words Alfred Döblin described his return to Germany after World War II (Döblin 1992, 334). Similar feelings soon became common among many of those Jewish intellectuals, writers, artists, and scholars who returned to an occupied country and to a society that had to "take off" from National Socialism but seemed paralyzed by the results of war, by physical and moral devastation. Alfred Döblin had come to southwest Germany as a French officer responsible for cultural affairs in the French occupied zone of Germany. Soon he became active in the reconstruction of a democratic culture; founded a literary journal, *Das Goldene Tor;* and promoted many young German writers. In the spring of 1945, the authors Stefan Heym and Hans Habe had arrived in American uniform and immediately had begun to work to establish new democratic media. In the East, the writer Friedrich Wolf returned from Moscow in civilian clothes while his son, Konrad, later to become one of the outstanding East German filmmakers, returned as a soldier with the Russian forces. The journalist Jacob Goldberg and the writer Wolfgang Hildesheimer returned with the British forces in 1946. Hildesheimer had emigrated with his family to Palestine, and he served until 1949 as an interpreter at the Nuremberg Trial. In 1950, he began to publish his first literary works.

German-Jewish literature returned with a number of German Jews. Their stories, the reception of their writing, and the silencing boycott are an intriguing part of the cultural ambiguities of the whole postwar period. Jewish intellectuals were never absent from German postwar culture. They were, of course, fewer than in the years of Weimar, fewer than the forceful voices of exile. They were a small intellectual minority. The question is whether the German literary public accepted these voices, and whether these voices resounded distinctively as German-Jewish reminders of a once prominent presence.

The names mentioned stand for those intellectuals who had left Germany and returned during the late 1940s and early 1950s. They went back to a Germany they did not know and whose citizens did not expect them. In mid-1945, the word "Germany" had many meanings, and it may not be accurate to define Germany under the occupation of the four allies as one political, social, and cultural entity. To return to German culture seemed dubious because the democratic traditions of German culture had been exiled, and its representatives had preserved this tradition outside the boundaries of the Nazi empire. The German-Jewish intellectuals looked from the outside at the rubble of the German cities and at the rubble in the German minds. A relevant number of

German Jews, however, were hoping for a new Germany. Recalling the last months of his exile in Switzerland, Hans Mayer, then a journalist and later an outstanding scholar of German literature and culture, wrote about the growing tensions among the Jewish and non-Jewish émigrés. The focus of many fierce discussions was the problem of return. In his autobiography he questions whether he really wanted to go back to Germany and writes that he did not ask this question back then. He participated in the activities of those exiles who were culturally and politically active, most of them with some leftist leaning. "I was not alone anymore," he remembers. "Somehow I belonged" (Mayer 1982, 298). He was active in the movement for a Free Germany in Switzerland and helped another émigré to publish his first poems. It was Stephan Hermlin who, through France, had escaped with his daughter. Brochures, journals, and newspapers were produced by these exiles. Poems by Bertolt Brecht, Else-Lasker Schüler, and others could now be read while heated debates concentrated on Germany's future and on the Zionist perspective of turning one's back on Germany forever. The Yalta Conference, in February 1945, and the pictures of Churchill, Roosevelt, and Stalin, seemed to represent a future in which the enemies of democracy and of cultural freedom would definitely be overcome. It was a vision that combined a democratic renewal of the Soviet Union with Roosevelt's New Deal in "a world," as Hans Mayer wrote in 1945, "that would not be bourgeois any more and establish new relations between the people and the arts."

One cannot overlook the fact that such hopes were a sort of cultural glue connecting many exiles with the communist activities in their countries of exile and at the time of their return. Hans Mayer says about himself in this period until the early 1950s that he was a communist but "outside the party" (Mayer 1982, 304). He describes the atmosphere among the exiles in 1945 as a mixture of uneasiness and heroic postwar planning. They had survived; now everything would begin anew. Nothing illustrates the bathos of this sentiment better than Stephan Hermlin's *Ballade von der Überwindung der Einsamkeit in den Großen Städten* (Ballad on overcoming the loneliness in the big cities), which was published by Mayer in Zürich. It speaks of the loneliness of exile, of the final defeat of the enemy, of the resolution to return with a future in mind, and—most important—it stresses the hope of never being alone again, the hope of belonging. This, in fact, has been a motif in the works of German-Jewish intellectuals since the time of the Enlightenment. Now, however, it was more related to a political and cultural vision of the future Germany than to a social environment or national community.

Other German-Jewish writers, some immediately and some reluctantly, returned from exile in England, Sweden, Switzerland, China, Palestine, Mexico, or the United States. Many, more cautious, delayed their return, and after observing political developments in Germany, settled in other states. Walter Mehring, Wolfgang Hildesheimer, Hermann Kesten, Robert Neumann, Jean Améry, Ludwig Marcuse, Carl Zuckmayer, and Peter Weiss—to name just a few intellectuals— lived only temporarily in Germany or became just visitors. Wolfgang Hildesheimer, in an autobiographical interview (1993, 51), said in 1989: "We are nowhere at home." In 1978, looking back, Hildesheimer defined the very loss of a homeland, *jene Heimatlosigkeit,* as his real home and the source of all his creativity. In a thoughtful vein he added that now, after all that had happened, there was no place for Jews in Germany. Jews, he wrote, still had to consider themselves as outsiders. Yet this perspective reflects cultural contradictions because, as he sums up his experience in the 1950s and 1960s, Jewish writers usually were not pushed into the role of outsiders. At least, he would never have accepted such an attitude. In a strange turnabout, such reasoning returns in the autobiographical writing of many German-Jewish writers after 1945. It seems that the term "inner emigration," as the returnee Arie Goral (since 1953 a student, artist, and publicist in Hamburg) has stressed, is applicable to a number of German Jews who lived and worked in the two Germanys. Very often they did not stress their Jewish roots, background, or shared imaginations—a fact that leads some scholars to believe that there was no German-

Jewish literature in the first two decades of post-war Germany.

The restrained discourse of the German-Jewish literary imagination in those years definitely had more to do with nineteenth and early twentieth century German-Jewish traditions and memory than with the failure of non-Jewish German writers to face the Holocaust. Much of this early postwar German-Jewish writing has been forgotten, and it took decades before some of the works published in the late 1940s or 1950s reached a new audience. In the 1950s, German culture quickly adapted to this solution of extended displacement and exile. In high schools, for example, Zuckmayer was taught as a Swiss author. It was easier to ward off memory if Jewish writers could largely be seen as outsiders. In the eyes of most postwar Germans, so it seemed, German literature was not represented by the humanist encyclopedia of those volumes that had been burned in May 1933, but through the hidden voices of the Germanic inner emigration that came proudly forward now, looking disdainfully down on writers like Thomas Mann, Alfred Döblin, and others who, for obvious reasons, had not been in the homeland, and who apparently did not know what had been going on inside the Reich. Consequently, most of the burned books were not reprinted in the first postwar years, although there were some serious efforts to do so in East Germany. With the new literary public sphere, the *cordon sanitaire* of German memory, as Primo Levi termed it years later, remained a delicate dividing line, a cultural twilight zone where it could be understood that not too many Jewish authors should be printed. In the 1950s, textbooks for schools and universities rarely contained texts by exiled Jewish authors. Besides, in these early years, one could always pretend that there was a lack of paper, and, particularly, a lack of interest among the German readers. Although some Jewish women and men returned, most of the Jewish voices of Weimar culture remained a distant and silenced memory. The cordon sanitaire of memory, after Hitler, even began to extend backward beyond the Nazi period into the rich cultural German-Jewish life of the past. At the same time, there also existed various Jewish perspectives on this specific situation. In January 1946, Hannah Arendt answered Karl Jaspers's invitation to publish in a new German periodical, *Wandlung:* "It is not an easy thing for me to contribute to a German journal. . . . Yet one thing seems clear to me: If the Jews are to be able to stay in Europe, then they cannot stay as Germans or Frenchmen, etc., as if nothing had happened. It seems to me that none of us can return (and writing is surely a form of return) merely because people again seem prepared to recognize Jews as Germans or something else. We can return only if we are welcome as Jews" (Arendt and Jaspers 1992, 31f.)

Others, particularly those who had been close to the socialist movements of Weimar and were in exile, returned as antifascists. Antifascist attitudes, at this point in time, ranged from the hope for the revival of the radical liberal temper in German culture to the dream of a socialist Germany that would cure all the failures and mistakes of the socialist and communist movements of the 1920s and 1930s. This is the background for those intellectuals among the approximately 3,500 German Jews who settled in East Germany. They were driven by the intellectual and emotional urge to participate in real history after they had so long participated in the shadowlike reproductions of memory. They wanted to participate in the economic, cultural, academic, and political reconstruction that, then, was defined as the creation of an antifascist-democratic order in the tradition of that other Germany, which was seemingly lost but envisioned by many.

To look at Germany after May 1945 means to look at a defeated people after the demise of the Nazi empire and the breakdown of the political system. The institutions of education and the whole cultural industry had to face an hour of truth. They were closed down. Denazification and reeducation were the allied order of the day. Everything that smacked of Nazi literature was banned by the occupation forces: libraries were cleansed and only later allowed to reopen. Allied postwar planning—which consisted of military directives by the responsible American, British, French, and Russian military leaders and the allied agreements of Yalta and Potsdam—concentrated on a cultural vision of a reborn democratic and humanist Germany that would forever erase militarism, chauvinism, racism, and anti-Semitism, that would in short overcome the antidemocratic burden of German history and culture. The written and the spoken word that was supposed to change the nationalist temper of the German people became of utmost importance in this period of transition from National Socialist Germany to a new postwar order. Everything that was going to be printed, whether a newspaper, a brochure, a book or a leaflet—and everything that was broadcasted on the air—was subject to censorship, political and cultural control. The occupation authorities, through their cultural, educational, and press officers, engaged in one of the most intriguing enterprises of modern history and contemporary culture. They set out to subject a whole nation—an outstanding body of cultural creativity, of aesthetic representations and works of art—to a profound and sometimes naive screening. The German culture became an overall comprehensive text for cultural criticism sponsored and conducted on a nationwide scale and, in the end, buried with the illusion of changing the German mind by way of directives. In this context, the cultural relevance and the influence of the returning intellectuals depended very much on the cultural politics of the military authorities in a Germany that was first divided into four zones and soon into two major cultural spheres—East and West.

A number of experienced and young writers had to realize that the audience for their works first had to be created. The practice of writing became a political virtue, not just a spiritual urge. Rather than turning to novels, to the lyrical working through of their experience, practical cultural lines of German-Jewish tradition came to the fore. It is amazing to see how many of these talented intellectuals turned to journalism in the new democratic media. Even among those who returned in the 1950s or early 1960s, the media proved to represent an openness that many other cultural fields were lacking. A number of journalistic genres received a rather literary touch, a feature that becomes obvious when looking at the first years of *Die Neue Zeitung, Frankfurter Rundschau, Süddeutsche Zeitung* or the *Jüdische Wochenzeitung*. The renewed project of cultural enlightenment was again on the agenda, after the Allies had returned political emancipation to the remnant of German Jewry. Among those who received this responsibility were Leon Brandt, who after returning in 1958 worked for Jewish institutions and then as a journalist and editor; Emil Carlebach, cofounder of the *Frankfurter Rundschau;* and Heinz Elsberg, who worked for various newspapers and the radio. Elsberg in particular wrote about the optimism of the first years. He described the disappointment, and the fact that many Jews kept a critical intellectual, emotional, and social distance from German everyday life. He recalled as most painful the actual lack, reminiscent of Weimar, of a significant number of representatives of an intellectual *Judentum* in postwar Germany (Broder and Lang 1979, 110). They were few, and they were scattered all over Germany, although the big cities attracted most. Hans Wallenberg came back with the allied forces and became an important figure in the Hamburg newspaper scene. Peter Finkelgruen returned to West Germany in 1954 and worked as a journalist. Peggy Parnass, who returned from Sweden, became a writer, an actor, and a journalist. Bruno Frei, who had been one of the famous journalists and editors of Weimar Germany, returned in 1947 to Vienna and edited a number of journals. He was not the only one to stay in Vienna. There the returning Georg Kreisler became a popular writer and cabaret performer, and Günther Anders, after his return to Europe, in 1950, became a prominent cultural critic. These are just some of those who worked in the media, very often with a typed volume of poems and plays in the drawer, or a novel waiting to be published. Ralph Giordano and Lotte Paepcke, who had survived inside Germany, published literary works decades after their journalistic activities began. They were more lucky than some of those authors who waited to return.

For writers like Arnold Zweig, Anna Seghers, Theodor Plievier, Ernst Bloch, Stephan Hermlin, Hans Mayer, and Friedrich Wolf, it was not at all easy to leave a place or country of exile and buy a ticket for Germany. For Arnold Zweig in Haifa, it turned out to be an almost impossible task.

The Allied authorities were more than reluctant in granting the necessary travel documents, and moving between the zones of occupation was almost impossible in the first months of the occupation period. Most of these exiles did not know very much about the concrete living conditions or the cultural and spiritual climate after May 1945. And only those who had come with the conquering armies had an idea of the political problems connected with the immense shift from fighting the Germans to administrating German society after Hitler. Sometimes, the question of return was related to very concrete problems of how to reacquire apartments in Berlin or somewhere else. Lion Feuchtwanger in America, and Arnold Zweig in Palestine, reflected such problems in their continuous correspondence. Zweig wrote that they as German writers should assist all efforts of German reconstruction, yet he added that one would have to check in person the situation inside Germany. Feuchtwanger, in December 1947, strongly advised Zweig not to travel to Germany but to stay in Haifa and continue with the plans for two new novels. Zweig, nonetheless, chose to return through Prague to East Germany, and together with Anna Seghers and other Jewish authors he became a cultural asset of the East German Republic.

Other émigrés, such as Hannah Arendt, began to correspond with former colleagues in Germany and made it clear that there could not be a return as if nothing had changed. Alfred Kerr, who in 1933 was among the first who had to flee hastily in order not to get caught by the Gestapo, returned for a short visit from London. Among those who considered returning existed the feeling of a cultural, intellectual, and emotional responsibility not just to return but to help in the building of another, new Germany. For years they had been involved in the debates of the German-Jewish and the left political exiles about a future Germany that would be democratic and would revitalize the humanism that had been fundamentally attacked by Nazism but that remained inherent in German culture and history. As Alfred Kantorowicz described it, they wanted to be part of this spiritual and moral reconstruction and to become active in the rebuilding of a new Germany that would be a social and spiritual home for everybody.

In the end, there were three distinct groups of Jewish writers who did return in more than one way. First were Jewish intellectuals who did not return to Germany to live there, but who visited and monitored political and cultural developments in Germany. They continued writing about Germany, and they even sought cooperation with intellectuals and publishers inside Germany. Lion Feuchtwanger and Herman Broch in the United States, Nelly Sachs and Peter Weiss in Sweden, Erich Fried in England, and Max Zweig in Israel were some of the most important of these writers. They did not come back in person, but some of their writings returned to Germany. Although these writings usually did not emerge in the late 1940s, Feuchtwanger published his short story *Der treue Peter* in 1946 in the Berlin journal *Aufbau,* and Carl Zuckmayer's play *The Devil's General* appeared in 1946. Hermann Kesten's piece *The Friend in the Closet* was published in Munich in 1949. In 1948, Franz Werfel's *Song of Bernadette* had already been published in Germany. Herman Broch published his novel *The Guiltless* in 1950 in Zurich. A number of writers, particularly in Israel, who kept writing in German could not find any publisher in Germany. Some of their works were published in the 1970s or 1980s, but they seldom found public resonance. Many, however, had adapted to the language of their new homeland. Interest in their writing was in later years (predominantly since the 1960s) related to generational changes in Germany and to a new book market with interest in translations. Others, writers, like Curt Riess, did not return in person but published continually in Germany.

A second group included those very few who had survived inside Germany, as well as those who had returned to Germany with the allied forces or during the occupation of Germany. Some of these writers stayed in the western parts of occupied Germany, and some decided to go east and help in the building of an antifascist Germany in the Soviet zone of occupation. Some writers who had begun working in the American zone and had published first works there, like

Stefan Heym and Stephan Hermlin, continued their journalistic and literary activities in the Soviet zone. Hans Mayer, Ernst Bloch, Arnold Zweig, Anna Seghers, and Stephan Hermlin looked for a new and promising home in East Germany. Friedrich Torberg returned in 1951 from the United States to Vienna, where he had already published two novels in 1948 and 1950. Theodor Plievier had come back from Moscow in 1945, and he published a first volume of stories in 1947. None of these intellectuals thought about contributing to the division of Germany, but they hoped to participate in the cultural revival of the German classical tradition and in the development of a progressive democratic, socialist alternative. With the cultural onslaught of the Cold War, however, they relived the old dilemma of the painful German discourse of *Geist und Macht*. Those political and cultural changes that had not been brought about at the end of the Weimar era haunted these writers and influenced their readiness for personal and intellectual compromise. They contributed willingly or unwillingly to the cultural divide between the two Germanys. Hans Mayer and Ernst Bloch, however, were not ready to adjust to a German version of Stalinist cultural politics in the 1950s. They left East Germany in the early 1960s and continued working in West Germany. Others stayed, and either kept their distance from party politics or became involved to an extent that must have seemed to some of them a betrayal of their former antifascist pledge. The debates about Anna Seghers, who had returned from Mexico, can serve as an example. Authors like Stephan Hermlin or Peter Edel who had become communists in the 1930s usually gave witness to persistent antifascist convictions that seemed outdated to many of those they tried to reach in both Germanys. The situation was different for a small group of future authors whose parents had decided to stay in Germany without feeling at home. Jurek Becker, who together with his father had been liberated in the Sachsenhausen concentration camp, and who grew up in East Germany, describes this basic sentiment: "So I owe the fact that I became a German to my father's belief that here, in this part of the world, he would be more or less safe

from persecution. It was this same belief . . . that also kept him from going to West Germany; he often became upset over the careers that Nazis were making for themselves there. . . . The only thing that interested him about the Soviet zone of occupation and, later, the German Democratic Republic, was that the Anti-Fascists were in charge there" (Becker 1994). Others believed that their future was in the West. Authors with a German-Jewish background, like Hilde Domin, returned to West Germany but did not publish works of literature in the first years. They remained in Germany because the presence of the German language combined in a creative way with the past in Jewish memory. Hilde Domin argued—and this sums up the thoughts and feelings of other returnees as well—that the main reason for return was to be able to write in German, to live their language. A test case of Jewish assimilation and literary involvement is Elisabeth Langgässer, who survived inside Germany and published a number of books from 1945 until her death in 1950.

The third and most complicated group encompasses those who had been exiled or murdered in the Nazi extermination camps and whose works were burned. Their books were usually not reprinted in the immediate postwar period. With some exceptions in the 1950s, only parts of their work have been rediscovered since the early 1960s. Else Lasker-Schüler belongs to this group of Jewish authors. Lion Feuchtwanger's work, previously printed only in East Germany, returned to the bookstores, and so did, among others, the writings of poet Rose Ausländer. One may even conclude that this late return of German-Jewish writers to Germany is not yet over. There are still many Jewish authors of the decades between 1920 and 1980 to be rediscovered. The future will show to what extent the Aryanization of German literature, at least concerning the generation of those authors, will be a lasting success of Nazi Germany.

At the same time, it has to be stressed that some of the returning writers reached a broader audience when working in the media. Hence, when looking at literary works written by authors of Jewish origin and published in postwar Germany one should not disregard one important aspect: in the age of electronic dissemination literature is not only printed or distributed in bookstores. In the immediate postwar period it was sometimes much more relevant—in terms of reaching an interested public—to be broadcasted by the big and influential radio stations. The stations in Baden-Baden, Stuttgart, Munich, Frankfurt, Hamburg, or Berlin reached millions of radio listeners. Hundreds of thousands may not have bought the novels by Alfred Döblin or the poems or plays of Nelly Sachs—which sometimes were not even printed—but they surely heard works of these authors and many others on the air. Long before the relevant printed editions of Nelly Sachs's mystery play *Eli* appeared in bookstores it was successfully broadcasted on Stuttgart radio and other German stations. In 1950, Alfred Döblin spoke on Radio Baden-Baden and argued in favor of the necessary German-French reconciliation. In 1952, he reviewed on the air novels of Hermann Kesten, who still lived in New York, and Lion Feuchtwanger's new novel *Goya*. The same held true for broadcasting stations in the American zone, and newspapers like *Frankfurter Rundschau* and *Süddeutsche Zeitung*. They tried to create a cultural presence of the exiled literature and their returned representatives. Sometimes the public could read about a work of literature but not the work itself. The media, in other words, were important in creating the new democratic literary sphere, although this took much more time than those who were active in the ambitious enterprise of reeducation had thought it would in 1945.

In short, one has to realize that the return of literature written by authors of Jewish origin to post-Hitler Germany has many faces. Sometimes the writers returned, sometimes just their works reappeared, sometimes the author chose the partial return of extended visits, and sometimes a writer returned without finding the audience he had been longing for in exile. When Alfred Döblin left Germany in 1953, he was deeply disappointed about the failure of German publishers and readers to accept his works. But, most ironically, at the time when he left to live in France, one of his books had just returned to the German

literary sphere. His *Tales of a Long Night* was printed in East Germany and was well received.

In the late 1940s, and particularly in the early 1950s, a strange dualism evolved. On the one hand, a new Germany had to be created culturally and politically. But those writers who had represented this new Germany in exile and had continued to write and publish were not welcomed enthusiastically. This rejection had much to do with the widespread antiexile sentiment, but it cannot be reduced to the rejection of the emigrants and their voices. Beyond the contradictions of the German-Jewish literature in exile and the German writers within Germany existed yet another conflict: opposing literary traditions clashed in the postwar period. There existed the continuity of popular right-wing authors, and of semantic forms that were highly indebted to fascist rhetoric. Young German authors searched for their literary roots either in Weimar expressionism or in the rationalism of the *Neue Sachlichkeit,* the new objectivity, of Erich Kästner and other writers. Most exiled authors, on the other hand, had continued their work in exile as if their contributions would be welcomed by a Weimar culture audience. Weimar as a cultural entity, however, did not exist anymore. This fact had led to a specific loss of tradition, to a rupture between the literature of exile and the writers' actual social and cultural frame of reference. It was thus understandable that most German-Jewish authors in exile looked upon Western culture and civilization as their new frame of reference. This outlook could be seen as a means of cultural transition, but it was not enough considering the spiritual and literary needs of the postwar Germans. Wolfgang Borchert's writings were closer to the mindset of the postwar Germans than was a novel about the Spanish Inquisition. The Jewish returnees, at the same time, were not able to accept the ongoing relevance of the literary production under National Socialism or the ambiguous experiences of the so-called inner emigration that were of eminent importance for the young generation of German postwar writers (Group 47 and others), at least in the West. Peter Weiss, in his *Abschied von den Eltern,* notes that emigration did not teach him anything—it just confirmed his not-belonging, his displacement. This displacement, in fact, has to be seen as a possible common denominator of the Jewish writers who stayed in West Germany, those who stayed in East Germany, and those who went on living in various other countries. Displacement and exile are not historical phenomena of those twelve years, but rather a state of mind, an emotional and spiritual attitude—and, as the writer Barbara Honigmann has shown in recent years, a productive force of ongoing creativity more than fifty years after 1945.

The literary sphere of the early postwar years did not belong to the exiled writers. Most of the German-Jewish writers were not even asked to return; their manuscripts were rejected, their books were not accepted by the public. The return of German-Jewish writers to Germany is an ongoing process, often interrupted, but not yet over. The year 1945, with all its historical and literary connotations, seems to be a literary project still in progress. The story of the novelist Konrad Merz illustrates this context. In 1934 he had fled to Amsterdam, where he published, in 1936, *Ein Mann fällt aus Deutschland,* a book that was praised by Klaus Mann. But during the following thirty-six years he did not publish. His novel had to wait until 1978 to be republished in Germany. In another example, Merz, living in Holland, returned only for visits. In 1992, he participated in a public reading in his native Berlin. A significant number of German-Jewish authors share the long-standing verdict of the "boycott of silence" that Döblin so sharply criticized in the early 1950s. Some exiled works returned, many were off limits owing to the differing cultural politics in East and West Germany, and even more still wait to be rediscovered in the evolving cultural sphere of Germany after unification.

But even the new Jewish voices that can be heard in Germany today reflect different shades of displacement and represent unique images of the centuries-old search for a German-Jewish dream that began with the youthful and creative poet Süßkind von Trimberg. Centuries later, two of the motives to be found in his songs resound in the writings of Barbara Honigmann and others: first, the endeavor to be understood (to write for a German audience in the most appropriate literary imagery), and second, the revitalization of a colorful and concrete Jewish identity as an answer to the alienating attitudes of German society. Since 1945, both literary paradigms characterize the German-Jewish ambivalence. The writers Peter Weiss, Wolfgang Hildesheimer, Stefan Heym, Ralph Giordano, Lotte Paepcke, and many others tried to capture this ambivalence, in their literary work or in their individual reflections on the tribulations of the German postwar societies. In the end, the German-Jewish returnees had only one thing in common: theirs was a community of shared dissent.

Bibliography

Hannah Arendt and Karl Jaspers, *Correspondence, 1926–1969* (New York: Harcourt: 1992); Jurek Becker, "My Father, the Germans, and Me," *Internationes* (winter 1994): 4–12; Henryk M. Broder and Michel R. Lang, eds., *Fremd im eigenen Land: Juden in der Bundesrepublik* (Frankfurt a. M.: Fischer, 1979); Alfred Döblin, *Destiny's Journey* (New York: Paragon, 1992); Lion Feuchtwanger and Arnold Zweig, *Briefwechsel, 1933–1958,* vol. 1, *1933–1948* (Berlin: Aufbau, 1984); Wolfgang Hildesheimer, *Ich werde nun schweigen* (Göttingen: Lamuv, 1993); Thomas Koebner, *Unbehauste: Zur deutschen Literatur in der Weimarer Republik, im Exil und in der Nachkriegszeit* (Munich: Text & Kritik, 1992); Hans Mayer, *Ein Deutscher auf Widerruf I* (Frankfurt a. M.: Suhrkamp, 1982); Mayer, *Die umerzogene Literatur: Deutsche Schriftsteller und Bücher, 1945–1967* (Berlin: Siedler, 1988); Peter Mertz, *Und das wurde nicht ihr Staat: Erfahrungen emigrierter Schriftsteller mit Westdeutschland* (Munich: Beck, 1985); Lotte Paepcke, *Unter einem fremden Stern* (Frankfurt a. M.: Frankfurter Hefte, 1952); Hans Jürgen Schultz, ed., *Mein Judentum* (Stuttgart: Kreuz, 1978); and Peter Weiss, *Notizbücher, 1960–1971* (Frankfurt a. M.: Suhrkamp, 1982).

FRANK STERN

1946 Edgar Hilsenrath and Jakov Lind meet at the employment office in Netanya, Palestine, discuss literature, and contemplate their recent past

After time had passed, some survivors of the Holocaust began to write down their versions of what had happened, attempting to reconstruct as literature an event that many felt was beyond words. As the scope of the disaster became evident, most of these authors felt compelled to treat this theme as virtually a sacred topic, not to be violated lightly by such potentially blasphemous literary devices as satire, irony, travesty, or black humor, which had often been used in fictional accounts of destructive events in Jewish history. For Yiddish-language writers, whose potential readership had been decimated during the war, this trend was especially apparent. Whereas the most famous character in all of Yiddish literature, Sholom Aleichem's Tevye the milkman, could discuss the devastating anti-Semitic pogroms in tsarist Russia around the turn of the century with a kind of bitter ironic humor, no such stance was possible with regard to the Holocaust.

Early literary attempts to deal with the Holocaust in the German language showed a strong tendency to attempt to depict, in as realistic a manner as possible, the incomprehensible viciousness to which the authors' personal, cultural, and religious worlds had been subjected. Such authors as Peter Weiss, Nelly Sachs, Paul Celan, Peter Edel, Ilse Aichinger, Grete Weil, and H. G. Adler, who had survived by luck or by exile, wrote works of unrelenting bleakness and despair to present the fate of European Jewry during World War II. In their descriptions of the Holocaust, there was no place for the arsenal of literary weapons that had been put to such effective use by their colleague Günter Grass in the most famous German work of this period, *Die Blechtrommel* (The tin drum; 1959). There were, however, a couple of glaring exceptions to this rule. In New York and London, two young men who had lived through the Holocaust and had subsequently met in Palestine, wrote phantasmagoric works of fiction in German about what they had experienced: Edgar Hilsenrath and Jakov Lind.

They were born within a year and a few hundred miles of each other, Hilsenrath in Leipzig in 1926 and Lind, whose real name was Heinz Landwirth, in Vienna in 1927. Hilsenrath's Orthodox Jewish paternal grandparents had emigrated just before the turn of the century from that part of Austrian Galicia that later became Polish, and his mother had come early in the new century from the Austrian Bukowina, which later became Romanian. Because his grandmother had followed tradition and returned to her parents' home to give birth, his father had been born in Galicia, making him an Austrian and then a Polish citizen, even though he had actually lived only in Germany. He won medals for bravery while fighting as an officer in the Austrian army in World War I, married in 1924, and was a reasonably successful merchant in Leipzig by the time of Edgar's birth. In 1929 he moved his business to Halle an der Saale, and in 1938 everything he owned was confiscated by the Nazis. Just before it was too late, he sent his wife and two sons to his wife's family in Siret, Romania, forty kilometers south of Chernovtsy. Almost ten years later, his family found out that his plans to get an American visa had come to nothing, and that he had escaped across the French border with the clothes on his back, ten marks in his pocket, and a packet of cigarettes.

Jakov Lind's father was born on the Polish side of the Tatra mountains, and his mother not far from the birthplace of Hilsenrath's mother in the Bukowina. They married in 1921 in Vienna, where his father was in the textile business in the Ninth District. In many ways Edgar and Jakov were raised in families very much like those of millions of other Orthodox, Yiddish-speaking, Eastern European Jews who had emigrated to the powerful urban centers to the west in search of improved economic conditions, and who were not interested in drawing attention to their backgrounds. In both cases, the children were brought up speaking German and had no formal religious training. In the first volume of his autobiography, *Counting My Steps* (1969), Lind writes that his father "loathed the Orthodox Jews . . . despised the righteous and the respectable, called them all 'hypocrites'" (33), and that he was, at the same time, "an ordinary father, an ordinary Viennese, and as a normal Viennese, he felt better than all the other normal Viennese. I loved my father and my Vaterland" (35). In 1938, the Nazis annexed a willing Austria, and Lind's father discovered that Jews were no longer considered to be Austrians. Shortly thereafter, Jakov found himself on a train to the Netherlands, where for a short time he was under the protection of the Jewish Refugee Committee, and his parents were on the boat to Bratislava en route to Palestine. Vienna became a city of the dead, he writes, but his family was tough, and "we probably lost only eighty-four uncles, aunts, and cousins in the last war. That's all" (58).

Away from Nazi Germany, Hilsenrath spent the happiest time of his childhood with his grandparents in Siret, a largely Jewish town where the old people spoke Yiddish and the young spoke German and where he, as a representative of the great German culture of the West,

was named captain of the youth soccer team. Then in the fall of 1941, Romania deported the Jews of Bessarabia and the Bukowina, including Edgar, his mother, and his brother, to the concentration camps of Transnistria, in the western part of Ukraine, which had been annexed by advancing German troops and then given to their Romanian allies. The Hilsenraths found themselves in the largest of these concentration camps, located in the ruins of the city of Moghilev-Podolsk. It quickly turned into a communal cemetery containing the victims of hunger, typhoid, and mass murder.

In the Netherlands, too, the Nazis eventually caught up with their Jewish refugees, sending most of them, along with the native Dutch Jews, to the killing centers in Poland. But young Jakov was intelligent, resourceful, healthy, and a native German speaker, and he decided that his safest course of action was to illegally cross back into Germany and to try to survive after having jettisoned his Jewish background. Armed with false papers, which identified him as the gentile Jan Gerrit Overbeek, a Dutch laborer with an Austrian mother, he spent what was for the European Jews the most dangerous part of the war working on the boats along the Rhine, occasionally playing the role of an anti-Semite, and eventually even becoming a cog in the Nazi bureaucracy as an assistant to an SS official in the air ministry.

When the war was over, Lind and Hilsenrath made their way to Palestine, the goal of the Zionist groups to which they both had once belonged. After an adventurous journey by foot and a convoy through Ukraine, Romania, Bulgaria, and Turkey, Hilsenrath crossed the Lebanese border with a forged passport on the Baghdad train in early January 1945; Lind arrived six months later, this time as Jakov Chachlan, on one of the overcrowded refugee ships from Marseilles. For both of them, Palestine proved to be a hot, dry, and occasionally violent land, full of people very different from themselves and who spoke languages they did not understand. They spent their time there wandering around the country with the semiemployed European survivors of the war, picking up any jobs that were offered and contemplating their prospects in an alien world. Lind soon found out that his mother had died of cancer in Tel Aviv in 1941, and that the Haganah had blown up the ship carrying all his father's belongings, leaving the father a wreck of the man he had been (Lind 1969, 194–95). Hilsenrath discovered, to his great surprise, that his father had survived the war and was alive in France. By then, both Hilsenrath and Lind had learned lessons about the fragility of individuality, and about the dubiousness of the concept of identity, not to mention nationality. These themes continually appeared in the prose accounts of their experiences that were beginning to form in their imaginations.

In the spring of 1946, Hilsenrath's and Lind's paths crossed for the first time in the construction employment office of the kibbutz in Netanya, a coastal town north of Tel Aviv. Lind recalls, with a fondness rare in his memories of Palestine, the cultural discussions with Hilsenrath, among nameless others, in the tin hut they shared in Netanya (Lind 1969, 207). In his recently published memoirs, "Die Sache mit dem toten Engländer (eine wahre Geschichte)" (The thing about the dead Englishman [a true story]), Hilsenrath describes his response to a request for an example of his supposedly heroic role in the liberation of Palestine. He simply recounts an incident that occurred when he and Lind, working together as stretcher bearers in the Hagassah hospital in Tel Aviv, had a dead British soldier, whom they were carrying down to the morgue after a terrorist attack, slide out of his blanket and land with his legs around Hilsenrath's neck. When asked "What does the fact that a dead British soldier crawls on the neck of a Jewish writer have to do with the liberation of Palestine? What sense does that make?" his answer is immediate: "None at all." It is a response that reverberates through all the stories that were about to be written by these two stretcher bearers.

Neither Hilsenrath nor Lind stayed very long in Palestine; both traveled back briefly to continental Europe before moving on to the English-speaking world. Following brief stops in Amsterdam and Vienna, Lind made his way to London, his principal place of residence after 1954. After writing and publishing half a dozen works in

German between 1962 and 1968, he changed languages, writing all of his subsequent works in English. Hilsenrath first traveled to France, where he joined his father and the rest of his family in emigrating to the United States, settling in New York in 1951. He would later use his quixotic adventures there as the basis of his novel *Bronskys Geständnis* (Bronsky's confession). In 1975, afraid that he was losing his ability to write in German, he returned to Berlin, where he has lived ever since.

In the 1960s, Hilsenrath and Lind published highly imaginative stories and novels that illustrated the macabre senselessness suggested by the fate of the dead Englishman, thus creating a dilemma for German publishers who suspected, correctly as it turned out, that their readers' interest in the Holocaust was limited to works of supposed "realism." Unconvinced that the Holocaust could be portrayed in the form of a surrealistic nightmare, they remained wary of any work in which the true intentions of the author might be masked behind a suspect narrative voice. Ultimately, these publishers were justifiably skeptical that their readers were prepared for the challenge of reading about this event in fictional works that demanded the same kind of creative response on the part of the readers as did *Die Blechtrommel*.

In 1962, Luchterhand Verlag published Jakov Lind's *Eine Seele aus Holz* (Soul of wood), a collection of seven short stories, of which the title story is also by far the longest and most famous. "Eine Seele aus Holz" begins with what appears to be an "acceptable" account of the fate of a Viennese Jewish couple, Mr. and Mrs. Barth, who board a train on what they have been told will be a journey back to their ancestral home, Odessa. After just one succinct page, Lind concludes his realistic, factual description of the fate of the Jews. "Of course, they didn't make it to Odessa. In the Polish city of Auschwitz, they were met by uniformed officers and on the same day burned" (8). If that's the way you want to hear this story, the author implies, then that's all there is to it. There's nothing more to be said.

But then he goes on to tell the story as he wants to tell it, the tale of the son Anton, who was left behind, suicidal, crippled, and dependent on the mercy of others who had been generously compensated by the departing parents to provide it. But Anton does not die, as he wishes, experiencing instead the most fulfilling and human moments of his whole life alone with the animals in the mountain hut where he has been deposited by his caretakers. Lind's tale contains elements of literary parody (of Oskar Matzerath in *Die Blechtrommel* and Menuchum in Joseph Roth's *Hiob* [Job]), satire (of the Austrian bourgeoisie), autobiography (his abandonment), and travesty (of the Nazis), and it was like nothing else written previously in German about the Holocaust. By interweaving the fate of the utterly helpless Anton with that of the Austrian Jews and Nazis, Lind managed to make a subversive commentary on both the senseless naiveté of the former and the boundless depravity of the latter. Lind's last laugh is particularly bitter. As the war nears its end, Anton is removed from his hut, and various Austrian Nazis and their accomplices fight over the suddenly invaluable right to claim to have saved him. When he wrote this novel, Lind was already living in London.

In *Landschaft in Beton* (Landscape in concrete; 1963), Lind employed a similar mixture of the grotesque, the macabre, and the perversely comic to tell the story of the German soldier Gauthier Bachmann, who claims to have seen his entire company sink into the swamps of the eastern front and to have spent months searching for his comrades. His adventures, ranging from the pathologically sadistic (the murder and decapitation of a Norwegian resistance family at the command of a crazed collaborator) to the grotesquely comic (his destruction of the subterranean home of a German deserter by stomping on the roof), provide an unrelieved bitter commentary on a world out of joint. But the novel, in which no Jews appear, also demands that the reader make the connection between the absurd caricatures of human beings who inhabit Lind's world and the absurdity of the Europe that had been ruled by such caricatures. In a novel that at times seems to be a vicious parody of popular German war novels, Lind never points out the correct interpretation for his readers, insisting that they draw their own conclusions.

During this period, Lind tested out the possibilities of his two languages, writing "imaginary" descriptions of his experiences in German and "realistic" ones in English. The fictional works, which went on to include another novel, *Eine bessere Welt* (Ergo; 1966) and three radio plays (1965–68), were quickly supplanted by "factual" English accounts in his two autobiographical works, *Counting My Steps* (1969) and *Numbers* (1972), and the journalistic report of his return to Israel, *The Trip to Jerusalem* (1973). Critical reaction in Germany, after some early positive response to *Eine Seele aus Holz,* became increasingly negative during the 1960s. This censure provided one major reason for his decision to eventually abandon German entirely and write exclusively in English, even in works of fiction.

Edgar Hilsenrath's *Nacht* (Night) was first published by the prominent Kindler publishing house in 1964, but in a run of only 1,000 copies, apparently because of in-house dissension on whether such a potentially offensive work should be published at all. *Nacht* was (and is) disturbing because it concentrates almost entirely on the captive Jewish inmates in the ruins of Prokow, the fictional version of Moghilov-Podolsk, and shows little interest in the captors. The reader is transported directly into the brutal daily routines of the veterans of the ghetto, who are determined to win the battle of survival in the disease-ridden ruins of a city with no food deliveries, even if it is at the expense of their fellow-prisoners.

The difficulty with Hilsenrath's novel is that it scarcely even addresses directly the terrifying historical fact that such a nightmare could be conceived and carried out by supposedly civilized people. Rather, it takes that as a given, and offers a story designed to illustrate Hilsenrath's dark conclusion that under such circumstances almost everyone becomes the predator that the authorities had always said they were, and that most generally civilized human beings, thrust into a landscape where only the fittest can survive, will go to any lengths to try to remain among the fittest. In the face of this riveting portrayal of nihilistic human behavior under pressure, one of the central themes of most standard accounts of the Holocaust—namely, the specific guilt of the

Nazis and their collaborators in the genocide of the Jews—is left for his readers to introduce.

Hilsenrath insists not only that this is an accurate description of what life really was like in Transnistria, but also that Prokow should be understood to be a ghetto symbolic of every once-civilized place that has been thrust back into barbarism, a truly somber view of the history of mankind. By identifying Van Gogh's first large painting, *The Potato Eaters,* as an inspiration for *Nacht,* however, he has also implied the potential for a kind of light in the darkness. Here, a group of poor people sit at a table before a meal of potatoes, and it is perhaps no coincidence that in both Van Gogh's painting and in Hilsenrath's novel there are figures who offer food and compassion to their fellow-sufferers despite personal consequences, thus defying the temptation to allow the grinding poverty, hunger, and disease to undermine their concept of ethical behavior.

Der Nazi und der Friseur (The Nazi and the barber), Hilsenrath's second novel, which no German publisher would touch until six years after the English translation had appeared in 1971, replaces the science-fiction wasteland of the historical Moghilev-Podolsk with the surrealistic landscape of a familiar German world placed totally out of its usual narrative context. The most shocking feature of *Der Nazi und der Friseur* is the sarcastic voice of the narrator—mass-murderer Max Schulz, as he likes to identify himself—the SS man who at the end of the war takes over the identity of his boyhood friend Itzig Finkelstein, whom he had murdered in concentration camp. Financed by a bag of gold teeth hammered out of the mouths of his victims, he journeys from Poland to the ruins of Berlin, taking advantage of the benefits offered a concentration camp survivor in black-market postwar Germany. Newly circumcised and tattooed, and armed with a knowledge of Yiddish and Judaism learned as a child in the Finkelstein home, the committed Zionist then starts a new life in Palestine, where he joins the war for Israeli independence, finding favor with the freedom fighters because of his experience with arms. It is a plot that has the potential to offend everyone involved—Germans, Jews,

Poles, and Israelis. (The first Hebrew and Polish translations appeared in 1994.)

Because the storyteller Max Schulz has profited greatly from the rise of the Nazis and his activities in the SS, and continues in his final years in Israel to look back nostalgically at that time, the novel presents an inverted literary version of the Holocaust. This narrator has nothing but fond memories of the Nazi period, and the unwary and uncritical reader, content with following the grotesquely comical, picaresque, sadistic, and occasionally pornographic adventures of Schulz as he enjoys his rise to the kind of power which he otherwise could never have experienced, may well find himself being either totally repelled or unwittingly entertained by the memoirs of the narrator, who is, among other things, a clever and provocative raconteur.

In his review of the first German edition of the novel, Heinrich Böll writes about the effort he had to expend in order to force himself to burrow beneath the repugnant surface of *Der Nazi und der Friseur* and to recognize the validity of the reverse fairy tale lurking below. In Hilsenrath's distorted story, argues Böll, Hans im Glück (Lucky Hans), an iconic figure of German folklore, goes out, finds his luck by reveling in the perverse bloodletting of World War II, and is proud of his skill in later escaping blame. It is enough to make you want to put the book down in disgust, Böll begins, but he concludes by recognizing that "this horrifying game was no game, it becomes reality through Hilsenrath and it really existed—didn't it?—these Nazis, who did what nobody knew about, which nobody wanted, and which everyone ought to forget: you don't forget the gold teeth and those who once carried them when Schulz-Finkelstein goes for a walk there in the forest of the six million" (Böll 1977).

During the 1960s, when the first works of Lind and Hilsenrath appeared, the Holocaust was still a punishing recent memory for most of their readers. Those who condemned the works did so because they seemed to prefer surrealism to realism, parody to veracity, black humor to moralism, lunacy to logic, nightmares to facts, and universals to specifics in translating into literature an event of intense personal pain. In doing so, they assembled a cast of characters who were too busy trying to survive to bother assigning specific guilt in a world void of spiritual and moral conviction.

When that happens, and Hilsenrath warns that it can happen anywhere, anytime, civilized conduct is limited to those threatened individuals, such as the saintly Debora in *Nacht,* who understand that their behavior is governed by ethical laws unaffected by the civic reversion to barbarism. In the stories of Lind such figures (perhaps the Norwegian resistance family in *Landschaft in Beton*) are hard to discern. *Der Nazi und der Friseur* offers almost no one who embodies such a hope, unless it is the Finkelstein family, who disappear quickly into the death camps in Poland. In *Bronskys Geständnis,* Hilsenrath presents a relatively light, comparatively harmless version of this desolate world, with New York serving as the setting for the homeless and the hungry, and his own alter ego Jakob Bronsky acting as the determined survivor. No one dies of hunger in Hilsenrath's postwar New York, however, and Bronsky's various financial schemes give this novel a comic edge, which tends to lighten the dark struggle between the occasionally altruistic castaways and a society uninterested in their dilemma. But in his 1989 novel, *Das Märchen vom letzten Gedanken* (The story of the last thought), Hilsenrath would test this idea once again in a deadly historical context, that of the Turkish treatment of the Armenians in World War I, an event he portrays as having directly influenced the Nazi decision to carry out the genocide of the European Jews. In this novel, as well, there is a total breakdown of civilized behavior on the part of those who wield power and strike laws. In Hilsenrath's dark and menacing world, there is either the moral determination of the individual, or there is nothing at all.

It is now more than fifty years since Lind and Hilsenrath met in the kibbutz at Netanya and more than a quarter century since they first published their shocking versions of the Holocaust.

Soon after Lind decided to abandon his career as one of the most promising young German writers, Hilsenrath chose to return to Germany, and has, with the publication of major novels in 1989 (*Das Märchen vom letzten Gedanken*) and 1993 (*Jossel Wassermanns Heimkehr* [The return of Jossel Wassermann]), confirmed his status as one of the few German writers who has been able to maintain his creativity and productivity throughout the postwar period. In 1989 he won the Döblin Prize, in 1993 the Galinski Prize, and in 1994 the Nossack Prize. For the author of *Der Nazi und der Friseur,* who has recently celebrated his seventieth birthday, it must seem macabre and ironically appropriate that he continually runs the risk of being honored as one of the grand old men of German literature.

Bibliography

Heinrich Böll, "Hans im Glück im Blut," *Die Zeit* 51 (Dec. 9, 1977); Sander L. Gilman, "Jüdische Literaten und deutsche Literatur: Antisemitismus und die verborgene Sprache der Juden am Beispiel von Jurek Becker und Edgar Hilsenrath," *Zeitschrift für deutsche Philologie* 107 (1988): 269–94; Edgar Hilsenrath, *Bronskys Geständnis* (Munich: Langen-Müller, 1980); Hilsenrath, *Das Märchen vom letzten Gedanken* (Munich: Piper, 1989); Hilsenrath, *Nacht* (Munich: Kindler, 1964); Hilsenrath, *Der Nazi und der Friseur* (Cologne: Literarischer Verlag Braun, 1977), first appeared as *The Nazi and the Barber* (New York: Doubleday, 1971); Hilsenrath, "Die Sache mit dem toten Engländer (eine wahre Geschichte)," *5734 Jüdischer Kalender, 1993/94* (Berlin: Lichtig Verlag, 1993); Peter Jokostra, "Bericht aus dem Inferno," *Echo der Zeit* (May 2, 1965); Jakov Lind, *Counting My Steps* (London: Macmillan, 1969); Lind, *Eine bessere Welt* (Berlin: Wagenbach, 1966); Lind, *Eine Seele aus Holz: Erzählungen* (Neuwied: Luchterhand, 1962); Lind, *Landschaft in Beton* (Neuwied: Luchterhand, 1963); and Peter Stenberg, *Journey to Oblivion* (Toronto: University of Toronto Press, 1991).

PETER STENBERG

1946 Jewish playwrights in the postwar German theater begin to break the taboos associated with German-Jewish relations and the Holocaust

It was soon after the end of World War II that Jewish playwrights and directors began to examine the fate of the Jews under the Nazis and to investigate the relationship between Jews and Germans in the light of what had happened. It would be wrong, both quantitatively as well as qualitatively, to maintain that the celebrated German-Jewish theater tradition was restored in the postwar era. Nonetheless, it appears in retrospect that Jewish playwrights and directors contributed substantially to the depiction of the German-Jewish relationship during and after the Holocaust. Moreover, some of these playwrights, such as George Tabori and Peter Zadek, helped to combat and remove preconceptions and taboos closely associated with this subject.

The first postwar play to pose the question of guilt and responsibility for the crimes perpetrated during the Third Reich was Carl Zuckmayer's *Des Teufels General* (The devil's general). Zuckmayer (1896–1977), born of a Jewish mother though raised as a Catholic, was well known before 1933 as a novelist and dramatist. He immigrated to Switzerland and later settled in the United States. Harras, the protagonist of his box-office success, is a well-known pilot modeled after the historical *Wehrmacht* General Udet, who dissociates professional duty from political involvement and shows sympathy for the Jewish victims. Writing the play in exile before the war had ended, Zuckmayer was the first Jewish playwright to repudiate the proposition of the collective guilt of Germans and to offer a portrayal of the "other Germany."

The suffering of the Jews during the war also preoccupied Zuckmayer in *Das kalte Licht* (The cold light; 1955), in which the religious Jew Friedländer is portrayed as a master of the art of survival, reminiscent of Werfel's protagonist Jacobowsky, and in the play *Gesang im Feuerofen* (The song in the fiery furnace; 1950). In the latter, Zuckmayer depicts the agony and suffering of a Jewish family trying to reach the shelter of safety in Switzerland. Strikingly, these harassed refugees remain anonymous. Indeed, Zuckmayer stylizes the historical case by means of allegorical elements and changing roles and identities so as to imply its universal quality. In other words, Zuckmayer is not so much concerned with the political or historical aspects of persecution as with the suffering inflicted by people, whomever they may be, on their fellow human beings.

An ahistorical approach supported by allegorical elements characterizes the plays of the Austrian Jewish writer Albert Drach (b. 1902). A practicing lawyer who joined the French Resistance and returned to his native Austria in 1947, Drach did not become known for his literary oeuvre until the 1960s. Justice and its miscarriage is the main theme underlying his literary work, whereby the crime against the Jews is seen as yet another instance of injustice in our world. In his satirical stage parable "Das I" (The I; written 1965), he suggests that the crime against the Jews may not possess that historical uniqueness some bestow upon it, but that it may in fact mark only one of the most horrendous stages in the eternal process of catastrophes brought upon humankind by evil men and men of power. The characters are literally dehumanized, puppets in a mask ("Maskenspiel"), and the play ends with the return of the arch-villain Ganstel-Hitler, who pops out as "Jack-in-the-box," this time as the Arab Ahmed Al Gangstel.

Some of the Jewish playwrights writing in German (Elias Canetti, for instance) avoided dealing with the German-Jewish past. Others, like Thomas Brasch (b. 1945) only touched upon it. Brasch, who was born in England to Marxist Jewish emigrants, started his career in East Germany, where the family had moved in 1947, and settled in West Berlin in 1976. His play *Rotter* (1977) depicts in a loose, episodic structure the life of a bystander in the Nazi period who later skillfully adapted himself to the Socialist regime, "the eternal time-server." Whereas the Jewish issue hardly plays a role in *Rotter*, Brasch's filmscript *Der Passagier—Welcome in Germany* (The passenger; 1988), which was written in collaboration with the Jewish author Jurek Becker, deals with the fate of Jewish actors who were promised freedom for their participation in an anti-Semitic propaganda film and who nonetheless were later murdered.

Still other Jewish playwrights tried to recapture the Jewish past or look for the origins of the Jewish tragedy. In his much-acclaimed documentary play about the Holocaust *Die Ermittlung* (The investigation; 1965), Peter Weiss (1916–83) examined the Nazi system of extermination, suggesting that its origins lay in the malaise of fascist capitalism. Confronting the spectator for the first time with Auschwitz as the region of hell in which the system reached its hideous perfection, Weiss's main interest lies with the perpetrators and their accomplices. The Nazi machinery, he implies, not only exterminated millions of Jews, but victimized others as well. The nameless Jewish survivors who are called to witness in the trial against the Nazi murderers describe the system from the point of view of the victims, whoever they may have been. "Auch wir Häftlinge / vom

Prominenten bis hin zum Sterbenden / gehörten dem System an" (Even we prisoners, prominent people as well as the dying, belonged to the system; 334–35). Indeed, the question may be asked whether this Jewish playwright, who survived the war in Sweden, did not break the first taboo in that he consistently avoided the word "Jew" in a play about the Final Solution. Moreover, Weiss seems to imply that under different circumstances the Jews themselves could have been the perpetrators.

Like Peter Weiss, the German-Jewish playwright Hans Sahl (1902–93) also attempts to investigate the past and to look for the origin of the catastrophe, yet his interest lies with the Jewish victims. Sahl, who emigrated in 1933 and returned to Germany in old age, insisted in the preface to his play *Hausmusik* (Music-making at home; 1984) that "the tone of the play should not be too heavy, not pregnant with meaning as is often the case on German stages when this theme [the Holocaust] is being treated." "Hausmusik" depicts the fate of the Rosengarten family during the Nazi period. Their story is to be seen as representative of the experience of the German-Jewish bourgeoisie—in their effort to assimilate, their devotion to the German *Heimat*, and the ensuing catastrophe. Sahl, like other Jewish playwrights, is aware of the uneasiness and guilt of German spectators and advocates a performance that would coalesce "joke and solemnity, tragedy and farce."

Hans Sahl is one of the few playwrights who, like Albert Drach, chose to return to his native home after years in exile. Fritz Hochwälder (1911–86), whose parents had been deported and murdered in Poland, was a writer who decided to stay away from his native Austria, although it had honored him with prizes. A writer dedicated to the theater, Hochwälder was one of the first to point out the lies that the postwar society spawned in order to protect itself from the harrowing truth. In his comedy *Der Himbeerpflücker* (The raspberry picker; 1965), he depicts a system of repression—"unbewältigte Gegenwart"— abetted by a whole village. The arrival of a fugitive taken to be a notorious SS officer in Bad Brauning (alluding to Hitler's Austrian birthplace) forces the villagers to face the past they have repressed. Each one of them has a skeleton in the closet, having once been actively involved in the Nazi machinery. Disappointed at the banal truth of the fugitive's identity, the villagers seek consolation in a new speculation, namely, that the thief must be a Jew. Indeed, Hochwälder is one of the first dramatists to show that clichés and prejudices associated with Jews have survived even where Jews are no longer present—anti-Semitism has lived on without Jews.

A portrait of Viennese society as having undergone little change in spite of the war was also offered by the prominent director and playwright Fritz Kortner (1892–1970), who chose to return to Germany—not to his native Vienna—soon after the war. In his first postwar play, *Donauwellen* (The waves of the Danube; 1949), which he had completed in the United States, Kortner depicts postwar Viennese society in a somewhat comic vein, as one in which people try to adapt to the demands of the moment just as they had accommodated themselves to the fascist regime. Although he rejected the notion of collective guilt, Kortner brought out the connection between the striving for a "fresh start" and the specter of the past. In his later marital drama *Die Zwiesprache* (The dialogue; 1964), the Jewish Professor Ewald is a key figure as Kortner's image of the Jew after Auschwitz. The survivor is a man haunted by suffering and the dread of adversity. He is hypersensitive, vulnerable, said to suffer from claustrophobia, and given to polemics when in company. In addition, he suffers pangs of remorse at having consented to accept reparations from the Germans, whom he unceasingly criticizes. At work in the figure of Professor Ewald are reverberations of those deep-seated and irresolvable tensions that were to be the lot of so many Jewish survivors—tensions born of their inability to come to terms with the crimes wrought upon them by a people with whom they had sought, almost pathetically, to identify; born, equally, of their failure to resign themselves to exile and the profound sense of disorientation, of belonging nowhere, that ensued. Expression of this anguish is, in fact, also to be found in Kortner's own autobiography *Aller*

Tage Abend (1959): "Whoever calls so many countries 'Heimat' has no fatherland, he is a wanderer without a homeland who only has one mother-tongue."

Most significant perhaps was Kortner's version of Shakespeare's *Merchant of Venice,* a play that German directors and actors avoided after the Holocaust. Whereas the Shylock of Ernst Deutsch (directed by Erwin Piscator, Berlin 1963) was an advocate, as it were, of reconciliation (*Wiedergutmachung*)—according to Piscator, the character is "tragic, pitiable and deeply, deeply human"—Kortner's sinister and vindictive Jew appeared as a mutilated angry old man, a lonely yet proud outsider—"a figure most human in its miserableness, cruelty, dignity and suffering," as Volker Canaris put it. (The last performance of Kortner's version of this play was for a German television production in 1968.) A few years later, in 1972, another Jewish director, Peter Zadek (b. 1926), who grew up as the son of émigré parents in England and launched an impressive career as a director in Germany in 1958, offered a highly controversial interpretation of the play. Hans Mahnke was a mean and malicious, almost monstrous Shylock, so much so that he appeared "in a frightening manner of conflicting and vindictive traits." As opposed to the dignified-looking Deutsch and Kortner, who wore the traditional black garment (caftan) and had side-locks and beards, Mahnke wore a shabby, partly torn garment. He spoke with a lisp, and his German was tinged with the sound of Yiddish. Zadek deliberately sought an exaggerated, almost grotesque Shylock who is indeed a compendium of anti-Semitic clichés. A philo-Semitic presentation of Shylock stems from a bad conscience, he argued, and his aim was clearly to shock the German public into awareness and to provoke them to reconsider preconceptions and prejudices. In a later production of *The Merchant of Venice* at the Vienna Burgtheater in 1989, Zadek presented yet another interpretation of the play. In an all glass and steel environment, amidst Venetian "yuppies" doing business with cordless phones, Shylock, middle-aged and blond, was a smart scheming dealer indistinguishable from the rest.

It was Zadek once again who, known for his provocative, nonconformist approach, for offending "good taste," decorum and moral principles, staged in 1984 the first German production of *Ghetto* by the Israeli playwright Yehoshua Sobol. In his spectacularly staged production, a spellbinding and brilliant revue about the liquidation of the Wilna ghetto, Zadek succeeded in provoking both spectators and critics, whose reactions ranged from embarrassment and bewilderment to resentment and anger. Is it right to stage a play in Germany in which Jewish victims are depicted in an ambivalent light, as human beings with virtues and faults? Does Sobol's drama not play into the hands of those Germans who untiringly try to exculpate themselves of responsibility and guilt by suggesting that the Jews were at least partly responsible for their own fate? No wonder then that many a well-known critic, who had been used to seeing the Jew as a noble and innocent victim, was alarmed and shocked by the numerous "taboo violations," which, they argued, might sustain a dangerous revision of history and nurture anti-Semitic sentiments.

It was Peter Zadek again, who in the highly controversial dispute over Fassbinder's *Garbage, the City, and Death* in 1985, argued that, although Fassbinder's play was clearly anti-Semitic, it had to be produced. Less provocative than Zadek and yet free of the German *Befangenheit* (awkwardness), other young Jewish directors followed him with puzzling productions that deviated from the prevailing conventions. This is true of Arie Zinger's 1979 production of *The Merchant of Venice* or Benjamin Korn's vexing staging (1981) of Lessing's *Nathan der Weise* (Nathan the wise), a play that had been staged time and again as a plea for reconciliation and tolerance, with Nathan as the sagacious and noble Jew.

No doubt the most significant contribution in postwar theater to the German-Jewish discourse has been that of George Tabori (b. 1914). A native of Budapest, Tabori sojourned in seventeen countries, writing novels, filmscripts for Hollywood, essays, and plays. A Jewish cosmopolitan carrying a British passport and writing all his works in English, he made his theater debut in

West Germany in 1969—and has troubled German audiences ever since by touching upon neuralgic issues in the relationship between Germans and Jews. Indeed, it took quite a while for Tabori to be recognized and duly appreciated by the establishment. Over a number of years he worked—out of conviction and a desire to change and vitalize the theatrical experience in the light of Lee Strasberg and the Living Theater—with his own fringe troupe as well as with lay actors before he was offered such traditional stages as the Viennese Burgtheater. One of his ardent admirers has been the influential critic of the German theater journal *Theater heute,* Peter von Becker, whose sustained support no doubt promoted Tabori's reception and recognition in Germany. Becker considers Tabori to be a unique figure in postwar German theater: "He is the only artist since Bertolt Brecht . . . who embodies the ideal union of playwright, director, theater-director and for a while also actor." Moreover, Tabori represents for Peter von Becker the last of a culturally eminent generation, an extinct species of great emigrants, and by virtue of his unique role, a reminder of "how very much we lack today in Central Europe the vitality of a cosmopolitan Jewish culture and intellectual life" (von Becker in Tabori 1994, xv).

It is not only Tabori's personality and his refreshing approach to the theater that acquired him a singular position on the German stage, but also his unconventional treatment of German-Jewish relationships. "There are taboos that must be broken or they will continue to choke us," Tabori said at the German premiere of *Die Kannibalen* (The cannibals) in 1969 (Tabori 1981, 37). The play, "a black mass," depicts the inmates of a concentration camp who cook and eat their inmate Puffi. The black mass evolves along unconventional structural and theatrical lines, discards the familiar scheme of victimizer and victimized, shatters the taboos relating to the presentation of Jewish figures in the theater after Auschwitz, and aims at the demythologization of the Holocaust victims. While concentrating on the special dynamics of the prisoners, Tabori exposes their fears and anguish, their suffering and behavior in the extreme conditions to which they have been condemned. (Such liminal stages—*Grenzsituationen*—have been a major concern of Tabori, signifying, as it were, the ontological position of modern man.) Tabori discards realism in favor of psychological and moral dimensions. The major question posed by the play is whether the hungry victims have the right to victimize a fellow prisoner in the hope of survival, and it is indeed this question that underlines their uncurbed free will. True resistance—so Tabori argues, very much like Primo Levi—lies in the individual decision making of the victim, or, in other words, in the preservation of human integrity even in a context deprived of moral values. The uncle, that figure in the play modeled on Tabori's father, who was murdered in Auschwitz, represents the principles of nonviolence and humaneness in his refusal to partake in the meal.

Tabori succeeded in provoking and infuriating audiences in his attempt to free the Jewish victim from heroic constraint—to take the Jew off the pedestal and show him as an individual of flesh and blood—as well as in his renouncing inculpation and the condemnation of the Germans, and the revue-like quality and black humor of the mass. The head of the Jewish community in Berlin, Heinz Galinski, himself a survivor of Auschwitz, even tried to prevent the performance of *Kannibalen.* This unconventional treatment of the Holocaust also posed great difficulties to the actors, Jews and Germans alike. Tabori defended his heretical approach, arguing that it would be offensive to try and enlist spectators' sympathy for the suffering of the Jews; piety and sentimentality produced the wrong sort of mourning. Gerhard Stadelmaier, a German theater critic, described the effect of the play in the following words: "Tabori stole from the Germans who had murdered eighty per cent of his family in Auschwitz and in other extermination camps the consternation, the shame, the zealous guilty conscience, the habitual, little, cozy kowtow to the outsized horror, these words, maxims, sermons, in which there was good will but no life and above all no emotion."

In his own idiosyncratic adaptation of Shake-

speare's *The Merchant of Venice* (1978), Tabori continued to provoke the spectator into rethinking clichés and stereotypes connected with the Jews, and in this way he totally broke away from Deutsch's or Kortner's Shylock. "True remembrance is possible only through sensory recollection: it is impossible to master the past without reliving it through the skin, nose, tongue, feet and belly," argued Tabori (1981, 202), and he tried to evoke compassion (*Mit-leid*) rather than pity (*Mitleid*) in spectators as well as actors. Tabori's compelling production concentrated exclusively on Shylock. Indeed, it multiplied the role: there were thirteen Shylocks in the play, alternately offering variations on the role. The subtext of this production was, as so often in Tabori's productions, the Holocaust, signified by puppets dressed as concentration camp prisoners, abandoned suitcases, and piles of clothes. It was not the original Shakespearean text that was at the heart of this extraordinary production, but rather the individual experience and grappling of each and every actor with Shylock (and also with a pound of "flesh" / meat), accompanied by jazz improvisations on the piano. "I wanted to find out what happens when actors grapple here and now with this material," wrote Tabori. "Shylock is victim and executioner; this polarity is inherent in every human being, beyond the historical circumstances. I wanted to show: so it was, so it is, time and again."

The Third Reich, postwar Germany, and the fiftieth anniversary of Hitler's seizure of power (*Machtergreifung*) set the historical frame of reference for Tabori's ironically titled play *Jubiläum* (Jubilee, 1983). The linear development is deliberately broken in favor of a theatrical collage made up of associations, or events relived through memory, reflection, and theatrical images: the incorporation of the Brechtian episode "die jüdische Frau," the reflective gravedigger image from "Hamlet," or the Beckettian metaphor of inaction and stagnation as Lotte bids farewell to her friends from a phone booth in which the water is continually rising. Tabori develops further in this play the proliferation of perspectives: he seeks no synthesis but rather endeavors to retain the theatrical polyphony as he explores how Germans and Jews respectively have (or have failed to) grapple with that chapter of history that ironically draws them together. Five figures present the world of the victims: the Jewish Lotte, deported and later murdered; her husband, the musician Arnold, who survived; the homosexual Helmut, who suffers from guilt feelings vis-à-vis the Jews; his beloved, Otto; and the spastic Mitzi. These perennial outsiders, stigmatized, scar-ridden, and vulnerable, are ironically the guards of society's humane image. As in *Kannibalen,* however, Tabori does not juxtapose victims and fascists but alludes through changing roles to the complexity of discrimination: "You would all like to do so, wumm, bang and slap," says the neo-Nazi Jürgen, "only you don't have the guts to let out the little N-a-z-i in you."

Tabori offered the German public the drama of his mother's last-minute rescue in *Mutters Courage* (My mother's courage; 1979), as well as the dramatic adaptation of Peter Sichrovsky's book on children of prominent Nazi figures, *Schuldig geboren* (Born guilty; 1987). One of his most daring and fascinating treatments of the German-Jewish relationship, however, is his play *Mein Kampf* (1987), in which he presented on stage a Viennese homeless shelter in the Blutgasse (blood street), where the would-be artist Hitler and the Jewish man of letters Schlomo Herzl meet. A weird yet intense relationship develops between the two, one of respect and hostility, dependence and rejection. Tabori's black humor, which underlined such plays as *Kannibalen* and *Mutters Courage,* finds here its "most clear-sighted and human" expression, as Peter von Becker put it (Tabori 1994, 1:xi). Compassion and extermination, joke and horror cannot be separated; indeed they are intertwined, suggests Tabori, who more than once shocked his public with the play on words about Auschwitz ("Ausch-Witz," or "Ausch-joke"), suggesting that it was the best joke.

Jewish playwrights and directors attracted a great deal of attention in postwar Germany, so much so that one sometimes wonders whether this keen reception rests solely on artistic merits.

The interest in all aspects of the German-Jewish discourse led not only to renewed productions of such popular works as the musical *Anatevka* (Fiddler on the roof), or to the stage adaptation of Anne Frank's diary by Goodrich and Hackett, but also to the "rediscovery" of plays such as Paul Kornfeld's *Jud Süß* (The Jew Süß) in 1988—or even to belated premieres, such as the first staging in 1979 of Else Lasker-Schüler's *Ichundich* (You and me). Significantly, there has also been a continuously growing interest in works by foreign Jewish playwrights, especially in plays that are related to the Holocaust and its repercussions (for example, Jacques Kraemer's *Uncle Jacob's Tales,* which had its German premiere in 1981; René Kalisky's *Falsch,* [German premiere 1986]; or the interest in plays by the Dutch-Jewish dramatist Judith Herzberg and the above-mentioned Israeli playwright Yehoshua Sobol).

The more challenging of those plays written by Jewish dramatists confront theater people and spectators with the problematics of a complex vision that is free of philo-Semitic clichés and of malignant prejudices and that attempts occasionally to break deeply rooted taboos. The question in this context is how far one may rely on the historical awareness of German spectators, on their common sense, or their powers of discrimination and discernment, to accurately interpret these daring visions.

Bibliography

Peter von Becker, "Diese Stücke—ein Leben: Über George Tabori," in George Tabori, *Theaterstücke,* vol. 1; Volker Canaris, "Die erste Juden, die ich kannte, waren Nathan und Shylock," *Theater heute* 2 (1973): 20–25; Anat Feinberg, *Wiedergutmachung im Programm: jüdisches Schicksal im deutschen Nachkriegsdrama* (Cologne: Prometh, 1988); Jörg W. Gronius and Wend Kässens, *Tabori* (Frankfurt a. M.: Athenäum, 1989); Fritz Kortner, *Aller Tage Abend* (Munich: Deutscher Taschenbuch-Verlag, 1959); Mechthild Lange, *Peter Zadek* (Frankfurt a. M.: Fischer, 1989); Gundula Ohngemach, *George Tabori* (Frankfurt a. M.: Fischer, 1989); Gerhard Stadelmaier, "Fürst des Feigenblatts," *Frankfurter Allgemeine Zeitung* 21 (1994); Marleen Stoessel, "Auf dem

Friedhof Theater?" *Theater Heute* 8 (1984): 4–13; George Tabori, *Ich wollte meine Tochter läge tot zu meinen Füßen und hätte die Juwelen in den Ohren, Improvisationen über Shakespeares Shylock* (Munich: Hanser, 1979); Tabori, *Theaterstücke,* 2 vols. (Munich: Hanser, 1994); Tabori, *Unterammergau oder Die guten Deutschen* (Frankfurt a. M.: Suhrkamp, 1981); Andrea Welker, *George Tabori—Dem Gedächtnis, der Trauer und dem Leben gewidmet* (Weitra: Verlag Bibliothek der Provinz, 1994); and Carl Zuckmayer, *Als wär's ein Stück von mir: Erinnerungen* (Frankfurt a. M.: Fischer 1969).

A N A T   F E I N B E R G

1946   Hans-Joachim Schoeps settles in Germany after eight years of exile in Sweden

Nationalism, that bugaboo of our time, shares in the dynamics inherent in the plurality of the human situation: the fundamental need to identify the self, on the one hand, and the equally necessary demand to locate that self in the world around it. This unending, because never finally resolved, imposition of identification burdens the human condition. The culture of German Judaism was keenly marked by this horizon, against which its representatives built themselves and their world. Hans-Joachim Schoeps (1909–80) must certainly be accounted not only one of German Judaism's most remarkable figures but also one of twentieth-century Germany's most provocative and fruitful scholars. From the world of the *Jugendbewegung* (youth movement) and Germany's Jewish community, it was Schoeps who, in the wake of the rise of National Socialism and eventually the holocaustal eradication of German Judaism, attempted to reconstruct a nationalism to which Germany would not be enslaved, but that instead would serve its culture as a medium of ever-changing, but always-linked, identity.

Born of Jewish parents in Berlin, Schoeps developed early those critical faculties and the astoundingly graceful pen that were to mark his work throughout his career. By the end of the 1920s—at age twenty—he had already collaborated with Max Brod on editions from Kafka's unpublished papers and had shaken the theological world of German Judaism with his attempts to use Barth's dialectical methodology to found a new, "modern" Jewish theology.

During the early years of the National Socialist hegemony in Germany, Schoeps worked hard at organizing resistance to what he saw, especially in Prussia, as a barbaric usurpation of traditional political structures and a threat to the continued presence of Jews in German culture and society. His Vortrupp publishing house and group; his debates with Scholem and other leading members of German Judaism; his role in a Jewish Jugendbewegung movement; and his constant appeals to German Jewry to reflect critically upon the meaning of existence in the twentieth century—all these activities marked him as one of German Judaism's and Germany's most stimulating cultural critics and intellectual historians.

In two volumes of memoirs, Schoeps has described the hair-raising years between the National Socialist assumption of power (1933) and his eventual flight into exile at the end of 1938 (Schoeps 1963; 1974). Increasingly isolated from his colleagues, slowly pushed into an underground life, and finally frozen out of all action, he fled to Sweden, where he became an active participant in the shadowy world of German emigration, writing under his own name, as well as a pseudonym. While penning thoughtful reflections on the future of Germany and German Jews, he also engaged in scholarship of the most detailed and profound kind: studies of baroque Jewry and investigations into the origins of Christianity took up the bulk of his time (Schoeps 1952; 1949).

At the conclusion of the war, Schoeps returned immediately to Germany in 1946—one of the very few German Jews to do so. Accepting an appointment at the University of Erlangen in 1947, he set to work reviving the world of German academia. His epoch-making study of Jewish Christianity appeared in 1949, an unsurpassed treatment of one of the most complicated elements in Christianity's story of origins. At the same time he was busy organizing a new interdisciplinary approach to historical studies that has left its mark throughout the world of scholarship: *Geistesgeschichte,* or a "history of consciousness," as he titled this effort, achieved a firm, though limited and disturbing, presence in German academia. Schoeps founded a society to promote this multi- and interdisciplinary attack on time-honored (but staid and restrictive) categorizations of historical reflection introduced into German universities. In addition, he cofounded the prestigious journal for the history of religion and consciousness *Zeitschrift für Geistes- und Religionsgeschichte* as a public organ for work in his new discipline-spanning efforts.

Throughout the 1950s and 1960s, Schoeps continued to work and publish in an astonishingly broad scope of fields: Prussian history; early Christianity; New Testament exegesis; nineteenth- and twentieth-century intellectual history; and contemporary cultural criticism. These are only the main disciplines to which he contributed. For ten years he was a member of the executive committee for the Preußischer Kulturbesitz foundation, and in 1969 he received the Adenauer Award of Scholarship, granted by the Germany Foundation. Controversy was never far from Schoeps and his direct, almost acidic pen. Charges and countercharges—surrounding his emigration to Sweden during the National Socialist period and the character of his writings during the 1930s—involved him during the 1960s in increasingly bitter and acrimonious public and private battles. Dismayed over developments in the structure and administration of German universities at the end of that decade,

Schoeps finally resigned an active role at the University of Erlangen and dedicated the final ten years of his life to ever-increasing scholarly productivity. His death in 1980 came as a surprise, and it silenced one of contemporary Germany's most stimulating, critical, and thought-provoking voices.

In characterizing his relationship to the German and Jewish worlds in which he came of age, Schoeps always saw the fundamental building blocks of his life contained in being "conservative, Prussian and Jewish" (Schoeps 1974, 11). And indeed his conception of nationalism, above all of a nationalism that could be termed "German," is summed up in those designations. For Schoeps, a German nationalism is *not* German in substance and origin, but rather takes its legitimacy from prior, more fundamental stances. His earliest writings, even before the ascendancy of the National Socialists to power in 1933, chart this position clearly, and it is a standpoint from which Schoeps did not deviate throughout his career. Sadly, it was also a conception of nationalism that gave rise to grave misunderstandings that haunted Schoeps throughout his life. Only late in his career did a renewed controversy over Schoeps's thought and writings in the 1930s focus attention on his unique position on the stage of nationalistic struggle prior to the National Socialist triumph.

At the end of 1969 an exhibition was organized to display a selection of works from German-Jewish authors in Europe's major cities. Initially Schoeps was included in this assemblage, and his many works were on display. When the exhibition reached Berlin, however, an "anonymous" German Jew protested publicly that the inclusion of Schoeps and his work in such a display was nothing less than a confirmation of Schoeps's "pro-Hitler" activities; his continued presence in the exhibit would mean an "insult to murdered Jews and all other martyrs of the Nazis." As a result, Schoeps was removed from the exhibit (Schoeps 1970). Well aware that this action was based on a profound misunderstanding of his concept of nationalism, Schoeps immediately issued a reprint of his major articles and addresses from the 1930s. To no avail. Just as he had been crassly misinterpreted at the time, so also did this ill-fitting exegesis follow him into the twilight of his life. A blistering critique from London brought forth an equally harsh reply from Schoeps; in the aftermath of that exchange another émigré recalled for Schoeps the 1935 remark of Heinrich Löwe that he, Schoeps, "is a Nazi" (H. F. Ashbrook to Schoeps, Oct. 10, 1978, in Schoeps 1926–80, box 37). And Robert Weltsch, a leading figure in the world of postwar German Jewry, characterized Schoeps as having offered "unwanted professions of supra-nationalist German loyalty (even to the Nazi-Regime)" (*Association for Jewish Refugees Information* 33 [Apr. 1970]: 6). Weltsch viewed Schoeps as belonging to a "fringe which could not be blamed for being psychologically disturbed by the complete collapse of its ideological structure." A few old friends came to his defense, but on the whole Schoeps's position regarding German nationalism remained misunderstood and indeed ignored in light of the destruction of German Jewry and his own anomalous position within twentieth-century Judaism. As a result, he came to doubt the wisdom of his return to Germany in 1946.

Schoeps's position on the identity of Germany, and how the members of that society were to identity themselves, progressed through two major stages, each anchored at its end and its beginning by his return to Germany from exile in 1946. In the first, under the strong influence of a fundamental religious experience (Schoeps 1970, 32–33; Schoeps 1963, 45–46), he wove together his early experiences in the *Jugendbewegung* (youth movement) and his perception of the "existential" dismantling of German society into a general call for inner and subjective reform, which would lie at the base of the *new* society for which he wished to be the herald. In October 1926—at the young age of seventeen—Schoeps published his first article in *Die Wegwarte,* Eberhard Arnold's journal for his Sannerz commune. Under the strong influence of Arnold's visionary version of Christianity and its reformatory tendencies, Schoeps called for the awakening of a "radical desire for self-liberation and a thirst for truth at any price" in every single member of German society, but above all in its youth (Schoeps 1926, 13–15). Reflecting

his own religious experience, he sketched the basic sinfulness and poverty of humanity, its abandonment before God precisely because humanity is not divine, and the lack of any access to that God; he drew, in other words, a Barthian-Lutheran picture of the human condition and matched it to the general existential misery of the time. The times, according to Schoeps, called for both prophetic and political action; one must be careful not to absolutize either knowledge or experience, but must always be a conduit for the divine spirit. There are many forms that such action can take: Schoeps called for one form, that of brotherhood, to realize the goals of "discipline and order, loyalty and service," which would characterize the reformed society of the future. This brotherhood, "whose spirit was poured out into the world by Christ," would be the very embodiment of a new Germany, a "free" Germany that would encompass both the German "Volk" and eventually the world. In one ringing appeal, Schoeps not only called for a "revolution" in the Jugendbewegung, but also revealed the basis of his nationalistic conception for Germany: behind his vision of the German nation lay a fundamental theology, albeit one still unformed in its details and still unfocused in its appeal to a "Christ" who stood in distinction to his own Jewish heritage.

Three years later (1929), with the founding of the *Freideutsche Kameradschaft* (free German fraternity), Schoeps developed and expanded on his earlier point of departure. Convinced that the fundamental question of the times—namely, the question of meaning asked in a *personal* and subjectively reforming way—had been posed only in Germany, Schoeps saw the national task of transcending the merely vegetative and bodily dimension as requiring that human beings' personhood become central. Only when the great spiritual questions had become, as "vital realities and established meanings," decisive for human existence, would there be a genuine national identification possible for Germany. The source of such a renewal was clear for Schoeps: the youth, and above all the Prussian youth. Though there was not, in his eyes, an essential difference between this youth and the masses of the middle class, nevertheless he predicted that through his young brotherhood a *Blutauffrischung* (a freshening of the blood) would occur that would benefit the entire nation. Thus Schoeps called upon both the youth in particular, and the German nation as a whole, to commit themselves to a "conversion" that would renew both the nation and the age. At the same time Schoeps sounded, at this very early date, a warning that would become louder as the years progressed: It is possible, he noted, that this position was "already lost"; nevertheless one must continue to fight a battle that may already be decided. This conclusion would, of course, have far-reaching consequences in a later, quite different context marked by the extermination of the German Jewish community, including Schoeps's parents.

Schoeps was fueled by the belief that the most profound and effective human revolution is also the quietest and least remarkable—the revolution that emerges from individual reflection upon the self and from the willingness to undergo "conversion" of that self from within. His new brotherhood, so he hoped, would be the "shock troops" for just such a "spiritual revolution." This process, according to Schoeps, is fundamental to all religions, and is based on the universal human experience of creatureliness; though Christianity, and perhaps even Judaism, know only a bond of equality under God, this world demands a prior level of identity that is national in scope. Without the acknowledgment of one's createdness, and thus dependence upon a transcendent source, the necessary reformation of humanity cannot be accomplished. In Schoeps's view, the attempt within Germany—indeed throughout Europe—to reject capitalism, Americanism, and Bolshevism could never succeed without this basic recognition. In other words, for the early youth leader Schoeps, nationalistic identification, so necessary for the renewal of German society, must proceed from a basic religious experience: nationalism, for Schoeps, always proceeds from and rests upon a theology.

This theological basis to Schoeps's German nationalism took on a distinct character in the development of its second, or Jewish, phase. By 1931 he had realized that the "mere appeal to the expression of faith in, or a confession to Germany" made access to the genuinely mythical content of such nationalism difficult, if not impossible. According to Schoeps, this mythical content, or the coherent unity with past but fulfilled reality, was not to be found in such nationalistic self-delusions as National Socialism, but rather in the true mythic conservatism represented by such entities as Prussia and Judaism. This shift in Schoeps's thought was occasioned not only by his own studies in Leipzig and his growing awareness that despite his deep involvement in the categories and directions of contemporary Protestant Christian thought he was bound inextricably to his Jewish heritage, but also by a deep division within the ranks of Jewish youth groups and leaders. Chief among these groups, besides Schoeps's own Vortrupp (shock troop), was the Schwarzes Fähnlein (Black flag), headquartered in Breslau and led by Günter Holzmann. Throughout 1933 and into 1934, these Jewish youth organizations debated a Jewish presence in a National Socialist Germany. Holzmann finally threw down the gauntlet in his radical statement "Entweder-Oder" (Either-or; 1934). In outlining a Jewish response to the simplified nationalism of Hitler's ruling party, he fell prey to the same confusion that had marked National Socialist doctrine. For him and his disciples there was only one unified community, bound together by fate, and that was the German nation. For them "there was neither an Arian nor a non-Arian race, but only a German race," to which all members of German society belonged by reason of *Blut und Boden* (blood and soil) (Schoeps 1926–80, box 38, folder 2, p. 6). Holzmann also drew out the consequences of his position: he called for his followers to withdraw from all Jewish organizations that did not provide for a nationalistic participation in his sense. Thus he also rejected any responsibility for the whole of German Jewry.

Schoeps, who through his friend Eberhard Beyer considered himself actually "converted" to Judaism, and who had just published his first book—an attempt to formulate a new Jewish theology based on conceptual categories taken from nineteenth-century Judaism (Steinheim) and twentieth-century Christian (Barth) thought systems (*Contemporary Jewish Faith,* 1932)—felt called upon to respond. Faced with the alternative of choosing between a confused German nationalism and the Prussian-Jewish traditions that he was now convinced were the content of his past, he forcefully rejected the former and sided with the latter. In a blistering handwritten statement to Holzmann and the Schwarzes Fähnlein, he made it clear that he, in turn, must abandon all ties to that organization; after the latest meeting, and Holzmann's memo, it had become clear to him that he could not remain in contact with a group that rejected Judaism:

These last days have mobilized within me the final remains of Jewish substance and Jewish self-determination. I can no longer represent a position whose supporters have as their goal, to abandon as quickly and extensively as possible everything Jewish, in order to legitimate themselves as *deutschvölkisch.* Today for the first time, or at least much more clearly than ever before, I feel convinced that my fathers have passed on to me the responsibility for Jacob's heritage, and that in this hour of need I must conserve and develop my Jewishness, a Jewishness which is not a conceptual outline, but rather a spiritual reality which also molds the body, and that I cannot ignore this heritage or throw it away. My concrete duty in this very moment is to speak to my comrades in faith to strengthen them for a spiritual rebellion. (Schoeps 1926–80, box 40, folder 3)

At the same time Schoeps made it clear that supporting his Jewish heritage and identity did not mean a surrender of his German identity; on the contrary, he found that both could be combined: "My own position concerning the German fatherland remains unchanged. I have no other fatherland than the one which is called Germany; and I cannot serve it in any other meaningful way than that as a full Jew I am also a German, rather than by means of a declaration of neutrality toward my Jewishness" (Schoeps 1926–80, box 40, folder 3).

Schoeps now held irrevocably to Judaism in the face of demands that he abandon it for a German identity, because he had come to identify his youthful but fundamental religious experience of creation (creature / creator) with that very Jewish

heritage (Lease 1984). He established that being Jewish does not depend upon one's will to do so or not; rather, being Jewish itself makes demands of one. "No one," he continued, "can remove himself from the fact of being Jewish, no one has the freedom to deny his Jewishness or to toss it away. One must instead confess and commit himself to Judaism because God committed himself in Israel" (Schoeps 1926–80). A more formal reply to Holzmann laid out the practical consequences of Schoeps's theological program: "We will not throw stones at anyone who leaves now because the very minimum for his existence is not guaranteed. We know that it is very often—though not always—fate which leads to this step—and indeed a tragic one. Who, however, and even under the harshest conditions and reduced living standards, wishes to remain in Germany no matter what—and there are young members of our society who are ready to do so, and I am their public leader—for such people the Jewish Question becomes mainly a spiritual question. . . . No one wants us, and we stay here. Our being German is denied us, and we continue to pledge our allegiance to Germany" ("Deutschjüdische Besinnung. 1V.33 1V.35 Schoeps 1926–80," ca. 1934). The problem was clear: one is a Jew because one is a child of the Sinaitic Covenant, and not because one is a member of a certain race, or even because one is a member of a Jewish nation. This question of Jewish identity—which for Schoeps was ultimately a religious question and thus elicited a theological response—lies at the basis of Schoeps's discussion of German identity: "Alles für Deutschland, aber Deutschland für Gott!" ("Everything for Germany, but Germany for God!"; Lease 1988).

This second stage in the development of Schoeps's thought on nationalism had its roots in the final conference of his *Freideutsche Kameradschaft,* which met in Eckartberga in the fall of 1932. There is little doubt that Schoeps and his colleagues were aware, as he put it, that the Germany that they represented and fought for could not survive the struggle ahead. And yet, against the temptation of resignation, they found the energy for one last attempt to formulate the rudiments of a theory of nationalism that would allow them to maintain their Jewish identity precisely as Germans. For Schoeps, the key rested in a concept of the state as the object of nationalism, as a servant of the people and society that it represents. Such a state is responsible to its culture and society for *order,* an order that has its origin in the divine order of creation. Such a function protects society against the many threats to meaning and substance in its life and makes transparent the transcendent realities that promise hope and support in moments of chaos and threatened existence. Where such questions arise, there the nation awakes (Eckartberga Protocoll, Schoeps 1926–80). Only when a nation acknowledges this genuine task to which it is charged within the broader framework of the order of creation can it be a legitimate nation, and only then can legitimate rule be exercised in the relationship of governor and governed. Only when Germany lives and functions as a nation with such a mission— the representation and fulfillment of the divine order anchored in creation—can a German nationalism thrive. To confuse this mission, to pervert the nation, is to run the risk of demonic misalignment. True, every nation strives for power and rule; but it can exercise them only within the broader order of creation. To do otherwise is to deny the myth of nationhood and ultimately to deny the nation itself.

For Schoeps a valid German identity was composed of two major parts: a religious, or *theological* dimension—which for him personally was made up of his Jewish identity with its firm grounding in the *facts* of God, creation, and the revelational covenant of Sinai (*not* an identity founded on race or a separate Jewish nation)—and his *Prussian identity,* which was a "confession" to the *idea* of societal order as reflecting the creational order, the state as responsible both to society and to God. Thus in Schoeps's conception, Prussia represented the one possible "authentic" nation in central Europe because among the German cultures it was the only one that provided a "faithful response" to the call of creation. In this version, "nationalism" is a multilayered concept capable of sustaining a wide variety of supports and sources. For Schoeps, Germany at the end of the 1920s was an *artificial* creation because it pro-

posed a national identity based on *race;* such a "tribal" unity was incapable, under the historical conditions, of producing a national identity. He contended that the only state ideology that might have supported such a national identity had disappeared in 1918 with the Prussian crown. National Socialism, among other ideologies, tried to fill precisely this vacuum, and to a degree it was successful. But in another and much deeper sense—which Schoeps attempted to make clear in his opposition—National Socialism destroyed forever the "state" to which a nationalistic confession could have been made.

From his exile in Sweden, Schoeps saw these consequences clearly. For him the whole Prussian tradition had been based on the acceptance of *conscience* as a ruling guide for political action, a consciousness of having been given an office by God. Hitler, of course, changed that radically; he demanded instead a political "confession" to himself as the "Messiah of all Germans." It is only from this standpoint that one can understand the political conservatism of Schoeps's postwar years and his attempts to reinstitute both the Prussian state and the monarchy (Schoeps 1973). Schoeps, of course, was not alone in taking a stand that was based on principle; Walter Laqueur has remarked that there were opponents to the National Socialists who belonged to a generation for which principles and values counted. If that can be said of anyone, it must be said of Schoeps.

Schoeps's vision of a German nation remained finally, and for all practical purposes, irrelevant—at the most one hundred or so followers actively pursued his model. But his provocative theory of nationalism for twentieth-century Germany—conservative, Prussian Jewry as the backbone of a reformed German nation—remains a vibrant witness to the variegated, even fractured state of German culture at the end of the Weimar Republic and on the eve of the National Socialist state.

Bibliography

Gary Lease, "Salomon Ludwig Steinheim's Influence— Hans-Joachim Schoeps, A Case Study," *Leo Baeck Insti-*

tute Yearbook 29 (1984): 383–402; Lease, "Wer war hier Christ, wer Jude? Das Gespräch zwischen Hans-Joachim Schoeps und Hans Blüher," *Das jüdisch-christliche Religionsgespräch,* ed. Heinz Kremers and Julius Schoeps (Stuttgart: Burg Verlag, 1988), 114–30; Hans-Joachim Schoeps, *Abschied von Deutschland* (Mainz: v. Hase & Kohler, 1973); Schoeps, *"Bereit für Deutschland!" Der Patriotismus deutscher Juden und der Nationalsozialismus* (Berlin: Haude & Spener, 1970); Schoeps, *Das andere Preußen* (Berlin: Haude & Spener, 1981); Schoeps, *Ja, Nein und trotzdem* (Mainz: v. Hase & Kohler, 1974); Schoeps, *Jüdischer Glaube in dieser Zeit* (Berlin: Philo Verlag, 1932); Schoeps, *Philosemitismus im Barock* (Tübingen: J. C. B. Mohr, 1952); Schoeps, *Rückblicke* (Berlin: Haude & Spener, 1963); Schoeps, *Rufmord 1970* (Erlangen: self-published, 1970); Schoeps, *Streit um Israel: Ein jüdisch-christliches Gespräch* (Hamburg: Hanseatische Verlagsanstalt, 1933); Schoeps, *Theologie und Geschichte des Judenchristentums* (Tübingen: J. C. B. Mohr, 1949); Schoeps, *Unpublished Papers* (Berlin State Library, ca. 1926–80); Schoeps, *Was ist und was will die Geistesgeschichte?* (Göttingen: Musterschmidt, 1970); Schoeps, "Zur freideutschen Fahne," *Die Wegwarte* (Oct. 1926): 13–15; and Julius Schoeps, ed., *Im Streit um Kafka und das Judentum: Der Briefwechsel zwischen Max Brod und Hans-Joachim Schoeps* (Königstein / Taunus: Athenäum, 1985).

GARY LEASE

1947 Anna Seghers returns to Germany from exile and makes her home in East Berlin

The life and work of Anna Seghers were marked by Nazi persecution and exemplified Cold War contradictions. Seghers is primarily known as a Communist writer. This meant that the work of a writer now regarded as one of the greatest female writers in the German language was for years ignored or derided in the West and uncritically revered in the East. Her Jewish origins and the way her Jewishness shaped both her life and her work have not been part of this equation. She, the rounded person, who despite her commitment to Communism remained deeply steeped in Jewish culture, was thereby rendered invisible by both sides of this false duality. Although West Germany failed to publish Seghers for over fifteen years after World War II because of her commitment to Communism, official German Democratic Republic (GDR) literary sources praised her in 1974 as having successfully sloughed off her bourgeois heritage through her commitment to "the liberation struggle of the proletariat and the construction of socialism" (*Lexikon deutschsprachiger Schriftsteller,* 1974). It is striking that Seghers's 1946 story "Post ins gelobte Land"—one of only two of her stories rooted in Jewish cultural and religious tradition—was published only once and remained virtually unknown in the GDR (Hermlin in Roehner 1995).

Her Jewishness is perhaps the most striking example, yet it is by no means the only aspect of Anna Seghers's life and work that remains shrouded in mystery. Her identity as a woman is equally elusive, because most of her early works and those written in exile feature men as central characters (Kaufmann 1988, 352). The first-person narrator of the novel *Transit* (1944) is one of two men in love with the same woman. Seghers deliberately avoided making revelations about her personal life; instead she hid behind the much-cited sentiment that the reader can glean all she or he needs to know about a writer's views—and even about the writer's life—from the work (1965 interview with Christa Wolf in: Seghers 1980 2:411; and Wolf 1987, 280). The publication of no fewer than four biographical studies between 1992 and 1994 and the devotion of the 1994 annual conference of the Anna Seghers Society to her biography point to a growing fascination with the enigmatic nature of Anna Seghers (or rather of Netty Reiling-Radvanyi, the woman behind the author) and a desire to fathom the relationship between writer and work. Speakers at the 1994 Seghers conference stressed that the existing biographies should be seen as mere first steps in understanding this unknown woman.

The bare bones of what *is* known about Anna Seghers include her family background in Mainz where her parents were members of the Orthodox Jewish community. There are a few clues scattered through her essays that suggest that the respectable middle-class family life she led as the only child of an antiques and art dealer introduced her to art and creativity, and to literature and fairy tales—both of which were to remain central influences in her writing. But it also seems that this lifestyle was inhibiting and stifling to someone of her imaginative depth and passion. In interviews given during the 1970s, she described as "terrible" what she calls the "typical bourgeois sitting room atmosphere" at home, which fueled an increasing "urge to leave home as early as possible, to fly away" (Roscher interview, 1983, cited in Zehl-Romero 1993, 8)—away too, one can assume, from what Isaac Deutscher called "the chains of orthodoxy" (1981, 13). In his essay "The Non-Jewish Jew," Isaac Deutscher describes "the Jewish heretic who transcends Jewry" as belonging "to a Jewish tradition." Jews who went beyond Jewry to the highest ideals of mankind— like Spinoza, Heine, Marx, Rosa Luxemburg, Trotsky, and Freud—"found Jewry, too narrow, too archaic and too constricting. They all looked for ideals and fulfillment beyond it, and they represent the sum and substance of much that is greatest in modern thought, the sum and substance of the most profound upheavals that have taken place in philosophy, sociology, economics and politics in the last three centuries. . . . as Jews they lived on the borderlines of various civilizations, religions and national cultures. . . . Each of them was in society and yet not in it, of it and yet not of it" (26–27).

Seghers studied art history and sinology in Heidelberg from 1920 to 1924, completing her doctoral thesis, "Jews and Judaism in Rembrandt's Work," in 1924. This is one of only three pieces of writing in which Seghers explicitly addressed the theme of Jewishness. In it, she makes a distinction between the rich Sephardic Jews in Amsterdam who had become assimilated into bourgeois society (and whom Rembrandt romanticizes, in her view, when he paints them in exotic costumes not true to the period) and the poor Eastern European "ghetto Jews" flocking to Amsterdam to escape pogroms. About the life of these latter, she claims, Rembrandt cannot have known much, and yet, she argues, he seems to have used the suffering faces of individual (rather than idealized) Eastern European Jews as models for many of his Christ figures.

It was at the University of Heidelberg that Seghers first came into contact with the ideas of socialism, which enabled her to articulate her previously inchoate feelings about social injustice (Seghers 1980, 2:338, 2:434; cited in Zehl-Romero 1993, 17). There too she met the Hungarian Jew Laszlo Radvanyi, whom she married in 1925. At some time between 1925 and 1927 it is thought that she explicitly left the Jewish community before becoming a member of the Communist Party in 1928 (the same year she received the Kleist Prize for two of her early stories) and the Association of Revolutionary Proletarian Writers (Bund Proletarisch-Revolutionärer Schriftsteller [BPRS]) in 1929.

Seghers's early desire to escape from the suffocating small-town atmosphere of her hometown, Mainz, became translated in exile into an enduring love for the town and the Rhine landscape where she received what she called, after Goethe, her lasting *Originaleindruck* (an "original impression" she linked with knowledge of social conditions). This *Heimatliebe* (love of the environment where one grew up) is a special attachment not unique to Seghers or to Jews who were forced into exile by the Nazis. It was particularly strong, however, according to Dr. Anton-Maria Keim, cultural senator of the city of Mainz, among Jews from that area, many of whom returned from exile after the end of World War II. Indeed there is some evidence that Seghers herself initially may have wanted to settle in the landscape of her youth when she returned to Germany in 1947, but that the American occupation forces refused her an entry permit because of her Communist party membership and activities in Mexico.

Seghers's short story "Ausflug der toten Mädchen" (Dead girls' outing; 1946), completed in Mexico in 1944, gives eloquent expression to her love for the Rhine landscape and her hometown. Interestingly, this is one of the very few stories in which Seghers writes in the first person. Returning, in her memory, from the school picnic on a Rhine ferry boat, she feels "apprehensive about turning into my street, as if I had a premonition of its destruction." On that boat trip, she conjures up a landscape in which—in contrast to the barren rocky hills of Mexico where the few trees "seem to burn more than they bloom" (173) in the relentless sun—"the afternoon sun slanting down on the hills and vineyards filled out the dotted pink and white fruit tree blossoms" (194). This story of homesickness is also a history of the Third Reich: all of the girls die—as Nazis or opponents of the regime, in detention or in bombing raids, but they exert individual choice and hence bear differing levels of responsibility for the events that bring about their deaths and that send Anna Seghers's wistfully portrayed mother (the Jewish teacher) and Sophie (a Jewish pupil) to inhuman deaths in Piaski, an outlying camp of the Auschwitz complex.

In a 1947 letter to a young girl who complains of the lack of tolerance in small towns, Anna Seghers appears to offer a revision of her earlier reaction against the stifling limits of life in a small town like Mainz. She advises always doing what you believe to be right as the recipe for overcoming the understandable mistrust that is the legacy of Nazi distortions. But she also draws out explicit advantages of small town life: "I'm a small town person myself, and I learnt more there which has stood me in good stead for my whole life than I did in the big city of Berlin. . . . In small towns, people still take the important things in life seriously" (Wagner, Emmerich, and Radvanyi 1994, 169). In the earlier *Transit,* the first-person narrator envies and longs for the "ordinary life" from which he feels shut out.

Anna Seghers distinguished, in many of the essays she wrote in exile, between a healthy Heimatliebe and its perversion into the "myth of blood and soil" by the Nazis. Her 1935 essay "Vaterlandsliebe" (Love of the fatherland) struggles with this painful reality, which she attributed to a mistaken lack of social or class consciousness. "There is no homeland as such, there is no apple tree in itself," she maintained: it depends who owns the land, and who works it. It is understandable that workers identify with the country in which they struggle for their rights, but writers who propagate the myth of a "community" united in love of the fatherland are ultimately stirring up war. Seghers situated herself in relation to patriotism, then, by redefining it in terms of her commitment to a society based on social justice.

In seeing herself as a German patriot of this

newly modified kind, Seghers was again not alone among her contemporaries of Jewish origin. Artur Joseph relates how, in the interwar years when he grew up in Cologne, he experienced being Jewish as a question of religion, so "in this way we grew up as loyal Germans and observant Jews. . . . Being German and Jewish seemed to me in those years neither a misfortune nor a contradiction" (Joseph 1991, 56). This phenomenon of educated, professionally successful German Jews whose religious affiliation was all that separated them from other Germans is cited by Völker Dahm (in Benz 1993, 76) as the legacy of a century of emancipation. In fact, Dahm claims that most such secularized German Jews had become, by the early part of the twentieth century, only nominally observant. Hence the term "German citizen of the Jewish faith," coined in the late nineteenth century, became increasingly inaccurate. Moreover, this distinction was, of course, to be shattered by the Nazis, under whom it was no longer a matter of personal choice whether one defined oneself and lived as a German or as a practicing Jew. "One was a Jew, whether one liked it or not, one was thrown back onto a form of existence which one hardly knew and indeed had always regarded as very backward" (Dahm, in Benz 1993, 78). Hans Mayer describes the accession to power of the Nazis on January 30, 1933 as the "retraction of what is known as the German-Jewish symbiosis" (Mayer 1994, 430).

For Anna Seghers too, it seems, being Jewish was a confessional question. In her 1944 essay on Tolstoy and Dostoevsky (Seghers 1980, 1:156) she writes: "Many people have renounced their religious affiliations, not because they saw their ethical dicta as invalid, but rather because they felt committed to new and broader ethical values, values which had arisen from their own times." The urge to abandon a minority culture, which even in the late 1920s in Mainz denied its women a voice in community affairs (Schütz 1993, 164), for an internationalist movement which promised an end to all forms of discrimination, is all too understandable. Many educated Jews followed this path at that time "in view of the increasingly obvious agony of the Weimar Republic" (Mayer 1994, 275).

At that time Socialism also represented an escape from tribalism and nationalism, what the writer Ben Okri calls the "best dream of them all . . . a beautiful vision" of a world in which "all tribes, all nations should celebrate their uniqueness," but within a "universal goal . . . [of] the realization of the human potential, the eradication of poverty, the enhancement of liberty, and the triumph of justice" (Okri 1995, 5). Or in Isaac Deutscher's words: Jews who transcended Judaism "like Marx, Rosa Luxemburg and Trotsky strove, together with their non-Jewish comrades, for the universal, as against the particularist, and for the internationalist, as against the nationalist, solutions to the problems of their time . . . all these men, from Spinoza to Freud, believed in the ultimate solidarity of man . . . the message of universal human emancipation" (Deutscher 1981, 33, 36, 41). In his doctoral dissertation, Seghers's husband, Laszlo Radvanyi, suggested that Bolshevism could be seen as the attempt to secularize chiliastic dreams of realizing the millennium, thereby creating a humane society in the empirical world.

But what Anna Seghers could not have foreseen when she joined the Communist Party in 1928, more than a decade after the October Revolution in Russia, was that only a few years later she would be joining another persecuted minority. Because she was a Jew, her desire to travel the world was to become involuntary banishment from her beloved Germany and her acclaimed early writings would be burned.

In exile she struggled to situate herself in relation to the misused concept of *Volk* ("race" or "people"): "Since 'Volk' is not simply nature, not blood and soil, it appears to the writer not as a natural phenomenon, but as a social one," she wrote. Her 1942 essay "Volk und Schriftsteller" (Writers and the people; *Essays* 1:117–18) goes on to speak of varying possibilities of multiple identities—Jewish writers in the Soviet Union, for example, can choose to write in the language and within the culture of Judaism, or as Russians. What is decisive, she claims, is not the accident of birth into a particular racial group, but the writer's identification with a particular social location and class, which in the case of an anti-fascist writer will be that social grouping that secures "progressive history, the freedom of his people." Yet after the Nazi-Soviet Pact of 1939, despair is not far from the surface of these years in exile. In 1941 she had written (in "Deutschland und Wir" [Germany and us], Seghers 1980, 1:91–93): "A people which attacks other peoples, in order to exterminate them, are they still our people?" The response to her own rhetorical question, given in the same essay, is that Germany and the German people are not the problem; it is the scourge of fascism which is to blame. "Germany . . . is the language, . . . is German music, the German landscape," to all of which Seghers remained passionately committed. Nevertheless, as early as 1941 she recognized that "the process of de-fascisization of the German people" would be a "terrible" and long-drawn-out undertaking.

Central to many of her essays written in exile is the question of how Nazism managed to take hold of (especially young) people's hearts and minds. The question of how it could happen is insistent, although it is worth noting that "it"—that is, fascism—is never defined in terms of racism or anti-Semitism, but solely as an affront to social justice, human dignity, or to humanity itself. Her essays "Eroberung der Jugend" (Winning over the young) and "Was wissen wir von Jugendcliquen?" (What do we know about youth gangs?) suggest as early as 1931 the failure of Communist Party propaganda to appeal to young people desperate for a chance to prove themselves, to experience life and to feel wanted. The appeal of Nazism to unemployed young people for whom society seems to offer no place is understandable. Seghers suggests in several of her fictional works as well as her essays that empty political sloganeering on the part of wooden Communist Party officials is inappropriate.

In April 1947 Anna Seghers returned to the Berlin she had fled shortly after Hitler came to power in 1933. It was not the same Berlin, nor was she the same person. She had spent fourteen years in exile, seven each in France and in Mexico, and had written many of her greatest works, including her two best known novels, *Das Siebte Kreuz* (The seventh cross, 1942) and *Transit* (1944). She had also lost both her parents—her father had died in Germany in 1940, and her mother had been deported to Piaski in Poland in 1942 and had been murdered there in 1943. Germany, that "country under an evil spell" as Seghers described it in letters written shortly after her return, was "horribly devastated, internally as well as externally, above all internally" (Wagner, Emmerich, and Radvanyi 1994, 159, 161), its people "internally as devastated as their cities were reduced to rubble externally" (167). Returning there gave Seghers the feeling, she wrote to her old friend Georg Lukács in 1948, that she had "returned to in the Ice Age" (167). Every German she met after her arrival proffered "an alibi in his outstretched hand" (interview with Delbert Clark, *New York Times,* Apr. 1947, in Seghers 1985, 111). No one, she implied, had wanted what happened, nor had they known about it when it did. Once again, "it" never explicitly included the Holocaust, but the Holocaust reverberated clearly as unspoken subtext.

Why did she return? What could possibly motivate Jews who had suffered so much at the hands of the Nazis to go back to the "scene of the crime"? This question is in part answered by the determination of the people living in the Russian-occupied eastern part of Germany to create a different Germany, a society committed to the egalitarian ideals of Communism. This determination led many Jewish Socialists to return in the early postwar years. Seghers's return to Germany was largely motivated by her commitment to re-educating the young, who had been so dreadfully misled by the Nazis. She writes in response to a young woman that in the Germany that "often seems more foreign to me than do foreign countries, . . . I like young people best. . . . Because you get the feeling that young people are still asking questions, they're not yet as encrusted with all kinds of nastiness, fear and prejudice as older people are" (Wagner, Emmerich, and Radvanyi 1994, 169).

Seghers's motivation was not confined to this "didactic impulse" (Bock 1986, 123), to her determination to be "teacher for an entire people" (Wolf 1987, 309), but had a lot to do with her dream of being able, in the new and different Germany she hoped to help build, to give up the eternal outsider position of the exile years. Just before returning to Germany, she wrote that in exile she had managed to combat the worst pain of homesickness by feeling, as did Heinrich Heine, solidarity with all those in every country fighting for freedom and human rights. Yet she shared with Heine the longing to write in harmony with the society within which she lived (Seghers 1980 1:198). Her wish to escape minority oppositional status was this time to be superficially fulfilled: Seghers became chairperson of the GDR Writers' Union and played a very public role as spokesperson for the new Germany. At a deeper level, however, her public reticence, out of party discipline, about the failings of the Communist Party during these years indicates she was aware of her ongoing status as outsider. The two novels written after her return testify to the uncomfortable truth that great literature is produced in conditions of adversity, not from a position of didactic acceptance of the ruling norms.

Hans Mayer speaks of the deep dualism in the life and work of Anna Seghers: of her attachment to her German origins and homesickness for the country of her language and culture, on the one hand, and the shattered hopes embodied in the reality of Stalinism in the GDR and a narrowly conceived Socialist Realism that she had always opposed, on the other. Beyond that, Mayer sees the experience of being German and Jewish, of belonging and not belonging to German culture, as quintessentially dualistic (Mayer 1994, 277, 282). Hans-Albert Walter (1988) suggests that for Jewish German socialists, Soviet Communism, warts and all, was the only real refuge from anti-Semitism and total persecution—the only hope of a better future. The alternative to total outcast status was this compromise, which meant Seghers had no real choice but to return to the GDR. Her life from then on was ruled by contradiction: she remained silent when she knew, claims Albrecht, that the emancipatory ideal of socialism had been betrayed by Stalinism. But considering the suffering she had endured, who could blame her?

With few exceptions, there is apparent silence on the subject of Judaism and her Jewishness in Seghers's work. A close reading of *Transit* reveals the image of the Wandering Jew in the old orchestra conductor who is desperate for his exit visa but meets death before reaching his destination. There is also the beautiful young Jewish girl, dragged off from her family by a French official because of inadequate papers; and the German-Jewish legionnaire who decides to return to his German home, even if this means certain death. It is striking, however, that concentration-camp prisoners and ex-prisoners are not Jewish in *Das siebte Kreuz* and *Transit*. It is true that the first inmates of concentration camps were overwhelmingly Communists and trade union leaders. It is equally true, however, that many of these were also Jewish (Eschwege 1989, 391–92). Commitment to the larger cause within which she had subsumed her Jewish identity may also explain why, in Seghers's 1952 speech to former Buchenwald inmates, Jews are also conspicuous by their absence. Instead, she paid homage to the suffering of "thousands of people [*Menschen*] from all nations whom the Nazis had tried to brand as un-people [*Untermenschen*]," and honored their solidarity, loyalty, and mutual supportiveness. She has asserted that in the GDR today, "for the first time in German history the younger generation is internalizing, along with their mother tongue, from their first school days, respect for other peoples, respect for human dignity and for human rights." Similarly, in a 1979 speech for World Peace Day (Sept. 1) Seghers asks the question: "Who were the women of Ravensbrück?" and answers not that they were Jews among others, but that they were "girls and women from the resistance groups of peoples conquered by the Nazis and from their own people: workers, housewives, artists, mothers, brides" (both speeches are in the Seghers Archive of the East Berlin Academy of Arts).

Mass arrests and deportations of Jews began after Kristallnacht in November 1938 and intensified after the Wannsee Conference in 1941. Anna Seghers was dependent on secondhand information, and *Das siebte Kreuz* was already completed in 1939. But this novel has often been praised for its accurate description of German society at the time. Moreover, in 1960 Alexander Abusch reminded Seghers, and she confirms elsewhere, that he and others visited her in Bellevue near Paris in order to bring her fresh snippets smuggled out of Germany to furnish *Das siebte Kreuz* with authenticity (Abusch letter to Seghers on her sixtieth birthday, in Gossow 1960, 5–8; Seghers, in conversation with Christa Wolf, 1965, in Wolf 1987, 285).

As she did with her own biography, Seghers appears to have maintained a silence on the fate of Jews under the Nazis. It is during her early exile period that she wrote to the publisher Hermann Kesten refusing to participate in an anthology of Jewish writing. Her reasoning suggests that this silence is politically motivated and that she did not want to demonstrate a "merely" or primarily Jewish allegiance: she says an anthology of *all* writers driven out by the Nazis would be one thing; she considers one exclusively containing Jewish writers inappropriate at that time (Seghers 1964).

Yet it is clear that Anna Seghers had by no means "buried" her Jewish identity. A browse through her personal library in her former apartment—now a museum—showed me how deeply steeped in Jewish culture she was. A battered Hebrew prayer book designed to teach children the language, published in 1907, has individual prayers marked in pencil, as if by a teacher marking homework. One can only speculate whether it was used by the young Netty Reiling, although it would seem logical that her Orthodox Jewish upbringing would have included learning Hebrew. Individual key words translated in the textbook read, in part, like a litany of leitmotif-like words describing the humanistic values and concerns that inform Anna Seghers's works: generous, good, forgiving, light, darkness, day, night, heaven, earth, our voice, the people, love, honor, our children, teaching, showing pity, healing, peace, mercy, justice, war, soul, heart, and thou shalt love, good deed, community, noble, mankind, strength, truth, joy, justice, trust, liberate, and constancy.

Seghers's love of myths and fairy tales is enriched by collections of Eastern European Jewish stories and legends by Buber and others. A small volume of beautiful Eastern European Yiddish love songs transliterated into German, given to

Seghers by her husband, speaks of the pain of love parted and fortitude in the face of adversity in terms that could almost be prophetic: "Wenn du kommen wirst in eine fremde Stadt, Liebele, Meine Red sollst du bedenken . . . / Und wenn du kommen wirst über ein Feuer, Liebele, / Vor Kummer sollst du dich nicht verbrennen" (If you come to a strange city, dear one, remember my words. . . . / And if you get into a fire, beloved, / don't burn to death with grief).

It is unclear when Anna Seghers heard about her mother's death. Her first documented mention of the "accursed news" comes in a January 1945 letter to Kurt Kesten, and in a 1946 letter written from Mexico to Lore Wolf, Seghers speaks of her mother's deportation to and murder in Piaski, and of having arranged visas for her, a matter of days too late (Wagner, Emmerich, and Radvanyi 1994, 143, 159).

The writer Stephan Hermlin, a long-time friend and colleague of Anna Seghers, has said on more than one occasion that she was "cut to the quick" by her mother's death—that, although she never spoke of it, it was a decisive influence in her inner development. He recounts an episode in Stockholm when they climbed a hill toward a restaurant together, in enervating heat. Suddenly Seghers said: "My beloved Jewish people." At that moment he knew, said Hermlin, that Seghers was thinking of her mother (Hermlin in Roehner 1995, 155–56).

If "Ausflug der toten Mädchen" has been seen as, among other things, a form of homage to Seghers's mother, "Post ins gelobte Land" (Mail to the promised land; 1946) portrays the exercise of the filial duty of "keeping the memory," to an extent that Anna Seghers was certainly unable to fulfill in real life. The book has been described as "both a reaffirmation and a statement of loss" about her Jewish roots (LaBahn 1986, 19). This exquisitely crafted and moving story embodies the different social roles available to Jews in Europe. It traces four generations in a family of Polish Jews who live in Paris after fleeing a pogrom in the last decade of the nineteenth century. The first generation lives as though back in the shtetel; they are religiously observant in a ghetto surrounded by familiar faces from their home area.

Their son Nathan Levi carries on the family fur trade and is a devout Jew. His son Jakob is brought up to be observant of orthodox practices, but he transcends ghetto mentality and its social and religious norms when he goes to a French lycée. He becomes a respected eye specialist, the pride of his father, and develops an assimilated persona as Jacques Levi. *His* son does not need to learn French in school; he is fluent from the outset. Unlike his father, who stood in the doorway watching children play in the street, marked as an outsider by his strange clothing, this child is one of the gang, completely assimilated.

When father Nathan chooses to spend his last days in the Promised Land, his son solemnly promises to write regularly. In this as in the earlier novel *Transit,* Seghers's passionate commitment to creating trust, to not abandoning people, operates on the level of personal relationships as well as in her wider political and literary credo. (Seghers in conversation with Chrisa Wolf, 1959, in Wolf 1987, 258). Faced himself with death before his father dies, Jacques writes a supply of letters that he entrusts to his wife. She does not escape the Nazi invasion of France but manages to get the last letter sent by a friend who does. Seghers suggests in this story the triumph of loyalty and humane values over persecution and repeated exile, in what Martin Kane describes as "that restrained but confident belief in the human spirit which characterizes all of Anna Seghers's work" (Kane 1991, 39).

Their devotion to family relationships, their care for others' well-being, are far more important characteristics of these four generations of Jews than their outward forms of social existence, and these attributes ultimately influence the other people with whom these characters come into contact. Rather than teaching by didactic method, Seghers shows here the power of example. The effect of the story also exemplifies her own early dictum that we writers "write not to describe, but by describing to change things" (Seghers 1980 1:31–32). Further, the loving descriptions of Jewish religious customs and festivals make it plain that Seghers never denied her Jewishness; it remained very much a part of her identity as writer and human being.

Stephan Hermlin once said that he and Anna Seghers never once spoke explicitly about Jewishness: it simply wasn't a topic; they were Communists and therefore had other concerns. He went on to say, however, that there are some things that are simply too painful to speak about, and that it is a long tradition within German-Jewish families not to articulate the unspeakable—the pain of 2,000 years of persecution. This self-imposed silence, Hermlin maintains—in a statement surprising for an East German writer, when Jewishness was simply not an issue in public discourse during the forty years of the GDR—is built on the deep "pessimism" arising from "2,000 years of experience that society is hostile to Jews. Even if sometimes the world appears benign toward Jews, so that things seem to have become normal, it is never truly normal; it can always turn into its opposite—the pogrom. That can always happen, it can always appear, quite suddenly, and there's no protection from it" (Hermlin in Roehner 1995, 155–56).

Perhaps it was this pessimistic knowledge engraved deep on her inner self, together with her experiences of exile and of Stalinism, that made Anna Seghers, the ostensibly powerful figure though she was, cautious, and led her to stay silent at the 1957 trial of Walter Janka. She, whose whole life was dedicated to creating a society based on truth and social justice, "was once silent where she ought to have spoken up." But it is easy to know best with hindsight, from the end of the Cold War rather than in its chilling midst. And as Hermlin went on to say, those who arrogate the right to accuse her "should ask themselves how they would have behaved in a similar situation. But they haven't ever experienced similar situations. . . . May self-righteousness shut up. Let justice speak" (Hermlin 1991, 29; Roehner 1995).

Bibliography

Sigrid Bock, "Seghers in der DDR oder Vom Lob des Erzählens," *Exil und Rückkehr: Emigration und Heimkehr,* ed. Anton-Maria Keim (Mainz: Schmidt, 1986), 121–35; Volker Dahm, "Jüdische oder deutsche Kultur: Die Suche nach Identität," *Die Juden in Deutschland, 1933–1945: Leben unter nationalsozialistsicher Herrschaft,* ed.

Wolfgang Benz (Munich: Beck, 1993), 75–82; Isaac Deutscher, *The Non-Jewish Jew and Other Essays* (London: Merlin, 1981); Helmut Eschwege, "Resistance of German Jews against the Nazi Regime," *The Nazi Holocaust 7: Jewish Resistance to the Holocaust,* ed. Michael R. Marrus (1989): 385–428; Karl Gossow, ed., *Anna Seghers: Briefe ihrer Freunde* (Berlin: Aufbau, 1960); Stephan Hermlin, "Nachdenken über Anna Seghers," *neue deutsche Literatur* 39 (1991): 1, 28–29; Artur Joseph, "Chanukka in Köln" [1970], *Der Wunderrabbi: Jüdische Geschichten* (Cologne: Kiepenheuer & Witsch, 1991), 50–63; Martin Kane, "Visions for a New Society," *Socialism and the Literary Imagination: Essays on East German Writers,* ed. Martin Kane (Oxford: Berg, 1991), 29–40; Eva Kaufmann, "Die Frau im Verborgenen," *Deutsche Literatur von Frauen,* ed. Gisela Brinker-Gabler, vol. 2 (Munich: C. H. Beck, 1988), 352–63; Kathleen J. LaBahn, *Anna Seghers' Exile Literature* (New York: Peter Lang, 1986); *Lexikon deutschsprachiger Schriftsteller,* 2 vols. (Leipzig: VEB Bibliographisches Institut, 1974); Hans Mayer, "Deutsche, Juden, Kommunisten," *Der Widerruf: Über Deutsche und Juden* (Frankfurt a. M.: Suhrkamp, 1994), 271–85; Ben Okri, "Time to Dream the Best Dream of All," *The Guardian* (Jan. 1995): 5; Ladislaus Radvanyi, *Der Chiliasmus: Ein Versuch zur Erkenntnis der chiliastischen Idee und des chiliastischen Handelns* [1923] (Budapest: Lukács Archivum, 1985), 77–81; Eberhard Roehner, "Nicht gleichartig, aber verwandt: Gespräch mit Stephan Hermlin," *Argonautenschiff* 4 (1995): 153–62; Friedrich Schütz, "Die Familie Seghers-Reiling und das jüdische Mainz," *Argonautenschiff* 2 (1993): 151–73; Anna Seghers (Netty Reiling), *Anna Seghers–Wieland Herzfelde: Ein Briefwechsel, 1939–1946,* ed. Ursula Emmerich and Erika Pick (Berlin: Aufbau, 1985); Seghers, "Der Ausflug der toten Mädchen" [1946] and "Post ins gelobte Land" [1946] in *Erzählungen* (Berlin: Aufbau, 1974); Seghers, "Eroberung der Jugend" [1931], "Was wissen wir von Jugendcliquen?" [1931], "Vaterlandsliebe" [1935], "Deutschland und Wir" [1941], "Volk und Schriftsteller" [1942], "Fürst Andrej und Raskolnikow" [1944], and "Inneres und Äußeres Reich [1946], *Essays,* 2 vols. (Berlin: Aufbau, 1980); Seghers, "Die Hochzeit von Haiti" [1949], in *Erzählungen 1948–1949* (Berlin: Aufbau, 1994); Seghers, *Jude und Judentum im Werke Rembrandts* [1924] (Leipzig: Verlag Philipp Reclam, 1983); Seghers, "Letter to Hermann Kesten" in *Deutsche Literatur im Exil: Briefe Europäischer Autoren, 1933–1949,* ed. Hermann Kesten (Vienna: Verlag Kurt Desch, 1964), 48–49; Seghers, *Das siebte Kreuz* [1942] (Hamburg: Rowohlt, 1965); Seghers, *Transit* [1944] (Berlin: Aufbau-Verlag,

1976); Frank Wagner, Ursula Emmerich, and Ruth Radvanyi, eds., *Anna Seghers: Eine Biographie in Bildern* (Berlin: Aufbau, 1994); Hans-Albert Walter, radio talk show on Anna Seghers (Oct. 1988) "Anna Seghers," *"Es ist ein Weinen in der Welt": Hommage für deutsche Juden,* ed. H. J. Schultz (Stuttgart: Kreuz, 1990), 406–29; Christa Wolf, *Die Dimension des Autors* (Neuwied: Luchterhand, 1987); and Christiane Zehl-Romero, *Anna Seghers* (Hamburg: Rowohlt, 1993).

BARBARA EINHORN

1947 Arnold Zweig begins to work on *Freundschaft mit Freud*

We think we know everything about Arnold Zweig. His decision to leave exile in Palestine to go into the Soviet occupied zone did not help the reception of his work. In the West, he was quickly seen as a notorious hard-liner who had long ago reached his peak as a writer; in the East he was promoted, but he couldn't achieve everything that he had imagined was part of antifascist cultural production. By the end of the 1940s, political freedom was becoming increasingly limited as show trials pervaded the cordon sanitaire of the Soviet Union. Stalin began his last years in power with new waves of oppression, of which the attack on cosmopolitanism stands out as especially horrible because it began in the same century that saw the Nazi mass-murder of European Jews. Old certainties were brought into question: "Only anti-Fascism and democracy secure the very existence of the Jews. Everywhere! Even in one's own camp. Don't fool yourselves! No dreams and fantasies in politics!" (Hermand 1990, 73). History foiled Zweig's good intentions of 1933. At the end of the 1940s, Germany found itself divided: in the West, there was democracy without anti-fascism; in the East, antifascism without democracy.

"And so we all did not know at the end of 1932 that partial fascism always grows into total fascism and that partial Socialism hardly ever grows into total Socialism." This statement appears on page 135 of the manuscript for *Freundschaft mit Freud*, completed in 1962 "in a cozy little house between parks and other residences," as the author Arnold Zweig assures us. Zweig had sent a "skeleton of the book" to his friend Lion Feuchtwanger in the United States on March 23, 1947. In the fourteenth year of his exile in Palestine, Zweig was in dire need of money—he could hardly survive in Palestine any longer. In order to gather more material for his Freud book and to find new contacts to have it published, Zweig planned a trip to England, but the Home Office denied him entry in 1948. He stayed for a while in Prague and took the opportunity to visit Freud's birthplace in Moravia. He already had an invitation to visit East Berlin, but he wanted only to go to the Soviet occupied zone "with several precautions so that I won't go to the dogs again, as I did in Palestine" (letter to Erich Weinert, May 31, 1947).

Arnold Zweig hoped to take charge of his life again. He thought he knew the great disrupters of mankind: Copernicus, Darwin, and Freud. He confidently added Karl Marx to the other three mentioned by Freud—with this designation, Zweig pointed to the economic disturbance of a people that idealized itself as autonomous. Zweig knew what he was talking about—he had expected things to be better in the coming years in East Germany: "I had it easy for only a few years before and after Hitler. The money-complex that otherwise made me produce has fallen away" (Zweig to Feuchtwanger, Apr. 2, 1949). The new East German government thanked him for his confidence and he thanked them in return. In one of his least critical texts, written in 1961, he asserted: "If I should say what I am, I am a yes-man. I am a pronounced yes-man who has returned from exile in Palestine after the main cause of our defeat had been done away with in 1945: the splitting of the workers through the creation of a closed German workers group, composed of Wilhelm Pieck, von Gratewohl, and Walter Ulbricht" (Zweig 1959, 446). Now one could close the door and let the voice of 1990 speak instead. One of the heroes of 1989, Vaclav Havel, president of the Czech Republic, uttered this dubious statement: "Nothing should remind us of the time that lies behind us." In contrast to the mood in Germany in 1990, one notes in these words the strong rejection of the need for revenge. But with this desire to forget the contradictions of past generations, the living punish all of the dead. We would best ask today: Why did Arnold Zweig leave Haifa in 1948 for the eastern section of Berlin?

Zweig's wife, Beatrice, known as Dita, became ill when she left Palestine in 1948. She did not want to go to Germany: "She doesn't want to go back, she must not live here, amidst the rubble and with these people who have committed such horrors. She wants only to go back to Israel to live in the young state and take part in its development." This statement was written by a "windblown Zweig" to Feuchtwanger in April 1949 (*Zweig* is the German word for branch). A contradiction presented itself and threatened to tear Zweig's life in two: "I will not give up either Berlin or Haifa as a place to work and perhaps must be separated from my wife for part of the year, since she clings unwaveringly to an extended return to Karmel." This was the mild version of the confusion that Zweig expressed to his old friend Walter Berendson in July. Zweig clung to a hope and an illusion: "a bridge from Berlin to Haifa that appears almost like a tender rainbow," as he wrote in the afterword to Hilde Huppert's *Fahrt zum Acheron* in December 1950. Arnold Zweig wanted to pull together a world that was breaking apart.

Zweig worked against forgetting the past. In 1958 he wrote a commentary on the unveiling of a memorial for the victims of Buchenwald:

"Among the 21 flags . . . there was none with the ancient symbol of the Star of David to represent the Jewish victims of fascist terror. Here, in this book, it is hoisted up next to the red flag" (cited in Wiznitzer 1983, 186). Zweig knew about the roots from which Israel and East Germany sprang. The politics of the two countries had long ago broken down what was once common to both. Close friendships fell apart in the conflict. In the West, Zweig had long been attacked as a dry Communist. In Israel, he was seen as a betrayer of Zionism. In East Germany, he atrophied as a classic. Zweig, the state-supported writer, would die with East Germany—twenty years after his biological death.

But his *Friendship with Freud* (*Freundschaft mit Freud*) gives us the opportunity to rediscover Arnold Zweig. In a conformist society, where labels are handed out like dog tags, individual achievements are destroyed through classification. This arbitrary classification is given the appearance of natural inevitability when it is declared to be "identity." One of the most horrible customs, which is every bit as arbitrary as the Marxist-Leninist classification by classes, consists in a posthumous assessment of individuals according to a contemporary notion of normative "common sense" identity. All of the labels that have been applied to Arnold Zweig border on nonsense or say nothing at all: Prussian Jew, cultural German, Marxist, pacifist, Freudian. These labels are not useful as guides; they lead us astray.

Freud did not allow himself to be aligned with existing Socialist systems. Interestingly, in 1930 Zweig presented in his critical articles on the Moscow executions the pattern for Freud's unequivocal position toward the Soviet Union. In Freud's words, the sorrow resonated with the changes in the world: "What you have written about the Soviet experiment has struck me. We have lost a hope and an illusion through that and now have nothing to take its place. We live in bad times; I ought to have dismissed the obtuseness of the age, but I can't help it that I feel sorry for my seven grandchildren" (Freud to Zweig, Dec. 7, 1932). Freud did not have to experience the worst that was yet to come.

In the last hours of Yom Kippur in 1939,

Freud died after a long period of suffering. In July 1939, Zweig had visited him in his London exile and described these last hours in the opening of his *Friendship with Freud*. Zweig saw an epoch end with Freud—Freud, the "high point and culmination of a liberal age." Zweig did not see himself as part of Freud's generation but rather as a son—the son of another time.

Anna Freud, as Jost Hermand reports, had requested that Zweig write her father's biography five years after his death. *Friendship with Freud*, which he worked on in 1947, 1948, and 1962, became something else; in Hermand's assessment the book is "less a biography or even a scholarly study of the founder of psychoanalysis" (Hermand 1990, 103). In 1936 Freud had already let "Master Arnold" know in no uncertain terms that he didn't want a biography: "Whoever writes a biography commits himself to lies, cover-ups, hypocrisy, whitewashing, and even to the suppression of his lack of understanding, for biographical truth cannot be achieved, and even if one were to find it, it would be useless" (Vienna, May 31, 1936).

In 1973, Johannes Cremerius still interpreted the relationship of Zweig to Freud without paying attention to its substance—as "the fate of exaggerated transference," which was a hindrance to a planned "novel of psychoanalysis." It is noteworthy that Cremerius saw Zweig's neurosis as being responsible for his turning away from Freud and "turning to Marxism" (Cremerius 1973, 658). Zweig's repeated returns to the manuscript *Friendship with Freud*, which still lies unpublished in the archives, counters this hypothesis. Zweig's correspondence with Feuchtwanger reveals Cremerius's theses to be bad speculation: "In the case of Freud, East Germany and apparently all of the people's democracies are twenty years behind. I will make it clear to them how great a scientific and German event this psychologist and writer Freud is and will continue to be and how he and Marx relate to one another" (to Feuchtwanger, Feb. 24, 1950).

To reproach Zweig for not paying attention to the debate between Marxism and psychoanalysis would not get us very far. Zweig was not a theorist of Marxism or psychoanalysis, and for that

very reason analysis could make the representation of a societal totality possible. The proposed psychoanalytic novel would have run aground just as the Freud biography did. The more than 200-page literary work on his experiences with Freud cannot be read simply as "operated love of exaggeration" (*agierte Übertragungsliebe*). But even without knowing this manuscript, the attentive reader of *Erziehung vor Verdun* or *Beil von Wandsbek* could not miss the fact that these books implicitly present psychic processes that formed the explicit arguments of Freud's works *Zeitgemäßes über Krieg und Tod* and *Totem und Tabu*. The productive reworking of psychoanalytic experiences is not clumsily performed as intellectual history; rather, the epic poet learns to articulate unconscious processes in a literary manner. Zweig's epic accomplishment made visible the barbaric effects of the killing taboo on human consciousness and the unconscious. The common origin of this cultural-critical position lies in war trauma. The unresolved experience of mass murder thrust him into a new world beyond the *Novellen um Claudius* and the *Familie Klopfer*. It was precisely this new subjective working-through of the war that forced Freud and his closest colleagues to step from psychology to critical cultural theory.

Zweig's choice of material stemmed neither from excitement over psychoanalytic theory nor from a Marxist world view. Arnold Zweig experienced over the course of his life a secular societal transformation that he sought to understand. The bourgeois drive to understand everything that arises when one is the victim of invisible societal mechanisms turned Zweig, who came from a lower-middle-class Jewish background, into a creator of epic worlds in which barbarism within civilization could be survived. A straight path runs from *Grischa* to *Beil von Wandsbek*. It is the dialectic of the matter itself that allowed Zweig to distance himself from the war experience: in the history of the lower-middle-class butcher who became an executioner, one finds the destruction of bourgeois culture—a Faustian tale of physical work that can be contrasted with Thomas Mann's Faustian drama of the German spirit. Zweig's great abstract achievement of showing the prehistory of the mass murder in the life story of a goy is developed in a remarkable letter to Freud that, for unknown reasons, is missing from the edition of their correspondence: "I see a Grischa-type here, in whom the old German springs up repulsively and breaks through layer after layer. And especially my wife, a Protestant, who agrees deep down that 'whoever spills human blood. . . .' It would be a true novel—and he would have to show the people buried in Nazism who are so often forgotten and overlooked. The violated German is not only in the concentration camps, but also in his executioners" (dated mid-1938).

As Hans Albert Walter so memorably noted (*Im Anfang war die Tat,* 1986), Zweig carried out this concept through well-informed psychoanalytical and critical social theory with exacting imagination. There is no comparable literary working-through of National Socialism in Germany. It is astonishing how little attention the world paid to *Beil.* Zweig did not fall into any camp: with the help of psychoanalysis, he refused the national model of perception and the Marxist-Leninist class model. The "Suicide of an Executioner," which he derived from a newspaper article, contained the history of a legal murderer as the pre-history of the machinery of mass murder. Aesthetic power ends in the approach to Auschwitz, in the history of a murderer—through holding back, through indirect view, there is no deception that the whole horror can be represented. Zweig conceived of the novel in 1938, shortly before the machinery of murder was set up. In full consciousness of Auschwitz he would not have been able to write this story.

After 1945, Zweig experienced the power of forgetting. He attempted to publish the "notes of Frau Hilde Huppert on her experience in the Nazi death land and her remarkable rescue from Bergen-Belsen." This report was smuggled into the Egyptian prisoner-of-war camp along with a preface and afterword by Arnold Zweig. It appeared officially in 1951 under Zweig's name, with the title *Fahrt zum Acheron.* "And not by chance, but according to internal necessity, I was led to suffer in words what life had spared me and which I hadn't ordained." Zweig became familiar with the horror; he tried to make it understand-

able through Marx and Freud: "That which is most repressed returns and becomes explosive, whether one looks at it with Karl Marx from the objective side or with Sigmund Freud from the side of spiritual, personal, and collective reality. And, therefore, wouldn't it be better to fight a repression right away, to confront it *ab ovo?* Certainly the outermost layer of our experiences testifies to the monstrous guilt that the German people brought upon themselves. But then the non-German world would not need a reason to close its ears when the reality of the Nazi-fascist epoch is given a voice and speaks." Zweig wrote these words in Haifa on May 20, 1947. They did not find a publisher.

Arnold Zweig's works ran up against collective amnesia, of which he had already found traces just after 1945. Moreover, history in the 1990s has become a media-manipulated event: a new era blind to history seems to be dawning. The demise of existing Socialism seems also to be burying the work of those who, after coming out of exile, bound themselves to this social system. The labels that were placed upon those returning from exile now serve as epitaphs that conceal their unread works. Zweig's epic life work mediates the transformation of the bourgeois world into a catastrophe of civilization. The bridge leads from *Grischa* to *Beil.* Like any bridge, one can also travel in the other direction to catch a glimpse of the origin of the contemporary world. Zweig's still unpublished *Freundschaft mit Freud* deserves to be finally made public today. Especially in a time when conformist views prevail, it remains an intellectual duty "to work against the repression" (Haifa, 1947).

I fear that everything considered to fall within the sphere of the Socialist system will be held responsible for its bankruptcy. The hatred for the defenseless dead, who embodied a hope for which we have no substitute, will continue to grow as our present society appears ever more to be without alternatives. Today one need only label someone a Marxist to throw him or her in league with Stalin. Zweig always attempted to uncover the consequences of societal catastrophes. He tried to do so with movements that promised to change the world: Zionism and Socialism. Both movements seemed to be answers to the disappointments that he had experienced in the bourgeois world. The display of the bourgeois spirit occurred in the form of bourgeois national cultures. Culture seemed to him to allow for an escape from petty bourgeois narrowmindedness in order to develop his own means of expression as an individual. This promise of cultural emancipation seduced many intellectuals in Imperial Germany into becoming propagandists for the "Ideas of 1914."

The reality of the war wiped these illusions away, but for the simple soldier Zweig, the security of assimilation that had held the floor since the *Novellen um Claudia* also fell apart with the census of the Jews in the army in 1916. Freud's disillusion was even greater when, in 1914, he was the victim of Austrian cultural chauvinism. All the correspondence between Zweig and Freud revolves around the collective escape from the culture bought out by barbarism. Freud was much more skeptical of collective solutions to cultural entanglements than was Zweig. On the bitter disappointment with Zionism that Zweig experienced in Palestine, Freud could only comment calmly, for he had long ceased to believe in a German-Jewish symbiosis. Freud greeted Zweig's literary self-interpretation that he wanted to reconcile German culture with Judaism with a refreshing disapproval: "If you tell me of your ruminations, I can free you from the madness that one must be a German. Shouldn't we leave this god-forsaken people to themselves?" (Freud to Zweig, Aug. 18, 1932).

Zweig's friendship with Freud reconciled him to the separation of life and theory, of storytelling and analysis. Zweig battled his whole life against the negativity of theoretical work; his theoretical social-psychology, such as he developed in *Caliban* (1927) did not reach the individual subject, the essence of mass-psychology: Zweig the epic poet—not Zweig the theorist—reached this level. During Freud's lifetime, Zweig placed his hopes in Zionism and was disappointed. Freud's response was so bitter that the editor of the correspondence in 1968, during a wave of anti-Zionist sentiment, felt it necessary to leave these comments out. That must be corrected in a new edi-

tion. Freud had argued remorselessly for the withdrawal from the collective, whereas Zweig found a new cause after Freud's death. The differences between these two thinkers and their views will become clearer when all of the material is finally published. Zweig never accepted Freud's strict critical individualism in theory, but artistically—in his best work, the great novels—he put it into practice.

Zweig's motive is understandable: he did not want the breakdown of civilization to be without consequences. The West wanted to know very little about the reconditioning of the past; the East seemed in 1948 to be the place where antifascism would be able to alter German reality. A cardboard box full of newspaper clippings from the years 1951–53 lies in the Arnold Zweig house. The campaign against cosmopolitanism appears to have been attentively followed in the Zweig household. Had he chosen the wrong side again? Zweig displayed courage: in his *Soviet Diary,* published in *Sinn und Form* in 1952, he refers to his friendship with Freud, "with whom I was closely joined by our common origin" (249). Zweig testified that Freud, who was an absolute nonperson in Stalin's anti-Semitic campaign, belonged among those who had recently been persecuted. It seemed self-evident to him to join the Jewish community rather than the Socialist Unity Party (SED) when he returned to Berlin. In 1958, after Lukács had returned to Budapest from Romania, he received a proud defense from Zweig: "Perhaps everything can be traced to the fact that I could never belong to a party and knew how to find my way and carry through as a maverick" (Mar. 11, 1958).

Freud warned us that biographical truth is only useful when discussed in relation to one's work. Biographical criticism that constructs the work from the life history destroys the work. The *Freundschaft mit Freud* that I have mentioned could be successful only because it did not subordinate self-reflection to autobiography and did not let Freud's work dissolve into his life story. We can learn from *Freundschaft mit Freud* something about the contradictions in Zweig himself—beneath the yes-man lay an individual who was no match for the ideal self, "Father Freud," but who could recognize the other. "The view he offered took more courage than joining any party or movement," Zweig notes right at the beginning of his manuscript. Zweig, who suffered from a loss of sovereignty as a result of his war experience, finally regained it through writing after many attempts at analysis. He simply could not live by writing in Palestine. He returned to cold-war Germany compelled once again to take the path to reconstitution through psychoanalysis. His *Freundschaft mit Freud* reveals an attempt to preserve the freedom to be different under the compulsion to be a yes-man. Zweig consciously smuggled contraband psychoanalysis and Jewish history into his East German novels. The best goods remain unknown, locked up in Berlin-Niederschönhausen.

Bibliography

Johannes Cremerius, "Arnold Zweig," *Psyche* 27 (1973); Lion Feuchtwanger, *Briefwechsel, 1933–1958,* 2 vols. (Berlin: Aufbau, 1984); Ernst L. Freud, ed., *Briefwechsel: Sigmund Freud {und} Arnold Zweig* (Frankfurt a. M.:Fischer, 1968); Freud, ed., *The Letters of Sigmund Freud and Arnold Zweig,* trans. Elaine and William Robson-Scott (New York: Harcourt, Brace & World, 1970); Günter Grass, *Der Fall Axel C. Springer am Beispiel Arnold Zweig* (Berlin: Voltaire Verlag, 1967); Jost Hermand, *Arnold Zweig: mit Selbstzeugnissen und Bilddokumenten* (Reinbek bei Hamburg: Rowohlt, 1990); Eberhard Hilscher, *Arnold Zweig: Brückenbauer vom Gestern ins Morgen* (Halle [Saale]: Verlag Sprache und Literatur, 1962); Hermann Kahler, *Arnold Zweig: Der Dichter und der Psychologe* (Berlin: n.p., 1987); Hans-Harald Müller, *Arnold Zweig und der Zionismus* (Munich: Dr. Rudolf Georgi, 1989); Johanna Rudolph, *Arnold Zweig* (Berlin: Deutscher Kulturbund, 1962); Rudolph, *Der Humanist Arnold Zweig: Ein Versuch* (Berlin: Henschelverlag, 1955); George Salamon, *Arnold Zweig* (New York: Twayne, 1975); Wilhelm von Sternburg, *Arnold Zweig* (Frankfurt a. M.: Hain, 1990); von Sternburg, *Arnold Zweig: Materialien zu Leben und Werk* (Frankfurt a. M.: Fischer, 1987); von Sternburg, ed., *Heinrich Mann, Arnold Zweig: Hilfsmaterial für den Literaturunterricht an den Ober- und Fachschulen* (Berlin: Volk und Wissen Volkseigener Verlag, 1954); George Wenzel, ed., *Arnold Zweig, 1887–1968: Werk und Leben in Dokumenten und Bildern; mit unveröffentlichten Manuskripten und Briefen aus dem Nachlaß* (Berlin: Aufbau, 1978); Manuel Wiznitzer, *Arnold Zweig: das Leben eines deutsch-jüdischen Schriftstellers* (Königstein/Taunus: Athenäum, 1983); Arie Wolf, *Grosse und Tragik Arnold Zweigs: Ein jüdisch-deutsches Dichterschicksal in jüdischer Sicht* (London: World of Books, 1991); and Arnold Zweig, *Essays* (Berlin: Aufbau, 1959).

DETLEV CLAUSSEN

TRANSLATED BY TODD HERZOG
AND HILLARY HOPE HERZOG

1948 Hannah Arendt appeals for Arab-Jewish reconciliation as the most plausible reaction to the German-Jewish catastrophe

The announcement on September 9, 1993, that Israel and the Palestine Liberation Organization (PLO) had signed an agreement of mutual recognition was more than a surprise. Coming forty-five years after the proclamation of the State of Israel—forty-five years of failed attempts to resolve the bitter Arab-Jewish conflict in the Middle East—it was an extraordinary moment in history, the crowning achievement of both parties' political good will. The leaders on both sides, old men who had fought many battles, were laying the bad past to rest and hoping for a good future to emerge. But Jews, looking at their history as tenacious entanglement of pasts and futures, have not been known to forget. Nor will all Palestinians find it easy to do so. Both might find useful the perspective on their shared difficult past of two contemporaries who forty-five years ago were deeply troubled about the brand new future they saw emerging.

For Hannah Arendt, the German-Jewish exile in the United States, and Judah L. Magnes, the American-born, German-educated president of Hebrew University, 1948 was a year of intense collaboration on proposals for an Arab-Jewish reconciliation, notably a confederation of a Jewish and an Arab state with Jerusalem as the capital. The sum of her thought on the Jewish-Arab question, Arendt's 1948 essay "Peace or Armistice in the Middle East?" was dedicated to the memory of Magnes, who "from the close of World War I to the day of his death in October 1948, had been the outstanding Jewish spokesman for Arab-Jewish understanding in Palestine." Unlike Arendt, who was unlikely to be labeled a "problematic Jew," Magnes has to this day been seen as a "Dissenter in Zion," rather than as a shrewd and perceptive voice in ongoing political debates among Zionists. His clear-headed critique of certain crucially important aspects of political Zionism in the 1930s and 1940s has been given very little attention in Israel—as has Arendt's, for that matter—though it remains thoroughly contemporary today and would be useful to the now ongoing process of Arab-Jewish political reconciliation.

Magnes's argument against an exclusive concept of Jewish statehood built on the proposal of a binational state in Palestine was made by "Brit Shalom," a group of intellectuals of mostly Central and West European origin, many of them German, who had come together in 1925 out of a shared concern for equal rights for Jews and Arabs. Considered by many Zionists to be severely lacking in political realism and national feeling, their proposal was essentially ignored after the 1929 disturbances, and when another Arab revolt began in 1936, most of the Brit Shalom members gave up hope for reaching a Jewish-Arab rapprochement. Yet as late as 1942, Magnes founded a party called Ihud (Unity) with the intention of furthering Jewish-Arab understanding and to call again and more urgently for a binational state. His view of the relation between

Eretz Israel and the *Galut* (Diaspora) and of the cultural mission of Judaism was influenced by the spiritual-cultural Zionism of Ahad Ha'Am, who had proposed a complicated synthesis between rejuvenation of the Jewish spirit and reestablishment of the Jewish body politic. For Ahad Ha'Am as well as Magnes, the spiritual center in the land of Israel was to unify and give meaning to the lives of Jews both in Palestine and on the periphery, in the Diaspora. But this cultural Zionism did not, as did political Zionism, clearly privilege one choice over the other.

Ahad Ha'Am's secular concept of Zionism emphasized the need for cultural-national rather than political-national unity: the land and Judaism do not in themselves represent values, but only in the service they render to the Jewish people. It was for this reason that Magnes saw Ahad Ha'Am as representative of "modern Judaism." Two decades later, on the occasion of the politically difficult inauguration of Hebrew University (1925), he appealed to Ahad Ha'Am as "one of the moral guides of our generation." The presence at the inauguration ceremony of Lord Balfour, which in Magnes's view was unwise and insensitive, had provoked nonviolent Arab demonstrations. In contrast to the prevailing Jewish reaction of disregarding the demonstrations, Magnes commented that the Arabs' laudable restraint was due not so much to the presence of government forces but to the conviction that he saw "growing in the Moslem world as elsewhere that understanding and reconciliation between peoples can come only through pacifist and nonviolent methods" (letter to Ahad Ha'Am, Apr. 1925, in Goren 1982, 235).

In *Like All the Nations?* (1930), Magnes emphasized the fact that "Jewish conscience" must realize "that the inhabitants of this country, both Arabs and Jews, have not only the right but the duty to participate, in equitable and practical ways, in the government of their common Homeland." In this context he singled out the political sphere as the focus for solutions—an argument that would greatly influence the development of Arendt's political philosophy. "The life of this unhappy country," he wrote, "will be much saner and much less hysterical the sooner its population

can exercise its political energies in legitimate and practical and constructive ways" (14, 16). Like Arendt, Magnes did not believe in Jewish uniqueness. There were historical reasons for the separateness of the Jewish people that made it imperative to learn how to live in the comity of other peoples. Magnes's utopian impulses, like Arendt's, were not fueled by a radical suspension of the reality of human limitations—as has been the case with so much twentieth-century intellectual utopianism. He was fully aware of the need to negotiate a compromise between unlimited fears and desires and limited resources and reassurances. The process needed to be supported by the coming together of adult people as political agents who, as they came together in the political sphere, were seen and saw each other as equals. This concept of political cooperation led Magnes to conclude, like Arendt, that neither a Jewish state, nor a binational state, nor a *Yishuv* in Palestine could be maintained, "if the whole surrounding world be our enemies" (21). If there is any significance in being in the world it is in sharing it—in this case most reliably and most enduringly through participation in government. The answer to the question "Like all the nations?" was an emphatic "yes."

Magnes introduced the policies of Ihud to American readers in his article "Towards Peace in Palestine" (*Foreign Affairs,* Jan. 1943). In contrast to many American Jews, Arendt respected the Ihud position as it was stated, though she had reservations regarding the proposal, supported by Martin Buber and Ernst Simon, of an Arab federation connected with an Anglo-American alliance. But in the "Testimony before the Anglo-American Inquiry Commission for the *Ihud* (Union) Association" given by Magnes, Buber, and Moses Smilanski in August 1946, the goals of Ihud were framed more clearly in political terms, a change that was reflected in the development of Arendt's critique of political Zionism. In his preface to the printed text, Magnes stated Ihud's intense disappointment that the movement of displaced persons to the home in Palestine had not yet begun *and* that the committee had not recommended an immediate increase of self-government for Palestine. He called for a policy "whose main objec-

tive is Jewish-Arab cooperation." Economic, social, and political conditions had to be "created"
that would require both sides to cooperate, and
"there is no part of life more important for this
than full participation together in government"
(Magnes 1946, preface). Magnes was emphatic in
his warning that if these conditions were not created, if Jews and Arabs were not helped to become
adults in political terms, violence would increase
and the results would be disastrous. His argument here influenced profoundly not only Arendt's political writings in the late 1940s on the
Arab-Jewish question, but also her later works,
The Human Condition (1958), *On Revolution*
(1963), and the counterpart to these two works,
Eichmann in Jerusalem (1963).

Magnes repeated this warning in his address
"A Solution Through Force?" given in New York
on July 17, 1946. During this speech, he appealed to his audience to be clear, in this complex
and emotional context, about the issue of domination: to the Arabs a Jewish state meant "the
rule by Jews of others who live in that Jewish
State." Having adopted much from the report of
Ihud, the Anglo-American Commission still
needed to grasp the absolute necessity for Jews
and Arabs "to come together in one of the most
important concerns of life, government" (Magnes
1947, 14–18).

At their annual convention in Atlantic City in
October 1944, however, American Zionists
across the political spectrum had demanded
unanimously a "free and democratic Jewish commonwealth . . . [that] shall embrace the whole of
Palestine, undivided and undiminished." Arendt,
in her article "Zionism Reconsidered," pointed
out that this was a deeply troubling "turning
point in Zionist history; for it means that the
Revisionist program, so long bitterly repudiated,
has proved finally victorious" (Feldman 1978,
131). A forceful critique of Zionist politics, the
essay seemed too disturbing to the editors of *Commentary,* to whom she had submitted the piece in
late 1944. It contained, in their opinion, "too
many anti-Semitic implications—not in the sense
that you intend them as such implications, but
that the unfriendly reader might intend them as
such" (Kohler and Saner 1992, 223). At issue was

precisely Arendt's claim of a close affinity in this
crisis between Revisionists and general Zionists—this was considered a "self-hating" argument, "exploitable" by "the enemy." She did acknowledge the tremendous pressures under
which Zionist leadership had to operate at that
time. But to Arendt Jewish nationalism did not
seem a good answer because it not only trusted in
nothing but "the rude force of the nation," but
also clearly depended on the "force of a foreign
nation." Like Magnes, Arendt argued here for the
practical need to coexist with the Arabs as well as
the other Mediterranean peoples. Unlike Magnes,
she alerted her readers also to the dangers of anti-
Semitism when others understandably resented
the interference by big outside powers. From historical experience, Jews ought to know that such
a state of affairs would provoke accusations "that
Jews not only profiteered from the presence of the
foreign big powers in that region but had actually
plotted it and hence are guilty of the consequences" (133). The editors of *Commentary* anticipated that statements like this could be misunderstood or misconstrued. But Arendt had done
nothing more than present Jewish experience as
located firmly in the realm of history. Like the
experience of all peoples, the historical experience
of Jews has been one of active and passive participation and therefore has not been inevitably fated
in its direction and outcome. Notwithstanding
the disproportionately large share of persecution
and suffering in Jewish history, it could be appealed to as a learning experience that might lead
to a more thoughtfully responsive and flexible
reaction to the situation in Palestine.

Arendt missed in contemporary Zionist politics a sober and detailed analysis of the Palestine
question, which would extend beyond the Jewish
Question. According to her, the dangerously apolitical nature of political Zionism was linked to
its nineteenth-century sources, Socialism and nationalism. These sources were never amalgamated
in the Zionist movement, which was split between the social-revolutionary energies of the
Eastern European masses and Herzl's and his followers' aspiration for national emancipation. Arendt's distinction here between political and social anti-Semitism—she was to develop it in

Origins of Totalitarianism (1951)—may or may not have been useful for an understanding of the situation of the Eastern Jewish masses. But it did support her attempt to trace the development of a less than realistic "political creed" of Zionist intellectuals. Seeing their national aspirations fulfilled by settling in the promised land of Palestine, Socialist Zionists did not foresee any possible national conflict with the already present inhabitants of the land. "They escaped to Palestine as one might wish to escape to the moon, to a region beyond the wickedness of the world. True to their ideals, they established themselves on the moon; and with the extraordinary strength of their faith they were able to create small islands of perfection" (Arendt 1978, 137).

But though the *chalutz* and kibbutz movements had contributed greatly to the creation of a "new type of Jew," their political influence had been negligible, precisely because their attention was focused too singlemindedly on the existing and future Yishuv. Because they did not attempt to develop a considered position on political anti-Semitism, they could not provide any fresh ideas concerning the Arab-Jewish conflict, notwithstanding their revolutionary background and ideology. Actual and pressing political conflicts in Palestine were dealt with in terms of the doctrine of a fated anti-Semitism that had, at all times and everywhere, controlled Jewish-gentile relations. Thus conceived, anti-Semitism explained (or explained away) a conflict that could not be explained. At the same time, it blocked attempts at understanding phenomena that, by their very historical political nature, would have been accessible to rational discussion. Arendt was to analyze the same problem in her report on the Eichmann trial, where she argued against a metahistorical discussion of evil and of the German catastrophe—arguments that she had started to develop in her correspondence with Jaspers immediately after the war. The motivation for her arguments was in both cases the political damage caused by such transcendence of historical political actuality. The ancient tradition of the Jewish people to distinguish so sharply between Jews and non-Jews tended to fortify "the dangerous, time-honored, deep-seated distrust of Jews for Gentiles."

To envision an "undivided and undiminished" Israel embracing "the whole of Palestine" as *the* answer to anti-Semitism presupposed an unquestioned solidarity of Jewish settlers in Palestine who would not be expected to analyze the political situation in which they acted. It presupposed, too, the assumption that anti-Semitism, a corollary of nationalism, would not be directed against an established Jewish nation. In this scenario, Palestine would appear as the (only) place where Jews could be permanently safe from the attacks of their enemies, because "their very enemies would miraculously change into their friends" (Arendt 1978, 148–50).

Arendt's concern was the political interdependence of peoples and nations. The destruction of European Jewry, in her view, called for a greater Jewish awareness of such interdependency rather than greater isolationism. The Zionist-nationalist solution of "Pan-Semitism" for Jews remaining temporarily in the Galut was the worst answer to anti-Semitism. The proposal of a Jewish state rather than a Jewish-Arab confederation seemed so problematic because it would mean that Jews established themselves from the very beginning as a "'sphere of interest' under the delusion of nationhood." But the Yishuv has not only been an asylum for persecuted Jews from Diaspora countries, it also has needed the support of other Diaspora Jewries, especially American Jews. And here Arendt predicted exactly the troubled future of a Jewish state founded with the help of the political influence of American Jews against the will of the Arabs and without the support of the Mediterranean peoples (Arendt 1978, 162).

Arendt's article "To Save the Jewish Homeland There Is Still Time" (*Commentary*, May 1948) established the personal connection with Magnes. After his long advocacy of binationalism had been ended by the proclamation of the Jewish state, Magnes set out to find a political formula that would calm Arab fears. His goal in coming to America in April 1948 had been to bring about a cease-fire in Jerusalem that could then be extended to the whole country, and to get support for a temporary United Nations trusteeship for Palestine—the plan favored by the United States over the immediate implementation of partition. Arriving in New York at a climactic moment in the battle for and against Jewish statehood, he had wanted above all to bring about peace "at nearly any price, surely at the price of statehood" (Goren 1982, 462). After May 15, Magnes continued to work on a plan for a confederation of a Jewish and an Arab state in which both parties were sovereign, but allied in defense and foreign policy. "The plan was, in a sense, a compromise," he wrote, "between binationalism and statehood, between partitioning Palestine and maintaining its unity" (463).

Magnes, whom Arendt finally met in person in the summer of 1948, was a man who deeply appealed to Arendt's sense of political integrity and rationality. She knew that he was seriously ill, and she admired his gallantry in continuing to fight for his political convictions, which she shared. He had been exhilarated by the fierce clarity of her dissection of an ominous Jewish unanimity on the Palestine issue—another testimony to the man's imaginative political realism that made him less sensitive than other Jewish readers to her notoriously aggressive rationality regarding such painful issues. Arendt wrote her essays "To Save the Jewish Homeland There Is Still Time" and "Peace or Armistice in the Middle East?" exactly when Magnes was negotiating patiently for a peaceful solution to the conflict. But though she too desired above all such a peaceful solution, she did not do so patiently. The often criticized "coldness" or remoteness of her discourse, her crisp conceptual arrangements, her rapid and sharp distinctions, and her ungentle irony derived from this impatience with solidarity and with separateness as a Jewish state of mind. But Arendt also sensed that it would be particularly important during this crisis—when the fate of the homeland seemed suspended in a balance no longer open to rational decision—to temper her appeals to political sanity. Analyzing the "sheer irrationality" of both the Arab and the Jewish peoples' desire "to fight it out at any price," she needed to find ways to help readers hostile to her argument to at least consider her criticism.

Arendt pointed out that peace between Jews and Arabs, like armistice generally, could not be imposed from the outside, but could only result from negotiation and mutual compromise. The declaration of a Jewish state and Jewish victories over Arab armies had not influenced Arab politics: "All hopes to the contrary notwithstanding, it seems as though the *one* argument the Arabs are incapable of understanding is force" (Feldman 1978, 194). Most upsetting was the unanimity of opinion growing among Jews both in America and in Palestine as to the conflict of Arab and Jewish claims: us against all Arabs; us against the hostile world. She feared the cultural consequences of a racist Jewish chauvinism inherent in contemporary Zionist understanding of "Israel's mission"—which she felt threatened to destroy the contributions made to the homeland by the collective settlements, the kibbutzim. These, in her view, constituted "perhaps the most promising of all social experiments made in the twentieth century," because they provided a fresh perspective on old cultural conflicts of central importance to modern mass democracies (185). Jews in Palestine needed to react to a recent traumatic history by looking at familiar conflicts and dilemmas in new ways. Only by emancipating—not separating—themselves from the past could they learn how to live as one people among others, and thus have a future. To continue with the concept of a unique—and uniquely significant—Jewish past would undermine this learning process irreparably.

The grave lack of political prudence or realism in Israel (the determination to regard the chancy outcome of the armed conflict as final—as having solved, once and for all, the social and political conflict) had a parallel in the Arabs' determination to see their defeat as merely an interlude and to not draw any conclusions from it. This shared refusal to take seriously the other's position meant that both sides shared, too, an ideological concept of history. History, a combination of accident and human action, must be responsible to the future precisely because the future is not known. Teleological messianic yearning and fatalism both transcend and thereby close off historical experience. In defending a state that had been established against the wishes of the Arab majority in Palestine and had resulted in a very serious Arab refugee problem, the Jews rationalized wronging the Arabs through the history of their own persecution—an argument that the Arabs could neither deny in general nor accept in particular terms. The Arabs, in their resistance to the Jewish state, used an argument that, as a general statement, the Jews could not deny, but that detracted from the fact that the Arabs had also resisted the building of the Jewish homeland in Palestine—despite the historical significance of this enterprise. In both cases the arguments lacked profoundly the political awareness that the world extends beyond the confused, conflicted present into the past and the future and that both sides have to give the other a chance to negotiate and to compromise.

Linking the Jewish-Arab conflict to the German-Jewish catastrophe, Arendt stressed the openness of the future over the closedness of the past. But in her analysis of the genesis of the Palestine conflict, she also demonstrated that both past and future needed to be questioned more rigorously: neither is the past fully known, nor is the future fully unknowable. The Zionist achievement of in-gathering could not be allowed to degenerate into another imperialist colonial enterprise. But the Yishuv as the home that had been built for and by a people without a country in a country (allegedly) without a people threatened to become just that (Arendt 1978, 202). Zionists stressing the "natural," inevitable logic of the achievement tended to emphasize the argument of blind and urgent necessity—eternal anti-Semitism—rather than of political challenges creatively met. Arendt thought it more helpful to understand the Yishuv in terms of the *kind* of response with which the challenges were met (207). As a social creation, the experiment of building up a Jewish homeland could and did provide new (and in important ways spontaneous), unpredictable answers to past experience, and in that it was indeed unique. The fact and the manner of change—the transformation of deserts into fertile land, and the design of political structures to ensure equality for heterogeneous

groups—could have been understood as a reaffirmation of the possibility of change for the world around them as well. The uniqueness of the achievement could have supported the desire to be one nation among other nations in a shared world. It should have provided a new perspective on the argument of Jewish uniqueness in the past. This is where Arendt faulted the Israeli leadership, whose Jewish nationalism, she thought, projected (and fed on) an unrealistic need to fight for everything against everybody (207f.). The only hope for peace in the Middle East in 1948 was indeed a *political* solution: two sovereign but allied states that would keep in check nationalistic anxieties and aggressions on both sides.

Bibliography

Hannah Arendt,"Peace or Armistice in the Near East?"193–222; Arendt, "To Save the Jewish Homeland There Is Still Time," *The Jew as Pariah,* 178–192; Arendt, "Zionism Reconsidered," *The Jew as Pariah* (New York: Grove, 1978), 131–177; Dagmar Barnouw, *Visible Spaces: Hannah Arendt and the German-Jewish Experience* (Baltimore, Md.: Johns Hopkins University Press, 1990), 72–134, 177–222; Ron H. Feldman, ed., *The Jew as Pariah: Jewish Identity and Politics in the Modern Age* (New York: Grove, 1978); Arthur A. Goren, *Dissenter in Zion: From the Writings of Judah L. Magnes* (Cambridge, Mass.: Harvard University Press, 1982); Lotte Kohler and Hans Saner, eds., *Hannah Arendt—Karl Jaspers Correspondence, 1926–1969,* trans. Robert and Rita Kimber Gordon (New York: Harcourt Brace, Jovanovich, 1992); Judah L. Magnes, *Like All the Nations?* (Jerusalem: Herod's Gate, 1930), 6–32; Magnes, "A Solution Through Force?" *Towards Union in Palestine: Essays on Zionism and Jewish-Arab Cooperation,* ed. Martin Buber, Judah L. Magnes, Ernst Simon (Jerusalem: Ihud Association, 1947), 14–21; Magnes, *Palestine: A Bi-National State* (New York: Ihud Association of Palestine, 1946); and Elisabeth Young-Bruehl, *Hannah Arendt: For Love of the World* (New Haven: Yale University Press, 1982).

DAGMAR BARNOUW

1949   The Frankfurt school returns to Germany

From the point of view of the international Jewish community, the return of the Frankfurt school to Germany in 1949—after more than a decade of exile in the United States—must have come as a surprise. After all, Max Horkheimer, Theodor W. Adorno, and Friedrich Pollock returned to the country and the people that organized the Holocaust. Not only was the number of German Jews who had survived the persecution very small, but also those who came to Germany from other countries (mostly in Eastern Europe) as displaced persons were, for the most part, only waiting to leave Germany for North America or Israel. For Adorno and Horkheimer, on the other hand, the United States always remained a foreign country—a place of exile that for cultural as well as political reasons marginalized their work, which was rooted in the German language and the continental neo-Marxist tradition. Although they might have readily agreed that the German-Jewish symbiosis had failed—in fact, that its idealized form had been an illusion from the very beginning—they felt a strong commitment to their country of origin. When they were approached by the city of Frankfurt and its university about rebuilding the Institute for Social Research in Frankfurt, they decided that this offer, which was primarily directed at Max Horkheimer, would give them the chance to significantly expand the influence of Critical Theory on intellectual life in postwar Germany. In 1949, when they actually arrived to resume their academic duties, the Federal Republic had just been founded, with Konrad Adenauer as its first chancellor. Although they had escaped the difficult postwar years, they were immediately confronted with the political climate of the Cold War, which defined the first decade of the Federal Republic. The recent political division of Germany had left its mark not only on political discourse but also on cultural tradition. Because anti-Communism assumed the status of a quasi-official ideology, any deviation from the conservative consensus (supplemented by a neo-liberal economic policy) was registered with apprehension by the state. Thus the official ban of the Communist Party in 1956 was only the logical conclusion of a process that had begun in 1949.

Given the Marxist past of the institute during the 1930s and its highly critical attitude toward late capitalism, as articulated in *Dialectic of Enlightenment* (1947), the return of the Frankfurt school was potentially fraught with serious philosophical and ideological problems: a common ground for the young Federal Republic and the Frankfurt school required a carefully worked-out compromise that would allow its members to do their research and teaching without provoking the hostility of the new political system. Clearly, Horkheimer, Pollock, and Adorno welcomed and supported the efforts of the new state to democratize Germany. Much of their post-1949 research was linked to this goal, including the so-called Gruppen Experiment of 1950–51, which attempted to assess public opinion in postwar Germany. Also, they shared with the West German government a highly critical attitude toward the political system of

East Germany, which they perceived as a Stalinist version of Communism. Adorno's sharp polemics against Lukács, for instance, in "Reconciliation under Duress" (1958), must be seen in this context, because Lukács represented the official voice of orthodox Marxism in East Germany. And, last but not least, Horkheimer, Pollack, and Adorno initially affirmed the dependence of the new Federal Republic on the United States—notwithstanding their strong criticism of the American culture industry in *Dialectic of Enlightenment*. In fact, a special relationship to the American high commissioner was a key element in the carefully prepared return of the institute to Frankfurt.

The immediate success of this operation was primarily due to the organizational skills of Horkheimer, who not only pressed for *Wiedergutmachung* (reparations) but also played the American card: the members of the institute came back as American citizens and would be involved in the project of German reeducation. Hence for the rebuilding of the institute, Horkheimer relied on funding from the city of Frankfurt as well as from the American high commissioner in West Germany. Although Horkheimer almost immediately became a prominent faculty member at the University of Frankfurt (first dean of the humanities and social sciences and later *Rektor*), Adorno's career moved much more slowly; initially he was given a fairly low rank and received a chair only in 1956. This treatment was indicative of the resistance of the German faculty to exiled Jewish colleagues. Reparations for losses in career opportunities were resented as preferential treatment. In other words, anti-Semitic tendencies, although officially shunned, continued to play a role in the public sphere of West Germany.

The members of the institute could not fail to realize that in spite of official support, their existence in Frankfurt remained somewhat precarious. As Adorno remarked some years later in an essay on Heinrich Heine: after Auschwitz it had become impossible to return to one's home. The concept of *Heimat* had lost its meaning. Still, especially for Adorno, the return to Germany was crucial, because it implied the return to the German language and to a cultural tradition that Adorno refused to conflate with National Social-

ism. In the short essay "On the Question: 'What Is German?'" (1965) Adorno briefly commented on his personal motivation: "I simply wanted to go back where I had spent my childhood, to where whatever was most specifically mine was mediated to the core." At the same time, Adorno underscored that his decision to return to Frankfurt should not be read as a critique of American civilization or as a preference for *Kultur* over civilization. Still, there is an anti-American moment in Adorno's explanation for his return: it comes to the fore when he discusses his own work and the question of translation. For Adorno, translation into English (as a form of reorganization) disfigures his writings to the point where they lose their authenticity. Ultimately, the loyalty to Germany is a loyalty to the German language, which is, according to Adorno, more appropriate for philosophical reflection than English. Emphasizing the expressive power of German, Adorno insists on its special nature and his personal need to rely on the complexity of German in his own writings. Historically speaking, it is of course the language of Kant and Hegel that Adorno wants to claim for the philosophical tradition in which he sees his own work.

The 1965 essay also reemphasizes what became clear in the early 1950s: those members of the Frankfurt school who returned to Germany meant to continue the work they had developed in the United States during the 1940s. They clearly did not want to return to the positions of the 1930s, which were grounded in Hegelian Marxism. The new environment, however, caused a shift in emphasis. To teach and write in postfascist Germany called for a different focus. The lack of any reliable cultural and academic tradition after 1945 that was unspoiled by fascism forced these intellectuals to reassess the very cultural tradition that had motivated them to return to Germany in the first place. Neither the cultural nor the philosophical restoration that defined the intellectual climate of the 1950s could be accepted as a solid ground. More specifically, neither Heidegger's ontology nor traditional German high culture—for example, the invocation of the German classics, could be trusted. Moreover, the traditional social sciences, among them

German sociology, had to be critiqued. In this context American empirical sociology played an important role as an antidote to the abstract German tradition, which was also compromised by its partial alliance with National Socialism. During the early 1950s in particular, the Frankfurt school championed empirical methods as part of a policy of reeducation. This course was revoked only during the 1960s, especially after the *Positivism Dispute* between Adorno and Popper. Although Adorno, and subsequently Jürgen Habermas, resumed the Frankfurt school's old hostility toward positivism as a form of reified rationality, they continued to criticize conservative German sociology. Habermas in particular offered a politically motivated critique of the German tradition from a leftist point of view.

The interventions of the Frankfurt school in postwar Germany, although they did not question the new democratic political system, underscored the burden of the fascist past and the ideological implications of cultural projects. They questioned the neat separation of periods that was used to cover up an inconvenient past. Both the German Democratic Republic and the Federal Republic of Germany, although with different arguments, claimed a new beginning for themselves. In its first major project, the "Gruppen Experiment," the new institute began to investigate the character of public opinion in West Germany. Although the investigation was based on empirical research, it deliberately deviated from standard procedures of public opinion polls because these polls merely reproduce superficial aspects of the public's self-definition. What Pollock, Horkheimer, and Adorno wanted to examine were the invisible parts of opinions— the problematic aspects that the new democracy could not acknowledge, and therefore carefully tried to repress in the political public sphere.

In order to open up the deep structure, Pollack, Horkheimer, and Adorno developed different methods based on group discussions that favored the expression of opinions and sentiments that conventional questionnaires would not retrieve. Quantitative analysis had to be supplemented by qualitative interpretations, for which Freudian psychoanalysis provided the methodological frame. Hence it is assumed that mechanisms like repression and displacement play an important role in the reactions of the German population. The result of the study, finally published in 1955, undermined the official self-understanding of the Federal Republic by demonstrating the continuity of German history beyond 1945, as well as the weakness of the democratic system in the minds of the German population. Most of all, however, it demonstrated that the past had not been worked through, that many of those participating in the guided discussions were either unwilling or unable to acknowledge responsibility. As Adorno points out, by and large the participants failed to accept responsibility; instead they claimed German innocence. In other instances more subtle defense mechanisms blocked the process of comprehension. One of them was an accounting system in which German crimes were balanced by those of the Allies. Moreover, the numerous discussions with selected groups confirmed that anti-Semitic attitudes survived the end of the Nazi state. Confrontation with the overwhelming evidence of the mass murder did not necessarily change one's attitude toward Jews.

The effect of this extensive empirical study remained rather limited, partly due, it seems, to its late publication (by the time it was released, the question of German guilt and responsibility had been superseded by new topics such as German rearmament and the threat of the Communist bloc). In addition, Austrian psychologist Peter Hofstätter criticized the entire project: his methodological reservations articulated the resistance of the German side toward criticism coming from émigrés. When Adorno came back to the issue of German guilt in his public lecture "Was bedeutet: Aufarbeitung der Vergangenheit?" in 1959, the intellectual climate in West Germany was already beginning to change, and Adorno could hope for a more favorable reception among the younger generation. He insisted again on the lack of a collective project of acknowledgment and mourning. In 1959, however, Adorno also emphasized the possibility of a return of fascism, because the social conditions that once made the Nazi regime possible had not changed.

For Adorno it is not the economic structure itself that operates as a cause for the totalitarian system; rather, he underscores the weakness of the individual, its need for conformity and identification with the state. Lack of autonomy contains the seed for the return of the fascist state. At the same time, Adorno calls for enlightenment—that is, a process of reflection on prejudices and stereotypes, to break through the psychological blockage and thereby overcome the social roots of fascism.

Although the work of the institute initially focused on empirical research projects, Adorno and Horkheimer were ultimately more interested in resuming their theoretical work. Because Horkheimer, as director of the institute and administrator of the University of Frankfurt, was largely preoccupied with administrative duties, however, the task of developing Critical Theory beyond *Dialectic of Enlightenment* fell mostly on Adorno's shoulders. For this reason, the notion of a theoretical school is somewhat misleading, especially because the majority of the members of the old institute, among them Herbert Marcuse, Otto Kirchheimer, and Franz Neumann, did not return to Frankfurt. As a result, we have to note a shift in the project of the Frankfurt group from social to cultural theory. The neo-Marxist framework of the 1930s and early 1940s became less visible, but it was not abandoned as a moment of critical intervention. At the same time, this epistemological position had to be distinguished from the Marxist orthodoxy (Diamat) of East Germany, where it legitimized a political system to which the members of the institute, including the younger generation, remained unsympathetic.

Although Horkheimer and Adorno did not develop a new political theory after 1943, they felt committed to a Western-style democracy based on an advanced capitalist society. But they also remained highly critical of advanced capitalism and the totally administered society it produced—because, among other things, this social formation contained a proclivity to fascism. This tension was not fully explained by the older members of the institute; it came to the fore in the mid-1960s when Adorno's disciples began to formulate a radical political critique of the Federal Republic that questioned the viability of liberal democracy under late capitalism. Confronted with the student revolution, Adorno refused to accept its radicalism as the logical result of his own work, which had stressed the problematic nature of collective political action. Clearly, however, the West German student revolt had made use of the Frankfurt school's theoretical apparatus, especially of its theory of mass culture and its critique of advanced capitalism, two strands that were, of course, intimately connected in Adorno's writings.

The Frankfurt school's understanding of modern mass culture as a culture industry (that is, a cultural formation determined by postliberal administrative capitalism), first formulated in *Dialectic of Enlightenment,* remained in place. In his essay "Culture Industry Reconsidered" (1963), Adorno reiterated the basic features of his former position and suggested only relatively minor adjustments for the postwar years. Once more Adorno underscored the moment of deception and antienlightenment tendencies that would necessarily undermine the possibility of emancipation. For Adorno the culture industry remained authoritarian and therefore politically regressive and dangerous. Aesthetically, mass culture as a mode of mechanically produced culture according to preestablished designs is seen and evaluated against the background of the modern work of art. Its autonomy, defended against commodity fetishism, contrasts with the complete commodification of the products of the culture industry. In the late 1960s, the student movement adopted this position for a large-scale political critique of the Federal Republic. Focusing on the concentration of the West German press and in particular on the concept of manipulation in the process of cultural reproduction, the student protest brought into the foreground Adorno's social theory, which remained politically diffuse because Adorno placed the emphasis on the aesthetic aspect of modernism rather than the politics of the collective. It is not accidental that Adorno's oeuvre came to a close with his posthumously published *Aesthetic Theory* (1997).

The contributions of the Frankfurt school to

social theory in West Germany were initially ambivalent. As part of the political agenda of the institute, Horkheimer wanted to introduce empirical sociology as it was taught in the United States to counter the conservative tendencies of German sociology. Empirical methodology was expected to give support to the new political system that was still in need of legitimation. In the long run, however, this position did not have the wished-for results. The positivism dispute of 1961 comes to mind as a turning point because the discussion with Karl Popper forced Adorno, who was then aided by Habermas, to focus on the critical moment of reason that he found undeveloped in the various schools of positivism. Specifically, Adorno charged that modern empirical methodology shied away from the category of totality for the exploration of the social. Consequently, Adorno suggested, sociology becomes a necessarily conservative force. Adorno's insistence on social totality brought back to the surface the Hegelian-Marxian dialectic, and with it the problem of a possible intervention—which Adorno himself viewed with considerable skepticism (in contrast to Popper, who had confidence in experimental rationality).

In the continuation of the debate (as a sharp polemic), it was the young Habermas who defended the position of the Frankfurt school against the members of the Cologne School (Hans Albert). Yet we have to note that Habermas's own theoretical position was by no means identical with that of Adorno. Already at this stage and still under the institutional umbrella of the Frankfurt school, he began to develop a critique of Popper that relied on a model of communicative rationality. Thus Habermas stressed the need for a reconsideration of empirical methods within the larger context of social interaction. This reformulation would ultimately lead Habermas away from Marxian theory, which is still very much present in Adorno's social and economic theory.

Adorno's sociological essays, in particular those written in the 1960s, emphasized the macro level of social analysis as a means of critical intervention. Returning to the rhetoric of earlier Critical Theory, Adorno insisted on the continuing importance of concepts like society or late capitalism for contemporary social analysis, and criticized the preference among West German sociologists for small-scale research as a form of misplaced realism that fails to grasp the structural interdependence of social phenomena. Hence the essay "Society" (1965) almost repudiates the Frankfurt school's empirical program of the 1950s by calling into question notions of scientific experiments. A critical concept of the social, Adorno argues, must begin with the mode of production and, specifically in the case of modern society, with the concept of market exchange. Human interaction as well as power relations between human agents are mediated through commodity exchange, and therefore are not reducible to the abstract category of social roles. For Adorno, postwar society (including West Germany) was marked by a continuing process of concentration of capital, a process in which the individual is relegated to a weak and dependent position. He argued that in contemporary society, social integration is achieved through the culture industry, which makes objective social antagonisms invisible.

Although Adorno insisted on the significance of Marxian theory for social analysis, he also stressed the need for theoretical revisions in order to analyze late capitalist societies. Not only did he emphasize in "Spätkapitalismus oder Industriegesellschaft?" (1968) the reduced relevance of social antagonism and traditional Marxist class theory, he also questioned the traditional theory of surplus value. At the same time, however, Adorno foregrounded the category of domination (through economic processes) and with it aspects of oppression and repression. Most importantly, Adorno underscored the static character of late capitalist society—in other words, the predominance of the state and its administration. Obviously, Pollock's theory of state capitalism introduced in the early 1940s is used once more to describe the situation of the 1960s. In this respect, Adorno's approach remained fixated on the modernist paradigm in Fordist capitalism.

To some extent this direction in the work of the Frankfurt school was defined by the restoration in the Federal Republic. The members of the institute had to deal with the conservative climate of the 1950s as it became evident not only in the field of social theory but also in philosophical and aesthetic debates. In these discussions the influence of the Frankfurt school became noticeable in the 1960s, when Horkheimer and especially Adorno found themselves surrounded by younger disciples. Adorno's interventions attempted to break up the rather self-contained academic discourse for both epistemological and political reasons. In the case of Adorno's polemic against Heidegger's ontology in *The Jargon of Authenticity* (1964), both aspects were, of course, intimately linked. Yet Adorno was less interested in Heidegger's personal involvement with the Nazi regime between 1933 and 1945 than in the effect of Heidegger's language and its truth claims on the intellectual scene of the Federal Republic. As a form of academic philosophy, it took for granted what Adorno wanted to question: the restoration of philosophy after 1945. For Adorno, the claim for a system of total knowledge, even in its advanced dialectical form, had become absurd. Consequently, philosophy was left with a critical task: an epistemological model that holds on to emphatic truth claims without confirming dogmatic knowledge of the absolute. What remains of the philosophical project of the modern age is the moment of critique. For Adorno, neither logical positivism nor ontology were compatible with critical reflection. His defense of a critical project quite consciously invoked the metaphysical tradition (put down by Heidegger as a loss of Being) insofar as this tradition enables conceptual work in the mode of dialectical oppositions. Yet this project by no means coincided with a theory of science that legitimates positive research.

For Adorno, philosophical reflection ultimately has to come to terms with its own impotence vis-à-vis a world that is moving toward catastrophe. Hence traditional philosophical contemplation has become as inadequate as revolutionary activism, which relies on the model of the young Marx. Thus the survival of philosophy is a paradox: only by radically undermining its continued legitimacy, by questioning its own function as a means of furthering progress, can it prove its viability. In terms of the mod-

ern / postmodern divide, Adorno maintained a metaphysical position precisely because it allowed him to undercut the modernist project and its articulation in the idealist tradition (including Marx and its materialist consequences). In *Negative Dialectics* (1966), he rigorously pursued the paradoxical character of this project—namely, a form of dialectic that has given up on the moment of synthesis and identity. In his words, "Dialectics is the consistent sense of non-identity" (Adorno 1980, 5). The insistence on nonidentity implied, at least for Adorno, the negation of firm positions and the need for the internal moment of contradiction. In *Negative Dialectics,* Adorno shifted the philosophical project to the side of non-conceptionality, individuality, and particularity, that is, precisely to those aspects that traditional philosophy had neglected or marginalized. But he accomplished this shift only with and through concepts that by themselves were inadequate for the task at hand because of their imposing nature.

Adorno's focus on particularity and individuality foregrounds two aspects that philosophy has traditionally shunned: the question of style and aesthetic theory. Although Horkheimer and Marcuse continued to use the conceptual apparatus of the 1940s in their writings, Adorno, after his return to Germany, began to emphasize the instability of language. His famous essay "The Essay as Form" (Adorno 1991–92, 8–23) of 1958 already announced an anti-Cartesian project of philosophical reflection. In the essay form, the search for truth takes on an anti-systematic character that explores and relies on the contingent moments of reality. Thought processes are not expected to proceed in a linear manner. Instead of imposing conceptual constraints derived from first principles, the essay absorbs experience through its linguistic configuration.

In Adorno's late writings, the essay becomes the model for the most differentiated articulation of experience—not only with respect to the discussion of literature and art, but also vis-à-vis the philosophy of art. Although *Negative Dialectics* still maintained the structure of a philosophical argument, in *Aesthetic Theory* Adorno resolutely organized the material according to its internal logic, which foregrounds the interwoven structure of the ideas. In his last work Adorno largely abandoned the pursuit of linear arguments. With few exceptions, the younger members of the Frankfurt school did not immediately appreciate the epistemological significance of this development. As one can glean from the initial reception of *Aesthetic Theory*, the New Left in Germany remained rather distant. It was not only the seemingly apolitical stance of the late Adorno that erected a barrier but also the language itself: its radical subversion of linearity made the younger members suspicious because it refused to serve political strategies.

The effect of the Frankfurt school on the intellectual climate of the 1960s was extraordinary. It ranged from philosophy to literary criticism, and from music theory to political theory. The writings of Horkheimer, Adorno, and Herbert Marcuse (who became a presence although he lived in the United States) helped the emerging New Left to formulate its project; more specifically, they politicized the West German intelligentsia, including the students. For the radical students of the mid-1960s, the rediscovery of *Dialectic of Enlightenment* marked a new phase in their political consciousness. It enabled them to articulate a political position outside the political system of the Federal Republic. The Frankfurt school's critique of commodified culture and the totally administered society provided the tools for a political opposition that between 1965 and 1967 moved from theoretical reflection to political action. Yet precisely at this juncture the teachers withdrew their support. Adorno rejected the activism of the student movement as a regressive move, because it relied on outmoded forms of collective organization. Even Jürgen Habermas, who was sympathetic to the struggle of the students, distanced himself from their radical activism. But this position was not shared by other members of the second generation—among them Oskar Negt, Claus Offe, and Wolfgang Lefèvre—who argued for a revolutionary strategy.

By 1969 it had become fairly clear that the history of the Frankfurt school had come to a close. With Adorno's unexpected death, the institute had lost its leader, a position that Haber-

mas, who had succeeded Horkheimer in 1965 at the University of Frankfurt, did not claim for himself. In fact, when Habermas left Frankfurt for Starnberg in 1970, the continuity of the school seemed to be broken. Habermas's project, which in its early stages seemed rather close to that of the older generation, moved in new and different directions. For him Adorno's conception of negative dialectics described an aporia that had to be overcome through a different grounding of rationality, namely, a theory of communicative action. Although other members of the second generation remained closer to the work of Horkheimer and Adorno, a sense of rupture was generally felt. In the field of aesthetic theory, Peter Bürger's *Theory of the Avant-Garde* (1974) captured that moment by radically historicizing Adorno's concept of autonomous art. In *Public Sphere and Experience* (1972), Alexander Kluge and Oskar Negt followed a different strategy. In their critique of Habermas they returned to Adorno's and Horkheimer's critique of instrumental rationality, but at the same time their own analysis of advanced electronic media broke away from traditional descriptions of the culture industry.

The relocation of the Frankfurt school to Frankfurt in 1949 became a major event in the intellectual history of the Federal Republic. Although the initial effect of the institute remained limited, during the 1960s the Frankfurt school became a dominant force on the Left, which helped reshape the Federal Republic.

Bibliography

Wolfgang Abendroth et al., *Die Linke antwortet Jürgen Habermas* (Frankfurt a. M.: Europäische Verlagsanstalt, 1968); Theodor W. Adorno, *Aesthetic Theory* [1970], ed. and trans. Robert Hullot-Kentor (Minneapolis: University of Minnesota Press, 1997); Adorno, *The Jargon of Authenticity* (Evanston, Ill.: Northwestern University Press, 1973a); Adorno, *Negative Dialectics* (New York: Continuum, 1973b); Adorno, *Notes to Literature*, 2 vols. (New York: Columbia University Press, 1991–92); Axel Honneth and Albrecht Wellmer, *Die Frankfurter Schule und die Folgen* (Berlin: W. de Gruyter, 1986); Max Horkheimer and Theodor W. Adorno, *Dialectic of Enlightenment* (New York: Herder and Herder,

1972); Martin Jay, *Permanent Exiles: Essays on the Intellectual Migration from Germany to America* (New York: Columbia University Press, 1985); Friedrich Pollock, ed., *Gruppenexperiment: Ein Studienbericht* (Frankfurt a. M.: Europäische Verlagsanstalt, 1955); Frank Stern, *The Whitewashing of the Yellow Badge: Antisemitism and Philosemitism in Postwar Germany* (Oxford: Pergamon, 1992); and Rolf Wiggershaus, *Die Frankfurter Schule: Geschichte, Theoretische Entwicklung, Politische Bedeutung* (Munich: Carl Hanser, 1986).

PETER UWE HOHENDAHL

1951 In his essay "Kulturkritik und Gesellschaft," Theodor W. Adorno states that it is barbaric to write poetry after Auschwitz

A tenaciously recurring leitmotif accompanying, at least implicitly, much West German discourse and criticism on lyric poetry after about 1960 has been the veritable possibility or impossibility of writing poetry after Auschwitz. Why lyric poetry should be singled out rather than, say, prose fiction or drama, has partially to do with the aporetic problem of representing the Shoah at all, but perhaps more with traditional German understanding of this particular genre. The question is fundamental, not merely academic; whether it is in fact relevant requires explication.

In 1949, the same year he returned to West Germany to teach temporarily at the University of Frankfurt after having lived in exile in the United States since 1938, Adorno wrote his essay "Kulturkritik und Gesellschaft" (Cultural criticism and society). The essay first appeared in print in 1951 and then again, more visibly, in 1955 in *Prismen* (Prisms). Drawing on a Central European notion of *Kultur* with its various repertoires of articulation, while at the same time pessimistically reaffirming the ossification of bourgeois understanding of what culture is and can mean, Adorno attempted to interpret the transformed meaning of the term and phenomenon in society after fascism and after the Shoah. This task became all the more complicated with the realization that culture had had no appreciably moderating effect on the conception and execution of the Final Solution. To the contrary, Adorno appears to suspect a moment of complicity in cultural criticism itself: "Such critical consciousness remains servile toward culture in that it distracts from the horrors, but it also determines culture as a complement of the horrors" (22). In its closing argument, this essay contained a provocative pronouncement that would occupy West German—and evidently only West German—literary critics throughout and beyond the 1960s, especially since a long overdue counterposition to conservative criticism had found articulation, and this articulation had reached a responsive critical awareness among increasingly influential younger critics. The statement in question reads: "By being neutralized and processed, traditional culture in its entirety today becomes insignificant. . . . Even the most extreme consciousness of the catastrophe threatens to degenerate into drivel. Cultural criticism exists in confrontation with the final level of the dialectic of culture and barbarism: to write a poem after Auschwitz is barbaric, and that also gnaws at the knowledge which states why it has become impossible to write poems today" (30).

In virtually every reference made to Adorno's postulate, critics confined themselves to what they understood to be its pithy essence: "to write a poem after Auschwitz is barbaric." The aphoristic reduction would seem to preclude interpretation, and thus critics irresponsibly or at least misleadingly abbreviated Adorno's thought to assert the impossibility of poetry at all after Auschwitz. This reduction, however, always occurred in reviews and discussions of poetry—often remarkable poetry, often sympathetic reviews—that had found their way to publication. The patent contradiction critics evoked here only to leave unresolved seemed strangely unworthy of further attention, as did a closer examination of what Adorno might have intended by such an absolute claim. Even recently Günter Grass has skeptically asked whether speaking about Adorno's sentence might have only satisfied a ritual of dismay, and whether the self-interrogations of writers in the 1950s and early 1960s only served as rhetorical exercises (Grass 1990, 10).

Certainly part of the responsibility for the limited understanding and the later superficial readings and resultant misunderstanding lies in Adorno's strained articulation of the problem of comprehending and representing or treating the Shoah in poetry. He does not indicate what he holds "poetry" to be, as if, even in cultural circles, a consensus existed. One may not assume that Adorno found the very genre of lyric poetry had become culturally insignificant or superfluous, given his major essays and the passages within other works written after 1949 and devoted to the poetry of George, Hofmannsthal, Borchardt, Eichendorff, Mörike, Heine, and others. Indeed, most of these names provide a key to aspects of poetry that Adorno held dear: with the exception of Heine, these poets belonged to a conservative poetic tradition in nineteenth- and twentieth-century Germany that helped define the poetic canon and formative mainstream bourgeois *Bildung* and mentality. Of great significance is the fact that the same year his essay "Kulturkritik und Gesellschaft" appeared—and not in 1957, as is commonly assumed—Adorno also published for the first time his later radio essay "Rede über Lyrik und Gesellschaft" (Talk on poetry and society). In constituting a retrospective analysis of earlier poetry and of the function of society in poetic utterance, this essay does not contradict Adorno's radical pronouncement, but it does open other and more differentiated vistas for a reading of poetry that went far beyond the non-historicizing intrinsic readings that were the norm at this time. In the essay, Adorno demon-

strates how individual poetic expression becomes artistic expression only when it participates in more general or more universally shared experience, and that implies society, social influence, and societal developments; the poetic subject represents, according to Adorno, a more general, collective subject (Adorno 1958, 74–75, 91).

In his dictum on poetry after Auschwitz, Adorno had himself inadvertently become distracted by the very phenomenon he feared—namely, the not unfounded expectation of a conservative continuation of pre-1933 poetic forms and themes that dominated poetic writing throughout the fascist years, both in Germany itself and even among prominent exile writers. By affirming traditional poetics, such writing would be unable to overcome impotence in reacting to the devastations of fascism. Poetry had been primarily thought of as originating in feeling, and, since Goethe's poetry of experience and Hegel's lectures on aesthetics, as the most subjective of literary genres. Adorno without doubt assumed such a non-response to the catastrophe to be severely inadequate, historically displaced and inappropriate, and potentially dangerous, not to mention a brutal disregard for the suffering and death of fascism's victims. He can only have based his verdict that writing poetry after Auschwitz is barbaric on his own previous understanding of what poetry was, rather than what its function and potential might be, both aesthetically and sociologically. Some consistency in his position remained, however. His defense of Stefan George in the "Rede über Lyrik und Gesellschaft" and the later essay "George" (1967), as well as his introduction to and selection of poems by Rudolf Borchardt (1968), document Adorno's effort to redeem these conservative poets critically—at a time that, remarkably, coincided with the beginnings of the student movement in the Federal Republic.

Beginning in 1945–46 and continuing into the early 1950s, a veritable deluge of new poetry flooded the journals and, in the form of individual volumes and anthologies, the bookstores. The bulk of this poetry, largely forgotten today, exhibited traditional themes from personal experience and nature in rhymed strophic forms, indicated no awareness of the avant-garde, and showed little interest in exploring the limitations of language even (or especially) where it occasionally thematized postwar realities. It corresponded to a deeply felt need among both poets and readers in the ruins after the war to seek out metaphysical havens of interiority and timelessness, rather than constructive introspection and a sense of the historicity of their own time. The designation "pure poetry" (*reine Dichtung* or *reine Lyrik*) became, not surprisingly, the supreme recognition of poetic accomplishment.

In intuiting this development and formulating his premise, Adorno failed to anticipate a counterdevelopment, to postulate or envision a poetic writing possible after Auschwitz. At present one can only speculate about the actual texts Adorno might have read during the fascist years and immediately thereafter by poets within and outside of Germany and how these texts might have affected his thinking. The few names he briefly mentions in his *Minima Moralia* (written 1944–47)—Hölderlin, Goethe, Verlaine, Liliencron, Trakl, Däubler, Stramm, George, and Rilke—only confirm his adherence to the canon and betray a characteristic reception of poets he and his educated contemporaries would have read in younger years. Brecht, the outstanding non-Jewish representative of poetic response to fascism, albeit not to the Shoah, did not become a paradigm of poetic voice for Adorno, even in view of such Brecht poems as "Schlechte Zeit für Lyrik" (Bad times for poetry, 1939), which, by lamenting the inopportuneness of writing poetry as usual, implicitly calls for a (political) poetry suited to defy fascism. Nonetheless, Adorno must have become aware of important Jewish writing by the early 1950s, primarily that by Nelly Sachs, whose collection *In den Wohnungen des Todes* (In the dwellings of death) appeared in Berlin (East) in 1947, and by Paul Celan, whose work he had read at least by the late 1950s, whom he planned (but failed) to meet in 1959 in Engadin, and to whom he dedicated the second publication of his essay "Valérys Abweichungen" (Valéry's divergences; 1961).

Hans Magnus Enzensberger appears to have become the first to challenge Adorno's pronouncement in eulogizing Nelly Sachs, who had lived in exile in Sweden since 1940 and whose work before 1961 had moved from publisher to publisher and received only irregular, if indeed favorable, attention by critics. In 1959 Enzensberger published in *Merkur* his essay on Sachs's poetry, "Die Steine der Freiheit" (The stones of freedom), which appeared again in an homage to Nelly Sachs in 1961. Here he counters Adorno: "Adorno has written a sentence which belongs to the most severe judgments that can be made about the time in which we live: after Auschwitz it is no longer possible to write a poem. If we want to continue living, we have to disprove this proposition. Only few [writers] are able to do so. Nelly Sachs belongs to these few. A moment of redemption is inherent in her language. In speaking, she gives back to us, sentence by sentence, what we have been in danger of losing: language" (Enzensberger 1961, 47).

Sachs, who saw herself as a quasi-depersonalized voice or mediator speaking for the remembered and mourned dead, attempted to place her work outside the confines of subjective expression. As early as 1948 Sachs had written to a friend that she had tried "to capture the apocalyptic time" in her most recent poems, while at the same letting "the eternal mysteries shine through." "Just as times past," she continued, "our time, as horrible as it is, does have to find its expression in art; it must be attempted with all new means, for the old means are no longer sufficient" (Sachs 1985, 98).

In his essay "Engagement" (Commitment; 1962), Adorno concurred with Enzensberger's rebuttal in principle by saying that a refutation of the verdict through poetry was necessary, lest the very existence of poetry commit itself to cynicism: "I am not inclined to mitigate the sentence that says it is barbaric still to write poetry after Auschwitz; in this statement the impulse is expressed that inspires *littérature engagée*. . . . But Enzensberger's rejoinder remains true that poetry has to stand up to precisely this verdict and hence has to be such that it does not surrender to cynicism through its very existence after Auschwitz. Poetry's own situation is paradoxical, not the manner in which one chooses to view poetry. The excesses of real suffering do not permit forgetting" (Adorno 1965, 125–26).

In his "Meditationen zur Metaphysik" (Meditations on metaphysics), first published in *Negative Dialektik* (Negative dialectics; 1966), Adorno contextualizes his pronouncement anew. The opening section, entitled "After Auschwitz," contains his final statement on poetry after Auschwitz: "Perennial suffering has just as much a right to receive expression as the tortured victim has to scream; hence it may have been wrong to say that poetry could not be written after Auschwitz. Not wrong, however, is the less cultural question as to whether living is at all possible after Auschwitz, as to whether whoever by chance escaped death and legitimately [*rechtens*] should have been killed has a right to live at all" (Adorno 1980, 355).

Adorno retracts his original statement, but even more he revises its radical gesture and places it in the more encompassing context of what culture and education, survival and life itself, could possibly mean after Auschwitz. At this point it is important to recall those Jewish poets such as Gertrud Kolmar and Selma Meerbaum-Eisinger who wrote anticipating the Shoah (and who perished in its wrath) and the poetry written in the ghettos and camps by many nameless and some remembered authors. Ruth Klüger (1992, 122–27) has written an eloquent personal testimony about the meaning of poetry for her as a young girl in the camps, poetry she recited to herself to pass the time and assuage fear, as well as poetry she herself wrote. Three pioneering lyric anthologies have collected verse by camp inmates and others: *Jüdisches Schicksal in deutschen Gedichten: Ein abschließende Anthologie* (Jewish fate in German poems: A final anthology, 1959), *An den Wind geschrieben: Lyrik der Freiheit. Gedichte der Jahre, 1933–1945* (Written in the wind: Poetry of freedom. Poems, 1933–1945; 1960), and *Welch Wort in die Kälte gerufen: Die Judenverfolgung des Dritten Reiches im deutschen Gedicht* (What a word called into the cold: The persecution of the Jews by the Third Reich in German poetry;

1968). Of these collections, the first evidently received little or no attention, and the last, an East German publication, disappeared from the bookstores and even certain libraries. Only the second, after the editor's initial difficulty in locating a willing publisher, found readers and is again in print today. Yet other poets such as Else Lasker-Schüler and Nelly Sachs, in exile, turned to poetic expression in German as the only vehicle remaining to them to explore the contemporary horrors they had suffered. In a poem written in 1944 in a work camp, "Nähe der Gräber" (Nearness of the graves), Paul Celan apostrophizes his murdered mother, seeking dispensation to continue writing in his mother-tongue: "Und duldest du, Mutter, wie einst, ach, daheim, / den leisen, den deutschen, den schmerzlichen Reim?" ("And can you bear, Mother, as you did back home, / the quiet, the German, the painful rhyme?") (Celan 1983, v., 20). The young Celan was aware of the same dilemma as Adorno; he questioned not the possibility of poetry, however, but the possibly of using the German language. This perhaps was the blind spot in Adorno's original argument, because he can hardly have proposed that poetry in any language was impossible.

Lyric poetry existed not in a time-eternity dichotomy, but on borrowed time; it had to discontinue now questionable traditions and become the direct product of historical experience (and perforce of redefined poetics). Adorno, who at the time of his death had planned an essay on Celan, recognized that this poet was one of the few capable of addressing the Shoah and indicated as much in his *Aesthetic Theory:* "This poetry is permeated by the shame of art in view of the suffering that evades both experience and sublimation. Celan's poems want to express extreme horror by maintaining silence [*Verschweigen*]" (Adorno 1973, 477). The silence to which Adorno perhaps misleadingly refers is not congruent with that of those who would silence the horror, but rather with the frequently hermetic language of poetry that cautiously moves toward the ineffable. Of German-language lyric poetry, Celan observed in 1958: "With dismal gloom in its memory and dubiousness surrounding it, it can, despite the presence of the tradition in which it stands, no longer speak the language which some sympathetic ears still appear to expect from it. Its language is more austere, more factual; it distrusts the "Beautiful"; it attempts to be true. . . . This language does not transfigure, does not "poeticize"; it names and constructs meaning; it attempts to measure the space of the given and the possible. To be sure, language itself, language per se is never at work here, but always only a voice speaking under the angle of its existential inclination, interested in contour and orientation. Reality does not exist as such; reality needs to be sought and attained" (Celan 1983, 3:167–68).

Celan did not claim to speak for all of his contemporaries, although he felt he could speak for many. Speaking from the periphery as a Romanian-born, German-speaking Jew living in Paris, whose works were published (with a few minor exceptions) exclusively in the Federal Republic and whose literary reception in the 1950s and 1960s was strongest in that country, he experienced reactions to his work ranging from perplexity to praise and from scandalous charges of plagiarism to misreadings destined to neutralize the poetry's efficacy. But part of this reception would seem to fulfill the foreboding Adorno had had in 1949. In an essay of 1960 in a pedagogical journal, a German teacher wrote about interpreting Celan's "Todesfuge" (Death fugue; 1944–45) in the school classroom: "One may not expect the pupils to have precise knowledge of the fate of the Jews under the Hitler regime. The pupil first has to learn as historical material what the teacher consciously experienced as a contemporary. Hence a discussion of 'Death Fugue' could easily lapse into an explanation of the persecution of the Jews, whereby the poem would then only be a pretext, not the constant focus of the discussion" (Butzlaff 1960, 42).

In this essay, a remarkable combination of didactic myopia, historical naïveté, and impudence sees the poem as a purely literary, historically irrelevant utterance that warns the reader not to politicize the text; in a tastelessly didactic gesture the author proceeds to compare the "fugal" technique in "Todesfuge" with that of a poem by Ernst Bertram, a poet and Germanist who lost his chair at the University of Cologne in 1945 because of his fascist activity. The mentality betrayed in this essay is not appreciably distant from the discussion of the mid-1960s concerning the aestheticization of the Shoah by precisely such poems as "Todesfuge." Using the negatively charged category of aestheticizing the catastrophe thus becomes a further strategy for silencing a victim's expression of having been terrorized.

The author of this didactic essay saw in Celan's "Death Fugue" a thematization of Auschwitz that would stand in the way of literary interpretation. But Auschwitz, a reality and incessant presence in his life (Grass 1990, 30), nowhere became a theme in Celan's writing, as Peter Szondi unequivocally pointed out. Celan's lyrical writing, Szondi wrote in 1964 in refuting a critique by Hans Egon Holthusen, disproves Adorno's dictum by recalling Auschwitz and the Shoah in virtually every text he wrote without merely "thematizing" it (Szondi 1993, 165–67). In a hermeneutically intense reading of Celan's "Engführung" (Stretto; 1958), Szondi sees this poem as the precise refutation of Adorno's earlier position: "No poem is possible after Auschwitz, unless it be conceived by reason of Auschwitz" (Szondi 1972, 102–3).

Without advocating an aesthetics of suffering, we can view poems after and about a metonymically understood Auschwitz as attempts to work through unspeakable personal and collective trauma, as long as their means break new ground and do not merely utilize worn forms, images, and gestures. Thus understood, poetry after Auschwitz is not only not barbaric by its very existence, but in certain of its manifestations vitally necessary. It may be significant that the correspondence between Celan and Sachs contains no mention of Adorno or of the controversy, presumably because these poets saw no reason to theorize about the ethical feasibility of texts they wrote as a necessity for survival. Even in the verse of a number of postwar poets who are not Jewish and who do not treat Auschwitz explicitly (for example, Ingeborg Bachmann, Enzensberger, and Günter Eich), one senses not only an intangible awareness of traditions and poetry's respon-

696 "Kulturkritik und Gesellschaft"

sibility toward history, but also a distrust of blithe indifference.

Bibliography

Theodor W. Adorno, *Ästhetische Theorie,* ed. Gretel Adorno and Rolf Tiedemann (Frankfurt a. M.: Suhrkamp, 1973); Adorno, "Engagement," *Noten zur Literatur III* (Frankfurt a. M.: Suhrkamp, 1965), 109–35; Adorno, "Kulturkritik und Gesellschaft," *Kulturkritik und Gesellschaft I: Prismen. Ohne Leitbild* (Frankfurt a. M.: Suhrkamp, 1977), 11–30; Adorno, "Meditationen zur Metaphysik," *Negative Dialektik* (Frankfurt a. M.: Suhrkamp, 1980), 354–61; Adorno, "On the Question: 'What Is German?'" *New German Critique* 36 (fall 1985): 121–31; Adorno, "Rede über Lyrik und Gesellschaft," *Noten zur Literatur I* (Frankfurt a. M.: Suhrkamp, 1958), 73–104; Wolfgang Butzlaff, "Paul Celan: 'Todesfuge,'" *Der Deutschunterricht* 12 (1960): 42–51; Paul Celan, *Gesammelte Werke in fünf Bänden,* ed. Beda Allemann and Stefan Reichert with Rolf Bücher, 5 vols. (Frankfurt a. M.: Suhrkamp, 1983); Hans Magnus Enzensberger, "Die Steine der Freiheit," *Nelly Sachs zu Ehren* (Frankfurt a. M.: Suhrkamp, 1961), 45–51; Günter Grass, *Schreiben nach Auschwitz: Frankfurter Poetik-Vorlesung* (Frankfurt a. M.: Luchterhand, 1990); Ruth Klüger, *Weiter leben: Eine Jugend* (Göttingen: Wallstein, 1992); Nelly Sachs, *Briefe der Nelly Sachs,* ed. Ruth Dinesen and Helmut Müssener (Frankfurt a. M.: Suhrkamp, 1985); Peter Szondi, *Briefe,* ed. Christoph König and Thomas Sparr (Frankfurt a. M.: Suhrkamp, 1993); and Szondi, "Durch die Enge geführt: Versuch über die Verständlichkeit des modernen Gedichts," *Celan-Studien,* ed. Jean Bollack with Henriette Beese et al (Frankfurt a. M.: Suhrkamp, 1972), 47–111.

LEONARD OLSCHNER

1952 Manès Sperber pursues the Jewish Question in *Wolyna*

Until the outbreak of World War II, Manès Sperber had shown little interest in the Jewish Question, which had gradually been turned into a program of extermination by the Nazis, otherwise known as the Final Solution. Yet as he became more aware of the fate of European Jews, Sperber was deeply shaken and concerned. By 1945 he began raising his own Jewish questions and focusing his attention on issues pertaining to Jewish identity, the Holocaust (or *Churban* as he preferred to call it), anti-Semitism, Zionism, and messianism. Though he had not begun his first novel, *Der verbrannte Dornbusch* (The burned bramble, part of his famous trilogy *Wie eine Träne im Ozean* [Like a tear in the ocean]), with these questions in mind, they rose to the fore by the time he had started conceiving the third novel in the series. In fact, these issues are all addressed in the momentous episode of *Wolyna*, which was first published as a separate book in 1952 under the title *Qu'une larme dans l'océan* in France. It was as if he had come full circle—from a deep belief in the Jewish religion, to devout Communism, and back to a fervent dedication to his Jewishness. Almost full circle but not quite, for Sperber combined elements of Jewish messianic thinking and Marxist philosophy in the post-war years to conceive his own peculiar, radical notion of Jewishness that formed the basis of his heretical socialism.

To understand why Sperber turned to Jewish questions after 1945 and how he arrived at his unique Jewishness and heretical socialism, it is important to review briefly the trajectory of his life up to his writing of the "Wolyna" episode.

Born 1905 in Zablotow, a tiny shtetel in Eastern Galicia, Sperber was brought up in a religious family and regarded his "Jewishness" as second nature. Already at the age of four, he began studying the Torah and the Old Testament. Though the shtetel life gave him a strong sense of Jewish identity as a child, he also wondered why God allowed the people of his village, Jews and Poles alike, to live in such decrepit conditions and suffer so much poverty. With the outbreak of World War I, Sperber's family moved to Vienna to avoid the Russian attacks on Zablotow, a town situated on the border between Poland and Russia. But the young Sperber still witnessed the havoc and pain caused by the war, and his doubts about the existence and omnipotence of God increased.

In Vienna, his family, which had been fairly prosperous in Zablotow, experienced a decline in social status. In addition, Sperber began encountering virulent anti-Semitism and class discrimination. During the war years he joined a Zionist Youth movement, but by 1920 he broke with Zionism and the Jewish religion because he believed that neither Judaism nor Jewish organizations were capable of dealing with the urgent problems of poverty and injustice he had been experiencing. Although Sperber himself was still in his teens, he was keenly sensitive to the deplorable living conditions among

Jews and gentiles alike and was critical of the social inequities in Austrian society. He felt compelled to get to the root of these problems, not only by theoretically grasping them, but also by actively pursuing political solutions.

In 1921, at age sixteen, Sperber gave a talk on "The Psychology of the Revolutionary" in a seminar attended by Alfred Adler, the founder of individual psychology. So impressed was Adler with his views that he asked the young Sperber to work with him. In turn, Sperber soon realized that Adler's revision of Freud might enable him to be effective in working with individuals and groups to improve social conditions in Vienna. Sperber's early religious zeal and belief in the coming of the Messiah, along with his personal desire to change the world, were channeled into Adler's notions of individual psychology. Adler had rejected Freud's emphasis on sexuality as the area in which disorders and neuroses originate. Instead he argued that physical deficiencies and the environment are what cause psychological disturbances, and that it is only by changing the material conditions of life that one can overcome individual psychological problems. Because Sperber, too, was particularly interested in the relationship between the individual and his or her social surroundings, he sought to develop programs with Adler that would lead to the mutual benefit of the individual and community.

For six years Sperber worked in youth homes and welfare organizations as Adler's chief disciple and wrote articles about socioeconomic causes of psychic disorders. Soon, however, he became too political for Adler, who had begun changing his own views about the significance of environmental factors in psychological development. On the other hand, Sperber had become increasingly convinced that society had to be radically changed if psychological treatment was to have an effect. His disagreements with Adler led Sperber to leave Vienna and move to Berlin in 1927, the same year that he joined the Communist Party.

In Berlin, Sperber established his own practice as a psychotherapist and was considered, along with Wilhelm Reich, a radical innovator who made important contributions to social psychology. Aside from his own practice, Sperber lec-

tured and wrote articles on the social causes of psychological disturbances and sought to influence the programs of the Communist Party. In 1933, however, he was arrested and interrogated by the Gestapo, and after a brief period of detention, he was fortunate to gain his release and make his way first to Vienna and later to Yugoslavia. By 1934, Sperber was sent to Paris by the Communist Party and became one of the primary advisers and lecturers at the Institute for the Study of Fascism. He also continued to work as a psychologist and established contact with most of the leaders of the Comintern outside the Soviet Union. He grew increasingly skeptical about the Communist Party's policies, however, which were essentially designed to serve the interests of totalitarianism within the Soviet Union. As he traveled throughout Europe to help organize Communist Party youth movements and to carry secret documents, he witnessed the party's brutal methods of eliminating or removing members who were critical of the "correct line." When the Moscow show trials began in 1937, Sperber finally broke with the party and became an "independent revolutionary."

During his stay in Paris (1934–39) Sperber joined other prominent émigré writers such as Arthur Koestler, Ludwig Marcuse, and Willi Münzenberg to contribute to the antifascist cause by writing political articles for a journal entitled *Die Zukunft.* His friendship with André Malraux provided him contact with French leftists and enabled him to obtain an editorial position with a French publishing house. In addition to his writing, Sperber continued to support the Popular Front and gave talks that dealt with analyses of fascism. In 1938 he published *Zur Analyse der Tyrannis* (The analysis of tyranny) and produced reviews of books by Anna Seghers and Bertolt Brecht. But it was not until he had served as a French soldier in the disastrous 1939 campaign against the Germans and had escaped to the south of France, where he started writing *Der verbrannte Dornbusch,* that he began to think somewhat about the Jewish Question and his own relationship to Judaism and revolutionary action. Indeed, it is not by chance that the two major figures of *Wie eine Träne im Ozean,* the trilogy in the making—Denis Faber, the dedicated communist revolutionary, and Edi Rubin, the Viennese biologist and pacifist—are Jewish, and that the positions they assume throughout the course of the trilogy represent the Sperber's own shifting perspectives about his role as a Jew committed to socialist change in Europe.

What is most significant at this point in Sperber's life and writing is that, for the first time, he begins to reconsider and analyze his "Jewishness" and the situation of Jews in Europe. Perhaps the turning point for him, as Sperber recorded in his essay "Une règle fondamentale de la diaspora" (1965), was a conversation that he had with a man who had escaped a concentration camp in Poland. This discussion took place in Switzerland in 1943, one year after Sperber himself had fled the south of France to take refuge in Geneva. Here the Polish refugee revealed to Sperber all the atrocities that he had witnessed in Treblinka and told him all he knew about the Nazi program. Not only did this conversation bring about Sperber's resolution never to resettle in Germany or Austria after World War II, but it also drew his attention to the destruction of European Jewry. At the same time he became upset that the Jews were not revolting and resisting the Nazi persecution.

In 1943, it must be remembered, Sperber could not know much about Jewish resistance groups and the various uprisings that had occurred in ghettos and camps. Nor did he learn much about actions by Jews until the late 1950s. Therefore, as a Jewish revolutionary, he was ashamed and puzzled by the apparently submissive attitude of European Jews, and this concern was clearly the driving force behind his writing the most poignant episode, *Wolyna*, in *Wie eine Träne im Ozean*. Indeed, this part of his trilogy was so significant and so moving that his friend André Malraux insisted that he publish it separately as a novella in 1952 with the title *Qu'une larme dans l'océan* before the third volume, *Die verlorene Bucht* (The lost bay), appeared in its entirety.

In his preface to the novella, Malraux made some remarks that pertain to the trilogy and perhaps to Sperber's future writings as a whole: "Manès Sperber is not a Jew because of his religious faith but through his heritage just in the same way that I am Catholic. The heritage links this agnostic writer with its greatness and darkness passed on through the incarnation of a great way of thinking. Therefore, this story (*Wolyna*) is Jewish just as *Port Montherlant* is Christian, but not like the *Annunciation of Mary* is Catholic. This story strives for universality. It is not concerned with rational syncretism but with the essential expression of religious experience that leads agnostics today to relativize the gods" (Sperber 1984, 10).

In order to understand why Malraux called *Wolyna* a Jewish story and why much of Sperber's writings after 1952 become Jewish, it is necessary to recall the key incidents and to consider carefully what questions Sperber, as secular Jewish writer, hoped to raise. As we know, *Wolyna* is entirely fictitious. That is, while writing about the events in this small Polish town in his novel, Sperber did not have a historical incident in mind, nor was he aware of Jewish uprisings. In short, Sperber artistically constructs this situation to explore what Jewishness is and what might be salvaged from the Jewish faith in light of fascism and the threat that totalitarianism posed everywhere to humanity.

Wolyna takes place during the summer of 1942. By this time Edi Rubin has lost his wife and son in the concentration camps and is traveling in Poland disguised as a German officer to warn Jews about their systematic annihilation and to relate all that he has witnessed in the camps. He journeys to the region of Wolyna because he had heard from his friend Faber that the Count Roman Skarbek works for the resistance, and Rubin hopes that Skarbek will help him in some way. At first, however, Rubin does not trust the count, and he goes directly to the *Zaddik* (head rabbi) in the shtetel of Wolyna, which is renowned for its carpet makers and musicians, to convince him that the Jewish inhabitants will be slaughtered if they do not join the resistance or flee the Nazis. The Zaddik, however, believes that the Jews must be patient and that God will somehow save them, for God has supposedly chosen them for their special role. Rubin is disgusted with the Zaddik, who enjoys power and privileges in Wolyna that make him oblivious to the sufferings of his people. On the other hand, the rabbi's son, Bynie, a sixteen-year-old wonder rabbi who reads Hegel's *Phenomenology of the Spirit* in secret, realizes that Rubin is right, and he leads twenty-eight other young Jews to join Rubin in the woods. Soon afterward they find refuge in Skarbek's castle with a large group of Polish resistance fighters.

In the meantime the Nazis invade Wolyna, humiliate and kill the Zaddik, and begin transporting the Jews to concentration camps. Bynie is now the official head of the Wolyna Jews, and he decides that they should fight with the Poles to obtain weapons from the Germans and Ukrainian militia. After they unite in a successful raid and capture weapons, they hide once again in Skarbek's castle. But when Skarbek goes off to have a rendezvous with a young woman, the Poles, who are anti-Semitic and jealous of the weapons that the Jews have captured, try to take the weapons. Rubin tries to organize the Jews to fight against the Poles, but the conflict takes place on the Sabbath, and Bynie orders the Jews not to fight on the Sabbath. Consequently, the Jews are slaughtered by their former allies with the exception of Bynie, Rubin, and Mendel Rojzen. When Skarbek returns, he is enraged and takes the wounded Jews to a cloister run by his sister. While Rubin and Mendel recover, Bynie, who is bedridden, receives Polish peasants and heals them in seemingly miraculous ways. Eventually, however, he dies, and Rubin makes his way to Warsaw with Skarbek. There they experience the uprising in the ghetto but cannot help the Jewish fighters. Rubin continues his wandering and eventually arrives in Palestine; Skarbek rejoins the Polish resistance.

Throughout the Wolyna episode, Rubin, who has lost his faith in God and Judaism, questions what it means to be Jewish. He is baffled and frustrated by the Wolyna Jews, angry about their anachronistic ways, overcome by hate for the Nazis and anti-Semites, and somehow healed by the "Jewish" wisdom and compassion of Bynie, who speaks the key words of the trilogy: "Since death is a void, it can be disregarded. And that is why killing is a meaningless act. I saw that so clearly during the battle in the forest and again in

the gallery. You can prove this to yourself, Dr. Rubin. Try, just once, to describe a battle and you will find that all those actions taken together are smaller and more shapeless than a tear in the ocean" (Sperber 1961, 89).

Rubin does not regain a belief in Judaism through his contact with the mysterious Bynie, nor does he stop fighting. He does, however, overcome the hate that had poisoned his soul. Somehow the Jewish parables that Bynie conveys to him provide him with a sense of hope that he had lost before the encounter with the young rabbi in Wolyna. In face of the senselessness of war, Rubin struggles to grasp his own identity, which had been shattered during the past decade.

Though it would be too simplistic to identify Rubin with Sperber himself, there is no doubt that Rubin and Faber constitute and carry on a probing dialectic throughout the trilogy—a dialectic that posed not one Jewish Question for Sperber but many Jewish questions that had a great importance for him after he had rejected the Communist Party. In fact, as we have seen, there was a series of rejections in Sperber's own life—of Jewish religion, of Adlerian psychology, and of Communism—that by 1952 led him to write his trilogy and to raise the Jewish Question in the particular manner that he did. Yet at the same time, it is clear that he also continued to use aspects of all three in his thinking and acting vis-à-vis Nazi fascism and Stalinist totalitarianism. This continuation was in keeping with Sperber's dialectical principle of never abandoning essential features of philosophical tenets that had served him well in his efforts to create a more just society. So by 1952, as he finished *Wie Eine Träne im Ozean,* he transformed the customary Jewish Question—What are we to do with the Jews? How can we improve the Jews so that they assimilate?—into his own personal questions that were intended to be voiced in public and to be provocative: How is a Diaspora Jew, who is an atheist and socialist, to contribute to the reformation of European society and to the formation of Israel in light of the Holocaust? How can a Diaspora Jew who no longer believes in the Jewish religion support the further development of the Jewish faith?

As Sperber pointed out in his essay on hate, "De la haine" (1956), and in other writings, he believed that hatred and bitterness would not benefit Jews, certainly not the kind of Jew that he was. Thus almost all his efforts after 1952 were intended to explore different positions that he could assume as a Jew who had lost his faith and did not perceive Israel as his home, for he carried a sense of Jewish messianic belief within him as his home. But, as a former revolutionary and an atheist, sitting "zwischen den Srühlen" (sitting on the fence), so to speak, how was he to align himself and intervene in political debates?

Clearly, after he had completed the trilogy in 1952, Sperber was at a crossroads in his life. As he stated in an interview, "Die Treue des Häretikers" (1976) in *Ex Libris,* he felt depressed and could not write a fourth part of *Wie eine Träne im Ozean* that he had planned. Instead he turned to writing essays and his autobiography. Although one cannot talk about a systematic development in his writings after 1952, it is possible to argue that Sperber sought to establish what his Jewishness meant to his heretical position as an independent socialist in the post-Holocaust age and to open up the traditional Jewish Question and provide new perspectives on it.

Sperber was very familiar with Jean-Paul Sartre's book *La Question juive* (1946) and with the writings of other intellectuals such as Raymond Aaron and Jean Améry, who wrote about the Holocaust and Jewish identity, and he sought to distinguish his views clearly from theirs. By 1967 he had fully developed most of his key notions and had succinctly voiced them in two essays: "Weil Wir Gott niemals aufgaben" and "Le Judaïsme, fardeau et promesse." For instance, in opposition to Sartre, he stated:

Now, what Sartre says and what so many Jews think is that we are Jews because the enemy forces us to be a Jew or to remain a Jew. I consider this assertion to be utterly intolerable nonsense and an insult at the same time. We entered into the most unique spiritual and haunting adventure of the world that took place at the very latest when Abraham distanced himself from human sacrifice. For the first time in history a God stopped being bloodthirsty and a killer of humans. A separation began here that the world has still not learned to bear even up to today. We took a position against the heathen world. It was clear and simple everywhere. When a people or a tribe was defeated, its god was also defeated, and one gave up the god or combined him with the god of the victors. We alone were continually defeated but never declared in the aftermath that our God had also been defeated—and thus never gave up God. (Sperber, Jan. 13, 1967, 5)

Curiously, Sperber argues that although he cannot retrieve his belief in God and the Jewish religion, it is important that contemporary Jews both maintain their Jewish faith and seek new ways to instill the young with pride in the Jewish culture. Otherwise, in his view, the young Jews will assimilate and abandon Judaism altogether. Sperber declares that Israel, as a state, will not resolve the Jewish Question in the world or the disaffection of young Jews in the Diaspora and in Israel itself. It is through reclaiming the Jewish intellectual tradition and Jewish history, Sperber argues, that Judaism can be revived and made more relevant. In other words, Judaism must seek a new authenticity, and it can only become authentic if Jews throughout the world see this as their burden, or *fardeau.*

As one can see in Sperber's own writings after 1952, he accepted this burden. Throughout the postwar period he went back to his roots as a Jew to bring out their significance in his writings and his political interventions as Jewish intellectual. For instance, in a 1978 interview with Hans Jürgen Schultz he fully outlined what the Bible meant to him. Entitled "Verwoben ins tägliche Leben," this interview reveals how Sperber had fully woven and integrated Jewish strands of thinking into his philosophy as a socialist and Diaspora Jew. From the very beginning it was the Bible that provided a "Jewish" pattern for the rest of his life: "Now the important thing was to live in such a way that the Messiah would find sufficient reason to come. Thus all life is in the Jewish people a life in the Diaspora, in dispersal—and not only are the Jewish people in the Diaspora but God, too, is in exile, indeed, humanity is in exile—and one must live so that sufficient reason arises for the Messiah to come and to bring salvation to the earth. And in this sense, it is only natural—let us say—that we lead our lives according to the Ten Commandments" (Sperber 1975, 136).

It is not simply the ethics of the messianic faith that were important to Sperber, however, but also its mode of reading, thinking, and acting. As he points out, reading was the art of learning how to question words and literal meanings. Learning never ended, and learning was interpretation. To read the Bible was to grasp a specific intellectual and cultural heritage created by human beings in the past and to interpret it in such a way that the present would take on significance and meaning through radical action. As a psychologist, revolutionary, and writer, Sperber sought to bring to light the hidden and mysterious meanings of life, and he saw this mode of thinking as specifically Jewish because it carried with it a set of ethical commandments:

I have remained true to the essential nature of the Jewish commandments, and I believe that they are not just valid for the Jews—Christianity has taken them over. My entire life has been determined by them, my political decisions, everything that I write is marked by the notion that when there is not the same justice for everyone, our existence is an unbearable challenge to the humane and (if you want) to the divine in us. Therefore, under the influence of this challenge to the people, to everyone, I took the side of revolution. . . . As I said, I am not religious, and I believe that the people will become mature when they do not need the thunder and lightning, the enormous authority of a god to act in the manner that the Bible demands they act. My morality is perhaps stricter than the strictest religious morality, but I do not justify it by calling upon a superhuman source. In this regard my position is more difficult. It is very hard; it is a daily regaining the ground that will—perhaps—be lost again in the night. (139–40)

Sperber's attachment to the Bible and to Jewish thinking is clearly what kept the spark of hope in his socialism alive after his disenchantment with Communism and his depression in 1952. Paradoxically, the more he began to write about the Holocaust, Israel, Jewish identity, and Zionism, the more he reinforced the deeply religious nature of his socialism. His three-volume autobiography, *Der Wasserträger Gottes* (God's water carrier; 1974), *Die vergebliche Warnung* (The futile warning; 1975), and *Bis man mir Scherben auf die Augen legt* (Until the fragments are placed on my eyes; 1977), records the events in his life that led Sperber to secularize and universalize his Jewish learning in political action and to distance himself from Stalinism and the student revolution of the late 1960s. *Churban oder die unfaßbare Gewißheit* (1979), a collection of essays, most of which were originally written in French from 1952 to 1979, reveals how Sperber continued to intervene in all questions that pertained to Jews in order to posit ethical principles of behavior that would serve as guidelines for political change. He did not, however, address just Jews, for his major goal was to transcend the Jewish religion and Jewish culture. He took as his motto Dostoyevsky's words, "We are all responsible for everything," and declared in his essay "Mein Judesein" (1979) that "from the very beginning my Jewishness has consisted of solidarity with the Jews, clear and unquestionable identification with them—how should it be otherwise after all that has happened to them during this century? And this, too, is my Jewishness: solidarity with those who are victims of injustice. That has been my socialism from the very beginning; it has remained my socialism despite the numerous unsuccessful and impatient efforts to bring about a world in which theory and practice would be united and would remain so forever" (Sperber 1979, 58).

Sperber makes clear in this essay that he does not believe that the Jews are a special *Volk,* nor does he identify with the Jewish religion and Israel. Nevertheless, he declares that his particular kind of Jewishness has been reinforced and hardened by the Holocaust and, as part of his Jewishness, he recalls the past every day in order not to demand revenge or to hate but to experience the times as they are and to live against the times. Moreover, his Jewish identity depends on reversing the Jewish Question as it is generally understood. As he wrote in a letter to a Christian colleague: "Yes, the philo-Semitism inherent in what you wrote worries me, and humiliates me as would a compliment based upon an absurd misunderstanding—a compliment that one would rather not have deserved. You dangerously overestimate us Jews. You insist on loving our entire people. I do not ask, I decidedly do not wish, that we be loved in this fashion (we, for that matter any other people). . . . The pitiless battle against anti-Semitism is your concern. Indeed, if this hatred is sometimes a mortal danger to us, for you it is a disease, a cancer, that you carry within yourselves. It has made us suffer horribly, but we continue to overcome it each day. The proof of this? We are free of all hatred towards you, and we feel ourselves fraternally linked with you in the defense of all those values which justify the presence of human beings on earth" (Sperber 1979, 64).

Clearly, Sperber's answer to this colleague cannot be considered a typical "Jewish" response to questions about the essence of Judaism and anti-Semitism. Nor were any of his theoretical positions intended to provide definitive answers for a reading public of gentiles and Jews. In fact, Sperber's great accomplishment in the postwar years cannot be found in the answers that he provided to the Jewish Question and to his own Jewishness, but in his disturbing questions that formed the paradox of his life: those concerning the Jew as heretical socialist.

Bibliography

Primary Documents

Manès Sperber, *Bis man mir Scherben auf die Augen legt* (Vienna: Europa Verlag, 1977); Sperber, *Churban oder Die Unfaßbare Gewißheit* (Vienna: Europa Verlag, 1979); Sperber, *Être Juif,* preface by Elie Wiesel (Paris: Editions Odile Jacob, 1994); Sperber, "Le Judaïsme, fardeau et promesse: Réflexions à l'ombre du hourban,"

Arche 122 (Apr. 1967): 20–25; Sperber, *Der verbrannte Dornbusch* (Mainz: Universum-Verlag, 1950); Sperber, *Die vergebliche Warnung* (Vienna: Europa Verlag, 1975); Sperber, *Die verlorene Bucht* (Cologne: Kiepenheuer & Witsch, 1955); Sperber, *Der Wasserträger Gottes* (Vienna: Europa Verlag, 1974); Sperber, *Wie eine Träne im Ozean* (Cologne: Kiepenheuer & Witsch, 1961); Sperber, "Weil wir Gott niemals aufgaben . . . " *Jüdische Rundschau* (Jan. 13, 1967): 5–7; Sperber, *Wolyna,* foreword by André Malraux (Vienna: Europa Verlag, 1984).

Interviews

"Dies Mein Judentum: Versuch eines Selbstporträts," *Mein Judentum,* ed. Hans-Jürgen Schultz (Stuttgart: Kreuz Verlag, 1978), 178–94, "Die Treue des Häretikers," *Ex Libris* 10 (Oct. 1976): 17–24; "Verwoben ins tägliche Leben," *Sie Werden Lachen,* ed. Hans-Jürgen Schultz (Stuttgart: Kreuz Verlag, 1975), 135–52.

Secondary Documents

Gisela Brude-Firnau, "Exil und Ethos: Zu Manès Sperbers Trilogie *Wie eine Träne im Ozean*" in *Das Exilerlebnis: Verhandlungen des vierten Symposium über deutsche und österreichische Exilliteratur,* eds. Donald Daviau and Ludwig Fischer (Columbia, S.C.: Camden, 1982), 297–306; Friedrich Heer, "Churban: Manès Sperbers bitteres Zeugnis," *Literatur und Kritik* 151 (1981): 1–3; Claudio Magris, "Ein Versuch aus dem Nirgends: Zu Manès Sperber und seinem Werk," *Modern Austrian Literature* 12 (1979): 41–66; Stéphane Moses, Joachim Schlor, and Julius H. Schoeps, eds., *Manès Sperber als Europäer: Eine Ethik des Widerstands* (Berlin: Hentrich, 1996); Peter Stenberg, "Remembering Times Past: Canetti, Sperber, and 'A World That Is No More,'" *Seminar* 17 (Nov. 1981): 296–311; Arnim Wallas, "Kindheit in Galizien: Das galizische Judentum im Spiegel der Autobiographien von Minna Lachs und Manès Sperber," *Sprachkunst* 24 (1993): 19–40; and Jack Zipes, "Manès Sperber's Legacy for Peace in *Wie eine Träne im Ozean,*" *German Quarterly* 61 (spring 1988): 249–63.

JACK ZIPES

1957 Hermann Levin Goldschmidt receives the first Leo Baeck Prize for *Das Vermächtnis des deutschen Judentums*

Born in 1914 in prewar Berlin, Hermann Levin Goldschmidt emigrated to Switzerland in February 1938. After a fourteen-year residence, he finally was granted official permission to remain and work in Switzerland. Soon thereafter he founded the Jüdisches Lehrhaus Zürich. For Goldschmidt, the "sacrifice of six million innocents," the greatest single disaster to befall the Jews in their 4,000-year history, created an entirely new situation. Auschwitz, according to Goldschmidt, requires above all else a recovery of the traces of Jewish tradition and an inventory of the remains of Jewish life that had flourished in Germany, which had been the center of advanced European culture. The crucial insight guiding the work of the Jüdisches Lehrhaus was that the present and future of Judaism depends on the past, and a working-through of that past. Critical in its attitude toward public opinion, the Lehrhaus did not look to mastering the past (*Vergangenheitsbewältigung*) as a solution, a term with negative connotations that gained wide currency in Germany, but that can also imply a wish to get rid of the past. The Lehrhaus's central idea was instead that the present situation called for a rigorous working through (*Aufarbeitung*) of the past. Opposed to the attempt to draw an historical divide between a lost world of the past and the present, the Lehrhaus emphasized the continuing importance and contribution of Jewish life in Germany. This emphasis on continuity instead of destruction led to a study of Judaism as something more than a relic of history. The Lehrhaus was thus able to address the reality of Jewish life in Germany after Auschwitz in a way that was free of the trammels of theologically fraught discourse and unhindered by the particularly unfortunate tropes of God-is-dead theology. The fact that, as Goldschmidt put it, "the six million dead are the part of us that is most alive" makes any ideological construction of Jewish identity impossible.

After the war, Zurich was the largest German-speaking Jewish community in Europe; thus it was an ideal site for such an undertaking. And it was here that Margarete Susman, who served as a kind of mentor to a circle of exiled Jewish intellectuals, published one of the first attempts to come to terms with what had occurred in Germany. That book, *Das Buch Hiob und das Schicksal des jüdischen Volkes* (1946), was republished in 1948 with a new preface that took into account the creation of the state of Israel. Along with Helmut Plessner's *The Belated Nation,* Max Horkheimer and Theodor Adorno's *Dialectic of the Enlightenment,* Erich Fromm's *Escape from Freedom,* Hannah Arendt's *The Origins of Totalitarianism,* and Martin Buber's *The Eclipse of God,* Susman's study was a groundbreaking attempt to come to terms with the destruction of Jewish life in Germany and German culture by reassessing the role of Judaism in history. Susman confronts the unspeakable by taking up the work of mourning—not by searching for a cause but by pursuing the existential question of how life itself would have to be conceived anew after Auschwitz.

If Franz Rosenzweig's *Jüdisches Lehrhaus* in Frankfurt had sought to address the predicament of Jewish identity in a Germany alienated by its recent confrontation with modernity, post-Auschwitz consciousness faced a radically different and deeper dilemma. Judaism was now called into question in the most existential way. The depth of this challenge posed all questions regarding Judaism and Jewish identity with a new and sharper sense of urgency. Life after Auschwitz could not avoid confronting the brute fact of Auschwitz. The sheer survival of Judaism required Jews to define their situation in a radically changed world.

The Jüdisches Lehrhaus began this task, and it was directed by Goldschmidt from 1951 until it closed its doors in 1961. It was here that Goldschmidt developed the material that became his trilogy published in the 1950s: *Das Vermächtnis des deutschen Judentums* (1957; largely expanded in 1965), *Die Botschaft des Judentums* (1960), and *Dialogik—Philosophie auf dem Boden der Neuzeit* (1964). In 1946, *Hermann Cohen und Martin Buber* appeared, which examines each writer as a theorist of Jewish modernity. This study's subtitle, *Ein Jahrhundert Ringen um Jüdische Wirklichkeit* (The struggle of a century for Jewish reality) indicates the direction in which Goldschmidt would take the interpretation of the role of Judaism for modernity. Two years later followed *Philosophie als Dialogik,* which casts the problem of delimiting autonomous spheres for philosophy and religion in dialogic terms. The move to dialogics preserves the intricate complexity of the interdependence of each realm, and resists a reduction of the argument to any simple formula; this approach was crucial to a new and critical conception of Judaism.

Unlike Buber's "dialogical principle," Goldschmidt's *Dialogik* operates as a purely philosophical argument without theological underpinnings. The dialogical procedure settles the dispute between philosophy and religion with the resources of epistemology alone, in a manner sharply distinguished from Buber's deeply metaphysical philosophic mode, which was part and parcel of his phenomenology of religion. Goldschmidt's sharp distinction between philosophy

and religion typifies his concept of modernity, which was one that remained committed to critical rationality while refusing to sacrifice the legitimacy of religious and spiritual life. His position argues for a critical conception of modernity that resists the one-dimensionality of instrumental reason, a critical perspective that in fact constitutes an unflagging commitment to scientific thought. In his early critique of Nietzsche's nihilism, *Der Nihilismus im Licht einer kritischen Philosophie* (1941) and in the project of *Dialogik,* Goldschmidt—always resistant to premature visions of dialectical solution—lay the groundwork for a modern understanding of Judaism. For the first time, it became possible to leave apologetics behind without having to resort to nationalistic or isolationist discourse. Instead, the history of the Jewish people was to be rethought. German-Jewish historiography, as well as the work of Simon Dubnow, set the parameters for this project. Rewriting Jewish history became the last, decisive step in the process of emancipation. This emancipation aimed at liberating the Jewish self-image from subjection to mythologized shadow histories of the other. Previously silenced "others" now stepped forward to reclaim their past and write their own history.

In the year of his death, Leo Baeck recommended that the Europäische Verlagsanstalt publish *Das Vermächtnis des deutschen Judentums*. The book appeared in 1957, and the press became Goldschmidt's publisher until 1968. The revolt of the sons against the fathers, who represented that Nazi past in the German cultural turmoil of 1968, had the ironic effect of leading those radical sons to discard and ignore important work of cultural memory and recovery that had already been done. Goldschmidt, swimming against this tide, came to see 1968 as Germany's final repression of its past. *Das Vermächtnis des deutschen Judentums* forcefully argues for a dynamic interpretation of this legacy, an interpretation that neither fixes nor hypostatizes the past but liberates its critical content. Critical appropriation of the past transforms history into a site for negotiating one's identity and its determinants. Legacy becomes the name for what is specific, yet it is a specificity that is realized only in the process of interpretation. *Das Vermächtnis des deutschen Judentums* and *Die Botschaft des Judentums* occupy the boundary between historiography and reflection on history's theoretical implications. Both books reject the normative conventions of historiography; Goldschmidt's writing keeps open the space in which the conditionality of historiography can be addressed. Goldschmidt's work forces us to recognize that history itself requires a firm grounding in theory, because reflection on history—when history is not being altogether ignored—is always contested ground. His first step in this project is to stake out the discursive and institutional bounds within which a history so long and effectively ignored can be represented for modernity.

In this view, culture transcends any univocal representation as "other,"and Jewish culture cannot be defined in the biological, deterministic image conjured by the myth of German-Jewish symbiosis. Now it can be recovered on its own terms, as a once thriving and vital reality. An experience exists beyond theological strictures, an experience of crucial significance not only for Judaism but for modernity itself. For Goldschmidt, Jewish modernity is not a theological problem, but it reflects the formative role of Jewish tradition in the constitution of modern culture. It was Spinoza who first made it possible to conceive of Judaism as something more than a theological issue; his sociological and political interpretation of biblical scripture led to a radically modern conception of Judaism. According to Spinoza, a critical reading of biblical scripture is naturally resistant to any attempt to support a dogmatic or doctrinal interpretation. The Bible's mandate, Spinoza argued, is legislative, prescribing rules and laws guiding moral action. Thus according to Spinoza, the Bible makes no truth claims whatsoever and is therefore free from theological pretension. This line of thought was carried on by Moses Mendelssohn, who formulated a modern liberal conception of Judaism whose fundamental outlines were shared by Leo Baeck. In his *Das Wesen des Judentums* (The essence of Judaism), Baeck defined a modern concept of Judaism at the start of the twentieth century. It was this line of thought that Goldschmidt continued.

Goldschmidt's argument is thus distinct from confessional attempts to read Jewish history in Christian terms, a trend so pervasive that even philosophers such as Hermann Cohen and Franz Rosenzweig find their positions determined by it. Judaism could now be treated in its own specific historical terms. Christianity was no longer the yardstick by which every other religion was to be measured. Only this assertion of the independence of Jewish historiography and hermeneutics made it possible to begin a Christian-Jewish dialogue that no longer sought to skirt the hard questions. A certain period during the postwar reconstruction of Germany made such a dialogue seem possible, and even salutary. Goldschmidt is active in numerous efforts to sustain such a serious dialogue between Christians and Jews. Yet the frankness born of his strong commitment to this project was not always met with congeniality.

Aside from the many essays Goldschmidt wrote for anthologies published by Christian presses, two books, *Heilvoller Verrat? Judas im Neuen Testament* and *Weil wir Brüder sind,* were published with Katholisches Bibelwerk, Germany's official Catholic publishing house. The press, however, made a less than full effort to promote its "Jewish" books. Goldschmidt's study of Judas interprets this figure as an attempt on the part of Christian theology to project onto the Jews the Church's guilt at having betrayed its Jewish heritage. Goldschmidt argued that the perpetuation of this myth served not only to fuel continued anti-Semitism (even in a secular, post-Christian world, where Christ may have disappeared but culprits are still called Judas), but also prevented well-meaning Christians from dealing with their religious genealogy. It was a critique that was largely ignored. (In the *Theologische Realenzyklopädie,* 17:304–7, Goldschmidt gives a brief summary of his position.) *Weil wir Brüder sind* argues for a *heilsgeschichtliche Arbeitsteilung* (a division of labor in history's march toward redemption). The admonition for Christians to become better Christians and for Jews to become better Jews strikes too close to home to be met with enthusiasm when what people prefer is talk of harmony and good will. The antifundamentalist thrust of Goldschmidt's critique may have lacked a certain appeal in this situation. But it is his statement "the holy land is everywhere" that radically refuses to attribute sacredness to land, nations, language, institutions, or whatever else might be considered itself part of the religious moment in modernity. For in modernity, Goldschmidt argues, Judaism's uncompromising rejection of idolatry in any form should be understood as a caution against any confused attempt to identify representation with what it represents.

But for Goldschmidt, as for Hermann Cohen, the essential contribution of Judaism is its call for universal liberation. Any kind of exclusivism or compromise with the powers that determine the status quo is a betrayal of the promise of historical redemption. So long as any people stands deprived of freedom, Judaism can neither forsake nor delegate its responsibility to bring messianic hope to fruition. As long as exploitation and subjection seem the unquestioned rule, the insistent call for liberation remains all the more necessary. Judaism, according to Goldschmidt, represents the intransigent, historically specific call to reject any compromise in the pursuit of universal freedom. Its messianic mission can therefore be fulfilled only by the universal establishment of peace on earth. Judaism is kept alive, so to speak, sometimes even despite the efforts of its representatives, by the sheer force of its radical message.

This future-oriented message is what defines the timeless relevance of Judaism's message, and the universal character of that message shapes the contingent particularity of each of its interpreters. A paradox informs the messianic power of this message: it is the particular alone, in all its contingency, that is capable of representing the hope and promise of the universal. This messianic conception keeps Judaism from falling into a temporal standstill. The Jewish and philosophical impulses of Goldschmidt's thought meet in this insight.

Freiheit für den Widerspruch, which began as a lecture in 1969 and became the title of a book in 1976, argues for the importance of contradiction to philosophy and thereby becomes an expression of the Jewish experience in modernity. The central tension of the experience that informs the book is the tension between the demands of the universal and the specific forms—in Judaism, for instance—that those universals took. *Freiheit für den Widerspruch* argues that any conceptual attempt to harmonize the particular and the universal, whether by dialectical means or otherwise, would claim to fix precisely that which defies fixity. The dynamics of this tension result in ever new instantiations of this contradiction. To resolve such a contradiction would be to misunderstand it completely, and would silence the insistent challenge and radical meaning of universalism. Judaism's aporetic solution to this existential contradiction stands as a signal contribution to this human struggle. To follow Jewish history is to observe an ongoing historical negotiation between the universal and the particular.

Thus although Jewish identity and philosophy mutually constitute one another, they do not do so in a way that leads to fixed definitions, but rather in a way that reveals the complex nature of modernity itself. Goldschmidt's dialogic argues that the practical import of contradiction needs to be recognized as a counterweight to the philosophical notion of some absolute ground for experience. Such certainty had already been successfully challenged by Nietzsche, but it was never fully abandoned by modern philosophical discourse. To acknowledge the insistence of contradiction offers a way out of the theoretical impasse that results from the hermeneutic circle—and grants legitimacy only to that which one has already presupposed. It is precisely Goldschmidt's grounding of his philosophical reflections in the historicity of Jewish experience that gives them an open and unhindered prospect on the possibilities of a human universalism.

If one of the consequences of 1968 has been the forgetting of the German-Jewish legacy (due in part to the institutionalization of Jewish Studies), or if such subject matter has become an ethnic enclave or another rubric among others—a collection of obsolete tales important only to the abandoned fathers—the increasing importance of cultural difference has brought Goldschmidt's work new attention. This growing interest in theorizing difference and contradiction as constitutive elements of the modern experience has led to the development of many new models for understanding alterity and identity in critical terms. Alterity and identity are now seen as central questions of philosophy. Goldschmidt's antidialectical impulse, like Theodor Adorno's *Negative Dialectics,* aims at redeeming contradictions rather than refashioning them into elements of a dialectical system. Whereas Adorno's critical method carries out dialectics to a point of implosion, Goldschmidt, like Jacques Derrida, challenges the manipulation of contradictions altogether. Adorno, Derrida, and Goldschmidt all argue for an epistemological aporia that forces us to reflect on the critical limits of the power of concepts. Pushing conceptual claims beyond such limits leads to monological thinking, and consequently to totalitarianism in theory and praxis. The persistence of this urge to do away with contradictions once and for all betrays some of the violence inherent in conceptual thought.

Goldschmidt's writing centers in this recognition that knowledge, as well as truth, is a process in which contradictory claims must constantly be rethought. Writing therefore becomes the space in which such renegotiations take place. Goldschmidt's *Ganzheitsbuch—Sefer Haschlemut* (1993) makes this point typographically. A collection of texts—all of equal length—portray the contingent bounds of space and time in which thoughts are expressed. Meditations though they are, these texts provoke a continual exchange between the reader and the text. The assertive character of these statements does not signify final certainty but instead opens up ever new occasions for reflection. Likewise, the German renderings of the *Tao-te-King* by Laotse (1982–92) suggest a bridge between Chinese and biblical antiquity. *Chinas kundige Weisheit—Judentums kündende Gewissheit* (1990) inaugurates a genuine culture challenge to Eurocentric closure. In such openness to the world as a whole (*Weltoffenheit*), Goldschmidt recognizes Judaism's vital capacity for change and, more importantly, its creative contribution to the world.

Goldschmidt's work combines a rare ability to reflect on the Jewish predicament after Auschwitz with systematic philosophic rigor. His decidedly liberal, middle position between Zionism and Orthodoxy makes him an exception in a postwar Europe characterized by increasing polarization. If the liberal tradition of German Judaism has for all practical purposes all but ceased to exist, and if Zionism and Orthodoxy have claimed to be the only valid choices for a viable Jewish identity, Goldschmidt's contribution stands as an insistent challenge to such claims. At a time when vicarious religiosity or vicarious patriotism have become a way of life for many Jews, Goldschmidt's reminder that there is more to Judaism than the privilege of the persecuted has not always been enthusiastically received.

Although Alain Finkielkraut's *The Imaginary Jew* (1980) describes the problem of postwar Jewish identity in this regard, Goldschmidt responds that the problem has indeed become one of Jews without Judaism. For Goldschmidt, the question of Jewish identity has always been secondary to the work of recovering Jewish history for modernity, not as something to wallow in, but as a way of realizing the Bible's promise. Goldschmidt's ability to be equally at ease in things Jewish, Christian, or secular flows naturally from a coherently developed Jewish position that has long superseded the need for apologetics or self-aggrandizement. Goldschmidt has instead fully integrated the message of Judaism into his concept of modernity. In tandem with this work, his anchoring in Swiss culture has led him to embrace and critically reformulate the progressive line of thought that runs from Rousseau to Pestalozzi, and to conceptualize Helvetian neutrality as a political space in which cultural and social tensions can be played out in a productive way. Goldschmidt therefore stands out as a German Jew who has defied, with outspoken persistence, the constraining prejudice that sees German Jews as incapable of taking any path but that of uprooted exile or wholehearted assimilation. This sets him apart from those who preferred to keep silent about their situation, and from those who have turned to one or another form of compensatory extremism. These life situations provide proof for Goldschmidt's insight that it is not synthesis that is productive and true, but rather the way contradictions are negotiated that is of lasting significance. Goldschmidt's mediation of the biblical with the contemporary asks us to examine and think through the dynamics of modern existence. Instead of offering another form of quiescent escapism, his work allows us to appreciate Judaism as a crucial contributor to the future validity and viability of modernity.

Bibliography

Alain Finkielkraut, *The Imaginary Jew,* trans. Kevin O'Neill and David Suchoff (Lincoln: University of Nebraska Press, 1994); Willi Goetschel, ed., *Wege des Widerspruchs: Festschrift für H. L. Goldschmidt* (Bern: Haupt, 1984), with a bibliography of Goldschmidt's writings; Goetschel, "'Gibt es eine jüdische Philosophie?' Zur Problematik eines Topos," *Perspektiven der Dialogik,* ed. W. Goetschel (Vienna: Passagen, 1994); Hermann Levin Goldschmidt, *Das Vermächtnis des deutschen Judentums: Werkausgabe,* vol. 2 (Vienna: Passagen, 1993); Goldschmidt, *Die Botschaft des Judentums: Werkausgabe,* vol. 3 (Vienna: Passagen, 1993); Goldschmidt, *Hermann Cohen und Martin Buber: Werkausgabe,* vol. 1 (Vienna: Passagen, 1993); Goldschmidt, *Weil wir Brüder sind: Biblische Besinnung für Juden und Christen* (Stuttgart: Katholisches Bibelwerk, 1975); Goldschmidt, *Heilvoller Verrat? Judas im Neuen Testament* (Stuttgart: Katholisches Bibelwerk, 1976); Goldschmidt, *Jüdisches Ja zur Zukunft der Welt: Eine schweizerische Dokumentation eigener Mitwirkung seit 1938* (Schaffhausen: Novalis, 1981); Goldschmidt, *Chinas kundige Weisheit-Judentums kündende Gewissheit* (Zurich: Goldschmidt, 1990); David Suchoff, "Widersprüchliche Identität: Judentum und Postmoderne im Denken Hermann Levin Goldschmidts," *Perspektiven der Dialogik;* and Margarete Susman, *Das Buch Hiob und das Schicksal des jüdischen Volkes* (Zurich: Steinberg, 1946).

WILLI GOETSCHEL

1959 Hilde Domin publishes *Nur eine Rose als Stütze* and Nelly Sachs publishes *Flucht und Verwandlung*, both of which deal with flight and exile

The 1950s were years of economic recovery and "normalization" in the history of the German Federal Republic. This normalization consisted of a nationwide denial and repression of the psychological experience of the Nazi era and its moral consequences, and it formed the basis of the "inability to mourn," to quote the title of the 1967 psychohistory by Alexander and Margarete Mitscherlich. That this experience ended at the end of the decade is indicated by the publication of three titles in 1959 that marked the beginning of an authentic post–World War II German literature: *Billard um halbzehn* (Billiards at half past nine) by Heinrich Böll, *Die Blechtrommel* (The tin drum) by Günter Grass, and *Mutmaßungen über Jakob* (Speculations about Jacob) by Uwe Johnson.

Until 1959, West German literature was still influenced by conservative, if not reactionary, writers who had been tolerated, and perhaps promoted, by the Nazi authorities and their aesthetics. In addition, literary discourse after 1945 had been polarized by the controversy over "inner emigration." When in September 1945 Thomas Mann refused to return from his exile in the United States and exonerate the German writers who had stayed behind in Nazi Germany, he was reviled by these authors, who claimed to have resisted the Nazis by withdrawing into this inner emigration. This controversy made German exile writers personae non gratae in West Germany.

Meanwhile, a new generation of writers had arrived who were willing to open themselves up to the experience of the Nazi past in order to derive from it some form of insight. Literature began to serve as a seismograph for the change of consciousness about the past and as a compass for the future direction of political culture in West Germany. Among the signs of this change was the fact that a new, select reading audience began to listen for the first time to voices from exile. Indeed, the most dramatic demonstration of this directional change was the awarding in 1960 of the Georg Büchner Prize to the Jewish exile poet Paul Celan by the West German Academy for Language and Literature in Darmstadt.

In 1959, Hilde Domin and Nelly Sachs were able to place their volumes of poetry with West German publishers and to find a receptive audience among critics and readers. For Hilde Domin, this was the first book publication and for Nelly Sachs, the fourth. Nelly Sachs's first volume of poetry, *In den Wohnungen des Todes* (In the dwellings of death), was published by the Aufbau Verlag in East Germany in 1947; the second, *Sternverdunklung* (Eclipse of the stars), was published by the exile publisher Berman-Fischer in Amsterdam in 1949. Only the third volume, entitled *Und Niemand weiß weiter* (And no one knows how to go on) was published by a German publisher—Ellermann in Hamburg distributed this work in 1957. *Sternverdunklung* had to be pulped, because there were no sales. *Flucht und Verwandlung* (Flight and metamorphosis), put out by Deutsche Verlagsanstalt in Stuttgart in 1959, was Nelly Sachs's first successful publication in West Germany. Whereas Nelly Sachs had written poetry throughout her life and had been published in the 1920s and 1930s (although she dated her legitimate poetry from 1945), Hilde Domin began writing poetry only late in life: her first poem is dated 1951. Domin's first volume of poetry, *Nur eine Rose als Stütze* (Only a rose as a support), published by the famous Fischer publishing house in Frankfurt, met with instant success. The unknown poet was heralded as one of the six best women writers in contemporary German literature. But what Nelly Sachs and Hilde Domin had in common was a Jewish background and a life of persecution and exile during the Nazi period. Both came from assimilated German-Jewish families, and both of them had to leave Germany under the threat of discrimination and persecution, which finally turned to extermination. Nelly Sachs was born in 1891 in Berlin as the only child of a Jewish manufacturer, and Hilde Domin was born in 1912 in Cologne as Hildegard Löwenstein, the daughter of a Jewish lawyer. Domin's married name was Hildegard Palm, and she chose Hilde Domin as her pen name, indicating her exile and her beginnings as a poet in Santo Domingo from 1940 to 1953. In Santo Domingo, Hilde Domin wrote her first poem, in German. She later translated it into Spanish.

Both poets were able to escape from Nazi Germany—Hilde Domin left early, in 1932, in a kind of pre-Hitler emigration; Nelly Sachs escaped at the last possible moment, in May 1940. As a student, Domin went with her husband Erwin Palm first to Italy, where she earned a doctoral degree in political science at the University of Florence. She then went via England to the Dominican Republic in 1940. In the same year, Nelly Sachs was able to emigrate with her mother to Sweden, where she stayed until her mother's death in Stockholm in 1970. Sachs returned to Germany only for two brief visits. Hilde Domin, however, returned in 1954 for the first time after her 1932 departure and, after a one-year stay in Spain from 1956–57, she and her husband returned to settle in West Germany. As of 1961, Domin considered Heidelberg, where her husband accepted a professorship, her permanent residence.

Although Domin's permanent return to Germany is not the only feature that distinguishes her from Sachs, it is one of the most critical. In Hilde Domin's case, it was not only a return to a spiritual Germany, a Germany existing in the language of her poetry—it was also an explicit affirmation of loyalty to the Federal Republic of Germany, its political system, its intellectual atmosphere, and its territory. "I love Germany," she said in 1968, when she received a literary prize. As one critic said, "Hilde Domin intones a paean or love song, sometimes muted, always tentative, to her once and present homeland" (G. Stern 1987, 136).

Although her first poems were written in exile, Domin became an established poet in her own right because of her return to West Germany. She spoke of the "happiness of her return to the country of her language, of her childhood." Her "homecoming, not the persecution, was the great experience of [her] life" ("Hineingeboren" [Born into Judaism; Domin 1982]). Any such statements would have been impossible for Nelly Sachs to utter. Sachs became a poet because of the Shoah. This was acknowledged by the award of the Nobel Prize in 1966, which recognized her for having "given voice to the world wide tragedy of the Jewish people" and for having interpreted "Israel's destiny." During her first return visit to Germany, in May 1960, Nelly Sachs was afraid to stay overnight; she attended an award ceremony at Meersburg at Lake Constance but stayed in a hotel in Zurich. Until the end of her life, she felt personally haunted by the images of mass murder and genocide of the Jewish people. Afraid of continued persecution, she was committed to a mental hospital between 1960 and 1963.

This critical difference in the personal lives of Domin and Sachs also formed and shaped the differences in their poetry. The Jewish experience of the twentieth century is at the center of Nelly Sachs's poetry, whereas for Hilde Domin existential exile provided the focal point of reference.

Domin's position becomes obvious from her four-stanza title poem "Nur eine Rose als Stütze" (Only a rose as a support), whose title also provides the last line. The speaker of the poem has selected and furnished "ein Zimmer in der Luft" (a room in the air / among acrobats and birds). There is no firm ground: her bed lies "on the trapeze of emotions / like a nest in the wind / at the extreme end of the branch." The two middle stanzas develop a sequence of images of warmth and protection, provided by gentle sheep "who drift in the moonlight like shimmering clouds over the solid earth." The speaker buys "a blanket of the softest wool" and wraps herself "in the fleece of the reliable animals." The sheep, as images of domesticity and security, are locked into the barn at night. Comforted by the knowledge that the sheep are protected, the speaker is, nevertheless, reminded in the last stanza of her own precarious position and feels vertigo. Grasping for something to hold onto, she finds "only a rose for a support." As a symbol of the autonomous aesthetic, the rose is the only support available to the existential exile who chooses her living space—which lacks firm footing—not out of political necessity, but of her own free will. In such a space, the only support left to the speaker is autonomous art (or poetry).

Nelly Sachs's response to exile in her collection *Flucht und Verwandlung* (Flight and metamorphosis) is a poem that is without a title of its own, yet is linked by two of its key words to the title of the book: "Fleeing, / what a great reception / on the way—." Fleeing is viewed not only as an ordeal, but also as a blessing: "a great reception" by people who open their homes. The exile is poor and afflicted: she has no garment in which to wrap herself but the "wind's shawl"—she has no firm ground under her feet, no secure place for her prayers, because the sand is blown in all directions before the "Amen" can be pronounced. "Sand" is associated with "fin" and "wing" as an additional image of swift motion and flight: sand is "compelled from fin to wing / and further—." The motion of the sea is also evoked, with the waves rolling toward the beach but returning to the sea. The straight line of fleeing is thus turned into an eternal cycle of fleeing and receiving. The

sea, too, becomes an image of constancy, with its promise of strengthening the sick butterfly—an image of the exiled soul. The waves leave stones on the beach from the depths of the sea; in one, a fly is encrusted in amber. Hundreds of years ago, a fly that tried to escape the dripping sap of a tree was trapped by the resin, and its flight was arrested by the yellowish gum that turned into stone, changing inconstancy and temporality into constancy and timelessness. The fly leaves an "inscription," a message for the speaker, on the stone: one can lose one's homeland; one is subject to change; yet existence and identity are not lost during the flight through time and space. The persona of the poem is no longer in need of a homeland: "I hold instead of a homeland / the metamorphoses of the world—." In the language of the poem the speaker has preserved her identity through change.

Both poets write about the same historical experience of exile, yet their responses are different. Although both turn to art or language as a means of coping, Hilde Domin's final answer is aesthetic and ahistorical. There are references to danger and vertigo, but very few to persecution and death. For her, the situation of exile is born out of an almost Nietzschean defiance of the bourgeois philistine world. Domin's poem of exile does not allow for an interpretation with reference to the Bible, whereas the first three lines of Nelly Sachs's poem require such a reading. Sachs's poem is not only about a biographical flight, but also the typological flight of the people of Israel from ancient past to modern times, from the biblical Exodus to the most recent persecution and flight of the Jews. The meaning of the first three lines rests on the flight of the people of Israel from Egypt and their reception by God—as well as on the understanding that they receive Him in the wilderness of Sinai. The sand is not only the sand of the desert; it is also an image of the people of Israel. In the Bible and in Jewish legends, Israel is compared to sand, to fish, and to a bird. According to Jewish legend, Moses wanted to be transformed into a fish or a bird in order to see the Promised Land. The sick butterfly, an image of the soul, is told that it "will soon learn again of the sea." In elucidating this line about the exiled soul learning again of the sea, the following passage from the *Zohar,* the most important book of Jewish mysticism, is helpful: "When the Holy One remembers His children, He drops them into the great Sea which is the Sea of Wisdom, in order to sweeten them, and He turns the attribute of Justice into the attribute of Mercy, and takes compassion on Israel" (3:62–63). Stones are tokens of God's compassion in the Bible and Jewish legends. Precious stones are given to the pious. In Nelly Sachs's poem, the "inscription" on the stone is clearly an allusion to the Tablets of the Law given to Israel on Mount Sinai. The biblical dimensions of exile and its relevance to the Jewish experience of the twentieth century are essential to this poem. The centrality of this poem to Nelly Sachs as a Jewish poet is indicated by the fact that she recited this poem at the Nobel Prize ceremony in 1966 instead of presenting a conventional address.

Although a reading of Nelly Sachs's poetry without the biblical level of interpretation and an exploration of its interrelationship with contemporary Jewish history is incomplete, the discourse of Hilde Domin's work, especially *Nur eine Rose als Stütze,* is removed from the Bible and contemporary Jewish life. The best example is her poem "Apfelbaum und Olive" (Apple tree and olive), which, in a manner reminiscent of Heinrich Heine's poem about a fir and a palm, juxtaposes the familiar tree of her homeland with the evergreen of the subtropics. In Domin's work, the trees of the subtropical regions signify not the exotic, but exile. Her three-page poem does not deal with dreams and longing for the exotic, as does Heine's poem, but with examples of everyday life in exile. These examples are comforting: "To know / where the cups and the plates are / in a house, where you are a guest," or "To share the trust of the cat and the dog / of a friend / and to know the secret trick of the bicycle / as if it were your own." This relationship to objects and animals is reminiscent of Bertolt Brecht's epigrams in his California exile. The speaker of Domin's poem addresses herself as "the wanderer / from day to day / and from country to country"; she incorporates the fact that "the word / of the transitoriness / of all existence / has become flesh."

The apple tree and the olive take the place of possessions for the exile, "and in foreign countries" she has a place at the table, "at the side of the hostess," and the family shares its meals with her and treats her "like a child that is late for dinner." This flow of exile images is suddenly interrupted by the revelation of a romantic German scene: "a deer stepping out of the forest / a small chapel on a hill / with a solitary churchyard" greeting the poem's persona. This greeting is regarded as an invitation she would like to accept one day. She realizes that she is "here a little bit more / than at other places / at home." The Christian imagery of this rustic scene, which seems to emerge from the pages of Eichendorff, made Hilde Domin the "Poet of Return" for West German critics such as the philosopher Hans-Georg Gadamer, who coined this phrase in 1971. Although the last lines include a sense of loss, which the German critic was ready to concede, they nevertheless signal a return to Germany, encapsulated in its most romantic and Christian imagery.

The Jewish experience of the twentieth century is present in Domin's poetry only in its most generalized form, especially in her first collection. There are only two biblical references, one to Abel and one to the "door post of the house" (Exod. 12) in *Nur eine Rose als Stütze,* but Cain and Abel are also part of the Christian tradition, and the latter reference to the doorpost is obscured by allusions to the notches cut in the wood to measure "the years of childhood / centimeter by centimeter." Symbols that are exclusively Christian prevail, as, for example, in her poem "Die Heiligen" (The saints), where the saints are tempted like Christ but refuse to leave the church because the children need miracles. In the same poem, there is a literal allusion to Christ's response to the tempter that "man shall not live by bread alone": "For we eat bread / but live of the light" (Matt. 4:1–4). In another poem of *Nur eine Rose als Stütze,* entitled "Die schwersten Wege" (The most difficult journeys), there is an unmistakable reference to the bread and wine of the Eucharist.

The number of Christian allusions increased in Domin's subsequent volumes of poetry, including references to Christ's crucifixion and resurrection. In a later poem of 1970, entitled "Ecce Homo," man appears as "one-armed forever" in juxtaposition to the crucified with "both arms / wide open / the Here-I-Am," always exposed and present. As Hilde Domin said in her autobiographical essay "Hineingeboren" (Born into Judaism), as a Jew she felt like "a direct heir of Jesus, disassociated from church and dogma: 'always crucified and burnt.'" Although in her imagery Domin drew heavily from the Christian tradition, she also incorporated images of death and the perils of exile and persecution. The focus of the central seven-page poem of *Nur eine Rose als Stütze,* entitled "Wen es trifft" (Whoever is selected), is not the experience of persecution; rather, the poem constitutes a plea to the survivors at home. The bystander is entreated to show compassion for the exile and never to lend his hand "to the construction / of the hells of barbed wire." German critics have compared this poem to Paul Celan's "Todesfuge" ("Death fugue") or to Nelly Sachs's "Chor der Geretteten" (Chorus of the rescued"); the essential difference, however, is that Domin's poem is not about the Shoah, but about the experience of exile (and return in general) and about searching for a basis of reconciliation with the bystanders. Furthermore, for Hilde Domin, unlike for Nelly Sachs, exile is not the central Jewish experience through the ages, but only the "extreme experience of the conditio humana" (Domin 1974).

For Sachs, it is the Shoah that forms the basis and beginning of her poetry in 1945. With her collection *In den Wohnungen des Todes,* written after the first breakthrough of the Allied forces in the winter of 1943–44, Nelly Sachs broke new ground by explicitly thematizing death in the extermination camps. In order to avoid any misunderstanding, she did not use metaphors for the first line of the introductory poem, but addressed the smoke stacks of the crematoria of the extermination camps: "O the chimneys / On the ingeniously devised habitations of death" (Sachs 1967). The buildings are deceptively constructed like houses, but they are not designed for living. The human craft of the construction of houses is totally estranged from its original function. By drawing attention to this separation, the perversion of the design of the gas chambers is exposed.

The third stanza addresses the body parts of the SS officers at the selection ramp used to direct the victims to extermination or forced labor: "O you fingers / Laying the threshold / Like a knife between life and death—." Whereas one usually points one's finger to help people find their way, here this gesture of assistance is perverted into the act of the assassin or murderer.

Although Hilde Domin never dealt with the Shoah in her poetry, Nelly Sachs's collections *In den Wohnungen des Todes* of 1947 and *Sternverdunklung* of 1949 had a cathartic effect on her, and she became one of the most sensitive and discerning interpreters of Sachs's work. As Domin said in 1966, Nelly Sachs lent her voice to the dead of the Shoah: "With your words they went the way which the dead go. Only a victim and exile who was also a German poet could do this. One familiar with the German language. . . . And one who shares the fate of the victims" (Domin 1966).

After 1933, Nelly Sachs began to identify with Judaism as a religion, reading the major texts of Hasidism and Jewish mysticism. Her poetry after 1945 is steeped in the symbolism of Jewish mysticism. Paul Celan and Hilde Domin considered and envied her as a "believer." For Hilde Domin, Judaism was neither religion nor nation, but a "community of fate" (*Schicksalsgemeinschaft*) into which she was born. As she said in the autobiographical "Hineingeboren," the truly emancipated person cannot evade this community of fate: "Human solidarity belongs to one's unconditional credo."

Although both Domin and Sachs spoke the languages of their countries of exile, the language of their poetry was German. In her "Open Letter to Nelly Sachs" of 1966, Domin dealt with this paradox, when she said that Sachs wrote for those whose mother tongue was German: "Therefore you are a German poet and cannot be anybody else. You who spoke of the victims and who had only a narrow escape. You who become sick to death again and again of this experience. Your poetry is based on this tension." Referring to the person exiled and persecuted, expelled from her community, who uses the language that is her own and that of her persecutors, Domin also spoke of her own situation: "Those who were persecuted because of racism were only the most unfortunate, the most negated of exile poets." For Domin, the "German poets of Jewish fate," as she called them, experienced only the extreme of the paradox that all poets have to live with. Defending the use of her native language, Domin offered the following explanation for her dilemma: "Language serves as humanity's memory. . . . The remembrance of man consists of all languages. The poet keeps that remembrance living and vivid. . . . This each poet can do with his or her own language. Ours happens to be German" (Domin 1966).

This "Open Letter" of 1966 summarizes the interrelationship between Nelly Sachs and Hilde Domin, and expresses the dilemma of the Jewish poet in the German language. Domin sent her first volume *Nur eine Rose als Stütze* to Sachs in 1959 and received her collection *Flucht und Verwandlung* in return with the dedication: "To Hilde Domin who sent me a rose as a support." They exchanged letters, and Domin addressed her "Lied der Ermutigung III" (Song of encouragement III) to Nelly Sachs, as a way of supporting Sachs after her nervous breakdown in 1960. Nelly Sachs and Hilde Domin were soul mates, yet they were very different. Sachs never confirmed Domin's analysis of the Jewish poet in the German language. When Sachs spoke of "her people," she meant the Jewish people and considered it her task to put the "tragedy of the Jewish people into words" (Dinesen and Müssener 1984, 175, 177). Domin was a poeta doctus—she published extensively on the theory of poetry—whereas Sachs said very little about her craft. And although Domin allowed for political engagement in poetry, she defended the autonomy of literature. (With the exception of her essays and her novel *Das zweite Paradies* [The second paradise] of 1968, Domin never became as politically outspoken in her poetry as did, for example, Erich Fried.) Nelly Sachs, on the other hand, transcended but never abandoned in her late poetry (1961–70) the theme of the Nazi genocide against the Jews.

Bibliography

Ehrhard Bahr, "Flight and Metamorphosis: Nelly Sachs as a Poet of Exile," *Exile: The Writer's Experience,* ed. John M. Spalek and Robert F. Bell (Chapel Hill: University of North Carolina Press, 1982), 267–77; Bahr, *Nelly Sachs* (Munich: Beck, 1980); Bahr, "'Meine Metaphern sind meine Wunden': Nelly Sachs und die Grenzen der poetischen Metapher," *Nelly Sachs: Neue Interpretationen,* ed. Michael Kessler and Jürgen Wertheimer (Tübingen: Stauffenburg, 1994), 318; Ursula Baltz, "Exil und Heimkehr: Biographische und religiöse Elemente in der Dichtung Hilde Domins," *Poesie wie Brot: Religion und Literatur: Gegenseitige Herausforderung* (Munich: Kaiser, 1989), 55–84; Michael Braun, *Exil und Engagement: Untersuchungen zur Lyrik und Poetik Hilde Domins* (Frankfurt a. M.: Peter Lang, 1993); Ruth Dinesen, *Nelly Sachs: Eine Biographie* (Frankfurt a. M.: Suhrkamp, 1992); Ruth Dinesen and Helmut Müssener, eds., *Briefe der Nelly Sachs* (Frankfurt a. M.: Suhrkamp, 1984); Hilde Domin, "Exil und Heimkehr," *Sinn und Form* 45 (1993): 335–40; Domin, "Exilerfahrungen: Untersuchung zur Verhaltenstypik," *Frankfurter Hefte* 29 (1974): 185–92; Domin, *Gesammelte Gedichte* (Frankfurt a. M.: Fischer, 1987); Domin, "Hineingeboren," *Aber die Hoffnung: Autobiographisches aus und über Deutschland* (Munich: Piper, 1982), 64–80; Domin, *Nur eine Rose als Stütze* (Frankfurt a. M.: Fischer, 1959); Domin, "Offener Brief an Nelly Sachs," *Nelly Sachs zu Ehren: Zum 75. Geburtstag am 10 Dezember 1966: Gedichte. Beiträge. Bibliographie* (Frankfurt a. M.: Suhrkamp, 1966), 191–97; Gabriele Fritsch-Vivié, *Nelly Sachs* (Reinbek: Rowohlt, 1993); Nelly Sachs, *Flucht und Verwandlung: Gedichte* (Stuttgart: Deutsche-Verlagsanstalt, 1959); Sachs, *O the Chimneys: Selected Poems, Including the Verse Play "Eli,"* trans. Michael Hamburger et al. (New York: Farrar, Straus and Giroux, 1967); Sachs, *Fahrt ins Staublose: Die Gedichte der Nelly Sachs* (Frankfurt a. M.: Suhrkamp, 1961); Dagmar C. Stern, *Hilde Domin: From Exile to Ideal* (Bern: Herbert Lang, 1979); Guy Stern, "In Quest of a Regained Paradise: The Theme of Return in the Works of Hilde Domin," *Germanic Review* 62 (1987): 136–42; and Bettina von Wangenheim, ed., *Heimkehr ins Wort: Materialien zu Hilde Domin* (Frankfurt a. M.: Fischer, 1982).

EHRHARD BAHR

1960 Paul Celan wins the Georg Büchner Prize

In Darmstadt on October 22, 1960, Paul Celan delivered an acceptance speech before the German Academy for Language and Literature, which had just awarded him the Georg Büchner Prize. This speech, later published under the title "Der Meridian" (The meridian), came to be regarded as Celan's most important poetological text. At the time of this publication, Paul Celan was almost forty years old. Born as Paul Antschel on November 23, 1920, in the city of Czernowitz, which was capital of the then Austro-Hungarian province of the Bukovina, Celan, like most of the Jews from that region, grew up in a linguistically and culturally German environment. During World War II he was interned in a Romanian work camp; his parents were murdered in a Nazi extermination camp. In 1945 he went first to Bucharest, then, in 1947, to Vienna, and one year later to Paris, where he lived until his death. On April 20, 1970, he threw himself into the Seine from the Pont Mirabeau, that same bridge made famous by Guillaume Apollinaire. In the meantime he had published a series of lyric collections that had made him the most significant German poet after 1945 and one of the greatest German poets of the twentieth century. Paul Celan's poetry grows out of the tension between the world-historical catastrophe to which he bears witness and the German language in which he writes. Paradoxically, there is much evidence that this tension that gave life to his writing also destroyed him.

In retrospect the Meridian speech appears both as the midpoint of Celan's poetic work and as the decisive turning point in his biography. Therefore we can use it as a point of departure for reconstructing his personal and poetic world. Even the external circumstances under which the speech was written and delivered reveal almost paradigmatically the problematic that governed his life and his art. On the one hand, the prize the academy had awarded him was an excellent indication of the recognition "official Germany" bestowed upon this Jewish poet, this Holocaust survivor whose parents had been murdered by the Nazis. On the other hand, the recognition from precisely this academy, which at that time had a considerable number of former Nazis among its members, could only have deeply disturbed him. Celan's anxiety comes out in the strangely convoluted rhetoric that characterizes the Meridian speech. The almost compulsive repetition of the address "Ladies and Gentlemen"; the complicated sentence structures with endless chains of clauses and dependent clauses; and the countless expressions of apology, retractions, and circumlocutions all attest to his inner discomfort on an occasion that must have reawakened his innermost doubts and deepest suffering.

The tension and anxiety occasioned by the Büchner prize was further exacerbated by another event. A few months earlier, in March 1960, Claire Goll, widow of the German Jewish poet Ivan Goll, had publicly accused Paul Celan of plagiarism. This accusation catalyzed a crisis for Celan that led to ever more acute psychological disturbances. At the time of the Darmstadt speech, he also began to connect the Goll affair with his fear of neo-Nazi tendencies in West Germany. But to what extent can these concerns explain the new emphasis he gave to his Jewish identity in numerous private statements during the 1960s? Regardless of the answer to this, for the first time in Celan's writings Jewish themes assume a central place in the 1963 collection *Die Niemandrose* (The no-one rose). In addition, in the collections *Atemwende* (Turn of breath; 1967), *Fadensonnen* (Threads of suns; 1968), and *Lichtzwang* (Force of light; 1970) there are many poems that—sometimes explicitly, sometimes implicitly—refer to motifs from Jewish mysticism, but above all to the ever-burning wound of the Jewish extermination. But the second part of the posthumously published volume *Zeitgehöft* (Timestead; 1976) constitutes the most significant corpus of Jewish-oriented poems and contains the poems Celan wrote after his visit to Jerusalem in the fall of 1969. Here, love poems, descriptions of Jerusalem landscapes, and meditations on themes from Jewish history and religious tradition combine in a way that lends the whole a tone of peace and tranquillity that is unusual for Celan.

It should be noted, however, that long before *Die Niemandrose* Celan had concerned himself directly with Jewish themes, and above all those related to his own biography—namely, the annihilation of the Jews in German extermination camps. This is apparent in the famous "Todesfuge" (Death fugue) from *Mohn und Gedächtnis* (Poppies and memory; 1952); the speech on the occasion of the Bremen literature prize (1958); the poem "Engführung" (Constriction), which concludes the volume *Sprachgitter* (Speech bars, 1959); and the prose text "Gespräch im Gebirg" (Conversation in the mountains), which was written a year before the Meridian speech.

All the more astonishing then is the fact that the theme of Judaism is not mentioned at all in the Meridian. The speech is dedicated from beginning to end to a single theme—namely, Celan's conception of poetry. At the center of this search for the essence of poetry stands the opposition Celan sets up between art and poetry. Art designates for Celan the sum of approaches, id-

ioms, tropes, and other technical means that lend the poem its "aesthetic" form. Over and against this general and impersonal aspect of the poem Celan places the uniqueness of the individual utterance, which for him characterizes poetry. For Celan every poem is a unique expression of a specific experience, and although the poem cannot circumvent the use of traditional modes of poetic language, it employs them only as a means to manifest itself as a completely personal expression. And in fact Celan's work cannot be traced back to a single common denominator. Every poem is an autonomous, unique construct that engenders its own language and its specific semantic code, so that each individual poem must be read *mit wechselndem Schlüssel* (with a changing key).

The opposition between the impersonal system of language and personal speech—that is, between the linguistic code and the particular subjective utterances of the speaking subject—was already the focus of "Gespräch im Gebirg." In this work, however, this opposition was portrayed in direct relation to the Jewish experience of language. By connecting the French linguist Emile Benveniste's theory of the difference between the impersonal system of language and its personalized appropriation via the speaking subject with Martin Buber's opposition between the language of the It and the language of the I-Thou, Celan reached an overarching antithesis between the anonymous language of nature, that language "without I and without Thou, only He, only It," and the language of dialogue in which one subject turns to another. This entirely subjective form of language, inscribed with the individual's personal experience, represented for Celan the traditional manner in which the Jews had always expressed themselves.

The French philosopher Emmanuel Lévinas interpreted this conception of speech as the turning toward an Other as the fundamental opposite to Heidegger's theory of language as the revelation of Being. This turn "from Being to the Other" (*de l'Être à l'Autre*) that Lévinas has highlighted in Celan's poetry is also at the center of the Meridian speech: "Das Gedicht steht im Geheimnis der Begegnung" (The poem stands in the mystery of the encounter), emphasizes Celan, and further: "Das Gedicht will zu einem Anderen, es braucht dieses Andere, es braucht ein Gegenüber" (The poem wants an Other, needs this Other, needs an opposite). By alluding to Buber—without mentioning him—and his philosophy of dialogue, Celan refuted the conception of the poem (advanced, for example, by Mallarmé) as a purely formal linguistic construct, and he opposed to that a different conception of poetic language, namely as a direct address of a speaking "I" to a listening "Thou." He thereby joined in the tradition of dialogical thinking from Eugen Rosenstock, Franz Rosenzweig, and Martin Buber up to Mikhael Bakhtin, Emile Benveniste, and Emmanuel Lévinas, which taken as a whole offers a position counter to the dominant semiotically oriented linguistic theories of the twentieth century.

All of Celan's poems thus appear as "substantiated language of an individual . . . , presence and present" (*gestaltgewordene Sprache eines Einzelnen . . . , Gegenwart und Präsenz*) (Celan 1983, 3:197). This means, first, that they are almost never written in the language of narration, which is grounded in the use of the third-person pronoun and the past tense, but rather in the language of discourse, which is characterized by the use of the pronouns "I" and "You" and is predominantly in the present tense. This "radical individuation" of language reflects an equally fundamental individuation of all tropes and metaphors that are more or less made anew in each poem in order to express "the uniqueness, the ever recurring uniqueness and only here and now perceived and perceptible" (*das einmal, das immer wieder einmal und nur jetzt und hier wahrgenommene und wahrzunehmende*) (3:1999).

If one follows the development of Celan's poetic language, one discovers that it became more and more compressed and elliptical over time. In *Mohn und Gedächtnis* (1952), his language is still situated in the realm of a modernism strongly influenced by Trakl and Rilke, in which traditional lyrical forms play a central role. This is also true to a certain extent in *Die Niemandrose* (1963), although the deconstruction of canonical forms of expression, the dissolution of traditional sentence structures, and the division of words already point toward the kind of poetic language that characterizes Celan's later work. From this point onward every poem generates its own language and becomes a unique example of its self-created new idiom. Each of these poems is like an elementary particle of language embodying an incredibly explosive poetic power.

It could well be that this gradual separation from the traditional forms of German lyric poetry expressed Celan's growing ambivalence toward the strictures of the German language itself. Two years prior to the Meridian speech, on the occasion of his acceptance of the Bremen literature prize, Celan had asked whether the German language was still capable of giving voice to true poetry and had answered this question affirmatively: "Attainable, near and not lost in the midst of loss this: language. It, language, remained, was not lost, yes, in spite of everything. But it had to go through terrible silence, go through the thousand darknesses of fatal speech. It went through and did not provide any words for what happened. But it went through this happening. Went through and was allowed to come back into light, enriched by it all" (Celan 1983, 3:185).

It is all the more surprising that this issue, so important for Celan, is not even touched upon in the Meridian speech. The question of his relationship to postwar Germany and the German culture industry occupied Celan so intensively that one could not assume that he had repressed it in the Meridian. It is more likely that this was a conscious avoidance, a decision not to reveal his most intimate doubts and concerns before a forum that would not understand them. Thus, if we want to use the Meridian speech as the basis for reconstructing the essence of Celan's poetics, we must also and perhaps above all take what is left unspoken in the speech as a point of departure.

Paul Celan's personal and poetic world can be understood only against the backdrop of the world-historical catastrophe whose witness and victim he was. The concept "world-historical" is used here in Heidegger's sense (cf. *Being and Time*, sec. 75), as that foundational dimension of historicity that unfolds beyond the division between external and internal history, and that reveals the fateful unity of Existence and World. It is precisely in this sense that Celan experienced and understood the Nazis' annihilation of the Jews: neither as the sum of the individual fates of the victims as reflected in the collective memory of the survivors, nor as the "objectively" describable historical event, but rather as a fundamental modality—namely that of the total destruction of the human in general—of the process in which the world "happens" in history. The world-historical extent of this catastrophe determines the ineradicability of the traces that it leaves in the soul of the poet. The wound that Celan's poems continually conjure up is this world-historical one: "Black / like the memory-wound" (Celan 1983, 2:57). As a metaphor of death and mourning but also as a metonymy of the burned, of ashes and of night, the color black in Celan's work always points toward the landscape of destruction: "Ashes. / Ashes, ashes. / Night-and-night" (1:199).

In the sense that Celan called up the memory of the victims and inscribed their names in his poetry, he cut a symbolic wound in the substance of language. The traces that the traumatic originary scene of destruction had left in his memory became graphic signs that subvert the written from inside. If the trauma continued to be influential for Celan and was able to crystallize into ever different poetic images it was because for him, as a historical and not as a private subject, something of the past dangers were still—or again—tangible. Like Walter Benjamin, Celan expressed historical commemoration in images "wherein the past comes together suddenly with the here-and-now." If "to articulate the past historically" meant for Benjamin "to seize hold of a remembrance that flashes in the moment of danger," then for Celan it meant not only to bring the past into immediate relationship with today's dangers, but also to perceive the present in light of (or rather in the shadow of) the trauma of the past.

Celan's correspondence with Nelly Sachs at the time of the Meridian speech reveals how intensely the suffering and mourning of the past lived on in his psyche. "The meridian of pain and consolation runs between Paris and Stockholm," Nelly Sachs wrote to him on October 28, 1959. What conjoined these two poets—besides the deep and genuine admiration that Sachs felt for the genius of her younger colleague—was a spiritual affinity grounded in their common experience as survivors of the genocide, as well as in their shared fascination with Jewish tradition and mysticism. But most of all their affinity was grounded in a similar sensitivity toward all indications of a possible renewed outbreak of persecution. In a letter of February 20, 1960, Paul Celan asked emphatically: "What still awaits us Jews?" Nelly Sachs, who herself suffered from tormenting delusions of persecution, responded to this a few months later as follows: "Yes, in actuality we belong to death." At that time Celan attempted to alleviate Sachs's fears with his friendship and empathy: "I sense that the evil that haunts you, that also haunts me, is gone, consigned to the substancelessness where it belongs." But he was unsuccessful in eluding his own anxiety. In "Voices," the first poem of the 1959 volume *Sprachgitter*, he relied on a traditional rabbinical saying to explain European anti-Semitism in light of the biblical story of the arch-enmity between Jacob and Esau, the two sons of Isaac. In this explanation, he traced the hatred of the Jews in the Christian West back to the primordial scene (Gen. 27:1–41) in which Jacob, the mythical forefather of the people of Israel, tricks his twin brother Esau, who in Jewish tradition represents the Roman Christian world, out of his birthright:

Jacob's voice:
The tears.
The tears in brother's eye.
One remained hanging, grew.
We live within it.
Breathe, so that
it falls.

Four years later, in the collection *Die Niemandrose*, this theme appears again, but this time in a completely different sense: the conciliatory interpretation of the biblical episode that characterizes the passage in the poem "Voices" has been displaced by a grim, even desperate one in the

poem "Eine Gauner- und Ganovenweise gesungen zu Paris emprès Pontoise von Paul Celan
aus Czernowitz bei Sadogora" (A manner of
crooks and thieves sung in Paris emprès Pontoise
by Paul Celan of Czernowitz near Sadogora). Here
Celan no longer takes Esau's perspective, but
rather that of Jacob, whose name in Hebrew can
also mean "the crooked one:" "Crooked was the
way that I went, / crooked it was, yes, / because,
yes, / it was straight."

The motto from Heinrich Heine's poem "To
Edom" that Celan uses as an epigraph to his own
poem also indicates the turn in Celan's perception
of European anti-Semitism: "Only sometimes, in
dark times." Edom, as one knows, is the biblical
name of a foreign kingdom that was situated on
the southern border of the land of Israel, but it is
also another name for Esau. Heine's poem "To
Edom" refers to the long tradition of Jewish persecution in Christian Europe and establishes the
context within which Celan's poem should be read:

Ein Jahrtausend schon und länger,
Dulden wir uns brüderlich,
Du, du duldest daß ich atme,
Daß du rasest, dulde Ich.

Manchmal nur, in dunklen Zeiten,
Ward dir wunderlich zu Mut,
Und die liebesfrommen Tätzchen
Färbtest du mit meinem Blut!

Jetzt wird unsre Freundschaft fester,
Und noch täglich nimmt sie zu;
Denn ich selbst begann zu rasen,
Und ich werde fast wie Du.

Paul Celan's position vis-à-vis Germany and
he Germans moves between these two attitudes:
the conciliatory (which comes out in the poem
"Voices") and the aggressive (which characterizes
the tone of "A Manner of Crooks and Thieves").
The poem "Todtnauberg" (from the 1970 volume
Lichtzwang) offers one of the most striking testi-
monials to this ambivalence. In this poem Celan
describes a visit with Martin Heidegger that took
place on July 25, 1967. Celan had long been a
reader of Heidegger's writings, and for his part,
Heidegger was a great admirer of Celan's poetry.

It would appear that during a stay in Freiburg
Celan let himself be persuaded to visit the German philosopher in his Black Forest retreat despite his awareness of Heidegger's pro-Nazi
stance. He had hoped that Heidegger would express words of responsibility, and in view of the
magnitude of the world-historical atrocity, perhaps even remorse, toward him as a Holocaust
survivor. This was obviously too much to be expected, and Celan's poem "Todtnauberg" (Celan
1983, 2:255), which mentions Heidegger's guest
book, clearly indicates that the hoped-for words
of responsibility and remorse were not spoken:

written into this book
this line of
a hope, today,
of a word
by a thinker
coming
in the heart.

Like most of the poems in the volume Lichtzwang, "Todtnauberg" was written immediately
after the event it depicts. There is much to indicate that Celan's poems almost always derive
from a direct experience, whether it be an encounter, a landscape, or something he had read. If
Mohn und Gedächtnis follows a predominantly aesthetic compositional principle, the series of
poems in his next volumes follow the chronology
in which they were written, so that one can read
Celan's lyric as a kind of poetic diary, inscribed
not only with the most diverse experiences but also
with daydreams, memories, and contemplations.

It is remarkable how well informed Celan was
in many areas—not only in world literature but
also in the sciences, where he had a knowledge of
physics, chemistry, biology, geology, and botany.
Above all, however, he was very familiar with
Jewish tradition and was an ardent reader of Ger-
shom Scholem's studies on Jewish mysticism.
Several of Celan's poems refer directly to specific
passages in Scholem's works (for example, "Of
Angel-Material" and "Orphaned in the Storm-
Trough"—which are both from the collection
Fadensonnen).

Celan's trip to Israel in October 1969 and especially his encounter with Jerusalem inspired a

series of poems where, for the last time, he expressed his doublerootedness in the world of Judaism and the world of Western culture. "I drink wine from two glasses" is how he described it. In an earlier poem "Hut-window" (from *Die Niemandrose*) he had coined the phrase "humans-and-Jews" in reference to the fate of the Jewish people. The double hyphen in this formula indicates the unavoidable duality of connection and separation that joins these two words together. Celan's poetry of memory moves within the realm of this duality: what has happened to the Jews has not only happened to them, but their fate exemplifies that of countless other human beings. In Celan's work the Jews stand for all of the nameless ones in whose memory "the historical construction is dedicated" (Benjamin 1972, vol. 1, no. 3, 1241).

Bibliography

Gerhart Baumann, *Erinnerungen an Paul Celan* (Frankfurt a. M.: Suhrkamp, 1986); Christiane Bohrer, *Paul Celan-Bibliographie* (Frankfurt a. M.: Peter Lang, 1989); Martine Broda, ed., *Contre-Jour: Études sur Paul Celan* (Paris: Cerf, 1986); Paul Celan, *Gesammelte Werke in fünf Bänden* (Frankfurt a. M.: Suhrkamp, 1983); Celan, *Paul Celan: Last Poems,* bilingual ed., trans. Kathrin Washburn and Margret Guillemin (San Francisco: North Point, 1986); Celan, *Paul Celan-Nelly Sachs: Briefwechsel* (Frankfurt a. M.: Suhrkamp, 1993); Israel Chalfen, *Paul Celan: Eine Biographie seiner Jugend* (Frankfurt a. M.: Insel, 1979); Amy D. Colin, ed., *Argumentum e Silentio: International Paul Celan Symposium* (Berlin: Walter de Gruyter, 1987); Jacques Derrida, *Schibboleth, pour Paul Celan* (Paris: Galilée, 1986); John Felstiner, *Paul Celan: Poet, Survivor, Jew* (New Haven: Yale University Press, 1995); Werner Hamacher and Winfried Menninghaus, eds., *Paul Celan* (Frankfurt a. M.: Suhrkamp, 1988); Dietlind Meinecke, ed., *Über Paul Celan* (Frankfurt a. M.: Suhrkamp, 1973); Winfried Menninghaus, *Paul Celan: Magie der Form* (Frankfurt a. M.: Suhrkamp, 1980); Peter Horst Neumann, *Wort-Konkordanz zur Lyrik Paul Celans* (Munich: Fink, 1969); Neumann, *Zur Lyrik Paul Celans* (Göttingen: Vandenhoeck und Ruprecht, 1968); Ilana Schmueli, "Denk dir: Paul Celan in Jerusalem," *Jüdischer Almanach 1995* (Frankfurt a. M.: Jüdischer Verlag bei Suhrkamp, 1994); Georg-Michael Schulz, *Negativität in der Dichtung Paul Celans* (Tübingen: Niemeyer, 1977); Thomas Sparr, *Celans Poetik des hermetischen Gedichtes* (Heidelberg: Carl Winter, 1989); and Peter Szondi, *Celan-Studien.* Frankfurt a. M.: Suhrkamp, 1975).

STÉPHANE MOSES

1964 On March 13, in the middle of rehearsals for the premiere of *Marat / Sade,* Peter Weiss attends the Frankfurt Auschwitz trial

Just like any other adolescent, young Peter Weiss wanted to fit in, he wanted to be like his friends and classmates, and he had the same goal as so many of them during the last years of the Weimar Republic: he wanted to be a part of the emerging new order. He was, after all, a regular German Protestant boy. His upbringing did not differ essentially from that of many of his generation. Born in 1916 in Nowawes near Berlin to cold, emotionally crippled parents, Weiss was raised in a repressive atmosphere, was humiliated by a sadistic teacher, and felt frightened and confused by the overheated homoerotic and sadistic activities prevalent among youth organizations, as well as by their paramilitary training (in which he nevertheless participated eagerly). Years later, in his autobiographical novels *Abschied von den Eltern* (Leave-taking; 1961) and *Fluchtpunkt* (Vanishing point; 1962), he described how elated he felt at being at one with power, at being at one with the new forces that were taking over the streets, and how he even participated in tormenting a Jewish classmate.

It was a short-lived elation. When, after January 1933, the Nazi salute was introduced in the schools, Peter Weiss was exempt from this regulation. All of a sudden, his identity as a normal and very German Christian schoolboy, an identity his parents had tried hard to construct, dissolved, leaving nothing but difference. For Weiss was not German after all: his father, originally a citizen of the Austro-Hungarian Empire, had chosen Czech citizenship after the war, and so had his family. Foreigners, it now turned out, were not allowed to give the Nazi salute. But his nationality was not the only aspect of Weiss's identity his parents had kept from him. Baptized and raised as a Christian, Weiss now had to learn that his father was a converted Jew. This did not make the son a Jew according to Jewish law, but by then the Jews' own definition of Jewishness had lost all relevance. Weiss was never to demonstrate any interest in the Jewish (or any other) religion, but he eventually developed a deep existential appreciation for his Jewish side, for it had prevented him from becoming a perpetrator and had linked him instead with the victims—of the Holocaust, as well as of the atrocities of colonialism, imperialism, and Stalinism.

In March 1935 the Weiss family went into exile to Chislehurst, near London. Weiss had started to paint at an early age and now decided, in spite of his difficult situation, to become a painter. In 1937 the family moved again, this time to Varnsdorf in the northern Bohemian region of Czechoslovakia. Thus, at age twenty, Peter Weiss came for the first time to the country whose citizenship he held, but whose language he did not speak. He was now an exile in his own country. He was studying painting at the Prague Art Academy when the Nazis occupied northern Bohemia (the Sudetenland) on October 1, 1938. The Weiss family escaped to Sweden.

In 1946 Peter Weiss obtained Swedish citizenship. Eventually, he became fluent in Swedish, the language in which he wrote his first significant literary works. Sweden is where he lived for the rest of his life, where he raised his family, and where he found a basis for his growing political commitment by joining the Swedish Communist Party in 1968. From Sweden he involved himself in the support of the struggle of the Vietnamese people and in the liberation movements in Angola, Central America, and South Africa. There he wrote all his important works. And there he remained, despite repeated plans for a (temporary) move to the Federal Republic of Germany. Never, though, was there a feeling of home. Sweden would remain exile, and exile would forever be experienced as an incurable affliction, as he once wrote in his notebooks. Together with the Austrian lyricist Erich Fried, Peter Weiss was among the youngest writers to be forced into exile by the rise of fascism, and, like Fried, he died in exile (in 1982).

For twenty years, until the mid 1950s, Weiss was a painter. This fact did not receive wide attention until the mid-1970s, when his work was exhibited in Sweden, in both Germanys, and in several European countries, and when several of his art books and articles were published. During his early years, Weiss experienced nearly insurmountable difficulties establishing himself on the Swedish art scene. Weiss's sense of self, continually undermined by his being a foreigner, a cultural outcast, and a Jew in a country that was sympathetic to Nazi Germany, remained fragile. He began to turn to writing. In a painstaking process, wherein at times he wrote his manuscripts simultaneously in Swedish, German, and even English, he eventually reclaimed his mother tongue. Still, it wasn't until 1959 that one of his texts, written eight years previously, was published in the Federal Republic of Germany by the prestigious Suhrkamp Verlag. *Der Schatten des Körpers des Kutschers* (The shadow of the coachman's body) gained Weiss, who was now forty-three, instant acclaim with the West German literati. Five years later his play *Marat / Sade* made him one of the few internationally famous writers in German during the postwar period.

On March 13, 1964, in the middle of rehearsals for the premiere of *Marat / Sade,* Weiss attended for the first time the proceedings of the "criminal case against Mulka et al.," which had gotten under way in Frankfurt am Main in December of the previous year. After the Allied trials at Nuremberg (1945–46) and the Eichmann trial in Jerusalem (1961), the Federal Republic finally held its own large-scale Nazi trial. It lasted for twenty months and ended in August 1965. Its main accomplishment, and indeed its main interest, lay not in the sentences eventually handed down to the twenty defendants, but rather in the interrogation of several hundred camp survivors and other witnesses. The trial produced the most minute, exhaustive testimony, corroborated over and over again, on the day-to-day workings of Nazi genocide.

It was not only the recognition of how easy it might have been for someone like himself to become one of the perpetrators that had brought Weiss to the Auschwitz trial. While in Prague, he had befriended a young fellow painter, Peter Kien, as well as a young woman, Lucie Weisberger. Weiss's last news of them, by which time he was long in Sweden, came from the Theresienstadt concentration camp. From Stockholm he attempted to rescue Lucie Weisberger, an effort that was bound to fail and that left him with indelible feelings of horror and guilt. After his insight into how close he had come to associating himself with the perpetrators, there was now the awareness of how close he had been to becoming a victim. The horror of both possibilities never again left him.

In the summer of 1964 Weiss wrote the fragment "Frankfurter Auszüge" (Frankfurt excerpts), his first attempt at finding a dramatic form for the Auschwitz trial. An almost verbatim transcription of some of the testimony from the actual trial, "Frankfurter Auszüge" was a first indication of the documentary style of the new play. In December of that year, Weiss visited Auschwitz. Shortly thereafter, he published his famous essay "Meine Ortschaft" (My place). In it, again using a documentary and seemingly emotionless style, Weiss registered what he saw at the former camp, down to the exact length and width of the spaces where the atrocities had been committed. Auschwitz, Weiss states here, "is a place for which I was destined but which I managed to avoid. I have had no experience of this place. I have no relation to it, except that my name was on the lists of the people who were supposed to be sent there forever" (Weiss 1967, 20). By the fall of 1965, Peter Weiss had become the world-famous dramatist of *Marat / Sade*. On October 19, his new play, *The Investigation,* opened simultaneously on more than a dozen stages in West Germany and—in a rare demonstration of unity—East Germany as well, which made that day a milestone not only in the history of the German theater, but also in the history of postwar Germany.

"We must drop the lofty view / that the camp world is incomprehensible to us." This not inappropriate demand of the present and future generations is made by the Third Witness in Peter Weiss's "Oratorio"—and became the subtitle of *The Investigation.* What, if not the hope of gaining some measure of understanding, would be the incentive for confronting the issue of mass extermination under fascism? *The Investigation* proceeds to destroy systematically any such hope. From one scene to the next, the play seems intent on revealing the complete and utter incomprehensibility of the events. In the face of a relentless succession of atrocities, any attempt at rational analysis appears to grow futile. But this dynamic is offset by a counter principle at work in *The Investigation,* one that Peter Weiss would formulate a few years later in the play *Trotzki im Exil* (Trotsky in exile; 1969): "When things are beyond rational comprehension, that's the very time we must apply our reason. It's our only weapon." *The Investigation* numbs one's faculties to reason while it encourages rational analysis.

From the outset Weiss was convinced that the events at Auschwitz defied portrayal on stage. This impossibility became even more evident when fellow dramatist Rolf Hochhuth's drama *Der Stellvertreter* (The deputy) premiered in 1963. The last act of this play about the pope's complicity in the extermination of the Jews takes place in Auschwitz. Hochhuth's attempt to shock by depicting mass extermination on stage natu-

ralistically, with crying children and barking guard dogs, appeared inadequate to many critics, including Weiss. Weiss's own solution took the opposite direction. He made every effort to dedramatize, deemotionalize, and formalize his play—to create distance between the events on stage and the viewers. *The Investigation* is not a historical drama about Auschwitz, but rather a play about the Frankfurt trial. There is no attempt to recreate events at the camp on stage, but only the present-day confrontation with them. There is no legal drama either, for Weiss had finished his play before the sentences were announced, and the play never mentions them. There is no plot, no action—there are no rounded characters, only people talking, most of whom use an impoverished, bureaucratic idiom.

In addition to his own notes of the trial, Weiss used a number of sources, chief among them Bernd Naumann's almost daily reports of the proceedings in the *Frankfurter Allgemeine Zeitung.* He adhered to his sources with great accuracy and often retained dialogue verbatim, down to the speech mannerisms of the trial participants. Because the events exceeded any superlative forms available in language, Weiss dispensed with the use of such forms, just as he dispensed with any attempts at artful linguistic characterization, as well as with images, metaphors, and even with the minimal dramatization provided by punctuation. All Weiss permitted himself was a slight rhythmization of the language. Even so, the material from 183 days of legal proceedings had to be reduced to a performable length: the hundreds of witnesses were reduced to nine; the number of judges, prosecuting attorneys, and counsels for the defense was reduced to one each. Still, it would be inaccurate to consider Weiss's artistic contribution in *The Investigation* minimal, as some critics at first suggested. The complex structure of the play has long since been revealed, specifically its debt to Dante's *Divine Comedy.* From the early 1960s until his death, Weiss attempted to create a *Divine Comedy* for his own time, and even though the project never materialized, it influenced all of his major works, foremost among them *The Investigation.*

Weiss's investigation of the hell of Auschwitz

begins with the arrival of the trains at the ramp and ends with the fire ovens. In between, witnesses and survivors describe in relentless detail the concrete, physical, material aspects of the Nazi genocide, from mass murder by gas, by shooting, by injection, and by starvation, down to individual cases of torture and death. And although the emphasis of the play is on the factory-like extermination of anonymous victims, at its exact center in acts five and six (of eleven) two individual fates are related: the death of a young woman, Lili Töffler; and the deeds of one Corporal Stark, a nineteen-year-old Nazi henchman who had not yet finished high school and who was just as easily inculcated with love of Goethe as with the most heinous behavior. The figure of Stark, in particular, draws attention to one of the main aspects of *The Investigation.*

The majority of victims in Auschwitz were Jews, as is known. Yet the word Jew is never uttered in the play, just as the word German, or the name Auschwitz, are ignored. Weiss systematically eliminated from his text any specific reference to nationality, race, or place. In early notes on the Frankfurt trial, Weiss still used words like Jews, Poles, Russians, and Gypsies. But his enduring awareness of how close he himself had come to being among the persecuted, as well as among the persecutors, ultimately affected the concept of the emerging play. In an interview given to the *New York Times* in October 1966, at the time of the opening of *The Investigation* on Broadway, Weiss insisted that Auschwitz could occur not only under German fascism. In *The Investigation,* he continued, it was not Jews who were being exterminated but human beings, and he added that given a "different twist of the historical kaleidoscope," many of the victims might have been on the side of the Nazis. This conviction is formulated in the play itself. The Third Witness, the most lucid and politically aware of all the figures in the play, states:

Many of those who were destined
to play the part of prisoners
had grown up
with the same ideas
the same way of looking at things

as those
who found themselves acting as guards

. . . .

And if they had not been designated prisoners
they could equally well have been guards
(Weiss 1966, 108).

The system of the camps, intended to destroy all humanity in the inmates, also destroyed the humanity of the camp personnel. This personnel consisted of average people, and if half of the defendants in Frankfurt were members of the working class, there also were physicians and dentists. None was ever accused of any sadistic or deviant behavior after the war had ended. In the Federal Republic they led normal lives, typically as train conductors or teachers. One of the most bestial became a nurse whom his patients trustingly called "Papa Kaduk" (Weiss 1966, 55). In interviews, Weiss repeatedly emphasized the averageness of these men, their banal and unremarkable lives. Weiss's position recalls Hannah Arendt's concept of the "banality of evil" in her book on the Eichmann trial in Jerusalem. In her introduction to Naumann's book on the Frankfurt trial she insisted once again that the atrocities in the camps had not been committed by "sadists in a clinical sense" but by "perfectly normal people" (Naumann 1965).

By insisting on the banality of the perpetrators, Weiss, like Arendt, draws attention to the system that produced such people and behind which they sought to hide by pleading "superior orders": "It was not my job / to question this purpose" (100), "I made no decisions / I had no such authority" (52), "But I only did what I had to do" (53). The accused reject the court's suggestion that they should have resisted or at least refused to carry out certain commands with their last and strongest argument, namely that they might have "risked the death penalty" (100), that anyone refusing to kill "would have been put up against the wall" (190). Had that indeed been true, all arguments would fail. Like their other excuses, however, these assertions are refuted. One witness states "that each one of the men in charge / could take a stand / against conditions in the camp / and change them" (58). The prosecuting attorney points out that there was no known instance of anyone having been punished for refusal to participate in the killings (195). Witnesses mention the names of individual guards who were able to preserve some degree of humanity as evidence that genocide could not have been carried out on such a scale, or at least could not have proceeded so smoothly, if there had been more such people. Absolute obedience, as Arendt has pointed out, indicates complete agreement with the laws and institutions of the state. In questions of morality, she insisted, there can be no appeal to obedience; it is one's duty to resist against, or at least withhold support from, an unlawful state. The same insight is conveyed by *The Investigation.*

Weiss did not entirely adhere to his concept of not mentioning nationalities. Most notable among the few exceptions is the mentioning, on several occasions, of "Soviet prisoners" (Weiss 1966, 149, 152 [twice], 225, 267). In a historical play about Auschwitz this might not have been remarkable. After all, the systematic decimation of the Soviet people under German fascism is beyond dispute. *The Investigation,* however, is to an important degree a play about the mid-1960s—a key period in the Cold War, which had become even more significant with the building of the Berlin Wall in 1961. In this atmosphere, the repeated reference to "Soviet prisoners" took on added significance, as Weiss intended. From his Swedish vantage point he wanted to draw attention to what he perceived as a disturbing continuity. The West Germans, he noted in a letter to fellow writer Hans Werner Richter, had never relinquished their hatred. In the Cold War they had merely switched its object from the Jews to the Communists of Eastern Europe and particularly of the Soviet Union. Weiss reminded Richter that the Nazis had intended to destroy the Communists even before they exterminated the Jews. The anti-Communism of the sixties, Weiss wrote, was but a continuation, under changed historical circumstances, of a paramount tenet of fascist ideology. The frequent reference to Soviet prisoners of war was intended to draw attention to this fact.

The similarities between the Nazi state and the Federal Republic of the sixties is one of the recurring themes of the play. These similarities reflected a continuity not only of anti-Communism but also of the economic institutions that had led to fascism. Industries had been set up in the vicinity of the camp where prisoners were forced to labor until their death (which usually occurred within a few weeks). Some of the companies are mentioned by name: "They were branch plants / of IG Farben / Krupp and Siemens" (Weiss 1966, 6). The yearly revenue of these firms, as revealed by the prosecutor, amounted to several billion marks (131). The industry also made profits from the extermination itself. Mentioned in the play is Degesch, the company that supplied the gas (229); the German version of the play also mentions Topf und Söhne, the firm that built the crematoriums. In addition to these "traditional" forms of profit-making, there was a third form of capitalist exploitation: the prisoners themselves were processed as industrial raw materials. After death, jewelry worth hundreds of millions of German marks was removed; the hair was shorn, bundled, and put into bags; and gold teeth were removed. Finally, flesh was cut out of some of the corpses (182) for use in bacteriological experiments (200). Surrounded by other factories, Auschwitz was itself a factory and, like the others, it supplied products necessary for the war.

In the course of the Auschwitz trial, Weiss's interest was increasingly directed toward the fact that these economic powers continued to exist and toward the profits they had derived from the extermination of human beings. In the play, witnesses for the defense, such as a former chairman of the board of one of the industries located in Auschwitz, are repeatedly revealed to be living in the Federal Republic in great comfort, even in extreme wealth. At the time of the trial the chairman was drawing a huge annual pension from his former company and living in a palace where he collected precious objects (Weiss 1966, 129). Examples like this eventually reveal a supra-individual pattern of continuities that extended to some of the most important industries of the Federal Republic. The investigation of the past turns into an investigation of the present of the year

1965; Weiss's critique of fascism becomes a critique of the role capitalism played in the camps, a critique that is emphatically extended to the capitalist system of the Federal Republic. All the facts about this continuity were in the public domain. But in the prevalent political climate, the play's arguments about economic continuity were exaggerated by some of Weiss's critics, and a strident public debate turned *The Investigation* into a key work of the Cold War.

Apparently, however, most spectators did not experience the play as a commentary on contemporary politics. At the end of performances of *The Investigation* in West Germany, there generally was no applause. Audiences often sat quietly for minutes, then slowly filed out. They had just seen a play about the Nazi Holocaust, the details and extent of which, at least until the Frankfurt trial, had been little known or debated by much of the population, who had been busy rebuilding the country and creating a *Wirtschaftswunder* (economic miracle). *The Inability to Mourn* is how in 1967 Alexander and Margarete Mitscherlich titled their well-known study of West German society, and this phrase fits the general reaction to *The Investigation*. Reviewers of the play in newspapers and journals, however, often neglected the play's main focus in order to attack Weiss's critique of capitalism and his accusations of economic continuity. The attacks were all the more vituperative because only a few weeks prior to the premiere of *The Investigation*, Weiss had published an essay entitled "10 Arbeitspunkte eines Autors in der geteilten Welt" (An author's ten working-points in the divided world), in which he had explained his turn toward socialism. He was now accused of disturbing the economic order of the Federal Republic, of abusing the Holocaust for political agitation, of having put Auschwitz in the service of the Cold War, and even of having placed "Auschwitz in the service of the Ulbricht Reich" (Walter Ulbricht was head of the German Democratic Republic [GDR] from 1960 to 1973).

In the GDR, too, as was inevitable at the time, the intentions of the play were at times distorted. The critique of West German capitalism was emphasized to the exclusion of most other aspects of *The Investigation*, and Auschwitz was treated as a problem that concerned mostly *West* Germans. Such pronouncements distracted from the GDR's own shortcomings in confronting anti-Semitism and the Holocaust. Still, it is worth noting that on the day of the premiere of *The Investigation*, the GDR held a quasi-official reading at the Academy of Arts in East Berlin in which leading writers, actresses, and politicians—such as Stephan Hermlin, Helene Weigel, and Alexander Abusch—participated. This act of state was fitting given the importance of *The Investigation* for both Germanys.

After its enormous initial success—subsequent to the premiere, *The Investigation* was staged in many more theaters in both West and East Germany—the play disappeared from German stages for a dozen years. It was not until 1979, on the occasion of the thirtieth anniversary of the Federal Republic, that *The Investigation* was staged again, in the small West German city of Moers. When this production was brought to Berlin in 1980, it once again provoked a scandal. It was set in a sleazy night club and performed as a kind of cheap TV talk show. The actors represented third-rate entertainers who, as the play proceeds, become increasingly drunk and end up showing obvious sympathy for the perpetrators. Expanding one of the play's main themes, this new staging focused almost exclusively on contemporary attitudes toward the Holocaust: of playing down its extent, of insisting that everybody merely did their duty, and of declaring that Germans had had enough of endlessly being reminded of the Nazi genocide. Of the critical voices that characterized this production as embarrassing, disgusting, and perverted, the most weighty was that of Heinz Galinski, head of the Jewish community of West Berlin, who termed it an insult to the millions of dead and called for its cancellation. This led to the intervention of Peter Weiss from Sweden, who, even though he had not seen the production (no more than had Galinski), declared valid this radical attempt at confronting Germans with their attitudes toward the Holocaust. Thus *The Investigation* had once again revealed its power to disturb, provoke, anger, and stir debate about the history of Germany, past and present.

Bibliography

Robert Cohen, *Understanding Peter Weiss* (Columbia: University of South Carolina Press, 1993); Sidra De-Koven Ezrahi, *By Words Alone: The Holocaust in Literature* (Chicago: University of Chicago Press, 1980); Manfred Haiduk, *Der Dramatiker Peter Weiss* (Berlin: Henschelverlag, 1977); Karl-Heinz Hartmann, "Peter Weiss: Die Ermittlung. Der Frankfurter Prozess und das Stück," *Deutsche Dramen,* ed. Harro Müller-Michaels, vol. 2 (Königstein / Taunus: Athenäum, 1981), 163–83; Andreas Huyssen, "The Politics of Identification: 'Holocaust' and West German Drama," *New German Critique* 19 (1980): 117–36; Rolf D. Krause, *Faschismus als Theorie und Erfahrung: 'Die Ermittlung' und ihr Autor Peter Weiss* (Frankfurt a. M.: Peter Lang, 1982); Bernd Naumann, *Auschwitz: Bericht über die Strafsache gegen Mulke und andere vor dem Schwurgericht Frankfurt* (Frankfurt a. M.: Athenäum, 1965); Alvin H. Rosenfeld, *A Double Dying: Reflections on Holocaust Literature* (Bloomington: Indiana University Press, 1980); Erika Salloch, *Peter Weiss' Die Ermittlung* (Frankfurt a. M.: Athenäum, 1972); Ernst Schumacher, "'Die Ermittlung' von Peter Weiss," *Über Peter Weiss,* ed. Volker Canaris (Frankfurt a. M.: Suhrkamp, 1976), 69–91; Thomas von Vegesack, "Dokumentation zur 'Ermittlung'," *Kürbiskern* 2 (1966): 74–83; Gerd Weinreich, *Peter Weiss: Die Ermittlung* (Frankfurt a. M.: Diesterweg, 1983); Peter Weiss, *The Investigation,* trans. Jon Swan and Ulu Grosbard (New York: Atheneum, 1966); Peter Weiss "My Place," trans. Christopher Middleton, *German Writing Today,* ed. Christopher Middleton (Harmondsworth: Penguin, 1967), 20–28; and James E. Young, *Writing and Rewriting the Holocaust: Narrative and the Consequences of Interpretation* (Bloomington: Indiana University Press, 1988).

ROBERT COHEN

1965 The premiere of Peter Weiss's *The Investigation: Oratorio in Eleven Songs,* a drama written from the documentation of the Frankfurt Auschwitz trial, is staged

On December 20, 1963, the city of Frankfurt am Main witnessed the beginning of the trial of twenty-two former SS members active in the concentration camp at Auschwitz-Birkenau. For over a year and a half, the court heard testimony from 409 witnesses relating to twenty-two defendants and their alleged actions. On August 19, 1965, the court convicted seventeen of the defendants to prison sentences ranging from three years and three months to life imprisonment. Three defendants were acquitted; one died before he could be brought to trial; another was excused because of illness. This trial was only one of many postwar juridical actions against perpetrators of National Socialist crimes, but it was surely one of the most infamous. The first Nuremberg trials, which had been conducted by the Allies after the war in 1946, had dealt with leaders of the Nazi criminal regime, as well as with industrialists who had participated in crimes against humanity. And the Eichmann trial in Israel from April 11 to December 15, 1961, had attracted worldwide attention because it brought to justice one of the foremost planners of the Holocaust, who had been spectacularly captured and furtively transported from Argentina in 1960. But the so-called Auschwitz trial, conducted entirely by the German judicial system, was perhaps more significant because it dealt in horrific and graphic detail with the concentration camp that has now become metonymically identified with the genocidal plans of Nazi Germany. The first major concentration camp trial, the proceedings in Frankfurt were the result of inquiries by the Central Office for Investigation of National Socialist Crimes, which had been established in Ludwigsburg in 1958. Until that time there was no coordinated effort by German authorities or by the individual ministers of justice in the separate German states to proceed against former Nazis. Even worse, there was little sympathy for pursuing persons involved in the mass murders of the Third Reich; before the Auschwitz trial, it seemed likely that the statute of limitation would not be extended for murders committed under the auspices of the National Socialists. In part, the notoriety surrounding the court proceedings in Frankfurt contributed to a new public consciousness concerning the Nazi past and initiated further concentration camp trials when the German parliament eventually voted to extend the statute of limitations for Nazi crimes.

In attendance at the Auschwitz trial on March 13, 1964, was the writer and dramatist Peter Weiss, whose play *Marat / Sade* (1964), then in the midst of rehearsals, was to become a German, and then an international success. Attracted to the drama of the court proceedings and fascinated by the possibility of condensing the masses of material into a structure suitable for the stage, Weiss determined shortly thereafter to compose a play based largely on the documents from the Frankfurt trial. He composed a first sketch during the summer of 1964, the *Frankfurter Auszüge* (Frankfurt excerpts). In

December 1964 he traveled to Poland to visit Auschwitz (Oświęcim) and composed a prose text, *Meine Ortschaft* (My place), which recounted his experiences and feelings. In contrast to *The Investigation, Meine Ortschaft* is a personal text: Weiss recognized that he, like millions of other Jews from across Europe, was destined for Auschwitz, but that he was able to escape the fate of his coreligionists. He left with a debt to those who perished to understand their deaths and to make their sufferings known to a broad public. Weiss, in short, determined to enhance the public nature of the discourse around Auschwitz and the crimes of National Socialism by making the documents of the trial known to a wider audience. His self-conceived task was originally to open discussion and debate around the German past; accordingly his play premiered simultaneously in fifteen German cities and was often followed by intense discussions with the audience.

Weiss's dramatic rendition of the Frankfurt trials is therefore a continuation and an intensification of the *Vergangenheitsbewältigung* (mastering of the past) that had occurred only sporadically in the German public sphere until the 1960s. In its initial phases, Germany dealt with the past in one of two ways: either the past was repressed and energies were devoted to the rebuilding of the divided nation, or the war and the Holocaust were viewed primarily as the result of a moral failing on the part of the German people or of individuals in key social and political positions. The former position was analyzed most consistently by the psychoanalysts Alexander and Margarete Mitscherlich, whose book *The Inability to Mourn* (1967) discusses the psychological mechanisms that have prevented Germans from facing their responsibilities for the war and the genocidal activities of the National Socialism regime. The Mitscherlichs postulated that the German people entered into a strong cathartic bond with Hitler, and that in the postwar era they lived in a collective state of denial. The consequence of this mass psychological neurosis is a failure to confront a precarious relationship to authority and a concomitant inability to mourn the true victims of the Third Reich. The moral response is typified in *The Question of German Guilt,* written

by Karl Jaspers in 1946. Jaspers opposed the collective guilt thesis and advocated an individual accountability based on a differentiated model of guilt. Most important for him, however, were the notions of moral and metaphysical guilt, over which the individual conscience and the deity have authority. In his view, only a personal soul-searching and a quasi-religious penance will bring about the requisite cleansing of Germany and enable a healthy national development. Jaspers was, however, a lonely voice in calling for a moral revival. Although we can find evidence that some German writers—for example, the early Heinrich Böll—shared his ethical concerns, his plea for accountability was largely ignored by the German populace.

Perhaps the relative lack of reflection on the atrocities of the Third Reich in the first decade and a half after the war contributed to the rise of documentary forms of cultural production in the 1960s. Documentation of the Holocaust in order to influence a targeted audience was, of course, not new. Immediately after the war Germans were made to watch films of concentration camps in order to impress on the incredulous populations the extent of the criminal behavior of their country. And among the first films dealing with the Holocaust was Alain Resnais's *Night and Fog* (1955), which used extensive documentation to acquaint its audience with the universe of concentration camps. Indeed, the postwar discussion of the Holocaust, more than any other event, has been intimately linked with data, facts, reports, film footage, eyewitness reports by survivors and perpetrators, and other forms of documentation. Part of this obsession with documentation is no doubt connected with the National Socialists' own fetishism with bureaucracy and files. In *The Investigation,* one of the witnesses tells of how the Germans insisted that their office personnel— women inmates—keep meticulous records of the genocide: "We had to keep the death lists up to date. . . . We had to enter the particulars . . . relating to date and cause of death. . . . The entries had to be made . . . with absolute accuracy. . . . Mr. Broad grew furious . . . if he found a single mistake in our typing." But the more salient reason for the reliance on documents, even in many "creative" works, was the feeling that the facts offered the best possible vehicle to a genuine understanding of events that were otherwise unbelievable. Documentation in written or pictorial form appeared to guarantee a fidelity to what actually occurred, and it simultaneously provided a testimony to those who suffered and perished. It was the most adequate mode of presentation for portraying to an audience the enormity and horror of the Shoah. With regard to the Holocaust more than with any other historical event, the facts appeared to speak for themselves.

The new provocative mood of the 1960s was inaugurated by a play that appeared two years before Weiss's *Investigation,* Rolf Hochhuth's *The Deputy.* Based on extensive documentation and drawing on real historical personages, *The Deputy* achieved international renown because of its implicit accusation that the pope had not intervened strongly enough on behalf of the Jews, and that he therefore shared a portion of the responsibility for the Holocaust. Facts were thus important for Hochhuth, because he was building a historical argument, and his drama is accordingly filled with them. To emphasize his documentary concerns, Hochhuth included at the close of his drama a section of "Historical Sidelights," in which he cited approximately forty sources for the preceding play and mentioned that these represent only "a fragment of the available collection of material." The materials that are cited give us an insight into Hochhuth's practice as a playwright. It is obvious that he studied the memoirs, biographies, diaries, letters, speeches, and legal protocols that pertain to the Jewish Question under the Third Reich before framing his play. What he wrote is therefore thoroughly documented in the sense that every major scene and action, every reference and allusion, has a basis in historical materials. Rather than composing a history of the Jewish Question with regard to the Catholic Church or a treatise on Pope Pius XII's positions on the extermination of the Jews during World War II, Hochhuth fashioned his "facts" into dramatic form, insisting that "the author of the play has only allowed free play to his imagination when it was necessary to transform the available historical raw material into a form suitable

for the stage" (Hochhuth 1963, 269). To an extent the documents become more important than the dramatic action; the lengthy stage directions, which include historical discussions and extensive descriptions of the history and fate of various chapters, indicate not only Hochhuth's obsession with historical accuracy, but also his inability to find a form adequate for his immense subject. Unwilling to compromise history for the sake of drama, Hochhuth was ultimately unable to accommodate his tale within the traditional forms of dramatic representation.

Weiss's play, by contrast, is both more faithful to documents and more innovative in formal terms. Hochhuth constructed a story based on conventional dramatic structures such as exposition, complication, climax, denouement, and tragic end. He employed his documents as ammunition in the speeches of the various characters, in stage directions, or in his lengthy prose conclusion. Weiss abandoned traditional dramatic structure and constructed his drama around a creative citation and adaptation of the documents themselves. He did not aim to reconstruct or to invent a narrative of events, but instead sought to recount in systematic form various aspects of the concentration camp. His eleven "acts," called "songs," start with testimony on the ramp and the physical structure of the camps, proceed through accounts of various persons, procedures, and instruments of death, and end with the crematorium.

Instead of recreating a possible historical occurrence during the war, as Hochhuth does, Weiss allowed the reports taken from the Auschwitz trial to reflect on the past, and his drama consists almost entirely of the speeches of the accused, witnesses, prosecutors, defense attorneys, and judges. There are almost no stage directions, and Weiss provided only a short authorial note at the beginning of the play. The method he used is one of condensation, a "concentration" (*Konzentrat*) of statements, as Weiss himself wrote, playing eerily on the word concentration camp (*Konzentrationslager*). The 409 witnesses are reduced to an anonymous nine; eighteen of the original twenty-two defendants appear in the play; and the year and a half of testimony, which totals thousands of pages, is presented in un-rhymed, unpunctuated, and largely arrhythmic verse on fewer than two hundred pages. To insure a variety of response, Weiss often took testimony from different parts of the trial, which sometimes related to different historical persons or occur-rences, and adapted it to create a more coherent event involving a single individual. For example, in the section on Lili Töffler, a young woman killed for passing a letter to a friend, the play attributes to her a remark actually made by Mala Zinetbaum, a woman who escaped from the camp, was captured, and, in defiance of her cap-tors, committed suicide before she could be hanged. At the end of the first part of the "Song of the Camp," the child that shouts to the SS guard, "You won't be forgiven / anything," is a compos-ite of two children drawn from Weiss's sources. The condensation and simplification is justified because Weiss believed that the experiences of the concentration camp inmates were largely in-terchangeable. In the brief introductory note he wrote: "Personal experience and confrontations must be steeped in anonymity. Inasmuch as the witnesses in the play lose their names, they be-come mere speaking tubes. The nine witnesses sum up what hundreds expressed." Although the defendants retain their identities, they too are more important as vehicles for establishing facts than as illustrations of moral depravity or of gross disregard for human life in Auschwitz: the ac-cused have merely "lent their names which, within the drama, exist as symbols of a system that implicated in its guilt many others who never appeared in court." Weiss was uninterested in the individuals, in individual psychology, and in personal histories; his use of three legal officials (a prosecutor, a defense attorney, and a judge), nine witnesses, and eighteen accused is arbitrary and related only to the multiples of three that abound in *The Investigation*. Weiss combined the testimony of actual witnesses to create characters who convey the nature of the system to which individuals belong.

There is thus a tension present in Weiss's play between empirical reality as recorded in docu-ments and supra-individual structures and ideol-ogies as they are constructed in Weiss's creative use of documents. This tension is manifested in the play on several levels. The title, for example, conveys very strongly the sense of facts and docu-mented occurrences. *Ermittlung* is the German word for police investigations that are conducted to ascertain whether or not a crime has been com-mitted. It conveys the meaning of finding some-thing out, of getting all the facts on the table so that a determination can be made about the possi-bility of prosecuting for an offense. The actual *Ermittlung* for the Auschwitz trials was done well before the case came before the court in 1963. In addition, Weiss usually did not cite from docu-ments created during the actual investigatory stage, but from the courtroom proceedings them-selves. His use of the term *Ermittlung* thus dis-tances his work from the trial: his play is obvi-ously investigating some other offense. It is therefore understandable that Weiss did not use the most obvious and accurate title for his drama: the trial (*der Prozeß*). Indeed, Weiss steered his production away from recreating not only Ausch-witz on stage, but also the Auschwitz trial. There are no opening statements or lists of alleged viola-tions of law—and at the close of the play there are no verdicts and sentencing of the convicted, no legal justification for the findings of the court. Weiss's goal was obviously not to accuse the per-petrators once again on stage; he was relatively unconcerned with the guilt and innocence of these men as individuals. Moreover, he did not want his play to simulate closure, as a trial does. Although he set up a rough narrative of experi-ence starting with the arrival in Auschwitz and ending with the crematories, the investigatory aspect of the play does not bring us to any conclu-sions. We are left instead with documented facts.

The subtitle, however, points to the other facet of Weiss's play—his creative employment of documents. The notion that the documents can be arranged into an "Oratorio in Eleven Songs" makes the reader aware of the constructed nature of the drama, and perhaps, by extension, of the constructed nature of the camps and the events that occurred there. An oratorio is a musical pro-duction of a sacred story using voice and orches-tra. It is dramatic, in the sense that it recounts a tale with various parts and personae, but in contrast to an opera, for example, it narrates without the use of scenery, costume, or actions on stage. Weiss's play conforms to the outer structure of an oratorio in that the various witnesses and defendants simply recite their speeches. In his introductory note, Weiss makes it clear that he is not striving to recreate the courtroom in which the trial took place, and that such a recreation would be just as impossible as the recreation of the concentration camp itself. The oratorio form also suggests a degree of seriousness that is appropriate for Weiss's theme. Like works in this religious tradition, Weiss is dealing with events and persons that should have a profound effect on the audience. But Weiss's oratorio is obviously a modern and a secular variant. There are no heroes or saints populating the pages of *The Investigation;* there is no redemption and salvation. The cast of characters is largely anonymous, and their actions are far removed from anything sacred or holy. Nonetheless, the suggestion that the play is an oratorio contrasts sharply with the juridical notion of the main title. Together title and subtitle reflect the dual use of the raw materials for the play: to document the facts of history and to construct a new, nonmimetic reality different from that history.

The play itself continues this tension between documentary evidence and the construction of an artistic work. On the most basic level, Weiss sought to emphasize Auschwitz in all its facticity. In "The Song of the Platform," for example, Weiss reproduced for us through testimony details about the length of the platform (850 yards long), the length of the trains that stopped there ("They usually took up about two thirds / of the platform"), the site of the selections ("In the middle of the platform") and the width of the platform ("about 30 feet wide"). In these passages we get an impression of the camp as a concrete, material entity. Similarly, in "The Song of the Swing," we receive a rather graphic description of this instrument of torture and how the prisoners were bound to it:

First the prisoner had
to sit down on the floor
and draw up his knees

His hands were tied in front
and then pushed down over his knees
Then they shoved the pipe in the space
between the arms and knees
Then the pipe was raised and set into the wood
    frame.

Like an investigator, Weiss appears to search out minute details in the reports; the text is filled with numbers and statistics concerning everything from the size of the bunks, the number of calories consumed, and the size of the trains, to the distance between prisoners being shot at the wall, the amount of Zyklon B delivered to the camp, and the dimensions of the crematories. The audience is bombarded with facts and figures, and although no amount of description can recreate the horrors of the camp or its experience, the documents on which Weiss draws seem to account for every detail.

This almost obsessive focus on the facticity of Auschwitz is situated within a structure that suggests the unreality of the documented occurrences. Weiss himself and numerous commentators have noted that *The Investigation* is modeled on Dante's *Inferno*. Weiss was not the first author to recognize the parallels between the hell portrayed by his illustrious Italian predecessor and the world of the concentration and extermination camps, but he may have been the writer who took the comparison most seriously—in particular with regard to form. Like Dante, Weiss wrote a work consisting of eleven cantos or songs, each of which is divided into three parts. As in the *Divine Comedy,* the number three and its multiples recur throughout *The Investigation,* determining, as we have already noted, the number of witnesses, accused, and court personnel.

But it is also evident that the *Inferno* is merely a structural device to assist Weiss in his work of condensation: his use of the Dantean framework is as an external framework, rather than a reflection of a world view. The symmetry in Dante's poem refers the reader to the harmonious universe maintained and ordained by the deity. The *terza rima* employed by the Italian poet is an intricate unifying device on the level of each line; it is a verse form that not only adds another structure of three, but also links each tercet to the next. Weiss did not attempt to follow Dante here: his "songs" are unrhymed and unmetered; lines and "songs" have different lengths. On the level of detail, Weiss appears to admit a chaos that diverges strongly from Dante's encompassing accord. In the modern drama, the exterior system is not matched by a harmonious interior. The secularized hell of Auschwitz may be cast in the form borrowed from a sacred model, but there is neither peace nor salvation as content or telos in the universe Weiss portrayed. The construction borrowed from medieval Italy exists in tension with the content drawn from Central Europe in the mid-twentieth century.

This tension between document and construction in the title and the structure is found on the level of message as well. Although the documents tell the story of Auschwitz, Weiss does not assemble them into a drama primarily for the purpose of admonishing Germany, publicizing the crimes committed against the Jews, or condemning the Nazi regime. The very fact that the words "Jew" or "Jewish" never occur in the play, and that there is a paucity of information about mechanisms of racism in Germany, is a good indication that Weiss's point lies in another realm. One of the indications of Weiss's intention in constructing this play is his frequent reference to the current activities of the accused. In the very first part of the initial song, we encounter a witness who is now the superintendent of the government railroads. During the war his job also had to do with trains; he was responsible for the delivery of "freight" to the death camps. He accomplishes his job with efficiency now, as he did then. In a later song, another witness relates that his "assignment was / to keep an eye on the guards / to see they carried out their charge / diligently and faithfully." He further claims that guards were not rewarded for shooting prisoners trying to escape, but the court produces a document with his signature that proves the contrary. Today this witness is the director of an insurance company, where he applies the same diligence that served him so well in Auschwitz. We learn in "The Song of Zyklon B II" that Dr. Capesius, the head of the dispensary that stored the Zyklon B death gas,

now owns his own pharmacy and a beauty parlor, probably purchased with money stolen from murdered prisoners. Kaduk, obviously one of the brutal guards, is today a hospital attendant, loved by his patients, who call him "Papa Kaduk." The people who ran the extermination machinery seem to have had little trouble adjusting to civilian life in the Federal Republic. Their unproblematic integration into postwar society indicates a fundamental similarity between the factories of death and those of the postwar economic miracle. Weiss is thematizing more than the banality of evil about which Hannah Arendt wrote after the Eichmann trial. He is connecting the logic of fascism with an underlying inhumanity in the capitalist order of Germany and the industrialized world.

It is not insignificant, therefore, that the central theme of *The Investigation* is articulated most clearly by the Third Witness, whose statements are not drawn from any documentary source. In the second part of the "Song of the Possibility of Survival," which Weiss himself called the "center of the play," this witness presents in condensed form the thesis crafted from the documents: the logical nature of oppression in the camps is an extension of oppression outside the camps. Auschwitz is thus not exceptional, but is a more drastic manifestation of what already existed in German (capitalist) society and what continues to exist to the present day. The Third Witness first notes the hermetic nature of the camp, the interchangeability of guards and prisoners, and their mutual implication in a system based on hierarchy and injustice. In contrast to the common contention that Auschwitz was an exceptional situation, incomprehensible to the world, he claims that it was an extension of what was—and is—familiar to everyone:

We must drop the lofty view
that the camp world
is incomprehensible to us
We all knew the society
that produced a government
capable of creating such camps
The order that prevailed there
was an order whose basic nature

we were familiar with
For that very reason
we were able to find our way about
in its logical and ultimate consequence
where the oppressor
could expand his authority
to a degree never known before
and the oppressed
was forced to yield up
the fertilizing dust of his bones.

Weiss's analysis of Auschwitz, placed in the mouth of the witness he would have been had he himself been a survivor, is that the extermination camps were an extreme manifestation of an order based on oppressed and oppressors, a limit case for what occurs on an everyday basis in our own world. His view is essentially the same as that of Theodor W. Adorno, who remarked in 1959: "We will not have come to terms with the past until the causes of what happened then are no longer active. Only because these causes live on does the spell of the past remain, to this very day, unbroken." For both Adorno and Horkheimer, the essence of Auschwitz lies in the society that produced it.

The tension between documentation and construction that permeates Weiss's drama has consequences for his message as well. Although Weiss carefully arranges the testimony, questions, and remarks from his sources to support his main thesis, and although he even invents a witness as his own mouthpiece, the documented testimony of the Nazi genocide winds up overwhelming the thesis connecting past crimes with present society and thereby indicting capitalist logic as the root cause of the Holocaust. The graphic descriptions of the torture, mutilation, and death of countless individuals; the sadistic brutality and inhumanity of the camp personnel; and the squalid, depraved circumstances in which the prisoners were compelled to live ultimately vitiate the ideological premise on which the drama is based. The voice of the Third Witness is drowned out by the din of those who testify and the silence of the millions unavailable for testi-

mony. Composed on a contrast between documentary facticity and constructed representation, *The Investigation* is itself a testimony to the power of the documentary form in dealing with the Holocaust and, simultaneously, to the impotence of documentation to convey an intelligible, cohesive story. Like prior and subsequent endeavors to harness this unique event as evidence for a political or ideological conviction, Weiss's play demonstrates again the impossibility of such an appropriation. With regard to the Holocaust, the very nature of the documented reality removes us temporarily from our historical situatedness—exploding time, place, and the prospect of coherent representation.

Bibliography

H. G. Adler et al., *Auschwitz: Zeugnisse und Berichte* (Frankfurt a. M.: Europäische Verlagsanstalt, 1962); Theodor W. Adorno, "What Does Coming to Terms with the Past Mean?" *Bitburg in Moral and Political Perspective*, ed. Geoffrey H. Hartman (Bloomington: Indiana University Press, 1986), 114–29; Hannah Arendt, *Eichmann in Jerusalem: A Report on the Banality of Evil* (New York: Viking, 1963); Ilan Avisar, *Screening the Holocaust: Cinema's Images of the Unimaginable* (Bloomington: Indiana University Press, 1988); Robert Cohen, *Understanding Peter Weiss* (Columbia: University of South Carolina Press, 1993); Rolf Hochhuth, *The Deputy* (New York: Grove, 1964); Hochhuth, *The Representative*, trans. Robert David MacDonald (London: Methuen, 1963); Karl Jaspers, *The Question of German Guilt* (New York: Capricorn, 1947); Rolf D. Krause, *Faschismus als Theorie und Erfahrung: "Die Ermittlung" und ihr Autor Peter Weiss* (Frankfurt a. M.: Peter Lang, 1982); Alexander and Margarete Mitscherlich, *The Inability to Mourn* (New York: Grove, 1975); Bernd Naumann, *Auschwitz: Bericht über die Strafsache gegen Mulka und andere vor dem Schwurgericht Frankfurt* (Frankfurt a. M.: Athenäum, 1965); Erika Salloch, *Peter Weiss' "Die Ermittlung": Zur Struktur des Dokumentartheaters* (Frankfurt a. M.: Athenäum, 1972); Peter Weiss, *The Investigation* (New York: Atheneum, 1966).

ROBERT HOLUB

1967 Alexander and Margarete Mitscherlich's *Die Unfähigkeit zu trauern* is published

In their efforts to enlist state support to reconstruct the institutional structures of psychoanalysis after the war, the founding members of the German Psychoanalytic Society (which included figures who had been active in the Nazi-sponsored Göring Institute during the Nazi period) were able to persuade governmental authorities of the need for trained psychotherapists; they would be needed, it was argued, to treat the enormous amount of psychic distress that the shock of defeat would engender in the population. When, some twenty years later, Alexander and Margarete Mitscherlich published their psychoanalytic interpretation of social and political behaviors in the postwar period, they argued that the salient feature of those behaviors was precisely an *absence* of the extreme psychic distress that had been anticipated. What struck the Mitscherlichs most was not the perhaps predictable absence of a sustained moral, political, juridical, and even emotional *confrontation* with the Nazi past (that is, individual and institutionally supported expressions of contrition, shame, and will to bear witness). Rather, they were impressed by the fact that the population of the new Federal Republic seemed to have avoided what might have been (and in a certain sense should have been) the psychological reaction to the defeat in 1945, to the widespread dissemination of the facts of the Holocaust, and, above all, to the loss of Hitler as führer—namely, a massive fall into depression and melancholy.

The Mitscherlichs argued that Hitler, along with the values he embodied, had occupied the place of the collective ego-ideal within the politicolibidinal economy of the German population, that group and individual identifications converged on the phantasm of this totalitarian leader, which had been "constructed," as later commentators would show, by a massive deployment of media technologies (above all, film and radio): "The loss of an object so highly cathected with libidinal energy . . . was indeed reason for melancholia. Through the catastrophe not only was the German ego-ideal robbed of the support of reality, but in addition the Führer himself was exposed by the victors as a criminal of truly monstrous proportions. With this sudden reversal of his qualities, the ego of every single German suffered a central devaluation and impoverishment. This creates at least the prerequisites for a melancholic reaction" (Mitscherlich and Mitscherlich 1975, 26). The theoretical basis for these claims, which together form a psychoanalytic theory of the phenomenon of *sudden and radical moral delegitimation*, was provided by Freud's metapsychological reflections on narcissism, group psychology, and his distinction between two different patterns of bereavement: mourning and melancholy.

According to Freud, mourning occurs when an object that one had loved for its intrinsic qualities as separate and distinct from oneself is lost. The pleasures that derive from this form of love depend on a capacity to tolerate the potentially painful awareness that "I" and "you" have edges, and that inscribed within the space of this interval are the possibilities of misunderstanding, disappointment, even betrayal. According to Freud, the loss of an object loved in this manner typically results in mourning. In the case of melancholy, the pattern by which loss is worked through is different because the loved object fulfilled a rather different function in the psychological life of the bereaved. A melancholic response to loss—the symptomology of which is a severe, often suicidal depression—ensues when the object was loved not as separate and distinct from oneself, but rather as a mirror of one's own sense of self and power. The predisposition to love in this manner—the Mitscherlichs actually spoke of a "German way of loving"—obtains when the self lacks sufficient strength and cohesion to tolerate, much less comprehend, the reality of separateness (this is the situation of both the primary narcissist, the infant, and the secondary narcissist, the adult melancholic).

The paradox of this narcissism is that the narcissist loves an object only insofar and as long as he or she can repress the otherness of the object; narcissistic love plays itself out in the (non-)space where "I" and "you" are not perceived as having hard edges. The grieving that occurs in melancholy is thus more primitive than what occurs in "healthy" mourning, because what is at stake is nothing less than the constitution of the boundaries between self and other and the integration of that painful awareness of the dangers of separateness (conflict, misunderstanding, betrayal, and so forth). What melancholy must work through is not so much the loss of a particular object that one had loved and cared for—an object that had appealed to one's pleasure principle—but rather the loss of a fantasy of omnipotence. The melancholic grieves not so much for the loss of the other as for the fact of otherness and all that that entails. Melancholy, one might say, is the rehearsal of the shattering or fragmentation of one's primitive narcissism, an event that predates the capacity to feel any real mourning for a lost object because for the narcissist other objects do not yet really exist. Because love inevitably includes an element of narcissism (understood in the most general sense

as a residual resistance to the perception of the separateness of self and other), it makes more sense to speak of a continuum or layering of more primitive and more mature modes of mourning in any specific experience of loss. The shock of mortal loss, which is the shock of definitive separateness, therefore necessarily recapitulates the more fundamental task of reestablishing the boundaries of the self.

The Mitscherlichs' core thesis was that the corporatist fantasy of the Aryan people's, or national, community—the *Volksgemeinschaft*—must be understood as an indication of the predominance of the narcissistic element in the communal fabric of Nazi Germany. Before Germans could really begin to perceive the full magnitude of the crimes committed in the name of the fatherland and to generate real empathy for the victims of Nazism, they would first have to work through the traumatic shattering of the specular relations they had maintained with Hitler and Volksgemeinschaft. A sense of self would first have to be reconstituted on the ruins of this narcissism, on the shocking realization of one's own psychic investments in the ideological fantasies that had sustained a murderous political system.

The Mitscherlichs argued that this process, which would have required a willingness to experience and work through a potentially debilitating melancholy, never took place in postwar Germany, thanks to a remarkably efficient deployment of institutionally supported defense mechanisms that served to burn affective bridges to the past. Foremost among these defenses were derealization of the past, the sudden and radical shift of (narcissistic) identifications with Hitler to the democratic allies, and finally, appropriation of the status of victim. Regarding the last mode of defense, the Mitscherlichs suggested that "identification with the innocent victim is . . . frequently substituted for mourning; this is above all a logical defense against guilt. . . . The past then appears as follows: We made many sacrifices, suffered the war, and were discriminated against for a long time afterward; yet we were innocent, since everything that is now held against us we did under orders. This strengthens the feeling of being oneself the victim of evil forces; first the evil Jews, then the evil Nazis, and finally the evil Russians. In each instance the evil is externalized. It is sought for on the outside, and it strikes one from the outside" (Mitscherlich and Mitscherlich 1975, 45–46). To this one could add that the real suffering experienced by the German population during and after the war—bombings, forced migrations, mass rapes, hunger, and so forth—was experienced by many as a more than sufficient moral and emotional counterweight to the suffering inflicted by the Germans on Jews, Russians, and others.

The cumulative effect of these defenses was, the Mitscherlichs claimed, widespread psychic numbing along with a social and political immobility that accompanied the successes of the "economic miracle": "That so few signs of melancholia or even of mourning are to be seen among the great masses of the population can be attributed only to a collective denial of the past. The very grimness with which the job of clearing away the ruins was immediately begun—which, in oversimplification, was taken as a sign of German efficiency—itself betrayed a manic element. Perhaps this manic defense also explains why news of the greatest crimes in Germany's history was received with so few indications of outward emotion" (Mitscherlich and Mitscherlich 1975, 28).

Many of these arguments had been anticipated by Theodor Adorno in a speech delivered in 1959, "What Does Coming to Terms with the Past Mean?" Apropos of Freud's argument in *Group Psychology and the Analysis of the Ego* that panic typically ensues upon the collapse of collective identifications, Adorno suggested that the absence of such panic in the postwar period allowed for "only one conclusion: secretly, unconsciously smoldering and therefore especially powerful, these identifications as well as a group narcissism were not destroyed but continue to exist" (Adorno 1986, 122). Like the Mitscherlichs, Adorno believed that the German population had narcissistically identified with Hitler and the ideological phantasms of National Socialism. This identification implied above all a conception of the "national community" as a seamless and harmonious interweaving of individual and collective interests and identifications; social, economic, political, even sexual antagonisms were accounted for by reference to the intrusion of foreign and "impure" elements, above all to the corrosive effects of a parasitic Jewish presence targeted at first for marginalization and eventually for utter annihilation.

This particular coupling of psychoanalytic theory with social, political, and cultural critique was based in part on collaborative work between members of the Sigmund Freud Institute, founded by Alexander Mitscherlich in 1960, and those of Adorno's new Institute for Social Research. These collaborations between psychoanalysis and Critical Theory had their roots in cooperative efforts begun in the 1930s between the Institute for Social Research and the Frankfurt Psychoanalytic Institute. Mitscherlich became particularly close to Jürgen Habermas, the most important representative of the tradition of Critical Theory after Adorno and Horkheimer. Habermas's notions of "communicative competence," "constitutional patriotism," and "postconventional identity" parallel in many ways the Mitscherlichs' conception of a psychological and ethical maturity achieved through a labor of mourning.

Some of these parallels might be understood in the light of Peter Homans's Weberian application of the Mitscherlichs' thesis to the prewar period. Faced with rapid, even traumatic transformations of their social structures, including the dissolution of a religiously grounded common culture that might have absorbed the shocks of those disruptions, Germans were, Homans suggests, faced with a moral choice between two basic options: the ability to mourn, represented by psychoanalysis, and the inability or refusal to mourn, represented by Nazism: "Because they were capable of mourning the loss of the past, Freud and his followers were subsequently able to transform a devastating historical situation into an instrument for its investigation and into a mode of self-understanding which made possible the tolerance of the chaos, both inner and outer, which was in and around them. On the other hand, by denying the painful psychological consequences of the social and historical changes that were taking place—in other words, by refusing to mourn—the German Nazis became intolerant of chaos" (Homans 1989, 338). Homans cites Leni Riefenstahl's *Triumph of the Will* as an example of the capacity of the Nazis to use new media technologies to generate a sense of a new and total common culture, to produce the national community as *Gesamtkunstwerk*. The persecutory activity that energized this corporatist fantasy abolished any moral or psychological willingness to feel the painful affects that form the inner lining of the mourning process. To return to the postwar situation, the impasse faced by Germans after 1945 was that they were expected to mourn as well as feel shame and contrition for devastation incurred in the name of a society that was paradoxically founded on a disavowal of mourning. The way out of this impasse, according to the Mitscherlichs, was a reconstitution of the *capacity* for mourning, which demands a willingness to endure and even to valorize disorientation and depression.

Although the great majority of German psychoanalysts in the postwar period were primarily clinically oriented, the Mitscherlichs' efforts to link therapeutics with ethics and politics, manifest in *The Inability to Mourn* (as well as in other books published by the Mitscherlichs independently of one another), had an enormous influence on political and cultural discourse in Germany, as well as on the reception of psychoanalysis in the postwar period. On the basis of the Mitscherlichs' study, the association of the very institution of psychoanalysis with the work of mourning—understood not only as a therapeutic paradigm but also as a moral imperative—was consolidated in postwar German political culture, a phenomenon that was bound to increase ambivalence and even hostility toward psychoanalysis. Indeed, one critique of the Mitscherlichs emerging from within the psychoanalytic community was that their "moralization" of therapeutic processes had the effect of reifying the very defenses they had set out to dismantle (other critiques focused on the slippage between some of the crucial terms of analysis in *The Inability to Mourn*, for example, from mourning to melancholy to working through of shame and guilt). Because of this mor-

alizing posture, Tilmann Moser (1992) has claimed, for example, that the Mitscherlichs' analyses of patterns of behavior in postwar Germany were largely perceived as persecutory attacks and insults rather than as genuine efforts at empathic understanding. The continual shifting between voices and modes of address—from therapist to cultural historian to national pedagogue to moral philosopher—along with the excessively utopian expectations about the social and political effects of psychoanalytic thinking in general, were bound, Moser argued, to limit the effect of the Mitscherlichs' intervention on individual behaviors or the larger political culture. Moser furthermore censures the Mitscherlichs for failing to appreciate the nonverbal, somatic expressions of depression and disorientation that were widespread in the perpetrator generation (such a failure would be particularly ironic given Alexander Mitscherlich's particular area of clinical and theoretical competence in psychosomatic illness) as well as for their androcentric theoretical bias— that is, a fixation on fathers and oedipal structures (one result of this bias was a blindness to the extent of women's involvement with the National Socialist movement).

Moser also argues that the efforts of the so-called generation of '68 to establish a social and cultural space in which the Nazi past could be confronted and worked through were doomed to failure because the student rebels adopted the arguments and inquisitorial stance of the Mitscherlichs' book. Moser's more general argument, however, was that the limits of the Mitscherlichs' work indicated that psychoanalysis as an institution was simply not prepared to deal with the complex transferential and countertransferential issues raised by individuals implicated in horrific crimes.

Some of these same objections to the Mitscherlichs' approach have entered into the idiom of larger and more problematic critiques of intellectual and aesthetic discourses in the postwar period. Perhaps the most extreme example of such a critique, made possible in large measure by the fall of the Berlin Wall and the collapse of Socialism in Eastern Europe, was articulated by the filmmaker Hans Jürgen Syberberg in his polemical reevaluation of postwar aesthetic and political culture, *Vom Unglück und Glück der Kunst in Deutschland nach dem letzten Kriege*. In effect, Syberberg blames the inability to mourn on the very combination of Freudian and Marxist traditions forged by the Frankfurt school and from which the Mitscherlichs drew in their analysis of postwar German society. The kernel of Syberberg's thesis was that the legacy of the Frankfurt school philosophers in postwar Germany was a series of cultural taboos that foreclosed access to the aesthetic and intellectual resources that would have made possible a genuine effort at coming to terms with the past. Apropos of Adorno's famous statement of the impossibility of poetry after Auschwitz, Syberberg wrote: "This was equivalent to an ancient prohibition of graven images, of poetic speech, of art as such. . . . Regardless of how it was meant or said, it had the effect of a general ban on poetry and even on emotion" (Syberberg 1990, 35–36). Through taboos of this sort, Syberberg argued, Germans were expropriated of the very aesthetic and psychic means and materials with which they might have been able to construct works of elegiac art and engage in an authentic labor of mourning: the inability to mourn was, in other words, imposed on the Germans from the outside. It is very clear that Syberberg considered this imposition a Jewish one, and indeed one primarily associated with the names of Freud and Marx: "The Jewish interpretation of the world follows upon the Christian, just as the Christian one followed Roman and Greek culture. Thus the predominance of those analyses, images, definitions in art, science, sociology, literature, politics, information media. . . . Marx and Freud are the pillars marking the path from east to west. Neither are conceivable without Jewishness. Their systems are defined by it. . . . This shapes the way people feel, think, judge, act, and pass information. We live in the Jewish epoch of European cultural history " (79). Syberberg's deeply disturbing appropriation of the thesis of the inability to mourn thus ultimately blames the limits of the Mitscherlichs' version of that thesis on a Jewish influence. Syberberg's own interpretation thereby culminates in a kind of perverse aporia: If only Germans could free themselves from the Jewish influence (above all via the Frankfurt school) on postwar German art and culture, they could begin in earnest the work of mourning for the disaster they brought on in their grandiose efforts to eliminate the Jewish influence on German art and culture.

Although very few German psychoanalysts or intellectuals would subscribe to such openly anti-Semitic formulations, it is clear that in Germany psychoanalysis and the reception of Freud have been powerfully informed by the Mitscherlichs' use of central Freudian categories to analyze the legacies of Nazism in postwar German society. For better or worse, Freud's thought thus continues to be associated in Germany with an at least in part German-Jewish tradition of critical theory aimed at illuminating and dismantling the psychic, social, and political structures associated with fascism.

Bibliography

Theodor W. Adorno, "What Does Coming to Terms with the Past Mean?" *Bitburg in Moral and Political Perspective,* ed. Geoffrey Hartman, trans. Timothy Bahti and Geoffrey Hartman (Bloomington: Indiana University Press, 1986); Martin S. Bergmann and Milton E. Jucovy, eds., *Generations of the Holocaust* (New York: Basic Books, 1982); Sigmund Freud, "Group Psychology and the Analysis of the Ego," *The Standard Edition of the Complete Psychological Works of Sigmund Freud,* ed. James Strachey, vol. 18 (London: Hogarth, 1953–74), 73–102; Freud, "Mourning and Melancholia," *Standard Edition,* vol. 14 243–60; Freud, "On Narcissism: An Introduction," *Standard Edition,* vol. 14, 67–144; Saul Friedländer, "Some German Problems with Memory," *Bitburg in Moral and Political Perspective,* ed. Geoffrey Hartman (Bloomington: Indiana University Press, 1986); Jürgen Habermas, *Eine Art Schadensabwicklung: Kleine Politische Schriften VI* (Frankfurt a. M.: Suhrkamp, 1987); Peter Homans, *The Ability to Mourn: Disillusionment and the Social Origins of Psychoanalysis* (Chicago: University of Chicago Press, 1989); Julia Kristeva, *Black Sun: Depression and Melancholia,* trans. Leon S. Roudiez (New York: Columbia University Press, 1989); Edith Kurzweil, *The Freudians: A Comparative Perspective* (New Haven: Yale University Press, 1989); Peter Kutter, ed., *Psychoanalysis International: A Guide to Psychoanalysis Throughout the World,* vol. 1 (Stuttgart: frommann-holzboog, 1992); Alexander Mitscherlich and Margarete Mitscherlich, *The Inability to Mourn: Principles of Collective Behavior,* trans. Beverley R. Placzek (New York: Grove, 1975); Margarete Mitscherlich, *Erinnerungsarbeit: Zur Psychoanalyse der Unfähigkeit zu trauern* (Frankfurt a. M.: S. Fischer, 1987); Tilmann Moser, "Gibt es die 'Unfähigkeit zu trauern'? Zur psychischen Verarbeitung des Holocaust in der BRD," *Erinnerung: Zur Gegenwart des Holocaust in Deutschland-West und Deutschland-Ost,* ed. Bernhard Moltmann (Frankfurt a. M.: Haag & Herchen, 1992); Eric L. Santner, *Stranded Objects: Mourning, Memory, and Film in Postwar Germany* (Ithaca, N.Y.: Cornell University Press, 1990); and Hans Jürgen Syberberg, *Vom Unglück und Glück der Kunst in Deutschland nach dem letzten Kriege* (Munich: Matthes and Seitz, 1990).

ERIC L. SANTNER

1968 The translation of Isaac Bashevis Singer's *Gimpel der Narr* appears in the Federal Republic of Germany

The enormous popularity in Germany of Isaac Bashevis Singer and Ephraim Kishon provides an interesting perspective on the relationship of non-German Jewish writing to the German (Jewish and non-Jewish) reading public. It inevitably points to the way in which Jewish writing in Germany is filtered through the United States, as in the case of Singer, and through Israel, where Kishon is generally considered the country's national satirist. The reception of the work of Singer and Kishon in the Federal Republic of Germany from 1968, the date of the German publication of Singer's *Gimpel der Narr* (Gimpel the fool), to the publication of Kishon's memoirs *Nichts zu lachen* (Not a laughing matter) in 1993, can shed light on the larger question of Jewish writing in Germany and the representation of Jewishness in the German context. It also brings up the question of what it means to "export" Jewish culture to Germany. Although there were Jewish authors writing in German in the 1960s and 1970s (such as Jurek Becker and Edgar Hilsenrath), that number is significantly small, and a good deal of the literary production by Jews writing in German took place in countries other than Germany (the cases of Paul Celan in Paris and Nelly Sachs in Stockholm come to mind).

Singer and Kishon are two radically different Jewish writers with radically different conceptions of what it even means to be one. In Germany, Singer's work is generally admired for the picture it paints of Eastern European Jewish life, whereas Kishon, often referred to in the German press as "Germany's favorite Israeli," is commonly seen as an exemplar of so-called Jewish humor. Both are writers in exile: Singer was a Polish Jew born in Warsaw who lived as of 1935 in New York, and Kishon was born in Budapest in 1924 and moved to Tel Aviv after surviving the war. Both became literary sensations in their country of exile and yet, for their German audience, both remain, or at least are marketed, as somehow quintessentially "Jewish." Although they have markedly different reading audiences, both Singer and Kishon provided a certain degree of definition for the German reader of what Jewishness and Jewish experience are all about. The reception of their work in the German popular and critical press can give insight into the discourse about Jews, Jewishness, and the Holocaust in Germany since 1968.

Although neither Singer nor Kishon's work could be classified as "Holocaust literature," the Holocaust is certainly the pivotal event when looking at the reception of both writers' work, from Singer's tales of seventeenth-century Poland to Kishon's "Tiergeschichten." For Kishon, the Holocaust remains a kind of *terra sancta,* the one event that he cannot and will not satirize, as he has repeatedly stated. The Holocaust also defines his relationship to the German reading public that so strongly endorses him. On the one hand, in interviews he repeatedly underscores that it is both a great irony and a "just revenge" that he should be the favorite writer of the descendants of his executioners (*Der Spiegel,* Sept. 27, 1993). On the other hand, he insists on exonerating Germans today and building, in the words of a Langen-Müller promotional release, "bridges between the two nations of Germans and Jews." The reception of Isaac Bashevis Singer in Germany was somewhat more complicated. He was cast by his German admirers as bearing likeness to such diverse figures from literature as Don Quixote and Nathan der Weise, and as providing the final peg in the trajectory of Yiddish luminaries that begins with Sabbatai Zevi (the seventeenth-century Hasidic false messiah who, in the glossary found in the dtv edition of *Verloren in Amerika,* is described as a "jüdischer Schwärmer") and extends to the triumvirate of Sholem Aleichem, Mendeles Mocher-Sforim, and Itzak Leib Peretz (*Die Zeit,* Oct. 13, 1978). Like Kishon, he too became a sort of all-purpose Jew for the German public.

Singer's reception in Germany was always filtered through the United States. The German editions of Singer's work have all been translated first from the American edition, and American-Jewish writing and the American publishing industry played a large role in Singer's success in Germany. In a review of *Satan in Goraj* in *Die Zeit,* Salcia Landmann stressed the pivotal role that Yiddish writing in the United States has played for Singer's work, pointing out that many of his novels, although written in Yiddish, were published first in their English translation and only later appeared in Yiddish (*Die Zeit,* Feb. 13, 1970). Singer's career in the American literary scene was launched overnight in 1953 with Saul Bellow's translation in *Partisan Review* of *Gimpel the Fool,* and it continued with his winning the National Book Award in 1970 for *A Warsaw Childhood* and again in 1974 for *Enemies: A Love Story.* In Germany, however, his reputation was established with the publication of *Gimpel der Narr* in 1968. Prior to that time, his novels had not sold well, and Rowohlt allowed four unsuccessful novels to go out of print. His reputation in Germany was considerably heightened when Hanser Verlag began to publish Ellen Otten's translations of his work. In 1978 he was awarded the Nobel Prize for Literature, thus becoming the first Yiddish writer ever to be honored with such high literary recognition.

Singer's Nobel Prize did not go unnoticed in Germany. In fact, Rowohlt continues to cash in on "its" author receiving the Nobel by adding, in press releases and advertisements, the label "Nobelpreisträger" under the bold print of his name. In this way, the German press continues to create, market, and sell a particular Isaac Bashevis Singer. The German press coverage of this landmark event for Yiddish writing is striking in its insistence on portraying the late Singer as the embodiment of the *Ostjude,* a sort of spokesperson for the shtetel. Singer as *Ostjude* par excellence: this trope had already been set with the translation of *Gimpel der Narr* in 1968. In countless German reviews, Singer was praised as a chronicler and a "Volksdichter" who successfully depicted the strong and "unbroken" Eastern European Jewish culture, but who also wove in the sensual and the modern (*Frankfurter Allgemeine Zeitung* [FAZ], Oct. 15, 1968). From the late 1960s—beginning with the publication of *Gimpel der Narr* in 1968—until he received the Nobel award in 1978, Singer was celebrated as a "master of local color, of the specific and the precise" (*Die Zeit,* Jan. 28, 1972). At the same time, he was seen as portraying "universal" experience—with the "simplicity" of the shtetel as backdrop—and providing characters with whom even the (non-Jewish) German reader can "identify." Singer's Yiddish-speaking audience, on the other hand, sharply criticized him for his departure from traditional narrative tradition, and for his sensual (often frankly sexual) and markedly modernist leanings. Singer's embrace of modernist aesthetics, and his subsequent difficulty with the Yiddish literary community, is rarely mentioned in the German reviews of his work, when, in fact, it was the basis (as Irving Howe and Cynthia Ozick, among others, have illustrated) of the enormous success he had in the (non-Yiddish) literary world, and of the suspicion and resentment he provoked in his Yiddish readers.

For many German critics, however, Singer remained largely a writer of the shtetel, a chronicler of the nobly decimated, forsaken world of the Eastern European Jew. Writing in *Die Zeit* on the occasion of Singer receiving the Nobel Prize, Horst Bienek states unequivocally that Singer, despite his immigration to the United States in

1935, never really left the world of the shtetel because the culture of the lower east side of Manhattan was, Bienek maintains, a resolutely Yiddish one. Furthermore, Bienek is adamant in his view that Singer not be considered an "intellectual" writer—that alongside other more "serious" Jewish writers such as Philip Roth, Saul Bellow, and Mordechai Richler, Singer represented the more popular, even "folksy," side of North American–Jewish writing. Bienek cites as Singer's greatest literary achievement his ability to fuse the world of the shtetel with the urban exile experience in New York: "the mixture of Galicia and Brooklyn, of the Talmud and drive-in-movie theaters, of the *dybbuk* and sexual slavery, of intellect and instinct" (*Die Zeit,* Oct. 13, 1978). Indeed, in many ways the "Amerikabild"—or rather, the distinctly *Jewish* "Amerikabild"—that Singer offered his German readers is another cause for the enormous success of these books in Germany.

An exception to this sentimental vision of Yiddish and Eastern European Jewish culture in the German reception of Isaac Bashevis Singer is Jorg von Uthman's thoughtful review in the *Frankfurter Allgemeine* of Singer's life and work, written on the occasion of his death in 1991 (*FAZ,* July 26, 1991). Von Uthman insisted that although Singer always placed the fate of Eastern European Jews and of shtetel life at the heart of his fiction, it is nonetheless reductive to characterize him as having been a Jewish propagandist or an "illuminator" of the ghetto. Although Singer wrote about messianism, Hasidism, and kabbalist mysticism, von Uthman quite correctly stresses Singer's vehement secularism and his conscious turn away from the Orthodoxy of his childhood. In this context, he cites the often-quoted Singer dictum "The truth is that there is no truth" and concludes that in this regard Singer was reminiscent of Lessing's figure Nathan der Weise.

The German press is forever comparing Singer to literary figures throughout history, creating the impression that Singer was as much a fictive construct as his own Gimpel (or Sholem Aleichem's Tevye)—that there is a sort of wholeness or continuity between Singer as an Eastern Eu-

ropean Jewish writer and the Jewish / Yiddish world he, along with other Yiddish writers, depicts in his writing. In his *Laudatio* to Isaac Bashevis Singer in the *Frankfurter Allgemeine* (written on the occasion of the "Woche der Brüderlichkeit"), Günter Kunert writes as well a sort of *Laudatio* to the *Ostjude* and the (now dead) culture of Eastern European Jewry. He describes the figures in Singer's fiction as people whose "thinking and feeling is not yet deformed or corrupted, whose spirit is not yet fully formed or limited, whose compassion is not yet crippled or perverted, whose souls have not been made into a dangerous vacuum by continuous discipline; in short, people who are still driven or consumed by passion" (*FAZ,* Mar. 11, 1981).

Singer himself, however, was certainly intent on throwing some kinks into this picture of happy, harmonious Yiddish culture. His reflections on the role of Yiddish writing provide a good counterpoint to the German critics: "Yiddish must strike out boldly in two directions. First of all it must become what it was intended to be—an instrument of Jewishness. And, secondly, it must go forth and encounter the vanities, illusions, temptations and risks of the world. . . . A contemporary literature intent on awakening and binding together all Jews dares not restrict itself to a vision of hamlets nor can it cultivate merely primitive attitudes. The Jew is not a primitive. He may come from a village, but he is not a villager. His nature is dynamic, not static" (Singer 1985a, 146–47). An insistence on the "static" nature of Eastern European Jewish life, however, dominates many of the German reviews. For instance, in a review of *Mein Vater der Rabbi* (1972) in *Die Zeit,* Gabriel Laub laments that the German translation via the American translation, and the fact of Singer's exile from Poland, causes the Polish place names in the novel to be somewhat imprecise—but he adds, with an oddly derisive tone, that this "imprecision" is about as significant as if they were the names of excavated Assyrian cities (*Die Zeit,* Jan. 28, 1972). In a review in the *Frankfurter Allgemeine* of *Gimpel der Narr,* one critic describes Yiddish culture as "strong and unbroken" yet at the same time laments that the German edition of *Gimpel der Narr* does not provide a glossary—the need for which, in fact, demonstrates that the continuity of the culture, the "static" quality to which Singer refers, has in fact been broken.

Singer's insistence on this fundamental split within the culture of the shtetel—that the Jew may come from the village or shtetel, but that he is not a villager—counters, complicates, and problematizes the inclination of many German critics, such as Horst Bienek and Günter Kunert, to relegate Yiddish writing—and the work of Isaac Bashevis Singer in particular—to the irretrievable, past, and harmonious world of the shtetel. Singer's renown in Germany as a literary figure is based partly on the fact that critics have been able to place him "there," in the shtetel that embodies and defines the (German) reconstruction of Eastern European Jewish experience. And yet the shtetel is also a mythical and fictive place, especially for the post-1968 German reading public. Contrary to Horst Bienek's belief that despite his 1935 immigration to New York Singer never really left the shtetel, the shtetel experience in Eastern Europe was not nearly as uniform as critics like Bienek would have us believe.

It is not the "unbrokenness" of Eastern European Jewish life that most clearly characterizes Singer's fiction, but rather the language in which he wrote, Yiddish. Singer repeatedly states the obvious but vital fact that "Yiddish is homeless," and this "homelessness" is what lies at the very heart of Isaac Bashevis Singer's work. For Bienek, the fact that Singer continues to write in Yiddish is his most marketable quality: "it [Yiddish] belongs to his authenticity, to his bearing witness" (*Die Zeit,* Oct.13, 1978). Yiddish is certainly *the* language of exile, in many ways a lost language. In his Nobel Prize speech, Singer observed that Yiddish is "a language of exile, without a land, without frontiers, not supported by any government, a language which possesses no words for weapons, ammunition, military exercises, war tactics: a language that was despised by both Gentiles and emancipated Jews" (Singer 1985b, 171). Again, Singer himself provides a more complex and interesting perspective than his critics. His Nobel Prize speech ends with the following:

"Yiddish has not yet said its last word. It contains treasures that have not been revealed to the eyes of the world. It was the tongue of martyrs and saints, of dreamers and kabbalists—rich in humor and in memories that mankind may never forget. In a figurative way Yiddish is the wise and humble language of us all, the idiom of the frightened and hopeful humanity" (172).

Isaac Bashevis Singer's political and aesthetic identities remained somewhat invisible, then, to his German readers and critics: he was first and foremost the *Ostjude* who writes of the shtetel. Kishon's acclaim in Germany, on the other hand, cannot be separated from his politics, in particular his avowedly conservative and anti-intellectual stance. If the Germans love him, then he in turn professes to love not only the German reading public that buys his books, but also the country, which he praises for being consistently pro-Israeli (in contrast to the United States, which he indirectly criticizes). In an article in the *Hamburger Abendblatt* in 1990, for example, he insists that Germany's pro-Israeli sentiment is the result neither of guilt nor of a desire to make reparations, but rather is due to the policies of its chancellor, Helmut Kohl, and the fact that millions of German tourists have visited Israel in the forty years of its existence. This in turn, says Kishon, has promoted a "friendly" spirit between Germany and Israel (*Hamburger Abendblatt,* May 12, 1990). This folksy sort of bonhomie not only about political matters, but also about questions of gender or sexual equality, is perhaps also a part of his appeal for this audience. For instance, he almost always appends the epithet "die beste Ehefrau von allen" (the best wife of all) when his wife Sara is mentioned, and in a questionnaire published in the *Frankfurter Allgemeine Zeitung* he responded to the question, "Welche Eigenschaften schätzen Sie bei einer Frau am meisten?" (Which qualities do you value most in a woman?) with "Die Hüften und die Beine" (The hips and the legs). In general, his appeal is predicated on precisely this sort of "boyish" and determinedly folksy—indeed, kitschy—kind of humor. His status as an Israeli author and Holocaust survivor is certainly a large part of his success in Germany, but one wonders why others who would fit this bill, such as Aharon

Appelfeld or S. Y. Agnon, are not the same sort of household words as Kishon. Indeed, Kishon is synonymous in Germany with a Jewishness that is palatable to the German reading public in part because of his endorsement of Helmut Kohl's belief in "the grace of being born late," and his prevailing desire for reconciliation between Germans and Jews.

In some respects, Kishon's journey has been an odd one, and ironically it has always included Germany in some form or other. Born Ferenc Hoffmann in 1924 to an assimilated Jewish family in Budapest, he describes himself as corresponding to Goebbels's Aryan prototype so much that under the Horthy regime in Hungary, he was summoned to an elite paramilitary unit until his Jewish identity was revealed (*FAZ*, Jan. 29, 1994). He credits his survival in a work camp to his skill as a chess player: while in Jolsva, a high-ranking camp official discovered this talent and granted him the special status that ultimately enabled him to flee the camp. In earlier years, Kishon expressed a greater ambivalence toward Germany than his recent statements might indicate: in 1952, for instance, as a recent immigrant to Israel, he actively opposed the establishment of cultural relations with Germany. His first book, published in Germany in 1961, was the volume *Drehn Sie sich um, Frau Lot!* (the English version, incidentally, was the *New York Times Book Review*'s "Book of the Month" selection in 1959). Since that time, his "Kishonsche Komik" has become familiar to the German reading public. He has been extremely prolific not only as a humorist and satirist, but also as a playwright and screenwriter, and his creative pursuits have earned him numerous awards and prizes, including the Israeli Herzl Prize, the Jabotinsky Prize, the Nordau Prize for Literature, and the Sokolov Prize for outstanding journalism. He is often compared to such politically diverse German-Jewish satirists as Kurt Tucholsky and Erich Kästner, as well as to James Thurber and Mark Twain.

Kishon, "the Germans' favorite Israeli," feels that the recent right-wing violence against foreigners in Germany has been overplayed in the media, and he claims not to have experienced any anti-Semitism in Germany, Austria, or Switzerland. This generous exoneration of Germans is perceptible in his work as well. As Martin Doerry observed in a recent *Spiegel* article on Kishon, "The colorful mixture of contemplative and cheery anecdotes enables the reader to decide whether he will be moved, amused, or both, all at the same time. There is not a single line where Kishon forces the reader to acknowledge guilt" (*Der Spiegel,* Sept. 27, 1993). The German-language press makes much of his second residence in Appenzell, Switzerland (whose peaceful surroundings he sees as a sort of refuge from the hectic pace of Tel Aviv), and of the fact that he learned German from collaborating on the translations of his own books. (Friedrich Torberg, and later Gerhard Bronner, were the original translators of his work, until Kishon felt he knew enough German to work on the translations himself.) And yet he forcefully disavows that Switzerland could ever be a "zweite Heimat" for him; he instead stresses his Israeli identity and that his relationship to Switzerland and Germany is ultimately that of a tourist: "I'm just a tourist in Germany" (*Der Spiegel,* Sept. 27, 1993). His relationship to Austria is also celebrated in the press as that of the native Hungarian exhibiting "monarchical feelings" for the "Habsburg" cities of Vienna and Budapest (*Illustrierte Neue Welt Wien,* Dec. 11, 1990). He has enjoyed a close friendship since 1967 with his publisher, Herbert Fleissner, the arch-conservative ("the rightist right winger"; *FAZ,* Jan. 29, 1994) owner of Ullstein Langen-Müller. Fleissner also published the confessional memoir *Ich war dabei* by Franz Schönhuber, the founder of the *Republikaner* party, whose book defends his career in the Waffen SS.

Kishon's complex position as a Jew in relation to Germany cannot be separated from the fact that his greatest success has come from his German, Swiss, and Austrian readers, and that Ullstein Langen-Müller is the publishing house that has brought Kishon to this reading audience. Of the roughly 38 million books by Kishon that have sold worldwide in thirty-one different languages, 24 million books have appeared in German translation. It is not insignificant that

Ullstein Langen-Müller, headed by Herbert Fleissner, has become Kishon's publisher. Axel Springer, who was, among other things, a strong supporter of Israel, bought Ullstein in the early 1960s, and his legacy lives on in scandals such as the one surrounding the publication of Schönhuber's book. Kishon, incidentally, defended Fleissner—and, indirectly, Schönhuber and the *Republikaner*—by claiming that if a member of the *Republikaner* party were to declare himself a Nazi or anti-Semite, he would be ousted from it immediately (*Der Spiegel,* Sept. 27, 1993). In light of this, the recent publication of Kishon's memoirs, *Nichts zu lachen,* and its reception in the German press become even more interesting. Because Kishon's greatest success as a writer has come from his German audience, the emergence of this volume in 1993, and with Ullstein Langen-Müller, comes as no surprise. There is already a German market for the Jewish and non-Jewish Holocaust memoirs, and the *Nichts zu lachen* entered this already established marketplace with, significantly, the Ullstein stamp on it.

Although this book stands apart from his others in that it deals directly with his Holocaust experience, some critics nonetheless see Kishon making the same tired jokes in this book—jokes about taxes, monogamy, and modern art that have become the staple of his writing. In a review of *Nichts zu lachen* in the *Frankfurter Allgemeine Zeitung,* Hannes Stein suggests the unique role that Kishon, as the "literary representative of Israel," has played for Germany in his insistence that the younger generation in Germany does not bear any direct responsibility for the crimes of the Nazis (*FAZ,* Jan. 29, 1994). Stein states that for many Germans, Kishon has long since embodied the "good Jew," which he aptly describes as the "Jew who does not bear a grudge." Kishon's memoirs, in which he openly asserts his identity as a Holocaust survivor, nonetheless display the same characteristic blend of sarcasm, self-irony, and, for Stein at least, the same tiresome tirades against modern art and intellectual life (*FAZ,* Jan. 29, 1994). There is a refrain throughout reviews of his autobiography that Kishon does not blame the Germans, that he believes the Hungarians and the Slovaks did not behave any better than

the Germans, and that he is not certain that he would have acted any differently than they did (*Der Spiegel,* Sept. 27, 1993).

Kishon's role as a writer whose greatest success has come from the descendants of those who once pinned the yellow star on his sleeve is, in a certain sense, both logical and predictable. Kishon makes things easy for a German audience, and it is for this, as much as for his merits, that he has been rewarded—with large book sales and even, one could argue, with the *Bundesverdienstkreuz* (the Federal Republic Cross of Service) that he received in 1993. Kishon is a Jewish writer who both asserts his Jewishness and denies the particular and automatic relationship that this Jewishness obtains in the German context. He is the model Jew, a sort of latter-day Jewish Axel Springer who not only refuses to blame the Germans but also provides this same German audience in his Holocaust memoir with an "unknown side of Kishon" (as a Langen-Müller press release states) that is somehow compatible with his previous work. Perhaps Kishon's restraint (if that is what it is) in not bringing the Holocaust into his earlier writing is why this volume has been so well received: it is as if Kishon, having proven his "good will" to Germany over and over again, can now tell the other, "unknown" side of his story. Despite—or perhaps precisely because of—his experience in World War II, he nonetheless exonerates the Germans by creating a cozy and folksy camaraderie between himself and his reader, between the now-Israeli Jew and the (largely) non-Jewish German reader. If he is in fact the tourist he claims to be in Germany, then he is a tourist who is not simply taking in the sights. In a sense, the reception of Kishon in Germany is relatively simple: as the embodiment of the *Ullstein-Autor,* he appeals to that segment of the German reading public that, while perhaps receptive to Jewish culture (in fact, at times even philo-Semitic), is comfortable with the sort of political stance once espoused by Axel Springer and now, conveniently perhaps, by a *Jewish* writer, Ephraim Kishon.

Perhaps the most significant and interesting aspect of the success in Germany of Ephraim Kishon and Isaac Bashevis Singer is the insight this success provides into the importing and marketing of "Jewish" literature (written in the two "Jewish" languages) in Germany from the late 1960s to the present. Rather than a harmless cultural exchange of the sort celebrated in media events such as the "Woche der Brüderlichkeit" (week of brotherhood), the success and endorsement of Hebrew and Yiddish writing in postwar Germany, and of Kishon and Singer in particular, ultimately points to the complex and difficult relationship the German reading public and German literary critics still have to the many aspects of Jewish life and culture. Despite a few critical voices to the contrary, the German press has played an instrumental role in maintaining the view that Kishon bridges the gap between Germans and Jews with his "befreiendes Lachen" (cathartic laughter), and that Singer paints the "unbroken" and somehow timeless or universal life of the shtetel. That an Israeli author would find his largest audience in Germany, and the works of a Yiddish writer would be so well received there, is ironic and yet, at the same time, entirely fitting.

Bibliography

Ephraim Kishon, *Drehn Sie sich um, Frau Lot!* (Munich: Langen-Müller, 1961); Kishon, *Essen ist mein Lieblingsspeise: Gesammelte Satiren. Satiren um die zweitschönste Sache der Welt* (Munich: Langen-Müller, 1992); Kishon, *Das Große Kishon-Buch* (Munich: Langen-Müller, 1993); Kishon, *Nichts zu lachen* (Munich: Langen-Müller, 1993); Kishon, *Über die Schweiz* (Munich: Langen-Müller, 1992); Kishon, *Undank ist der Welten Lohn* (Munich: Langen-Müller, 1990); Kishon, *Wie unfair, David!* (Munich: Langen-Müller, 1967); Isaac Bashevis Singer, *Eine Kindheit in Warschau* (Munich: dtv, 1976); Singer, *Feinde, die Geschichte einer Liebe* (Munich: Hanser, 1974); Singer, *Gimpel der Narr: Ausgewählte Erzählungen* (Reinbek bei Hamburg: Rowohlt, 1968); Singer, *Ich bin ein Leser: Gespräche mit Richard Burgin* (Munich: dtv, 1988); Singer, *Jakob der Knecht* (Reinbek bei Hamburg: Rowohlt, 1965); Singer, *Mein Vater der Rabbi* (Reinbek bei Hamburg: Rowohlt, 1971); Singer, "New Yiddish Frontiers," *Yiddish* 6 (1985a): 141–48; Singer, "Nobel Lecture," *Yiddish* 6 (1985b): 169–72; Singer, *Satan in Goraj* (Reinbek bei Hamburg: Rowohlt, 1969); Singer, *Verloren in Amerika* (Munich: Hanser, 1983); and Singer, *Der Zauberer von Lublin* (Reinbek bei Hamburg: Rowohlt, 1967).

LESLIE MORRIS

1971 *Ein Sommer in der Woche der Itke K.* by American-born author Jeannette Lander is published

Gaining momentum in the mid-1970s, the West German women's movement discovered Ingeborg Bachmann relatively late and celebrated in the non-Jewish writer's aesthetically complex texts the depiction of woman as victim. In its crassest form, this mode of reception equated the victimization of women in patriarchal societies with that experienced by Jews under National Socialism or by indigenous peoples under European colonialism. In contrast, literature written by Jewish women—whether survivors of the Holocaust or members of subsequent generations—went largely ignored by many German feminists and literary critics. For the critics such authors were only marginally talented, their "Jewish" themes of only peripheral interest to a public sphere in which living Jews who actually wanted to problematize the Holocaust in the present (rather than merely memorialize it) were an uncomfortable reminder of cultural and political taboos in postwar Germany. Focused on sisterly bonds of universal victimization, feminists of the 1970s and early 1980s were ill equipped to challenge these taboos, something that would have required them to look at profound experiential differences between Jewish and non-Jewish women in Germany, especially in the Third Reich.

This situation began to change with a spate of public media events that commenced with the television broadcast of *Holocaust* in 1979, and it peaked with President Reagan and Chancellor Kohl's controversial visit to the military cemetery in Bitburg in 1985, President Richard von Weizsäcker's much-quoted speech in the same year commemorating the end of World War II in Europe, and the heated newspaper debates in 1986 among prominent historians concerning the singularity of Nazi genocide. The shift extended into the late 1980s as the fiftieth anniversary of one war-related event after another was commemorated. Yet discussions about the proper way to memorialize the Jews murdered by the Nazis did not necessarily increase the awareness or understanding of an extremely heterogeneous Jewish population that was living in West (or East) Germany in the present. It is perhaps the greatest collective contribution of Jewish women writers of contemporary German literature that they have repeatedly unsettled the taboos and stereotypes of postwar German culture in a number of different ways (and with varying degrees of success).

One potentially surprising feature of this literature is that much of it is written in German by authors who do not come from a German-speaking country. (This applies particularly to younger generations.) Public focus on authorial background and the concomitant authority accorded to such life experience reveal a great deal about the cultural politics that determine who will be recognized, marketed, and read as a "Jewish" author in Germany. In this reading economy, gender issues are customarily relegated to the periphery of the dominant discursive dichotomy between "Germans" and "Jews."

Among the older generation, Grete Weil (b. 1906) may stand as representative of a certain type of German Jewish Holocaust survivor. Raised with educational privilege and bourgeois comfort in her native Munich, Weil (née Dispeker) considered herself and her family fully assimilated Germans, not Jews. Her father, a successful lawyer, adored Wagnerian opera. Although the family had never converted to Christianity, Christmas and Easter were commonly celebrated in the household, whereas Jewish religious practices and beliefs remained foreign to the young Grete. After pursuing university studies in German literature in Frankfurt am Main, Berlin, and Munich, she married the Jewish dramaturge Edgar Weil in 1932. The Nazi rise to power in the following year and Edgar Weil's subsequent brief imprisonment led the Weils to emigrate in the mid-1930s to Holland, which was as yet unoccupied. When their country of refuge fell to the Nazis in 1940, they were unable to escape. One year later Edgar Weil and several hundred other Jewish men were seized from the streets of Amsterdam and deported by the Nazis to the concentration camp of Mauthausen. Within three months they had all been murdered. For roughly two years the traumatized widow was able to save her mother and herself from deportation by working as a secretary for the controversial Jewish Council of Amsterdam. When in 1943 even those associated with the Jewish Council were scheduled for deportation, Grete Weil went into hiding, where she survived the end of the war. Much to the consternation of many other Jews, Weil returned to (then occupied) Germany, first illegally in 1946 and then permanently in 1947. Nearly thirty years later she resettled in her beloved Munich, a city that rewarded her with two literary prizes in the 1980s.

Weil's biography is important to recount here because it figures so significantly in all of her novels and short stories. She is one of the many German Jews who acquired a "Jewish" identity only after the Nazis had targeted them for humiliation, persecution, and death. Although she herself was never sent to a concentration camp, Weil knows, as one of her characters says, "it was

meant for me." Her failure to prevent her husband's capture and brutal death is a traumatic site to which her writer's imagination returns again and again. The author and many of the figures in her autobiographically encoded tales see their primary purpose in the postwar German public sphere as bearing witness to the horrors of the Nazi regime. And yet these texts circle like insatiable vultures around the guilt of having survived, the guilt of bearing inadequate witness, the guilt of loving life in spite of it all.

All of Weil's work attests to the ongoing presence, however submerged in public consciousness, of a sorrowful past that refuses to go away and that, like all trauma, retains its haunting, tormenting power. These themes were present as recently as 1992, when Weil published her newest collection of short stories, *Spätfolgen* (Delayed aftereffects). In the final story in this volume, Weil poignantly rejects the basis of her life's work: "For over forty years I have fooled myself into thinking that I was a witness, and that enabled me to live as I have done. I am no longer a witness. I knew nothing. When I read Primo Levi, I know that I am not really able to imagine a concentration camp. My fantasy wasn't sick enough." Whereas much of her earlier writing drew its creative sustenance from her feeling that she died with her husband in Mauthausen and from her anguish over having survived him in reality, Weil ultimately concedes in guilt-ridden bitterness that she was spared too much to bear witness to the worst forms of persecution. Because she had seen this as her mission, the one that legitimated her continued existence, she effectively and ironically questioned her life's endeavor at a time when the octagenarian was touted as a grande dame of German-Jewish letters.

Although Weil wrote literary manuscripts throughout her life, *Ans Ende der Welt* (Toward the end of the world) was her first prose piece to be published—in 1949 by an East German publishing house. The brief account of two Dutch-Jewish families who were brought against their will to the Schouwburg theater in Amsterdam, the gathering point (where Weil actually worked for the Jewish Council) for Jews marked for deportation to "the East," went virtually unnoticed. (Forty years later, the West German publisher of a paperback edition felt compelled to liken this story to Anne Frank's diary, even claiming that Weil wrote it "in close proximity to Anne Frank's hiding place." This type of marketing highlights the trope of victimized innocence, as if to say—as late as 1989—that Germans are willing to read only those Holocaust stories that mimic Anne Frank's diary!)

Although the shock of transition from respected citizen to denigrated prisoner provides the focus for Weil's literary debut, her first novel, published in 1963 in the West, explores the radical jolt that a non-Jewish German journalist experiences in occupied Amsterdam when he realizes that hundreds of Jews are being deported every night from the streetcar stop outside his window. *Tramhalte Beethovenstraat* (Streetcar stop Beethoven street) details the agony of this German protagonist, who considers it his primary responsibility to bear witness to the fate of murdered Jews and yet finds, after the war, that there are no words with which he could write about the only subject worth his efforts. In what would become her characteristic narrative style, Weil moves back and forth between the 1940s and the present to underscore the tormented quest for solutions that neither she nor her protagonist ever finds. This first novel is in many ways a treatise about the need for survivors and witnesses to write about the Holocaust and the impossibility of adequately doing so.

Weil has repeatedly been compelled to return to precisely this dilemma. Although a slim volume of short stories, *Happy, sagte der Onkel* (Happy, said the uncle) appeared in 1968, Weil's big breakthrough did not come until 1980, when she published *Meine Schwester Antigone* (My sister, Antigone). The author was seventy-four at the time. This is the novel that won her widespread acclaim among German critics. Tormented by the details of Weil's traumatic biography, the first-person narrator conjures a personal relationship with the mythical Greek persona of Antigone, the exemplary figure of decisive resistance. Serving as the negative counterpart to Antigone's fatal but morally pure defiance, the

protagonist in fact relies heavily on this mythical "sister," who acted as she herself did not, in order to be able to tell her own story of guilt-ridden survival. The complicated structure of the novel reveals that this Holocaust survivor cannot be Antigone, whose presence in the narrative nonetheless legitimizes the story that the survivor has to tell. Ironically, Weil achieved this major literary success by returning to the bourgeois humanist repertoire of German classical education; in the view of some critics, the Antigone motif "elevated" the Holocaust narrative by giving it intellectual rigor.

In subsequent years Weil published two additional novels, in each of which the author's by now familiar life story figures prominently. *Generationen* (Generations; 1983) traces the everyday emotional torture that three women of different generations inflict upon themselves and each other as they experiment with living together in one house. The eldest of the three narrates in Weil's voice: "My illness is called Auschwitz, and it is terminal." Her housemates are no more interested in her personal sorrows than is the outside world. *Antigone* figures even here, for the book on which the narrator has been toiling becomes a success. This causes her to reflect on two contradictory developments: First, for a long time no one in the German public sphere was interested in what she had to say, and now "that has changed"; and second, she has become "a case study for them."

The additional themes of weakness and isolation in old age form a link with the earlier Antigone novel as well as *Der Brautpreis* (The bride price; 1988), for which the Association of Bavarian Publishers and Bookdealers and the City of Munich awarded Weil the Geschwister-Scholl Prize—a prize named in honor of the Scholl siblings, two Catholic teenagers who were executed by the Nazis for distributing antifascist leaflets. (Weil received this award in November 1988, the same month in which parliamentary president Philipp Jenninger gave his controversial speech commemorating the so-called Night of Broken Glass. Public response to this speech subsequently led to Jenninger's resignation.) This novel represents Weil's only attempt to foreground traditionally Jewish material—in this case, the story of King David and his first wife. The narration alternates between "I, Grete" and "I, Michal," a character whom Grete envies because she has no knowledge of the Holocaust to come and because she was able to save her husband's life once, even if she was not able to prevent him from becoming a mighty warrior and ruthless tyrant. Michal herself admires Antigone, for the king's wife regrets many moments in her life when she was too weak to resist political injustice. (Similarities to Christa Wolf's *Kassandra* [1983] are striking. Michal sees herself as "a daughter of kings, trading commodity for men" and inwardly decries the growing militarism of the nation that David leads.) Written shortly after Weil's first trip to Israel and published subsequent to the outbreak of the Palestinian uprising in 1987 (the Intifada), the novel could perhaps be read as a veiled critique of Israeli militarism. The intertwining themes of old age and Holocaust survival in Weil's three novels of the 1980s point of course to the author's increasing awareness of her physical vulnerability and the inescapability of death. On another level they suggest her concern for the fragility of Holocaust remembrance in German culture.

If Weil's work revolves around the unresolved trauma of Nazi persecution experienced firsthand and defines Jewish identity in terms of faith in Yahweh, bonds with Israel, or a "collective of suffering," younger writers turn to more multidimensional notions of Jewish identity as the actual historical events of the Holocaust recede from the view of the present. Of these writers, Jeannette Lander presents a particularly interesting case. Born in New York in 1931 and raised in Atlanta, this American-Jewish writer of Polish extraction emigrated to West Berlin in 1960. Early prize-winning essays in English on Herman Melville and Nathaniel Hawthorne were followed by academic treatises on W. B. Yeats and Ezra Pound. Between 1971 and 1980, Lander published several novels and two collections of short stories (in German), in addition to writing countless essays for the print media, plays and commentaries for radio broadcast, and documentary films for West German television. Although

three of her novels were published by the prestigious publishing house of Suhrkamp/Insel (an East German edition of her first novel was also published in 1974) and she was awarded the competitive Villa-Massimo Fellowship for writers in 1976, Lander's expressive, creative style offended many critics, who thought she might eventually become a good writer if she ever learned "proper" German. Her efforts to unsettle the language of contemporary German literature in productive and critical ways thus went largely unnoticed, as did the fact that her texts did not simply mirror "Jewish-American" themes, but raised provocative questions about contemporary German culture and, specifically, the place of heterogeneous Jewish experience within it. Although Lander continued to write for German newspapers, radio, and television throughout the 1980s, Suhrkamp allowed the titles that she had published with them to go out of print. It was not until 1993 that Lander published another novel, *Jahrhundert der Herren* (Century of the masters), this time with the reconfigured, postunification Aufbau Press (formerly an East German publishing house).

Set against the civil wars of Sri Lanka in the early 1980s, this most recent publication could be considered a German-language contribution to the growing body of postcolonial world literature. In the context of the British colonial legacy of Singhalese nationalism, the narrator probes the transferability of European culture as the protagonist, a (non-Jewish) German woman, seeks to establish an independent existence on the island. In effect, the novel asks what it means to speak of cultural identities in an arena of transnational histories and myths that migrate in both political and imaginary terms. The inclination to traverse or transgress conventional boundaries profoundly influences Lander's earlier novels as well, texts in which Jewish characters and issues are of pivotal significance.

Whereas *Ich, allein* (I, alone; 1980)—much like Weil's *Generationen*—depicts the struggles of an older, single woman who bucks social convention in everyday life, Lander's three earlier novels—*Ein Sommer in der Woche der Itke K.* (A summer in the week of Itke K.; 1971), *Auf dem Boden der Fremde* (On strange ground; 1972), and

Die Töchter (The daughters; 1976)—could easily be seen as a kind of trilogy in which Lander undermines the traditional binary constellation of "Jews and Germany." She does this by displacing the centrality of the Holocaust in temporal, geographical, national, political, cultural, generational, and psychological terms. Lander thus tackles some of the hardest questions concerning Jewish identity in German politics and culture today. Reading her work, one must recall that only a small percentage of Jews living in present-day Germany are of *German*-Jewish descent; that most of them do not have first hand memories of the Holocaust; and that those survivors who do have been scattered to many corners of the world, where diverse local cultures have affected the ways in which these memories have been processed, recorded, publicized, and honored (or not). Writers of the younger generations must confront the slippage of meaning that accompanies the slippage of memory as the German public sphere—and those Jews who participate in it—renegotiate the relationship between Jews and Germany today.

Over twenty years ago, Lander began this process of renegotiation with her wonderfully rich first novel, *Itke*. A daughter of Polish-Jewish immigrants, the teenage protagonist explores what it means to be white, Jewish, and female in a predominantly African-American neighborhood in early 1940s Georgia, where the Holocaust is a distant, mediated horror. Lander intelligently uses various forms of stylistic estrangement to set staid notions of any type of identity into critical motion. Departing from Weil's fixation on Jewish identity (which Weil herself claims not to have) as defined by faith in God and Israel, Lander opts for a prophetic tradition of Judaism, which expresses itself in Itke's quest for social justice. Attention to factors such as race, gender, and eroticism further challenges the common static views of Jews as Jewish *only* or as victims *only*. (It is interesting to note that the themes of bisexuality and incest, which run throughout Weil's work, are almost never mentioned in public responses to it. Critics prefer to focus on "the courageous survivor.") *On Strange Ground* continued to problematize an alleged absolute dichotomy

between Germans and Jews by dissecting the relationship between a young Jewish-American woman who marries a non-Jewish German prisoner of war and returns with him to the ruins of West Berlin in the early postwar years. Flashbacks to this time are interspersed with scenes from the 1960s that address racism in the United States, militarism in Israel, and anti-Semitism in Germany.

The historical specificity of divergent Jewish experiences in different configurations of power and in various cultural contexts figures even more prominently in *The Daughters,* when the plot and its Jewish characters travel back and forth between 1940s France and 1960s West Berlin, Atlanta, Haifa, and Poland. The presence of disenfranchised African Americans (in the United States) and Arabs (in Israel) precludes any one-dimensional appropriation of victim status for the three women protagonists, the geographically scattered daughters of a Polish Jew who set off in 1941 to find their father's grave in Poland. Their collective journey to Poland, years later, to find traces of their own dead father highlights the haunting legacy of the Holocaust, which functions for each of the daughters as an elusive imaginary construct (however real in historical terms) that clearly shapes their lives in the present, though not in an unmediated fashion or in predetermined ways.

Lander's keen predilection for rupture and contradiction serve to demythologize both Jewishness and the Holocaust in contemporary German culture, unsettling in the process both poles of an all too rigidly formulated "German-Jewish" question. In contrast, the Israeli-born Ronnith Neumann cultivates a hunger for harmony and reconciliation between Germans and Jews in spite of an awareness that such hunger cannot be sated. The autobiographically informed *Heimkehr in die Fremde: Zu Hause in Israel oder zu Hause in Deutschland?* (Home to strangeness: At home in Israel or at home in Germany?; 1985) relates the anguish of a young woman born in Israel after the war to German-Jewish parents who escaped to Palestine in the late 1930s and migrated back to Germany in 1958. "I was emigrated," complains the protagonist, who resents being forcefully removed from Israel, her "childhood paradise." The tendency to structure her texts in metaphorical, oddly ahistorical terms similarly informs *Nirs Stadt* (Nir's city; 1991), in which Neumann weaves a story of a woman prisoner, her child daughter, and a brutal prison guard. Prose texts written since 1986 by Barbara Honigmann, who was born in the German Democratic Republic and emigrated to Strasbourg in 1984 to find a viable Jewish community, and by Esther Dischereit, whose Jewish mother survived the Third Reich in hiding, do considerably more to illuminate the many different facets, tensions, and faces of Jewish life in the three German states that this postwar generation has known.

Between Lander, who was born before the war, and Neumann, Honigmann, and Dischereit, who belong to the post-Holocaust generation, there is Katja Behrens, born in the Third Reich in Berlin in 1942. Aside from two years spent in Israel (1968–70) and various travels to South America, India, and the United States, this author has lived most of her life in West Germany. An acclaimed translator of American novels (notably works by William S. Burroughs and Henry Miller), she did editorial work for the West German publishing house of Luchterhand before becoming a freelance literary writer in 1978, when she published her first collection of short stories. (Earlier that year Behrens had been awarded the coveted Ingeborg Bachmann Prize for as yet unpublished work.) *Die weiße Frau* (The white woman; 1978) met with rave reviews. Critics celebrated Behrens as a female "German storyteller" who offered a welcome alternative to the then-popular *Frauenliteratur* (women's literature), which the critics decried as whining and strident. One critic lauded a second collection of short stories (*Jonas;* 1981) for addressing "the human condition as such"; this publication won Behrens the Thaddäus Troll Prize for German authors in 1982. As Behrens continued to publish short stories (and one novel) throughout the 1980s and into the 1990s, subsequent literary honors included the Villa Massimo Fellowship in 1986 and a literary sabbatical sponsored by German television (ZDF) and the city of Mainz in 1992.

Although Behrens's early stories could be read (and were marketed) as tales of existential loneliness and human callousness that an independent woman feels or observes as she travels through "exotic" (South American) or "familiar" (German) settings, one could also recognize in them early signs of themes that haunt the author's entire oeuvre: the fearful repression of painful knowledge and the refusal of that knowledge to go comfortably away. The story of a middle-age woman who becomes infatuated with a young thief who invades her home (*Liebe;* Love) and the tale of an adult woman who must hide in a hole in her basement because she has been displaced by her double (*Kein Platz für zwei;* No room for two) thus emerge as allegorical precursors to Behrens's lone, semiautobiographical novel, *Die dreizehnte Fee* (The thirteenth fairy; 1983). This was the first of the author's publications to address Jewish-German experiences explicitly and the first to elicit any negative reviews ("too sentimental," "too hackneyed," "no positive solution"). The anti-Semitic past is always psychologically present for the three main characters of this novel, the syntactically elliptical style of which further underscores the threat of that which goes unspoken. Marie, the German-Jewish grandmother—herself an illegitimate daughter—bore two illegitimate children by non-Jewish men and lives in postwar West Germany with her adult daughter Hanna and her troubled granddaughter, Anna, who is also the child of a German-Jewish mother and a non-Jewish German father. For these three women, however, all of whom survived living in the Third Reich only by passing as Christian Aryan Germans, Jewishness has no religious or cultural content but is reduced instead to "the nose question." The double brand of being born out of wedlock and being Jewish creates a chain of shame and terror that torments the generations in different ways as it binds them together in a traumatized female collective. Retreating to the shelter of her bed, Marie succumbs to nightly nausea and ultimately dies in a mental hospital imagining that all the Nazi threats she escaped in reality will now be visited upon her. Long after the Third Reich has been supplanted by the Federal Republic of Germany, two dead flies on a window sill strike paranoid panic to Hanna's heart. The youngest of this female trinity, "Anna had to step lightly in order not to wake what slept in dark corners, lightly and carefully. Something hidden behind grimly quiet pieces of furniture did not want to be disturbed, could break out at any moment, fall upon [her], no time left to scream." The fickle affection of non-Jewish husbands and lovers in the Third Reich exacerbates life in a delicate balance, because it lends a particular urgency to solidarity among women who dare not reveal their true selves.

Similarly, it is the combined longevity of psychological trauma, the tenacity of historical repression, and the presence of hidden dangers—rather than any particular notion of Jewish identity—that motivate the short stories that Behrens published in later anthologies. Even those labeled "Jewish Stories" (*Salomo und die anderen,* 1983; Solomon and the others) focus on the silences, both personal and collective, that perpetuate the trauma of twentieth-century anti-Semitism in Germany, Russia, and Israel. Although the longest story in this volume relates the obstacles and animosity that the author encountered among non-Jewish Germans as she tried to research the fate of a Jewish doctor who died in Auschwitz—of "homesickness," according to one of the few German villagers willing to talk to the writer—Behrens also thematizes her own as well as an Israeli aversion to acknowledging the details that concentration camp survivors know no one wants to hear. (The central story here is especially reminiscent of Michael Verhoeven's film *Das schreckliche Mädchen* [The nasty girl; 1989], except that the filmic protagonist is a non-Jewish Bavarian schoolgirl.)

Perhaps the most controversial author of "Jewish" literature in Germany today is an American woman born in New York City in 1952 to Jewish-born parents who converted to Catholicism and fled the Third Reich in the early years of World War II. Raised as a strict Catholic with no knowledge of her Jewish family history, Irene Dische traveled as a rebellious teenager to Libya, Iran, and Kenya, where she allegedly worked for Louis Leakey. With the help of this famous mentor, Dische was admitted to anthropological studies at Harvard University. Shortly after

Leakey's death in 1972, the independent-minded student turned her thoughts to literature instead. Although she has lived in West Berlin since 1980, Dische did not become known as a "cult figure" in the German literary establishment until 1989, when she published her first collection of short stories under the tutelage of Hans Magnus Enzensberger. Prior to this, Dische had produced a television documentary in 1986 about her father, a Nobel Prize-winning scientist (*Zacharias*), and published a little-known article in 1981 entitled "The Rich Jews in Germany." This finely researched piece of journalism clearly reveals Dische's early interest in undermining both anti-Semitic and philo-Semitic stereotypes in postwar Germany. By delving into the particular life histories of Polish Jews involved in the real estate and construction industries in Frankfurt am Main since World War II, the author attacks biases and blind spots that led German media as well as literary authors to reproduce in the late 1970s and early 1980s either the philo-Semitic stereotype of morally superior Jewish victims or the anti-Semitic stereotype of the conniving rich Jew. (In this sense, the article critically illuminates the public controversy over Rainer Werner Fassbinder's play about a wealthy Jewish real estate speculator in Frankfurt, a production that took many of its cues from an earlier novel by Gerhard Zwerenz.) Dische concludes this piece by noting that the postwar era has brought no normalization of life for Jews in Germany.

Even though she speaks German well, Dische nonetheless insists on writing all her literary compositions in English before having them translated into German for publication. A similar element of estrangement characterizes the author's focus on the discourse of anti-Semitism rather than the facts of history. Despite occasional autobiographical elements in her stories—a mother who conducted autopsies in the city morgue, a father who won the Nobel Prize and suffered from Alzheimer's disease—Dische's texts are not concerned with bearing witness for those immediately affected by the Holocaust. Neither do they depict a struggle to maintain Jewish identity in spite of fears that accompany disclosure, nor do they seek to honor the cultivation of historical memory. Rather, the stories for which Dische has become a bestselling, rising star in the German literary firmament (Christoph Hein has compared her talents with those of Molière, Kafka, and Shakespeare) are tales of deception where truth is elusive, history a fiction, and memory unreliable. This is most obvious in Dische's second splash on the literary scene, a short story entitled *Der Doktor braucht ein Heim* (The doctor needs a home; 1990), which could be read as a sensitive but unsentimental account of an aging scientist with Alzheimer's, narrated from the perspective of the afflicted man himself. Because this nonagenarian is a Jewish survivor whose relatives were murdered by the Nazis, however, this coolly tender text might also be read as an indictment of flawed Jewish memory. At a time when the first generation of Holocaust survivors is actually dying out and the factuality of the Holocaust is questioned by historical revisionists, this slim publication is hardly an innocent portrait of a dying man.

With only an occasional short story or essay in the *Frankfurter Allgemeine Zeitung* or *Die Zeit* (two major German newspapers) in 1990 and 1992, Dische sparked international press debates in January 1993 when it became known that the author, wife of one of Erich Honecker's defense lawyers, was the only journalist admitted to a legal hearing for the former East German leader. The year 1993 also saw the publication of *Esterhazy: Eine Hasengeschichte* (Esterhazy: A rabbit story), a children's book written by Dische and Enzensberger about the fall of the Berlin Wall. For her adult readers, Dische addressed the effects of German unification in a lengthy novel entitled *Ein fremdes Gefühl oder Veränderungen über einen Deutschen* (original English title: A violent chord; 1993). This piece, alternately called "the kitsch that came in from the cold" and "the great German novel of the season," relegates explicitly Jewish concerns to the periphery of German public awareness, much as the recent unification has done. The homosexual protagonist, Count Waller von Wallerstein, becomes incurably ill the night the Wall falls and yearns to adopt a child to ensure his progeny. In passing he remarks that Auschwitz makes him "extremely embarrassed,"

yet when a seven-year-old Russian refugee and his mother respond to the count's advertisement, the aristocrat is revolted by the odor of "decay" that emanates from them, the smell of dirty clothes and "the giant toilet, the East." Although it is only once implied that the Russian woman might be Jewish, the count initially sees her as his personal punishment for the sins of the nation before he realizes, hundreds of pages later, that he does not want to live without this mysterious woman who smells and acts so "foreign."

Dische's willingness, even eagerness, to probe cultural taboos, especially those concerning the representation of Germans and Jews, is strikingly evident in *Fromme Lügen* (1989; the English version was published in 1991 as *Pious Secrets*). This was the collection of short stories that catapulted her to star status in Germany and won her the acclaim of the Association of German Critics. (Two years later the city of Bremerhaven awarded her the Jeanette Schocken Prize in memory of a citizen sent to her death by the Nazis.) In the opening story, "A Jewess for Charles Allen," an adult child of German-Jewish emigrants who has been raised as an American Catholic returns to Berlin to settle the inheritance bequeathed to him by his father. What Charles Allen finds is an illegal business operation run by a loud, domineering "spoiled German Jewess," who is later unmasked as the daughter of a high-ranking member of the Nazi Party who merely pretends to be Jewish in Germany and manipulates that designation to her advantage. In a flurry of erotic attraction and revulsion, Charles rapes the woman and rejects his inheritance while remaining hopelessly embroiled in his father's historical legacy. The "pious secrets" of the title story are deceptions that people—in this case, Jews—live and die by. While a blond, buxom forensic pathologist has sex with a male colleague in a labyrinthine basement underneath the New York City morgue, her eight-year-old daughter reads the *National Enquirer* and concludes that her anti-Semitic, Austrian-born grandfather is none other than Adolf Hitler in disguise. (She knows that he hates Jews because he despises her own father, a Polish Jew with bad table manners and too much intellect.) In contrast to the precise dissection of cadavers in the morgue, the amateur investigation into Carl Bauer's "real" identity is a messy affair in a text that thrives on a fascination with life secrets, erotic fantasies, and hidden pathogens. When the reader finally learns that the Bauers converted to Catholicism to escape persecution as Jews under the Nazis and clung to their Catholic identity as they clung to their Jewish fears in the United States, uncomfortable questions arise. Does Dische draw from the repertoire of anti-Semitic stereotypes in order to dismantle them? Or does she mimic anti-Semitic discourse so well that no critical vantage point is discernible? *Pious Secrets* in particular seems to derive its suspense from the tension between two anti-Semitic assumptions: (1) that Jews are readily identifiable by physical characteristics, and (2) that Jews are skilled and dangerous masters of disguise who threaten to infiltrate and subvert the non-Jewish world around them. Judgments are left to the reader.

This readerly dilemma makes the marketing of this author in Germany singularly unsettling. Although Dische herself has repeatedly said that she is not Jewish and that she knows nothing about Jewishness, she also knows that in Germany she is *considered* to be Jewish. Dische even claims that the German media have made her into a Jew. This public fixation on the writer as a talented "Jewish" author of German literature clearly privileges a notion of Jewish identity defined by blood. This might itself be seen as anti-Semitic in the postwar German context, in which issues of "Jewish" representation remain inextricably tied to supposed rights of legitimizing genealogy. Furthermore, the implications are that this Catholic author has not been influenced by church doctrine regarding Jews and that she intuitively knows what Jews are "really" (genetically?) like. Consequently, she can write with impunity stories that might otherwise be condemned as anti-Semitic. As one critic has written of other critics' responses to Dische: "Their guilty conscience comforts itself by bestowing exaggerated praise." From Dische's own point of view, however, her texts are not anti-Semitic but her readers are. Rejecting philo-Semitic stereotypes while mimicking anti-Semitic ones is a delicate balancing act. What exactly hangs in the balance is never made entirely clear in these early publications. Among her contemporaries, Dische is perhaps most skilled at digging her finger into the German-Jewish wound of discursive representation and making her readers squirm. Whereas authors such as Weil, Lander, and Behrens have explored the haunting legacy of the historical past (and Lander has begun to explode some of the discursive impasses that attend this legacy), Dische unsettles the ground of discursive certainty on which Germans or Jews propose to make definitive moral judgments about themselves or each other. Without condoning or denying the Holocaust, America's youngest author of "German-Jewish" literature has cultivated a postmodern distrust of constructed identities that lay claim to fixed historical truths. Reminiscent in this respect of Edgar Hilsenrath's 1977 novel, *The Nazi and the Barber*, Dische's work otherwise breaks ranks with the multifaceted tradition of Jewish literature in postwar Germany.

Bibliography

Leslie A. Adelson, *Making Bodies, Making History: Feminism and German Identity* (Lincoln: University of Nebraska Press, 1993); Adelson, "There's No Place Like Home: Jeannette Lander and Ronnith Neumann's Utopian Quest for Jewish Identity in the Contemporary West German Context," *New German Critique* 50 (1990): 113–34; Katja Behrens, *Die weiße Frau* (Frankfurt a. M.: Suhrkamp, 1978); Behrens, *Jonas* (Pfaffenweiler: Pfaffenweiler Presse, 1981); Behrens, *Die dreizehnte Fee* (Düsseldorf: Claassen, 1983); Behrens, *Salomo und die anderen: Jüdische Geschichten* (Frankfurt a. M.: Fischer, 1993); Behrens, *Von einem Ort zum anderen* (Pfaffenweiler: Pfaffenweiler Presse, 1987); Behrens, *Im Wasser tanzen: Ein Erzählzyklus* (Frankfurt a. M.: Luchterhand, 1990); Irene Dische, "Brahms Intermezzo," trans. Robin Cackett, *Frankfurter Allgemeine Zeitung* (Mar. 17, 1990); Dische, *Der Doktor braucht ein Heim,* trans. Reinhard Kaiser (Frankfurt a. M.: Suhrkamp, 1990); Dische, *Ein fremdes Gefühl oder Veränderungen über einen Deutschen,* trans. Reinhard Kaiser (Berlin: Rowohlt, 1993); Dische, *Fromme Lügen,* trans. Otto Bayer and Monika Elwenspoek (Frankfurt a. M.: Eichborn, 1989); Dische, *Die intimen Geständnisse des Oliver Weinstock: Wahre und erfundene Geschichten,* trans.

Robin Cackett, Reinhard Kaiser, and Bernd Samland (Berlin: Rowohlt, 1994); Dische, *The Jewess: Stories from Berlin and New York* (London: Bloomsbury, 1992); Dische, *Pious Secrets* (New York: Viking, 1991); Dische, "Die reichen Juden in Deutschland," *Trans Atlantik* 6 (1981): 14–25; Dische, "Wirtschaftsflüchtling," trans. Karin Graf, *Frankfurter Allgemeine Zeitung* (Oct. 2, 1992); Irene Dische and Hans Magnus Enzensberger, *Esterhazy: Eine Hasengeschichte* (Frankfurt a. M.: Sauerländer Aarau, 1993); Jeannette Lander, *Auf dem Boden der Fremde* (Frankfurt a. M.: Insel, 1972); Lander, *Die Töchter* (Frankfurt a. M.: Insel, 1976); Lander, *Ich, allein* (Munich: Autoren Edition, 1980); Lander, *Jahrhundert der Herren* (Berlin: Aufbau, 1993); Lander, *Ein Sommer in der Woche der Itke K.* (Frankfurt a. M.: Suhrkamp, 1971); Elena Lappin, ed., *Jewish Voices, German Words: Growing Up Jewish in Postwar Germany and Austria,* trans. Krishna Winston (North Haven, Conn.: Catbird, 1994); Dagmar C. G. Lorenz, *Verfolgung bis zum Massenmord: Holocaust-Diskurse aus der Sicht der Verfolgten* (New York: Lang, 1992); Ronnith Neumann, *Heimkehr in die Fremde: Zu Hause in Israel oder zu Hause in Deutschland?* (Göttingen: Bernt Schlender, 1985); Neumann, *Nirs Stadt* (Frankfurt a. M.: Fischer, 1991);

Karen Remmler, "En-gendering Bodies of Memory: Tracing the Genealogy of Identity in the Work of Esther Dischereit, Barbara Honigmann, and Irene Dische," *Reemerging Jewish Culture in Germany: Life and Literature Since 1989,* ed. Sander L. Gilman and Karen Remmler (New York: New York University Press, 1994), 184–209; Inge Stephan, Sabine Schilling, and Sigrid Weigel, eds., *Jüdische Kultur und Weiblichkeit in der Moderne* (Vienna: Böhlau, 1994); Sigrid Weigel, *Die Stimme der Medusa: Schreibweisen in der Gegenwartsliteratur der Frauen* (Dölmen-Hiddingsel: tende, 1987); Grete Weil, *Ans Ende der Welt* (Frankfurt a. M.: Fischer, 1987); Weil, *The Bride Price,* trans. John Barrett (Boston: Godine, 1991); Weil, *Generationen* (Zürich: Benziger, 1983); Weil, *Happy, sagte der Onkel* (Frankfurt a. M.: Fischer, 1982); Weil, *Meine Schwester Antigone* (Frankfurt a. M.: Fischer, 1982); Weil, *My Sister, Antigone,* trans. Krishna Winston (New York: Avon, 1984); Weil, *Spätfolgen* (Zürich: Nagel & Kimche, 1992); and Weil, *Tramhalte Beethovenstraat* (Zürich: Nagel & Kimche, 1992).

LESLIE A. ADELSON

1973   Stefan Heym's *Der König David Bericht,* which fictionalizes the biblical account of David's reign to comment on the contemporary situation in the German Democratic Republic, is published

Born Helmut Flieg in Chemnitz in 1913, Stefan Heym fled Germany for political reasons in 1933; emigrated to Czechoslovakia and then in 1935 to the United States where he studied, worked as an anti-Nazi journalist, and began to write novels; returned to liberate Europe as a U.S. soldier; and pursued his literary career in the United States until such factors as the McCarthy hysteria and Heym's opposition to the Korean War led him to seek asylum in the German Democratic Republic, where he received citizenship. There he quickly irritated the government by speaking his mind in his journalistic activities and political-social novels. Eventually his work was banned.

Despite being Jewish, Heym seldom treated Jewish issues in his early and middle literary career. Sometimes Jewish characters played major roles in his novels, for example, Sergeant Bing in *Der bittere Lorbeer* (The crusaders; 1966, Eng. ed. 1948) and the title figure in *Lassalle* (Uncertain friend; 1969), but they were less important as Jews than as representatives of the political-social milieu and concerns he was portraying. Heym departed radically from this practice, however, in *Der König David Bericht* (The King David report), his only novel that featured almost exclusively Jewish characters and a Jewish setting. (He recorded the genesis of this book in his *Nachruf* [Eulogy; 1981].) After his first wife's death in 1969, he picked up the King James Bible, started reading the story of David, and immediately realized the novelistic possibilities in it. The caesura this moment represented in his career is evident in his words, "I've wondered more than once whose hand was in play here; S. H. could just as easily have opened to the book of Esther or Job, and the rest of his life would have turned out differently" (Heym 1988, 760). There was more than a little chance involved, for Heym had just finished *Die Schmähschrift oder Königin gegen Defoe* (The Queen against Defoe; 1970, Eng. trans. 1975), and the linguistic and narrative techniques used in that satire proved to be excellent preparation for his *König David Bericht*. Besides studying the biblical text, he consulted with Professor Walter Beltz, a specialist from the German Democratic Republic (GDR) on religious history of the Middle East, and utilized the commentaries in the Kautzsch edition of the Bible (Heym 1988, 763–64).

Heym wrote the novel in English first. It was his practice to compose many of his works in English and then translate them into German (Hutchinson 1992, 74), but this time he had to immerse himself in the German of the Luther Bible in order to produce a good translation (Heym 1988, 764). By late 1972 *Der König David Bericht* was published in Munich, and the work appeared in English in New York and London in 1973. In the GDR, publication was often problematic. Heym was not in favor, and several of his

759

works composed in the GDR had not been published there. Many writers were experiencing difficulties because of the state's anxiety about their loyalty, expressed in an attack on Heym and other artists at the Eleventh Plenary of the SED Central Committee in 1965. Fortunately, a thaw in the relationship of the state and writers occurred about the time Heym completed his King David novel, so it was approved for publication in the GDR in 1973 (Hutchinson 1992, 161).

The content of *Der König David Bericht* contributed to the GDR's reluctance to publish it. Solomon commands the first-person narrator, the writer Ethan ben Hoshaja, to join the royal commission charged with compiling the authoritative report on David's life. From his own research and the reports of other commission members, Ethan soon realizes that the tales about David's exploits may not accurately reflect historic fact. An ethical historian, he tries to discover the truth, but he is repeatedly stymied by the cabals of certain commission members and by the king's resolve that a glowing report on his father legitimize his own reign and claim to the throne. Though Ethan learns the truth about David, he can never reveal it openly. He reluctantly limits himself to planting a word here and there in the official report that may alert posterity to the facts (Heym 1972, 12). Even that circumspect behavior leads to his downfall; he is dismissed from the commission, declared a non-person, and sent away with his life intact, but with little else.

The King David novel is significant in Heym's oeuvre and in GDR literary history for several reasons, one of which is his use of a biblical story as the basis for the work. Although it has not been uncommon for a Jewish author to adapt biblical stories or themes, Heym had never before shown any inclination to do so—although this was not the last time that the Bible served him as a source of novelistic inspiration. It was, moreover, a most unusual step for a writer in a Socialist country that was officially atheistic and discriminated against citizens who practiced a religion. Although the censors surely realized that this novel not only had no religious agenda but also skillfully satirized biblical revelation, it is nevertheless remarkable that a work set in biblical times and focusing on the lives of Saul, David, and Solomon could be published in the GDR, especially because its author had long been persona non grata for expressing views the authorities considered dangerous.

In this novel, Heym availed himself of a time-honored literary technique: the use of a historical or mythological setting and plot to comment on the contemporary situation in his own country. Although he claims to have hoped this would be his first work "in which everything is solely fictitious . . . but then the present crept in after all" (Heym 1990, 94, my trans.), this remark is disingenuous, for Heym has stated: "Literature is nothing but fictionalized history of the time into which the author was born, . . . and even if he tells of a time other than his own, it is still his, just in different costume and with different stage sets" (111). Despite fears about the danger dissident writers posed for the stability of the state, GDR censors, like most censors, often failed to recognize the political subtext. Thus Heym's David novel was published in the GDR, just as Christa Wolf's Cassandra story was; the biblical and mythological guises of these works finally led the censors to conclude that criticism of the GDR need not be assumed.

Having commented on conditions in the GDR by portraying historical characters in another land in his Defoe story, Heym was able to exploit his experience for *Der König David Bericht*. Here almost everything reflects critically on similar situations in the GDR and other Eastern bloc countries. By revealing the oppression of ordinary citizens in the realm of Saul, David, and Solomon—the ruthlessness of these rulers and their minions in doing anything necessary to achieve their ends even in contravention of their religious principles, and the sang froid with which they conceal their crimes and their successors maintain the cover-up—the narrator effectively depicts the corruption and abuse of power in any dictatorship, but implicitly in Heym's own country and its Soviet master. Hutchinson (1992, 153) enumerates many parallels between this Israel and the Soviet Union, particularly the analogy of Saul, David, and Solomon to Lenin, Stalin, and Khrushchev. Benaja ben Jehojada and his Krethi and Plethi remind the reader not just of the Soviet secret police (153), but also of the GDR's ministry for state security, the infamous Stasi. Heym's anachronisms skillfully indicate the target of his criticism: the word "non-person" and the phrase "to silence to death" (Hutchinson 1992 153, 160; Zachau 1982, 78–79), for example, show that he is decrying nefarious practices of "really existing socialism."

Another central facet of this novel is its focus on the problems of writing history. The very concept of a King David report parodies the effort "to produce a definitive history" and the "numerous projects launched over the years with the aim of legitimizing aspects of the GDR's status" (Hutchinson 1992, 154). Ethan's plight in his attempts to record the truth about David despite Solomon's determination to suppress all undesirable facts reflects the dilemma of authors and other intellectuals in the GDR who were trying to speak the truth under censorship (159–60), and the parallels between Ethan's situation and Heym's own are unmistakable (Hutchinson 1992, 151; Milfull 1991, 191; Zachau 1982, 75). Heym (1988, 764) himself has alluded to similarities he shares with Ethan.

Although *Der König David Bericht* is a work that portrays the problems of "socialist historiography" (Hutchinson 1992, 156), this widely held view has perhaps tended to obscure or draw attention from an important facet of the novel: the depiction by a Jewish writer (Heym) of a Jewish writer (Ethan) whose intent is to discover and convey historic truth for the edification of future generations. Thus Heym thematizes the necessity of remembering and recording the past, a pursuit that has always been a concern of Jewish writers, but has become even more vital since the Holocaust. Because almost all the novel's characters are Jews and it treats contemporary matters in historic guise, it is easy to overlook and difficult to recognize this significant Jewish theme of the work.

On the other hand, two critics' attempts to define the Jewish nature of this novel seem rather forced. Roland Smith claims (1991) that the book illustrates one of two facets that Jewishness has for Heym: "the emerging monotheistic faith . . .

with its concept of a supreme, jealous God, . . . lending itself to manipulation and abuse by the powerful and unscrupulous" (52). In fact, the novel's intent is political, not religious, and religion, a necessary component of the setting in ancient Israel, contributes primarily to the political plot. Likewise, John Milfull's statement that Heym uses "the perspective of the Jewish outsider" here (Milfull 1991, 192) needs elucidation. Ethan's perspective is certainly that of an outsider because he strives to discover and record the truth despite the intrigue and perfidy around him, but he is not an outsider as a Jew because he lives in Israel surrounded by other Jews. Thus the usual meaning of the concept "the Jewish outsider" does not apply to him.

Of course, a work like *Der König David Bericht* requires more of its author than research and reading the biblical story of David. Because Heym himself says that only a Jew could have written this novel (Koelbl 1989, 115), it is imperative to examine his Jewish background and his views on Jewish identity. His family was liberal and relatively unobservant religiously. They attended the synagogue on holy days, and the boy learned Jewish history and Hebrew (Heym 1988, 16). Although Heym claims he did not really believe in God and regarded his religious life as "very unimportant," he concedes that "the impressions that the child received sank in more deeply than one generally imagines" (Kuschel 1985, 102–3, my trans.). Although his parents counseled assimilation (Heym 1990, 193), the anti-Semitism of the times forced him to confront his Jewishness (Kuschel 1985, 103; Koelbl 1989, 115). Unlike religious belief and ethnic background, culture and tradition contributed significantly to his sense of Jewish identity: he received hospitality from Jewish families as an émigré in Prague and a scholarship to the University of Chicago from a Jewish fraternity, and he has cited the importance of German literature as a conduit of Jewish tradition for him in the works of Lessing, Mendelssohn, and Heine (Kuschel 1985, 102–3), the latter of whom was the subject of his master's thesis.

Another central factor in Heym's awareness of his Jewish identity was the Nazi era, particularly the Holocaust. He followed the plight of the Jews attentively, and though he brought his immediate family to the United States, he lost many relatives to the death camps, including a daughter of whose existence he had been unaware (Heym 1988, 650). Like many whom the Holocaust forced to confront their Jewishness, Heym continues to regard himself as a Jew and to identify with Holocaust victims, as evidenced by frequent remarks like "If I had stayed [in Nazi Germany], in all probability . . . I would have ended as a little cloud of smoke in the Polish sky, Jew that I am" (Heym 1990, 25). Ironically, the Jewish identity that would likely have doomed him in the Third Reich may have protected Heym from imprisonment for his outspoken positions in the proudly antifascist GDR (Hutchinson 1992, 137).

Characteristic of Heym's activist personality, his acceptance of his Jewishness and his love of the Jewish tradition did not remain solely intellectual. Before writing *Der König David Bericht,* he participated in Jewish affairs in several ways. His strong anti-Nazi stance, derived as much from his opposition to the persecution of the Jews as from his political views, manifested itself in journalistic work for several German-American anti-Nazi newspapers and an exposé on Nazis in the United States (Hutchinson 1992, 25–27). As an American soldier trained in psychological warfare, he fought the Nazis with flyers and radio broadcasts in Europe and interrogated captured Germans. At war's end he tried to focus the military government on the need to eradicate Nazi views among the German authorities and populace, and as the political editor of an occupation newspaper, he covered the Belsen war crimes trial in Lüneburg (47). Back in the United States, he made speeches for the United Jewish Appeal (UJA) about the Holocaust and the postwar plight of the survivors, and he took his first trip to Israel because that country was the new topic of interest to UJA audiences (Heym 1988, 426). Israel confronted him with existential questions he could not yet answer: "Is this country his [Heym's] country, are these Jews his people . . . ? And to whom does he feel tied anyway, to what nation, race, group? Where does he belong?" (448).

Some of Heym's journalistic work on Jewish issues has appeared in several collections. *Wege und Umwege* (Paths direct and roundabout; 1980) includes two 1938 newspaper articles on the situation of the European Jews: "Der Flüchtlingsplan" (The refugee plan) calls for the rescue of Jewish refugees from Germany and Austria and rails against the American quota system, and "Schlimmer als der Zar" (Worse than the czar) speaks of the German pogroms and begs the countries assembled at Evian to permit refugees to immigrate. *Reden an den Feind* (Broadcasts to the enemy; 1986) contains the texts of two 1945 radio broadcasts about the concentration camps: "Im Konzentrationslager Auschwitz" (In the Auschwitz concentration camp) and "Buchenwald"—and *Stalin verläßt den Raum* (Stalin leaves the room; 1990) includes a report on the 1945 Belsen trial, "Wir alle starben in Auschwitz" (We all died at Auschwitz). Interestingly, Heym mentions in *Nachruf* that he conceived, but never wrote, a novel on camp survivors before he even landed in Nazi Europe or met any such people (Heym 1988, 283–84), and that he quickly lost the notes of his interviews with Holocaust survivors on an immigrant ship to Israel, a loss he implicitly attributes to inability to deal with such traumatic memories (441).

This, then, is the Jewish context of the author of *Der König David Bericht.* Clearly, this novel did not spring merely from a chance encounter with the biblical story of David, but also from Heym's long interest in Jewish identity, Jewish concerns, and the situation of the Jews. But did this work represent a one-time major novelistic immersion in Jewish matters, or did it significantly influence his later writing? As the 1981 West German publication of *Ahasver* (The wandering Jew; 1984) shows, the latter is the case, for here Heym again uses the Bible as a source of literary inspiration and a Jew, as a Jew, as a central character. He reports that, while writing his David novel, he started a period of intense concern with God that continued after finishing the book, when he began reading the New Testament to prepare for depicting Jesus in *Ahasver* (Kuschel 1985, 106). To Heym, both products of his "Marxist Bible reading" (108, my trans.) reflect his interest in "this God who is also my God" (Heym 1990, 135).

Ahasver treats the story of its title character, an angel cast out of heaven with Lucifer for rebelling against God. Ahasver and Lucifer appear in various historical and biblical contexts in several incarnations. Evoking the words that gave rise to the legend of the Wandering Jew, Ahasver refuses to let Jesus rest by his door on the way to Calvary. Heym's Ahasver suffers anti-Semitic prejudice and persecution in Luther's Germany, fights beside the Warsaw Ghetto heroes, and helps Lucifer seize men who make pacts with him in sixteenth-century Germany and in the GDR. He finally spurs Jesus to action and joins him in an attempt to bring about Armageddon early and to reform creation, for which rebellion God casts them both out.

Clearly, Heym here goes beyond his use of the Bible as a source in *Der König David Bericht*. This time he avails himself of Old Testament stories about creation and the legend of the fall of Lucifer, which he adapts by adding a second fallen angel. His primary biblical sources in *Ahasver*, however, are the New Testament accounts leading up to the crucifixion—from part of which the legend of the Wandering Jew is drawn—and the prophecies of Armageddon. He even utilizes information from the Dead Sea Scrolls. Heym employs historical research and the folklore of "sightings" of the Wandering Jew to place his Ahasver in several historical contexts, including Luther's Germany and the Warsaw Ghetto, in the latter of which the Wandering Jew never "appeared" in tradition. As usual, Heym's novel comments on the present and this time even includes contemporary settings (the GDR and modern Israel) and issues, such as the GDR's views on Israel and the threat of nuclear and ecological destruction of the earth.

In the Wandering Jew, Heym has chosen a Jewish character with roots in Christian legend. The figure is so familiar in European folk tradition and literature that Heym remembers having known about him in his youth in Germany (Kuschel 1985, 106). Yet although some previous writers have stressed Jewish aspects of the Wanderer (Ecker 1987, 32–33), Heym, more than any of them, essentially re-Judaized this character: although the Wanderer has often been used for anti-Semitic purposes, Heym restores him to a Jewish context by not limiting him to the legend and by giving him roles as a Jew in various settings. His Ahasver debates with God, Jesus, and Lucifer as an ardent Jewish social reformer, defends the Jewish position in a sixteenth-century scholarly religious disputation, and symbolizes the Jewish victims in sixteenth- and twentieth-century Europe. Thus Heym transformed a stereotype of the Jew into a genuine representative of Jewish reality.

Heym regards both *Der König David Bericht* and *Ahasver* as works that could only be written by a Jewish writer "who can understand the mentality of a person like David or Ahasver or even Jesus. . . . from the history of a minority that is constantly oppressed" (Koelbl 1989, 115). In fact, Smith identifies historical victimization as one of two major aspects of Jewishness for Heym and sees it as the author's purpose in *Ahasver* to portray "the image of the Jew as outcast . . . [and] perpetual victim" (1991, 52–53). Heym's Ahasver does represent the Jew as victim, as persecuted by anti-Semites down through the ages. The anti-Semitism of Luther and Eitzen points to that of Hitler and the Holocaust, the latter of which Heym treats both implicitly and explicitly: Ahasver's fate at Eitzen's hands foreshadows the Holocaust (Milfull 1991, 198), whereas his participation in the Warsaw Ghetto uprising permits a brief depiction of this event. Yet this Ahasver is no passive sufferer, but a militant activist who repeatedly tries to spur Jesus—whom he calls the Rabbi or Reb Joshua, thus placing him in an appropriate, but often forgotten, Jewish context—and even God to social, political, and ecological reform. Thus the image of the Jew that Ahasver conveys is paradigmatic of Heym's concept of Jews and himself as a Jew: he sees them and himself as historic objects of persecution (Heym 1988, 646; 1990, 134), although he rejects those who bask in the role of victim (Smith 1991, 52), and he admires and emulates those who become subjects by involvement in progressive reforms.

Since the publication of *Ahasver,* the topic of

the Germans' treatment of Jews has appeared more often in Heym's writing and speaking, perhaps because of his being confronted with this while writing his memoirs, as Hutchinson (1992, 222) postulates. His depiction in *Schwarzenberg* (1984) of Max Wolfram, a Jewish idealist who had been imprisoned by the Nazis, reflects this concern. In *Nachruf,* in a 1982 address to the International Council of Christians and Jews included in *Einmischung,* and in a 1988 speech at the writers' conference "Vom Schreiben nach Auschwitz" (On writing after Auschwitz), Heym discusses several aspects of this topic, such as anti-Semitism, coming to terms with the past, and neo-Nazism. The brief history of anti-Semitism in the two speeches illuminates and is illuminated by *Ahasver,* especially in regard to the Luther period (see also Hutchinson 1992, 200). To Heym, modern anti-Semitism begins with the economic anti-Semitism of that time, and Luther's diatribes against the Jews lead directly to the Holocaust (Heym 1989, 21–23). Clearly alarmed by neo-Nazism in today's Germany, he calls on Germans to consider their attitudes and actions toward the Jews both now and in the past and urges renewed efforts to come to terms with the past effectively (17, 21).

Such comments, as well as *Ahasver* and *Der König David Bericht,* must be seen as Heym's attempts to put into practice his views on the author's role and responsibility after Auschwitz. Though the Holocaust has taxed "the limits of literature's efficacy," Heym believes that writers have a vital post-Holocaust role because "they are . . . predestined by their calling . . . to formulate the questions with which those in authority and private citizens are confronted after Auschwitz" (Heym 1989, 19, 25). He does not favor constant lamentations and warnings but insists that the knowledge of what happened must be "in the back of their [writers'] mind with every word that they write" so that their work will fulfill the responsibility bequeathed to them by the Holocaust dead (26). Heym takes this responsibility very seriously, as his depiction of the perennial victimization of the Jews in *Ahasver* shows. Yet works need not be directly or even indirectly related to the Holocaust to satisfy Heym's dictum.

In a broader sense, *Der König David Bericht* itself reflects his understanding of the writer's role after the Holocaust, especially because it thematizes the need to remember and record the truth about the past.

The David novel, then, represents the crucial moment in Heym's development from a Jewish writer by accident of birth into an author whose work is significantly affected by the Jewish experience and Jewish concerns. The moment was prepared for by his family and cultural heritage, personal encounters with anti-Semitism, the Holocaust, and his engagement for Jewish causes, but *Der König David Bericht* marks his "literary rediscovery of his Jewishness" (Milfull 1991, 191). Although he has never immersed himself so completely in a Jewish world since, his literary involvement with Jewish issues in his David novel has been fruitful for his subsequent work, most notably *Ahasver.*

Bibliography

Hans Peter Ecker, *Poetisierung als Kritik: Stefan Heyms Neugestaltung der Erzählung vom Ewigen Juden* (Tübingen: Narr, 1987); Stefan Heym, *Ahasver* (Munich: Bertelsmann, 1981); Heym, *Der bittere Lorbeer* (Munich: List, 1966), prev. pub. as *Kreuzfahrer von heute: Roman unserer Zeit* (Munich: List, 1950); Heym, *The Crusaders: A Novel of Only Yesterday* (Boston: Little, Brown, 1948); Heym, *Einmischung: Gespräche, Reden, Essays,* ed. Inge Heym and Heinfried Henniger (Munich: Bertelsmann, 1990); Heym, *The King David Report* (New York: G. P. Putnam's Sons, 1973); Heym, *Der König David Bericht* (Munich: Kindler, 1972); Heym, *Lassalle: Ein biographischer Roman* (Munich: Esslingen, 1969), later published as *Lassalle* (Berlin: Verlag Neues Leben, 1974); Heym, *Nachruf* (Munich: Bertelsmann, 1988); Heym, "The Queen Against Defoe: From the Notes of One Josiah Creech," *The Queen Against Defoe and Other Stories* (New York: Lawrence Hill, 1974), 15–62; Heym, *Reden an den Feind,* ed. Peter Mallwitz (Munich: Bertelsmann, 1986); Heym, *Die Schmähschrift oder Königin gegen Defoe: Erzählt nach den Aufzeichnungen eines gewissen Josiah Creech von Stefan Heym* (Zurich: Diogenes, 1970); Heym, *Schwarzenberg* (Munich: Bertelsmann, 1984); Heym, *Uncertain Friend* (London: Cassell, 1969); Heym, *The Wandering Jew* (New York: Holt, Rinehart, and Winston, 1984); Heym, *Wege und Um-*

wege: Streitbare Schriften aus fünf Jahrzehnten, ed. Peter Mallwitz (Munich: Bertelsmann, 1980); Heym, "Wir alle starben in Auschwitz: Korrespondentenberichte vom ersten KZ-Prozeß in Lüneburg," *Stalin verläßt den Raum: Politische Publizistik,* ed. Heiner Henniger (Leipzig: Reclam, 1990), 32–45; Heym, "Wo stehe ich, geboren nach Auschwitz, geheißen Soundso?" *Schreiben nach Auschwitz,* ed. Peter Mosler (Cologne: Bund, 1989), 16–26; Peter Hutchinson, *Stefan Heym: The Perpetual Dissident* (Cambridge: Cambridge University Press, 1992); Herlinde Koelbl, "Stefan Heym," *Jüdische Porträits,* photos and interviews by Herlinde Koelbl (Frankfurt a. M.: Fischer, 1989), 115–17; Karl-Josef Kuschel, "Die Bibel als Stoff für Schriftsteller: Über Marxismus und Judentum. Gespräch mit Stefan Heym," *Weil wir uns auf dieser Erde nicht ganz zu Hause fühlen: 12 Schriftsteller über Religion und Literatur* (Munich: Piper, 1985), 102–12; Nancy A. Lauckner, "Stefan Heym's Revolutionary Wandering Jew: A Warning and a Hope for the Future," *Studies in GDR Culture and Society 4,* ed. Margy Gerber (Lanham: UPA, 1984), 65–78; John Milfull, "The Wandering Jew and the Sense of History: Stefan Heym and the Ahasveric Principle," *The Modern German Historical Novel: Paradigms, Problems, Perspectives,* ed. David Roberts and Philip Thomson (New York: Berg, 1991), 191–99; Roland Smith, "Stefan Heym: A Question of Identity," *German Literature at a Time of Change, 1989–1990: German Unity and German Identity in Literary Perspective,* ed. Arthur Williams et al. (Bern: Herbert Lang, 1991), 47–64; and Reinhard Zachau, *Stefan Heym* (Munich: C. H. Beck, 1982).

NANCY A. LAUCKNER

November 17, 1976 Stephan Hermlin and Günter Kunert protest the expulsion of Wolf Biermann from the German Democratic Republic

When Adolf Hitler assumed power in Germany in January 1933, Stephan Hermlin (b. 1915) was nearly eighteen years old, Günter Kunert (b. 1929) had not quite reached his fourth birthday, and Wolf Biermann (b. 1936) had not even been born. Yet Hitler's ascension to power, which led to war and the Holocaust, had a profound influence on all three authors. As Stephan Hermlin wrote in 1975 in "Mein Friede" (My peace), the war began for him on January 30, 1933, not on September 1, 1939, as it did for most other Germans. In a speech at a PEN club meeting in 1988 commemorating Primo Levi, Kunert divided our time into two periods: "before Hitler and after Hitler" (Kunert 1991b, 214).

Because all three matured as writers in the German Democratic Republic (GDR) and were thus subjected to its cultural policies, another decisive date in their lives and careers was Biermann's expatriation from the GDR on November 16, 1976. One day later, both Hermlin and Kunert were among the first group of thirteen writers and artists who openly protested this infamous decision; indeed, it was Hermlin who initiated the petition to the GDR authorities demanding that they reconsider Biermann's expulsion (Kunert 1992, 146–50). The repercussions of the expulsion continued during the dissolution of the GDR in 1989–90 and beyond because it led to reprisals by GDR officials against those who signed the petition, and, at the same time, opened up an unbridgeable gulf between those writers and artists who supported the state's decision and those who opposed it. Hermlin's and Biermann's careers had already directly intersected at an earlier date; in fact it was Hermlin who "discovered" Biermann. As secretary of the section for poetry and language of the East German Academy of Arts, Stephan Hermlin arranged a public reading of young poets in the academy on December 11, 1962, where at that time "unknown" poets such as Wolf Biermann, Sarah and Rainer Kirsch, and Volker Braun first reached a wider audience. Because Hermlin made no attempt to direct or control the readings and discussions, he was severely criticized by narrow-minded cultural functionaries. As a result he lost his positions in the academy and in the directorate of the East German writers' union.

The demise of the GDR in 1989–90 affected Hermlin more than it did Kunert and Biermann, who had long before moved to the West and pretty much given up on the GDR. For Biermann in particular, the Gulf War in February 1991 had a much greater effect on his life and career.

Although Hermlin, Kunert, and Biermann are half Jewish, they were more devoted to their Socialist beliefs than to their Jewish faith. In an interview with Robin Ostow, Thomas Eckert said about Jewish émigrés returning to the Soviet occupation zone and the GDR after 1945: "The Jewish émigrés who came back to the GDR were, for the most part, Jews and Communists, both to-gether. They came to the GDR as Communists to build a Socialist Germany in the Soviet Occupied Zone. They regarded their Jewishness as inciden-tal" (*New German Critique* 38 [spring–summer 1986]: 76); they were what Isaac Deutscher called "non-Jewish Jews." This statement certainly ap-plies to Stephan Hermlin, who spent his exile from fascist Germany in Egypt, England, France, Palestine, Spain, and Switzerland. But the claim also includes Biermann and Kunert. To be sure, neither Biermann nor Kunert were émigrés, but they deliberately chose the GDR as the more pro-gressive Germany. Similar to other Jewish Social-ists, "their commitment and identity were pri-marily socialist, and they kept their distance from the Jewish communities" (Ostow 1994, 62).

Stephan Hermlin (pseudonym of Rudolf Leder) grew up in a comfortable middle class fam-ily in Chemnitz and Berlin. In 1931, as a gymna-sium student in Berlin, he joined the Communist Youth League, worked against the Nazis in the underground, left Germany in 1936, fought in the Spanish civil war on the Republican side, lived in hiding in France after Franco's victory, escaped to Switzerland, and returned to East Ger-many in 1947. From his largely autobiographical work "Abendlicht" (Evening light; 1978–79), we learn that his father was taken to the concen-tration camp Sachsenhausen after Kristallnacht (the Night of Broken Glass, in November 1938) and that his younger brother died as a pilot in the Royal Air Force. In this book, Hermlin describes his home (his businessman-father was an accom-plished pianist, famous musicians visited, and Lovis Corinth painted a portrait of his parents), his classmates and friends (some switched from Communism to fascism like Eric M.), and his entry into the Communist Party in Berlin in 1931 (as he noted "in the street" and—with a stab at the Socialist Unity Party [SED]—"that was still possible then," that is, without elaborate procedures [Hermlin 1990, 509]). He also recalls his disagreements with cultural dogmatists in the GDR and his inability "to recognize and accept their simple universal truths" when "new inter-preters tried to outdo each other with condemna-tions and restrictions." He decried their narrow-

mindedness when "great names in literature, mu-sic, and the arts were declared personifications of evil while third rate academic epigones were pro-moted to geniuses . . . even Flaubert and Bau-delaire were declared decadent" (514). In "Mein Friede" and "Rückkehr" (Return; 1982–83), he describes his feelings on returning to Germany at the end of June to early July 1945. Friends had urged him not to come back. Through the good offices of his English mother he could have re-ceived a home and citizenship in Britain. But throughout his nine years in exile, Germany had always been on his mind. He chose to return to Germany because he felt he was needed there in the reconstruction of a new society—the country where his ancestors had lived for almost 2,000 years, the country whose language and culture he knew better than any other, the country whose glories and crimes he understood better than many others, the country he regarded "with lov-ing reverence" ("mit liebender Ehrfurcht") de-spite everything it had done to him. In these texts, he records the excuses of his countrymen in the face of the Nazi crimes and his impressions as a reporter at the Nuremberg trials, and we learn about the working conditions at the Frankfurt radio station under the tolerant supervision of Hermlin's American control officer Golo Mann—as well as the difficulties Hermlin had with Mann's ignorant successor that caused him to resign his position and move to East Berlin. He goes on to describe the problems the ensuing Cold War brought for him, and he remembers his friends who were executed at Plötzensee as resis-tance fighters against Hitler and those who died in the Spanish civil war at the Jarama and the Ebro. He reminds his readers of the innocent victims in Auschwitz—as he does in his cycle of poetry entitled *Erinnerung* (Remembrance), which was written between 1943 and 1953 and concludes with the hopeful poem "Die Asche von Birkenau" (The ashes of Birkenau):

But those who remember,
Are there, are many, grow more.
No murderer will escape,
No fog will surround him.
Wherever he attacks people,

He will be caught.
Seed of iron suns,
Ashes fly over the world.
To all, young and old,
Ash is given to throw,
Heavy as memories
And light as forgetfulness.

("Doch die sich entsinnen, / Sind da, sind viele,
    werden mehr. / Kein Mörder wird
    entrinnen, / Kein Nebel fällt um ihn
    her. / Wo er den Menschen angreift, / Da
    wird er gestellt. / Saat von eisernen
    Sonnen, / Fliegt die Asche über die
    Welt. / Allen, Alten und Jungen, / Wird
    die Asche zum Wurf gereicht, / Schwer wie
    Erinnerungen / Und wie Vergessen leicht")
                                (Hermlin 1979, 85)

In an interview with Silvia Schlenstedt conducted in the summer of 1983, Hermlin discussed his relationship to Jewish culture at some
length. "Jewish culture is practically unknown to
me; it has played no part in my life except for the
Bible, and here both the Old and the New Testament. I have also read some eastern Jewish authors
in translation; I have read Peretz and Scholem
Aleichem; I am aware of Marc Chagall's and Kaplan's art" (Schlenstedt 1985, 20). For him Jewish
culture was synonymous with Eastern Jewish culture, and that was virtually destroyed by the
Nazis. In this interview, he expressed his outrage
about when the Nazis declared Heinrich Heine
an "un-German" poet but conceded that from
their debased point of view, the Nazis may
well have been correct: "From the point of view
of the final human degeneration, namely anti-
Semitism, which I call the lowest humiliation of
mankind in general—when I lower myself for a
moment to the level of those people, then, indeed,
I refuse to have anything in common with what
they call German. In this context, Heine is indeed
an un-German poet." The Nazis' anti-humanistic
definition of "German-ness" left no room for him
or for Heine, however; it likewise excluded many
other "aryan" writers: "In reality, the Fascist
'Entjudung' [making Germany free of Jews] of
Germany includes so-called aryan artists as
well. When taking Fascism to its logical con-

clusion, Goethe and Hölderlin are just as un-
German as Heine. In that case I will gladly be
counted among the number of un-Germans together with Bach, the freemason Mozart, the freemason Goethe and similar people." And yet,
he admitted, there is something special about
Heine, "something the others do not have,"
which can be found in works such as *Rabbi von
Bacherach*.

Fascism, Jews, and anti-Semitism occupy an
important place in Hermlin's work. In 1983,
Hermlin published the short story "Ein Mord in
Salzburg" (A murder in Salzburg), which deals
with Salzburg's long tradition of anti-Semitism
from the Middle Ages to the present. The story is
centered around the murder of a man who boasted
of having personally killed numerous Jews and of
being willing to do it again if the opportunity
arose. The narrator of the story, a journalist, discovered that the man's claims were pure invention. Because he had many interested listeners,
however, the story illustrates that anti-Semitism
is always present; it lurks barely hidden under the
surface, even if not openly displayed.

In the story "Zeit der Gemeinsamkeit" (Time
of togetherness; 1949) the narrator traveled
to Warsaw to commemorate the uprising of
the Jewish ghetto in 1944 that was brutally
squelched by the Nazis. The story receives its
powerful immediacy from its narrative device: it
is written in the form of a letter from one of the
participants in the uprising. At the core of this
narrative are Mlotek, one of the leaders of the
uprising, and his story of how he came to be a
Communist first and a Jew second. Mlotek had
once visited Israel illegally, but he is not a Zionist; he calls the country Palestine rather than
Eretz Israel. While in Palestine, he joins the
Communist Party and finds himself confronted
with the choice of either being beaten at home in
Poland by the Pilsudski police because he is a
Jew, or by the British and Jewish police in Palestine because he is a Communist. He is first
jailed, then deported from Palestine. It is only
after his experience in Palestine that he realizes
his identity as a Communist and a Jew; for him
both were oppressed people: "One could say . . .
that before [his experience in Palestine] I was not

much interested in Communism. Since I had become a Communist, the Jews concerned me more than ever before, and indeed, not only the Jews alone" (Hermlin 1990, 296). Hermlin's own strong identification with Mlotek is obvious, particularly when it comes to the last sentence of the quote; it in particular seems to reflect closely Hermlin's own views.

In a manner similar to that used by Peter Weiss in *Ästhetik des Widerstands* (Aesthetics of resistance; 1975–81), Hermlin commemorates a number of antifascist fighters in a series of individual portraits entitled "Die erste Reihe" (The first row), including Communists who bravely gave their lives for the cause, such as John Sieg, a German-American from Detroit, and Walter Husemann, a member of both the "Rote Kapelle" (Red chapel), a resistance group dominated by leftists, and the "Weiße Rose" (White rose), a resistance group made up mostly of university students, among them Hans and Sophie Scholl. "Die Gruppe Baum," a group of about a hundred Jewish boys and girls in Berlin in 1942, also sacrificed themselves to the cause under the leadership of Herbert Baum. Baum reminded this group of young people that they were Jews and good German patriots at the same time, and that they belonged to the best Germany had produced. He had them read Marx, Engels, Lenin, and Bebel, and he explained to them that fascism was not only directed against Jews but against all workers. Anti-Semitism was, in Baum's (and Hermlin's) view, only a devilish smokescreen to divert attention from the real enemy, the exploiters of the oppressed working class (Hermlin 1990, 113) In the above-mentioned interview with Klaus Wagenbach in 1979, Hermlin acknowledged his indebtedness to these resistance fighters: "Even today I am strongly influenced by the deeds of those dead people. I have always felt indebted to them because I was undeservedly spared while others died" (Kunert 1982, 138).

Among Hermlin's best known stories is "Der Leutnant Yorck von Wartenburg," which was written in the fall of 1944 and published in 1945. This work was inspired by Ambrose Bierce's short story from the American Civil War entitled "An Occurrence at Owl Creek Bridge." In Bierce's story, a Confederate spy imagines his escape in the brief time span between the adjustment of the noose for his execution and the plunge to his death. Hermlin transposes this illusionary escape to the main conspirator of the failed assassination attempt on Hitler on July 20, 1944. In a fantastic illusion, moments before his execution Lieutenant von Wartenburg—modeled after Count von Stauffenberg, who placed the bomb that was supposed to kill Hitler—escapes from prison and to the Soviet Union, where he establishes contact with the Komitee Freies Deutschland (Committee of Free Germany), an organization of Communists and former Wehrmacht officers who had turned against Hitler, while at home Germany openly revolts against the Nazis. But alas, in all cases, it was only a dream, that of the Confederate spy, von Wartenburg, and Stephan Hermlin himself.

Hermlin regards himself as a Socialist and a German patriot. He is steeped in German music and literature; among his favorite authors are Heinrich Heine, a German Jew who was persecuted in his homeland and who while living in exile longed for Germany, and Friedrich Hölderlin, a "belated Jacobean" (in the words of Georg Lukács) like Hermlin. Hermlin deliberately chose the GDR as his home, but he is also an internationalist who has lived in many countries, speaks several languages, and has translated poetry from many different languages into German. Throughout his years in the underground and in exile, he carried with him books from only three authors: Baudelaire, Hölderlin, and Shelley. Although he had his difficulties and differences with the GDR regime, he never once considered leaving the country of his choice as so many of his compatriots did—not even after the Biermann expulsion, which he severely criticized. In a speech that he delivered at the Eighth Congress of the East German Writers' Union in East Berlin on May 30, 1978, he emphatically rejected the attacks on his friends and on fellow writers such as Christa Wolf, Günter Kunert, Stefan Heym, and Franz Fühmann ("Lacking real arguments, they [the functionaries] resort to demagoguery which has a long and ignominious history when it comes to vilifying intellectuals" [Kunert 1978b]) and pleaded for open-mindedness and tolerance. He countered the accusation that those writers had cooperated with the class enemy by stressing that he, although a GDR writer, considers himself a late-bourgeois ("spätbürgerlicher") writer influenced by a number of different cultures, and he maintained that "the existence of literature is not congruent with the existence of states" (34–35).

The Biermann case "also played a decisive role" in Günter Kunert's life (Kunert 1992, 146). November 16, 1976, the date of Biermann's expulsion, constitutes, in Kunert's words, "a date like a turning point in history: before Biermann and after Biermann" (Kunert 1992, 136.) As Kunert pointed out, the case went far beyond Biermann, the person. It was a demonstration of absolute power on the part of a government totally uninterested in any kind of dialogue. In a prepared statement, Kunert explained why he signed the Biermann petition: "My motivation for opposing Biermann's expatriation is quite simple: it is widely known that at the root of my work is my rigorous anti-Fascism. For me, the GDR is one of the genuine anti-Fascist states— therefore the stronger my shock about a measure that is bound to taint the image of the GDR, an image that I, too, helped to shape and propagate." The implication is clear: the action against Biermann is reminiscent of fascist practices because "it is designed for the sole purpose of causing fear and anguish." Kunert had deliberately chosen the GDR as his home because for him this German state seemed to be the best guarantee against a revival of fascism in Germany. Now this illusion was shattered and his hopes utterly destroyed: "There are norms of morality that cannot be breached without doing irreparable harm to man. I have been deeply hurt by the expatriation measure; I will continue to oppose it, and I am prepared to take all the consequences." Seeing no change in GDR policies and unable to write, Kunert finally gave up on the GDR and left for Itzehoe in West Germany in 1979. He explained the reasons for his departure in an article in the weekly *Die Zeit* (Nov. 2, 1979), under the heading "Now it is finally enough: About the unbearable life of writers in the GDR." Criticized in the past as a "skepticist" on numerous occasions,

Kunert was no longer willing to accept the shabby treatment by cultural functionaries and literary critics that made life in the GDR unbearable for him and for many other GDR writers who saw no alternative but to turn their backs on the GDR.

The half-Jewish Kunert, of course, was no stranger to persecution, albeit by a much more brutal and ruthless authoritarian system. As a child in Berlin during the Nazi period, he had seen the "Baruchs, Caros, Falckensteins and Warschauers," including his grandfather, killed. Although he and his mother, née Warschauer, were protected by his Aryan father, they always wondered how long that protection would last (Reich-Ranicki 1982, 238). Before World War I, Kunert's father, Adolf Aloys Paul Franz Kunert, the owner of a small business, had migrated from Bohemia to Berlin and married Edith Warschauer. Although urged to do so, he refused to divorce her during the Third Reich, and thereby took upon himself all the consequences that it entailed. Kunert had his disagreements with his father on the topic of Socialism, but he admired his father's moral courage: "What remains is the decency of a man who with a single signature on a divorce paper could have considerably improved his status and might have prolonged his life, but he did not do it" (Kunert 1974, 144).

Kunert did not particularly like his school in the workers' district of Berlin-Kreuzberg, but his teachers and fellow students—most of whom were apolitical, some even openly anti-Nazi— left him in relative peace. He was considered an outsider, "a stranger one puts up with" ("ein geduldeter Fremdling") whose religion was listed as "dissident" in the school records, a term "which was filled with real meaning for me only some forty years later" (Reich-Ranicki 1982, 235). The air raids, which increased in frequency and severity toward the end of the war, left him strangely untouched, even elated, although their own house was hit, because he felt that they were not directed against him but against the "others," the Germans, which he regarded as a "just punishment" (240).

Kunert's Jewishness is defined not by tradition or religion, let alone "race," but by political and social circumstances. Similar to Jean Améry, he is Jewish because he is not non-Jewish. Yet Auschwitz had eliminated his sense of security and became a determining factor in his life and work: "Confidence in the world and meaning in existence were the invisible components which also went through the chimneys of Auschwitz and disappeared without a chance for their renewal" (Kunert 1991b, 245). As Heidelberger-Leonard noted, "The presence of the past . . . dominates his [Kunert's] entire thinking, even his entire work from his novel *Im Namen der Hüte* [1967] to his recently published volume of essays *Die letzten Indianer Europas* (1991)" (Reich-Ranicki 1988, 257). For Kunert, the past means Auschwitz and the Holocaust; they constitute a recurring theme in his work. The uninvited guest of his poem "The Uninvited Guest," who hailed from the area around Warsaw and became a victim of the Holocaust, keeps coming back. In a sermon with the significant title "Ungemeinsame Geschichte—erinnern und weiterleben" (Separate history—to remember and continue living) that he delivered in Lübeck's St. Petri church in 1989, Kunert traces the history of anti-Semitism from medieval religious Christianity to a modern nationalistic chauvinism that finally led to the "Holocaust"—a term Kunert rejected because it implies an element of inevitable fate (Kunert 1991b, 222–35). According to Kunert, the search for a German national identity after World War II cannot bypass the Holocaust, a fact that led the German-Jewish journalist Henrik Broder to the conclusion that "the Germans will never forgive the Jews for Auschwitz." Kunert warns, therefore, that the memory of Auschwitz could lead to a new wave of anti-Semitism in the efforts to establish a renewed German nationalism. For a while, at least, Kunert sincerely believed that the Socialist system of the GDR would change the course of German history for the better.

Karl Wolf Biermann was born on November 15, 1936, in Hamburg, a son of Emma and Dagobert Biermann, two active and committed Communists. Dagobert Biermann worked in the Hamburg shipyard of Blom & Voss; he lost his job and was jailed because of his political activ-

ities. Released in 1935, he secretly collected information for the Franco troops about ships sailing for Spain with weapons and ammunition; he was subsequently caught, convicted, sent to prison, and murdered in Auschwitz in 1943. Wolf believed that his father might have survived the Nazi period had he not volunteered at his trial that he was a Jew; being both a Jew and a Communist sealed his fate. Biermann's father, however, was not a practicing Jew. Dagobert Biermann, his parents, and all of his relatives died in Nazi concentration camps; only Wolf and his mother survived the war. This, then, is the legacy with which Wolf Biermann grew up, a legacy he never forgot. In numerous poems, songs, and articles he commented on daily events and criticized the Communist authorities in the East as well as politicians and politics in the West. But time and again, he returned to his origins, especially his father and his fate, and wherever he lived he hung an enlarged picture of him on his wall, a "mug shot" that was sent to his mother from Nazi prison.

Having been raised a Communist, it was only natural that young Biermann, eager to help build an antifascist, Socialist society, would leave the conservative Adenauer republic in the west and move to East Germany two months after Stalin's death in May 1953, and a month before the ill-fated uprising in East Germany on June 17. Later, in 1990, he remembered: "In 1953, when I came to Gadebusch, a small town in Mecklenburg, I found Communism thoroughly healthy and a Communist state almost a reality. Our beloved Stalin had just died, and 17 June 1953 had left this place untouched. I felt great because I understood nothing" (Biermann 1990b, 330). In Gadebusch he composed a few songs and poems that later in life he preferred to forget, such as "Soldatenlied" (Soldiers' song), in which he advised youngsters to join the East German Peoples' Army. As a young student in Gadebusch full of ideals (and delusions), Biermann seemed easy prey even for the Stasi (the East German state security service), which attempted but failed to recruit him only because were too clumsy (Biermann 1990a).

It did not take Biermann long, however, to

realize that his idea of Socialism differed substantially from the officially decreed Socialism in the GDR. He refused to follow the official line of Socialist realism and sing the praises of happy Socialists: "I should sing to you of the happiness of a new age / But your ears are deaf from speechmaking. / Make more happiness in reality! / Then you won't need so much Ersatz in my words" ("Tischrede des Dichters," in Bentley 1968, 62). Biermann was never one to mince words, and he accused the GDR functionaries, those "inquisitors of happiness," of repressing freedom and avoiding reality: "Would you chop your foot off / Rather than wash it?" (Biermann 1972, 53; Bentley 1968, 51) He openly declared that he was "dissatisfied with the new order" (Biermann 1972, 67; Bentley 1968, 68).

Naturally, the GDR functionaries were not particularly pleased, and Klaus Höpke, deputy minister of culture, took Biermann to task in a lengthy article in the party newspaper *Neues Deutschland* on December 5, 1965: "Biermann refuses to fulfill the beautiful and noble social task of a writer in our society, that of depicting the construction of a new and just society. . . . He repeats the meager demands of bourgeois individualism and approaches Nietzsche's ideology of superman" (Schubbe 1972, 1066). Even Erich Honecker, himself a victim of fascism and, from 1971 to 1989, the last significant leader of the GDR, joined the attack on Biermann in a speech before the eleventh plenary session of the politburo of the SED's Central Committee, the highest policymaking body in the GDR. The result was that beginning in 1965 Biermann was not allowed to perform inside or outside the GDR— until November of 1976, when GDR authorities permitted him to perform in West Germany only to prevent him from returning to the GDR. Because Biermann's tapes and books were widely distributed underground in the GDR—he had become, in his own words, a kind of "plebeian Orpheus in a totalitarian underground"—he had obviously become such a problem for GDR officials that they saw no other way to silence him. Conscious of the fact that his father died as a Jew and a Communist in Auschwitz, jailing his son would have been too embarrassing, even for GDR

politicians. As the subsequent furor over Biermann's expatriation indicated, however, they had miscalculated; instead of silencing a "troublemaker," they had unwittingly driven one more nail into the coffin that was to hold the GDR state in 1989.

In the West, Biermann joined the peace movement and remained a critical Socialist who was not always in tune with West German leftists. These leftists by and large closed their eyes to realities in the Eastern bloc and turned more and more pro-Palestinian and anti-Zionist; many of them even came to regard Israel as a fascist state oppressing Palestinians and took to wearing Palestinian shawls in solidarity with Palestinians. When the end came for the GDR, Biermann did not mourn the loss, and he ridiculed those who tried to breathe new life into a dead corpse, as many of the speakers (including the writers Stefan Heym and Christa Wolf, as well as the spymaster Markus Wolf) attempted to do with their speeches during a rally on the Alexanderplatz in Berlin on November 4, 1989. Biermann was forced to admit that Communism was "stillborn" and that his lifelong dream of a better Socialism (see, for example, "Das Thälmann-Lied" [Thälmann Song]) and his Oma Meume's prayer that Communism should win ("Großes Gebet der Oma Meume in Hamburg" [Great Prayer of Grandma Meume in Hamburg]) would not be realized.

Throughout the years, Auschwitz was never far from Biermann's mind. In "Gesang für meine Genossen" (Song for my comrades), he dedicated one stanza to his "comrade Dagobert Biermann who was turned into smoke from the chimneys" (Biermann 1991, 80 and 78). In his poetic search of graves of victims and victimizers in various parts of the world, he does not have to look far for his father's grave: "My fathers' grave stone / is everywhere. I need / Not look for his grave / It is so easy to find / There, where a chimney smokes." (Biermann 1982, 41) His poem "Nach Auschwitz" (After Auschwitz) is his answer to the German philosopher Theodor Adorno, who claimed in 1951 that writing poetry after Auschwitz was barbaric, even impossible. "There was no death knell in Auschwitz, when my father burnt," but there are poems written to remember, even after Auschwitz: "Yes, there are poems after Auschwitz. And / there are even merry songs. That's / The way we are. We perish completely / And we rise again" (47). Interpreting Fritz Brügel's "Flüsterlied" (Whisper song; 1936), an antifascist song from the Spanish Civil War, Biermann cannot help but read this poem with hindsight after Auschwitz: "Those gassed in the smoke above the camp are already burnt; nothing worse can happen to them. I can hear my murdered father sing this song into the wind, and then every fragmented word assumes cruel truth: 'We are unseen, we are unknown / we do not wear a sign. / The enemy's cunning burns us not, / We can be reached no more.' The dead of Auschwitz are secure for the time being . . . but they are in danger of being killed again by our forgetting them" (Biermann 1992, 46–47). Similar to Kunert's work, much of Biermann's work is written so that we remember.

No other event in postunification German history caused so much acrimonious debate as the Gulf War in early 1991. The peace movement, long dormant after the threat of a nuclear holocaust seemed to have evaporated with the demise of the Soviet Union, came to vigorous life again protesting this "American war for oil." The war against Saddam Hussein "opened a pacifistic religious war in the German media" that divided Germans into "bellicists" (those for the war) and "pacifists" (those against the war). Both sides claimed they had learned the lesson of World War II: no more war, no more Auschwitz.

Biermann entered this debate with an article in the weekly *Die Zeit* (reprinted in Biermann 1992), in which he unabashedly supported the war and thereby confounded his friends on the left and in the peace movement. Biermann did not arrive at his momentous decision lightly; he knew the brutalities of war from personal experiences in the Hamburg firestorm of 1943 that cost 40,000 lives. And yet as a Jew, like Kunert, he approved of those raids because they were directed not against himself but against the Nazis: "And because I was born in Germany / Under the yellow star / We accepted the British bombs / As presents from Heaven" (Biermann

1992, 4). He realized that the motives behind the American strategy in the Gulf War may not have been entirely altruistic. And yet he declared, "I am for this war" (3). For Biermann, Saddam Hussein had demonstrated on numerous occasions that he was a brutal dictator who would not hesitate for a minute to destroy Israel (with weapon systems delivered by the Americans, the French, the Russians, and, last but not least, the Germans): "He will gas my father a second time" (19). In his opinion, there are times when it takes a war to prevent an Auschwitz. Remembering Auschwitz and the fate of his father, he did not want to see Jews gassed again: "Forty-five years after Auschwitz, Jews sit at home in their cozy gas chambers behind plastic covers and scotch tape, that is progress. In Tel Aviv and Jerusalem, with German gas masks over their Jewish noses, they are waiting for the moment when poison gas is thrown in from above. That is progress: this time it is no SS man filling in the grainy Zyclon B by hand from a can manufactured by IG Farben. Today Jewish people are waiting for the modern sarin gas, for tabun gas, thrown by a Soviet scud missile via the Jordanian air corridor" (6).

It seems that in the fires of the Gulf War, Biermann for the first time truly discovered his Jewish roots: "For me, the circle comes back to my childhood" (Biermann 1992, 18) Under attack from "genuine rightists and false leftists," supported only by a few Jewish friends (among them the writer Hans Sahl), and consoled by Manès Sperber's writings, he felt "returned to the coldness of a familiar hostile alienation" (18). He parted with German pacifists ("fasten your Palestinian neck scarfs, we have nothing in common" [19]) and turned to translating Yiddish songs, including those of Mordecai Gebirtig. In a letter to his Jewish friend Arno Lustiger in Frankfurt he asked for a Yiddish-German dictionary: "Now that you have made so much of a Jew out of me, you can supply the language as well" (29). And he thought about recording these songs with a klezmer band, "like those young New York Jews playing the music of their Polish great grandfathers" (30).

Clearly, the Gulf War was another watershed for Biermann; Biermann after the war was different from Biermann before the war. And yet he did remain consistent: as Dagobert Biermann's son, his position in the Gulf War was only a logical extension of his previous antifascist stance, except that now he had also discovered his Jewish roots more clearly than ever before. One of his latest songs, dating from 1991 and dedicated to Arno Lustig, is characteristic for the old and new Biermann: "I remain what I have always been / Half goy and half Jew / But one thing I know for sure: / *Only he who changes to himself remains true*" (Biermann 1991, 440)

Hermlin, Kunert, and Biermann, although belonging to different generations, shared a belief in a Socialist utopia; their lives and views were greatly influenced by their Jewish origins, by Nazi rule in Germany, by the foundation of the GDR, by the repressive cultural policies in the GDR (most notably demonstrated by the expatriation of Biermann), by the demise of the GDR, and (especially for Biermann) the Gulf War. All of them were also shaped by the German cultural heritage, from Friedrich Hölderlin, Heinrich von Kleist, and Heinrich Heine to Bertolt Brecht. Their relationship to Germany, however, was as complicated and complex as that of those German writers from the past.

Bibliography

Eric Bentley, trans., *The Wire Harp* (New York: Harcourt, Brace & World, 1968); Wolf Biermann, *Alle Lieder* (Cologne: Kiepenheuer & Witsch, 1991); Biermann, "Auch ich war bei der Stasi," *Die Zeit* 19 (May 11, 1990a): 18–19; Biermann, *Die Drahtharfe* (Berlin: Wagenbach, 1972); Biermann, *Klartexte im Getümmel* (Cologne: Kiepenheuer & Witsch, 1990b); Biermann, *Der Sturz des Dädalus* (Cologne: Kiepenheuer & Witsch, 1992); Biermann, *Verdrehte Welt—das seh' ich gerne* (Cologne: Kiepenheuer & Witsch, 1982); Irene Heidelberger-Leonard, "'Auschwitz werden die Deutschen den Juden nie verzeihen!' Überlegungen zu Günter Kunerts Judesein," *Günter Kunert: Beiträge zu seinem Werk,* ed. Manfred Durzak and Helmut Steinecke (Munich: Hanser, 1992), 253; Jeffrey Herf, "Der Geheimprozeß," *Die Zeit* 41 (Oct. 14, 1994): 7; Stephan Hermlin, *Aufsätze, Reportagen, Reden, Interviews,* ed. Ulla Hahn (Munich: Hanser, n.d.); Hermlin, *Erzählende Prosa* (Berlin: Weimar, 1990); Hermlin, *Gesammelte Gedichte* (Munich: Hanser, 1979); Dietmar Keller and Matthias Kirchner, eds., *Biermann und kein Ende: Eine Dokumentation zur DDR-Kulturpolitik* (Berlin: Dietz, 1991); Michael Krüger, ed. *Kunert lesen* (Munich: Hanser, 1979); Günter Kunert, *Die Beerdigung findet in aller Stille statt* (Munich: Hanser, 1968); Kunert, *Camera Obscura* (Munich: Hanser, 1978a); Kunert, *Diesseits des Erinnerns: Aufsätze* (Munich: Hanser, 1982); Kunert, "In den Kämpfen dieser Zeit," *Tintenfisch* 14 (1978b): 32; Kunert, *Fremd daheim* (Munich: Hanser, 1990); Kunert, *Die letzten Indianer Europas* (Munich: Hanser, 1991a); Kunert, *Die letzten Indianer Europas: Kommentare zum Traum, der Leben heißt* (Munich: Hanser, 1991b); Kunert, *Der Sturz vom Sockel* (Munich: Hanser, 1992); Kunert, *Tagträume in Berlin und andernorts* (Frankfurt a. M.: Fischer, 1974); Kunert, *Der ungebetene Gast* (Berlin: Aufbau, 1965); Robin Ostow, "Becoming Strangers: Jews in Germany's Five New Provinces," *Reemerging Jewish Culture in Germany: Life and Literature Since 1989,* ed. Sander L. Gilman and Karen Remmler (New York: New York University Press, 1994); Ostow, "Being Jewish in the Other Germany: An Interview with Thomas Eckert," *New German Critique* 38 (spring–summer 1986): 73–87; Marcel Reich-Ranicki, "Die Geschichte einer zunehmenden Verfinsterung," *Ohne Rabatt* (Stuttgart: Deutsche Verlags-Anstalt, 1991), 157–58; Reich-Ranicki, ed., *Meine Schulzeit im Dritten Reich: Erinnerungen deutscher Schriftsteller* (Cologne: Kiepenheuer & Witsch, 1982); Nicolai Riedels, *Internationale Günter Kunert Bibliographie. I* (Hildesheim: Olms, 1987); Jay Rosellini, *Wolf Biermann* (Munich: Beck, 1992); Silvia Schlenstedt, *Stephan Hermlin* (Berlin: Volk und Wissen, 1985); and Elimar Schubbe, ed., *Dokumente zur Kunst-, Literatur- und Kulturpolitik der SED* (Stuttgart: Seewald, 1972).

KARL-HEINZ J. SCHOEPS

October 1978   Jean Améry takes his life

At age sixty-six, in a Salzburg hotel room, Jean Améry took his own life. The act—in which he had reflected from his first, unpublished novel (*Die Schiffbrüchigen;* 1934) to his phenomenological examination of suicide (*Hand an sich legen;* 1976)—took place six months after Améry had delivered the official speech at the opening of the Lessing House at Wolfenbüttel. In that text, "The Spirit of Lessing and the World of Today," Améry had given a breathtaking demonstration of the life remaining not only in the beleaguered notion of Enlightenment, but in the apparently moribund idea of Providence. The speech, in which he "refused to accept resignation, however deadly, erotically seductive it might be," was to be his last.

Introductions to authors, normally and sensibly, do not begin by discussing their ends. And much has been written of Améry's death: some of it vulgar, some merely false. But this aversion to focusing on Améry's death is as it should be, for it is clear to anyone who has encountered Améry's work that the nature of his death could not be a merely biographical question. This is partly because nothing, for Améry, was merely biographical. One of his last essays describes all his books as autobiographical; moreover, questions about the nature and meaning of the subject, the relation of subjective experience to a reality which is impervious to it, are probably the most central in Améry's work. As with other questions, Améry did not address this through the metaphysical abstractions he often considered to be elusive, but radically and directly: by taking himself as the subject of each of his major texts.

For some, it may be this more than other qualities that removes Améry's writing from the realm of the philosophical. But to isolate his writing in this way would be to forget the role of self-examination not only in the origins of Greek philosophy, but also in the thought of Kant and Wittgenstein—two of the philosophers in whose work Améry was most steeped. Améry himself was surely more unrelenting in following Socrates' injunction to self-knowledge than any philosopher before him. He saw the right to use his life as a text not in any of its remarkable features, but in its representative ones. A life that began in provincial romanticism and led through exile, resistance, torture, and Auschwitz can well be said to have crossed what was crucial in the twentieth century, and all the more so if it is a life accompanied by the widest sort of erudition; Améry's knowledge of modern thought was intimate, in the most exacting sense of the word. Améry's exercise in self-knowledge was successful not only because of the way in which his life could be seen as archetypal or because it was conducted with an intelligence exhibited in constant dialogue between the concrete and the theoretical, but also because of his commitment to searing self-criticism. Fond of the word "lucid," he had no use for the more stylish "authentic"; what can be shown cannot be said.

In describing his writing as autobiographical, he denied that it was personal. Still less does it display anything that might be called exhibitionistic, though it was characteristic of Améry to raise this question himself. His sense of fineness is shown in his use of several voices to carry out the work of autobiography: he describes himself in the third person in certain moments of irony and addresses himself in the second person when the need for self-critique seemed greatest. Only when describing his life in Auschwitz (which he did very rarely) or his visits to postwar Germany (which he did more often) does he consciously, sometimes jarringly, choose the first person. And this choice should not surprise: Améry's exploration of the self began in the experience of its absolute negation. Long after the war was over, the Auschwitz tattoo that turned Hans Mayer into Prisoner 172364 shook him anew every morning and was inscribed on his Vienna tombstone. Améry's assertion of subjectivity is part of a search for self-knowledge that has a very old philosophical tradition; it is also an act of defiance.

But Améry's death raises questions about his work not only because action and reflection were, for him, always tested against each other—even more directly, his suicide would become the fact through which his work is perceived. Améry's death, it was claimed, showed that it was impossible to maintain that principle of hope of which he spoke so often; his work must therefore be viewed as defeatist, despairing, even nihilistic. It was said that his uncompromising rejection of those elements of life that he judged unacceptable to reason left him nothing to accept but his own death. Primo Levi wrote that "Améry's courageous decision to leave the ivory tower and go down onto the battlefield left him incapable of finding joy in life, indeed of living. Those who 'trade blows' with the entire world achieve dignity but pay a very high price for it because they are sure to be defeated."

As Améry would insist in his discourse on suicide, every death that is freely chosen remains partly mysterious just because it is free. It cannot be the task of this essay to explain Améry's death or, even more impossibly, to justify it. It is also not my intent to touch the veil of the indestructibly private that, as Améry wrote, must cover every suicide. The final years of his life offered Améry sufficient reason for depression. The

writer who defended—indeed reveled in—absolute individuality was never without the most acute regard for the political. The literary recognition that his work received in the 1970s could not compensate for the growing sense that his words were wasted. His essays increasingly excoriated the breakdown of the Left: in the third world, the transformation of revolutionary movements into dictatorships (which he ruthlessly denounced without ever being tempted by anti-Communist positions); in Europe, the transformation of a critical commitment to utopian Socialism into an empty radicalism that could only choose between elite and impotent language games, and blind terrorism.

This movement was discouraging enough in post-1968 France, the place Améry described not only as his own spiritual home, but the home of spirit outright. Matters were even worse in Germany. There the postwar generation in whom Améry had placed much hope was failing in a manner that seemed barely conceivable. Not only was the German Left unable to confront the Nazi past with the seriousness the task demanded; it was increasingly prey to, and preoccupied with, what it called anti-Zionism. It did not take the sound of young German "anti-fascists" shouting "Death to the Jewish People!" at a rally for the Palestine Liberation Organization for Améry to hear leftist support for what he feared could become another Auschwitz on the Mediterranean. Such support must have been truly world-shattering. Améry wrote often of the exhilaration of the early postwar years during which there was, finally, mutual understanding between himself—as a Jewish resistance member who had survived Auschwitz—and the rest of the world, which seemed committed to destroying whatever vestiges remained of a universally hated regime. In the years that followed, not only did the Left fail in its attempt to turn resistance into revolution; throughout Europe, Nazis and their collaborators were also reinstated in positions of power while resistance heroes were politely consigned to oblivion. Améry described this process as a source of deepest disorientation as well as dismay; but it was, at least, explicable, carried out by global reactionary forces in the service of the Cold War.

To watch the *Left* transform itself into a well-spring of anti-Semitism may have been unbearable. In the preface to the second edition of *At the Mind's Limits,* Améry wrote that he "would never have dreamed it when the first edition of my book appeared in 1966 and I had no other enemies except my natural ones: the Nazis, old and new, the irrationalists and fascists, the reactionary pack that had brought death to the world. That today I must stand up against my natural friends, the young women and men of the Left, is more than overtaxed 'dialectics.' It is one of those bad farces of world history that make one doubt the sense of all historical occurrence and in the end despair."

Yet even more was at stake than Améry expressed here. As Henryk Broder put it, more than a little condescendingly, Améry retained a "touching" belief that the anti-Semitism of the German Left was a failure of consciousness; if one could only explain matters properly, one could turn them back toward a reasonable path. Améry never abandoned this belief, neither in regard to the German Left nor in regard to anything else, and it is this fact that leads us from personal to philosophical despair. Améry heard the sweet voice of reason as composers hear music, and his death raised questions threatening to silence the force of his work. His is sometimes mentioned as an instance of post-Holocaust suicide—the fate of some survivors who, it is suggested, had looked too hard, thought too clearly, seen too far to allow them to live further. Like Celan and Levi, Améry had experienced the sense that his own survival was not only monstrously accidental, but thereby illegitimate. Unlike Celan and Levi, he placed that survival squarely in the service of the Enlightenment. Hence the issue becomes whether those who have struggled too directly with certain questions must eventually succumb, paying for that struggle with their sanity or their lives. Are there things that cannot be faced? Are there thoughts that cannot be borne?

Enlightenment, Améry never tired of telling us, is a key word. His understanding of the Enlightenment was as clear as his allegiance to it. The early student of Schlick and the *Tractatus* became the late critic of Adorno, Foucault, and lesser proponents of what he viewed to be an irrationalism as frivolous as it was fashionable. Asked to place himself philosophically, Améry called himself an existentialist-positivist. The answer underscores his commitment to the rigorous use of thought, especially a stern regard for the distinction between the empirical and the ideal, to examine real questions that the Vienna Circle had too quickly dismissed as illusory. Enlightenment grounded his political belief in the principles of the French Revolution, which he viewed as the foundation of a Socialism that invoked both common sense and utopia. Enlightenment was a matter of content and practice; how else to establish a society devoted to the material realization of liberty, equality, and fraternity except by patiently showing that thinking clearly leads to acting decently, education to democracy? Enlightenment was expressed in the demand that the sharpest critical intelligence be cultivated not in order to distance its possessors from the common lot, but to establish its conditions for everyone.

Améry's understanding of Enlightenment was classical, finally, in its relentless use of reason to probe the very hardest questions, to strain at the limits of reason itself. Améry's first major book was devoted to the exploration of Auschwitz and torture, and it was followed by treatises on aging and suicide. The list would be daunting were it not for Améry's uncanny ability to write about decay, ruin, and death itself without a trace of the morbid. His project is imbued with the tone as well as the zeal of the old Encyclopedists; as Alfred Andersch noted in *Über Jean Améry,* Améry's discourse on aging is his "Poem on the Lisbon Earthquake." Though describing himself as radically old-fashioned, his own century forced him to carry this project further than Voltaire could have foreseen. Not the Thirty Years' War but Auschwitz, not sudden senseless natural death but the naturalness of death itself, would be called into question from the standpoint of reason. These are thoughts from which many will shrink; Améry's suicide seemed to confirm their reluctance. That the eighteenth century raised just these questions in regard to Améry's beloved Lessing could not have been unknown to this very literate thinker. The word nihilism was invented by F. H. Jacobi during a far-reaching debate in which he claimed it to be the direct consequence of Lessing's practice of radical Enlightenment; reason, Jacobi argued, should be abandoned for the sake of what might be saved of the human soul. This challenge would be central to Améry's work.

Améry was born Hans Mayer in 1912 to an assimilated Austrian-Jewish father and an Austrian mother who raised him in the Catholic traditions of the province. After his father's death in the Kaiser's army in 1916, his mother supported herself and her son by innkeeping in a small Austrian resort. Poverty was always a threat, and Améry was often forced to interrupt his university studies in Vienna to work variously as a porter, a salesman, and a barroom pianist. His study of philosophy and literature brought him to Moritz Schlick and Rudolf Carnap, whom he saw as deeply connected to the German emigrant writers he admired. He was later to criticize himself for believing that Carnap's ridicule was an appropriate means of dispensing with Heidegger. Although positivism was far more honest than the provincial romanticism that was his earlier base, it proved equally ineffectual in combating, or even recognizing, the catastrophe about to engulf them.

Améry could not have been quite as politically unsuspecting as he later portrayed himself. While studying positivism and writing literature, he also participated in the Viennese workers' brief attempt to resist the clerical-fascist Dollfuss government's suppression of social democracy in 1934. But his life took an unchangeable course with the publication of the Nuremberg Laws, through which he recognized that he was "a dead man on leave." Améry, whose connections to the Jewish community had been hitherto nonexistent, was given the opportunity to obtain "Aryan" papers. With his usual honesty, he wrote that he might have succumbed to that temptation were it not for his love for the Jewish woman who was to become his first wife. If his Jewish identity was forced on him by the Nazis, however, it was one he henceforth resolved to choose as his own.

Or did he? Améry returned to the question of his own Jewishness many times because he felt caught between what he called the simultaneous necessity and impossibility of being a Jew. To be a Jew seemed impossible: his childhood memories were of neither secular nor religious Jewish culture, but of midnight masses in a snow-covered village. The intellectual influences he later chose for himself showed no particularly Jewish slant: Améry mentions Heine less often than Trakl, Joseph Roth leaves him less in awe than Thomas Mann. Of course Améry could, he noted, move to Israel, learn Hebrew and its literature, and call himself Jochanan, but such an attempt would involve as much bad faith as his youthful cultivation of lederhosen and knee socks in the attempt to masquerade as a pure provincial Austrian. (His only trip to Israel, two years before his death, seemed to call this view into question: in one interview Améry said that, were he young enough to "be of use there," he would probably move to Israel despite the difficulties he had noted.) Améry believed that it was too late for him to acquire a Jewish identity with positive content; that identity could be expressed only in his understanding of himself as a victim of anti-Semitism, and in his consequent solidarity with every Jew threatened by it.

Améry's readers will doubt his claim that only Hitler made him a Jew. He himself later noted that, without any scientific way of understanding it, he was convinced that his intellectual and spiritual constitution were Jewish by birth, though his upbringing and milieu were not. That constitution is evident throughout his work and not only in his magnificent use of irony or in the sense of permanent restlessness that pervades even his repeated return to the question of what it means to be a Jew. Améry's work also revives the old Jewish love for that Enlightenment which, historically, had raised—some will say emptied—the people from the category of Jewish to that of the simply human. In his commitment to being "a Jew without Judaism," Améry rejected the more treacherous versions of such love. But his often-expressed solidarity with the state of Israel itself was also a piece of the very classic Jewish commitment to the "insuperable and trivial truth that 'where some are stronger, always stand on the side of the weaker,'" which he took as the unwritten moral law of the Left. Améry's affirmation of universalism and Jewishness was—to risk a word he used only with caution—dialectical; perhaps only his keen understanding of the condition of homelessness would be able to unite them both.

None of these feelings of solidarity with the Jewish people were apparent when Améry read the Nuremberg Laws that were to change his life. His early connections to Austria led him to assure a friend, while looking over the Vienna hills, that nothing could force them to leave. In December 1938 he and his wife fled Vienna for Belgium, where he would live until his 1940 internment as a "foreign enemy" in the infamous camp at Gurs. He escaped from Gurs and made his way back to Brussels, living in hiding until he was arrested for distributing Resistance propaganda. Tortured by the Gestapo during months of solitary confinement, he was sent to Auschwitz in 1943 after it was discovered that he was not only a political prisoner but also a Jew.

After the liberation of Bergen-Belsen in 1945, Hans Mayer returned to Brussels to learn that his wife had died of heart failure during the war. His discovery of Sartre's work in the first months after the war seemed to justify his past and offer him a future: "Existentialism became for me a wholly personal philosophy of the hunger for life which had gnawingly returned after so many deaths, so many provisional resurrections." He would eventually remarry, choose a French-sounding anagram of his very German original name, and turn to freelance writing for the Swiss press as a source of income. Améry turned out essays and monographs on jazz, Pascal, Marilyn Monroe, NATO, Gerhart Hauptmann, and anything else that his editors requested. Those pieces do not deserve the disparaging judgment he later reserved for them, but they do not yet exhibit the qualities that would win him recognition as a master of twentieth-century German prose: clarity, passion, irony, courage, and a never-failing sense of taste.

These qualities emerged when Améry agreed to produce a series of radio pieces about his experience at Auschwitz, after a chance meeting with a German critic made him hope that writing for a German audience might not be in vain. The series was published as the book *Jenseits von Schuld und Sühne*. In the twelve years between the publication of that book and his death in Salzburg, Améry wrote an impressive number of books and essays on a wide range of topics, yet all of them can be seen as attempts to answer the questions this first book raised.

At the Mind's Limits (the English translation of *Jenseits*) was Améry's exploration of the confrontation between Auschwitz and the intellect. Through reflections on the lives of intellectuals in the concentration camp, Améry attempted to understand what happens when pure reason is set against absolute evil. His answer was grim. Absolute evil not only triumphed but virtually abolished the intellect, and in very short order. The consolations of philosophy may have worked in a Roman prison, but they withstood only a few weeks at Auschwitz. There, as under Gestapo torture, what had been human beings were transformed into sheer flesh. "A slight pressure by the tool-wielding hand is enough to turn the other—along with his head, in which are perhaps stored Kant and Hegel, and all nine symphonies, and *The World as Will and Representation*—into a shrilly squealing piglet at slaughter." The ease with which everything we call mind, soul, or spirit could be destroyed left Améry with an amazement he never lost.

Reason failed him in Auschwitz on several counts. He had passed time in the freezing Gurs prison camp by composing an anthology of German poetry from memory, and by coauthoring a tract of neo-positivist epistemology. In Auschwitz the intellect abruptly lost its basic quality, transcendence: a remembered line of poetry "brought at most pain or derision, then trickled away in a feeling of complete indifference. . . . Nowhere else in the world did reality have as much effective power as in the camp, nowhere else was reality so real. In no other place did the attempt to transcend it prove so hopeless and so shoddy" (Améry 1980a). If the intellect was unable to transcend reality, it failed even more miserably in its attempts to comprehend it. Améry suggests that it was not only foolish to use reason to understand Auschwitz, but that it may also be a moral error to try. "S'expliquer n'est pas justifier" is a maxim that is always used on the defensive: to explain oneself is merely the attempt to make oneself intelligible. And where intelligibility is within reach, justification cannot be far behind.

Reason could not make Auschwitz more bearable; it should not try to make it comprehensible. Instead reason was left, in the camp, with one remaining task: to abolish itself, by shattering all its frameworks of belief. What makes *At the Mind's Limits* more painful than more graphic or gruesome descriptions of the concentration camp is the fact that in it, a man of the highest intellect does just that which he learned at Auschwitz: he uses that intellect to undermine itself and thereby shows the impotence and self-betrayal of reason at the point when it was needed most. Nor does Améry allow himself to find any later meaning in the experience he underwent: Auschwitz did not, he insists, make its survivors wiser, or deeper, or ethically mature. On the contrary, in the terrible thought of the final sentence: "The word always dies where the claim of some reality is total. It died for us a long time ago. And we were not even left with the feeling that we must regret its departure."

Those who are not themselves survivors cannot forget Améry's warning that their most thoughtful efforts to understand the catastrophe will be like a blind man's attempts to talk about color. Nevertheless, Améry's work is also always a call to dialogue. His readers will be forced to question the last sentence quoted—if only because its bitter coldness could only have been formulated by someone who regrets the loss of the word so deeply that he cannot in fact let it go. And this sense is more than confirmed by his later work. If anyone had the right to maintain the impossibility of poetry after Auschwitz it must be Améry—not perhaps, because of his suffering during the war, but because of what he showed in *At the Mind's Limits*. If Adorno's aphorism has meaning at all it would seem to be that expressed in Améry's claim that "to reach out beyond concrete reality with words became before our very eyes a game that was not only a worthless and impermissible luxury but also mocking and evil." Yet Améry wrote that Adorno's claim is nonsense.

Even more puzzling can be passages like these: "What happened that the Enlightenment became a relic of intellectual history, good enough at best for the diligent but sterile exertions of scholars? What sad aberration has brought us to the point where modern thinkers do not dare to employ concepts such as progress, humanization and reason except within damning quotation marks?"

One's reaction to such passages—which can be found in nearly every one of Améry's later texts—is liable to be surprise. Didn't Améry himself tell us precisely what happened? Shouldn't he know better than anyone why no modern thinker feels free to use those ideas in good faith? Améry's work seems threatened not by simple contradiction, but by outright antinomy. He maintained that the only hope for fulfilling the one truly human task—giving meaning to the meaningless—lies in "the benevolent optimism of the Enlightenment with its constant values of freedom, reason, justice and truth." Human value, he argued, is found in the protest against every occurrence that is unacceptable to reason; this revolt against reality is all that allows us to make history, to create sense and dignity. But if Améry's defense of these ideas is profoundly moving, his demonstration of their antithesis is at least as compelling. For no other author has combined reflection and experience so successfully to convince us that, since Auschwitz at the very latest, the attempt to create meaning by using reason to confront reality is bound to be forlorn.

If antinomies have solutions, they will not be straightforward ones. All of Améry's later work can be seen as a struggle to resolve this paradox—and his realization that if resolution is to be found it will only be in the struggle itself. He is not the only philosopher of this century whose work resists systematization, summary, or even paraphrase: one wants, simply, to quote. In Améry, this difficult feature of his style stems not merely from the fact that it is so very good, but from his own awareness of the philosophical importance of ambiguity. Without it, not only our empirical reality, but also our dreams, will be falsified. Ambiguity, and the permanent self-criticism permitted by it, allow us to steer a course between dogmatism and nihilism. Like his greatest predecessor, Améry held these to be twin results of the same error: the attempt to seek certainty at the cost of freedom.

The remaining space cannot survey Améry's work as a whole, but his last book may give some indication of its range. He had always blended genres, and invented them. *Charles Bovary, Landarzt* combines essay and fiction to retell Flaubert's novel from the standpoint of Emma's pitiful husband. In giving Charles a voice, Améry succeeds in conveying Charles's passion for Emma with more feeling and intensity than Flaubert describes the desire of Emma for her lovers: Améry's attention to the political dimensions ignored by Flaubert results in a portrait that is not only more realistic than that drawn by the creator of realism, but more aesthetically compelling as well. Reconceiving Charles Bovary permits Améry to extend the right to self-determination from the wretched of the earth to those most wretched of spirit, the banal. By taking up this unlikely hero, Améry showed that the self can be asserted from starting points we have yet to imagine. For if Améry could reclaim himself after the war, surely he could recover the country doctor's soul as well.

In the insightful essay already cited, Andersch wrote that in Améry's writing, ideas become persons. The claim is imprecise. In Améry's writing ideas are cherished, and mourned, and loathed, with the ardor others normally reserve for human beings. Yet Améry always insists we be utterly clear about the differences between them. The attention to the ordinary he shared with other contemporaries is at once a philosophical, a political, and an aesthetic principle. Améry could describe with equal compassion the psychological pain that may be initiated by a toothache and the happiness of factory workers at a Saturday night dance. His sharpest scorn was reserved for those who lose sight of the beauty, justice, and goodness to be found in the world in the singleminded search for their ideal forms. The ability to combine respect for the ordinary with faithfulness to the ideal is evident in Améry's political writings, but it reaches its full expression in *Charles Bovary.*

The book's final chapter is titled "J'accuse." Améry had a penchant for allusion, subtle or otherwise; here the reference is particularly crucial.

When asked to discuss the practical value of intellectual work, Améry often remarked that while it is given to few to be a Robespierre or a Trotsky, anyone could be a Zola. In his own "J'accuse," Charles Bovary turns from expressions of love and despair to those of rage: first toward Emma's lovers but finally toward his creator, Gustave Flaubert. For Charles, and ultimately Emma too, were denied the right to the boundless sensuality, and extreme emotion, that were to remain a privilege of the elite. In refusing to grant Charles the dignity that is only achieved through real passion, Flaubert "refused him the chances that are inscribed in the principles of 1789." Bovary's indictment is an attempt to recover the honor of all those "who are not ugly because they are not beautiful, not contemptible because they possess little, not stupid because they serve the reasonableness of the everyday." Flaubert's contempt for such people is a "violation of the pact which you made with reality before you sat down to write my story: for I was more than I was, like every human being, who in resistance against the others and the world daily and hourly steps out of himself to negate what he was, and to become what he will be." In indicting the fictional Bovary's creator, Améry found a way to indict that Creator in whom he never believed. For if *Über das Altern* is his "Lisbon Earthquake," *Charles Bovary* is his Book of Job.

Like Job, Charles Bovary withdraws his indictment in a few final mysterious lines. That withdrawal is not, I believe, an indication of Améry's own resignation, but it is essential to his work. This work is concerned to preserve both sides of a conflict in all their urgency, and to make apparent that there is no middle ground without deception. The attempt to escape this tension by seeking final answers is fatal to thought itself. Only by acknowledging the force of competing claims and moving between them can reason be kept alive. Améry's work confronts the claims made by the most important opposing moments of modern thought while recognizing fully the impulses giving rise to each. This is perhaps clearest in regard to the conflict between Enlightenment and nihilism, but it is equally evident in his discussions of Marxism and humanism, analytic and continental philosophy; in his exploration of the demands of reason and emotion, theory and practice, the political and the erotic. Améry's anti-Hegelianism is far too decided to seek unity in these forces. Here unity would entail compromise, and his thought is uncompromising. The search is rather one for balance. That such balance will be precarious should be clear from the start; perhaps it was only the thorough destruction of his own sense of being at home in the world that gave Améry a standpoint from which to admit the pervasiveness of deepest disharmony.

Nowhere does Améry's apparently endless sympathy for two sides of a contradiction achieve more startling expression than in the final page of his treatise on suicide. "But the survivors are right; for what are dignity, humanity and freedom next to smiling, breathing, striding? Dignity against the conditions of every possibility of being dignified? Humanity against the human being as living, smiling, breathing, striding reality?"

This coda follows a stunning tribute to the ideas of dignity, humanity, and freedom—one that goes so far as to defend the act of suicide as a means that may be chosen to protect them. Unlike the philosophers of the classical Enlightenment, Améry never asked whether one would, or should, choose to live again. (Nearly all the representatives of that allegedly optimistic age answered in the negative.) The question has gone out of fashion. Yet it seems likely that he would have answered it differently than did the thinkers he admired. For Améry as for Kant, hope was a moral obligation, but for Améry it was something else as well. Not only because he could write with insight and wonder about toothaches, or the concept of kitsch, or a man's hunger for his dead wife; but also because he held death to be "the absolutely unreasonable." Like Charles Bovary's love for the faithless Emma, Améry's love for reason was profound enough to sustain even the knowledge of its betrayal. And his death by his own hand does not change this understanding; instead it perhaps affirms that he would have chosen to live again as he died—freely, consciously, in the conviction that "the belief in the human as the goal of the human doesn't let itself be crushed by conceptual contradiction."

Bibliography

Jean Améry, *At the Mind's Limits,* trans. Sidney Rosenfeld and Stella P. Rosenfeld (Bloomington: Indiana University Press, 1980a); Améry, *Im Banne des Jazz: Bildnisse grosser Jazz-Musiker* (Vienna: Albert Müller, 1961); Améry, *Bücher aus der Jugend unseres Jahrhunderts* (Stuttgart: Klett-Cotta, 1981); Améry, *Charles Bovary, Landarzt: Porträt eines einfachen Mannes* (Stuttgart: Klett-Cotta, 1978); Améry, *Cinema: Arbeiten zum Film* (Stuttgart: Klett-Cotta, 1994); Améry, *Geburt der Gegenwart: Gestalten und Gestaltungen der westlichen Zivilisation seit Kriegsende* (Olten: Walter, 1961); Améry, *Gerhart Hauptmann: Der ewige Deutsche* (Stieglitz: E. Handle, 1963); Améry, *Hand an sich Legen* (Stuttgart: Klett, 1976); Améry, *Der integrale Humanismus: Zwischen Philosophie und Literatur. Aufsätze und Kritiken eines Lesers, 1966–1978* (Stuttgart: Klett-Cotta, 1985); Améry, *Jenseits von Schuld und Sühne: Bewältigungsversuche eines Überwältigten* (Munich: Szczesny, 1966); Améry, *Karrieren und Köpfe: Bildnisse berühmter Zeitgenossen* (Zurich: Thomas, 1955); Améry, *Lefeu oder Der Abbruch: Roman-Essay* (Stuttgart: Klett, 1974); Améry, *Örtlichkeiten* (Stuttgart, Klett-Cotta, 1980b); Améry, *Radical Humanism: Selected Essays,* ed. and trans. Sidney Rosenfeld and Stella P. Rosenfeld (Bloomington: Indiana University Press, 1984); Améry, *Teenager-Stars: Idole unserer Zeit* (Vienna: Albert Müller, 1960); Améry, *Über das Altern: Revolte und Resignation* (Stuttgart: Klett, 1968); Améry, *Unmeisterliche Wanderjahre* (Stuttgart: Klett, 1971a); Améry, *Weiterleben—aber wie? Essays, 1968–1978* (Stuttgart: Klett-Cotta, 1982); Améry, *Widersprüche* (Stuttgart, Klett, 1971b); Améry, *Winston S. Churchill: Ein Jahrhundert Zeitgeschichte* (Frankfurt a. M.: Bucher, 1965); Irene Heidelberger-Leonard, ed., *Über Jean Améry* (Heidelberg: Carl Winter Universitätsverlag, 1990); *Hermannstraße 14: Halbjahrsschrift für Literatur: Sonderheft Jean Améry* (Stuttgart: Klett-Cotta, 1978); *Jean Améry, der Grenzgänger: Gespräch mit Ingo Hermann in der Reihe "Zeugen des Jahrhunderts"* (Göttingen: Lamuv, 1992); *Text und Kritik, Heft 99: Jean Améry* (Munich: Text & Kritik, 1988); and *Über Jean Améry: Zum 65. Geburtstag von Jean Améry* (Stuttgart: Klett-Cotta, 1977).

SUSAN NEIMAN

1979 The American television series *Holocaust* is shown in West Germany

April 16, 1978. After weeks of intense promotion and publicity, more than a hundred million viewers were eagerly awaiting the premiere of NBC's television miniseries *Holocaust,* the first Hollywood-produced film to depict the persecution and systematic slaughter of millions of European Jews. In four two-hour installments on consecutive evenings, the record audience (every other American!) watched a chronicle that traced the lives of two fictional German families—one Jewish, one Nazi—during Hitler's reign of terror. The film uses personal stories to exemplify a fateful history that began with anti-Semitic practices of exclusion and discrimination in the 1930s and ended in the industrial mass murder of millions of Jews ten years later. The advertising slogan for the miniseries described the project succinctly: "Holocaust: A Story of Two Families. Of terror and murder. Of love and triumph." The Holocaust recast as the story of two families? The inexpressible reduced to a predictable melodrama of love and murder? Holocaust made in Hollywood? The daring gamble paid off for NBC: *Holocaust* became the most successful program ever for the network, topping even ABC's immensely popular 1977 TV miniseries *Roots.* The series was sold to television networks in more than fifty countries around the globe; it was also widely disseminated as a movie on videocassette. It is estimated that today more than 500 million people have seen the Holocaust film. Its phenomenal success here and abroad has indelibly influenced the way in which we reflect on mass media and their power to shape popular memory.

Not surprisingly, *Holocaust* aroused particular interest in West Germany, where it was shown less than nine months after the American premiere. From the beginning, German film critics and news reporters covered the media event and castigated the Holocaust movie—even before it was broadcast in Germany—for its commercial motives, its sentimentality, and its tasteless blend of concentration camp scenes and pantyhose commercials. Many West German newspapers reprinted a German translation of Elie Wiesel's thunderous attack on the movie in lieu of their own criticism. As a Nobel Prize winner and survivor of Auschwitz, Wiesel could speak with unassailable authority against Hollywood's version of the Holocaust. Under the title "The Trivialization of the Holocaust: Semi-Fact and Semi-Fiction," he wrote in the *New York Times* on the day of the film's premiere: "As a TV production, the film is an insult to those who perished and to those who survived. In spite of its name, this 'docu-drama' is not about what some of us remember as the Holocaust. . . . It tries to show what cannot even be imagined. It transforms an ontological event into soap-opera. Whatever the intentions, the result is shocking. Contrived situations, sentimental episodes, implausible coincidences: If they make you cry, you will cry for the wrong reasons. . . . Holocaust, a TV drama. Holocaust, a work of semi-fact and semi-fiction. Isn't this what so many morally deranged 'scholars' have been claiming recently all over the world? That the Holocaust was nothing else but an 'invention?' The Holocaust *must* be remembered. But not as a show." Wiesel's argument that the Holocaust as event resists representation on principle was warmly welcomed by those who wanted to forget altogether this "darkest chapter" of German history.

The television miniseries *Holocaust* is based on the eponymous novel by Gerald Green, who also wrote the screenplay. It depicts the step-by-step disintegration and destruction of an amicable and respected Jewish middle-class family—a doctor, his wife, and their four children—all of whom except one die in concentration camps. Only the youngest member of the Weiss family, Rudi, who had joined the resistance movement, survives. This story line, with its inexorable downward spiral, is interwoven with the ascendancy of a German Nazi, Eric Dorf, who, prodded by his ambitious wife, rises from poverty as an unemployed lawyer to wealth and fame as a high-ranking officer in the SS. The German version of *Holocaust* ends with Dorf's suicide, whereas the original closes with Rudi's departure for Israel. This uplifting "American" ending was cut in the West German adaptation.

Holocaust follows the classical narrative pattern of historical fiction by weaving the private stories of invented figures into a dense fabric of known and verifiable historical events. The series uses these fictional figures to demonstrate the persecution and annihilation of fully assimilated German Jews in the Third Reich between 1933 and 1945. The viewer learns about the Nuremberg Laws, the Kristallnacht, the euthanasia program, Buchenwald, Theresienstadt, Babi-Yar, Sobibor, the Warsaw uprising, and Auschwitz through the personal lives of these characters. Their coincidental meetings and forced partings are obvious fictions, staged and artificial, but the history that intervenes in their lives is real. This commingling of historical events with invented characters, of political *Geschichte* (history) with private *Geschichten* (stories), leads necessarily to a blurring of the borders between fiction and documentable fact— a blurring that is characteristic of television in general. "Is fact watched as fiction? And fiction as fact?" asked Gerald Green, fully aware that *Holocaust* exploits this very indeterminacy. The care-

fully reconstructed historical mise-en-scène, the realistic acting, the large number of interconnected life stories, and the occasional intercutting of documentary photographs and authentic film footage from the concentration camps lend the film a strong "reality effect." This effect is intensified by the film's appeal to the visual memory of the spectator. The pictures of concentration camps are well known, even clichéd; no one would fail to recognize them. Seeing these images again as part of the television series produces a déjà-vu effect that implicitly validates the historical "correctness" of the film.

As a consumer commodity, *Holocaust* offered something for everyone: love, ambition, humiliation, fear for one's life, incarceration, war, rebellion, death, and liberation—all narrative tropes whose universality guaranteed the broadest possible public appeal. After its popular success in the United States, the broadcast of this series in the "land of the guilty" promised to draw strong reactions, yet the extent of the collective preoccupation with this film exceeded all predictions. Dubbed into German, *Holocaust* was shown on four evenings between January 22 and 26, 1979. *Holocaust,* the movie, was preceded by an intense information campaign about Holocaust, the event. Government agencies, schools, churches, television and radio stations, newspapers, and magazines were all involved in disseminating information about the Final Solution. The whole country was mobilized and ready to watch the American recounting of a tabooed period of German history.

Holocaust—the word entered the German language in 1979—encountered a sensitive political situation. It coincided with the ongoing Majdanek trial, which lasted from 1975 to 1981, the most extensive trial for concentration camp crimes in the history of the Federal Republic. It also coincided with the so-called Filbinger affair, wherein the governing president of Baden-Württemberg was exposed as having sentenced a deserter to death in the last days of the war. And, above all, it coincided with heated debates in parliament about extending the statute of limitations for Nazi crimes. Even so, the statistics are startling: over 20 million West Germans—

which means every other adult—watched *Holocaust* on television.

The television station responsible for the broadcast, WDR, received more than 30,000 telephone calls and thousands of letters. Without exception, all West German media addressed the issue of German war crimes in the wake of *Holocaust*. The publishers of the two largest weekly magazines in the Federal Republic, *Der Spiegel* and *Stern,* wrote editorials confessing that they too had taken part in discriminating against German Jews because they had looked the other way. During all four episodes, telephone numbers were superimposed over the film, inviting viewers who wanted to share their experiences to call in and talk before the whole nation with experts from the press and academia. These discussions followed each segment of *Holocaust* and ran for several hours. "An American television series," wrote *Der Spiegel* on January 29, 1979, "accomplished what hundreds of books, plays, films, and television programs, thousands of documents, and all the concentration camp trials have failed to do in the more than three decades since the end of the war: to inform Germans about crimes against Jews committed in their name so that millions were emotionally touched and moved. . . . Only since, and thanks to, *Holocaust* does a large majority of the nation know what was hidden behind the seemingly innocuous bureaucratic phrase, 'the final solution.' They know it because U.S. filmmakers had the courage to free themselves from the crippling precept that it is impossible to portray mass murder."

It is true that films before and after *Holocaust* were fearful of turning the unimaginable horror of millions of innocent people into easily consumable entertainment for the masses. One of the first filmic attempts to represent the Holocaust, Alain Resnais's *La nuit et brouillard* (Night and fog, 1958; shown on German television only twenty years later, in 1978) is more a meditation on the memory of Auschwitz than a reconstruction of the historical events. Eberhard Fechner's four-hour documentary of the Majdanek trial, *Der Prozeß* (The trial; 1984) and Claude Lanzmann's magisterial documentary film *Shoah* (1986), which consists of nine-and-one-half hours of in-

terviews with Holocaust victims and perpetrators, were praised by the critics but made no noticeable impression on the West German public. Although both films were shown on television, their self-reflexivity, their modernist montage techniques, and their withholding of visual and narrative pleasure did not appeal to the audience of *Holocaust.*

The West German intellectual elite in particular was disturbed by the overwhelming popular success of the American television series. The traditional German distinction between "high culture" and commercial "mass culture," which goes back to debates in the Weimar Republic, suddenly seemed highly problematic. German pride in classical high culture—an essential part of its national identity since the eighteenth century—had to face the question of its actual effect and social function. Those who felt responsible for the state of German culture chastised themselves publicly. Even someone as enmeshed in tradition as the literary critic Marcel Reich-Ranicki asked testily why none of the German filmmakers had managed to produce a popular work like *Holocaust.* And Marion von Dönhoff, publisher of the influential weekly *Die Zeit,* made fun of her own aesthetic objections: "The league of film critics, led last year by the *New York Times,* raised many critical objections in this country as well: it is a melodramatic tearjerker, a trivial entertainment cliché, an impermissible mixture of love story and horror story—as if these aesthetic categories had even the slightest significance in the face of the moral dimension and the message of this series. Some critics overvalue the aesthetic at the expense of the moral in a truly horrifying way" (*Die Zeit,* Feb. 2, 1979). She went on to note that valuing only the purely aesthetic was a typical feature of fascism: "Even during the Hitler business the aesthetic perfection of the flag parades or the grandiose choreography of the Nuremberg Party Congresses infected many and made them 'fellow travelers.'" Such extreme statements that posit a rigid, undialectical opposition between aesthetics and morality, between quality and popularity were part of the media hype that Hollywood's *Holocaust* elicited in Germany.

The shifts in press response before and after

the event are especially telling. Sabina Lietz-
mann, writing for the *Frankfurter Allgemeine
Zeitung,* was one of the first to criticize the American broadcast of *Holocaust* on April 20, 1978,
using the pejorative headline, "The Annihilation
of the Jews as Soap Opera." Much like Wiesel, she
described her discomfort with the trivialization
of suffering and the watering-down of history
writing into storytelling. By September 28,
1978, however, she had revised her opinion, now
convinced that the theme was so central to national self-awareness that it

provokes constant thought, which sometimes, as
in this case, can lead to a total rethinking: Why?
The response of the American public to *Holocaust,*
many of them delayed reactions, taught us that
intellectual and political reaction is one thing,
whereas the spontaneous effect on the emotions is
something altogether different. For millions of
viewers throughout the country, *Holocaust* was
their first and only access to that otherwise unimaginable phenomenon of the destruction of the
Jews. We still consider a good, objective documentary to be a superior instrument of information, but we know that 'in people terms,' the
television series compelled the mass audience to
watch and to empathize. This is a power that no
documentary has, however well made. If we are
faced with the choice whether to allow no information to be presented or to permit information
tailored for easy access as a 'story' and produced
for people who want entertainment, today, re-
signing ourselves to the realities, we choose the
story. In this sense *Holocaust* has a purpose, however much our taste and our critical purism rebel
against it.

The *Holocaust* television movie opened the flood-
gates. It seemed as if for the first time an entire
nation dared to remember and to look at its own
past.

Collective mourning in the Federal Republic
itself became a public spectacle, played out, consciously or unconsciously, before the eyes of the
world. The Germans knew the world would be
waiting with bated breath for their reception of
this film. The influential American columnist
Mary McGrory, for instance, intimated this in her

commentary on *Holocaust:* "What would be most
encouraging, perhaps, to those who are drained
from watching this harrowing and often inept recreation of recent history would be the news that
Germany had ordered a print of the film" (*Los
Angeles Times,* Apr. 20, 1978). Günter Rohrbach,
the person mainly responsible for showing the
film in Germany, echoed this sentiment: "It
would be remarkable if the Germans, who as protagonists proceeded so purposefully in the annihilation of the Jews, were to raise special objections to the treatment of this theme by others"
(Märtesheimer and Frenzel 1979, 45). Similarly,
Heinz Werner Hübner, director of WDR, admitted candidly: "The film is a political event, and if
it is shown in the land of those who were affected
by the Holocaust, in Israel, then we should expect
the people in Germany who participated in those
events and their successors to view it as well"
(*Süddeutsche Zeitung,* Sept. 22, 1978). From this
perspective, the *Holocaust* series seemed to challenge the Germans to recognize themselves in the
mirror held up by Hollywood. One advantage of
the "right" reaction would be the chance to show
the rest of the world that the Germans had
learned from history, that they had finally
changed.

Small wonder that this confrontation with a
long-repressed history met with resistance and
criticism. Peter Schulz-Rohr, director of the TV
station SWR, spoke about the "almost exhibitionist German inclination to engage in self-
abnegation," which "fatally goes hand in hand
with the performance of public acts of atonement
and exemplifies the kind of moral gesture that is
meant to impress others. For anyone with a sensitive conscience, this calls into question the very
morality it is meant to demonstrate" (*Die Zeit,*
June 23, 1978). For Edgar Reitz, even worse than
the dreaded spectacle of guilt and atonement was
the fact that the "commercial aesthetic of America" had taken charge of German history, had
even "ripped" German history "out of the hands"
of the Germans (Reitz 1984, 102). This insistence on retaining one's own history, even in its
most inhuman form, introduces a new, highly
problematical note in the chronicle of West Germany's coming to terms with its own past—a

note that became unmistakable a few years later during Reagan's controversial visit to the military cemetery at Bitburg in May 1985 and in the so-called Historians' Debate in 1986. Both events highlight the new revisionist struggle over German history, memory, and national identity.

Even with several empirical studies at our disposal, it remains difficult to assess the actual effect of *Holocaust* on the German public. Like any television event, it "hits home" because unlike film, which is experienced collectively at a special public site, television images are delivered into the privacy of one's living room. Constantly blending fiction and facts—soap operas, sitcoms, and action movies are offered side by side with news, documentaries, and live coverage—television has blurred the distinction between truth and lie, between representation and simulation. In both the imaginary and the factual areas, television's forte is the private and personal, the small (commensurate with the screen) and the everyday. *Holocaust* succeeded because it placed the terror of persecution and murder into the matrix of everyday life. Furthermore, the sheer length of the series promoted identification with the victimized characters; the story itself became an integral part of the viewer's life experience. Letters from German viewers ranged from aggressive rejection to demonstrative, self-chastising confessions of guilt. Whatever the individual strategies for dealing with *Holocaust*, however short-lived the tears it provoked, one thing is certain: the film ignited a new, broad-based interest in the images and stories of the German past, in new filmic representations of German history.

The *Holocaust* series also inspired renewed discussion about the various ways in which history should be presented on film. Innovations in narrative technique and film aesthetics that characterize several of the films following *Holocaust* can be seen as responses to the aesthetic and dramatic structure of the American television series. If the political crisis of the German Autumn of 1977 (terrorism and sweeping countermeasures by the police that reminded many of fascism) had produced a "surplus of motivation" (in the words of Alexander Kluge) among intellectuals and filmmakers to address German history, the broad reception of *Holocaust* and the interest in German history it engendered provided the numerous films about the Third Reich with a ready-made audience. The collective film *Germany in Autumn* (1978) presented impressions of a country on which the past weighed heavily; the German reaction to *Holocaust* showed how much remained to be done in coming to terms with that past.

In 1979, it seemed as though the Germans were finally able to look their history in the eye. *Holocaust* allowed the Germans to work through their most recent past, this time from the perspective of the victims, by proxy, in the innocuous form of a television show that viewers could switch off at any time. Because the collective catharsis experienced by many viewers was brought about by a *film* (that is, by fiction and simulation), one might well suspect that the catharsis, if indeed there was one, rested on self-deception. Still, no matter how skeptical one may be about the long-term effect of a fiction like *Holocaust,* it cannot be denied that a new historical consciousness had emerged in the Federal Republic. The past suddenly seemed very present. Influenced by the enormous outpouring of sympathy for Holocaust victims, and pressured by political concerns, the Bundestag eliminated the statute of limitations for war crimes or genocide; trials of concentration camp guards or administrators may now still proceed more than forty years after these crimes. *Holocaust* also stirred up an intensive public debate that included books and essays on the Holocaust, new documentaries, and new educational materials for the schools. Several German filmmakers felt encouraged to make films about the German past—always, however, in programmatic opposition to the aesthetics of *Holocaust*. Feminist filmmakers like Helma Sanders-Brahms in *Deutschland, bleiche Mutter* (Germany, pale mother; 1980) and Jutta Brückner in *Hungerjahre* (Years of hunger; 1980) emphasized the subjective, autobiographical, and incomplete memory of the past rather than linear narrative history. On the other hand, Kluge's essay film *Die Patriotin* (The patriot; 1980) focused almost exclusively on Stalingrad and the repressed memory of it rather than on Auschwitz—thereby in effect foreshadowing a heated debate among historians about the status of Auschwitz in German historiography.

It is no secret that Edgar Reitz conceived his own sixteen-hour television series *Heimat* as a counterproduction to *Holocaust*. He justified it repeatedly in public as the German answer to the American attempt to write German history. For Reitz, *Holocaust* was a "glaring example" of an "international aesthetics of commercialism," for which the "misery produced by the Nazis in the original" is nothing but a "welcome background spectacle for a sentimental family story" (Reitz 1984, 98). Films in the style of *Holocaust,* Reitz wrote, prevent us from "taking narrative possession of our past, from breaking free of the world of judgments and dealing with it through art" (100). Reitz claimed Germany's right to its own history when he declared: "The most radical process of expropriation there is, is the expropriation of one's own history. The Americans have stolen our history through *Holocaust*" (102).

This polemic of making the Americans responsible for robbing Germany's most recent history, both as subject matter for a film and as part of German identity, seems audacious: the Germans now asserted vehemently their ownership of German history, which they had readily disavowed in the 1950s and 1960s. For Reitz, the real scandal was "German history—Made in Hollywood." His response was a film bearing the sarcastic working title, "Made in Germany." The American import was to be confronted with a German product. *Heimat* provided what Reitz considered lacking in the *Holocaust* television series, namely the "authentic atmosphere of individual images." Reitz's 1979 project coincided with a general interest in regionalism and rural life, and with a new focus on everyday experience that had emerged since the mid-1970s. "Large-scale" politics was to be prismatically refracted in the limited consciousness of the "little people." Reitz's "history from below" not only attacks the claim to totality made by official historiography, which radically reduces the multiplicity of stories to a single history, but it also legitimizes the exclusion of all those experiences about which "simple" people either knew nothing or preferred to know nothing. What Sanders-Brahms, Reitz,

and Kluge share is the fact that they ascribe to Germans the role of victims—victims of a criminal leadership, victims of the devastating war, victims of the American and Russian liberators. It seemed only a matter of time before a German Nazi could become a movie hero. Ironically, it was again Hollywood that broke the ice, and the German public responded positively.

March 1, 1994. Steven Spielberg's three-hour feature film *Schindler's List* opened in Frankfurt with a gala premiere in the Opera house, attended by Spielberg himself, Germany's president Richard von Weizsäcker, and many dignitaries from politics and the business world. The event honored Oskar Schindler, a resident of Frankfurt until his death in 1974, who, as an industrialist and member of the Nazi Party, had saved nearly eleven hundred Jewish lives from extermination in Polish concentration camps. The film tells the story of Schindler's slow recognition of the Nazis' genocidal aims and focuses on his attempts to subvert the death machinery with cunning, bribery, and courage. An adventurer not unlike Spielberg's other famous hero, Indiana Jones, Schindler managed to convince the Nazis it would be more cost-effective to employ Jews in his bogus weapons factory than to kill them. After the war, Schindler was revered by those who had been saved because their names had appeared on his list of employees. The film concludes with Holocaust survivors, the so-called Schindler Jews and their children, visiting his grave—a tribute to the film's claim to authenticity, which is further supported by its mostly black-and-white photography and its realistic-documentary style. The media hype that surrounded the opening of this film in Germany reminded reviewers immediately of the reception of *Holocaust* in 1979: "Not since the American-made television miniseries 'Holocaust' provoked widespread rumination by Germans about their dark past, has a cultural event here uncorked such painful memories," wrote the *Washington Post* on March 4, 1994. Headlines in American newspapers uncannily resembled those of fifteen years earlier; again the film's reception was a gauge to measure Germany's progress in coming to terms with its past: "Breaking the Big Silence: 'Schindler's List' Forces Germans to Look at Their History" (*Los Angeles Times*), "Germany Revisits Its Nazi Past in Spielberg's Holocaust Film" (*Christian Science Monitor*), and "The German Premiere of 'Schindler's List' Brings Tears and Praise" (*New York Times*). Once again Germany watched itself perform under the watchful eyes of the world. As in the case of *Holocaust,* any criticism of *Schindler's List* on aesthetic or ideological grounds was muted by the overriding assumption (not shared by everyone) of the film's ethical and educational value. And once again, as in the case of *Holocaust,* the question was raised as to why no German filmmaker was able or willing to take on the task of representing the Holocaust in a feature film.

Bibliography

Ilan Avisar, *Screening the Holocaust: Cinema's Images of the Unimaginable* (Bloomington: Indiana University Press, 1988); Michael Geisler, "The Disposal of Memory: Fascism and the Holocaust on West German Television," Framing the Past: The Historiography of German Cinema *and Television,* ed. Bruce A. Murray and Christopher J. Wickham (Carbondale: Southern Illinois University Press, 1992), 220–60; Annette Insdorf, *Indelible Shadows: Film and the Holocaust* (New York: Random House, 1983); Anton Kaes, *From "Hitler" to "Heimat": The Return of History as Film* (Cambridge, Mass.: Harvard University Press, 1989); Friedrich Knilli and Siegfried Zielinski, eds., *Holocaust zur Unterhaltung: Anatomie eines internationalen Bestsellers* (Berlin: Elefanten Press, 1982); Claude Lanzmann, "From the Holocaust to 'Holocaust,'" *Dissent* 28 (1981): 188–94; Peter Märthesheimer and Ivo Frenzel, eds., *Im Kreuzfeuer: Der Fernsehfilm Holocaust. Eine Nation ist betroffen* (Frankfurt a. M.: Fischer 1979); Anson G. Rabinbach and Jack Zipes, eds., *Germans and Jews Since the Holocaust: The Changing Situation in West Germany* (New York: Holmes & Meier, 1986); Edgar Reitz, "Unabhängiger Film nach Holocaust?" *Liebe zum Kino: Utopien und Gedanken zum Autorenfilm, 1962–1983* (Cologne: KÖLN 78, 1984); and Wilhelm van Kampen, ed., *Holocaust: Materialien zu einer amerikanischen Fernsehserie über die Judenverfolgung im "Dritten Reich"* (Düsseldorf: Landeszentrale für politische Bildung, 1978).

ANTON KAES

1979 Peter Lilienthal makes *David,* the first "post-Shoah German-Jewish film"

Peter Lilienthal refers to his 1979 film *David* as "the first German-Jewish film, that is, the first film to focus on the everyday life of the Jews during the Third Reich" (Layton 1984, 224). To be sure, the screenplay of *David* was written by a prominent trio of German Jews, namely, Lilienthal, Jurek Becker, and Ulla Ziemann, and it was based on an autobiographical novel by Joel König (Ezra Ben Gershon). But although there is no doubt that Lilienthal's film is one of the most powerful attempts to address the Third Reich from a Jewish perspective, he is perhaps overstating his case. Lilienthal's remark ignores a large body of work and a tradition of filmmaking that begins immediately after 1945.

His assertion remains interesting, however, on a different level. It reflects a long-standing tension among Jews regarding assimilation and cultural production. Although *David* is certainly a film and screenplay consciously constructed as a German-Jewish production, one need not move far from the beginning of postwar German film history to find a series of important screenwriters and directors who were Jewish and whose work confronts the range of issues surrounding the German-Jewish politics of identity in the wake of the Holocaust.

Artur Brauner, a concentration camp survivor, was one of the first Germans to emerge out of the destruction of World War II and the Shoah to begin making films. Although he later become a successful producer, he began his postwar career by writing a screenplay, *Morituri* (1947), based on his experiences in the Lodz ghetto. The film depicts a group of camp and ghetto escapees—Russians, Poles, Serbs, Canadians, and Danes—all on the run from the Gestapo. The Jews, some non-Jewish Poles, and some Russian prisoners of war end up hiding themselves in a forest, creating a little community organized around the common struggle to survive. Insofar as it refuses to present itself strictly as a story about Jews' struggle for survival, it differs from Lilienthal's project. In fact, what is interesting about Brauner's story is that it is almost utopian in its belief in nonidentity, or at least identity based on something other than ethnicity. It is a gesture often repeated by Brauner's generation and one later rejected by Lilienthal's.

Another film of the era is *Lang ist der Weg* (The way is long; 1948), written by Israel Becker and directed by Marek Goldstein and Herbert Fredersdorf. It is the story of David Jelin, a Warsaw Jew who jumps from the train that is meant to take him and his family to Auschwitz. The film traces him through his underground resistance to and survival of National Socialism and the injustices of the early postwar years. It ends with a reunited Jelin family finding a new home in Palestine. As much as any film in the postwar era, *Lang ist der Weg* struggles to tell a history of the Holocaust and its early aftermath through the eyes of German and Polish Jewish survivors. Becker thematizes survival and its implications in his screenplay while leaving aside a number of other issues that will arise in subsequent attempts at providing testimony to the Shoah. Yet there is no question that this is a German-Jewish film in the sense that Lilienthal articulates it.

Disproving Lilienthal's statement does not initially prove much in itself. What these films show is that there was a deliberate attempt in the early postwar years to contend with questions of Jewish identity and the telling of history that all but disappear from the German landscape in the 1950s. This is true at least in the West and most certainly for German gentiles. Whether in Hollywood or Bavaria, writing the history of the Shoah for the screen is still done to this day almost solely by Jewish screenwriters. But in Germany (East and West) even Jewish screenwriters, who were otherwise extremely active in the 1950s, strove to reassimilate themselves to the extent that their identities as Jews (or partial Jews) were secondary.

Filmmaking in what would become the German Democratic Republic took on a different face, albeit not necessarily a more friendly one. This difference was due, in part, to the dominance of the East German film company, Deutsche Film Aktiv (DEFA), by two men, Kurt Maetzig and Konrad Wolf, whose own personal histories and identities differ radically from those of many of their Western counterparts. For both men, their Jewishness is something that is all but invisible in their public personae, but something that erupts all over the place in their screenplays.

Few people affected postwar filmmaking in Germany, East or West, as did Kurt Maetzig. A founding member of the collective that started up DEFA out of the ruins of the Universal Film Agentur (UFA) film studios in Babelsberg, Maetzig was the dominant director during the first twenty years of East German filmmaking. Like many of the Jews and half-Jews who settled in the German Democratic Republic after the war, Maetzig's identification with his Jewish cultural heritage is generally overshadowed by his being a Communist. Although this conflict is apparent in his autobiographical interviews, it is less visible in his films.

Maetzig's first film, *Ehe im Schatten* (Marriage in the shadows; 1947), is the story of a German-

Jewish–gentile mixed marriage in the Third Reich, based on the biography of the famous Berlin stage actor Joachim Schalk and a novella by Hans Schweikart. The couple is traced from their work in the Berlin theater just before the Nazi takeover, through their difficult marriage "in the shadows" of the Third Reich, and finally to the couple's Romeo and Juliet–like demise.

Maetzig claims to have identified heavily with the story of a *Mischehe* (mixed marriage) very similar to that of his parents. The differences between the decisions his family made and those made by the Schalk family impressed him even more than did the similarities. By exploring the process of survival undertaken by so many Jews, the screenplay actually becomes an interrogation of Maetzig's own personal history. Effectively, the screenwriter and director questions the actions of his non-Jewish father as well as the value of a marriage that became increasingly undignified and demeaning for his mother and, as much as anything, contributed to her untimely death at the hands of the Gestapo: "The question of human dignity in such situations played a big role for me. Therefore, I think the film became not only a discussion with the spectator but also a polemic with my father" (Agde 1987, 37).

Thus one of the first films to deal with the personal narratives involved in the Nazi persecution of Jews is intimately tied to the screenwriter / director's own attempt to come to terms with his own cultural heritage and family history. Although it is both Maetzig's first film and his first screenplay, he shows much more skill in the latter, due arguably in great part to his own personal stake in the narrative. In fact, the most compelling thing about this film is that with which Maetzig identifies so closely. The immediacy of the dialogue and the personal dilemma faced by a couple confronted with nonchoices creates a certain empathy that salvages a film to which Brecht referred as "terrible kitsch" (Agde 1987, 37). In retrospect at the end of his career, Maetzig distinguishes between the *Ehe im Schatten* screenplay that he thinks is sensitive to the problems of representation and his direction of the film and the actors, which is bound entirely to the UFA film tradition. Maetzig discovers a dilemma that is prevalent throughout Germany and the United States during this period, namely, the problem of transforming a written depiction of Jews that is sensitive to difference into a "graven image."

The difficulties of transforming the written word into an image is a dominant theme with a variety of German-Jewish or half-Jewish screenwriters and directors of the early postwar years. The strategies for overcoming this problem vary tremendously. Maetzig assumes that it is a question of performance and that the agency of the director can intervene in the problem. If this is true, it is more evident in Maetzig's most famous protégé, who became East Germany's most dominant director, Konrad Wolf. A member of perhaps the most fascinating Communist family of twentieth-century Germany, Wolf was generally able to waltz around questions of public identity, not only in his films but in his public behavior. For instance, Wolf was able to avoid many of the censorship questions that plagued other directors, in part due to his membership on the Central Committee of the SED, the East German ruling party and, more important, his role as president of the Academy of Arts of the German Democratic Republic (GDR). A latecomer to East German politics (he joined the party in the mid-sixties, well after having established himself as a filmmaker), Wolf never had a problem legitimating himself politically. For not only was Wolf the son of the famous Communist playwright Friedrich Wolf, but his brother, Markus Wolf, was also until 1990 the most powerful member of the East German security elite, as minister of state security. Few families enjoyed as many privileges of power as did the Wolf family in the GDR. Arguably due to this lack of need to exert an identity for himself, Wolf remained able to float among various subject positions.

Wolf's strongest early film, *Sterne* (1958–59), with a screenplay written by Angel Wangenstein, is the first of his films to address the issues of Jewish survival in Nazi-occupied Europe. It is a love story between a young German soldier and a Bulgarian-Jewish girl who is deported to Auschwitz. In 1961 Wolf rewrote his father's drama *Professor Mamlock* for the screen. It is the story of a German-Jewish medical professor struggling to be recognized as both German and Jewish in 1920s Germany. What is most fascinating about Konrad Wolf's screenplay of his father's drama is the struggle over Jewish identity versus class identity that Wolf the younger writes into the film. Professor Mamlock wavers between being identified and identifying himself as a Jew versus identifying himself as a German and as an injured war veteran. In fact, the latter identity is the one that ushers in Mamlock's success as a practicing physician. The film organizes itself around identification and the choices that it entails. Mamlock's hope is that his choice of a German identity will take precedence over his Jewish heritage.

The question of identity is not one that Wolf negotiates simply. Unlike Maetzig, his Jewish identity does not get effaced by his Communist one; they are interwoven in a manner unique among East German intellectuals. Throughout his body of works is not only an attempt to reach some accord with the questions of German-Jewish identity, but also a rigorous interrogation of the very possibilities of cultural identification. Rather than assimilating one identificatory possibility into another, Wolf's films from the earlier *Mamlock* to the later *Ich war neunzehn* (I was nineteen; 1967) and *Solo Sunny* (1979–80) (both co-written with Wolfgang Kohlhaase) layer the possibilities of identifying with cultural or religious heritage along with identification with a state, vocation, or personal history. One can perhaps tie Wolf's sophisticated treatment of the question of Jewish (or any other, for that matter) identity to his own complicated personal history—a history that hardly allows for stable or overdetermined identification.

An actor and screenwriter whose attempts to grapple with similar problems predate Wolf's is Fritz Kortner (Fritz Nathan Kohn). Kortner rose to fame in the twenties as an actor in Max Reinhardt's Deutsches Theater ensemble as well as in various silent films of the 1920s. Unlike Maetzig or Wolf, whose Jewishness was only a part of how they imagined themselves, Kortner always thematized his cultural and religious background openly. Despite the fact that he took on an assimilated stage name, Kortner's Jewishness always remained a part of his public persona.

Kortner left Germany immediately after the National Socialist takeover, landing first in England and then a few years later in the United States. He received some work in film both in England and in Hollywood, but his tentative grasp of English stifled his ability to rise above supporting roles in B films. Although he belonged to the elite class of exiles who found themselves in southern California at this time—a group that included Theodor Adorno, Arnold Schoenberg, Thomas Mann, and Bertolt Brecht—Kortner was unable to reorganize his identity around his vocation as easily as many of the others. He was displaced as a Jew, a German, and an actor.

Although there are many facets of Kortner's work as an actor and stage director that would merit treatment, what is most relevant to the topic of German-Jewish screenwriters is Kortner's 1949 screenplay for the film in which he also starred, *Der Ruf* (The call). Of the early postwar German films, the so-called *Trümmerfilme*, the screenplay for *Der Ruf* is the most sophisticated and ambitious. In it, Kortner attempts, more so than the Becker-Lilienthal-Ziemann screenplay, to narrate the ambiguities of the relationship between Germanness and Jewishness, between exiled German-American identity and that of those who stayed behind.

The film's main character, Professor Mauthner, is a fusion of all of these identities. He is a Jewish professor of philosophy who at the beginning of the film is celebrating fifteen years in beautiful exile. He is having a party at which all of those in attendance are stereotypes, from the race-sensitive black servant, to the homesick German nanny, to the German-Jewish intellectual who thinks of California as the promised land, to the totally assimilated German Jew whose Swabian characteristics appear much stronger than his Jewish ones. Professor Mauthner is set up as the character who has absorbed all of these traits that circulate around him. This story line becomes more complicated when Mauthner is called back to his professorship in Frankfurt. What ensues is a heated argument among the

exiled German Jews about the nature of national identity and possibility of German Jews reclaiming their German heritage. The stereotypical figures form a sort of Greek chorus for whom the tragic figure of Mauthner must play out his fate.

Not unlike Greek tragedy, the film sets up Professor Mauthner's subjective confusions in terms of varying love triangles and quadrangles. He falls in love with his young student at the same time that he wants to go back to Germany and seek out his ex-wife and child. This love triangle is set up so that Mary, the young American, comes to represent all of his experiences of a young and bright America, whereas his ex-wife, Lina, marks his emotional and troublesome past abroad. When he takes with him three assistants from his California university, including Mary, the fresh-faced American attitude is juxtaposed against a dark and resentful Germany.

Mauthner returns to a Germany that is in the throes of a bitter defeat. Far from being destroyed by the war, anti-Semitism becomes the idea around which the young students organize their generational opposition. They are led by a pitiful old academic who presumed himself to be in line for the position to which Mauthner had been called. The leader among the students is a charismatic young man, Walter, who turns out to be Mauthner's son. Walter, who is part of a plot to kill Mauthner, also falls in love with Mary, thus setting up a sort of Oedipal quadrangle. It gradually becomes clear that any sort of reconciliation of Mauthner's Germanness and Jewishness is impossible. He begins to die of heartbreak. Walter shows up to kill Mauthner, not knowing he is his father, only to find his mother there. Mauthner, aware of the plot against him, dies with an image of his wife in his murderous son's arms.

Thus Kortner calls upon the Oedipal narrative in order to bring together the complicated strands of a German-Jewish subjectivity. The critical reception of the film at the time noted that the screenplay was strong but that the film depended too much on dialogue. Indeed, most of the film unfolds in the dialogue and not in the construction of images. It is noteworthy, however, that that is what makes it Kortner's film rather than that of the director, Josef v. Baky. The difference between *Der Ruf* and *Ehe im Schatten* lies on the level of that medium in which the narratives seem most comfortable. Both draw heavily upon a series of written texts in constructing their film. Yet whereas Maetzig quickly draws these texts into the production of images that will correspond to the text, Kortner's screenplay has an almost confrontational relationship to the medium. The only time in the entire film that the narrative draws upon specifically filmic mechanisms is in the penultimate sequence as Mauthner lies dying. At that point, the film cuts to a series of circulating images and flashbacks, the last of which is his son in his wife's arms.

Kortner's is a theatrical text, one that depends heavily on the written word and one that, at the same time, is cautious about the production of images. It is, in a stricter sense, therefore the most Jewish of German-Jewish films. It is a screenplay that is difficult to turn into a film but one that is easily imaginable on stage. The stereotypes that Kortner sets up in the beginning are constructed much more through what they say than what they look like. Kortner attempts to give them the language of the German and German-Jewish diaspora as it was constituted during the war. We cannot see this; we can only hear it in the text.

Peter Lilienthal, in contrast, comes to screenwriting as a filmmaker. Although the Kortner screenplay seems aware of the possibility of adequately representing experience, Lilienthal and his colleagues constructed a narrative that tries to reproduce on film the horror and desperation of David's life in the Third Reich. The film does not rely so much on the spoken text for this representation as on the production and juxtaposition of images. By having the entire film assume the perspective of the protagonist, the screenplay attempts to put the spectator into the immediacy of David's experience. Lilienthal goes even further in his attempt to reproduce lived experience by casting primarily survivors and children of survivors of the Shoah. (Curiously enough, my reading of the screenplay is precisely the opposite of that of the German Federal Film Board, which refused to fund the project, claiming it was uncinematic.)

The difference between the Becker, Lilienthal, and Ziemann screenplay and Kortner's conceptualization of *Der Ruf* can be understood most clearly through reference to Adorno and Horkheimer's "Kulurindustrie" chapter of *Dialektik der Aufklärung*. Gertrud Koch (1992) has argued that it is the tension between the commandment against the production of likenesses in the second commandment as handed down by Moses and the breaking of the commandment by his deputy Aaron that is at the heart of the Frankfurt school's modernist aesthetics. Although I do not want to approach this problem in detail here, I would suggest that a similar tension is at work between these two works, which are perhaps the most significant among postwar German-Jewish screenplays and films.

Both *Der Ruf* and *David* imagine themselves as historical films. Yet Kortner, who was a friend and confidant of Adorno's in their California exile, adheres perhaps more closely to the notion that the filmic medium will always distort the perception of experience. Lilienthal and his colleagues belong to a different generation, one no less directly affected by the horrors of the genocide, but one much less beholden to a modernist aesthetic. In fact, it could be argued that Jurek Becker (along with the much earlier screenwriters Marek Goldstein, Israel Becker, or Artur Brauner, all of whom were camp survivors) actually comes to the script with a more urgent sense that this is a story that must be told, an experience that must somehow be relayed. Kortner (and, for that matter, Adorno and Horkheimer), by contrast, did not experience the camps directly; they are therefore skeptical of any attempt to reproduce that experience or even its aftereffects, as in the case of *Der Ruf*.

However we might perceive the range of differences that manifest themselves in these two films, it is fair to say that they mark the parameters of a certain type of screenwriting in the postwar era: screenwriting by German Jews that attempts to narrate (however problematically) the experience of Jewishness during and in the wake of the Holocaust. The tradition is constituted of many German-speaking Jews who have contributed to the medium. They include, among others, Peter Lorre, Ralph Giordano, and

George Tabori. The intent of this article is not to include them all in my discussion as much as it is to take issue with the Lilienthal comment that begins this essay. For if much of German-Jewish screenwriting has been concerned with the reconstruction of memory in an amnesiac culture, such comments serve to undermine even Lilienthal's more productive efforts. What has actually developed as a tradition of German-Jewish screenwriting and filmmaking in postwar Germany has created some of the most important calls to memory in the wider history of postwar German filmmaking, a tradition that continues to struggle against amnesia.

Bibliography

Günter Agde, ed., *Kurt Maetzig, Filmarbeit: Gespräche, Reden, Schriften* (Berlin: Henschelverlag, 1987); Gerd Albrecht, *Konrad Wolf* (Frankfurt a. M.: Deutsches Institut für Filmkunde, 1983); Gertrud Koch, *Die Einstellung ist die Einstellung: Visuelle Konstruktion des Judentums* (Frankfurt a. M.: Suhrkamp, 1992); Claus Landsittel, *Kortner Anekdotisch* (Munich: Kindler, 1967); and Lynne Layton, "Peter Lilienthal: Decisions Before Twelve," *New German Filmmakers: From Oberhausen Through the 1970s,* ed. Klaus Phillips (New York: Frederick Ungar, 1984), 230–45.

ROBERT R. SHANDLEY

1980 The "Third Generation" of Jewish-German writers after the Shoah emerges in Germany and Austria

For many Jewish-German writers living in the Federal Republic of Germany, the fall of the Berlin Wall on November 9, 1989, was more than the uncanny coincidence of the end of the two postwar German states and the fifty-first anniversary of the November Pogrom in 1938. It was the culmination of a decade of controversial events that coincided with a growing literature by Jewish writers living in Germany about Jewish identity in contemporary Germany. In the 1980s the explosion of commemorative events dedicated to the remembrance of the victims of the Shoah was accompanied by an increase in media attention to Jewish culture and history. At the same time as "rites of memorialization" mushroomed, especially in the Federal Republic of Germany, some Jews living in Germany feared a growing indifference among younger generations of Germans and a recurrence of anti-Semitic attacks (Hartman 1986, 1). In addition, Germans of Jewish descent began to engage in debates about the meaning of Jewish culture in present-day Germany and about the ramifications of a changing Jewish community that had become increasingly Russian-Jewish. Before 1980 German Jews and those non-German Jews who had emigrated to the former Federal Republic after the war had been relatively reticent about their Jewish background except as commentators on issues related to the remembrance of the Shoah or in discussions about the literary heritage of German-Jewish writers. As Jack Zipes points out in his article "The Contemporary German Fascination for Things Jewish," Jews began to take a more active role in the cultural life of Germany shortly after the television film *Holocaust* (1979) raised new questions about present-day anti-Semitism in Germany (Gilman and Remmler 1994, 15–45). The broadcast of *Holocaust* in West Germany and the overwhelming response to it by viewers served as the catalyst that transformed the interactions between members of the Jewish communities and their non-Jewish counterparts. Jews born after World War II began to speak out publicly about their identity as Jews in Germany, a country in which they felt increasingly alienated, even as they wrote in German and participated in German society as Germans. Ironically, at the same time as the increase in local and oral history projects encouraged Germans to take an interest in the legacy of Jewish life and death in their villages, towns, and cities, public events such as the Bitburg affair (1985), the boycott of Fassbinder's allegedly anti-Semitic play *Garbage, the City, and Death* (1985), the *Historikerstreit* ([Historians' Debate] 1985–86), and Philip Jenninger's speech in May 1988 before the German parliament commemorating the fiftieth anniversary of the November Pogrom in 1938 brought about increased tensions between Germans and Jews and were also emotionally debated within Jewish organizations and publications.

Keeping the above events in mind, this article focuses on the writing of four Jewish writers, Barbara Honigmann, Esther Dischereit, Rafael Seligmann, and Maxim

Biller, Jews who write in German and who first published in the former Federal Republic of Germany after 1980. Their writing by no means represents German-Jewish writing per se. As the recent collection of contemporary writing by Jews living in Germany *Jewish Voices, German Words: Growing Up Jewish in Postwar Germany and Austria* (1994) shows, Jewish playwrights, artists, and journalists often write semiautobiographical accounts of their experiences in present-day Germany. They are certainly not the only Jews writing in Germany today—a wave of emigration from the former Soviet Union, for example, has reshaped the ethnic make-up of Jewish communities throughout the country, particularly in Berlin, where more than half of the 10,000 members of the Jewish community are from the former Soviet Union. Better known Jewish authors such as Jurek Becker, Katja Behrens, Edgar Hilsenrath, or George Tabori are discussed at length in other essays in this volume.

The four authors under discussion here were all born after 1945. Although they share the decision to identify as Jews in Germany, their diverse life histories and ambiguous relationship to their Jewish heritage, as well as their relationship to Germany, point to the heterogeneity of Jewish culture in present-day Germany. In particular, their country of origin and gender distinguish their approach to Jewish experience as depicted in their writing. Esther Dischereit was born in the former Federal Republic in 1952 and lives in Berlin. Her mother, a Jew, survived Nazi Germany in hiding. Her father was a non-Jewish German. In addition to a number of radio plays that deal with issues of alienation, xenophobia, and sexism, Dischereit has published two novels, *Joëmis Tisch: Eine jüdische Geschichte* (Joëmi's table: A Jewish story; 1988) and *Merryn* (1992). Writing from a decidedly feminist standpoint, Dischereit argues that the alienation she experiences as a German-Jewish woman is a combination of anti-Semitism and sexism in both German and Jewish culture.

Barbara Honigmann, born in 1949 to German Jews who identified as Socialists and who settled in East Berlin after the war, grew up in the former German Democratic Republic but left in 1984 to live in Strasbourg. She has written a novel, *Eine Liebe aus Nichts* (A love out of nothing; 1991), and a collection of short stories, *Roman von einem Kinde* (Novel from a child; 1986). Although Honigmann's work can only be seen within the context of the former German Democratic Republic (GDR) and thus under the perspective of the GDR's specific emphasis on Communist, rather than Jewish, victims of the Shoah, her work is nevertheless representative of the dilemma facing self-identified Jewish writers who write for a German public. Her writing calls for a reassessment of the meaning of Jewish identity in German society not only as it is formed out of the remembrance of the Shoah, but also out of present experience. Not surprisingly, both Honigmann and Dischereit turned to their Jewish heritage without having grown up in religious households.

Unlike their female counterparts, Rafael Seligmann and Maxim Biller were born outside of Germany. Seligmann was born in 1947 in Israel, but moved to Munich in 1957 with his parents, who were German Jews. His two novels, *Rubensteins Versteigerung* (Rubenstein's auction; 1989) and *Die jiddische Mamme* (The Yiddish mama; 1990), are often compared to Philip Roth's books in light of their humorous depictions of Jewish male sexual anxiety. Maxim Biller arrived in Hamburg in 1970 from Prague where his family had been living. He has written two collections of short stories, *Wenn ich einmal reich und tot bin* (When I am for once wealthy and dead; 1990) and *Land der Vater und Verräter* (Land of the fathers and traitors; 1992).

What distinguishes the writing of these authors from one another? What are the common themes in their writing? Under what circumstances have they published their work in the Federal Republic, and how do they perceive their role as Jewish writers in Germany today? The answer to these questions lies in part within the political and cultural context of the 1980s in the Federal Republic and in the consequences of those public events that brought about a stronger self-awareness and self-definition of Jewish identity and its mediation in the writing of the four authors.

The fall of the Berlin Wall on November 9,

1989 and the subsequent call by major German politicians and many German citizens for a new era free of the burden of the past accentuated previous attempts by both conservative and liberal political factions to establish a positive German national identity throughout the 1980s. In extreme cases, attacks against people who were perceived to be foreign brought home to many potential targets of the violence how acute the tension had remained in a country that had supposedly dealt with its past through numerous rituals of *Vergangenheitsbewältigung* (coming to terms with the past), a term that sums up the conflicts and tensions of an impossible task. The fall of the Wall (on the very anniversary, as mentioned, of the November Pogrom of 1938) may have been a major turning point in the relationship between non-Jewish Germans and German Jews, but it does not fully explain the increase in publications and public statements by Jews during the 1980s. What were the factors that brought about the stronger voice of Jewish writers, journalists, and intellectuals of the postwar generation?

Clearly, there is no one Jewish "voice" in Germany, but rather a diverse chorus of individuals whose work receives attention by both Jewish and non-Jewish readers. In contrast to the previous decades in which survivors of the Shoah and those who returned from exile struggled to speak about their pain under the Nazis, German Jews writing in the 1980s and born after 1945 represent a new generation of Jewish Germans whose decision to remain in or to leave Germany is as much a statement about their German identity as it is about their ambivalence toward official, mostly religious Jewish organizations in Germany. As Seligmann points out in an essay about the apparent taboo among Jews living in Germany to express hatred toward Germans, most of the literature published in Germany by Jewish writers until the 1980s was composed of autobiographical accounts of the Holocaust or of life in exile (Gilman and Remmler 1994, 173). Not until the mid-1980s did contemporary Jewish writers living in Germany begin to write about their lives in present-day Germany.

The effect of the controversial events of the 1980s that were both catalysts for and expressions of a new-found Jewish voice should not be underestimated. This phenomenon coincided with a growing collection of essays and articles on issues affecting the everyday life of Jews in Germany that appeared not only in mainstream German publications, but also in journals geared specifically to issues affecting Jewish life in Germany. The two journals founded in the 1980s and dedicated to German Jewish life and culture in present-day Germany—*Babylon* and *Semittimes*—contain analyses of the political and cultural structures that both obscure and encourage anti-Semitism; discussions by Jewish intellectuals on the behavior and policies of the German government toward the commemoration of the victims of the Shoah; and, more recently, the controversial reaction to the Gulf War of many self-proclaimed Leftists in the German Peace Movement.

The discussions evoked by the provocative work of Henryk Broder or Dan Diner demonstrate the influence of living Jews within Germany who have established themselves not only as Jews, but also as leading voices in contemporary German society. On the one hand, journalists such as Broder or Lea Fleischmann have written polemical critiques of the hypocrisy and ignorance of the Germans toward Jews. Broder and Lang's *Fremd im eigenen Land* (Foreign in one's own country; 1979) and Fleischmann's *Dies ist nicht mein Land: Eine Jüdin verläßt die Bundesrepublik* (This is not my country: A Jewish woman leaves the Federal Republic; 1980) express not only the sense of alienation, but also a growing insistence among Jews that non-Jewish Germans learn to accept "that there were *live* Jews in Germany who wanted to be known for who they were and what they were doing" (Zipes in Gilman and Remmler 1994, 19). On the other hand, the historian Michael Wolffsohn's book *Ewige Schuld?* pleads for a reassessment of the centrality of the Shoah in Germany's present and calls for a less polemical relation between Germans and Jews.

As many second-generation Jews living in

Germany began to participate more fully in the cultural life and public debates of the 1980s, a parallel generation of non-Jewish Germans sought to break with the past in the hopes of establishing a German national identity that was free of the burden of the past. Consequently, much of the dialogue between Germans of Jewish descent and their non-Jewish counterparts revolves around the difficulty that German society has in dealing with living Jews and the ambivalence of some Jews toward their German heritage. The four Jewish writers mentioned above reflect upon this dialogue in their writing, although not all agree on what the value or outcome of a continued dialogue with their non-Jewish German counterparts should be.

The events that took place in the 1980s formed the backdrop against which a new self-awareness of second-generation Jews emerged. Jews active in the cultural arena began to take part in public debates as Jews, though often reluctantly. At times they found themselves faced with the expectation of the German media and their German counterparts that they serve as spokespersons whenever an issue related to Jewish existence in Germany came up, although they themselves emphasized that they could only represent an individual point of view. Nevertheless, Jewish writers, journalists, and cultural figures responded critically to the controversial visit of President Reagan and Chancellor Kohl to the German military cemetery outside of Bitburg in 1985, to the planned premiere of Fassbinder's allegedly anti-Semitic play *Garbage, the City and Death* in the same year in Frankfurt, to the Historikerstreit in 1985–86, to Philip Jenninger's politically irresponsible speech commemorating the fiftieth anniversary of the 1938 November Pogrom, and to the unification in 1990.

A case in point is the political symbolism of the commemoration of German soldiers in which German and American politicians gathered at the military cemetery at Bitburg to remember the fortieth anniversary of the end of the war. By laying a wreath at the grave of German soldiers, Reagan announced his intention to lay the past to rest as well. His decision to visit the cemetery and his initial refusal to visit a concentration camp received heavy criticism from Jewish leaders from around the world and from U.S. veterans. (Reagan did agree to lay a wreath at Bergen-Belsen, which he did on May 5, 1985.) In discussing his reasons for visiting the cemetery, Reagan claimed that the German soldiers (some of whom were members of the Waffen SS) were victims of the Holocaust "just as surely as the victims in the concentration camps" (Hartman 1986, xiv). More recently, the demand by German veteran organizations and others to properly bury the skeletons of German soldiers killed in the battle of Stalingrad has raised the question of how both Germans and Jews can mourn their dead from World War II without erasing the different circumstances under which the respective groups were killed. The dedication of an enlarged replica of Käthe Kollwitz's sculpture *Pietà* to commemorate all victims of World War II at the site of the neoclassical memorial the Neue Wache in Berlin was perceived by some as an affront to Jews whose ancestors had been killed in concentration camps and whose death was not to be compared with the death of German soldiers fighting on the front.

The increase in blatant anti-Semitism that ran parallel to the above controversies made it clear to a new generation of Jews living in Germany that the commemoration of Jewish victims in the Nazi death camps continued to be a partially artificial imperative in German society—more ceremony than deep contemplation or active interaction—and new concerns about the safety and role of Jews in Germany began to take root. Jewish intellectuals such as Dan Diner and Micha Brumlik began to write articles that analyzed the social and psychological structures of the relations between non-Jewish Germans and their Jewish "co-citizens" (*Mitbürger*) in present-day German society that make it difficult for Jews to feel comfortable in Germany even as they participate in ordinary public life on a regular basis as German citizens. Concurrently, Jewish writers such as Honigmann, Dischereit, Seligmann, and Biller gave body to the theoretical and political discussions about Jewish identity in their work by raising questions about the inadequacy of official designations to express the experience of Jews living in Germany. What did it mean to have a hyphenated identity? How could they establish themselves in the public realm as Jews *and* Germans? Are Jews by definition outsiders in German society regardless of their "Germanness"? As Honigmann wrote in a 1992 essay entitled "Selbstporträt als Jüdin" (Self-portrait of a Jewish woman), "I am also a writer, and one can say lightly, a Jewish one. But I am not so sure about that, because what I have said does not make me into a Jewish writer. It means that I belong existentially more to Jewish culture than to the German one, but culturally I belong to Germany and to nothing else." She, like Dischereit and Seligmann, struggles with the meaning of her conflicted heritage. Honigmann sums up the dilemma in this essay by saying that it seems as though the German-Jewish symbiosis, this "inability to come free of one another," had finally come about "because the Germans and the Jews had now become a pair in Auschwitz, whom even death could not separate."

As Katharina Ochse notes in her article "The Representation of Jews in the German Media after 1989," terms such as "German citizens of Jewish faith" or "Jewish fellow citizens" are not only inadequate but also indicative of the "impossibility of grasping the relations between the two groups linguistically in a way that would be accepted by everybody" (Gilman and Remmler 1994, 113). Therefore, the relation itself remains controversial and precarious. Accordingly, much of the writing of Jews in Germany runs parallel to a discussion among Germans who are not of Jewish descent about how to establish a less burdened German identity, one formed by the *Nachgeborene*—Germans born after World War II who are reluctant to take responsibility for the atrocities that their fathers and mothers committed against the Jews and other victims of Nazi genocide.

Dischereit, for example, writes about the tendency in contemporary Germany of Germans to see themselves as indirect victims of the Shoah because the remembrance of the Nazi past continues to occupy the German present. Thus the lack of distinction between how and under what circumstances victims of Nazi atrocities were killed has moved some Jewish writers to reassess their place in German society. The work of the four authors expresses the desire to break down monolithic images of "The Jew" as victim, yet questions the continued sense of alienation that many Jews feel in Germany. Honigmann, Dischereit, Seligmann, and Biller question the possibility of reestablishing a Jewish culture in Germany despite the legacy of the killing of the Jews under the Nazis. In addition, the diversity of their writing reminds readers of the heterogeneity of Jewish life in Germany today. Their writing deals not only with the question of Jewish identity per se, but with the vicissitudes of Jewish male and female identities, the experience of emigration, and inter-generational conflict.

As sites of Jewish history in Berlin such as the Scheunenviertel or the Spandauer Vorstadt are being rebuilt and documented by local historians with little direct attachment to the sites, Jewish writers continue to question the feasibility of a Jewish renaissance in a contemporary Germany in which anti-Semitism is not relegated to scattered acts of violence against Jews (or those people who are perceived to be Jewish), but rather continues to be pervasive in everyday conversations, as texts by Dischereit problematize. Given that estimates of the total Jewish population in unified Germany are of approximately 80,000 Jews in a total population of approximately 79 million, it is important to recall that the reception of the work by Jewish writers and journalists is foremost by *Germans*. Thus the preoccupation with things Jewish in German society cannot be separated from the particular needs of many non-Jewish Germans to engage with Jewish culture at the same time they avoid the reality of its absence in Germany today. Simultaneously, the diversity of opinions about what exactly constitutes Jewish identity and / or culture within the specific historical context of Germany's past and present provides for an ongoing dilemma among German Jews about how to define themselves. In addition, they are being defined by their publishers and a non-Jewish reading public as *Jewish,* not simply *German,* writers.

Interestingly, the marketing of the literature

emphasizes the Jewish identity of the authors even when the themes of the works are not related to the experience of Jews. Tellingly, emphasizing the Jewish identity of an author, whether that author accepts this designation or not, does have an effect on the sales and reception of the books. Often the literary quality of the text itself receives little attention, whereas the "Jewish" content or biography of the author is highlighted in the press releases and reviews. Recent series in Jewish literature by major German publishing companies such as Suhrkamp, however, frequently include translations or reprints of texts by Jews who live outside of Germany (Gilman and Remmler 1994, 119) and few works by younger authors living and writing in Germany. As Dischereit comments in her essay "No Exit from This Jewry" (Gilman and Remmler 1994), publishers have a difficult time categorizing her work when the "Jewish" content is treated in conjunction with other issues of identity or when the images require a differentiated view of "The Jew." She calls for a recognition that Jews are contributing to German culture, not as outsiders or Mitbürger ("fellow citizens") but as Germans. Writing for an audience that is predominantly non-Jewish, Dischereit has compared this phenomenon to "prostitution" (Gilman and Remmler 1994, 128, n. 7).

Similarly, Seligmann, whose first novel portrays the often petty and nasty interchanges between a Jewish protagonist and his mother, had difficulty getting the novel published and often encountered the ignorance and discomfort of editors who refused to publish his works on grounds that they placed Jews in a negative light (Gilman and Remmler 1994, 179). Like Seligmann's writing, Biller's texts have been received with mixed feelings among both Jewish and non-Jewish readers. As the publisher Kiepenheuer & Witsch's blurb for his second collection of short stories announces, Biller is both condemned and celebrated as an "inconsiderate breaker of taboos" because his texts deal with "our country [Germany] . . . its present and its past, the crimes of the perpetrators, the deeds of the victims and above all with the children and grandchildren of those that have survived all that." Clearly, "our country" creates distance between Biller and the society in which he lives, thus indicating that he observes as an outsider, even as he is presented as a German writer.

Consequently, Jewish *and* German identity play a major role in his work, as they do in Dischereit's attempts both to interact with non-Jewish Germans despite the specter of the past and to serve as an oppositional voice against the rise in xenophobia, a rise that became accentuated by the call for a break with the Nazi past and a movement toward a positive national German identity as the Berlin Wall fell.

For many Jews, living in contemporary Germany means juggling the remembrance of the past with the building of a future in which Jewish communities can become a vital, central part of German society. Instead of concentrating on the past, the writers address the events of the 1980s as signs that many non-Jewish Germans are incapable of dealing with the presence of living Jews, even as they go to great lengths to commemorate their victimization in the past. In Dischereit's writing, for example, she examines the present-day attitudes and beliefs toward Jews not as outsiders to German society, but as major participants within that society, in which "Jewishness" or "Germanness" are but two definers of identity.

Although Jewish identity is a major theme in most of the works represented here (as are Jewish relations to non-Jewish Germans), the experience of being female and Jewish distinguishes the writings of these women from that of the men. Whereas texts by Seligmann and Biller often address the anxiety over the stigma of circumcision, the double stigma of femaleness and Jewishness is an implicit theme in the works of the Jewish women writers. In addition, the choice of narrative perspective and textual structure of the work of the four authors—as well as the choice of style—differentiates their writing. It seems, then, that there is no unified body of contemporary Jewish writing in Germany today.

Nevertheless, in addition to the dilemma of identity, a shared characteristic in the texts discussed here is the development of a genealogical memory that recalls the destruction of the Shoah as a process that can only take place in confrontation with non-Jewish Germans. Given that the

German heritage of the authors complicates the divisions between Jewish and German identity, the interactions with Germans brings more confusion than clarity. Reading Biller's stories, one learns as much about the contemporary cultural scene in Germany and the attitudes of Germans toward Jews as about the vicissitudes of being Jewish and German. The texts engage with the present and make no attempt to separate fact from fiction. The events of the 1980s, such as the protest by members of the Frankfurt Jewish community that blocked the premiere of Fassbinder's play or the polemical and heated discussions within the Jewish community about the conservative politics of Heinz Galinski (the former director of the Jewish community in West Berlin), are filtered through the subjective experiences of mostly male Jewish and German protagonists. In Biller's (1990) short story "Harlem Holocaust," for example, the narrator is not Jewish, but becomes obsessed with his own inner struggle to enter the world of the Jews even as he is unable to overcome his resentment at being excluded. By presenting differentiated images of Jewish figures modeled after real figures in contemporary Germany, Biller breaks down the dichotomy that fixes the Jew as victim and the German as perpetrator. Further, he does so without erasing the context in which the dubious business transactions of a Jewish businessman in "Meine Tage mit Frenkel" can only be judged in light of the effects of the Shoah upon postwar relations between Jews and Germans. Whereas one survivor becomes a successful businessman, in the story "Horwitz erteilt Lubin eine Lektion," another survivor suffers isolation, paranoia, and impoverishment (Biller 1990). In other words, Biller does not paint a one-sided picture of Jews or Germans, but rather a portrait of human beings torn apart by individual needs, the legacy of history, and the absence of a moral system after the ravaging of the Shoah: "The anarchy of violence that had captured Europe and Asia, excused every act. All the value systems appeared to be canceled, including that of the National Socialists. Ideologies and ethics were no longer utopian drafts of reality, instead the earth was cold and cold corpses were still lying on this earth" (66).

As Sander Gilman has discussed at length in his article "Male Sexuality and Contemporary Jewish Literature in German: The Damaged Body as the Image of the Damaged Soul" (Gilman and Remmler, 210–52), the stigma of circumcision, as both a physical and metaphorical marker of male Jewish identity, plays a major role in the work of Biller and Seligmann. In *Rubensteins Versteigerung,* for example, the constant anxiety of Rubenstein, the main protagonist, about his sexual performance and virginity at the age of twenty-one is linked to his condemnation of his German-Jewish parents for returning to "Naziland" from Israel. As he attempts to sleep with a number of Jewish and German women, he sees his failure to achieve erection as a consequence of his parents' decision, a decision that subjects him to perpetual alienation and the predicaments of being a German Jew without a homeland. Frequently, the description of sexual encounters and identity crises focuses on the male experience. The female characters are objectified as clichés and / or feared—as in the case of Seligmann's antagonistic relations to his mother. As Gilman has shown, the male Jewish body functions in these texts as both a sign of difference and as a stigma of illness. The male protagonists are often ill in the work of Biller and Seligmann, an indication both of the no-win situation of being Jewish in Germany and of being an outsider obsessed with the tasks of being Jewish and observing the Germans observing the Jews.

Gertrud Koch and other critics have associated the writing of Biller and Seligmann with the Jewish-American tradition of Philip Roth and Saul Bellow; Dischereit and Honigmann, by contrast, create their own models, based as much on German literary tradition as on Jewish female tradition. In contrast to the writing of the two male writers, the texts by Honigmann and Dischereit represent Jewish identity as not only defined by the circumcised male organ, but also as a sign of the lack of presence for a Jewish female identity that itself does not solely function as a metaphor for absence. In Dischereit and Honigmann's writing the representation of remembering, Jewish identity, and the female body create a genealogical practice that questions fixed notions of identity and expresses the desire to recover lost or thwarted moments of a female Jewish subject based on experience, not metaphor. As a remembering process, the genealogical approach of texts such as *Joëmis Tisch* by Dischereit and *Eine Liebe aus Nichts* by Honigmann allows for the expression of the deep loss caused by the atrocities of the Shoah, while at the same time attesting to the strength of genealogical ties that have survived the Shoah (even though these ties are constantly on the verge of breaking apart). By engendering a female Jewish identity that is neither fixed nor homogeneous, but rather fragmented and heterogeneous, Dischereit and Honigmann present a differentiated picture of the oppression of women within Jewish culture and German society.

Instead of dwelling on her position as other within German society, the female Jewish protagonist in Dischereit's *Joëmis Tisch* questions the "normalcy" of the dominant culture in which she lives. The novel intersperses images of the narrator's dead Jewish mother, Hannah, with the narrator's encounters with Germans, with whom she engages in conversations about the German past and present-day society. The narrative of more than fifty scenes moves between the past and present, between individual and historical experience, and between third- and first-person narration. The daughter imagines her mother's history against the backdrop of her own sense of alienation in postwar Germany and her decision to reclaim her Jewish identity "after twenty years of being an un-Jew [*Un-Jude*]" (Dischereit 1988, 9). The process of "coming out" as a Jew in Germany takes place through the reconstruction of the narrator's mother's life in conjunction with present-day confrontations with non-Jewish Germans.

Taking on a lost or repressed Jewish identity in Germany after the Shoah suggests the impossibility of remembering in isolation. The ritual of conjuring the past in order to live in the present is a practice undertaken not just in the company of the Jewish community, but also in the company of Germans. The "German" Germans are the "resident other" (in the words of Karl Planck) with whom Jewish Germans must reckon. By objecting to the prejudices and misconceptions

that reduce living Jews in contemporary Germany to images, the female Jewish narrator listens to and comments on the patronizing words of German counterparts, whose insensitivity and tendency to complain about the Shoah's "curse" of guilt implies the impossibility of a symbiosis between Jews and Germans.

Dischereit's text exposes the unwillingness of many Germans to name the perpetrators or to take responsibility for the remembrance of the Shoah. By inserting quotation marks around statements by Germans that are interrupted by the narrator's sarcastic monologues about the blindness of many Germans to their false piety, Dischereit exposes the lack of communication between Germans and Jews. In one conversation, for example, a Sudeten German complains about the hardship he experienced as a refugee in 1945. While he remembers the "beautiful May day" and having to leave the family dog behind as they left the Sudetes, the narrator interjects the description of the deportation of her Jewish relatives. The juxtaposition of the experiences exposes not only the abyss between most Germans and Jews based on history but also the inner conflicts experienced by the narrator as she attempts to come to terms with her Germanness despite her Jewish heritage.

By describing the situation of being both other and German in German society, Honigmann also addresses the dilemma of juggling Jewish and female identity, as well as the difficulty of incorporating the experiences of her parents (who did not primarily identify as Jews) within her own search for Jewish identity. Her collection of short stories, *Roman von einem Kinde* (1986), retrospectively dissects the ambiguities of Jewish identity from the vantage point of Strasbourg, a city with a thriving Jewish community, which did not exist in the GDR. In her short story "Doppeltes Grab" (Double grave), Honigmann describes Gershom Scholem's visit to the site of his family's tomb in the Jewish cemetery in Berlin-Weißensee. After clearing the tombstones of branches and vines, "until the entire stony order grew back to a forest and not only the body of the dead, but also this entire work of remembering the body, became earth again" (89), Scholem remarks that "one needs an ax to cut a path through the overgrowth of time" (89). Indeed, time's choking of the graves of Jewish relatives and obscuring of the memorial inscription of their names has an ambiguous connotation in Honigmann's story. It is not the "natural" passing of time that has obstructed the inscriptions of names, but the rapid consolidation of Jewish memory within German culture—a merging that leaves little room for the different experiences of Jewish life in Germany.

In her novel *Eine Liebe aus Nichts,* Honigmann describes the transience of Jewish existence within the borders of the former GDR, and within German culture per se—a culture in which family ties and language create a semblance of *Heimat* not necessarily bound by national borders. The protagonist in Honigmann's novel seeks to write the life of her past by reconnecting with her father after his death. As part of her research, she retrieves his mostly blank diary from his room in the Belvedere Schloß in Weimar. By filling in the dates of his death, his funeral, and her last encounter with him, the narrator takes leave of her father by bringing her father's autobiography up to date, thus making his presence felt even as it has faded. The scenes of railroad stations, of the experience of forced exile under the Nazis (her parents' experience), and of her own chosen exile constitute the experience of a Jewish woman in the process of rediscovering her Jewish heritage and coming to terms with her German identity.

As in the texts by Biller, Seligmann, and Dischereit, the famous packed suitcase, the tense encounters with Germans, and the sense of alienation are responses not only to the destruction wrought by the Nazis against Jews but also to present-day anti-Semitism, real physical danger, and the continual reminders that Germans and Jews are bound by history now more than ever. The writing of German Jews in the 1980s suggests that this dilemma will continue to occupy Jewish writers and their readers in Germany for many years to come.

Bibliography

Jurek Becker, *Bronsteins Kinder* (Frankfurt a. M.: Suhrkamp, 1986); Ruth Beckermann, *Unzugehörig: Österreicher und Juden nach 1945* (Vienna: Locker, 1989); Katja Behrens, *Die dreizehnte Fee* (Frankfurt a. M.: Fischer, 1985); Maxim Biller, *Wenn ich einmal reich und tot bin* (Cologne: Kiepenheuer & Witsch, 1990); Dirk Blasius and Dan Diner, eds. *Zerbrochene Geschichte: Leben und Selbstverständnis der Juden in Deutschland* (Frankfurt a. M.: Fischer, 1991); Henryk Broder, *Der ewige Antisemit* (Frankfurt a. M.: Suhrkamp, 1986); Henryk M. Broder and Michel Lang, eds., *Fremd im eigenen Land* (Frankfurt a. M.: Suhrkamp, 1979); Erica Burgauer, *Zwischen Erinnerung und Verdrängung—Juden in Deutschland nach 1945* (Reinbek bei Hamburg: Rowohlt, 1993); Esther Dischereit, *Joëmis Tisch: Eine jüdische Geschichte* (Frankfurt a. M.: Suhrkamp, 1988); Lea Fleischmann, *Dies ist nicht mein Land: Eine Jüdin verläßt die Bundesrepublik* (Hamburg: Hofmann und Campe, 1980); Sander L. Gilman and Karen Remmler, eds., *Reemerging Jewish Culture in Germany: Life and Literature Since 1989* (New York: New York University Press, 1994); Geoffrey H. Hartman, ed. *Bitburg in Moral and Political Perspective* (Bloomington: Indiana University Press, 1986); Barbara Honigmann, *Eine Liebe aus Nichts* (Berlin: Rowohlt, 1991); Honigmann, *Roman von einem Kinde: Sechs Erzählungen* (Frankfurt a. M.: Luchterhand, 1986); Gertrud Koch, "Corporate Identities: Zur Prosa von Dische, Biller und Seligmann," *Babylon* 7 (1990): 139–42; Elaine Lappin, ed., *Jewish Voices, German Words: Growing Up Jewish in Postwar Germany and Austria,* trans. Krishna Winston (New Haven, Conn.: Catbird Press, 1994); Anson Rabinbach and Jack Zipes, eds., *Germans and Jews Since the Holocaust* (New York: Holmes & Meier, 1986); Rafael Seligmann, *Rubensteins Versteigerung* (Frankfurt a. M.: Eichborn, 1989); and Michael Wolffsohn, *Ewige Schuld? 40 Jahre deutsch-jüdisch-israelische Beziehungen* (Munich: Piper, 1991).

KAREN REMMLER

1985 Rainer Werner Fassbinder's play *Garbage, the City and Death,* produced in Frankfurt, marks a key year of remembrance in Germany

Such a bad play as Rainer Werner Fassbinder's *Garbage, the City and Death* is hardly worth mythologizing and memorializing. It does not even warrant questioning whether this dubious work of art was truly anti-Semitic or not. The public acrimony, protests, and heated parleys in the press surrounding its attempted staging are significant, however, for what they reveal about political culture in West Germany in the mid-1980s, when the transition was already well under way from Bundesrepublik to Deutschland. The Fassbinder affair aroused those same questions of national identity, confrontation of the past, and the relationship of Germany to its Jewish citizens and its own history that would become urgent with the coming of unification. Though written in 1975 and *almost* performed on numerous subsequent occasions, it was not until 1985 that the production of the play resulted in sit-ins and nationwide, even international, attention. This vociferous reaction to an otherwise brief, forgettable work about Frankfurt real estate speculation in the 1970s, replete with obscenities and anti-Semitic slurs, illustrates the changing relationship between Germans and Jews in the 1980s. "In the context of the West German reality," wrote Dan Diner, "it [the play] has an anti-Semitic effect, which does not necessarily mean that it is anti-Semitic" (Töteberg and Lensing 1992, 65).

It is in the broader context of the increasing acerbity in the relationship between non-Jewish Germans and Jews during the 1980s and in the wake of conservatism's triumph in West Germany's public discourse that this single incident must be regarded. One faux pas followed another in the efforts of chancellors Helmut Schmidt and Helmut Kohl to normalize Germany's past and improve relations with Israel. Against the wishes of his own Social Democratic Party, Schmidt fought in parliament to sell some of Germany's Leopard tanks to Saudi Arabia. Defending his position in the late 1970s, he insisted that Germany must act according to its interests and not its past. In Schmidt's view, Menahem Begin, whom Schmidt was known to dislike, abused his position as an Eastern European Jew and took advantage of German Holocaust guilt to further his political aims. In the end, Schmidt's effort proved unsuccessful. The Federal Republic did not sell its tanks to Saudi Arabia.

The issue of guilt influencing Germany's leadership emerged once again in January 1984 during Helmut Kohl's visit to Israel. In a much criticized speech, Kohl exempted himself and his generation from responsibility for the Holocaust by virtue of having been born too late to have participated in the Nazi regime's reign of terror. This syndrome was to become known as the "grace of belated birth" (*Gnade der späten Geburt*). During the same trip, Kohl's spokesman, Peter Boenisch, clad in a full-length black SS-type leather coat, told his Israeli hosts upon his arrival at Ben Gurion Airport that Jews should not always confront Germans with Auschwitz.

During December of the same year, a delegation from the Green Party visited the key participant countries in the Middle East conflict. Israel received the harshest criticism, whereas abuses committed by the other countries were barely mentioned. Indeed, it had become known that some of the position papers voicing this criticism had, in fact, been written in West Germany *prior* to the delegation's departure, thereby clearly conveying that its mission was less the amassing of new information than the condemnation of Israel. To their credit, however, the Greens were the only political party to condemn the Bitburg affair.

In the spring of 1985 the Bundestag passed the so-called Auschwitz lie law, in which the Social Democratic Party (SPD) and the Greens succeeded in making it criminal to claim that Auschwitz never existed. This act, however, was severely diluted by the Christian Democratic Union (CDU) and its conservative allies, who tied its passage to the inclusion of a clause that made it equally criminal to deny the expulsions of Germans from the German Reich's former Eastern territories. In other words, the law as it currently stands equates the denial of Auschwitz with that of the fate of Germans expelled from Europe's east.

The Fassbinder scandal fell in the middle of these events and just before the outbreak of the 1986 Historians' Debate (*Historikerstreit*) over revisionism in the writing of Holocaust history. The conservatism of the government precipitated the desire to reassess the attitude in Germany toward the nation's Jews and, at the same time, was itself indicative of a trend already long in currency with the German public. In the case of the Fassbinder affair, in particular, the unease over the issue of anti-Semitism became obvious not only from the Right but from the traditionally philo-Semitic Left as well. Despite the latter's normal willingness to deal with accusations of anti-Semitism, in this well-publicized media affair members of all political camps shied away from, and even denied, the issue's clear and

obvious relevance. This is because it was not anti-Semitism per se that was regarded as threatening but the issues of Holocaust, German-Jewish relations, and the German past, which seem naturally to segue from the discussion of anti-Semitism.

The political Right, which on the whole opposed the play, decried its tastelessness. The Left, most elements of which supported the performance, supported it in the name of free speech and endorsed its anticapitalist message. Anti-Semitism, though central to the fabric of the work, was deliberately made secondary in an argument polarized along Left-Right political lines. The denial by critics of the play's obviously anti-Semitic content suggested the public's yearning for a normalization of the past. Such normalization had already been promulgated by the government, which wanted to erase the stain of the Holocaust from German history and prove the lasting efficacy of the conservative administration and its would-be contribution to posterity. At the same time, the Jews' protest of the play qua Jews, a first in the political history of modern Germany, revealed their isolation on the question of anti-Semitism and the abrupt end to the once "special" relationship between Germans and Jews. It was the charge of anti-Semitism made by the protesters, more than the play itself, that was at the source of the protracted argument and that put pressure on old wounds. But the allegation of anti-Semitism in the play, as we shall see, was eagerly dismissed as irrelevant, outmoded, and unwanted by all but a handful of protesters.

In the early 1970s, a period of economic boom and massive construction in Frankfurt, the city's New and Old Left were at loggerheads. The former had long desired the modernization of Germany's cities. But this new generation felt angered by what it considered to be a selling-out, the construction of ahistorical "monstrosities" and perpetration of "technological determinism." In the midst of this debate, Rainer Werner Fassbinder, the left-wing filmmaker and author, arrived in Frankfurt from Munich in 1974 to join the avant-garde Theater am Turm (TAT). *Garbage, the City and Death* represents the main work of his Frankfurt interlude. Based loosely on Gerhard Zwerenz's 1973 novel, *Die Erde ist unbewohnbar wie der Mond* (The Earth is uninhabitable like the moon), the play, which he wrote on a round-trip flight from Frankfurt to New York, was published by Suhrkamp, the elite Frankfurt press, in 1976. The publication met with rabid attacks, however, and was discontinued.

Between 1976 and 1985 there were seven aborted attempts to stage the play. Günter Rühle, then the leading feuilletonist of the prestigious *Frankfurter Allgemeine Zeitung,* played a major role in preventing its production. But in early 1985 Rühle left the newspaper to become head of Frankfurt's renowned Schauspielhaus theater. Shortly after his arrival there, Rühle suddenly and inexplicably shifted course and scheduled *Garbage, the City and Death* for production.

Despite heated debate in the culture columns of the country's most influential newspapers, the premiere was set for October 31, 1985, and seemed likely to go ahead. But on that evening a thousand protesters crowded the streets outside the theater. A candlelit church vigil in protest of the play's obscenity, anti-Semitism, and vulgarity had been scheduled for after the show. Between twenty and twenty-five individuals led by Hermann Alter, member of the board of directors of the Jewish Community of Frankfurt, occupied the stage. Even though the name of the main character in the play had been changed from the original "A Rich Jew" to "The Rich Jew," *Garbage, the City and Death* was deemed by the protesters to be so anti-Semitic as to be offensive and unworthy of production in the country that had perpetrated the Final Solution. The notorious line uttered by one of the play's characters, Hans von Gluck, is usually cited as the classic example: "He sucks us dry, the Jew. He drinks our blood and puts us in the wrong because he's a Jew and we carry the blame. If he had stayed where he came from, or if we had gassed him, I could sleep better today."

Three hours of discussion and peaceful protest, in the most democratic aspect of the tradition of 1968, delayed the performance before Rühle and Hilmar Hoffmann, the city's culture minister, capitulated and canceled the show. During that time protesters, members of the audience, and the cast debated whether or not the curtain should rise.

Rühle insisted that all arguments with regard to the nature and merit of the play had already been presented in the press and that the final judgment must come after its production. One of the protesters, Micha Brumlik, shouted to Rühle: "You know, the way and manner, the inconsiderate decisiveness with which you run through this here, reminds me of Helmut Kohl at Bitburg. For me, you are the Kohl of culture!" (Kiderlen 1985, 18). Daniel Cohn-Bendit, the charismatic Jewish "sponti" who was a member of the audience that evening, remained committed to the premiere but welcomed the Jewish community's active stance, which he assessed as its first "decisively public stand in any political controversy in the postwar period." Though a Jew, he argued against the protesters, applauding Fassbinder's gall to say "Reicher Jude," to make Jews real instead of metaphorical victims by letting them be criminal, evil, and distasteful.

Garbage, the City and Death is hardly typical of Fassbinder's oeuvre, with regard to either its quality or its anti-Semitic content. Primarily, Fassbinder was concerned in his work with the portrayal of marginalized groups such as blacks, gypsies, gays, and dwarves. Whereas he left something to be desired as a dramaturge, he can be considered one of the major figures of twentieth-century German film, to which he contributed tremendously as a director along with his contemporaries Volker Schlöndorff, Wim Wenders, and Werner Herzog.

Beyond the shock value of the curses, sex, sadism, and nudity, there is not much of a story line to *Garbage, the City and Death.* The "Rich Jew," who uses various unsavory schemes to destroy Frankfurt in his unstoppable quest to make money and modernize the city in his image, becomes a customer of the prostitute, Roma B. Her pimp and husband, Franz B., a homosexual, is brutalized by certain characters for being gay. Among his tormentors is the chief of police, Müller II. The Jew takes up with Roma B. because he believes her father, Mr. Müller, to have been the Nazi responsible in the war for the murder of his parents. Mr. Müller is himself a transvestite who takes his clothes off the back of his wheelchair-ridden wife. The Rich Jew is arrested for the murder of Müller, but it is Franz B. who is punished for it, thrown out a window by the other characters. In addition to "he sucks us dry," *Garbage, the City and Death* also thematizes all the traditional anti-Semitic prejudices: the Jew as modernizer who in his wanton lust for profit destroys German values and tradition; the Jew as a rootless cosmopolitan devoid of loyalties; and the Jew as a being whose essence is profoundly alien to the German people.

The depiction of gays, prostitutes, transvestites, and pimps sprang from Frankfurt's notorious underworld and, at the same time, was intended as a deliberate shock to the conservative establishment. The play's anticapitalist message emerged from Fassbinder's political convictions and from the aftermath of the true-to-life real estate speculation scandal that rocked Frankfurt in the late 1960s and early 1970s.

The city of Frankfurt, together with a business consortium led by the large banks, had developed a plan to transform the old patrician west end into commercial property. This conglomerate bought many residential buildings and either evicted tenants, often by violent means, or allowed buildings to decay until they could be torn down. In 1972, 40 percent of the occupants (9,000 of 23,000) in this district were forced out to make room for temporary *Gastarbeiter* (guest workers) and, later, for the high-rise construction projects (Kiderlen 1985). Squatters occupied sites, resulting in frequent skirmishes between left-wing protesters and the police. Despite the contentious and aggressive push to clear the land, it was to remain unused for years.

Complicating the issue were the actual Jewish origins of most of the speculators who, in addition to being non-Christian, had also grown up abroad. In other words, they were foreign as well as Jewish. This phenomenon had its forerunner in German history. For just as there existed a preponderance of Jews in the banking and finance professions before World War II, a fact that was distorted by Nazis to portray Jews as mercenary usurpers, so, too, was the Jewishness of the real estate world a source of anti-Semitic sentiment in modern Frankfurt.

The Fassbinder scandal divided German public opinion; it split the press and even the German Jewish community. In the debate before and after the interrupted premiere of *Garbage, the City and Death,* certain distinct camps emerged that can, albeit roughly, be described as follows. In the camp supporting the play's production were the center Left to far Left, the Greens, parts of the Social Democratic Party, and a small portion of the Jewish Left. In support of these groups were two prominent left-wing papers, the *Frankfurter Rundschau* and the *Tageszeitung.* Individual journalists at *Die Zeit* and *Der Spiegel* belonged to this coalition as well. In the middle of the controversy stood Walter Wallmann, the yuppie mayor of Frankfurt, who, though opposed to the play, refused to use state power to prevent its presentation. Of course, there were also those with the viewpoint similar to that of Daniel Cohn-Bendit, who urged for presentation but applauded the vociferous actions of the Jewish protesters for their own sake. In the camp against the play were the Christian Democratic Union, the Free Democratic Party, parts of the Social Democratic Party, the Church and its clergy, and the majority of the Jewish community. To back them, they had the voice of the prestigious, established conservative *Frankfurter Allgemeine Zeitung,* as well as the *Süddeutsche Zeitung,* which remained staunchly opposed. In addition, individuals at *Die Zeit* and *Der Spiegel,* which represented both sides in their reportage, opposed Fassbinder's play.

Whereas the coalitions break down rather neatly into Left and Right, the arguments within each camp were by no means harmonious. In short, the arguments invoked against production rested on two pillars: the obscenity of *Garbage, the City and Death* and its anti-Semitism. But both of these views, although touted by social critics in the press and in government, masked more complicated relations with the issue of anti-Semitism. Conservatives denounced the obscenity first and the anti-Semitism second, as part and parcel of the work's general vulgarity. It was only the Jewish community that decried the blatant anti-Semitism first and foremost.

The Jewish attitude was the most straightforward. Henryk Broder insisted that the anti-

Semitism provoked by the play, by breaking old taboos, was not in defiance of old traditions but the result of them. In other words, this was anti-Semitism because of Auschwitz, not in spite of it. The play and the denial of its anti-Semitism were symptoms of German impatience with the albatross of their history and the overwhelming desire to reclaim it from the Jews whose Holocaust had come to define this past. The play represented, to Broder, a blatant attack against Jews, because it meant an end to the *Schonzeit* "no-hunting season" and a return to "normalcy" much too soon after the Holocaust. The normalcy euphemism sanctioned socially acceptable anti-Semitism in German public discourse. "What has remained is an unresolved anti-Semitic potential, a platonic hatred of the Jews, so to speak, on the one hand, without Jews, and on the other, without anti-Semites. So it seems. The good old anti-Semitism is a nostalgic remembrance of those days when Veit Harlan staged his *Jud Süß* and German girls and women were warned about intimate contact with Jews" (Lichtenstein 1986, 211).

The mainstream conservative position, however, complicated the picture. Although those on the Right joined with the Jewish protesters in denouncing Fassbinder's play, it was not for the same reasons. Ironically, the Right, in this case the ally of the Jews against Rühle, had never been known as the great friend of Jewish causes in Germany. Having had a less than stellar track record with normalization in the past, the forces opposed to the play made suspicious bedfellows for the Jewish community. Their stated argument against the play rested on its poor quality and the hype that surrounded it. Conservatives were offended by *Garbage*'s affront to middle-class decency. But despite apparent common interest, the reasoning behind its opposition had little to do with anti-Semitism. Quite the opposite: vulgarity was still considered the play's primary transgression by shocked conservatives, whose moral outrage and concern allowed them to appear philo-Semitic as well. Conservatives in this camp earned a "freebie" opportunity to be on the politically correct side of the Jewish issue.

It must be added that there were non-Jews on the Right who did oppose the play on anti-Semitic grounds. "After Auschwitz, human decency, tact, style or whatever one calls it should simply forbid this, as the consequences are clear. The anti-Semites become more anti-Semitic and the few Jews who returned to this country or fled here from the East are worriedly asking themselves if it really will reach such a point again" (Marion Gräfin Dönhoff in Lichtenstein 1986, 116). This criticism, however, was merely part of an attempt to silence the play, because the Right feared that the scandal the play would create would expose the latent and insidious normalization being furthered by Bonn authorities. Those conservatives who opposed the performance of the play certainly did not do so out of philo-Semitic sentiment. Rather, their opposition stemmed from distaste for all the reforms wrought by "1968," of which Rainer Werner Fassbinder was a prime protagonist. They dismissed the play as yet another excess of a movement that they detested. By opposing the play's anti-Semitism, they found an excellent fig leaf with which to cover their own anti-Semitic attitudes.

Perhaps more surprising were the views expressed by those, primarily on the Left, who endorsed the production of the play. Again the arguments spanned a wide spectrum and, as with the contra camp, the rhetoric in the press reflected a specific, evident view of the issue of anti-Semitism and the image of the Jew as portrayed in *Garbage, the City and Death*. Despite the deliberate confluence in Fassbinder's play of anti Semitism and anticapitalism—a rhetorical technique frequently invoked by the Left in the past to reprove Jews for belonging primarily to the capitalist classes—German left-wing critics denied the existence of anti-Semitism in the work. This reaction suggested deep emotional discomfort with the issue. The Left, by not addressing the anti-Semitism, seemed to flip-flop on the position it had taken with regard to Bitburg, when members of its camp vehemently denounced the anti-Semitic efforts of conservatives to deny the past. Traditionally more philo-Semitic than the Right—albeit not Zionist—the Left's stance on *Garbage, the City and Death* revealed that both ends of the leftist political spectrum felt troubled by the issues aroused in the play.

First among these on the Left was a minority of Jews who supported the production. Peter Zadek admitted that the play was anti-Semitic but advocated its performance for this very reason. "Indeed the statement of the theater (if it really is the statement of the theater and not that of the reporting journalists) that the play is not anti-Semitic is absurd. Naturally it is anti-Semitic. Everyone who reads it notices that. For exactly this reason, it must be performed" (Lichtenstein 1986, 65). Similarly, Daniel Cohn-Bendit vocally endorsed *Garbage, the City and Death* for its confrontation with anti-Semitism and the glorification of the right to free speech upheld by allowing its production. Esther Schapira remonstrated that the issue at stake was not the verity of Fassbinder's anti-Semitism but that of each individual confronting his own (Kiderlen 1985, 58).

There were also those criticisms from the Left that denied the anti-Semitism of the play or rejected its relevance for the question of the play's production. In the former category there were two variants, those who denied that the Left was even capable of anti-Semitism, declaring it to be a right-wing phenomenon, and those who simply dismissed the notion altogether. Gerhard Zwerenz, the author of the original book on which Fassbinder based his play, advocated the former position and wrote: "Anti-Semitism was and is right-wing, nationalistic, 'biologistic' [*biologistisch*], racist . . . a left-wing anti-Semite is impossible. Left-wing criticism cannot argue racially, 'biologistically,' or nationalistically. Where the criticism, as in Frankfurt, affects Jews or Israelis, it is not against the Jews, but against failed and inhuman politics of construction. . . . If eight out of ten important realtors in Frankfurt are of Jewish origin, I cannot write about a Persian. . . . To saddle Fassbinder and the young Germans with some guilt or other for anti-Semitism is crazy" (Lichtenstein 1986, 37). Since the Six-Day War in Israel, the German Left had turned increasingly toward an anti-Zionist stance, under whose guise, despite its complete denial, it masked anti-Semitic sentiments as well.

Those in favor of the play appealed to the right to freedom of speech and praised the open, honest discussion of anti-Semitism that would result from its production. To limit any freedom, they contended, is to limit political freedom and thereby the freedom and security of Germany's Jews. Only the Greens focused exclusively on the theme of real estate speculation and exploitation in Frankfurt and picked up on the play's anti-capitalist message. A loose alliance of Frankfurt's literati and the left-wing intelligentsia agreed with Günter Rühle that it was high time to abandon the Schonzeit of the Jews, which supposedly had defined West Germany's public discourse for far too long. After all, the most basic characteristics of any successful liberal democracy are complete artistic freedom and free speech. Thus the Holocaust simply could not be used to protect the Jews indefinitely. Such excessive consideration— so the argument goes—undermines the fundamentally democratic character of the Federal Republic. Curiously, it was the Right—certainly no friend to the Jews—that argued against the play's performance, though mainly on the grounds of its tastelessness and sensationalism, rather than its blatant anti-Semitism.

The rhetoric that emerged from left-wing critics and their press posits that the play was not anti-Semitic at all. After all, in addition to the "Rich Jew" character, Fassbinder included two old Nazis as well. Fassbinder himself went so far as to say that the piece was philo-Semitic: "You know exactly that for many anti-Semites, Jews are rich, business-oriented and potent. Hence the important, rich Jew so that one holds one's breath in order to listen better. My 'Rich Jew' dismantles himself. . . . My 'Rich Jew' is just a person and does not embody abstract, Jewish capital" (Töteberg and Lensing 1992, 35).

On a certain level the Germans' discomfort with anything related to Jews, anti-Semitism, the Holocaust, and Israel is understandable, for any of these topics cannot help but remind them of their unresolved but deeply troubled relationship with Germany's recent past. Thus, it is not surprising to witness the periodic recurrence of events throughout postwar German history in which the debate about the whole complex of Jewish causes also entailed a cathartic dimension in the sense that one was finally permitted to blurt out one's feelings. Moreover, by treating the Jews as "normal," the Germans could finally regain a sense of calm and self-identity, a welcome respite from a sense of being constantly judged. Paradoxically, an expression of open anti-Semitism yielded a certain emancipation and liberation for virtually all Germans, regardless of political allegiance.

What is interesting about the Fassbinder affair is not whether the play or its author actually are anti-Semitic but the public discussion it awakened about the relationship between Germans and Jews. Considered to be a "special relationship" since Auschwitz, in the mid-1980s, when the mood of introspection and searching for a sense of national self-identity had gripped the Federal Republic, the Jews' status ceased to be unique. Nonetheless, neither group will ever relate to any other ethnicity, nation, or culture in quite the same way as each relates to the other. This is not to say that German-Jewish relations of the past fifty years have been particularly bad. Quite the contrary, they have seemed rather good on the surface, at least on the official and formal level, and in a comparative context. The changing nature of Germany's European presence and the passage of time, however, have begun the erosion of the "special" nature of the old *Bundesrepublik*'s relationship with the Jews.

Fassbinder himself said in an interview: "The hysterical tone of the discussion surrounding this play strengthens me in the fear of a 'new anti-Semitism' that moved me to write this play in the first place" (Töteberg and Lensing 1992, 119). One critic's comment, which met with widespread public approval, was: "Do they not through their clumsiness provoke the anti-Semitic consequences: now the rich, all powerful Jews have also succeeded in blocking a premiere? Even if they are not beloved, don't they still have only themselves to blame?" (Georg Hensel in Lichtenstein 1986, 95).

Does this so-called normalization, this right to break old taboos and criticize the Jews, reflect the development of an ideological democracy and flexibility or the emergence of ideological narrow-mindedness, rigidity, and the infiltration of public opinion by a new, socially permissible anti-Semitism? Whatever the intent of the author, the anti-Semitic content of *Garbage, the City and Death* concretized the issue of anti-Semitism by putting it into words. Many argued that open discussion or pronouncement of anti-Semitic ideas diffuses their danger. But isn't this claim of "coming out," of needing to be able to say that there are Jewish speculators, spurious? Should it be said that Jews participated in the destruction of inner-city Frankfurt real estate? Of course. But what does such reprehensible behavior have to do with religious affiliation, an ethnic allegiance, a cultural identity, or any of the other characteristics defining the Jews as a special minority in the German context? Rather, is this not perhaps an attempt to blame the Jews and hence imply that "they had it coming to them"? The construction of an image of the guilty victim fulfills an exculpatory function for those Germans eager to rid themselves of the burden of their past.

Bibliography

Janusz Bodek, *Die Fassbinder-Kontroversen: Entstehung und Wirkung eines literarischen Textes* (Frankfurt a. M.: Peter Lang, 1991); Rainer Werner Fassbinder, *Der Müll, die Stadt und der Tod* (Frankfurt a. M.: Verlag der Autoren, 1981); Elisabeth Kiderlen, *Deutsch-jüdische Normalität: Fassbinders Sprengsätze* (Frankfurt a. M.: Pflasterstrand, 1985); Heiner Lichtenstein, ed., *Die Fassbinder Kontroverse oder das Ende der Schonzeit* (Königstein/Taunus: Athenäum, 1986); Andrei Markovits, Seyla Benhabib, and Moishe Postone, "Rainer Werner Fassbinder's *Garbage, the City and Death*: Renewed Antagonisms in the Complex Relationship Between Jews and Germans in the Federal Republic of Germany," *New German Critique* (fall 1986): 3–27; and Michael Töteberg and Leo A. Lensing, eds., *The Anarchy of the Imagination: Interviews, Essays, Notes of Rainer Werner Fassbinder*, trans. Krishna Winston (Baltimore, Md.: Johns Hopkins University Press, 1992).

ANDREI S. MARKOVITS AND
BETH SIMONE NOVECK

1986   The Historians' Debate (*Historikerstreit*) takes place over the status and representation of the Nazi period, and more specifically of the Holocaust, in Germany's past

The Historians' Debate was conducted not in professional journals but in the popular press and large-circulation periodicals. It thus raised the question of the relation between the public sphere and the work of specialized professionals. Appropriately enough, it was catapulted to the status of a heated public controversy, if not a cause célèbre, by two articles in *Die Zeit* by the philosopher Jürgen Habermas, which were written in response to a June 6 article in the *Frankfurter Allgemeine Zeitung* by the historian Ernst Nolte. By the end of 1986, contributions had been made by a long list of scholars, especially historians, whose names read like an honor roll of the profession in Germany: Karl Dietrich Bracher, Joachim Fest, Imanuel Geiss, Klaus Hildebrand, Andreas Hillgruber, Eberhard Jäckel, Jürgen Kocka, Christian Meier, Horst Möller, Hans Mommsen, Wolfgang J. Mommsen, Thomas Nipperdey, Hagan Schulze, Michael Stürmer, and Heinrich August Winkler. A close reading of their contributions reveals often subtle differences in position as well as lines of argument that are not easy to summarize. But the crux of the debate on a popular level was the extent to which certain interpretive procedures, notably the comparison of Nazi crimes with other modern genocidal phenomena (particularly Stalin's Gulag), tended to relativize, normalize, or even "air-brush" Auschwitz in order to make it fade into larger historical contexts and out of conscious focus, thereby helping to foreground acceptable continuities in German history as a basis for an affirmative, pro-Western identity.

One irony of the debate, which the present commentary will perforce compound, is that its major participants were for the most part non-Jews writing about the problem of the elimination of Jews and other oppressed groups. The fact that forty years after the fall of the Nazis, Jews had to be represented by others attested to the effectiveness of the Nazi genocide in Germany and central Europe, and it forced even those who insisted on the duty to remember and mourn the victims of a "past that will not pass away" to become involved, however unintentionally, in a scenario that on some level repeated the suppression or repression of Jewish voices. Manifest in the debate was the intense involvement of all participants in the attempt to come to terms with a traumatic, highly "cathected" past—an undertaking perhaps best understood through the medium of psychoanalytic concepts such as transference, repression, denial, acting out, and working through. Indeed, one prominent feature of the debate was the spontaneous use by participants themselves of psychoanalytic categories. The pertinence of these categories becomes particularly pronounced with respect to drastic events whose traumatizing potential varies with the different subject-position of participants, witnesses, and commentators.

"Transference" in this context has as a primary meaning the tendency to repeat, in one's own analysis, forces that are active in one's object of investigation. With reference to the Holocaust or Shoah, this problem arises even on the basic level of terminology, for no terms are innocent, and there is the danger of using dubious terms in one's own voice. Thus there is an ineluctable difficulty in naming the events in question. "Holocaust" connotes a sacrificial offering, and its use threatens to sacralize events, although this possibility is counteracted at present by the prevalent use of the term in ordinary contexts. "Shoah" seemingly places events in one religious and ethnic tradition and has an exoticizing potential. (It also brings out the cultural and even linguistic power of the film in the recent past.) Other terms, such as "final solution" or "annihilation," repeat Nazi terminology, and neologisms such as "Judeocide" recall neutralizing bureaucratic jargon favored by the Nazis. "Genocide" may have a leveling effect, but "Nazi genocide" may be one of the better terminological compromises. Still, the best option may be to use various terms with an awareness of their problematic nature and not to become riveted on any one of them. In any case it is significant that, particularly with respect to extremely traumatic events, the transferential problem arises on the elementary discursive level of naming.

To act out a transferential relation is to compulsively repeat the past as if it were fully present, typically in a manic or melancholic manner. Acting out may be necessary with respect to trauma, especially in the case of victims, but fixation on the past blocks mourning and working through in general. To work through problems is to counteract the tendency to deny, repress, or blindly repeat them, and doing so enables one to acquire critical perspective that allows for a measure of control and responsible action, notably including the renewal of life in the present. Working through, which may never fully transcend acting out or totally heal the wounds of a traumatic past, should be distinguished from the phantasm of total mastery (evoked in the unfortunate term *Vergangenheitsbewältigung* [mastering the past]).

The two principal protagonists in the Histo-rikerstreit, with reference to whose writings other participants framed issues, were Ernst Nolte and Jürgen Habermas. Although certain nuances are lost in the procedure, it is worthwhile to examine in some detail their position-setting views. Acting out the past in a rather uncontrolled manner marked important aspects of Ernst Nolte's "Vergangenheit die nicht vergehen will" (The past that will not pass), whereas Habermas in limited ways at least broached problems of working through a traumatic past and warned of the dangers of denying, repressing, or acting it out.

One issue that was often stressed by participants in the debate was that of the comparability or singularity of Nazi crimes. This issue could easily become diversionary, in that all events are both comparable and singular or unique. In addition, the historical question concerns the nature and function—including the function in the historian's own context of enunciation—of comparisons that delineate a specific configuration of similarities and differences. Nolte at times stressed similarities to the virtual exclusion of differences and, through a sophistic use of rhetorical questions, took comparison in the dubiously metaphysical (perhaps magical) direction of making Nazi crimes derivative or mimetic of a more basic original—Stalinist crimes. In a move that made the Shoah seem old hat and assimilated it to other genocidal phenomena with only a seemingly negligible qualification, he asserted that "a notable shortcoming of the literature about National Socialism" was the failure to admit that all Nazi deeds "had already been described in the voluminous literature of the 1920s . . . with the sole exception of the technical process of gassing" (Nolte 1987, 21–22). He even suggested that Hitler's policies were preemptive with respect to an archetypal Bolshevik menace. He thereby brought to life the hackneyed apologetic claim that at least the Nazis opposed the Bolsheviks and defended the interests of the West: "The following question must seem permissible, even unavoidable: Did the National Socialists or Hitler perhaps commit an 'Asiatic' deed merely because they considered themselves and their kind to be potential victims of an 'Asiatic' deed? Was not the Gulag Archipelago primary to [or more original (*ursprünglicher*) than] Auschwitz? Was the Bolshevik murder of an entire class not the logical and factual prius of the 'racial murder' of National Socialism? Cannot Hitler's most secret deeds be explained by the fact that he had *not* forgotten the rat cage? Did Auschwitz in its root causes not originate in a past that will not pass?" (Knowlton and Cates 1993, 22; trans. modified).

Nolte thus used the ploy of posing presumably daring, experimental questions—questions that the norms of liberalism and pluralism would require one to entertain in open-minded scholarship. But the ploy is deceptive because the apparent questions are rhetorically converted into pseudo-interrogatives whose dogmatic, incantatory effect is to suggest the actuality of an implausible, if not historically absurd, postulation.

For Nolte the Gulag may have "caused" Auschwitz, although precisely how is unclear. Somehow, the Nazis did it because the Russians did it first, and the Nazis were afraid that the Russians might do it to them. Given his discursive style, it is unclear whether Nolte takes up the racial slur concerning an "Asiatic deed" in his own voice. As Eberhard Jäckel observed in a September 12 article in *Die Zeit*, Nolte's arguments "are not only unconvincing—they can be disproven with some certainty" (Knowlton and Cates 1993, 78). For Jäckel, the underlying reasons for the Holocaust were clear: "Hitler often said why he wished to remove and to kill the Jews. His explanation is a complicated and structurally logical construction that can be reproduced in some detail. A rat cage, the murders committed by the Bolsheviks, or a special fear of these are not mentioned. On the contrary, Hitler was always convinced that Soviet Russia, precisely because it was ruled by Jews, was a defenseless colossus standing on clay feet. Aryans had no fear of Slavic or Jewish subhumans. The Jew, Hitler wrote in 1926 in *Mein Kampf*, 'is not an element of an organization but a ferment of decomposition. The gigantic empire in the East is rife for collapse.' Hitler still believed this in 1941 when he had his soldiers invade Russia without winter equipment" (78).

In part to offset Nolte's exaggerated emphasis on similarities between Nazi and Bolshevik poli-

cies, Jäckel offered an oft-quoted delineation of the singularity of Nazi crimes: "I, however, claim (and not for the first time) that the National Socialist murder of the Jews was unique because never before had a nation with the authority of its leader decided and announced that it would kill off as completely as possible a particular group of humans, including old people, women, children, and infants, and actually put this decision into practice, using all the means of governmental power at its disposal" (Knowlton and Cates 1993, 76). Jäckel also noted that Nolte's point about the rat cage, which for Nolte referred to a technique of torture evoked in George Orwell's *1984*, was interpreted by Hitler himself as referring to Lubjanka prison, and that Orwell's novel did not appear until 1949 (77). In a more sober follow-up article in *Die Zeit* of October 31, Nolte asserted that he believed Hitler was referring not to the prison per se but to a process in Lubjanka that had become known worldwide through Orwell's novel—a process that had been reported in the press during the early post–World War I years as a reality in the prisons of the Cheka (150). Whether or not these reports were true, Hitler, for Nolte, "was apparently convinced of their validity," although once again Nolte provided no proof. Nolte also specified that "the Gulag Archipelago is primary to Auschwitz precisely because the Gulag was in the mind of the originator of Auschwitz; Auschwitz was not in the minds of the originators of the Gulag" (151). He did not tell the reader what evidence enabled him either to read Hitler's mind or to assume that Hitler shared his own obsessions.

The rat cage is a detail that reveals much about the nature and effects of Nolte's discursive and argumentative procedures. Although his postulation of some sort of causal priority for Bolshevism is gratuitous, it is conceivable that there is an element of validity in Nolte's speculations about Hitler's own confused stereotypes and anxieties concerning rats and Jews. The rat has long been a marker of subterranean filthiness and at times of homophobic anxiety, and Hitler did see Jews as vermin. Moreover, one may qualify Jäckel's argument by pointing out that Hitler may have had a paranoid fear of Jews and Jewish "contamination," including the possibility that he himself had some Jewish "blood." But the basic point is that Nolte did not carefully frame his views as speculations but presented them as seeming facts (or at least as solidly based conclusions), and he inserted them into dubious associative trains of thought rhetorically constructed as pseudo-interrogatives or as tendentious arguments that could easily serve apologetic purposes. He thus did more to reinforce paranoid anxieties and questionable inferences than to provide a basis for their critical analysis. In an earlier essay, he even went to the extreme of suggesting that Hitler might have been justified in interning Jews as prisoners of war because of Chaim Weizmann's "official declaration in the first days of September 1939, according to which Jews in the whole world would fight on the side of England" ("Between Myth and Revisionism? The Third Reich in the Perspective of the 1980s," in Koch 1985, 27). Here Nolte's rhetorical strategy is based on a blatantly projective inclination to blame the victim.

Nolte nonetheless warned against indiscriminate conceptions of German "guilt" that unconsciously replicate the kind of thinking by which the Nazis convinced themselves of the "guilt" of the Jews. He also did not deny the prevalence of atrocity in the twentieth century. But Nolte insists on this prevalence not so much to emphasize its importance as to mitigate, if not evade, the anti-Semitism of specifically Nazi behavior. In light of his premise (or fixation) whereby Communism is the ultimate cause of all modern evil, Nolte's argument itself takes on a circular, paranoid structure that makes it impermeable to counterevidence. His argument also has the earmark of uncontrolled transference in its uncritical repetition of features of his object of study.

Nolte's views are often opposed to those that Jürgen Habermas has championed. In his initial response to Nolte, "A Kind of Settlement of Damages" of July 11, Habermas saw revisionist tendencies not only in professional historiography but in plans for the German Historical Museum in Berlin and the House of History of the Federal Republic in Bonn. He may have associated Nolte with such other historians as Hillgru-

ber and Stürmer to give an insufficiently qualified and overly unified view of a movement in the profession toward apologetic revisionism. Moreover, Habermas's own self-image and his understanding of the tradition of critical rationality he wishes to defend led him to make allowance in his own approach only for rather reduced variants of notions that disorient rationality without simply denying it (such as Freud's notion of the unconscious). But Habermas's intervention in the Historikerstreit enabled him to bring important problems to public attention and even to elaborate in more telling fashion certain of his basic arguments.

One may also note that the Bitburg incident forms part of the larger context in which the Historikerstreit must be seen. In 1985 Ronald Reagan tried to justify a decision not to visit a concentration camp during his trip to Germany commemorating the fortieth anniversary of the end of the war—a decision he changed only because of public pressure. And he persisted in his determination to visit Bitburg cemetery despite the revelation that it contained SS graves. He regressed to immediate post–World War II tendencies by demonizing events and attributing "the awful evil . . . an evil that victimized the whole world" primarily to one man, Hitler. He also asserted: "I think that there is nothing wrong with visiting that cemetery where those young men are victims of Nazism also, even though they were fighting in German uniform, drafted into service to carry out the hateful wishes of the Nazis. They were victims, just as surely as the victims in the concentration camps" (*New York Times,* Apr. 19, 1985). The indiscriminate generalization of victimhood and the dissociation of the army and even the SS from Nazism were among the more egregious initiatives in the attempt to provide Germany with a positive identity as an ally of the United States. In the article he wrote on Bitburg, Habermas prefigured some of the points he would make in the salvo that opened the Historikerstreit (see "Die Entsorgung der Vergangenheit: Ein kulturpolitisches Pamphlet," *Die Zeit,* May 24, 1985; trans. Thomas Levin as "Defusing the Past: A Politico-Cultural Tract," in Hartman 1986, 43–51.)

In the second of his interventions, Habermas put forth a striking formulation of the relationship between collective responsibility and the public role of memory: "There is first of all the obligation that we in Germany have—even if no one else any longer assumes it—to keep alive the memory of the suffering of those murdered by German hands, and to keep it alive quite openly and not just in our own minds. These dead justifiably have a claim on a weak anamnestic power of solidarity, which those born later can only practice in the medium of memory which is constantly renewed, often desperate, but at any rate alive and circulating. If we brush aside this Benjaminian legacy, our Jewish fellow citizens, the sons, the daughters, the grandchildren of the murdered victims, would no longer be able to breathe in our country. That also has political implications" (Knowlton and Cates 1993, 165; trans. modified).

Habermas also argued for a critical rather than a blind appropriation of traditions—a critical appropriation that would validate only traditions that "stand up to the suspicious gaze made wise by the moral catastrophe" (Knowlton and Cates 1993, 166; trans. modified). Instead of a particularistic nationalism, Habermas called for a "postconventional identity" based on universal norms and a constitutional patriotism. In themselves these ideals may seem rather ineffective and overly indebted to the abstract aspirations of the Enlightenment and German Idealism. But one may argue that the larger project is to join these ideals to the selective appropriation of traditions, including those of the Enlightenment, that in their own way also carry historical sedimentation and concrete commitments.

In a still further intervention in the debate—an address delivered in Denmark (reprinted in Habermas 1989)—Habermas extended his inquiry into the complex transformations of embeddedness in a traditional "life-world." While insisting on a complementary rather than analogical relation between individual and collective identity, he stressed the postconventional implications of Kierkegaard's notion of a conversion-like existential choice that consciously and responsibly transforms one's life history. This

choice puts the individual in the ethical position of an editor deciding what should be considered essential and worth passing on in his or her past. The counterpart in the life of a people would be the decision, conscious of the ambivalence in every tradition, that publicly and critically determines which traditions or aspects of traditions one wanted to continue and which one did not. The reference to Kierkegaard might itself be read to indicate that, with respect to the tense conjunction of universalizing constitutional principles, and more specifically to some extent non-reflective bonds, there is a need for continual rethinking and renegotiation rather than speculative synthesis, or *Aufhebung*.

Habermas strongly criticized the kind of uncritical, customary identity that seeks an affirmative conception of the past and self-confirming normalization or national identity even at the price of denial and distortion. The power of the following questions is enhanced when they are contrasted with the earlier quoted questions raised rhetorically by Ernst Nolte:

Can one continue the tradition of German culture without taking over the historical liability for the way of life in which Auschwitz was possible? Can one be liable for the context of the origins of such crimes, with which one's own existence is historically woven, in any other way than through common remembrance of that for which one cannot atone other than in a reflective, testing attitude toward one's own identity-endowing traditions? Can it not be generally said that the less commonality a collective life-context has afforded, and the more it has maintained itself outwardly by usurpation and destruction of alien life, the greater will be the burden of repentance imposed on the mourning and self-critical examination of the following generations? And does not precisely this sentence prohibit downplaying the weight of the burden with which we are saddled by making leveling comparisons? This is the question of the singularity of the Nazi crimes. (Knowlton and Cates 1993, 167)

Habermas saw no simple dichotomy between memory and history. His arguments indicated that a historical consciousness ideally performs critical work on memory in order to avoid being misled by its ideological lures and to determine what in it deserves to be passed on as a living heritage. It would, moreover, be mistaken to identify Habermas's specific and limited notions of historical liability and solidarity of memory with an indiscriminate conception of German guilt that is visited on each and every German as irrational fate or pathogenic stain, even though those "born later" at times may unjustifiably feel guilty about the past.

There were questionable aspects of Habermas's argument, including a tendency to conflate or at least implicitly to correlate a normative conception of Western democratic values with the existing Western political alliance. Moreover, in view of his defense of modernity as an uncompleted project of Enlightenment, Habermas had strategic as well as more deep-seated philosophical reasons for not placing too much emphasis on the ambivalence of Western traditions and the possibly dubious role of a critique of revisionism in lessening the implication of other Western countries in massively destructive or even genocidal processes. Given the history of the United States, this danger is clear and present for an American, and identification with Habermas's position may be facilitated by the narcissistic and self-justificatory gains it brings. It would nonetheless be a mistake simply to process all of Habermas's arguments in the Historians' Debate in terms of a preset conception of his politics or philosophy. Such a response to Habermas is itself rather leveling and leads one to miss or underplay significant, contextually important features of his interventions, not least of which was his role in triggering the Historians' Debate itself.

"I think that the debate initiated by Habermas is unfortunate," asserted Thomas Nipperdey. Nipperdey was writing as a professional historian and perhaps as a conservative thinker for whom "the areas under discussion are highly sensitive, the moral and political commitment of the participants is strong, the difficult distinctions and differentiations will get lost in the fray" (Knowlton and Cates 1993, 146). In retrospect other professional historians (for example, Ian Kershaw and Richard Evans) noted that the Historians'

Debate unearthed no new facts about the Nazi period and provided no genuinely revised interpretation of it; they therefore tended to downplay its significance and saw it as generating more heat than light. Nipperdey himself impatiently called for a return to "real" history and objectivity: "We must historicize National Socialism. . . . Beyond apologetics and criticism, beyond conservative and progressive partisanship, there is objective history, which we, despite the limitations of our—transnational—scholarly endeavor, are closing in on. Everyone knows it: There simply is, beyond our bickering about values, history writing that is more or less valuable, outmoded or merely provisionally valid" (145).

Even Habermas, whom Nipperdey took to task, defended the ability to debate public issues in the press in terms that tended to confirm and reveal the prevalence of Nipperdey's assumptions, for Habermas sharply divided if not dichotomized between the public "arena" involving a "public use of history"—an "arena" in which "there can be no impartial ones among us"—and "the discussion of scholars who in their work must assume the perspective of an outside observer" (Knowlton and Cates 1993, 167–68). Yet two broader questions raised by the Historians' Debate itself were whether one could neatly separate between arenas or spheres in modern life (the professional from the public sphere, for example) and whether one could define history in purely professional, objective, third-person terms under the aegis of a strictly differentiated or even autonomized paradigm of research. The debate pointed to the problematic nature of boundaries, the possibly valid status of hybridized roles (such as the historian-intellectual), and the need to argue for the relative strength or weakness of problematic but crucial distinctions that could not simply be conflated with comfortable dichotomies or binary oppositions. It also indicated the need for a psychoanalytically informed approach to problems in which one did not assume that objectivity was a mere given or taken-for-granted professional characteristic in relation to which there might be biased deviations that could always be corrected for, thereby allowing a return to (third-person) objectivity. Rather, objectivity could be seen as a difficult, never fully achieved objective that was not even desirable in its imaginary total state and that in its justifiable, desirable forms (related to accuracy, meticulous empirical research, and rigorous argumentation) had to be elaborated by working through transferential relations, resistances, denials, and repressions. Also required were the explicit acknowledgement and the possible transformation of subject-positions as one engaged problems in historical research and self-understanding.

The Historians' Debate, which delivered relatively little in terms of new facts or particular interpretations of events, may have contributed a great deal to historical self-understanding by disclosing the importance of the problem of one's relation to the past and its implications for the present and future. In this light it may have also indirectly stimulated questions for research and interpretation—such questions as the positionality of the historian, the bearing of present contexts on research, and the nature of the very language used by the historian in his or her accounts. The problem it posed was how to negotiate the relation between the specific demands of representing the Nazi period and the Shoah, on the one hand, and, on the other, the more general questions raised by one's differential implication in a controversial, traumatizing past.

In the more immediate post–World War II period, there was the danger that the events of the Nazi period would be demonized and that their predominant cause would be found in the personality of Hitler and the manipulations of his regime. The Nuremberg trials also created the temptation to emphasize the criminality of a diabolical elite and to use it as a stereotypical counterimage to the virtues of "our side." These simplifying responses were to some extent understandable as immediate reactions to extremely traumatic events, but their deficiencies became readily apparent. Yet their effects were intensified by the German "economic miracle" that furthered avoidance, denial, or repression of the Nazi past and provided manic outlets for those marked by an "inability to mourn."

The events culminating in 1968 provided an opportunity to confront the past, especially on the part of younger Germans who had no direct acquaintance with the Nazi period but who might not experience their own "born-later" status as altogether fortunate because of displaced guilt feelings and distrust of their parents' generation's silences, evasions, and impatient dismissals concerning the past. But 1968 and its aftermath were at best ambivalent in their bearing on the attempt to work through the past, and the emergence of conservative forces in the 1970s, which provisionally culminated in the political victory of the Tendenzwende in the 1980s, often seemed to bring a renewed avoidance of the past. The effects of the broadcast in 1979 of the TV series *Holocaust* is itself an almost textbook illustration of displacement in the classical Freudian sense, for a minor event that was broadly recognized as a commercialized, offensively Hollywood–type production nonetheless triggered a traumatizing return to the past that perhaps functioned either as a transitory catharsis or, in the best of circumstances, as the occasion for critical reflection upon events. The return of the repressed during the Historikerstreit in 1986 was heated and disorienting, and some of its participants (notably Nolte) threatened to overreact against the earlier tendency (for example, in Friedrich Meinecke's *German Catastrophe* or even in Thomas Mann's *Doktor Faustus*) to represent the Nazi past as singular, demonic, and centered on Hitler by going to the opposite but complementary extreme of normalizing it through potentially leveling comparisons and modes of contextualization. Unfortunately, the debate's potential for a more effective and valid reckoning with the past was easily lost.

Aside from narrowly professional or neopositivistic attempts to downplay the significance of the debate, since 1989 the Historikerstreit has been eclipsed by the uncertainties as well as the promise of German reunification in the wider context of the movement for European integration. The recrudescence of scapegoating tendencies, the hostility toward immigrants, and the rise of neo-Nazi groups are the most negative aspects of the recent configuration. Yet the debate over the so-called failure of the intellectuals in responding to the challenge of reunification—

and especially the controversy centering around Christa Wolf—indicate that problems rehearsed in the Historians' Debate have not been transcended. The East German past arose to create difficulties not only through the heretofore avoided issue of complicity in the Nazi regime but through the more clear and present dangers to stability created by disclosure of the shockingly unexpected extent of spying, informing, and intimidation under the former Communist government. Indeed it has been argued that the ultimate goal of both the Historikerstreit and the debate over the "failure of the intellectuals" is similar: "One wants to get away from a past that is considered either a burden or an embarrassment in order to construct an alternative agenda for the future. While the attempt to overcome the German past in the name of 'normalization' was not successful in the historians' debate, it may very well end up successful in its more removed and diluted form in the current culture debate" (Huyssen 1991). In any case, whatever the more immediate effects of reunification, the problems raised in the Historians' Debate must return in a different way in the new context of a unified German nation-state insofar as the manner in which one comes to terms with the past affects the attempt to construct the present and future.

Bibliography

Peter Baldwin, ed., *Reworking the Past: Hitler, the Holocaust, and the Historians' Debate* (Boston: Beacon, 1990);
Richard J. Evans, *In Hitler's Shadow: West German Historians and the Attempt to Escape from the Nazi Past* (New York: Pantheon, 1989); Saul Friedländer, ed., *Probing the Limits of Representation: Nazism and the "Final Solution"* (Cambridge, Mass.: Harvard University Press, 1992); Jürgen Habermas, *The New Conservatism: Cultural Criticism and the Historians' Debate* (Cambridge, Mass.: MIT Press, 1989); Geoffrey Hartman, ed., *Bitburg in Moral and Political Perspective* (Bloomington: Indiana University Press, 1986); Andreas Huyssen, "After the Wall: The Failure of German Intellectuals," *New German Critique* 52 (1991): 109–43; Ian Kershaw, *The Nazi Dictatorship: Problems and Perspectives of Interpretation,* 2d ed. (London: Edward Arnold, 1989); James Knowlton and Truett Cates, trans., *Forever in the Shadow of Hitler? Original Documents of the Historikerstreit, the Controversy Concerning the Singularity of the Holocaust* (Atlantic Highlands, N.J.: Humanities Press, 1993); H. W. Koch, ed., *Aspects of the Third Reich* (London: Macmillan, 1985); Dominick LaCapra, *Representing the Holocaust: History, Theory, Trauma* (Ithaca, N.Y.: Cornell University Press, 1994); Charles Maier, *The Unmasterable Past* (Cambridge, Mass.: Harvard University Press, 1988); *New German Critique,* vol. 52, *Special Issue on German Unification* (winter 1991); *New German Critique,* vol. 44, *Special Issue on the Historikerstreit* (spring–summer 1988); Ernst Nolte, *Das Vergehen der Vergangenheit: Antwort auf meine Kritiker im sogenannten Historikerstreit,* 2d rev. ed. (Berlin: Ullstein, 1987); and Eric Santner, *Stranded Objects: Mourning, Memory, and Film in Postwar Germany* (Ithaca, N.Y.: Cornell University Press, 1990).

DOMINICK LACAPRA

1990 Jenny Aloni's *Das Brachland* is published as volume 1 of her *Gesammelte Werke in Einzelausgaben*

Jenny Aloni's novel *Das Brachland* was published in 1990. It was the first volume of her *Gesammelte Werke in Einzelausgaben,* which actually is the first complete edition ever dedicated to a German-speaking writer living in Israel. The beginning of the publication of her works (by 1994 they consisted of six volumes, a third of which had never been published before) marks a climax for writers within the "second chapter" of this literature—those male and female authors who had not been prominent as writers *before* their immigration. The complete edition of her works not only renewed readers' interest in Aloni's work, it also attracted the attention of literary juries: she won two renowned literature awards in 1991, the Internationaler Droste-Preis, awarded by the city of Meersburg, and the Westfälischer Literaturpreis (Annette von Droste Hülshoff Preis). In 1993 the critic of the *Neue Zürcher Zeitung* drew the following conclusion under the title "Späte Ehre" (Late honor): "There can be no doubt: the most famous German-speaking writer in present-day Israel is a woman—Jenny Aloni. Moreover she is one of the most prominent female story-tellers of her generation, but her work was never really appreciated until her old age. She had to reach the age of seventy before she could recognize a change in the public estimation of her work."

The history of German-language writing in Israel began with the first wave of the *Aliya* (Rise) in the early twentieth century. The first chapter of this history was characterized by male and female authors who were already known as writers in Europe during the first decades of the century; they even gained some fame before they immigrated to Palestine, mainly in the thirties. Of these authors, Else Lasker-Schüler, Max Brod, Arnold Zweig, Martin Buber, Josef Kastein, Ludwig Strau, and Werner Kraft are the most important names out of a far greater number. The difficulties of these authors have repeatedly been discussed during the last few years, most extensively and learnedly by Margarita Pazi from Tel Aviv. As a first step these difficulties will be illustrated in three individual cases.

Else Lasker-Schüler (1869–1945) lived in exile in Switzerland. Her work had been known since the turn of the century, but she became famous during the expressionistic era. She visited Palestine twice during the thirties before settling there in 1939. Although she wrote the *Hebräische Balladen* (1913) and many other poems dealing with "Jewish topics," throughout her life, the *Hebräerland*, as she called it in her account of her first visit (1937), remained a religious-intellectual idea rather than a political reality to her; she never felt at home in Palestine. In her last play, *Ichundich,* written in Jerusalem, one can find the sentence: "Only eternity is no exile."

Max Brod (1884–1968) was already fifty-five years old when he emigrated from Prague to Palestine in 1939. He had been a Zionist and defender of a Jewish state since the beginning of the century. He understood his salvation as a favor and was thankful to his new home country. He tried—most of the time successfully—to get used to the circumstances of his new life, and he was to a certain extent acknowledged as a writer. But nevertheless he did not write and publish a lot during his first decade in Palestine.

Arnold Zweig (1887–1968), one of the first immigrants, arrived in 1933. By that time the forty-six-year-old was already a well-known author. The upper-middle-class lifestyle he was used to caused him problems in the new country. So did his attitude toward the Eastern Jews, for whom he had fought in the past by writing pamphlets, but whose dominating role in society he disliked. He often complained about the unfamiliar life and the lack of appreciation for his writing; thus he was considered to be arrogant. After the end of World War II he took the first opportunity to return to Germany (to the Soviet occupied zone).

As unique as the careers of these three authors in Palestine may be, they still have some basic commonalities. The central problem is that the language in which these authors wrote, to which they owed their success as artists, and in which they felt at home and which formed a main part of their identity, suddenly became the language of persecutors and murderers and therefore was ostracized or even forbidden in their new home country.

Nevertheless, most of them could not and did not want to abandon the German language. It had been this language that had formed an intellectual home for them in Europe. Werner Kraft emphasized that he never "betrayed the [German] language," and he considered it to be his duty to "lead a life in the German spirit." In his essay "Sprache als Heimat" (1980), Schalom Ben Chorin still talks about his native language as the "language of the soul. . . . One can emigrate from one's country, but not from one's native language." This attachment to the German language not only caused indignation in the new home, it also grew more and more problematic as the German language became more and more isolated. On the one hand, it turned out to be much

more difficult to perceive from such distance how the words that one used without any uneasy feelings began to lose their "innocence" through Nazi usage; on the other hand, these authors often used German grammar and syntax that seemed outdated after only a short time.

Quite frequently these insecurities affected the authors' concepts of themselves. For most of the writers, mainly for the Zionists, emigration did not mean exile but return, the *Aliya* to their home Israel (*Erez Israel*). But these authors in particular suffered enormously from their situation, because for them their commitment to Judaism and their new home was closely connected not only with an adherence to the German language but also with a high esteem for German culture, which in many ways stood in contrast to the majority culture of Eastern Jews, not to mention "oriental" culture. Traditional Eastern Jewish culture was hardly recognized, let alone valued, in these authors' new homes.

Another difficult realization was that European literary fame seldom translated into appreciation in Palestine. They had to earn their living by other means, mostly unaccustomed manual work. Many of these writers had no command of *Ivrit* (Hebrew) or had great difficulties with it. (Ludwig Strauss was a remarkable exception.) This lack not only resulted in their inability to write literature in this language, so that they were to the greatest extent excluded from the literary life—it also restricted their participation in everyday life and limited their ability to understand the problems of people and society in detail. Because of this such issues rarely became the subject of their writing; instead, the authors continued to focus on traditional subjects imported from their former lives and from contemporary Europe.

During Hitler's regime, German-speaking authors in Palestine had very little opportunity to publish their works: some pieces were published in periodicals with tiny circulation, others were published by the authors themselves; translations into Hebrew (such as of Zweig's *Das Beil von Wandsbek*) remained exceptional. These multiple restrictions still remained for the older writers after the foundation of Israel. Only a few of them were prepared to jump into the newspaper and book markets in the German-speaking countries, which redeveloped in the decade after the war.

The second generation of German-speaking writers in Israel had to face even greater difficulties. It was especially hard for them to get in touch with the German market, because from a literary point of view they had not emerged and were completely unknown. Because the ban on the German language persisted after the war, authors writing in German remained to a large degree excluded from the literary life. They had only a few advantages compared with the older authors: writing was only a part-time occupation for them; consequently they were involved in the professional world and the everyday life in Israel, and most of them were able to speak Hebrew. This was the reason for a great number of this circle to write and publish in Ivrit. In any case literature played a different, less important role in the lives and self-conceptions of this second generation, as compared with the older authors.

The bad conditions for German authors from Israel gradually changed in Germany during the 1960s, but this improvement did not last long. During this period, interest in Israel and German-Jewish literature grew, probably due to the public sensation caused by the great trials (such as the Eichmann and Auschwitz trials). It is telling that Jenny Aloni was writing stories during the 1930s, but she was able to publish one in a German newspaper for the first time only in 1960 ("Die Begegnung" [The encounter] in the *Frankfurter Allgemeine Zeitung;* in this story she describes a fictitious conversation between a Jew and a National-Socialist mass-murderer in a prison cell in Israel). In addition, a great number of Israel's German-speaking writers had the opportunity during this decade to publish poems, stories, and autobiographical texts in German newspapers—in rare cases they were even able to publish them in book form. Thus authors tended to steer away from genres depending on the book form—like the novel and drama.

When during the 1970s the interest of the German readers and publishers decreased, writers, critics, and publicists took the initiative: they formed a writers union in 1975, and their chairman, Meir M. Faerber, published an anthology of works written by members of the union (*Stimmen aus Israel: Eine Anthologie deutscher Literatur in Israel* [Gerlingen: Bleicher, 1979]). Because of the attention this volume achieved, another four anthologies could be published during the 1980s: Margarita Pazi, ed., *Nachrichten aus Israel: Deutschsprachige Literatur in Israel* (New York: Hildesheim, 1981); Alice Schwarz-Gardos, ed., *Heimat ist anderswo: Deutsche Schriftsteller in Israel. Erzählungen und Gedichte* (Freiburg: Herder, 1983) and *Hügel des Frühlings: Deutschsprachige Autoren Israels erzählen* (Freiburg: Herder, 1984); and Meir M. Faerber, ed., *Auf dem Weg: Eine Anthologie deutschsprachiger Literatur in Israel* (Gerlingen 1989).

These five anthologies contain more than one hundred texts by fifty authors, both male and female. They show a fairly representative sampling of works by the most important Israeli authors during the past two or three decades. According to the above-mentioned criteria, about forty writers belong to the "second phase" of the literature written in the German language in Israel. A few of them are included in several different anthologies and can therefore be considered the most prominent members of the group. For this reason their names are mentioned here. Their biographical data and birthplaces are included as well to demonstrate the diverse composition of their group: Jenny Aloni (1917–93, Paderborn), Werner Bukofzer (1903–85, Berlin), Schalom Ben Chorin (b. 1913, Munich), Alexander Czerski (1920–85, Katowice), Meir Marcel Faerber (1908–94, Maehrisch-Ostrau), Benno Fruchtmann (b. 1913, Meuselwitz / Thuringia), Erich Gottgetreu (1903–81, Chemnitz), Nora Hauben (b. 1918, Chemnitz), Frieda Hebel (b. 1904, Darmstadt), Leopold Marx (1889–1985, Stuttgart), Fritz Naschitz (b. 1900, Vienna), Ephraim Pistiner (b. 1906, Bukowina), Alice Schwarz-Gardos (b. 1916, Vienna), Hans Josef Speer (b. 1920, Vienna), Heinz Weissenberg (b. 1908, Gießen).

Between 1956 and 1969, Jenny Aloni published six books in Germany. Furthermore more than forty stories of hers have been published in about fifteen different newspapers, magazines, and anthologies in the Federal Republic of Germany, Switzerland, and Austria since 1960. If one adds the selective anthology from 1987 and the volumes of the *Gesammelte Werke,* one can draw the conclusion that no other German-language author of that generation from Israel was more prominent in Germany than Jenny Aloni. Her work, which, as was mentioned before, was acknowledged only very lately, is therefore one of the most representative examples for the "second chapter" of literature written in the German language in Israel.

Jenny Aloni's life history can be called exemplary. The daughter of the Jewish merchant Rosenbaum was born in 1917, left the lyceum of her hometown in 1935, and began to prepare herself—with support from the Youth Aliya—for the emigration to Palestine. She worked on farms, learned Hebrew, studied Jewish history and regional differences, and graduated from a Jewish high school in Berlin in 1939. During her time as a youth worker, she taught children and teenagers who were waiting for emigration. She led a children's transport via Trieste to Palestine in November 1939. There she studied at the Jewish University in Jerusalem and later worked in the hospital service of a Jewish unit of the British army from 1942 to 1946. She visited a school for social work in 1946; in 1948 she participated as first-aid attendant in the Jewish-Arabic War; and afterward she worked in the youth welfare and as a nurse. Jenny Rosenbaum married Esra Aloni (formerly Erich Eichgrün; he changed his name to sound more Hebrew), who was born in the Sauerland and emigrated in 1934. In 1957 the Alonis moved to Ganei Jehuda near Tel Aviv, where Jenny Aloni died in 1993.

Jenny Rosenbaum started writing in Germany, mainly poems, a genre she also preferred for a long time in her new home country. A volume of poetry (*Gedichte*) was published in Germany in 1956. It showed her dependence on many models and traditional forms. A tone of her own can be recognized in her depictions of the rugged nature or the strange culture of her new home country, Israel. Her poetic voice also emerged when she described the first visit to her German hometown in 1955: here she complains about the disappearance of her parents' house and portrays her fright about the strangeness of the people. The poem "Stadt der Kindheit" ends with the words: "Drowned is the vision of the long years. / Whatever you meant to me, you are it no longer." The hard formulation of these final words, which deny a harmonious rhythm, underlines the disruption from a transfigured past.

Not many prose texts by Jenny Aloni from her time in Germany and her first decade in Israel have survived. During the 1950s she turned mainly to short prose and the novel. What was already indicated in her poems was now fully revealed: her work was established around two poles: her German native country, which had become strange to her, and her new home, Israel, which remained strange for a long time. Strangeness became the great leitmotif in Jenny Aloni's imagination and writing.

During this period, Jenny Aloni began to convert the experience of her own life into her prose. In her story "Die Synagoge und der Dom," she depicts the atmosphere in a German provincial town during February 1933 from the point of view of a fifteen-year-old girl: to do so, she creates a mood of insecurity and hostility and depicts the feeling of gradually being excluded. She recognizes that the reason for the growing distance between her and her friends was her Jewishness, of which she had been hardly conscious until then.

One of the most impressive stories by Jenny Aloni, "Kristall und Schäferhund," deals with the incidents during the night of the pogroms in Berlin and Paderborn on November 9, 1938. Here her return to the parent's devastated house combines distance and sensation in a very vivid way. This loss becomes a symbol for her that will recur in her life and writing: "There is no home in this world, only darkness and strangeness."

In spite of the autobiographical traits in these and many other pieces, Jenny Aloni also made use of the reports and experiences of others. She used the deportation of children from the Jewish orphanage in Paderborn during the summer of 1942, for example, as background for the impressive short story "Zwei Inschriften" (Two inscriptions). The story is organized around the principle of duality—a concept that is not only featured in the title, but also reaches into the structure of single sentences: on the walls of both the Jewish orphanage and the Christian monastery, one could read the same inscription: "Thou shalt love thy neighbor as thyself." This commandment, which Jews and Christians share, shows its own fragility in the course of the story: the inhabitants of the monastery watch the transports and do nothing. In addition to the structure of contrast and the pointed way of storytelling, one can find intertextual references in this story to the most famous narration of the nineteenth century dealing with a "Jewish" subject, namely, *Die Judenbuche* by Annette von Droste-Hülshoff. Here, as in Aloni's story, an inscription—a Hebrew quotation that is translated in the last sentence of the narration—takes a key position. With her reference to the *Judenbuche* Jenny Aloni at the same time mentions another literary model: the *Sittengemälde aus dem gebirgigten Westfalen,* which is situated near Paderborn, already fascinated the schoolgirl by its "rough, almost meagre language."

Jenny Aloni, like most Jews living in Palestine, only learned about the Nazi horrors—the deportations, the concentration camps, and the mass extermination—after the end of the war. Only then did she discover the fate of her relatives, and their end is never directly mentioned in her work. Only decades later, in her second volume of poems (*In den schmalen Stunden der Nacht* [In the early hours of the night; 1980]), did she include the dedication: "In memory of my parents and sister, killed in Theresienstadt and Auschwitz." Although accusation is almost completely missing in Jenny Aloni's work, narrations that return to Germany as a subject—such as *Fahrt in die Erinnerung, Besuch 1947, Der weiße Kittel*—show her scars of continuity and repression.

Although the pole of Paderborn and Germany remained present in Aloni's work until the end, the other pole—the new home country, Israel— became ever more important to her during the 1950s: the majority of her stories are set there, and her four novels that have been published thus far are situated there.

Unlike most European writers, Jenny Aloni has considered the historical process in Israel from the mandated territory to the foundation of the state as an important subject of her writing, and she features it by weaving an autobiographical thread through her novels and narrations. Her first novel, *Zypressen zerbrechen nicht* (Cypress trees do not break; 1961), for example, begins with the arrival of a young girl in Palestine and her first experiences in her new home country. *Das Brachland* mirrors the conflict between city and the rural areas in Israel in the late fifties. *Der blühende Busch* (The blossoming bush; 1964) depicts life in a Kibbutz, in particular the relationships between immigrants from various other nations and native-born Israelis. And *Der Wartesaal* (The waiting room; 1969) is influenced by author's impressions during her work for the mentally ill. (Indeed, a great number of her narrations focus on a young social worker.)

But the past is always present in Aloni's works about everyday life in Israel. The heroine of the first novel, for example, learns that the adoption of a Jewish name still cannot erase the past. She realizes that one cannot escape from one's memory and one's own self, as "one can escape from one's own shadow." The inability to forget remains a leitmotif in Jenny Aloni's work. Not infrequently this theme is intensified to a traumatic self-accusation about having survived: "Where others died, were shot, beaten to death, gassed, starved . . . millions of others except me. . . . But why? Why especially me?" Jenny Aloni considers it a duty of those who accidentally survived to write down what they saw and experienced.

Everyday life as illustrated by Jenny Aloni mainly shows places where people in need— social outcasts and socially weak people—live: hospitals, social-welfare stations, detention homes, cheap cafes, and poor cabins. Nature at most forms a counterpart to the poorness and harshness of the country by offering impressive pictures. The blooming desert, the fallow land, and the sea are shown as the shaping powers of the landscape. As little as in Droste is nature depicted for its own sake; the image that inspired the title of the first novel, for example, becomes a sign of the immigrant generation's ability to survive in Israel.

These suggestive images comprise some of the few ornamental elements of language and style in Jenny Aloni's work. Although one can still often find a "polished," sometimes even pathetic, tone in the early poems and novels, the style of her later works becomes simpler, less pretentious, short, and often almost meager. Her quest for the truth penetrates the neglect of life—it is harsh and merciless, linguistically correct, lapidary, laconic, and painfully apt.

Jenny Aloni's themes and language show what the writing of German texts in Israel meant for this "second generation" in a country where fewer and fewer people speak German. The consequences of such linguistic isolation are obvious: language and style often sound preserved from a distant epoch, whereas at the same time they are mixed with forms and grammatical constructions borrowed from Hebrew and English. This dilemma does not have to remain a drawback; it can become a virtue or at least an idiosyncrasy. Jenny Aloni's language can also be seen as a result of this twin tension: the uncomfortable relationship both to her former native language and to her Hebrew and English environment.

While I was writing this essay, Jenny Aloni died. So the circle of authors who wrote the "second chapter" of German-language literature written in Israel diminishes again. Already in 1987 Margarita Pazi wrote that the number of German-speaking writers in Israel had continually decreased since the foundation of the association of German-speaking writers in 1975: "And these authors 'will have no heirs' to quote Rilke. This means an end, the end of the German-Jewish symbiosis, which was cited quite often, but was doubted by many people and probably never existed. At any rate the end of a cultural relationship which undoubtedly enriched Jews and Germans" (Pazi 1993).

Does the appreciation of Jenny Aloni that climaxed with the publication of her works and the literary awards at the same time mark the end of our interest in this unique group of writers? Perhaps there will be another, a "third chapter." Margarita Pazi herself indicated that a few younger writers are again writing in German. Elazar Benyoetz (b. 1937 in Wiener Neustadt), for example, grew up in Israel, but still thought that certain aspects of Jewish fate could only be described in German: "Hebrew and Auschwitz don't get along well, therefore I had to expatriate myself to German"; he also believed that "an adequate poem after Auschwitz could only be written in German, because it influenced Auschwitz." In addition to the few writers who have grown up in Israel, there are others who do not want to live in Germany or prefer to spend a significant part of their lives in Israel: Lea Fleischmann (b. 1947, Ulm), Henryk Broder (b. 1946, Katowice, Poland) and Inge Deutschkron (b. 1922, Finsterwalde) are the most prominent of a still small number of names. During the 1980s younger poets who immigrated to Israel during the 1960s (for example, Annemarie Koenigsberger and Manfred Winkler) formed a union and published fascicles of poems under the title *Lyris*. For some of these writers, especially the younger ones, various taboos no longer exist: it is now deemed acceptable to write, for example, about Arab-Israeli relations, the debate on Jewish Orthodoxy, and the role of the Shoah in establishing Jewish identity in Israel and the United States, considering the decline in religious observance. With the critical treatment of such subjects these authors picked up on developments that have played an important role in Hebrew literature in Israel since the beginning of the eighties. In the same way, these authors returned—in terms of language and spelling—to the literature of the German-speaking areas. Although the second generation was deeply influenced by the growing isolation from literature and the literary business in Germany and the German-speaking countries, these younger authors are involved in a natural exchange with these (and other) literatures. This development could be an important basis for starting a third chapter of literature written in the German language in Israel.

Bibliography

Jenny Aloni, *Ausgewählte Werke,* ed. Friedrich Kienecker and Hartmut Steinecke (Paderborn: Schöningh,

1987); Aloni, *Gesammelte Werke in Einzelausgaben,* ed.
Friedrich Kienecker and Hartmut Steinecke (Paderborn: Schöningh, 1990–97); Sabina Becker, "Zwischen Akkulturation und Exkulturation: Anmerkungen zu einem vernachlässigten Autorinnentypus—Jenny Aloni und Ilse Losa," *Exilforschung: Ein internationales Jahrbuch* 13 (1995): 114–36; Rüdiger Bernhardt, "Fremd in zwei Heimaten—die jüdische Schriftstellerin Jenny Aloni," *Exil: Forschungen, Erkenntnisse, Ergebnisse* 13 (1992): 17–26; Schalom Ben Chorin, "Sprache als Heimat," *Germania Judaica: Beiträge zum Verhältnis von Deutschen und Juden* (Gerlingen: Bleicher, 1982), 33–54; Klaus Müller-Salget, "Deutschsprachige Schriftsteller in Palästina und Israel: Ein Forschungsprojekt," *Kontroversen, alte und neue: Akten des VII. Internationalen Germanisten-Kongresses, Göttingen 1985,* ed. Albrecht Schöne, vol. 5, *Auseinandersetzungen um jiddische Sprache und Literatur. Jüdische Komponenten in der deutschen Literatur—die Assimilationskontroverse,* ed. Walter Röll and Hans-Peter Bayerdörfer (Tübingen: Niemeyer, 1986), 244–50; Müller-Salget, "'Und doch!' Die deutschsprachige Literatur Israels seit 1945," *"Wir tragen den Zettelkasten mit den Steckbriefen unserer Freunde": Acta-Band zum Symposion "Beiträge jüdischer Autoren zur deutschen Literatur seit 1945,"* ed. Jens Stüben and Winfried Woesler (Darmstadt: Häusser, 1993), 74–84; Müller-Salget, "Zur Identitätsproblematik deutschsprachiger Schriftsteller in Palästina und Israel," *Begegnung mit dem "Fremden": Grenzen—Traditionen—Vergleiche. Akten des VIII. Internationalen Germanisten-Kongresses, Tokyo 1990,* vol. 8 (Munich: Judicium, 1991), 149–57; Jürgen Nieraad, "Deutschsprachige Literatur in Israel," *Deutschsprachige Literatur des Auslandes,* ed. Erwin Theodor Rosenthal (Bern:

Herbert Lang, 1989): 83–100; Margarita Pazi, "Die deutschsprachige Literatur Israels," *Deutsch-jüdische Exil- und Emigrationsliteratur im 20. Jahrhundert,* ed. Itta Shedletzky and Hans Otto Horch (Tübingen: Niemeyer, 1993), 81–94; Pazi, "Deutschsprachige Literatur und Autoren in Israel," *Kontroversen* 5, ed. Walter Röll and Hans-Peter Bayerdörfer (1986), 251–60; Pazi, "Jenny Aloni, eine deutschschreibende, israelische Autorin," in Aloni, *Ausgewählte Werke,* 162–73; Pazi, "Staub und Sterne: Deutschschreibende Autorinnen in Erez-Israel und Israel," *Deutsche Literatur von Frauen,* ed. Gisela Brinker Gabler, vol. 2 (Munich: Beck, 1988), 317–33; Claudia Schoppmann, "Jenny Aloni," *Im Fluchtgepäck die Sprache: Deutschsprachige Schriftstellerinnen im Exil* (Berlin: Orlanda, 1991), 161–68; Alice Schwarz, "Die Einsamkeit der deutschsprachigen Schriftsteller in Israel," *Literatur und Kritik* 105 (1976): 302–5; Hartmut Steinecke, "Jenny Aloni," *Kritisches Lexikon zur deutschsprachigen Gegenwartsliteratur,* ed. Heinz Ludwig Arnold (Munich: Text & Kritik), loose-leaf ed.; Steinecke, "Jenny Aloni—Ein Porträt zum 75. Geburtstag," *Literatur in Westfalen: Beiträge zur Forschung 2,* ed. Walter Gödden and Winfried Woesler (Paderborn, 1992), 237–46; Steinecke, *". . . man müßte einer späteren Generation Bericht geben." Ein Literarisches Lesebuch zur deutsch-jüdischen Geschichte und eine Einführung in Leben und Werk Jenny Alonis* (Paderborn: Schöningh, 1995); and Steinecke, "' . . . nur Finsternis und Fremde': Das Thema Einsamkeit in den Erzählungen von Jenny Aloni," *"Wir tragen . . . ,"* 105–11.

HARTMUT STEINECKE

1992 Robert Schindel's novel *Gebürtig* continues the development of Jewish writing in Austria after the Shoah

The enormous loss to Austrian culture caused by the expulsion and murder of Austria's Jewish population cannot possibly be recovered. An idea of its dimensions can be gained from pertinent accounts that give a survey of those who were expelled. Specifically, I should like to recommend Harry Zohn's documentation *". . . ich bin ein Sohn der deutschen Sprache nur . . ."* (I am just a son of the German language).

The following pages, then, cannot aim for completeness, but will try to demonstrate by way of examples how the menace of Nazism and its extermination machinery was dealt with by Jewish-Austrian writers. The experience of the Holocaust that became constitutive of these writers' identity distinguishes them fundamentally from other Austrian writers, but they also differ in both their artistic treatment and their theoretical reflection of the conditions and consequences of National Socialism.

Unfortunately, one cannot help stating that writing in Austria after 1945 essentially did not need to, nor was supposed to, work through the horrible events of 1938 to 1945. Established Austrian writers like Karl Heinrich Waggerl and Max Mell passed lightly and nonchalantly over the facts. Austria's insistence after World War II on its status as the first victim of Nazi Germany impeded a confrontation with its atrocities; there was no need for such a confrontation because Austria, unlike Germany, did not consider itself "defeated" and "occupied" but "liberated."

Although in Germany, partly due to the country's division, the confrontation with Nazism was not shunned, and (as Erich Fried describes) an attempt was made for a new beginning, in Austria, because of Austrians' ostensible status as victims, such a new beginning seemed unnecessary, and old traditions were resumed. "That not all the old values were that good, that they had in part already served in the education of young Adolf Hitler, was forgotten," wrote Fried (1987, 23). According to Fried, the quick resumption of old traditions in Austria was in accordance with the fact that in Austria city centers and library buildings were less destroyed than those in Germany, so that "the structure of traditional conventional literature" (24) remained intact as well.

In particular, it was the reabsorption into the government of cultural officials from the period of Austro-fascism that enabled this structure to be reoccupied in conventional ways. This process is illustrated by Karl-Markus Gauß in his description of Albert Ehrenstein's short return to Austria: "The post-war director of the Austrian Broadcasting Corporation was a man who, before the war, as a high ranking cultural official in the period of Austro-Fascism, had known how to, let's say, fill responsible positions with verve. Someone like him, his shadow Rudolf Henz, could surely have been encountered by Albert Ehrenstein if, in 1949, he had gone on Viennese walks through the realm of culture, rehabilitation and oblivion. Rudolf Henz had been a leading scribbler and cultural functionary of the Christian *Ständestaat*" (Gauß 1988,

11). Henz is a good example of the appointment policy as well as of the general consciousness of the time. The war apparently had little effect on him, and he did not feel challenged to rethink or change matters. As he writes in his autobiography: "For me, as I saw, work would now be resumed where it had ended in 1938" (11).

A similarly cozy passage that sums up the Zeitgeist from a historical distance, yet perpetuates it by its lack of criticism, can be found in Paul Kruntorad's contribution in *Kindlers Literaturgeschichte der Gegenwart*: "For the most part, in the first years after the war, Austrian fiction writers were busy continuing where they had left off before the war—if the war meant a caesura to them at all" (165). Thus, prominent Jewish writers in exile were excluded from Austrian literature. The section of Kruntorad's book elegantly labeled "Emigrés—Rémigrés" commemorates Ernst Lothar, Ernst Weigel, and Friedrich Torberg; "others," we are told, "remained in emigration or, if they returned, did not go back to Austria" (157). Yet even those, Kruntorad suggests, were not essentially shaken in their writing: "In a sense, like Vicki Baum, Robert Neumann, and even Alfred Polgar, they only continued along the lines that had already characterized their work before the war" (157).

The situation is described very differently by Jean Améry: "1945, 'risen from the dead,' as the apostolic profession of faith puts it, the head still heavy from the beating and one's own useless pondering, I fancied that the world would belong to us: the beaten ones who had become victors, the utopians . . . , the visionaries. . . . Radical evil, we believed, was now eliminated" (Améry 1982, 279). Yet this was "Spoken to the Wind," as the title of his essay has it. When Friedrich Theodor Csokor, for instance, having returned from exile, opposed the professorship of a Nazi Germanist, he was asked by Victor Reimann, "What gives you the right to set yourself up as a judge now?" Nor does Albert Drach, in 1950, at the end of his *Unsentimental Journey,* meet with a friendly reception; instead he has to win back his own apartment, room by room and piece by piece. No wonder then that, given more detailed information, many did not want to return or, if they

did, they went back into exile—like Theodor Kramer, they felt "banished from Austria" (*Verbannt aus Österreich,* 1943), or even considered themselves homeless.

And yet as early as 1946, the first antifascist exhibition, planned only a few weeks after the war and entitled "Never Forget!" had been accomplished and was exceptionally well attended. Wolfgang Kos, however, attributes this success partly to the exhibition's basic concept: externalization of guilt and nontreatment of Austrofascism. Already then, the purpose was not to serve the "perpetuation of hatred" but to enlighten "those who, seduced by irresponsible propaganda and pressed by the troubles of the times, had as mere followers joined the front-lines of doom" (Kos 1994, 12). This official phraseology created the paradigm of an Austrian innocence derived from ignorance and want—a paradigm that complied so well with contemporary needs and established itself so strongly in the minds of the following generation that a federal president was later able to draw upon this pattern and be understood.

Considering these circumstances, it is not surprising that if the past is considered at all, it is the political prisoners who are given prominence whereas the Jewish victims are ignored. As Brigitte Bailer stated in her study on reparations in Austria: "The largest group of victims, the Austrian Jews, were publicly repressed or at best mentioned as the dead to be deplored. Surviving Jews had no place in public discourse" (Bailer 1993, 24).

Of the writers expelled, the writers whose homeland was Austria, many remained in exile: Rose Ausländer, Herman Broch, Elias Canetti, Albert Ehrenstein, Johannes Urzidil, Erich Fried, Hilde Spiel, Franz Werfel, and Richard Beer-Hofmann, for example, stayed in the United States and Great Britain; Fritz Hochwälder remained in Switzerland; and Max Brod and Leo Perutz kept their homes in Israel. For most of these authors, taking up permanent residence outside of Austria meant that they not only had to start over financially; they also had to come to terms psychically and artistically with the "deadening" (*Ertötnis*) of exile (*Oskar Jellinek*). This is how Albert Drach, for instance, in his *Unsentimental Journey* (1966), describes his experience in exile: He has saved a French mountain village from the Germans by his ready wit; the villagers want to make him their mayor; when he later asks why they never turned him over to the Germans, he is told: "Because a reward was only offered in the beginning, but then we didn't know enough about you. First it was 5000 francs, then 500, then 150. In the end, they said we would only get half of the person's belongings. What do you think we could have done with a couple of lousy books?" (Drach 1966, 356).

As can be seen in most biographies, this exile was not over with the end of Nazism and, due to the bad reception in Austria, it often threatened to turn into internal exile. Still, a number of writers, such as Günther Anders, Hans Weigel, Friedrich Torberg, and Berthold Viertel, did return, although they never felt at home again there. Erich Fried, for example, was reminded in 1984 that he "has been in possession of an Austrian passport for one year." He once again concluded: "It is by no means a matter of my own assessment. As long as others still regard me as an outsider or at best a newcomer, my literary *homecoming* has despite all my successes not really succeeded. Is there really such a thing as coming home?" (Fried 1987, 60–61). Hilde Spiel shared this sentiment. In 1963 she returned from her exile in England, regarding her "return to Vienna" (*Rückkehr nach Wien,* 1968) as "inevitable," but she eventually went back yet again to England.

Both those writers who remained in exile and those who tried to return home were confronted not only with the problem of dealing with the circumstances of their external lives but also with the necessity of dealing and possibly coming to terms with the situation that was brought upon them. Thus even during the war Elias Canetti began to write his anthropological and sociohistorical study *Crowds and Power* (*Masse und Macht,* published in German in 1960); in Paris in 1938, Manès Sperber published his socio-psychological study on tyranny, *Zur Analyse der Tyrannis*; and Hermann Broch, from 1939 on, wrote several studies in mass psychology and, in the

United States in the 1940s, tried to establish a "research institute in mass psychosis." Günther Anders fundamentally and extensively explored the social system that enabled and allowed for the extermination machinery of Auschwitz. His reflections on the mediatization of society, on the menace of the atomic age, and on the Holocaust can be found in his study about the obsoleteness of humans (*Die Antiquiertheit des Menschen,* 1956, 1980), in his theses on the atomic age (*Thesen zum Atomzeitalter,* 1959), in his correspondence with Hiroshima pilot Claude Eatherly (*Off limits für das Gewissen,* 1961 [Burning conscience, 1989]), in his *Visit Beautiful Vietnam—das ABC der Aggressionen heute* (1968), and in his *Besuch im Hades: Auschwitz und Breslau 1966. Nach "Holocaust" 1979* (1979).

In *Besuch im Hades,* Anders defends the TV miniseries *Holocaust,* or, indeed, any artistic treatment of the subject, because he feels it is necessary "to down scale the truth in its incomprehensible enormity so as to not remain completely excluded from it." Anders himself had written an antifascist novel as early as 1930–32, although it has been published only recently (*Die molussische Katakumbo,* 1992). Most other novelistic treatments of the subject by Jewish writers belong to a later period and are partly autobiographical in content. Examples are Ernst Lothar's *Die Rückkehr* (The return; 1949), Hans Weigel's *Unvollendete Symphonie* (Uncompleted symphony; 1951), Robert Neumann's *Ein leichtes Leben* (An easy life; 1963), and Albert Drach's already mentioned *Unsentimentale Reise* (Unsentimental journey; 1966). Ilse Aichinger, in her novel *Die größere Hoffnung* (The greater hope; 1949), draws on her own experience to describe the fate of Jewish children under National Socialism. Hermann Broch, in his novel *Die Schuldlosen* (The guiltless; 1950), tries to trace the social changes that enable individuals to experience themselves outwardly without guilt; as a solution to the conflict of ideologies, he speaks of the need for "plain decency," for a "militant duty of decency" beyond ideology but also beyond hope. Manès Sperber's novelistic trilogy, *Wie eine Träne im Ozean* (Like a tear in the ocean), which started to appear in 1949, also raises the question of the individual's responsibility for and complicity with history. "How shall we live without be-coming guilty? The heroes of my trilogy try to answer this question through actions," he wrote, summing up his purpose. Jean Améry's studies, *Jenseits von Schuld und Sühne: Bewältigungsversuche eines Überwältigten* (Beyond guilt and penance: An overpowered one tries to master; 1966), *Über das Altern: Revolte und Resignation* (About aging: Re-volt and resignation; 1968), and *Unmeisterliche Wanderjahre* (Unmasterly years of travel; 1971) are intended as "essayistic autobiographical novels" that are supposed to testify in a subjective way to the "limits of the mind," and the "disaster" of history.

By contrast, Leo Perutz's attempt to erect a memorial to the old Prague ghetto in *Nachts unter der steinernen Brücke* (Night under the stone bridge; 1953) is more of an exception, because most writers feel obliged to reflect their Jewish-ness in relation to the most recent events. Because of this tendency, attempts to come to terms with the extermination machinery of the Nazis gained a new dimension when, in 1960, Adolf Eichmann was arrested and convicted. For, as Manès Sperber wrote in his essayistic history of Judaism *Churban oder Die unfaßbare Gewißheit* (Churban, or the in-comprehensible certainty; 1979), Eichmann's conviction and execution by the state of Israel could be understood as a contribution to the "res-toration of the dignity of every survivor" (Sperber 1979, 97). Csokor treated the subject of the mass murderer in his play *Das Zeichen an der Wand* (The sign on the wall; 1962), Fritz Hochwälder dealt with it in *Der Himbeerpflücker* (The raspberry picker; 1965) and *Der Befehl* (The command; 1967), and Günther Anders wrote an open letter to Eichmann's son Klaus, "Wir Eichmannsöhne" (Us sons of Eichmann; 1964), where he considers responsibility and complicity.

Apart from the languages of the countries of exile, the language of these reflections continued to be German. Elias Canetti gives the following reason for it: "The language of my mind will always be German *because* I am a Jew. What is left of that country which is in every way devastated, I, the Jew, want to preserve within me. Even *their* fate is mine; but in addition, I bring along a universally human heritage. I want to return to

their language what I owe to it. I want to contrib-ute to their having something to thank for" (Ca-netti 1978, 73). This perspective depends, apart from other personal factors, surely on the age of the émigré; Jakov Lind, who had to leave Austria at the age of eleven and has lived ever since in England, writes both in German and English, with the English allowing for more distance, as he explains with regard to *Counting My Steps* (1969; *Selbstporträt,* 1970). At a symposium held in Vienna in January 1995, he specified: "My En-glish is a kind of Esperanto. To write in Austrian is no longer possible for me" (*Der Standard,* Jan. 14–15, 1995, p. 22).

For most writers it was not only a matter of being faced with the task of reflecting the histori-cal situation—the menace to and near extermina-tion of the Jews—but also of being forced to think about their Jewishness, because many of them no longer regarded themselves as Jews in a religious sense. The experience of belonging to a "community of fate" (Zohn 1986, 9), among whom they would not have numbered them-selves, forced many to perceive themselves as "Jewish" because of this external attribution. As Albert Ehrenstein describes this process in his story "Ruapehu" (formerly entitled "Views of an Exterritorial"; 1912): "Only the others call him a Negro and Jew, about which he then contem-plates, yet still fails to arrive at a sense of his Jewishness or negritude except in a fictive or real dialogue with himself and others" (401).

Although being a society's Other does not in any case mean exclusion and extermination, the Holocaust gives it an unequivocal, indelible di-mension. As Manès Sperber writes in *Churban oder Die unfaßbare Gewißheit:* "I am a European Jew, who is at every moment aware of being a survivor, and who will never forget the years when being a Jew was a deathly crime" (Sperber 1979, 42). Still, he tries to work out a positive meaning and comes to attest a specific "impermeable Jewish optimism": "It is less an unbreakable *will to hope* than the categorical rejection of hopelessness and hence a *resistance against resignation,* which in times of despair so easily becomes a temptation. Ultimately, my entire writing—which began in the shadow of horrible disappointments—has been, and still is, resistance" (159). On the other hand, for Sperber this will to resistance is accompanied by a sense of guilt: the insurgents in the Warsaw ghetto "had no longer any hope because even despair was denied to those young people: They died in some nowhere. But we live—helpless, guiltlessly guilty of their doom, of everything" (60).

Universally, then, Jewishness for the writers of this generation is determined by the experience of the Holocaust; as Jean Améry sketches the situation in an essay entitled "On the Obligation and Impossibility of Being a Jew": "For them, for me being a Jew means to feel burdened by yesterday's tragedy. On my left forearm I wear the Auschwitz number; it reads shorter than the Pentateuch or the Talmud and yet supplies more exhaustive information. . . . If I tell myself and the world, including the religious and nationally minded Jews who do not consider me as one of them: I am a Jew, then I mean the realities and possibilities summed up in the Auschwitz number" (Améry 1966, 146). Moreover, there is a sense of being one of the last ones, as Anders writes, because no one will any longer feel as or call oneself a "German Jew" and the chapter of German-Jewish intellectual history has been closed (Anders 1978).

Although this type of Jewish identity, according to Améry, is certainly not defined by positive experiences—"the Jew without positive determination," he wrote, "the catastrophic Jew, as we shall safely call him, will have to live without reliance in the world" (Améry 1966,147)—he also asserted a stance that goes beyond this experience and involves a positive, operative aspect: "I became a human being not by internally invoking my abstract humanity, but by finding and fully realizing myself within the given social reality as a revolting Jew" (142).

This stance, as well as Sperber's "impermeable Jewish optimism," is understood by the younger generation of Jewish writers in Austria as an obligation to resistance and to maintaining a keen eye on power relations. Among the women writers, specifically, this position emerges as the look toward the stranger, toward the uneven distribution of power implied in sexual difference. This outlook can be seen, for example, in Anna Mit-

gutsch's novel *Abschied von Jerusalem* (Farewell to Jerusalem; 1995), where, in a series of historicizing excursions, she explores Judaism and, at the same time, has the young Jewish woman, Dworah, confront the stranger, the Arab man.

The obligation to be wary is also shared by Elfriede Jelinek, who, especially in interviews, addresses her situation as a daughter of a Jewish scientist. Her notions of Judaism, however, can be rather stereotypical when she talks, for example, of her "Jewish proletarian" father and of originating in the "Slavic depressive, Jewish culture," or when she claims to write in the tradition of the "Eastern, Jewish urban culture of Austria." In her book *Die Kinder der Toten* (The children of the dead; 1995), she is, according to the prospectus, now also dealing in an explicitly literary manner with the subject of Austria's denial of its history and its involvement with Nazism.

Alienation and identity are the subjects Robert Schindel has pursued throughout his works, also with regard to his Jewishness. In *Gebürtig* (Born; 1992), Jewish protagonists of various generations strive to overcome their alienation by finding a position vis-à-vis their Jewishness—a position ranging from the acceptance of the external attribution to the denial of its importance. The difficulty of avoiding common notions is revealed not only in Schindel's representations of Jewish bodies, which follow the old stereotype, but also in the stigmatizing ironical employment of names. Whereas the Jewish protagonists cannot free themselves from their past—their Otherness—the son of a convicted and executed Nazi manages to shed his guilt-laden past and becomes "identical with himself."

Thus in Schindel we encounter the question of guiltless guilt raised by Sperber, as well as the question of the identity of an assimilated Jew who is in danger of getting lost in society. Yet Schindel apparently also draws on Jean Améry's concept of the revolting Jew when, in "Judentum als Erinnerung und Widerstand" (Jewishness as memory and resistance; *Illustrierte Neue Welt,* Oct. 1989), he explains why Jewishness per se can mean resistance. Because in Europe anti-Semitism is the archetypal form of persecution, Jewishness can mean resistance as a remembrance of the traditions of the Enlightenment and as a union with all those who were expelled, abused, or exterminated. By this, Schindel hopes to also productively restore his own roots; for non-religious, non-Zionist Jews, this act can restore their own Jewish identity so as to not render this question superfluous by continued assimilation. Resistance is "obstinacy, a sense of one's own, and as such is capable of resisting both anti-Semitism and assimilation by forming one's own idea both for establishing an identity and as a political agenda: The tradition of the enlightenment has not been discarded, not even in the age of inwardness" (5). Although resistance alone is not specifically Jewish, "for me [Schindel] this agenda is part of my union with myself as an annihilated ancestor, as a forward-directed survivor of my own death, and in such union constitutes my Jewishness" (6).

Bibliography

Jean Améry, *Jenseits von Schuld und Sühne: Bewältigungsversuche eines Überwältigten* (Stuttgart: Klett, 1966); Améry, *Weiterleben—aber wie? Essays, 1968–1978,* ed. Gisela Lindemann (Stuttgart: Klett-Cotta, 1982); Günther Anders, "Mein Judentum," *Mein Judentum,* ed. Hans Jürgen Schultz (Stuttgart: Kreuz, 1978), 58–76; Brigitte Bailer, *Wiedergutmachung—kein Thema: Österreich und die Opfer des Nationalsozialismus* (Vienna: Löcker, 1993); Elias Canetti, *Die Provinz des Menschen: Aufzeichnungen, 1942–1972* (Munich: Hanser, 1973), trans. as *The Humane Province* (New York: Seabury, 1978); Albert Drach, *Unsentimentale Reise: Ein Bericht* (Munich: Hanser, 1966); Erich Fried, *Nicht verdrängen, nicht gewöhnen: Texte zum Thema Österreich,* ed. Michael Lewin (Vienna: Europa, 1987); Karl Markus Gauß, *Tinte ist bitter: Literarische Porträts aus Barbaropa* (Klagenfurt: Wieser, 1988); Elfriede Jelinek, *Die Kinder der Toten* (Reinbek: Rowohlt, 1995); Wolfgang Kos, *Eigenheim Österreich: Zu Politik, Kultur und Alltag nach 1945* (Vienna: Sonderzahl, 1994); Theodor Kramer, *Verbannt aus Österreich* (London: Austrian PEN, 1943); Paul Kruntorad, "Prosa," *Kindlers Literaturgeschichte der Gegenwart: Autoren, Werke, Themen, Tendenzen seit 1945.* Vols. 5, 6: *Die zeitgenössische Literatur Österreichs. I, II,* ed. Hilde Spiel (Frankfurt a. M.: Fischer, 1980), 135–323; Joseph MacVeigh, *Kontinuität und Vergangenheitsbewältigung in der Österreichischen Literatur nach 1945* (Vienna: Braumüller, 1988); Anna Mitgutsch, *Abschied von Jerusalem* (Berlin: Rowohlt, 1995); Robert Schindel, *Gebürtig* (Frankfurt a. M.: Suhrkamp, 1992); Hans Schütz, *Juden in der deutschen Literatur: Eine deutschjüdische Literaturgeschichte im Überblick* (Munich: Piper, 1992); Manès Sperber, *Churban oder Die unfaßbare Gewißheit: Essays* (Vienna: Europaverlag, 1979); Sperber, *Nur eine Brücke zwischen Gestern und Morgen* (Vienna: Europaverlag, 1980); Hilde Spiel, "Einführung," *Kindlers Literaturgeschichte der Gegenwart,* 3–133; and Harry Zohn, ". . . ich bin ein Sohn der deutschen Sprache nur . . . " *Jüdisches Erbe in der Österreichischen Literatur: Darstellungen und Dokumentation* (Vienna: Amalthea, 1986).

INGRID SPÖRK

Contributors

Leslie A. Adelson
Cornell University

Jeremy Adler
University of London

Arthur Tilo Alt
Duke University

Mark M. Anderson
Columbia University

Steven E. Aschheim
Hebrew University

Ehrhard Bahr
University of California at Los Angeles

Dagmar Barnouw
University of Southern California

David Bathrick
Cornell University

Hans-Peter Bayerdörfer
University of Munich

Delphine Bechtel
University of Paris

Ruth Beckermann
Freelance writer and filmmaker, Vienna

Nitsa Ben-Ari
Tel Aviv University

Klaus L. Berghahn
University of Wisconsin, Madison

Michael Berkowitz
Ohio State University

Albrecht Betz
University of Aachen

David Biale
Graduate Theological Union
Berkeley, California

Dorothy Bilik
University of Maryland

John Bormanis
University of Arizona

Michael Brenner
Brandeis University

Mordechai Breuer
Bar-Ilan University
Israel

Stephen Eric Bronner
Rutgers University

Gisela Brude-Firnau
University of Waterloo

Micha Brumlik
Jüdische Hochschule, Heidelberg

Marcus Bullock
University of Wisconsin, Milwaukee

Anita Bunyan
Gonville and Caius College
Cambridge, England

Robert Chazan
New York University

Detlev Claussen
Independent scholar, Frankfurt am Main

Robert Cohen
New York University

Amy Colin
University of Pittsburgh

Joseph Dan
Hebrew University

John M. Efron
Indiana University

Barbara Einhorn
University of Sussex

Peter R. Erspamer
Independent scholar, St. Paul, Minnesota

Anat Feinberg
Jüdische Hochschule, Heidelberg

Sterling Fishman
University of Wisconsin, Madison

Kristie A. Foell
Bowling Green State University

Jerold C. Frakes
University of Southern California

Thomas Freeman
Beloit College

Harriet Freidenreich
Temple University

Ken Frieden
Syracuse University

Eike Geisel
Independent scholar, Berlin

Mark H. Gelber
Ben Gurion University of the Negev

Katharina Gerstenberger
University of Cincinnati

Sander L. Gilman
University of Chicago

Willi Goetschel
Columbia University

Simha Goldin
Tel Aviv University

Jost Hermand
University of Wisconsin, Madison

Deborah Hertz
State University of New York at Binghamton

Susannah Heschel
Case Western Reserve University

Marianne Hirsch
Dartmouth College

Frank D. Hirschbach
University of Minnesota

Dierk O. Hoffmann
Colgate University

Peter Uwe Hohendahl
Cornell University

Robert Holub
University of California at Berkeley

Hans Otto Horch
University of Aachen

Wilma A. Iggers
State University of New York, Buffalo

Noah W. Isenberg
Wesleyan University

Jack Jacobs
John Jay College

Martin Jay
University of California at Berkeley

Anton Kaes
University of California at Berkeley

Edward K. Kaplan
Brandeis University

Marion Kaplan
Queens College

Ephraim Kanarfogel
Yeshiva University

Douglas Kellner
University of Texas

Dominick LaCapra
Cornell University

Nancy A. Lauckner
University of Tennessee

Gary Lease
University of California at Santa Cruz

Leo A. Lensing
Wesleyan University

Meira Likierman
Tavistock Institute

Michael Löwy
National Center for Scientific Research, Paris

Dagmar C. G. Lorenz
Ohio State University

Paul Michael Lützeler
Washington University

Ivan G. Marcus
Yale University

Andrei S. Markovits
University of California at Santa Cruz

Paul Mendes-Flohr
Hebrew University

Leslie Morris
Bard College

Stéphane Moses
Hebrew University

Karl Müller
University of Salzburg

Brian Murdoch
University of Stirling, England

Susan Neiman
Tel Aviv University

Beth Simone Noveck
Yale Law School

Laureen Nussbaum
Portland State University

Kenneth H. Ober
University of Illinois

Katharina L. Ochse
Goethe Institute, Sarajevo

Leonard Olschner
University of London

Moshe Pelli
University of Central Florida

Uwe Henrik Peters
University of Cologne

Peter C. Pfeiffer
Georgetown University

Anson Rabinbach
Princeton University

Karen Remmler
Mount Holyoke College

Ritchie Robertson
University of Oxford

Alexis P. Rubin
Independent scholar, Saratoga, California

Eric L. Santner
University of Chicago

Marc Saperstein
Washington University

Julius H. Schoeps
University of Potsdam

Karl-Heinz J. Schoeps
University of Illinois

Egon Schwarz
Washington University

Ruth Schwertfeger
University of Wisconsin, Milwaukee

Robert R. Shandley
Texas A & M University

Zohar Shavit
Tel Aviv University

Rima Shichmanter
Tel Aviv University

David Sorkin
University of Wisconsin, Madison

Ingrid Spörk
University of Graz

Michael P. Steinberg
Cornell University

Hartmut Steinecke
University of Paderborn

Peter Stenberg
University of British Columbia

Frank Stern
Ben Gurion University of the Negev

Guy Stern
Wayne State University

Heidi Thomann Tewarson
Oberlin College

Céline Trautmann-Waller
University of Paris

Brigitta van Rheinberg
Princeton University Press

Annegret Völpel
Johann-Wolfgang-Goethe University
Frankfurt am Main

Marc A. Weiner
Indiana University

Liliane Weissberg
University of Pennsylvania

Irving Wohlfarth
University of Reims, France

Susanne Zantop
Dartmouth College

Klaus Zelewitz
University of Salzburg

Jack Zipes
University of Minnesota

Harry Zohn
Brandeis University

Index

47, 352–53; Lukács's correspondence with, 288; in Palestine, 820; and the Philosophy of Life, 396; translation of the Bible into German, 397, 398; and Vienna, 232; *Die Welt* edited by, 227; and Zionism, 191, 339, 344, 345, 487, 678. Works: *The Eclipse of God*, 704; *Gog und Magog*, 350; *I and Thou*, 341, 343; "Jewish Renaissance," 421; *The Legend of the Baal Schem*, 288

Buber, Paula (Winkler), 190, 191, 233

Buche, Die, (anthology), 627–28, 631

Buchenwald, 602, 672, 784

Buchholz, Friedrich, 81

Büchner, Georg, 269; *Woyzek*, 269, 559, 566

Buckwitz, Harry, 510

Bühler, Charlotte Malachowski, 284

Bukofzer, Werner, 822

Bukowina, 627–33

Buonarroti, Filippo, 174

Bürger, Peter. *Theory of the Avant-Garde*, 689

Bürgerliche Revolution. See Revolution of 1848–49

C. V.-Zeitung (journal), 532

Cabala. *See* Kabbalah

Cabaret, political, 458

Caesarius of Heisterbach, 18

Cambridge Codex ("Dukus Horant"), 42

Canaris, Volker, 650

Canetti, Elias, 464–70, 602; in exile, 468, 555, 828; as loyal to the German language, 468, 545, 830. Works: *Die Blendung*, 466–67, 566, 600; *Comedy of Vanity*, 467; *The Conscience of Words*, 469; *Crowds and Power*, 465–66, 469–70, 829; *Die Fliegenpein*, 470; *The Numbered*, 467–68; *The Play of the Eyes*, 468, 600; *The Tongue Set Free*, 468, 549; *The Torch in My Ear*, 468; *The Voices of Marrakesh*, 469; *The Wedding*, 467

Cantor, Georg, 294

Capitalism: and anti-Semitism, xxiv, 413, 479; and art, 132; fascism linked to, 686; Fromm's critique of, 483–84; and Holocaust profit-making, 726–27, 734; as "Jewish," 130, 133, 413; Marxist cri-

tique of, 175; and Protestantism, 291; and World War I, 290

Caricatures of Jews: in anti-Semitic humor, 81–83; as backward people, 75–83; as Bolsheviks, 368; as degenerate, 273–78; as diseased, 258, 428–29; of Eastern Jews, 127, 297; in Fassbinder's *Garbage, the City and Death*, 805–11; as lascivious, 444–47; as mentally unsound, 297–98; as money handlers, 77, 82, 184, 313, 437; as pariahs, 606–12; physiognomy, 302, 388, 439; as ritual murderers, 153, 313; Social Darwinist caricatures, 412; on Yiddish as *Jargon*, 127, 244, 245, 416, 461

Carlebach, Joseph, 206, 528

Carmely, Klara, xxvii

Cassirer, Ernst, 403–4, 528

Castellio, Sebastian, 88

Catholic Church: German Empire and, 205; and the Holocaust, 731. *See also* Christianity

Celan, Paul, xxiii, xxiv, 615, 642, 693, 716–21; on Bukowina, 629; on the problem of language, 631, 632, 694–95, 717; receives the Georg Büchner Prize, 710, 716; suicide of, 716, 777. Works: *Atemwende*, 717; "Engführung," 695, 717; *Fadensonnen*, 717; "Gespräch im Gebirg," 717; *Lichtzwang*, 717; "Der Meridian," 716–19; *Mohn und Gedächtnis*, 717, 718, 720; "Nähe der Gräber" (Nearness of the graves), 694; *Die Niemandrose*, 717, 718, 719–20; *Sprachgitter*, 717, 719; "Todesfuge" (Fugue of death), 550, 695, 717; "Todtnauberg," 720; *Zeitgehöft*, 717

Centralverein deutscher Staatsbürger jüdischen Glaubens (Central Organization of German Citizens of the Jewish Faith), 532–36

Chagall, Marc, 421

Chamberlain, Houston Stewart, 313, 500

Chaplin, Charlie, 580; as pariah, 606, 609

Chasan, Bella, 306

Chasidic movement. *See* Hasidic movement

Children: and *Bildung*, 127; psychoanalysis of, 591–98; socialization of, 35–38; and sexuality, 276

Children's literature, 38–41; histori-

cal novels, 144; *Jewish Children's Calendar*, 485–86; *Lesebuch für jüdische Kinder*, 68–73; Nazi era reflected in, 512–18, 532–36; in the Weimar Republic, 486–91

Chosenness of Jews, 97; and Jewish education, 36; and sexuality, 275

Christian Democratic Union, xxv, 806, 808

Christian Socialists: anti-Semitism among, 336, 444, 446; Austrian, 212, 417

Christianity: and anti-Semitism, 79, 80–83, 183, 573; Fromm's interpretation of, 481; German Jews' ideological construct of, 193–98; and the Holocaust, 731; Judaic origins of, 193–96; and mass psychology, 465–66; Mendelssohn on the role of churches, 91; Nazi de-Judaization of, 197–98; Protestantism linked with Judaism, 338–39; and psychoanalysis, 445; Schoeps's study of, 656; and sexual pathology, 275. *See also* Catholic Church; Christian-Jewish relations; Conversion to Christianity

Christian-Jewish relations: and conversion to Judaism, 186–91; in the Crusades, 1–7; disputations, 78–79, 337–39; Enlightenment friendship cult, 61–67, 136, 611; and independent Jewish historiography, 706; and Jesus scholarship, 193–98; and modernization of Jews, 80; toleration debates, 75–83

Chutzpah, 584

Cinema. *See* Filmmaking

Circumcision: and conversion to Judaism, 188–89; scientific writing on, 295

Civil rights of Jews, 76, 77, 79–80, 84, 90; in France, 161. *See also* Emancipation, Jewish

Claussen, Detlev, 82

Clermont-Tonnerre, Count, 90

Cohen, Hermann, 91, 304, 322–23, 331, 395, 397, 706, 707; Buber's debate with, 347; on Christianity, 196; on humanity, 340–42; on the Jewish Question, 336–39; as neo-Kantian, 403–4; on the *Neue Jüdische Monatshefte*, 353; on *Offenbarungsglaube*, 322–23; and Science of the Jews, 203; World War I supported by, 339, 348. Works: